LARGE PRINT PUBLISHER'S NOTE

This Large Print edition of *The Little Oxford Dictionary* will hopefully fill a 'void' for those readers who are unable to read normal size small print and who now rely upon Large Print since its introduction and development over the last fourteen years.

The choice of a suitable Dictionary for Large Print purposes was a formidable task. The very nature of a Large Print edition necessitates it being unavoidably larger and more cumbersome to handle, than a normal small print edition.

After careful consideration and consultation with various bodies of librarians and educationalists, it became apparent that The Little Oxford Dictionary (which in its original size fits into one's pocket) was held in the highest esteem by everyone. It was therefore decided to reprint this version for the Ulverscroft Large Print series.

This explanation is intended to clarify the ensuing 'Publisher's Note' and 'Preface' which refer to size and dimensions, and which could otherwise confuse the reader.

The Publishers wish to express gratitude to Oxford University Press for allowing the use of their version to help fulfil the worldwide need for a Large Print Dictionary.

This Large Print Edition
of *The Little Oxford Dictionary of Current English*
(fourth edition 1969)
is published by arrangement with
Oxford University Press.
© Oxford University Press 1969

THE
LITTLE OXFORD
DICTIONARY
OF CURRENT ENGLISH

Compiled by
GEORGE OSTLER

FOURTH EDITION

Edited by
JESSIE COULSON

Complete and Unabridged

ULVERSCROFT
Leicester

PUBLISHER'S NOTE

WHEN the demand arose for a dictionary which should be still smaller than the *Pocket Oxford Dictionary*, and yet cover the same or even a wider vocabulary, it soon became clear that the problem of compression required not merely lexicographical accuracy, but the technical skill of an experienced compositor. Mr. George Ostler, who served for forty-four years on the composing and reading staff of the Clarendon Press, and whose encyclopaedic knowledge had been of service to two generations of compositors and authors, was therefore entrusted with the task of packing all that could be packed into 640 of these pages. He had completed the Dictionary proper, revised all the proofs, and prepared the appendix of Abbreviations, when his death on 21 April 1929 prevented him from carrying through its last stages a work to which he had given his best energies. The publishers are grateful to Mrs. J. Coulson, of the staff of the Oxford Dictionary, for reading the early proofs with the editor, for preparing the appendix of Difficult Proper Names, and for finishing the work after Mr. Ostler's death. It is not possible to make more than a general acknowledgement of the helpful suggestions received from many quarters; but particular thanks are due to Sir William Craigie, the organizing editor of the forthcoming great *Dictionary of American English*, and to his assistant, Mr. M. M. Mathews, for their help in selecting and distinguishing words and meanings that have their origin or principal use in the United States.

NOTE TO THE FOURTH EDITION, 1969

THIS fourth edition has been completely revised and reset. Words that have recently made good their claim to inclusion will be found in the Addenda.

First edition 1930
Second edition 1937   Third edition 1941
Fourth edition 1969
Twelfth impression 1977

First Large Print Edition
published October 1977

SBN 0 7089 0118 2

Published by
F. A. Thorpe (Publishing) Ltd.
Anstey, Leicestershire
Printed in England

PREFACE

THIS work was originally based on the *Pocket Oxford Dictionary* edited by F. G. and H. W. Fowler and, like it, rests ultimately upon the authority of the great Oxford Dictionary (1884–1928) edited by J. A. H. Murray, Henry Bradley, W. A. Craigie, and C. T. Onions. The choice of words was in the main that of the *Pocket Oxford Dictionary*, but new words and phrases, whose place and dignity in the language were less assured, were admitted rather more freely. Such elements of the vocabulary have, in the course of nearly forty years of revision, come to occupy a greater proportion of the available space; those years have seen an immense expansion in science and technology, and increased interest in and knowledge of these advances have been fostered by the growing number, rapidity, and frequency of means of communication.

In a work of such small dimensions as the *Little Oxford Dictionary*, the inclusion of the largest possible number of words has meant the adoption of various devices to save space. When, for example, the meaning of derivatives is sufficiently clear from the definition of the main word, the definition of the derivatives is omitted; and obvious derivatives (e.g. *happily, sharpness*) are usually excluded. Generally words are given in their alphabetical order; but for brevity compounds and derivatives are often grouped under the main word.

In order to save space, the tilde ~ may be substituted in compounds and derivatives for the main word or some part of it; e.g. under **hook, ~-up** = *hook-up*, **~er** = *hooker*. It should be noted that where ~ stands for less than the whole of the main word, the last letter or letters common to the word and the derivative are repeated after the tilde, e.g. under **petulant, ~ance** = *petulance*. Pronunciation and stress may be assumed to be unchanged unless a change is indicated; e.g. **admiss'ible, ~bil'ity ; enu'merate, ~ā'tion, ~ative.**

FOREIGN WORDS AND PHRASES are entered among English words in their alphabetical order, those which are not yet fully naturalized in English being printed in italic type.

P. This dictionary includes some words which are or are asserted to be proprietary names or trade marks. Their inclusion does not imply that they have acquired for legal purposes a non-proprietary or general significance, or any other judgement concerning their legal status. In cases where the editor has some evidence that a word is used as a proprietary name or trade mark this is indicated by the symbol **P**, but no judgement concerning the legal status of such words is implied thereby.

PRONUNCIATION

1. Accent. The accentuation mark ' is usually placed at the end of the stressed syllable.

2. Phonetic System. Where the pronunciation of a word or part of a word cannot be shown by the ordinary spelling and markings, a phonetic spelling is given in round brackets immediately after the black-type word. The phonetic scheme is as follows:

CONSONANTS: b; ch (ch*i*n); *ch* (lo*ch*); d; e; dh (dh*e* = the); f; g (g*o*); h; j: k; l; m; n; ng (s*i*ng); ngg (*fi*ng*er*); p; r; s (s*i*p); sh (sh*i*p); t; th (th*i*n); v; w; y; z; zh (*vi*zh*n* = vision).

VOWELS: ā ē ī ō ū o͞o (mate mete mite mote mute moot)
        ă ĕ ĭ ŏ ŭ o͝o (rack reck rick rock ruck rook)
        ār ēr īr ūr ȳr (mare mere mire mure byre)
        är ėr ör (part pert port)
        ah aw oi oor ow owr (bah bawl boil boor brow bower).

The symbol ṅ indicates French nasalization of the preceding vowel.
Vowels printed in italic within the brackets indicate vague sounds.

3. Pronunciation without Respelling. As far as possible pronunciation is shown without respelling by placing symbols over the words (e.g. ā, ĕ, ār, ėr, o͞o, etc.) in black type.

(*a*) The ordinary spelling often coincides with the phonetic system described in par. 2.

(*b*) The following additional symbols are used in the black type:
ė = ĭ (nā'kėd, rėlȳ', cŏll'ėge, prĭv'ėt, rė'al)
īr, ūr = ėr (bīrth, būrn)
ȳ, y̆ = ī, ĭ (implȳ', sŭnn'y̆)

c) final *e* when unmarked is mute, i.e. not to be pronounced. Thus **ape** is to be pronounced āp. Where final *e* is pronounced, it is marked as in rĕ'cĭpė.

(*d*) Unless another pronunciation is indicated, the following letters and combinations have the usual values in English spelling which are shown alongside them:

Vowels

ae = ē (aegis)	eu, ew = ū (feud, few)
ai = ā (pain)	ie = ē (thief)
air = ār (fair)	ier = ēr (pier)
au = aw (maul)	oa = ō (boat)
ay = ā (say)	oe = ē (amoeba)
ea, ee = ē (mean, meet)	ou = ow (bound)
ear, eer = ēr (fear, beer)	oy = oi (boy)
ei = ē (ceiling)	

Consonants

c is 'hard' and = k (cob, cry, talc) *but*	n before k, 'hard' c, q, x = ng (zinc, uncle, tank, banquet, minx)
c before e, i, y, is 'soft' and = s (ice, icy, city)	ph = f (photo)
dg = j (judgement)	qu = kw (quit)
g before e, i, y, is 'soft' and = j (age, gin, orgy)	tch = ch (batch)
	x = ks (fox)

Thus in gĕm the pronunciation of g is not marked because it comes under the rule above: 'g before e, i, y, is soft and = j'; but gĕt is followed by (g-) to show that here exceptionally g before e is 'hard' as in *go*.

(*e*) The following terminations have the values shown:

-**age** = -ĭj (garbage)
-**ate** = -ĭt or -at (mandate)
-**cean, -cian, -sian, -tian** = shan (cetacean, musician, Prussian, Venetian)
-**ceous, -cious, -tious** = sh*u*s (siliceous, delicious, ambitious)
-**cial, -sial, -tial** = -sh*a*l (commercial, controversial, palatial)
-**ey** = -ĭ (donkey)
-**geous, -gious** = -j*u*s (gorgeous, religious)
-**igh, -ight, -ign** = -ī, -īt, -īn (sigh, fight, resign)

-**le** after consonant(s) = -*e*l (axle, buckle, eagle, kettle, muffle)
-**our** = -*e*r (clamour)
-**ous** = -*u*s (furious)
-**re** after consonants = -*e*r (centre, lucre, meagre)
-**sion** = -zh*o*n (division)
-**sion** after consonant(s) = -sh*o*n (passion, recension)
-**sm** = -zm (atheism, spasm)
-**tion** = -sh*o*n (salvation)
-**ture** = -ch*e*r as well as -tūr, esp. in common words.

ABBREVIATIONS

a., aa., adjective(s)
abbr., abbreviation
abs., absolute
acc., accusative
adj., adjj., adjective(s)
adv., advv., adverb(s)
advb., adverbial
Afr., African
alg., algebra
Amer., American
Amer.-Ind., American Indian
anat., anatomy
Anglo-Ind., Anglo-Indian
Anglo-Ir., Anglo-Irish
ant., antiquities
approx., approximately
arch., archaic
archaeol., archaeology
archit., architecture
astrol., astrology
astron., astronomy
attrib., attributive(ly)
Austral., Australian
bibl., biblical
biol., biology
bot., botany
c., cc., century, -ies
Camb., Cambridge
C.-Amer., Central American
Can., Canadian
Ch., Church

chem., chemistry
cine., cinema
collect., collective(ly)
colloq., colloquial
comb., combination, combining
commerc., commercial
comp., comparative
cond., conditional
conj., conjunction
contempt., contemptuous
contr., contraction
crick., cricket
cu., cubic
dem., demonstrative
derog., derogatory
dial., dialect
dist., distinguished
Du., Dutch
E., east(ern)
E.-Afr., East African
eccl., ecclesiastical
E.-Ind., East Indian
electr., electricity
emphat., emphatically
erron., erroneously
esp., especially
euphem., euphemism
Eur., European
exc., except
excl., exclamation
expr., expressing
F, French
fem., feminine

fig., figurative(ly)
footb., football
Fr., French
freq., frequently
ft., foot, feet
G., German
gal., gals., gallon(s)
G.B., Great Britain
geol., geology
geom., geometry
Ger., German
Gk., Greek
gram., grammar
gym., gymnastics
her., heraldry
hist., historical
imper., imperative
impers., impersonal
in., inch(es)
ind., indicative
inf., infinitive
int., interjection
interrog., interrogative(ly)
Ir., Irish
iron., ironically
It., Italian
joc., jocular(ly)
L, Latin
lb, pound(s)
log., logic
math., mathematics
mech., mechanics
med., medicine
metaphys., metaphysics

viii

meteor., meteorology
mil., military
min., mineralogy
mus., music
myth., mythology
n., *nn.*, noun(s)
N., north(ern)
N.-Amer., North American
nat. hist., natural history
naut., nautical
nav., naval
neg., negative
n. fem., noun feminine
north., northern
n. pl., noun plural
N.T., New Testament
N.Z., New Zealand
obj., objective
obs., obsolete
occas., occasionally
opp., (as) opposed to
opt., optics
orig., originally
O.T., Old Testament
P., proprietary (see p. iii)
paint., painting
parl., parliament(ary)
part., participle
pass., passive
path., pathology
pers., person
philos., philosophy
phonet., phonetics
phot., photography
phr., phrr., phrase(s)
phys., physics
physiol., physiology
pl., plural
poet., poetic
pol., politics

pol. econ., political economy
pop., popular
poss., possessive
p.p., past participle
pr., pronounced
pred. a., predicative adjective
pref., prefix
prep., *prepp.*, prepositions
pres., present
pres. p., present participle
print., printing
pron., pronoun
prop., proper(ly)
pros., prosody
Ps., Psalm
psycho-anal., psycho-analysis
psychol., psychology
p.t., past tense
R.A.F., Royal Air Force
R.C. (Ch.), Roman Catholic (Church)
ref., reference
refl., reflexive
rel., relative
repr., representing
rhet., rhetoric
Rom., Roman
Rom. ant., Roman antiquities
s., singular
S., south(ern)
S.-Afr., South African
S.-Amer., South American
Sc., Scottish
Scand., Scandinavian
sch. sl., school slang
sculp., sculpture

SE., south-east
sent., sentence
S.-Eur., southern European
sing., singular
Skr., Sanskrit
sl., slang
Sp., Spanish
Sp.-Amer., Spanish American
sq., square
st., stone(s)
St. Exch., Stock Exchange
subj., subjective, subjunctive
sup., superlative
surg., surgery
theatr., theatrical
theol., theology
trans., transitive
transf., in transferred sense
typ., typography
univ., university
U.S., United States
usu., usually
v., *vv.*, verb(s)
var., variant
v.aux., verb auxiliary
vb., vbl., verb(al)
v.i., verb intransitive
v.impers., verb impersonal
voc., vocative(ly)
v.refl., verb reflexive
v.t., verb transitive
vulg., vulgar
W., west(ern)
W.-Afr., West African
W.-Ind., West Indian
yd., yds., yard(s)
zool., zoology

SPECIAL SIGNS

~ : see above, p. iii   **P.** = proprietary term (see p. iii)

CONTENTS

CONTENTS

A

A¹ (ā), (mus.) 6th note in scale of C major.

a², an¹ (*a, an*; emphat. ā, ăn) *a.* one, some, any; each.

a³ *prep.* on, to, in (now chiefly pref. in *abed, afoot,* etc.).

A. *abbr.* adult; alto; answer; *avancer* [F], accelerate.

A.A. *abbr.* anti-aircraft; Automobile Association.

A.A.A. *abbr.* Amateur Athletic Assoc.

A.A.A.S. *abbr.* American Association for Advancement of Science.

aard'vark (ārd-) *n.* S.-Afr. quadruped between armadillos and ant-eaters.

Aar'on's beard, rod (ār-) *nn.* kinds of plant.

A.A.U. *abbr.* Amateur Athletic Union. (U.S.)

A.B. *abbr.* able-bodied seaman.

abăck' *adv.* backwards, behind; *taken* ~, disconcerted, surprised.

ăb'acus *n.* (pl. -cī), frame used for calculating; (archit.) upper member of capital supporting architrave.

abaft' (-ah-) *adv.* in stern of ship. *prep.* nearer stern than.

abăn'don *v.t.* give up; desert. *n.* careless freedom. ~ed *a.* profligate. ~ment *n.*

abăndonee' *n.* underwriter to whom salvage of wreck is abandoned.

abāse' *v.t.* humiliate, lower, degrade. ~ment *n.*

abăsh' *v.t.* put out of countenance. ~ed *a.*; ~ment *n.*

abāte' *v.* diminish, make or become less; (law) put an end to, quash. ~ment *n.*

ăb'atis *n.* defence made of felled trees.

ăb'attoir (-twār) *n.* slaughter-house.

Abb'a (ă-) *n.* Father.

ăbb'acў *n.* office of abbot.

abbé (ăb'ā) *n.* French ecclesiastic.

ăbb'ess *n.* head of nunnery.

ăbb'ey *n.* (pl. -*eys*), body of monks or nuns; monastic buildings; church of abbey.

ăbb'ot *n.* head of abbey.

abbrē'viate *v.t.* shorten. ~ā'tion *n.*

ABC (ā'bē'sē') *n.* alphabet; rudiments; alphabetical railway guide.

ăb'dĭcāte *v.* renounce formally or by default; renounce throne etc. ~ā'tion *n.*

ăbdō'men (*or* ăb'-) *n.* belly; hinder part of insect etc. **ăbdŏm'inal** *a.*

abdŭct' *v.t.* carry off illegally; (of muscle etc.) draw from normal position. **abdŭc'tion,** ~**or** *nn.*

abeam' *adv.* on line at right angles to ship's length.

abēle' *n.* white poplar.

Aberdeen' (ă-). ~ **Ang'us** (ăngg-), breed of beef cattle. ~ **terrier,** Scotch terrier.

ăberdevine' *n.* siskin.

ăberrā'tion *n.* wandering; straying; (astron.) apparent displacement of heavenly body; (opt.) non-convergence of rays to one focus.

abĕt' *v.t.* countenance or assist. ~ment, ~tor *nn.*

abey'ance (-bā-) *n.* suspension, temporary disuse.

ăb ĕx'tra, from outside. [L]

abhor' *v.t.* regard with disgust and hatred, detest. **abhŏ'rrence** *n.*; **abhŏ'rrent** *a.*

abīde' *v.* (*abōde*), dwell; remain, continue; submit to; bear. **abī'dance** *n.*; **abī'ding** *a.*

ăb'igail *n.* lady's-maid.

abĭl'itў *n.* power or capacity (*to* do); cleverness, talent.

ăb inĭt'iō, from the beginning. [L]

ăbiōgĕn'esis *n.* spontaneous generation.

ăb'jĕct *a.* craven, degraded. *n.* abject person. **abjĕc'tion** *n.*

abjure' (-joor) *v.t.* renounce on oath. **abjurā'tion** *n.*

abl. *abbr.* ablative.

ăb'lative *a. & n.* (case) expressing source, agent, etc.

ăb'laut (-owt) *n.* vowel-change in related words.

ablāze' *adv. & pred. a.* on fire; excited; glittering.

ā'ble *a.* having power or ability (*to* do); talented. **~-bodied**, robust; skilled. **ā'blў** *adv.*

ablu'tion (-loo-) *n.* ceremonial or (pl.) ordinary personal washing; (pl.) military building or part of ship used for toilet.

ăb'nĕgāte *v.t.* deny oneself; renounce. **~ā'tion** *n.*

abnôr'mal *a.* exceptional, deviating from type. **~ăl'itў** *n.*

aboard' (-ôrd) *adv. & prep.* on board.

abōde'[1] *n.* dwelling-place.

abode[2], *p.t. & p.p.* of **abide**.

abŏl'ĭsh *v.t.* do away with. **~ment** *n.*

ăboli'tion *n.* abolishing, esp. of Negro slavery. **~ism, ~ist** *nn.*

A-bomb *abb.* atomic bomb.

abŏm'inable *a.* detestable, revolting.

abŏm'ināte *v.t.* loathe, detest. **~ā'tion** *n.* (object etc. deserving) loathing or disgust.

ăbori'ginal *a.* indigenous, existing at dawn of history. *n.* aboriginal inhabitant, plant, etc.

ăbori'ginēs (-z) *n.pl.* aboriginal inhabitants.

abôrt' *v.i.* miscarry; become sterile, remain undeveloped.

abôr'tion *n.* premature expulsion of foetus, procuring of this; dwarfed or misshapen creature. **~ist** *n.* one who procures abortion.

abôr'tive *a.* premature; fruitless.

abound' *v.i.* be plentiful; be rich *in*; teem *with*.

about' *adv. & prep.* all round; somewhere round, here and there; astir; approximately; facing round; in connexion with, concerning.

above' (-ŭv) *adv.* higher up, overhead, up stream; in addition. *prep.* over, higher than; more than; of higher rank etc. than. **~-board**, without concealment.

Abp. *abbr.* Archbishop.

ăbracadăb'ra *n.* cabalistic word used as spell; gibberish.

abrāde' *v.t.* scrape off, injure, by rubbing.

abrā'sion *n.* rubbing or scraping (off); wound made by this.

abrā'sive *a.* causing abrasion. *n.* abrasive substance.

abreast' (-ĕst) *adv.* on a level and facing same way; **~** *of*, not behind.

abridge' *v.t.* condense, shorten; curtail. **~ment** *n.*

abroad' (-awd) *adv.* widely, in different directions; out of one's country.

ăb'rogāte *v.t.* repeal, cancel. **~ā'tion** *n.*

abrŭpt' *a.* sudden, hasty; disconnected; steep.

A.B.S. *abbr.* American Bible Society.

abs. *abbr.* absolute.

ăb'scess (-sĕs) *n.* collection of pus in cavity of body.

abscŏnd' *v.i.* go away secretly, fly from law.

ăb'sence *n.* being away; non-existence; abstracted state.

ăb'sent[1] *a.* not present; not existing; abstracted in mind. **~ly** *adv.*

absĕnt'[2] *v. refl.* go or keep away.

ăbsentee' *n.* person not present, esp. at work or on his property. **~ism** *n.* (esp.) habitual absence from work.

ăb'sinth *n.* (liqueur flavoured with) wormwood.

ăb'sit ō'mĕn! may suggested foreboding not be realized. [L]

ăb'solūte (*or* -oot) *a.* complete, pure, perfect; unrestricted; despotic, ruling arbitrarily; not in (usual) grammatical relation with other words; real, unqualified, self-existent. **~ alcohol**, containing at least 99% pure alcohol. **~ pitch**, ability to remember pitch of notes. **~ temperature**, measured on centigrade scale with zero at absolute zero. **~ zero**, temperature at which all substances have lost all available heat ($-273°$ C). **~lў** *adv.* (esp., colloq.) quite so, yes.

ăbsolū'tion (*or* -oo-) *n.* forgiveness, esp. ecclesiastical declaration of remission of sins.

ăb′solūtism (or -ōot-) n. principle of absolute government. ~tist n. & a.

absŏlve′ v.t. set or pronounce free of guilt or blame.

absŏrb′ v.t. swallow up; assimilate; suck in; engross attention of.

absŏr′bent a. tending to absorb. n. absorbent substance.

absōrp′tion n. absorbing, being absorbed. ~tive a.; ~tiv′ity n.

abstain′ v.i. refrain, esp. from alcohol. ~er n.

abstē′mious a. sparing or moderate in food, drink, etc.

abstĕn′tion n. refraining, holding back.

abstĕr′gent a. cleansing. n. cleansing substance. abstĕr′sion n.

ăb′stinence n. refraining from food, pleasure, etc.; total ~, abstaining from alcohol. ăb′stinent a.

ăb′străct[1] a. not concrete; ideal, theoretical. n. essence, summary.

abstrăct′[2] v.t. take away; steal; summarize. ~ed a. withdrawn in thought.

abstrăc′tion n. withdrawal; stealing; abstractedness.

abstruse′ (-ōos) a. hard to understand; profound.

absŭrd′ a. unreasonable, ridiculous. ~ity n.

abŭn′dance n. plenty, more than enough; affluence, wealth.

abŭn′dant a. plentiful, rich.

abūse′ (-z) v.t. make bad use of; revile. n. (-s), misuse; corrupt practice; reviling.

abū′sive a. insulting, using bad language. ~ness n.

abŭt′ v. border upon; touch upon, lean against. abŭtt′er n. owner of adjoining property.

abŭt′ment n. support from which arch etc. springs.

abȳ(e)′ v.t. (arch.) pay penalty of.

abȳsm′ (arch.), abȳss′ nn. bowels of earth; bottomless or deep chasm. abȳs′mal (-z-) a. bottomless. abȳss′al a. of or living at more than 300 fathoms below sea-surface.

A.C. abbr. Alpine Club; alternating current; ante Christum [L], before Christ.

acā′cia (-sha) n. kinds of tree some of which yield gum arabic.

ăcadĕm′ic a. of academy; scholarly; abstract, unpractical. n. member of university; (pl.) academic arguments. ~al a. of college or university; n.pl. college costume.

acădĕmī′cian n. member of academy, esp. Royal Academy of Arts.

acăd′emȳ n. place of study; (pretentious) school; place of special training; society for cultivating art, learning, etc.

acăn′thus n. kinds of plant with ornamental leaves; (archit.) conventional acanthus leaf.

acc. abbr. account; accusative.

accēde′ (aks-) v.i. enter into office, come to throne; join party; assent.

accĕlerăn′dō (ăks-) adv. (mus.) with gradually increasing pace. a. & n. (passage) so performed. [It.]

accĕl′erāte (aks-) v. increase speed, increase speed of; cause to happen earlier. ~ā′tion n. ~ātor n. thing that increases speed, esp. device opening car's throttle.

ac′cent (ăks-) n. prominence given to syllable by stress or pitch; mark indicating stress, vowel quality, etc.; national or other peculiar mode of pronunciation; (pl.) speech; rhythmical stress. v.t. (-ĕnt′), pronounce with accent upon; mark with accents; emphasize, dwell on. accĕn′tūal a.; accĕn′tūāte v.t.; ~ūā′tion n.

accĕpt′ (aks-) v. consent to receive (gift etc.); answer affirmatively (offer etc.); receive as true; agree to meet (bill); express acceptance. ~able a. worth accepting, welcome. ~abil′ity n. ~ance n. accepting or being accepted; accepted bill. ~ā′tion n. sense in which word is used. ~or n. one who accepts bill.

ac′cĕss (ăks-) n. admission, approach; attack (of illness etc.) accĕss′ible a. able to be reached. ~ibil′ity n.

accĕss′arȳ (aks-) n. helper in, one privy to, (esp. criminal) act.

accession (aksĕ′shn) n. acceding esp. to throne; addition.

accĕss′orȳ (aks-) a. additional, extra. n. accessory thing, accompaniment.

ac′cidence (ăks-) *n*. part of grammar dealing with inflexions.

ac′cident (ăks-) *n*. event without apparent cause; unexpected event; unintentional act; mishap; attribute, non-essential quality or property. ~děn′tal *a*.; ~děn′tally *adv*. ~děn′tal *n*. (mus.) sharp, flat, or natural not in key signature.

acclaim′ *v.t.* welcome loudly; hail. *n*. shout of applause.

ăcclamā′tion *n*. loud and eager assent; (pl.) shouting.

ăcc′limāte (U.S.), accli′matize *vv.t.* habituate to new climate. acclimā′tion, acclimatizā′tion *nn*.

accliv′ity *n*. upward slope.

ăcc′olāde (*or* -ahd) *n*. ceremony of conferring knighthood; (mus.) vertical line or brace coupling staves.

accŏmm′odāte *v.t.* adapt, harmonize; reconcile; find lodging for. ~āting *a*. obliging.

accŏmmodā′tion *n*. adaptation, adjustment; convenience; lodging; loan. ~ address, to which letters etc. may be sent for person not living there. ~ ladder, up ship's side for entering or leaving small boat.

accom′pany (-ŭm-) *v.t.* go with, escort, attend; (mus.) support by performing subsidiary part. ~niment *n*. accompanying thing; (mus.) subsidiary part. ~nist *n*.

accŏm′plice (*or* -ŭm-) *n*. partner in crime or guilt.

accŏm′plish (*or* -ŭm-) *v.t.* perform, carry out, succeed in doing. ~ment *n*. achievement, fulfilment; (pl.) social attainments.

accŏrd′ *v.* agree, be consistent, *with*; grant, give. *n*. consent; harmony, agreement. ~ance *n*.; ~ant *a*.

accŏr′ding *adv.* ~ as, in proportion as. ~ to, in manner consistent with; on authority or in opinion of.

accŏr′dingly *adv.* in accordance with what preceded; therefore.

accŏr′dion *n*. portable musical instrument with bellows, keys, and metal reeds.

accŏst′ *v.t.* approach and speak to; solicit.

account′ *v.* regard as; ~ *for*, give reckoning for, answer for, explain.

n. reckoning; statement of money received and paid; explanation; ground; reason; narration; *on* ~, in part payment.

accoun′table *a*. responsible, liable: explicable. ~abil′ity *n*.

accoun′tancy *n*. profession, duties, of accountant. accoun′tant *n*. keeper or inspector of accounts.

accou′trements (-ōōt-) *n.pl.* equipment, trappings. accou′tred (-ōōterd) *a*. equipped, attired.

accrĕd′it *v.t.* send out with credentials.

accrē′tion *n*. growth, esp. by external addition; adhesion; extraneous addition.

accrue′ (-ōō) *v.i.* fall *to*, arise, as natural increase or result.

accū′mūlāte *v.* heap up, acquire in increasing amounts; grow numerous, go on increasing. ~ā′tion *n*.; ~ative *a*.

accū′mūlātor *n*. apparatus for storing electricity.

ăcc′ūrate *a*. precise, exact, correct. ăcc′ūracy *n*.

accūr′sed *a*. detestable, annoying; (also *accurst*) lying under curse.

accū′sative (-z-) *a. & n.* (gram.) (case) used to indicate goal of motion or object of action.

accūse′ (-z) *v.t.* indict, charge; lay blame on. ~sā′tion *n*.; ~satory *a*.

accŭs′tom *v.t.* habituate. ~ed *a*.

āce *n*. one on dice, cards, etc.; one point at racquets etc.; (tennis) service that beats opponent; distinguished airman, player, etc.

acer′bity *n*. bitterness of speech, temper, etc.; sourness, harsh taste.

ă′cetāte *n*. salt of acetic acid, esp. cellulose acetate, used for textile fibre etc.

acē′tic (*or* -ĕt-) *a*. of vinegar, sour. ~ acid, acid contained in vinegar.

acĕt′ify *v.* turn into vinegar, make or become sour. ~ficā′tion *n*.

acĕt′ylēne *n*. colourless gas burning with bright flame.

Achates (akā′tēz) *n*. faithful friend.

ache (āk) *v.i. & n.* (suffer) continuous or prolonged pain or longing.

achieve′ *v.t.* accomplish, perform; attain, acquire, reach. ~ment *n*. feat achieved; escutcheon, hatchment.

achromă'tĭc (ăk-) *a*. free from colour; transmitting light without decomposing it. **achrō'matĭsm** *n*. achromatic quality. **achrō'matīze** *v.t.* make achromatic.

ă'cĭd *a*. sour, sharp; of acid(s). *n*. (chem.) any of class of compounds of other elements with hydrogen, most of which are sour. ~ **test**, (esp., fig.) severe or conclusive test. **acĭd'ĭfў** *v*.; **~ificā'tion, acĭd'itў** *nn*.

ăcĭdō'sĭs *n*. (med.) reduced alkalinity of blood etc.

acĭd'ūlous *a*. somewhat acid. **acĭd'ūlātĕd** *a*. made acidulous.

acknowledge (aknŏl'ĭj) *v.t.* admit truth of, admit, own; announce receipt of (letter etc.); express appreciation of (services etc.). **acknow'ledg(e)ment** *n*. acknowledging; thing given or done in return for service etc.

aclĭn'ĭc līne *n*. magnetic equator, on which magnetic needle has no dip.

ăc'mĕ *n*. highest point.

ăc'nĕ *n*. skin eruption with red pimples esp. on face.

ăc'olўte *n*. inferior officer in church attending priest.

ăc'onīte *n*. (dried poisonous root of) kinds of plant including monk's--hood.

ā'cōrn *n*. fruit of oak. **~-shell**, cirriped allied to barnacles.

acŏtўlē'don *n*. plant with no distinct cotyledons. **~ous** *a*.

acou'stĭc (-ōō- *or* -ow-) *a*. of sound; of acoustics. **~al** *a*.

acou'stĭcs (-ōō- *or* -ow-) *n*. science of sound; properties of room etc. in respect of audibility of sounds.

acquaint' *v.t.* make aware or familiar; inform; **~ed with**, having personal knowledge of.

acquain'tance *n*. being acquainted; person one knows but not intimately. **~ship** *n*.

ăcquĭĕsce' *v.i.* agree, esp. tacitly; not object. **~cence** *n*.; **~cent** *a*.

acquīre' *v.t.* gain, get, come to have. **~d** *a*. not inherited; not innate. **~ment** *n*.

ăcquĭsĭ'tion (-z-) *n*. thing acquired; useful addition. **ăcquĭs'ĭtĭve** *a*. desirous of or given to acquiring.

acquĭt' *v.t.* declare not guilty, free *of* blame etc.; **~ oneself**, perform one's part. **acquĭtt'al** *n*. deliverance from charge by verdict etc. **acquĭtt'ance** *n*. payment of or release from debt; receipt in full.

ā'cre *n*. measure of land (4,840 sq. yds); (pl.) lands, fields. **~age** *n*. (ā'kerĭj) *n*. number of acres.

ăc'rĭd *a*. bitterly pungent; of bitter temper etc. **acrĭd'itў** *n*.

ăc'rĭmonў *n*. bitterness of temper or manner. **ăcrĭmō'nĭous** *a*.

ăc'robăt *n*. performer of spectacular gymnastic feats. **ăcrobăt'ĭc** *a*.

ăc'ronўm *n*. word made from syllables or initial letters of other words.

acrŏp'olĭs *n*. citadel or elevated part of Greek city, esp. Athens.

acrŏss' *prep. & adv.* from side to side (of), to or on other side (of); across one another.

acrŏs'tĭc *n*. poem etc. in which first or first and last letters of lines form word(s).

ăct *n*. thing done, deed; decree of legislative body; main division of play; item in variety or circus programme. *v*. perform, play part (of), be actor; do things, perform functions; take action; serve *as*.

ăc'tĭnĭsm *n*. property of radiant energy that produces chemical changes, as in photography. **actĭn'ĭc** *a*.

ăctĭn'ĭum *n*. radioactive metallic element.

ăc'tion *n*. doing, working, exertion of energy; thing done; mode or style of movement of horse, machine, batsman, etc.; mechanism of instrument; legal process; battle; **take ~**, begin legal process, take steps, begin to act. **~able** *a*. affording grounds for legal action.

ăc'tĭvāte *v.t.* make (radio-)active; aerate (sewage).

ăc'tĭve *a*. working, acting, operative; consisting in or marked by action; energetic, diligent. **~ voice**, (gram.) all forms of intr. and those forms of trans. verbs attributing verbal action to person etc. whence it proceeds.

ăctĭv'itў *n*. being active; sphere or kind of operation.

ăc′tor *n.* dramatic performer; doer. ăc′trĕss *n.*

ăc′tūal *a.* existing, real; present, current. ăctūăl′itў *n.* ~ly *adv.* in actual fact, really; as a matter of fact.

ăc′tūарў *n.* insurance expert calculating risks and premiums. ăctūār′ial *a.*

ăc′tūāte *v.t.* serve as motive to; communicate motion to. ~ā′tion *n.*

acū′itў *n.* sharpness, acuteness.

acū′mĕn *n.* keen perception, penetration.

ăc′ūpŭncture *n.* (med.) puncture of tissues with needles as treatment for rheumatism etc.

acūte′ *a.* sharp, keen, penetrating; clever; (of disease) coming sharply to crisis, not chronic; (of angle) less than right angle. ~ accent, the accent ′.

ăd *n.* (colloq.) advertisement.

A.D. *abbr. anno Domini* [L], in the year of our Lord.

ăd′age *n.* proverb, saw.

adagio (adah′jyō) *adv.* and *a.* (mus.) slow(ly). *n.* slow movement. [It.]

Ad′ăm (ă-) *n.* first man. ~′s apple, cartilaginous projection of throat.

ăd′amant *n.* & *a.* impenetrably hard (substance), unyielding (person). ădamăn′tīne *a.*

adăpt′ *v.t.* suit, fit; modify, alter. ~able *a.* (esp.) able to adapt oneself to new surroundings etc. ~abil′itў, ădaptā′tion, ~or *nn.*

A.D.C. *abbr.* aide-de-camp; Amateur Dramatic Club.

ădd *v.* join by way of increase or supplement; ~ *together*, ~ *up*, find sum of, amount *to.*

addĕn′dum *n.* (pl. -da), something to be added, appendix.

ădd′er *n.* small venomous snake.

ădd′ĭct *n.* one addicted to drug etc. addĭc′tĕd *a.* devoted *to* or enslaved by drug etc. addĭc′tion *n.*

addĭ′tion *n.* adding; thing added. ~al *a.* added, extra.

ădd′ĭtive *n.* & *a.* (substance) added to impart specific qualities to mixture etc.

ădd′le *v.* make or grow addled. ~-headed, ~-pated, confused in mind. ~d *a.* (of egg) rotten, producing no chick; muddled, crazy.

addrĕss′ *v.t.* speak or write to; direct in speech or writing; write directions for delivery on (envelope etc.); apply (one*self*). *n.* speech delivered to audience; manner, bearing; superscription of letter etc.; place of residence; (pl.) courtship. ~ee′ *n.* person to whom letter etc. is addressed.

addūce′ *v.t.* (-*cible*), cite as proof or instance.

addŭct′ *v.t.* (of muscles) draw to common centre. ~tion, ~tor *nn.*

ăd′enoids (-z) *n.pl.* spongy tissue at back of nose, often hindering breathing.

ăd′ĕpt (*or* -ĕpt′) *a.* thoroughly proficient. *n.* adept person.

ăd′ĕquate *a.* sufficient, such as meets need. ~acў *n.*

à deux (ah dẽr′), for two. [F]

ad fin. abbr. ad finem [L], towards the end.

adhēre′ (-h-) *v.i.* stick fast; give support or allegiance *to.* adhēr′ence *n.*; ~ent *a.* & *n.*

adhē′sion *n.* adhering, sticking. adhē′sive *a.* sticking, sticky; *n.* adhesive substance.

ăd hŏc, for this purpose. [L]

ădiăn′tum *n.* kinds of fern, esp. black maidenhair.

adieu (adū′) *int.* & *n.* good-bye.

ăd infīnī′tum, for ever. [L]

ad init. abbr. ad initium [L], at the beginning.

ăd in′terim, for the meantime. [L]

ăd′ipōse *a.* of fat, fatty. ădipŏs′itў *n.*

ăd′ĭt *n.* horizontal entrance to or passage in mine.

adj. *abbr.* adjective.

Adjt. *abbr.* Adjutant.

adjā′cent *a.* lying near *to*, contiguous. ~encў *n.*

ădj′ĕctive *n.* name of attribute added to name of thing to describe it more fully. *a.* additional, not standing by itself. ~ī′val *a.*

adjoin′ *v.t.* be adjacent to.

adjourn (ajẽrn′) *v.* break off till another time; suspend; move *to* another place.

adjŭdge′ *v.t.* pronounce or award judicially.

adju′dĭcāte (ajoo-) *v.* try and determine judicially; act as judge. ~ā'tion, ~ātor *nn*.

ădj'ŭnct *n*. subordinate or incidental thing, accompaniment; (gram.) amplification of predicate, subject, etc.

adjure (*a*joor') *v.t.* charge or request solemnly or earnestly. ~rā'tion *n*.

adjŭst' *v.t.* arrange, put in order; harmonize; adapt. ~ment *n*.

ădj'utant (-ōō-) *n*. officer assisting superior by communicating orders, conducting correspondence, etc.; large Indian stork. ~ancў *n*.

ăd-lĭb' *v.* (colloq.) improvise. *a*. improvised.

ăd lĭb.(*ĭtum*), to desired extent or amount. [L].

Adm. *abbr.* Admiral; Admiralty.

admĭn'ĭster *v.t.* manage (affairs etc.); dispense; apply, give. ~trā'tion *n*. administering; management (esp. of public affairs); executive part of legislature; Government. ~tratīve *a*.; ~trātor *n*.

ăd'mirable *a*. worthy of admiration; excellent.

ăd'miral *n*. (hist.) commander-in-chief of navy; naval officer commanding fleet or squadron; ship carrying admiral; commander of fishing or merchant fleet; *red* ~, *white* ~, kinds of butterfly.

ăd'miraltў *n*. office of admiral; *the* (*Lords Commissioners of*) *A*~, branch of executive superintending navy; (rhet.) command of seas.

admīre' *v.t.* approve warmly of; look with wonder and pleasure at; (colloq.) compliment person on. ădmirā'tion *n*. admīr'er *n*. one who admires; lover.

admĭss'ible *a*. capable of being admitted or allowed. ~bĭl'itў *n*.

admĭ'ssion *n*. admitting, being admitted; acknowledgement of error etc.

admĭt' *v.* let in, allow entrance of; accept as valid or true; acknowledge, confess; ~ *of*, lie open to. admĭtt'ance *n*.; ~tĕdly *adv*.

admĭx' *v.t.* add as ingredient, mix *with*. ~ture *n*.

admŏn'ĭsh *v.t.* exhort, warn, remind; reprove. ~ment *n*.

ădmoni'tion *n*. warning; reproof. admŏn'ĭtorў *a*.

ăd nau'sĕăm, to disgusting extent. [L]

ado (adōō') *n*. fuss; difficulty.

adō'bĕ (*or* -ōb) *n*. unburnt brick sun--dried.

ădolĕs'cent *a*. between childhood and manhood or womanhood. *n*. adolescent person. ~ence *n*.

Adō'nĭs *n*. beautiful youth.

adŏpt' *v.t.* take into relationship, esp. as one's own child; take over; accept; take up, choose. ~īve *a*. adopted, by adoption.

adōr'able *a*. worthy of love; (colloq.) charming, delightful.

ădorā'tion *n*. homage; worship.

adōre' *v.t.* regard with deep respect and affection; worship; pay divine honours to; like very much. ~r *n*. (esp.) admirer, lover.

adōrn' *v.t.* add beauty or lustre to, furnish with ornaments.

ăd rĕm, to the purpose. [L]

adrē'nal *a*. at or near kidney. ~ glands, two ductless glands on upper surface of kidneys. adrĕn'alin *n*. hormone secreted by adrenal glands.

adrĭft' *adv.* drifting; at mercy of wind and tide or of circumstances; loose.

adroit' *a*. dexterous, skilful.

ădscĭtĭ'tious *a*. added from without; supplemental.

ăd'sŭm, I am here. [L]

ăd'ūlāte *v.t.* flatter basely. ~ā'tion *n*.: ~ā'tory *a*.

ăd'ult (*or* -ŭlt') *a*. grown up; mature. *n*. grown-up person.

adŭl'terāte[1] *v.t.* falsify by mixing with baser ingredients. ~ant *a*. & *n*. (substance) used in adulterating. ~ā'tion *n*.

adŭl'terate[2] *a*. spurious, counterfeit; stained by, born of, adultery.

adŭl'terў *n*. sexual intercourse of man with woman not his wife, either or both being married. adŭl'terer, ~eress *nn*. ~erīne (*or* -ĭn) *a*. of adultery. ~erous *a*.

ăd'umbrāte *v.t.* sketch in outline; indicate faintly; foreshadow. ~ā'tion *n*.

adŭst' *a*. parched; scorched.

adv. *abbr.* adverb.

ăd valōr'ĕm, in proportion to (estimated) value of goods. [L]

advance' (-vah-) *v.* move or put forward; help on; make (claim etc.); hasten (event); lend (money); raise (price); rise (in price). *n.* going forward; progress; overture; rise in price; loan; *in ~*, in front, ahead, beforehand. **~d** *a.* ahead of times, others, etc.; far on in progress. **~ment** *n.*

advan'tage (-vah-) *n.* better position, superiority; favouring circumstance; (tennis) next point won after deuce. *v.t.* be advantage to; help, profit.

ădvantā'geous *a.* giving advantage; beneficial.

ăd'vent *n.* coming of esp. important person or thing; *A~*, season including four Sundays immediately before Christmas; coming of Christ. **Ad'ventist** *a. & n.* (member) of sect believing in imminent second coming of Christ.

ădventi'tious *a.* accidental, casual.

advĕn'ture *n.* unexpected or exciting experience; daring enterprise. *v.* risk; venture.

advĕn'turer *n.* one who seeks adventures; one who lives by his wits. **~ėss** *n.*

advĕn'turous *a.* venturesome, enterprising.

ăd'vĕrb *n.* word qualifying adjective, verb, or other adverb. **advĕr'bial** *a.*

ăd'versarў *n.* antagonist, enemy.

ăd'vĕrse *a.* opposed, hostile. **advĕr'sative** *a.* (of word) expressing opposition.

advĕr'sitў *n.* trouble; misfortune.

advĕrt'[1] *v.i.* refer or allude *to*.

ăd'vert[2] *n.* (colloq.) advertisement.

ăd'vertīse (-z) *v.* make generally or publicly known; proclaim merits of, esp. to encourage sales; ask *for* by public notice. **advĕr'tisement** *n.*

advīce' *n.* opinion given as to action; information, notice.

advī'sable (-z-) *a.* expedient, judicious. **~bĭl'itў** *n.*

advīse' (-z) *v.* give advice to; recommend; take counsel *with*; notify. **advī'ser** *n.* counsellor, esp. person habitually consulted.

advīsed' (-zd) *a.* deliberate; judicious. **advī'sėdly** *adv.*

advī'sorў (-z-) *a.* giving advice.

ăd'vocate *n.* one who pleads for another; professional pleader; one who supports or speaks in favour of policy etc. **ăd'vocāte** *v.t.* plead for or support (policy etc.). **ăd'vocacў** *n.* advocate's function; pleading in support *of*.

advow'son (-z-) *n.* right of presentation to benefice.

advt. *abbr.* advertisement.

ăd'ўtum *n.* (pl. *-ta*), innermost part of temple; sanctum.

ădze *n.* axe-like tool with arched blade at right angles to handle.

ae'dīle *n.* Roman magistrate superintending public works etc.

ae'gĭs *n.* shield of Zeus or Athene; protection, impregnable defence.

aegrō'tăt (*or* ē'-) *n.* (degree awarded on) certificate that candidate is ill.

Aen. *abbr.* Aeneid.

Aeō'lĭan *a.* of Aeolus, god of winds. *~ harp*, instrument producing musical sounds in current of air.

ae'on, ē'on *n.* immense period.

ā'erāte (*or* ār-) *v.t.* expose to action of air; charge with carbon dioxide. **~ā'tion** *n.*

aer'ĭal (ār-) *a.* of air, gaseous; ethereal; existing in air. *n.* wire(s) or rod(s) transmitting or receiving radio waves.

aerie, aery (ār'ĭ *or* ēr'ĭ) *n.* nest of bird (esp. eagle) that builds high; house etc. perched high up.

ā'erifórm *a.* gaseous; insubstantial.

aer'o- (ār- *or* āer-) in comb., air-, of aircraft. **aerobăt'ics** *n.pl.* feats of expert and spectacular flying. **~drōme** *n.* taking-off and landing ground for aircraft, with auxiliary buildings etc. **~foil** *n.* any lifting surface in aircraft. **~līte, -lĭth** *n.* meteorite. **~sŏl** *n.* system of minute particles suspended in gas; device for producing fine spray.

aerodўnăm'ics (ār-) *n.pl.* dynamics of solid bodies in motion in air. **~mic** *a.*

aeronau'tics (ār-) *n.pl.* science or practice of flying. **~ical** *a.*

aer'oplāne (ār-) *n.* heavier-than-air aircraft with wings.

Aes. *abbr.* Aesop.

Aesch. *abbr.* Aeschylus.

Aescŭlā′pĭus *n.* god of medicine; physician.

aes′thēte *n.* professed lover of beauty.

aesthĕt′ĭc *a.* of appreciation of beauty. ~**ĭsm,** ~**s** *nn.*

aet., aetat., aetā′tis, of or at age of. [L]

aetĭŏl′ogÿ *n.* assignment of cause; science of causes of disease. **aetiolŏ′gĭcal** *a.*

A.E.U. *abbr.* Amalgamated Engineering Union.

A.F., a.f. *abbr.* audio-frequency.

afar′ *adv.* at or to a distance; *from* ~, from a distance.

A.F.C. *abbr.* Air Force Cross.

ăff′able *a.* easy of address, courteous. ~**bĭl′itÿ** *n.*

affair′ *n.* business, concern; temporary relationship between people in love; (colloq.) thing, happening.

affĕct′[1] *v.t.* pretend to have or feel or *to* do.

affĕct′[2] *v.t.* attack (as disease); move, touch; produce effect on. *n.* (ăf′-) feeling, emotion.

ăffĕctā′tion *n.* artificial manner; pretentious display.

affĕct′ĕd *a.* full of affectation.

affĕc′tion *n.* warm or kindly feeling (*for*), fondness, love; malady, disease. ~**ate** *a.* loving.

affī′ance *v.t.* promise in marriage.

ăffĭdā′vit *n.* written statement on oath.

affĭl′ĭāte *v.* adopt, attach *to*, connect *with*; become affiliated; fix paternity of (illegitimate child) for maintenance. ~**ā′tion** *n.*

affĭn′itÿ *n.* relationship; resemblance; attraction; (chem.) tendency of substances to react together.

affĭrm′ *v.* state as fact; make affirmation. **ăffĭrmā′tion** *n.* (esp.) declaration by one who conscientiously declines oath. ~**ative** *a.* affirming; *n.* affirmative word etc.; *in the* ~, yes.

affĭx′ *v.t.* fasten, append, attach. *n.* (ăf′-), thing affixed, addition; prefix or suffix.

afflā′tus *n.* inspiration.

afflict′ *v.t.* distress, trouble; cause mental or bodily suffering to.

afflĭc′tion *n.* thing that afflicts; distress, pain.

ăff′luence (-lŏŏ-) *n.* wealth, abundance.

ăff′luent (-lŏŏ-) *a.* rich, abundant. *n.* tributary stream.

ăff′lŭx *n.* flow towards point; accession.

affŏrd′ *v.t.* spare money for; manage to spare (time etc.); supply, furnish.

affŏ′rest *v.t.* convert into forest; plant with trees. ~**ā′tion** *n.*

affray′ *n.* breach of peace by fighting or riot.

affright′ (-īt) *v.t.* frighten. *n.* alarm, terror.

affront′ (-ŭnt) *v.t.* insult openly. *n.* open insult.

afield′ *adv.* on, in, or to field; away, at a distance.

afīre′ *a.* and *adv.* on fire.

A.F.L. *abbr.* American Federation of Labour.

aflāme′ *adv.* in flames; glowing.

afloat′ *adv.* floating; at sea; out of debt.

A.F.M. *abbr.* Air Force Medal.

afŏŏt′ *adv.* on foot, in progress.

afōre′ *adv.* & *prep.* before. ~**named,** ~**said,** previously named or mentioned. ~**thought,** premeditated.

ā fŏrtĭŏr′ī, with stronger reason. [L]

afraid′ *a.* in fear, feeling fear or dread; sorry to say or anticipate.

afrĕsh′ *adv.* with fresh start.

Afrĭkaans′ (ă-, -ahns) *n.* form of Dutch spoken in S. Africa.

Afrĭka′ner (ă-, -kah-) *n.* native of S. Africa of European (esp. Dutch) origin.

Af′rō (ă-) *a.* African.

aft (ahft) *adv.* in, near, to, or towards stern of ship.

af′ter (ah-) *adv.* behind; later. *prep.* behind; in pursuit or quest of; about, concerning; later than; according to; in imitation of. *conj.* after time at which. *a.* later, hinder. ~**birth,** placenta etc. extruded after birth. ~**-care,** care or attention after treatment etc. ~**crop,** second crop. ~**damp,** gas left in mine after fire-damp explosion. ~**glow,** glow in west after sunset. ~**math,** results, consequences. ~**-pains,** pains caused by uterine contractions after birth. ~thought, later expedient, explanation, etc.

af'termōst (ah-) *a.* furthest aft.

afternoon' *n.* time between noon and evening.

af'terwards (ah-, -z) *adv.* later, subsequently.

A.G. *abbr.* Adjutant-General.

again' (*or* -ĕn) *adv.* another time, once more; further, besides.

against' (*or* -ĕnst) *prep.* in opposition to; in contrast to; in anticipation of; in opposite direction to; into collision with.

agāpe' *adv. & pred. a.* gaping.

ā'gar(-ā'gar) *n.* gelatinous substance got from seaweeds and used in culture media for bacteria etc.

ăg'ate *n.* kinds of semi-pellucid variegated often banded semiprecious stone; (U.S.) size of type (5½-point).

agā'vē (*or* -āv) *n.* kinds of plant including American aloe.

āge *n.* length of life or existence; duration of life required for purpose; latter part of life; great period; (colloq.) long time. *v.* (cause to) grow old; show signs of age. ~**less** *a.* never growing old.

aged *a.* (ājd) of the age of; (of horses) over six years old; (ā'jĭd) old.

ā'gencў *n.* active operation, action; instrumentality; office of agent; business establishment.

agĕn'da *n.* items of business to be considered at meeting.

ā'gent *n.* person or thing producing effect; one acting for another in business, politics, etc.

agent provocateur (ah'zhahṅ prŏvŏkahtēr') *n.* person employed to detect suspected offenders by tempting them to overt action. [F]

agglŏm'erāte *v.* collect into mass. ~**ā'tion** *n.*; ~**ative** *a.*

agglu'tĭnāte (-loo-) *v.* unite as with glue; join (simple words) into compounds. ~**ā'tion** *n.*; ~**ative** *a.*

aggrăn'dīze *v.t.* increase power, rank, or wealth of. ~**ĭzement** *n.*

ăgg'ravāte *v.t.* increase gravity of; (colloq.) annoy. ~**ā'tion**, ~**ātor** *nn.*

ăgg'rėgate *a.* collected, total. *n.* whole collection, sum total; sand,

broken stone, etc. for concrete. *v.* (-gāt), collect together, unite. ~**ā'tion** *n.*; ~**ative** *a.*

aggrĕ'ssion *n.* unprovoked attack. **aggrĕss'ive** *a.*; **aggrĕss'or** *n.*

aggrieved' (-vd) *a.* injured, having grievance.

aghast (agahst') *a.* amazed and horrified.

ă'gīle *a.* quick-moving; nimble, active. **agĭl'itў** *n.*

ă'gīō *n.* (pl. -os), charge for changing paper-money into cash or one currency into another. ~**tage** *n.* exchange business.

ă'gĭtāte *v.* shake about; disturb, excite; stir up (public) disquiet and unrest. **ăgĭtā'tion**, ~**ātor** *nn.*

ăg'lĕt, ai'glĕt *n.* metal tag of lace; tag or spangle as ornament of dress.

ăg'nail *n.* torn skin at root of finger-nail, resulting soreness.

ăg'nāte *a.* descended from same male ancestor; of same clan or nation. *n.* agnate person etc.

ăgnō'mĕn *n.* additional name.

agnŏs'tĭc *n.* one who holds that nothing is known of existence of God or any but material phenomena. *a.* of or holding this theory. ~**ism** *n.*

Ag'nus Dē'ī (ă-) *n.* part of Mass.

agō' *adv.* in the past.

agŏg' *adv. & pred. a.* eager, expectant.

ăg'onīze *v.i.* suffer agony; make desperate efforts.

ăg'onў *n.* intense bodily or mental suffering; severe struggle. ~ **column**, of personal advertisements in newspaper etc.

ăgoraphō'bĭa *n.* morbid dread of open spaces.

agrār'ian *a.* relating to landed property; of cultivated land. *n.* advocate of redistribution of landed property. ~**ism** *n.*

agree' *v.* consent; concur; be in harmony or concord (*with*); settle etc. by agreement; ~ *with*, be beneficial to.

agree'able (-rĭa-) *a.* pleasing; well disposed; conformable.

agree'ment *n.* mutual understanding; legal contract; concord.

agrĕs'tĭc *a.* rural, rustic.

ăg′rĭcŭlture n. cultivation of the soil. ~cŭl′tural a.; ăgricŭl′tur(al)ist nn.

aground′ adv. & pred. a. on bottom of shallow water.

ā′gūe n. malarial fever with cold, hot, and sweating stages; fit of shivering.

ah int. expr. sorrow, surprise, entreaty, etc.

aha (a-hah′) int. expr. surprise, triumph, mockery, irony.

ahead (ahĕd′) adv. in advance, in front; forward.

ahoy (a-hoi′) int. (naut.) used in hailing.

A.I.(D.) abbr. artificial insemination (by donor).

aid v. help, assist, promote. n. help, helper; helpful thing.

aide n. aide-de-camp; assistant.

aide-de-camp (ā′dekahn′) n. (pl. aides-de-camp), officer assisting general by carrying orders etc.

ai′grĕtte (or -ĕt′) n. tuft of feathers or hair; spray of gems etc.

aiguille (ā′gwēl) n. sharp peak.

A.I.H. abbr. A. I. by husband.

ail v. trouble, afflict, in body or mind; ~ing, (slightly) ill. ~ment n.

ai′leron n. lateral-control hinged flap on trailing edge of aircraft wing.

aim v. direct or point (at); aim gun etc.; direct one's ambition etc. n. aiming; object aimed at; purpose. ~less a. purposeless.

air n. gaseous mixture of oxygen and nitrogen enveloping earth; atmosphere; open space; appearance; confident bearing; melody; (pl.) affected manners; on the ~, (in process of being) broadcast by radio-transmission; by ~, in or by aircraft. v.t. expose to air, ventilate; make known, show off. ~borne, (of troops) carried by aircraft; (of aircraft) having left ground. ~-brake, brake operated by compressed air. ~brick, perforated brick for ventilation. ~-conditioning, control of temperature, moisture, etc. of air in room etc. ~cooled, (of engine) cooled by current of air. ~drop, dropping of persons or supplies by parachute. ~ force, branch of armed forces using aircraft. ~ hostess, stewardess in aircraft. ~-lift, carriage of supplies etc. by air to area otherwise inaccessible. ~-liner, large passenger aircraft. ~-lock, stoppage of flow of liquid by air-bubble in tube etc.; airtight compartment in vessel etc. under pressure. ~plane, aeroplane. ~-raid, attack by aircraft. ~ship, lighter-than-air flying-machine; dirigible balloon. ~-speed, aircraft's speed relative to air through which it is moving. ~strip, strip of ground for taking off and landing aircraft. ~tight, impermeable to air.

air′craft (-ahft) n. aeroplanes, airships, and balloons; any one of these. ~-carrier, ship that carries and serves as base for aircraft.

Aire′dāle (terrier) n. large brown rough-coated terrier.

air′less a. stuffy; still, calm.

air′-līne n. line of passenger aircraft; tube supplying air to diver; (U.S.) direct line.

air′-mail n. mail carried by aircraft.

air′man n. aviator; member of air force.

air′pŏrt n. aerodrome for aircraft carrying passengers, goods, etc.

air′way n. ventilating passage in mine; route regularly followed by aircraft.

air′ў a. breezy; light, thin; sprightly.

aisle (īl) n. division of church parallel to nave, choir, or transept; passage between rows of pews; (U.S.) passage-way in building or train.

ait : see eyot.

aitch′-bōne n. rump-bone; cut of beef lying over this.

ajar′ adv. (of door etc.) slightly open.

akĭm′bō adv. (of arms) with hands on hips and elbows out.

akĭn′ pred. a. related; similar.

à la (ah lah), in manner of. [F]

Ala abbr. Alabama.

ăl′abaster (-bah-) n. kinds of translucent carbonate or sulphate of lime. a. of alabaster, resembling it in whiteness or smoothness.

à la cărte′ a. (of meals etc.) ordered by separate items.

alăck′ int. (arch.) expressing sorrow.

alăc′rity n. briskness, readiness.

à la mōde', in the fashion. [F]

alārm' *n.* call to arms, warning sound; warning; excited anticipation of danger. *v.t.* give alarm to; disturb, frighten. ~-clock, one that can be set to give warning sound at predetermined time. ~ist *n.* & *a.* (person) causing esp. unnecessary or excessive alarm.

ală'rum *n.* signal of alarm; alarm-clock.

alăs' (*or* -ahs) *int.* expressing grief.

ălb *n.* white vestment reaching to feet worn by priests etc.

ăl'bacōre *n.* large sea-fish of tunny kind.

Alban. *abbr.* (Bishop) of St. Albans.

ăl'batrŏss *n.* kinds of long-winged oceanic bird allied to petrel.

albē'ĭt (awl-) *conj.* although.

ălbi'nō (-bē-) *n.* (pl. -os), person or animal (almost) without natural pigment in skin and hair. ăl'bĭnism *n.*

ăl'bum *n.* blank book for insertion of autographs, photographs, etc.

ălbū'mĕn *n.* proteinous constituent of animal cells etc. forming white of egg etc. ălbū'mĭnoid, ~mĭnous *aa.*

ălbūr'num *n.* soft recently formed wood.

ăl'chĕmў (-k-) *n.* precursor of chemistry; transmutation of baser metals into gold. ~mĭst *n.*; ~mīze *v.t.*

ăl'cohŏl *n.* pure spirit of wine; liquor containing alcohol. ălcohŏl'ĭc *a.* of or containing alcohol; *n.* person suffering from alcoholism. ~ism *n.* addiction to alcohol; effect of alcohol on human system.

ăl'cōve *n.* vaulted recess in room; recess in garden-wall or hedge.

al'der (awl-) *n.* tree related to birch.

al'derman (awl-) *n.* civic dignitary next below mayor. aldermăn'ic *a.*

Al'derney (awl-) *n.* cow etc. from Alderney.

Al'dīne (awl-) *a.* of or by Aldus Manutius, Venetian printer who introduced italic type.

āle *n.* malt liquor, beer. ~house, place where ale is retailed.

alĕm'bĭc *n.* apparatus used by alchemists in distilling.

alĕrt' *a.* watchful, vigilant; nimble.

n. warning, esp. of air-raid; *on the* ~, vigilant. *v.t.* rouse to vigilance.

Alĕxăn'drīne (ă-) *a.* & *n.* (line) of six iambic feet.

ălfăl'fa *n.* lucerne.

ălfrĕs'cō *adv.* & *a.* in open air.

ăl'ga *n.* (pl. -gae, pr. -jē), kinds of primitive aquatic cryptogam including seaweeds.

ăl'gĕbra *n.* branch of mathematics dealing with relations and properties of numbers by means of general symbols. ălgĕbrā'ĭc(al) *aa.*

ā'lĭas *adv.* on other occasions. *n.* (pl. -ases), assumed name.

ā'lĭbī *n.* (pl. -bis), plea of being elsewhere; excuse.

ā'lien *a.* not one's own; foreign; out of harmony. *n.* stranger, foreigner.

ā'lienāte *v.t.* estrange; transfer; divert. ~ā'tion *n.* estrangement; insanity.

ā'lienĭsm *n.* study and treatment of mental diseases. ~ist *n.*

alight'[1] (-īt) *v.i.* dismount, descend; descend and settle.

alight'[2] (-īt) *pred. a.* kindled, on fire, lighted up.

align' (-īn) *v.* place in, bring into, or form line. ~ment *n.* (esp.) formation in straight line.

alīke' *a.* similar, like. *adv.* similarly, in like manner.

ăl'ĭment *n.* food.

ălĭmĕn'tarў *a.* nourishing, concerned with nutrition. ~ canal, channel through which food passes from mouth to anus.

ăl'ĭmonў *n.* allowance to divorced or separated wife for support.

ăl'ĭquŏt *a.* & *n.* (part) contained exact number of times in whole.

alīve' *pred. a.* living; brisk, active; fully susceptible *to.*

ăl'kalī *n.* caustic soda, potash, etc.; (chem.) any of class of compounds forming caustic or corrosive solutions in water that neutralize acids. ~līne *a.*; ~lĭn'itў *n.* ăl'kaloid *n.* any of large group of nitrogenous organic substances, many used as drugs.

all (awl) *a.* whole amount, extent, or number of. *n.* whole number; every one; whole world; everything. *adv.* entirely, quite. All

Fools' Day, 1 April. ~ fours, hands and knees. All Hallows, All Saints' Day. ~ in, quite exhausted; everything included. ~-in, (of wrestling) with few or no restrictions. ~ out, involving all one's strength or resources; at top speed, with maximum effort. ~ right, in good state, satisfactory; well enough; satisfactorily; (as sent.) very well, I consent. ~-round, having ability and skill in all departments, esp. of game. ~-rounder, all-round person. All Saints' Day, 1 Nov. All Souls' Day, 2 Nov. ~ there, sane, in one's right mind. ~ the same, in spite of that. ~-up, (of weight) inclusive of crew, pay-load and fuel.

Allah (ăl'a) n. Moslem name of God.

allay' v.t. repress; alleviate.

allège' v.t. state or advance as fact, esp. without proof. ăllēgā'tion n.

allē'giance (-jans) n. duty of subject to sovereign or government; loyalty.

ăll'ėgorў n. narrative describing one subject under guise of another. ăllēgŏ'ric(al) aa.; ~rist n.; ~rīze v.

ăllėgrĕtt'ō adv., a., & n. (mus.) (passage etc. played) in somewhat lively time. ălle'gro (-lā-) adv., a., & n. (passage etc. played) in quick lively time.

ăllėlu'ia (-lōōya) int. & n. (song of) praise to God.

ăll'ergў n. constitutional liability to acute reaction to certain proteins. allêr'gĭc a. having, caused by, allergy; ~ to, sensitive to, repelled by.

allē'vĭāte v.t. mitigate, lessen (pain, evil). ~ā'tion n.; ~atorў a.

ăll'ey n. (pl. -eys), narrow street, passage; (U.S.) back street; enclosure for skittles etc.

alli'ance n. relation of allies; confederation; union by marriage.

ăll'ĭgātor n. kinds of American reptile of crocodile family. ~ pear, avocado.

allĭterā'tion n. commencement of two or more words in close connexion with same letter or sound. allĭt'erāte v.; allĭt'erative a.

ăll'ocāte v.t. assign (to). ~ā'tion n.

ăllocū'tion n. formal hortatory address, esp. by Pope.

allŏt' v.t. assign; distribute by lot. ~ment n. assignment; small plot of land let for cultivation.

allow' v. admit, admit of; permit; give periodically; add or deduct in consideration of something. ~able a. ~ance n. fixed sum allowed; deduction, discount.

ăll'oy (or aloi') n. mixture of two or more metallic elements; (arch.) baser metal mixed with gold or silver; base admixture. v.t. (-oi'), mix with another metal; mix (metals); debase, spoil, by admixture.

all'spĭce (awl-) n. (aromatic spice got from) dried unripe berry of W. Ind. tree.

allūde' (or -ōōd) v.i. make indirect or passing reference to.

allūre' v.t. entice, tempt; charm. n. charm, fascination. ~ment n.

allū'sion (or -ōō-) n. indirect reference, hint. allu'sĭve a.

allū'vĭon (or -lōō-) n. wash of sea or river against shore; matter deposited by flood. allu'vĭum n. deposit of flood. allu'vĭal a.

allŷ'[1] v.t. join in confederation or marriage or for special object. n. (or ăl'ī), allied State or person.

ăll'ў[2] n. choice playing-marble.

Al'ma Mā'ter (ă-) n. one's university or school.

al'manăc (awl-) n. yearly calendar of months and days with other data.

almighty (awlmī'tĭ) a. infinitely powerful; (colloq.) very great; the A~, God.

al'mond (ahm-) n. edible kernel of fruit allied to plum; tree bearing this.

ăl'moner (or ahm'ner) n. official distributor of alms; social worker in hospital etc.

al'mōst (awl-) adv. very nearly, all but.

alms (ahmz) n. charitable relief of poor; donation. ~-house, founded by charity for reception of aged poor. ~man, one supported by alms.

ăl'ōe n. kinds of plant with erect spikes of flowers and bitter juice;

(pl.) purgative drug from aloe juice.

aloft' *adv.* high up, overhead.

alone' *pred. a.* solitary, by or to oneself. *adv.* only, exclusively.

along' *prep.* through (any part of) length of. *adv.* within limits of thing's length; in company or conjunction *with*; onward, in progress. ~side *adv.* and *prep.* close to side of.

aloof' *adv. & a.* away, apart; not showing or feeling sympathy; unconcerned.

alopē'cia *n.* (med.) baldness.

aloud' *adv.* in normal voice, not silently or in whisper; loudly.

alp *n.* mountain-peak; mountain meadow.

alpac'a *n.* llama with long wool; its wool, fabric made from it.

al'penstock *n.* staff with iron point used in climbing.

al'pha *n.* first letter of Greek alphabet; chief star of constellation. ~ **and omega**, beginning and end. ~ **plus**, superlatively good. ~ **particles, rays**, kinds emitted by radioactive substances.

al'phabet *n.* set of letters used in language; first rudiments. **alphabet'ic(al)** *aa.*

al'pine *a.* of the Alps; lofty. **al'pinist** *n.* mountain-climber.

already (awlrĕd'ĭ) *adv.* beforehand; by this time, thus early.

Alsā'tian (ăl-) *n.* German sheep-dog.

al'sō (awl-) *adv.* besides, too.

alt *n.* (mus.) high note; *in* ~, in octave beginning with G above treble stave.

Alta *abbr.* Alberta.

al'tar (awl-) *n.* flat-topped block for offerings to deity; Communion table. ~-**piece**, painting or sculpture above back of altar.

al'ter (awl-) *v.* change in character, position, etc.; modify. ~**ā'tion** *n.*

altercā'tion (awl-) *n.* dispute, wrangle, noisy controversy.

al'ter ĕg'ō *n.* other self. [L]

alter'nate (awl-) *a.* (of things of two kinds) occurring each after one of other kind; (of series or whole) composed of alternate things. *v.* (awl'ternāt), arrange, occur, in alternate order. **alternating current,**

(electr.) whose direction is regularly reversed. ~**ā'tion** *n.*

alter'native (awl-) *a.* (of two things) mutually exclusive. *n.* choice between two (or more) things or courses. ~**ly** *adv.*

although (awldhō') *conj.* though.

al'timēter *n.* aeronautical instrument showing altitude.

al'titūde *n.* vertical height; height above sea-level; (usu. pl.) high place.

al'tō *n.* (pl. *-os*), highest male voice; female voice of similar range. ~ **clef**, clef indicating middle C on central line of stave.

altogether (awltogĕdh'er) *adv.* entirely; on the whole.

al'tō-rèlie'vō *n.* (pl. *-os*), (sculp.) high relief.

al'truism (-roo-) *n.* regard for others as principle of action. ~**ist** *n.*; ~**ist'ic** *a.*

al'um *n.* kinds of mineral salt.

alū'mina *n.* oxide of aluminium. **alūmin'ium** *n.* very light silvery-white metallic element. **alū'minous** *a.* of alum or alumina.

alū'minum *n.* (U.S.) aluminium.

alŭm'na *n.* (pl. *-nae*), (U.S.) fem. of alumnus.

alŭm'nus *n.* (pl. *-nī*), (former) pupil of school or university.

al'ways (awl-) *adv.* at all times, on all occasions.

ăm, 1st pers. sing. pres. of **be.**

A.M. *abbr.* Master of Arts; audio-modulation.

a.m. *abbr. ante meridiem* [L], before noon.

amain' *adv.* (arch.) with force; in haste.

amăl'gam *n.* alloy of metal with mercury; plastic mixture.

amăl'gamāte *v.* mix; unite, combine. ~**ā'tion** *n.*

amănuĕn'sis *n.* (pl. *-nsēs*), clerk who writes from dictation.

ăm'arănth *n.* kinds of plant with coloured foliage; imaginary unfading flower. **ămarăn'thīne** *a.*

ămarȳll'ĭs *n.* kinds of flowering plant.

amăss' *v.t.* heap together, accumulate.

ăm'ateur (-ēr; *or* -ūr) *n.* one who

practises esp. art or sport as pastime. ~ish *a.* like amateur; unskilful.

ăm'atĭve *a.* disposed to loving.

ăm'atorў *a.* of lovers or sexual love.

amāze' *v.t.* overwhelm with wonder. amā'zing *a.* astonishing. ~ment *n.*

Am'azon (ă-) *n.* one of fabulous race of female warriors; masculine woman. Amazō'nĭan *a.*

ămbăss'ador *n.* minister sent to foreign State as permanent representative or on mission. ămbăssadōr'ĭal *a.*; ămbăss'adréss *n.*

ăm'ber *n.* yellow translucent fossil resin.

ăm'bergris (-ēs) *n.* wax-like substance from sperm-whale used in perfumery.

ăm'bĭdĕxter *a.* & *n.* (person) able to use both hands alike. ămbĭdextĕ'ritў *n.*; ămbĭdĕx'trous *a.*

ăm'bĭent *a.* surrounding.

ămbĭg'ūous *a.* of double meaning; doubtful, uncertain. ămbĭgū'itў *n.*

ăm'bĭt *n.* confines, scope.

ămbĭ'tion *n.* desire for distinction; aspiration; object of this. ămbĭ'tious *a.* full of or showing ambition.

ămbĭv'alent *a.* having either or both of two contrary values or qualities. ~ence *n.*

ăm'ble *v.i.* move, ride, at easy pace. *n.* easy pace.

ămbrō'sĭa (-z-) *n.* (myth.) food of gods; thing delightful to taste or smell. ~ĭal *a.*

ăm'būlance *n.* moving hospital following army; conveyance for sick or wounded persons.

ăm'būlatorў *a.* of or for walking. *n.* place for walking, esp. round east end of church behind altar; cloister.

ămbuscāde' *n.* and *v.t.* ambush.

ăm'bush (-ŏŏsh) *n.* concealment, troops concealed, in wood etc.; concealment, person(s) lying in wait. *v.t.* lie in wait for; lie concealed in or near.

A.M.D.G. *abbr. ad majorem Dei gloriam,* to the greater glory of God. [L]

amē'lĭorāte *v.* make or become better. ~ā'tion *n.*; ~atĭve *a.*

amĕn' (ah- *or* ā-) *int.* & *n.* (saying etc. of) so be it (at end of prayer etc.).

amē'nable *a.* tractable, responsive (*to*). ~bĭl'itў *n.*

amĕnd' *v.* correct, improve; make improvements (in), alter in detail. ~ment *n.*

amende honorable (ămahṅd' ŏnŏŕah'bl) *n.* public apology and reparation. [F]

amĕnds' (-z) *n.* reparation, restitution; *make* ~, make up (*for*).

amē'nitў (*or* -ĕn-) *n.* pleasantness; (usu. pl.) agreeable feature.

amĕŕce' *v.t.* fine; punish. ~ment *n.*

Amĕ'rĭcan *a.* of America or United States. *n.* (esp.) citizen of U.S. ~ cloth, cotton cloth with surface resembling shiny leather. ~ism *n.* word or usage peculiar to U.S.; adherence to American principles etc. ~īze *v.* make or become American in character etc.

ămeri'cium (-ĭshĭ-; *or* -ĭsĭ-) *n.* transuranic radioactive metallic element.

ăm'ĕthўst *n.* purple or violet semi--precious stone. ămĕthўst'īne *a.*

ā'mĭable *a.* feeling and inspiring friendliness. ~bĭl'itў *n.*

ăm'ĭcable *a.* friendly. ~bĭl'itў *n.*

ăm'ĭce[1] *n.* square of white linen on shoulders of celebrant priest.

ăm'ĭce[2] *n.* cap, hood, badge, of some religious orders.

amĭd', amĭdst' *prep.* in middle of. among.

amĭd'ships *adv.* in middle of ship.

amĭss' *adv.* & *pred. a.* wrong(ly), bad(ly).

ăm'itў *n.* friendly relations.

ămm'ĕter *n.* instrument for measuring electric currents.

ammō'nĭa *n.* (aqueous solution of) strongly alkaline colourless pungent gas. ~ĭăc, ~ī'acal, ~ĭātéd *aa.* ~ĭum *n.* radical of ammonia salts.

ămm'onīte *n.* fossil shell of coiled flat spiral shape.

ămmūnĭ'tion *n.* military stores (now only of powder, shot, etc.); supply of cartridges etc. for gun. ~ boots, kind issued to soldiers.

ămnē'sĭa (-z-) *n.* loss of memory.

ăm'nĕstў *n.* pardon, esp. for political offence(s). *v.t.* grant amnesty to.

amoe'ba *n.* (pl. -bae, -bas), primitive

microscopic single-celled animal-cule.

amŏk′, amŭck′ *adv.* in phr. *run* ~, run about in frenzied thirst for blood; get out of control.

among′, amongst′ (-mŭ-) *prep.* in midst of, in number of; between; by joint action of.

amŏ′ral *a.* non-moral.

ăm′orous *a.* of or showing (sexual) love; in love.

amōr′phous *a.* shapeless; non-crystalline.

amōr′tīze *v.t.* extinguish (debt, usu. by sinking-fund). ~**zā′tion** *n.*

amount′ *v.i.* be equivalent in quantity, value, importance, etc. *to*; add up *to* (total). *n.* total quantity.

amour′ (-oor) *n.* love affair, intrigue.

amour-propre (ăm′oor-prŏp′r) *n.* self-esteem. [F]

ămpĕlŏp′sis *n.* kinds of climbing plant.

ăm′pēre *n.* unit of electric current.

ăm′persănd *n.* the sign & (= 'and'):

ămphĭb′ĭan *a.* & *n.* (animal) living both on land and in water; (aircraft, tank, etc.) able to operate on both land and water.

ămphĭb′ĭous *a.* living etc. both on land and in water; amphibian.

ăm′phitheatre (-ĭater) *n.* oval or circular building with tiers of seats surrounding central space; semicircular gallery in theatre.

ăm′phora *n.* (pl. -ae, -as), Greek or Roman two-handled vessel.

ăm′ple *a.* spacious, extensive; abundant; quite enough. **ăm′plў** *adv.*

ăm′plĭfȳ *v.* enlarge; increase strength of (electric current, signal, etc.); add details (to). ~**fĭcā′tion** *n.* **ăm′plĭfier** *n.* (esp.) appliance for increasing strength of signals etc.

ăm′plĭtūde *n.* spaciousness.

ăm′poule (-ool) *n.* small sealed vessel holding solution for injection.

ămpŭll′a (or - oola) *n.* (pl. -ae), Roman globular two-handled flask; eccl. vessel for oil etc.

ăm′pūtāte *v.t.* cut off (limb etc.). ~**ā′tion** *n.*

ăm′ūlĕt *n.* thing worn as charm against evil.

amūse′ (-z) *v.t.* excite risible faculty of; be or find diversion or light

occupation for; entertain. ~**ment** *n.*

ā′mȳl (*or* ăm′ĭl) *n.* (chem.) radical of various alcohols.

ămȳlā′ceous *a.* starchy.

an¹: see **a²**. **ăn²** *conj.* (arch.) if.

ā′na *n.* (pl. *anas*), collection of sayings of or literary gossip about person.

ănabăp′tĭst *n.* member of sect believing in rebaptism of adults. ~**ĭsm** *n.*

anăb′olĭsm *n.* synthesis of complex molecules by organism.

ană′chronĭsm (-k-) *n.* chronological error; thing out of harmony with period. ~**ĭs′tĭc** *a.*

ănacŏn′da *n.* large tropical S.-Amer. aquatic and arboreal boa.

anae′mĭa *n.* deficiency of haemoglobin or of red blood cells. **anae′mĭc** *a.* having or liable to anaemia; bloodless.

ănaesthē′sia (-zĭa) *n.* insensible condition. ~**thĕt′ic** *a.* & *n.* (drug etc.) producing anaesthesia. **anae′sthĕtĭst** *n.*; **anae′sthĕtīze** *v.t.*

ăn′agrăm *n.* word or phrase formed from letters of another.

ā′nal *a.* of anus.

ănalĕc′ta *n.pl.* literary gleanings.

ănălgē′sia (-z-) *n.* absence of pain. ~**gĕt′ic**, ~**gē′sic** *aa.* & *nn.* (drug) giving analgesia.

anăl′ogous *a.* similar, parallel.

ăn′alŏgue (-g) *n.* analogous thing; ~ **computer**, operating with numbers represented by measurable quantities.

anăl′ogy *n.* parallelism, similarity; reasoning from parallel cases. **ănalŏ′gical** *a.*

ăn′alўse (-z) *v.t.* ascertain elements, minutely examine constitution, of

anăl′ўsĭs *n.* (pl. -*ysēs*), resolution into simple elements.

ăn′alўst *n.* one who analyses.

ănalўt′ĭc, ~**al** *aa.* of or employing analysis.

ăn′apaest *n.* metrical foot of three syllables (∪ ∪ −). **ănapae′stic** *a.*

ăn′archĭsm (-k-) *n.* system or theory conceiving of society without government. ~**ĭst** *n.* & *a.*; ~**ĭs′tĭc** *a.*

ăn′archў (-k-) *n.* absence of government; disorder, political and social confusion. **anăr′chĭc**(al) *aa.* lawless.

anastĭg′măt *n.* anastigmatic lens.

ănastĭgmăt'ĭc *a.* (of lens) with astigmatism corrected.

anăth'ema *n.* solemn curse; accursed thing. ~tīze *v.t.*

anăt'omў *n.* (science of) bodily structure; dissection. ănatŏm'ical *a.*; ~mĭst *n.* ~mīze *v.t.* dissect; analyse.

ăn'cĕstor *n.* any of those from whom one's father or mother is descended. ăncĕs'tral *a.* inherited from ancestors. ~trĕss *n.* ~trў *n.* ancestors; ancient descent.

ănch'or (-k-) *n.* heavy iron appliance with barbed arms for mooring ship to bottom of water. *v.* secure (ship) with anchor; cast anchor; fix firmly. ~age *n.* place where ship(s) may lie at anchor.

ănch'orĕss (-k-) *n.* female anchorite.

ănch'orĕt, ănch'orīte (-k-) *n.* hermit, recluse.

ănchō'vў (*or* ăn'-) *n.* small pungent--flavoured fish of herring family.

ancien régime (ahn'syan rāzhĕm') *n.* time before French Revolution. [F]

ā'ncient[1] (-shent) *a.* of times long past; old. A~ of Days, God.

ā'ncient[2] (-shent) *n.* (arch.) ensign.

ăncĭll'ary (*or* ăn'-) *a.* subordinate.

and (and; *emphat.* ănd) *conj.* connecting words, clauses, and sentences.

ăndăn'tĕ *adv., a. & n.* (mus.) (passage) in moderately slow time.

ăn'diron (-īrn) *n.* stand for supporting logs on hearth.

ăndrŏ'gўnous *a.* hermaphrodite.

ăn'ĕcdōte *n.* narrative of detached incident. ~tage *n.* garrulous old age. ănĕcdō'tal *a.*; ~tĭst *n.*

anēle' *v.t.* anoint; give extreme unction to.

anĕmŏm'ĕter *n.* instrument for measuring force of wind. ănĕmo-mĕt'ric *a.*; ănĕmŏm'ĕtrў *n.*

anĕm'onĕ *n.* kinds of flower of buttercup family; *sea* ~, kinds of zoophyte.

anĕnt' *prep.* (arch.) concerning.

ăn'eroid *a. & n.* (barometer) measuring air-pressure by its action on lid of metal box exhausted of air.

ăn'eurўsm, -ĭsm *n.* localized dilatation of artery.

anew' *adv.* again, once more.

ăng'ary (-ngg-) *n.* (law) belligerent's right of seizing or destroying neutral property.

ā'ngel (-j-) *n.* divine messenger; attendant spirit; kind or innocent person; old English gold coin. ăngĕl'ic *a.*

ăngĕl'ĭca (-j-) *n.* (candied root of) aromatic plant.

ăn'gĕlus (-j-) *n.* (bell rung for) R.-C. devotional exercise said at morning, noon, and sunset.

ang'er (ăngg-) *n.* hot displeasure. *v.t.* make angry, enrage.

ăngī'na (pĕc'torĭs) (-j-) *n.* painful spasm of chest due to over-exertion when heart is diseased.

angle[1] (ăng'gl) *n.* space between two meeting lines or planes, inclination of two lines to each other; corner; (colloq.) point of view.

angle[2] (ăng'gl) *v.i.* fish with hook and bait. ăng'ler *n.*

Ang'lican (ăngg-) *a. & n.* (member) of reformed Church of England.

Anglice (ăng'glĭsē), in English. [L]

Ang'lĭcĭsm (ăngg-) *n.* English idiom. ~cīze *v.t.* make English.

Ang'lo- (ăngg-) in comb., English. Anglo-Căth'olic *a. & n.* (adherent) of section of Church of England that insists on its catholicity. ~-In'dian *a. & n.* (person) of British birth but living or having lived long in India. ~mā'nĭa *n.* excessive admiration of things English; ~mā'nĭăc *n.* ~phīle, ~phĭl *n. & a.* (person) well-disposed towards English. ~phō'bĭa *n.* dread of English; ~phōbe *n.* ~-Săx'on *a. & n.* English (person, language) before Norman Conquest; (person) of English origin or descent.

angōr'a (ăngg-) *n.* fabric made from hair of Angora goat. A~ cat, goat, rabbit, varieties with long silky hair. A~ wool, sheep's wool mixed with Angora-rabbit hair.

angŏstūr'a (ăngg-) *n.* (tonic made from) aromatic bitter bark of S.--Amer. tree.

ang'rў (ăngg-) *a.* feeling or showing anger; (of sore etc.) inflamed, painful. ăng'rilў *adv.*

Ăng'ström (ū'nĭt) (ă-) *n.* hundred--millionth of centimetre (used in measuring wave-lengths of light).

ang'uish (ănggw-) *n.* severe mental or bodily pain.

ang'ūlar (ăngg-) *a.* having angles; sharp-cornered. ~ **distance**, distance between two points in terms of angle they make with third. ~**ă'rity** *n.*

ănhy'drous *a.* without water, esp. water of crystallization.

ăn'ilĭne (*or* -ēn *or* -ĭn) *n.* organic base used in manufacture of many dyes etc. ~ **dye**, synthetic dye.

ănĭmadvẽrt' *v.i.* pass criticism or censure *on*. ~**vẽr'sion** *n.*

ăn'ĭmal *n.* being endowed with life, sensation, and voluntary motion; (pop.) animal other than man. *a.* of (nature of) animals; carnal; sensual. ~**ism** *n.* (mere) animal activity or enjoyment. **ănimăl'ity** *n.* (merely) animal nature.

ănimăl'cūle *n.* microscopic animal.

ăn'ĭmāte *v.t.* breathe life into; encourage, inspirit. *a.* (-*at*), living, not inanimate. ~**ĕd** *a.* lively, vivacious; (cine., of drawings etc.) having apparent motion.

ăn'ĭmĭsm *n.* attribution of soul to inanimate objects and natural phenomena. ~**mĭst** *n.*; ~**mĭs'tĭc** *a.*

ănĭmŏs'ity *n.* hostility, enmity.

ăn'ĭmus *n.* bitter feeling (*against*).

ăn'ĭse *n.* plant with aromatic seeds. **ăn'ĭseed** *n.* seed of anise.

ănk'le *n.* joint connecting foot with leg. **ănk'lĕt** *n.* fetter, ornament, protective band, etc. round ankle.

ănkўlō'sis *n.* stiffening of joint by uniting of bones.

ănn'a *n.* (hist.) sixteenth part of rupee.

ănn'als (-z) *n.pl.* narrative of events year by year; historical records. **ănn'alĭst** *n.*

anneal' *v.t.* toughen by gradually diminishing heat; temper.

ănn'ĕlĭd *n.* segmented worm, e.g. earth-worm, leech.

annĕx' *v.t.* add, append, attach; take possession of. **ănn'ex(e)** *n.* supplementary building, addition to document etc. ~**ā'tion** *n.*

anni'hilāte (-nĭï-) *v.t.* destroy utterly. ~**ā'tion** *n.*

ănnivẽr'sary *n.* yearly return of date; celebration of this.

ănn'ō aetā'tis sū'ae in the — year of his age, [L]

Ann'ō Dŏm'ĭnī (ă-) *adv.* in the year of our Lord, of the Christian era. *n.* (colloq.) advancing age.

ănn'otāte *v.t.* add notes to (book etc.); make notes on. ~**tā'tion**, ~**tātor** *nn.*

announce' *v.t.* proclaim, give notice of. ~**ment** *n.* **announ'cer** *n.* (esp.) broadcaster reading news, announcing programme, etc.

annoy' *v.t.* irritate; molest. ~**ance** *n.* molestation; vexation.

ănn'ūal *a.* reckoned by year; recurring yearly. *n.* plant living only one year; yearly periodical.

annū'ĭty *n.* yearly grant or sum; investment entitling one to fixed annual sum. **annū'ĭtant** *n.*

annŭl' *v.t.* abolish, cancel; declare invalid. ~**ment** *n.*

ănn'ūlar *a.* ring-like. **ănn'ūlate, -ātĕd** *aa.* furnished or marked with, composed of, rings.

annŭncĭā'tion *n.* announcement, esp, to Virgin Mary of Incarnation; **A~.** Lady Day.

ăn'ōde *n.* positive electrode.

ăn'odỹne *a.* pain-killing, soothing. *n.* drug to allay pain.

anoint' *v.t.* apply ointment or oil to esp. as religious ceremony.

anŏm'alous *a.* irregular, abnormal.

anŏm'aly *n.* irregularity.

anŏn' *adv.* soon, presently.

anon. *abbr.* anonymous.

anŏn'ỹmous *a.* of unknown name or authorship. **ănonỹm'ity** *n.*

anŏph'ĕlēs (-z) *n.* kinds of (esp. malarial) mosquito.

ăn'orăk *n.* hooded wind-proof jacket or pullover.

anoth'er (-ŭdh-) *a.* an additional; a different. *pron.* another one.

ăn'serĭne *a.* of geese; silly.

answer (ahn's*e*r) *v.* speak, write, act, etc. in reply or response (to); be responsible *for*; correspond to; fulfil (purpose etc.). *n.* thing said, written, or done in reply; defence. ~**able** *a.* responsible.

ănt *n.* small social hymenopterous insect proverbial for industry. ~**-eater**, kinds of animal living on ants. ~**-hill**, mound over ants' nest.

ăntă′cĭd *a. & n.* preventive of acidity, esp. in stomach.

ăntăg′onĭsm *n.* active opposition. ~ĭst *n.* opponent. ~ĭs′tĭc *a.* antăg′onīze *v.t.* evoke hostility in.

ăntâr′ctĭc *a. & n.* (of) south polar regions.

ăn′tė *n.* (poker etc.) stake put up before drawing new cards.

ăn′tė- in comb., before.

ăntėcĕ′dent (*or* ăn′-) *a.* previous. *n.* preceding event or circumstance; (gram.) noun, clause, etc. to which following adv. or pron. refers; (pl.) person's past history. ~ence *n.*

ăn′tėchāmber *n.* room leading to chief apartment.

ăn′tėchăpel *n.* outer part at west end of chapel.

ăntėdāte′ (*or* ăn′-) *v.t.* affix or assign earlier than true date to; precede; anticipate.

ăntėdĭlū′vĭan (*or* -loō-) *a.* before Flood; antiquated.

ăn′tėlōpe *n.* deer-like ruminant.

ăn′tė mĕrĭd′ĭem, before noon. [L]

ăntėnā′tal *a.* previous to birth.

ăntĕnn′a *n.* (pl. -ae), sensory organ like horn on heads of insects and crustaceans; (radio) aerial.

ăntėpĕnŭlt′, ~ĭmate *aa. & nn.* (syllable) last but two.

ăntēr′ior *a.* prior *to*; further to front.

ăn′tė-rōōm *n.* room leading to another.

ăn′them *n.* composition for church use sung antiphonally; song of praise.

ăn′ther *n.* part of stamen containing pollen.

ănthŏl′ogў *n.* literary collection esp. of small choice poems. ~ogĭst *n.*

ăn′thracīte *n.* hard glossy kind of coal. ~cĭt′ĭc *a.*

ăn′thrăx *n.* acute infectious disease of sheep and cattle that may be transmitted to man.

ăn′thropo- in comb., man. anthropocĕn′trĭc *a.* regarding man as central fact of universe. ănthropŏm′etrў *n.* (part of anthropology concerned with) measurements of human body. ~mŏr′phĭsm *n.* attribution of human form or personality to God etc.; ~mŏr′phic *a.* ~mŏr′phous *a.* having human form. anthropŏph′agi (-gī) *n. pl.* cannibals; ~phagous *a.*

ăn′thropoid *a. & n.* manlike (ape).

ănthropŏl′ogў *n.* whole science of man; study of man as animal. ~olŏ′gical *a.*; ~ŏl′ogĭst *n.*

ăn′tĭ- in comb., opposite, against. anti-air′craft *a.* for defence against hostile aircraft. ~bĭŏt′ĭc *a. & n.* (substance) produced by living organism and destroying or injuring bacteria. ~bŏdў *n.* substance formed in reaction to foreign substance in body. An′tĭchrĭst (-k-) *n.* great enemy of Christ expected before end of world. ~chrĭs′tĭan (-k-) *a.* opposed to Christianity; ~chrĭs′tĭanĭsm *n.* ~gĕn *n.* substance stimulating production of antibodies. ~-mătter *n.* matter whose properties are negative of those of ordinary matter. Antĭnō′mĭan *n. & a.* (person) holding that moral law is not binding on Christians. antĭn′omў *n.* contradiction in law, authorities, or conclusions. ~pōpe *n.* opposition pope. ~pȳrĕt′ĭc *a. & n.* (drug) allaying or preventing fever. ~scôrbū′tĭc *a. & n.* (medicine etc.) preventing or curing scurvy. ~-Sē′mīte (*or* -sĕ-) *n.* person hostile to Jews; ~-Sĕmĭt′ĭc *a.*, ~-Sĕm′ĭtĭsm *n.* ~sĕp′tĭc *a. & n.* (agent) counteracting putrefaction. ~tŏx′ĭn *n.* serum etc. serving to neutralize toxin; ~tŏx′ĭc *a.* ~-trāde *n.* wind blowing in opposite direction to trade wind.

ăn′tĭc *n.* grotesque posture or trick. *a.* grotesque; fantastic.

ăntĭ′cĭpāte *v.t.* look forward to, expect; forestall; use in advance. ~ā′tion *n.*; ~atĭve, ~ā′torў *aa.*

ăntĭclī′măx *n.* lame conclusion to anything promising climax.

ăntĭcȳ′clōne *n.* rotatory outward flow of air from atmospheric area of high pressure.

ăn′tĭdōte *n.* medicine used to counteract disease or poison.

ăntĭmacăss′ar *n.* protective covering for chair-back.

ăn′tĭmonў *n.* brittle bluish-white metallic element.

ăntĭp'athў *n.* constitutional or settled aversion.. ăntĭpathĕt'ĭc *a.*

ăn'tĭphon *n.* passage sung by one choir in answer to another; composition consisting of such passages. ăntĭph'onal *a.* sung alternately.

ăntĭp'odēs (-z) *n.pl.* region of earth diametrically opposite, esp. to our own. ăntĭpodē'an *a. & n.*

ăn'tĭquarў *n.* student or collector of antiquities. ~ār'ĭan *a. & n.*; ~ār'ĭanĭsm *n.*

ăn'tĭquāted *a.* very old; out of date.

ăntique' (-ēk) *a.* of or dating from old times; old-fashioned. *n.* antique relic, esp. work of art.

ăntĭ'quĭtў *n.* old times, esp. before Middle Ages; (pl.) customs etc. of ancient civilized peoples; (pl.) ancient relics.

ăntĭrrhi'num (-rī-) *n.* snapdragon.

ăntĭs'trophė *n.* lines recited during returning movement from left to right in Greek chorus.

ăntĭth'ėsĭs *n.* (pl. -*thesēs*) contrast of ideas marked by parallelism of contrasted words; direct opposite. ăntĭthĕt'ĭc(al) *aa.*

ănt'ler *n.* branched horn of deer.

ăn'tonўm *n.* word of contrary meaning to another.

ā'nus *n.* terminal opening of alimentary canal.

ăn'vĭl *n.* block on which smith works metal.

anxī'ėtў (ăngz-) *n.* troubled state of mind; uneasiness.

anxious (ăngk'shus) *a.* troubled; uneasy in mind; desirous *to* do.

any (ĕn'ĭ) *a. & pron.* one or some, no matter which. *adv.* at all, in any degree. ~body *n.* any person; person of importance. ~how *adv. & conj.* in any way; in any case; at random. ~thing *n.* any thing, any whit. ~way *adv. & conj.* anyhow. ~where *adv.* in or to any place.

An'zăc (ă-) *n. & a.* (belonging to, member of) Austral. and N.Z. Army Corps in war of 1914–18.

ā'orĭst *n.* (gram.) tense denoting simply occurrence.

āōr'ta *n.* great artery issuing from left ventricle of heart. āōr'tĭc *a.*

à outrance (ah ōō'trahns), to the death. [F]

apāce' *adv.* swiftly.

apache' (-ahsh) *n.* Parisian street ruffian.

ăp'anage, ăpp- *n.* provision for younger children of kings etc.; dependency; perquisite.

apărt' *adv.* aside, separately.

apărt'heid (-hāt) *n.* policy of racial segregation in S. Africa.

apărt'ment *n.* single room; (U.S.) flat; (pl.) set of rooms.

ăp'athў *n.* insensibility, indifference; mental indolence. ăpathĕt'ĭc *a.*

āpe *n.* tailless monkey; imitator. *v.t.* imitate.

aperçu (ah'pārsū) *n.* summary exposition. [F]

apĕ'rĭent (*or* -ēr-) *a. & n.* laxative.

apéritif (apĕ'rĭtēf) *n.* alcoholic drink as appetizer before meal. [F]

ăp'erture *n.* opening, gap; space through which light passes in camera etc.

ā'pĕx *n.* (pl. -*ĭcēs*, -*exes*), tip, topmost point, pointed end.

aphā'sĭa (-z-) *n.* loss of speech.

aphē'lĭon *n.* (pl. -*ia*), point of orbit farthest from sun.

ăph'ĭs (*or* ā-) *n.* (pl. *aphidēs*), minute insect infesting stems and leaves of plants.

ăph'orĭsm *n.* short pithy maxim. ăphorĭs'tĭc *a.*

ăphrodĭs'ĭăc (-z-) *n. & a.* (drug) provoking sexual excitement.

ā'pĭarў *n.* place where bees are kept. ā'pĭarĭst *n.* bee-keeper.

ā'pĭcal (*or* ă-) *a.* of or at apex.

ā'pĭcŭlture *n.* bee-keeping.

apiece' *adv.* severally, each.

ā'pĭsh *a.* of or like an ape.

aplŏmb' (-m) *n.* self-possession.

A.P.O. *abbr.* Army Post Office.

apŏc'alўpse *n.* revelation, esp. that of St. John. apŏcalўp'tĭc(al) *aa.*

apŏc'opė *n.* cutting off of end of word.

Apocr. *abbr.* Apocrypha.

Apŏc'rўpha *n.* O.T. books not counted genuine. apŏc'rўphal *a.* doubtful; spurious.

ăpodei'ctĭc (-dī-),-dĭc'tĭc *a.* established on incontrovertible evidence.

apŏd'osĭs n. (pl. -sēs), consequent clause in conditional sentence.

ăp'ogee n. point of moon's or planet's orbit furthest from earth; highest point.

Apŏll'ō n. Greek sun-god; sun; man of great beauty.

apŏlogĕt'ĭc a. regretfully acknowledging fault; of nature of apology. ~s n.pl. reasoned defence, esp. of Christianity. **apŏl'ogĭst** n. one who defends by argument. **apŏl'ogīze** v.i. make apology.

ăp'ologue (-ŏg) n. moral fable.

apŏl'ogў n. regretful acknowledgement of offence; explanation, vindication.

ăp'ophthegm (-o(f)thĕm) n. terse or pithy saying. ~măt'ic (-gm-) a.

ăp'oplĕxў n. seizure caused by blockage or rupture of artery in brain. **ăpoplĕc'tic** a.

ăposīopē'sĭs n. (pl. -sēs), (rhet.) breaking off short for effect.

apŏs'tasў n. abandonment of religious faith, party, etc. ~tate n. & a. (one) guilty of apostasy. ~tatīze v.i.

ā postĕrĭor'ĭ, (reasoning) from effect to cause. [L]

apŏst'le (-sl) n. one of twelve sent forth by Christ to preach gospel; first Christian missionary in country etc.; leader of reform. **ăpostŏl'ĭc** a. of Apostles; of pope as successor of St. Peter.

apŏs'trophė n. exclamatory address; sign (') of omitted letter(s) or of possessive case. **apŏs'trophīze** v.t.

apŏth'ėcarў n. (arch.) druggist.

apŏthēō'sĭs n. (pl. -osēs), deification; transformation; deified ideal. **apŏth'ėosīze** v.t.

app. abbr. appendix; apparently.

appal' (-awl) v.t. dismay, terrify.

appanage : see **apanage**.

apparā'tus (pl. -tuses) n. mechanical requisites, appliance, for scientific or other work.

appă'rel v.t. dress, attire. n. dress, clothing.

appă'rent (or -ār-) a. manifest; seeming. ~ly adv.

ăpparī'tion n. appearance, esp. of startling kind; ghost.

appă'ritor n. officer of ecclesiastical or civil court.

appeal' v.i. apply to higher court for revision of lower court's decision; make earnest request; be attractive to. n. act or right of appealing; Court of A~, one hearing cases previously tried in inferior court.

appear' v.i. become visible; present oneself; be published; seem.

appear'ance n. appearing; seeming; look, aspect; (pl.) outward show (of prosperity, friendly relations, etc.)

appease' (-z) v.t. pacify, soothe; satisfy. ~ment n. policy of making concessions to aggressor.

appĕll'ant a. concerned with appeals. n. one who appeals to higher court.

appĕll'ate a. (of court) hearing appeals.

ăppellā'tion n. name, title.

appĕnd' v.t. attach as accessory; add. ~age n.

appĕndĭcī'tis n. inflammation of vermiform appendix of intestine.

appĕn'dĭx n. (pl. -ixes or -icēs), subsidiary addition (to book etc.); small process developed from organ, esp. vermiform appendix.

ăppertain' v.i. belong or relate to.

ăpp'ėtīte n. desire, inclination (for food, pleasure, etc.); relish. **ăpp'ėtīzer** n. thing taken to give appetite for meal. **ăpp'ėtīzing** a. inviting.

applaud' v. express approval (of), esp. by clapping; commend.

applause' (-z) n. loud approbation.

ăpp'le n. rounded firm fleshy fruit. ~-cart : upset one's ~-cart, upset one's plans. ~-jack, (U.S.) spirit distilled from cider. ~ of one's eye, cherished object. ~-pie bed, with sheets so folded that one cannot get one's legs down. ~-pie order, perfect order.

applī'ance n. applying; thing applied as means to end; device.

ăpp'licable a. that applies or may be applied. ~bĭl'itў n.

ăpp'licant n. one who applies.

ăpplicā'tion n. applying; request; diligence; relevancy.

ăppli'qué (-ēkā) n. cut-out material applied to surface; needlework made thus. v.t. apply (material) to surface.

applў' v. put close to, put in contact; administer (remedy); devote to;

use, esp. as relative or suitable *to*; set one*self* closely (*to*); be relevant (*to*); address oneself (*for* help, situation, etc., *to*).

appoint' *v.t.* fix (time etc.); prescribe, ordain; assign *to* post.

appoint'ment *n.* engagement, assignation; appointing, office assigned; (pl.) outfit.

ăpp'ŏrt *n.* material thing produced at spiritualist seance etc.

appŏr'tion *v.t.* assign as share; portion out. **~ment** *n.*

ăpp'osĭte (-z-) *a.* to the point, appropriate.

ăpposĭ'tion (-z-) *n.* (gram.) placing of word etc. syntactically parallel to another; *in* ~, so placed, in same case etc.

appraise' (-z) *v.t.* fix price for: estimate. **apprai'sal, ~ment** *nn.*

apprē'ciable (-sha-) *a.* perceptible.

apprē'ciāte (-shĭ-) *v.* set high value on; estimate rightly; rise in value. **~ā'tion** *n.*; **~atĭve** *a.*

ăpprehĕnd' *v.t.* seize, arrest; understand; anticipate with fear.

ăpprehĕn'sĭble *a.* perceptible to senses. **ăpprehĕn'sion** *n.* arrest; understanding; dread. **ăpprehĕn'sĭve** *a.* afraid, fearful.

apprĕn'tĭce *n.* learner of craft bound to employer for specified term. *v.t.* bind as apprentice. **~ship** *n.*

apprīse' (-z) *v.t.* give notice *of*, inform.

appro. *abbr.* approval.

approach' *v.* come nearer (to); make overtures to. *n.* (way of) approaching; access, way towards; (golf) shot intended to reach green. **~able** *a.* (esp.) friendly to advances.

ăpp'robāte *v.t.* (U.S.) approve, sanction.

ăpprobā'tion *n.* sanction, approval. **ăpprobā'torў** (*or* ăp'-) *a.*

apprō'priate *a.* suitable, proper. *v.t.* (-āt), take possession of; devote to special purposes. **~ā'tion, ~ātor** *nn.*

approve' (-ōōv) *v.* confirm, sanction; pronounce good, have favourable opinion *of*. **appro'val** *n.* favourable opinion; *on* ~, without obligation to purchase.

approx'imate *a.* fairly correct, very near. *v.* (-āt), bring or come near *to*. **~ā'tion** *n.*

appûr'tĕnance *n.* appendage; (usu. pl.) belonging.

Apr. *abbr.* April.

ā'prĭcŏt *n.* orange-pink stone-fruit.

A'prĭl (ā-) *n.* fourth month of year, noted for frequent showers. ~ **fool**, person hoaxed on 1 April.

ā priōr'ī, (reasoning) from cause to effect; deductive(ly). [L]

ā'pron *n.* garment worn in front of body to protect clothes etc.; (theatr.) advanced strip of stage for playing scenes before proscenium arch; hard-surfaced area on airfield for aircraft on ground.

ăpropos' (-pō) *adv.* & *a.* to the point or purpose. ~ **of**, in connexion with.

ăpse *n.* arched or domed recess esp. at end of church.

ăp'sĭdal *a.* of form of apse; of apsides.

ăp'sĭs *n.* (pl. **ăp'sĭdēs** *or* **ăpsī'dēs**), aphelion or perihelion of planet, apogee or perigee of moon.

ăpt *a.* suitable, appropriate; quick, ready; inclined. **~ly** *adv.*; **~ness** *n.*

ăp'terŷx *n.* kiwi.

ăp'tĭtūde *n.* fitness, talent.

ā'qua-fŏr'tĭs *n.* nitric acid.

ā'qualŭng *n.* diver's portable breathing-apparatus.

ăquamarine' (-ēn) *n.* bluish-green beryl; colour of this.

ăquarĕlle' *n.* painting with transparent water-colours.

aquār'ĭum *n.* tank for aquatic plants or animals; place with such tanks.

Aquār'ĭus, Water-carrier, eleventh constellation and sign of zodiac.

aquăt'ĭc *a.* living in or near water; conducted in or on water.

ā'quatĭnt *n.* (print produced by) method of etching on copper.

ā'quĕdŭct *n.* artificial channel, esp. elevated structure, for water.

ā'quĕous *a.* of water, watery; produced by action of water.

ā'quĭlīne *a.* eagle-like; (of nose) hooked.

A.R.A. *abbr.* Associate of Royal Academy.

A'rab (ă-) *n.* & *a.* (person, horse) of Arabia or Arabian descent.

ărabĕsque' (-k) *n.* & *a.* (of, resembling) decoration of fancifully intertwined scrolls, leaves, etc.; musical composition suggesting this; ballet-dancers' pose on one foot with other leg extended behind.

Arā'bian *a.* & *n.* (native) of Arabia. ~ **bird**, phoenix.

A'rabĭc (ă-) *a.* & *n.* (language) of Arabia or Arabs. **a~ numerals**, those now in common use in all western countries.

ă'rable *a.* fit for tillage.

arăch'nĭd (-k-) *n.* member of class comprising spiders etc.

Aramā'ĭc (ă-) *n.* & *a.* (of) Semitic language of Aram or Syria.

ăr'balĕst *n.* machine crossbow.

ăr'bĭter *n.* judge; one in control *of*. **ăr'bĭtrĕss** *n.*

ărbĭt'rament *n.* decision.

ăr'bĭtrary *a.* capricious; despotic.

ăr'bĭtrāte *v.* determine; settle dispute. **ărbĭtrā'tion** *n.* ~**ātor** *n.* one appointed to settle dispute.

ăr'bor *n.* main support of machine; axle or spindle of wheel.

ărborā'ceous *a.* tree-like.

ărbōr'ĕal *a.* of, living in, trees.

ărbōr'ĕous *a.* abounding in trees.

ărborĕs'cent *a.* tree-like in growth or form. ~**ence** *n.*

ărborē'tum *n.* (pl. *-ta*), tree-garden.

ăr'borĭcŭlture *n.* cultivation of trees or shrubs. **ărborĭcŭl'tural** *a.*

ăr'bour (-*er*) *n.* leafy nook.

ărbū'tus *n.* kinds of evergreen.

ărc *n.* part of circumference of circle; luminous discharge between two electric poles. ~-**lamp**, using electric arc.

ărcāde' *n.* covered walk lined with shops; row of arches supporting or attached to wall. **arcā'dĕd** *a.*

Arcā'dian (är-) *a.* ideally rustic.

ărcā'num *n.* (pl. *-na*), mystery.

ărch[1] *n.* curved structure supporting bridge etc.; curve, vault. *v.* furnish with arch; form (into) arch. ~**way**, arched passage or entrance.

ărch[2] *a.* roguish, saucy.

ărchaeŏl'ogy (-kĭ-) *n.* study of antiquities or of prehistoric remains. ~**lŏ'gĭcal** *a.*; ~**logĭst** *n.*

ărchā'ĭc (-k-) *a.* primitive, antiquated. **ăr'chāism** *n.* archaic quality; use of what is archaic; archaic word etc. **archāis'tic** *a.*

ăr'chāngel (-k-; -j-) *n.* angel of highest rank. **ărchăngĕl'ĭc** *a.*

ărchbĭsh'op *n.* chief bishop, metropolitan. ~**rĭc** *n.*

ărchdea'con *n.* church dignitary next below bishop and holding lowest ecclesiastical court.

ărchdī'ocĕse *n.* archbishop's see.

ărch'dūke *n.* son of Emperor of Austria. ~**dū'cal** *a.*; ~**dŭch'ĕss**, ~**dŭch'y** *nn.*

ăr'cher *n.* one who shoots with bow and arrows. **ăr'chery** *n.* use of bow and arrows.

ăr'chetȳpe (-k-) *n.* original model.

ărch'fiend' *n.* Satan.

ărchidĭăc'onal (-kĭ-) *a.* of archdeacon.

ărchiĕpĭs'copal (-kĭ-) *a.* of archbishop.

ărchimăn'drīte (-k-) *n.* superior of Orthodox monastery.

ărchipĕl'agō (-k-) *n.* (pl. *-os*), sea with many islands; group of islands.

ăr'chĭtĕct (-k-) *n.* designer of buildings, ships, etc.

ărchĭtĕctŏn'ic (-k-) *a.* of architecture; of systematization of knowledge.

ăr'chĭtĕcture (-k-) *n.* science of building. **ărchĭtĕc'tural** *a.*

ăr'chĭtrāve (-k-) *n.* beam resting on abacus of column; moulded frame round doorway, arch, etc.

ăr'chives (-kīvz) *n.pl.* public records; place for these. ~**vĭst** *n.*

ărc'tĭc *a.* of north pole.

ăr'dent *a.* eager, zealous, fervent; burning. ~**ency** *n.*

ăr'dour (-d*er*) *n.* zeal; warmth.

ăr'dūous *a.* hard; strenuous.

are : see **be**.

ār'ĕa *n.* extent of surface; region; scope, range; sunk court in front of basement of house.

ă'rĕca (*or* arē'-) *n.* kinds of palm. ~-**nut**, astringent seed of areca.

arē'na *n.* centre of amphitheatre; scene of conflict.

ărēnā'ceous *a.* sandy.

arête (ărāt') *n.* sharp ridge of mountain. [F]

ăr'gent *n.* & *a.* silver (colour). ~**ĭf'erous** *a.* yielding silver.

ăr'gĭl *n.* (potter's) clay. **argĭllā'ceous** *a.* of or like clay.

ăr'gol *n.* tartar from wine.

ăr'gon *n.* almost inert gaseous element present in small quantities in air.

ar'gosў *n.* richly laden ship.

ar'got (-ō) *n.* (esp. thieves') slang.

ar'gūe *v.* maintain by reasoning; prove; reason; contend, wrangle.

ar'gūment *n.* reason advanced; debate; summary of subject-matter of book etc. **~ā'tion** *n.* **argūmĕn'tative** *a.* fond of arguing.

Ar'gus (ār-) *n.* (Gk. myth.) fabulous person with hundred eyes. **~-eyed** *a.* vigilant.

Argyl. *abbr.* Argyllshire.

ar'ia *n.* song for one voice in opera, oratorio, etc.

Ar'ian (ār-) *a.* & *n.* (holder) of heretical doctrine of Arius, denying consubstantiality of Christ. **~ism** *n.*

ă'rid *a.* dry, parched. **ărid'itў** *n.*

Ar'iēs (ār-), Ram, first constellation and sign of zodiac.

aright' *adv.* rightly.

arīse' (-z) *v.i.* (arōse, arĭsen), appear, spring up, occur.

Arist., Aristot. *abbr.* Aristotle.

ărĭstŏc'racў *n.* nobility; supremacy of privileged order. **ă'rĭstocrăt** *n.* member of aristocracy. **ăristocrăt'ĭc** *a.*

Aristoph. *abbr.* Aristophanes.

Aristotē'lian (ă-) *a.* of Aristotie.

arith'mĕtĭc *n.* science of numbers; computation, use of numbers. **ărithmĕt'ical** *a.*; **~tĭ'cian** *n.*

Ariz. *abbr.* Arizona.

ark *n.* covered floating vessel in which Noah was saved in Flood; wooden coffer containing tables of Jewish law.

Ark. *abbr.* Arkansas.

arm[1] *n.* upper limb of human body; sleeve; branch; armlike thing. **~-chair,** chair with arms. **~pit,** hollow under arm at shoulder.

arm[2] *n.* particular kind of weapon; (pl.) weapons; (pl.) heraldic devices. *v.* furnish with arms; take up arms; provide, furnish, *with.*

Arma'da (-mah-) *n.* Spanish fleet sent against England in 1588.

** armadill'o** *n.* (pl. *-os*), S.-Amer. burrowing mammal with body cased in bony plates.

Armagĕdd'on (ār-, -g-) *n.* supreme battle at end of world.

ar'mament *n.* military equipment; equipping for war.

ar'mature *n.* framework of iron bars; piece of soft iron connecting poles of magnet; part of electric generator or motor in which currents are induced by action of field.

Armĭn'ian (ār-) *a.* & *n.* (adherent) of doctrine of Du. Protestant theologian Arminius.

ar'mĭstice *n.* cessation of hostilities; short truce.

arm'lĕt *n.* band worn round arm.

armōr'ial *a.* of heraldic arms.

ar'mour (-mer) *n.* defensive covering worn in fighting; steel plates etc. protecting ship, train, car, etc.; armoured vehicles etc. **~ed** *a.* furnished with armour, equipped with armoured vehicles. **~er** *n.* maker of arms; official in charge of arms.

ar'mourў (-mer-) *n.* place where arms are kept; arsenal; (U.S.) place where arms are manufactured.

ar'mў *n.* organized body of men armed for war; vast number; organized body. **~-list,** official list of commissioned officers.

ar'nĭca *n.* kinds of plant including mountain tobacco; tincture of this used for sprains, bruises, etc.

arō'ma *n.* fragrance, sweet smell; subtle quality. **ăromăt'ic** *a.*

arose, *p.t.* of **arise.**

around' *adv.* & *prep.* on every side (of), all round; about.

arouse' (-z) *v.t.* rouse.

ārpe'ggio (-ĕjĭō) *n.* (pl. *-os*), striking of notes of chord in rapid succession; chord so struck. [It.]

arquebus : see **harquebus.**

arr. *abbr.* arrives etc.

ă'rrack (*or* arăk') *n.* alcoholic spirit made in East, esp. from rice.

arraign' (-ān) *v.t.* indict, accuse; find fault with. **~ment** *n.*

arrānge' (-nj) *v.* put in order; settle; form plans; (mus.) adapt (composition). **~ment** *n.*

ă'rrant *a.* downright, notorious.

ă'rras *n.* (hangings of) tapestry.

array' *v.t.* dress, esp. with display; marshal (forces). *n.* dress; imposing series; martial order.

arrears' (-z) *n.pl.* outstanding debts; work etc. in which one is behindhand; *in* **~,** behindhand.

arrĕst' *v.t.* stop; seize by authority; apprehend; catch attention of. *n.* legal apprehension; stoppage.

arrière-pensée (ă'rĭār pahn̈'sā) *n.* ulterior motive; mental reservation. [F]

ă'rrĭs *n.* sharp edge where two planes or curved surfaces meet.

arrīve' *v.i.* come to destination or end of journey; attain object; establish one's position. **arrī'val** *n.*

ă'rrogant *a.* overbearing; presumptuous. **ă'rrogance** *n.*

ă'rrogāte *v.t.* claim unduly. **~ā'tion** *n.*

arrondissement (ărawn̈'dēsmahn̈) *n.* French administrative subdivision. [F]

ă'rrow (-ō) *n.* pointed missile shot from bow; mark etc. shaped like (head of) arrow, freq. used to indicate direction etc.

ă'rrowroot *n.* nutritious starch got from W.-Ind. plant.

ărse *n.* (vulg.) buttocks.

ăr'senal *n.* place for storage or manufacture of war material.

ăr'senĭc *n.* brittle steel-grey chemical element; its violently poisonous trioxide. **ărsĕn'ical** *a.*

ăr'sĭs *n.* (pl. *arsēs*), accented syllable in English scansion.

ăr'son *n.* wilful setting on fire of houses or other property.

art[1]: see **be.**

ărt[2] *n.* skill, esp. applied to representation, design, or imaginative creation; cunning; (pl.) branches of learning traditionally supposed to prepare for life or advanced studies; *fine ~s.* music, painting, etc.

ărtēr'ĭal *a.* of or in or like artery. **~ road,** main highway.

ărtērĭōsclerō'sĭs *n.* hardening of walls of arteries.

ăr'terȳ *n.* muscular-walled blood-vessel conveying blood from heart; important channel of supplies etc.

ărtē'sian (-zhn) **well** *n.* deep well in which water rises to surface through intervening impervious strata.

ărt'ful *a.* sly, crafty.

ărthrī'tĭs *n.* inflammation of joint. **ărthrĭt'ic** *a.*

ăr'tichōke *n.* thistle-like plant of which bases of flower-bud and surrounding scales are edible; Jerusalem artichoke.

ăr'tĭcle *n.* clause of agreement, treaty, etc.; literary composition forming part of magazine etc.; thing; (gram.) *definite ~,* 'the', *indefinite ~,* 'a, an'. *v.t.* bind by articles of apprenticeship.

ărtĭc'ūlar *a.* of joints.

ărtĭc'ūlate *a.* having joints; divided into words or syllables, distinct; capable of verbal expression. *v.* (-āt), speak distinctly, express clearly; connect by joints. **ărtĭcūlā'tion** *n.*

ăr'tĭfĭce *n.* device; cunning; skill.

ărtĭf'ĭcer *n.* craftsman.

ărtĭfĭ'cial *a.* produced by art; not natural, not real. **~ insemination,** insemination by injecting semen into uterus. **~ respiration,** manipulation etc. to restore suspended natural breathing. **ărtĭfĭcĭăl'itȳ** (-shĭ-) *n.*

ărtĭll'erȳ *n.* cannon; ordnance branch of army. **~man,** one serving in artillery, gunner.

ărtĭsăn' (-z-) *n.* mechanic, craftsman.

ăr'tĭst *n.* one who practises fine art, esp. painting; highly gifted practiser of any craft; artiste. **artis'tĭc** *a.*; **~rȳ** *n.*

ărtiste' (-tē-) *n.* professional singer, dancer, etc.

ărt'less *a.* guileless, simple; lacking art, crude.

ăr'tȳ *a.* having artistic pretensions.

ăr'um *n.* kinds of plant including cuckoo-pint. **~ lily,** white arum.

Ar'ȳan (ār-) *a. & n.* (esp. Eastern) Indo-European (language, speaker); (loosely) non-Jewish, esp. fair-haired blue-eyed (person).

as[1] (*az or ăz*) *adv. & conj.* in same degree; similarly; while, when; since, seeing that. *rel. pron.* that, who, which.

ăs[2] *n.* Roman copper coin.

A.S. *abbr.* Anglo-Saxon.

ăsafoe'tĭda *n.* resinous gum with smell of garlic.

Asaph. *abbr.* (Bishop) of St. Asaph's.

asbĕs'tŏs (ăz-) *n.* fibrous mineral; incombustible fabric woven from this.

ascĕnd' *v.* go or come up; rise, mount, climb.

ascĕn'dancў, -encў *n.* sway, powerful influence.

ascĕn'dant, -ent *a. & n.* rising, rising towards zenith; (point of ecliptic or degree of zodiac) just rising above eastern horizon; *in the* ∼, becoming predominant.

ascĕn'sion *n.* ascent, esp. of Christ into heaven; rising of celestial body. **A∼ Day**, sixth Thursday after Easter.

ascĕnt' *n.* ascending, rising; upward path or slope.

ăscertain' *v.t.* find out. ∼**ment** *n.*

ascĕt'ĭc *a.* severely abstinent, severe in self-discipline. *n.* ascetic person. ∼**ĭsm** *n.*

ascŏr'bĭc ă'cĭd *n.* antiscorbutic vitamin, vitamin C.

ascrībe' *v.t.* attribute, impute; assign.

ascrĭp'tion *n.* ascribing.

As'dĭc (ăz-) *n.* echo-sounding device for detecting under-water objects.

āsĕp'sĭs (*or a-*) *n.* absence of putrefactive matter or harmful bacteria; aseptic method in surgery.

āsĕp'tĭc (*or a-*) *a.* preventing putrefaction by securing absence of bacteria; surgically sterile, sterilized. *n.* aseptic substance.

āsĕx'ūal (*or a-*) *a.* without sex.

ăsh[1] *n.* (wood of) kinds of forest tree. ∼**en**[1] *a.* of ash.

ăsh[2] *n.* powdery residue left after combustion of any substance; (pl.) remains of human body after cremation; *the Ashes*, symbol of victory in series of cricket test--matches between England and Australia. **Ash Wednesday**, first day of Lent. **ăsh'en**[2] *a.* ashy.

ashāmed' (-md) *a.* abashed or upset by feeling of shame.

ăsh'lar *n.* square hewn stone(s); masonry of this. ∼**ing** *n.* short upright wall in garret cutting off angle of rafters.

ashŏre' *adv.* to or on shore.

ăsh'ў *a.* of or like ashes; pale.

A'sian (ā'shan), **Asiăt'ĭc** (āshĭ-) *aa. & nn.* (native) of Asia.

asīde' *adv.* to or on one side, away, apart. *n.* words spoken aside, esp. by actors.

ăs'inīne *a.* of asses; stupid.

ask (ah-) *v.* inquire, put question (to); make request (for); invite, demand.

askănce' *adv.* sideways; *look* ∼ *at*, view suspiciously.

askew' *adv.* obliquely, awry.

aslant' (-ahnt) *adv.* obliquely. *prep.* slantingly across.

asleep' *adv. & pred. a.* in state of sleep; (of limbs) benumbed; (of top) spinning without apparent motion.

ASLIB, As'lĭb (ăz-) *abbr.* Association of Special Libraries and Information Bureaux.

aslōpe' *adv. & pred. a.* sloping, crosswise.

ăsp *n.* small venomous snake.

aspă'ragus *n.* plant whose vernal shoots are table delicacy.

ăs'pĕct *n.* way thing presents itself to eye or mind; direction in which thing fronts, side fronting in stated direction; (astrol.) relation of planet etc. to other heavenly bodies.

ăs'pĕn *n.* kind of poplar with tremulous leaves.

ăspĕ'ritў *n.* harshness; roughness.

aspĕrse' *v.t.* attack reputation of, calumniate. **aspĕr'sion** *n.*

ăs'phălt *n.* pitch resulting from evaporation of petroleum; mixture of this with sand etc. for surfacing roads etc. *v.t.* surface with asphalt.

ăs'phodĕl *n.* kinds of lily; (poet.) immortal flower covering Elysian meads.

ăsphўx'ĭa *n.* suffocation. ∼**ĭal** *a.* ∼**ĭāte** *v.* suffocate. ∼**ĭā'tion** *n.*

ăs'pĭc *n.* savoury jelly, usu. with cold game, eggs, etc. in it.

ăspĭdĭs'tra *n.* foliage plant with broad taper leaves.

ăs'pĭrate *n.* sound of *h*, consonant blended with this. *v.t.* (-āt), pronounce with *h*.

aspīre' *v.i.* feel earnest desire or ambition; reach high. **ăs'pĭrant** *n.* one who aspires. **ăspĭrā'tion** *n.*

ăs'pĭrĭn *n.* kind of analgesic and febrifuge.

asquĭnt' *adv. & pred. a.* with squint.

ăss (*or* ahs) *n.* long-eared quadruped of horse family; stupid fellow.

assail' *v.t.* attack, assault. ∼**ant** *n.*

assăss'ĭn *n.* one hired to kill another treacherously; murderer. ∼**āte** *v.t.*

kill by treacherous violence. ~ā'tion *n.*

assault' *n.* attack on fortress etc. by sudden rush; unlawful personal attack; (euphem.) rape. *v.t.* make attack upon; rape.

assay' *n.* trial of ore for quantity of metal, bullion for fineness, etc.; testing. *v.t.* make assay of; attempt.

ăss'ĕgai (-gī) *n.* throwing spear of S.-Afr. peoples.

assĕm'blage *n.* collection, concourse.

assĕm'ble *v.* bring or come together; collect; fit together parts of (machine etc.).

assĕm'blў *n.* gathering of persons, esp. of deliberative body; assembling of parts, parts assembled. ~ line, sequence of machines, workers, etc. for assembly of product.

assĕnt' *v.i.* agree (*to*). *n.* concurrence; sanction.

assĕrt' *v.t.* maintain claim to; declare; ~ oneself, insist on one's rights. assĕr'tion *n.* ~tive *a.* positive, dogmatic.

assĕss' *v.t.* fix amount of (fine, tax, etc.); value, esp. for taxation. ~mĕnt *n.* ~or *n.* one who assesses taxes; adviser to judge or magistrate.

ăss'ĕt *n.* (pl.) all available property of person or company; (sing.) item of this; any possession or useful quality.

assĕv'erāte *v.t.* declare solemnly. ~ā'tion *n.*

ăssĭdū'ĭtў *n.* constant attention.

assĭd'ūous *a.* diligent, unremitting.

assign' *v.t.* make over formally; allot; appoint, ascribe. *n.* one to whom property or right is legally transferred. ~ee' *n.* one appointed to act for another; assign. ~ment *n.* (esp.) task, commission.

ăss'ĭgnăt *n.* paper money secured on State lands, esp. in Fr. Revolution.

ăssĭgnā'tion *n.* assigning; appointment.

assĭm'ĭlāte *v.* make or become like; absorb, be absorbed, into system. ~ā'tion *n.*; ~ative, ~atorў *aa.*

assĭst' *v.* help, aid; take part (*in*). ~ance *n.*

assĭs'tant *n.* helper; subordinate worker, esp. serving customers.

assīze' *n.* (usu. pl) periodical sessions held by judges on circuit; (hist.) statutory price (*of* bread and ale).

Assoc. *abbr.* Association.

assō'cĭāte (-shĭ-) *v.* join, unite together; have intercourse (*with*); connect in idea. *n.* (-at), partner, companion, subordinate member of association. *a.* (-at) allied.

assōcĭā'tion *n.* organized body of persons; connexion of ideas; intercourse. A~ football, kind played with round ball which may be handled only by goalkeeper.

ăss'onance *n.* resemblance of sound between two syllables; rhyme depending on similarity of vowel-sounds only. ~ant *a.*

assōrt' *v.* arrange in sorts; suit, harmonize (*with*). ~ed *a.* of different sorts put together. ~ment *n.*

Asst. *abbr.* Assistant.

assuāge' (-sw-) *v.t.* soothe, allay. ~ment (-jm-) *n.*

assūme' *v.t.* take upon oneself; simulate; take for granted.

assŭmp'tion *n.* assuming; arrogance; the A~, reception of Virgin Mary into heaven, feast (15th Aug.) in honour of this.

assure (ashoor') *v.t.* make safe, make certain; make sure (of), tell confidently; insure (life). assur'ance *n.* positive assertion; self-confidence; impudence; (life) insurance. assur'edlў *adv.* certainly.

ăs'ter *n.* kinds of plant with showy radiated flowers; (U.S.) Michaelmas daisy.

ăs'terĭsk *n.* mark of reference (*).

astĕrn' *adv.* in, at, towards, stern; behind; backwards.

ăs'teroid *n.* any of numerous small' planets between orbits of Mars and Jupiter.

ăsth'ma (-sm-) *n.* disorder marked by paroxysms of difficult breathing. asthmăt'ic *a.* & *n.*

astĭg'matĭsm *n.* defect in eye or lens preventing rays of light from being brought to proper focus. ăstĭg-măt'ĭc *a.*

astĭr' *adv.* & *pred. a.* in motion; out of bed.

astŏn'ĭsh *v.t.* amaze, surprise. **astŏn'- ĭshment** *n.*

astound' *v.t.* shock with surprise.

ăstrakhan' (-kăn) *n.* (cloth imitating) Persian lamb.

ăs'tral *a.* of or connected with stars. **~ body**, (theosophy) spiritual counterpart of human body.

astray' *adv.* & *pred. a.* out of right way.

astrīde' *adv.* & *pred. a.* with legs wide apart or one on each side (*of*).

astrĭn'gent (-nj-) *a.* & *n.* (substance) contracting or drawing together organic tissues. **~encў** *n.*

ăs'trolābe *n.* instrument formerly used in taking altitudes etc.

astrŏl'ogў *n.* study of occult influence of stars on human affairs. **~loger** *n.* **~lŏ'gical** *a.*

ăs'tronaut *n.* traveller in space. **~nau'tĭc(al)** *aa.* · **~nau'tĭcs** *n.* science of navigation in space.

astrŏn'omў *n.* science of heavenly bodies. **~nomer** *n.* student of astronomy. **~nŏm'ĭc(al)** *aa.* of or concerned with astronomy; very big, immense.

astūte' *a.* shrewd; crafty.

asŭn'der *adv.* apart, in pieces.

asȳ'lum *n.* institution for afflicted, esp. insane, persons; refuge; sanctuary.

asȳmm'ĕtrў (*or* ā-) *n.* want of symmetry or proportion. **ăsȳmmĕt'rĭcal** *a.*

at (*at or* ăt) *prep.* expressing position or time of day; **~** *all*, in any way, of any kind; **~** *that*, moreover.

ăt'avĭsm *n.* resemblance to remote ancestors; reversion to earlier type. **ătavĭs'tic** *a.*

ăt'elier (-*elyā*) *n.* studio, workshop.

ā'thĕĭsm *n.* disbelief in existence of God. **~ĭst** *n.*; **~ĭs'tic** *a.*

ăthĕnae'um *n.* literary or scientific club.

athĭrst' *pred. a.* thirsty; eager (*for*).

ăth'lēte *n.* one who competes or excels in physical exercises or some sports (running, jumping, etc.).

athlĕt'ĭc *a.* physically powerful; of athletes. *n.* (pl.) athletic sports. **~ĭsm** *n.*

athwart' (-ôrt) *adv.* & *prep.* across, esp. obliquely.

ăt'las *n.* volume of maps.

ăt'mosphēre *n.* spheroidal gaseous envelope, esp. that surrounding earth; mental or moral environment; air. **atmosphĕ'ric** *a.* **atmosphĕ'rics** *n.pl.* electrical disturbances in air interfering with radio or telephone reception.

atŏll' (*or* ăt'ŏl) *n.* ring-shaped coral reef enclosing lagoon.

ăt'om *n.* body too small to be divided; minute thing; smallest particle of element that can exist alone or in combination with similar particles. **~ bomb**, atomic bomb. **~īze** *v.t.* reduce to atoms; reduce (liquid) to fine spray. **~īzā'tion**, **~īzer** *nn.*

atŏm'ĭc *a.* of atom(s); resulting from or utilizing disintegration of atomic nucleus. **~ number**, that determining position of element in periodic table, number of unit positive charges carried by nucleus of atom. **~ weight**, ratio between weight of one atom of element and $\frac{1}{16}$ atom of oxygen.

ăt'omў *n.* atom, tiny being; emaciated body.

atō'nal *a.* (mus.) without conscious reference to any scale or mode. **~ăl'itў** *n.*

atōne' *v.t.* make amends; **~** *for*, expiate. **~ment** *n.*

atŏn'ic *a.* unaccented.

ătrabĭl'ĭous *a.* melancholy, gloomy; splenetic.

atrō'cious *a.* heinous, gross. **atrō'citў** *n.* atrocious deed; (colloq.) hideous object.

ăt'rophў *n.* wasting away for lack of nourishment or use. *v.* cause atrophy in; suffer atrophy.

ăt'ropĭne (*or* -ēn) *n.* poisonous alkaloid got from deadly nightshade.

attăch' *v.* fasten, join; attribute *to*; adhere, be incident *to*; bind in friendship; seize by legal authority. **~ment** *n.*

attaché (atăsh'ā) *n.* junior official attached to ambassador's suite. **~ case** *n.* small rectangular case for documents etc.

attăck' *v.t.* fall upon with (esp. armed) force; set upon with hostile action or words; act harmfully on. *n.* act of attacking; assault; onset.

attain' *v.* reach, gain, accomplish; ~ *to*, arrive at. ~ment *n.* (esp., pl.) personal accomplishments.

attain'der *n.* punishment by loss of civil rights etc.

attaint' *v.t.* subject to attainder.

ătt'ar *n.* fragrant oil distilled from flowers, esp. roses.

attĕmpt' *v.t.* try; try to accomplish or master. *r.* attempting; endeavour.

attĕnd' *v.* apply mind or oneself (*to*); be present at; accompany, wait on.

attĕn'dance *n.* attending; body of persons present.

attĕn'dant *a.* waiting on; accompanying. *n.* one who attends.

attĕn'tion *n.* attending; consideration, care; (mil.) formal attitude of troops on parade etc.; (pl.) ceremonious politeness, courtship. **attĕn'tĭve** *a.* heedful, observant; polite.

attĕn'ūāte *v.t.* make slender or thin; reduce in force or value. *a.* (-at), slender; rarefied. ~ā'tion *n.*

attĕst' *v.t.* bear witness to, certify; put on oath or solemn declaration. **ăttĕstā'tion** *n.* ~ĕd *a.* (of cattle) officially certified free from disease.

ătt'ĭc *n.* (room in) storey immediately under roof.

Att'ĭc (ă-) *a.* of Athens or Attica. ~ **order**, square column of any of five orders of architecture.

attīre' *v.t.* & *n.* dress, array.

ătt'ĭtūde *n.* posture of body; settled behaviour as showing opinion; ~ (*of mind*), settled mode of thinking. **ăttĭtū'dĭnīze** *v.i.* assume attitudes; show affectation.

attor'ney (-tẽr-) *n.* business or legal representative (appointed by *letter* or *power of* ~); solicitor. **A~-General**, chief legal officer appointed to act in cases in which State is party.

attrăct' *v.t.* draw to oneself; allure, charm. **attrăc'tion** *n.* attracting; thing that attracts; charm, inducement. ~ĭve *a.* inviting, pleasing.

attrĭb'ūte *v.t.* ascribe as belonging or appropriate *to*: assign. *n.* (ăt'-), quality ascribed to person or thing; characteristic quality; object regarded as appropriate to person or

office. **ăttrĭbū'tion** *n.* **attrĭb'ūtĭve** *a.* expressing an attribute, qualifying.

attrĭ'tion *n.* friction; abrasion; wearing out.

attūne' *v.t.* bring into musical accord; adapt; tune.

aubergine (ō'berzhēn) *n.* fruit of egg-plant used as vegetable.

aubrie'tia (-brēsha) *n.* spring-flowering dwarf perennial rock-plant.

au'burn *a.* reddish brown.

A.U.C. *abbr.*, *ab urbe condita, anno urbis conditae* [L], from, in year of, founding of Rome.

auc'tion *n.* sale in which articles are sold to highest bidder; (cards) form of bridge. *v.t.* sell (*off*) by auction. ~**eer'** *n.* conductor of auctions.

audā'cious *a.* daring, bold; impudent. **audă'cĭtў** *n.*

au'dĭble *a.* that can be heard. **audĭbĭl'ĭtў** *n.*

au'dĭence *n.* formal interview; hearing; assembly of listeners or spectators.

au'dĭt *n.* official examination of accounts. *v.t.* examine (accounts) officially.

audĭ'tion *n.* trial hearing of actor, singer, etc. *v.* give audition to; hold audition(s).

au'dĭtor *n.* one who audits accounts; hearer. ~**ōr'ĭal** *a.*

audĭtōr'ĭum *n.* part of building occupied by audience.

au'dĭtorў *a.* of hearing.

au fait (ō fā'), conversant, instructed. [F]

au fond (ō fawn'), at bottom. [F]

Aug. *abbr.* August.

au'ger (-g-) *n.* boring-tool with long shank and screw point.

aught (awt) *n.* anything.

augmĕnt' *v.t.* make greater, increase; prefix augment to. *n.* (aw'-) (gram.) vowel prefixed to past tenses in some languages. **augmĕntā'tion** *n.* ~**atĭve** *a.* increasing force of idea of original word. ~**ĕd** *a.* (mus., of interval) increased by semitone.

au'gur (-er) *n.* Roman religious official who predicted events by omens; soothsayer. *v.* foretell; betoken, give promise (of). **au'gurў** *n.* divination; omen; prophecy.

augŭst'[1] *a.* venerable, imposing.

Au'gust² *n.* eighth month of year.

auk *n.* kinds of sea-bird including puffin and guillemot, esp. extinct flightless *great* ~.

aunt (ahnt) *n.* parent's sister or sister-in-law. **A~ Sally**, game of throwing balls at wooden head.

au pair¹ (ō pār'), (of arrangement) on basis of mutual services, without monetary payments. [F]

au-pair'² (ō-; *or* ō'-) *a.* (colloq., esp. of foreigner) performing domestic duties in return for instruction in language etc.

aur'a *n.* subtle emanation; atmosphere diffused by or attending person etc.

aur'al *a.* of ear.

aur'ēōle *n.* gold disc or circle of light depicted round and behind head; halo, esp. that seen in eclipses.

au revoir (ōrevwahr'), (good-bye) till we meet again. [F]

aur'ïcle *n.* external ear of animals; small appendage of either upper cavity of heart.

aurïc'üla *n.* kinds of alpine primula.

aurïc'ülar *a.* of ear or hearing. **~ confession**, made privately to priest.

aurif'erous *a.* yielding gold.

aur'öchs (-ks) *n.* extinct wild ox.

aurōr'a *n.* (*A~*) Roman goddess of dawn; luminous electrical radiation from northern (~ bōrēā'lïs) or southern (~ austrā'lïs) magnetic pole.

auscultā'tion *n.* listening to sound made by heart, lungs, etc.

au'spïces *n. pl.* (good) omens; patronage. **auspï'cious** *a.* of good omen, promising.

austēre' *a.* morally strict; severely simple; stern. **austě'rïty** *n.*

au'stral *a.* southern.

Australā'sian *a. & n.* (native) of Australia and S.-W. Pacific islands.

Austrā'lïan *a. & n.* (native) of Australia.

au'tarchy (-kï) *n.* absolute sovereignty.

au'tarkÿ *n.* (esp. economic) self-sufficiency.

authěn'tïc *a.* trustworthy, reliable; of undisputed origin, genuine. **authěn-tï'cïtÿ** *n.*

authěn'tïcāte *v.t.* establish truth, authorship, or validity of. **~ā'tion** *n.*

au'thor *n.* writer of book etc.; originator. **~ess, ~ship** *nn.*

authörïtār'ïan *a. & n.* (person) favouring obedience to authority as opp. individual liberty.

authö'rïtative *a.* having or claiming authority.

authö'rïtÿ *n.* power or right to enforce obedience; personal influence; person etc. having authority; (book etc. referred to for) conclusive opinion or statement; expert.

au'thorïze *v.t.* sanction; give ground for or authority to. **Authorized Version** (of Bible), English translation of 1611. **~zā'tion** *n.*

autïs'tïc *a.* morbidly self-absorbed and out of contact with reality.

autobīŏg'raphÿ *n.* (writing of) one's own life. **autobīŏg'rapher** *n.*; **~grăph'ïc(al)** *aa.*

autŏch'thonous (-k-) *a.* aboriginal, indigenous.

autŏc'racÿ *n.* absolute government. **au'tocrăt** *n.* absolute ruler. **~crăt'ïc** *a.*

auto-da-fé (aw'todahfā') *n.* (pl. *autos--da-fé*), sentence of Inquisition; execution of this. [Port.]

au'tograph (-ahf) *n.* own handwriting, esp. signature. *v.t.* write autograph on or in, sign.

automăt'ïc *a.* mechanical; unconscious, involuntary; self-acting. *n.* automatic pistol. **autŏm'atism** *n.* involuntary or unconscious action.~

automā'tion *n.* automatic control of manufactured product through successive stages. **au'tomātěd** *a.*

autŏm'aton *n.* (pl. *-ta, -tons*), piece of mechanism with concealed motive--power and lifelike actions.

au'tomobile' (-ēl) *n.* motor-car.

autŏn'omous *a.* self-governing. **autŏn'omÿ** *n.*

autŏp'sÿ (*or* aw'-) *n.* post-mortem examination. **autŏp'tïc** *a.*

autō-suggěs'tion *n.* hypnotic suggestion proceeding from subject himself.

au'tumn (-m) *n.* third season of year, between summer and winter;

season of incipient decay. **autŭm'-nal** *a.*

auxĭl'iarў *a.* helpful; subsidiary; (of verbs) serving to form tenses etc. of other verbs. *n.* assistant; (pl.) troops not belonging to regular establishment.

A.V. *abbr.* Authorized Version.

avail' *v.* be of use or assistance (to); help, benefit; ~ *oneself of*, use, take advantage of. *n.* use, profit. ~**able** *a.* capable of being used, at one's disposal. ~**abil'itў** *n.*

ăv'alanche (-ahnsh) *n.* mass of snow, earth, and ice falling down mountain.

ăv'arice *n.* greed of gain, cupidity. **ăvari'cious** *a.*

avast' (-ahst) *int.* (naut.) stop.

ăv'atār *n.* (Hindu myth.) descent to earth and incarnation of deity.

avaunt' *int.* (arch.) begone.

avdp. *abbr.* avoirdupois.

ā've (*or* ah-) *int.* & *n.* (cry of) welcome, hail. **A~ Maria**, devotional recitation and prayer to Virgin.

avĕnge' (-j) *v.t.* inflict retribution on behalf of; exact retribution for.

ăv'ĕnūe *n.* roadway, approach to house, bordered by regularly spaced trees etc.; way of approach.

avēr' *v.t.* assert, affirm.

ăv'erage *n.* arithmetical mean; ordinary standard; generally prevailing degree etc. *a.* estimated by average; of usual standard. *v.* estimate average of; amount on average (to).

averse' *a.* opposed, disinclined, unwilling. **avēr'sion** *n.* dislike or antipathy; object of dislike.

avĕrt' *v.t.* ward off; turn away.

ā'viarў *n.* large cage or building for keeping birds.

āviā'tion *n.* flying in aircraft. **ā'viator** *n.*

ăv'ĭd *a.* eager, greedy. **avĭd'itў** *n.*

ăvoca'dō (-kah-) *n.* succulent pear-shaped tropical fruit.

ăvocā'tion *n.* vocation, calling.

avoid' *v.t.* shun, keep away from; (law) annul. ~**ance** *n.*

avoirdupois (ăverdŭpoiz') *n.* system of weights with ounces etc. as units; weight, heaviness.

avouch' *v.t.* vouch for; affirm.

avow' *v.t.* admit, confess. ~**al** *n.*; ~**ėdly** *adv.*

avŭnc'ūlar *a.* of or like uncle.

await' (a-) *v.t.* wait for.

awāke' (a-) *v.* (p.t. *awōke*, p.p. *awaked* or *awoke*), cease to sleep; become active, be aroused *to*; rouse from sleep. *pred. a.* not asleep; vigilant. **awā'ken** *v.* awake, arouse (*to*).

award (awŏrd') *v.t.* adjudge; grant, assign. *n.* judicial decision; thing awarded.

awāre' (a-) *a.* conscious, not ignorant (*of*). ~**ness** *n.*

awash' (awŏ-) *pred. a.* flush with or washed by waves.

away' (a-) *adv.* to or at distance; constantly, continuously.

awe *n.* reverential fear. *v.t.* inspire with awe. ~**struck**, struck with awe. ~**some** *a.* dread, terrible.

aweigh (awā') *adv.* (of anchor) just lifted from ground.

aw'ful *a.* inspiring awe; (colloq.) notable in its kind. ~**ly** *adv.* (esp., colloq.) very.

awhile (awīl') *adv.* for a time.

aw'kward *a.* ill-adapted for use; hard to deal with; clumsy.

awl *n.* small pricking-tool.

awn *n.* beard of grain.

aw'ning *n.* canvas roof; shelter.

A.W.O.L. *abbr.* absent without leave.

awry (arī') *adv.* crookedly; amiss.

ăxe *n.* tool for chopping.

ăx'ial *a.* forming, belonging to, axis.

ăx'iom *n.* self-evident truth; established principle. **ăxiomăt'ic** *a.*

ăx'is *n.* (pl. *axēs*), line about which body rotates; line dividing regular figure symmetrically.

ăx'le *n.* spindle on or with which wheel revolves; (end of) axle-tree. ~**-tree**, bar connecting pair of wheels.

Ax'minster (ă-) (**carpet**) *n.* machine-made tufted carpet.

ay (ī) *int.* yes. *n.* (pl. *ayes*), affirmative answer or vote.

ayah (ī'a) *n.* white children's native Indian nurse.

aye (ā) *adv.* always.

azā'lea *n.* kinds of flowering shrubby plant.

ăz'imuth *n.* arc of heavens from

zenith to horizon; arc of horizon between meridian and vertical circle passing through heavenly body.

azure (ā'zh*er*; *or* ă-) *n. & a.* unclouded blue (sky); (her.) blue; sky--blue.

B

B, b (bē), (mus.) 7th note in scale of C major.

B. *abbr.* bass; *Beatus, -ta* [L], Blessed; black.

b. *abbr.* born; bowled; bye.

B.A. *abbr.* Bachelor of Arts; British Academy; British Association.

baa (bah) *n. & v.i.* (*baaing, baa'd*), bleat.

baas (bahs) *n.* (S.-Afr.) boss.

băbb'le *v.* talk or say half articulately or foolishly; (of stream) murmur. *n.* idle talk; prattle.

bābe *n.* baby.

bā'bel *n.* (scene of) confusion and uproar.

baboon' *n.* large monkey.

bā'bў *n.* very young child, esp. one not yet able to walk; childish person. ~ **car**, very small motor-car. ~ **grand**, small grand piano. ~-**sitter**, person employed to remain with children while parents are out. ~**ĭsh** *a.*

băccalaur'ēate *n.* degree of bachelor.

băcc'arat (-rah) *n.* gambling card--game.

băcch'anal (-ka-) *a.* of Bacchus or his rites. *n.* Bacchant; reveller. ~**ā'lĭa** *n.pl.* festival of Bacchus. ~**ā'lĭan** *a.*

Băcch'ant (-k-), **Bacchăn'tē** (*or* -t) *nn.* priest, priestess, votary, of Bacchus.

Băcch'us (-k*u*s) *n.* Greek god of wine. **băcch'ĭc** *a.* bacchanal; drunken.

băch'elor *n.* unmarried man; holder of university degree below Master. ~ **girl**, unmarried girl living independently.

bacĭll'us *n.* (pl. -*llī*) straight rod--shaped bacterium. **bacĭll'arў** *a.*

băck *n.* hinder surface of human body; upper surface of animal's body; hind part of things; rear;

football player stationed behind forwards. *a.* situated behind; covering past period. *adv.* to rear; in(to) earlier or retired or remote position; ~ *of*, (U.S.) behind. *v.* put or be back or lining or background to; support with money, argument, etc.; bet on; endorse (cheque etc.); ride (horse); cause to move back; go backwards; ~ *out of*, withdraw from; ~ *up*, support, (cause to) move back. ~**blocks**, (Austral.) furthermost fringe of settlement. ~-**chat**, back talk. ~-**cloth**, ~**drop**, painted cloth at back of scene or stage. ~**door**, door at back of house; underhand or secret (means or approach). ~**fire**, (produce) premature explosion in cylinder, explosion in hot exhaust-pipe, of internal combustion engine. ~**log**, arrears (of work etc.). ~ **number**, (sl.) out-of-date method, person, etc. ~ **room**, place where (esp. secret) research or other work goes on. ~**stage**, behind the scenes. ~ **talk**, (sl.) impudent answer(s). ~**wash**, motion of receding wave, wash behind vessel.

băck'bīte *v.t.* slander. ~**r** *n.*

băck'bōne *n.* spine, main support; firmness of character.

băck'er *n.* one who backs or supports.

băckgămm'on *n.* game for two played on special double board with draughts and dice.

băck'ground *n.* back part of scene; obscurity, retirement; person's social surroundings, education, etc.

băck'hănd, -hăn'dĕd *aa.* delivered with back of hand, or with back of hand turned in direction of stroke; equivocal. **back-hănder** *n.* backhand blow

băckslīde' *v.i.* relapse into sin, error, etc.

băck'stairs' *n.pl.* back or secondary stairs. *a.* secret, underhand.

băck'stĭtch *v.* sew by inserting needle each time behind place where it was brought out. *n.* stitch made thus.

băck'ward(s) *adv.* back foremost; back towards starting-point; reverse way. **băck'ward** *a.* directed backwards; slow in learning.

băck'water (-waw-) *n.* still water

beside stream and fed by its back flow.

băck'woŏds *n.pl.* remote uncleared forest land. **~man** *n.* settler in this; peer who rarely attends House of Lords.

bā'con *n.* cured back and sides of pig.

băctērĭŏl'ogў *n.* study of bacteria, esp. as branch of medicine. **~lŏ'gĭcal** *a.*

băctēr'ĭum *n.* (pl. *-ia*), kinds of microscopic unicellular organism found almost everywhere, some causing disease, decay, etc. **bactēr'ĭal** *a.*

băd *a.* (comp. *worse*, sup. *worst*), worthless, defective, inefficient, not valid; wicked, depraved; corrupt, decayed; injurious; painful; ill, injured, in pain.

bade, *p.t.* of bid.

bădge *n.* emblem or mark as sign of office, membership, etc.

bădg'er *n.* nocturnal burrowing quadruped intermediate between weasel and bear. *v.t.* worry, pester.

băd'ĭnage (-ahzh) *n.* banter.

băd'lў *adv.* defectively, unsuccessfully; to serious extent.

băd'mĭnton *n.* game like lawn-tennis played with shuttlecocks.

băff'le *v.t.* foil, frustrate, perplex. *n.* plate etc. hindering or regulating passage of fluid, sound, etc.

băg *n.* receptacle of flexible material with opening usu. at top; sac in animal body for honey, poison, etc.; all sportsman has shot; (pl., sl.) trousers. *v.* put in bag; secure (game); (colloq.) take possession of, steal; bulge; hang loosely. **băgg'ў** *a.* loose-hanging.

băgatĕlle' *n.* mere trifle; game of billiards kind.

băgg'age *n.* portable equipment of army; luggage; (joc.) saucy girl.

bagnio (băn'yō) *n.* Oriental prison; brothel.

băg'pīpe(s) *n.* musical instrument with wind-bag held under arm. **băg'pīper** *n.*

bail¹ *n.* security for prisoner's appearance for trial; person who becomes surety. *v.t.* become bail for and secure liberation of; deliver (goods) in trust. **~ee'** *n.* one to

whom goods are entrusted. **~ment, ~or** *nn.*

bail² *n.* (crick.) either cross-piece resting on top of stumps.

bail³ : see **bale³**.

bai'ley *n.* open space enclosed by fortification: *Old B~*, Central Criminal Court in London.

bai'lie *n.* Scottish municipal officer corresponding to English alderman.

bai'liff *n.* sheriff's officer who distrains, arrests, etc.; agent collecting rents, steward managing estate, etc.

bai'liwick *n.* district of bailie or bailiff.

bairn *n.* (Sc.) child.

bait *v.t.* worry (animal) by setting dogs at it; worry (person) by jeers; give (horse etc.) food; put bait on or in (fish-hook, trap, etc.). *n.* food to entice prey; allurement.

baize *n.* coarse woollen usu. green stuff used for covers etc.

bāke *v.* cook by dry heat; harden by heat; be or become baked. **~house,** place for baking bread etc. **baking--powder,** used to make cakes etc. rise.

bā'kelīte (-ke-) *n.* kind of plastic. **P.**

bā'ker *n.* professional bread-maker. **~'s dozen,** thirteen. **~ў** *n.* bakehouse; trade of baking.

băk'sheesh *n.* gratuity, tip.

bălalai'ka (-līka) *n.* Russian guitar--like musical instrument.

băl'ance *n.* weighing apparatus; regulating gear of clock etc.; equilibrium; preponderating weight or amount; excess of assets over liabilities or vice versa; remainder. *v.* weigh; equalize, match; bring or come into equilibrium. **~-sheet,** statement of assets and liabilities.

băl'as *n.* rose-red spinel ruby.

balăt'a (*or* băl'-) *n.* dried milky juice of some tropical Amer. trees as substitute for gutta-percha.

băl'conў *n.* outside balustraded or railed platform with access from upper-floor window; (seats in) gallery of public building, in theatre usu. between dress-circle and gallery.

bald (bawld) *a.* with scalp wholly or partly hairless; without feathers etc.; bare; meagre, dull.

băl'dachin (-k-), **-quin** n. canopy over throne etc.

bal'derdash (bawl-) n. jumble of words, nonsense.

bal'dric (bawl-) n. belt for sword, bugle, etc.

bāle[1] n. evil, destruction, woe.

bāle[2] n. & v.t. (make up into) large bundle or package of merchandise, hay, etc.

bāle[3], **bail**[3] v. throw water out of boats etc. with bowls etc.; ~ **out**, bale, abandon aircraft in air.

baleen' n. whalebone.

bāle'ful (-lf-) a. pernicious, destructive, malignant.

balk, baulk (bawk) n. roughly squared timber beam; stumbling--block; sanctuary area on billiard table; ridge left unploughed between furrows. v. thwart, hinder; foil; jib, shy.

ball[1] (bawl) n. solid or hollow sphere, esp. one used in game; rounded mass of snow, string, etc.; (crick.) single delivery of ball by bowler; missile for cannon, rifle, etc.; ~ *of foot* rounded part of sole at base of big toe. v.i. (of snow etc.) form lumps. ~**-bearing**, (ball of) bearing in which revolving parts turn on loose metal balls. ~**-cock**, valve in cistern etc. opened or shut by falling or rising of floating ball. ~**point (pen)**, pen whose writing point is small ball-bearing.

ball[2] (bawl) n. social assembly for dancing.

băll'ad n. simple sentimental song; (esp. traditional) narrative poem in short stanzas. ~**rӯ** n.

băllade' (-ahd) n. poem of 7- or 8-lined stanzas each ending with same line, followed by envoy.

băll'ast n. heavy material carried in ship's hold, balloon, etc., for stability; steadying element in character etc.; unscreened gravel, coarse stone, clinker, etc., esp. forming bed of railroad. v.t. furnish with ballast.

bălleri'na (-ēna) n. female solo ballet--dancer.

băll'et (-lā) n. stage entertainment telling story or expressing idea in dancing and mime.

ballis'ta n. (pl. -ae), ancient military engine for hurling stones etc. **ballis'tic** a. of projectiles. **ballis'tics** n.pl. science of these.

balloon' n. large air-tight envelope inflated with gas lighter than air; small usu. rubber envelope inflated with air as toy; outline containing words etc. represented as those of figure in cartoon etc. ~ **barrage**, anti-aircraft barrier of steel cables supported by captive balloons. ~**ist** n.

băll'ot n. (ball, paper, etc. used in) secret voting; drawing of lots. v.i. vote by ballot; draw lots.

băll'ӯ a. & adv. (sl.) mild or joc. euphemism for bloody.

băllyhoo' n. noisy or vulgar or misleading publicity.

balm (bahm) n. fragrant exudation; ointment; healing or soothing influence; tree yielding balm.

bălmŏ'ral n. kind of Sc. regimental cap.

balmy (bah'mi) a. of or like balm; fragrant, mild, soothing; silly.

băl'sa (or bawl-) n. (tropical Amer. tree yielding) extremely light wood.

bal'sam (bawl-) n. balm; kinds of ointment; tree yielding balm; kinds of flowering plant. **balsăm'ic** a.

băl'uster n. short pear-shaped pillar; post supporting handrail of staircase, (pl.) posts and handrail. **bălustrāde'** n. row of balusters with rail or coping as parapet.

bămboo' n. (hollow jointed stem of) kinds of tropical giant grass.

bămboo'zle v.t. hoax, mystify.

băn v.t. prohibit, interdict, forbid. n. formal or authoritative prohibition.

banal' (-ahl; or bā'-) a. commonplace, trite. **banăl'ity** n.

bana'na (-nah-) n. tropical fruit-tree; its finger-shaped fruit.

banau'sic a. fit (only) for artisans.

bănd n. flat strip of thin material; hoop of iron, rubber, etc.; belt connecting wheels; body of musicians; group of persons; stripe of colour etc.; (radio) group of frequencies that may be tuned together. v.t. form into league; put band on. ~**box**, box for millinery.

~master, conductor of musical band. ~-saw, endless saw running over wheels. ~sman, ~stand, member of, platform for, military or brass band. ~wagon, one carrying band at head of procession etc.; leading, popular, or winning side, cause, etc.

băn'dage *n.* strip of material for binding up wound etc. *v.t.* tie up with bandage.

băndănn'a *n.* yellow- or white--spotted coloured handkerchief.

băn'deau (-dō) *n.* (pl. -*x*, pr. -z), band of ribbon etc. round head; band inside woman's hat.

băn'dĭcōot *n.* kinds of rat-like Austral. insectivorous marsupial.

băn'dit *n.* (pl. -*its*, -*ĭtt'ĭ*), outlaw; brigand; lawless and violent robber, gangster. ~rў *n.*

băndoleer', -ier (-ēr) *n.* shoulder--belt with cartridge-loops.

băn'dў *v.t.* throw or pass to and fro; discuss; exchange. *n.* hockey. *a.* (of legs) wide apart at knees.

bāne *n.* ruin; poison. ~ful *a.* pernicious.

băng[1] *v.* strike or shut noisily; make sound as of blow or explosion; treat roughly, knock about. *n.* sharp blow; loud noise. *adv.* with bang, abruptly; ~ *on* (colloq.) right on, exactly right.

băng[2] *n.* front hair cut straight across forehead.

băng'le (-nggl) *n.* ring bracelet or anklet.

băn'ĭsh *v.t.* condemn to exile; dismiss from one's presence or mind. ~ment *n.*

băn(n)'ister *n.* baluster.

băn'jō *n.* (pl. -*os*), musical instrument like guitar with tambourine body. băn'jōĭst *n.*

bănk[1] *n.* raised shelf of ground, slope; ground at edge of river; (flat--topped) mass of cloud etc. *v.* contain, confine, as or with bank(s); build up outer edge of (road etc. at bend); incline aircraft, be inclined, laterally for turning; ~ *up*, heap or rise into bank(s), pack (fire) tightly for slow burning. ~ĭng[1] *n.*

bănk[2] *n.* establishment for custody of money; money before keeper of gaming-table. *v.* keep bank; deposit money at bank; count or rely *on*. ~-bill, bill drawn by one bank on another; (U.S.) bank-note. ~-book, book showing state of customer's bank-account. ~ holiday, public holiday when banks are closed. ~-note, banker's promissory note payable to bearer on demand. ~-rate, rate at which Bank of England will discount bills of exchange, used as basis for fixing some interest rates. ~ĭng[2] *n.* business of bank.

bănk[3] *n.* galley-rower's bench; tier in galley; row of organ keys.

bănk'er *n.* proprietor, director, etc. of bank; keeper of money staked at gaming-table; gambling card-game.

bănkĕt' *n.* auriferous conglomerate rock found in S. Africa.

bănk'rŭpt *n.* insolvent person. *a.* insolvent; bereft *of* (quality etc.). *v.t.* make bankrupt. ~cў *n.*

bănk'sĭa *n.* kinds of flowering shrub. ~ rose, kinds of climbing rose.

bănn'er *n.* flag of king, country, army, friendly society, etc.

bănn'erĕt *n.* knight with vassals under his banner; one knighted on field for valour.

bănn'ock *n.* Sc. home-made loaf, usu. unleavened and flat.

bănns (-z) *n.pl.* notice of intended marriage read three times in church.

băn'quĕt *n.* sumptuous feast; dinner with speeches. *v.* regale with, take part in, banquet.

bănquette' (-kĕt) *n.* firing-step in trench.

băn'shee *n.* spirit whose wail portends death in a house.

bănt *v.i.* reduce weight by dieting.

băn'tam *n.* small variety of fowl, of which cock is pugnacious; small but spirited person. ~-weight, boxing-weight (not over 8 st. 6 lb.).

băn'ter *n.* humorous ridicule. *v.* make good-humoured fun of; jest.

Băn'tu (-ōō) *n.* (pl. same), large group of Afr. negroid races; their language(s).

băn'yan (tree) *n.* Indian fig whose branches root themselves over large area.

bā′obăb *n.* African tree with extremely thick stem and edible fruit.

băp′tĭsm *n.* religious rite of immersing in or sprinkling with water in sign of purification and admission to (Christian) church. **băptĭs′mal** *a.* **Băp′tĭst** *n.* one of sect objecting to infant baptism and practising immersion. **băp′tĭst(e)rў** *n.* part of church where baptism is administered. **băptīze′** *v.t.* administer baptism to, christen; name.

bār[1] *n.* long-shaped piece of rigid material; slip of silver below clasp of medal as extra distinction; rod or pole or rail used to limit or confine or obstruct; barrier; broad line or band; (mus.) (vertical line marking off) one of sections of fixed time-value into which piece is divided; (room containing) counter at which refreshments are served; barristers, their profession. *v.t.* fasten with bars, keep in or out thus; obstruct, prevent; exclude. *prep.* except, excluding. **~maid, ~man, ~tender,** attendant at refreshment bar. **~room,** bar. **~ sinister** (erron.) badge of bastardy.

bār[2] *n.* unit of atmospheric pressure.

bărathė′a *n.* fine cloth of wool, wool and silk, etc.

bārb *n.* recurved point of arrow, fish-hook, etc. *v.t.* furnish with barb. **barbed wire,** for fences etc., with short pointed wires twisted in.

bārbār′ĭan *a.* uncivilized, wild, uncultured. *n.* such person.

bārbă′rĭc *a.* rude, rough; of barbarians.

bār′barĭsm *n.* rude or uncultured state; uncultured expression.

bārbă′rĭtў *n.* savage cruelty.

bār′barīze *v.* make or become barbarous. **~zā′tion** *n.*

bār′barous *a.* uncivilized.

bār′bėcūe *n.* framework for smoking or roasting or broiling; (freq. portable) fireplace with such framework; barbecued meat or fish; hog, ox, etc. roasted whole; (esp. open-air) social gathering where barbecue is served. *v.t.* cook on barbecue or with barbecue sauce. **~ sauce,** highly seasoned sauce of vinegar, spices, etc.

bār′bel *n.* fresh-water fish with fleshy appendages at mouth.

bār′ber *n.* one who shaves beards and cuts hair, hairdresser.

bār′berrў *n.* yellow-flowered shrub; its oblong red sharply acid berry.

bār′bĭcan *n.* outer defence to city or castle, esp. double tower over gate or bridge.

bārbĭt′ūrate (*or* -tūr′-) *n.* sedative derived from barbituric acid.

bārcarōl(l)e′ *n.* gondolier's song.

bārd *n.* Celtic minstrel; poet recognized at Eisteddfod. **bār′dĭc** *a.*

bāre *a.* unclothed, uncovered; exposed; unadorned; scanty; mere. *v.t.* make bare, strip, expose. **~back,** on unsaddled horse. **~faced,** shameless, impudent. **~lў** *adv.* scarcely, only just.

bār′gain (-gĭn) *n.* agreement on terms of purchase; compact; thing acquired cheap or by bargaining. *v.i.* haggle; stipulate; be prepared *for.*

bārge *n.* flat-bottomed freight-boat; large oared vessel for ceremonial occasions. *v.i.* lurch or rush heavily. **bārgee′** *n.* bargeman.

bārge′-board *n.* board or ornamental screen under edge of gable.

bă′rĭtōne *a.* between tenor and bass. *n.* baritone voice or singer.

bār′ĭum *n.* white metallic element.

bārk[1] *n.* outer sheath of tree trunk and branches; tan. *v.t.* strip bark from; abrade (shins etc.).

bārk[2], **bārque** (-k) *n.* vessel with fore- and main-masts square-rigged, mizen fore-and-aft rigged; (poet.) ship, boat.

bārk[3] *v.* (of dog etc.) utter sharp explosive cry; speak petulantly; cough. *n.* sound of barking; report of gun; cough. **~er** *n.* auction-room or side-show tout. **~ing deer,** Indian muntjak.

bār′ley *n.* (grain of) awned cereal used as food and in preparation of malt. **~corn,** grain of barley. **~-meal,** flour ground from barley. **~-sugar,** sweetmeat of boiled sugar. **~-water,** decoction of pearl barley.

bārm *n.* froth on fermenting malt liquor, yeast.

Bär'mecīde feast *n*. imaginary or illusory benefits.

bärn *n*. covered building for storing grain etc.

bär'nacle[1] *n*. (usu. pl.) pincers put on horse's nose to keep him still for shoeing etc.

bär'nacle[2] *n*. Arctic goose visiting Britain in winter; kinds of crustacean clinging to ships' bottoms etc.

barŏm'eter *n*. instrument measuring atmospheric pressure and used to forecast weather. bărŏmĕt'rĭc(al) *aa*.

bă'ron *n*. (hist.) great noble; member of lowest rank in British peerage. ~ of beef, double sirloin. ~age *n*. barons collectively. ~ess *n*. baron's wife; female baron. barō'nĭal *a*. of baron(s).

bă'ronĕt *n*. member of lowest hereditary titled order. ~age *n*. list of baronets. ~cў *n*. baronet's rank or patent.

bă'ronў *n*. baron's rank or domain; division of Irish county; large manor in Scotland.

barōque' (-k; *or* -ŏk) *a*. (of pearl) irregular in shape; of 17th–18th c. style esp. of architecture developed from that of late Renaissance; grotesque, whimsical. *n*. baroque style.

barouche' (-ōōsh) *n*. four-wheeled carriage for four occupants.

barque: see bark[2].

bär'quentine (-kentēn) *n*. vessel with foremast square-rigged, main and mizen fore-and-aft rigged.

bă'rrack *n*. (usu. pl.) building for lodging soldiers; building of severely plain or dull appearance. *v*. (sl.) jeer (at), cheer ironically.

bărracu'da (-ōō-) *n*. large voracious fish of W.-Ind. etc. seas.

bă'rrage (-ahzh) *n*. obstacle to enemy action, esp. line or area on which heavy gunfire is concentrated; heavy fire *of* questions etc.

bă'rrator *n*. litigious person.

bă'rratrў *n*. vexatious litigation; fraud of master or crew to prejudice of ship's owners.

bă'rrel *n*. cylindrical wooden vessel of hooped staves; contents of such vessel; metal tube of gun; cylinder;

cylindrical body of object. *v.t.* put in barrels. ~-organ *n*. musical instrument with pin-studded cylinder turned by handle and operating pipe-opening mechanism.

bă'rren *a*. not bearing, incapable of bearing (children, fruit, etc.); unprofitable. *n*. tract of barren land; (pl.) elevated unproductive land without large trees.

bărrĭcāde' *n*. improvised or hastily erected barrier, esp. of trees, paving-stones, etc., across street. *v.t.* block or defend or shut in (as) with barricade.

bă'rrĭer *n*. fence, rail, etc. barring advance or access; obstacle, circumstance, etc., that keeps apart.

bă'rrĭster *n*. lawyer entitled to practise as advocate in superior courts.

bă'rrow[1] (-ō) *n*. prehistoric grave--mound, tumulus.

bă'rrow[2] (-ō) *n*. frame with short shafts used for carrying load; wheelbarrow; two-wheeled hand--cart.

Bart. *abbr*. Baronet.

bär'ter *v*. exchange goods, rights, etc. for things of like kind. *n*. traffic by exchange.

bär'ton *n*. farmyard.

Bart's *abbr*. (colloq.) St. Bartholomew's Hospital, London.

barȳ'tēs (-z) *n*. native sulphate of barium, heavy spar.

basalt (băs'awlt, basawlt') *n*. dark--coloured freq. columnar igneous rock. basalt'ĭc *a*.

băs'cūle bridge *n*. kind of draw-bridge worked by counterpoise.

bāse[1] *a*. morally low, mean, ignoble; debased; of inferior value. ~-born *a*. of low birth; illegitimate.

bāse[2] *n*. foundation, bottom, ground-work, principle, starting-point; town or other area in rear of army where drafts, stores, hospitals, etc. are concentrated; (chem.) substance that combines with acid to form salt. *v.t.* found or rest *on*; establish. bā'sal *a*. of or at or forming base; fundamental.

bāse'ball *n*. (ball used in) U.S. national field-game between teams of nine players.

bāse′less (-sl-) *a.* groundless, un-founded.

bāse′ment (-sm-) *n.* lowest part of structure; storey below ground level.

basĕn′jĭ *n.* small barkless African dog.

băsh *v.t.* strike so as to smash (*in*). *n.* heavy blow; (sl.) try.

băshaw′ *n.* pasha.

băsh′ful *a.* shy; sheepish.

băshĭ-bazouk′ (-ōōk) *n.* mercenary of Turkish irregulars.

bā′sic *a.* of, at, forming, serving as, or resembling base or basis; funda-mental. **~ slag**, slag from certain steel-manufacturing processes used as fertilizer. **~allў** *adv.*

băs′ĭl (-z-) *n.* aromátic herb.

basil′ĭca *n.* oblong hall with double colonnade and apse; church with apse at one end.

băs′ĭlĭsk (-z-) *n.* fabulous reptile blasting by its breath or look; lizard with crest inflated at will.

bā′sin *n.* round vessel with sloping or curving sides for holding water etc.; hollow depression; tract drained by river; dock with flood-gates; land-locked harbour.

bā′sis *n.* (pl. *basēs*), foundation, thing to work upon, main ingredient or principle.

bask (bah-) *v.i.* expose oneself to, revel in, flood of warmth or light.

bas′kĕt (bah-) *n.* wicker vessel of plaited or interwoven canes, osiers, etc. **~-ball**, game in which goals are scored by tossing ball into baskets suspended from posts.

basque (bahsk) *n.* continuation of bodice below waist.

băs-rélief′ (*or* băs′-) *n.* carving or sculpture projecting only slightly from background.

băss[1] *n.* kinds of fish of perch family, including common perch.

băss[2], **băst** *n.* inner bark of lime-tree, other similar fibre. **~ broom**, coarse fibre broom.

băss[3] *a.* deep-sounding; of lowest part in music. *n.* bass voice or singer or part.

băss′ĕt *n.* short-legged dog used in unearthing badgers etc.

băssĭnĕt′ *n.* hooded wicker cradle or perambulator.

bassōōn′ *n.* double-reed bass wood-wind instrument.

băst: see **bass**[2].

băs′tard *a.* born out of wedlock; hybrid, counterfeit. *n.* illegitimate child, counterfeit thing. **~īze** *v.t.* declare bastard. **~ў** *n.*

bāste[1] *v.t.* sew together with long loose stitches, tack.

bāste[2] *v.t.* moisten (roasting meat etc.) with fat etc.; thrash, cudgel.

băstille′ (-ēl) *n.* fortress; prison.

băstĭnā′dō *n.* (pl. *-oes*), caning on soles of feet. *v.t.* cane thus.

băs′tion *n.* pentagonal projection from fortification.

băt[1] *n.* small nocturnal mouse-like winged mammal.

băt[2] *n.* wooden implement for striking ball in cricket, baseball, etc.; bats-man. *v.i.* use bat, have innings. **~sman**, **~ting** *nn.* performer, per-formance, with bat.

băt[3] *n.* (sl.) pace.

băt[4] *v.t.* wink or blink.

bătch *n.* loaves baked at one time; group or collection or set.

bāte[1] *v.t.* restrain; deduct.

bāte[2] *n.* (sch. sl.) rage.

bath (-ah-; pl. -dhz) *n.* washing, im-mersion; vessel or place for bathing in; (pl.) bathing-place. *v.* wash in bath.

Bath (bahth) *n.* town in Somerset named from hot springs. **~-brick**, preparation for cleaning metal. **~ bun**, kind of bun with sugar-icing. **~ chair**, invalid's wheel chair. **~-chap**, pickled lower half of pig's cheek. **~ Oliver**, kind of unsweetened biscuit. **~ stone**, building stone quarried at Bath.

bāthe (-dh) *v.* immerse in water etc.; moisten all over; take bath or bathe; (of sunlight etc.) envelop. *n.* immersion in water esp. of sea or river or swimming-bath. **bathing-machine**, wheeled dressing-box formerly used for sea-bathing.

Bath. et Well. *abbr.* (Bishop) of Bath and Wells.

bā′thŏs *n.* fall from sublime to ridicu-lous. **bathĕt′ic** *a.*

băth′ўscăphe (*or* -āf), **băth′ўsphēre** *nn.* vessels for deep-sea diving and observation.

bătˈĭk *n.* (material patterned by) Javanese method of painting parts with wax and then dyeing.

bătiste' (-ēst) *n.* fine light cotton fabric.

băt'man (-an) *n.* member of army etc. acting as officer's servant.

băt'on *n.* staff of office; conductor's wand for beating time.

batrā'chĭan (-k-) *a.* of frogs or other animals that discard gills and tail. *n.* such animal.

battăl'ion (-yon) *n.* large body of men in battle array; infantry unit forming part of regiment or brigade.

bătt'els *n.pl.* college account at Oxford esp. for provisions.

bătt'en¹ *n.* board for flooring; strip of wood esp. to secure hatchway tarpaulin. *v.t.* strengthen or fasten with battens.

bătt'en² *v.i.* feed; grow fat.

bătt'er *v.* strike repeatedly so as to bruise or break. *n.* mixture of flour and eggs beaten up with liquid for cooking. ~ing-ram, military engine for assailing walls.

bătt'erў *n.* (law) infliction of blows or menacing touch to clothes or person; (mil.) emplacement for one or more guns, artillery unit of guns and men and vehicles or horses; set of similar or connected instruments etc.; series of cells for generating or storing electricity; series of cages in which laying hens etc. are confined.

bătt'le *n.* combat, esp. of organized forces. *v.i.* struggle *with*, *for*, etc. ~-axe, medieval weapon. ~-cruiser, heavy-gunned ship of higher speed and lighter armour than battleship. ~dress, soldier's etc. uniform of belted blouse and trousers. ~field, scene of battle. ~ship, warship of most heavily armed and armoured class.

bătt'ledōre (-tld-) *n.* bat like small racket for striking shuttlecock.

bătt'lement (-lm-) *n.* (usu. pl.) indented parapet (and enclosed roof) at top of wall.

băttūe' (*or* -ōō) *n.* driving of game by beaters to sportsmen; wholesale slaughter.

bau'ble *n.* showy trinket.

baulk : see balk.

bau'xīte *n.* earthy mineral, chief source of aluminium.

baw'bee *n.* (Sc.) halfpenny.

bawd *n.* procuress. ~ў *a.* obscene.

bawl *v.* shout or weep noisily; ~ out, (U.S.) reprimand severely.

bay¹ *n.* kind of laurel with deep-green leaves; (pl.) conqueror's or poet's bay wreath. ~berry, W.-Ind. tree. ~ rum, perfume distilled from bayberry leaves.

bay² *n.* part of sea filling wide-mouthed opening of land. ~ salt, got from sea-water by evaporation.

bay³ *n.* division of wall between buttresses etc.; recess; projecting window-space. ~ window, window filling bay.

bay⁴ *n.* bark of large dog, esp. chorus of pursuing hounds; *at* ~, (of hunted animal) surrounded by dogs and unable to escape; *keep at* ~, ward off; *turn at* ~, turn on pursuers. *v.* (of large dog) bark (at).

bay⁵ *a.* & *n.* reddish-brown (horse).

bay'onet *n.* stabbing blade attached to rifle. *v.t.* stab with bayonet.

bayou (bī'ū) *n.* marshy inlet or creek in southern U.S.

bazaar' (-zär) *n.* Oriental market; sale of needlework, fancy goods, etc. esp. for charity.

BB, BBB *abbr.* (of pencil) double-black, treble-black.

B.B.C. *abbr.* British Broadcasting Corporation.

B.C. *abbr.* before Christ; British Columbia.

B.C.L., B.Com., B.D. *abbr.* Bachelor of Civil Law, of Commerce, of Divinity.

bds *abbr.* boards.

be (bē, bǐ) *v.i.* (pres. ind. *am*, *art*, *is*, pl. *are*; past ind. 1 & 3 *was*, 2 *wast*, pl. *were*; pres. subj. *be*; past subj. *were*, imper. *be*; part. *being*; p.p. *been*), exist, occur; remain, continue; have specified state or quality. *v. aux.* forming (with p.p.) pass, or expr. (with pres. p.) incomplete action.

B.E.A. *abbr.* British European Airways.

beach *n.* sandy or pebbly shore of sea, lake, etc. *v.t.* run (boat etc.) ashore, haul up. ~-comber, long rolling wave; white man in Pacific islands etc. who lives by collecting jetsam etc. **~-head**, fortified position of troops landed on beach.

bea'con *n*. signal-fire on hill or pole; signal; signal-station.

bead *n*. small ball pierced for threading with others; small knob in front sight of gun; drop of liquid; narrow cylindrical moulding. *v.t.* furnish or ornament with bead or beading; string together. **bea'ding** *n*. bead moulding. **bea'dy** *a.* (of eyes) small and bright.

bea'dle *n*. (hist.) parish officer appointed to keep order in church etc. **~dom** *n*. stupid officiousness.

bea'gle *n*. small hound for hunting hares, followed on foot. **bea'gling** *n*. hunting with beagles.

beak *n*. horny projecting part of bird's jaws; hooked nose; prow of warship; (sl.) magistrate.

bea'ker *n*. large drinking-cup; wide-mouthed pottery drinking-cup found in early Bronze-Age graves; straight-sided lipped glass for scientific experiments.

beam *n*. long piece of squared timber supported at each end; bar of balance; horizontal cross-timber of ship, extreme width of hull; ray or pencil of light, sound, electrons, etc.; directional radio signal for aircraft, course indicated by it; radiance, bright smile; *on the* **~-ends**, (of ship) lying on its side and in danger of capsizing, (of person) extremely hard-up. *v.* emit light; shine; smile radiantly; direct, aim (radio signals etc.).

bean *n*. plant with kidney-shaped seed in long pods; seed of this or of coffee and other plants; (sl.) coin. **~-feast**, work-people's annual outing; frolic, spree. **bea'no** *n*. (sl.) bean-feast.

bear[1] (bār) *n*. heavy thick-furred quadruped; rough surly person; (St. Exch.) speculator for fall in price of stocks. **~-garden**, scene of tumult. **~-leader**, travelling tutor to rich young man. **~-skin**, Guards' tall furry cap. **~ish** *a.* rough-mannered, surly; (of stock-market or prices) tending to fall.

bear[2] (bār) *v.* (p.t. *bōre*, arch. *bāre*; p.p. *bōrne* or *born*) carry or support; endure, tolerate; give birth to; produce, yield. **~able** *a.* endurable.

beard *n*. hair of lower part of face; chin tuft of goat etc.; awn of grasses. *v.t.* oppose openly, defy. **~ėd** *a.* **~less** *a.* youthful, immature.

bear'er (bār-) *n*. bringer of letter etc., presenter of cheque; carrier of coffin; (hist., India) palanquin-carrier, domestic servant. **~ bonds, securities**, unregistered securities, title to which is vested in possessor.

bear'ing (bār-) *n*. behaviour; heraldic charge; relation, aspect; direction, relative position; part of machine bearing friction, support on which shaft or axle turns. **~-rein**, rein forcing horse to arch its neck.

beast *n*. animal; quadruped; bovine animal; brutal man; person one dislikes. **~ly** *a.* dirty, disgusting; (colloq.) annoying.

beat *v.* (p.t. *beat*, p.p. *beaten* or *beat*) strike repeatedly; flog, whip, batter; hammer (metal); (of sun, rain, etc.) strike persistently; pulsate; move to and fro; defeat, overcome; forestall; perplex; mark (time etc.) with regular strokes; rouse game; **~ *it***, (sl.) go, get out. *n*. stroke on drum; movement of conductor's baton; measured sequence of strokes etc., e.g. in verse; emphatic or exaggerated rhythm in music etc.; throbbing; appointed round; pulsation caused by combination of waves etc. of different frequencies; (U.S.) newspaper success against rivals. *a.* of or like beatniks. **~er** *n*. man employed to rouse game.

bēatif'ic *a.* making blessed; blissful. **bėăt'ify** *v.t.* make supremely happy; (R.C.Ch.) pronounce to be Blessed as step towards canonization. **~fica'tion** *n*.

bėăt'itūde *n*. blessedness; (pl.) blessings in Matt. v. 3–11.

beat'nik *n*. young person rebelliously unconventional in dress, attitude, self-expression, etc.

beau (bō) *n*. (pl. -*x*, pr. -z), dandy; suitor.

Beau'fort (bō-) **scāle** n. scale of numbers indicating force of wind.

beau geste (bō zhĕst') n. display of magnanimity. [F]

beau īdė'al (bō) n. one's highest type of excellence.

beau monde (bō mawṅd) n. fashionable society. [F]

beau'tėous (bū-) a. (poet.) beautiful.

beau'tĭful (bū-) a. having beauty; capital, excellent.

beau'tĭfy̆ (bū-) v.t. make beautiful.

beauty (bū'tĭ) n. combination of qualities that delights sight or mind; person or thing possessing this. ~-sleep, that before midnight. ~-spot, small patch stuck on woman's face as foil to complexion; beautiful scene.

bea'ver[1] n. amphibious broad-tailed soft-furred rodent; its fur; hat of this.

bea'ver[2] n. lower face-guard of helmet; (sl.) bearded person.

bėcalm' (-ahm) v.t. deprive (ship etc). of wind.

bėcause' (-kŏz, -kawz) adv. by reason. conj. for the reason that.

bĕck[1] v. beckon. n. significant nod or gesture.

bĕck[2] n. brook, mountain stream.

bĕck'on v. make mute signal; summon thus.

bėcloud' v.t. cover (as) with clouds.

bėcome' (-ŭm) v. (p.t. *became*, p.p. *become*), come to be, begin to be; suit, befit, look well on. **bėcom'-ingly̆** adv. suitably, gracefully.

bĕd n. couch to sleep on; animal's resting-place, litter; flat base on which thing rests; garden plot for plants; bottom of sea, river, etc.; stratum. v.t. prepare bed for (horse etc.); plant in bed. ~-clothes, sheets, blankets, etc. ~-fellow, sharer of bed. ~-pan, invalid's chamber utensil for use in bed. ~-plate, base of machine etc. ~ridden, confined to bed by infirmity. ~-rock, solid rock below superficial formations; (fig.) foundation, bottom. ~room, for sleeping in. ~-spread, coverlet. ~stead, framework of bed. ~time, hour for going to bed.

bedăbb'le v.t. splash with liquid.

bėdaub' v.t. daub over.

bĕdd'ĭng n. mattress and bed-clothes; litter for cattle etc.

bėdĕck' v.t. adorn.

bė'del(l) n. university official with duties now chiefly processional.

bėdĕv'il v.t. treat diabolically, bewitch. ~ment n. maddening trouble or confusion.

bėdew' v.t. sprinkle (as) with dew.

bėdĭm' v.t. make dim.

bėdī'zen (or -ĭz-) v.t. deck out gaudily.

bĕd'lam n. madhouse; scene of uproar. ~īte n. lunatic.

Bĕd'lington (terrier) n. long-legged curly-haired grey terrier.

bĕd'ouĭn (-ōō-) n. (pl. same), Arab of the desert.

bėdrăgg'le v.t. make limp or wet or dirty by trailing.

Beds. abbr. Bedfordshire.

bĕd'straw n. kinds of plant.

bee n. social insect producing wax and honey; busy worker; meeting for combined work etc. ~hive, hive. ~line, straight line between two points. ~s-wax, (polish with) wax secreted by bees.

beech n. smooth-barked glossy-leaved tree; its wood. ~-mast, fruit of beech.

beef n. meat of ox, bull, or cow; beef animal. v.i. (sl.) complain. ~eaters, Yeomen of Guard or Warders of Tower of London. ~-tea, stewed beef juice for invalids. **bee'fy̆** a. solid, muscular.

been, p.p. of be.

beer n. alcoholic liquor made from fermented malt etc. flavoured with hops etc. ~-house, one licensed for beer but not for spirits. ~-money, allowance in lieu of beer. **beer'y̆** a. of or betraying influence of beer.

bees'tings (-z) n. pl. first milk of cow after parturition.

bees'wing (-z-) n. filmy scales of tartar on old port etc.

beet n. kinds of plant with succulent root used for salads etc. and sugar--making. ~root, root of beet.

bee'tle[1] n. heavy-headed tool for ramming, crushing, etc.

bee'tle[2] n. coleopterous insect. a. projecting, shaggy, scowling. v.i. overhang.

bĕfall' (-awl) *v.* happen, happen to.

bĕfĭt' *v.t.* be suited to.

bĕfŏg' *v.t.* envelop in fog; obscure.

bĕfōol' *v.t.* make fool of.

bĕfōre' *adv.* ahead; in front; previously, already. *prep.* in front of, ahead of; in presence of; earlier than. *conj.* sooner than; rather than.

bĕfōre'hănd *adv.* in anticipation, in readiness, before time.

bĕfoul' *v.t.* make foul.

bĕfriend' (-rĕnd) *v.t.* help, favour.

bĕg *v.* ask for as alms, live by begging; ask earnestly; entreat; ~ *the question*, assume by implication what one is trying to prove.

began, *p.t.* of **begin.**

bĕgĕt' (-g-) *v.t.* (past *begŏt,* arch. *begăt,* p.p. *begŏtten*), procreate (usu. of father); give rise to. **~ter** *n.*

bĕgg'ar *n.* one who begs or lives by begging; poor or penniless person; (colloq.) fellow. *v.t.* reduce to poverty. **~-my-neighbour,** cardgame. **~ly** *a.* poor, needy; mean. **~ў** *n.* extreme poverty.

bĕgĭn' (-g-) *v.* (*begăn, begŭn*), set about, make start (*with*); originate. **~ner** *n.* (esp.) learner. **~ning** *n.* time at which thing begins; source, origin.

bĕgīrd' (-g-) *v.t.* (*begirt*), gird, encircle.

bĕgŏne' *int.* away with you!

bĕgō'nĭa *n.* plant with petal-less flowers and ornamental foliage.

begot, begotten, *p.t.* & *p.p.* of **beget.**

bĕgrīme' *v.t.* make grimy.

bĕgrŭdge' *v.t.* grudge.

bĕguile' (-gīl) *v.t.* delude, cheat; charm, amuse; cause (time etc.) to pass easily. **~ment** *n.*

bē'gum *n.* Moslem queen or lady of high rank.

begun, *p.p.* of **begin.**

bĕhalf' (-ahf) *n.* part or account *of.*

bĕhāve' *v.i.* & *refl.* conduct oneself, act in specified manner.

bĕhā'viour (-yer) *n.* manners, conduct, way of behaving. **~ism** *n.* study and analysis of behaviour as method of psychology. **~ist** *n.*; **~is'tic** *a.*

bĕhead' (-hĕd) *v.t.* cut off head of; execute thus.

beheld, *p.t.* & *p.p.* of **behold.**

bĕhē'moth (*or* bē'ĭ-) *n.* huge creature.

bĕhĕst' *n.* command.

bĕhĭnd' *adv.* & *prep.* in or to rear (of); hidden (by); in arrears (with); in support of. *n.* posterior. **~hand** *a.* & *adv.* in arrears, behind time, too late.

bĕhōld' *v.t.* see; take notice, observe.

bĕhō'lden *a.* under obligation *to.*

bĕhōof' *n.* use, advantage.

bĕhōve', -hōove' *v.t.* be incumbent on; befit.

beige (bāzh) *n.* fine woollen fabric left undyed and unbleached; colour of this. *a.* of this colour.

bē'ĭng *n.* existence; what exists; person; constitution.

bĕlā'bour (-b*er*) *v.t.* thrash.

bĕlā'tĕd *a.* overtaken by darkness; (too) late.

bĕlaud' *v.t.* heap praises on.

belay' *v.t.* coil (rope) round cleat etc. to secure it. **~ing-pin,** fixed pin for belaying on.

bĕlch *v.* emit wind noisily from stomach through mouth; (of volcano, gun, etc.) emit (fire, smoke, etc.). *n.* belching.

bĕl'dam(e) *n.* hag; virago.

bĕlea'guer (-g*er*) *v.t.* besiege.

bĕl'emnīte *n.* common fossil of pointed bullet shape.

bĕl'frў *n.* bell tower; room etc. in which bells are hung.

bĕlīe' *v.t.* fail to justify or act up to; give false notion of.

bĕlief' *n.* trust, confidence; acceptance as true or existing; what is believed.

bĕlieve' *v.* accept as true; have faith (in), trust word of; think. **belie'ver** *n.*

bĕlīke' *adv.* (arch.) probably; perhaps.

bĕlĭtt'le *v.t.* disparage.

bĕll *n.* hollow esp. cup-shaped metal body emitting musical sound when struck; bell-shaped thing; (naut., pl.) half-hours of watch. *v.* furnish with bell; widen *out* like lip of bell. **~-bottomed,** (of trousers) widening from below knee to bottom of leg. **~-founder,** caster of bells. **~-hop** (U.S. sl.) hotel page. **~man,** town-crier. **~-metal,** alloy of copper and tin. **~-pull,** cord etc. attached to bell wire. **~-ringer, ~-ringing,**

(person) ringing changes etc. on church bells. ~-tent, conical tent. ~-wether, leading sheep of flock, with bell on neck.

belladŏnn'a n. poisonous plant, deadly nightshade; drug got from this.

belle n. handsome woman; reigning beauty.

belles-lettres (bĕl lĕtr) n. studies, writings, of purely literary kind. [F]

bĕll'icōse a. inclined to fight.

bĕlli'gerent a. & n. (nation or party or person) waging regular war; of or suited to such nation etc. ~ency n.

bĕll'ow (-ō) v. roar as bull; roar or cry with pain. n. bellowing sound.

bĕll'ows (-ōz) n.pl. contrivance for driving air into fire, organ, etc.; expansible part of photographic camera.

bĕll'y n. abdomen, stomach; cavity or bulging part of anything. v. swell out. ~ful n. as much as one wants.

belŏng' v.i. ~ to, be property of; be proper to or connected with, be rightly placed or classified. ~ings n.pl. one's property or relatives or luggage.

beloved a. (-ŭv'ĭd) & p.p. (-ŭvd'), dearly loved. n. beloved person.

below' (-ō) adv. at or to lower level; in lower position or rank. prep. lower in position, amount, degree, rank, etc., than; unworthy of, beneath.

bĕlt n. strip of leather etc. worn round waist; endless strap connecting wheels etc.; sash; zone or disstrict. v.t. put belt round; thrash.

bĕl'vedēre n. raised turret or lantern, summer-house, to view scenery from.

bemīre' v.t. besmirch.

bemoan' v.t. lament.

bemūse' (-z) v.t. stupefy.

bĕnch n. long seat of wood or stone; judge's or magistrate's seat; court of law; carpenter's or laboratory table; level stretch on mountain--side. ~-mark, surveyor's mark indicating point in line of levels. ~er n. (esp.) senior member of Inns of Court.

bĕnd v. (bent), force into curve or angle; receive such shape; incline

from vertical, bow, stoop; (force to) submit. n. bending, curve; bent part of thing; (naut.) kinds of knot. ~ sinister (her.) parallel lines indicating bastardy. ~er n. (sl.) sixpenny-bit.

beneath' adv. & prep. below, under.

bĕn'edick n. newly married man.

Bĕnedic'tine a. & n. (monk) of Order of St. Benedict. b~ (-ēn) n. kind of liqueur.

benedic'tion n. (utterance, service, of) blessing. ~tory a.

benedic'tus n. canticle; (R.C.Ch.) part of mass. [L]

benefac'tion n. doing good; charitable gift. bĕn'efactor, -tress nn. patron of or donor to cause etc.

bĕn'efice n. church living. bĕn'eficed (-st) a. holding benefice.

benef'icent a. doing good; actively kind. benef'icence n.

benefi'cial a. advantageous, serviceable.

benefi'ciary (-sha-) a. holding by feudal tenure. n. holder of living; receiver of benefits.

bĕn'efit n. advantage, profit; allowance etc. to which person is entitled; performance, game, etc., of which proceeds go to particular player or charity. v. do good to; receive benefit.

benĕv'olent a. desirous of doing good; charitable. ~ence n.

Bengal' (-awl) a. ~ light, firework used as signal. ~ tiger, tiger proper. ~i a. & n. (native or language) of Bengal.

benigh'ted a. overtaken by night; involved in intellectual or moral darkness.

benign' (-īn) a. kindly, gentle; favourable, salutary; (med.) mild, not malignant. benig'nancy, benig'nity nn. benig'nant a. kindly, gracious.

bĕn'ison (-zn) n. benediction.

bĕnt[1] n. kinds of stiff-stemmed grass; stiff flower-stalk or old stalk of grass.

bĕnt[2] n. inclination, bias.

bĕnt[3], p.t. & p.p. of bend.

Bĕn'thamism (-ta-) n. greatest happiness of greatest number as guiding principle of ethics.

běn′thŏs n. fauna and flora of sea-bottom.

bĕnŭmb′ (-m) v.t. make numb or torpid; paralyse.

bĕn′zēne n. aromatic hydrocarbon got from coal-tar.

bĕn′zine (-ēn) n. mixture of hydrocarbons got from mineral oils and used as solvent etc.

bĕn′zōin n. fragrant aromatic resin.

bėqueath′ (-dh) v.t. leave by will; transmit to posterity.

bėquĕst′ n. thing bequeathed.

bėrāte′ v.t. scold.

bėreave′ v.t. (bereaved or bereft), rob, deprive; leave desolate. ∼ment n. loss by death.

bě′ret (-ā) n. (cap like) Basque peasant's flat round woollen cap.

bĕrg n. iceberg.

bĕr′gamot[1] n. tree of orange kind; perfume from its fruit.

bĕr′gamot[2] n. kind of pear.

bĕrĭbĕ′rĭ n. deficiency disease affecting chiefly rice-eating populations.

bĕrkē′lĭum (or bĕrkl-) n. metallic radioactive transuranic element.

Berks. abbr. Berkshire.

Bĕrlĭn′ n. four-wheeled covered carriage with hooded seat behind.

Bermū′da rĭg n. yacht rig with very high tapering mainsail.

bě′rrў n. any small roundish juicy stoneless fruit. **bě′rrĭed** a.

bĕrsĕrk′ (-s- or -z-) pred. a. frenziedly or insanely violent, wild.

bĕrth n. sea-room; ship's place at wharf; sleeping-place; situation. v.t. moor (ship) in berth; provide sleeping-berth for.

bě′rўl n. kinds of (esp. green) precious stone; mineral species including emerald.

bĕrўll′ĭum n. white very light metallic element.

bėseech′ v.t. (-sought, pr. -sawt), entreat; ask earnestly for.

bėseem′ v.t. suit, be fitting for.

bėsĕt′ v.t. hem in, assail.

bėshrew′ (-rōō) int. (arch.) plague on.

bėsīde′ prep. at side of, close to; compared with; wide of.

bėsīdes′ (-dz) prep. in addition to; otherwise than. adv. also, as well; else; except.

bėsiege′ v.t. lay siege to; crowd round; assail with requests.

bėslăv′er v.t. slaver on or over; flatter fulsomely.

bėsmear′ v.t. smear.

bėsmĭrch′ v.t. soil, sully.

bē′som (-z-; or bě-) n. long-handled broom made of twigs.

bėsŏt′ v.t. stupefy mentally or morally. **bėsŏtt′ėd** a.

besought, p.t. & p.p. of **beseech.**

bėspătt′er v.t. spatter all over; cover with abuse.

bėspeak′ v.t. (p.t. -spōke; p.p. -spōken), engage beforehand; order (goods); be evidence of.

bėsprinkle (-ĭng′kl) v.t. sprinkle.

Bĕss′ėmer prō′cĕss n. method of making steel by passing current of air through molten pig-iron.

bĕst a. & adv. (sup. of good, well) of or in most excellent kind or way. v.t. (colloq.) get better of. ∼ **man,** bridegroom's supporter. ∼**-seller,** (author of) book with large sale.

bĕs′tial a. of beasts; brutish. ∼**ăl′itў** n.; ∼**alīze** v.t. **bĕs′tiarў** n. medieval treatise on beasts.

bėstĭr′ v.refl. exert, rouse, oneself.

bėstow′ (-ō) v.t. confer as gift; deposit. ∼**al,** ∼**ment** nn.

bėstrew′ (-rōō) v.t. (p.p. -ewed, -ewn), strew; lie scattered over.

bėstrīde′ v.t. (p.t. -ōde; p.p. -ĭdden) sit astride on; stand astride over.

bĕt v. risk one's money etc. against another's on result of event; be assured. n. wager.

bėtāke′ v.refl. (-tōōk, -tāken), go (to); have recourse to.

bē′tatrŏn n. apparatus for accelerating electrons.

bē′tel n. leaf chewed in some eastern countries with areca nut. ∼**-nut,** areca nut.

bête noire (bāt nwahr) n. (one's) abomination. [F]

bĕth′el n. hallowed spot; Nonconformist chapel.

bėthink′ v.refl. (-thought, pr. -awt), reflect, stop to think.

bėtīde′ v. happen; happen to.

bėtīmes′ (-mz) adv. in good time.

bėtō′ken v.t. be sign of.

bĕt′onў n. purple-flowered plant.

betook, p.t. of **betake.**

bĕtray′ *v.t.* give up or reveal treacherously; be disloyal to; reveal involuntarily. ∼al *n.*

bĕtrōth′ (-dh) *v.t.* bind with promise to marry. ∼al *n.*

bĕtt′er *a.* (comp. of *good*) having good qualities in higher degree. *n.* better thing or person; superiority or mastery. *adv.* (comp. of *well*) in higher degree; in better way. *v.* improve; improve upon, surpass. ∼ment *n.* improvement.

bĕtween′ *prep.* in or into space or interval; to and from; in shares among; (*choose* etc.) one or other of. *adv.* between two or more points; between two extremes. ∼-maid, servant helping two others. ∼whiles, in intervals.

bĕtwixt′ *prep.* between.

BEV *abbr.* billion (= 1,000 million) electron volts.

bĕv′el *n.* tool for setting off angles; slope, face sloped, from right angle or horizontal or vertical. *v.* impart bevel to; slant.

bĕv′erage *n.* drink.

bĕv′y̆ *n.* company.

bĕwail′ *v.t.* mourn for.

bĕwāre′ *v.* take heed *of*, be on one's guard (against).

bĕwil′der *v.t.* perplex, confuse. ∼ment *n.* state of confusion.

bĕwitch′ *v.t.* cast magic spell on; delight; captivate. ∼ment *n.*

bewray (bĭrā′) *v.t.* (arch.) reveal.

bey (bā) *n.* Turkish governor.

bĕyŏnd′ *adv.* at or to further side, further on. *prep.* at or to further side of; more than; except. *n. the* future life; *back of* ∼, out-of-the-way place.

bĕz′el *n.* sloped edge of chisel etc.; groove for watch-glass etc.

bĕzique′ (-ēk) *n.* card-game for two; combination of queen of spades and knave of diamonds in it.

B.F.B.S. *abbr.* British and Foreign Bible Society.

b.h.p. *abbr.* brake horse-power.

bĭănn′ūal *a.* occurring etc. twice a year.

bī′as *n.* (in bowls) bowl's curved course due to its lopsided form or (orig.) lead loading; predisposition, prejudice; diagonal across material. *v.t.* give bias to; prejudice.

bĭb *v.* drink much or often; tipple. *n.* cloth worn under child's chin to keep clothes clean; apron-top.

bĭbb′er *n.* one who drinks frequently.

Bī′ble *n.* (copy or edition of) sacred books of Christianity; sacred book. bĭb′lical *a.* of Bible.

bĭblĭŏg′raphy̆ *n.* history of books, their editions, etc.; list of books of any author, subject, etc. ∼pher *n.*; bĭblĭŏgrăph′ic(al) *aa.*

bĭblĭomā′nĭa *n.* rage for collecting books. ∼ĭăc *n. & a.*

bĭb′lĭophīle *n.* book-lover.

bĭb′ūlous *a.* addicted to drink.

bĭcăm′eral *a.* with two (legislative) chambers.

bĭcȧr′bonate *n.* salt of carbonic acid in which metal replaces only one hydrogen atom.

bīce *n.* dull blue or green pigment.

bĭcĕntē′nary̆ *a.* pertaining to 200 years. *n.* two hundredth anniversary or its celebration.

bĭcĕph′alous *a.* two-headed.

bī′cĕps *n.* muscle with double head or attachment, esp. that at front of upper arm.

bĭck′er *v.i.* quarrel, wrangle; (of stream, rain, etc.) brawl, patter.

bĭcŭs′pĭd *a. & n.* two-cusped (tooth).

bī′cy̆cle *n.* two-wheeled pedal-driven vehicle. *v.i.* ride bicycle.

bĭd *v.* (past *băde, bĭd*; p.p. *bĭdden, bĭd*), command; invite; offer (price); make bid; proclaim (defiance etc.). *n.* offer of price; (bridge) statement of number of tricks player hopes to make. bĭdd′able *a.* obedient. bĭdd′ing *n.* (esp.) command.

bīde *v.t.* await (one's *time*).

bĭĕnn′ial *a.* two-year long, two-yearly. *n.* plant that flowers and fruits in second year.

bier (bēr) *n.* movable stand on which coffin is taken to grave.

bĭff *n.* (sl.) smart blow. *v.t.* strike.

bī′fĭd *a.* divided by cleft into two parts.

bīfō′cal *a.* (of spectacle-lenses) with two segments of different focal lengths. ∼s *n.pl.* bifocal spectacles.

bīfō′lĭate *a.* of two leaves.

bī′furcāte *v.* divide into two branches, fork. *a.* (-at), forked. ∼ā′tion *n.*

big *a.* & *adv.* large; grown up; pregnant; important; boastful(ly). ~ **business**, large-scale commerce. ~ **end**, crank-pin end of engine connecting-rod. ~**-horn**, Rocky Mountain sheep. ~ **noise**, bigwig. ~ **top**, circus marquee. ~**wig**, important person.

big'amy̆ *n.* second marriage while first is still valid. ~**mist** *n.*; ~**mous** *a.*

bight *n.* loop of rope; curve, recess, of coast, river, etc.

big'ot *n.* obstinate and unreasonable adherent of creed or view. ~**ėd** *a.*; ~**ry̆** *n.*

bijou (bē'zhōō) *n.* (pl. -*oux*, pr. -ōō), jewel, trinket. *a.* small and elegant.

bīke *n.* & *v.i.* (colloq.) bicycle.

biki'nĭ (-kē-) *n.* woman's scanty two-piece bathing-suit.

bīlā'bĭal *a.* & *n.* (consonant) produced with (nearly) closed lips.

bīlăt'eral *a.* of or on or with two sides; between two parties.

bil'berry̆ *n.* dwarf shrub of heaths etc.; its deep-blue edible fruit.

bil'bō *n.* (pl. -*os*), (hist.) sword.

bīle *n.* bitter fluid secreted by liver to aid digestion; derangement of bile; peevishness.

bilge *n.* nearly horizontal part of ship's bottom; foulness that collects in this; (sl.) rubbish, rot. ~**-water**, foul water in bilge.

bilhăr'zĭa *n.* (disease caused by) flat-worm parasitic in veins of human urinary organs etc., esp. in Egypt.

bil'iary̆ (-lya-) *a.* of bile.

bīling'ual (-nggw-) *a.* of or in or speaking two languages.

bil'ious (-lyus) *a.* arising from or liable to or affected by derangement of bile; peevish. ~**ly** *adv.*; ~**ness** *n.*

bilk *v.t.* evade payment of, cheat.

bill[1] *n.* halberd; (also ~*hook*) concave-edged pruning-instrument.

bill[2] *n.* beak (of bird); narrow promontory; point of anchor-fluke. *v.i.* (of doves etc.) stroke bill with bill; ~ *and coo*, exchange caresses.

bill[3] *n.* draft of proposed Act of Parliament; (law) written statement of case; indictment; note of charges for goods, work done, etc.; promissory note; (U.S.) bank-note; poster, programme. *v.t.* announce, put in programme; (U.S.) present or submit bill to, charge to. ~**-broker**, dealer in bills of exchange. ~**-head**, printed account form. ~ **of exchange**, written order to pay sum on given date. ~ **of fare**, menu. ~ **of health**, certificate regarding infectious disease on ship or in port at time of sailing. ~**-poster**, ~**-sticker**, man who posts up bills.

bill'abŏng *n.* (Austral.) branch of river that comes to dead end.

bill'ėt[1] *n.* place where soldier etc. is lodged; appointment, job. *v.t.* quarter (soldiers etc. *on* town etc., *in*, *at* place). ~**ee'** *n.* person billeted.

bill'ėt[2] *n.* thick piece of firewood; (archit.) short roll at intervals in hollow moulding.

billet-doux (bĭlĭdōō') *n.* (joc.) love-letter.

bill'iards (-lyardz) *n.* game played with cues and balls on cloth-covered table. **billiard-marker**, attendant marking score.

bill'ingsgate (-z-) *n.* foul language.

bill'ion (-yon) *n.* million millions; (U.S.) thousand millions.

bill'ow (-ō) *n.* great wave. *v.i.* rise or move in billows. ~**y̆** *a.*

bill'y̆, bill'ycăn *n.* tin can serving as kettle etc. in camping.

bill'y̆cŏck *n.* bowler hat.

bill'y̆-goat *n.* male goat.

bil'tŏng *n.* (S.-Afr.) sun-dried meat in strips.

bīmĕt'allism *n.* use of both gold and silver as currency. **bīmėtăll'ic** *a.*

bin *n.* receptacle for corn, coal, bottled wine, refuse, etc.; canvas receptacle used in hop-picking.

bī'nary̆ *a.* dual, of two. ~ **scale**, (math.) using two, not ten, as basis of notation.

bind *v.t.* (*bound*), tie, fasten, attach together; wreathe or edge (with); fasten *round* etc.; be obligatory on; impose obligation on; fasten (sheets or book) into cover. ~**er** *n.* bookbinder; sheaf-binding machine; anything that binds. ~**ery̆** *n.* bookbinders' workshop. ~**ing** *a.* obligatory (*on*); *n*. book-cover; braid etc. for binding raw edges of fabric.

bïnd'weed *n*. convolvulus.

bïne *n*. flexible shoot; stem of climbing plant, esp. hop.

bïnge (-j) *n*. (sl.) drinking-bout, spree.

bïng'ō (-ngg-) *n*. variety of lotto.

bïnn'acle *n*. box of ship's compass.

bïnŏc'ūlar *a*. for two eyes. **~s** *n.pl.* binocular field- or opera-glasses.

bïnō'mïal *a*. & *n*. (algebraic expression) consisting of two terms joined by + or −.

bīochem'istrў (-kĕ-) *n*. chemistry of living organisms.

bīogĕn'ĕsĭs *n*. hypothesis that living matter arises only from living matter.

bīŏg'raphў *n*. written life of person. **~pher** *n*.; **bīogrăph'ical** *a*.

bīŏl'ogў *n*. science of physical life of animals and plants. **bīolŏ'gĭcal** *a*.; **~gĭst** *n*.

bīpär'tīte *a*. consisting of two parts; in which two parties are concerned.

bī'pĕd *a*. & *n*. two-footed (animal).

bī'plāne *n*. aeroplane with two pairs of wings one above the other.

bïquadrăt'ĭc *a*. of fourth power. *n*. fourth power of number.

bïrch *n*. smooth-barked forest tree; bundle of birch twigs for flogging. *v.t.* flog with birch.

bïrd *n*. feathered vertebrate; (sl.) girl. **~-fancier**, dealer in birds. **~-lime**, sticky stuff set to catch birds. **~-seed**, kinds of seed given to caged birds. **~ of passage**, migrant. **~'s-nesting**, hunting for nests.

bïrd's'-eye (-zī) *n*. kinds of plant with small bright flowers; tobacco in which ribs are cut as well as fibre. **~ maple**, wood of sugar maple. **~ view**, of landscape etc. as seen from above; résumé.

bïrĕtt'a *n*. square cap of R.C. and other clerics.

bïrth *n*. bringing forth of offspring; being born; origin, beginning; descent. **~ control**, prevention of undesired conception. **~day**, anniversary of birth. **~-mark**, blemish on body from birth. **~-place**, where one was born. **~-rate**, births per thousand of population. **~-right**, rights to which one is born.

bĭs *adv*. (in references) in two places [L]; (mus.) twice, repeat. [It.]

B.I.S. *abbr*. Bank for International Settlement(s).

bĭs'cuit (-kĭt) *n*. kinds of unleavened bread, usu. dry and crisp; flat thin cake of this; (U.S.) small scone; porcelain etc. after first firing and before being glazed.

bīsĕct' *v.t.* divide into two (usu. equal) parts. **bīsĕc'tion**, **~tor** *nn*.

bīsĕx'ūal *a*. of two sexes.

bish'op *n*. clergyman consecrated as ecclesiastical governor of diocese; piece in chess; mulled and spiced wine. **~rĭc** *n*. office of bishop.

bĭs'muth (-z-) *n*. reddish-white brittle metallic element.

bī'son *n*. wild ox; buffalo.

bĭsque[1] (-k) *n*. right of scoring unearned point at tennis or playing extra turn at croquet etc.

bĭsque[2] (-k) *n*. unglazed white china for statuettes.

bĭsque[3] (-k) *n*. rich soup.

bĭssĕx'tïle *a*. & *n*. leap(-year).

bĭs'tre *n*. brown pigment made from soot; colour of this.

bĭt *n*. small piece or amount; cutting part of tool etc.; part of key engaging with levers of lock; mouth-piece of bridle. *v.t.* put bit into mouth of (horse); restrain.

bĭtch *n*. female dog, fox, or wolf; abusive term for woman.

bīte *v*. (p.t. *bĭt*; p.p. *bĭtten*, occas. *bĭt*), seize, cut into or off, with teeth; penetrate; grip; corrode. *n*. act of biting; wound so made. **bī'tïng** *a*. cutting; severe.

bĭtt'er *a*. tasting like wormwood etc.; virulent; biting, harsh.

bĭtt'ern *n*. marsh bird allied to heron.

bĭt'ūmĕn *n*. mineral pitch; any natural (esp. solid) hydrocarbon. **bĭtū'mĭnous** *a*.

bī'vălve *a*. & *n*. two-valved; (mollusc) with hinged shell.

bĭv'ouăc (-o͞o-) *n*. & *v.i.* (remain esp. for night in) temporary encampment without tents.

bizärre' *a*. of fantastic appearance or effect; grotesque.

B.L. *abbr.* Bachelor of Law.

b.l. *abbr.* bill of lading.

blăb *v.* talk or tell foolishly or indiscreetly.

blăck *a.* opposite to white, colourless from absence or complete absorption of light, very dark-coloured; dark-skinned; dusky, gloomy; wicked; sullen; produced or handled or operated by blackleg or non-union labour. *n.* black colour, paint, clothes, speck; Negro. *v.t.* make black; polish with blacking; ~ *out,* obscure (window etc.) so that no light is visible from outside or from air, suffer black-out. ~ **art,** magic. ~**ball,** exclude from club, society, etc. ~-**beetle,** dark-brown beetle-like nocturnal insect infesting kitchens etc. ~-**board,** for chalking on in class-room etc. ~ **cap,** put on by judge in sentencing to death. ~ **coffee,** without milk. ~ **eye,** discoloured with bruise. ~-**fellow,** Australian aboriginal. ~ **flag,** used by pirates as ensign etc. ~ **friar,** Dominican. ~ **frost,** hard frost without snow or rime. ~ **grouse,** British species of grouse. ~**head,** black-headed pimple caused by dirt in pore. ~ **hole,** dark hole or deep cell, esp. (hist.) punishment cell. ~-**jack,** tarred-leather wine-bottle; (U.S.) short heavy club with pliable shaft. ~-**lead,** (polish with) graphite. ~--**letter,** kind of type used by early printers. ~ **list,** of undesirable persons etc. ~-**list,** enter on black list. ~ **market,** illegitimate traffic in controlled goods or currencies or commodities in short supply. ~--**out,** (period of) obscuration of windows etc., material for this; temporary esp. sudden or momentary loss of vision or consciousness. ~ **pudding,** sausage of blood, suet, etc. **B~ Rod,** chief usher of House of Lords. ~ **sheep,** scoundrel; disreputable member *of.* ~-**shirts,** fascists. ~ **velvet,** mixture of stout and champagne.

blăck'amoor *n.* Negro.

blăck'berry̆ *n.* bramble or its fruit.

blăck'bĭrd *n.* European song-bird; captive Negro on slave-ship.

blăck'căp *n.* kind of warbler with top of head black.

blăck'cŏck *n.* male of black grouse.

blăck'en *v.* make or grow black(er); speak evil of, defame.

blackguard (blăg'ȧrd) *n.* scoundrel, foul-mouthed fellow. *v.t.* abuse scurrilously. **black'guardly** *a.*

blăck'ĭng *n.* paste or liquid for blacking boots.

blăck'lĕg *n.* worker who works while fellow-workers are on strike.

blăck'mail *n.* extortion by threats or pressure. *v.t.* extort money from thus.

blăck'smith *n.* smith working in iron.

blăck'thŏrn *n.* thorny shrub bearing small bluish-black fruits.

blădd'er *n.* membranous bag in human or other animal body, esp. urinary bladder; inflated thing. ~-**wrack,** seaweed with air-bladders in substance of fronds.

blāde, *n.* flat narrow leaf of grass and cereals; leaf-like part of bat, oar, spade, etc.; cutting-part of knife etc.; flat bone of shoulder; gay dashing fellow.

blah *n.* (colloq.) high-sounding nonsense.

blain *n.* inflamed sore.

blāme *v.t.* find fault with; fix blame on. *n.* censure; responsibility for bad result. ~**worthy** *a.* deserving blame. ~**less** *a.* innocent.

blanch (-ah-) *v.* make white by peeling, immersing in boiling water, etc.; make or grow pale.

blancmange (blȧmah̐zh') *n.* opaque jelly of cornflour etc. and milk.

blănd *a.* polite, suave, mild; balmy.

blăn'dĭshment *n.* (usu. pl.) flattering attention; attraction.

blănk *a.* not written or printed on; void of interest, result, etc. *n.* void; empty space in document etc. blank ticket in sweepstake. ~ **cartridge,** without ball. ~ **cheque,** one with amount left for payee to fill in. ~ **verse,** unrhymed verse.

blănk'ĕt *n.* large woollen sheet as bed-covering, horse-cloth, etc. *a.* (U.S.) covering, inclusive. *v.t.* cover (as) with blanket.

blănk'ly̆ *adv.* without expression.

blāre v. make sound of trumpet; trumpet forth. n. blaring sound.

blȧr'ney n. cajoling talk. v. cajole, use blarney.

blasé (blah'zā) a. cloyed or exhausted with pleasure.

blăsphēme' v. talk impiously; profane in words. **blăs'phēmous** a. **blăs'phēmy̆** n. impious speech, profanity.

blast (-ah-) n. strong gust; blowing or sound of wind instrument; current in blast-furnace; destructive wave of compressed air spreading outwards from explosion. v.t. blow up with explosive; blight, shrivel. ~-furnace, one into which draught of compressed hot air is driven.

blăs'todĕrm n. cellular layer in some fertilized ova from which embryo develops.

blā'tant a. loudly obtrusive.

blāze[1] n. bright flame or fire; violent outburst of passion. v.i. flame; burn with excitement etc.

blāze[2] n. white mark on face of horse or chipped in bark of tree. v.t. mark (tree, path) with blaze(s).

blāze[3] v.t. proclaim (abroad, forth).

blā'zer n. unlined jacket worn with sports clothes etc.

blā'zon n. heraldic shield, coat of arms, etc. v.t. describe or paint (arms) heraldically; proclaim. ~ry̆ n. heraldic devices, art of blazoning.

bleaoh v. whiten in sunlight or by chemical process. n. bleaching process or substance. ~ers n. pl. (U.S.) unroofed plank-seats at sports ground etc.

bleak[1] n. kinds of small fish.

bleak[2] a. dreary; bare; chilly.

blear a. dim, rheumy, misty. v.t. dim (eyes); blur. ~y̆ a.

bleat v. utter bleat; speak foolishly. n. cry of sheep, goat, etc.; similar sound.

blĕb n. small blister or bubble.

bleed v. (bled), emit blood; draw blood surgically from; extort money from; feel pity. ~er n. (esp.) haemophiliac; (vulg.) obnoxious person.

blĕm'ish v.t. spoil beauty of, mar. n. flaw, defect, stain.

blĕnch v.i. flinch, quail.

blĕnd v. (blended; also blent), mix (esp. sorts of tea etc. to produce certain quality); mingle intimately; become one. n. blending; mixture.

blĕnde n. native zinc sulphide.

Blĕn'heim (-nĭm) **Orange** n. kind of apple.

blent : see blend.

blĕss v.t. (blessed, pr. usu. -st; also blest), consecrate; praise; invoke God's favour on; make happy; thank. **blĕss'ĕd, blĕst** aa. consecrated; revered; in paradise; blissful; (pr. -st or -sed) cursed. ~ing n. declaration, invocation, or bestowal of divine favour; grace at meals; thing one is thankful for.

blĕth'er (-dh-) v.i. & n. (talk) nonsense.

blew, p.t. of blow.

blight n. fungoid disease of plants; kinds of aphis; malignant withering influence. v.t. affect with blight; mar, frustrate. ~er n. (sl.) annoying person; fellow.

blī'mey int. (vulg.) expr. surprise.

blind a. without sight; without moral or mental discernment; reckless; drunk. v. deprive of sight, make mentally blind; go blindly or recklessly. n. obstruction to sight or light; screen for window. ~ alley, closed at one end, not leading anywhere. ~ corner, round which driver on road cannot see. ~-man's-buff, game in which blindfold player tries to catch others. ~ spot, spot on retina insensitive to light; limited area where vision, judgement, etc. fails. ~-worm, slow-worm.

blind'fōld a. & adv. with eyes bandaged; reckless(ly). v.t. deprive of sight with bandage.

blind'ly̆ adv. without seeing, recklessly.

blink v. shut eyelids momentarily and involuntarily; cast sudden or momentary light; ignore or shirk (facts). n. blinking; momentary gleam; shining white reflection on horizon of distant ice-masses; on the ~, (sl.) nearly extinguished, worn out, etc. ~er n. screen on bridle preventing horse from seeing sideways. ～ing *a.* (sl.) blooming, bloody.

blĭp *n.* image on radar-screen.

bliss *n.* heavenly joy. ～ful *a.*

blĭs'ter *n.* vesicle on skin filled with serum; any swelling resembling this. *v.* raise blister on; become covered with blisters.

blīthe (-dh) *a.* gay, joyous. ～some *a.*

blĭth'ering (-dh-) *a.* blethering; (sl.) consummate.

B.Litt. *abbr.* Bachelor of Letters.

blĭtz *n.* intensive (esp. air-) attack. *v.t.* damage or destroy in blitz.

blĭzz'ard *n.* blinding snowstorm.

bloat[1] *v.t.* cure (herring) by salting and smoking. **bloa'ter** *n.* bloated herring.

bloat[2] *v.* inflate, swell. ～ĕd *a.*

blŏb *n.* drop of liquid; small round mass or spot.

blŏc *n.* combination of parties to form government or of groups etc. to forward some interest.

blŏck *n.* log, tree-stump; large piece of wood or stone; mould for shaping hats on; piece of wood etc. engraved for printing; obstruction; spot on which batsman rests bat before play; buildings surrounded by (usu. four) streets; large number or quantity; number of sheets of paper fastened together at edge(s). *v.t.* obstruct; stop (ball) with bat; shape on block; ～ *out,* sketch roughly. ～capitals, letters, (writing with) detached letters as in printing. ～ĕd *a.* (of currency) not freely convertible.

blŏckāde' *n.* shutting-up of place by hostile forces. *v.t.* subject to blockade.

blŏck'head (-hĕd) *n.* dolt.

blŏck'house *n.* detached fort; timber building with loopholes.

blōke *n.* (sl.) man, fellow.

blŏnd, blŏnde *a.* & *n.* fair-skinned and fair-haired (person).

blood (blŭd) *n.* red liquid circulating in arteries and veins of vertebrates, analogous liquid in invertebrates; murder, bloodshed; race, descent; relationship; man of fashion. *v.t.* give first taste of blood to (hound); smear face of (hunting novice) with blood of fox after kill. ～bank,

reserve of blood for transfusion. ～-count, count of red corpuscles in blood. ～-donor, giver of blood for transfusion. ～-feud, feud involving bloodshed. ～hound, large keen--scented dog used for tracking. ～orange, orange with red-streaked pulp. ～-pressure, pressure of blood against walls of arteries; abnormally high blood-pressure. ～relation, one related by virtue of common descent. ～shed, spilling of blood, slaughter. ～shot, (of eye) suffused or tinged with blood. ～sports, those involving killing of animals. ～stock, thoroughbred horses collectively. ～stone, kinds of precious stone spotted or streaked with red. ～sucker, leech; extortioner, sponger. ～thirsty, eager for bloodshed. ～-vessel, vein or artery conveying blood. ～less *a.* without blood or bloodshed.

bloody (blŭd'ĭ) *a.* of or like blood; blood-stained, running with blood; involving bloodshed; cruel; (in foul language) damned. *adv.* confoundedly, very. *v.t.* make bloody.

bloom[1] *n.* flower; florescence; prime; freshness. *v.i.* bear blooms; be in flower; flourish. ～ing *a.* (esp.) bloody.

bloom[2] *n.* mass of puddled iron hammered into thick bar.

bloo'mer *n.* (sl.) blunder.

bloo'mers (-z) *n.pl.* (woman's undergarment of) loose drawers reaching to knee.

blŏss'om *n.* flower; mass of flowers on tree. *v.i.* open into flower.

blŏt *n.* spot of ink etc.; blemish; disgraceful act. *v.t.* make blot on; stain (character); dry with blotting--paper; obliterate.

blŏtch *n.* inflamed patch etc. on skin; dab of ink etc. ～ed, ～y̆ *aa.*

blŏtt'er *n.* pad of blotting-paper.

blŏtt'ing-pāper *n.* absorbent paper for drying inkmarks.

blouse (-owz) *n.* (French) workman's loose upper garment; woman's loose upper garment tucked into skirt at waist; upper part of battledress; jacket of U.S. army uniform. *v.* arrange, be arranged, in loose light folds like blouse.

blow[1] (-ō) v. (*blew,* **pr.** -ōō; *blown*), move as wind does; puff, pant; make or shape or work or sound by blowing; (of fly) deposit eggs on; (of electric fuse) melt when overloaded; (sl., p.t., -*ed*) curse, confound; spend; ~ *in,* come in unexpectedly or casually; ~ *up,* inflate, enlarge, shatter or be shattered by explosion, reprove violently. n. blowing, puff of fresh air. ~**fly,** meat-fly, bluebottle. ~**-lamp,** portable apparatus for directing intensely hot flame on limited area. ~**-out,** (sl.) large meal; burst in pneumatic tyre. ~**-pipe,** tube through which dart or arrow is projected by blowing. ~**-torch,** (U.S.) blow-lamp. ~**er** n. sheet of iron increasing draught of fire; (sl.) telephone. ~**y** a. windy.

blow[2] (-ō) v.i. (*blew,* **pr.** -ōō; *blown*), come into, be in, flower. n. flowering condition.

blow[3] (-ō) n. hard stroke with fist, hammer, etc.; disaster, shock.

blowzed (-zd), **blow'zy** aa. red-faced, coarse-looking; dishevelled.

blŭb v.i. (sch. sl.) shed tears.

blŭbb'er n. fatty tissue of aquatic mammals; weeping. a. (of lips) swollen, protruding. v.i. sob, weep noisily.

blŭdg'eon (-jn) n. heavy stick. v.t. strike heavily or repeatedly (as) with bludgeon.

blue (blōō) a. coloured like sky or deep sea; livid; low-spirited; indecent, obscene. n. blue colour, cloth, etc.; blue powder used in laundering; sky, sea; (award to) athlete representing university; (pl.) dumps; B~s (pl.) Royal Horse Guards; (pl.) kind of melancholy song of Amer. Negro origin. v.t. make blue; (sl.) spend extravagantly. ~**bell** n. wild hyacinth; (north.) harebell. ~ **blood,** high birth. ~ **book,** Parliamentary or Privy-Council report. ~**bottle,** blowfly; blue cornflower. ~**-coat boy,** scholar of charity school, esp. Christ's Hospital. ~ **grass,** kinds of field-grass esp. of Kentucky and Virginia. ~ **gum,** kind of eucalyptus. ~**-jacket,** seaman in Royal Navy ~**-pencil,** censor. **B~ Peter,** blue flag with central white square, hoisted before sailing. ~**print,** photographic print with white lines on blue ground, usu. of engineering plans or drawings; detailed plan. ~ **ribbon,** ribbon of Garter; highest honour or distinction; badge of teetotalism. ~**-stocking,** woman having or affecting literary tastes and learning. ~ **tit,** titmouse with blue and yellow plumage.

blŭff[1] a. with perpendicular broad front; blunt, frank, hearty. n. bluff headland.

blŭff[2] v. deceive opponent as to value of one's hand at poker; make pretence of strength to gain advantage etc. n. bluffing.

blŭn'der v.i. move blindly; make gross mistake. n. stupid or careless mistake.

blŭn'derbŭss n. short gun with large bore firing many balls.

blŭnt a. dull, not sensitive; without edge or point; plain-spoken. v.t. make blunt.

blŭr n. smear; dimness, confused effect. v.t. smear with ink etc.; make indistinct; dim.

blŭrb n. (sl.) publisher's commendation of book printed on jacket etc.

blŭrt v.t. utter abruptly or tactlessly.

blŭsh v.i. be or become red (as) with shame or other emotion; be ashamed. n. blushing; (*first*) glance.

blŭs'ter v. storm boisterously. n. blustering; self-assertive talk.

B.M., B.M.A. abbr. British Museum, Medical Association.

B.Mus. abbr. Bachelor of Music.

Bn abbr. Battalion.

B.N.C. abbr. Brasenose College.

B.O. abbr. body odour.

bō'a n. large non-poisonous crushing S.-Amer. snake; woman's long round fur or feather throat-wrap. ~**-constrictor,** Brazilian species of boa; any great crushing snake.

B.O.A.C. abbr. British Overseas Airways Corporation.

boar (bōr) n. male swine.

board (bōrd) n. thin plank; wooden or cardboard slab used in games, for posting notices, etc.; thick stiff paper used in bookbinding; (pl.) stage; table; daily meals; council--table, councillors, committee; *on* ~, on ship, train, etc. *v.* cover with boards; provide, be provided, with meals at fixed rate; come alongside (ship), embark on. ~-fence, (U.S.) close fence of boards. ~ing-house, house in which persons board and lodge. ~ing-school, school in which pupils live during term. ~-school, public elementary school managed by school-board (1870–1902). ~ wages, servant's pay while masters are away from home. ~-walk, (U.S.) footway of boards. ~er *n.* (esp.) one who is lodged and fed at a fixed rate; child at boarding-school.

boast *n.* vainglorious statement; thing one is proud of. *v.* make boast(s), brag (*of*); have as proud possession. ~ful *a.* apt to boast.

boat *n.* small open oared or sailing vessel; (small) ship; boat-shaped receptacle. *v.i.* sail or row or go in boat, esp. for amusement. ~-hook, long pole with hook and spike. ~-house, shed at water's edge for boats. ~man, one who lets out boats; waterman. ~ train, train timed to connect with ship. ~er *n.* hard flat straw hat.

boatswain (bō'sn) *n.* ship's officer in charge of sails etc.

bŏb[1] *n.* weight on pendulum etc.; bobbed hair; knot of hair, curl; horse's docked tail; bob-sled. *v.t.* cut (hair) to hang short of shoulders. ~-sled, ~-sleigh, (either of) two short sleds coupled together. ~tail, docked tail, horse or dog with this; *rag, tag, & ~tail*, rabble. ~-wig, short-curled, not full-bottomed.

bŏb[2] *v.* move up and down, rebound. *n.* bobbing movement; curtsy; kinds of change in bell-ringing.

bŏb[3] *n. dry* ~, *wet* ~, cricketing, boating, Etonian.

bŏb[4] *n.* (pl. same), (sl.) shilling.

bŏbb'in *n.* cylinder for holding thread etc., reel, spool; small bar and string for raising door-latch.

bŏbb'ish *a.* (sl.) brisk, well.

bŏbb'ÿ *n.* (sl.) policeman.

bŏb'olink *n.* N.-Amer. song-bird.

bŏb'stay *n.* rope holding bowsprit down.

bŏck *n.* strong dark German beer.

bōde *v.* portend; augur. ~ful *a.* ominous.

bŏd'ïce *n.* upper part of woman's dress down to waist; under-garment for same part of body.

bŏd'kin *n.* blunt thick needle for drawing tape etc. through hem; (hist.) dagger-shaped hairpin; dagger; pointed instrument for piercing holes in cloth.

bŏd'ÿ *n.* material frame of man or animal; corpse; trunk apart from head and limbs; main part; part of vehicle etc. fitted to receive load; person; aggregate of persons or things, collection; solidity, substance; thing perceptible to senses. ~guard, retinue, escort; personal guard. ~ politic, State ~-snatcher, stealer of corpses for dissection. **bŏd'ïless** *a.* incorporeal, separated from body. **bŏd'ïlÿ** *a.* of or affecting body; *adv.* in person, as whole.

Bō'er (*or* boor *or* bôr) *n.* Dutch--descended S.-African.

bŏg *n.* wet spongy ground, morass. *v.t.* trap or submerge in bog; hamper; ~*ged down*, unable to move or make progress.

bō'gey (-gǐ) *n.* score that good golfer should do hole or course in; bogy.

bŏgg'le *v.i.* demur or hesitate (*at*).

bŏgg'ÿ (-g-) *a.* marshy, spongy.

bō'gie (-gǐ) *n.* under-carriage pivoted below end of locomotive etc.

bō'gle *n.* goblin; scarecrow.

bō'gus *a.* sham, spurious.

bō'gÿ (-gǐ) *n.* devil; goblin; bugbear.

bōhea' (-hē) *n.* black tea of lowest quality.

Bohē'mian *a.* socially unconventional; of free-and-easy habits. *n.* Bohemian person, esp. artist or writer. ~ism *n.*

boil[1] *n.* hard inflamed suppurating tumour on skin.

boil[2] *v.* bubble up with heat; be agitated like boiling water; subject to heat of boiling water; cook thus. *n.* boiling heat. ~ed shirt, dress shirt. ~ed sweet, sweetmeat made of boiled sugar. ~ing hot, (colloq.)

very hot. ~ing-point, temperature at which liquid boils. ~ing n. (esp.) *the whole* ~*ing*, (sl.) all.

boi'ler n. vessel for boiling, esp. for making steam in engine; tank heating water for domestic use.

boi'sterous a. violent, rough; noisily cheerful.

bōld a. courageous, enterprising, confident; impudent, immodest; vigorous, well-marked, clear; ~(-face, -faced), (of type) with thick or 'fat' face.

bōle n. stem, trunk.

bolēr'ō (*or* -ār-) n. (pl. -os), Spanish dance; (also bŏl'erō) short jacket barely coming to waist.

bōll n. round seed-vessel of flax, cotton, etc. ~-weevil, ~-worm, attacking cotton bolls.

bŏll'ard n. post on ship or quay for securing ropes to; short thick post in street etc.

Bŏl'shévĭk n. & a. (member) of Russian revolutionary party that seized power in October Revolution of 1917; revolutionary. ~vĭsm n.; ~vĭst n. & a.

bō'lster n. long stuffed (under-)pillow. v. support with bolster, prop up.

bōlt[1] n. short heavy arrow of cross-bow; discharge of lightning; door--fastening of sliding bar and staple; headed metal pin secured with rivet or nut; running away; length of fabric woven in one operation. v. dart off, run away, (of horse) break from control; gulp down un-chewed; fasten with bolt. ~ upright, erect.

bōlt[2], boult (bōlt) v.t. sift. bo(u)l'ter n. sieve, boulting-machine.

bō'lus n. large pill.

bŏmb (-m) n. case of explosive, gas, etc. fired from gun or dropped from aircraft or thrown by hand. v. assail with or throw bombs. ~-proof, safe from bombs. ~-shell, shattering or devastating event etc. ~er (-mer) n. soldier, aircraft, using bombs.

bŏmbărd' v.t. batter with shot and shell; assail with abuse etc.; subject to impact of electrons or other rapidly moving particles. ~ment n.

bŏmbardier' (*or* bŭ-) n. artillery N.C.O. below sergeant; (U.S.) air-man releasing bombs from aircraft.

bŏm'bardon n. (organ-stop imitating) low-pitched brass musical instrument.

bŏm'basine (-zēn; *or* bŭ-) n. twilled dress-material of worsted, or silk or cotton with worsted weft.

bŏm'bast n. hollow and inflated language. bombăs'tĭc a.

bō'na fī'dė a. & adv. genuine(ly), sincere(ly). bō'na fī'dēs (-z) n. honest intention, sincerity. [L]

bonăn'za, n. rich mine; source of great wealth.

bŏn'bŏn n. sweetmeat; Christmas cracker.

bŏnd[1] n. that which binds or unites; covenant or binding agreement; document binding person or government or company to pay or repay money, debenture; bond paper; (pl.) fetters, chains; *in* ~, in bonded warehouse. v.t. bind or connect together; put in bond. ~ed ware-house, place in which importer's dutiable goods are stored to await Customs duty. ~-holder, person holding bond(s). ~ paper, superior kind of writing paper.

bŏnd[2] a. (arch.) in slavery, not free. ~man, ~maid, ~servant, ~slave, ~sman, serf or slave.

bŏn'dage n. serfdom, slavery; confinement, constraint.

bōne n. any of separate parts of vertebrate skeleton; (thing made of) substance of which these consist; (pl.) skeleton, mortal remains. v.t. rid of bones; (sl.) steal. ~-dry, quite dry. ~ china, fine semi-trans-lucent earthenware resembling porcelain. ~head, stupid person. ~-setter, person who treats frac-tures etc., esp. without being qualified surgeon. ~-shaker, (colloq.) bicycle without pneumatic tyres.

bŏn'fīre n. large open-air fire.

bŏng'ō (-ngg-) n. large striped African antelope.

bŏn'homie (-nomē) n. geniality.

bon mot (bawṅ mō) n. (pl. bons mots, bawṅ mō), witty saying. [F]

bŏnn'ét n. woman's brimless out-door head-dress with strings; (Sc.)

man's cap; hinged cover over engine of motor-vehicle.

bŏnn'ў a. comely, healthy-looking.

bŏn'spiel (-ēl) n. curling-match.

bō'nus n. something extra, esp. addition to dividends or wages.

bon vivant (bawṅ vē'vahṅ) n. gourmand. [F]

bō'nў a. of or like or abounding in bone(s); big-boned.

bŏnze n. Japanese or Chinese Buddhist priest.

bŏn'zer a. (Austral. sl.) excellent, splendid.

bōō int., n. & v. (make) sound of disapproval or contempt, hoot.

bōō'bў n. silly or awkward fellow; kinds of gannet. **~ prize**, for last or lowest competitor. **~-trap**, things balanced on door ajar to fall on head of first comer; apparently harmless object designed to explode when disturbed; v.t. set booby-trap(s) in or on.

bōōk n. number of sheets of paper, written or printed on, folded, fastened together, and bound in cover; series of written sheets fastened together in long roll etc.; literary composition that would fill book; number of cheques, stamps, blank sheets of paper, etc., fastened together in shape of book; main division of literary work or of Bible; libretto; record of bets made; (pl.) account-books. v. enter in book or list; secure (seat etc.) in advance; obtain ticket for journey etc. **~-case**, case with shelves for books. **~-ends**, pair of props to keep row of books upright. **~-keeper**, one who keeps business accounts. **~-maker**, (esp.) professional betting man. **~-muslin**, fine muslin folded like book when sold. **~-plate**, label with owner's name, crest, etc., for pasting in books. **~-worm**, book-destroying maggot; great reader.

bōōk'ie n. (sl.) book-maker.

bōōk'ish a. literary, studious, knowing only books.

bōōm¹ n. spar stretching sail-foot and attached at one end to mast; floating timber barrier across harbour etc.

bōōm² n. deep resonant sound; sensational activity in commerce etc. v. emit, utter with, boom; increase greatly and rapidly in prosperity, popularity, etc.

bōō'merăng n. Australian missile of curved wood that can be so thrown as to return to thrower.

bōōn¹ n. request; favour, blessing, thing to be thankful for.

bōōn² a. convivial.

boor n. peasant; uncouth or ill-bred fellow. **~ish** a.

bōōst v.t. help (up, over) by shove or lift from below; produce (esp. sudden or temporary) increase or improvement in, raise (voltage, pressure, etc.). n. boosting; hoist, lift-up. **~er** n. (esp.) first stage in multi-stage rocket.

bōōt¹ n. advantage (now only in phr. to **~**, as well, into the bargain). v.i. impers. (arch.) be of avail. **~less** a. unavailing.

bōōt² n. foot-covering of leather etc. reaching above ankle; (hist.) instrument of torture; luggage-receptacle in coach, car-body, etc. v.t. kick. **~-jack**, appliance for pulling boots off. **~-tree**, mould for keeping boot in shape. **bōō'tėd**, a. wearing boots. **bōōtee** n. infant's woollen boot, woman's lined boot.

booth (-dh) n. temporary structure of canvas or wood.

bōōt'lĕg a. (of liquor) illicit. **~ger**, **~ging** (-g-) nn. illicit trader, trading, in liquor.

bōōts n. hotel-servant who cleans boots, carries luggage, etc.

bōō'tў n. plunder or profit acquired in common; prize, plunder.

bōōze v.i. drink hard, go on drinking. n. drinking-bout; drink. **bōō'zer** n. hard drinker; (sl.) public-house. **bōō'zў** a. given to drink; fuddled.

borắ'cĭc a. of borax. **~ acid**, boric acid.

bŏ'rage (or bŭ-) n. blue-flowered plant used to flavour claret-cup etc.

bŏr'ăx n. salt of boric acid.

bŏr'der n. side, edge, boundary or part near it; frontier; distinct edging round anything. v. put or be border to; adjoin. **~line**, boundary between areas or classes; a. lying (nearly) on border line.

bŏr'derer *n.* dweller on English- -Scottish border.

bore[1], *p.t.* of bear[2].

bōre[2] *v.* make hole, esp. with revolving tool; (of horse) push (another) out of course. *n.* hollow of gun- -barrel, its calibre; ~(hole), small deep hole made to find water, oil, etc.

bōre[3] *n.* tiresome person or thing; nuisance. *v.t.* weary by tedious talk or dullness.

bōre[4] *n.* great tide-wave moving up some estuaries.

Bōr'ĕăs *n.* north wind. bōr'ĕal *a.* of north wind or north.

bōre'cōle (-ōīk-) *n.* kale.

bore'dom (bōrd-) *n.* being bored.

bōr'ic acid *n.* mild antiseptic used as ointment etc.

bōrn, *p.p.* of bear[2]; chiefly in *be* ~, come into world. *a.* destined from birth (*to be* etc.); arrant, utter.

bŏr'ŏn *n.* non-metallic solid element.

borough (bŭ'ro) *n.* town with municipal corporation; town electing M.P.(s).

bŏ'rrow (-ō) *v.* get temporary use of (something to be returned); adopt or use as one's own (idea, word, etc.).

Bōr'stal *n.* institution to which young offenders may be sent for reformative training.

bōr(t)sch (-sh) *n.* Russian beetroot soup.

bōr'zoi *n.* Russian wolf-hound.

bŏs'cage *n.* shrubs or trees.

bŏsh *n.* nonsense, rubbish.

bŏs'kў *a.* wooded, bushy.

bo'som (bŏŏz-) *n.* breast; enclosure formed by breast and arms; space between breast and dress; surface of water etc.; midst; heart, thoughts. ~ friend, intimate friend.

bŏss[1] *n.* master, manager, overseer. *v.t.* be boss of, control; ~ *about*, domineer over. ~ў *a.* domineering.

bŏss[2] *n.* protuberance, round knob or stud.

bŏss[3] *a.* (sl.) ~-eyed, cross-eyed. ~ shot, failure, bungle.

B.O.T. *abbr.* Board of Trade.

bŏt'anīze *v.i.* study plants, esp. by seeking them where they grow.

bŏt'anў *n.* science of plants. botăn'- ic(al) *aa.*; bŏt'anĭst *n.*

bŏtch *v.t.* patch, mend clumsily bungle. *n.* botched work, bungle.

bōth *a.* & *pron.* the two (not only one of them), the pair (*of*). *adv.* ~ . . . *and* . . ., not only . . . but also.

bŏth'er (-dh-) *v.* give trouble to; perplex; take trouble. *n.* worried state, fuss. *int.* of impatience. ~ā'tion *n.* & *int.* bother. ~some *a.* annoying, troublesome.

bŏth'ў, -ie *n.* (Sc.) (one-roomed) hut.

bŏtt *n.* parasitic larva of ~-fly, causing disease (~s) in horses and cattle.

bŏtt'le[1] *n.* narrow-necked usu. glass vessel for storing liquid; liquid in bottle. *v.t.* put into bottle(s); ~ *up*, restrain (feelings etc.). ~-green, dark green. ~-holder, pugilist's attendant at fight. ~-neck, narrow stretch or restricted outlet of road etc.; anything obstructing even flow of production etc. ~-party, party to which guests contribute drinks. ~-washer, underling.

bŏtt'le[2] *n.* bundle (*of* hay or straw).

bŏtt'om *n.* lowest part; posterior; ground under water of sea etc.; low-lying land; less honourable end of table, class, etc.; bottom of ship's hull; ship; basis, essential character. *a.* lowest; last. *v.* put bottom to; touch bottom (of); sound. ~less *a.* unfathomable. ~rў *n.* borrowing of money on security of ship.

bŏt'ūlism *n.* usu. fatal food-poisoning caused by micro-organism.

bouclé (bŏŏ'klā) *n.* & *a.* (textile) with looped surface.

boudoir (bŏŏ'dwār) *n.* lady's small private room.

bough (bow) *n.* branch of tree.

bought, *p.t.* & *p.p.* of buy.

bouillon (bŏŏl'yawṅ) *n.* broth.

boul'der (bōl-) *n.* detached rock; large water-worn stone.

boulevard (bŏŏl'vahr) *n.* broad tree- -lined street.

boult : see bolt[2].

bounce *v.* (of ball etc.) spring back after striking ground etc.; (of person) jump up, esp. in anger; boast; hustle or bluff; (sl., of cheque) be returned to drawer. *n.* rebound; boastfulness, assurance. boun'cer *n.* (U.S.) chucker- -out. ~cing *a.* big and hearty.

bound[1] *n.* (usu. in pl.) encircling boundary, limit; *out of* ~*s*, beyond prescribed limits. *v.t.* be boundary of; set bounds to. ~**less** *a.*

bound[2] *v.i.* (of ball etc.) recoil from wall or ground; spring, leap. *n.* recoil of ball etc.; springy upward or forward movement.

bound[3] *a.* ready to start or having started (*for*).

bound[4], *p.t.* & *p.p.* of **bind**.

boun'dary *n.* line etc. indicating bounds or limits; (crick.) hit to limit of field, runs scored for this.

boun'der *n.* (colloq.) cheerfully or noisily ill-bred person.

boun'téous, boun'tiful *aa.* showing bounty, generous, profuse.

boun'ty *n.* liberality in giving; gift, gratuity; subsidy.

bouquet (bookā') *n.* bunch of flowers; perfume of wine; bunch of herbs for flavouring.

bour'bon (ber-) *n.* whisky distilled from maize and rye.

bourgeois[1] (boor'zhwah) *a.* & *n.* (person) of shop-keeping or mercantile middle-class. ~**ie** (-zē) *n.* middle class.

bourgeois[2] (berjois') *n.* size of printing-type (approx. 9-point).

bourn(e)[1] (boorn) *n.* stream.

bourn(e)[2] (boorn) *n.* bound, limit; goal.

bourse (boors) *n.* French money-market.

bout *n.* spell or turn or fit of work, illness, etc.; round, contest.

bō'vine *a.* of oxen; dull, inert.

bow[1] (bō) *n.* weapon for shooting arrows; curve, rainbow; rod with horsehair stretched from end to end for playing violin etc.; slip-knot with one loop or two, ribbon etc. so tied. ~**-compass(es)**, compass with jointed legs. ~**-legged**, bandy. ~**man**, archer. ~**-window**, curved bay window.

bow[2] *v.* bend or kneel in sign of submission, reverence, greeting, or assent; express, usher *in* or *out*, by bowing; incline head in salutation. *n.* bowing of head or body.

bow[3] *n.* fore-end of boat or ship; rower nearest bow.

bowd'lerīze *v.t.* expurgate.

bow'el *n.* intestine; (pl.) entrails, tender feelings, inside.

bow'er[1] *n.* anchor at ship's bow.

bow'er[2] *n.* dwelling, lady's room; arbour, leafy nook. ~**-bird**, kinds of Austral. bird building 'bowers' adorned with feathers etc. ~**y** *a.* leafy.

bow'er[3] *n.* knave of trumps (*right* ~) or other suit of same colour (*left* ~) at euchre.

bowie-knife (bō'ï) *n.* large knife with long blade curved and double-edged near point.

bowl[1] (bōl) *n.* basin, esp. for drink or food; hollow of tobacco-pipe, spoon, etc.

bowl[2] (bōl) *n.* biased wooden ball; (pl.) game played on green with such balls; ball used in skittles. *v.* play bowls or skittles; roll; go along at smart even pace; (crick.) deliver ball, dismiss (batsman) by knocking off bails in bowling. ~**er**[1] *n.*

bow'ler[2] (bō-) *n.* hard felt hat with round crown and narrow brim.

bow'line (bō-) *n.* knot for making fixed loop at end of rope.

bow'ling (bō-) *n.* (esp.) skittles. ~**-alley**, long enclosure for playing skittles. ~**-crease**, line from behind which ball is bowled in cricket. ~**-green**, **-rink**, lawn for playing bowls.

bow'sprit (bō-) *n.* spar running forward from ship's bow.

bŏx[1] *n.* kinds of evergreen shrub or small tree. ~**wood**, wood of box.

bŏx[2] *n.* receptacle, usu. rectangular, lidded, and for solids; driver's seat in vehicle; separate compartment in theatre, stable, etc.; jury-box, witness-box, signal-box, sentry-box; protective case for piece of mechanism etc.; (typ.) space enclosed by rules etc. *v.* put in or provide with or confine as in box; partition *off*; (naut.) rehearse points of (compass) in correct order. ~**-bed**, that can be shut in with hinged or sliding panels. ~**-camera**, box-shaped photographic camera. ~**-car**, (U.S.) enclosed railway goods-wagon. ~**-kite**, with light rectangular frame at each end.

BOX 57 BRAKE

~-office, for booking theatre etc. seats. **~-pleat,** two parallel contrary pleats forming raised band. **~-spanner,** with socket-head fitting over nut etc.

bŏx³ *v.* slap (person's *ears*); fight with fists, usu. in padded gloves. *n.* slap *on the ear.* **~er** *n.* one who boxes; smooth-coated dog of bull--dog type; *B~* (hist.) member of Chinese anti-foreign secret society.

bŏx-calf′ (-ahf) *n.* chrome-tanned calfskin with hatched grain.

bŏx′ing *n.* act or sport of fighting with fists. **~-gloves,** padded gloves used in boxing. **~-weight,** at which boxers are matched against each other.

Bŏx′ing-day *n.* 26 Dec., when Christmas-boxes are traditionally given.

boy *n.* male child or youth, son; man with boy's tastes etc.; male native servant. **B~ Scout,** member of boys' organization for practising open--air skills and developing character. **~hood** *n.* boyish age. **~ish** *a.* of or like boy(s).

boy′cott *v.t.* refuse all relations or dealings with (person, goods, etc.) for purpose of coercion or punishment. *n.* boycotting.

B.P. *abbr.* British Pharmacopœia.

Bp. *abbr.* Bishop.

b.p. *abbr.* boiling-point.

B.R. *abbr.* British Rail(ways).

bra (-ah) *n.* (colloq.) brassière.

brāce *v.t.* strengthen or tighten, make taut; invigorate. *n.* thing that braces or connects; (pl.) trouser-suspenders; pair or couple.

brāce′lĕt (-sl-) *n.* ornamental band, chain, etc. for arm or wrist; (pl., sl.) handcuffs.

brā′cer *n.* wrist-guard in archery and fencing.

brăck′en *n.* fern abundant on heaths; mass of this.

brăck′ĕt *n.* projection from wall serving as support, corbel; angular support for something fastened to wall; marks used in pairs for enclosing words or figures, viz. ( ), [ ], { }. *v.t.* support with bracket; enclose in brackets; couple together; fire shots beyond and short of (target) in finding range.

brăck′ĭsh *a.* saltish (of water).

brăct *n.* (bot.) small leaf or scale below calyx.

brăd *n.* thin small nail.

brăd′awl *n.* small boring-tool.

brāe *n.* (Sc.) hill-side, steep bank.

brăg *v.* talk boastfully, boast. *n.* boastful statement or talk; card--game like poker.

brăggadō′cio (-shĭō) *n.* bragging talk; boaster.

brăgg′art *n.* & *a.* (person) given to bragging.

Brah′ma *n.* supreme Hindu deity.

Brah′mĭn *n.* member of Hindu priestly (highest) caste; (U.S., usu. derog.) highly cultured or intellectual person.

braid *n.* plaited tress of hair; silk or thread or wire woven into band. *v.t.* form into braid; trim with braid; interweave.

brail *n.* (pl.) trussing-cords along sail-edge. *v.t.* truss (sail).

braille *n.* system of writing or printing for blind with embossed characters.

brain *n.* convoluted mass of nervous tissue contained in skull, controlling processes of sensation, learning, and memory; (pl.) substance of this; intellectual ability. *v.t.* dash out brains of. **~-fag,** nervous exhaustion. **~-fever,** inflammation of brain. **~-pan,** cranium. **~storm,** sudden cerebal disturbance. **~s trust,** group assembled to answer questions impromptu. **~-washing,** systematic elimination of person's established ideas by persistent indoctrination etc. **~wave,** bright idea. **brai′nў** *a.* mentally smart, inventive.

braise (-z) *v.t.* steam (meat) slowly with vegetables, herbs, etc.

brāke¹ *n.* bracken.

brāke² *n.* thicket, brushwood.

brāke³ *v.t.* crush (hemp, flax) by beating. *n.* toothed braking-instrument; heavy harrow.

brāke⁴ *n.* apparatus for checking motion of wheel or vehicle. *v.* apply brake; check with brake. **~sman,** man in charge of brake; (U.S.) guard of train. **~-van,** guard's compartment containing train-brakes.

brāke[5] *n.* large wagonette.

brăm'ble *n.* rough prickly shrub with long trailing shoots, blackberry.

brăm'blïng *n.* mountain finch.

brăn *n.* husks separated from flour after grinding. ~-pie, ~-tub, tub of bran into which children dip for toys.

branch (-ah-) *n.* limb growing from stem or bough of tree; lateral extension or subdivision of river, railway, family, etc.; (U.S.) small stream. *v.i.* put *out* branches; divide, diverge, strike *off, out,* etc. in new path.

brănd *n.* piece of burning or smouldering wood, torch; (poet.) sword; iron stamp used red-hot, mark left by it; stigma; goods of particular make or trade-mark. *v.t.* stamp with brand; impress indelibly; stigmatize. ~ĕd *a.* sold under particular name or trade-mark. brăn(d)'-new' *a.* conspicuously new.

brăn'dïsh *v.t.* wave or flourish.

brănd'lïng *n.* red worm used as bait by anglers.

brăn'dў *n.* strong spirit distilled from wine or grapes. ~-snap, crisp rolled-up gingerbread wafer.

brănt'-gōōse *n.* brent-goose.

brăsh[1] *n.* loose broken rock or ice; hedge clippings etc.

brăsh[2] *a.* vulgarly assertive; impudent.

brass (-ahs) *n.* yellow alloy of copper with zinc; (hist.) bronze; monumental or sepulchral brass tablet; brass wind-instruments; (fig.) effrontery; (sl.) money; (sl.) brass hats. ~ band, of musicians with brass instruments. ~ hat, (sl.) officer of high rank. ~ tacks, (sl.) actual details, real business.

brăss'ard *n.* badge on arm.

brăss'ière (-yār) *n.* woman's undergarment supporting breasts.

brăss'ў (-ah-) *a.* like brass in colour or sound or taste; brazen. *n.* (also ~ïe) brass-soled golf-club (no. 2 wood).

brăt *n.* (contempt.) child.

brava'dō (-ah-) *n.* ostentatious or simulated boldness.

brāve *a.* ready to confront and steady in enduring danger or pain; showy,

excellent. *n.* Red-Indian warrior. *v.t.* defy, dare, challenge.

brā'verў *n.* brave conduct or temper; bright colours, fine clothes.

bra'vō (-ah-) *n.* (pl. -os), hired assassin or bully; cry of bravo! *int.* excellent! well done!

bravur'a (-oora) *n.* (attempt at) brilliant performance; (mus.) passage requiring brilliant execution.

brawl *n.* noisy quarrel. *v.i.* engage in brawl; (of stream) be noisy.

brawn *n.* muscle, lean flesh; meat of pig's head. ~ў *a.* muscular.

bray[1] *n.* ass's cry; loud harsh jarring sound. *v.* emit bray, utter harshly.

bray[2] *v.t.* pound in mortar.

brāze *v.t.* solder with alloy of brass and zinc.

brā'zen *a.* of or like brass; shameless. *v.t.* carry off shamelessly.

brā'zïer (*or* -zher) *n.* cage or iron basket for charcoal fire.

brazïl' *n.* (now usu. ~-wood), hard brownish-red wood of various tropical trees. ~-nut, large three--sided edible seed of Brazilian tree.

breach *n.* breaking or neglect of rule, duty, promise, etc.; breaking off of relations, quarrel; fissure; gap made in fortifications by artillery etc. *v.t.* make breach in.

bread (-ĕd) *n.* flour kneaded into dough, made into loaves, and baked; this as staple food. ~-fruit, large round tropical fruit with whitish pulp. ~-winner, person who supports family.

breadth (-ĕd-) *n.* broadness, distance from side to side; freedom from mental limitations or prejudices. ~ways, ~wise *advv.*

break (-āk) *v.* (brōke, brō'ken) divide or split or separate otherwise than by cutting; tame, subdue; lay open; fall to pieces; make or become bankrupt; interrupt, transgress, violate; come, produce, etc. with suddenness or violence; (of ball) change direction after touching ground; (boxing) come out of clinch; ~ *down,* fail or collapse, itemize, analyse; ~ *even,* emerge with neither gain nor loss; ~ *through,* (esp.) burst through or surmount obstacle or barrier; ~ *up,* become feeble, dismiss, disperse, break small. *n.* breaking; broken place, breach, gap; pause in work etc.; deviation of ball on pitching, ball that breaks; (billiards) points scored in one sequence. **~down**, collapse, stoppage; failure in health or power; analysis (*of* statistics etc.); Negro dance. **~neck**, headlong, dangerous. **~-up**, disintegration, collapse, dispersal. **~water**, mole etc. to break force of waves. **~able** *a.* that can be broken; *n.pl.* things easily broken. **~age** *n.* breaking.

brea′ker (-āk-) *n.* heavy wave breaking on coast or over reef.

breakfast (brĕk′fast) *n.* first meal of day. *v.i.* take breakfast.

bream *n.* yellowish fresh-water or (*sea-~*) sea-fish.

breast (-ĕst) *n.* either milk-secreting organ in woman; (fig.) source of nourishment; chest; seat of affections. *v.t.* oppose breast to, struggle with (waves etc.). **~-bone**, that connecting ribs in front. **~plate**, piece of armour for breast.

breath (-ĕth) *n.* air as used by lungs; breathing, one respiration; slight movement of air; mere word.

breathe (-dh) *v.* use lungs; live; allow to take breath or rest; inhale or exhale or instil; speak or utter softly. **~r** *n.* spell of rest.

brea′thing (-dh-) *n.* respiration; (Gk. gram.) sign (′,′) indicating that initial vowel is, is not, aspirated. **~-space**, time to breathe, pause.

breath′less (-ĕth-) *a.* panting; unstirred by wind; holding one's breath.

bred, *p.t.* & *p.p.* of **breed**.

breech *n.* buttocks; back end of gun or gun-barrel. **~loader**, gun loaded at breech, not through muzzle.

breeches (-ĭch′ĭz) *n.* short trousers fastened below knee; (colloq.) trousers. **~ buoy**, lifebuoy with canvas supports for legs.

breech′ing (-ĭch-) *n.* strap round horse's breech for backing; rope securing gun to ship's side.

breed *v.* (brĕd), produce offspring, propagate, give birth to; raise (cattle etc.); train; (phys., of nuclear reactor) produce new fissile material during fission of element. *n.* race, strain; family with hereditary qualities.

bree′ding *n.* nurture, good manners.

breeze[1] *n.* gadfly.

breeze[2] *n.* gentle wind; wind off sea during day or land at night; (sl.) quarrel. **bree′zў** *a.* pleasantly windy; lively, irresponsible.

breeze[3] *n.* small cinders, coke-dust, etc. used to make concrete blocks for building etc.

Brĕn gun *n.* magazine-fed light automatic rifle.

brĕnt′-gōōse *n.* smallest kind of wild goose.

brĕř *n.* (U.S. Negro dial.) brother.

brĕth′rėn (-dh-) *n.pl.* (arch.) brothers, esp. (fellow-) members of religious order, guild, etc.

Brĕt′on *n.* & *a.* (native, language) of Brittany.

brev. *abbr.* brevet.

brēve *n.* (mus.) note equal to two semibreves; mark (˘) over vowel to show it is short.

brĕv′ĕt *n.* document conferring nominal rank on army officer.

brē′vĭarў *n.* book containing R.C. Divine Office for each day.

brévier′ *n.* size of type (approx. 8 pt.)

brĕv′ĭtў *n.* conciseness, shortness.

brew (-ōō) *v.* make beer etc. by fermenting malt; make punch, tea, etc. by infusion. *n.* amount brewed; liquor brewed. **~er** *n.* one who brews beer or malt liquors. **~erў** *n.* commercial brew-house.

brews′ter (-ōō-) *n.* (arch.) brewer. **B~ Sessions**, for issue of licences to trade in alcoholic liquors.

briar : see **brier**.

brībe *n.* inducement offered to procure esp. dishonest or illegal service to giver. *v.t.* persuade by bribery. **brī′berў** *n.*

brĭc′-à-brăc *n.* antiquarian or artistic odds and ends.

brĭck *n.* building-material of baked clay in oblong blocks; brick-shaped block; toy building block; (sl.) warmly approved person. *v.t.* block *up* with brickwork. **~-bat**, piece of brick, esp. as missile. **~-dust**, powdered brick. ~-field, ~-kiln, places for making and baking bricks. ~layer, workman building in brick.

brī'dal *n.* wedding feast or ceremony. *a.* of bride or wedding.

brīde *n.* woman on her wedding day and shortly before and after it. ~groom, man on wedding day etc. ~smaid, unmarried woman or girl attending bride.

bride'well (-dw-) *n.* (arch.) gaol.

bridge¹ *n.* structure carrying road or path across stream, ravine, etc.; (naut.) platform amidships for officer in charge; upper bony part of nose; prop under strings of violin etc. *v.t.* make bridge over, span (as) with bridge. ~-head, position held on enemy's side of water-barrier as starting-point for future attack.

bridge² *n.* kinds of card-game developed from whist.

brī'dle *n.* head-gear of harness; restraint, curb. *v.* put bridle on; control, curb; draw one's head up in offence etc. ~-path, ~-road, fit or meant for riders but not vehicles.

brief *a.* of short duration; concise. *n.* solicitor's summary for guidance of barrister; pl. very short knickers or trunks. *v.t.* instruct by brief, employ (barrister); give instructions, necessary information, etc. to. ~-case, flat handbag for carrying papers etc.

brī'er¹, brī'ar¹ *n.* wild-rose bush. ~-rose, wild rose.

brī'er², brī'ar² *n.* heath with root used for pipe-bowls; brier pipe.

brig¹ *n.* (Sc.) bridge.

brig² *n.* two-masted square-rigged vessel with additional lower fore- -and-aft sail on mainmast; (U.S. Navy sl.) guardhouse.

brigāde' *n.* military sub-unit of division, usu. three battalions; organized band of workers etc.

brigadier' *n.* brigade-commander; officer next above colonel.

brig'and *n.* member of robber gang. ~age *n.*

brig'antine (-ēn) *n.* two-masted vessel with square-rigged foremast and fore-and-aft rigged mainmast.

bright *a.* shining, brilliant; cheerful; vivacious, quick-witted.

brigh'ten *v.t.* make bright.

Bright's disease *n.* granular degeneration of kidneys.

brill *n.* flat-fish resembling turbot.

brill'iant (-lya-) *a.* bright, sparkling, highly talented, distinguished. *n.* diamond of finest quality; size of type (approx. 3½ pt.). ~ance *n.* ~antine (-ēn) *n.* cosmetic for hair.

brim *n.* edge of cup, hollow, channel, etc.; projecting edge of hat. *v.* fill or be full to brim. ~ful *a.*

brim'stone *n.* sulphur; fuel of hell- -fire.

brin'dled (-dld) *a.* brown with streaks of other colour.

brine *n.* salt and water for pickling; salt water, sea; tears. *v.t.* treat with brine.

bring *v.t.* (*brought*, pr. -awt), cause to come with one, come with, convey; result in; prevail upon; cause to come *in*, *out*, etc.; prefer (charge); ~ *to bear*, apply; ~ *to mind*, recall; ~ *to pass*, cause to happen; ~ *about*, cause to happen; ~ *off*, succeed in; ~ *round*, restore to consciousness; ~ *up*, educate, rear, sue in court; ~ *up the rear*, come last.

brink *n.* edge of precipice etc.

brī'nȳ *a.* of brine or sea, salt. *n.* (joc.) *the* sea.

briquette' (-kĕt) *n.* block of compressed coal-dust.

brisk *a.* active, lively, quick.

bris'kĕt *n.* animal's breast, esp. as joint of meat.

bris'tle (-sl) *n.* short stiff hair. *v.* (of hair etc.) stand up; make bristle; show temper; be thickly set (*with* obstacles etc.).

bris(t)'ling *n.* sardine-like fish.

Bris'tol board *n.* fine pasteboard for drawing on.

Britănn'ia (-ya) *n.* Britain personified. ~ metal, silvery alloy.

Britănn'ic *a.* of Britain.

Brit'ish *a.* of Britain or British Commonwealth. *n.pl.* people of Britain. ~er *n.* native of Great Britain.

Brit'on *n.* one of race found by Romans in S. Britain; (poet., rhet.) native of Great Britain.

Britt. *abbr. Brittanniarum* [L]. of the Britains.

britt'le *a.* apt to break, fragile.

broach *n.* roasting-spit; kinds of boring-bit. *v.t.* bore or begin drawing from (cask); start using; bring up for discussion.

broad (-awd) *a.* large across, extensive; comprehensive, tolerant; of specified breadth; full, clear; downright, coarse, crude; (of accent) marked, strong. *n.* expanse of water formed by widening of stream; broad part. *adv.* broadly. **~ a,** that heard in father. **~ arrow,** mark cut or stamped on Government stores. **~ bean,** common flattened variety. **~loom,** (carpet) woven of greater width than 54 in. **~tail (lamb),** fur of very young Persian lamb.

broad'cast (-awd-) *v.* (p.t. -*cast*(*ed*), p.p. -*cast*), sow (seed) by scattering freely, not in drills or rows; disseminate widely; transmit (news, musical performance, etc.) to public by radio or television; perform etc. for such transmission. *a.* & *adv.* (sown, transmitted) by broadcasting. *n.* act or practice of, matter intended for or transmitted by, broadcasting. **~er, ~ing** *nn.*

broad'clŏth (-aw-) *n.* fine close twilled or plainly woven cloth.

broa'den (-aw-) *v.* make or become broader.

broad'sheet (-aw-) *n.* large sheet of paper printed on one side only.

broad'sīde (-aw-) *n.* ship's side above water; (discharge of) all guns on one side of ship. **~ on,** with broadside presented (*to*).

broad'sword (-awdsŏrd) *n.* sword with broad straight blade.

brocāde' *n.* fabric with raised patterns woven in. **brocā'dĕd** *a.*

brŏcc'olĭ *n.* kinds of cauliflower.

brō'chure (-shoor) *n.* stitched booklet, pamphlet.

brŏck *n.* badger.

brō'derĭe anglaise (ahṅ'glāz) *n.* usu. white openwork embroidery on fine cotton etc. fabric.

brōgue (-g) *n.* rough shoe of untanned leather; strong shoe for sports and country wear; marked local esp. Irish accent.

broil[1] *n.* & *v.i.* (engage in) quarrel or tumult.

broil[2] *v.* cook on fire or gridiron; make or be very hot. **~er** *n.* (esp.) young chicken suitable for broiling; **~er-house,** building in which chickens are reared in close confinement.

broke[1] *p.t.* of **break**.

brōke[2] *a.* ruined, penniless.

brō'ken *a.* in pieces, shattered; ruined, despairing; (of colour) mixed with another; imperfect, interrupted, uneven, infirm, incomplete. **~-hearted,** crushed by grief. **~-winded,** (of horse) disabled by ruptured air-cells. **~ly** *adv.* spasmodically; with breaks.

brō'ker *n.* middleman, agent; stockbroker; dealer in second-hand furniture etc.; appraiser and seller of distrained goods. **~age** *n.* broker's fees or commission. **brō'king** *n.*

brō'mīde *n.* compound of bromine; potassium bromide as sedative; commonplace or conventional remark etc. **~ paper,** photographic printing-paper with silver bromide in coating.

brō'mine (-ēn) *n.* (chem.) reddish-black heavy liquid non-metallic element.

brŏn'chĭal (-ngk-) *a.* of two main divisions of windpipe or their ramifications in lungs.

brŏnchī'tĭs (-ngk-) *n.* inflammation of bronchial mucous membrane.

brŏn'co *n.* wild or half-tamed horse of California etc.

brŏntosaur'us *n.* (huge reptile of) genus of dinosaurs.

brŏnze *n.* brown alloy of copper and tin; its colour; work of art in it; (attrib.) made of or coloured like bronze. *v.* give bronze-like surface to; make or grow brown, tan. **B~ Age,** stage of culture (between Stone and Iron Ages) when tools etc. were of bronze.

brooch (-ō-) *n.* ornamental safety-pin worn as fastening of dress etc.

brood *n.* birds or other animals produced at one hatch; (contempt.)

children of family, gang or crew; (attrib.) for breeding. *v.i.* sit on eggs; meditate deeply, fret *over*. ~ỹ *a.* (of hen) wishing to sit.

brook¹ *v.t.* tolerate; admit of.

brook² *n.* small stream. ~let *n.*

broom *n.* yellow-flowered shrub; long-handled sweeping-brush. ~stick, broom-handle.

Bros. *abbr.* Brothers.

broth *n.* thin meat soup.

broth'el *n.* house of prostitution.

broth'er (-ŭdh-) *n.* son of same parents; companion, equal; (pl. ~s, *brethren*) member of religious order; (pl. *brethren*) fellow member of church, guild, order, etc. ~-in--law *n.* wife's or husband's brother, sister's husband. ~hood *n.* (esp.) association for mutual help etc. ~lỹ *a.* of or like brother or brother's.

brough'am (-ooam) *n.* short closed four-wheeled one-horse or electric carriage.

brought, *p.t.* & *p.p.* of bring.

brow *n.* arch of hair over eye (usu. in pl.); forehead; edge of cliff, hill, etc.; summit of pass. ~beat *v.t.* bully, bear down, with looks and words.

brown *a.* of colour produced by mixing orange and black pigments; dark, dark-skinned. *n.* brown colour or pigment; brown butterfly, clothes, etc. *v.* make or become brown. ~ bread, of unbolted flour. ~ paper, unbleached kind used for packing etc. ~stone, dark-brown sandstone used for building. ~ sugar, partially refined kinds. ~ study, reverie.

brow'nie *n.* benevolent sprite haunting house; junior member of Girl Guides.

browse (-z) *v.* feed on leaves and young shoots; (fig.) read for enjoyment. *n.* browsing.

Bru'in (-oo-) *n.* (name for) bear.

bruise (-ooz) *n.* injury caused by blow or pressure discolouring skin. *v.* pound, grind small, batter; inflict bruise on; be susceptible to bruises. brui'ser *n.* prize-fighter.

bruit (-oo-) *v.t.* spread *about, abroad.*

Brŭmm'agėm *a.* counterfeit, cheap and showy.

brunětte' (-oo-) *n.* & *a.* dark-skinned and dark-haired (woman).

brŭnt *n.* stress of shock or attack.

brŭsh *n.* cleaning or hair-dressing or painting implement of bristles etc. set in holder; fox's tail; (act of) brushing; skirmish; (electr.) strip of carbon etc. for making and breaking contact; brushwood; (Austral.) dense trees and undergrowth. *v.* touch lightly, graze in passing; use brush on. ~wood, undergrowth, bushes and saplings. ~-work, painter's way of using brush.

brŭsque (*or* -oosk) *a.* blunt, offhand.

Brŭss'els (-z). ~ carpet, ~ lace, kinds made at Brussels. ~ sprouts, edible buds of kind of cabbage.

bru'tal (-oo-) *a.* as of brutes; coarsely sensual or callously cruel. brutăl'itỹ *n.* ~īze *v.t.* make brutal.

brute (-oot) *a.* not gifted with reason. *n.* animal other than man, large or formidable beast; human being of low type; (colloq.) person one dislikes.

brỹ'onỹ *n.* climbing hedge plant.

B.Sc. *abbr.* Bachelor of Science.

B.S.I., B.S.T. *abbr.* British Standards Institution, Summer Time.

Bt *abbr.* Baronet.

B.Th.U. (*or* **B.T.U.**) *abbr.* British thermal unit.

bŭbb'le *n.* globe or half-globe of liquid or glass enclosing air or gas; visionary project. *v.i.* send up or rise in bubbles; boil (*over*) *with* joy, anger, etc. ~-and-squeak, cooked potatoes and cabbage fried together. ~-car, small motor-car with glass-like dome.

bŭbb'lỹ *a.* full of bubbles. *n.* (sl.) champagne.

bū'bō *n.* (pl. -*oes*), inflamed swelling in groin or armpit. būbŏn'ĭc *a.* characterized by buboes.

bŭccaneer' *n.* sea-rover esp. of S.-Amer. coasts.

bŭck¹ *n.* male of fallow-deer, chamois, hare, etc.; dandy. *a.* (sl.) male. ~-bean, pinkish-flowered water--plant. ~-hound, small staghound. ~shot, large coarse shot. ~skin, soft leather made from skin of deer, goat, etc.; (pl.) breeches of this. **~-tooth**, projecting tooth.

bŭck² v. (of horse) jump vertically with back arched and feet drawn together; throw *off* thus. **~ -jumper**, horse given to bucking.

bŭck³ v. (sl.) **~up**, hurry, become or make cheerful or vigorous.

bŭck⁴ n. (U.S. sl.) dollar.

bŭck⁵ n. small object placed before dealer at poker; *pass the* **~**, shift responsibility (*to*).

bŭck⁶ n. (sl.) boastful talk.

bŭck'board n. (U.S.) (light vehicle consisting of) plank slung between wheels.

bŭck'ĕt n. vessel for drawing, carrying, or holding water etc.; socket for whip, carbine, etc.; scoop for hoisting, dredging, etc. v.i. row hurried stroke; make jerky or bumpy progress. **~ seat**, seat in car etc. with high rounded back. **~-shop**, office for speculative dealing in stocks etc.

bŭck'le n. clasp with hinged tongue used for straps etc. v. fasten with buckle; put *on*; bend one's energies *to* work; crumple (*up*).

bŭck'ler n. small round shield; protector or protection.

bŭck'ram n. coarse linen or cloth stiffened with paste etc.

Bucks. *abbr.* Buckinghamshire.

bŭck'shee a. & adv. (sl.) free, gratis.

bŭck'wheat n. cereal plant.

būcŏl'ĭc a. of shepherds, rustic, pastoral.

bŭd n. projection from which branch or leaf-cluster or flower develops; flowers or leaf not fully open; (zool.) reproductive growth attached to parent and developing into new individual. v. put forth buds, sprout as buds; begin to grow or develop; graft bud on alien stock.

Buddhism (bŏŏd'ĭzm) n. religion founded by Buddha. **~ĭst** n.

bŭdd'leia (-lĭa) n. shrub with lilac or yellow flowers.

bŭdd'ŷ n. (U.S.) brother; mate.

bŭdge v. move in slightest degree.

bŭdg'erĭgar n. Australian love-bird.

bŭdg'ĕt n. contents of bag, bundle of letters, etc.; Chancellor of Exchequer's annual estimate of revenue and expenditure, private person's similar estimate; amount of money required or available. v.i. allow or arrange *for* in budget.

bŭff n. stout velvety dull-yellow leather; colour of this. a. of this colour. v.t. polish with buff.

bŭff'alō n. (pl. -oes), kinds of ox; (pop.) Amer. bison.

bŭff'er¹ n. apparatus for deadening or sustaining concussions, esp. on railways; also *fig.* **~ State**, between two possible belligerents, reducing chance of hostilities.

bŭff'er² n. (usu. *old* **~**), fellow.

bŭff'ĕt¹ n. blow with hand; blow dealt by wave etc. or by fortune. v.t. deal blows to, knock about.

bŭff'ĕt² n. sideboard for china, glass, etc.; (pr. bŏŏ'fā) refreshment bar.

buffōōn' n. person who makes himself ridiculous to raise laughter, coarse jester. **~erŷ** n.

bŭg n. small blood-sucking insect infesting beds; any insect. **~-hunter**, (sl.) entomologist.

bŭg'abōō, bŭg'bear (-bār) nn. fancied object of fear.

bŭgg'er n. sodomite; (vulg.) term of abuse. v. (vulg. sl.) mess *about*, clear *off*. **~ŷ** n. sodomy.

bŭgg'ŷ n. light horse-drawn vehicle for one or two persons.

bū'gle¹ n. kinds of plant.

bū'gle² n. tube-shaped glass bead sewn on dress etc. as ornament.

bū'gle³ n. brass instrument like small trumpet. v.i. sound bugle. **~r** n.

bū'glŏss n. kinds of plant allied to borage.

buhl (-ōōl) n. inlaid work of brass and tortoise-shell.

build (bĭ-) v. (*built*), construct or erect by successive additions; be engaged in building; base hopes *on*; **~ up**, establish, make or become or increase gradually, surround or cover with houses etc. n. style of construction, proportions. **~-up**, favourable publicity to popularize person, product, etc. **~er** n. (esp.) contractor for building houses.

buil'ding (bĭ-) n. house or other structure with roof and walls. **~ society**, company lending money to build or buy house.

built (bĭ-) *a.* made or constructed; made *for*. ~-in, forming integral part of structure. ~-up, covered with buildings; increased in height, thickness, etc.

bŭlb *n.* globular base of stem of some plants; roundish swelling in cylindrical organ or tube; glass container of electric-light filament.

bŭl'bous *a.* bulb-shaped, having bulb or bulbs; swollen.

bulbul (bŏŏl'bŏŏl) *n.* Eastern song--thrush.

bŭlge *n.* irregular swelling out of surface or line; (sl.) advantage, upper hand; (temporary) increase in numbers or volume. *v.i.* form or show bulge.

bŭlk *n.* contents of ship's hold, cargo; *the* mass or greater part; size, magnitude, volume; *in* ~, in large quantities, not in package(s). *v.i.* seem in respect of size or importance. ~ buying, buying in bulk. ~head, upright partition in ship's hull between cabins or watertight compartments.

bŭl'kў *a.* large, unwieldy.

bull¹ (-ŏŏ-) *n.* Papal edict.

bull² (-ŏŏ-) *n.* statement so made as to imply absurdity.

bull³ (-ŏŏ-) *n.* male of ox, elephant, whale, and other large animals; bull's-eye in shooting; (St. Exch.) speculator for rise in prices. ~-calf, young bull. ~doze, clear (ground), make (one's way), (as) with bull-dozer; intimidate, bully. ~dozer, powerful tractor pushing broad steel blade in front, for clearing ground etc. ~-fight, (esp. Spanish) sport of baiting bulls with horsemen etc. ~frog, kinds of large frog with loud bellowing note. ~-ring, arena for bull-fight. ~-terrier, heavily built smooth-haired cross between bulldog and terrier.

bullace (bŏŏl'ĭs) *n.* small wild plum.

bull'dŏg (-ŏŏ-) *n.* powerful and courageous large-headed smooth-haired dog; tenacious person; (sl.) university proctor's attendant.

bull'ĕt (-ŏŏ-) *n.* spherical or conical missile for rifle, pistol, etc. ~-head(ed), (with) round head.

bull'ĕtĭn (-ŏŏ-) *n.* short official statement of invalid's condition etc.

bull'fĭnch (-ŏŏ-) *n.* fine-plumaged song-bird; quickset hedge with ditch.

bullion (bŏŏl'yon) *n.* gold or silver in lump or by weight.

bull'ock (-ŏŏ-) *n.* gelded bull.

bull's-eye (bŏŏl'zī) *n.* (lantern with) hemispherical lens; centre of target; large peppermint sweetmeat.

bull'ў (-ŏŏ-) *n.* hired ruffian, blusterer, browbeater; schoolboy tyrant; tinned beef; scrummage in Eton football; (hockey) bullying off. *v.* play bully, browbeat, persecute physically or morally; ~ (*off*), (hockey, of centre-forwards) put ball in play. *a.* (sl.) first-rate.

bul'rush (-ŏŏ-) *n.* kinds of tall rush; (bibl.) papyrus.

bul'wark (-ŏŏ-) *n.* earthwork or other material defence; person or principle that protects; ship's side above deck.

bŭm¹ *n.* (vulg.) backside, buttocks. ~-bailiff, sheriff's officer for arrests etc. ~-boat, plying with fresh provisions for ship.

bŭm² *n.* (U.S. colloq.) loafer, dissolute person, tramp. *a.* worthless, poor. *v.* loaf or wander (*around*); lead life of bum; cadge.

bŭm'ble-bee *n.* large loud-humming bee.

bŭm'bledom (-ld-) *n.* consequential minor officials and their ways.

bŭm'ble-pŭppў *n.* unskilled whist, tennis, etc.; game with tennis-ball slung to post.

bŭmm'alō *n.* small fish of S. Asia, dried and used as relish.

bŭmp *n.* dull-sounding blow, collision, swelling caused by it; protuberance; (faculty supposed to be indicated by) prominence on skull; (variation of air pressure causing) irregularity in motion of aircraft. *v.* inflict bump(s) on; strike or come bump against; jolt; (of cricket-ball) rise abruptly; ~ *off*, (sl.) murder with violence. *adv.* with a bump, suddenly, violently. bŭmp'ў *a.*

bŭm'per *n.* brimming glass; anything unusually large or abundant; ball that bumps; fender at front or rear of motor-car etc. to take first shock of collision.

bŭmp′kĭn n. country lout.

bŭmp′tious a. self-assertive, conceited.

bŭn n. small soft currant cake; small coil of hair at back of head.

bŭnch n. cluster of things growing or fastened together; lot; (sl.) gang, group. v.i. arrange in bunch(es); gather in folds; come or cling or crowd together. **bŭnch′y** a.

bŭnd n. embankment, embanked causeway, quay.

bŭn′dle n. odds and ends tied up in cloth etc.; sticks etc. bound up together. v. tie in bundle; throw confusedly in(to) receptacle; go or send unceremoniously away, out, etc.

bŭng n. stopper, esp. large cork stopping hole in cask. v.t. stop with bung; stop up; (sl.) throw.

bŭng′alow (-nggalō) n. one-storeyed house, orig. lightly built. **bŭng′aloid** a. of or like bungalow(s).

bungle (bŭng′gl) v. go awkwardly to work; mismanage, fail to accomplish. n. piece of bungling.

bŭn′ion (-yon) n. inflamed swelling on foot.

bŭnk[1] n. sleeping-berth, bed, freq. one of two or more in tiers. v.i. sleep esp. in bunk. **~-house**, with bunks for gang of workmen etc.

bŭnk[2] v.i. (sl.) make off, vanish. n. (sl.) do a ~ run away.

bŭnk[3] n. (U.S.) humbug, nonsense.

bŭnk′er n. large bin or compartment for storing fuel etc.; sand-pit or hollow as hazard on golf-course; underground shelter esp. of reinforced concrete. v. fill bunkers of (ship etc.), fuel; (pass.) be hit into or have one's ball in bunker.

bŭnk′um n. bunk, claptrap.

bŭnn′y n. childish name for rabbit.

Bŭn′sen bŭr′ner n. gas-burner producing very hot non-luminous flame.

bŭnt[1] n. cavity or baggy part of sail, fishing-net, etc.

bŭnt[2] v.t. block (baseball) with bat without swinging. n. bunting.

bŭn′tĭng[1] n. kinds of small bird allied to finch.

bŭn′tĭng[2] n. (flags made from) open--weave worsted or cotton material.

buoy (boi) n. anchored float as navigation mark etc.; lifebuoy. v.t. mark with buoy(s); ~ up, keep afloat, sustain.

buoy′ant (boi-) a. apt to float, light; cheerful. **~ancy** n.

bŭr, bŭrr[2] n. clinging seed-vessel or other part of plant, plant producing burs; person hard to shake off; knot in wood.

bŭr′berry n. waterproof material; garment made of it. **P.**

bŭr′bot n. eel-like freshwater fish.

bŭr′den n. load, task, weight of grief, obligatory expense; (freq. *burthen*) ship's tonnage; refrain of song, theme. v.t. load, encumber, lie heavy on. **~some** a. imposing burden, oppressive.

bŭr′dock n. plant with prickly flowers and dock-like leaves.

bŭreau′ (-rō) n. (pl. -*eaux*, pr. -ōz), escritoire; (U.S.) chest of drawers; office, esp. of Government department.

bŭreau′cracy (-rŏ- *or* -rō-) n. government by bureaux, centralization; officialism; officials. **~crăt** n.; **~crăt′ic** a.

bŭrgee′ n. swallow-tailed triangular pennant of yacht etc.

bŭr′geon (-jn) n. & v.i. bud, shoot.

bŭr′gess n. freeman of borough, citizen; M.P. for borough, university, etc.

burgh (bŭ′ru) n. Sc. borough.

bŭr′gher (-ger) n. citizen esp. of foreign town.

bŭr′glar n. person breaking into house by night with felonious intent. **burglar′ious** a.; **~y** n. **bŭr′gle** v. (colloq.) commit burglary; enter or rob thus.

bŭr′gomaster (-mah-) n. Dutch or Flemish mayor.

bŭr′gundy n. kinds of wine produced in or resembling those of Burgundy.

bu′rĭal (bĕ-) n. burying, esp. of dead body; funeral.

bŭr′ĭn n. engraver's tool.

bŭrke v.t. smother, stifle.

bŭrl n. knot in wool or cloth or (U.S.) wood.

bŭr′lăp n. coarse canvas, sacking.

burlĕsque′ (-k) *a.* of derisively imitative kind. *n.* dramatic or literary parody; (U.S.) broadly humorous variety show. *v.t.* make or give burlesque of, travesty.

bŭr′lў *a.* of stout sturdy build.

bŭrn[1] *n.* (Sc.) brook, stream.

bŭrn[2] *v.* (*burnt*, occas. *-ed*), consume or be consumed by fire, blaze or smoulder; feel intense heat or emotion; injure or make by burning; brand. *n.* sore or mark made by burning; (U.S.) burnt area in forest etc. **~er** *n.* part of lamp etc. that shapes flame.

bŭr′nĕt *n.* brown-flowered plant. **~(-moth)**, dark-coloured red-spotted moth. **~-rose**, wild rose of sand-dunes etc.

bŭr′nĭsh *v.* polish by friction.

burnt, *p.t.* & *p.p.* of **burn**.

bŭrr[1] *n.* rough edge left by cutting metal etc.; rough sounding of *r*.

burr[2]: see **bur**.

bŭ′rrō (*or* boŏ-) *n.* small donkey used as pack-animal.

bŭ′rrow (-ō) *n.* hole excavated by animals as dwelling. *v.* make or live in burrow; excavate.

bŭr′sar *n.* treasurer of college etc.; holder of bursary. **bŭrsār′ial** *a.* **~ў** *n.* bursar's office; exhibition.

bŭrst *v.* fly violently asunder or give way suddenly, explode; rush, move, speak, be spoken, etc. suddenly or violently. *n.* bursting, explosion, outbreak; spurt. **~ing** *a.* full to overflowing.

burthen : see **burden**.

bŭr′ton *n.* light handy two-block tackle.

bu′rў (bĕ-) *v.t.* commit (corpse) to earth or tomb or sea, celebrate burial rites over; inter, hide in earth; consign to oblivion.

bŭs *n.* (pl. *buses*), large public passenger-carrying vehicle plying on fixed route; vehicle carrying passengers, luggage, etc. to or from airport, hotel, etc. *v.i.* go by bus. **~man**, bus-driver; *~man's holiday*, leisure spent in same occupation as working hours.

bŭs′bў (-z-) *n.* tall fur cap of hussars etc.

bush[1] (-oŏ-) *n.* shrub, clump of shrubs; (Austral. etc.) woodland, untilled land; luxuriant growth (*of* hair etc.); bunch of ivy as old vintner's sign. **~-baby**, small Afr. long-tailed thick-furred big-eyed lemur. **~buck**, small African antelope. **~-hog**, wild pig of southern Africa. **~ lawyer**, N.Z. bramble. **~man**, member or language of S.-Afr. aboriginal tribe; dweller or traveller in Australian bush. **~-ranger**, Australian brigand living in bush. **~-telegraph**, rapid spreading of information, rumour. etc. **~-veldt**, veldt composed largely of bush. **bushed** *a.* lost in bush.

bush[2] (-oŏ-) *n.* perforated plug; metal lining of axle-hole etc.

bush′el (-oŏ-) *n.* measure of capacity (8 gals.) for corn, fruit, etc.

bush′ў (-oŏ-) *a.* growing thickly or like bush; abounding in bushes.

business (bĭz′nĭs) *n.* one's occupation or affairs; one's province or duty; work, employment; (theatr.) dumb show; commercial transactions; firm. **~-like** *a.* systematic, practical, prompt, well-ordered.

bŭsk *n.* stiff rib at corset-front.

bŭs′ker *n.* (sl.) wandering actor etc.; street performer.

bŭs′kin *n.* high boot; ancient tragic actor's boot; tragic drama.

bŭss *n.* & *v.t.* kiss.

bŭst[1] *n.* sculptured head, shoulders, and chest; upper front of (woman's) body.

bŭst[2] *n.* (sl.) burst; spree. *v.* burst, break; go bankrupt. *a.* broke. **~-up**, violent break; explosion, excitement, quarrel.

bŭs′tard *n.* large running bird.

bŭs′tle[1] (-sl) *v.* make show of activity, hurry about; make (others) hurry. *n.* excited activity.

bŭs′tle[2] (-sl) *n.* pad or framework puffing out top of woman's skirt behind.

busy (bĭz′ĭ) *a.* working with concentrated attention, fully employed; fussy, meddlesome. *v.t.* engage, occupy, keep busy. **~-body**, meddlesome person, mischief-maker.

bŭt *adv.*, *prep.* & *conj.* only; except, without, outside of or apart from; unless, if not, yet, still.

bū'tāne *n.* colourless hydrocarbon gas used as illuminant etc.

butch'er (-ŏŏ-) *n.* slaughterer of animals for food, meat-dealer; one who delights in bloodshed. *v.t.* slaughter or destroy or ruin mercilessly or wantonly. ~ў *n.*

bŭt'ler *n.* man-servant in charge of wine, plate, etc.

bŭtt[1] *n.* large cask (108–140 gals.).

bŭtt[2] *n.* mound behind target; grouse-shooter's stand behind low turf or stone wall; (pl.) shooting-range; object of ridicule, person habitually teased.

bŭtt[3] *n.* thicker end esp. of tool or weapon; square end of plank.

bŭtt[4] *v.* push with head; meet end to end; ~ *in*, intervene, meddle. *n.* (violent) push or blow with head or horns.

bŭtte (-t) *n.* isolated abrupt flat-topped hill in western U.S.

bŭtt'er *n.* yellow fatty food-substance made from cream. *v.t.* spread, cook, etc. with butter; (colloq.) flatter. ~ **bean**, dried large flat white kind. ~-**fingered**, **fingers**, (person) given to letting things slip. ~**milk**, liquid left after butter-making. ~ **muslin**, thin loosely woven fine-meshed cloth. ~-**nut**, (large oily fruit of) N.-Amer. white walnut. ~**scotch**, sweetmeat of butter and sugar. ~**wort**, violet-flowered bog-plant. ~ў[1] *a.*

bŭtt'ercŭp *n.* kinds of yellow-flowered ranunculus.

bŭtt'erflў *n.* diurnal insect with large wings, often of brilliant colours; showy person, trifler.

bŭtt'erў[2] *n.* place in college etc. where provisions are kept.

bŭtt'ock *n.* either protuberance of rump; (pl.) seat, rump.

bŭtt'on *n.* disc sewn to garment etc. as fastening or for ornament; (pl. as sing.) page with many-buttoned coat; small knob or projection; unopened flower-bud. *v.* fasten with button(s); enclose in buttoned garment etc. ~**hole**, hole into which button fits; flower(s) to be worn in buttonhole; *v.t.* seize or detain (reluctant listener). ~**hole stitch**,

used for finishing raw edges. ~**hook**, for fastening buttons.

bŭtt'rėss *n.* support built against wall etc.; buttress-like projection of hill. *v.t.* support or strengthen.

bŭtt'ў *n.* (dial.) slice of bread.

bŭx'om *a.* plump, comely.

buy (bī) *v.t.* (*bought*, pr. -awt), obtain in exchange for money or other consideration; gain (over) by bribery. *n.* bargain. ~**er** *n.* (esp.) one who buys stock for (department of) shop etc.; ~**ers' market**, in which goods are plentiful and prices low.

bŭzz *n.* humming (as) of bee etc.; confused low sound. *v.* make buzz; throw hard; (sl.) go quickly *off*; (of aircraft etc.) warn, annoy, etc. by flying close to.

bŭzz'ard *n.* kinds of hawk; (U.S.) turkey-buzzard.

bŭzz'er *n.* steam-whistle; electric buzzing-machine for sending signals.

B.V.M. *abbr. Beata Virgo Maria* [L], Blessed Virgin Mary.

by (bī) *adv.* near, at hand; aside, in reserve; past. *prep.* near to, beside, within reach of; along, via, past; through action, agency, means, or instrumentality of; as soon as, not later than; in accordance with. ~ **and by**, before long; *n.* future. ~-**blow**, bastard child. ~-**election**, caused by death, resignation, etc. of member. ~-**name**, nickname. ~**pass**, secondary gas-jet alight when main supply is cut off; road providing alternative route for through traffic, esp. round town etc.; *v.t.* furnish with bypass, make detour round. ~-**path**, unfrequented path. ~**play**, action, usu. dumb show, carried on aside, esp. on stage. ~-**product**, substance etc. produced incidentally in making of something else. ~-**road**, side road. ~-**street**, side street. ~ **the by**, ~ **the way**, incidentally, parenthetically. ~-**way**, secluded road etc.; less known department of subject.

bўe *n.* (crick.) run made from ball that passes batsman and wicket-keeper; (in tournament) position of competitor left without opponent in round; (golf) hole(s) unplayed when match is finished.

bȳ'gŏne *a.* past, departed. **~s** *n.pl.* past; past offences.

bȳ'-law, bȳe'-law *n.* regulation made by local authority etc.

bȳre *n.* cow-house.

bȳ'stănder *n.* spectator.

bȳ'word (-ērd) *n.* proverb; thing or person as type of (usu. bad) quality.

Bȳzăn'tīne (*or* bĭ-) *a.* of Byzantium or Constantinople; of architectural etc. style developed in Eastern Roman Empire.

C

C, c (sē), as Roman numeral, 100; (mus.) first note of natural major scale.

C. *abbr.* Centigrade; Conservative.

c. *abbr.* caught; cent(s); century; chapter; *circa, circiter* [L], about; cubic.

căb *n.* hackney carriage, taxi; shelter for crew of locomotive or driver of lorry, crane, etc. *v.i.* go by cab. **~man**, driver of cab. **~-rank**, row of cabs on **~-stand**, where cabs stand for hire.

C.A.B. *abbr.* Citizens' Advice Bureau.

cabăl' *n.* secret intrigue; political clique.

căb'aret (-ā) *n.* French tavern; entertainment in restaurant etc. while guests are at table.

căbb'age *n.* kinds of green vegetable with round heart or head of unexpanded leaves. *v.i.* form head like cabbage. **~ rose**, double rose with large round compact flower. **~ white**, kinds of white butterfly.

căb(b)'ala *n.* Jewish oral traditions; occult lore. **căb(b)'alism, ~list** *nn.*; **căb(b)alis'tic** *a.*

căbb'ȳ *n.* (colloq.) cabman.

cā'ber *n.* pine-trunk used in Sc. sport of *tossing the ~*.

căb'ĭn *a.* small dwelling, esp. of wood; hut; private or public room on ship. **~-boy**, boy waiting on ship's officers or passengers. **căb'ĭned** (-nd) *a.* cramped in small space.

căb'ĭnėt *n.* closet, private room; body of Ministers attending councils with Prime Minister; case with drawers or shelves or compartments. **~-maker**, skilled joiner. **~ pudding**, steamed pudding usu. made in moulds and containing dried fruit.

cā'ble *n.* anchor rope or chain; (as measure) 100 fathoms; thick rope of wire or hemp; insulated submarine or underground line containing telegraph or telephone wires; cablegram. *v.* send (message), communicate, by submarine cable. **~gram**, message sent by submarine cable. **~ railway**, funicular railway. **~-stitch**, knitting stitch producing rope-like pattern.

căb'ochŏn (-sh-) *n.* precious stone polished but not cut into facets.

cabōō'dle *n.* (sl.) group, lot, set.

cabōōse' *n.* cook-room on ship's deck; (U.S.) trainmen's or workmen's van on goods train.

căb'otage *n.* (right of) trade or carriage in coastal waters or between two points within country's territory.

căb'riole *n.* kind of curved leg in 17th- and 18th-c., esp. Chippendale, furniture.

căbriolet' (-lā; *or* kăb'-) *n.* kind of chaise.

ca'cănn'ȳ (kah-) *n.* 'going slow', policy of limiting output.

cacā'ō *n.* (seed of) tropical Amer. tree yielding cocoa and chocolate.

căch'alŏt (-sh-) *n.* kinds of whale.

căche (-sh) *n.* hidden store of provisions etc. *v.t.* place in cache.

cachet (kăsh'ā) *n.* mark of authenticity; distinctive stamp; flat capsule for medicine.

căch'innāte (-k-) *v.i.* laugh loudly. **~ā'tion** *n.*

cachou (kăsh'ōō) *n.* small scented lozenge, esp. for sweetening breath.

căck'le *n.* clucking of hen, calling of geese; glib inconsequent talk; loud silly laughter. *v.* emit cackle; utter or express with cackle.

căcōē'thēs (-z) *n.* itch for doing something unadvisable.

cacŏph'onȳ *n.* ugly sound, esp. of words or music. **~nous** *a.*

căc'tus *n.* (pl. -tī, -tuses), kinds of

succulent plant with thick fleshy stem, clusters of spines and usu. no leaves. **~ dahlia**, dahlia with ray florets recurved at edges.

căd *n.* low ill-bred fellow. **~dĭsh** *a.*

cadăv′erous *a.* corpse-like.

cădd′ĭe, cădd′y[1] *n.* golfer's attendant carrying clubs etc. *v.i.* act as caddy.

cădd′ĭs(-worm) *n.* larva of mayfly etc. living in water and making cylindrical case of hollow stems, shells, etc.

cădd′y[2] *n.* small box for tea.

cā′dence *n.* measured movement esp. of sound; intonation; close of musical phrase.

cadĕn′za *n.* (mus.) florid passage for solo instrument or voice.

cadĕt′ *n.* younger son; student in naval, military, etc. college; schoolboy etc. receiving military training.

cădge *v.* get by begging or sponging, beg. **cădg′er** *n.*

ca′dĭ (kah-) *n.* (pl. *-s*), Moslem judge.

căd′mĭum *n.* soft bluish-white metallic element.

cadre (kah′der) *n.* permanent expandable esp. military establishment.

cadū′ceus *n.* (pl. *-eī*), ancient herald's wand, esp. Mercury's.

cae′cum (sē-) *n.* (pl. *-ca*), (biol.) tube with closed end, esp. at beginning of large intestine.

Caes. *abbr.* Caesar.

Caesār′ean, -ĭan (sēz-) *a.* of Caesar. **~ operation, section**, delivery of child by cutting walls of abdomen.

cae′sĭum (sēz-) *n.* rare metallic element of sodium group.

caesūr′a (sĭz-) *n.* point of natural pause near middle of metrical line.

cafe (kăf′ā) *n.* coffee-house or tea-shop or restaurant.

căfėtēr′ĭa *n.* self-service restaurant.

căff′eine (-ēn) *n.* vegetable alkaloid found in coffee and tea plants.

căf′tan *n.* long girdled under-tunic of Turkey etc.

cāge *n.* prison of wire or with bars, esp. for animals; open framework, mineshaft car, etc. *v.t.* confine in cage.

cā′gey *a.* (sl.) wary, non-committal, reserved.

căhōōts′ *n.* (sl.) *in ~*, in league or partnership.

caiman : see **cayman**.

caique (ka-ēk′) *n.* Levantine sailing-vessel.

cairn *n.* pyramid of stones. **~ (terrier)**, small short-legged shaggy-haired terrier.

cairn′gŏrm *n.* yellow or wine-coloured gem-stone.

caiss′on (*or* kasōōn′) *n.* watertight chamber used in laying foundations under water etc.; ammunition chest or wagon.

cai′tĭff *n. & a.* (arch.) coward(ly), rascal(ly).

cajōle′ *v.t.* persuade or soothe by flattery or deceit. **~ment, cajō′lery** (-erĭ) *nn.*

cāke *n.* small flat loaf; sweet mixture of flour, butter, eggs, dried fruit, etc. or some of these, baked freq. in flattish round shape; flattish compact mass. *v.* form into cohesive mass, harden. **cā′ky** *a.*

Cal. *abbr.* California.

căl′abăsh *n.* (vessel made from) kinds of gourd or hard-shelled fruit of tropical Amer. tree.

călabōōse′ *n.* (U.S. colloq.) prison.

călamăn′der *n.* hard cabinet wood of Ceylon and India.

căl′amīne *n.* native zinc carbonate used as skin lotion etc.

calăm′ĭty *n.* grave disaster. **~ĭtous** *a.* causing or marked by calamity.

calăsh′ *n.* low light hooded carriage; (Can.) two-wheeled one-seated vehicle with driver's seat on splash-board; (hist.) woman's hooped silk hood.

călcār′eous *a.* of or containing calcium carbonate or limestone.

călcėolār′ĭa *n.* S.-Amer. plant with slipper-shaped flower.

căl′cĭfy *v.* harden by deposit of calcium salts. **~fĭcā′tion** *n.*

căl′cĭne *v.* reduce, be reduced, to quicklime or friable substance by burning or roasting. **~ĭnā′tion** *n.*

căl′cĭum *n.* light silver-white malleable metallic element. **~ carbide**, calcium salt yielding acetylene when treated with water.

căl′cūlāte *v.* compute by figures, ascertain by exact reckoning; plan deliberately; (U.S.) suppose, believe; (*p.p.*) intentional, cold-blooded. ~ā'tion, ~ātor *nn*.

căl'cūlus *n*. (pl. -lī), (med.) stone, concretion in some part of body; (math.) particular method of calculation, esp. differential and integral calculus.

caldron : see cauldron.

Călēdō'nĭan *a*. & *n*. (native) of (prop. ancient) Scotland.

căl'ĕndar *n*. system fixing civil year's beginning etc.; almanac or table exhibiting year's arrangement; register or list, esp. of saints. *v.t.* enter in list; arrange, analyse, and index (documents).

căl'ĕnder¹ *n*. roller-machine for glazing or smoothing paper, cloth, etc. *v.t.* press in calender.

căl'ĕnder² *n*. mendicant dervish in Persia etc.

căl'ĕnds, k- *n.pl.* first of month in ancient-Roman calendar.

calf¹ (kahf) *n*. (pl. -*ves*), young of cow, elephant, whale, etc.; stupid fellow; calf-leather. ~-love, immature romantic affection.

calf² (kahf) *n*. (pl. -*ves*), fleshy hinder part of leg below knee.

căl'ĭbrāte *v.t.* find calibre of; determine or correct graduations of (gauge). ~ā'tion *n*.

căl'ĭbre *n*. internal diameter of gun or projectile or any tube; degree of merit or importance.

căl'ĭcō *n*. (pl. -*oes*), cotton cloth, esp. plain white kinds; (U.S.) printed cotton cloth. *a*. (U.S.) variegated, piebald. ~ printer, ~ printing, (one whose trade is) printing coloured patterns on cotton cloth.

Calif. *abbr.* California.

călĭfôr'nĭum *n*. transuranic element.

căl'ĭpăsh, căl'ĭpee *nn*. gelatinous green and yellow substances in turtle(-soup).

căl'ĭph (*or* kā-) *n*. chief civil and religious ruler in Moslem countries.

calk (kawk) *n*. sharp iron to prevent horse-shoe or boot from slipping. *v.t.* provide with calk.

calkin (kaw'kĭn) *n*. turned-down edge of horse-shoe.

call (kawl) *v*. speak in loud tone; utter characteristic note; summon; pay brief visit; convoke; name, describe as; ~ *forth*, elicit; ~ *in*, summon (doctor); ~ *off*, cancel, abandon (project); ~ *up*, summon to serve in army etc., ring up. *n*. shout, bird's cry, signal on bugle etc.; summons; short visit; (summons to) telephone conversation. ~-box, public telephone booth. ~-boy, attendant summoning actors to stage. ~-girl, prostitute who can be rung up. ~-sign, conventional sign identifying source of radio message etc.; ~-up, summons to serve in armed forces.

căll'a (lily) *n*. white arum lily of southern Africa.

căll'er *a*. (Sc.) fresh.

callĭg'raphy *n*. (beautiful) handwriting. călligrăph'ic *a*.

call'ing (kaw-) *n*. profession, occupation.

căll'ĭper *n*. (pl.) compasses for measuring diameter of convex bodies, cavities, etc.; support for weak or injured leg. *v.t.* measure with callipers.

căllĭsthĕn'ĭcs *n.pl.* exercises to develop strength and grace.

callŏs'ĭty *n*. hardness of skin, hardened part, insensible lump.

căll'ous *a*. hardened, horny; unfeeling, unsympathetic.

căll'ow (-ō) *a*. unfledged; raw, inexperienced.

căll'us *n*. thickening of skin or soft tissue.

calm (kahm) *a*. tranquil, windless, unagitated; (colloq.) impudent. *v*. make or become calm, pacify. *n*. calm state.

căl'omĕl *n*. mercurous chloride, used as purgative.

căl'orĭe *n*. unit of heat, amount required to raise temperature of one kg. (*large* ~) or one g. (*small* ~) of water 1° C.; unit for measuring heat-producing capacity of food.

călorĭf'ic *a*. heat-producing.

călorĭm'ĕter *n*. heat-measuring apparatus.

căl'trop *n*. four-spiked iron ball thrown down to maim cavalry horses; (usu. pl.) kinds of plant.

căl'ūmĕt *n*. Amer.-Ind. tobacco-pipe.

calŭm'niāte *v.t.* slander, utter calumny about. ~ā'tion *n.*

căl'umnў *n.* defamation, slander.

căl'varў *n.* place, representation, of Crucifixion.

calve (kahv) *v.i.* produce calf.

Căl'vĭnĭsm *n.* Calvin's theology, esp. his doctrine of predestination; adherence to this. ~ĭs'tĭc *a.*

călx *n.* (pl. *calcēs*), friable residue after calcination.

calўp'sō *n.* West-Indian song, usu. topical and extempore.

cā'lўx (*or* -ă-) *n.* (pl. *-cēs, -xes*), whorl of leaves called sepals forming outer case of bud.

căm *n.* sliding or rotating part of machinery bearing on and imparting particular kind of motion to lever etc.

cămara'derie (-ahd*er*ē) *n.* comradeship.

căm'ber *n.* slight convexity, arch, of deck, road, etc. *v.t.* construct with camber.

Căm'brĭan *a.* & *n.* Welsh(man); (of) lowest system of Palaeozoic.

cā'mbrĭc *n.* fine white linen or cotton.

Cambs. *abbr.* Cambridgeshire.

came, *p.t.* of come.

căm'el *n.* large ruminant domesticated quadruped with one hump or two used as beast of burden in arid regions.

camē'llĭa (*or* -ĕ-) *n.* kinds of tropical Asian evergreen flowering shrub.

cămĕl'opărd *n.* (rare) giraffe.

Căm'embert (-ār) *n.* small rich soft Normandy cheese.

căm'ĕo *n.* (pl. *-os*), onyx or similar stone carved in relief.

căm'era *n.* apparatus for taking photographs. ~man, user of esp. film or television camera. ~ obscura, apparatus projecting on paper etc. image of distant object.

căm'ĭon *n.* low flat four-wheeled horse- or motor-truck.

căm'ĭsōle *n.* under-bodice.

căm'omīle *n.* aromatic herb. ~ tea, infusion of camomile flowers.

căm'ouflage (-ōōflahzh) *n.* disguise of guns, ships, etc., by obscuring outlines etc.; means of throwing people off scent. *v.t.* conceal (as) by camouflage.

cămp[1] *n.* place where troops etc. are lodged in tents etc.; temporary quarters of gipsies etc.; (remains of) ancient entrenched and fortified site. *v.* encamp, be in camp; ~ out, sleep in tent or in open. ~-bed, ~-chair, ~-stool, portable folding kinds. ~-follower, non-military hanger-on of camp. ~-meeting, (U.S.) religious open-air meeting.

cămp[2] *a.* (sl.) homosexual, 'queer', perverted; extravagant, bizarre.

cămpaign' (-ān) *n.* series of military operations; organized course of action in politics etc. *v.i.* serve on or conduct campaign.

cămpani'lě (-nē-) *n.* detached bell-tower.

cămpanŏl'ogў *n.* subject of bells.

cămpăn'ūla *n.* kinds of plant with bell-shaped flowers.

căm'phor *n.* whitish crystalline aromatic bitter substance. ~āte *v.t.* impregnate with camphor.

căm'pĭon *n.* kinds of red- or white-flowered plant.

căm'pus *n.* (U.S.) grounds of university or college.

căn[1] *n.* metal vessel for liquids; tin-plate vessel in which food etc. is sealed for preserving. *v.t.* preserve (food etc.) in can; (colloq.) record (music etc.) for reproduction; (U.S. sl.) discharge, suppress.

căn[2] *v. aux.* (2 s. *canst*, 3 *can*; neg. *cannot, can't*, pr. kahnt; past & cond. *could*, pr. kŏŏd, *couldst* or *couldest*), be able to; have the right to; be permitted to.

Can. *abbr.* Canada.

Cā'naanīte (-n*a*n-) *a.* & *n.* (non--Jewish native) of ancient W. Palestine.

Canā'dĭan *a.* & *n.* (native) of Canada. ~ canoe, open canoe with single--bladed paddle.

canăl' *n.* duct esp. in animal body for food, air, etc.; artificial watercourse. căn'alīze *v.t.* make into canal; direct into course or channel.

căn'apé (-ā) *n.* piece of fried bread etc. on which anchovies etc. are served as hors-d'œuvre etc.

canărd' (*or* kă'-) *n.* unfounded rumour.

canār'ў *n.* cage songbird of yellow

plumage; wine from Canary Islands. *a.* bright yellow.

canăs'ta *n.* card-game resembling rummy.

canăs'ter *n.* coarsely broken tobacco.

cancan (kahn'kahn) *n.* high-kicking dance. [F]

căn'cel *v.* cross out, annul, countermand, neutralize; (arith.) strike out (same factor) from two sides of equation etc.; (print.) suppress and reprint (sheet etc.); ~ *out*, neutralize or balance each other. *n.* (print.) suppressed or substituted page, leaf, etc. **căncellă'tion** *n.*

Căn'cer, Crab, fourth constellation and sign of zodiac; *Tropic of* ~, northern tropic.

căn'cer *n.* malignant tumour tending to spread indefinitely; (fig.) corruption. **căn'cerous, căn'croid** *aa.*

căndèla'brum (-lah-; *or* -lă-) *n.* (pl. -a), large, usu. branched, candlestick.

căn'dĭd *a.* unprejudiced; free from dissimulation; outspoken. ~ **camera,** for taking informal unposed photographs.

căn'dĭdate *n.* one who seeks or is nominated etc. for election, office, position, etc.; one who undergoes examination etc. ~**acy̆,** ~**ature** *nn.*

candied : see **candy.**

căn'dle *n.* cylinder of wax, tallow, etc. enclosing wick for giving light. ~**light,** artificial light. ~**-power,** unit of light-measure. ~**stick,** stand for holding candle. ~**wick,** thick soft loosely-twisted cotton yarn used for raised, usu. tufted, embroidery.

Căn'dlemas *n.* feast of Purification of Virgin Mary, 2 Feb.

căn'dour (-d*er*) *n.* candidness.

căn'dy̆ *n.* sugar crystallized by repeated boiling and evaporation; kind of soft toffee; (U.S.) sweetmeat, (pl.) sweets. *v.* make or become candy; preserve (fruit etc.) by impregnating with sugar. ~**-floss,** sweetmeat of fluffy spun sugar. **căn'dĭed** *a.* (fig.) sugared, honeyed.

căn'dy̆tŭft *n.* plant with flowers in flat clusters.

cāne *n.* hollow jointed stem of giant reeds and grasses, stem of slender palms, used as walking-stick, instrument of punishment, etc.; stem of raspberry etc. *v.t.* beat with cane; weave cane into (chair etc.). ~**-brake,** (U.S.) tract of land overgrown with canes. ~ **sugar,** obtained from sugar-cane.

căn'īne (*or* -ā-) *a.* of or as of dog(s). *n.* canine tooth. ~ **tooth,** one of four strong pointed teeth between incisors and molars.

căn'ĭster *n.* small usu. metal box for tea etc.

cănk'er *n.* ulcerous sore or disease; disease of fruit-trees etc.; larva or caterpillar destroying leaves or buds; (fig.) corrupting influence. *v.t.* consume with canker; corrupt.

cănn'a *n.* kinds of bright-flowered ornamental-leaved plant.

cănn'el (coal) *n.* hard bright-flamed coal rich in oil and gas.

cănn'ĭbal *n.* man or animal that eats own species; (attrib.) having this habit. ~**ism** *n.*; ~**ĭs'tĭc** *a.* ~**īze** *v.t.* take parts from (machine) as spares for others.

cănn'ĭkĭn *n.* small can.

cănn'on *n.* mounted gun throwing projectile larger than bullet; (billiards) hitting of two balls successively by player's ball. *v.i.* make cannon at billiards; run or strike (obliquely) *against, into,* etc. ~**-ball,** round shot. **cănnonāde'** *n.* continuous gunfire; *v.* fire continuously, bombard.

cannot : see **can²**.

cănn'y̆ *a.* shrewd, quiet, circumspect.

canoe' (-nōō) *n.* light boat propelled with paddle(s). *v.i.* go in or paddle canoe.

căn'on¹ *n.* Church decree; criterion; list of Bible books accepted by Church; work(s) accepted as belonging to author etc.; part of Mass containing words of consecration; (mus.) composition with parts taken up successively in strict imitation; large size of printing--type (48-point). ~ **law,** ecclesiastical law.

căn'on² *n.* member of cathedral chapter. ~**ry̆** *n.*

cañon : see **canyon.**

canŏn'ical *a.* appointed by canon

law; of canon of Scripture; of (member of) cathedral chapter; authoritative or accepted. ~ **dress**, dress of clergy. **~s** *n.pl.* canonical dress.

căn'onīze *v.t.* admit to calendar of saints. **~īzā'tion** *n.*

Canō'pic *a.* of ancient Egyptian town of Canopus. ~ **jar, vase**, urn for entrails of embalmed body.

căn'opў *n.* covering hung or held up over throne, bed, person, etc.; roof- -like projection; (fig.) sky or over- hanging shelter. *v.t.* supply or be canopy to.

cănt[1] *n.* bevel, slanting surface; tilted position; oblique push or jerk. *v.* push or jerk or hold out of level; tilt, slant; bevel.

cănt[2] *n.* thieves' slang; jargon of class, profession, etc.; temporary catchwords; insincere pious or moral talk. *v.i.* use cant.

can't : see **can**[2].

Cant. *abbr.* Canticles.

Cantab. *abbr.* of Cambridge Univer- sity.

căn'taloup (-ōōp) *n.* small round variety of musk-melon.

căntănk'erous *a.* cross-grained, quarrelsome.

cănta'ta (-ah-) *n.* choral work like oratorio but usu. shorter.

cănteen' *n.* camp or barrack shop for liquor, provisions, etc.; refresh- ment-room in works etc.; soldier's mess-tin or water-bottle; case hold- ing table cutlery.

căn'ter *n.* easy gallop. *v.* (make) go at a canter.

Căn'terburў běll *n.* kind of cam- panula.

cănthă'rĭdēs (-z) *n.pl.* (med.) pre- paration of dried Spanish fly used as counter-irritant etc.

căn'tĭcle *n.* biblical hymn used in church services.

căn'tĭlēver *n.* overhanging or projec- ting beam etc. with one end fixed to wall, pier, etc., and the other free. ~ **bridge**, with span(s) formed by two cantilevers meeting or joined by suspended central member.

căn'tle *n.* slice cut off; hind-bow of saddle.

căn'tō *n.* (pl. *-os*), division of long poem.

căn'ton (*or -ŏn'*) *n.* State of Swiss confederation. *v.t.* (-ōōn'), quarter (troops). **canton'ment** (-ōōn-) *n.* lodgings assigned to troops.

căn'tŏr *n.* precentor in church or synagogue.

cantŏr'ĭal *a.* of precentor's (usu. north) side of choir.

Cant. T. *abbr.* Canterbury Tales.

Cantuar. *abbr.* (Abp.) of Canterbury.

Canŭck' *n.* (French-)Canadian.

căn'vas *n.* strong unbleached cloth of flax, hemp, etc., used for sails, tents, embroidery, painting on, etc.; picture; covered end of racing- -boat. **~-back**, N.-Amer. duck.

căn'vass *v.* discuss; solicit votes or custom (of), try to ascertain views of. *n.* canvassing.

canyon, cañon (kăn'yon) *n.* deep gorge cut by river.

căp *n.* soft brimless outdoor head- -dress; woman's (indoor) head- -dress; cap worn as sign of inclusion in team, its wearer; non-subscri- ber's payment for day's hunting; cap-like explosive device, esp. of paper for toy pistol. *v.t.* put or confer cap on, cover (as) with cap; surpass; touch or take off one's cap to.

cap. *abbr.*, *caput* [L], chapter.

cā'pable *a.* able, competent; suscep- tible (*of*). **~abĭl'itў** *n.*

capā'cious *a.* roomy, of large content.

capā'cĭtance *n.* ability of apparatus to store electric charge.

capā'cĭtў *n.* cubic content; mental power; function or character; capacitance.

căp-à-pie' (-pē) *adv.* from head to foot.

capā'rĭson *n.* harness, trappings. *v.t.* put caparison upon.

cāpe[1] *n.* short sleeveless cloak.

cāpe[2] *n.* headland, promontory; *the C~*, Cape of Good Hope. **C~ Coloured**, S. African of mixed black and white descent.

cā'per[1] *n.* S.-Eur. bramble-like shrub; (pl.) its pickled flower-buds.

cā'per[2] *n.* frisky movement, leap. *v.i.* make capers.

căpercai'llie (-lyĭ), **-cail'zĭe** *n.* largest bird of grouse kind.

capill'ary *a.* of hair; of hair-like fineness. *n.* capillary tube, minute blood-vessel. ~ **attraction**, effect of surface tension in raising level of liquid in capillary tube.

căp'ital *a.* of chief importance, principal, primary, leading, first-class, excellent; fatal, vital; punishable with death. *n.* capital city; capital letter; head or cornice of pillar; stock with which company etc. starts; accumulated wealth used in producing more; money invested or loaned. ~ **goods**, goods (to be) used in producing commodities. ~ **letter**, letter of form and size used at beginning of sentence etc.

căp'italĭsm *n.* economic system with ownership and control of capital in private hands. ~**ĭst** *n.* owner of (esp. large amounts of) capital. ~**ĭs'tĭc** *a.*

căp'italīze *v.* use as capital; compute or realize present value of; print in capitals; ~ *on*, profit by, turn to account or advantage. ~**zā'tion** *n.*

căpĭtā'tion *n.* attrib., of so much a head.

Căp'itol *n.* temple of Jupiter in Rome; building of U.S. Congress or State legislature.

capĭt'ūlar *a.* of cathedral chapter.

capĭt'ūlāte *v.i.* surrender on terms; yield. ~**ā'tion** *n.*

cā'pon *n.* castrated cock.

capŏt' *n.* taking of all tricks in piquet. *v.t.* score capot against.

caprice' (-ēs) *n.* unaccountable change of mind or conduct; freakish fancy. **capri'cious** *a.* guided by whim, inconstant.

Căp'ricŏrn, Goat, tenth constellation and sign of zodiac; *Tropic of* ~, southern tropic.

căp'riŏle *n.* trained horse's high leap and kick. *v.i.* make capriole.

caps. *abbr.* capital letters.

căp'sicum *n.* (fruit of) kinds of plant with pungent capsules.

căpsīze' *v.* overturn, esp. on water.

căp'stan *n.* revolving barrel for winding in cable etc.

căp'sūle *n.* enclosing membrane; plant's seed-case; (med.) gelatine envelope for drug etc.; compact usu. detachable container or com-partment, esp. part of rocket etc. holding scientific instruments etc.

Capt. *abbr.* Captain.

căp'tain (-tĭn) *n.* chief, leader; naval or military officer; master of merchant ship; leader of side in games. ~**cy̆** *n.*

căp'tion *n.* heading, title; wording on cartoon, cinema screen, etc.

căp'tious *a.* given to carping, quibbling.

căp'tivāte *v.t.* fascinate, charm. ~**ā'tion** *n.*

căp'tive *a.* taken prisoner; in confinement; unable to escape. *n.* captive person or animal. **căptĭv'ity** *n.*

căp'tor *n.* one who takes captive. **căp'trĕss** *n.*

căp'ture *n.* seizing, taking possession. *v.t.* take prisoner; seize.

Căp'ūchĭn *n.* Franciscan friar of new order of 1528. **c**~ **monkey**, Amer. monkey with hair like black cowl.

căr *n.* wheeled vehicle; motor-car, tram-car; (U.S.) railway carriage or van; pendant of airship holding passengers.

cărabineer' *n.* soldier with carbine.

că'racal *n.* (fur of) kind of lynx.

că'racōle *n.* trained horse's half turn to right or left. *v.i.* perform caracole(s).

că'racul (-ōol) *n.* Persian lamb.

carafe' (-ahf) *n.* table bottle for water etc.

că'ramĕl *n.* brown substance got by heating sugar or syrup; soft toffee made with this.

că'rapāce *n.* upper shell of tortoises and crustaceans.

că'rat *n.* unit of weight for gems and of fineness for gold.

căravăn' (*or* kă'-) *n.* company travelling together for safety in N. Africa or East; house on wheels.

căravăn'serai (-rī; *or* -ĭ) *n.* Eastern inn with large courtyard for caravans.

că'ravel, căr'vel *n.* (hist.) small light fast ship.

că'raway (-a-wā) *n.* plant with small aromatic fruit (~-*seeds*) used in cakes etc.

căr'bīde *n.* compound of carbon with metal.

căr'bīne *n.* kind of short rifle.

cărbohy̆'drate *n.* kinds of compound

of carbon, hydrogen, and oxygen essential to living organisms.

carbŏl'ic (ă'cĭd) *n.* disinfectant and antiseptic.

car'bon *n.* non-metallic element occurring as diamond, graphite, charcoal, etc.; carbon rod used in arc-lamp; sheet of carbon paper, carbon copy. **~ copy,** copy made with **~ paper,** thin paper with coating of wax preparation for duplicating writing etc. **~ā'ceous** *a.* containing carbon. **~ate** *n.* salt of carbonic acid.

carbŏn'ic *a.* of carbon. **~ acid,** compound of carbon dioxide and water. **~ acid gas,** carbon dioxide.

carbonif'erous *a.* producing coal; *C~* (of) system or period of Upper Palaeozoic rocks between Devonian and Permian.

car'bonīze *v.t.* reduce to charcoal or coke by burning. **~zā'tion** *n.*

carborŭn'dum *n.* silicon carbide used for polishing etc. **P.**

car'boy *n.* large globular wicker--covered glass bottle.

car'bŭncle *n.* cabochon garnet; inflamed skin-tumour; red pimple esp. on nose. **carbŭnc'ūlar** *a.*

carbūrĕtt'or, -er *n.* apparatus mixing air with petrol vapour for combustion in motor engines etc.

car'cass *n.* dead body of beast or (contempt.) person; framework or skeleton or worthless remains.

card[1] *n.* toothed instrument, wire brush, etc. for combing wool etc. *v.t.* treat with card.

card[2] *n.* (piece of) thick paper or thin pasteboard; ticket of admission, invitation, label, etc.; one of 52 pieces of pasteboard making pack for playing games; (pl.) card-playing; (sl.) odd or original person. **~board,** pasteboard for making boxes etc. **~ index,** index with each item on separate card. **~-sharp(er),** professional swindler at card-games. **~ vote,** system by which delegate's vote counts for number of his constituents.

Card. *abbr.* Cardinal.

car'damom *n.* E.-Ind. spice.

car'dan *a.* **~ joint,** universal joint. **~ shaft,** with cardan joint at end(s).

car'dĭăc *a.* of heart.

car'dĭgan *n.* close-fitting usu. knitted jacket with or without sleeves.

car'dĭnal *a.* fundamental, central; of deep scarlet. *n.* one of seventy eccl. princes forming pope's council and electing new pope; cardinal colour or number; (U.S.) scarlet grosbeak. **~ numbers,** one, two, etc.

cāre *n.* anxiety, concern; task, thing to be seen to; serious attention. *v.i.* feel concern or interest or affection.

careen' *v.* turn (ship) on one side for repair; heel over.

career' *n.* swift course; course through life; way of making livelihood. *v.i.* go swiftly or wildly. **~ diplomat,** (U.S.) professional diplomatist. **~ist** *n.* person intent mainly on personal advancement.

cāre'free (-rf-) *a.* free from anxiety.

care'ful (-ārf-) *a.* painstaking, watchful, cautious, solicitous.

care'lèss (-ārl-) *a.* unconcerned, thoughtless, negligent, inaccurate.

carĕss' *n.* fondling touch, kiss. *v.t.* bestow caress(es) on.

că'rĕt *n.* omission-mark ($\wedge$).

cāre'tāker *n.* person hired to take charge of house in owner's absence, or of school etc. *a.* (only) temporarily in control.

cāre'wŏrn *a.* worn by trouble and anxiety.

car'gō *n.* (pl. *-oes*), ship's freight.

Că'rĭb *n.* aboriginal native of some W.-Ind. islands; their language.

că'rĭbou (-bōō) *n.* N-Amer. reindeer.

că'rĭcatūre *n.* grotesque or ludicrously exaggerated representation. *v.t.* make or be caricature of. **~rĭst** *n.*

cār'ĭēs (-z) *n.* decay (of tooth or bone).

că'rĭllon (-lyon) *n.* (air played on) set of bells sounded mechanically or from keyboard.

cār'ĭous *a.* affected with caries.

cār'kĭng *a.* burdensome.

Carliol. *abbr.* (Bp.) of Carlisle.

cār'man (-an) *n.* van-driver.

Cār'mĕlīte *n. & a.* (member) of order of mendicant friars or of nuns.

cār'mĭnatĭve *a. & n.* (drug) curing flatulence.

cär′mine n. vivid crimson pigment and colour. a. of this colour.

cär′nage n. great slaughter.

cär′nal a. sensual; sexual; worldly. **~ism, ~ăl′itў** nn.

cärnā′tion[1] a. & n. (of) light rosy pink.

cärnā′tion[2] n. cultivated clove pink.

carnelian : see **cornelian**.

cär′nival n. festive days preceding Lent; riotous revelry.

cärniv′ora n.pl. carnivorous order of mammals. **cär′nivōre** n. animal that feeds on flesh. **~orous** a.

cä′rol n. joyous song, esp. Christmas hymn. v.i. sing joyfully.

carŏt′id n. & a. (of, near) either of two main pairs of arteries carrying blood to face etc.

carouse′ (-z) n. & v.i. (engage in) drinking-bout.

cärp[1] n. fresh-water fish freq. bred in ponds.

cärp[2] v.i. find fault, cavil.

cär′pal a. of carpus.

cär′pel n. (bot.) unit of compound ovary.

cär′penter n. artificer in (esp. rough solid) woodwork. v. do, make by, carpenter's work. **~trў** n.

cär′pĕt n. textile fabric for covering floors etc.; covering or expanse of grass etc. v.t. cover with carpet. **~-bag**, travelling bag made of carpet material. **~-bagger**, person interfering in politics of place he is not connected with.

cär′pus n. (pl. -pī), small bones uniting hand to fore-arm, wrist.

cä′rriage (-rĭj) n. (cost of) conveying, transport; carrying; bearing, deportment; wheeled, esp. private, vehicle drawn by horse(s); railway coach or compartment; gun-carriage; sliding etc. part of machinery shifting position of other parts. **~way**, (part of) road used by vehicles.

cä′rrier n. (esp.) person conveying parcels by cart etc. for hire; part of bicycle etc. for carrying luggage etc.; person etc. conveying germs of disease; aircraft-carrier; paper bag for carrying parcels etc. **~ pigeon**, homing pigeon used for carrying letters etc. **~ wave**, high-frequency oscillations emitted by transmitter.

cä′rrion n. dead flesh; garbage, filth.

cä′rrot n. (plant with) tapering orange-red sweet fleshy root; (pl., sl.) (person with) red hair. **~ў** a.

cä′rrў v. convey, transport, bear; support; be bearer of; have specified range; (make) pitch beyond; succeed in establishing, passing, etc.; capture; (arith.) transfer (figure) to column of higher notation; **~ away**, inspire, transport, make lose self-control; **~ forward**, transfer (figure) to new page or column; **~ off**, (esp.) make brave show of; **~ on**, (esp.) continue, flirt; **~ out**, put in practice. n. (mil.) position of carrying sword etc. at salute; (golf) ball's flight before pitching; range.

cärt n. strong two- or four-wheeled vehicle for heavy work; light two-wheeled one-horse vehicle for driving in. v. carry in cart, use cart. **~-horse**, horse of heavy build. **~wheel**, wheel of cart; large coin; sideways somersault. **~wright**, maker of carts. **~age** n. (cost of) carting. **~er** n.

cärte blanche (-ahṅsh), full discretionary power. [F]

cärtĕl′ (or kär′-) n. manufacturers' union to control prices etc.

Cärthū′sian (-zĭan or -zhn) n. & a. (member) of severe order of monks or of Charterhouse School.

cär′tilage n. firm elastic skeleton-tissue of young vertebrates. **cärtilā′ginous** a.

cärtŏg′raphў n. map-drawing. **~grapher** n.; **~grăph′ĭc(al)** aa.

cär′tomancў n. divination by playing-cards.

cär′ton n. cardboard box, cardboard.

cärtōon′ n. drawing for painting of same size, tapestry, etc.; humorous topical illustration; film, usu. comic, made by photographing series of drawings. **~ist** n.

cärtouche′ (-ōōsh) n. scroll ornament; oval enclosing name and title of ancient Egyptian king etc.

cär′tridge n. charge of explosive made up in case. **~-paper**, thick rough paper for drawing etc.

cǎ'rŭncle n. fleshy excrescence.

cǎrve v. cut, make by cutting; cover or adorn with cut figures etc.; cut up meat at or for table; subdivide. **~r** n. (esp.) knife, (pl.) knife and fork, for carving meat. **cǎr'ving** n. carved work or figure or design; **carving-fork, -knife,** for carving meat.

carvel: see **caravel**. **~-built,** (of boat) with planks flush with side.

cǎrўǎt'ĭd n. female figure used as pillar.

cǎscāde' n. waterfall; wavy fall of lace etc. v.i. fall in or like cascade.

cāse¹ n. instance of thing's occurring; hypothetical or actual situation; instance or condition of disease; plight or condition; (law) suit or cause; (relation expressed by) inflected form of noun etc.; *in ~,* in event (of), if; *in any ~,* in any event, anyhow. **~book,** record of doctor's or other cases. **~-law,** law as settled by decided cases. **~-work,** social work, sociology, in reference to individual cases.

cāse² n. box, cabinet, crate, bag, or sheath designed to hold something. v.t. enclose in case; surround (*with*); (sl.) inspect or examine closely, esp. for criminal purpose. **~-bottle,** square bottle to fit in case with others. **~-harden,** harden surface of (esp. steel); (fig.) render callous.

cā'sėin n. main protein of milk.

cāse'māte (-sm-) n. embrasured room in wall of fortress.

cāse'ment (-sm-) n. hinged (part of) window. **~ cloth,** kinds of plain--woven usu. cotton fabric.

cǎsh¹ n. money in form of coin or bank-notes. v.t. give or obtain cash for (cheque etc.). **~ register,** till recording sums put in.

cǎsh² n. (pl. same), kinds of coin of very low value in China etc.

cǎsh'ew (-ōō; or -ōō') n. W.-Ind. tree bearing kidney-shaped edible nut.

cashier'¹ n. person in charge of cash in bank or other business firm.

cashier'² v.t. dismiss from service.

cǎsh'mēre n. fine soft material of wool of goats of Kashmir etc.; imitation of this.

cā'sĭng n. enclosing material, framework, etc.

casi'nō (-ē-) n. (pl. -os), public building for gambling etc.

cask (-ah-) n. cylindrical bulging vessel for holding esp. beer, wine, and cider.

cas'kėt (kah-) n. small box for holding valuables; coffin.

cǎsque (-k) n. (arch.) helmet.

cassā'tion n. act of annulling.

cassa'va (-sah-) n. W.-Ind. plant; starch or flour obtained from its roots.

cǎss'erōle n. vessel in which food is cooked and served. v.t. cook in casserole.

cǎss'ĭa n. inferior kind of cinnamon; kinds of plant yielding laxative substances.

cǎss'ock n. long close usu. black tunic worn by clergy.

cǎss'owarў (-o-w-) n. kinds of large running bird related to ostrich.

cast (kah-) v. (p.t. & p.p. *cast*), throw; give (vote); throw off, lose; form (molten metal) in mould; give (part) to actor, assign part to, assign parts in (play etc.); add *up*; reckon (horoscope etc.); *~ down,* depress; *~ off,* abandon, (knitting) pass (stitch) over next and drop from needle, cast off stitches of, (print.) estimate printed size of (MS.). n. throw of missile, lead, fishing-line, etc.; mould for casting, thing cast in it; moulded copy of sculpture etc.; earth excreted by worm; set of actors in play etc.; slight squint; tinge, type, quality. *~ iron,* iron shaped by casting. **~-iron,** of cast iron; hard, rigid, unshakeable.

cǎs'tanĕt (*or* -ĕt') n. one of pair of small concave wooden or ivory shells held in palm of hand and clicked or rattled in time with dancing.

cast'away (-ah-) n. & a. shipwrecked (person).

caste (-ah-) n. Indian hereditary class with members shunning intercourse with other castes; exclusive class elsewhere.

cǎs'tellan n. governor or constable of castle.

căs′tellātèd *a.* built like castle, battlemented.

caster : see **castor²**.

căs′tigāte *v.t.* punish, chastise. **~ā′tion** *n.*

Căstile′ (-ēl) **soap** *n.* fine hard white or mottled soap.

ca′sting (kah-) *n.* (esp.) piece of metal etc. shaped by melting and pouring into mould. *a.* (of vote) deciding between two equal parties.

castle (kah′sl) *n.* building designed to serve as both residence and fortress; (chess) piece with battlemented top, rook. *v.i.* (chess) make combined move of king and rook.

cas′tor¹ (-ah-) *n.* substance from beaver used in perfumery etc.; (sl.) hat.

cas′tor², -er (kah-) *n.* vessel with perforated top for sprinkling sugar etc.; small swivelled wheel enabling heavy furniture to be moved. **~ sugar**, finely granulated white sugar.

cas′tor oil (kah-) *n.* vegetable oil used as purgative and lubricant.

căstrāte′ *v.t.* remove testicles of, geld. **~ā′tion** *n.*

că′sual (-zhŏŏ- *or* -zū-) *a.* due to chance; not permanent; careless, unconcerned. **~ labourer**, doing occasional or casual jobs. **~ ward**, (of workhouse), for tramps etc.

că′sualty (-zhŏŏ- *or* -zū-) *n.* mishap; person killed, wounded, or injured. **~ department, ward**, for treatment of accidental injuries.

căsūarī′na (-z-; *or* -ēna) *n.* kinds of tree with jointed leafless branches.

că′suĭst (-zhŏŏ- *or* -zū-) *n.* theologian etc. who studies and resolves cases of conscience etc.; sophist, quibbler. **~ĭs′tic(al)** *aa.*; **~istry** *n.*

cā′sus běll′ī *n.* act (regarded as) justifying war. [L]

căt *n.* small furry domestic quadruped; any feline animal; spiteful woman; cat-o′-nine tails; piece of wood used in tip-cat. **~call**, shrill whistle. **~fish**, kinds of fish. **~head**, horizontal beam at ship′s bow for raising and carrying anchor. **~-o′-nine-tails**, whip of nine knotted cords. **~′s-cradle**, child′s game with string. **~-′s-eye**,

precious stone; reflector stud on road etc. **~′s-meat**, horseflesh prepared for cats. **~′s-paw**, person used as tool by another; slight breeze rippling water. **~walk**, narrow footway along bridge, over engine-room, etc.

Cat. *abbr.* Catullus.

C.A.T. *abbr.* College of Advanced Technology.

cătachrē′sĭs (-k-) *n.* misapplication of words. **~ĕs′tĭc** (*or* -ē-) *a.*

căt′aclўsm *n.* deluge; political or social upheaval. **~clўs′mĭc** *a.*

căt′acōmb (-m; *or* -ōōm) *n.* subterranean cemetery.

căt′afălque (-k) *n.* stage for display of coffin at funeral.

cătalěc′tĭc *a.* a syllable short.

căt′alěpsў *n.* disease with recurrent trances. **cătalěp′tĭc** *a.* & *n.* (person) having catalepsy.

căt′alŏgue (-g) *n.* complete list, usu. in alphabetical or other systematic order. *v.t.* make catalogue of; enter in catalogue.

catăl′pa *n.* kinds of tree with trumpet-shaped flowers.

catăl′ўsĭs *n.* effect of substance that aids chemical change without itself changing. **căt′alўst** *n.*; **~ўt′ĭc** *a.*

cătamarăn′ *n.* (esp. sailing-)boat or raft with two hulls side by side.

căt′amīte *n.* boy kept for homosexual practices.

căt′apŭlt *n.* ancient engine for hurling stones or darts; boy′s shóoting contrivance of forked stick and elastic; mechanical device for launching aircraft etc. *v.* shoot, hurl, launch, (as) with catapult; be catapulted.

căt′arăct *n.* waterfall; downpour; progressive opacity of crystal lens of eye impairing vision.

catarrh′ (-ǎr) *n.* inflammation of mucous membrane esp. of nose etc. **~al** *a.*

catăs′trophė *n.* denouement of drama; subversive event; great disaster. **cătastrŏph′ĭc** *a.*

căt′boat *n.* sailing-boat with single forward mast and one sail.

cătch *v.* (*caught*, pr. kawt), capture, lay hold of, seize; hold; overtake; be infected with; become entangled; grasp; surprise, trick; check suddenly. *n*. act of catching; thing or person caught or worth catching; question designed to trick; hidden trap; (chance of) catching ball; musical round. ~-crop, one grown between rows of another crop, two crops in sequence, etc. ~penny, got up merely to sell. ~pole, (hist.) sheriff's officer. ~word, word placed at corner of page, head of dictionary article, etc.; word(s) caught up and repeated, slogan. ~ing *a*. (esp.) infectious; captivating. ~ment area *n*. whole area from which water flows into river, reservoir, etc. ~y̆ *a*. (of tune etc.) readily caught up.

cătĕchĕt'ical (-k-) *a*. teaching orally; proceeding by question and answer; of catechism.

căt'ĕchĭsm (-k-) *n*. piece of catechizing; form of (esp. religious) instruction drawn up by way of question and answer. ~ist *n*.

căt'ĕchīze (-k-) *v.t*. instruct by question and answer; put questions to.

cătĕchū'mĕn (-k-) *n*. convert under instruction before baptism.

cătĕgō'rical *a*. unconditional, absolute, explicit.

căt'ĕgory̆ *n*. class, rank, or order of ideas or things.

catē'na *n*. connected series.

catē'nary̆ *n*. & *a*. (like) curve formed by hanging chain.

cā'ter *v.i*. purvey food; provide amusement etc. *for*.

căt'eran *n*. (Highland) irregular fighting-man, marauder.

căt'erpillar *n*. larva of butterfly or moth; endless articulated steel band with treads passing round wheel(s) of vehicle to be used on rough ground (**P**).

căt'erwaul *v.i*. squall like cats. *n*. cry (as) of cat in rut.

căt'gŭt *n*. dried and twisted intestines of sheep etc. used for fiddle--strings etc.

cathăr'sĭs *n*. (pl. -*ēs*), purgation; purification or release of emotion.

cathăr'tĭc *a*. & *n*. purgative (drug).

cathē'dral *n*. principal church of diocese, with bishop's throne.

Căth'erĭne-wheel *n*. rotating firework.

căth'ĕter *n*. tube for passing into hollow organs of body.

căth'ōde *n*. (electr.) negative pole. ~ ray, beam of electrons issuing from cathode of high-vacuum tube under impulse of electron field.

căth'olĭc *a*. universal, all-embracing; broad-minded; C~, including all Christians or all of Roman Church. *n*. member of Catholic, esp. R.C., church. cathŏl'ĭcĭsm *n*. adherence to Catholic church. cătholĭ'cĭty̆ *n*. comprehensiveness; accordance with Catholic church doctrine. cathŏl'ĭcīze *v.t*.

căt'īon *n*. positively charged ion.

căt'kĭn *n*. hanging flower of willow, hazel, etc.

căt'mĭnt, (U.S.) căt'nĭp *n*. aromatic plant.

catŏp'trĭc *a*. of reflector or reflection. ~s *n*. part of optics dealing with reflections.

căt'sup *n*. ketchup.

cătt'le *n*. livestock, esp. oxen; (sl.) horses.

cau'cus *n*. local political party committee.

cau'dal *a*. of or at or like tail.

cau'date *a*. tailed.

cau'dle *n*. (arch.) warm spiced gruel.

caught, *p.t*. & *p.p*. of catch.

caul *n*. membrane occas. found enclosing child's head at birth.

caul'dron *n*. large boiling-vessel.

caul'ĭflower (kŏl-) *n*. kind of cabbage with edible white flower-head.

caulk (kawk) *v.t*. stop up (ship's seams) with oakum and pitch.

cau'sal (-z-) *a*. of nature of cause and effect. ~ăl'ĭty̆ *n*. relation of cause and effect; doctrine that everything has cause(s).

causā'tion (-z-) *n*. causing, causality.

cause *n*. what produces effect; ground or reason or motive for action; justification; case of party in lawsuit; side in struggle etc. *v.t*. effect; induce, make (*to* do etc.).

cause célèbre (kōz sălĕbr), lawsuit that excites much interest. [F]

cause'lĕss (-zl-) *a*. groundless, without justification.

cause'way (-zw-) *n*. raised road across

low or wet ground; raised footway at side of road.

cau'stĭc *a.* that burns or corrodes; sarcastic, biting. *n.* caustic substance. **causti'cĭtў** *n.*

cau'terīze *v.t.* sear with caustic or cautery. **~zā'tion** *n.*

cau'terў *n.* (hot iron for) surgical searing.

cau'tion *n.* avoidance of rashness, attention to safety; warning; (sl.) strange person, staggering event. *v.t.* warn, admonish. **~arў** *a.* conveying warning or admonition.

cau'tious *a.* disposed to or exhibiting caution.

căvalcāde' *n.* company of riders.

căvalier' *n.* horseman; gallant; lady's protector or escort; 17th-c. royalist. *a.* brusque, discourteous.

căv'alrў *n.* horse-soldiers.

căvati'na (-tē-) *n.* (mus.) short simple song; smooth melodious air.

cāve[1] *n.* underground hollow, usu. with horizontal entrance. *v.* hollow out; **~** *in*, subside or give inwards, yield to pressure, submit. **~-dwellers**, prehistoric men living in caves. **~man**, cave-dweller.

cā've[2] *int.* (sch. sl.) look out!

cā'vĕăt (*or* kă-) *n.* (law) process to suspend proceedings; warning.

căv'endĭsh *n.* kinds of strong cake tobacco.

căv'ĕrn *n.* (vast) cave.

căv'ĕrnous *a.* full of caverns; huge or deep as cavern.

căv'iāre *n.* pickled sturgeon-roe; **~** *to the general*, good thing unappreciated by ignorant.

căv'ĭl *v.i.* take exception *at*, find fault. *n.* frivolous objection.

căv'ĭtў *n.* hollow place.

cavõrt' *v.i.* prance.

caw *n.* cry of rook etc. *v.i.* utter caw.

cayenne (kāĕn') *n.* hot red pepper.

cay'man, cai- *n.* (esp. tropical S.-Amer.) alligator.

C.B. *abbr.* Companion of the Bath; confinement to barracks.

C.B.E. *abbr.* Commander of the (Order of the) British Empire.

C.C. *abbr.* County Council, Councillor; cricket club.

cc *abbr.* cubic centimetre(s).

C.C.C. *abbr.* Corpus Christi College.

Cd *abbr.* Command Paper.

C.D. *abbr.* Civil Defence; Contagious Diseases (Acts).

c.d., c. div. *abbr.* cum dividend.

C.E. *abbr.* Church of England.

cĕanō'thus *n.* blue-flowered shrub.

cease *v.* desist *from*; stop; come or bring to an end. *n.*, *without* **~**, unceasingly.

cease'lĕss (-sl-) *a.* incessant.

cĕ'dar *n.* (fragrant fine-grained wood of) evergreen tree.

cēde *v.t.* give up, yield, surrender (territory).

cĕdĭll'a *n.* mark (ʕ) written under c to show sibilance.

ceil *v.t.* line roof of (room etc.).

cei'ling *n.* lining of roof concealing timbers; maximum altitude of aircraft; upper limit.

ceilidh (kā'lĭ) *n.* informal Highland gathering for song and story.

cĕl'adon *n.* & *a.* pale grey-green.

cĕl'andĭne *n.* kinds of yellow spring flower.

cĕl'ĕbrant *n.* officiating priest.

cĕl'ĕbrāte *v.* duly perform (rite etc.); keep festival or commemorate event; publish abroad, extol; (*p.p.*) famous. **~ā'tion** *n.*

cĕlĕb'rĭtў *n.* fame; widely known person.

cĕlĕ'rĭăc *n.* turnip-rooted celery.

cĕlĕ'rĭtў *n.* dispatch, swiftness.

cĕl'erў *n.* plant of which blanched stems are used as salad and vegetable.

cĕlĕs'ta *n.* keyboard musical instrument of metal plates struck with hammers.

cĕlĕs'tĭal *a.* of sky; heavenly, divinely good or beautiful; *C***~**, Chinese. *n.* *C***~**, Chinese.

cĕl'ĭbacў *n.* unmarried state. **cĕl'ĭbate** *a.* & *n.* unmarried (person); (person) bound or resolved not to marry.

cĕll *n.* hermit's one-roomed dwelling; (single person's) small room in monastery or prison; unit of voltaic battery; sac or cavity or interstice in natural structure; (biol.) unit of organic structure, mass of protoplasm bounded by membrane and containing nucleus; small group as nucleus of political activity.

cĕll'ar *n.* underground room for

storage etc.; wine-cellar, stock of wines. **~age** n. cellar accommodation. **cĕll'arer** n. keeper of monastery's wine and food. **~ĕt'** n. case etc. for wine-bottles in dining--room.

cĕll'ō, 'cĕll'ō (ch-) n. violoncello. **cĕll'ist** n.

cĕll'ophāne n. tough glossy transparent plastic for wrapping etc. **P.**

cĕll'ūlar a. of or having or consisting of cells; porous, of open texture.

cĕll'ūle n. small cell.

cĕll'ūloid n. plastic made from cellulose nitrate and camphor.

cĕll'ūlōse n. carbohydrate forming chief constituent of cell-walls of plants; derivatives of this used in making rayon, plastics, glossy paints, etc.

Cĕl'sĭus a. Centigrade.

cĕlt[1] n. chisel-edged prehistoric tool.

Cĕlt[2] (k- or s-), **Kĕlt** n. member of one of ancient peoples of W. Europe or of peoples speaking languages related to those of ancient Gauls. **~ic** a. & n. (language) of Celts.

cĕmĕnt' n. substance of lime and clay setting like stone; adhesive material; binding agency. v.t. apply cement to; unite firmly.

cĕm'ĕterў n. burial-ground other than churchyard.

cĕn'otaph (-ahf) n. monument to one whose remains are elsewhere.

cĕnse v.t. worship or perfume with incense. **cĕn'ser** n. incense-burning vessel.

cĕn'sor n. official who examines plays, books, news, etc. to suppress what is immoral or seditious or inopportune; person assuming right of judging others. v.t. act as censor of. **censôr'ĭal** a.; **~ship** n.

censôr'ious a. severely critical, fault--finding.

cĕn'sure (-sher) n. expression of disapproval or blame. v.t. criticize unfavourably; reprove.

cĕn'sus n. official numbering of population.

cĕnt n. hundredth of dollar; per **~**, for, in, to, every hundred.

Cent. abbr. Centigrade.

cent. abbr. century.

cĕn'tal n. 100 lb.

cĕn'taur (-tôr) n. (Gk. myth.) fabulous creature with man's head, trunk, and arms on horse's body and legs.

cĕn'taurў n. kinds of plant.

cĕntenār'ian n. & a. (person) hundred years old.

cĕntē'narў a. centennial. n. hundredth anniversary.

cĕntĕnn'ial a. of, having lived or lasted, 100 years. n. centenary.

cĕntĕs'ĭmal a. reckoning or reckoned by hundredths.

cĕn'tigrāde a. having 100 degrees; (of thermometer) with freezing--point of water at 0 and its boiling--point at 100°.

cĕn'tigrăm, cĕn'tĭlitre (-ēter), **cĕn'tĭmètre** nn. hundredth part of gram, litre, metre.

centime (sahn'tēm) n. hundredth part of franc. [F]

cĕn'tĭpēde n. many-footed crawling wormlike animal.

cĕn'tō n. (pl. -os), work composed of quoted scraps.

cĕn'tral a. of, in, at, etc. centre; leading, principal. **~ heating**, heating of building from central source.

cĕn'tralīze v. come or bring to centre; concentrate (administrative powers) in one centre, bring (State etc.) under this system. **~zā'tion** n.

cĕn'tre n. middle point or part; point of concentration or dispersion; (pol.) holders of moderate views; (games) (position of) player in centre of field or line; **~ of gravity**, point about which all parts of body exactly balance each other. v. have centre, concentrate, in, at, etc.; place (as) in centre; find centre of. **~bit**, tool for making cylindrical holes. **~board**, (sailing-boat with) board or plate that can be lowered to deepen keel. **~(-)forward**, (position of) middle player in forward line. **~(-)half**, (player with) central position among half-backs.

cĕntrif'ūgal (or -fū'-) a. flying or tending from centre. **~ force**, tendency away from centre of body moving round it. **cĕn'trifūge** n. machine using centrifugal effect, e.g. to separate cream from milk.

cĕntrip'etal a. tending towards centre.

cĕn'tūple a. hundredfold. v.t. multiply by 100.

cĕntūr'ĭon n. commander of century in Roman army.

cĕn'tūrў n. (Rom. hist.) army company; 100 years; any set of 100. ~ plant, American aloe.

cephăl'ĭc a. of or in head. ~ index, ratio of width to length of skull.

cĕph'alopŏd n. kinds of mollusc with tentacles attached to head.

cĕrăm'ĭc a. of (art of) pottery. ~s n. ceramic art.

Cĕr'berus n. (Gk. myth.) three--headed dog guarding Hades.

cēre n. naked waxlike membrane at base of beak in some birds.

cēr'ĕal a. of edible grain. n. any plant cultivated for seed as human food; food, esp. breakfast dish, made from cereal.

cĕrĕbĕll'um n. posterior part of brain.

cĕ'rĕbral a. of brain.

cĕrĕbrā'tion n. working of brain.

cĕrĕbro-spī'nal a. of brain and spinal cord.

cĕ'rĕbrum n. anterior and in man largest part of brain.

cere'cloth (sērk-) n. waxed cloth as winding-sheet.

cere'ment (sērm-) n. (usu. pl.) grave--clothes.

cĕrĕmō'nĭal a. with or of ceremony, formal. n. system of rites or ceremonies.

cĕrĕmō'nĭous a. addicted or showing addiction to ceremony, punctilious.

cĕ'rĕmonў n. religious rite, piece of formal procedure, polite observance; punctilious behaviour; stand (up)on ~, insist on observance of formalities.

cerise' (-ēs) n. & a. cherry-red.

cēr'ĭum n. element of rare-earth group.

CERN, Cĕrn abbr. Centre Européen de Recherche Nucléaire [F], European Nuclear Research Centre.

cĕrt n. (sl.) event or result certain to happen; horse sure to win.

cĕr'tain (-tn) a. settled, unfailing; unerring; reliable; indisputable; sure; a definite, some. ~lў adv. (esp.) I admit it, no doubt, yes. ~tў n. undoubted fact; absolute conviction.

cĕr'tĕs (-z) adv. (arch.) assuredly.

certĭf'ĭcate n. document formally attesting fact. v.t. (-āt), furnish with certificate.

cĕr'tĭfў v.t. attest formally; declare insane by certificate.

cĕr'tĭtūde n. feeling certain.

cĕru'lĕan (-ōō-) a. sky-blue.

cĕr'use (-ōōs) n. white lead.

cĕr'vĭcal (or -vī'-) a. of cervix.

cĕr'vĭx n. (anat.) neck; neck-like structure, esp. neck of womb.

cĕssā'tion n. ceasing.

cĕ'ssion (-shn) n. ceding.

cĕss'pōōl n. well sunk to receive house-drainage.

Cestr. abbr. (Bp) of Chester.

cĕtā'cean a. & n. (member) of order of marine mammals including whales.

cĕt'erăch (-k) n. kinds of fern.

C.F. abbr. Chaplain to the Forces.

cf. abbr., confer [L], compare.

cg. abbr. centigram.

C.G.M. abbr. Conspicuous Gallantry Medal.

c.g.s. abbr. centimetre-gram-second.

C.G.T. abbr., Confédération Générale du Travail [F], General Confederation of Labour.

C.H. abbr. Companion of Honour.

ch. abbr. chapter.

Chablis (shăb'lē) n. kind of dry white wine.

chăcŏnne' (sh-) n. stately old Spanish dance; (mus.) instrumental composition in $\frac{3}{4}$ time with unchanging ground-bass.

chāfe v. rub (skin etc.) to restore warmth; make or become sore by rubbing; irritate; show irritation, fret. n. rubbing, chafing.

chā'fer n. cockchafer.

chaff (-ahf) n. separated grain-husks; chopped hay and straw; worthless stuff; banter, raillery. v.t. banter.

chăff'er v.i. & n. bargain, haggle.

chăff'ĭnch n. common kind of finch.

chā'fing-dish n. vessel for keeping warm or heating food esp. at table.

chagrin (shagrĕn' or shăg'rĭn) n. acute disappointment, mortification. v.t. mortify, vex.

chain n. series of links; sequence, connected series (of proof, events, mountains, etc.); fetters, binding influence; measuring line, its length (66 ft.). *v.t.* secure with chain. ~-**armour**, armour of interlaced links. ~-**gang**, convicts chained together at work etc. ~-**mail**, chain-armour. ~ **reaction**, self-propagating esp. nuclear reaction. ~-**smoker**, one who lights cigarette etc. from stump of last one smoked. ~-**store**, one of series of shops belonging to one firm and selling same goods.

chair *n*. seat for one, usu. movable; seat of authority; professorship; chairman; sedan; socket holding rail of railway in place. *v.t.* install in chair; carry aloft (as) in chair. ~**man**, person who presides over meeting, board, or committee. ~**woman**, woman chairman.

chaise (shāz) *n*. pleasure- or travelling-carriage. ~-**longue** (-lawngg), kind of chair with seat long enough to support sitter's legs.

chălcĕd'onў (k-; *or* kăl'sĭ-) *n*. precious stones of quartz kind.

chalet (shăl'ā) *n*. Swiss peasant's wooden house; villa in this style.

chăl'ĭce *n*. goblet (poet.); eucharistic wine-cup.

chalk (-awk) *n*. white soft limestone; coloured substance used for drawing. *v.t.* rub, draw, or write with chalk. ~ў *a*.

chăll'ĕnge (-j) *n*. calling to account, esp. demand for pass-word etc.; exception taken (to juryman etc.); invitation to contest. *v.t.* call to account; take exception to, dispute; claim (attention etc.); invite to contest.

chalўb'ĕate (ka-) *a*. (of water) impregnated with iron salts.

chā'mber *n*. room, esp. bedroom; (pl.) set of rooms; deliberative body; house of parliament or its debating-room; enclosed space in mechanism etc.; part of gun containing charge; chamber-pot. ~ **music**, for performance in room rather than hall. ~-**pot**, vessel for urine.

chā'mberlain (-lĭn) *n*. officer managing royal or princely household, treasurer of corporation, etc.

chā'mbermaid *n*. inn housemaid.

chamē'lĕon (ka-) *n*. lizard with power of changing colour.

chăm'fer *n*. & *v.t.* groove, bevel.

chamois *n*. (shăm'wah), small mountain antelope; (shăm'ĭ), soft leather from sheep, goats, etc.

chămp *v*. munch (fodder) or mouth (bit) noisily; make chewing noise.

champagne (shămpān') *n*. kinds of sparkling wine.

chăm'paign (-ān) *n*. open country.

chăm'pertў *n*. offence of assisting in suit with view to sharing proceeds.

chăm'pion *n*. person who fights for another or for cause; athlete, beast, etc. that has defeated all competitors. *a*. that is a champion. *v.t.* maintain cause of. ~**ship** *n*.

champlevé (shahṅlevā') *a*. & *n*. (enamel work) in which colours are filled into hollows made in surface.

chance (-ahns) *n*. way things fall out, accident; probability or prospect of any occurrence; possible catch at cricket. *a*. fortuitous. *v*. befall, happen; risk.

chan'cel (-ah-) *n*. railed-off eastern part of church.

chan'cellerў (-ah-) *n*. chancellor's department or staff or offices; office attached to embassy.

chan'cellor (-ah-) *n*. kinds of State or law official; titular head of university; *Lord C~*, highest English judicial functionary, presiding over House of Lords; *C~ of the Exchequer*, British cabinet minister who prepares Budget.

Chan'cerў (-ah-) *n*. division of High Court of Justice.

chan'cў (-ah-) *a*. risky.

chăndelier' (sh-) *n*. branched hanging support for lights.

chand'ler (-ah-) *n*. dealer in candles, oil, etc. ~ў *n*.

chānge (-j) *n*. variation, alteration; substitution of one for another; money in small coins; (pl.) different orders in which peal of bells can be rung. *v*. make or become different, alter; change gear; interchange or exchange; give or get other coin(s) etc. for. ~**able** *a*. inconstant, given to change. ~**abil'itў** *n*.; ~**ful**, ~**less** *aa*.

chānge′lǐng (-jl-) *n.* elf-child; child substituted for another.

chǎnn′el *n.* bed in which water runs; passage for liquid; groove or flute; medium or agency; narrow piece of water connecting two seas; *the C~*, English Channel. *v.t.* form channel(s) in; groove.

chant (-ah-) *n.* song; melody for psalms; droning music, sing-song talk. *v.* sing; intone, sing to chant.

chan′ter (-ah-) *n.* melody-pipe of bagpipe.

chan′ticleer (-ah-) *n.* (arch.) domestic cock.

chan′trў (-ah-) *n.* endowment for singing of masses for founder's soul; chapel or priests so endowed.

chanty : see **shanty²**.

chā′ŏs (k-) *n.* formless welter of matter conceived as preceding creation; utter confusion. **chāŏt′ic** *a.* utterly without order.

chǎp¹ *n.* (colloq.) fellow; boy.

chap², **chǒp³** *n.* (pl.) jaws, cheeks; (sing.) lower jaw esp. of pig as food. **~-fallen**, dispirited, dejected.

chap³ *n.* crack, fissure, caused by frost, wind, etc. in skin. *v.* (cause to) develop chaps.

chap. *abbr.* chapter.

chǎparrǎl′ *n.* (U.S.) dense tangled brushwood.

chǎp′bŏŏk *n.* (hist.) cheap book of tales, ballads, tracts, etc.

chǎp′el *n.* place of worship attached to institution or private house; oratory with altar in church; Nonconformist place of worship; printing-office; journeyman printers' association or meeting.

chǎp′erōn (sh-) *n.* older woman in charge of young unmarried woman on social occasions. *v.t.* act as chaperon to. **~age** *n.*

chǎp′lain (-lǐn) *n.* clergyman of institution, private chapel, ship, regiment, etc. **~cў** *n.*

chǎp′lĕt *n.* wreath or circlet for head; string of beads, one-third of rosary.

chǎp′man *n.* hawker, pedlar.

chǎps *n.* (U.S.) horseman's stout leather trousers without seat.

chǎp′ter *n.* division of book; (general meeting of) body of resident clergy of cathedral under dean, (assembly of) members of monastic or religious order. **~-house**, room in which chapter meets.

chār¹ *n.* & *v.i.* (act as) charwoman.

chār² *n.* fish of trout kind.

chār³ *v.* burn to charcoal; scorch or blacken with fire.

chār⁴ *n.* (sl.) tea.

charabanc (shǎ′rabǎng) *n.* long vehicle with rows of seats looking forward.

chǎ′racter (k-) *n.* distinctive mark; letter, sign; mental or moral nature, reputation; testimonial; person in novel, play, etc.; odd or eccentric person.

chǎracterǐs′tǐc (k-) *a.* & *n.* typical or distinctive (trait, mark, quality).

chǎ′racterīze (k-) *v.t.* describe *as*; be characteristic of. **~īzā′tion** *n.*

charade (sharahd′) *n.* game of guessing word from acted clue.

chār′coal *n.* black porous residue of partly burnt wood etc. **~-burner**, maker of charcoal.

chārd *n.* kind of beet with succulent leaf-stalks and large leaves used like spinach.

chārge *n.* load; quantity of propellant for gun or explosive for blasting etc.; (accumulation of) electrical energy; (her.) device, bearing; task, duty; price, expenses; liability; exhortation; trust, custody; thing or person entrusted; accusation; impetuous attack; *in ~*, having charge or care (*of*), in(to) custody of police. *v.* supply with charge of explosive etc.; fill (*with*); entrust *with*; solemnly urge; demand as price or sum (*for*); enter cost of *to*, make liable for; attack at gallop or run. **~-hand**, workman etc. in charge of others. **~-sheet**, police-station record of persons charged etc. **~able** *a.*

chargé d'affaires (shār′zhā dǎfār′) *n.* (pl. *-gés*, pr. as sing.), deputy ambassador, ambassador at minor court.

chār′ger¹ *n.* horse ridden in cavalry charge or by officer in field.

chār′ger² *n.* (arch.) large flat dish.

chǎ′riot *n.* stately vehicle; (hist.) kind of carriage; (hist.) car used in ancient warfare and racing. **~eer′** *n.*

charis′ma (k-; -z-) *n.* divine gift or talent; capacity to inspire followers or disciples with devotion and enthusiasm. ∼**măt′ic** *a.*

chă′ritable *a.* of or connected with charity; liberal in giving to poor; lenient in judging others.

chă′rity *n.* Christian good feeling; kindness; lenience in judging others; almsgiving; institution, foundation, etc. for benefit of others, esp. poor or helpless.

chăr′latan (sh-) *n.* impostor pretending to knowledge or skill. ∼**ism** *n.*

chăr′lock *n.* field mustard.

chăr′lotte (sh-) *n.* pudding of cooked fruit under bread-crumbs etc. ∼ **russe** (rōōs), mould of whipped cream in sponge-biscuits etc.

chărm *n.* word(s) or act(s) or object having occult power; object supposed to bring luck or avert evil; quality etc. exciting love or admiration; (pl.) beauty. *v.t.* subject to spell, bewitch, protect by magic; captivate, delight. **chăr′ming** *a.* (esp.) very pleasing, delightful.

chăr′nel-house *n.* place containing corpses or bones.

chărt *n.* map esp. for sea or air navigation or showing weather conditions etc.; sheet of tabulated or diagrammatic information, graph. *v.t.* make chart of.

chăr′ter *n.* written grant of rights by sovereign or legislature; privilege or admitted right. *v.t.* grant charter to; hire (ship) by charter-party; hire (vehicle etc.). ∼**-party**, indenture between ship-owner and merchant. ∼**ed** *a.* having charter; privileged; belonging to chartered body.

Chăr′tism *n.* working-class reform movement of 1837–48. ∼**ist** *n.*

chartreuse (shärtrĕrz′) *n.* green or yellow liqueur of brandy etc.

chăr′woman *n.* woman hired by day or hour for housework.

chăr′y *a.* cautious; sparing *of.*

chāse[1] *v.t.* emboss or engrave (metal).

chāse[2] *v.t.* try to overtake, pursue. *n.* hunting; attempt to catch by pursuit; unenclosed park-land. **chā′ser** *n.* pursuer; gun in bow or stern for use during chase; (sl.)

water or beer drunk after spirit; horse for steeplechasing.

chāse[3] *n.* frame holding sheet or page of type.

chăsm (k-) *n.* deep cleft, gulf, fissure; wide difference.

chassé (shăs′ā) *n.* & *v.i.* (make) gliding dance-step.

chassis (shăs′ē) *n.* (pl. same), base-frame of carriage, motor-car, etc.

chāste *a.* pure from (unlawful) sexual intercourse; pure in taste or style.

chā′sten (-sn) *v.t.* discipline by suffering; refine, temper.

chăstīse′ (-z) *v.t.* punish, beat. ∼**ment** *n.* punishment.

chăs′tity *n.* chasteness.

chăs′ūble (-z-) *n.* celebrant's sleeveless vestment.

chăt *v.i.* & *n.* (indulge in) easy familiar talk. **chătt′y** *a.* talkative, fond of chat; of nature of chat.

château (shăt′ō) *n.* (pl. -*x*, pr. -z), French castle or mansion.

chăt′elaine (sh-) *n.* appendage to woman's belt for carrying keys etc.; mistress of country house.

chătt′el *n.* movable possession; piece of property.

chătt′er *v.* talk fast, incessantly, trivially, or indiscreetly; (of teeth) rattle together. *n.* chattering. ∼**box**, talkative child. **chatty** : see **chat**.

chauffeur (shō′fĕr) *n.* professional driver of private or hired car.

chau′vinism (shō-) *n.* bellicose patriotism. ∼**ist** *n.*; ∼**is′tic** *a.*

chaw *v.t.* (vulg.) chew. ∼**-bacon**, (sl.) bumpkin.

Ch.B. *abbr.* Bachelor of Surgery.

Ch. Ch. *abbr.* Christ Church.

cheap *a.* inexpensive; easily got; of little account. ∼**jack**, hawker at fairs etc.

chea′pen *v.* make or become cheap.

cheat *v.* trick, defraud; deal fraudulently. *n.* deception; swindler; unfair player.

chĕck[1] *n.* position of king at chess when exposed to attack; sudden arrest of motion, stoppage; rebuff; slight military reverse; restraint; control to secure accuracy etc.; token of identification for left luggage etc.; (U.S.) counter at cards. *v.* (chess) subject (opponent or his king) to check; arrest motion of, restrain; (of hound) stop on losing scent; test accuracy of.

check² n. (fabric woven or printed with) pattern of cross-lines forming squares. ~ed a.

check³ n. (U.S.) cheque.

checker : see **chequer**.

chĕck'māte n. check at chess from which there is no escape; final defeat. v.t. defeat at chess; discomfit or frustrate.

chĕdd'ar n. kind of cheese.

cheek n. side of face below eye; (colloq.) saucy speech, effrontery; (pl.) jaws of vice, paired side-pieces in machine. v.t. (colloq.) address impudently. ~y̆ a. (colloq.) impudent.

cheep v.i. & n. (utter) shrill feeble note as of young bird.

cheer n. shout of encouragement or applause; (arch.) frame of mind; (arch.) comfort. v. comfort, gladden; urge *on* by shouts etc.; applaud, shout for joy; ~ *up*, comfort, be comforted. ~ful a. in good spirits; pleasant; willing, not reluctant. ~less a. gloomy, dreary. ~y̆ a. lively, genial.

cheese (-z) n. food made by pressing curds, cake or ball of this within rind; thick conserve of damsons etc.; heavy wooden disc used in skittles. ~-cake, tart filled with mixture of curds, sugar, etc. ~-paring, stingy; stinginess. **chee'sy̆** a. like cheese.

chee'tah n. kind of leopard used for hunting.

chĕf (sh-) n. male head cook.

chef-d'œuvre (shāder'vr) n. (pl. *chefs-* pr. as sing.), masterpiece. [F]

chĕm'ical (k-) a. of or made by chemistry. n. substance obtained by or used in chemical process. ~ **warfare**, use in war of chemicals other than explosives.

chemise (shĭmēz') n. woman's shirt-like undergarment worn next skin; chemise-like dress.

chem'ist (kĕ-) n. person skilled in chemistry; dealer in medical drugs.

chem'istry̆ (kĕ-) n. science of elements and their laws of combination and behaviour.

chenille (shĭnēl') n. (fabric with weft of) velvety yarn.

chĕque (-k) n. written order to banker to pay sum of money.

chĕ'quer (-ker), **chĕck'er** (chiefly U.S.) n. (pl.) chess-board as inn-sign; (freq. pl.) chequered pattern; (pl.) game of draughts. v.t. divide or mark like chess-board with squares esp. of alternating colours; diversify. ~**board**, chess-board. **chĕ'quered** a. (fig.) marked with alternating light and dark.

chĕ'rish v.t. tend lovingly; keep in one's heart, cling to.

chĕrōōt' (sh-) n. cigar with both ends open.

chĕ'rry̆ n. small stone-fruit, tree bearing it, wood of this. a. cherry-coloured, bright red. ~-**pie**, the plant heliotrope.

chĕ'rub n. (pl. -*s*, -*im*), angelic being; beautiful child. **chĕru'bĭc** (-ōō-) a.

chĕr'vĭl n. garden herb used to flavour salads etc.

Ches. *abbr.* Cheshire.

chess n. game for two players with 32 ~**men** on chequered ~-**board** of 64 squares.

chĕst n. large box of wood or other material; coffer; upper front part of body. ~ **of drawers**, frame with set of drawers.

chĕs'terfield n. kinds of overcoat and sofa.

chĕst'nŭt (-sn-) n. glossy brown seed or nut of edible and non-edible kinds, tree bearing either; bright brown; chestnut-coloured horse; stale anecdote. a. chestnut-coloured.

chĕvăl'-glass (sh-; -ahs) n. tall mirror swung on uprights.

chĕvalier' (sh-) n. member of certain orders of knighthood etc.

chevaux-de-frise (shevōdefrēz') n. pl. projecting spikes or sharp points to check cavalry, prevent climbing of walls, etc.

chĕv'iot n. cloth of Cheviot sheep's wool.

chĕv'ron (sh-)n. inverted V-shaped bar in heraldry etc.; V-shaped mark of rank or long service on uniform sleeve.

chew (-ōō) v. work about between

teeth; grind to pulp or indent by repeated biting; meditate *on*, ruminate *over*. *n*. spell of chewing; quid of tobacco. **~ing gum**, preparation of gum(s), esp. chicle, for prolonged chewing.

Chiăn'tĭ (kĭ-) *n*. dry usu. red Italian wine.

chiaroscuro (kyȧrŏskoor'ō) *n*. treatment of light and shade in painting; use of contrast in literature etc.

chĭbouk' (-ook) *n*. long Turkish tobacco-pipe.

chic (shēk) *a*. stylish, in fashion.

chicāne' (sh-) *n*. chicanery; (bridge-hand with) void in suit; (esp. temporary or movable) barrier or obstacle on road, race-course etc.

chĭcā'nerў (sh-) *n*. legal trickery; underhand dealing; sophistry.

chĭck *n*. young bird or child . **~weed**, kinds of small weed.

chĭck'ĕn *n*. young domestic bird, esp. fowl; its flesh as food; youthful person. **~-hearted**, cowardly, fearful. **~pox**, mild eruptive disease.

chĭck'-pea *n*. dwarf pea.

chĭ'cle (-ē-) *n*. tough elastic gum from sap of tropical S.-Amer. tree.

chĭc'orў *n*. (salad plant with) root ground and used with or instead of coffee; (U.S.) endive.

chīde *v*. (chĭd, p.p. chĭdden or chĭa), rebuke, scold.

chief *n*. leader or ruler; head of tribe or clan; (colloq.) head of department etc. *a*. first in importance or influence; prominent, leading.

chief'lў *adv*. above the rest: mainly but not exclusively.

chief'tain *n*. military leader; chief of clan or tribe or robber-band. **~cў**, **~ship** *nn*.

chiff'-chăff *n*. bird of warbler kind.

chiff'ŏn (sh-) *n*. diaphanous silky fabric.

chiffonier' (sh-) *n*. movable low cupboard used as sideboard.

chignon (shē'nyŏn) *n*. large coil, plait, etc. of hair at back of head.

chigoe : see **jigger**[1].

chĭhua'hua (-wahwah) *n*. tiny short-haired orig. Mexican dog.

chĭl'blain *n*. itching blain on hand, foot, ear, or nose.

chīld *n*. (pl. *chĭldren*), young human being; descendant or follower or product (*of*). **~hood** *n*. time from birth to puberty; *second* **~hood**, dotage. **~ish** *a*. of or like child. **~like** *a*. innocent, frank, etc. like child.

Chĭl'dermas *n*. festival of Holy Innocents (28 Dec.).

chĭl'ĭ *n*. (pl. *-ies*), red acrid pungent dried pod of kinds of capsicum.

chill *n*. cold sensation; slight esp. feverish cold; unpleasant coldness of air etc. *a*. lacking warmth. *v*. make or become cold; depress, dispirit.

chill'ў *a*. rather cold; sensitive to cold; cold-mannered.

chime *n*. (series of sounds given by) set of attuned bells; harmony; agreement, correspondence. *v*. make (bell) sound, ring chimes (on); show (hour) by chiming; agree (*with*), join *in*.

chimēr'a (kī- *or* kĭ-) *n*. bogy; wild impossible scheme or fancy. **chimĕ'rĭcal** *a*.

chim'ney *n*. structure by which smoke or steam is carried off; glass tube protecting lamp-flame. **~piece**, mantel. **~pot**, pipe at top of chimney. **~sweep**, one who cleans chimneys of soot.

chĭmpanzee' *n*. manlike African ape.

chĭn *n*. front of lower jaw.

chī'na *n*. & *a*. (of) hard fine semi-transparent porcelain. **~clay**, kaolin. **~man** *n*. (crick.) left-handed bowler's off-break to right-handed batsman.

chĭnchĭll'a *n*. (fine soft grey fur of) small S.-Amer. rodent. **~ rabbit**, long-haired kind bred for its fur.

chīne[1] *n*. deep narrow ravine.

chīne[2] *n*. backbone; joint of meat from backbone; hill-ridge. *v.t.* cut or slit along or across chine.

Chīnēse' (-z) *n*. & *a*. (native, language) of China. **~ lantern**, collapsible lantern of coloured paper. **~ white**, zinc oxide as pigment. **Chīnee'** *n*. (sl.) Chinese.

chĭnk[1] *n*. sound as of glasses or coins striking together. *v*. (cause to) make chink.

chink² _n._ crevice, long narrow opening.

Chink³ _n._ (sl.) Chinese.

chink'apin, chin'quapin (-ngk-) _n._ N.-Amer. dwarf chestnut.

chintz _n._ colour-printed glazed cotton cloth.

chionodŏx'a (k-) _n._ small blue-flowered early-blooming bulbous plant.

chip _v._ cut or break (_off_) at surface or edge; shape thus; suffer chipping. _n._ piece cut off, chipped place; (basket made of) wood split into thin strips; (pl.) stick-shaped pieces of potato fried crisp; counter in games of chance.

chip'mŭnk _n._ N.-Amer. striped ground-squirrel.

chipola'ta (-lah-) _n._ kind of thin sausage.

Chipp'endāle _n._ & _a._ (furniture) in style of 18th-c. London cabinet-maker.

chir'omancy (k-) _n._ palmistry.

chirŏp'ody (kīr- _or_ kǐ-) _n._ treatment of feet, corns, etc. **~dist** _n._

chīroprăc'tic (k-) _n._ & _a._ (U.S.) (of) manipulation of spinal column as way of curing disease. **chīr'oprăctor** _n._

chirp _n._ short sharp thin note as of small bird. _v._ utter chirp(s); express thus; talk merrily. **~y** _a._ cheerful.

chis'el (-zl) _n._ edged tool for cutting. _v.t._ cut with chisel; (sl.) defraud, cheat _out of._

chit¹ _n._ written note.

chit² _n._ young child, little woman.

chit'-chăt _n._ small-talk, gossip.

chitt'erlings _n.pl._ smaller intestines of pig etc. as food.

chiv'alry (sh-) _n._ medieval knightly system; inclination to defend weaker party; knights or gallant gentlemen. **~rous** _a._

chīve _n._ herb of leek kind.

chiv'y _v.t._ (colloq.) chase, harry.

chlōr'al (kl-) _n._ oily liquid used as hypnotic and anaesthetic.

chlōr'īde (kl-) _n._ compound of chlorine.

chlōr'ināte (kl-) _v.t._ impregnate, purify (water etc.) with chlorine. **~ā'tion** _n._

chlorine (klōr'ēn) _n._ heavy yellowish-green non-metallic gaseous element with irritating smell and powerful bleaching and disinfecting properties.

chlŏ'rofŏrm (kl-) _n._ heavy volatile liquid whose inhaled vapour produces insensibility. _v.t._ render insensible with this.

chlŏ'rophўll (kl-) _n._ colouring matter of green parts of plants.

chŏck _n._ block of wood, wedge. _v.t._ make fast, wedge, with chocks. **~-a-block**, jammed together, crammed _with._ **~-full**, crammed, stuffed.

chŏc'olate _n._ paste, cake, etc. of roasted, ground, and sweetened cacao seed; drink made of this; (pl.) sweets made with it; dark brown colour. _a._ chocolate-coloured.

choice _n._ act of choosing; preference; variety to choose from; thing chosen. _a._ of picked quality; exquisite.

choir (kwīr) _n._ band of esp. church singers; chancel. _v.i._ (poet.) sing in chorus. **~-boy**, boy who sings in choir. **~-organ**, part of organ used for accompanying choir.

chōke _v._ stop breath of, suffocate; block up; have coughing-fit. _n._ valve for closing air-inlet of petrol engine; (electr.) coil with low resistance and large inductance inserted in circuit; downy scaly heart of artichoke. **~-cherry**, astringent N.-Amer. wild cherry. **~-damp**, carbon dioxide in mines etc.

chō'ker _n._ (esp.) clerical or high stand-up collar.

chŏl'er (k-) _n._ bile; anger, irascibility. **chŏl'eric** (_or_ kolě'rĭk) _a._ irascible.

chŏl'era (k-) _n._ infectious and freq. fatal endemic & epidemic disease; summer diarrhoea.

cholĕs'terol (k-) _n._ white waxy-looking crystalline alcohol present in human tissues.

chōose (-z) _v._ (_chōse, chōsen_) select out of greater number; make choice _between_; decide or think fit _to_ do; (theol.) destine to be saved.

chŏp¹ _v._ cut with axe or heavy edge-

-tool; mince; cut short; strike (ball) with or make short heavy edgeways blow. *n.* chopping stroke; small thick slice of meat usu. including rib; short broken motion (of waves etc.). **chŏpp'er** *n.* large-bladed short axe. **chŏpp'y** *a.* (of wind, sea, etc.) jerky, rough.

chŏp² *v.i.* ~ *and change*, vacillate; ~ *logic*, bandy arguments.

chop³: see **chap²**.

chŏp'stick *n.* (pl.) pair of small sticks held in one hand and used by Chinese in eating.

chŏp-su'ey (-soõi) *n.* Chinese dish of meat or chicken, rice, onions, etc.

chōr'al¹ (k-) *a.* of, for, or sung by choir; of or with chorus.

choral(e)² (korahl') *n.* (metrical hymn set to) simple tune.

chōrd¹ (k-) *n.* string of harp etc. (poet.; also fig. of mind etc.); straight line joining ends of arc.

chōrd² (k-) *n.* (mus.) combination of simultaneous notes.

chōre *n.* odd job; (usu. pl.) daily light work of house, farm, etc.

chŏrēŏg'raphy (k-) *n.* arrangement of dancing in ballet; art of dancing. ~**grapher** *n.*; ~**grăph'ic** *a.*

chōr'ic (k-) *a.* of, for, or like Greek chorus.

cho'rister (kŏ-) *n.* member of choir; choir-boy.

chōr'tle *v.i.* (sl.) chuckle loudly.

chōr'us (k-) *n.* organized band of singers and dancers in Gk. dramatic performance, freq. commenting on action; song sung by these; explainer of or commentator on action of play; band of singers, choir; thing sung or said by many at once; refrain of song. *v.* speak or say or sing in chorus.

chose(n), *p.t.* & *p.p.* of **choose**.

chough (chŭf) *n.* red-legged crow.

chow *n.* heavily built thick-coated black-tongued Chinese breed of dog; (sl.) food; (Austral. sl.) Chinese.

chow'der *n.* N.-Amer. dish of clams etc. stewed with bacon, onions, etc.

chri'sm (k-) *n.* consecrated oil.

christen (krĭs'n) *v.t.* baptize and give name to; name. ~**ing** *n.* ceremony of baptism.

Christendom (krĭs'n-) *n.* Christians, Christian countries.

Christian (krĭs'tyan) *a.* & *n.* (person) believing in or professing or belonging to religion of Christ or resembling Christ or following his teachings; civilized or decent (person). ~ **era**, era counted from supposed year of Christ's birth. ~ **name**, name given at christening. ~ **Science, Scientist,** (believer in) doctrine that matter is an illusion and bodily disease an error of mind. ~**ize** *v.t.* make Christian.

Christiăn'ity (k-) *n.* Christian faith, quality, or character.

Christ'like (k-) *a.* partaking of nature and attributes of Christ.

Christmas (krĭs'm-) *n.* Christmas Day or Christmas-tide. ~**-box**, small present given at Christmas. ~ **card**, sent as Christmas greeting. ~ **Day**, festival of Christ's birth, 25 Dec. ~ **rose**, white-flowered winter-blossoming hellebore. ~**-tide**, season of Christmas. ~**-tree**, small fir hung with candles and presents. **Christ'mas(s)y** *a.*

chromăt'ic (k-) *a.* of colour, in colours; (mus.) of or having notes not belonging to prevailing key. ~ **scale**, proceeding by semitones (12 to octave).

chromăt'ics (k-) *n.* science of colour.

chrōme (k-) *n.* yellow pigment got from lead chromate. ~ **leather**, tough waterproof leather tanned with potassium bichromate. ~ **steel**, tough alloy of chromium and steel. ~ **yellow**, chrome.

chrō'mium (k-) *n.* metallic element used esp. in electro-plating and making of stainless steel alloys.

chrōmolith'ograph (k-; -ahf) *n.* picture lithographed in colours.

chrō'mosōme (k-) *n.* one of rods or threads occurring in pairs in cell-nucleus and carrying genes.

Chron. *abbr.* Chronicles.

chrŏn'ic (k-) *a.* constantly present or recurring; confirmed, permanent; (vulg.) bad, intense.

chrŏn'icle (k-) *n.* register of events in order of time. *v.t.* enter in chronicle or record. ~**r** *n.*

chrŏnolŏ'gĭcal (k-) *a.* according to sequence of time.

chrŏnŏl'ogў (k-) *n.* science of computing dates; arrangement or table of events with dates.

chronŏm'ēter (k-) *n.* time-measuring instrument, esp. one unaffected by temperature changes.

chrўs'alĭs (k-) *n.* form taken by insect in stage between larva and imago; case enclosing it.

chrўsăn'thėmum (k-) *n.* kinds of composite plant, esp. cultivated varieties.

chrўs'obĕrўl (k-), **chrўs'olīte, chrўs'oprāse** (-z) *nn.* yellowish-green, olive-green, apple-green, precious stones.

chŭb *n.* river fish of carp kind.

chŭbb'ў *a.* plump, round-faced.

chŭck[1] *n.* part of lathe holding work; cut of beef including part of neck and shoulder and some ribs. *v.t.* fix in chuck.

chŭck[2] *v.t.* give gentle blow *under the chin*; (colloq.) fling, throw carelessly; give *up*; ~ *it*, (sl.) stop; ~ *out*, expel. *n.* act of chucking; (colloq.) dismissal. **~-farthing,** kinds of game with coins pitched at mark. **~er-out,** person employed to expel intruders etc.

chŭck[3] *n.* (arch.) darling.

chŭck[4] *n.* (sl.) food.

chŭck[5] *int.* calling fowls or urging horse. *v.i.* utter this.

chŭck'le *n.* & *v.i.* (make) suppressed inarticulate sound of mirth etc.

chŭck'le-headėd (-hĕd-) *a.* doltish, stupid.

chŭg *v.i.* make or progress with intermittent explosive sound.

chŭkk'er *n.* each period of play in game of polo.

chŭm *n.* (colloq.) familiar friend; *new* ~, (Austral.) recent immigrant, greenhorn. *v.i.* share rooms *with*; strike *up* friendship.

chŭmp *n.* (colloq.) lump of wood; thick end of loin of mutton; (sl.) head; (colloq.) blockhead.

chŭnk *n.* (colloq.) lump cut or broken off. **~ў** *a.* short and thick or stout, stocky.

chupătt'y *n.* thin round cake of unleavened bread in N. India etc.

chûrch *n.* building for public Christian worship; collective body of Christians; body adhering to one particular form of worship; clerical profession. *v.t.* bring (woman after childbirth) to church for thanksgiving service. **~man, ~woman,** member of established Church. **~warden,** elected lay representative of parish; long clay pipe. **~yard,** enclosed ground round church.

chûrl *n.* ill-bred or cross-grained fellow; niggard; (arch.) peasant, low-born person. **~ish** *a.*

chûrn *n.* butter-making vessel or machine; large milk-can. *v.* make butter by agitating cream in churn; stir or wash about, seethe.

chute (shōot) *n.* slide for conveying things to lower level; rapid smooth fall of water over slope.

chŭt'ney *n.* strong pungent relish of fruits, chilies, etc.

chyle (kīl) *n.* milky fluid into which chyme is converted.

chyme (kīm) *n.* pulp into which gastric secretion converts food.

chypre (shēpr) *n.* kind of scent. [F]

Cic. *abbr.* Cicero.

cĭca'da (-kah- *or* -kā-) *n.* winged chirping insect.

cĭc'atrĭce *n.* scar of healed wound. **cĭc'atrīze** *v.* skin over, heal. **~zā'tion** *n.*

cĭ'cėlў *n.* kinds of flowering plant allied to parsley and chervil.

cicerō'nė (chĭche- *or* sĭse-) *n.* (pl. *-ni,* pr. -nē) person acting as guide.

Cĭcerō'nĭan *a.* eloquent, classical.

Cicestr. *abbr.* (Bishop) of Chichester.

C.I.D. *abbr.* Criminal Investigation Department.

cĭ'der *n.* fermented drink made from apple-juice.

ci-devant (sē devahn') *a.* former. [F]

c.i.f. *abbr.* cost, insurance, and freight.

cĭgãr' *n.* roll of tobacco-leaf for smoking. **cĭgarĕtte'** *n.* cut tobacco rolled in paper for smoking.

C.I.G.S. *abbr.* Chief of Imperial General Staff.

cĭl'ia *n.pl.* eye-lashes; similar fringe on leaf or insect's wing. **~rў** *a.*

Cĭmmēr'ian *a.* extremely dark.

C.-in-C. *abbr.* Commander-in-Chief.

cǐnch *n.* (U.S.) saddle-girth used in Mexico etc.; (sl.) sure or easy thing, certainty. *v.t.* put cinch on.

cǐnchō'na (-k-) *n.* kinds of tree with bark yielding quinine etc.

cǐnc'ture *n.* girdle, belt, fillet.

cǐn'der *n.* slag; residue of coal etc. that has ceased to flame; (pl.) ashes. ~-track, running- or racing--track laid with cinders. ~ў *a.*

Cǐnderěll'a *n.* neglected or despised member of group etc.

cǐn'ė- in comb., cinema. cǐn'ė--cămera *n.* motion-picture camera.

cǐn'ėma *n.* cinematography; making or showing of motion pictures; theatre for showing them. ~măt'ic *a.*

cǐnėmăt'ograph (-ahf) *n.* apparatus for making or projecting motion pictures. ~ográph'ic *a.*; ~ŏg'ra-phў *n.*

cǐnerār'ia *n.* kinds of flowering plant with downy leaves.

cǐn'erarў *a.* of ashes (esp. of urn holding cremated ashes).

Cǐngalese' (-nggalēz) *a.* & *n.* (obs.) Sinhalese.

cǐnn'abăr *n.* red mercuric sulphide; vermilion.

cǐnn'amon *n.* E.-Ind. tree; (colour of) its aromatic yellowish-brown inner bark used as spice. *a.* cinnamon--coloured.

cǐnque'foil (-kf-) *n.* plant with five--lobed leaves.

Cǐnque (-k) Pŏrts *n.pl.* certain ports (orig. five) on SE. coast of England, with ancient privileges.

C.I.O. *abbr.* (U.S.) Congress of Industrial Organizations.

cǐ'pher *n.* arithmetical symbol 0; worthless or unimportant person or thing; any Arabic numeral; secret or disguised way of writing; monogram. *v.* do arithmetic; write in cipher.

circ. *abbr.*, circa, circiter [L]), about.

cǐr'ca *prep.* about. [L]

Cǐr'cė *n.* (Gk. legend) enchantress whose victims were turned into swine. Cǐrcė'an *a.*

cǐr'cle *n.* perfectly round plane figure, line enclosing it; roundish enclosure, ring; curved tier of seats in theatre etc.; set or coterie or

class; period or cycle. *v.* move in circle (round).

cǐr'clět *n.* small circle; circular band as ornament for head etc.

cǐr'cuit (-kǐt) *n.* circular or cir-cuitous course; judge's progress through district to hold courts, such district; (electr.) course or path of current. circū'itous *a.* roundabout, indirect.

cǐr'cūlar *a.* of, in form of, moving in, passing over, circle. *n.* letter, advertisement, etc. sent round in same form to several people. ~ saw, revolving toothed disc. ~ tour, returning to starting-point by different route. ~īze *v.t.* send circular to.

cǐr'cūlate *v.* go or send round; give currency to. ~ā'tion *n.* movement of blood from and back to heart; movement in more or less circular course; transmission, distribution; number of copies of newspaper etc. sold. ~atorў *a.*

cǐrcumăm'bient *a.* surrounding.

cǐr'cumcīse (-z) *v.t.* cut off foreskin of.

cǐrcumci'sion (-zhn) *n.* act or religious rite of circumcising; festival of circumcision of Christ, 1 Jan.

circǔm'ference *n.* line enclosing circle; distance round thing.

cǐr'cumflĕx (accent) *n.* mark (^) over vowel to indicate contraction, length, etc.

cǐrcumfūse' (-z) *v.t.* pour round; bathe or surround.

cǐrcumjā'cent *a.* situated around.

cǐrcumlocū'tion *n.* use of many words where few would do; evasive speech. ~lŏc'utorў *a.*

cǐrcumnăv'igāte *v.t.* sail round. ~ā'tion, ~ātor *nn.*

cǐrcumpō'lar *a.* about or near one of earth's poles.

cǐr'cumscrībe *v.t.* draw line round; enclose; mark or lay down limits of; confine, restrict.

cǐrcumscrip'tion *n.* limitation; inscription round coin etc.

cǐrcumsō'lar *a.* moving round or situated near sun.

cǐr'cumspĕct *a.* wary; taking everything into account. ~spĕc'tion *n.* exercise of caution.

cĭr'cumstance *n.* (pl.) time, place, manner, etc. of act; (pl.) person's material welfare or situation; occurrence or fact or detail; formality, fuss.

cĭr̄cumstăn'tial *a.* of or dependent on circumstances; (of evidence) tending to establish disputed point by reasonable inference; accidental, incidental; full of detail.

cĭr̄cumvĕnt' *v.t.* overreach, outwit.

cĭr'cus *n.* arena for equestrian and other exhibitions, entertainment given in it; travelling show of riders, acrobats, trained animals, etc.; open space in town with streets converging on it.

cirrho'sis (sĭrō-) *n.* chronic progressive disease of liver.

cĭ'rrĭpĕd *n.* kinds of crustacean.

cĭ'rrus *n.* (pl. -rī), form of cloud with diverging woolly filaments.

Cĭstêr'cian *n.* & *a.* (monk) of strict Benedictine order founded 1098.

cĭs'tern *n.* reservoir for water.

cĭs'tus *n.* kinds of flowering shrub, rock-rose.

cĭt'adel *n.* fortress protecting or dominating city.

cīte *v.t.* summon at law; adduce as instance, quote in support. **cītā'tion** *n.* summons; reference; mention in official dispatch, recommendation for honour.

cĭth'ern, cĭtt'ern *n.* old musical instrument resembling lute.

cĭt'ĭzen *n.* burgess or freeman of city; townsman, civilian; enfranchised member of State. **~ship** *n.*

cĭt'rāte *n.* salt of citric acid.

cĭt'rĭc ă'cĭd *n.* sharp-tasting acid found in juice of lemon, orange, etc.

cĭt'ron *n.* fruit of lemon kind but larger; tree bearing it.

cĭtronĕll'a *n.* (grass yielding) fragrant ethereal oil.

cĭt'rus *n.* & *a.* (of) genus including orange, lemon, etc. **cĭt'rous** *a.*

cĭt'y̆ *n.* important town; town created city by charter; *Eternal C~*, Rome; *Holy C~*, Jerusalem, Heaven; *the C~*, part of London governed by Lord Mayor and Corporation, business part of this; commercial and financial circles.

~ editor, editor of financial part of newspaper.

cĭv'ĕt *n.* (unctuous musky-smelling substance got from) kinds of carnivorous quadruped, esp. central Afr. **~-cat.**

cĭv'ĭc *a.* of city or citizenship. **cĭv'ics** *n.* study of civic rights and duties.

cĭv'il *a.* of citizen community; non--military; non-ecclesiastical; not criminal or political; polite, obliging. **~ engineering,** all branches of engineering except military, mechanical, and electrical. **C~ List,** Parliamentary allowance for Sovereign's household and royal pensions. **~ marriage,** solemnized without religious ceremony. **C~ Service,** all public State departments or services except armed forces. **~ war,** war between sections of one State.

cĭvil'ian *a.* & *n.* (person) not in or of armed forces.

cĭvil'ĭty̆ *n.* readiness to oblige; (pl.) acts of courtesy.

cĭvĭlīzā'tion *n.* making or becoming civilized; (esp. advanced) stage of social development; civilized conditions or society.

cĭv'ĭlīze *v.t.* bring out of barbarism; enlighten, refine.

C.J. *abbr.* Chief Justice.

cl. *abbr.* centilitre; class; clause.

clăck *n.* sharp sound; clatter of tongues. *v.i.* make clack; chatter.

clad, *p.t.* & *p.p.* of **clothe.**

claim *v.t.* demand as one's due; have right to; assert. *n.* demand; right or title (*to*); (mining etc.) piece of ground marked out or allotted.

clai'mant *n.* claiming party, esp. in law-suit.

clairvoy'ance *n.* faculty of seeing mentally what is out of sight; second sight. **~ant** *n.* & *a.*

clăm *n.* kinds of edible bivalve; uncommunicative person. *v.i.* (U.S. sl.) shut *up.*

clā'mant (*or* klă-) *a.* noisy, insistent.

clăm'ber *v.i.* climb with help of hands or with difficulty.

clămm'y̆ *a.* stickily moist.

clăm'our *n.* shouting, confused noise; loud protest or demand. *v.i.* vociferate, make clamour. **clăm'orous** *a.*

clămp *n.* brace or band of iron etc.; gripping appliance tightened by screw etc. *v.t.* strengthen or fasten with clamp.

clăn *n.* Scottish Highlanders with common ancestor; family holding much together; party or coterie. **clănn'ish** *a.*; **~ship** *n.*

clăndĕs'tine *a.* surreptitious, secret.

clăng *n.* loud resonant metallic sound. *v.i.* make clang. **~our** (-ngg-) *n.* continued clanging.

clănk *n.* sound as of heavy pieces of metal struck together. *v.* (cause to) make clank.

clăp *v.* strike palms loudly together, applaud; strike, apply, put, etc. quickly or energetically or with clap; flap (wings) audibly. *n.* explosive noise, esp. peal of thunder; sound or act of clapping. **~board**, (U.S.) weatherboard. **~net**, net closed by pulling string.

clăpp'er *n.* tongue or striker of bell; bird-scaring rattle.

clăp'trăp *n.* trick, device, language, to catch applause.

claque (-ahk) *n.* hired body of applauders in theatre etc.

clă'rendon *n.* thick-faced type.

clă'ret *n.* red Bordeaux wine.

clă'rĭfӯ *v.* make, become, clear or pure or transparent.

clărĭnĕt' (*or* klă'-) *n.* wood-wind single-reed musical instrument with holes and keys; organ-stop of like quality.

clă'rĭon *n.* shrill trumpet; organ-stop of like quality; rousing call. *a.* loud and clear.

clă'rĭonĕt' *n.* clarinet.

clă'rĭtӯ *n.* clearness.

clăr'kĭa *n.* kinds of showy-flowered annual garden-plant.

clăsh *n.* loud broken sound as of cymbals; collision, conflict; discord of colours etc. *v.* make clash; be at variance with; bring together with clash.

clasp (-ah-) *n.* contrivance of two interlocking parts for fastening; grip of arms or hand, embrace, hand-shake; silver bar on medal-ribbon. *v.* fasten, fasten clasp of; encircle, embrace, grasp. **~-knife**, large folding knife.

class (-ahs) *n.* rank or order of society; set of students taught or (U.S.) graduating together; any set of persons or things differentiated by quality from others. *v.t.* assign to class. **~-conscious**, conscious of one's own social class (and hostile to others).

clăss'ĭc *a.* of allowed excellence; standard; of first order or rank; of ancient Greek and Latin literature or art or culture; in classic style. *n.* classic writer or artist; great literary work; classic race; (pl.) study of ancient Greek and Latin. **~ races**, five chief English horse-races.

clăss'ĭcal *a.* of or based on ancient Greek and Latin authors or art; of ancient Greece and Rome; standard, model, first-class; in or following restrained style of classical antiquity; (of music) not light, popular, jazz, etc.

clăss'ĭcism *n.* following of classic(al) style; classical scholarship; advocacy of classical education. **~cist** *n.*

clăss'ĭfӯ *v.t.* arrange in classes, class. **~fĭcā'tion** *n.*; **~fĭcatorӯ** *a.*

class'ӯ (-ah-) *a.* (sl.) superior.

clătt'er *n.* rattling sound; noisy talk. *v.* (cause to) make clatter, fall with clatter.

clause (-z) *n.* single proviso in treaty, law, or contract; (gram.) subordinate part of sentence including subject and predicate.

claus'tral *a.* of cloister.

claustrophō'bĭa *n.* morbid dread of confined places.

clave, *p.t.* of **cleave**[1].

clăv'ĭchŏrd (-k-) *n.* earliest stringed key-board instrument.

clăv'ĭcle *n.* collarbone. **clavĭc'ūlar** *a.*

claw *n.* pointed horny nail of beast's or bird's foot; ugly hand; grappling-iron. *v.* scratch or maul or seize or pull with claws or fingernails.

clay *n.* stiff tenacious earth usẹd for bricks, pottery, etc.; earth; earth as material of human body; *yard of* **~**, long clay pipe. **clay'ey** *a.*

clay'mŏre *n.* ancient Scottish two-edged broadsword.

clean *a.* free from dirt; unsoiled; free of defilement or disease; complete, decisive. *adv.* completely, altogether. *v.* make, make oneself, clean; undergo cleaning process; ~ *out*, empty, strip (esp. of money); ~ *up*, (esp.) acquire as profit, make profit. *n.* cleaning.

clean'lў¹ *adv.* in clean manner.

clean'lў² (-ĕn-) *a.* habitually clean; attentive to cleanness.

cleanse (-ĕnz) *v.t.* purify from sin; make clean.

clear *a.* transparent; not clouded; distinct, intelligible, manifest; not dim; complete, net; free *of*; well--defined, unobstructed, open; unhampered. *v.* make or become clear; show or declare innocent; remove, remove encumbrance etc. from; make sum as net gain; settle (debt etc.), free from debt; pass (cheque) through Clearing House; ~ *away*, remove meal from table; ~ *off*, *out*, get rid of, go away.

clear'ance *n.* clearing; clear space, room to pass. ~ **sale**, shop's sale to get rid of surplus stock.

clear'ing *n.* (esp.) piece of land cleared for cultivation. **C~ House**, place where bankers exchange cheques and bills.

clear'way *n.* road where vehicles may not stop on carriageway.

cleat *n.* tightening-wedge; projecting piece to give footing, fasten ropes to, etc.

clea'vage *n.* (esp.) way in which thing tends to split.

cleave¹ *v.i.* (*cleaved* or *clāve*; p.p. *cleaved*), be faithful, adhere *to*.

cleave² *v.* (*clōve* or *clĕft*; p.p. *clōven* or *clĕft*), split, divide; chop asunder; make way through.

clea'ver *n.* butcher's chopper.

clea'vers (-z) *n.* goose-grass.

clĕf *n.* (mus.) symbol showing pitch of stave.

cleft¹ *p.t.* & *p.p.* of **cleave²**. ~ **stick**, position allowing neither advance nor retreat.

clĕft² *n.* fissure, split.

clĕm'atĭs *n.* kinds of twining freq. showy-flowered plant.

clĕm'encў *n.* merciful treatment or feeling.

clĕm'ent *a.* merciful; mild.

clĕnch *v.* secure (nail) by hammering point sideways; close tightly, grasp firmly. *n.* clenching or clenched state.

clere'stŏry (-ērs-) *n.* windowed part of wall of cathedral etc. above aisle roof.

clĕr'gў *n.* all persons in holy orders. ~**man** *n.*

clĕ'rĭc *n.* clergyman.

clĕ'rĭcal *a.* of clergy(man), of clerk(s). ~**ĭsm** *n.* (esp.) (support of) clerical rule or influence. ~**ĭst** *n.*

clĕ'rĭhew *n.* witty or humorous four-line verse on (usu.) biographical subject.

clerk (-ärk, U.S. -ērk) *n.* person employed to keep accounts etc.; lay officer of parish church; man of business and keeper of records in municipal and other public offices; clergyman; scholar or penman. *v.i.* act as clerk. ~**ly** *a.* skilled in penmanship.

clĕv'er *a.* adroit, dexterous; talented, skilful, ingenious.

clew *n.* ball of thread or yarn; sail--corner to which tacks and sheets are fastened. *v.t.* draw *up* lower ends of (sails) to upper mast or yard for furling.

cliché (klē'shā) *n.* stereotyped or hackneyed expression.

clĭck *n.* slight sharp hard non--ringing sound; sharp non-vocal articulation in some Afr. languages. *v.* (cause to) make click; (sl.) have luck, secure one's object.

clī'ent *n.* person using services of lawyer or other professional person; customer.

clī'entēle (*or* klēawǹtĕl') *n.* clients; customers or frequenters of shop, theatre, etc.

cliff *n.* steep rock-face, esp. overhanging sea.

clīmăc'terĭc (*or* -tĕ'rĭk) *a.* constituting turning-point, critical. *n.* critical point in physical development.

clī'mate *n.* (region with specified) prevailing weather conditions. ~**ăt'ĭc** *a.*; ~**atŏl'ogў** *n.*

clī'măx *n.* (series arranged in) ascending scale; peak, apex.

climb (-m) *v.* make way up hill, tree, ladder, etc.; (of sun, aeroplane, etc.)

mount slowly; (of plant) go up wall or other support by clinging; rise in social scale. *n.* piece of climbing; place to be climbed. **cli′mber** (-m*er*) *n.* (esp.) mountaineer; person climbing socially; climbing plant.

clime *n.* region, tract.

clinch *v.* clench; (naut.) fasten (rope) with half-hitch; drive home, settle conclusively; (of boxer) come to quarters too close for any but short--range blows. *n.* clinching, resulting state or position.

cling *v.i.* (*clŭng*), maintain grasp, keep hold, adhere closely.

cling′stone *n.* peach, nectarine, with pulp adhering to stone.

clin′ic *n.* clinical method of teaching; class so taught; institution giving (esp. regular) medical and other treatment or advice to outpatients etc.

clin′ical *a.* of or at sick-bed. **~ thermometer,** for taking patient's temperature.

clink¹ *n.* abrupt clear ringing sound, chink. *v.* (cause to) emit clink; touch (glasses) together in toasts etc.

clink² *n.* (sl.) prison.

clink′er¹ *n.* brick vitrified on surface; slag, fused ash.

clink′er² *n.* (sl.) first-class specimen; good shot or stroke.

clink′er-built (-bǐ-) *a.* with external planks overlapping downwards.

clink′ing *a.* (sl.) excellent.

clip¹ *v.t.* grip tightly; fasten or attach with clip. *n.* appliance for attaching something or holding things together; set of cartridges held together at base. **~board,** board with spring clip for holding papers etc.

clip² *v.t.* cut with shears or scissors; pare edge of (coin); remove small piece from (bus-ticket etc.) to show it has been used; cut short. *n.* clipping; yield of wool; smart blow. **clipp′er** *n.* (esp.) instrument for clipping (usu. pl.); swift mover; ship of raking build. **clipp′ing** *n.* (esp.) small piece clipped off; cutting from newspaper etc.

clique (-ēk) *n.* exclusive set of associates. **cli′quy** (-ēkǐ) *a.*

clit′oris *n.* rudimentary female sexual organ, homologue of penis.

cloak *n.* loose usu. sleeveless outdoor garment; pretext. *v. t.* cover with, wrap in, cloak; cover, hide. **~room,** room where hats, coats, luggage, etc. may be left; lavatory etc.

cloche (-sh) *n.* bell-shaped glass, glass frame, for protecting plant(s); woman's close-fitting deep-crowned hat.

clock¹ *n.* instrument measuring time and indicating it on dial; clock--like device showing readings on dial; downy seed-head of dandelion etc. *v.* time by clock or stop-watch; travel at (specified speed), cover distance in (specified time); **~** *in, out, on, off,* register time of arrival or departure, beginning or ending work, etc., by mechanical device. **~wise,** moving in curve from left to right as seen from centre. **~work,** mechanism on clock principle; (attrib.) regular, mechanical.

clock² *n.* ornamental pattern on side of stocking or sock.

clod *n.* lump of earth or clay; lout. **~hopper,** bumpkin, lout.

clog *n.* log fastened to leg to impede motion; wooden-soled shoe. *v.* confine with clog; be encumbrance to, impede; choke up.

cloisonné (klwahzŏn′ā) *a.* & *n.* (enamel) with colours separated by thin metal outline plates.

cloi′ster *n.* convent, monastic house; covered walk, esp. of convent, college, or cathedral buildings. *v.t.* shut up in convent, immure. **cloi′stral, cloi′stered** (-*erd*) *aa.*

clop *n.* & *v.i.* (make, go with) sound (as) of hoofs on road etc.

close¹ *a.* shut; tight; stifling; secret; niggardly; near together; compact, dense; nearly equal. *adv.* closely. *n.* enclosed place; passage or entry; small enclosed field. **~-stool,** chamber-pot mounted in stool with cover. **~-up,** part of cinema picture etc. taken at short range.

close² (-z) *v.* shut; be declared shut; finish, settle, complete; draw near (to); grapple (*with*); come to terms *with. n.* conclusion, end. **~d shop,** industrial etc. concern restricted to members of particular trade union.

clŏs'ĕt (-z-) *n.* private or small room; cupboard; water-closet. **~ĕd** *a.* in private conference etc.

clō'sure (-zh*er*) *n.* closing, closed state; closing of debate. *v.t.* apply closure to.

clŏt *n.* lump of adhesive matter; coagulated mass; (sl.) stupid person. *v.* form into clots; curdle.

clŏth *n.* woven or felted stuff; table--cover; woollen material for clothes.

clōthe (-dh) *v.t.* (*clothed* or *clăd*), provide with clothes, put clothes upon, be as clothes to.

clōthes (-ōz, -ōdhz) *n.pl.* wearing--apparel, garments.

clō'thĭer (-dh-) *n.* dealer in cloth and men's clothes.

clō'thĭng (-dh-) *n.* clothes.

cloud *n.* visible (mass of) condensed watery vapour floating in air; mass of smoke or dust; great number moving together; louring look. *v.* overspread or darken with clouds, gloom, trouble, or imbecility; become overcast. **~berry**, mountain raspberry. **~scape**, picture of clouds. **~lĕss** *a.* **~ў** *a.* obscured with clouds; lacking clearness.

clough (klŭf) *n.* ravine.

clout *v.t.* patch (shoe, garment); hit or rap. *n.* cloth; piece of clothing; rap or blow; iron plate on boot etc. to save wear.

clōve[1] *n.* pungent aromatic dried bud of tropical tree. **~ pink**, clove--scented pink.

clōve[2] *n.* one sector of bulb of garlic etc.

clove[3], **cloven**, *p.t.* & *p.p.* of **cleave**[2].

clōve hĭtch *n.* hitch securing rope round spar etc. at right angles.

clō'ver *n.* kinds of trefoil used as fodder.; *in* **~**, in ease and luxury.

clown *n.* rustic, lout; jester in pantomime or circus. *v.* act or perform as or like clown. **~ĭsh** *a.*

cloy *v.t.* satiate or weary by richness, sweetness, etc.

clŭb *n.* heavy stick used as weapon; kinds of stick used in golf etc.; playing-card of suit marked with black trefoils; (premises of) body of persons associated for social or other purposes. *v.* strike with club; bring or come *together*, contribute to common expense. **~-house**, building of (esp. golf-) club. **~-root**, disease of cabbages and turnips. **clŭbb'able** *a.* sociable.

clŭb'fŏŏt *n.* (foot with) kinds of malformation giving foot thick stunted appearance.

clŭck *n.* & *v.i.* (make) abrupt hollow guttural sound (as) of hen.

clue (-ōō) *n.* guiding or suggestive fact; thread of story; train of thought.

clŭm'ber *n.* breed of spaniel.

clŭmp *n.* cluster *of* trees; thick extra sole on shoe. *v.* tread heavily and clumsily; plant in clump; keep or mass together; put clump ŏń (shoe).

clŭm'sў (-z-) *a.* awkward iń movement or shape; ill-contrived, ill--conceived; tactless.

clung, *p.t.* & *p.p.* of **cling**.

clŭs'ter *n.* group of similar things; swarm or group of persons, stars, etc. *v.* form, arrange in, cluster.

clŭtch[1] *v.* seize eagerly, grasp tightly; snatch *at*. *n.* tight or (pl.) cruel grasp; device for coupling and uncoupling driving and driven parts of mechanism.

clŭtch[2] *n.* set of eggs; brood of chickens.

clŭtt'er *n.* crowded confusion, confused mass. *v.t.* litter, crowd untidily.

C.M. *abbr.* common metre.

cm. *abbr.* centimetre.

C.M.B. *abbr.* (certificated by) Central Midwives Board.

Cmd *abbr.* Command Paper.

C.M.G. *abbr.* Companion of (Order of) St. Michael and St. George.

Cmnd *abbr.* Command Paper.

C.M.S. *abbr.* Church Missionary Society.

C.N.D. *abbr.* Campaign for Nuclear Disarmament.

C.N.V.A. *abbr.* (U.S.) Committee for non-Violent Action.

C.O. *abbr.* Colonial Office; Commanding Officer; conscientious objector.

Co. *abbr.* company; county.

c/o *abbr.* care of.

coach *n.* state carriage; large four--wheeled closed carriage with seats inside and on roof carrying fare-

-paying passengers on fixed route; long-distance bus; railway carriage; tutor or trainer. *v.* train, tutor; travel by coach. **~man**, driver of horse carriage. **~work**, (esp. wooden parts of) body of motor-car.

cōădj′utor (-ōō-) *n.* assistant.

cōăg′ūlant *n.* coagulating agent.

cōăg′ūlāte *v.* change from fluid to solid state; clot, curdle, set. **~ā′tion** *n.*

coal *n.* black or blackish sedimentary rock used as fuel etc.; (pl.) pieces of coal. *v.* put coal into (ship etc.); take in coal. **~ face**, surface of coal seam exposed by mining. **~-field**, district in which coal is found. **~-gas**, gases extracted from coal and used for lighting and heating. **~-heaver**, one who carries and loads coal. **~-hole**, small place for keeping coal. **~-master**, **~-owner**, owner or lessee of colliery. **~ measures**, seams of coal with intervening strata. **~-scuttle**, portable vessel for coal. **~er** *n.* (esp.) ship for supplying others with coal.

cōălĕsce′ *v.i.* come together and form one; combine in coalition. **cōălĕs′cence** *n.*; **~ent** *a.*

cōăli′tion *n.* fusion into one whole; temporary combination between parties. **~ist** *n.*

coal′mouse, coal′tĭt *nn.* dark species of titmouse.

coa′ming *n.* raised border round ship's hatches etc.

coarse (kōrs) *a.* common, inferior; rough; lacking delicacy, unrefined; vulgar, obscene. **coar′sen** *v.* make or become coarse.

coast *n.* sea boundary, line of shore. *v.i.* sail along coast; travel downhill on toboggan or on bicycle without pedalling or in car with engine idle. **~guard**, man, body of men, employed to report wrecks, prevent smuggling, etc. **~line**, configuration of coast. **~al** *a.* **~er** *n.* (esp.) coasting vessel; low round stand for decanter. **~wise** *adv. & a.* along coast.

coat *n.* sleeved outer body garment; overcoat; jacket; beast's hair, fur, etc.; skin, rind, husk; layer of paint etc.; **~** (*of arms*), heraldic bearings, (hist.) tabard. *v.t.* cover with surface layer or coating. **~ armour**, heraldic arms. **~-hanger**, curved hanger fitting shoulders of coat etc. **~ee′** *n.* short coat. **~ing** *n.* cloth for coats; layer of paint etc.

cōa′tĭ (-ah-) *n.* tropical Amer. raccoon-like mammal with long flexible snout.

coax *v.t.* use blandishments on, persuade; manipulate gently.

cōăx′ial *a.* with common axis.

cŏb[1] *n.* stout short-legged riding-horse; male swan; large kind of hazel-nut; stalk of maize-ear; (pl.) coal in roundish lumps; small roundish loaf.

cŏb[2] *n.* composition of clay, gravel and straw for building walls.

cō′balt (-awlt) *n.* silver-white malleable metal; deep-blue pigment made from it.

cŏbb′er *n.* (Austral. sl.) mate.

cŏbb′le *n.* rounded fragment of rock bigger than pebble; (pl.) these used for paving; (pl.) coals of cobble size. *v.t.* mend, patch coarsely.

cŏbb′ler *n.* mender of shoes; clumsy workman; iced drink of wine, lemon, sugar, etc.

cŏb′le *n.* kind of fishing-boat.

cō′bra *n.* venomous hooded snake.

cŏb′wĕb *n.* spider's network or thread; anything frail or flimsy; (pl.) musty rubbish. *a.* delicate, flimsy.

cō′ca *n.* (dried leaves used as nerve stimulant etc. of) S.-Amer. shrub.

cocaine′ *n.* alkaloid got from coca used as local anaesthetic etc.

cŏc′cўx (-ks-) *n.* bone ending spinal column.

cŏch′ĭn-chī′na *n.* breed of fowl.

cŏch′ĭneal *n.* dried insects yielding scarlet dye.

cŏck[1] *n.* male of domestic fowl; any male bird; spout or short pipe with tap etc. for controlling flow of liquid or gas; lever in gun raised to be released by trigger. *v.* erect or stand *up* jauntily; raise cock or hammer of (gun); **~** one's *eye*, glance knowingly. **~-a-hoop**, exultant.

~-crow, dawn. ~-eyed, (sl.) squinting; set aslant, one-sided. ~ of the walk, dominant person in any company. ~shot, ~shy, object set up to be thrown at; throw at this.

cŏck² *n.* small conical heap of hay. *v.t.* put (hay) in cocks.

cockāde' *n.* rosette etc. worn in hat.

cŏck-a-lee'kĭe *n.* Scotch dish of chicken broth with leeks.

cŏckatōō' *n.* crested parrot.

cŏck'atrĭce (*or* -ĭ-) *n.* basilisk.

cŏck'boat *n.* small boat, esp. towed behind ship.

cŏck'chāfer *n.* large chestnut-coloured loud-humming beetle.

cŏcked hat *n.* hat with very wide brim permanently turned up at sides or front and back.

cŏck'er¹ *v.t.* pamper, coddle.

Cŏck'er² *n. according to* ~, correct, regular.

cŏck'er³ *n.* breed of spaniel.

cŏck'erel *n.* young cock.

cŏck'le¹ *n.* plant growing in corn.

cŏck'le² *n.* (shell of) edible bivalve found on sandy coasts; ~s *of the heart*, innermost feelings. ~-shell, shell of cockle; small frail boat.

cŏck'le³ *n.* bulge, pucker. *v.* (cause to) wrinkle or pucker.

cŏck'ney *n.* native of London; London English. *a.* of cockneys. ~ĭsm *n.* cockney idiom etc.

cŏck'pĭt *n.* enclosure in which game-cocks are set to fight; place of many battles; (hist.) part of orlop deck on man-of-war, used as hospital in action; space for pilot etc. in aeroplane, driver in racing-car, etc.

cŏck'roach *n.* blackbeetle.

cŏcks'cōmb (-m) *n.* cock's crest; kinds of plant.

cŏck'sure (-shoor) *a.* quite convinced; dogmatic, confident.

cŏck'tail *n.* horse of racing stamp but not thoroughbred; drink of spirit with bitters, sugar, etc.

cŏck'ў *a.* conceited, pert; cock-a-hoop.

cō'cō *n.* (pl. -os), tropical palm bearing coconut. ~nut, seed of coco with edible white lining enclosing liquid called *coconut milk.* ~nut matting, made from fibre of outer husk of coconut.

cō'coa (-kō) *n.* powder of crushed cacao seeds, drink made from this.

cocōōn' *n.* silky case spun by larva (esp. of silkworm) to protect it as chrysalis.

C.O.D. *abbr.* cash on delivery; Concise Oxford Dictionary.

cŏd¹ *n.* large sea fish. ~-liver oil, medicinal oil rich in vitamins.

cŏd² *v.* (sl.) hoax, fool.

cŏdd'le *v.* treat, treat oneself, as invalid; pamper; cook gently in water just below boiling-point.

cōde *n.* systematized body of laws; set of rules; system of signals; arbitrary symbols used for brevity or secrecy. *v.t.* put into code symbols.

cō'dĕx *n.* (pl. -*dicēs*), MS. volume esp. of ancient texts.

cŏdg'er *n.* (sl.) fellow.

cŏd'ĭcĭl *n.* supplement modifying or revoking will etc.

cŏd'ĭfy̆ (*or* kō-) *v.t.* reduce to code or system; code. ~ficā'tion *n.*

cŏd'lĭn(g)¹ *n.* variety of apple.

cŏd'lĭng² *n.* small cod.

cō-ĕdūcā'tion *n.* education of both sexes together.

cōĕffĭ'cient (-shnt) *n.* (alg.) expression of quantity standing before and multiplying another; number used as measure of some property etc.

coe'lacănth (sē-) *n.* fish of nearly extinct group of SE.-Afr. seas.

cōē'qual *a. & n.* equal.

cōērce' *v.t.* constrain into obedience. ~cĭve *a.* cōēr'cion (-shn) *n.* compulsion; use of force.

cōĕssĕn'tial (-shl) *a.* of same substance or essence.

cōĕtêr'nal *a.* alike eternal.

cōē'val *a. & n.* (person etc.) of same age, duration, or epoch.

cōĕxĭst' (-gz-) *v.i.* exist together or *with.* ~ence *n.* (esp.) mutual toleration between States with differing ideologies. ~ent *a.*

cōĕxtĕn'sĭve *a.* extending over same space or time.

C. of E. *abbr.* Church of England.

cŏff'ee (-fĭ) *n.* shrub of Arabia etc.; its seeds, powder made from them; infusion of this as drink. ~-grounds, granular sediment in coffee after infusion. **~-room,** dining-room of inn etc.

cŏff'er *n.* box esp. for valuables; (pl.) funds or treasury; sunk panel in ceiling etc. **~-dam,** caisson.

cŏff'in *n.* chest in which corpse is buried or cremated.

cŏg *n.* one of series of projections on wheel etc. transferring motion by engaging with another series.

cō'gent *a.* forcible, convincing. **~encў** *n.*

cŏ'gĭtāte *v.* ponder; form conception of. **~ā'tion** *n.*; **~atĭve** *a.*

cognac (kŏn'yăk) *n.* French brandy.

cŏg'nāte *a.* descended from same ancestor or root or origin. *n.* cognate word or person.

cŏgnĭ'tion *n.* knowing or perceiving or conceiving; notion. **cŏg'nĭtĭve** *a.*

cŏg'nĭzable *a.* within cognizance of court; knowable.

cŏg'nĭzance *n.* being aware; judicial notice; crest or other badge.

cŏg'nĭzant *a.* having cognizance (*of*); having cognition.

cŏgnō'mĕn *n.* nickname, surname.

cōhăb'ĭt *v.i.* live together as husband and wife. **~ā'tion** *n.*

coheir (kōār'), **coheir'ess** *nn.* joint heir, joint heiress.

cohēre' *v.i.* stick together, remain united; be well knit or consistent. **~ence** *n.* **~ent** *a.* holding together; not inconsequent or rambling; (of light etc.) having waves in phase. **~er** *n.* device using coherence of metal filings etc. to detect electric waves.

cohē'sion (-zhn) *n.* force with which parts cohere; union; dependence. **cohē'sive** *a.*

cō'hŏrt *n.* tenth part of Roman legion; (pl.) troops; band.

C.O.I. *abbr.* Central Office of Information.

coif *n.* (hist.) kind of close cap.

coiffeur (kwafẽr'), **coiffeuse'** (-ẽrz) *nn.* male, female, hairdresser. [F]

coi'ffūre (kwă-) *n.* way hair is dressed. *v.t.* dress (hair), dress hair of.

coign (koin) *n.* **~** *of vantage,* advantageous position.

coil *v.* dispose in concentric rings; take or twist into spiral or circular shape. *n.* coiled length of rope, wire, etc.

coin *n.* piece of stamped metal money; (collect.) money. *v.t.* make (money) by stamping metal; turn into money; invent, fabricate.

coi'nage *n.* (right of) coining; coins, currency; invention, fabrication; coined word.

cōĭncīde' *v.i.* occur simultaneously; agree or be identical *with.* **cōĭn'cidence** *n.* notable concurrence of events etc. **cōĭn'cĭdent, ~ĕn'tal** *aa.*

coi'ner *n.* (esp.) maker of false coin.

coir *n.* fibre of coconut husk used for ropes etc.

cōĭ'tion *n.* copulation.

cōke[1] *n.* residue of coal after distillation of volatile parts. *v.t.* make into coke.

cōke[2] *n.* (sl.) cocaine; coca-cola (proprietary non-alcoholic drink).

cŏl *n.* depression in summit-line of mountain-chain.

Col. *abbr.* Colonel; Colossians.

col. *abbr.* column.

cō'la *n.* kinds of orig. W.-Afr. tree. **~-nut,** bitter seed of one of these, chewed as mild stimulant.

col'ander (kŭ-) *n.* perforated vessel used as strainer in cookery.

cŏl'chicum (-kĭ-) *n.* meadow-saffron; drug got from it.

cōld *a.* of low temperature; feeling or suggesting cold; not heated; having cooled; lacking ardour, undemonstrative, apathetic; chilling; (of hunting-scent) faint. *n.* prevalence of low temperature; sensation produced by loss of body-heat; inflammation of mucous membrane of nose and throat. **~ cream,** unguent for skin. **~ feet,** (sl.) fear, cowardice. **~ snap,** sudden spell of cold weather. **~ storage,** (building for) storage or preservation in refrigerating chambers. **~ war,** pursuit of ends of war by means other than fighting.

cōle *n.* kinds of cabbage. **~-slaw,** (U.S.) salad of sliced cabbage.

cŏléŏp'terous *a.* with front wings forming hard sheaths for hind pair.

cŏl'ic *n.* griping belly-pain.

colī'tis *n.* inflammation of colon.

Coll. *abbr.* College.

collăb'orāte *v.i.* work in combination (*with*). ~ā'tion, ~ātor *nn.*

collăpse' *n.* tumbling down or falling to ruin; physical or mental break-down. *v.i.* suffer collapse; fall to ruin; break down.

collăp'sible *a.* folding.

cŏll'ar *n.* part of garment, separate piece, turned back near or encircling neck; leather band round dog's neck; part of harness round horse's neck; chain forming part of insignia of knighthood. *v.t.* seize by collar, capture; (footb.) tackle; (sl.) lay hold of, appropriate.

cŏll'arbōne *n.* bone joining breast--bone with shoulder-blade.

collāte' *v.t.* compare in detail; place (sheets of book) in order; appoint to benefice.

collăt'eral *a.* side by side; subordinate but from same source; connected but aside from main line. *n.* collateral kinsman; collateral security. ~ **security,** property pledged in addition to principal security.

collā'tion *n.* collating; light repast.

cŏll'eague (-g) *n.* associate in office etc.; member of same profession etc.

cŏll'ĕct[1] *n.* short prayer in prayer--book, esp. appointed for particular day etc.

collĕct'[2] *v.* assemble, accumulate, bring or come together; gather contributions, rates, etc.; concentrate (one's thoughts etc.).

collĕc'tion *n.* collecting; collecting of money at church service etc.; sum so collected; set of collected specimens.

collĕc'tive *a.* representing or including many; combined, aggregate, common; worked, managed, conducted, etc., by (esp. organized) group acting together for common good. *n.* (gram.) collective noun; collective farm or other enterprise. ~ **noun,** used in sing. to denote number of individuals. ~ **owner-ship,** by all for common benefit. ~ **security,** system by which all, or group of, countries guarantee security of each.

collĕc'tivism *n.* (theory of) collective ownership or control of means of production. ~**ist** *n.* & *a.*

collĕc'tor *n.* one who collects specimens, curiosities, revenue, etc.

cŏll'een *n.* (Anglo-Ir.) girl.

cŏll'ege *n.* organized society of persons having certain functions, rights, and privileges; corporation of scholars forming part of university; school with similar foundation; (Sc., U.S., etc.) university; place of professional study; (name assumed by) other educational institutions; buildings of college. **collē'gian** *n.* member of college. **collē'giate** *a.* constituted as college.

collīde' *v.i.* come into collision.

cŏll'ie *n.* Scotch sheep-dog.

cŏll'ier *n.* coal-miner; coal-ship, member of its crew.

cŏll'iery (-yerĭ) *n.* coal-mine.

colli'sion *n.* violent encounter of moving bodies; clash of opposed interests etc.

collō'dion *n.* colourless gummy rapid--drying liquid.

collōgue' (-g) *v.i.* (colloq.) talk confidentially.

cŏll'oid *n.* substance in or readily assuming colloid state; such substance with medium through which it is dispersed. *a.* of colloid(s). ~ **state,** of substance in very fine particles, freq. dispersed through gaseous, liquid, or solid medium. **colloi'dal** *a.*

cŏll'op *n.* slice of meat etc.

collō'quial *a.* proper or peculiar to everyday talk; not literary, formal, etc. ~**ism** *n.* colloquial word or idiom; use of these.

cŏll'oquy *n.* talk, dialogue.

cŏll'otype *n.* (printing, print made, from) gelatine photographic plate.

collū'sion (*or* -ōō-) *n.* fraudulent secret understanding esp. between ostensible opponents. ~**sive** *a.*

cŏll'ywŏbbles *n.pl.* (colloq.) belly-ache, diarrhoea.

Colo. *abbr.* Colorado.

cŏl'ocynth *n.* (plant bearing, purgative made from) gourd with bitter fruit.

cologne' (-ōn) *n.* eau-de-Cologne.

cō'lon[1] *n.* greater part of large intestine. **colon'ic** *a* cŏ'lon² *n.* punctuation-mark (:).

colonel (kẽr'nl) *n.* army officer next in rank to brigadier; (courtesy title for) lieutenant-colonel. ~cў *n.*

colo'nial *a.* of colony or colonies; of period before 13 British colonies of America became U.S. *n.* inhabitant of colony. ~ism *n.* (belief in) establishment or retention of colonies.

cŏl'onist *n.* settler in or part-founder of colony. ~ize *v.* establish or join colony (in). ~izā'tion *n.*

cŏlonnāde' *n.* row of columns supporting entablature.

cŏl'onў *n.* settlement, settlers, in new territory remaining subject to parent State; persons of foreign nation or of one trade forming community in town etc.; birds etc. similarly congregated.

cŏl'ophon *n.* tail-piece in book.

colŏph'onў *n.* kind of dark resin.

Cŏlora'dō bee'tle (-rah-) *n.* small beetle with larva destructive to potato.

colorā'tion (kŭ-) *n.* colouring, disposition of colours.

cŏloratur'a (-oora) *n.* florid ornament in singing. [It.] ~ soprano, (singer with) high flexible voice capable of this.

colŏss'al *a.* like colossus, huge; (colloq.) splendid, glorious.

colŏss'us *n.* (pl -*i*, -*uses*), statue of gigantic size; gigantic person or personified power.

colŏs'tomў *n.* formation of, artificial anus formed by, opening through abdominal wall into colon.

colour (kŭl'*er*) *n.* sensation produced in eye by rays of decomposed light; any particular hue; pigment; hue of darker, esp. Negro, races; complexion; (pl.) flag of regiment or ship; show of reason; pretext. *v.* give colour to; paint or stain or dye; blush; make plausible. ~-blind, unable to distinguish some colours. ~able *a.* specious, plausible, counterfeit. ~ed *a.* (esp.) Negro, of Negro origin. ~ful *a.* ~ing *n.* coloration; artist's use of colour. ~ist *n.* artist skilful in use of colour. ~less *a.* wanting in character or vividness.

cŏlpŏrteur' (-tẽr) *n.* book-hawker, esp.

one employed to distribute bibles and religious literature.

cōlt *n.* young horse; tyro, esp. cricket professional in first season.

cō'ltsfŏŏt *n.* large-leaved yellow-flowered weed.

Cŏlŭm'bia *n.* America.

cŏl'umbīne *n.* garden plant.

cŏl'umn (-m) *n.* round pillar, esp. one with base and capital; column-shaped thing; narrow vertical division of sheet of paper, esp. newspaper; printed matter in this; formation of troops, ships, etc. one behind other. ~ist *n.* journalist writing column of general comments.

cŏl'za-oil *n.* lamp oil got from rape seed.

cō'ma *n.* prolonged loss of consciousness; lethargy, stupor. cō'matōse *a.* in or like coma.

cōmb (-m) *n.* toothed strip of rigid material for disentangling, arranging, etc. hair; thing of similar shape or function, esp. for dressing wool; red fleshy crest of cock etc.; honeycomb. *v.t.* draw comb through (hair), dress (wool etc.) with comb; search thoroughly.

cŏm'bat (*or* kŭ-) *n.* fight, struggle. *v.* do battle; contend with, oppose.

cŏm'batant (*or* kŭ-) *a.* fighting. *n.* fighter.

cŏm'batĭve (*or* kŭ-) *a.* pugnacious or disputatious.

cŏmbinā'tion *n.* set of things or persons combined; united action; chemical union; (pl.) under-garment for body and legs.

combīne' *v.* join together, unite; enter into chemical union (*with*). *n.* (kŏm'-), combination esp. of business firms etc. to influence prices or course of trade. ~(-harvester), combined reaping- and threshing-machine.

combŭs'tible *a.* capable of burning, easily set alight. *n.pl.* combustible things. ~bil'itў *n.*

combŭs'tion (-chn) *n.* consumption by fire; oxidation.

come (kŭm) *v.i.* (*cāme*, p.p. *come*), draw near, advance; be brought; arrive; occur; become; prove, turn out; ~ *about*, happen; ~ *across*, meet; ~ *by*, obtain; ~ *off*, succeed; extricate oneself; ~ *out*, be revealed, show itself, make début; ~ *round*, recover from ill temper, swoon, etc.; ~ *to*, revive, recover; ~ *up*, come to or *to* capital, university, etc.; ~ *up to*; rise to level or height of. **~-back**, retort; return. **~-down**, descent, downfall.

come-ăt'-able (kŭ-) *a*. accessible.

comē'dĭan *n*. actor; comic performer or writer.

comēdĭĕnne' *n*. comedy actress.

comēdĭĕtt'a *n*. short comedy.

cŏm'ĕdў *n*. light amusing play; branch of drama concerned with comedies; life etc. regarded as comic spectacle.

comely (kŭm'lĭ) *a*. pleasant to look at; proper, decent.

comĕs'tĭbles *n.pl.* things to eat.

cŏm'ĕt *n*. heavenly body with star-like nucleus and 'tail' of light. **cŏm'ĕtarў** *a*.

com'fĭt (kŭ-) *n*. sweetmeat.

com'fort (kŭ-) *n*. relief in trouble, consolation; (pl.) things that make life easy. *v.t.* soothe, console; make easy.

com'fortable (kŭ-) *a*. at ease in body or mind; promoting comfort.

com'forter (kŭ-) *n*. one who comforts, esp. (*C~*), Holy Ghost; woollen scarf; (U.S.) quilted bed-cover; baby's dummy teat.

com'fortless (kŭ-) *a*. without provision for comfort.

com'frey (kŭ-) *n*. tall bell-flowered ditch-plant.

com'fў (kŭ-) *a*. (colloq.) comfortable.

cŏm'ĭc *a*. of or like comedy; facetious, burlesque, funny. *n*. comic actor or person; children's or other periodical etc. consisting largely of pictorial narratives. ~ **strip**, set of usu. humorous drawings in newspaper etc., esp. forming part of series.

cŏm'ĭcal *a*. mirth-provoking; queer, odd. **cŏmĭcăl'itў** *n*.

cŏm'ĭtў *n*. courtesy. ~ **of nations**, (nations practising) friendly recognition of other nations' law and customs.

cŏmm'a *n*. punctuation-mark (,).

command' (-ah-) *v*. order; issue orders; be in command; restrain or hold in check; have at disposal; look down over, dominate. *n*. order given; exercise or tenure of authority; troops, district, etc. under commander; *in* ~, having or exercising authority.

cŏmmandănt' *n*. commanding officer of depot, fortress, etc.

cŏmmandeer' *v.t.* impress or seize for military purposes; take arbitrarily.

comman'der (-ah-) *n*. one who commands or has command; naval officer ranking next to captain. **~-in-chief** *n*. commander of all land-forces of State, etc.

comman'ding (-ah-) *a*. in command; exalted or impressive; dominant.

command'ment (-ah-) *n*. divine command; mandate, order.

comman'dō (-ah-) *n*. (pl. -*os*), unit of Boer army in Boer War; picked soldier etc. trained for special missions.

commĕm'orāte *v.t.* celebrate in speech or writing or by ceremony; be memorial of. **~ā'tion** *n*. commemorating; ceremony etc. commemorating event etc. **~ative** *a*.

commĕnce' *v*. begin. **~ment** *n*. beginning, start.

commĕnd' *v.t.* entrust, commit; praise. **~able** *a*. praiseworthy. **~ā'tion** *n*.; **~atorў** *a*.

commĕn'surable (-sher-) *a*. measurable by same standard. **~bĭl'itў** *n*.

commĕn'surate (-sher-) *a*. coextensive; proportionate.

cŏmm'ĕnt *n*. explanatory or critical remark; observation; annotation. *v.i.* annotate, expound; make remarks (*upon*).

cŏmm'entarў *n*. running comments on book, performance, etc.

cŏmm'entātor *n*. maker of comments; writer or speaker of commentary.

cŏmm'ĕrce *n*. exchange of merchandise; intercourse, dealings; card game.

commĕr'cial *a*. of or engaged in commerce. *n*. (vulg.) commercial traveller; advertiser's announcement or programme. ~ **traveller**, agent sent out to solicit custom for firm.

cŏmminā'tion n. cursings, denunciation. **cŏmm'inatorў** a. threatening, denunciatory.

comming'le (-nggl) v. mix, unite.

cŏmm'inūte v.t. reduce to minute particles. **~ū'tion** n.

commĭs'erāte (-z-) v. show or express commiseration for; condole with.

commĭserā'tion (-z-) n. compassion, pity. **commĭs'erative** a.

cŏmmissār'iat n. food and stores department of army; food-supply.

cŏmm'issarў n. person deputed by superior power; head of commissariat. **cŏmmissār'ial** a.

commĭ'ssion n. act of committing; task committed to person; body or board of persons constituted to discharge task; warrant appointing commissioned officer; brokerage; percentage on sales etc.; in ~, (of ship) manned, armed, and ready for sea; on ~, (selling, salesman, etc.) remunerated only by commission on sales; out of ~, (of ship) laid up, not equipped etc. for sea, not fit for use or service or activity; Royal C~, body appointed by Crown with duties and powers of holding inquiry. v.t. empower or appoint by commission; commit task etc. to (person), give (artist etc.) commission, give commission for (piece of work); order (ship) for active service.

commissionaire' n. pensioned soldier employed as porter etc.

commĭ'ssioner n. member of permanent government board or other commission; representative of supreme authority in district etc.

commĭt' v.t. entrust; consign, imprison; perpetrate; pledge, involve. **~ment** n. engagement that restricts freedom of action; liability; being committed to a doctrine, cause, or course of action. **~tal** n. committing to prison, grave at burial, etc.

committ'ee (-tĭ) n. body to which consideration or ordering of any matter is referred.

commōde' n. chest of drawers; close-stool.

commō'dious a. roomy.

commŏd'itў n. useful thing, article of trade.

cŏmm'odōre n. naval officer above captain and below rear-admiral; courtesy-title for senior captain of ships cruising together, president of yacht-club, etc.; Air C~ air-officer next above Group Captain.

cŏmm'on a. shared by all; of ordinary kind; occurring often; of inferior quality; vulgar; (of name, noun, etc.) applicable to every individual of class etc., of either gender or sex; (math.) belonging to two or more quantities. n. land belonging to community, esp. unenclosed waste land; right over another's land or water; in ~, in joint use, shared; in ~ with, like. **~ chord,** (mus.) note with its third and perfect fifth (and octave). **~ law,** unwritten law of England derived from ancient usage. **~-law marriage,** of parties not united by ecclesiastical or civil ceremony. **~ metre,** four-lined hymn-stanza, with eight syllables in first and third lines and six in second and fourth. **C~ Prayer,** liturgy prescribed by Church of England. **~-room,** room in school etc. to which members of staff etc. have common access. **~ sense,** good practical sense in everyday matters. **~ soldier,** private. **~ time,** (mus.) with four crotchets in bar.

cŏmm'onage n. right of common; land held in common.

cŏmm'onaltў n. general community, common people.

cŏmm'oner n. person below rank of peer; person with right of common; at Oxford, student not on foundation.

cŏmm'onlў adv. usually, frequently.

cŏmm'onplāce n. trite quotation or everyday saying; platitude. a. lacking originality or individuality.

cŏmm'ons (-z) n.pl. common people; C~, lower house of Parliament; food, diet; short ~, insufficient fare.

cŏmm'onwealth (-wĕl-) n. independent community; C~, republican government in England 1649–1660; (British) C~ (of Nations), association of Great Britain and certain self-governing nations, with their dependencies.

commō'tion n. agitated stir.

cŏmm'ūnal a. of commune or Paris Commune; of community; for community or common use; public; of antagonistic communities in district. **~ism** n.; **~is'tic** a.

cŏmm'ūne[1] n. smallest administrative division in France etc.; (Paris) C~, insurrectionary communalistic government of 1871.

commūne'[2] v.i. hold intimate intercourse with.

commū'nicant n. receiver of Holy Communion; imparter of information.

commū'nicāte v. impart to, have communication with; receive Holy Communion.

commūnicā'tion n. imparting or exchange of information; connexion between places; (mil., pl.) connexion between base and front; (pl.) means of communicating. **~-cord**, chain etc. partially braking passenger train when pulled.

commū'nicative a. given to talking openly; not reserved.

commū'nion (-yon) n. intercourse; fellowship; (Holy) C~, (participation in) Eucharist.

commū'niqué (-kā) n. official intimation or report.

cŏmm'ūnism n. (advocacy of, party etc. advocating) social system based on common ownership of means of production, distribution, and exchange. **~ist** n. & a.; **~is'tic** a.

commū'nity n. joint ownership; body of people forming political or social unity, or living together and practising community of goods, or having race, religion, etc. in common.

cŏmm'ūtātor n. device for altering course of electric current.

commūte' v. exchange, interchange; change (esp. punishment) for, into, to another; travel regularly, esp. daily to and from work etc.

comp. abbr. comparative.

cŏm'păct[1] n. binding agreement or understanding.

compăct'[2] a. close, dense; well-knit; terse. v.t. make compact.

n. (kŏm'-), small case for compressed face-powder, rouge, etc.

compăn'ion[1] (-yon) n. comrade, mate; associate; thing that matches another; member of lowest grade of order of knighthood; person (usu. woman) paid to live with another. **~able** a. sociable. **~ship** n. fellowship.

compăn'ion[2] (-yon) n. (naut.) raised frame on quarter-deck to light cabins etc. below. **~-ladder**, from deck to cabin. **~-way**, staircase to cabin.

com'pany (kŭ-) n. being with another or others; persons assembled together; guests; body of persons combined for commercial or other end; (naut.) entire crew; (mil.) subdivision of infantry battalion.

cŏm'parable a. susceptible of comparison (with); fit to be compared (to).

compă'rative a. of or involving comparison; (gram., of derived form of adj. etc.) expressing higher degree of quality etc. denoted by simple form; that is so when compared with something else. n. comparative degree or form. **~ly** adv.

compāre' v. liken to; estimate similarity of; bear comparison (with). n. comparison.

compă'rison n. comparing; simile; degrees of ~, (gram.) positive, comparative, superlative.

compărt'ment n. division or space partitioned off, esp. in railway-carriage.

com'pass (kŭ-) n. circuit, extent, area, range; instrument with magnetic needle indicating magnetic north and bearings from it; points of the ~, 32 equidistant points marked on card with compass-needle's pivot at centre; (usu. pl.) instrument for describing circles, with two legs jointed together at one end. v.t. go round, surround, hem in; attain or bring about.

compă'ssion n. pity. **~ate** a. feeling or showing compassion. **~āte** v.t. regard or treat with compassion.

compăt'ible a. consistent, able to coexist (with). **~bil'ity** n.

compăt'rĭot *n.* fellow-countryman.

cŏm'peer *n.* (*or* -pēr') equal; comrade.

compĕl' *v.t.* force or constrain; bring about irresistibly.

compĕn'dĭous *a.* abridged; brief.

compĕn'dĭum *n.* (pl. -*s*, -*dia*) abridgement or summary.

cŏm'pĕnsāte *v.* counterbalance; recompense. **~ā'tion** *n.* compensating; amends (*for*). **~ātorў** *a.*

cŏm'père (-ār) *n.* person introducing and commenting on performers in entertainment. *v.* act as compère (to).

compēte' *v.i.* strive against others; vie (*with*), contend (*for*).

cŏm'pĕtence *n.* sufficiency of means; ability; legal capacity.

cŏm'pĕtent *a.* having qualifications required by law or by work in hand.

cŏmpĕtĭ'tion *n.* competing; rivalry, esp. in market; contest. **compĕt'itĭve** *a.*; **compĕt'itor** *n.*

cŏmpīlā'tion *n.* compiling; thing compiled.

compīle' *v.t.* collect together (facts, quotations, etc.).

complā'cency *n.* tranquil pleasure; self-satisfaction.

complā'cent *a.* self-satisfied; in pleasant mood.

complain' *v.i.* emit mournful sound; make complaint.

complaint' *n.* statement that one is aggrieved or dissatisfied; formal protest; bodily ailment.

complai'sance (-z-) *n.* civility; desire of pleasing.

complai'sant (-z-) *a.* disposed to please; obliging.

cŏm'plĕment *n.* what completes or necessarily coexists with; complete set or provision; full number. *v.t.* complete, form complement to. **cŏmplĕmĕn'tarў** *a.*

complēte' *a.* having all its parts; finished; thorough. *v.t.* make whole or perfect; finish.

complē'tion *n.* completing.

cŏm'plĕx *a.* consisting of parts; complicated, involved. *n.* complex whole; (psychol.) repressed group of linked strongly emotional ideas etc. **complĕx'itў** *n.*

complĕ'xion (-kshn) *n.* natural colour and texture of skin, esp. of face; character.

compli'ance *n.* complying.

compli'ant *a.* ready to comply.

cŏm'plĭcāte *v.t.* make complicated, entangle. **cŏm'plĭcātèd** *a.* intricate, involved, hard to unravel. **~ā'tion** *n.* complicated state; complicating circumstances.

compli'citў *n.* accompliceship.

cŏm'plĭment *n.* polite expression or implication of praise; (pl.) formal greetings. *v.t.* pay compliment to; flatter. **~mĕn'tarў** *a.* expressing or conveying compliment; presented as courtesy.

cŏm'plĭn(e) *n.* (eccl.) last service of day.

complў' *v.i.* act in accordance (*with*).

compō'nent *a.* going to making of whole; constituent. *n.* component part.

compôrt' *v. refl. & i.* behave or conduct (oneself); agree or accord *with*.

compōse' (-z) *v.t.* form or constitute; produce in literary or (esp.) musical form; arrange artistically; settle, adjust; make tranquil; reconcile; set up (type), set up in type. **~ed** *a.* quiet, calm. **~èdlў** *adv.* calmly.

compō'ser (-z-) *n.* one who composes, esp. music.

cŏm'posite (-zĭt *or* -zīt) *a.* consisting of different parts or materials; of natural order of plants with 'flowers' resembling daisy; *C~*, (archit.) of fifth (mixed Ionic and Corinthian) order. *n.* composite thing or plant.

cŏmposi'tion (-z-) *n.* composing; thing composed; agreement or compromise; compound artificial substance

compŏs'ĭtor (-z-) *n.* type-setter.

cŏm'pŏst *n.* mixture of natural fertilizing agents. *v.t.* treat with or make into compost.

compō'sure (-zher) *n.* calmness.

cŏm'pōte *n.* fruit in syrup.

compound'¹ *v.* mix or combine into whole; settle by mutual concession; come to terms; *~ a felony*, forbear prosecution for private motive.

cŏm'pound² *a.* composite; compounded; not simple; (chem.) consisting of elements chemically united in fixed proportions. *n.* mixture; compound word or thing; compound substance.

cŏm'pound[3] *n.* enclosure, esp. round buildings.

cŏmpréhĕnd' *v.t.* grasp mentally; be inclusive of, comprise.

cŏmpréhĕn'sible *a.* intelligible.

cŏmpréhĕn'sion *n.* understanding; inclusion; grasp.

cŏmpréhĕn'sive *a.* embracing much, of wide scope; (of school) providing all types of secondary education.

compréss'[1] *v.t.* squeeze together; bring into smaller compass. **compré'ssion** *n.* (esp., in motor engines) compressing of explosive mixture before combustion; **~ion ratio,** ratio of volume of compressed charge to its volume on entering engine.

cŏm'préss[2] *n.* pad for compressing artery etc.; wet cloth applied to relieve inflammation.

comprīse' (-z) *v.t.* contain; include.

cŏm'promīse (-z) *n.* agreement attained by mutual concession. *v.* adjust by mutual concession; bring under suspicion or into danger; make compromise.

comptrō'ller *n.* controller.

compŭl'sion *n.* compelling or being compelled; *under* **~,** because one is compelled.

compŭl'sory *a.* done or acting under compulsion; compelling.

compŭnc'tion *n.* pricking of conscience.

compūte'*v.t.* calculate, reckon, count. **~tā'tion** *n.* **compū'ter** *n.* (esp.) electronic apparatus for making calculations etc.

cŏm'rade (*or* kŭ-) *n.* mate or fellow; companion or associate; (fellow) communist, socialist, etc. **~ship** *n.*

cŏn[1] *v.t.* study or learn.

cŏn[2] *v.t.* direct steering of (ship).

cŏn[3] *n.* (sl.) confidence. *v.t.* dupe, persuade (as) by confidence trickery.

cŏn amōr'e, with enthusiasm. [It.]

conā'tion *n.* desire and volition; exertion of will.

cŏn brio (brē'ō), (mus.) with spirit. [It.]

concāténā'tion *n.* connexion as of

chain-links; string or series of ideas, events, etc.

cŏn'cāve *a.* curved like interior of circle or sphere; hollow. **concăv'ity** *n.*

conceal' *v.t.* hide or keep secret. **~ment** *n.*

concēde' *v.t.* grant; admit as true; allow.

conceit' *n.* one's notion of oneself; vanity; far-fetched comparison. **~ėd** *a.* vain.

conceive' *v.* become pregnant; form in mind, imagine, think; formulate, express.

cŏn'centrāte *v.* bring to or towards common centre; focus (mind, attention, etc.) keep attention etc. fixed *on*; increase strength of (solution etc.) esp. by evaporation. *n.* product of concentration. **~ā'tion** *n.*; **~ation camp,** for detention of internees, political prisoners, etc.

concĕn'tric *a.* having common centre. **cŏncĕntri'city** *n.*

cŏn'cĕpt *n.* idea of class of objects; general notion. **concĕp'tual** *a.* of concepts or mental conception.

concĕp'tion *n.* conceiving, being conceived; thing conceived; idea. **~al** *a.*

concērn' *v.t.* relate to; affect; be relevant to; interest or involve (oneself). *n.* thing that concerns one; (pl.) one's affairs; solicitude, anxiety; firm or enterprise. **~ed** *a.* involved, taking part; troubled. **~ing** *prep.* about. **~ment** *n.*

cŏn'cert *n.* agreement, union; combination of voices etc.; musical entertainment. *v.t.* (-sērt'), arrange by mutual agreement. **concēr'tėd** *a.* (esp.) done in concert.

cŏncerti'na (-tē-) *n.* portable wind-instrument consisting of bellows with finger-studs at ends.

concer'tō (-chār-) *n.* (pl. -os), musical piece for (usu.) solo instrument with orchestral accompaniment.

concé'ssion *n.* conceding; thing conceded; monopoly or similar privilege. **~aire'** *n.* holder of concession.

concĕss'ive *a.* of or tending to or (gram.) expressing concession.

cŏnch (*or* -k) *n.* shellfish; mollusc's shell, esp. spiral shell of large gastropod as triton's trumpet. **~ŏl'ogy** (-k-) *n.* study of shells and shellfish.

concil'iāte *v.t.* propitiate; win over from hostility; reconcile. **~ā'tion** *n.*; **~atory** *a.*

concīse' *a.* brief, condensed.

cŏn'clāve *n.* assembly, meeting-place, of cardinals for papal election; private or secret assembly.

conclude' (-ōōd) *v.* bring or come to end; finish, settle; infer.

conclu'sion (-ōō-) *n.* ending, close; inference; final opinion. **~sive** *a.* convincing.

concŏct' *v.t.* compound; fabricate; make in concert. **~tion** *n.* concocting, concocted thing.

concŏm'itant *a.* going together, accompanying. *n.* concomitant circumstance. **~ance** *n.*

cŏn'cŏrd *n.* agreement, harmony; (mus.) chord satisfactory to ear without other(s) to follow; (gram.) formal agreement between words in gender etc. **concŏr'dant** *a.*

concŏr'dance *n.* agreement; index of words used by author or in book, esp. Bible.

concŏr'dat *n.* compact between church and state.

cŏn'course (-ôrs) *n.* flocking together; crowd, throng; large central open space of building or (esp.) railway-station.

cŏn'crēte *a.* having objective reality; not abstract; made of concrete. *n.* (esp.) composition of gravel, cement, etc. used for building, paving, etc. *v.* build, pave, etc. with concrete; (-krēt'), form into mass, solidify.

concrē'tion *n.* (mass formed by) aggregation esp. of solid particles round nucleus. **~ary** *a.*

cŏn'cūbīne *n.* woman who cohabits with man without marriage; (among polygamous peoples) secondary wife. **concū'binage** *n.*

concū'piscence *n.* sexual lust. **concū'piscent** *a.* lustful.

concūr' *v.i.* coincide; agree. **concū'rrence** *n.*; **concū'rrent** *a.*

concŭss' *v.t.* shake violently; (pass., colloq.) suffer concussion.

concŭ'ssion *n.* violent shaking;

injury to brain, spine, etc. by shock of fall, heavy blow, etc.

condĕmn' (-m) *v.t.* censure, blame; give judicial decision against; sentence (*to*); doom *to*; pronounce unfit for use etc. **cŏndĕmnā'tion** *n.*; **condĕm'natory** *a.*

condĕnse' *v.* make denser or briefer; compress; reduce or be reduced from gas or vapour to liquid. **condensā'tion** *n.* (liquid formed by) condensing.

cŏndĕscĕnd' *v.i.* deign, stoop. **~ing** *a.* (esp.) patronizing.

cŏndĕscĕn'sion *n.* affability to inferiors, patronizing manner.

condign' (-īn) *a.* adequate, fitting.

cŏn'diment *n.* relish or seasoning for use with food.

condi'tion *n.* quality; state; attribute; (pl.) circumstances; stipulation; social rank. *v.t.* stipulate; qualify or limit as condition; be necessary condition of; bring to desired condition, make fit; modify (character, response, etc.) by training etc. **~al** *a.* not absolute; (gram.) expressing condition.

condōle' *v.i.* express sympathy in sorrow. **condō'lence** *n.*

cŏn'dom *n.* contraceptive sheath.

cŏndomin'ium *n.* joint control of State by two or more others; territory so controlled.

condōne' *v.t.* forgive, overlook. **cŏndonā'tion** *n.*

cŏn'dor *n.* large S.-Amer. vulture.

cŏndŏttier'e (-ārī) *n.* (pl. -ri, pr. -rē), leader of troop of mercenaries. [It.]

condūce' *v.i.* lead or contribute *to*. **~cive** *a.*

cŏn'duct *n.* behaviour, manner of conducting oneself, business, etc. *v.t.* (-ŭkt'), lead, escort; control, manage; behave (oneself); transmit (heat etc.) **condŭc'tion** *n.* (phys.) conducting of heat, electricity, etc. **condŭc'tive** *a.*; **~tiv'ity** *n.*

condŭc'tor *n.* leader, guide; director of orchestra or chorus during performance; official in charge of passengers; thing that conducts heat, electricity, etc.

cŏn'duit (-dit *or* -dūit; *or* kŭn-) *n.* channel or pipe, aqueduct.

cōne *n.* tapering figure with circular base; dry scaly more or less cone-shaped fruit of pine, fir, etc.; cone-shaped thing, esp. hoisted as storm-warning, to show wind-direction, etc.

cŏn'făb *n.* (colloq.) confabulation.

confăb'ūlāte *v.i.* talk together. ~ā'tion *n.*

confĕc'tion *n.* mixing, making up; prepared dish; sweetmeat; fashionable or elegant article of dress. ~er *n.* dealer in pastry, sweets, etc. ~erў *n.*

confĕd'eracў *n.* league, conspiracy; league of confederate States.

confĕd'erate *a.* allied; C~ *States* of America, those seceding from Union, 1861. *n.* ally, accomplice. *v.* (-āt), bring or come into alliance. ~ā'tion *n.* permanent union of sovereign States for common external action.

confĕr *v.* bestow; take counsel; meet for discussion.

cŏn'ference *n.* (formal, esp. annual, meeting for) consultation or discussion.

confĕr'ment *n.* conferring.

confĕss' *v.* acknowledge, admit; make formal confession (of); (of priest) hear confession of.

confĕss'ĕdlў *adv.* avowedly.

confĕ'ssion (-shn) *n.* acknowledgement of fact, sin, guilt, etc.; statement of principles. ~al *a.* of confession; *n.* cabinet or stall where priest hears confession.

confĕss'or *n.* one who avows his religion in face of persecution; priest who hears confession.

confĕtt'ĭ *n.pl.* scraps of coloured paper used as missiles in carnival, at wedding, etc.

cŏnfidănt', -ănte' *nn.* person, woman, trusted with private affair.

confīde' *v.* repose confidence *in*; impart secret(s) etc.; entrust *to*. ~dĭng *a.* trustful, unsuspicious.

cŏn'fĭdence *n.* firm trust; imparting of private matter, thing imparted; boldness, impudence. ~ trick, swindle worked by practising on credulous person's trust.

cŏn'fĭdent *a.* feeling or showing assurance; positive.

cŏnfĭdĕn'tial *a.* written etc. in confidence; enjoying confidence.

configūrā'tion *n.* aspect as produced by relative position of parts.

confīne'[1] *v.t.* keep *within, to,* limits; imprison, hold in custody; (pass.) be brought to bed of child.

cŏn'fīne[2] *n.* (usu. pl.) boundaries.

confīne'ment *n.* being confined; imprisonment; childbirth.

confĭrm' *v.t.* make stronger; ratify; corroborate; administer confirmation to. ~ănd' *n.* candidate for confirmation. ~ā'tion *n.* corroborating circumstance or statement; rite in which persons confirm vows made for them at baptism. ~ative, ~atorў *aa.*

cŏn'fĭscāte *v.t.* seize (private property) for public treasury; seize as by authority. ~ā'tion *n.*

cŏnflagrā'tion *n.* great and destructive fire.

cŏn'flict *n.* fight; collision; clashing; *in* ~, discrepant. *v.i.* (-ĭkt'), be at odds or inconsistent (*with*); struggle.

cŏn'fluent (-ŏŏent) *a.* merging into one. *n.* one of confluent streams etc. ~ence *n.*

confôrm' *v.* adapt; make like; comply with rules or general custom. ~able *a.* adapted or corresponding (*to*). ~ā'tion *n.* conforming; structure. ~ĭst *n.* conformer to Anglican usages. ~itў *n.* likeness; compliance.

confound' *v.t.* mix up, confuse; astound; baffle; (imper., as mild oath) curse; (*p.p.*) accursed, disagreeable.

cŏnfratĕr'nitў *n.* brotherhood.

confront' (-ŭnt) *v.t.* bring face to face *with*; face esp. in hostility or defiance. ~ā'tion *n.*

confūse' (-z) *v.t.* throw into disorder; obscure, mix up.

confū'sion *n.* confused state; tumult; discomfiture.

confūte' *v.t.* prove false or wrong. cŏnfūtā'tion *n.*

congé (kawṅ'zhā) *n.* dismissal without ceremony. [F]

congeal' (-j-) *v.* solidify by cooling; stiffen, coagulate. cŏngélā'tion *n.*

cŏn'géner (-j-) *n.* thing or person of same kind.

congē′nĭal (-j-) *a.* of kindred temper; suiting one's disposition; pleasurable *to.* **~ăl′ĭtў** *n.*

congĕn′ĭtal (-j-) *a.* belonging to one from birth.

cŏng′er (-ngg-) *n.* large sea eel.

cŏnge′ries (-jĕrĭēz; *or* -rēz; *or* kŏn′-) *n.* (pl. same), collection; mass, heap.

congĕs′tėd (-j-) *a.* overcrowded; over--charged with blood.

congĕs′tion (-jĕschon) *n.* abnormal accumulation of blood in organ, population in district, etc.

conglŏm′erate *a. & n.* (rock) formed of rounded pebbles etc. cemented together. *v.* (-āt), collect into coherent mass. **~ā′tion** *n.*

congrăt′ūlāte *v.t.* address with expression of sympathetic joy (*on* occasion etc.). **~ā′tion** *n.* congratulating; (pl.) congratulatory expressions. **~atorў** *a.*

cŏng′rėgāte (-ngg-) *v.* flock together, assemble.

cŏngrėgā′tion (-ngg-) *n.* assemblage; general assembly of members of university; body of persons assembled or habitually assembling for religious worship. **~al** *a.* of congregation; *C~*, of Congregationalism. **C~alism** *n.* system of ecclesiastical government under which legislative, disciplinary, and judicial functions are vested in individual congregation. **C~alist** *n.*

cŏng′rėss (-ngg-) *n.* formal meeting of delegates for discussion; *C~*, (session of) national legislative body of U.S. etc. **C~man**, member of (esp. lower house of) Congress. **congrė′ssional** *a.*

cŏng′ruence (-nggrŏō-), **congru′ĭtў** (-nggrōō-) *nn.* accordance; harmonious relation; correspondence. **cŏng′ruent, cŏng′ruous** *aa.*

cŏn′ĭc *a.* cone-shaped, of cone. **~ section**, figure formed by section of right circular cone by plane. **~al** *a.* cone-shaped. **cŏn′ĭcs** *n.* study of cones and conic sections.

cō′nĭfer *n.* coniferous tree.

conĭf′erous *a.* cone-bearing.

conj. *abbr.* conjugation; conjunction.

conjĕc′ture *n.* guessing, guess. *v.* make conjecture, guess. **conjĕc′tural** *a.* depending on conjecture.

conjoin′ *v.* make into or become single whole. **conjoint′** *a.* conjoined, combined.

cŏn′jugal (-ŏŏ-) *a.* of marriage; between married persons.

cŏn′jugāte (-ŏŏ-) *v.* inflect (verb); join in conjugation. *a.* (-ĭt), conjoint; growing in pairs.

cŏnjugā′tion (-ŏŏ-) *n.* joining together; (biol.) fusion of two cells etc. for reproduction; scheme of verbal inflexion.

conjŭnct′ *a.* joined, joint, associated.

conjŭnc′tion *n.* conjoining; simultaneous occurrence; word used to connect sentences or clauses or to co-ordinate words in same clause.

cŏnjunctī′va *n.* mucous membrane lining inner eyelid. **~tĭvī′tĭs** *n.* inflammation of this.

conjŭnc′tĭve *a.* joining, uniting; (gram.) of nature of or acting as conjunction.

conjŭnc′ture *n.* position of affairs at particular moment.

cŏnjurā′tion (-ŏŏ-) *n.* solemn entreaty; incantation.

conjure′[1] (-oor) *v.t.* appeal solemnly to.

conjure[2] (kŭn′jer) *v.* produce magical effects; do sleight-of-hand tricks; **~ up**, cause to appear to mind, fancy, etc.

conjuror (kŭn′jerer) *n.* adept at sleight-of-hand.

cŏnk *n.* (sl.) nose.

cŏnk *v.i.* (sl.) break down, give *out.*

cŏnk′er *n.* horse-chestnut; (pl.) children's game in which horse--chestnuts are struck together until one is broken.

cŏn′-măn *n.* (sl.) confidence trickster.

Conn. *abbr.* Connecticut.

cŏnn′āte *a.* congenital; (of leaves) united at base.

connĕct′ *v.* join, link, unite; (*p.p.*, of narrative etc.) having internal connexion, coherent. **~ĭve** *a.* serving as connexion.

connĕc′tion (-kshon), **connĕ′xion** *n.* being linked together or in communication or intercourse; connecting part; connecting train, steamer, etc.; family relationship.

cŏnn′ing-tower *n.* pilot-house of warship; superstructure of submarine used for navigation etc. on or near surface.

connive' *v.i.* wink *at* (what one ought to oppose). **conni'vance** *n.*

connoisseur' (-nosēr) *n.* critical judge, esp. of fine arts.

connōte' *v.t.* imply, betoken; mean; include in its meaning. **~tā'tion** *n.*; **~tative** *a.*

connū'bial *a.* connected with marriage.

cō'noid *a.* more or less conical. *n.* conoid object; solid generated by revolution of conic section about its axis.

con'quer (-ngker) *v.* overcome; acquire by conquest; master one's difficulties or passions. **~or** *n.*

con'quest *n.* conquering, what is won by it; winning of person to affection, person so won.

consanguin'eous (-nggw-) *a.* related by birth; near of kin.

consanguin'ity (-nggw-) *n.* kinship.

con'science (-shens) *n.* moral sense of right and wrong; consciousness of moral quality of one's actions or motives. **~ money**, paid to relieve conscience, esp. in respect of evaded tax etc. **~-stricken**, overcome with remorse.

conscien'tious *a.* obedient to conscience; scrupulous. **~ objector**, person who pleads conscience as reason for objecting to taking of oath or to military service.

con'scious (-shus) *a.* aware, knowing, with mental faculties awake or active; consciously performed, felt, etc.; self-conscious. **~ly** *adv*; **~ness** *n.*

conscribe' *v.t.* enrol by conscription.

con'script *n.* conscripted person. *a.* conscripted. *v.t.* (-ipt'), conscribe.

conscrip'tion *n.* compulsory enlistment for national service, esp. in armed forces.

con'secrate *v.t.* set apart as sacred (*to*); sanctify; devote *to*. **~ā'tion** *n.* consecrating, being consecrated; ordination to sacred office, esp. of bishop; devotion.

consec'ūtive *a.* following continuously; (gram.) expressing consequence.

consen'sus *n.* agreement (*of* opinions etc.).

consent' *v.i.* agree *to*; acquiesce. *n.* agreement; compliance; permission.

consen'tient (-shnt) *a.* agreeing.

con'sequence *n.* that which follows from any cause or principle; importance; influential position.

con'sequent *a.* that results; following as consequence.

consequen'tial (-shl) *a.* following as result or inference; self-important. **~tial'ity** (-shi-) *n.*

con'sequently *adv.* as a result; accordingly; therefore.

conser'vancy *n.* board controlling river, port, etc.

conserva'tion *n.* preserving, conserving; **~ of energy**, principle that total energy of any system of bodies can be neither increased nor diminished.

conser'vative *a.* of conserving tendency, opposed to change; (of estimate) moderate; *C~*, of or belonging to English political party believing in maintenance of existing institutions. *n.* member of Conservative party; conservative person. **~tism** *n.*

conser'vatoire (-twahr) *n.* public institution in France etc. teaching music and declamation.

con'servātor *n.* conserver; member of conservancy; official custodian.

conser'vatory *n.* greenhouse for tender plants; conservatoire.

conserve' *v.t.* preserve; keep from harm, decay, or loss. *n.* (usu. pl.) preserve.

consid'er *v.* contemplate; deliberate thoughtfully; reckon with, take into account; show consideration for. **consid'ering** *prep.* in view of.

consid'erable *a.* of some importance; much, no small.

consid'erate *a.* thoughtful for feelings or rights of others.

considera'tion *n.* considering; thing worth considering; thing given or done as inducement; considerateness.

consign' *v.t.* commit or hand over; transmit, send by rail etc. **~ee'**, **~or** *nn.* person to whom, by whom, goods are consigned. **~ment** *n.* consigning, goods consigned.

consist' *v.i.* be composed *of*; be comprised *in*; be compatible *with*. **~ence** *n.* degree of density, esp. in thick liquids; firmness, solidity. **~ency** *n.* being consistent; consistence. **~ent** *a.* compatible, not contradictory; constant to same principles.

consis'tory (or kŏn'-) *n.* senate of all cardinals presided over by Pope; *C~ (Court)*, Anglican bishop's court for ecclesiastical offences etc.; Lutheran supervisory clerical board; court of presbyters.

consolā'tion *n.* alleviation of grief or disappointment. **~ prize, race,** etc., for unsuccessful competitors.

consō'latory (*or* -ŏl-) *a.* giving consolation.

console'[1] *v.t.* bring consolation to.

cŏn'sōle[2] *n.* tall bracket supporting cornice; frame containing key-boards, stops, etc. of organ. **~ mirror, table,** supported against wall by bracket.

consŏl'idāte *v.* solidify; strengthen; combine (statutes, debts, etc.) into one. **~ā'tion** *n.*

consŏls' (-z) *n.pl.* Government consolidated stock.

cŏnsŏmm'é (-ā) *n.* clear soup.

cŏn'sonance *n.* agreement in sound, musical concord; agreement in meaning, taste, etc.

cŏn'sonant *a.* agreeable, concordant, consistent. *n.* (letter etc. expressing) non-vowel sound produced by stoppage or constriction of air-stream in mouth-cavity or by lips. **cŏnsonăn'tal** *a.*

cŏn'sōrt *n.* spouse; partner; ship sailing with another. *v.i.* (-ŏrt') associate or keep company (*with*); be in harmony.

conspĕc'tus *n.* general view; synopsis.

conspic'ūous *a.* striking to eye, readily seen; outstanding.

conspī'racy *n.* plot or plotting for evil-doing. **~ator** *n.*

conspīre' *v.i.* take part in conspiracy; agree together.

con'stable (kŭ-) *n.* (hist.) great officer of royal household; policeman of lowest rank; *Chief C~,* head of police force of county etc.

constăb'ūlary *a. & n.* (organized body) of police.

cŏn'stancy *n.* faithfulness; tenacious adherence; steadiness.

cŏn'stant *a.* not subject to variation; continual; firm. *n.* quantity that does not vary. **~ly** *adv.* always; often.

cŏnstellā'tion *n.* fixed stars forming group to eye.

cŏnsternā'tion *n.* paralysing sense of calamity.

cŏn'stipāte *v.t.* affect with constipation. **~ā'tion** *n.* difficulty in evacuating bowels.

constit'ūency *n.* body electing representative; place represented.

constit'ūent *a.* making part of whole; appointing, electing. *n.* constituent part; member of elective body; voter.

cŏn'stitūte *v.t.* appoint, make into; establish; be essence or components of.

cŏnstitū'tion *n.* constituent parts, essential nature; bodily predisposition; form in which State is organized; system of laws and customs.

cŏnstitū'tional *a.* of or due to one's constitution; in harmony with constitution of State. *n.* walk taken as healthy exercise. **~ism, ~ist** *nn.*

cŏn'stitūtive *a.* having power to constitute; constituent.

constrain' *v.t.* compel, force; confine. **~ed** *a.* forced, embarrassed.

constraint' *n.* compulsion; confinement; repression of feeling; embarrassment.

constrict' *v.t.* compress, contract, narrow; encircle and squeeze. **~tion** *n.*; **~tive** *a.* **~tor** *n.* constrictive muscle; boa-constrictor.

construct' *v.t.* fit together, frame, build; (geom.) draw.

construc'tion *n.* thing constructed; syntactical connexion between verbs or prepositions and their objects etc.; interpretation. **~al** *a.*

construc'tive *a.* of construction; tending to construct, not destructive.

construe' (-ōō) *v.t.* combine grammatically *with*; interpret; translate word for word.

cŏnsubstăn'tial *a.* of one substance,

esp. of three Persons of Trinity. **cŏnsubstăntia′tion** (-shĭă-) *n.* doctrine of presence of body and blood of Christ together with bread and wine in Eucharist.

cŏn′sul *n.* either of two elected magistrates exercising supreme power in Roman republic; State's agent in foreign town. **cŏn′sūlar** *a.* of consul.

cŏn′sūlate *n.* office of consul; consul's official residence.

consŭlt′ *v.* take counsel (*with*); seek information or advice from. **~ant** *a.* & *n.* (physician etc.) to whom others refer their patients for advice; (engineer etc.) giving professional advice to others or to public. **cŏnsultā′tion** *n.*; **~ative** *a.*

consūme′ *v.* destroy, use up, eat or drink; waste away; be exhausted.

consū′mĕdlў *adv.* excessively.

consū′mer *n.* user of product. **~ goods**, those directly satisfying human needs or desires.

consŭmm′ate¹ *a.* of highest perfection or completeness.

cŏn′summāte² *v.t.* complete (esp. marriage by sexual intercourse). **~ā′tion** *n.*

consŭmp′tion *n.* consuming; wasting disease, esp. pulmonary tuberculosis.

consŭmp′tive *a.* tending to or affected with tuberculosis etc. *n.* consumptive person.

cŏn′tact *n.* touch; connexion; (med.) person who has been exposed to contagious disease; (usu. pl.) person with whom one comes into touch. *v.t.* get into touch with. **~ lens**, small lens worn on eyeball.

contā′gion (-jn) *n.* communication of disease by contact; corrupting influence. **~gious** *a.*

contain′ *v.t.* have within, include; comprise; restrain; enclose; keep (enemy force) to limited area. **~ment. ~er** *nn.*

contăm′ĭnāte *v.t.* pollute, infect. **~ā′tion** *n.*

contăng′ŏ (-ngg-) *n.* (pl. *-os*), percentage paid by buyer of stock for postponement of transfer.

contĕmn′ (-m) *v.t.* feel contempt for; scornfully disregard.

cŏn′templāte *v.t.* survey steadily with eyes or mind; have in view. **~ā′tion** *n.* meditative state.

cŏn′templātive (*or* kontĕm′-) *a.* meditative; devoted to religious contemplation and prayer.

contĕmporā′néous *a.* belonging to or existing at same time.

contĕm′porarў *a.* of these times; equal in age; contemporaneous. *n.* contemporary person or newspaper.

contĕmpt′ *n.* feeling of scorn; disrespect; disobedience to lawful authority.

contĕmp′tĭble *a.* deserving contempt.

contĕmp′tūous *a.* feeling or showing contempt; apt to despise.

contĕnd′ *v.i.* strive, struggle; compete; argue (*with*), maintain (*that*).

contĕnt′¹ *a.* satisfied (*with*); willing (*to* do). *v.t.* satisfy; **~ oneself**, be satisfied (*with*). *n.* contented state, satisfaction. **~ĕd** *a.*; **~ment** *n.*

cŏn′tĕnt² *n.* capacity, amount contained; substance (of art etc., opp. *form*); (pl.) what is contained, esp. in book, document, etc.

contĕn′tion *n.* strife, controversy, rivalry; point etc. contended for in argument etc.

contĕn′tious *a.* given to or involving contention.

contĕr′minous *a.* having common boundary or end.

cŏn′tĕst *n.* contending; competition. *v.t.* (-ĕst′), dispute; contend or compete for. **contĕs′tant** *n.*

cŏn′tĕxt *n.* what precedes and follows word or passage. **contĕx′tūal** *a.*

cŏntĭgū′itў *n.* contact; nearness.

contĭg′ūous *a.* adjoining, next (*to*); neighbouring.

cŏn′tĭnent¹ *a.* temperate; chaste. **~ence** *n.*

cŏn′tĭnent² *n.* mainland of Europe; any of main land masses of earth.

cŏntĭnĕn′tal *a.* of or characteristic of continent, esp. mainland of Europe. *n.* inhabitant of continent.

contĭn′gencў *n.* being contingent; contingent event etc., chance occurrence.

contĭn′gent (-j-) *a.* of uncertain occurrence; incidental; dependent (*on*); conditional. *n.* body or group contributed to army, larger group, etc.

contin'ūal *a.* occurring on every occasion; seeming incessant.

contin'ūance *n.*. continuing in existence or operation; duration.

continūā'tion *n.* going on with or resuming something; thing that continues something else. **contin'ūative** *a.*

contin'ūe *v.* go on with; remain in existence; take up again. **continū'ity** *n.* uninterrupted connexion or series.

contin'ūous *a.* connected without break; uninterrupted.

contin'ūum *n.* (philos.) continuous whole.

contôrt' *v.t.* twist or force out of normal shape. ~**tion** *n.* ~**tionist** *n.* gymnast adopting contorted postures.

cŏn'tour (-oor) *n.* outline of figure, object, coast, etc.; line representing horizontal contour of earth's surface at given elevation.

cŏn'trabănd *n.* prohibited traffic; smuggled goods. *a.* forbidden to be imported or exported.

cŏntracĕp'tion *n.* prevention of uterine conception. ~**tive** *a.* & *n.* of or (means of) procuring contraception.

cŏn'trăct[1] *n.* mutual, esp. business, agreement; agreement enforceable by law; (bridge) declarer's undertaking to make so many tricks; ~ (*bridge*), form of bridge in which only tricks bid count towards game.

contrăct'[2] *v.* make contract; incur (disease, debt); form (habit etc.); draw together; make or become smaller; shorten.

contrăc'tile (*or* -ī-) *a.* capable of or producing contraction.

contrăc'tion *n.* shrinking; diminution; word-shortening or contracted word.

contrăc'tor *n.* one who undertakes contract, esp. in building, engineering, etc. or for public body; contracting muscle.

contrăc'tūal *a.* of (nature of) contract.

cŏntradict' *v.* deny; oppose verbally; be at variance with.

cŏntradic'tion *n.* verbal denial; direct opposition; inconsistency.

cŏntradic'tory *a.* given to contradiction; conflicting.

cŏntradistinc'tion *n.* distinction by contrast.

cŏntradisting'uïsh (-nggw-) *v.t.* distinguish by contrast.

contrăl'tō *n.* (pl. -*os*), lowest female voice; contralto singer.

cŏntrăp'tion *n.* (sl.) queer machine or appliance.

cŏntrapŭn'tal *a.* of or in counterpoint.

cŏntrarī'ĕtў *n.* contrariness.

contrār'iwīse (-z) *adv.* on the other hand; in the opposite way.

cŏn'trarў *a.* opposed in nature or tendency or direction; (-ār'ĭ) perverse, vexatious. *n. the* opposite. *adv.* in opposition (*to*).

cŏn'trast (-ah-) *n.* difference between things as shown by placing them against each other; thing in marked contrast to another. *v.* (-ahst'), put in or subject to or be in contrast. ~**as'tў** *a.* having marked contrasts of light and shade.

cŏntravēne' *v.t.* infringe, conflict with. ~**vĕn'tion** *n.* infringement.

contretemps (kawn'trĕtahn) *n.* unlucky accident; embarrassing occurrence. [F]

contrĭb'ūte *v.* give to common stock; ~ *to*, have part or share in.

cŏntribū'tion *n.* payment made in aid of common fund or collection; something contributed.

contrĭb'ūtor *n.* one who contributes (esp. literary work).

contrĭb'ūtorў *a.* that contributes, contributing.

cŏn'trīte *a.* sorrowing for sin.

contrī'tion *n.* sorrow for sin.

contrī'vance *n.* contriving; contrived article or appliance.

contrīve' *v.* devise, think out; plan, manage.

contrōl' *n.* restraint; check, means of checking, supervision; (spiritualism) personality controlling medium's words etc.; place where vehicles etc. in race must stop for official examination; (usu. pl.) apparatus by which machine, esp. car or aircraft, is controlled. *v.t.* have control of; govern; restrain.

contrō'ller *n.* officer controlling expenditure; one that governs.

controvēr'sial *a.* of, open or given to, controversy. ~ist *n.*

contrŏv'ersy (*or* kŏn'-) *n.* disputation; dispute; argument, esp. conducted in writing.

controvērt' *v.t.* call in question; dispute truth of.

cŏn'tūmacў *n.* stubborn disobedience. ~ā'cious *a.*

cŏn'tūmelў *n.* insulting language or treatment. ~ē'lious *a.*

contūse' (-z) *v.t.* bruise.

contū'sion *n.* bruise.

conŭn'drum *n.* riddle.

cŏnūrbā'tion *n.* group of towns united by expansion.

cŏnvalĕsce' *v.i.* be convalescent.

cŏnvalĕs'cence *n.* convalescent state.

cŏnvalĕs'cent *a.* recovering from sickness. *n.* convalescent person.

convenances (kawn'venahns) *n.pl.* conventional propriety. [F]

convēne' *v.* convoke, assemble.

convē'nience *n.* what suits one; useful appliance; water-closet; (pl.) material comforts.

convē'nient *a.* fit, suitable; not troublesome; conveniently near.

cŏn'vent *n.* religious community, esp. of women; its house.

convĕn'ticle *n.* meeting or meeting-house, esp. of dissenters.

convĕn'tion *n.* convening; assembly for transaction of business; (esp. formal and artificial) accepted usage.

convĕn'tional *a.* depending on convention(s); not natural or spontaneous or (of weapons etc.) nuclear. ~alism, ~alist, ~ăl'itў *nn.*

convĕn'tūal *a.* of convents.

convērge' *v.i.* tend to meet in point; approach nearer together; ~ on, tend or move towards from different points. ~ent *a.*; ~ence *n.*

convēr'sable *a.* pleasant, easy, in conversation.

cŏn'versant (*or* -vēr'-) *a.* well acquainted *with.*

conversā'tion *n.* talk, interchange of thoughts and words. ~ piece, portrait of group of figures. ~al *a.* of or in conversation; colloquial. ~alist *n.* practised talker.

cŏnversazĭō'nė (-săts-) *n.* social meeting of scientific or artistic kind.

convērse'[1] *v.i.* talk. *n.* (kŏn'-), (arch.) talk, communion.

cŏn'vērse[2] *a.* turned round or upside down; put the other way. *n.* converse statement or position.

convēr'sion *n.* converting, being converted.

convērt' *v.t.* change (*into*); cause to turn (*to* faith, opinion, etc.); (Rugby footb.) kick goal from (try). *n.* (kŏn'-), person converted, esp. to religious faith.

convēr'tible *a.* that may be converted; (of currency) freely exchangeable for gold etc. at fixed price; (of car) with collapsible hood. *n.* convertible car.

cŏn'vĕx *a.* curved like outside of sphere or circle. convĕx'itў *n.* convex surface.

convey' (-vā) *v.t.* transport, carry; transmit; impart; seem to mean; transfer by deed or legal process.

convey'ance (-āans) *n.* vehicle, carriage; (document effecting) transference of property. ~ancing *n.* branch of law dealing with titles and their transference.

convĭct'[1] *v.t.* prove or declare guilty.

cŏn'vĭct[2] *n.* sentenced criminal.

convĭc'tion *n.* convicting; verdict of guilty; firm belief.

convince' *v.t.* bring to a belief; produce conviction in.

convĭv'ial *a.* of or for feast; festive. convĭviăl'itў *n.*

cŏnvocā'tion *n.* convoking; assembly, esp. ceremonial or deliberative or legislative assembly of qualified members of university.

convōke' *v.t.* call together; summon to assembly.

cŏn'volūte(d) *aa.* coiled or spiral.

cŏnvolū'tion *n.* coiled state; one turn of coil or spiral.

convŏl'vūlus *n.* kinds of twining plant.

cŏnvoy' (*or* kŏn'-) *v.t.* escort, esp. ships etc. with armed force. *n.* (kŏn'-), escort; company, number of ships, etc., under escort.

convŭlse' *v.t.* affect with convulsions.

convŭl'sion *n.* (usu. pl.) bodily seizure with muscular spasms, esp. as disorder of infants; violent agitation; (pl.) uncontrollable laughter.

convŭl'sive *a.* as in convulsions.

cō'nў, -ey *n.* (pl. *-ies, -eys*), rabbit; hyrax.

coō *n. & v.* (make) soft murmuring sound (as) of doves.

coo'ee' *n. & v.i.* (make) call adapted as signal from Australian aborigines.

cook *v.* prepare food, prepare (food) by heat; undergo cooking; (colloq.) tamper with or falsify (accounts etc.). *n.* one whose business is to cook food; one who cooks; (chess) second solution to problem. ~-book, (U.S.) cookery-book. ~-house, camp kitchen; ship's galley. ~shop, eating-house. ~er *n.* stove or vessel for cooking; fruit etc. suitable for cooking.

cook'erў *n.* art of cooking. ~-book, of recipes and instructions in cookery.

cook'ie *n.* (U.S.) sweet biscuit.

cool *a.* cold to slight degree; unperturbed, self-possessed; lacking zeal or cordiality. *v.* make or become cool; ~ *one's heels*, be kept waiting. ~er *n.* (esp., sl.) prison.

coo'labah *n.* kinds of Australian gum-tree.

coo'lant *n.* liquid used to lessen friction of cutting-tool; motor-cooling medium.

coo'lie *n.* native hired labourer in India, China, etc.

coomb, combe (koōm) *n.* hollow on flank of hill; steep valley.

coōn *n.* raccoon; (U.S. colloq.) Negro.

coōp *n.* cage or pen for confining fowls. *v.t.* put in coop; shut up in narrow compass.

cō-ŏp' *n.* (colloq.) co-operative society or shop.

coo'per *n.* maker or repairer of casks, pails, etc. *v.t.* repair (casks etc.). ~age *n.* cooper's work(-shop) or charges.

cō-ŏp'erāte *v.i.* work together; concur in producing effect. ~ā'tion, ~ātor *nn.*

cō-ŏp'erative *a.* co-operating, willing to co-operate, helpful; of co-operation or co-operators; jointly owned by and managed for use and profit of members of organized group. *n.* co-operative association or enterprise. ~ **society**, trading etc. organization in which profits are shared among members esp. as dividend on purchases. ~ **store**, belonging to co-operative society.

cō-ŏpt' *v.t.* elect into body by votes of existing members. ~tion *n.*; ~tive *a.*

cō-ôr'dinate *a.* equal in status. *n.* (pl.) set of distances from known points etc. sufficing in combination to fix thing's position. *v.t.* make co-ordinate, bring into proper relation. ~ā'tion, ~ātor *nn.*; ~ative *a.*

coōt *n.* kinds of water-bird.

cŏp *v.t.* (sl.) catch. *n.* capture; policeman.

cō'pal *n.* kinds of resin used for varnish.

cōpârt'ner *n.* partner, associate. ~ship *n.* (esp.) system of profit-sharing with employees.

cōpe¹ *n.* vestment like long semi-circular cloak. *v.t.* furnish with coping.

cōpe² *v.i.* contend on even terms or successfully (*with*).

cō'pĕck *n.* hundredth of rouble.

cō'ping *n.* top course of masonry or brickwork, usu. sloping. ~-**stone**, stone used in coping; finishing touch.

cō'pious *a.* plentiful; abounding in words; exuberant.

cŏpp'er¹ *n.* (sl.) policeman.

cŏpp'er² *n.* metal of brownish-pink colour; bronze coin; (attrib.) of copper. *v.t.* cover with copper. ~plate, copper plate for engraving or etching; print taken from it; sloping rounded cursive handwriting.

cŏpp'eras *n.* ferrous sulphate.

cŏpp'ice, cŏpse *n.* small wood of undergrowth and small trees.

cŏp'ra *n.* dried coconut kernels.

cŏp'rolīte *n.* fossil dung.

coprŏph'agous *a.* feeding on dung.

copse : see **coppice**.

Cŏpt *n.* native Egyptian or Ethiopian Christian. ~ic *a.*

cŏp'ūla *n.* part of verb *be* connecting subject with predicate.

cŏp'ūlāte *v.i.* unite sexually. ~ā'tion *n.*; ~ātorў *a.*

cŏp′ūlatĭve *a*. serving as copula, connecting predicate with subject; of sexual union.

cŏp′ў *n*. reproduction, imitation; pattern of handwriting; matter to be set up in type; written or printed specimen (of book etc.). *v*. make copy of; imitate; crib. ~-book, book of handwriting exercises. ~-writer, composer of wording of advertisements.

cŏp′ўhōld *n*. land tenure resting on custom of manor. *a*. held by this tenure. ~er *n*.

cŏp′ўist *n*. imitator, transcriber.

cŏp′ўright *n*. exclusive right to produce or reproduce literary, musical, etc. work by making copies, performance, etc. *a*. protected by copyright. *v.t*. secure copyright of.

cō′quetrў (-kĭt-) *n*. coquetting, coquettish behaviour.

coquette′ (-kĕt) *n*. woman who trifles with men's affections. *v.i*. play coquette; trifle *with*. coquĕtt′ish *a*.

Cor. *abbr*. Corinthians; Coriolanus.

cŏ′racle *n*. boat of canvas- or skin--covered wicker.

cŏ′ral *n*. hard substance secreted by kinds of sea polyp; piece of coral as ornament etc.; unimpregnated roe of lobster. *a*. of, of (red) colour of, coral. ~-island, one formed by growth of coral.

cŏ′rallīne *a*. of or like coral.

cŏr anglais (ahng′glā) *n*. tenor oboe.

cŏr′bel *n*. stone or timber projection from wall. ~-table, projecting course resting on corbels.

cŏr′bĭe *n*. (Sc.) raven, carrion crow.

cŏrd *n*. thin rope or thick string; measure of cut wood; (pl.) corduroy breeches. *v.t*. secure with cord; make (wood) into cords. ~age *n*. cords or ropes.

cŏr′date *a*. heart-shaped.

cŏr′dĭal *a*. stimulating; heartfelt, sincere, hearty, warm. *n*. cordial drink; liqueur; heartening influence. cŏrdĭăl′itў *n*.

cŏr′dīte *n*. smokeless explosive.

cŏr′don *n*. line or ring of police etc.; ornamental cord or braid; fruit--tree trained to grow as single stem.

cŏr′duroy *n*. ribbed cotton velvet; (pl.) corduroy trousers; corduroy road. ~ road, made of tree-trunks laid transversely.

cŏrd′wainer *n*. shoemaker.

cŏre *n*. heart or innermost part of anything; horny capsule containing seeds of apple etc.; central part cut out, esp. of rock in boring; *hard* ~, irreducible minimum. *v.t*. remove core of.

cō-relĭ′gionist (-jo-) *n*. person of same religion.

cŏreŏp′sĭs *n*. plant with rayed usu. yellow flowers.

cō-respŏn′dent *n*. person proceeded against together with respondent in divorce suit.

cŏr′gi (-gi) *n*. small Welsh breed of dog.

cŏriā′ceous *a*. leathery.

cŏriăn′der *n*. plant with fruit (~ *seed*) used as flavouring.

Corin′thian *a*. of Corinth; (archit.) of most ornate of five orders.

cŏrk *n*. thick light tough elastic bark of ~-oak ; piece of this as bottle--stopper, float, etc. *a*. made of cork. *v.t*. stop (*up*) with or as with cork. ~age *n*. charge for serving bottles of wine etc. in restaurant etc. ~ed *a*. (of wine) spoiled by defective cork. ~er *n*. (sl.) something astounding, esp. notable lie.

cŏrk′screw (-ōō) *n*. implement for extracting corks. *v*. twist or (cause to) proceed spirally.

corm *n*. swollen underground base of stem in crocus etc.

cŏr′morant *n*. voracious sea-bird; rapacious person.

cŏrn[1] *n*. grain or seed of cereal plant; (collect.) cereals (esp. wheat) in growth, their seed after threshing; (U.S.) maize. *v.t*. preserve (meat) by sprinkling with salt. ~-chandler, retail dealer in corn. ~-cob, (centre of) ear of maize. ~-crake, landrail. ~-factor, corn merchant. ~-flour, fine-ground maize flour. ~-flower, blue-flowered plant growing among corn. ~-meal, (U.S.) maize meal. ~-pone, (U.S.) kind of maize-bread. ~-starch (U.S.) starch made from maize, esp. as fine cornflour.

cŏrn[2] *n*. horny tender place with hard centre, esp. on foot.

Corn. *abbr.* Cornwall.

cŏr′nĕa *n.* horny transparent structure in front of iris.

cŏr′nel *n.* kinds of hedgerow shrub and small tree.

cŏrnē′lĭan, cȧr- *n.* red or reddish variety of chalcedony.

cŏr′ner *n.* angle of room, box etc.; remote place; humble niche; monopolistic buying up of whole of commodity; *drive into a* ~, force into position from which there is no escape. *v.t.* drive into corner; establish corner in (commodity). ~**-boy,** street loafer. ~**-stone,** one of those forming salient angle of wall; indispensable thing or part.

cŏr′nĕt[1] *n.* (player of) brass musical instrument of trumpet class with piston-operated valves; conical wafer of ice-cream.

cŏr′nĕt[2] *n.* (hist.) junior officer of cavalry troop.

cŏr′nĭce *n.* horizontal moulded projection crowning (part of) building; moulding of room-wall just below ceiling; overhanging mass of hardened snow on mountain precipice.

cŏrnūcō′pĭa *n.* horn of plenty.

cŏr′nў *a.* (colloq.) old-fashioned; trite, sentimental.

corŏll′a *n.* flower's inner envelope consisting of whorl of petals.

corŏll′arў *n.* proposition that follows from one proved; natural consequence.

corō′na[1] *n.* halo of light round sun or moon, esp. that seen in total eclipse of sun.

corō′na[2] *n.* brand of Havana cigar. **P.**

cŏ′ronăch (-k) *n.* Highland dirge.

cŏ′ronal *n.* circlet for head. *a.* of crown of head.

cŏ′ronary *a.* resembling, encircling like, crown. ~ **artery,** one supplying blood to heart tissues. ~ **thrombosis,** blockage of coronary artery by blood-clot.

cŏronā′tion *n.* ceremony of crowning sovereign.

cŏ′roner *n.* officer holding inquest on corpse to ascertain cause of death.

cŏ′ronĕt *n.* peer's or peeress's small crown. ~**ĕd** *a.*

Corp. *abbr.* Corporal.

cŏr′poral[1] *n.* non-commissioned officer below sergeant.

cŏr′poral[2] *a.* of body. ~ **punishment,** whipping etc. ~**ăl′itў** *n.* being or having body.

cŏr′porate *a.* of or forming or having or organized into corporation(s).

cŏrporā′tion *n.* body of persons authorized to act as individual; civic authorities; mayor, aldermen and councillors of borough etc.; (colloq.) large belly.

cŏr′porative *a.* of corporation; (of State) organized in professional, industrial, etc. corporations.

cŏrpŏr′ĕal *a.* having body; material, tangible. ~**ăl′itў** *n.*

corps (kōr) *n.* (pl. same, pr. kōrz), military force; organized body.

cŏrpse *n.* dead (usu. human) body.

cŏr′pūlence *n.* bulkiness of body.

cŏr′pūlent *a.* fleshy, bulky.

cŏr′pus *n.* body of writings of particular kind; collection.

cŏr′puscle (-sl) *n.* microscopic or minute body; atom, particle.

cŏrpŭs′cūlar *a.* of corpuscles.

corrăl′ *n.* enclosure for horses, cattle, etc. in U.S. etc., or for capturing wild animals. *v.t.* confine (as) in corral; (colloq.) capture, get hold of.

correct′ *a.* in accordance with the facts; true, accurate; proper, in good taste, of good standard. *v.t.* set right; admonish for fault; counteract or neutralize. ~**tion** *n.* correcting; thing substituted for what is wrong; punishment. ~**titūde** *n.* correctness. ~**tive** *a.* serving to correct; *n.* corrective measure or drug. ~**tor** *n.*

cŏ′rrĕlāte *n.* either of two things or words necessarily implying each other. *v.* have or bring into mutual relation (*with, to*). ~**ā′tion** *n.*

corrĕl′ative *a.* having reciprocal relation, naturally occurring together (*with, to*); (gram.) corresponding and regularly used together. *n.* correlative thing or word.

cŏrrĕspŏnd′ *v.i.* be congruous or similar or analogous (*to, with*); agree in some respects (*to*); exchange letters (*with*). ~**ing** *a.*; ~**inglў** *adv.*

cŏrrĕspŏn′dence *n.* relation between

things that answer to each other in some respect; analogy; exchange of letters; letters.

cŏrrĕspŏn'dent *a.* corresponding. *n.* one who writes letter(s) to another or for newspaper, or contributes to newspaper esp. from abroad.

cŏ'rridŏr *n.* passage or gallery with doors leading into many rooms etc.; passage in railway coach into which compartments open; strip of territory etc. running through or over territory of another state etc.

cŏrrigĕn'dum *n.* (pl. -*da*), thing to be corrected, esp. in book.

cŏ'rrigĭble *a.* that can be corrected.

corrŏb'orāte *v.t.* give support to, confirm. ~ā'tion *n.*; ~ative, ~atorў *aa.*

corrŏb'oree *n.* Australian aboriginal dance.

corrōde' *v.* affect with or suffer corrosion; eat into.

corrō'sion *n.* wearing away or gradual destruction from surface inwards.

corrō'sive *a.* producing corrosion. *n.* corrosive agent.

cŏ'rrugāte (ŏŏ-) *v.* contract into wrinkles; bend into wavy ridges. ~ā'tion *n.*

corrŭpt' *a.* rotten; depraved; venal. *v.* make corrupt, deprave, bribe; rot, decompose. ~ĭble *a.*; ~ĭbil'itў *n.*

corrŭp'tion *n.* corrupting; corrupt state; depravity.

cŏr'sage (-ahzh *or* -ĭj) *n.* bodice; flower(s) worn on bodice or shoulder.

cŏr'sair *n.* privateer, esp. of Barbary; pirate.

cŏr'sĕt *n.* woman's tight-fitting and freq. stiffened inner garment round waist and hips.

cŏrs(e)'lĕt *n.* piece of armour covering body; undergarment combining corset and brassière.

cŏrtège' (-āzh) *n.* train of attendants; (esp. funeral) procession.

Cŏr'tĕs *n.* Spanish or Portuguese parliament.

cŏr'tĕx *n.* outer covering of some organs, esp. outer grey matter of brain; inner bark. cŏr'tical *a.*

corŭn'dum *n.* crystallized native alumina used as abrasive.

cŏ'ruscāte *v.i.* sparkle, flash. ~ā'tion *n.*

cŏr'vée (-vā) *n.* (hist.) unpaid labour exacted by feudal lord etc.

cŏrvĕtte' *n.* (hist.) flush-decked warship with one tier of guns; small fast naval escort-vessel.

cŏr'vīne *a.* of raven or crow.

Cŏ'rўbănt *n.* priest of Cybele performing rites with frenzied dances and cries. cŏrўbăn'tic *a.*

cŏ'rўmb *n.* raceme with flat or flattish top. •

corȳ'za *n.* nasal catarrh.

cŏs[1] *n.* crisp long-leaved lettuce.

cŏs[2] *abbr.* cosine.

cŏsh *n.* (colloq.) short heavy stick. *v.t.* strike with cosh.

cō-sig'natorў *n.* person or State signing document with others.

cō'sīne *n.* sine of complement of given angle.

cŏsmĕt'ic (-z-) *a. & n.* (preparation) designed to beautify complexion etc. ~ surgery, surgery undertaken to correct defects in or alter features etc. cŏsmĕtĭ'cian *n.*

cŏs'mic *a.* of cosmos. ~ rays, high-energy radiations originating in outer space.

cŏs'mo- (-z-) in comb., cosmos. cosmŏg'onў *n.* (theory of) genesis of universe. cosmŏg'raphў *n.* description or mapping of universe or earth; ~grăph'ic(al) *aa.* cosmŏl'ogў *n.* study or philosophy of universe as ordered whole; ~lŏ'gical *a.* ~naut *n.* astronaut.

cŏsmopŏl'itan (-z-) *a.* of all parts of world; free from national limitations. *n.* cosmopolitan person. ~ism *n.*

cŏs'mŏs[1] (-z-) *n̂.* universe as ordered whole; ordered system of ideas etc.; all stars in existence.

cŏs'mŏs[2] (-z-) *n.* kinds of plant with flower like single dahlia.

Cŏss'acks *n.pl.* (descendants of) settlers on Russian (esp. Ukrainian and Siberian) frontiers, famous as horsemen.

cŏss'ĕt *v.t.* pamper, pet.

cŏst *v.t.* involve payment or sacrifice of; have as price. *n.* what thing costs; (pl.) legal expenses.

cŏs'tal *a.* of ribs.

cŏs'tard *n.* large ribbed apple.

cŏs'ter(monger) (-mŭngg-) *n.* street--seller of fruit etc. from barrow.

cŏs'tive *a.* constipated.

cŏst'lў *a.* costing much, expensive; sumptuous.

cŏs'tūme *n.* outer clothes; style of dress etc. of particular period etc. ~ **jewellery,** showy artificial jewellery.

cŏstū'mier *n.* dealer in, maker of, costumes.

cō'sў (-z-) *a.* snug, comfortable. *n.* quilted cover to retain warmth in teapot or boiled egg.

cŏt[1] *n.* (poet.) small cottage; small erection for shelter, cote.

cŏt[2] *n.* light bedstead; swinging bed on board ship; child's bed.

cŏt[3] *abbr.* cotangent.

cōtăn'gent *n.* tangent of complement of given angle.

cōte *n.* shelter for animals.

cō'terie *n.* set of persons with exclusive interests; select circle.

cōtêr'minous *a.* conterminous.

cothûr'nus *n.* (pl. -nī), buskin of Greek tragic actor.

cotĭll'ion -llon (-lyon) *n.* (music for) ballroom dance with elaborate series of steps and figures.

cotōnĕăs'ter *n.* kinds of sḥrub or small tree, many with red or orange berries.

cŏtt'age (-ĭj) *n.* small house, esp. in country; (U.S.) summer residence. ~ **hospital,** small hospital without resident medical staff. ~ **loaf,** loaf with smaller round mass of bread on top of larger. ~ **pie,** of minced meat covered with potatoes. ~r *n.* one who lives in cottage.

cŏtt'ar *n.* Scottish peasant occupying cottage on farm.

cŏtt'er *n.* kinds of wedge or (esp. split) pin or bolt. ~-**pin,** to hold cotter in place.

cŏtt'on[1] *n.* white downy fibrous covering of seeds of ~-*plant*; thread spun, cloth made, from this. ~**tail (rabbit),** N. Amer. rabbit with white fluffy tail. ~**wood,** (U.S.) kinds of poplar; downy-leaved Austral. tree. ~ **wool,** raw cotton, esp. as prepared for wadding etc.

cŏtt'on[2] *v.i.* be drawn *to*; ~ *on (to),* understand.

cŏtўlē'don *n.* primary or seed leaf in plant embryos.

couch *n.* bed; piece of furniture made for reclining on. *v.* have one's bed or lair; lie ready to spring; express *in* specified terms.

couch'-grass (*or* kōō-) *n.* grass with long creeping underground stems.

cou'chant *a.* (her.) in couching attitude.

cou'gar (kōō-) *n.* puma.

cough (kŏf) *v.* expel air from lungs with violent effort and characteristic noise; ~ *out, up,* eject by, say with, cough; ~ *up,* (sl.) produce (esp. money). *n.* (sound of) coughing; tendency to cough; condition of throat etc. resulting in coughing.

could, *p.t.* of can[2].

couloir (kōōl'wahr) *n.* steep gully in mountain-side.

coulomb (kōōlŏm') *n.* quantity of electricity conveyed in one second by current of one ampere.

coul'ter (kōl-) *n.* vertical blade in front of share in plough.

coun'cil *n.* any deliberative or administrative body; esp. local administrative body of corporate town etc.

coun'cillor *n.* member of council.

coun'sel *n.* deliberation or debate; advice; barrister.

coun'sellor *n.* adviser.

count[1] *v.* reckon (*up*); repeat numerals in order; include or be included in reckoning; account, consider; be reckoned; ~ *down,* count seconds etc. backwards to zero as point where something is done; ~ *on,* depend or rely on; ~ *out,* exclude, end sitting of (House of Commons) by counting members present and finding less than 40, declare (fallen boxer) loser by counting 10 seconds before he rises. *n.* counting; reckoning; total; each charge in indictment; number indicating fineness of textile yarn; (boxing) counting of seconds before fallen boxer rises to resume fight.

count[2] *n.* foreign title of nobility.

coun'tenance *n.* expression of face; face; favouring look; moral support. *v.t.* sanction; encourage.

coun'ter[1] *n.* small disc etc. used in

scoring at cards etc.; token; piece at draughts etc.; banker's or shop-keeper's table. ~-jumper, (contempt.) shop assistant.

coun'ter² n. part of horse's breast between shoulders and under neck; curved part of stern of ship; depressed part of face of coin etc.

coun'ter³ a. opposed; opposite. adv. in opposite direction; contrary. n. (fencing) circular parry; (boxing) blow delivered as adversary leads; counter-move etc. v. meet or baffle with, make, counter-move, blow, etc.

counteráct' (or kown'-) v.t. neutralize or hinder by contrary action.

coun'ter-attáck v. & n. attack in reply to enemy's attack.

coun'ter-attrác'tion n. attraction of contrary tendency; rival attraction.

coun'terbálance n. weight balancing another. v.t. act as counterbalance to.

coun'terblast (-ah-) n. energetic declaration against something.

coun'ter-chárge n. & v.t. charge in answer to another.

coun'ter-claim n. claim set up against another.

coun'terfeit (-fĭt or -fēt) a. & n. (thing) made in imitation; forged; not genuine. v.t. imitate; forge; simulate.

coun'terfoil n. part of cheque, receipt, etc. retained as record.

counter-ĭ'rrĭtant n. (esp.) irritant diverting attention from troublesome thing etc.

coun'termand (-ah-) n. order issued in revocation of previous one. v.t. revoke order; recall by countermand.

coun'termárch n. & v. (cause to) march in contrary direction.

coun'termīne n. mine made to intercept that of besiegers etc.; (fig.) counterplot. v. make, oppose by, countermine.

coun'ter-move (-ōōv) n. move in opposition, contrary move.

coun'terpāne n. coverlet or quilt of bed.

coun'terpárt n. duplicate; complement; corresponding part.

coun'terplŏt n. plot contrived to defeat another. v.i. make counterplot.

coun'terpoint n. (mus.) melody added as accompaniment to given melody or plain-song; combination of parts or melodies each retaining its identity.

coun'terpoise (-z) n. counterbalancing weight or force; equilibrium. v.t. counterbalance; bring into or keep in equilibrium.

coun'ter-rĕformā'tion, ~-rĕvolū'tion (or -ōō-) nn. movement running counter to or undoing previous reformation or revolution.

coun'tershaft n. secondary shaft driven from main shaft.

coun'tersign (-īn) n. word to be given in answer to sentry's challenge. v.t. add confirming signature to.

coun'tersink v.t. bevel edge of (hole) to allow screw or bolt to lie flush with surface; sink, (screw etc.) in such hole.

coun'tertĕnor n. male alto.

countervail' v. counter-balance; avail against.

coun'tĕss n. wife or widow of, lady ranking with, count or earl.

coun'tĭng-house n. building or room devoted to book-keeping.

count'lĕss a. too many to count.

coun'trĭfied (kŭn-; -īd) a. rustic, rural.

coun'trў (kŭn-) n. region; territory of nation; land of one's birth or citizenship; rural districts. ~ dance, folk-dance. ~ gentleman, with landed property in country. ~man, ~woman, man, woman of one's own or specified country or living in rural parts. ~ seat, residence of country gentleman. ~side, rural district or its inhabitants.

coun'tў n. territorial division of G.B. and Ireland, shire; political and administrative division of State of U.S. etc.; people, esp. gentry, of county. ~ borough, ranking as administrative county. ~ council, elective governing body of county. ~ court, local judicial court (in England for civil actions). ~ seat (U.S.), ~ town, (former) seat of county administration.

coup (kōō) n. successful stroke or move.

coup d'état (kōō dātah') n. (esp.) violent or illegal change of government by ruling power. [F]

coup de grâce (kōō de grahs) n. finishing stroke. [F]

coup de théâtre (kōō de tāah'tr) n. dramatically sudden or sensational act etc. [F]

coupé (kōō'pā) n. closed carriage for two; half-compartment at end of railway-carriage; closed two-seater car.

coup'le (kŭ-) n. leash for two hounds; married or engaged pair; two, brace. v. link or fasten or associate together. ~r n. (esp.) device in organ for connecting two manuals etc.

coup'let (kŭ-) n. pair of successive lines of rhyming verse.

coup'ling (kŭ-) n. link connecting railway-carriages or parts of machine.

cou'pon (kōō-) n. detachable ticket or form entitling holder to something.

cou'rage (kŭ-) n. bravery, boldness; fortitude. courā'geous a.

cou'rier (kōō-) n. servant, official of travel agency, making travelling arrangements, esp. on Continent; official carrying documents.

course (kōrs) n. going on in space or time; line of conduct or action; series; ground on which race is run; one of successive divisions of meal; continuous layer of stones etc. in building etc. v. pursue (game); run about, run (esp. of liquids); chase; use hounds in coursing.

cour'ser (kōr-) n. swift horse.

court (kōrt) n. space enclosed by wall or buildings; confined yard; area within walls or marked boundaries used in some games; sovereign's residence, his establishment and retinue; assembly of judges or other persons acting as tribunal; place in which justice is administered; (meeting of) qualified members of corporation; attention paid to attract favour, affection, etc. v.t. pay court to; seek favour or love of; invite. ~-card, king, queen, knave.

~ martial, (trial of offence against military law by) court of officers. ~-martial, try by court martial. ~ shoe, woman's low-cut light shoe without fastening. ~yard, space enclosed by walls or buildings.

cour'teous (kêr-) a. polite or considerate in manners etc.

cour'tesan (kôr-, -z-; or -zăn') n. refined or high-placed prostitute.

cour'tesy (kêr-) n. courteous behaviour or disposition.

cour'tier (kôr-) n. frequenter of royal court.

court'ly (kôr-) a. in manner of royal courts; ceremonious; flattering.

court'ship (kôr-) n. courting, wooing, esp. of intended wife.

cousin (kŭz'n) n. child of one's uncle or aunt. ~hood, ~ship nn.; ~ly a.

cove[1] n. small bay or inlet of coast; sheltered nook; (archit.) concave arch, curved junction of wall with ceiling. v.t. provide (room etc.) with cove; slope (fireplace sides) inwards.

cove[2] n. (sl.) fellow, chap.

coven (kŭ-) n. (Sc.) assembly of witches.

co'venant (kŭ-) n. compact, bargain; sealed contract, clause of this. v. make covenant ~ed a. bound by covenant. ~er n. one who covenants, esp. (Sc. hist.) adherent of Covenants of 1638 and 1643.

Cŏv'entry n. send to ~, refuse to associate with.

co'ver (kŭ-) v.t. be over whole top of; overlie or lie above; conceal or shield; have within range (of gun etc.); suffice to defray (expenses); protect by insurance; report for newspaper etc. n. thing that covers; shelter; screen or pretence; covert; funds to meet liability etc.; cover--point. ~-point, (crick.) fielder behind point; his place in field. ~age n. area or amount or risk covered; section of community reached by advertising medium. ~let n. cover lying over other bedclothes.

co'vert (kŭ-) a. secret, disguised; not open or explicit. n. wood or thicket affording cover for game; (pl.) feathers covering base of wing and tail feathers. ~ **coat**, short light overcoat. ~ **coating**, usu. waterproof material for covert coats etc.

co'verture (kŭ-) *n.* covering; wife's position under husband's care.

co'vet (kŭ-) *v.t.* long to possess; desire eagerly. ~**ous** *a.* avaricious, grasping.

co'vey (kŭ-) *n.* brood of partridges etc.; family, set.

cow[1] *n.* (pl. -*s*, arch. *kīne*), female ox, esp. of domestic kind; female of elephant, rhinoceros, whale, seal, etc. ~**boy**, boy in charge of cows; man in charge of cattle on ranch. ~**-catcher**, (U.S.) fender in front of locomotive. ~**heel**, stewed foot of cow or ox. ~**herd**, one who tends cows at pasture. ~**-hide**, leather or whip of cow's hide. ~**-puncher**, (U.S. & Austral.) cowboy. ~**shot**, (crick. sl.) violent pull made in crouching position.

cow[2] *v.t.* intimidate.

cow'ard *n. & a.* faint-hearted, pusillanimous (person). ~**ice** *n.* cowardly conduct. ~**lў** *a.*

cow'er *v.i.* crouch or shrink with fear or with cold.

cowl *n.* monk's hooded cloak; its hood; hood-shaped top of chimney or shaft.

cow'rie *n.* sea-shell of Indian Ocean, used as money in parts of Asia etc.; kinds of small gastropod.

cow'slip *n.* yellow-flowered plant growing in pastures etc.

cŏx *n.* coxswain. *v.* act as cox (of).

cŏx'cōmb (-m) *n.* person given to showing off; (hist.) jester's cap like cock's comb. ~**rў** *n.*

coxswain (kŏk'sn) *n.* boat's helmsman, esp. one in charge of ship's boat; steersman of racing boat. ~**less** *a.*

coy *a.* (affectedly) modest, shy.

Coy *abbr.* Company.

coy'ōte (*or* kī-; *or* -ō'tǐ) *n.* N.-Amer. prairie-wolf.

coy'pu (-ōō) *n.* S. Amer. aquatic rodent.

co'zen (kŭ-) *v.* cheat; beguile. ~**age** *n.*

C.P. *abbr.* Clerk of the Peace; Common Pleas; Communist Party.

Cp. *abbr.* Corporal.

cp. *abbr.* compare.

c.p. *abbr.* candle power.

C.P.O. *abbr.* Chief Petty Officer.

C.P.R. *abbr.* Canadian Pacific Railway.

C.P.R.E. *abbr.* Council for Preservation of Rural England.

C.R. *abbr.* Caledonian Railway.

Cr. *abbr.* creditor.

crăb[1] *n.* crustacean with ten legs, esp. edible species; *the C~*, Cancer; *catch a ~*, get oar-blade jammed under water by faulty rowing-stroke. *v.* cry down, depreciate; criticize with intent to frustrate.

crăb[2], **crăb'-ăpple** *nn.* (sour harsh astringent fruit of) wild (or similar cultivated) apple-tree.

crăbb'ed *a.* cross-grained, perverse, cantankerous; (of handwriting) ill-formed and hard to decipher.

crăck *n.* sudden sharp noise; sharp blow; fissure; partial fracture (with parts still cohering); (sl.) cutting or witty remark; good player etc. *a.* (colloq.) first-rate. *v.* break partially (esp. with crack); break down; (cause to) make crack; utter (joke); make (voice), become, dissonant esp. at puberty; split up (oil etc.) to produce lighter hydrocarbons; drink (*a bottle*); ~ *a crib*, (sl.) break into house. ~**-brained**, crazy. ~**-jaw**, difficult to pronounce. ~**pot**, crazy (person).

crăcked (-kt) *a.* (colloq.) crazy, insane.

crăck'er *n.* (esp.) firework; paper cylinder containing small toy etc. and exploding with crack when ends are pulled; thin crisp biscuit; (U.S.) thin unsweetened biscuit. ~**jack**, (U.S. sl.) splendid (person or thing).

crăck'le *n.* sound of repeated slight cracking. *v.i.* emit crackle.

crăck'ling *n.* cracking sound; crisp skin of roast pork.

crăck'nel *n.* crisp soft biscuit.

crăcks'man *n.* burglar.

cră'dle *n.* infant's bed esp. on rockers; place in which thing is first nurtured; framework resembling cradle; gold-washing trough on rockers. *v.t.* place in cradle; contain or shelter as cradle.

craft (-ah-) *n.* skill, cunning; art, trade; boat(s), vessel(s).

crafts'man (-ahf-) *n.* one who practises craft. ~**ship** *n.*

craf'ty (-ah-) *a.* cunning, artful.

crăg *n.* steep rugged rock.

crăgs'man (-*an*) *n.* rock-climber.

crăm *v.* fill to repletion; fill mind with facts etc. required for examination etc.; pack tightly; eat greedily. *n.* cramming for examination. ~**mer** *n.* one who crams examinees.

crăm'bō *n.* game of finding rhymes to given word; *dumb* ~, game of guessing word from dumb-show of rhyming words.

crămp[1] *n.* sudden painful contraction of muscles from chill, strain, etc. *v.t.* restrict; enclose too narrowly; affect with cramp. **crămped** *a.* (esp., of handwriting) too small or close.

crămp[2] *n.* & *v.t.* (fasten with) kinds of clamp for holding masonry etc. together.

crăm'pon *n.* spiked iron plate fixed to boot for walking etc. on ice.

crăn *n.* measure (37½ gal.) for fresh herrings.

crā'nage *n.* use of crane; dues paid for this.

crăn'berry *n.* (small dark-red acid berry of) dwarf shrub.

crāne *n.* large wading bird; machine for moving heavy weights. *v.* stretch (neck), stretch neck, like crane. ~**-fly,** two-winged long--legged fly. ~**'s-bill,** kinds of wild geranium.

crā'nium *n.* (pl. *-ia*), bones enclosing brain, skull. **crā'nial** *a.*

crănk[1] *n.* part of axis bent at right angles for converting rotary into reciprocal motion and vice versa. *v.t.* start (motor-engine) by turning crank.

crănk[2] *n.* eccentric idea; eccentric person, esp. one enthusiastically possessed by idea etc. ~**y** *a.*

crănn'y *n.* chink, crevice, crack. **crănn'ied** *a.*

crāpe *n.* gauzy wrinkled fabric, usu. of black silk, esp. as (part of) mourning wear.

crăps *n.* (U.S.) game of chance played with dice.

crăp'ūlence *n.* state following intemperate drinking or eating. ~**lent,** ~**lous** *aa.*

crăsh[1] *n.* loud noise as of thunder, violent breakage, etc.; violent fall or impact; sudden downfall or collapse. *v.* move or go or drive or throw with crash; make crash; (cause to) come *into* violent collision, fall heavily, etc.; fail, esp. financially. ~**-dive,** (of submarine) dive suddenly and steeply. ~**-helmet,** protective helmet of motor-cyclists etc. ~**-land,** (of aircraft etc.) land hurriedly, esp. without lowering undercarriage.

crăsh[2] *n.* coarse linen cloth.

crăss *a.* grossly stupid; without sensibility.

crāte *n.* open-work case of wooden bars or basket-work.

crā'ter *n.* volcano-mouth; bowl--shaped cavity.

crăvăt' *n.* (hist.) ornamental band with bow or long flowing ends, worn round neck.

crāve *v.* long or beg for; long *for*. **crā'ving** *n.* intense longing (*for*).

crā'ven *a.* & *n.* cowardly, abject (person).

craw *n.* crop of bird or insect.

crawfish: see **crayfish.**

crawl *v.i.* move slowly with body on or close to ground, or on hands and knees; move slowly; creep abjectly; swim with crawl stroke; swarm *with* crawling things. *n.* crawling; fast swimming-stroke.

cray'fish, craw'- *n.* lobster-like freshwater crustacean; spiny lobster.

cray'on *n.* stick or pencil of coloured chalk, usu. mixed with wax; picture drawn with crayons.

crāze *v.t.* drive crazy; produce small cracks in glaze of (pottery). *n.* mania; temporary fashion.

crā'zy *a.* unsound, shaky; mad; half--witted; madly eager; (of quilt, paving, etc.) of irregular pieces fitted together.

creak *n.* harsh grating noise as of unoiled hinge. *v.i.* emit creak.

cream *n.* fatty part gathering on top of milk; fancy dish etc. like or made of cream; cream-like esp. cosmetic preparation; best part of anything; yellowish-white colour of cream. *v.* form cream or scum; take cream from, take best part of; apply cream to; add cream or cream sauce to in cooking; work into creamy consistency. ~ **cheese,** soft rich cheese made with added cream. ~-**laid,** ~-**wove,** laid, wove, (paper) of cream colour. ~ў *a.*

crease *n.* line made by folding; wrinkle; (crick.) white line defining position of bowler or limit of batsman's ground. *v.* make creases in; develop creases.

creāte' *v.* bring into existence; invest with rank; originate; (sl.) make fuss. **creā'tive** *a.*

creā'tion *n.* creating (esp. of the world); all created things; production of human mind.

creā'tor *n.* one who creates; *the C*~, God.

crea'ture (krē'cher) *n.* human being or animal; dependant or tool; contemptible person.

crèche (-āsh) *n.* public day-nursery for infants; nursery school.

crē'dence *n.* belief; credit.

crēdĕn'tials *n.pl.* letters of recommendation (also fig.).

crĕd'ible *a.* believable; worthy of belief. ~**bĭl'itў** *n.*

crĕd'it *n.* belief, trust; good reputation; allowing of deferred payment; sum at person's disposal in bank etc., or entered on credit side of account; kind of distinction awarded in examination etc.; acknowledgement of authorship, performance, direction, etc., esp. at beginning or end of film etc.; *give* (person) ~ *for,* enter (sum) to his credit, ascribe (quality) to him. *v.t.* believe; carry to credit side of account; ~ *with,* give credit for. ~**able** *a.* praiseworthy.

crĕd'itor *n.* person or body to whom debt is owing.

crē'dō *n.* (pl. -*os*), creed.

crĕd'ūlous *a.* too ready to believe. **crēdū'litў** *n.*

creed *n.* formal summary of Christian doctrine; system of (esp. religious) belief.

creek *n.* inlet on sea-coast or arm of river; small stream.

creel *n.* angler's fishing-basket.

creep *v.i.* (*crĕpt*), crawl; move steathily or timidly or slowly; (of plants) grow along ground, wall, etc.; (of skin etc.) feel as if things were creeping over it; (of metal etc.) undergo creep; proceed or exist abjectly. *n.* creeping; gradual movement, expansion, distortion, etc., under pressure or tension; (colloq. pl.) shrinking dread or horror. ~**er** *n.* (esp.) creeping plant. ~ў *a.* having or producing creeping of flesh.

crēmāte' *v.t.* consume (esp. corpse) by fire. ~**ā'ticn** *n.* ~**atōr'ium** (pl. -*s,* -*ia*), **crĕm'atorў** *nn.* establishment for cremation.

Crēmō'na *n.* violin made at Lombardy town of Cremona.

crĕn'ĕllātĕd *a.* having battlements or loopholes. ~**ā'tion** *n.*

crē'ōle *n.* descendant of European or Negro settlers in W. Indies etc.; French-speaking descendant of early French settlers in Louisiana etc. *a.* of or characteristic of creoles; naturalized in W. Indies etc.

crē'osōte *n.* oily antiseptic liquid distilled from wood-tar.

crēpe (-āp) *n.* textile fabric with wrinkled surface. ~ **de Chine** (dešēn), fine silk crêpe. ~ **paper,** thin crinkled paper. ~ **rubber,** crude rubber with wrinkled surface.

crĕp'itāte *v.i.* make crackling or grating sound. ~**ā'tion** *n.*

crept, *p.t.* & *p.p.* of **creep.**

crĕpŭs'cūlar *a.* of twilight; (zool.) active etc. at twilight.

cres. *abbr.* crescendo.

crĕscĕn'dŏ (-sh-) *adv., n.* & *a.* (mus.) (passage to be performed) with gradually increasing volume.

crĕs'cent (*or* -znt) *n.* figure of moon in first or last quarter; representation of this, esp. as symbol of Turkish or Moslem power; crescent--shaped thing, esp. row of houses. *a.* (of moon) waxing, between new and full; crescent-shaped.

crĕss *n.* kinds of plant with pungent edible leaves.

crĕss'ĕt *n.* fire-basket slung to give light.

crĕst *n.* comb or tuft on animal's

head; plume or central ridge of helmet; mane of horse etc.; top esp. of mountain; curl of foam on wave; heraldic device above shield or used separately. *v.t.* serve as crest to; crown; reach top of. **~fallen,** mortified, dejected.

crětā'ceous *a.* & *n.* chalky; *C~,* (of) system of rocks at top of Mesozoic.

crět'ĭn *n.* deformed idiot. **~ĭsm** *n.* idiocy combined with physical deformity. **~ous** *a.*

crětŏnne' (or krě'-) *n.* unglazed colour-printed cotton cloth.

crěvăsse' *n.* deep fissure in ice of glacier.

crěv'ice *n.* chink, fissure.

crew[1] (-ōō) *n.* body of men engaged in particular piece of work, esp. manning ship, boat, or aircraft (sometimes excluding ship's officers); gang, mob. *v.* act as crew (for); assign to crew. **~ cut,** (hair) cut very short all over.

crew[2]: see **crow**[1].

crew'ĕl (-ōō-) *n.* thin worsted yarn for embroidery. **~ needle,** blunt-ended embroidery needle.

crĭb *n.* barred rack for fodder; child's bed; model representing infant Jesus etc. at Bethlehem; (thieves' sl.) house; discard from other hands given to dealer at cribbage; plagiarism; translation for (esp. illegitimate) use of students. *v.* confine in small space; plagiarize, copy, use cribs.

crĭbb'age *n.* card-game for two, three, or four persons, with pegged board for scoring.

crĭck *n.* spasmodic affection of muscles of neck etc., sudden stiffness. *v.t.* produce crick in.

crĭck'ĕt[1] *n.* jumping insect producing shrill chirrup by rubbing parts of forewings together.

crĭck'ĕt[2] *n.* open-air game played with ball, bats, and wickets between two teams of 11; *not ~,* (colloq.) unfair, infringing code of fair play. **~er** *n.*

cried, *p.t.* & *p.p.* of **cry.**

crī'er *n.* officer who makes public announcements in judicial court, streets of town, etc.

crī'key *int.* (sl.) expressing astonishment.

crīme *n.* act punishable by law; wicked act; sin. **~-sheet,** record of soldier's offences against regulations.

crĭm'inal *a.* of (nature of) crime. *n.* person guilty of crime. **~ăl'itў** *n.*

crĭm'ināte *v.t.* impute crime to; prove guilty of crime; censure. **~ā'tion** *n.*

crĭmĭnŏl'ogў *n.* study of crime. **~logist** *n.*

crĭmp *v.t.* press into small folds; frill, corrugate.

crĭm'son (-z-) *a.* & *n.* rich deep red (colour). *v.* turn crimson.

crĭnge (-j) *v.i.* cower; behave obsequiously. *n.* act of cringing.

crĭnk'le *n.* & *v.* wrinkle. **crĭnk'lў** *a.*

crĭn'oline (*or* -ēn) *n.* stiff fabric of horsehair etc.; hooped petticoat used to expand skirt; (dress with) such skirt.

crĭpp'le *n.* lame person. *v.t.* lame, disable; impair.

crī'sĭs *n.* (pl. -ēs), turning-point; time of acute danger or difficulty.

crĭsp *a.* brittle; bracing; brisk, decisive; curly. *n.* thing dried or shrivelled by heat; (pl.) very thin slices of potato fried crisp. *v.* make or become crisp.

crĭss'-crŏss *n.* (network of) crossing lines etc. *a.* crossing, in crossing lines. *adv.* crosswise. *v.t.* mark with criss-cross lines.

crĭs'tāte *a.* crested, like crest.

crĭtēr'ion *n.* (pl. -*ia*), principle taken as standard in judging.

crĭt'ĭc *n.* person who attempts or is skilled in criticism.

crĭt'ical *a.* censorious, fault-finding; skilled in criticism; of nature of crisis; involving risk or suspense; (phys. etc.) marking transition from one state etc. to another.

crĭt'icĭsm *n.* judging of merit esp. of literary or artistic work; animadversion; critical observation; *textual ~,* concerned with establishing authentic' text and meaning of author etc.

crĭt'icīze *v.* discuss critically; find fault (with).

critique' (-ēk) *n.* critical essay.

croak *n.* (sound resembling) deep hoarse note of frog or raven. *v.*

utter croak, be hoarse; talk or say gloomily; (sl.) kill, die.

crō'chet (-shǐ) *n.* kind of knitting with single hooked needle. *v.* (-*cheted*, pr. -shǐd), do crochet, make by crochet.

crŏck[1] *n.* earthen pot or jar; broken piece of earthenware. **~erӯ** *n.* earthenware vessels, esp. for domestic use.

crŏck[2] *n.* (colloq.) worn-out or broken-down or disabled person or thing; broken-down horse. *v.* (cause to) give way or break down or collapse.

crŏck'ĕt *n.* ornament on inclined side of pinnacle etc.

crŏc'odīle *n.* large amphibious reptile; children walking two and two. **~ tears**, hypocritical tears.

crō'cus *n.* dwarf plant with corm and usu. yellow or purple flowers.

crŏft *n.* small piece of arable land close to house; small agricultural holding worked by peasant tenant.

crŏm'lĕch (-k) *n.* dolmen or (esp. in France) stone circle.

crōne *n.* withered old woman.

crō'nӯ *n.* intimate friend.

crŏok *n.* hooked staff, esp. of shepherd or bishop; bend, curve; (sl.) swindler, criminal. *v.* bend, curve. *a.* (Austral. sl.) unwell.

crooked *a.* (krŏokt), having crook; (krŏok'ĭd), not straight, bent, twisted, deformed; dishonest.

crōon *n.* low monotonous singing. *v.* utter croon; hum softly.

crŏp *n.* pouch in bird's gullet where food is prepared for digestion; whip-handle; short whipstock with loop instead of lash; produce of cultivated (esp. cereal) plants or land; cropping of hair. *v.* cut off, (of animal) bite off; gather, reap; cut short; raise crop on, bear crop; turn *up* unexpectedly.

crŏpp'er *n.* (esp., sl.) heavy fall.

crō'quet (-kǐ) *n.* lawn game with hoops, wooden balls, and mallets; croqueting. *v.t.* (-*ting*, -*ted*, pr. -kǐing, -kǐd), drive away (player's ball) by striking one's own ball placed in contact with it.

croquette' (-kĕt) *n.* fried ball of meat, potato, etc.

crō'sier, ~zier (-zhy*er*) *n.* pastoral staff of bishop or abbot.

crŏss *n.* stake used by ancients for crucifixion, usu. with transverse bar; representation of this as emblem of Christian religion; figure, mark, etc. of two roughly equal lines etc. crossing near their centres; cross-shaped thing; decoration in some orders of knighthood; sign of cross as religious act; affliction; trial or annoyance; intermixture of breeds; hybrid; *on the ~*, diagonally, on the bias. *a.* transverse; reaching from side to side; intersecting; (colloq.) peevish, out of humour; *be at ~ purposes*, misunderstand one another. *v.* place crosswise; make sign of cross on or over; draw line across; make two lines across (cheque etc.), which may then be paid only through bank; go across (road, sea, etc.); meet and pass; thwart; interbreed, cross-breed; *~ off, out*, cancel.

crŏss'bĕlt *n.* belt for cartridges etc. from shoulder to opposite hip.

crŏss'bill *n.* bird whose mandibles cross when bill is closed.

crŏss'bōnes *n.pl.* figure of two thigh--bones crossed.

crŏss'bow (-ō) *n.* weapon formed of bow fixed across wooden stock.

crŏss'-breed *v.* breed from individuals of different species etc. *n.* breed so formed; cross-bred individual. **~-brĕd** *a.*

crŏss-bŭtt'ock *n.* wrestling throw over hip.

crŏss-coun'trӯ (-kŭn-) *a.* across fields, not following roads.

crŏss'cŭt *a.* adapted for cutting across grain.

crŏsse *n.* netted crook used in lacrosse.

crŏss-exămĭnā'tion (-ėgz-) *n.* examination with view to checking or casting doubt on previous examination. **~-exăm'ĭne** *v.t.* subject to this.

crŏss'-grained *a.* (of wood) with grain running irregularly; (fig.) perverse, intractable.

crŏss'-hătch *v.t.* shade with intersecting parallel lines.

crŏss'ing *n.* intersection; place where street etc. is crossed.

cross'patch n. ill-tempered person.

cross-ques'tion n. question put in cross-examination. v.t. cross--examine.

cross-ref'erence n. reference from one part of book etc. to another. v.t. provide with cross-reference(s).

cross'-road n. road that crosses another or joins two; (pl.) inter-section of roads.

cross'-section n. transverse section; representative sample.

cross'-stitch n. needlework stitch of two straight stitches crossing each other. v. work (in) cross-stitch.

cross'wise (-z) adv. in shape or manner of cross.

cross'-word (-ẽrd) (puzzle) n. puzzle in which words crossing horizontally and vertically in chequered pattern are to be filled in from clues.

crotch n. fork, esp. of human body where legs join trunk.

crotch'et n. (mus.) black-headed note with stem, equal to half minim; whim or fad. ~y a.

cro'ton n. kinds of mainly tropical plant.

crouch v.i. stoop, bend, esp. timidly or servilely; (of animal) lie close to ground. n. act or position of crouching.

croup[1] (-oo-) n. laryngitis in children, with sharp cough.

croup(e)[2] (-oo-) n. rump, hind-quarters, esp. of horse.

crou'pier (-oo-) n. raker-in of money at gaming-table.

croûton (kroo'tawn) n. (cookery) small piece of fried or toasted bread. [F]

crow[1] (-ō) v.i. (past crowed, arch. crew, pr. -oo), utter cock's cry; (of infants) utter joyful sounds; exult. n. cock's cry; infant's crowing.

crow[2] (-ō) n. kinds of large black glossy-plumaged bird; crowbar. ~berry, black-berried heath shrub; (U.S.) cranberry. ~foot, kinds of buttercup etc. ~'s-foot, wrinkle at outer corner of eye. ~'s-nest, barrel etc. at masthead for look--out man.

crow'bar (-ō-) n. bar of iron used as lever.

crowd n. throng, dense multitude; (colloq.) set, lot. v. collect in crowd; fill, cram (with); force way into, through, etc. confined space etc.; ~ out, exclude by crowd-ing.

crown n. wreath for head; monarch's head-covering or circlet; supreme governing power in monarchy; British coin of 5s.; top of head or hat; completion. v.t. put crown on; make king or queen; be consumma-tion or reward of; put finishing touch to.

C.R.T. abbr. cathode-ray tube.

cru'cial (-oo-) a. decisive, critical; (anat.) cross-shaped.

cru'cian (-ooshn) (carp) n. deep--yellow fish allied to carp.

cru'cible (-oo-) n. vessel in which metals can be fused.

crucif'erous (-oo-) a. with four equal petals arranged crosswise.

cru'cifix (-oo-) n. image of Christ on Cross. **crucifi'xion** (-kshon) n. crucifying, esp. of Christ. **cru'ciform** (-oo-) a. cross-shaped. **cru'cify** (-oo-) v.t. put to death on cross; mortify or chasten.

crude (-oo-) a. in natural or raw state; not digested; unripe; (fig.) ill--digested, unpolished, lacking finish. **cru'dity** n.

cru'el (-oo-) a. callous to or delighting in others' pain; painful, distressing. ~ty n.

cru'et (-oo-) n. small stoppered bottle for vinegar, oil, etc., for table; cruet-stand. ~-stand, one holding cruets, mustard-pot, etc.

cruise (-ooz) v.i. sail about (esp. for pleasure) making for no particular port; travel at cruising speed. n. cruising voyage. **crui'sing speed**, suitable for maintaining for long periods.

crui'ser (-ooz-) n. warship faster than battleship and less heavily ar-moured. ~-weight, boxing weight (12 st. 7 lb.).

crumb (-m) n. small fragment, esp. of bread; soft inner part of bread. v.t. cover with crumbs; break into crumbs. **crumb'y** (-mi) a.

crum'ble v. break or fall into crumbs or fragments. ~bly a.

crumm'y a. (sl.) rubbishy, inferior.

crŭmp n. sound of heavy shell etc. exploding.

crŭm′pėt n. flat soft cake eaten toasted with butter; (sl.) head.

crŭmp′le v. crush together into creases; become creased; give way, collapse.

crŭnch n. sound made by chewing crisp food or treading on gravel. v. crush with teeth, esp. noisily; make or emit crunch. **~y̆** a. fit for being crunched.

crŭpp′er n. strap looped under horse's tail from back of saddle; hind-quarters of horse.

crur′al (-oor-) a. (anat.) of leg.

crusāde′ (-ōō-) n. medieval military expedition to recover Holy Land; campaign or movement against recognized evil. v.i. take part in crusade.

cruse (-ōōz) n. earthenware jar.

crŭsh v. compress with violence so as to break, bruise, or crumple; (be liable to) crumple; subdue, over-whelm. n. crowded mass (esp. of persons); (colloq.) group or set of people; drink made of juice of crushed fruit; (sl.) infatuation. **~-bar**, bar used during intervals in theatre etc. **~-barrier**, (esp. temporary) barrier for controlling crowd. **~ hat**, opera hat.

crŭst n. hard outer part of bread etc.; pastry covering pie; surface of earth etc.; deposit of tartar etc. inside wine-bottle. v. cover with, form into, crust; become covered with crust.

crŭstā′cean n. & a. (animal) of mainly aquatic group, many with hard shell and many jointed legs.

crŭs′ty̆ a. with much or hard crust; irritable, surly.

crŭtch n. staff, usu. with cross-piece fitting under armpit, for lame person; support, prop; crotch.

crŭx n. knotty point, puzzle; point at issue.

cry̆ n. loud inarticulate utterance of grief, fear, joy, etc.; loud excited utterance; call, esp. of birds; fit of weeping; appeal; watchword; yelp-ing of hounds; a far ~, a long way; in full ~, in full pursuit. v. (cried), utter cry or cries; utter loudly,

exclaim; weep; ~ off, withdraw; ~ up, praise. **~-baby**, one given to childish crying. **~ing** a. (esp., of evils) flagrant, notorious.

cry̆′o- in comb., freezing. **cry̆′ogėn** n. refrigerant. **~gėn′ic** a. of or produc-ing very low temperatures. **~stăt** n. apparatus for maintaining low temperature. **~sūr′gery̆** n. surgery performed at very low temperature.

cry̆pt n. vault, esp. one below church used as burial-place.

cry̆p′tic a. of mysterious import; veiled in obscurity.

cry̆p′togăm n. plant without stamens or pistils; non-flowering plant. **cry̆ptŏg′amous** a.

cry̆p′togrăm n. thing written in cipher. **~grăph′ic** a.

cry̆s′tal n. transparent mineral like ice or glass; glass of especial trans-parency; fine cut glass; watch--glass; substance solidified in definite geometrical form; crystal used as radio rectifier. a. made of, like, clear as, crystal.

cry̆s′tallīne a. of or like or clear as crystal.

cry̆s′tallīze v. form into crystals or definite or permanent state. **~zā′-tion** n.

C.S.C. abbr. Conspicuous Service Cross.

C.S.M. abbr. Company Sergeant--Major.

C.T.C. abbr. Cyclists' Touring Club.

C.U. abbr. Cambridge University.

cu. abbr. cubic.

cŭb n. young of fox or other wild beast; ill-mannered child or youth.

cŭbb′y̆-hōle n. very small confined room, cupboard, etc.

cūbe n. solid figure contained by six equal squares; product of number or quantity multiplied by its square. v.t. find cube of.

cū′bic a. of three dimensions; involv-ing cube of quantity. **~ content**, volume expressed in cubic feet, inches, etc. **~ foot** etc., volume of cube whose edge is one foot etc.

cū′bical a. cube-shaped.

cū′bicle n. small compartment or room or partitioned-off space for sleeping, dressing, etc., in.

cū′bifōrm a. cube-shaped.

cū′bĭsm *n.* style of painting in which objects are reduced to geometrical forms. ~**ĭst** *n.* & *a.*

cū′bĭt *n.* ancient measure of length (18–22 in.).

cŭck′old *n.* husband of adulterous wife. *v.t.* make cuckold of.

cuck′ōō (kŏŏ-) *n.* migratory bird appearing in spring; its call. *a.* (sl.) crazy.

cū′cŭmber *n.* (creeping plant with) long fleshy fruit eaten as salad etc.

cŭd *n.* ruminant's half-digested food.

cŭdd′le *v.* fondle; lie close and snug; nestle. *n.* hug, embrace.

cŭdg′el *n.* thick stick as weapon. *v.t.* beat with cudgel.

cūe[1] *n.* actor's words etc. as signal for speech, action, lighting-change, etc.; similar guide for musical performer; signal, hint. *v.t.* give cue to; ~ *in,* insert cue for.

cūe[2] *n.* long straight rod for striking ball in billiards etc. *v.t.* strike with cue.

cŭff[1] *n.* ornamental etc. band, lace, etc. at bottom of sleeve; (stiffened) wrist-band of linen etc.; (pl.) hand-cuffs; (U.S.) trouser turn-up; *off the* ~, extempore, without preparation.

cŭff[2] *n.* blow with open hand. *v.t.* strike thus.

cui bō′nō? (kī), who profits by it? (erron.) to what purpose? [L]

cuirăss′ (kw-) *n.* breast and back plate forming body armour. **cuirassier′** (kwĭ- *or* kūr-) *n.* cavalryman with cuirass.

cuisine (kwĭzēn′) *n.* style of cooking.

cŭl′-de-săc (*or* kŏŏ-) *n.* blind alley.

cŭl′ĭnarў *a.* of or for cooking.

cŭll *v.t.* pick (flowers); select.

cŭl′mĭnāte *v.i.* reach highest point of development; (astron.) reach meridian. ~**ā′tion** *n.*

cŭl′pable *a.* blameworthy, criminal. ~**bĭl′itў** *n.*

cŭl′prĭt *n.* prisoner at bar; offender.

cŭlt *n.* system of religious worship; devotion, homage; fad.

cŭl′tĭvāte *v.t.* prepare and use (soil) for crops; raise, produce (plant etc.); improve, develop; pay attention to, cherish. ~**ā′tion** *n.* ~**ātor** *n.* (esp.) agricultural implement for breaking up ground etc.

cŭl′ture *n.* cultivating; production; development of bacteria etc., bacteria etc. developed, in specially prepared medium; refinement · or improvement of mind, tastes, etc. by education and training; form or type of civilization. *v.t.* cultivate. **cŭl′tural** *a.* ~**d** *a.* (esp.) refined, well-educated.

cŭl′verĭn *n.* (hist.) small firearm; large cannon.

cŭl′vert *n.* channel or conduit for water crossing road, canal, etc.

cum. *abbr.* cumulative.

Cumb. *abbr.* Cumberland.

cŭm′ber *v.t.* hamper, hinder; burden. ~**some,** **cŭm′brous** *aa.* hampering; inconveniently large or heavy.

cŭm′ĭn *n.* fennel-like plant with aromatic seed.

cŭmm′erbŭnd *n.* waist-sash.

cū′mūlatĭve *a.* tending to accumulate; increasing etc. by successive additions.

cū′mūlus *n.* (pl. -lī), cloud in heaped-up rounded masses.

cū′nĕĭfŏrm *a.* & *n.* (writing, character) composed of wedge-shaped marks.

cŭnn′ĭng *n.* skill, dexterity; skill in deceit or evasion. *a.* possessed of or displaying cunning.

cŭp *n.* drinking-vessel of any material or form; (fig.) draught of sorrow or joy; trophy in wine-cup shape as prize; rounded cavity, socket, etc.; cupful; (usu. iced) drink of sweetened and flavoured wine, fruit-juice, etc. *v.t.* (hist.) bleed by applying open-mouthed glass vessel to skin.

cupboard (kŭb′erd) *n.* (usu. shelved) closet or cabinet.

cū′pĭd *n.* representation of Roman god of love as beautiful winged naked boy carrying bow and arrows.

cūpĭd′itў *n.* greed of gain.

cū′pola *n.* rounded dome forming roof; small dome above roof; kind of furnace; ship's or fort's revolving gun-turret.

cū′prēous *a.* of copper, coppery.

cū′prĭc, cū′prous *aa.* of copper.

cŭr *n.* worthless or snappish dog; ill-bred or cowardly fellow.

cūr′açao (-sō) *n.* orange-peel liqueur.

cūr′acў n. curate's office.

cūrār′é n. vegetable poison paralysing motor nerves.

cūr′ate n. parish priest's salaried clerical assistant.

cūr′ative a. tending to cure. n. curative drug or measure.

cūrā′tor n. person in charge esp. of museum or library.

cūrb n. chain or strap passing under horse's lower jaw; (fig.) constraint, check; kerb. v.t. apply curb to; restrain.

cūrd n. coagulated substance formed by action of acids on milk; (pl.) broken-up curd as food.

cūr′dle v. coagulate, form into curd.

cūre n. remedy; course of treatment; spiritual charge. v.t. restore to health, heal, remedy; preserve (meat etc.).

cūr′é (-ā) n. parish priest in France etc.

cūrĕtte′ n. surgeon's scraping instrument. v.t. scrape with this.

cūr′few n. ringing of bell at fixed evening hour; prohibition of being in streets during specified hours.

cūr′ie n. standard unit of radium emanation.

cūr′iŏ n. (pl. -os), object prized for its rarity, beauty, etc.

cūriŏs′itў n. desire to know; inquisitiveness; strange or rare thing.

cūr′ious a. eager to learn; inquisitive; strange, surprising.

cūrl v. bend; coil into spiral shape; proceed in curve; play at curling. n. spiral lock of hair; spiral or incurved form. **~ў** a.

cūr′lew n. long-billed wading bird with musical cry.

cūr′ling n. game of hurling large polished stones on ice.

cūrmŭdg′eon (-jn) n. churlish or miserly fellow.

cŭr′rant n. dried fruit of small seedless grape; (small round black or red or white berry of) kinds of shrub.

cŭr′rencў n. time during which thing is current; circulation; prevalence; money in actual use in country.

cŭr′rent a. in general circulation or use; (of time) now passing; belonging to current time. n. water, air, etc. moving in given direction; transmission of electric force, electric force transmitted, through body; general tendency or course. **~ account**, (at bank) that may be drawn on by cheque.

cŭ′rricle n. (hist.) light open two-wheeled two-horse carriage.

cŭrric′ulum n. (pl. -la), course (of study).

cŭrric′ulum vī′tae n. brief account of one's life. [L]

cŭ′rrier n. leather-dresser.

cŭ′rrў¹ n. dish of meat etc. cooked with bruised spices and turmeric and usu. served with rice. v.t. make into or flavour like curry.

cŭ′rrў² v.t. rub down or dress (horse etc.) with comb; dress (leather). **~-comb**, comb for horses etc.

cūrse n. invocation of destruction or punishment; profane oath; great evil, bane. v. utter curse against; afflict *with*; utter curses. **cūr′sĕd** a. damnable.

cūr′sive a. & n. (writing) done without lifting pen between letters.

cūr′sorў a. without attention to details; rapid, desultory.

cūrt a. noticeably or rudely brief; over-concise.

cūrtail′ v.t. cut down, shorten, reduce. **~ment** n.

cūr′tain (-tn) n. cloth etc. suspended as screen, esp. at window or between stage and auditorium; curtain-call; plain wall connecting two towers etc. of fortified place; barrage. v.t. provide, shut *off*, with curtains. **~-call**, (theatr.) applause calling for actor etc. to appear after curtain has been lowered. **~-raiser**, short piece before principal play etc. in theatre.

cūrt′s(e)y n. feminine movement of respect or salutation, made by bending knees. v.i. make curtsy (*to*).

cūr′vature n. curving; curved form.

cūrve n. line of which no part is straight; curved form or thing. v. bend or shape so as to form curve.

cūrvĕt′ n. horse's frisky leap. v.i. perform this.

cŭr'vĭlĭn'ẻar *a.* of curved line(s).

cŭ'sĕc *n.* unit of flow of water (one cubic foot per second).

cushion (kŏŏ'shn) *n.* bag of silk, cloth, etc. filled with soft material; elastic lining of billiard-table's sides. *v.t.* furnish with cushions; protect against shock etc., mitigate effects of, (as) with cushion.

cush'ў (kŏŏ-) *a.* (sl.) (of job etc.) easy, comfortable.

cŭsp *n.* point of meeting of two curves. **~ĭdal, ~ĭdate** *aa.*

cŭss *n.* (U.S. colloq.) curse; person, creature. **cŭss'ẻd** *a.* perverse.

cŭs'tard *n.* dish or sauce of beaten eggs and milk; sweet sauce of corn-flour and milk. **~-apple,** (W.-Ind. & S.-Amer. tree bearing) fruit with yellowish custard-like pulp.

cŭstō'dĭan *n.* curator, guardian.

cŭs'todў *n.* keeping, guardianship; imprisonment.

cŭs'tom *n.* usual practice; established usage; business patronage or support; (pl.) duties levied on imports. **~-house,** office at which customs are collected.

cŭs'tomarў *a.* usual; based on custom rather than law.

cŭs'tomer *n.* purchaser at shop etc., client of bank; (colloq.) person to have to do with.

cŭt *v.* divide or wound with edged instrument; detach by cutting; cross, intersect; reduce (hair etc.), shape, by cutting; have (tooth) appear through gum; (crick.) hit ball to off with chopping movement of bat; strike ball across its line of flight; divide pack of cards; decline to recognize (person); (sl.) *~ no ice,* effect nothing; *~ both ways,* serve both sides; *~ in,* interpose in conversation, join in card-game in place of player cutting out, obstruct overtaken car by returning to near side too soon; *~ off,* (esp.) intercept, interrupt, exclude (*from*); *~ out,* (esp.) shape by cutting, be excluded from card-game by cutting pack, (of engine etc.) stop working abruptly; *~ up,* (esp.) greatly distress; *~ up rough,* show resentment. *n.* act of cutting, wound made by it; stroke with

sword, whip, or cane; cutting of ball; cutting of acquaintance; excision; joint or piece of meat etc.; way thing is cut; *a ~ above,* a degree or stage above; *short ~,* way that shortens distance. **~-and-dried,** planned out, prepared, ready-made, lacking freshness. **~-out,** device for automatically disconnecting electric circuit, by-passing exhaust, etc.; figure etc. cut out of paper etc. **~-purse,** (arch.) thief. **~-throat.** murderer, murderous; (of competition etc.) intensive, merciless; (of card-game) three-handed.

cŭtā'nẻous *a.* of the skin.

cūte *a.* (colloq.) clever, ingenious; (U.S.) attractive (esp. of child).

cū'tĭcle *n.* outer skin, epidermis; skin at base of finger-nail.

cŭt'lass *n.* sailor's short broad-bladed sword.

cŭt'ler *n.* knife-maker or -dealer.

cŭt'lerў *n.* knives, scissors, etc.

cŭt'lẻt *n.* neck-chop of mutton; small piece of veal etc. for frying; minced meat etc. in cutlet shape.

cŭtt'er *n.* person or thing that cuts; tailor's cutting-out hand; war-ship's rowing and sailing boat; small sloop-rigged vessel.

cŭtt'ĭng *n.* excavation of high ground for railway, road, etc.; piece cut from newspaper etc.; piece cut from plant for replanting. *a.* (esp.) biting, wounding to mind or feelings.

cŭtt'lefish *n.* ten-armed marine cephalopod ejecting black fluid when pursued.

cŭt'water *n.* edge of ship's stem; wedge-shaped projection pointing up-stream from bridge-pier.

C.V.O. *abbr.* Commander of Royal Victorian Order.

cwm (kŏŏm) *n.* cauldron-shaped mountain hollow.

C.W.S. *abbr.* Co-operative Wholesale Society.

cwt. *abbr.* hundredweight.

cў'anĭde *n.* salt of hydrocyanic acid.

cўanō'sĭs *n.* dark bluish discoloration of skin etc.

cўbernĕt'ĭcs *n.* study of communication and control in living organisms or machines.

cўc'lamen *n.* plant of primula kind

with pink or purple or white flowers.

cȳ'cle *n.* recurrent period; complete performance of vibration, oscillation, etc.; frequency of electric current etc.; complete set or series; bicycle, tricycle, or similar machine. *v.i.* move in cycles; use bicycle etc. **cȳ'clist** *n.*

cȳ'clic(al) *aa.* recurring in cycles; of or forming cycle or circle.

cȳ'cloid *n.* curve traced by point on circumference of circle rolling along straight line. **cȳcloi'dal** *a.*

cȳclŏm'èter *n.* instrument for measuring circular arcs; instrument recording distances travelled by bicycle etc.

cȳ'clōne *n.* system of winds rotating around low-pressure region; violent destructive form of this. **cȳclŏn'ic** *a.*

cȳclopae'dia *n.* encyclopaedia.

cȳclora'ma (-ahma) *n.* circular panorama; curved wall or cloth forming back of stage.

cȳ'clostȳle *n. & v.t.* (reproduce by) device for making copies of written document from stencil--plate.

cȳ'clotrŏn *n.* apparatus for accelerating charged atomic particles by passing them repeatedly through same electro-magnetic field.

cȳg'nèt *n.* young swan.

cȳl'ĭnder *n.* solid or hollow roller--shaped body. **cȳlin'drĭcal** *a.*

cȳm'bal *n.* (mus.) one of pair of brass plates clashed together.

cȳm'balō *n.* (pl. *-os*), dulcimer.

Cȳm'rĭc (k-) *a.* Welsh.

cȳn'ĭc *n. C~,* philosopher of ancient Greek sect despising ease, pleasure, etc.; sarcastic disbeliever in human sincerity or goodness. *a.* of Cynics; cynical. **~al** *a.* incredulous of human goodness; sneering. **~ism** *n.*

cȳ'nosure (-shoor; *or* sĭ-) *n.* centre of attraction or interest.

cȳ'près *n.* coniferous tree with dark foliage, symbolic of mourning.

cȳst *n.* bladder or sac containing liquid secretion, morbid matter, etc. **~ic** *a.*

czar etc.: see **tsar** etc.

D

D, d (dē), as Roman numeral, 500; (mus.) second note in scale of C major.

d. *abbr.* daughter; dele; *denarii, denarius* [L], pence, penny; density; departs etc.; died.

D.A. *abbr.* (U.S.) District Attorney.

D.A.A.G. *abbr.* Deputy Assistant Adjutant-General.

dăb[1] *n.* slight or undecided blow; brief application of soft thing to surface without rubbing; moisture, colour, etc. so applied. *v.* make dab(s) at; make dab (*at*); apply by dabbing; **~ off**, remove by dabbing.

dăb[2] *n.* small flat fish.

dăb[3] (hănd) *n.* expert *at.*

D.A.B. *abbr.* Dictionary of Amer. Biography.

dăbb'le *v.* wet slightly or partly; soil, splash; move in shallow water, mud, etc. with splashing; engage in desultory or dilettante way (*in*). **dăbb'ler** *n.*

dăb'chick *n.* little grebe.

dăb'ster *n.* dab hand.

da ca'pō (dahkah-), (mus.) repeat from beginning. [It.]

dāce *n.* small freshwater fish.

dachshund (dahks'ho͝ond) *n.* small short-legged long-bodied German dog.

dacoit' *n.* (hist.) member of Burmese or Indian armed robber band. **~y** *n.* (act of) gang-robbery.

dăc'tȳl *n.* metrical foot (—◡◡).

dăd, da (dah), **dăd'a** *nn.* (colloq., childish) father.

da'daïsm (dah-) *n.* 20th-c. artistic movement repudiating tradition, reason, etc. **~ist** *n. & a.*

dădd'ȳ *n.* (colloq. & familiar) father. **~-long-legs**, crane-fly.

dā'dō *n.* block forming body of pedestal; lower part (of different material or colour) of interior wall.

dae'dal *a.* skilful; complex, intricate, labyrinthine.

dae'mon *n.* indwelling or attendant spirit, genius. **daemŏn'ic** *a.* of or like supernatural power or genius.

dăff'odil *n.* yellow-flowered bulbous plant.

daft (-ahft) *a.* foolish, wild, crazy.

D.A.G. *abbr.* Deputy Adjutant--General.

dag. *abbr.* decagram.

dăgg'er (-g-) *n.* short two-edged pointed weapon; obelus (†).

dā'gō *n.* (contempt.) Spaniard or Portuguese or Italian.

dague'rreotȳpe (-gĕro-) *n.* (photograph made by) early photographic process.

dahabee'yah (dah-h-) *n.* large lateen--rigged Nile sailing-boat.

dah'lïa (dā-) *n.* kinds of composite plant cultivated for their many--coloured flowers.

dai'ly *adv.* every day, constantly. *a.* done, occurring, published, etc., every day or weekday; doing non-resident domestic work. *n.* daily newspaper or domestic worker. ~ **bread**, necessary food.

dain'tȳ *n.* choice morsel, delicacy. *a.* choice; prettily neat; hard to please.

daiquiri (dī'kǐrǐ; *or* dăk'-) *n.* drink of rum, lime-juice, and sugar.

dair'ȳ *n.* place for dealing with or in milk etc. **~-farm**, producing chiefly milk, butter, etc. **~maid**, woman employed in dairy. **~man**, dealer in milk etc.

dā'ïs *n.* low platform, usu. at upper end of room or hall.

dai'sȳ (-z-) *n.* kinds of composite field and garden flower; (sl.) first-rate specimen. **~-chain**, string of field daisies fastened together.

Dak. *abbr.* Dakota.

dal. *abbr.* decalitre.

dāle *n.* valley. **dāles'man** (-zman) *n.* dweller in dales of N. England.

dăll'ȳ *v.i.* spend time in idleness or vacillation. **dăll'ïance** *n.* love--making; delay.

Dălmā'tian *n.* large white dark--spotted dog.

dălmăt'ĭc *n.* wide-sleeved slit-sided loose long vestment.

dăl segno (sā'nyō), (mus.) repeat from point indicated by sign. [It.]

dal'tonïsm (daw-) *n.* congenital colour-blindness.

dăm[1] *n.* barrier checking flow of water in stream etc. *v.t.* confine with dam; block (*up*) or restrain (as) with dam.

dăm[2] *n.* mother (usu. of beast).

dam. *abbr.* decametre.

dăm'age *n.* harm; injury; loss; (pl.) sum claimed or adjudged in compensation for loss or injury; (sl.) cost. *v.t.* do harm to; injure.

dămascēne' *v.t.* ornament (metal, esp. steel) with inlaid gold or silver or watered pattern.

dăm'ask *n.* & *a.* (of) reversible figured woven fabric; (of) blush--red colour of damask rose. ~ **rose**, old sweet-scented variety orig. from Asia Minor.

dāme *n.* lady; (hist.) keeper of private elementary school (~-*school*); keeper of Eton boarding-house; female character in pantomime played by male actor; title of woman D.B.E., G.B.E., etc.

dămn (-m) *v.* doom to eternal torment; condemn with curses; censure or condemn, curse. **dăm'nable** *a.* deserving damnation, hateful. **dămnā'tion** *n.* damning; eternal punishment in hell. **dămned** (-md) *a.* & *adv.* damnable, damnably.

dăm'nifȳ *v.t.* (legal) cause injury to. **~ficātion** *n.*

dăm'osĕl (-z-) *n.* (arch.) damsel.

dămp *n.* moisture in air or on surface or diffused through solid; choke--damp or fire-damp. *a.* slightly wet; moist. *v.t.* stifle, dull, extinguish; discourage, depress; (mus.) stop vibration of (string etc.); make damp. **~-course**, layer of slate etc. in wall to keep damp from rising. **~en** *v.t.* damp.

dăm'per *n.* person or thing that depresses; metal plate in flue controlling combustion; small pad to stop vibration of piano strings; (Austral.) cake of unleavened bread baked in wood ashes.

dăm'sel (-z-) (arch.) young unmarried woman.

dăm'son (-z-) *n.* small dark-purple plum; tree bearing it. ~ **cheese**, solid conserve of damsons.

Dan. *abbr.* Daniel.

dance (dah-) *v.* move with rhythmic steps, glides, etc., usu. to music; jump about, move in lively way *n.* piece of dancing; dancing-party. **~r** *n.* (esp.) one who dances in public for pay.

dăn′dėlĭon *n.* yellow-flowered wild plant.

dăn′der *n.* (sl.) fighting spirit.

Dăn′die Din′mont *n.* breed of short--legged rough-coated terrier.

dăn′dle *v.t.* dance or nurse (child) in arms.

dăn′druff *n.* dead skin in small scales among hair.

dăn′dy *n.* man paying excessive attention to smartness in dress etc., fop. *a.* (U.S.) splendid. **~-brush**, stiff brush for cleaning horses. **~ism** *n.*

Dāne *n.* native of Denmark; (hist.) Northman invader of England; *great* **~**, large powerful short--haired breed of dog.

dān′ger (-j-) *n.* liability or exposure to harm; thing that causes peril. **~-money**, extra payment for dangerous work. **~ous** *a.*

dangle (dăng′gl) *v.* hang loosely; hold or carry swaying loosely; keep hanging alluringly (*before*); hang about *after*.

dănk *a.* oozy; damp and cold.

dăph′nė *n.* kinds of flowering shrub.

dăpp′er *a.* neat, precise.

dăpp′le *v.t.* variegate with rounded spots. **~-grey** *a.* & *n.* (horse) of grey dappled with darker spots.

dāre *v.* venture; have courage or impudence (to); defy, challenge; *I* **~** *say*, very likely, I am prepared to believe. **~devil**, reckless (person).

dār′ing *n.* (esp.) adventurous courage. *a.* bold, fearless.

dă′rĭōle *n.* savoury dish cooked and served in small mould.

dărk *a.* with little or no light; gloomy; obscure, secret; (of colour) deep, approaching black in hue; brown-complexioned or dark--haired. *n.* absence of light; want of knowledge; dark colour. **D~ Ages**, Middle Ages, esp. period between break-up of Roman Empire and end of 8th c. **D~ Continent**, Africa. **~ horse**, horse of whose racing form little is known (freq. fig. of persons). **~ lantern**, one of which light may be con-

cealed. **~room**, one lighted only by light not appreciably affecting photographic materials. **~en** *v.* make or become dark; perplex. **~(e)y** *n.* (colloq.) Negro. **~ish** *a.* **~ling** *a.* & *adv.* in the dark. **~nėss** *n.* **~some** *a.* gloomy; obscure.

dār′ling *n.* beloved person or animal. *a.* beloved or prized.

dărn[1] *v.t.* mend (esp. knitted fabric or hole) by interweaving yarn or thread across hole. *n.* place so mended. **~ing-stitch**, large running stitch for embroidery.

dărn[2] *n.* & *v.t.* damn.

dăr′nel *n.* grass growing as weed among corn.

dărt *n.* pointed missile thrown by hand; arrow; (pl.) game in which darts are thrown at target; sudden rapid motion; stitched tapered fold or seam for shaping garment. *v.* throw (missile); emit suddenly and sharply; spring or move with sudden rapid motion, shoot; make dart in. **~board**, board marked with circles divided into segments as target in darts.

Dăr′win′ian *a.* & *n.* (follower) of Darwin or his theories esp. of evolution by natural selection. **Dăr′winĭsm, Dăr′winĭst** *nn.*

dăsh *v.* shatter *to pieces*; knock, drive, fling, thrust, rush *away, off*, etc.; bespatter *with*; frustrate, discourage; write or throw *off* hastily and vigorously; fall, move, collide, run, etc. with violence; damn. *n.* rush, onset; (capacity for) vigorous action; showy appearance or behaviour; horizontal stroke in writing or printing (—); splash, slight infusion; dashboard. **~board**, mud-shield in front of vehicle; board or panel in front of driver of car etc. carrying indicators, gauges, etc. **~er** *n.* (esp.) contrivance for agitating cream in churn.

dăsh′ing *a.* spirited; showy.

dăs′tard *n.* brutal coward. **~ly** *a.*

data : see **datum.**

dāte[1] *n.* oblong stone-fruit; tree bearing this.

dāte[2] *n.* (specification of) day or year of writing, happening, etc. of anything; season, period; duration, term of life or existence; (colloq.) appointment, person with whom one has appointment; *out of ~*, antiquated; *up to ~*, up to standard, requirements, etc. of time. *v.* mark with date; refer to its time; bear date; reckon, have origin, *from*; be or become recognizable as of past or particular date; (colloq.) make appointment with. **~-line**, line in Pacific Ocean at which calendar day is reckoned to begin and end. **~less** *a.* undated; endless; immemorial.

dā'tive *a.* & *n.* (gram.) (case) denoting indirect or remoter object of verb's action.

dā'tum *n.* (pl. *-ta*) thing known or granted as basis for inference; fixed starting-point of scale etc.

datūr'a *n.* kinds of strongly narcotic plant.

daub *v.* coat or smear or soil (*with* clay etc.); smear *on*; paint, lay on (colours etc.), crudely and clumsily. *n.* material for daubing walls etc.; patch or smear of grease etc.; coarse clumsy painting.

daughter (daw'ter) *n.* female child or descendant; female member *of* family etc. **~-in-law**, son's wife.

daunt *v.t.* discourage, intimidate. **~less** *a.* not to be daunted.

dau'phin *n.* king of France's eldest son.

dăv'enpŏrt *n.* writing-table with drawers and hinged writing-slab; large sofa.

dăv'it *n.* one of pair of curved uprights for suspending or lowering ship's boat.

Dā'vy̆ (lămp) *n.* miner's safety lamp.

Dā'vy̆ Jones's lŏck'er (jōn'zĭz) *n.* bottom of sea esp. as grave.

daw *n.* jackdaw.

daw'dle *v.i.* idle, waste time.

dawn *v.i.* begin to grow light; appear faintly. *n.* first light, daybreak; incipient gleam.

day *n.* time during which sun is above horizon; daylight, dawn; twenty--four hours, esp. from midnight to midnight; period, time, era; specified or appointed day; part of day allotted for work. **~-book**, one in which sales etc. are noted for later transfer to ledger. **~-boy**, schoolboy living at home. **~-dream**, dream indulged in while awake. **~light**, light prevailing from sunrise to sunset; dawn; visible space or interval (*between*); **~light saving**, putting clock forward to secure longer period of daylight in evening. **~-school**, school for day-pupils only. **~spring**, (poet.) dawn. **~time**, time of daylight.

dāze *v.t.* stupefy, bewilder. *n.* dazed state.

dăzz'le *v.t.* confuse sight by excess of light, intricate motion, etc.; confound or surprise by brilliant display. *n.* bright confusing light.

D.B.E. *abbr.* Dame Commander of (the Order of) the British Empire.

D.C. *abbr.*, *da capo* [It.], repeat from beginning; direct current; District of Columbia.

D.C.L. *abbr.* Doctor of Civil Law.

D.C.M. *abbr.* Distinguished Conduct Medal; District Court Martial.

D.D. *abbr.* Doctor of Divinity; *dono dedit* [L], gave as a gift.

D.D.D. *abbr.*, *dat dicat dedicat* [L], gives, devotes, and dedicates.

D.D.S. *abbr.* Doctor of Dental Surgery.

D.D.T. *abbr.*, dichlor-diphenyl-tri-chlorethane (insecticide).

D.E.A. *abbr.* Department of Economic Affairs.

dea'con *n.* clergyman below priest; layman dealing with secular affairs of church. **~ess** *n.* female deacon; woman with functions resembling deacon's.

dead (dĕd) *a.* no longer alive; numb; without spiritual life; obsolete; not effective; inanimate; extinct; dull, inactive, idle; out of play; not live; abrupt; complete; exact; absolute; *~ to*, unconscious or unheeding of. *n.* dead person(s); time of greatest darkness, cold, etc. *adv.* profoundly, absolutely, completely. **~-alive**, dull, spiritless. **~-beat**, utterly exhausted. **~ end**, end of passage etc. through which there is no way. **~-end**, leading nowhere. **~head**, non-paying member of audience etc. **~ heat**, race etc. in which winners finish exactly even. **~ letter**, law etc. no longer observed; undelivered or unclaimed letter. ∼light, shutter inside porthole or cabin window. ∼-line, fixed time-limit. ∼lock, position from which no progress is possible. ∼ march, funeral processional music. ∼ men, empty bottles. ∼-nettle, non-stinging nettle-like plant. ∼-pan, (sl.) expressionless. ∼ reckoning, estimation of position of ship etc. without taking observations. ∼ shot, unerring marksman. ∼ weight, heavy inert weight. ∼en v. deprive of or lose vitality, force, etc.; make insensible (to).

dead'ly (děd-) a. causing fatal injury or death; intense. ∼ nightshade, shrub with poisonous black berries.

deaf (děf) a. wholly or partly without hearing; inattentive; insensible (to). ∼-aid, small sound amplifier carried or worn by deaf person. ∼-mute, deaf and dumb person.

deaf'en (děf-) v.t. deprive of hearing.

deal[1] n. amount, quantity.

deal[2] n. (sawn) fir or pine wood.

deal[3] v. (dealt, pr. dělt), distribute among several; assign as share; deliver (blow); associate or do business or occupy oneself with; behave in specified way (with). n. dealing, turn to deal; business transaction, bargain; raw ∼, unfair treatment. ∼er n. ∼ings n.pl. (esp.) conduct or transactions.

dean n. head of cathedral chapter; (rural ∼), clergyman with authority over group of parishes; fellow of college with disciplinary functions; head of faculty or department in university. ∼ery n. dean's house or office; rural dean's division of archdeaconry.

dear a. beloved, loved (freq. merely polite); precious to; costly; not cheap. n. beloved one; charming person or thing. adv. at high price, dearly. int. expressing surprise, distress, etc.

dearth (děr-) n. scarcity and dearness of food; scanty supply of.

death (děth) n. dying, end of life; being dead; end, destruction; cause of death. ∼-duties, tax levied before property passes to heir. ∼-mask, cast taken from dead person's face. ∼-rate, proportion of deaths. ∼-roll, list of those killed. ∼'s-head, skull as emblem of mortality. ∼-trap, unwholesome or dangerous place etc. ∼-warrant, order for execution (also fig.). ∼-watch (beetle), small beetle boring in old wood and making sound like watch-tick. ∼less a. immortal. ∼ly a. & adv. deadly; like death.

děb n. (colloq.) debutante.

débâcle (dābah'-) n. utter collapse or downfall. [F]

debar' v.t. exclude; preclude.

debark' v. disembark.

debase' v.t. lower in character, quality, or value; depreciate (coin).

debate' v. dispute about, discuss; engage in (formal) argument or discussion (of); consider, ponder. n. controversy; discussion; public argument. **deba'table** a. subject to dispute.

debauch' v.t. pervert from virtue; vitiate (taste etc.); seduce. n. bout of sensual indulgence. ∼ee' (-shē) n. viciously sensual person. ∼ery n. indulgence in or prevalence of sensual habits.

deběn'ture n. bond etc. of corporation or company acknowledging sum on which fixed interest is due (esp. as prior charge on assets); (pl.) debenture stock. ∼ stock, debentures as fixed-interest stock.

debil'itate v.t. cause debility in.

debil'ity n. feebleness, weakness.

deb'it n. entry in account of sum owing. v.t. charge with sum, enter (sum) against or to.

debonair' a. genial, unembarrassed.

debouch' (or -ōōsh) v.i. issue from ravine, woods, etc. into open ground.

deb'ris (-rē; or dā-) n. strewn fragments, drifted accumulation.

debt (dět) n. what is owed; state of owing something.

debt'or (dět-) n. person in debt.

debŭnk' v.t. (colloq.) remove false sentiment from.

debŭs' v. (mil.) unload or alight from motor vehicles.

début (dā'bū *or* -ōō) *n.* first appearance in society or as performer etc.

dĕb'ūtante (-ahnt; *or* dā-) *n.* girl making first appearance in society.

Dec. *abbr.* December.

dĕc'a- in comb., ten. **dĕc'agon** *n.* plane figure with ten sides and angles; **dĕcăg'onal** *a.* **~grăm** *n.* ten grams. **~hē'dron** *n.* ten-sided solid. **~litre** (-lē-) *n.* ten litres. **~lŏgue** (-g) *n.* ten commandments. **~mētre** *n.* ten metres. **~pŏd** *n.:* ten--footed crustacean. **~sўll'able** *n.* line of ten syllables; **~sўllăb'ĭc** *a.*

dĕc'āde (*or* -ad) *n.* ten-year period; set or series of ten.

dĕc'adence *n.* (period of) decline, esp. of art or literature. **~ent** *a.* in state of decay or decline; belonging to decadent age; *n.* decadent person.

dĕcămp' *v.i.* break up or leave camp; take oneself off, go away suddenly.

dĕcā'nal *a.* of dean; of dean's or south side of choir.

dĕcā'nī, (mus. direction) to be sung by decanal side. [L]

dĕcănt' *v.t.* pour off (wine etc.) leaving sediment behind.

dĕcăn'ter *n.* stoppered bottle in which wine etc. is brought to table.

dĕcăp'ĭtāte *v.t.* behead. **~ā'tion** *n.*

dēcăr'bonīze *v.t.* (esp.) remove carbon deposit from (engine of car etc.).

dĕcăth'lon *n.* composite athletic contest of ten events.

dĕcay' *v.* rot, decompose; decline in power, wealth, energy, etc. *n.* decline, falling off; ruinous state; decomposition.

dĕcease' *n.* (legal or formal) death. *v.i.* die. **dĕceased'** (-st) *a. & n.* dead (person).

dĕceit' (-sēt) *n.* piece of deception; deceitfulness. **~ful** *a.* given to or marked by deceit.

dĕceive' (-sēv) *v.t.* persuade of what is false; mislead, take in; disappoint.

dĕcĕl'erāte *v.* decrease speed (of).

Dĕcĕm'ber *n.* twelfth month of year.

dē'cencў *n.* being decent; compliance with recognized notions of propriety; (pl.) decent or becoming acts or observances.

dĕcĕnn'ĭal *a.* of or lasting for or recurring in ten years. *n.* tenth anniversary.

dē'cent *a.* seemly; not immodest or obscene; respectable; passable; good enough; (colloq.) kindly, not severe.

dēcĕn'tralīze *v.t.* divide and distribute (government etc.) among local centres.

dĕcĕp'tion *n.* deceiving or being deceived; thing that deceives.

dĕcĕp'tĭve *a.* apt to mislead.

dē'cĭ- in comb., one-tenth. **dē'cĭgrăm, ~litre** (-lē-), **~mētre** *nn.* one-tenth of gram, litre, metre.

dē'cĭbĕl *n.* unit for measuring intensity of sound.

dĕcīde' *v.* settle by giving victory to one side; give judgement; bring or come to resolution or decision.

dĕcī'dĕd *a.* definite or unquestionable; not vacillating. **~lў** *adv.* undeniably, undoubtedly.

dĕcĭd'ūous *a.* shed periodically or normally; (of plant) shedding leaves annually.

dē'cĭmal *a.* of tenth parts or number ten; proceeding by tens. *n.* decimal fraction or figure. **~ coinage,** in which each denomination is worth ten times that next below. **~ figure,** figure to right of decimal point. **~ fraction,** one whose denominator is power of ten, expressed in figures to right of units figure after a dot (**~ point**) and denoting tenths, hundredths, etc. **~ system,** system of weights and measures with each denomination ten times that immediately below. **~īze** *v.t.* express as decimal or in decimal system.

dē'cĭmāte *v.t.* kill tenth or large proportion of. **~ā'tion** *n.*

dĕcī'pher *v.t.* make out (cipher, bad writing, hieroglyphics, etc.); make out meaning of. **~ment** *n.*

dĕcī'sion *n.* act of deciding; settlement; formal judgement; resolve; decided character.

dĕcī'sĭve *a.* deciding, conclusive; decided.

dĕck *n.* platform extending from side to side of (part of) ship or boat; floor of bus etc.; (sl.) *the* ground; pack (of cards). *v.t.* array, adorn; cover as or with deck.

~-chair, folding reclining chair.
~-hand, ordinary sailor.

děck'le-edge n. rough uncut edge of sheet of paper.

děclaim' v. speak rhetorically; recite; deliver impassioned speech. **děclamā'tion** n.; **děclăm'atorў** a.

děclarā'tion n. declaring; emphatic or deliberate or formal statement. **děclă'ratorў** a.

děclāre' v. proclaim or announce publicly, formally, or explicitly; acknowledge possession of (dutiable goods); (crick.) declare innings closed; (bridge) name trump suit or bid 'no trumps'.

děclǎss'é (dā-; -sā) a. (fem. -ée), that has sunk in social scale.

děclěn'sion n. declining or deviation from vertical or horizontal position or from standard; deterioration; (gram.) (class in which noun or adj. or pron. is grouped by) variation of form constituting cases. ~al a.

děclinā'tion n. inclination from vertical or horizontal; angular distance from celestial equator; deviation of magnetic needle from true N. and S.

declīne' v. show downward tendency; decrease, deteriorate; refuse; rehearse or make case-forms of (nouns etc.). n. gradual decrease or deterioration; decay; wasting disease.

děcliv'itў n. downward slope.

děclŭtch' v.i. disengage clutch.

děcǒc'tion n. extraction, liquid obtained, by boiling.

dēcōde' v.t. decipher.

dēcōke' v.t. (colloq.) decarbonize.

décolletage (dākǒl'tahzh) n. (exposure of neck and shoulders by) low-cut neck. [F]

décolleté (-ltā) a. (fem. -ée), low--necked; wearing low-necked dress. [F]

dēcompōse' (-z) v. separate or resolve into elements; rot. **dēcǒmposi'-tion** n.

dēcomprěss' v.t. relieve pressure on (person etc.) by air-lock etc.; reduce compression in (esp. engine of car etc.). ~ion n.

dēcontăm'ināte v.t. rid of (esp. radio-active) contamination. ~ā'tion n.

dēcontrōl' v.t. release from (esp. Government) control.

décor (dā'kōr) n. all that makes up appearance of room, stage, etc.

děc'orāte v.t. adorn, beautify; paint, paper, etc. (room etc.); invest with order, medal, etc. ~āted a. (esp.) of English Gothic architectural style c. 1250-1350. ~ative a. ~ātor n. (esp.) tradesman who decorates houses.

děcorā'tion n. decorating; badge, medal etc.; (pl.) flags etc. put up on festive occasion. **D~ Day,** (U.S.) annual commemoration (30th Mar.) of soldiers who fell in Civil War.

děcōr'ous (or děk'-) a. not offending against decency or seemliness.

děcōr'um n. seemliness, propriety, etiquette.

děcoy' n. netted pond into which wild duck may be enticed; bird etc. used to entice others; enticement, trap. v.t. entice into place of capture, esp. with decoy; ensnare.

děcrease' v. lessen, diminish. n. (dē'-) diminution, lessening.

děcree' n. authoritative order; judicial decision. v.t. ordain by decree. ~ ni'sī, order for divorce remaining conditional for period.

děcrěp'it a. enfeebled with age; infirm. **děcrěp'itūde** n.

děcrē'tal n. Papal decree.

děcrУ' v.t. disparage, cry down.

děc'ūple a. tenfold. n. tenfold amount. v. multiply by ten.

děd'icāte v.t. devote or give up (to God, person, purpose, etc.); inscribe (book etc.) to patron etc. ~ā'tion n. (esp.) dedicatory inscription. ~ā'tory a.

dědūce' v.t. (-cible), infer; draw as conclusion (from).

dědŭct' v.t. subtract; take away or withhold. ~tion n. deducting, amount deducted; inference by reasoning from general to particular; thing deduced. ~tive a.

deed n. thing consciously done; fact, reality; legal document. v.t. convey or transfer by deed. ~-poll, deed made and executed by one party only.

deem v.t. believe, consider, judge. **Deem'ster** n. Manx judge.

deep *a.* going far down or far in; immersed *in*; profound; heartfelt; hard to fathom. *n.* abyss, pit; *the* sea. *adv.* far down or in. **dee'pen** *v.*

deer *n.* kinds of ruminant quadruped with deciduous branching horns. **~-hound,** large rough-haired greyhound. **~stalker,** cloth cap with peak before and behind.

deface' *v.t.* disfigure; make illegible. **~ment** *n.*

de facto, in fact, whether by right or not. [L]

de'falcāte *v.i.* be guilty of defalcation. **~ā'tion** *n.* misappropriation of funds; breach of trust concerning money.

defāme' *v.t.* attack good fame of. **defamā'tion** (*or* dē-) *n.*; **defăm'atory** *a.*

default' *n.* failure to act or appear or pay. *v.i.* fail to meet obligations. **~er** *n.* (esp., mil.) soldier guilty of military offence.

defeat' *v.t.* worst in battle or other contest; frustrate, baffle. *n.* lost battle or contest; frustration. **~ism** *n.* tendency to accept defeat. **~ist** *n.* & *a.*

de'fecāte *v.* clear of impurities, refine; void excrement.

defĕct' *n.* failing; shortcoming, blemish. *v.i.* desert.

defĕc'tion *n.* abandonment of leader or cause.

defĕc'tive *a.* incomplete, faulty; wanting, deficient.

defĕnce' *n.* defending from or resistance against attack; (mil., pl.) fortifications; defendant's case in law-suit. **~less** *a.*

defĕnd' *v.* ward off attack from; keep safe, protect; conduct defence (of) in law-suit.

defĕn'dant *n.* person accused or sued in court of law.

defĕn'der *n.* one who defends.

defĕn'sible *a.* easily defended; justifiable. **~ibil'ity** *n.*

defĕn'sive *a.* serving for defence. *n.* state or position of defence.

defĕr'¹ *v.t.* put off, postpone. **~ment** *n.*

defĕr'² *v.i.* submit or make concessions *to* (person etc.).

dĕf'erence *n.* compliance with advice etc. of another; respectful conduct;

in ~ to, out of respect for. **dĕferĕn'tial** *a.*

defī'ance *n.* challenge to fight; open disobedience or disregard.

defī'ant *a.* expressing defiance.

defī'ciency (-shn-) *n.* lack or shortage; thing wanting; deficit. **~ disease,** disease caused by deficiency of vitamins etc. in diet.

defī'cient (-shnt) *a.* insufficient in quantity, force, etc.

dĕf'icit *n.* deficiency in sum of money etc.; excess of liabilities over assets.

dē'file¹ *n.* narrow gorge or pass. *v.i.* (-īl') march in file, go one by one.

defile'² *v.t.* make dirty, pollute; profane. **~ment** *n.*

define' *v.t.* mark out (limits, boundary); fix or show clearly; state precise meaning of.

dĕf'inite *a.* with exact limits; determinate, distinct, precise. **~ article,** demonstrative adj. *the.* **~ly** *adv.* clearly, plainly; (colloq.) yes indeed.

dĕfini'tion *n.* statement of precise meaning; making or being distinct, degree of distinctness.

defin'itive *a.* to be regarded as final; not subject to revision.

deflāte' *v.* let air out of (tyre etc.); reduce inflation of (currency), practise deflation. **~tion** *n.*; **~tionary** *a.*

deflĕct' *v.* bend or turn aside from straight line. **deflĕ'xion** (-kshn), **~ĕc'tion** *n.*

dēflorā'tion *n.* deflowering.

deflow'er *v.t.* deprive of virginity; ravage; strip of flowers.

defŏ'rest *v.t.* clear of forest. **~ā'tion** *n.*

defōrm' *v.t.* spoil aspect or shape of; disfigure; (*p.p.*) misshapen. **defōrmā'tion** *n.* **~ity** *n.* deformed state; malformation.

defraud' *v.t.* cheat, fraudulently deprive (*of*).

defray' *v.t.* provide money for.

defrŏck' *v.t.* unfrock.

defrŏst' *v.t.* remove frost or ice from, unfreeze.

dĕft *a.* dextrous, adroit.

defŭnct' *a.* dead; obsolete.

defȳ' *v.t.* challenge *to* do or prove something; resist openly; present insuperable obstacles to.

deg. *abbr.* degree.

dĕgĕn'eracў *n.* degenerate state.

dĕgĕn'erate *a.* having lost qualities proper to race or kind, debased. *n.* degenerate person. *v.i.* (-āt), become degenerate. **~ā'tion** *n.*

dĕgluti'tion (-lọō-) *n.* swallowing.

dĕgradā'tion *n.* degrading; disgrace; thing that degrades.

dĕgrāde' *v.t.* reduce to lower rank; debase. **~ding** *a.* dishonouring, humiliating.

dĕgree' *n.* stage in ascending or descending scale; unit of angular or of thermometric measurement; academic rank given for proficiency in scholarship or as honour.

dĕhīs'cent *a.* (of seed-vessels) gaping, bursting open.

dĕhū'manīze *v.t.* divest or deprive of human qualities.

dĕhŷ'drāte *v.* deprive of or lose water.

dē-īce' *v.t.* prevent formation of ice on, remove ice from (wings etc. of aircraft).

dē'īcīde *n.* killing, killer, of god.

dē'īfŷ *v.t.* make a god of; worship. **~ficā'tion** *n.*

deign (dān) *v.i.* condescend.

dē'ī grā'tia (-shĭā), by God's grace. [L]

dē'ism *n.* belief in existence of God with rejection of revelation. **dē'ist** *n.*; **dēīs'tĭc** *a.*

dē' itŷ *n.* divine status or nature; god.

dĕjĕct' *v.t.* dispirit, cast down. **dĕjĕc'tion** *n.*

dē jur'ē (joor-), rightful, by right. [L]

Del. *abbr.* Delaware.

del. *abbr.*, *delineavit* [L], drew this.

dĕlā'tion *n.* informing against person.

dĕlay' *v.* put off; hinder, frustrate; be tardy. *n.* lack of dispatch; hindrance.

dē'lĕ *imper.* delete.

dĕlĕc'table *a.* delightful.

dēlĕctā'tion *n.* enjoyment.

dĕl'ĕgacў *n.* body of delegates.

dĕl'ĕgāte *v.t.* send as representative(s) to council or conference; commit (authority) to representative(s). *n.* (-ĭt) such representative.

dĕlĕgā'tion *n.* delegating; delegacy; representatives of State in U.S. Congress.

dĕlēte' *v.t.* strike out (word, passage, etc.). **~tion** *n.*

dĕlētēr'ious *a.* harmful.

dĕlf(t) *n.* kind of earthenware.

dĕlĭb'erāte *v.* take counsel, hold debate; weigh, consider. *a.* (-ĭt), intentional, fully considered. **~ā'tion** *n.* deliberating; being deliberate. **~ative** *a.* of or appointed for deliberation or debate.

dĕl'icacў *n.* delicateness; refined feeling; choice kind of food.

dĕl'icate *a.* dainty, luxurious; tender or easily harmed; fastidious; slender, fine, exquisite; sensitive.

dĕlicatĕss'ĕn *n.* (shop selling) delicacies for table.

dĕlĭ'cious *a.* highly delightful esp. to taste or smell.

dĕlight' *v.* please highly; take intense pleasure *in. n.* (thing giving) great pleasure. **~ful** *a.*

dĕlim'ĭt *v.t.* determine limits or boundaries of. **~ā'tion** *n.*

dĕlin'ĕāte *v.t.* portray by drawing or description. **~ā'tion**, **~ātor** *nn.*

dĕlin'quencў *n.* being delinquent; neglect of duty; guilt; misdeed.

dĕlin'quent *n.* person who fails in duty or commits offence. *a.* defaulting, guilty.

dĕliquesce' (-ĕs) *v.i.* become liquid, esp. by absorbing moisture from air. **~cence** *n.*; **~cent** *a.*

dĕlī'rious *a.* affected with delirium; raving; wildly excited.

dĕlī'rium *n.* disordered state of mind; wildly excited mood. **~ trē'mĕns** (-z), form of delirium due to heavy drinking.

dĕlĭv'er *v.t.* rescue, save, set free; transfer or hand over; convey (letters, goods) to addressee or purchaser; aim (blow, cricket-ball, attack); utter (speech); assist (female) in giving birth, assist in birth of; *be ~ed of,* give birth to.

dĕlĭv'erance *n.* rescue; emphatically delivered opinion; verdict.

dĕlĭv'erў *n.* delivering or being delivered; periodical distribution of letters or goods; manner of delivering.

dĕll *n.* little wooded hollow.

Dĕl'phĭc *a.* oracular, ambiguous.

dĕlphĭn'ĭum *n.* (esp. cultivated kinds of) larkspur.

dĕl'ta *n.* Greek letter D, written Δ; triangular alluvial tract at mouth of river. **~ wing,** triangular swept--back wing of some aircraft.

dĕl'toid *a.* delta-shaped. *n.* deltoid muscle in shoulder.

dĕlūde' *v.t.* fool, deceive.

dĕl'ūge *n.* great flood; downpour. *v.t.* inundate.

dĕlū'sion (*or* -ōō-) *n.* false belief esp. as symptom or form of madness.

dĕlū'sĭve (*or* -ōō-) *a.* deceptive, disappointing.

de lūxe *a.* sumptuous; of superior kind. [F]

dĕlve *v.* (arch.) dig; make laborious research.

dĕm'agŏgue (-g) *n.* orator or agitator appealing to passions of mob. **~gŏg'ic** (-gĭk) *a.*; **~gŏgy** (-gĭ) *n.*

dĕmand' (-ah-) *n.* request made as of right; call for commodity; urgent claim. *v.t.* make demand for.

dĕmārcā'tion *n.* marking of boundary or limits of anything.

démarche (dā'mársh) *n.* political step or proceeding. [F]

dĕmean'[1] *v.t.* lower dignity of.

dĕmean'[2] *v.refl.* conduct or bear oneself. **dĕmea'nour** *n.* bearing.

dĕmĕn'tĕd *a.* beside oneself.

démenti (dāmahń'tē) *n.* official denial. [F]

dĕmĕn'tĭa (*or* -sha) *n.* failure or loss of mental powers as form of insanity. **~ prae'cox,** schizophrenia.

dĕmerār'a (*or* -ār'a) *n.* yellowish--brown raw cane sugar.

dĕmē'rĭt *n.* fault, defect; mark for bad conduct etc.

dĕmesne' (-ān, -ēn) *n.* possession of land with unrestricted rights; territory; landed estate.

dĕm'ĭgŏd *n.* being half divine and half human.

dĕm'ĭjohn (-ŏn) *n.* large wicker-cased bottle.

dĕm'ĭ-mŏnde *n.* class of women of doubtful reputation on outskirts of society. [F]

dĕmīse' (-z) *v.t.* convey by will or lease; transmit by death or abdication. *n.* demising; death.

dĕm'ĭsĕm'ĭquāver *n.* (mus.) note equal to half semiquaver.

dĕm'ĭûrge *n.* (Platonic philos.) creator of world.

dēmō'bĭlīze *v.* disband, release from, armed forces. **~īzā'tion** *n.*

dĕmŏc'racy *n.* (State practising) government by people as whole, esp. through elected representatives.

dĕm'ocrăt *n.* advocate of democracy; *D~,* member of U.S. Democratic party. **dĕmŏc'ratīze** *v.t.*; **~īzā'tion** *n.*

dĕmocrăt'ĭc *a.* of, practising, etc., democracy; *D~,* of U.S. Democratic political party, opposed to Republican party.

dĕmŏg'raphy *n.* statistical study of life in human communities. **dĕmogrăph'ĭc** *a.*

dĕmŏl'ĭsh *v.t.* pull or throw down (building); destroy; (colloq.) eat up. **dēmoli'tion** (*or* dĕ-) *n.*

dē'mon *n.* devil or evil spirit; person of great energy, skill, etc. **dĕmŏn'ic** *a.* **~ŏl'atrў** *n.* worship of demons. **~ŏl'ogў** *n.* study of beliefs about demons.

dĕmō'nĭăc *n.* person possessed by evil spirit. *a.* possessed by demon; of or like demons; devilish; frenzied.

dĕm'onstrable *a.* capable of being shown or proved.

dĕm'onstrāte *v.* give or be proof of; establish truth of; make or take part in demonstration. **~ā'tion** *n.* proving or proof; setting forth of case; show of feeling; display of armed force or organized expression of opinion. **dĕmŏn'stratĭve** *a.* conclusive; given to or marked by open expression of feelings; (of pron. or adj.) serving to point out or identify; *n.* demonstrative word. **~ātor** *n.* (esp.) scientific (assistant) teacher doing practical work with students.

dĕmŏr'alīze *v.t.* ruin morals or morale of. **~īzā'tion** *n.*

Dē'mŏs *n.* democracy personified.

Demosth. *abbr.* Demosthenes.

dĕmōte' *v.t.* (colloq.) reduce to lower rank or grade.

dĕmūr' *v.i.* raise objections; take exception. *n.* raising of objections.

demūre′ *a.* quiet or undemonstrative; affectedly coy.

dĕmŭ′rrage *n.* (amount payable for) detention or delaying of ship or railway truck; Bank of England charge for changing notes or coins into bullion.

dĕmŭ′rrer *n.* legal exception to relevance of opponent's point.

dĕmȳ′ *n.* size of paper (printing, 22½ × 17½ in.; writing, 20 × 15½ in.).

dĕn *n.* wild beast's lair; small private room.

dĕnār′ĭus *n.* (pl. -*ĭĭ*), ancient-Roman silver coin.

dē′narȳ *a.* of ten; decimal.

dēnă′tionalīze *v.t.* (esp.) return (nationalized industry etc.) to private ownership. **~izā′tion** *n.*

dēnā′ture *v.t.* change essential qualities of; make (alcohol) unfit for drinking.

dēne *n.* deep wooded valley.

dĕng′ue (-nggĭ) *n.* infectious eruptive fever with acute pain in joints.

dĕnī′al *n.* denying or refusing; contradiction.

dĕn′ĭer (*or* dĭnēr′) *n.* unit of fineness of silk etc. yarn.

dĕn′ĭgrāte *v.t.* blacken.

dĕn′im *n.* twilled cotton fabric; (pl.) (usu. blue) denim overalls.

dĕn′ĭzen *n.* inhabitant; naturalized foreign species.

dĕnŏm′ĭnāte *v.t.* give specified name to; designate. **~ātor** *n.* number below line in vulgar fraction; divisor.

dĕnŏmĭnā′tion *n.* name, title; class of units in money etc.; distinctively named Church or sect. **~al** *a.* of religious denominations.

dēnotā′tion *n.* denoting; term's primary meaning; designation. **dēnō′tative** *a.* denoting.

dēnōte′ *v.t.* stand for; be sign of; indicate; signify.

dénouement (dānōō′mahṅ) *n.* issue, final solution.

dēnounce′ *v.t.* inform or inveigh against; give notice of termination of (treaty etc.).

dē nō′vō, afresh; once more. [L]

dĕnse *a.* closely compacted; crowded together; stupid.

dĕn′sitȳ *n.* closeness of substance; crowded state; stupidity.

dĕnt *n.* depression left by blow. *v.t.* mark with dent.

dĕn′tal *a.* of tooth, teeth, or dentistry; (of sound) made with tongue-tip against front teeth. *n.* dental sound or letter.

dĕn′tāte *a.* toothed, notched.

dĕn′tĭfrĭce *n.* preparation for cleaning teeth.

dĕn′tine (-ēn *or* -ĭn) *n.* hard dense tissue forming main part of teeth.

dĕn′tĭst *n.* one who treats diseases of teeth. **~rȳ** *n.*

dĕntĭ′tion *n.* teething; characteristic arrangement of teeth.

dĕn′ture *n.* set of (artificial) teeth.

dēnūdā′tion *n.* stripping; (geol.) disappearance of forests or surface soil.

dēnūde′ *v.t.* make naked or bare; strip *of*.

dēnŭncĭā′tion *n.* denouncing; invective. **dēnŭn′ciatorȳ** *a.*

dēnȳ′ *v.t.* declare untrue or non-existent; disavow; refuse; **~** *one-self*, be abstinent.

dē′odār *n.* Himalayan cedar.

dēō′dorant *n.* & *a.* deodorizing (substance).

dēō′dorīze *v.t.* rid of smell. **~izā′-tion** *n.*

Dē′ō volĕn′tė, if God wills, if nothing prevents. [L]

dep. *abbr.* departs.

dēpārt′ *v.* go away (from); die; diverge or deviate. **~ure** *n.*

dēpārt′ment *n.* separate part of complex whole, esp. of business or of municipal or State administration; French administrative district. **~ store**, large shop selling great variety of goods. **dēpārtmĕn′-tal** *a.*

dēpĕnd′ *v.i.* be suspended; be contingent or dependent; rely, reckon confidently; *it* (*all*) **~s**, it depends on circumstances. **~able** *a.* reliable.

dēpĕn′dant, -ent *n.* dependent person; servant.

dēpĕn′dence *n.* depending; reliance; thing relied on.

dēpĕn′dencȳ *n.* something subordinate; dependent State.

dēpĕn′dent *a.* depending; contingent,

subordinate, subject; maintained at another's cost; (gram.) in subordinate relation.

dĕpĭct' *v.t.* represent in picture or words. ~**tion** *n.*

dĕp'ĭlāte *v.t.* remove hair from. ~**ā'tion** *n.*; **dĕpĭl'atorў** *a. & n.*

dĕplēte' *v.t.* empty out; (nearly) exhaust. ~**tion** *n.*

dĕplôr'able *a.* lamentable; to be regretted; blameworthy.

dĕplôre' *v.t.* grieve over; regret; deprecate.

dĕploy' *v.* spread out, put into or take up position, for most effective action etc. ~**ment** *n.*

dĕpō'nent *n.* maker of legal deposition; deponent verb. *a.* (of verbs) of passive form but active meaning.

dĕpŏp'ūlāte *v.t.* reduce population of. ~**ā'tion** *n.*

dĕpôrt' *v.t.* remove into exile; banish (alien); behave or conduct oneself. **dēpôrtā'tion** *n.* ~**ment** *n.* behaviour, bearing.

dĕpōse' (-z) *v.* remove from office, dethrone; state, testify.

dĕpŏs'ĭt (-z-) *n.* thing stored for safe keeping; sum placed in bank; earnest money; layer of accumulated matter. *v.t.* lay or set down; leave as deposit; entrust for keeping. ~**arў** *n.* person to whom thing is entrusted. ~**or** *n.* ~**orў** *n.* storehouse.

dĕposĭ'tion (-z-) *n.* deposing; removing; (giving of) sworn evidence.

dĕp'ot (-ō) *n.* storehouse; (mil.) place for stores, head-quarters; place where buses etc. are kept; (U.S., dĕ'-), railway or bus station, air terminal.

dĕprāve' *v.t.* corrupt morally. ~**d** *a.* wicked, dissolute.

dĕprăv'ĭtў *n.* wickedness, moral corruption.

dĕp'rĕcāte *v.t.* advise avoidance of; plead against. ~**ā'tion** *n.*; ~**atorў** *a.*

dĕprē'ciāte (-shĭ-) *v.* disparage; lower in value. ~**ā'tion** *n.* depreciating; fall in value. ~**atorў** *a.* disparaging.

dĕprĕdā'tion *n.* spoliation; (pl.) ravages.

dĕprĕss' *v.t.* lower or reduce; affect with economic depression; dispirit, deject. ~**ĭble** *a.*

dĕprĕ'ssion *n.* part of surface below general level; low spirits; lowering of barometric pressure, centre of low pressure; reduction in economic activity, period of reduced activity, slump.

dĕprĭvā'tion *n.* (esp.) felt loss.

dĕprĭve' *v.t.* dispossess or strip *of*; debar from enjoyment *of*; depose from (esp. ecclesiastical) office.

dept. *abbr.* department.

dĕpth *n.* being deep, measurement from top down or from front to back or from surface inwards; profundity, intensity; (usu. pl.) deep or lowest or inmost part; deep region; middle (of winter, night). ~**-charge**, explosive charge set to explode at certain depth under water.

dĕpūtā'tion *n.* body of persons sent to represent others.

dĕpūte' *v.t.* commit (task, authority) to another; appoint as substitute.

dĕp'ūtīze *v.t.* act as deputy (*for*).

dĕp'ūtў *n.* person acting as substitute; member of representative legislature. *a.* deputed; acting instead of or as subordinate to; vice-.

dĕrail' (*or* dē-) *v.t.* make (train etc.) leave rails. ~**ment** *n.*

dĕrānge' (-j) *v.t.* throw into confusion, disorganize; make insane; disturb. ~**ment** *n.*

dĕrāte' *v.t.* lower or abolish rates on.

Der'bў (där-) *n.* annual flat race for three-year-olds run at Epsom; other important horse-races etc. **dĕr'bў** *n.* (U.S.) bowler hat.

dĕ'rĕlĭct *a.* left ownerless (esp. of ship at sea); abandoned by society; (U.S.) neglectful of duty. *n.* derelict ship or article or person.

dĕrĕlĭc'tion *n.* neglect (*of* duty etc.); sin of omission.

dĕrīde' *v.t.* scoff at.

de rigueur (rēgĕr'), required by etiquette. [F]

dĕrī'sion *n.* ridicule, scoffing.

dĕrī'sĭve *a.* mocking, scoffing.

dĕrī'sorў *a.* mocking, ridiculing.

dĕrĭvā'tion *n.* (esp.) source to which thing is traced; descent.

dĕrĭv'atĭve *a.* of derived kind. *n.* derivative word or substance; offshoot.

derīve' v. obtain or have (from source); have origin from; trace or show descent, origin, or formation of.

dĕrmatī'tĭs n. inflammation of skin.

dĕrmatŏl'ogy n. study of skin. ~lŏ'gĭcal a. ~logĭst n. (esp.) specialist in diseases of skin.

dĕ'rogāte v.i. detract from; do something derogatory. ~ā'tion n. **dĕrŏg'atory** n. involving impairment or disparagement or discredit to; unsuited to one's dignity or position.

dĕ'rrick n. kinds of hoisting apparatus with pivoted or adjustable beam or arm; framework over deep bore-hole, esp. oil-well.

dĕ'rris n. kinds of tropical plant with tuberous root yielding insecticide.

dĕrv n. diesel fuel for road vehicles.

dĕr'vish n. Moslem friar vowed to poverty and austerity.

dĕscănt' v.i. talk at large, dwell upon. n. (dĕs'-) melody added above plain-song melody, hymn-tune, etc.

dĕscĕnd' v. come or go down; slope downwards; stoop (to meanness etc.); swoop on; be derived or descended or transmitted from. ~ant n. person or thing descended (of). ~er n. esp. (part of) letter descending below line.

dĕscĕnt' n. descending; slope; way down; sinking in scale; sudden attack; lineage.

dĕscrībe' v.t. give description of; mark out or draw or move in (esp. geom. figure).

dĕscrip'tion n. verbal portrait or portraiture; sort or kind or class (of thing). ~tive a. full of description; graphic.

dĕscry' v.t. make out dimly; succeed in discerning.

dĕs'ecrāte v.t. violate sanctity of. ~ā'tion, ~ātor nn.

dĕsĕrt'¹ (-z-) n. (usu. pl.) (conduct or qualities deserving) recompense.

dĕsĕrt'² (-z-) v. abandon, depart from, forsake; run away. a. & n. (dĕz'-) uninhabited and barren, esp. waterless (region). ~er n. (esp.) soldier etc. who leaves service without permission.

dĕsĕr'tion (-z-) n. deserting or being deserted.

dĕsĕrve' (-z-) v. be entitled by conduct or qualities to; have rightful claim to be well or ill treated at hands of. ~vĕdly adv. ~ving a. meritorious; worthy of.

dĕs'iccāte v. exhaust of moisture; dry. ~ā'tion n.; ~ative a.

dĕsĭd'erāte v.t. feel want of. ~ative a. & n. (verb or form) expressing desire. ~ā'tum n. (pl. -ta) something required or desired.

dĕsign' (-zīn) n. plan, purpose; preliminary sketch or plan; general idea, construction, etc., faculty of evolving these; pattern. ~ v. form or make design(s) for; be designer. **dĕsign'ĕdly** adv. on purpose, intentionally. ~er n. (esp.) one who designs theatrical settings and costumes, manufactured articles, etc.

dĕs'ignate (-z-) a. (placed after noun), appointed but not yet installed. v.t. (-āt), style or describe as; specify; appoint to office.

dĕsignā'tion (-z-) n. appointing to office; name, title; description.

dĕsign'ing (-zīn-) a. crafty, artful, scheming.

dĕsīr'able (-z-) a. worth wishing for; pleasing. ~bĭl'ity n.

dĕsīre' (-z-) n. craving, longing; eagerness to obtain; expressed wish or request: lust, object of desire. v.t. wish, long, feel sexual desire, for; request. **dĕsīr'ous** a. wishful, desiring.

dĕsist' (or -zĭ-) v.i. abandon course, cease.

dĕsk n. piece of furniture with (esp. sloping) top or rest for reading, writing, etc.; subdivision of (esp. newspaper) office.

dĕs'olate a. left alone; uninhabited; dreary, dismal, forlorn. v.t. (-āt) depopulate; devastate. ~ā'tion n.

dĕspair' v.i. lose all hope; despond. n. (cause of) want of hope.

despatch : see **dispatch**.

dĕsperā'dō (or -ah-) n. (pl. -oes), person who will stick at nothing.

dĕs'perate a. hopelessly bad; difficult or dangerous; reckless. **dĕsperā'tion**

n. reckless state of mind; hopelessness.

dĕs'pĭcable *a.* contemptible; vile.

dĕspīse' (-z) *v.t.* regard with contempt; look down upon.

dĕspīte' *n.* malice, spite: offended pride. *prep.* in spite of. **~ful** *a.* malicious, cruel.

dĕspoil' *v.t.* plunder or strip. **~ment, dĕspōlĭā'tion** *nn.*

dĕspŏnd' *v.i.* lose heart or hope; be dejected. **~encў** *n.*; **~ent** *a.*

dĕs'pot *n.* tyrant, oppressor; absolute ruler. **dĕspŏt'ĭc** *a.* subject to no constitutional checks; tyrannous. **~ism** *n.* tyrannical conduct; autocratic government.

dĕs'quamāte *v.i.* come off in scales. **~ā'tion** *n.*

dĕssĕrt' (-z-) *n.* course of fruit, sweetmeats, etc. at end of dinner; (U.S.) sweet course. **~-spoon,** one between tablespoon and teaspoon in size.

dĕstĭnā'tion *n.* place for which person or thing is bound.

dĕs'tĭne *v.t.* foreordain or mark out beforehand.

dĕs'tĭnў *n.* what is destined to happen, fate; power that foreordains.

dĕs'tĭtūte *a.* in want of necessaries; resourceless. **~ū'tion** *n.*

dĕstroy' *v.t.* make away with; make useless, spoil utterly; kill.

dĕstroy'er *n.* one that destroys; small fast warship orig. for attacking torpedo-boats.

dĕstrŭc'tĭble *a.* destroyable.

dĕstrŭc'tion *n.* destroying.

dĕstrŭc'tĭve *a.* causing destruction; pulling to pieces.

dĕstrŭc'tor *n.* furnace for refuse.

dĕs'uetūde (-swĭ-) *n.* passing into, state of, disuse.

dĕs'ultorў *a.* changing from one thing to another; unmethodical.

dĕtăch' *v.t.* unfasten and separate (*from*); send off on separate mission. **~ed** *a.* standing apart or aloof; separate, not joined to another. **~ment** *n.* (esp.) body of troops etc. separately employed.

dē'tail *n.* dealing with things item by item; item, small or subordinate particular; small party detailed for duty etc. *v.t.* (*or* dītāl'), give

particulars of, relate in detail; tell off for special duty etc.

dĕtain' *v.t.* keep in custody or under restraint; withhold; keep waiting, keep from proceeding.

dĕtĕct' *v.t.* discover; find out. **~tion** *n.*

dĕtĕc'tĭve *n.* person, esp. policeman, employed in investigating criminal etc. activities. *a.* of or concerned with detectives or detection.

dĕtĕc'tor *n.* (esp., radio) device for detecting signals or rectifying high-frequency oscillations.

détente (dā'tahnt) *n.* relaxing of strained diplomatic relations. [F]

dĕtĕn'tion *n.* detaining, being detained; confinement.

dĕtēr' *v.t.* discourage, hinder.

dĕtēr'gent *n.* & *a.* cleansing (agent), esp. substance other than soap emulsifying oils and holding dirt in suspension.

dĕtēr'iorāte *v.* make or grow worse. **~ā'tion** *n.*

dĕtēr'mĭnant *n.* decisive factor.

dĕtēr'mĭnate *a.* limited; of definite scope or nature.

dĕtērmĭnā'tion *n.* (law) cessation of interest etc.; decision, settlement; fixing, definition, exact ascertainment; settling of purpose; settled intention; resoluteness.

dĕtēr'mĭne *v.* end; ascertain or fix with precision; resolve; bring to decision. **~d** *a.* resolute.

dĕtēr'mĭnĭsm *n.* theory that action is determined by forces independent of will. **~ist** *n.*; **~is'tic** *a.*

dĕtĕ'rrent *a.* serving to deter. *n.* deterrent agent etc.; esp. weapon intended to prevent recourse to (nuclear) war.

dĕtĕst' *v.t.* hate, loathe; abhor. **~able** *a.* abominable. **dētestā'tion** *n.*

dĕthrōne' *v.t.* depose (sovereign). **~ment** *n.*

dĕt'onāte (*or* dē-) *v.* (cause to) explode with report. **~ā'tion, -ātor** *nn.*

detour (dā'toor *or* dītoor') *n.* deviation, roundabout way or course. *v.* (cause to) make detour.

dĕtrăct' *v.* take away *from*; **~ from,** diminish, depreciate. **~tion** *n.* **~tor** *n.* disparager.

dētrain' v. alight, make (troops) alight, from train.

dĕt'rĭment n. harm, damage.

dĕtrĭmĕn'tal a. harmful, causing loss or damage.

dĕtrī'tion n. wearing away by rubbing.

dĕtrī'tus n. matter produced by detrition, esp. gravel etc. washed away by water.

de trop (trō), not wanted, in the way; unwelcome. [F]

deuce[1] n. two at dice and cards; (tennis) state of score at which either side must gain two successive points or games to win.

deuce[2] n. (*the*) devil. deu'cėd a. & adv. confounded(ly), surprising(ly).

Deut. abbr. Deuteronomy.

deutēr'ĭum n. heavy hydrogen, hydrogen of atomic weight 2. deu'teron n. nucleus of deuterium atom.

dēvăl'ūe v.t. cheapen (currency) in terms of gold or of other currencies. ~ūā'tion n.

dĕv'astāte v.t. lay waste, ravage. ~ā'tion n.

dĕvĕl'op v. unfold, bring or come from latent to active or visible state; make or become more elaborate or systematic, bigger, or fuller; bring or come to maturity; make usable or profitable or accessible, esp. build on (land). ~er n. (esp.) chemical agent for developing photographs. ~ment n.

dē'vĭāte v.i. turn aside (*from*); digress. ~ā'tion n. (esp.) divergence from standard, normal position, etc.; departure from orthodox Communist doctrine. ~ā'tionist n. one who deviates from Communist orthodoxy.

dĕvīce' n. plan, scheme, trick; design, figure; motto; (usu. simple) mechanical contrivance.

dĕv'il n. personified spirit of evil; any cruel or malignant being; person of notable energy; person who devils for author or barrister. v.t. do work for author or barrister; grill with hot condiments. ~-may--care, happy-go-lucky; irrepressible. ~'s advocate, one who puts case against canonization; one who urges wrong course etc. dĕv'ilish a. monstrously cruel or wicked; adv. (colloq.) very. dĕv'ilment n. mischief; wild spirits; wizardry. dĕv'ilry n. black magic; iniquity; reckless daring.

dē'vĭous a. winding, circuitous; erring.

dĕvīse' (-z) v.t. leave by will; think out; contrive.

dĕvoid' a. destitute, empty *of*.

dĕv'oirs (-vwärz) n. pl. dutiful respects, courteous attentions.

dĕvolū'tion (*or* -ōō-) n. descent through series of changes; delegation of work or power.

dĕvŏlve' v. throw (task, duty), be thrown, *upon* another; descend or pass.

Dēvō'nian a. & n. (of) system of Palaeozoic rocks lying below Carboniferous.

dĕvōte' v.t. consecrate, dedicate; give up exclusively *to*. ~ėd a. (esp.) zealously loyal or loving. dĕvotee' n. votary; zealously or fanatically pious person.

dĕvō'tion n. devotedness; devoutness; self-surrender; (pl.) religious exercises. ~al a.

dĕvour' (-owr) v.t. eat up; eat greedily or fast; destroy or consume; take in greedily with eyes or ears.

dĕvout' a. earnestly religious, reverent, prayerful.

dew n. atmospheric vapour condensed in droplets during night; beaded moisture resembling it. v.t. bedew; moisten. ~berry, kind of blackberry. ~-claw, rudimentary claw on inside of dog's leg. ~pond, shallow pond fed by atmospheric condensation. dew'y a.

dew'lăp n. fold of loose skin hanging from throat esp. in cattle.

dĕx'ter a. on right-hand side (her., to spectator's left).

dĕxtĕ'rĭty n. dextrousness.

dĕx't(e)rous a. neat-handed, adroit; clever.

D.F. abbr. direction finder, finding.

D.F.C., D.F.M. abbr. Distinguished Flying Cross, Medal.

D.G. abbr., *Dei gratia* [L], by the grace of God; Dragoon Guards.

dg. *abbr.* decigram.

dho'tĭ (dō-) *n.* loin-cloth worn by Hindus.

dhow (d-) *n.* lateen-rigged Arabian--Sea ship.

dīabē'tēs (-z) *n.* disease with excessive accumulation of glucose in blood.

dīabĕt'ĭc (*or* -ē-) *a.* of or having diabetes. *n.* diabetic patient.

dīabŏl'ĭc(al) *a.* of the devil; monstrously cruel or wicked.

dīăb'olĭsm *n.* sorcery; diabolical conduct; devil-worship.

dīăc'onal *a.* of deacon.

dīăc'onate *n.* deacon's (term of) office; body of deacons.

dīacrĭt'ĭcal *a.* distinguishing, distinctive; (of mark) indicating that written letter has particular sound.

dī'adĕm *n.* crown.

dīaer'ĕsĭs (-ēr-) *n.* (pl. -*esēs*), mark (¨) placed over vowel to show it is not part of diphthong.

dīagnōse' (-z) *v.t.* determine nature of (disease).

dīagnō'sĭs *n.* (pl. -*osēs*), identification of disease by means of symptoms etc.

dīagnŏs'tĭc *a.* of or assisting diagnosis. *n.* symptom.

dīăg'onal *a.* traversing obliquely from angle to angle. *n.* line so drawn; any oblique line.

dī'agrăm *n.* graphic representation by lines etc. of process etc. **dīagrammăt'ĭc** *a.*

dī'al *n.* sun-dial; face of clock or watch; circular plate marked with figures etc.; ring of figures, letters, etc. on telephone by manipulating which calls may be made. *v.t.* ring up (number etc.) by manipulating dial.

dial. *abbr.* dialect(al); dialogue.

dī'alĕct *n.* form of speech peculiar to district or class. **dīalĕc'tal** *a.*

dīalĕc'tĭc *n.* (often pl.) art of investigating truth by logical discussion etc.; criticism dealing with metaphysical contradictions and their solutions. **~al** *a.*; **dīalĕctĭ'cian** *n.*

dī'alŏgue (-g) *n.* conversation esp. on stage or as form of literary composition.

dīamanté (dĕamahn'tā) *n.* textile fabric sparkling with powdered glass etc.

dīăm'ĕter *n.* straight line passing from side to side of any body or figure through its centre; transverse measurement.

dīamĕt'rĭcal *a.* of or along diameter; (of opposition etc.) direct.

dī'amond *n.* very hard and brilliant precious stone; (playing-card bearing) four-sided figure with diagonals vertical and horizontal; size of printing-type (4½ point). *a.* made of or set with diamond(s); rhomb--shaped.

dīapā'son (-zn) *n.* grand swelling burst of harmony; organ-stop.

dī'aper *n.* fine linen towelling; small towel, baby's napkin; reticulated decorative work. **~ed** *a.* with diaper decoration.

dīăph'anous *a.* transparént.

dīaphorĕt'ĭc *a.* & *n.* (drug etc.) inducing perspiration.

dī'aphragm (-ăm) *n.* partition between thorax and abdomen in mammals; vibrating membrane etc. in acoustic instrument; device for varying aperture of camera lens. **dīaphrăgmăt'ĭc** *a.*

dī'archy (-kĭ) *n.* government by two independent authorities.

dī'arĭst *n.* keeper of diary.

dīarrhoe'a (-rēa) *n.* excessive looseness of bowels.

dī'arў *n.* daily record of events etc.; book for keeping this or noting engagements etc.

Dīăs'pora *n.* dispersion of Jews, Jews dispersed, among Gentiles.

dī'astāse *n.* (chem.) enzyme converting starch to sugar.

dīăs'tolĕ *n.* dilatation alternating with systole in pulsation.

dīăth'ĕsĭs *n.* (pl. -*esēs*), constitutional predisposition, habit.

dī'ătom *n.* kinds of minute one-celled water-plant. **~ā'ceous** *a.*

dīatŏm'ĭc *a.* of two atoms.

dīatŏn'ĭc *a.* (mus., of scale) proceeding by notes proper to key without chromatic alteration.

dī'atrībe *n.* bitter criticism; denunciatory harangue.

dĭbb'er *n.* dibble,

dibb'le *n.* & *v.t.* (plant with) tool for making holes in ground.

dibs (-z) *n.pl.* (sl.) money.

dice *n.*: see **die**[1]. *v.* gamble with dice; cut into small cubes.

dichŏt'omў (-k-) *n.* division into two, esp. in logical classification.

dichromăt'ic (-k-) *a.* of two colours.

dick *n.* (U.S. sl.) detective.

dick'ĕns (-z) *n.* (colloq.) *the* deuce.

dick'er *v.i.* chaffer, haggle.

dickў, -ey *n.* dicky-bird; false shirt--front; seat at back of carriage or car. *a.* (sl.) shaky, rickety. **~-bird,** child's word for small bird.

dicŏtўlē'don *n.* flowering plant with two cotyledons. **~ous** *a.*

dic'taphōne *n.* machine recording for subsequent transcription words spoken into it. **P.**

dictāte' *v.* say aloud matter to be written down; give peremptory orders; lay down authoritatively. *n.* (dĭk'-), (usu. pl.) bidding *of* conscience, reason, etc. **dictā'tion** *n.*

dictā'tor *n.* absolute ruler; person in position of supreme authority. **~ship** *n.*

dictatŏr'ial *a.* absolute or free of checks; despotic or overbearing.

dic'tion *n.* choice and use of words in speech or writing; manner of speaking, enunciation.

dic'tionarў *n.* book dealing with words of language etc., their meanings, equivalents in other languages, etc.; book of reference with items arranged alphabetically.

dic'tum *n.* (pl. *-ta*), pronouncement; maxim, current saying.

did, didst, *p.t.* of **do.**

didăc'tic (*or* dī-) *a.* meant or meaning to instruct. **~ism** *n.*

didd'le *v.t.* (sl.) cheat, take in.

die[1] *n.* (pl. *dice*), small cube with faces marked with 1–6 spots used in games of chance, (pl.) game played with these; (pl. *dies*), engraved stamp for impressing design etc. on softer material. **~-casting,** process of making castings from metal mould(s). **~-sinker,** die--engraver.

die[2] *v.i.* (*dying*), cease to live; suffer spiritual death; fade away; cease to exist; (of fire) go out; **~** *with* or *of*

laughing, be exhausted by laughing; *be dying for,* *to,* long, desire keenly or excessively. **~-away,** languishing. **~-hard,** one who resists to the end.

dĭĕlĕc'tric *a.* & *n.* insulating or non--conducting (substance etc.).

diesel (dē'zl) *n.* diesel engine, loco-motive etc. **~-electric,** of or using electric generator driven by diesel engine. **~ engine,** internal-com-bustion engine in which oil is ignited by air compressed in cylinders. **~ fuel, ~ oil,** heavy mineral oil used in diesel engines.

Dī'ēs īr'ae (-z), hymn ('day of wrath') sung as part of mass for dead. [L]

di'et[1] *n.* congress, esp. as Eng. name for foreign parliaments etc.

di'et[2] *n.* way of feeding; prescribed course of food; habitual food. *v.* keep to special diet. **~arў** *n.* course of diet; allowance or character of food provided; *a.* of diet or dietary. **~ĕt'ic** *a.* of diet esp. as branch of medical science. **~ĕt'ics** *n.pl.* **~ĭ'cian** *n.* expert in dietetics.

diff'er *v.i.* be unlike; be distinguish-able; diverge in opinion.

diff'erence *n.* unlikeness; degree or amount of unlikeness; disagree-ment.

diff'erent *a.* dissimilar; not the same; of diverse qualities.

dĭfferĕn'tia (-shĭa) *n.* (pl. *-ae*), dis-tinguishing mark, esp. of species within genus.

dĭfferĕn'tial *a.* varying with circum-stances; distinctive; (math.) of infinitesimal differences between consecutive values of continuously varying quantities. *n.* (math.) in-finitesimal difference; differential gear; agreed difference in wage--rates in different industries etc. **~ calculus,** method of calculating differentials. **~ gear,** arrangement of gears allowing two connected shafts or axles to revolve at different speeds.

dĭfferĕn'tiāte (-shĭ-) *v.* constitute difference between or of or in; develop into unlikeness; discrimi-nate. **~ā'tion** *n.*

diff'icult *a.* hard to do, deal with, or understand; troublesome.

diff'icultў *n*. difficultness; difficult point or situation; obstacle.

diff'idence *n*. self-distrust; shyness.

diff'ident *a*. wanting in self-confidence.

diffract' *v.t.* break up (beam of light) into series of dark and light bands. **diffrac'tion** *n*.; **~ive** *a*.

diffūse' (-z) *v*. shed or spread around, disperse; (cause to) intermingle. *a*. (-s), dispersed, not concentrated; not concise, wordy. **~sible** (-z-), **~sive** *aa*.; **~sion** *n*.

dig *v*. (*dŭg*), turn up soil with spade etc.; thrust or plunge *in* or *into*; prod, nudge, poke; **~** one*self in*, prepare or occupy defensive position. *n*. piece of digging; (colloq.) archaeological excavation; thrust, poke; gibe; (pl., colloq.) lodgings.

digamm'a *n*. letter (F) of early Greek alphabet, later disused.

digest' (*or* dī-) *v*. reduce into systematic or assimilable form; summarize; absorb and assimilate; (of food) undergo digestion. *n*. (dī'-), compendium, esp. of laws. **~ible** *a*.; **~ibil'itў** *n*.

diges'tion (*or* dī-) *n*. digesting; power of digesting food.

diges'tive (*or* dī-) *a*. of or promoting digestion.

digg'er (-g-) *n*. one who digs, esp. for gold; (sl.) Australian.

digg'ing *n*. act of digging; (usu. pl.) gold-field; (pl. colloq.) lodgings.

dight *a*. (arch.) clad, adorned.

di'git *n*. each numeral from 0 to 9; finger or toe. **~al** *a*. of digits; operating on data in form of digits or other discrete elements.

digitā'lis *n*. heart stimulant made from foxglove.

di'gitigrāde *a.* & *n*. (animal) walking on toes, not touching ground with heel.

dig'nifў *v.t.* give dignity to. **~fied** *a*. stately, marked by dignity.

dig'nitarў *n*. holder of high rank or office, esp. in Church.

dig'nitў *n*. claims to respect; office or title; dignified behaviour.

di'graph *n*. two letters expressing single sound.

digress' *v.i.* diverge temporarily from main track, esp. in discourse. **~ion** *n*.; **~ive** *a*.

dihē'dral *a*. having two plane faces. **~ angle**, that between two meeting or intersecting plane faces.

dike, dўke *n*. long ridge of earth, embankment; channel or ditch. *v.t.* protect with dike.

dilăpidā'tion *n*. state of bad repair; falling into decay. **dilăp'idātĕd** *a*. in decay or disrepair.

dilāte' *v*. widen or expand; expatiate or enlarge. **dilatā'tion, dilā'tion** *nn*.

dil'atorў *a*. tending, designed, to cause delay; tardy.

dilĕmm'a (*or* dī-) *n*. position involving choice between evils; perplexing or doubtful situation.

dilĕttăn'tĕ *n*. (pl. -*ti*, pr. -tē), lover of fine arts; amateur, smatterer. *a*. amateur; desultory. **~tism** *n*.

dil'igence *n*. persistent effort or work. **dil'igent** *a*.

dill *n*. herb with seeds used in pickles.

dill'ў-dăllў *v.i.* (colloq.) procrastinate or vacillate.

dilūte' (*or* -ōōt) *v.t.* reduce in strength by addition of water, etc.; thin down. *a*. diluted. **~tion** *n*. diluting, being diluted; substitution of (proportion of) unskilled for skilled workers.

dilū'vial (*or* -ōō-) *a*. of flood, esp. Flood in Genesis.

dim *a*. deficient in brightness or clearness; obscure; indistinct. *v*. make or grow dim.

dim. *abbr*. diminuendo; diminutive.

dīme *n*. (U.S.) ten-cent coin; ten cents.

dimĕn'sion (*or* dī-) *n*. any of the three linear measurements, length, breadth, and depth; (pl.) size or extent. **~al** *a*.

dimin'ish *v*. make or become less; impair.

diminuĕn'dō *adv*. (mus.) with decreasing volume of sound. *n*. (pl. -*s*), (passage played with) such decrease.

diminū'tion *n*. lessening.

dimin'ūtive *a*. (of words etc.) denoting or implying smallness; tiny, undersized. *n*. diminutive word.

dim'itў *n*. cotton fabric with woven stripes for hangings etc.

dimôr'phic *a*. occurring in two distinct forms. **~ism** *n*.

dĭm′ple *n.* small hollow, esp. in cheek or chin; ripple in water. *v.* mark with, break into, dimples or ripples.

dĭn *n.* continuous roar of confused noise. *v.* make din; repeat continuously so as to deafen or weary.

dīne *v.* take dinner; entertain at dinner; accommodate (specified number of diners). **dī′ner** *n.* one who dines; dining-car. **dining-car, -room,** railway coach, room, in which meals are served.

dĭng-dŏng *adv.* & *n.* (with) sound of bell or alternate strokes of two bells; downright, desperate, neck--and-neck.

dĭnghy (-ng′ĭ) *n.* kinds of small boat.

dingle (dĭng′gl) *n.* deep dell.

dĭng′ō (-ngg-) *n.* (pl. *-oes*), Australian wild dog.

dĭn′gy (-jĭ) *a.* dull-coloured; grimy; dirty-looking.

dĭnk′um *a.* (Austral. sl.) genuine, real.

dĭnk′ў *a.* (colloq.) pretty, neat, of engaging appearance.

dĭnn′er *n.* chief meal of day; formal, esp. public, (evening) meal with distinct courses. **~-jacket,** less formal dress-coat without tails. **~-wagon,** wheeled trolley for holding dishes etc.

dī′nosaur (-ôr) *n.* kinds of usu. large extinct saurian reptile.

dĭnt *n.* dent; *by* ~ *of,* by force or means of. *v.t.* dent.

dĭŏ′cèsan (-z-) *a.* of diocese. *n.* bishop in relation to diocese.

dī′ocèse (*or* -ēz) district under bishop's pastoral care.

dī′ōde *n.* electronic valve with two electrodes.

Dīonŷs′ian (*or* -nĭ-) *a.* of (worship of) Dionysus, Gk. god of wine; riotous, orgiastic.

dĭŏp′tric *a.* of, assisting sight by, refraction; of dioptrics. **~s** *n.* part of optics dealing with refraction.

dīora′ma (-rah-) *n.* (building exhibiting) landscape etc. with atmospheric effects produced by changing lighting, usu. viewed through aperture. **~ăm′ic** *a.*

dīŏx′īde *n.* oxide with two atoms of oxygen to one of metal etc.

dĭp *v.* put or let down into liquid,

immerse; go under water and emerge quickly; lower (flag etc.) for instant; lower beam of (headlights); ~ (*into*), read or study cursorily. *n.* act of dipping; downward slope; short bathe; tallow candle; vermin-killing liquid into which sheep are dipped.

Dip. *abbr.* Diploma.

dĭphthēr′ia *n.* acute infectious disease with inflammation of mucous surface (usu. of throat).

dĭph′thŏng *n.* union of two vowels in one sound. **dĭphthŏng′al** (-ngg-) *a.*; **~īze** *v.t.*

dīplō′ma *n.* document conferring honour, privilege, or licence, esp. educational institution's certificate.

dīplō′macў *n.* management of international relations; tact.

dĭp′lomăt *n.* diplomatist.

dĭplomăt′ĭc *a.* of diplomacy; engaged or skilled in diplomacy; (of statements etc.) uncandid.

dĭplō′matĭst *n.* member of diplomatic service; adroit negotiator.

dĭpp′er *n.* (esp.) kinds of diving bird; utensil, esp. long-handled ladle, for dipping up water.

dĭpsomā′nia *n.* morbid craving for alcohol. **dĭpsomā′nĭăc** *n.* & *a.*

dĭp′terous *a.* two-winged.

dĭp′tўch (-k) *n.* pair of pictures or carvings on panels hinged together.

dīre *a.* dread, terrible.

dīrĕct′ (*or* dĭ-) *a.* straight, not crooked or devious; frank. *adv.* by direct route; without intermediaries. *v.t.* put in direct way by instructions; tell way *to* (place etc.); address (letter etc. *to*); command, order. ~ **action,** (esp.) exertion of pressure on community by strikes etc. instead of through parliamentary representatives. ~ **current,** electric current flowing in one direction only. ~ **method,** way of teaching foreign language through use of language itself without translation etc. ~ **speech,** (gram.) words as actually spoken, not reported in third person.

dīrĕc′tion (*or* dĭ-) *n.* directing; (pl.) orders or instructions; address of letter etc.; course; aim. **~al** *a.* (esp., radio) sending signals in one direction only; detecting direction from which signals are received.

dĭrĕc'tĭve (*or* dīr-) *a.* giving guidance. *n.* statement for guidance of subordinates etc.

dĭrĕct'lў (*or* dĭ-) *adv.* in direct manner; at once, without delay.

dĭrĕc'tor (*or* dĭ-) *n.* superintendent, manager, esp. member of board directing affairs of company etc.; person supervising production of play etc. ~**ate** *n.* board of directors. **dĭrĕctōr'ĭal** *a.*; ~**ship** *n.*

dĭrĕc'torў *n.* book of directions; list of inhabitants of town etc., telephone subscribers, members of profession, etc.

dĭre'ful (-īrf-) *a.* dire, dreadful.

dĭrge *n.* song of mourning.

dĭ'rĭgĭble *a.* that can be steered. *n.* dirigible balloon or airship.

dĭrk *n.* (esp. Sc. Highlander's) small dagger.

dĭrn'dl (skirt) *n.* woman's full gathered skirt with tight waistband.

dĭrt *n.* mud, filth, mire; earth, soil; worthless things or people; foul talk. ~-**cheap**, extremely cheap. ~-**road**, (U.S.) unmade road. ~-**track**, racing track with surface of earth or cinders etc.

dĭr'tў *a.* soiled, foul; unclean; obscene, filthy; mean, despicable; wet and windy; muddy-looking. *v.* foul, soi ; make or become dirty.

dĭsabĭl'ĭtў *n.* thing that incapacitates or disqualifies.

dĭsa'ble *v.t.* make unable to act or move, cripple, maim. ~**ment** *n.*

dĭsabūse' (-z) *v.t.* undeceive; relieve of illusion.

dĭsaccōrd' *n.* disagreement.

dĭsadvan'tage (-vah-) *n.* unfavourable condition or circumstance. ~**tā'geous** *a.*

dĭsaffĕc'tĕd *a.* discontented; ill-disposed; disloyal. ~**fĕc'tion** *n.* (esp.) political discontent, disloyalty.

dĭsagree' *v.i.* differ; fail to agree; quarrel. ~**ment** *n.*

dĭsagree'able (-rĭ-) *a.* unpleasant; ill-tempered.

dĭsallow' *v.t.* reject; prohibit.

dĭsappear' *v.i.* pass from sight; vanish, be lost, depart. ~**ance** *n.*

dĭsappoint' *v.t.* fail to fulfil desire or expectation of; belie, frustrate. ~**ment** *n.*

dĭsăpprobā'tion *n.* disapproval.

dĭsapprove' (-ōōv) *v.* have or express unfavourable opinion of or *of.* **dĭsappro'val** *n.*

dĭsărm' *v.* deprive of weapons; pacify hostility or suspicions of; abandon or reduce military establishment. ~**mament** *n.*

dĭsarrānge' *v.t.* put into disorder; disorganize. ~**ment** *n.*

dĭsarray' *n.* disorder, confusion.

dĭsa'ster (-zah-) *n.* sudden or great misfortune. ~**trous** *a.*

dĭsavow' *v.t.* disown; deny knowledge of; repudiate. ~**al** *n.*

dĭsbănd' *v.* break up, disperse. ~**ment** *n.*

dĭsbăr' *v.t.* deprive of status of barrister. ~**ment** *n.*

dĭsbĕlieve' *v.* refuse credence to; not believe (*in*). ~**bĕlief'** (*or* dĭs'-) *n.*

dĭsbūr'den *v.t.* relieve of burden.

dĭsbūrse' *v.* pay out; expend money. ~**ment** *n.*

disc, dĭsk *n.* round flat or apparently flat plate or surface or part; gramophone record. ~-**jockey**, compère of gramophone-record programme. ~ **wheel**, solid wheel without spokes.

dĭscărd' *v.* throw out (card from hand), play (card not of trump suit) when unable to follow suit; give up, cast aside; dismiss. *n.* (dĭs'-) discarding; discarded card(s).

dĭscĕrn' *v.t.* perceive clearly with mind or senses; make out. ~**ing** *a.* having quick or true insight, penetrating. ~**ment** *n.*

dĭschărge' *v.* disburden; unload; disembark; dismiss, cashier; release; let flow; send as missile; fire; acquit oneself of (duty, debt). *n.* (*or* dĭs'-) discharging or being discharged; matter issuing from sore etc.

dĭscī'ple *n.* one who takes another as his teacher or leader. **dĭscĭp'ūlar** *a.*

dĭscĭplĭnăr'ĭan *n.* maintainer of strict discipline.

dĭs'cĭplĭnarў *a.* of or promoting discipline.

dis'cipline *n.* branch of instruction; order maintained (as) among persons under control or command; chastisement. *v.t.* train to obedience and order; chastise.

disclaim' *v.t.* disown, disavow. **~er** *n.* disavowal.

disclōse' (-z) *v.t.* expose to view, reveal. **disclō'sure** (-zh*er*) *n.* disclosing; thing disclosed.

discol'our (-ŭl*er*) *v.* impair colour of; suffer such impairment. **discolorā'tion** *n.*

discom'fit (-ŭm-) *v.t.* defeat; thwart; disconcert. **~ure** *n.*

discom'fort (-ŭm-) *n.* uneasiness of body or mind.

discompōse' (-z) *v.t.* disturb composure of. **~pō'sure** (-zh*er*) *n.*

disconcĕrt' *v.t.* derange or upset; embarrass.

disconnĕct' *v.t.* sever connection of or between. **~ĕd** *a.* incoherent, not connected. **disconnĕc'tion, -ĕxion** (-kshn) *n.*

discŏn'solate *a.* inconsolable; unhappy, disappointed.

discontĕnt' *n.* want of contentment. *v.t.* make dissatisfied.

discontin'ūe *v.t.* leave off; not go on with. **~ūance, ~ū'itў** *nn.*; **~ūous** *a.*

dis'cōrd *n.* disagreement, strife; harsh noise; want of harmony. **~ance** *n.*; **~ant** *a.*

dis'cōthèque (-tāk), *n.* club etc. where dancing is accompanied by recorded music.

dis'count *n.* deduction from nominal value or price or amount; *at a ~*, below par, not in demand. *v.t.* (-ownt'), give or get value after deduction of discount of (bill of exchange not yet due); allow for exaggeration in; lesson effect of (news etc.) by anticipation.

discoun'tĕnance *v.t.* refuse to countenance; discourage.

discou'rage (-kŭ-) *v.t.* reduce confidence or spirits of; deter. **~ment** *n.*

dis'course (-ōrs) *n.* lecture or sermon or other exposition; talk or conversation. *v.i.* (-ōrs'), utter discourse; converse, talk.

discour'tĕous (-kĕr- *or* -kōr-) *a.* rude, uncivil. **discour'tĕsў** *n.*

disco'ver (-kŭ-) *v.t.* find out, detect; make known. **~er** *n.* **~ў** *n.* discovering; thing discovered.

discrĕd'it *v.t.* refuse belief to; bring discredit on. *n.* (thing involving) loss of repute or credit. **~able** *a.* bringing discredit, shameful.

discreet' *a.* prudent; cautious in speech or action.

discrĕp'ancў *n.* difference; failure to tally. **~ant** *a.*

dis'crēte (*or* -ĕt') *a.* separate; distinct.

discrē'tion *n.* liberty of deciding as one thinks fit; prudence, judgement; *age or years of ~*, age at which person is presumed capable of exercising discretion. **~arў** *a.*

discrim'inate *v.* draw or make distinctions (*between*); **~ against**, distinguish unfavourably. **~ā'tion** *n.*; **~ative** *a.*

discūr'sive *a.* rambling, not sticking to main subject.

dis'cus *n.* heavy disc thrown in athletic exercises.

discŭss' *v.t.* examine by argument; debate; (joc.) eat or drink. **~ible** *a.*; **~ion** *n.*

disdain' *v.t.* scorn; treat as unworthy of notice or of oneself. *n.* contemptuous neglect or dislike. **~ful** *a.*

disease' (-zēz) *n.* morbid condition; (specific) disorder, illness. **~d** *a.* affected with disease; morbid, depraved.

disĕmbark' *v.* put or go ashore. **~ā'tion** *n.*

disĕmbǎ'rrass *v.t.* free from embarrassment; disentangle; rid or relieve (*of*). **~ment** *n.*

disĕmbŏd'ў *v.t.* divest of body.

disĕmbōgue' (-g) *v.* (of river etc.) discharge, pour forth.

disĕmbow'ĕl *v.t.* remove entrails of; rip up belly of.

disĕmbroil' *v.t.* extricate from confusion or entanglement.

disĕnchant' (-ah-) *v.t.* free from enchantment or fascination; disillusion. **~ment** *n.*

disĕncŭm'ber *v.t.* disburden; free from encumbrance.

disĕndow' *v.t.* strip of endowments. **~ment** *n.*

disĕngāge' *v.* detach; liberate; loosen;

withdraw (troops) from action, break off action. ~ment *n.*

disêngãged' (-jd) *a.* at leisure; vacant; not occupied.

disêntail' *v.t.* free from entail.

disêntǎng'le (-nggl) *v.t.* extricate; unravel; untwist. ~ment *n.*

disêntomb' (-ōom) *v.t.* disinter.

disêstǎb'lish *v.t.* deprive of established character or status. ~ment *n.*

diseuse (dēzễrz') *n.* woman entertainer with monologues. [F]

disfǎ'vour *n.* dislike; disapproval.

disfea'ture *v.t.* disfigure.

disfig'ure (-ger) *v.t.* mar appearance of; sully. ~ment *n.*

disfrǎn'chise (-z) *v.t.* deprive of franchise. ~ment (-izm-) *n.*

disfrǒck' *v.t.* deprive of clerical status.

disgôrge' *v.t.* eject; give up; (of river) discharge.

disgrǎce' *n.* loss of favour. downfall from position of honour; shame; cause of reproach. *v.t.* dismiss from favour; bring shame or discredit on. ~ful *a.*

disgrǔn'tled (-ld) *a.* discontented.

disguise' (-gīz) *v.t.* make unrecognizable; pass off *as* something else; cloak or hide. *n.* disguised state; device or garb used to disguise.

disgǔst' *n.* loathing, strong aversion. *v.t.* excite loathing or aversion or indignation in. ~ing *a.* distasteful; sickening, loathsome; repellent.

dish *n.* shallow flat-bottomed vessel for holding food; food served in dish or prepared for table; anything dish-shaped, esp. concavity of wheel. *v.* put (food) into dish for serving; make concave; (colloq.) circumvent, do for, defeat completely; ~ *up,* serve, serve meal. ~water, in which dirty dishes etc. have been washed. ~ed *a.* (of wheel) concave.

dishǎr'monў (-s-h-) *n.* lack of harmony, discord.

dishear'ten (-hǎr-) *v.t.* discourage; deject. ~ment *n.*

dishěv'elled (-ld) *a.* with disordered hair; unkempt, untidy.

dishon'ěst (dǐsǒn-) *a.* not honest; fraudulent; insincere. ~ў *n.*

dishon'our (-sǒn-) *v.t.* treat with contumely; bring dishonour upon. *n.* dishonoured state; loss of repute. ~able *a.* shameful; unprincipled.

disillū'sion, ~ize (*or* -ōo-) *vv.t.* open eyes of; wake to (disappointing) realities. ~ment *n.*

disincěn'tive *a.* & *n.* discouraging, deterrent (fact etc.).

disinclinā'tion *n.* slight dislike or unwillingness.

disinclīne *v.t.* make averse or unwilling.

disinfěct' *v.t.* cleanse of infection. ~ant *a.* having disinfecting qualities; *n.* disinfectant substance. ~ion *n.*

disinflā'tion *n.* reduction of inflation.

disingěn'ūous *a.* insincere; not candid.

disinhě'rit *v.t.* deprive of right to inherit. ~ance *n.*

disin'těgrāte *v.* separate into component parts; lose cohesion. ~ā'tion *n.*

disintễr' *v.t.* dig out; unearth. ~ment *n.*

disin'terěstěd *a.* not influenced by self-interest or partiality; (colloq.) not interested.

disjěc'ta měm'bra *n. pl.* fragments, scattered remains. [L]

disjoin' *v.t.* separate, disunite.

disjoint' *v.t.* separate at joints; dislocate. ~ed *a.* incoherent, desultory.

disjǔnc'tion *n.* disjoining, separation. ~ive *a.* disjoining; alternative; involving or expressing choice between two statements etc.

disk : see **disc.**

dislike' *v.t.* have aversion or objection to. *n.* aversion.

dis'locāte *v.t.* put out of joint; put out of gear; displace. ~ā'tion *n.*

dislǒdge' *v.t.* remove, turn out, from position. ~ment *n.*

disloy'al *a.* unfaithful; untrue to allegiance; disaffected. ~tў *n.*

dis'mal (-z-) *a.* cheerless, dreary.

dismǎn'tle *v.t.* deprive of defences, equipment, etc.

dismast' (-ah-) *v.t.* deprive (ship) of mast(s).

dismay' *n.* loss of courage; horrified amazement. *v.t.* affect with dismay; reduce to despair.

dĭsmĕm′ber *v.t.* tear or cut limb from limb; partition (country etc.) **~ment** *n.*

dĭsmĭss′ *v.t.* send away, disband; discharge, cashier; put out of one's thoughts; (crick.) put (batsman, side) out. **~al** *n.*; **~ible** *a.*

dĭsmount′ *v.* (cause to) alight from horseback etc., unseat; remove from its mount.

dĭsobē′dĭence *n.* disobeying; rebelliousness. **~ent** *a.*

dĭsobey′ (-bā) *v.* disregard orders; break rules; not obey.

dĭsoblīge′ *v.t.* refuse to consult convenience or wishes of. **~oblī′gĭng** *a.*

dĭsŏr′der *n.* confusion; bodily or mental ailment; tumult, riot. *v.t.* disarrange; disturb healthy working of. **~lў** *a.* untidy; riotous or ill-disciplined.

dĭsŏr′ganīze *v.t.* destroy system etc. of; throw into disorder. **~zā′tion** *n.*

dĭsŏr′ientāte *v.t.* confuse (person) as to his bearings.

dĭsown′ (-ōn) *v.t.* refuse to own; repudiate, disclaim; renounce.

dĭspă′rage *v.t.* speak slightingly of; depreciate. **~ment** *n.*

dĭs′parate *a.* essentially different.

dĭspă′rĭtў *n.* inequality, difference.

dĭspă′ssionate *a.* free from emotion; impartial.

dĭspătch′, dĕs- *v.t.* send off; kill; get (business etc.) done promptly; eat quickly; (arch.) make haste. *n.* dispatching; rapidity; official communication on State affairs. **~-box, -case,** case for dispatches and other papers. **~-rider,** motor-cyclist etc. carrying military messages.

dĭspĕl′ *v.t.* dissipate; disperse.

dĭspĕn′sarў *n.* place where medicine is dispensed.

dĭspensā′tion *n.* distributing, dealing out; exemption; management, esp. of world by Providence; provision of Providence or Nature.

dĭspĕnse′ *v.* distribute; administer; make up (medicine) from prescription or formula; **~ with,** do without. **~r** *n.* (esp.) one who dispenses medicines.

dĭspĕrse′ *v.* (make) go various ways, scatter; (optics) spread (light) so as to produce spectrum. **~sal, ~sion** *nn.*

dĭspĭ′rĭt *v.t.* make despondent.

dĭsplāce′, *v.t.* shift from proper position; oust, remove from office. **~d person,** one removed from and unable to return to native place, esp. after annexation etc. **~ment** *n.* (esp.) amount or weight of fluid displaced by body floating or immersed in it.

dĭsplay′ *v.t.* spread out to view; exhibit. *n.* displaying; exhibition; ostentation.

dĭsplease′ (-z) *v.t.* offend; make angry; excite disapprobation of.

dĭsplea′sure (-lĕzher) *n.* resentment; annoyance; vexation.

dĭspŏrt′ *v.* (arch.) frolic, enjoy oneself.

dĭspō′sable (-z-) *a.* that can be disposed of or disposed.

dĭspō′sal (-z-) *n.* disposing (of); bestowal; sale; control.

dĭspōse′ (-z) *v.* place suitably or in order; bring into certain state; incline (*to*); determine course of events; **~ of,** do what one will with, get rid of, finish, kill, sell.

dĭsposĭ′tion (-zĭ-) *n.* disposing or arrangement; temperament.

dĭspossĕss′ (-oz-) *v.t.* oust or dislodge. **~ion** *n.*

dĭspraise′ (-z) *v.t.* disparage, censure. *n.* disparagement, blame.

dĭsproōf′ *n.* refutation.

dĭspropŏr′tion *n.* want of proportion. **~ate** *a.* relatively too large or too small.

dĭsprove′ (-ōov) *v.t.* prove false; show fallacy of; refute.

dĭs′pūtable *a.* open to question.

dĭs′pūtant *n.* person engaged in controversy.

dĭspūtā′tion *n.* argumentative debate, discourse, or treatise. **~ā′tious** *a.*

dĭspūte′ *v.* hold debate; quarrel, controvert; contend; resist. *n.* controversy, debate; quarrel; difference of opinion.

dĭsqual′ĭfў (-ŏl-) *v.t.* make unfit or ineligible. **~fĭcā′tion** *n.*

dĭsquī′et *n.* uneasiness, perturbation, anxiety. *v.t.* perturb. **~ūde** *n.*

disquisi'tion (-zĭ-) *n.* long or elaborate treatise or discourse.

disrĕgård' *v.t.* ignore, be uninfluenced by. *n.* neglect.

disrĕl'ish *n.* want of liking for. *v.t.* regard with distaste.

disrĕpair' *n.* bad state for want of repairing.

disrĕp'ūtable *a.* bearing bad character; not respectable.

disrĕpūte' *n.* ill repute; discredit.

disrĕspĕct' *n.* want of respect. **~ful** *a.* showing disrespect.

disrōbe' *v.* undress.

disrŭpt' *v.t.* shatter; separate forcibly. **~tion** *n.* violent severance; split, schism. **~tive** *a.*

dissătisfăc'tion *n.* discontent.

dissăt'isfy̆ *v.t.* fail to satisfy; make discontented.

dissĕct' *v.t.* cut in pieces; anatomize; examine or criticize. **~tion, ~tor** *nn.*

dissĕm'ble *v.* conceal or disguise; be hypocritical.

dissĕm'ināte *v.t.* spread abroad. **~ā'tion, ~ātor** *nn.*

dissĕn'sion *n.* discord arising from difference in opinion.

dissĕnt' *v.i.* differ in opinion, express different opinion (*from*); esp. differ from established, national, or orthodox church. *n.* dissenting; nonconformity. **~er** *n.* (esp.) member of dissenting church or sect.

dissĕn'tient (-shĭ-) *a.* not agreeing, dissenting. *n.* dissentient person.

dissertā'tion *n.* spoken or written discourse treating subject at length.

dissĕr'vice *n.* ill service, ill turn.

dissĕv'er *v.* sever, divide.

diss'idence *n.* disagreement.

diss'ident *a.* not in agreement; conflicting. *n.* dissentient.

dissim'ilar *a.* unlike. **~lă'rity̆** *n.*

dissim'ilāte *v.* make or become unlike. **~lā'tion** *n.* (esp.) alteration of one of two similar sounds occurring near each other in word.

dissim'ūlate *v.* dissemble. **~ā'tion, ~ātor** *nn.*

diss'ipāte *v.* dispel; squander or fritter away. **diss'ipatĕd** *a.* (esp.) given to dissipation, dissolute.

~ā'tion *n.* (frivolous) amusement; waste *of*; intemperate or vicious living.

dissō'ciāte (-shĭ-) *v.t.* cut off from association or society. **~ā'tion** *n.* (esp.) disintegration *of* personality etc.; co-existence of distinct personalities in same person.

diss'olūte *a.* loose-living, debauched

dissolū'tion *n.* dissolving; dissolved state.

dissŏlve' (-z-) *v.* mix with liquid, solid, or gas without chemical action to form homogeneous liquid or solution; mix thus *in* liquid; undo, destroy; fade *away, into, out,* etc.; disperse, bring (esp. Parliament), or come to end. *n.* (cine.) gradual replacement of one picture by another superimposed on it.

diss'onant *a.* jarring, clashing, discordant. **diss'onance** *n.*

dissuade' (-wād) *v.t.* advise to refrain (*from*), persuade against. **~ā'sion** *n.*; **~ā'sive** *a.*

dis'taff (-ahf) *n.* cleft stick holding wool etc. used in spinning. **~ side,** female branch of family.

dis'tance *n.* length from one point to another; remoteness; distant behaviour. *v.t.* leave behind in race etc.

dis'tant *a.* at considerable or specified distance; reserved.

distāste' *n.* dislike; aversion. **~ful** *a.* exciting distaste.

distĕm'per[1] *v.t.* upset, derange. *n.* catarrhal disease of dogs; ailment.

distĕm'per[2] *n.* (pigment used for) painting on plaster etc. with powder colours mixed with size etc. *v.t.* paint with distemper.

distĕnd' *v.* swell out by pressure from within. **distĕn'sible** *a.*; **distĕn'sion** *n.*

dis'tich (-k) *n.* verse couplet.

distil' *v.* subject to, undergo, distillation; make, produce, extract, drive *off*, etc., by distillation. **dis'tillāte** *n.* product of distillation. **distill'er, ~lery̆** *nn.* maker of, establishment for distilling, alcoholic spirit.

distillā'tion *n.* vaporizing and subsequent condensation of substance to purify or decompose it, extract spirit or essence, etc.

distĭnct′ *a.* clearly perceptible, definite, positive; separate, different in quality or kind.

distĭnc′tion *n.* difference; thing that differentiates; mark of honour; excellence; individuality. **~tive** *a.* distinguishing; characteristic.

distĭng′ué (-ănggā) *a.* of distinguished air, manners, etc. [F]

distĭng′uish (-nggw-) *v.* draw or make distinctions between; characterize; recognize; make prominent or eminent. **~ed** *a.* eminent, having distinction.

distôrt′ *v.t.* pull or twist out of shape; misrepresent. **distôr′tion** *n.*

distră̆ct′ *v.t.* divert; draw away or in different directions; bewilder; (chiefly *p.p.*) drive mad or infuriate. **distră̆c′tion** *n.* diversion; frenzy; perplexity; confusion, dissension.

distrain′ *v.* seize (chattels), seize chattels of person, in satisfaction of debt etc. **distraint′** *n.*

distrait′ (-rā) *a.* absent-minded, not attending. [F]

distraught′ (-awt) *a.* crazed with grief etc.; distracted.

distrĕss′ *n.* mental pain; pressure of want, danger, or fatigue; (law) distraining. *v.t.* subject to severe strain, exhaust; vex, make anxious or unhappy.

distrĭb′ūtary *n.* river branch not returning to main stream after leaving it.

distrĭb′ūte *v.t.* deal out, give share of to each of number; spread abroad; arrange, classify; put into proper place or category; (print.) separate (type) and return letters to their proper boxes. **~ū′tion** *n.* (esp.) dispersal among consumers; way in which particular character etc. is spread over individuals, members of class, etc. **~ūtive** *a.* of or concerned with or effecting distribution; (of word etc.) referring to each individual of class, not collective.

dĭs′trĭct *n.* region; administrative division; province; territory. **~ attorney,** (U.S.) public prosecutor of district. **~ nurse,** nurse employed to visit patients in their homes. **~ visitor,** worker assisting clergyman in parish.

distrŭst′ *n.* want of trust; doubt, suspicion. *v.t.* have no confidence in. **~ful** *a.*

distŭrb′ *v.t.* break rest or quiet of; worry; disorganize.

distŭr′bance *n.* disturbing; disturbed state, tumult, disorder.

dĭsū′nion *n.* separation; want of union; dissension.

dĭsūnīte′ *v.* separate; divide.

dĭsūse′ (-z) *v.t.* cease to use. *n.* (-s), discontinuance, want of use.

dĭsy̆ll′able *n.* word or metrical foot of two syllables. **~ăb′ic** *a.*

dĭtch *n.* long narrow excavation serving to drain land etc. *v.* make or repair ditches; provide with ditches; drive (vehicle) into ditch or off road; (sl.) make forced landing, land (aircraft), on sea; (sl.) leave in the lurch, abandon.

dĭth′er (-dh-) *v.i.* tremble, quiver; vacillate. *n.* tremulous excitement.

dĭth′y̆rămb (-m) *n.* (usu. pl.) outpouring of ecstatic kind, wild eulogy or invective. **dĭthy̆răm′bĭc** *a.*

dĭtt′ō, substitute for repetition of word or phrase.

dĭtt′y̆ *n.* short simple song.

dĭtt′y̆-bă̆g *n.* sailor's bag for odds and ends.

dīūrē′sĭs *n.* passing of urine in large amounts. **dīūrĕt′ĭc** *a.* & *n.* (substance) promoting urination.

dīūr′nal *a.* in or of day; (astron.) occupying one day.

div. *abbr.* dividend.

dī′va (dē-) *n.* prima donna. [It.]

dī′vagāte *v.i.* stray. **~ā′tion** *n.*

divă̆n′ (*or* dī-) *n.* oriental council or council-room; long seat against wall of room, low bed without head-board.

dīve *v.i.* plunge, esp. head foremost, into water etc.; seek *for* by diving; go down or out of sight suddenly; (of aircraft) descend steeply; (of submarine) submerge. *n.* diving; plunge, precipitate fall; (U.S. sl.) disreputable resort; (sl., boxing) pretence of being knocked out. **~r** *n.* (esp.) one who descends into deep water; kinds of diving-bird. **~-bomb,** bomb from diving aircraft. **~-bomber,** aircraft for dive-bombing.

dĭvẽrge′ (or dĭ-) v. (cause to) proceed in different directions from point or each other; become progressively further apart. ∼ence n.; ∼ent a.

dī′vers (-z) a. sundry, several.

dĭvẽrse′ (or dĭ-) a. of differing kinds; unlike.

dĭvẽr′sĭfy̆ (or dĭ-) v.t. introduce variety into; vary.

dĭvẽr′sion (or dĭ-) n. diverting, deviation; amusement.

dĭvẽr′sĭty̆ (or dĭ-) n. diverseness; variety.

dĭvẽrt′ (or dĭ-) v.t. turn in another direction; ward off; draw off attention of; entertain, amuse. dĭvẽr′t-ing a. amusing.

divertissement (dēvẽr′tēsmahṅ; or -tēs′-) n. short dance in ballet programme. [F]

dĭvẽst′ (or dĭ-) v.t. unclothe, strip, lay bare. ∼ment n.

dĭvīde′ v. separate into parts; sunder, cut off; set at variance; distribute; share with others; find how many times one number contains another, contain or be contained exact number of times; (of legislative assembly) separate into two sets for voting; cause to divide thus. n. water-shed; dividing-line. dĭvī′ders n.pl. pair of measuring compasses.

dĭv′idend n. number to be divided by another; sum payable as interest or profit or share.

dĭvĭnā′tion n. divining, esp. by supernatural means.

dĭvīne′ a. of or from or like God or a god; sacred; superhumanly beautiful or excellent. n. theologian. v. make out by intuition or magic or inspiration; foresee, predict, conjecture; practise divination. ∼service, public worship of God. divining-rod, dowser's forked twig.

dĭvī′ner n. expert in divination; dowser.

dĭvĭn′ity̆ n. divineness; god; theology; the D∼, God.

dĭvĭs′ĭble (-z-) a. that can be divided. ∼bĭl′ity̆ n.

dĭvī′sion n. dividing or being divided; one of parts into which thing is divided; (mil.) unit of two or more brigades; part of county or

borough returning member of parliament. ∼al a.

dĭvī′sor (-z-) n. number by which another is to be divided.

dĭvõrce′ n. dissolution of marriage; separation between things that should go together. v.t. separate by divorce; sunder. dĭvõrcee′ n. divorced person.

dĭv′ot n. (golf) piece of turf cut out in making stroke.

dĭvŭlge′ (-lj; or dĭ-) v.t. let out (secret); make public.

dĭvv′y̆ n. (colloq.) dividend. v. divide (usu. up), share.

dĭx′ie, dĭx′y̆ n. large iron pot for making stew, tea, etc.

D.I.Y. abbr. do it yourself.

dĭzz′y̆ a. giddy, dazed, unsteady; causing dizziness. v.t. make dizzy.

djĭnn (j-) n. genie.

dkg., dkl., dkm. abbr. decagram, decalitre, decametre.

dl. abbr. decilitre.

D.Lit. abbr. Doctor of Literature.

D.Litt. abbr. Doctor of Letters.

dm. abbr. decimetre.

D.M. abbr. Deutsche Mark; Doctor of Medicine.

D.M.I. abbr. Director of Military Intelligence.

D. Mus. abbr. Doctor of Music.

DNA abbr. deoxyribonucleic acid.

D.N.B. abbr. Dictionary of National Biography.

D.N.I. abbr. Director of Naval Intelligence.

dō,[1] doh n. (mus.) first note of scale in tonic sol-fa.

do[2] (dōō, dŏŏ, do) v. (dĭd, done pr. dŭn; 2 sing. pres. dost pr. dŭ-, & doest pr. dōō′ĭst; 3 sing. pres. does pr. dŭz, & arch. doth pr. dŭ-; 2 sing. past dĭdst), perform, effect, execute; deal with, set in order, solve; (colloq.) outwit, cheat; exhaust; (sl.) cater for (well etc.); act or proceed, succeed, make an end; fare, be suitable, suffice; ∼away with, abolish; ∼by, treat, deal with; ∼down, get the better of; ∼for, ruin, destroy, kill, (colloq.) do housework for; ∼in, (sl.) kill, exhaust; ∼up, restore, repair, wrap up, fasten, exhaust; ∼with, get on with, tolerate, be pleased to have etc.; ∼ *without,* dispense with. *v. aux.* used esp. in questions and negative or emphatic statements and commands; also as vbl. substitute to avoid repetition of verb just used. *n.* (sl.) swindle, hoax; (colloq.) entertainment, show, party, etc.

do³ *abbr.* ditto.

dŏbb'ĭn *n.* draught- or farm-horse.

Dō'bermann pĭn'scher (-sh-) *n.* large smooth-coated German terrier.

dō'cīle *a.* easy to teach and willing to obey. **docĭl'ĭtў** *n.*

dŏck¹ *n.* tall coarse weed.

dŏck² *v.t.* cut short (tail, money, etc.).

dŏck³ *n.* basin for loading and repairing of ships; enclosure in theatre etc. for scenery; (usu. pl.) range of docks with wharves, warehouses, etc. *v.* bring or come into dock. ∼-**yard,** enclosure for building and repairing ships, collecting stores, etc. **dŏck'er** *n.* labourer in dock.

dŏck⁴ *n.* enclosure in court for prisoner on trial.

dŏck'ĕt *n.* endorsement or label on letter etc. indicating contents etc.; file or set of documents; document recording payment of customs, nature of goods delivered, jobs done, etc.; voucher. *v.t.* enter in or endorse with docket.

dŏc'tor *n.* holder of highest university degree in any faculty; qualified medical practitioner. *v.t.* treat medically; patch up; garble; castrate. ∼**al** *a.* of doctor or doctorate. ∼**ate** *n.* doctor's degree.

dŏctrĭnaire' *n. & a.* (person) applying principles pedantically with no allowance for circumstances.

dŏctrī'nal (*or* dŏk'trĭ-) *a.* of or inculcating doctrine.

dŏc'trĭne *n.* what is taught; religious etc. belief, dogma, or tenet.

dŏc'ūment *n.* something written, inscribed, etc. that furnishes evidence or information on any subject. *v.t.* prove or support by, provide with, documents. **dŏcūmĕn'tarў** *a. & n.* (esp. film etc.) based on fact, not fiction. ∼**ā'tion** *n.*

dŏdd'er¹ *n.* kinds of parasitic plant like tangled threads.

dŏdd'er² *v.i.* shake with palsy; totter or potter with senility.

dōdĕca- in comb., twelve. **dōdĕc'agon** *n.* twelve-sided plane figure. ∼**hĕd'ron** *n.* solid figure of twelve faces. ∼**sўll'able** *n.* verse of twelve syllables.

dŏdge *n.* swerving or zigzag movement; piece of duplicity; wrinkle or ingenious method. *v.* elude; make dodge; treat evasively. **dŏdg'er** *n.* shifty person.

dō'dō *n.* (pl. -*os*), large extinct flightless bird.

dōe *n.* female of fallow deer, hare, or rabbit. ∼**skin,** leather made from doe's skin.

does, 3 pers. sing. pres. of **do.**

dŏff *v.t.* take off (hat etc.).

dŏg *n.* carnivorous domesticated or wild quadruped of many breeds; male of this or fox or wolf; (esp. gay or rascally) fellow; (pl.) metal supports for grate or fire-irons. *v.t.* follow closely; pursue, track. ∼-**cart,** two-wheeled driving-cart with cross seats back to back. ∼-**collar,** clergyman's stiff collar fastening at back. ∼-**days,** hot season variously dated with reference to dog-star. ∼-**eared,** (of book) having leaves crumpled or turned down at corner. ∼-**fight,** fight between dogs; general mêlée. ∼-**fish,** kinds of small shark. ∼-**leg,** bent like dog's hind leg. ∼-**rose,** wild hedge-rose. ∼**sbody,** (sl.) drudge, factotum. ∼-**star,** Sirius. ∼-**tired,** tired out. ∼-**tooth,** canine tooth; pointed ornament or moulding. ∼-**watch,** (naut.) each of two short watches of two hours between 4 and 8 p.m. ∼**wood,** (wood of) wild cornel.

dōge *n.* (hist.) Venetian or Genoan chief magistrate. **dō'gate** *n.* office of doge.

dŏgg'ĕd (-g-) *a.* tenacious.

dŏgg'erel (-ge-) *n.* slipshod or unpoetic verses (freq. attrib.).

dŏgg'ō *adv.* (sl.) *lie* ∼, make no sign, lie low.

dŏgg'ў (-g-) *a.* (esp.) devoted to dogs.

dŏg'ma *n.* (pl. -s, rarely -*ata*), principle, tenet; doctrinal system. ∼**ăt'ic** *a.* of dogma; based on *a priori* principles; authoritative; arrogant. **~atǐsm** *n.* dogmatizing temper or habit. **~atīze** *v.i.* make dogmatic assertion(s).

doh : see **do**[1].

doi'lў *n.* small mat placed under dish, finger-bowl, etc.

do'ings (dōō-; -z) *n.pl.* (esp.) performance, proceedings; (sl.) anything lying about or wanted.

dol. *abbr.* dollar(s).

dǒl'drums (-z) *n.pl.* equatorial ocean region of calms and light variable winds; *in the* **~**, becalmed, depressed.

dōle[1] *n.* charitable gift, esp. of measured amount; unemployment benefit; *on the* **~**, (colloq) unemployed. *v.t.* deal *out* sparingly.

dōle[2] *n.* (arch.) woe. **~ful** *a.* dreary, dismal, melancholy.

dǒlǐchocèphǎl'ic *a.* long-headed.

dǒll *n.* child's toy representing human figure; pretty woman or child. *v.* dress *up* finely.

dǒll'ar *n.* unit of currency in U.S., Canada, etc. **~ area**, where currency is linked to U.S. dollar.

dǒll'op *n.* (colloq.) great quantity, clumsy or shapeless lump or blob.

dǒll'ў *n.* (pet-name for) doll; various contrivances for clothes-washing, pile-driving, etc.; wheeled platform esp. for television etc. camera. *v.* move (camera), move camera on dolly.

dǒl'man *n.* hussar's uniform jacket worn like cape; woman's mantle with capelike sleeves.

dǒl'men *n.* megalithic structure of large flat stone lying horizontally on upright ones.

dǒl'omīte *n.* magnesian limestone.

dǒl'orous *a.* painful, sad, dismal.

dǒl'our (-ler) *n.* sorrow, distress.

dǒl'phǐn *n.* porpoise-like sea mammal; bollard or mooring-post or buoy.

dōlt *n.* stupid fellow. **~ish** *a.*

Dǒm *n.* title of some R.C. dignitaries, Carthusian and Benedictine monks, Portuguese noblemen, etc.

D.O.M. *abbr. Deo optimo maximo* [L], to God the best and greatest.

domain' *n.* lands as held or ruled over; estate or realm; (rhet.) sphere or scope.

dōme *n.* rounded vault as roof; natural vault or canopy; dome-shaped thing. **dōmed** *a.* vaulted; having dome(s).

Domesday (**Bōōk**) (dōō'mz-) *n.* William the Conqueror's record of English lands.

domĕs'tǐc *a.* of home, household, or family affairs; of one's own country; home-keeping. *n.* household servant.

domĕs'tǐcāte *v.t.* naturalize; tame, accustom to live near men; attach to home and its duties. **~ā'tion** *n.*

dǒmĕstǐ'cǐtў (*or* dō-) *n.* home life or privacy; homeliness.

dǒm'ǐcīle (*or* -ǐl) *n.* place of permanent residence. **~d** *a.* having domicile *at* or *in.* **domicǐl'ǐarў** *a.* of dwelling-place.

dǒm'ǐnant *a.* dominating, prevailing, established in power; that is a dominant. *n.* (mus.) 5th note of scale; (biol.) that one of pair of opposite characters that appears when both are inherited. **~ance** *n.*

dǒm'ǐnāte *v.* have commanding influence over; overlook, occupy commanding position in. **~ā'tion** *n.*; **~atǐve** *a.*

dǒmǐneer' *v.i.* behave overbearingly; tyrannize (*over*).

domǐn'ǐcal *a.* of Sunday.

Domǐn'ǐcan *a. & n.* (friar or nun) of order founded by St. Dominic.

dǒm'ǐnie *n.* (Sc.) schoolmaster.

domǐn'ǐon *n.* sovereignty or lordship; domination; territory of sovereign or government; self-governing territory of British Commonwealth; *Old D~*, (U.S.) Virginia.

dǒm'ǐnō *n.* (pl. *-oes*), hooded cloak worn with half-mask to conceal identity; (pl.) game played with 28 pieces marked with pips; one of these pieces.

dǒn[1] *v.t.* put on (garment).

dǒn[2] *n.* member of college or university staff; Spanish gentleman. **dǒnn'ǐsh** *a.* of university don.

dō'na(h) *n.* (sl.) woman, sweetheart.

donāte' *v.t.* make donation of. **donā'tion** *n.* gift (esp. money given to fund or institution).

done *p.p.* of **do.**

dŏn′jŏn *n.* keep of castle.

dŏnk′ey *n.* ass. ~ **engine,** small auxiliary steam-engine. ~ **work,** drudgery.

dŏnn′a *n.* Italian or Spanish or Portuguese lady.

dō′nor *n.* giver, bestower.

dŏn′t *v.* (imper.) do not. *n.* prohibition. ~**-care,** careless, reckless.

dōō′dle, *v.i.* scrawl aimlessly while one's attention is engaged elsewhere. *n.* such scrawl.

dōōm *n.* fate, destiny; judicial sentence. *v.t.* condemn, sentence, consign to misfortune or destruction (esp. in *p.p.*). **dooms′day** *n.* Last Judgement.

door (dōr) *n.* hinged or sliding or revolving barrier of wood etc. closing passage into building etc.; doorway; *at death's* ~, on point of dying; *next* ~, (in) next house or building, very near *to*; *out of* ~*s*, abroad, in the open air; *within* ~*s*, in the house. ~**-mat,** for wiping shoes on; (fig.) spiritless or subservient person. ~**-post,** either of uprights on each side of doorway. ~**way,** opening filled by door. ~**-yard,** (U.S.) yard or garden about door of house.

dōpe *n.* thick liquid used as lubricant etc.; kinds of varnish; (sl.) drug, esp. narcotic; (sl.) (esp. 'inside') information; (sl.) stupid person. *v.t.* drug; take drugs; apply dope to. **dō′p(e)y** *a.* slow-witted; sleepy.

Dŏpp′ler effect, shift *nn.* apparent change in frequency of sound or other waves due to relative motion between source and observer.

Dŏ′rĭc *a.* rustic, (of dialect) broad; (archit.) of oldest and simplest of five orders. *n.* Doric order; rustic, esp. Sc., dialect.

dŏr′mant *a.* inactive, in abeyance; sleeping; (her.) with head on paws. ~**ancy** *n.*

dŏr′mer (window) *n.* upright window set in sloping roof.

dŏr′mĭtorў *n.* sleeping-room with number of beds; suburban or country district of city workers' residences.

dŏr′mouse *n.* (pl. -*mīce*), small hibernating rodent.

dŏr′mў *a.* (golf) as many holes ahead as there are holes to play.

dŏr′sal *a.* of or on back.

dŏr′ter, -tour *n.* (hist.) bedroom, dormitory.

dŏr′ў *n.* edible sea-fish.

dō′sage *n.* giving of medicine etc. in doses; amount of dose.

dōse *n.* amount of medicine etc. administered at one time. *v.* administer dose(s) to, take doses.

dŏss *v.i.* (sl.) sleep in dosshouse; ~ *down,* sleep on makeshift bed. ~**house** *n.* common lodging-house.

dŏss′ier *n.* set of documents relating to person or happening.

dost, 2 pers. sing. pres. of **do.**

dŏt[1] *n.* small spot, point; (mus.) point after note etc. lengthening it by half its value; *on the* ~, punctually. *v.t.* mark or scatter with dot(s); scatter like dots; place dot over (letter *i*) or after (note etc.); ~ (person) *one,* (sl.) hit him. **dŏtt′ėd crotchet** etc., with time-value increased by half. **dŏtt′ėd line,** line of dots for signature etc. on document.

dŏt[2] *n.* woman's marriage-portion. [F]

dō′tage *n.* feeble-minded senility.

dō′tard *n.* man in his dotage.

dōte *v.i.* be feeble-minded or silly; ~ *on,* be passionately fond of.

doth, 3 pers. sing. pres. of **do.**

dŏtt′(e)rel *n.* kind of plover.

dŏtt′le *n.* tobacco left in pipe after smoking.

dŏtt′ў *a.* dotted; (sl.) silly.

doub′le (dŭ-) *a.* twofold; consisting of two parts; of twice amount or intensity; of two kinds; (of flower) with petals multiplied by conversion of stamens etc.; deceitful. *adv.* twice the amount; two together. *n.* person or thing mistakable for another; game between two pairs of players; twice the amount; (mil.) regulation running pace; (darts) score in outer ring of board, in which value is doubled; (racing) cumulative bet on two horses; double event, bed(room), tot of whisky, etc. *v.* make or become double; increase twofold; fold over upon itself; clench (fist); run; turn sharply; (naut.) get round; play two parts in same play etc. ~-barrelled, (of gun) with two barrels; (of surname) compound. ~-bass, largest and lowest-pitched musical instrument of violin kind. ~ bed, for two people. ~-breasted, (of garment) having fronts overlapping across breast. ~ chin, roll of fat below chin. ~-cross, betray, sell to both sides. ~-dealing, duplicity. ~-decker, (bus etc.) with two decks; (sandwich) of several layers. ~ eagle, figure of eagle with two heads. ~-edged, (of argument etc.) damaging to user as well as opponent. ~ event, winning of two races etc. in one season or meeting. ~ figures, numbers from 10 to 99. ~-stopping, simultaneous sounding of two strings of violin etc. ~-tonguing, rapid vibration of tongue in playing flute etc. ~ton n. (cards) two cards only of suit in one hand.

double entendre (dōo'bl ahn̈-tahn̈'dr) *n.* phrase with two meanings, one usu. indecent. [F]

doub'let (dŭ-) *n.* man's close body-garment in 14th–18th centuries; one of pair, esp. of words of same origin but different form or sense.

doubloon' (du-) *n.* (hist.) Spanish gold coin.

doubt (dowt) *n.* feeling of uncertainty, undecided frame of mind, inclination to disbelieve; uncertain state; *give benefit of the* ~, assume innocence of; *no* ~, certainly, admittedly. *v.* be in doubt or uncertainty; call in question, mistrust.

doubt'ful (-owt-) *a.* feeling or giving rise to doubt; uncertain.

doubt'less (-owt-) *adv.* no doubt.

douceur (dōo'sĕr) *n.* gratuity, bribe. [F]

douche (dōosh) *n.* jet of water applied to body externally or internally. *v.* administer douche to, take douche.

dough (dō) *n.* flour etc. kneaded into paste to be baked into bread etc. (U.S. sl.) money. ~-boy, (U.S. sl.) infantry soldier. ~nut, small spongy cake of dough fried in deep fat. doughy (dō'ĭ) *a.* like dough.

doughty (dow'tĭ) *a.* valiant.

dour (-oor) *a.* (Sc.) grim, stubborn.

douse *v.t.* extinguish (light); drench.

dove (dŭv) *n.* pigeon; type of gentleness or innocence. ~cŏt(e), pigeon-house.

dove'tail (dŭv-) *n.* joint made with tenon shaped like dove's tail. *v.* fit together (as) with dovetails.

dow'ager *n.* woman with title or property derived from her late husband.

dow'dy *a.* lacking smartness, ill-dressed. *n.* dowdy woman.

dow'el *n.* headless pin fastening together two pieces of wood etc. *v.t.* fasten with dowel(s). dow'elling *n.* round wooden rods for cutting into dowels.

dow'er *n.* widow's share for life of husband's estate; dowry; natural gift or talent. *v.t.* give dowry to; endow *with* talent etc.

dow'las *n.* kind of strong calico.

down[1] *n.* open high land; esp. (pl.) treeless undulating chalk uplands of S. England.

down[2] *n.* fine soft short hair or feathers or fluff.

down[3] *adv.* towards or in lower place or state or number; from earlier to later time; on ground; away from capital or university. *prep.* downwards along or through or into; at lower part of. *a.* directed downwards. *n.* reverse of fortune; throw in wrestling etc.; (Amer. footb.) (end of) attempt to advance ball; *have a* ~ *on*, (colloq.) dislike, be prejudiced against. *v.t.* (colloq.) put, throw, knock, bring, etc. down. ~ and out, beaten, done for, destitute. ~ east, (U.S.) in(to) eastern sea-coast districts of New England, esp. Maine. ~-grade, descending slope. ~-hearted, despondent. ~ south, (U.S.) in(to) southern States. ~-town, in(to) business part of town. ~ train, train going away from capital. ~trodden, crushed by oppression or tyranny. ~ under, at or to Antipodes, in Australia etc. ~ward *a.* & *adv.*; ~wards *adv.*

down'cast (-ah-) *a.* (of eyes) looking down; dejected.

down'fall (-awl) *n.* fall from prosperity or power; downpour.

down'hill *a.* sloping down, declining. *adv.* (-hĭl') in descending direction; on a decline.

down'pour (-pōr) *n.* heavy fall of rain etc.

down'right *a.* plain, straightforward, blunt. *adv.* thoroughly, quite.

downstairs'- *adv., n. & a.* (to, in, of) lower floor of house etc.

dow'nў *a.* of or like or covered with down; (sl.) knowing, sly.

dowr'ў *n.* property brought by wife at marriage.

dow'ser (*or* -z-) *n.* person able to locate hidden water or minerals by use of forked twig. **dow'sing** *n.*

dŏxŏl'ogў *n.* liturgical formula of praise to God.

doyen (dwah'yahn̄ *or* doi'en) *n.* senior member *of* body esp. of ambassadors.

doz. *abbr.* dozen.

dōze *v.i.* sleep lightly, be half asleep; ~ *off*, fall into doze. *n.* short light sleep.

do'zen (dŭ-) *n.* set of twelve.

D.P. *abbr.* displaced person; double pole.

D.P.H. *abbr.* Diploma in Public Health.

D.Ph., D.Phil. *abbr.* Doctor of Philosophy.

Dr. *abbr.* debtor; Doctor.

D.R. *abbr.* dead reckoning.

dr. *abbr.* drachm.

drăb[1] *a.* of dull light brown; dull, monotonous. *n.* drab colour.

drăb[2] *n.* (arch.) slut; prostitute.

drachm (-ăm) *n.* unit of weight (60 grains).

drăch'ma (-k-) *n.* (pl. -*ae*, -*as*), ancient and modern Greek coin.

Dracō'nĭan, -ŏn'ĭc *aa.* rigorous as laws of Draco.

draft (-ah-) *n.* (selection of) detachment of troops from larger body; (U.S.) conscription; order for drawing money; bill or cheque drawn; sketch of work to be done; rough copy. *v.t.* select as draft; (U.S.) conscript; prepare, make

rough copy of (esp. parliamentary Bill). ~**sman** *n.*

drăg *v.* draw along with force; trail or go heavily; search bottom of water with grapnels, nets, etc. *n.* check on progress, retarded motion; iron shoe to retard wheel and vehicle; coachlike four-horse vehicle; hunt using lure drawn before hounds; kinds of sledge, rake, net, etc.; (sl.) women's clothes worn by man.

dragée (drah'zhā) *n.* chocolate drop, sugar-coated almond, etc.

drăgg'le *v.* make dirty and wet by trailing; hang trailing. ~(-)**tail(ed).** (woman) with draggled skirts.

drăg'oman *n.* (pl. -*ans*, -*en*), interpreter and guide in Arab etc. countries.

drăg'on *n.* fire-breathing mythical monster like winged crocodile or snake; vigilant person, duenna.

drăg'onflў *n.* long-bodied gauze-winged insect.

dragōon' *n.* cavalryman of certain regiments; (hist.) mounted-infantry man. *v.t.* subject to oppression; force *into* course.

drain *v.* draw off (liquid) by ditches, pipes, etc., dry (land etc.) thus; drink to dregs; exhaust; flow *through* or *off* or *away*; be drained or dried by flowing off of water etc. *n.* channel or pipe carrying off water, sewage, etc. ~**age** *n.*

drāke *n.* male duck.

drăm *n.* drachm; small draught of strong drink.

dra'ma (-ah-) *n.* stage play; dramatic art; play-like series of events.

dramăt'ĭc *a.* of drama; forcible, theatrical; striking.

drăm'atĭs pērsō'nae *n. pl.* characters of drama. [L]

drăm'atĭst *n.* playwright.

drăm'atīze *v.* convert into play; admit of such conversion; make dramatic. ~**ā'tion** *n.*

Dram. Pers. *abbr., dramatis personae* [L], characters of the play.

drank, *p.t.* of **drink.**

drāpe *v.* cover, hang, adorn, with cloth etc.; arrange, hang, in graceful folds. *n.* fold; (pl.)

draperies, (U.S.) curtains. **drā′per** n. dealer in cloth, linen, etc. **drā′perў** n. draper's wares or trade; clothing or hangings disposed in folds.

drăs′tĭc a. strongly operative; vigorous; violent.

drăt v.t. curse. **drătt′ĕd** a. cursed.

draught (-ahft) n. traction; one drawing of net; one continuous act of drinking; dose of medicine; depth of water ship draws; current of air; (pl.) game played on chess--board; artist's sketch for picture etc.; draft; drawing of liquor. **~ beer**, drawn from cask, not bottled. **~ў** a. abounding in currents of air.

draughts′man (-ahft-) n. person employed to make drawings or plans; one skilled in drawing or designing; person who drafts documents; one of pieces in game of draughts.

draw[1] n. act of drawing; thing that draws custom or attention; drawing of lots, lottery; drawn game.

draw[2] v. (*drew*, pr. -ōō; *drawn*), pull, drag, haul; attract; derive, deduce, infer; inhale; extract; entice; extort, force; elicit; take from or out; pull into or out of position; make picture by tracing lines; describe in words; write out (bill, cheque, etc.); bring (game etc.) to undecided conclusion; (of ship) require (stated depth of water) to float; reach chance decision by taking one from number of things, obtain by lot; search (covert) for game etc.; make way, come, move; **~** *back*, withdraw; **~** *in*, (of days etc.) become shorter; **~** *out*, prolong, induce to talk, (of days) become longer; **~** *up*, come to stand, bring or come into regular order, compose (document etc.); **~** *oneself up*, assume stiff attitude.

draw′băck n. thing that qualifies satisfaction; amount of excise or import duty remitted or repaid on exports.

draw′brĭdge n. bridge hinged at one end for drawing up.

draw′er n. one who draws; sliding receptacle in table, chest, etc.; (pl.) two-legged undergarment.

draw′ĭng n. act of pulling, dragging, or hauling; delineation with pencil, pen, etc., esp. without colour; sketch. **~-board**, for stretching drawing-paper on. **~-pin**, flat--headed pin for fastening paper to drawing-board etc.

draw′ĭng-room n. reception-room; court reception.

drawl n. indolent or affected slowness of speech. v. speak or utter with drawl.

draw′-wĕll n. well with rope and bucket for drawing water.

dray n. low cart for heavy loads, esp. beer-barrels. **~-horse**, large heavy horse. **~man**, driver of brewer's dray.

dread (-ĕd) v. anticipate with terror; be in great fear of; be afraid (*to*). n. great fear; awe. a. dreaded, dreadful.

dread′ful (-ĕd-) a. terrible; troublesome, disagreeable, very bad.

dread′nought (drĕdnawt) n. (cloth used for) thick coat; powerful battleship.

dream n. sleeping vision; indulgence in fancy; day-dream, reverie. v. (*-eamt*, pr. -ĕmt, or *-ed*), experience dream; allow oneself to believe (*that*) or think *of*; fall into reverie. **~er** n. (esp.) unpractical person. **~less**, **~like** aa. **~ў** a. fanciful, unpractical; dreamlike.

drear (poet.), **drear′ў** aa. dismal, gloomy, dull.

drĕdge[1] n. apparatus for bringing up oysters etc. or clearing out mud etc. from bottom of sea etc. v. use dredge; clean or fetch up with dredge. **drĕdg′er**[1] n. boat employed in dredging.

drĕdge[2] v.t. sprinkle *with* flour etc., sprinkle (flour etc.) *over*. **drĕdg′er**[2] n. box for sprinkling flour etc.

drĕgs n.pl. sediment, grounds; refuse.

drĕnch v.t. wet all over; force (beast) to take dose. n. dose for beast. **~ing** n. & a. soaking.

Drĕs′den (-z-). **~ china**, **~ porcelain**, kind produced in Saxony, esp. in 18th c.

drĕss v. (mil.) take up exact alignment; clothe, clothe oneself; put dressing on (wound etc.); prepare (food); trim. *n*. clothing, esp. external; woman's or child's outer garment of bodice and skirt. ~ **circle**, first gallery in theatres. ~ **coat**, swallow-tailed coat for formal evening wear. ~**maker**, woman making women's dresses. ~ **rehearsal**, final one in costume. ~**-shirt**, (esp. stiff-fronted) shirt for evening wear.

drĕss'age (-ahzh) *n*. training of horse in obedience and deportment.

drĕss'er[1] *n*. surgeon's assistant; person who helps actor to dress for stage.

drĕss'er[2] *n*. kitchen sideboard with shelves; (U.S.) dressingtable.

drĕss'ing *n*. ointment etc. applied to wound; manure; sauce or stuffing. ~**-case**, case with toilet requisites. ~**-down**, scolding, reprimand. ~**-gown**, garment worn while making toilet etc.

drĕss'ў *a*. given to smart dress.

drew, *p.t.* of **draw**.

drey (-ā), *n*. squirrel's nest.

dribb'le *v*. flow or let flow in drops; run at the mouth; (footb. etc.) work ball forward with repeated touches of feet etc. *n*. dribbling flow; piece of dribbling.

drĭb'lĕt *n*. small quantity.

dried, *p.t.* & *p.p.* of **dry**.

drī'er *n*. thing, person, that dries; substance that expedites drying.

drĭft *n*. being driven by current; deviation due to current, wind, etc.; inaction; purpose, meaning, tenor; deposit or accumulation of sand, snow, etc. by action of wind or current; (mining) horizontal passage following vein; (S. Afr.) ford. *v*. be carried (as) by current; (of current) carry; heap or be heaped into drifts; go aimlessly; fish with drift-net. ~**-net**, large net allowed to drift with tide, for catching herring etc. ~**wood**, wood washed ashore by sea. ~**er** *n*. boat used for drift-net fishing.

drill[1] *n*. boring tool or machine; exercising of soldiers etc.; seed--sowing machine; small furrow. *v*. bore (hole etc.); subject to or undergo drill; sow in rows.

drill[2] *n*. coarse twilled fabric.

drill[3] *n*. kind of baboon.

drĭnk *v*. (*drănk*; *drŭnk* & *drŭnken*), swallow liquid; absorb moisture; take *in* with eager delight; drink alcoholic liquor, esp. to excess; ~ *to*, toast. *n*. liquid drunk or for drinking; intemperance; glass or portion of liquor; *the* ~, (sl.) the sea.

drĭp *v*. fall or let fall in drops. *n*. process of dripping; (sl.) boring or dreary person. ~**-dry**, (of fabric etc.) that may be hung up to dry and needs no ironing. ~**stone** projecting moulding over window etc. to throw off rain etc.

drĭpp'ing *n*. fat melted from roasting meat.

drīve *v*. (*drōve, driven*), urge onwards by force; chase (game etc.) from large area into small; direct course of (vehicle etc.); convey or be conveyed in vehicle; impel, propel, carry along. *n*. excursion in vehicle; carriage road, esp. private road to house; forcible blow at cricket etc., (golf) hit with driver, esp. from tee; energy, push, energetic campaign; social gathering to play card-games etc., changing partners and tables; ~ *at*, have as one's drift or aim; ~ *off*, (golf) drive ball from tee. ~**-in** *n*. standing for car etc.; drive-in bank, restaurant, etc.; *a*. that may be used without alighting from car.

drĭv'el *v.i.* slaver; talk silly stuff. *n*. silly nonsense. **drĭv'eller** *n*.

drī'ver *n*. one who drives; (golf) wooden-headed club for sending ball long distance.

drī'ving-wheel *n*. wheel communicating motion to other part of machine; wheel to which driving power is applied.

drĭzz'le *n*. & *v.i.* (fall in) fine dense rain.

drōgue (-g) *n*. sea-anchor; windsock.

drōll *a*. amusing, odd, queer. ~**erў** *n*. quaint humour.

drŏm'ėdarў (*or* -ŭm-) *n*. swift usu. one-humped camel bred for riding.

drōne *n*. male or non-worker bee; idler; (continuous tone emitted by)

bass-pipe of bagpipes; deep monotonous hum. v. buzz like bee or bagpipe; talk or utter monotonously.

drool n. & v. drivel.

droop v. incline or hang down;
languish, lose heart. n. drooping
state.

drop n. small quantity of liquid that
falls or hangs down or detaches
itself in spherical or pear-shaped
form; (pl.) medicinal preparation
to be used in drops; pendant of
metal, glass, etc.; sweetmeat; fall,
abrupt descent, distance through
which anything falls; platform in
gallows withdrawn from under feet
of condemned man; drop curtain.
v. fall or shed in drops; let fall;
lose (money); leave hold of; sink
to lower level; lower (eyes etc.);
sink to ground; (footb.) make
(goal) by drop-kick; allow oneself
to fall *behind* etc.; end, stop; break
off acquaintance etc. with; ~ *in*,
pay casual visit; ~ *off*, fall asleep,
become less numerous etc. ~ **curtain**, curtain let down between
acts etc. in theatre. ~**-kick**,
kicking of football as it bounds
after being dropped from hands.
~**-shot**, tennis-stroke causing ball
to drop abruptly after clearing net.
~**let** n. small drop. **dropp'ings**
n.pl. (esp.) dung of beasts etc.

drop'sy n. disease with watery fluid
collecting in body. **drop'sical** a.

dross n. scum of molten metal; impurities; refuse. **dross'y** a.

drought (-owt), (poet.) **drouth** nn.
thirst; continuous dry weather,
lack of rain. ~**y** a.

drove[1] n. moving herd or flock; crowd
in motion. **dro'ver** n. driver of or
dealer in cattle.

drove[2] p.t. of **drive**.

drown v. be suffocated or suffocate
by submersion; drench or flood;
overpower (sound) by greater
loudness; overcome (grief etc.)
with or *in* drink.

drowse (-z) v.i. be half asleep.

drow'sy (-z-) a. half asleep.

drub v.t. thrash, whack. ~**bing** n.

drudge v.i. work hard at distasteful
tasks. n. person who drudges.
drudg'ery n.

drug n. substance used in medicine;
substance taken or administered as
stimulant, narcotic, etc. esp. one
causing addiction; unsaleable commodity. v. adulterate or stupefy
with drugs; take drugs. ~**-store**,
chemist's shop selling many other
goods.

drugg'et (-g-) n. coarse woollen stuff
for floor covering etc.

drugg'ist (-g-) n. dealer in drugs.

Dru'id (-oo-) n. ancient Gallic or
British priest; officer of Welsh
Gorsedd or national assembly.
~**ess**, ~**ism** nn.

drum n. percussive musical instrument, sound of this; drummer;
cylindrical structure or object;
tympanum of ear; (arch.) large
evening party. v. play drum; tap
or thump continuously; expel,
drive *out*, (as) with drumbeats;
solicit orders; ~ *up*, obtain or
summon (as) by beating drum.
~**fire**, heavy continuous rapid
artillery fire. ~**head**, stretched
membrane of drum; (attrib.) of
kind held on active service.
~**-major**, regimental band-leader.
~**stick**, stick for beating drum;
lower joint of cooked fowl's leg.

drumm'er n. player of drum; (U.S.)
commercial traveller.

drunk, p.p. of **drink**. pred. a. in-
toxicated; overcome by strong
drink. n. (sl.) drinking-bout;
drunken man; drunkard. ~**ard** n.
person often drunk. ~**en** a. drunk;
given to drinking; caused by or
showing drunkenness.

drupe (-oo-) n. stone-fruit.

dry a. without or deficient in moisture; without rain; thirsty; stiff,
cold, matter-of-fact; (of wall etc.)
built without mortar; teetotal, free
from sale of intoxicants; uninteresting. v. make or become dry.
~**-clean**, clean without using water,
e.g. with spirit. ~**-fly**, (fish with)
artificial fly resting lightly on
water. ~ **goods**, (U.S.) drapery
etc. as opp. groceries. ~ **ice**, solid
carbon dioxide, used as refrigerant.
~**-nurse**, woman tending but not
suckling child. ~**-point**, engraving
tool not requiring use of acid; (print

made by) process of engraving on copper plate with this. ~ rot, decay in wood not exposed to air; moral or social decay. ~-shod, without wetting feet.

drȳ'ad n. nymph inhabiting tree.

drȳ'salter (-awl- or -ŏl-) n. dealer in tinned foods, drugs, oils, etc.

D.S. abbr., dal segno [It.], (repeat) from the mark.

D.Sc. abbr. Doctor of Science.

D.S.C., D.S.M., D.S.O. abbr. Distinguished Service Cross, Medal, Order.

D.T., d.t.(s) abbr. delirium tremens.

D.Th., D.Theol. abbr. Doctor of Theology.

dū'al a. of two; twofold, double, divided in two; shared by two; (of carriageway) with contrary streams of traffic kept separate. n. (gram.) dual number or form. ~ism 'n. duality; recognition of two independent principles or powers. ~ist, dūăl'itȳ nn.; ~is'tic a.

dŭb[1] v.t. make (person) into knight; give title or nickname to.

dŭb[2] v.t. add sound effects etc. or new sound track, esp. in different language, to film etc.

dŭbb'in(g) n. grease for suppling and waterproofing leather.

dūbī'etȳ n. feeling of doubt.

dū'bious a. doubtful; of questionable or suspected character.

dū'cal a. of or like duke.

dŭc'at n. gold coin formerly current in Italy etc.

dŭch'ess n. duke's wife or widow; lady holding duchy.

duchesse (dōōshĕs') n. ~ satin, soft kind of satin. ~ lace, kind of Brussels pillow-lace.

dŭch'ȳ n. reigning duke's territory.

dŭck[1] n. kinds of swimming bird; darling; (crick.) duck's-egg. ~bill, ~-billed platypus, ornithorhyncus. ~board, slatted board as pathway over muddy ground. ~'s-egg, batsman's score of 0. ~weed, plant covering surface of still water like carpet.

dŭck[2] v. dip head under water and emerge; push head of (person) under water; bob down to avoid blow etc.; drop curtsy; (bridge etc.)

avoid taking trick. n. quick dip below water; bob of head.

dŭck[3] n. strong linen or cotton material; (pl.) trousers of this.

dŭck'ling n. young duck.

dŭct n. conduit; (anat.) tube conveying secretions etc. ~less a. (of gland) of which secretion passes directly into blood.

dŭc'tile (or -il) a. capable of being drawn into wire; plastic; docile. dŭctil'itȳ n.

dŭd n. (sl.), (pl.) clothes, rags; shell etc. that fails to go off; futile plan or person. a. counterfeit; useless; futile.

dūde n. (U.S. sl.) fop, dandy; Eastern visitor in West. ~ ranch, ranch used as holiday centre.

dŭdg'eon (-jn) n. resentment; state of wrath or indignation.

dūe a. owing or payable as debt or obligation; proper, rightful, adequate; under engagement or contract to be ready, arrive, etc. at defined time; to be ascribed or attributed to (cause etc.). adv. exactly, directly. n. what is owed or due to person; (usu. pl.) toll or fee legally demandable.

dū'el n. fight with weapons between two persons; contest. v.i. fight duel(s). dū'ellist n.

dūenn'a n. governess, female guardian, chaperon.

dūĕt' n. musical composition for two performers.

dŭff n. boiled pudding.

dŭff'er n. (colloq.) inefficient or stupid person.

dŭff'le, dŭff'el n. heavy woollen cloth with thick nap; (U.S.) kit for camping etc. ~-bag, cylindrical bag for carrying kit etc. ~ coat, short heavy overcoat with toggle fastenings.

dŭg[1] n. udder, beast's teat.

dug[2], p.t. & p.p. of dig.

du'gŏng (-ōō-) n. large aquatic herbivorous mammal of Indian etc. seas.

dŭg'-out n. underground shelter esp. for troops in trenches; hollowed tree as canoe.

dūke n. sovereign prince, ruler of small State; British peer of highest rank; *royal* ~, duke who is member of royal family. ~**dom** *n*. duchy; duke's dignity.

dŭl′cĕt *a*. sweet, soothing.

dŭl′cĭmer *n*. musical instrument with strings struck by hammers held in hands.

dŭll *a*. lacking intelligence; not bright; blunt; wanting liveliness. *v*. make or grow dull; lose keenness. **dŭll′ard** *n*. slow-witted person.

dū′lў *adv*. properly, fitly, rightly; sufficiently; punctually.

Du′ma (dōō-) *n*. Russian parliament, 1906–17.

dŭmb (-m) *a*. unable to speak; silent, taciturn; (U.S. colloq.) dull, stupid. ~-**bell**, short bar with heavy knob at each end, used in pairs to exercise muscles.

dŭmbfound′ (-mf-) *v.t*. strike dumb, confound, nonplus.

dŭm′dŭm (**bullet**) *n*. soft-nosed expanding bullet.

dŭmm′ў *n*. sham article; mere tool; lay figure; (hand of) declarer's partner at bridge or imaginary whist-player whose cards are exposed and played by partner. *a*. that is a dummy, sham.

dŭmp *v.t*. shoot or deposit (rubbish); throw down; send (surplus goods) to foreign market at low price. *n*. rubbish-heap; (mil.) temporary depot of munitions etc.; depressing place; (pl.) depression, melancholy.

dŭmp′lĭng *n*. ball of dough boiled in stew etc.

dŭm′pў *a*. short and stout.

dŭn¹ *a*. of dull greyish brown. *n*. dun colour; dun horse etc.

dŭn² *n*. importunate creditor. *v.t*. importune for payment.

dŭnce *n*. bad learner; dullard.

dŭn′derhead (-ĕd) *n*. blockhead.

dūne *n*. mound of dry shifting sand esp. on coast.

Dunelm. *abbr*. (Bishop) of Durham.

dŭng *n*. excrement of animals; manure. *v.t*. manure (land). ~**hill**, manure-heap.

dŭngaree′ (-ngg-) *n*. coarse Indian calico; (pl.) overalls.

dŭn′geon (-jn) *n*. subterranean cell for prisoners.

dŭnk *v.t*. dip (bread etc.) into soup etc. while eating.

dŭn′lĭn *n*. red-backed sandpiper.

dŭnn′age *n*. light material stowed under or among cargo to protect it; (colloq.) miscellaneous baggage.

dū′ō *n*. pair of performers; duet.

dūodĕ′cĭmal *a*. of twelve or twelfths; proceeding by twelves.

dūodĕ′cĭmō *n*. (abbr. 12 mo.), (size of) book with sheets folded into 12 leaves or 24 pages.

dūodē′num *n*. part of small intestine next stomach. ~**nal** *a*.

dū′olŏgue (-g) *n*. dialogue of two speakers.

dūpe *v.t*. deceive and make use of. *n*. duped person.

dū′ple *a*. (of ratio) double; (mus.) of two beats to bar.

dŭ′plĕx *a*. of two parts; twofold; (U.S., of flat) on two floors.

dū′plĭcate *a*. double; exactly like thing already existing. *n*. one of two things exactly alike. *v.t*. (-āt), make exact copy of; repeat; double. ~**ā′tion** *n*. ~**ātor** *n*. apparatus for making copies.

dŭplĭ′cĭtў *n*. deceitfulness.

dūr′able *a*. capable of lasting; resisting wear. ~**bĭl′ĭtў** *n*.

dūrăl′ūmĭn *n*. hard tough aluminium alloy. **P.**

dūr′a mā′ter *n*. outer membrane of brain.

dūr′ance *n*. (arch.) imprisonment.

dūrā′tion *n*. time thing lasts.

dūr′bar *n*. public levee of Indian ruler, viceroy, etc.

dūrĕss(e)′ (*or* dūr′-) *n*. forcible restraint; threats or other illegal compulsion.

dūr′ĭng *prep*. throughout or at point in duration of.

dūrst, arch. *p.t*. of **dare**.

dŭsk *n*. partial darkness; obscurity. **dŭs′kў** *a*. shadowy, dim; dark-coloured.

dŭst *n*. light fine powder of earth or other solid matter; household refuse; mouldered corpse, man's mortal remains; *bite the* ~, fall slain. ~**bin**, receptacle for household refuse. ~-**bowl**, area denuded of forest and reduced to desert. ~-**cover**, book's paper jacket.

~man, man who carts away refuse etc. from dustbins; sleep personified. ~-up, (sl.) shindy. v. sprinkle (dust, flour, etc.), sprinkle *with* powder; clear of dust, brush or wipe dust away. ~er n. cloth for dusting.

dŭs′tў a. powdery, dust-covered.

Dŭtch[1] a. of Holland or its people or in their language. n. Dutch people or language; *double* ~, incomprehensible jargon. ~ auction, sale in which price is reduced till purchaser is found. ~ barn, one consisting of roof supported on poles. ~ courage, (courage due to) strong drink. ~man, native of Holland; (U.S. colloq.) German. ~ oven, metal box with open side attachable to grate. ~ treat, (U.S. colloq.) one in which each pays his own way.

dŭtch[2] n. (coster sl.) wife.

dū′tèous a. dutiful.

dū′tìable a. liable to customs or other duties.

dū′tìful a. regular and willing in discharge of duty.

dū′tў n. moral or legal obligation; office or function; tax levied on article or transaction.

dūŭm′vir (-er) n. (pl. -rs, -rī), (Rom. hist.) one of pair of co-equal magistrates etc. ~ate n.

D.V. abbr., Deo volente [L], God willing.

dwarf (-ôrf) n. person, plant, etc., much below ordinary size; small star of great density; (Scand. myth.) small supernatural being skilled in metal-working. a. stunted; undersized. v.t. stunt in growth; make look small. ~ĭsh a.

dwĕll v.i. (dwĕlt), reside, live; keep attention fixed on, write or speak at length on.

dwĕll′ĭng n. house, residence. ~-house, (part of) house used as residence, not as shop etc.

dwĭn′dle v.i. waste away; diminish; lose importance.

dwt. abbr. pennyweight.

dўe v. (dyed, dyeing), colour, tinge; make of specified colour; take dye. n. hue; colouring-matter used for, colour produced by, dyeing.

dying, pres. p. of die[2].

dyke : see dike.

dўnăm′ic a. of motive force or force in operation; of dynamics; potent, forceful. n. energizing force; (usu. pl. used as sing.) branch of applied mathematics treating of motion and of action of forces. ~al a. of dynamics or dynamism. dў′namism n. dynamic quality; (philos.) system or theory explaining all phenomena by immanent force or energy.

dў′namīte n. high explosive of nitro-glycerine contained in absorbent substance. v.t. blow up with this.

dў′namō n. (pl. -os), machine converting mechanical into electrical energy.

dўnamŏm′ėter n. instrument for measuring energy.

dўn′ast (or dў-) n. member of dynasty.

dўn′astў n. line of hereditary rulers. dўnăs′tĭc (or dў-) a.

dўne n. (phys.) unit of force.

dўs′enterў n. disease with inflammation of large intestine. dўsentĕ′rĭc a.

dўsgĕn′ic a. exerting detrimental effect on race.

dўslogĭs′tic a. used to express disapprobation.

dўspĕp′sĭa n. indigestion.

dўspĕp′tĭc a. having or subject to dyspepsia. n. dyspeptic person.

E

E, e (ē) n. (mus.) third note in scale of C major.

E. abbr. East; Egyptian; Engineering.

each a. & pron. (of two or more) every (one) taken separately. ~ way, (backed) for win or place.

ea′ger (-g-) a. full of keen desire; ardent; impatient.

ea′gle n. large bird of prey; figure of eagle as Roman ensign, church lectern, etc.; (golf) score of 2 under par for hole. ea′glĕt n. young eagle.

eagre (ā′ger, ē-) n. large tidal wave in river.

E. & O.E. *abbr.* errors and omissions excepted.

ear[1] *n.* (esp. external) organ of hearing; sense of hearing; faculty of recognizing musical intervals; ear--like object as handle etc. **~-ache,** pain in internal ear. **~mark** *n.* owner's mark on ear of sheep etc.; *v.t.* mark with this, assign (fund etc.) to some definite purpose. **~-phone,** telephone or radio receiver held to ear by band passing over head; small microphone worn in ear. **~ring,** ornament worn in lobe of ear. **~shot,** hearing distance. **~-trumpet,** trumpet-shaped tube held to ear to aid hearing.

ear[2] *n.* spike or head of corn etc. containing flowers or seeds.

earl (ẽrl) *n.* nobleman ranking next below marquis. **E~ Marshal,** officer of State with ceremonial duties. **~dom** *n.*

ear'lў (ẽr-) *a. & adv.* soon; betimes; in advance of others. **~ door(s),** in theatre, admitting audience before usual hour.

earn (ẽrn) *v.t.* obtain as reward of work or merit. **ear'nings** *n.pl.* money earned.

ear'nest[1] (ẽr-) *a.* serious, not trifling; ardent, zealous. *n.* seriousness.

ear'nest[2] (ẽr-) *n.* money paid as instalment to confirm contract; foretaste.

earth (ẽr-) *n.* planet we live on; dry land; soil, mould; ground; hole of foxes etc.; (electr.) (wire etc. as) connexion with earth; *run to ~,* chase (quarry) to earth, find after long search. *v.t.* heap earth over (roots etc.); (electr.) connect with earth. **~-closet,** privy in which dry earth is used to cover contents. **~work,** bank of earth in fortification. **~worm,** worm living in earth.

ear'then (ẽr-) *a.* made of earth or of baked clay. **~ware,** baked clay; vessels made of this.

earth'lў (ẽr-) *a.* of earth, terrestrial; *no ~ use* etc., (colloq.) no use etc. at all; *not an ~,* (sl.) no earthly chance.

earth'quāke (ẽr-) *n.* convulsion of earth's surface.

ear'thў (ẽr-) *a.* of or like earth or soil; grossly material.

ear'wig *n.* insect formerly thought to enter head by ear; (U.S.) kind of small centipede.

ease (ēz) *n.* freedom from pain or trouble or constraint; quiet, rest; facility. *v.* relieve from pain; etc.; relax, slacken; move gently or gradually; *~ (off),* become less burdensome, take things easily, (of prices etc.) fall slightly. **~ful** *a.*

ea'sel (-z-) *n.* frame to support painting, blackboard, etc.

ease'ment (-zm-) acquired right or privilege.

east *adv., n. & a.* (towards, at, near, blowing from) point of horizon where sun rises; (towards, in) eastern part of world, country, town etc., or altar-end of church. **E~ End,** eastern part of London. **E~ Side,** eastern part of New York City. **~ward** *adv., a. & n.* **~wards** *adv.*

Ea'ster *n.* festival of Christ's resurrection. *~ egg,* painted or imitation egg as Easter gift.

ea'sterly *a.* from or to east.

ea'stern *a.* of or in east. **E~ Church,** Orthodox Church. **Ea'sterner** *n.* inhabitant of eastern part esp. of U.S.

ea'sў (-z-) *a.* free from bodily or mental pain, worry, etc.; not difficult or burdensome or painful; easily obtained; not ceremonious; compliant; tranquil. *adv.* in comfortable fashion; gently; *~ all!* stop rowing. **~-chair,** chair designed for comfort. **~-going,** not fussy; content with things as they are.

eat *v.* (p.t. *ate,* pr. ĕt; p.p. *eaten,* pr. ētn), masticate and swallow (food); consume food, have meal; destroy, consume. **~ing-house,** restaurant, cook-shop. **~able** *a.* **~ables** *n.pl.* articles of food.

eau-de-Cologne (ōdĕkolōn') *n.* perfume first made at Cologne.

eaves (ēvz) *n.pl.* projecting lower edge of roof. **eaves'drŏp** *v.i.* listen secretly to private conversation.

ĕbb *n.* reflux of tide; decline, decay. *v.i.* flow back; decline.

ĕb'on *a.* (poet.) ebony.
ĕb'onīte *n.* vulcanized rubber.
ĕb'onў *n.* kinds of hard black wood. *a.* made of, black as, ebony.
Ebor. *abbr.* (Archbishop) of York.
ĕbŭll'ĭent *a.* boiling; exuberant. ~ence, ~encў *nn.*
ĕbulli'tion *n.* boiling; outburst.
E.C. *abbr.* East Central.
écarté (ākär'tā) *n.* card-game for two players.
ĕccĕn'trĭc (-ks-) *a.* not concentric; not placed, not having axis etc. placed, centrally; not circular; irregular; odd, whimsical. *n.* eccentric person; device for changing rotary into reciprocal motion. ĕccentrĭ'cĭtў *n.*
Eccles. *abbr.* Ecclesiastes.
ĕcclēsiăs'tĭc (-zĭ-) *n.* clergyman. ~al *a.* of church or clergy.
ĕcclēsiŏl'ogў (-zĭ-) *n.* science of church building and decoration. ĕcclēsiolŏ'gĭcal *a.;* ~gĭst *n.*
Ecclus. *abbr.* Ecclesiasticus.
ĕcdўs'ĭast (-z-) *n.* (joc.) strip-teaser.
E.C.G. *abbr.* electrocardiogram.
ech'elon (ĕsh-) *n.* formation of troops in parallel divisions, each with its front clear of that in advance; any similar formation. *v.* form or form into echelon.
echo (ĕk'ō) *n.* (pl. -oes), repetition of sound by reflection of soundwaves; close imitation. *v.* resound with echo; be repeated; repeat, imitate.
Ecl. *abbr.* Eclogues.
é'clair (ā-) *n.* finger-shaped cake filled with cream and iced.
éclat (ā'klah) *n.* brilliant success; prestige. [F]
ĕclĕc'tĭc *a.* & *n.* (ancient philosopher) selecting doctrines from every school; (person) borrowing freely from various sources.
ĕclipse' *n.* interception of light of sun, moon, etc. by another body; loss of brilliance or splendour. *v.t.* intercept light of; outshine, surpass.
ĕclĭp'tĭc *a.* of eclipse. *n.* (plane of) sun's apparent orbit.
ĕc'lŏgue *n.* pastoral poem.
ēcŏl'ogy *n.* (branch of science dealing with) living organisms in relation to their surroundings etc. ēcolŏ'gĭcal *a.;* ~gĭst *n.*

ēconŏm'ĭc *a.* of economics; maintained for profit; practical, utilitarian; paying for expenses or costs. ~al *a.* thrifty, not wasteful. ~s *n.pl.* science of production and distribution of wealth; country's condition in regard to material prosperity. ecŏn'omist *n.*
ecŏn'omīze *v.* use sparingly; practise economy; avoid expense.
ecŏn'omў *n.* management of concerns and resources of state or business or household; frugality, frugal use.
écru (ā'krōō) *n.* & *a.* (of) colour of unbleached linen.
E.C.S.C. *abbr.* European Coal and Steel Community.
ĕc'stasў *n.* exalted state of feeling; trance; poetic frenzy.
ĕcstăt'ĭc *a.* of or in ecstasies.
ĕc'toblast (-ah-) *n.* outer membrane of cell.
ĕc'toplăsm *n.* supposed viscous substance exuding from body of spiritualistic medium during trance.
E.C.U. *abbr.* English Church Union.
ēcūmĕn'ĭc *a.* of or representing whole Christian world, catholic; worldwide. ~al *a.*
ĕc'zėma *n.* kinds of inflammation of skin.
Ed. *abbr.* Edward.
ed. *abbr.* edited; edition; editor.
ĕdā'cious *a.* of eating; greedy.
E.D.D. *abbr.* English Dialect Dictionary.
ĕdd'ў *n.* small whirlpool; smoke etc. moving like this. *v.* move in eddies.
edelweiss (ā'dlvīs) *n.* white-flowered Alpine plant.
E'den (ē-) *n.* abode of Adam and Eve; delightful place or state.
ĕdĕn'tāte *a.* toothless.
ĕdge *n.* cutting side of blade; sharpness; crest of ridge, line where two surfaces meet abruptly; rim, narrow surface of thin or flat object; boundary, brink; *on* ~, excited or irritable; *the* ~ *on,* the advantage of. *v.* sharpen; border; move almost imperceptibly. ~-tool, cutting-tool. ~ways, ~wise *advs.* with edge foremost; edge to edge.

ĕdg'ĭng *n.* border, fringe, etc. on or at edge. ĕdg'ў̆ *a.* irritable, testy.

ĕd'ĭble *n.* eatable. ~bĭl'ĭtў̆ *n.*

ē'dĭct *n.* order proclaimed by authority.

ĕd'ĭfĭce *n.* building, esp. large and stately one.

ĕd'ĭfў̄ *v.t.* instruct; improve morally. ~fĭcā'tion *n.*

Edin. *abbr.* Edinburgh.

ĕd'ĭt *v.t.* prepare for publication; act as editor of; modify, garble. ĕdĭ'tion *n.* form in which literary work is published; whole number of copies of book etc. issued at one time. ĕd'ĭtor *n.* one who edits, esp. one who conducts (section of) newspaper etc.; publisher's literary manager. ~tôr'ĭal *a.* of or written by editor; *n.* newspaper article written by or under responsibility of editor.

E.D.S. *abbr.* English Dialect Society.

ĕd'ūcāte *v.t.* bring up (child); train mentally and morally; instruct. ~ā'tion, ~ātor *nn.*; ~able, ~ā'tional, ~atĭve *aa.* ~ā'tion(al)-ist *nn.* advocate of, person concerned with, education.

ĕdūce' *v.t.* bring out, develop; infer; extract. ĕdū'cĭble *a.*

Edwar'dian (ĕ-; -wôr- *or* -wâr-) *n.* & *a.* (person) belonging to or characteristic of reign of Edward VII.

E.E.C. *abbr.* European Economic Community.

E.E.G. *abbr.* electroencephalogram.

eel *n.* snake-like fish.

e'en, e'er, poet. for even, ever.

eer'ĭe, eer'ў̆ *a.* strange; weird.

E.E.T.S. *abbr.* Early English Text Society.

ĕffāce' *v.t.* rub or wipe out; eclipse; make one*self* inconspicuous. ~ment *n.*

ĕffĕct' *n.* result, consequence; impression; (pl.) property. *v.t.* bring about; accomplish.

ĕffĕc'tĭve *a.* operative; striking; fit for service; existing.

ĕffĕc'tūal *a.* answering its purpose. ~ly *adv.* efficaciously.

ĕffĕc'tūāte *v.t.* bring about, fulfil.

ĕffĕm'ĭnate *a.* unmanly, womanish; voluptuous. ~acў̆ *n.*

ĕffĕn'dĭ *n.* Turkish title of respect.

ĕffervĕsce' *v.i.* give off bubbles of gas. ~ent *a.*; ~ence, ~encў̆ *nn.*

ĕffēte' *a.* worn out; feeble.

ĕffĭcā'cious *a.* producing desired effect. ĕff'ĭcacў̆ *n.*

ĕffĭ'cient (-shnt) *a.* competent, capable; producing desired result. ~encў̆ *n.*

ĕff'ĭgў̆ *n.* portrait, image.

ĕffloresce' (-ĕs) *v.i.* (come to surface and) turn to fine powder on exposure to air; (of surface) become covered with powdery saline crust. ~ĕs'cence *n.*; ~ĕs'cent *a.*

ĕff'luence (-loo-) *n.* flowing out (of liquid etc.); what flows out.

ĕff'luent (-loo-) *a.* flowing out. *n.* stream flowing from lake etc.; outflow from sewage tank etc.

ĕfflu'vĭum (-loo-) *n.* (pl. -*ia*), noxious or offensive exhalation.

ĕff'lŭx *n.* effluence.

ĕff'ort *n.* exertion; endeavour. ~less *a.* (esp.) without effort, easy.

ĕffron'terў̆ (-ŭn-) *n.* impudence.

ĕffŭl'gence *n.* lustre, brightness.

ĕffŭl'gent *a.* bright, radiant.

ĕffūse' (-z) *v.t.* pour forth. ~sion *n.* (literary) outpouring. ~sĭve *a.* demonstrative, gushing.

ĕft *n.* newt.

E.F.T.A. *abbr.* European Free Trade Association.

e.g. *abbr.*, *exempli gratia* [L], for instance.

ĕgălĭtār'ĭan *a.* & *n.* (person) asserting equality of mankind.

ĕgg[1] *n.* spheroidal body produced by female of birds etc., containing germ of new individual within shell or membrane; ovum. ~head, (U.S. sl.) intellectual. ~-plant, plant with oval purple or white fruit. *v.t.* ~ *and* (bread-)*crumb*, coat with (yoke of) egg and bread-crumbs.

ĕgg[2] *v.t.* incite, urge *on.*

ĕg'lantĭne *n.* sweet-brier.

ĕg'ō *n.* the I, self; esp. conscious thinking subject. ~cĕn'trĭc *a.* & *n.* self-centred (person).

ĕg'ōĭsm *n.* systematic selfishness; self-opinionatedness; egotism. ~ĭst *n.*; ~ĭs'tĭc(al) *aa.*

ĕg'otĭsm *n.* practice of talking about oneself; self-conceit. ~ĭst *n.*; ~ĭs'tĭc(al) *aa.*

ėgrē'gious *a.* notable, distinguished (now derog.).

ē'grĕss *n.* going out; way out.

ē'grĕt *n.* lesser white heron.

Egyptian (ĭjĭp'shn) *a.* & *n.* (native) of Egypt.

Egÿptŏl'ogÿ (ē-) *n.* study of Egyptian antiquities. **~ogist** *n.*

eh (ā) *int.* expressing inquiry, surprise, etc.

ei'der (ī-) *n.* northern species of duck. **~down**, (quilt stuffed with) small soft breast-feathers of eider.

eight (āt) *n.* & *a.* one more than seven (8, VIII); (rowing-boat with) crew of eight. **eighth** (ātth) *a.* & *n.* **~some** *a.* (Sc., of reel) for eight persons.

eighteen' (āt-) *n.* & *a.* one more than seventeen (18, XVIII). **~th** *a.* & *n.*

eighty (ā'tĭ) *n.* & *a.* eight times ten (80, LXXX). **~tieth** *a.* & *n.*

eisteddfod (āstĕdh'vod) *n.* Welsh congress of bards.

ei'ther (īdh-; *or* ē-) *a.* one or other of two. *pron.* each of two. *adv.* introducing first alternative; (with neg. or interrog.) any more than the other.

ėjăc'ūlāte *v.* utter suddenly, cry out; eject (fluids etc.) from body. **~ā'tion** ; **~atorÿ** *a.*

ėjĕct' *v.t.* throw out, expel; emit. **ejĕc'tion, ~ment** *nn.* **~or** *n.* (esp.) device ejecting cartridge from gun, pilot from aircraft, etc.

ēke[1] *v.t.* **~ out**, supplement; contrive to make (living) or support (existence).

ēke[2] *adv.* (arch.) also.

ėlăb'orate *a.* minutely worked out; highly finished. *v.t.* (-āt), work out in detail. **~ā'tion, ~ātor** *nn.*; **~ative** *a.*

élan (ālahṅ') *n.* vivacity, dash. [F]

ē'land *n.* large S.-Afr. antelope.

ėlăpse' *v.i.* (of time) pass away.

ėlăs'tĭc (*or* -lah-) spontaneously resuming normal bulk or shape after dilation etc.; buoyant; flexible; made of thin strips etc. of usu. fabric-covered rubber. *n.* elastic fabric or band or string. **ėlăstĭ'citÿ** *n.*

ėlāte' *v.t.* raise spirits of, excite. **elā'tion** *n.*

ĕl'bow (-ō) *n.* (outer part of) joint between fore- and upper arm; elbow-shaped thing. *v.t.* thrust, jostle. **~-grease**, vigorous polishing, hard work. **~-room**, sufficient space to move or work in at ease.

ĕl'der[1] *n.* white-flowered black--berried tree or shrub. **~berrÿ** *n.* (fruit of) elder.

ĕl'der[2] *a.* of greater age; senior. *n.* person of greater age; lay official in some Protestant churches. **E~ Brethren**, senior members of Trinity House. **~ship** *n.*

ĕl'derlÿ *a.* growing old.

ĕl'dĕst *a.* first-born or oldest surviving (son, daughter, etc.).

ĕldora'dō (-ah-) *n.* (pl. *-os*), fictitious region rich in gold.

ĕl'drĭtch *a.* (Sc.) weird, hideous.

ėlĕct' *v.t.* choose, pick out; choose by vote; choose for salvation. *a.* chosen; elected but not yet installed.

ėlĕc'tion *n.* choosing, esp. by vote. **~eer'** *v.i.* busy oneself in political election(s).

ėlĕc'tive *a.* appointed or filled by election; entitled to elect; (U.S., of course of study) optional.

ėlĕc'tor *n.* person entitled to vote in election; *E~*, (hist.) German prince qualified to take part in election of Emperor. **~al** *a.* **~ate** *n.* body of electors.

ėlĕc'trĭc *a.* of, charged with, or worked by electricity; startling. **~ chair**, used for electrocution. **~ current**, flow of electricity from positive to negative pole or from high to low potential. **~ eel**, eel--like freshwater fish capable of giving electric shock. **~ shock**, effect of sudden discharge of electricity. **~ torch**, portable electric lamp. **~al** *a.* relating to or connected with electricity; electric.

electrĭ'cian *n.* one skilled in or dealing with electricity or electrical apparatus.

ėlĕctrĭ'citÿ *n.* (study of) form of energy present in protons and electrons.

ėlĕc'trĭfÿ *v.t.* charge with electricity; convert to electric working; startle, excite. **~fĭcā'tion** *n.*

ėlĕc'tro- in comb., of, by, etc. electricity. elĕctrocăr'dĭogrăm n. record of electrical waves generated by heart-beats; ~căr'dĭograph (-ahf) n. ~cūte v.t. kill by electricity, esp. as capital punishment; ~cū'tion n. ~ĕncĕph'alogrăm n. record of electrical impulses inside brain; ~encĕph'alograph (-ahf) n. electrŏ'lўsis n. chemical decomposition by action of electric current; ~lўse v.t.; ~lўt'ic a. ~-mag'nĕt n. magnet consisting of piece of soft iron surrounded by electric coil. ~-magnĕt'ic a. with both electrical and magnetic effects etc. (esp. of waves etc. travelling with velocity of light). ~plāte v.t. plate by electrolysis; n. electroplated ware. ~tуpe n. printing plate made by depositing copper by electrolysis on mould; v.t. copy thus.

ėlĕc'trōde n. either pole or terminal of source of electricity.

ėlĕc'tron n. (phys. etc.) ultimate indivisible unit of charge of negative electricity, revolving (in numbers constant for each element) about positive nucleus of every atom; free ~, not bound within atom. ~ŏn'ic a. of electron(s) or electronics; worked, controlled, produced, etc. by electronic devices. ~ŏn'ics n. science of control of free electrons; its technological applications.

ėlĕc'trum n. alloy of silver and gold used by ancients; (min.) native argentiferous gold.

ėlĕėmŏs'ўnarў (or -z-) a. of or dependent on alms; charitable.

ėl'ėgance n. grace, refinement.

ėl'ėgant a. graceful, tasteful; of refined luxury; (chiefly U.S.) excellent.

ėlĕgī'ăc a. suited to elegies, mournful.

ėl'ėgў n. song of lamentation, esp. for dead.

ėl'ėment n. (chem.) any of substances which cannot be decomposed chemically and which alone or in combination constitute all matter; one of four substances (earth, water, air, fire) formerly supposed to make up all matter; (pl.) atmospheric agencies; ordinary range of activity, congenial surroundings; component part; (pl.) rudiments, first principles.

ėlĕmĕn'tal a. of or like the four elements or the powers of nature; essential. n. supposed sub-human spirit or entity.

ėlĕmĕn'tarў a. rudimentary, introductory; unanalysable.

ėl'ėphant n. huge mammal with proboscis and ivory tusks. ėlėphăn'tīne a. (esp.) clumsy, unwieldy.

ėlėphăntī'asĭs n. tropical disease with enlargement of legs etc. and thickening of skin.

ėl'ėvāte v.t. lift up, raise.

ėlėvā'tion n. raising aloft; exaltation, dignity; height above given level; drawing of building made in projection on vertical plane.

ėl'ėvātor n. that which elevates; (U.S.) lift; hoisting-machine; warehouse for storing grain.

ėlĕv'en n. & a. one more than ten (11, XI); side of eleven persons at cricket etc. ~sės n. (sl.) mid-morning refreshments. ~th a. & n.

ĕlf n. (pl. elves), dwarfish supernatural being; small or mischievous creature. ~-lock, tangled mass of hair. ~ĭsh a.

ėl'fĭn a. of elves, elf-like; fairy-like, full of strange charm.

ėlī'cĭt v.t. draw out.

ėlīde' v.t. omit in pronunciation.

ėl'ĭgĭble a. fit or qualified or entitled to be chosen etc. (for); desirable, suitable. ėlĭgĭbĭl'itў n.

ėlĭm'ĭnāte v.t. remove, get rid of; expel, exclude. ~ā'tion, ~ātor nn.

ėlī'sion (-zhn) n. suppression of vowel or syllable in pronouncing.

élite (ālēt') n. the choice part (of); select group or class. [F]

ėlĭx'ir (-er) n. alchemist's preparation designed to change metal into gold or prolong life indefinitely.

Elĭzabē'than (ĭ-) a. & n. (person, writer) of time of Elizabeth I.

ĕlk n. largest existing animal of deer kind. ~-hound, grey shaggy-coated Scandinavian breed of dog.

ĕll n. obs. measure of length (45 in.).

ėllĭpse' n. regular oval. ėllĭp'tĭc(al[1]) aa.

ėllĭp'sĭs n. (pl.-pses, pr. -ēz), omission

of words needed to complete construction or sense. ĕllĭp'tĭcal[2] a.

ĕlm n. tree with rough doubly serrated leaves and rough bark.

ĕlocū'tion n. mode or art of oral delivery. ~arў a.; ~ĭst n.

E. long. abbr. East longitude.

ē'lŏngāte (-ngg-) v.t. lengthen, extend, draw out. ~ā'tion n.

ĕlōpe' v.i. run away with lover, esp. to be married. ~ment n.

ĕl'oquence n. fluent and powerful speech. ĕl'oquent a.

ĕlse adv. besides; instead; otherwise; if not. ~where adv. in or to some other place.

ĕlū'cĭdāte (or -ōō-) v.t. throw light on, explain. ~ā'tion, ~ātor nn.; ~ātĭve, ~ātorў aa.

elūde' (or -ōō-) v.t. escape adroitly from; avoid; baffle.

ĕlū'sĭve (or -ōō-) a. difficult to grasp or perceive or define.

elves : see elf.

Elys'ĭum (ĭlĭz-) n. (Gk. myth.) abode of blessed after death; (place of) ideal happiness. ~ĭan a.

ĕm n. letter M; (print.) unit of measurement (about ⅙ in.).

ĕmā'cĭāte (-shĭ-) v.t. make lean, waste. ~ā'tion n.

ĕm'anāte v.i. issue, originate, proceed from. ~ā'tion n. (esp.) person or thing emanating from Divine Essence.

ĕmăn'cĭpāte v.t. set free (esp. slave) from legal or social or political restraint. ~ā'tion, ~ā'tionĭst, ~ātor nn.

ĕmăs'cūlāte v.t. castrate; enfeeble; weaken by excisions. a. (-at), castrated; effeminate. ~ā'tion n.; ~ātĭve, ~ātorў aa.

ĕmbalm' (-ahm) v.t. preserve (corpse) with spices; preserve from oblivion; make fragrant. ĕmbalm'ment n.

ĕmbănk' v.t. enclose, retain, support, etc. with embankment. ~ment n. mound of earth, stone structure, etc. for confining river etc., carrying road, etc. ~ment wall, retaining wall.

ĕmbăr'gō n. (pl. -oes), order forbidding ships to enter or leave port; suspension of commerce; stoppage, prohibition.

ĕmbărk' v. put or go on board ship; enter on (course etc.). ~ā'tion, ĕmbărcā'tion n. embarking on ship.

ĕmbă'rrass v.t. encumber, esp. with debt; make confused or constrained. ~ing a.; ~ment n.

ĕm'bassў n. ambassador's function or office or residence.

ĕmbăt'tle v.t. set in battle array.

embay' v.t. enclose (as) in bay.

ĕmbĕd', ĭmbĕd' v.t. fix in surrounding mass.

ĕmbĕll'ĭsh v.t. beautify, adorn; enrich. ~ment n.

ĕm'ber n. (usu. pl.) small piece of fuel in dying fire.

Em'ber-day (ĕ-) n. (eccl.) any of appointed days of fasting and prayer in each of four seasons. Em'ber-week n. week containing Ember-days.

ĕmbĕzz'le v.t. appropriate fraudulently. ~ment n.

ĕmbĭtt'er v.t. make bitter; aggravate; exasperate. ~ment n.

ĕmblā'zon v.t. adorn with figures of heraldry; celebrate, extol.

ĕm'blĕm n. symbol, type; distinctive badge. ~ăt'ic a.

ĕmbŏd'ў v.t. clothe (spirit) with body; give concrete form to; cause to become part of body, incorporate, include.

ĕmbō'lden v.t. encourage.

ĕm'bolĭsm (-zm) n. blockage of artery etc. by blood-clot etc.

embonpoint (ahṅbawṅpwăṅ') n. plumpness, usu. of women. [F]

ĕmbos'om (-ōōz-) v.t. enclose, shelter (usu. pass.).

ĕmbŏss' v.t. carve or mould in relief. ~ment n.

ĕmbow'er v.t. enclose (as) in bower.

ĕmbrāce' v.t. fold in arms, clasp, enclose; accept, adopt; include. n. folding in arms.

ĕmbrā'sure (-zher) n. bevelling of wall at sides of window etc.; opening in parapet for gun.

ĕmbrocā'tion n. liniment.

ĕmbroi'der v.t. ornament with or work in needlework; embellish. ~ў n.

ĕmbroil' v.t. bring into state of confusion; involve in hostility. ~ment n.

ĕm'brўō n. (pl. -os), unborn offspring;

thing in rudimentary stage.
~ŏl'ogy, ~ŏl'ogĭst *nn.*; ~ŏn'ĭc *a.*

ĕmbŭs' *v.* (mil. etc.) put or get into
motor vehicle.

ĕmĕnd' *v.t.* correct, remove errors
from (text of book etc.). ēmendā'tion
n.; ~atorў *a.*

ĕm'erald *n.* bright-green precious
stone; colour of emerald; size of
printing-type (6½-point).

ĕmê̆rge' *v.i.* come up or out into
view or notice (*from*); come out.
~ence *n.* ~ent *a.* emerging, esp.
into nationhood.

ĕmê̆r'gencў *n.* sudden juncture
needing prompt action.

ĕmĕ̆'rĭtus *a.* retired, holding title
after retirement.

ĕmê̆r'sion *n.* emerging; reappearance
after eclipse.

ĕm'erў *n.* coarse corundum for
polishing metal etc.

ĕmĕt'ĭc *a.* that causes vomiting.
n. emetic medicine.

e.m.f. *abbr.* electromotive force.

ĕm'ĭgrāte *v.i.* leave one country to
settle in another; change place of
abode. ~ant *a.* & *n.*; ~ā'tion *n.*

émigré (ĕm'ĭgrā) *n.* emigrant, esp.
refugee from French or Russian
Revolution. [F]

ĕm'ĭnence *n.* recognized superiority;
rising ground; cardinal's title of
honour.

ĕm'ĭnent *a.* distinguished, notable.
~ly *adv.* notably, decidedly.

ĕmir' (-ē̆r) *n.* Arab etc. prince or
ruler. ~ate *n.* territory ruled by
emir.

ĕm'ĭssarў *n.* one sent on (esp. odious
or underhand) mission.

ĕmĭ'ssion *n.* emitting; what is
emitted. ĕmĭss'ĭve *a.*

ĕmĭt' *v.t.* give out, send forth (esp.
what is subtle or imponderable).

ĕmm'ĕt *n.* (dial.) ant.

ĕmŏll'ĭent *a.* softening; suppling.
n. emollient substance.

ĕmŏl'ūment *n.* (usu. pl.) profit from
employment; salary.

ĕmō'tion *n.* feeling; vehement or
excited mental state, agitation.
~al *a.* of emotion(s); given to
emotion.

ĕmō'tĭve *a.* tending or designed to
excite emotion.

ĕmpăn'el *v.t.* enter on panel; enrol.

ĕm'pathў *n.* power of projecting one's
personality into object of contemplation.

ĕm'peror *n.* ruler of empire.

ĕm'phasĭs *n.* significant stress on
word(s); vigour of expression etc.;
importance, prominence. ĕm'pha-
sĭze *v.t.* lay stress on.

ĕmphăt'ĭc *a.* forcible, strong; (of
words) bearing emphasis.

ĕmphўsē'ma *n.* (path.) abnormal
swelling caused by pressure of air
or gas in tissue esp. of lungs.

ĕm'pīre *n.* supreme and wide
dominion; extensive territory (esp.
aggregate of many States) ruled by
emperor or sovereign State; *E*~
(attrib.) of or in style of Empire of
Napoleon I. **E~ City, State,** (U.S.)
New York.

ĕmpī'rical *a.* based or acting on
observation and experiment, not
on theory. ~cĭsm, ~cĭst *nn.*

ĕmplāce'ment (-sm-) *n.* situation,
placing; platform for gun(s).

ĕmplāne' *v.* go or put on board
aircraft.

ĕmploy' *v.t.* use (thing, time, energies
etc.); use services of; find occupation for. *n.* (arch.) employment;
in the ~ *of*, employed by. ~ee *n.*
person employed for wages. ~er *n.*
(esp.) one who employs servants,
workmen, etc. for wages.

ĕmploy'ment *n.* (esp.) regular occupation or business; state of being
employed.

ĕmpôr'ĭum *n.* centre of commerce;
(vulg.) shop.

ĕmpow'er *v.t.* authorize; enable.

ĕm'press *n.* wife of emperor; female
ruler of empire.

ĕmp'tў (-mt-) *a.* containing nothing;
devoid (*of*); vacant; (colloq.)
hungry; frivolous, foolish. *n.*
empty truck etc.; emptied box,
bottle etc. *v.* remove contents of;
transfer contents of, discharge,
into; become empty.

ĕmpûr'ple *v.t.* make purple.

ĕmpўrĕ'an *a.* & *n.* (of) highest
heaven as sphere of fire or abode
of God; (of) sky.

ē'mū *n.* large Austral. running bird
with rudimentary wings.

ĕm'ūlāte v.t. try to equal or excel; imitate. **~ā'tion** n.; **~ative** a. **ĕm'ūlous** a. desirous or zealously imitative of; moved by spirit of rivalry.

ĕmŭl'sion n. suspension of oil etc. in aqueous liquid or of aqueous liquid in oil. **ĕmŭl'sifȳ** v. convert or be converted into emulsion.

ĕn n. letter N; (print.) unit of measurement (½ em).

ĕnā'ble v.t. empower; supply with means (to do).

ĕnăct' v.t. make into legislative act; ordain; play (part). **~ment** n. law enacted.

ĕnăm'el n. glass-like coating on metal; any hard smooth coating; hard and usu. glossy oil paint. v.t. coat with enamel.

ĕnăm'our v.t. inspire with love; make fond of.

en blŏc (ahṅ), in a lump, whole-sale. [F]

ĕncae'nĭa (-sēn-) n. (at Oxford) annual commemoration of univer-sity's founders and benefactors.

ĕncāge' v.t. put in cage.

ĕncămp' v. settle in camp; lodge in tents. **~ment** n.

ĕncāse' v.t. put into or surround as with case.

encau'stic a. (of tile etc.) inlaid with coloured clays burnt in; (of paint-ing) with wax colours fixed by heat. n. (method of) encaustic painting.

ĕncĕphalī'tĭs n. inflammation of brain.

ĕnchain' v.t. chain up; hold fast.

ĕnchant' (-ah-) v.t. bewitch; delight. **~er, ~ment, ~rĕss** nn.

ĕncīr'cle v.t. surround. **~ment** n.

ĕnclāve' (or ĕn'-) n. territory sur-rounded by foreign dominion.

ĕnclĭt'ĭc a. & n. (gram.) (particle) without accent.

ĕnclōse' (-z) v.t. surround, fence in; shut up or seclude (esp. monastic order etc.); hem in; insert in frame etc., esp. put (something other than letter) in envelope etc.

ĕnclō'sure (-zher) n. enclosing; en-closed land; thing enclosed.

ĕncō'mĭăst n. composer of enco-mium. **~ăs'tic** a.

ĕncō'mĭum n. formal or high-flown expression of praise.

ĕncom'pass (-ŭm-) v.t. shut in, surround, encircle.

encore (ŏng'kōr) int. & n. (call for performance to be repeated) again, once more. v.t. call for repetition of or by.

ĕncoun'ter v.t. meet hostilely; meet with (person, obstacle, etc.). n. hostile or casual meeting.

ĕncou'rage (-kŭ-) v.t. make bold; urge; further, promote. **~ment** n.

ĕncroach' v.i. intrude on others' territory etc. **~ment** n.

ĕncrŭst' v.t. cover with crust; overlay with ornamental crust.

ĕncŭm'ber v.t. hamper, impede; burden with debt. **~brance** n. burden, impediment; mortgage etc. on property.

ĕncȳ'clical (or -sĭk-) a. & n. (pope's letter) for wide circulation.

ĕncȳclop(a)e'dĭa (-pē-) n. (pl. -as), book of information on all branches of knowledge or of one subject. **~dic** a.; **~dist** n.

ĕncȳst' v.t. enclose in cyst.

ĕnd n. limit; extreme point or part; conclusion; destruction; death; result; object. v. bring or come to end. **~ game**, last stage in game of chess. **~-papers**, blank leaves at beginning and end of book. **~-product**, final product of process of manufacture etc. **~-stopped**, (of verse) with pause or stop at end of line(s). **~ways, ~wise** advv.

ĕndā'nger (-j-) v.t. bring into danger.

ĕndear' v.t. make dear. **~ing** a. winning affection. **~ment** n. word(s) etc. showing affection.

ĕndeav'our (-dĕver) v.i. try, strive. n. attempt, effort.

ĕndĕm'ĭc a. & n. (disease) regularly found among (specified) people, in (specified) area, etc.

ĕn'dĭng n. (esp.) concluding part (of book etc.); inflexional etc. suffix.

ĕn'dĭve n. curly-leaved plant used as salad; (U.S.) chicory.

ĕnd'lĕss a. unending, continual.

ĕn'dō- in comb., within. **ĕndo-cărdī'tis** n. inflammation of endo-cardium. **~căr'dĭum** n. lining membrane of heart. **~cărp** n.

inner fleshy, membranous, etc. layer of pericarp. **~crĭne** *a.* secreting internally, ductless. **endŏg'amў** *n.* custom of marrying only within clan or tribe; **endŏg'amous** *a.* **endŏ'gĕnous** *a.* growing, formed, etc. (from) within. **~spĕrm** *n.* albumen enclosed with embryo in some seeds. **~thē'lium** *n.* layer of cells lining blood-vessels etc.

endôrse' *v.t.* write on back of (document); esp. sign name on back of (cheque etc.), make payable *to* another thus; enter particulars of offence on (driving-licence etc.); vouch for, confirm; express approval of. **~ment** *n.*

endow' *v.t.* give permanent income to; invest *with* powers, qualities etc. **~ment** *n.*

endūe' *v.t.* clothe or invest (*with*).

endūr'ance *n.* habit or power of enduring.

endūre' *v.* undergo; bear; last.

ĕn'ėma (*or* inē'-) *n.* (syringe used for) introduction of liquid etc. into rectum.

ĕn'ėmў *n.* hostile person, opponent; hostile force or ship. *a.* of or belonging to enemy.

ĕnergĕt'ĭc *a.* forcible; vigorous; full of energy.

ĕn'ergīze *v.t.* infuse energy into.

ĕn'ergў *n.* force, vigour, activity; capacity for work.

ĕn'ervāte *v.t.* impair vigour or nervous tone of. **~ā'tion** *n.*

enfant terrible (ahǹ'fahǹ tĕrēbl') *n.* child who asks awkward questions, repeats talk, etc. [F]

ĕnfee'ble *v.t.* make feeble. **~ment** *n.*

ĕnfeoff' (-fĕf; *or* -ēf) *v.t.* invest with fief. **~ment** *n.*

en fête (ahǹ fāt), in festive array or mood. [F]

ĕnfilāde' *n.* fire from guns etc. sweeping line from end to end. *v.t.* subject (troops etc.) to enfilade.

ĕnfōld' *v.t.* wrap; embrace.

ĕnfôrce' *v.t.* press, urge; compel observance of. **~ment** *n.*

ĕnfrăn'chīse (-z) *v.t.* set free; give electoral franchise to. **~ĭsement** (-zm-) *n.*

engāge' (ĭn-g-) *v.* bind by contract or promise (esp. of marriage); pledge oneself; hire, bespeak; fit, interlock (*with*); cause parts of (gear) to engage; take part *in*; employ, occupy; bring or come into conflict with enemy. **~ment** *n.*

ėngĕn'der (-j-) *v.t.* give rise to.

ĕn'gĭne (-j-) *n.* complex mechanical contrivance esp. for converting fuel etc. into mechanical power; locomotive; means, instrument. **~-driver,** driver of locomotive. **~-room,** room containing esp. ship's engine(s). **~-turned,** ornamented with symmetrical pattern engraved by machine.

ĕngĭneer' (-j-) *n.* one skilled in construction, maintenance, etc. of military works (*military* ~), works of public utility (*civil* ~), machines (*mechanical* ~), electrical apparatus (*electrical* ~), etc.; soldier of branch of army called *Engineers*; one in charge of engine(s); engine-driver. *v.* construct, manage, etc., as engineer; contrive, bring about.

Eng'lish (ĭngg-) *a.* of England or the English or their language. *n.* English people or language; size of printing-type (14-point). **~man,** **~woman** *nn.*

engraft (ĭn-grahft') *v.t.* graft in; insert or incorporate *into,* (*up*)*on.*

engrain' (ĭn-g-) *v.t.* (usu. fig.) cause (dye etc.) to sink deeply in.

engrāve' (ĭn-g-) *v.t.* cut on metal plate etc. for printing; carve; impress deeply (*on* memory etc.). **ĕngrā'vĭng** *n.* (esp.) print made from engraved plate.

engrŏss' (ĭn-g-) *v.t.* write in large letters or in legal form; monopolize; absorb. **~ment** *n.*

engŭlf' (ĭn-g-) *v.t.* swallow up.

ėnhănce' *v.t.* heighten, intensify; exaggerate. **~ment** *n.*

ėnig'ma *n.* riddle; puzzling person or thing. **ĕnigmăt'ĭc(al)** *aa.*

ėnjoin' *v.t.* prescribe; command.

ėnjoy' *v.t.* find pleasure in; have use or benefit of; **~** one*self,* find pleasure, be happy. **~able** *a.*; **~ment** *n.*

ėnkin'dle *v.t.* set on fire.

ėnlāce' *v.t.* encircle; entwine.

ėnlârge' *v.* expand; grow larger; expatiate; reproduce on larger scale. **~ment** *n.*

ènligh'ten v.t. instruct; inform; shed light on. ~ment n.

ènlist' v. engage, enrol, for military service; get co-operation or support of. ~ment n.

ènli'ven v.t. animate, inspirit, brighten. ~ment n.

en mässe (ahṅ), all together. [F]

ènmĕsh' v.t. entangle (as) in net.

ĕn'mitў n. hatred, hostility.

ènnō'ble v.t. make noble. ~ment n.

ennui (ŏn'wē) n. boredom.

ènōr'mitў n. great wickedness; crime, monstrous offence.

ènōr'mous a. very large.

enough (ĭnŭf') a., adv. & n. (in) not less than required quantity, number or degree (of).

ènounce' v.t. enunciate.

enquire : see inquire.

ènrāge' v.t. make furious.

en rapport (ahṅ răpōr') adv. in harmony or sympathy. [F]

ènrăp'ture v.t. delight intensely.

ènrich' v.t. make rich(er). ~ment n.

ènrōbe' v.t. put robe on.

ènrōl' v.t. insert name in list, esp. of army; incorporate as member; register (deed etc.), record. ~ment n.

en route (ahṅ rōot) adv. on the way. [F]

ènscŏnce' v.t. establish safely.

ensemble (ahṅsahṅbl') n. thing viewed as whole; woman's dress, hat, etc. as complete whole; (mus.) united performance of voices, instruments, etc.

ènshrīne' v.t. enclose (as) in shrine; cherish.

ènsăng'uined (-nggw-) a. blood--stained, bloody.

ènshroud' v.t. cover completely.

ĕn'sign (-sīn, -sn) n. badge, emblem; banner, flag; (hist.) lowest commissioned officer in infantry; (U.S Navy, pr. -ĭn) lowest commissioned officer.

ĕn'sĭlage n. silage.

ènsīle' v.t. convert into silage.

ènslāve' v.t. make slave of. ~ment n.

ènsnāre' v.t. entrap.

ènsūe' v. happen later, result (from); (bibl.) seek after.

ensure (ĭnshoor') v.t. make safe or certain; secure.

 èntăb'lature n. architrave, frieze, and cornice of column.

èntail' v.t. settle (landed estate) on persons successively so that it cannot be bequeathed at pleasure; impose (on); necessitate. n. (ĕn'-) entailing; entailed estate.

èntăng'le (-nggl) v.t. catch in snare etc.; involve in difficulties; make tangled; complicate. ~ment n.

entente (ahṅtahṅt' or ŏntŏnt') n. friendly understanding between States. [F]

ĕn'ter v. go or come in or into; penetrate; come on stage; become member of; put (name, fact, etc.) into list, record, etc.; name, name oneself, as competitor for; admit, procure admission for; ~ into, engage in, sympathize with, form part of, bind oneself by; ~ (up)on, assume possession of, begin, begin to deal with; ~ up, enter in regular form, make entries in.

èntĕ'rĭc a. of intestines. n. enteric fever. ~ fever, typhoid.

ènterī'tĭs n. bowel inflammation.

ĕn'terprīse (-z) n. bold undertaking; readiness to engage in enterprises. ~sĭng a. full of enterprise.

èntertain' v.t. receive as guest; amuse; harbour; admit to consideration. ~ment n. hospitality; amusement; public performance.

ènthral' (-awl) v.t. enslave; captivate. ~ment n.

ènthrōne[1] v.t. place on throne. ~ment n.

ènthū'siăsm (-zĭ-) n. ardent zeal.

ènthūse' v.i. (colloq.) show enthusiasm, gush. ~iăst n.; ~iăs'tic a.

 èntīce' v.t. allure. ~ment n.

èntīre' a. complete; not broken; not castrated; of one piece.

èntire'ly (-īrlĭ) adv. wholly.

èntire'ty (-īrtĭ) n. completeness; sum total.

èntī'tle v.t. give (book etc.) title of; give right or claim to.

ĕn'titў n. thing with real existence; thing's existence.

èntomb' (-ōom) v.t. place in tomb; serve as tomb for. ~ment n.

èntomŏl'ogў n. study of insects. ~lŏ'gĭcal a.; ~logĭst n.

entourage (ŏn′toorahzh) *n*. attendant persons; surroundings. [F]

entracte (ŏn′trăkt) *n*. (performance in) interval in theatre etc. [F]

ĕn′trails (-z) *n.pl.* inner parts.

ĕntrain′ *v*. put or get into train.

ĕntrance′[1] (-ah-) *v.t.* overpower with strong feeling, esp. of delight etc.

ĕn′trance[2] *n*. coming or going in; right of admission; door or passage for entering.

ĕn′trant *n*. one who enters.

ĕntrăp′ *v.t.* catch (as) in trap.

ĕntreat′ *v.t.* ask earnestly; beg.

ĕntrea′tў *n*. earnest request.

entrée (ŏn′trā) *n*. right or privilege of admission; made dish served between fish and joint.

ĕntrĕnch′ *v.t.* surround or fortify with trench; encroach. **~ment** *n*.

entrepreneur (ŏntreprenĕr′) *n*. manager or organizer, esp. of musical entertainments; contractor. [F]

en′tresŏl (ŏn-), *n*. low storey between first and ground floors. [F]

ĕn′tropў *n*. measure of degree of molecular disorder in system, or of thermal energy not available for doing work.

ĕntrŭst′ *v.t.* charge *with* (duty, object of care); confide *to*.

ĕn′trў *n*. coming or going in; entrance; alley; entering, item entered.

ĕntwīne′ *v.t.* interweave; wreathe.

ent. Sta. Hall *abbr.* entered at Stationers′ Hall.

ĕnū′merāte *v.t.* count; mention separately. **~ā′tion**, **~ātor** *nn.*; **~ative** *a*.

ĕnŭn′ciāte (*or* -shĭ-) *v.t.* state definitely; proclaim; pronounce. **~ā′tion**, **~ātor** *nn.*; **~ative** *a*.

ĕnūrē′sis *n*. involuntary passing of urine.

ĕnvĕl′op *v.t.* wrap up, cover; surround (enemy). **~ment** *n*.

ĕn′vĕlōpe (*or* ŏn-) *n*. wrapper, covering, esp. folded (and gummed) cover for letter etc.

ĕnvĕn′om *v.t.* put poison on or into; infuse venom into.

ĕn′viable *a*. calculated to excite envy. **ĕn′vious** *a*. full of envy.

ĕnvīr′on *v.t.* form ring round, surround. **~ment** *n*. surroundings;

surrounding objects or circumstances. **~mĕn′tal** *a*. **ĕn′virons** (-z; *or* ĭnvīr′-) *n.pl.* surrounding districts (*of* town etc.).

ĕnvĭ′sage (-z-) *v.t.* face; visualize; contemplate.

ĕn′voy[1], **ĕn′voi** *n*. short final stanza of ballade etc.

ĕn′voy[2] *n*. diplomatic minister ranking below ambassador; messenger.

ĕn′vў *n*. bitter contemplation of another′s success etc.; object of this. *v.t.* feel envy of.

ĕnwrăp′ *v.t.* wrap, enfold.

ĕn′zўme *n*. (chem.) substance produced by living cells and acting like catalyst in promoting reactions in organism.

ē′ocēne *a*. (geol.) of lowest system of Tertiary rocks.

ē′olĭth *n*. unworked flint used by early man as weapon etc. **ēolĭth′ĭc** *a*. of age preceding palaeolithic.

E.P. *abbr.* electroplate.

ē′păct (*or* ĕ-) *n*. excess of solar over lunar year; age of moon on 1 Jan.

ĕp′aulĕt(te) (-pŏl-) *n*. ornamental shoulder-piece of uniform.

Eph. *abbr.* Ephesians.

ĕph′ĕdrĭn(e) *n*. stimulant drug.

ĕphĕm′era[1] (*or* -fē-) *n*. (pl. -ae, -as), ephemeron.

ephemera[2] : see **ephemeron**.

ĕphĕm′eral *a*. short-lived, transitory. **~ăl′itў** *n*.

ĕphĕm′eron *n*. (pl. -ra), may-fly; anything transitory or short lived.

ĕph′od (*or* ē-) *n*. Jewish priestly vestment.

ĕp′ĭc *a*. narrating heroic deeds of tradition or history; of heroic type or scale. *n*. epic poem.

ĕp′ĭcēne *a*. for or having characteristics of both sexes.

ĕp′ĭcĕntre *n*. point on earth′s surface nearest to centre of earthquake.

ĕp′ĭcūrė *n*. one with refined taste in food and drink. **~rĭsm** *n*.

ĕpĭcūrė′an *a. & n*. (person) devoted to refined sensuous enjoyment. **~ĭsm** *n*.

ĕp′ĭcўcle *n*. (geom.) small circle rolling on circumference of greater. **ĕpĭcў′clic** *a*. (esp. of gear). **ĕpĭcў′cloid** *n*. curve traced by point on circumference of epicycle.

ĕpĭdei'ctĭc (-dī-) *a*. meant for display.

ĕpĭdĕm'ic *a*. & *n*. (disease) spreading rapidly through community for period.

ĕpĭdēmĭŏl'ogy *n*. study of epidemics.

ĕpĭdēr'mĭs *n*. outer layer of skin.

ĕpĭdī'ascōpe *n*. optical lantern projecting images of both opaque and transparent objects.

ĕpĭgăs'trĭum *n*. part of abdomen above stomach. ~**tric** *a*.

ĕpĭglŏtt'ĭs *n*. erect cartilage at root of tongue, depressed in swallowing. ~**tic** *a*.

ĕp'ĭgōne *n*. one of later (and less distinguished) generation.

ĕp'ĭgrăm *n*. short poem with witty ending; pointed saying. ~**măt'ic** *a*.; **ĕpĭgrămm'atĭst** *n*.

ĕp'ĭgraph (-ahf) *n*. inscription. **ĕpĭgrăph'ĭc** *a*.; **ĕpĭg'raphў** *n*.

ĕp'ĭlĕpsў *n*. nervous disorder with recurrent attacks of unconsciousness, convulsions, etc.

ĕpĭlĕp'tĭc *a*. of or subject to epilepsy. *n*. epileptic person.

ĕp'ĭlŏgue (-g) *n*. concluding part of book etc.; short speech at end of play etc.

Epĭph'anў *n*. festival (6 Jan.) commemorating manifestation of Christ to Magi.

ĕp'ĭphўte *n*. plant growing on another; vegetable parasite on animal.

ĕpĭs'copacў *n*. government of church by bishops; bishops collectively.

ĕpĭs'copal *a*. of or governed by bishop(s); *E~ Church*, esp. (U.S. etc.) Church of England. ~**ā'lĭan** *a*. & *n*. (adherent) of episcopacy; (member) of Episcopal Church. ~**ate** *n*. bishop's office or see or tenure; bishops collectively.

ĕp'ĭsōde *n*. incidental narrative or digression; incidental happening. **ĕpĭsŏd'ĭc(al)** *aa*.

ĕpĭstēmŏl'ogy *n*. theory of method or grounds of knowledge. ~**lŏ'gĭcal** *a*.

ĕpĭs'tle (-sl) *n*. letter; poem etc. in form of letter.

ĕpĭs'tolarў *a*. of or carried on by letters.

ĕp'ĭtaph (-ahf) *n*. words inscribed on or suitable for tomb.

ĕpĭthalā'mĭum *n*. (pl. -*ums*, ,-*a*), nuptial song or poem.

ĕpĭthē'lĭum *n*. (biol.) layer of cells covering body surface or lining cavity.

ĕp'ĭthĕt *n*. adjective expressing quality or attribute; appellation.

ĕpĭt'omė *n*. summary, abstract. **ĕpĭt'omize** *v.t*.

E.P.N.S. *abbr*. electroplated nickel silver.

ē'pŏch (-k; *or* ĕ-) *n*. beginning of era; period marked by special events. **ĕp'ochal** *a*.

ĕpŏn'ўmous *a*. whose name has been given to people, place, etc.

ĕp'ŏs *n*. early unwritten epic poetry; epic poem.

ē'quable (*or* ē-) *a*. uniform, even; not easily disturbed. ~**abil'itў** *n*.

ē'qual *a*. same in number, size, merit, etc.; adequate; evenly matched. *n*. person etc. equal to another. *v.t*. be equal to.

ēqualĭtār'ĭan (-ŏl-) *a*. & *n*. (adherent) of doctrine of equality of mankind ~**ĭsm** *n*.

ēqual'itў (-ŏl-) *n*. being equal.

ē'qualīze *v*. make equal; (in games) equal opponent's score. ~**zā'tion** *n*.

ē'quallў *adv*. in equal degree or equal shares; uniformly.

ēquanĭm'itў (*or* ĕ-) *n*. composure, calm.

ēquāte' *v.t*. state equality of; treat as equivalent.

ēquā'tion *n*. making equal, balancing; (amount or process of) compensation for inaccuracy; formula affirming equivalence of two quantitative expressions, representing chemical reaction by means of symbols, etc. ~**al** *a*.

ēquā'tor *n*. great circle of earth equidistant from poles, or of celestial sphere with plane perpendicular to earth's axis. **ēquatōr'ĭal** *a*. of or near equator.

ē'querrў *n*. officer of prince etc. in charge of horses; officer of British royal household.

ēquĕs'trĭan *a*. of horseriding; representing person on horseback. *n*. rider or performer on horseback.

ēquĕstrĭĕnne' *n*. horsewoman, esp. female circus-rider.

ēquĭăng′ūlar (-ngg-) *a*. having equal angles.

ēquĭdis′tant *a*. at equal distance(s).

ēquĭlăt′eral *a*. having all sides equal.

ēquĭli′brāte (*or* ĭkwĭl′ĭ-) *v*. balance; counterpoise. ~ā′tion *n*.

ēquĭlĭb′rĭum *n*. state of balance; mental balance.

ĕ′quĭne (*or* ē-) *a*. of or like horse.

ĕquĭnŏc′tial (*or* ē-) *a*. of, happening at or near, equinox. *n*. celestial equator; (pl.) equinoctial gales.

ĕ′quĭnŏx (*or* ē-) *n*. time of year at which day and night are of equal length; either point where sun's path crosses equator.

ĕquĭp′ *v.t*. supply with requisites; provide (one*self* etc.) for journey etc. ĕ′quĭpage *n*. carriage, horses, and attendants; requisites, outfit. ~ment *n*.

ĕ′quĭpoise (-z; *or* ē-) *n*. equilibrium; counterpoise.

ĕ′quĭtable *a*. fair, just; valid in equity.

ĕquĭtā′tion *n*. riding.

ĕ′quĭtў *n*. fairness; principles of justice supplementing law; system of law suspending common and statute law; equitable right; net value of property etc. after deduction of charges; (pl.) stocks and shares not bearing fixed interest; *E*~, actors' trade union.

ĕquĭv′alent *a*. equal in value, meaning, etc.; corresponding. *n*. equivalent amount etc. ~ence, ~encў *nn*.

ĕquĭv′ocal *a*. of double or doubtful meaning; dubious. ~cāte *v.i*. use words ambiguously, esp. to conceal truth. ~cā′tion *n*.

E.R. *abbr*. East Riding; Elizabeth Regina (Queen Elizabeth).

ēr′a *n*. system of chronology starting from particular point; historical or other period.

ĕrăd′ĭcāte *v.t*. root out, extirpate. ~ā′tion *n*.

ĕrāse′ (-z) *v.t*. rub out, obliterate. ~r *n*. (esp.) preparation of rubber etc. for rubbing out writing etc.

Erăs′tĭan (-ĭ-) *a*. & *n*. (adherent) of doctrine of subordinating ecclesiastical to secular power. ~ĭsm *n*.

ĕrā′sure (-zh*er*) *n*. rubbing out; word etc. rubbed out.

ĕr′bĭum *n*. (chem.) metallic element of rare-earth group.

ere (ār) *prep*. & *conj*. (arch.) before.

ĕrĕct′ *a*. upright, vertical. *v.t*. raise, set upright; build. ~tĭle (*or* -ĭl) *a*. (esp., of animal tissue) capable of becoming distended and rigid under excitement. ~tion, ~tor *nn*.

ĕ′rĕmīte *n*. hermit.

ĕ′rĕthĭsm *n*. abnormal excitability.

ĕrg *n*. unit of work or energy.

ẽr′gō *adv*. therefore. [L]

ẽrgonŏm′ics *n*. study of efficiency of workers and working arrangements.

ẽrgŏs′terol *n*. substance yielding vitamin D₂ on exposure to ultraviolet radiation.

ẽr′got *n*. (fungus causing) disease of rye etc. ~ĭsm *n*. condition resulting from eating cereals affected with ergot.

Erin (ĕ′rĭn *or* ēr-) *n*. (poet.) Ireland.

ẽr′mĭne *n*. animal of weasel kind; its white winter fur.

ẽrne *n*. sea eagle.

ĕrōde′ *v.t*. gnaw away, destroy surface of.

ĕrŏ′gĕnous *a*. of, giving rise to, sexual desire.

Er′ŏs (ēr-; *or* ĕ-) *n*. god of love, Cupid.

ĕrō′sion *n*. eroding; (geol.) wearing away of earth's surface by wind or water or ice. ~sĭve *a*.

ĕrŏt′ic *a*. of or arousing sexual passion or excitement. ~a *n.pl*. erotic books etc.

ĕrōtogĕn′ĭc *a*. erogenous.

ẽrr *v.i*. make mistakes; be incorrect; sin.

ĕ′rrand *n*. short journey on which inferior is sent with message etc.; business on which one is sent, object of journey.

ĕ′rrant *a*. roaming in quest of adventure; itinerant; erring.

ĕrrăt′ĭc *a*. irregular or uncertain in movement, conduct, etc.

ĕrrā′tum (*or* -ah-) *n*. (pl. -ta), error in printing etc.

ĕrrō′nĕous *a*. incorrect.

ĕ′rror *n*. mistake; wrong opinion; transgression; deviation from accurate result, observation, etc.

ẽrst′whĭle *adv*. & *a*. (arch.) former(ly).

ĕrŭctā′tion *n*. belch.

ĕ'rudīte (-rōō-) a. learned.

ĕrudǐ'tion (-rōō-) n. learning.

ĕrŭpt' v.i. break out or through. erŭp'tion n. outbreak of volcano etc.; breaking out of rash etc.; rash. ~ive a.

ĕrўsǐp'ĕlas n. acute febrile disease with local inflammation of skin etc.

ĕscalāde' n. scaling of walls with ladders. v.t. scale thus.

ĕs'calāte v. increase or expand by degrees. ~ā'tion n.

ĕs'calātor n. moving staircase.

ĕs'cal(l)ŏpe (or -ōp') n. thin round steak of veal.

ĕs'capāde (or -ād') n. breaking loose from restraint; flighty piece of conduct.

ĕscāpe' v. get free; find way out; elude, avoid. n. escaping; leakage; outlet; fire-escape. ~ clause, releasing contracting party from obligation in specified circumstances. ~pee' n. one who has escaped. ~pǐsm n. tendency or desire to escape from realities into fantasy. ~pǐst a. & n. affording, (person) seeking, escape from realities of life.

ĕscāpe'ment (-pm-) n. mechanism regulating motion of watch etc.

ĕscãrp'ment n. steep bank below rampart; abrupt face of ridge etc.

ĕschatŏl'ogў (-k-) n. doctrine of death, judgement, heaven, and hell. ~lŏ'gǐcal a.

ĕscheat' n. lapse of property to crown etc.; property so lapsing. v. confiscate; revert by escheat.

ĕschew' (-ōō) v.t. abstain from.

eschschol(t)zia (ĭskŏl'sha or ĕshŏl'tsĭa) n. kinds of plant of poppy family.

ĕs'cõrt n. body of armed men as guard; person(s) accompanying another for protection, out of courtesy, etc.; ship(s) etc. so employed. v.t. (-õrt') act as escort to.

ĕs'crǐtoire (-twahr) n. writing-desk with drawers etc.

ĕs'cūlent a. & n. (thing, esp. vegetable) fit for food.

ĕscŭtch'eon (-chon) n. shield with armorial bearings; pivoted keyhole cover.

Es'kǐmō (ĕ-) n. (native, language) of Arctic coasts of N. America etc.

ĕsotĕ'rǐc (or ē-) a. meant for, intelligible to, initiates only.

esp. abbr. especially.

ĕspăl'ǐer n. framework for tree etc.; tree trained on espalier.

ĕspãr'tō n. kind of grass used in paper-making.

ĕspĕ'cial (-shal) a. chief; more than ordinary; particular. ~ly adv. chiefly; more than in other cases.

Esperăn'tō (ĕ-) n. artificial universal language.

ĕspī'al n. espying; spying.

ĕs'pǐonage (-ahzh) n. spying or using spies.

ĕsplanāde' (or ĕs'-) n. level space, esp. in front of fortress or used as public promenade.

ĕspou'sal (-z-) n. espousing; (usu. pl.) marriage, betrothal.

ĕspouse' (-z) v.t. marry; support (cause).

ĕsprĕss'ō n. apparatus for making coffee under pressure.

esprit de corps (ĕs'prē de kõr') n. regard for honour and interests of body one belongs to. [F]

ĕspў' v.t. catch sight of.

Esq. abbr. Esquire.

ĕsquīre' n. title of courtesy appended to man's name; (arch.) squire.

ĕss'ay n. literary composition of moderate length; attempt. v.t. (ĕsā'), attempt; test. ĕss'ayǐst n. writer of essays.

ĕss'ence n. existence or entity; reality underlying phenomena; all that makes thing what it is; indispensable quality or element; extract distilled from plant etc.; alcoholic solution esp. of essential oil used for flavouring etc.; perfume.

ĕssĕn'tial a. of or constituting or like essence. n. indispensable element. ~ oil, volatile oil giving characteristic odour etc. to (part of) plant.

ĕstăb'lǐsh v.t. set up; settle; place beyond dispute; place (church) in position of State or national Church.

ĕstăb'lǐshment n. establishing; church system established by law; established Church; staff, household, house of business; the E~, upper ranks of Church, Civil Service, etc. regarded as embodying established traditions and interests.

estāte' n. status, condition; order or class forming part of body politic; interest in lands etc.; landed property; housing estate; person's collective assets and liabilities. **~ agent,** person whose business is sale or letting of houses and iand.

esteem' v.t. think highly of; consider. n. favourable opinion.

Esth. abbr. Esther.

es'timable a. worthy of esteem.

es'timate n. approximate judgement of value etc.; price quoted for specified work. v.t. (-āt), form estimate of; fix by estimate at. **~ā'tion** n. judgement; opinion; esteem.

estŏp' v.t. (law) bar, preclude. **~pel** n. being precluded from course by one's own previous act.

estrānge' (-j) v.t. turn away feelings or affections of. **~ment** n.

es'tūarў n. tidal mouth of river.

esūr'ient a. hungry; starveling.

etc. abbr. etcetera.

etcĕt'era, and the rest; and so on. **~s** n.pl. extras, sundries.

etch v. make (picture etc.) or portray (subject) or prepare (printing--plate) by corroding with acid lines scratched through waxy covering of metal plate; practise this art; corrode (as) with acid; impress deeply; (of acid) corrode. **~er** n. **~ing** n. (esp.) print made from etched plate.

etĕr'nal a. that always (has existed and) will exist; incessant. **~īze** v.t.

etĕr'nitў n. being eternal; infinite time; future life.

ē'ther n. clear sky, upper air; medium assumed to permeate space; volatile liquid used as anaesthetic and solvent.

ethēr'eal a. light, airy; heavenly; of unearthly delicacy of appearance etc.; of or like ether. **~ăl'itў** n.; **~alīze** v.t.

eth'ical a. relating to or treating of morals or ethics; moral, honourable; (of drug etc.) sold only on prescription.

eth'ics n.pl. science of or treatise on morals; moral principles.

eth'nĭc(al) aa. of race.

ethnŏl'ogў n. science of races and peoples. **ethnolŏ'gĭc(al)** aa.

ethŏl'ogў n. study of animal behaviour.

ē'thŏs n. characteristic spirit of community, people, or system.

ē'tĭolāte v.t. make pale by excluding light; give sickly hue to. **~ā'tion** n.

ētĭŏl'ogў n. study or science or philosophy of causation (esp. of disease).

ĕt'ĭquette (-kĕt) n. conventional rules of manners; unwritten code of professional conduct.

et seq(q)., et sq(q). abbr., et sequentia [L], and what follows.

E.T.U. abbr. Electrical Trades Union.

é'tūde (ā-) n. musical composition designed to improve execution.

etym. abbr. etymology etc.

etўmŏl'ogў n. (account of) word's formation and sense-development. **etўmŏlŏ'gical** a.

ĕt'ўmŏn n. primary word whence another is derived.

eucalўp'tus n. (pl. -uses), kinds of plant, esp. Australian gum tree; (pop.) eucalyptus oil. **~ oil,** essential oil of kind of eucalyptus, with strong characteristic odour.

Eu'charĭst (-k-) n. central Christian sacrament of body and blood of Christ; consecrated elements, esp. bread. **~ĭs'tĭc** a.

eu'chre (-ker) n. Amer. card-game for 2, 3 or 4 players.

Eu'clĭd n. (pop.) geometry, esp. as school subject; geometry of ordinary experience, accepting Euclid's axioms as indisputable. **Euclĭd'ean** a.

eugĕn'ĭc a. of production of fine offspring. n.pl. study of improvement of human race by control of mating. **eu'gĕnĭst** n.

eu'logīze v.t. extol, praise highly. **eu'logĭst** n.; **eulogĭs'tĭc** a.

eu'logў n. speech or writing in praise or commendation.

eu'nuch (-k) n. castrated person.

eupĕp'tĭc a. of, having, resulting from, good digestion.

euphem. abbr. euphemism etc.

eu'phěmǐsm n. substitution of mild for blunt expression; such substitute. ~**ǐst'ǐc** a.

euphō'nǐum n. large brass wind instrument of tuba kind.

eu'phonў n. pleasantness or smoothness of sounds, esp. in words. **euphǒn'ǐc, euphō'nǐous** aa.

euphōr'ǐa n. sense of well-being. **euphǒ'rǐc** a.

eu'phūǐsm n. affectedly high-flown style of writing. ~**ǐst** n.

Eurasian (ūrā'shan) a. of mixed European and Asian parentage; of Europe and Asia. n. Eurasian person.

eurē'ka (ūr-) int. I have found it!

eurhyth'mǐc (ūrǐdh-) a. in or of harmonious proportion; of eurhythmics. ~**s** n.pl. system of expressing musical rhythm in bodily movement.

Eurip. abbr. Euripides.

Europė'an (ūr-) a. & n. (native) of Europe.

eurō'pǐum (ūr-) n. metallic element of rare-earth group.

Euseb. abbr. Eusebius.

Eustā'chǐan tube (-k- or -sh-) n. passage between middle ear and back of throat.

euthanā'sǐa (-z-) n. (bringing about of) gentle and easy death.

ěvăc'ūāte v.t. make empty, clear; withdraw or remove from (place, esp. one considered dangerous). ~**ūā'tion, ~ūee'** nn.

evāde' v.t. escape from, avoid; elude, baffle.

ěvăl'ūāte v.t. find or state amount or value of. ~**ā'tion** n.

ěvaněsce' v.i. fade from sight; disappear. **ěvaněs'cence** n. ~**cent** a. quickly fading.

ěvăngěl'ǐc(al) (-j-) aa. of or according to Gospel teaching; (usu. -ical) of Protestant or Low-Church school. n. member of evangelical school. ~**alism** n. doctrine of evangelical school.

ěvăn'gelǐst (-j-) n. one of writers of four Gospels; preacher of Gospel. ~**ǐsm** n. preaching of Gospel; evangelicalism. ~**ǐs'tǐc** a.

ěvăn'gelīze (-j-) v.t. preach Gospel to. ~**zā'tion** n.

ěvăp'orāte v. turn into vapour; pass away, drive off, cause to lose liquid, as or like vapour. ~**ā'tion** n.

ěvā'sion n. act or means of evading; shuffling excuse. **ěvā'sǐve** a. (esp.) seeking to evade.

ēve n. evening or day before festival etc.; time just before event; evening.

ē'ven[1] n. evening. ~**song**, evening prayer in Church of England. ~**tide**, evening.

ē'ven[2] a. level, smooth; uniform; equal; equable, calm; divisible by two. v.t. make even. adv. inviting comparison with less strong assertion, negation, etc., that might have been made.

ē'venǐng (-vn-) n. close of day, esp. time from sunset to bedtime.

ěvěnt' n. (actual or contemplated) occurrence, (esp. important) happening; item of programme, esp. in sports; result; in any ~, at all ~s, in any case.

ěvěnt'ful a. full of incidents.

ěvěn'tūal a. that will happen in certain circumstances; ultimately resulting. ~**ăl'itў** n. possible event.

ěvěn'tūāte v.i. turn out; end; happen, come to pass.

ěv'er adv. at all times; always; at any time; ~ **so**, (colloq.) very.

ěv'ergreen a. always green or fresh. n. tree or shrub having green leaves all year round.

ěverlas'tǐng (-ah-) a. lasting for ever, perpetual. n. eternity; flower retaining colour when dried.

ěvermōre' adv. for ever; always.

ěv'erў (-vr-) a. each; all taken separately. ~**day**, occurring every day; ordinary. ~**man**, ordinary or typical human being. ~ **other**, each alternate. ~**body** pron. every person. ~**one** pron. everybody. ~**thing** pron. all things; all; thing of first importance. ~**where** adv. in every place.

ěvǐct' v.t. expel by legal process. **ěvǐc'tion** n.

ěv'ǐdence n. indication, sign; information given to establish fact etc.; statement etc. admissible in court of law. v.t. be evidence of; indicate.

ěv'ǐdent a. obvious, manifest.

ĕvĭdĕn'tial *a*. of or based on or furnishing evidence.

ē'vil *a*. bad, harmful, wicked. *n*. evil thing; sin; harm. **~-doer**, sinner. **~ eye**, supposed power of doing harm by look.

ĕvince' *v.t*. show, indicate.

ĕvis'cerāte *v.t*. disembowel.

ĕvocā'tion (*or* ĕ-) *n*. evoking. **ĕvŏc'a-tive** *a*.

ĕvōke' *v.t*. call up (feeling etc.).

ĕvolū'tion (*or* ĕ-; *or* -ōō-) *n*. evolving; origination of species by development from earlier forms; change of position of troops or ships. **~al, ~arў** *aa*.; **~ĭsm, ~ĭst** *nn*.

ĕvŏlve' *v*. unfold, open out; produce (heat etc.); develop; produce or modify by evolution.

ewe (ū) *n*. female sheep. **~ lamb**, most cherished object.

ew'er *n*. pitcher; water-jug.

ĕx[1] *prep*. (commerc.) out of, sold from (warehouse etc.). **~ dividend**, not including next dividend.

ĕx[2] *n*. (colloq.) former husband, wife, etc.

ĕx- in comb., formerly. **ĕx-prĕ'sĭdent** (-z-) *n*. former president.

Ex(x)., ex(x). *abbr*. example(s).

ĕxă'cerbāte *v.t*. aggravate; irritate. **~ā'tion** *n*.

ĕxăct' (-gz-) *a*. precise, accurate, strictly correct. *v.t*. enforce payment of (fees, obedience, etc.).

ĕxăc'tion (-gz-) *n*. exacting; illegal or exorbitant demand.

ĕxăc'tĭtūde (-gz-) *n*. exactness.

ĕxăct'lў (-gz-) *adv*. (esp.) quite so.

exa'ggerāte (ĭgzăj-) *v.t*. carry beyond truth; overstate. **~ā'tion** *n*.; **~ative** *a*.

exalt (ĭgzawlt') *v.t*. raise in rank, power, etc.; praise, extol.

ĕxaltā'tion (-awl-) *n*. elevation, raising on high; elation.

ĕxăm[1] (-gz-) *n*. (colloq.) examination.

ĕxămĭnā'tion (-gz-) *n*. minute inspection, investigation; testing of knowledge or ability by questions; (statements made in) formal interrogation of witness etc.

ĕxăm'ĭne (-gz-) *v*. investigate or inquire into; test knowledge or proficiency of (pupils etc.) by questions; interrogate formally. **~ee', ~er** *nn*.

exam'ple (ĭgzah-) *n*. fact etc. illustrating general rule; model, pattern; specimen; precedent; warning to others.

ĕx'ărch (-k) *n*. (Byzantine empire) governor of distant province; (Eastern Ch.) bishop next in rank to patriarch. **~ate** *n*. office, province, of exarch.

ĕxăs'perāte (-gz-; *or* -ahs-) *v.t*. irritate (person); aggravate (pain etc.). **~ā'tion** *n*.

exc. *abbr*. except; *excudit* [L], engraved.

ĕx căthē'drā adv. & *a*. authoritative(ly), official(ly). [L]

ĕx'cavāte *v.t*. hollow out; make (hole etc.), unearth, get out, by digging. **~ā'tion, ~ātor** *nn*.

exceed' *v*. go beyond; be greater than; surpass; be immoderate.

excee'dĭnglў *adv*. very.

excĕl' *v*. surpass; be pre-eminent.

ĕx'cellence *n*. surpassing merit.

ĕx'cellencў *n*. title of ambassadors, governors, etc.

ĕx'cellent *a*. extremely good.

ĕxcĕl'sĭor *n*. (U.S.) fine wood-shavings for packing etc.

ĕxcĕpt' *v*. exclude from general statement etc.; make objection against. *prep*. & *conj*. not including, with exception of, but; (arch.) unless. **~ for**, if it were not for. **~ĭng** *prep*. & *conj*. except.

ĕxcĕp'tion *n*. excepting; thing or case excepted; objection. **~able** *a*. open to exception.

ĕxcĕp'tional *a*. forming exception; unusual.

ĕxcĕrpt' *v.t*. extract, quote (passage *from* book etc.). *n*. (ĕks'-) excerpted passage. **~tion** *n*.

ĕxcĕss' *n*. fact of exceeding; amount by which thing exceeds; unreasonable indulgence. **~ĭve** *a*.

ĕxchānge' *n*. giving one thing and receiving another in its place; exchanging of money for equivalent in other currency; *rate of ~*, price at which another country's money may be bought; building where merchants, stockbrokers, etc. assemble to do business; central office where telephone connexions are made. *v.* give or receive in exchange; interchange. ~able *a.*; ~abil'itў *n.*

exchĕq'uer (-k*er*) *n.* public department charged with receipt and custody of revenue; royal or national treasury; money of private person etc. ~-bill, bill of credit issued by authority of parliament.

ĕx'cīse[1] (-z) *n.* (government office collecting) duty on home-produced goods, various licences, etc. ~man, (arch.) officer collecting excise and enforcing excise laws.

excīse'[2] (-z) *v.t.* cut out or away. excī'sion *n.*

excī'table *a.* (esp.) easily excited, unbalanced. ~abil'itў *n.*

ĕx'cĭtant *a.* & *n.* stimulant.

ĕxcĭtā'tion *n.* exciting, rousing; stimulation.

excīte' *v.t.* set in motion; stir up; stimulate to activity; move to strong emotion. ~tatĭve, ~tatorў *aa.*; ĕxcĭtā'tion, excīte'ment (-tm-) *nn.*

exclaim' *v.* cry out, esp. in anger, delight, etc.; ~ *against*, protest or make outcry against.

ĕxclamā'tion *n.* exclaiming; word(s) etc. exclaimed; interjection. ~-mark, punctuation mark (!). exclăm'atorў *a.*

exclude' (-lōōd) *v.t.* shut out (*from*), leave out; make impossible, preclude.

exclu'sion (-lōōzhn) *n.* excluding; being excluded.

exclu'sĭve (-lōō-) *a.* excluding; not inclusive; (of society etc.) disposed to exclude outsiders; not to be had, not published, etc. elsewhere. *n.* (colloq.) exclusive item of news, film, etc. ~ of, not including, not counting.

ĕxcŏ'gĭtāte *v.t.* think out, devise. ~ā'tion *n.*

ĕxcommū'nicāte *v.t.* cut off from sacraments or communication with Church. ~ā'tion, ~ātor *nn.*; ~atĭve, ~atorў *aa.*

ĕxcŏr'iāte *v.t.* remove skin or bark from; remove (skin, bark). ~ā'tion *n.*

ĕx'crĕment *n.* waste matter discharged from bowels, dung. ~mĕn'tal *a.*

ĕxcrĕs'cence *n.* abnormal or morbid outgrowth. ~ent *a.*

ĕxcrē'ta *n.pl.* waste expelled from body.

ĕxcrēte' *v.t.* separate and expel (waste matters) from system. ~tion *n.*; ~tĭve, ~torў *aa.*

ĕxcru'ciāte (-krōōshĭ-) *v.t.* pain acutely; torture. ~ā'tion *n.*

ĕx'culpāte *v.t.* free from blame. ~ā'tion *n.*; excŭl'patorў *a.*

ĕxcūr'sion *n.* short journey or ramble; pleasure-trip, esp. one made by number of persons; excursion train or ticket; (arch.) sortie. ~ ticket, for journey at reduced fare. ~ train, train for persons making pleasure-trip, usu. at reduced rates. ~ist *n.*

ĕxcūr'sĭve *a.* desultory; digressive.

ĕxcūr'sus *n.* (pl. -*uses*), detailed discussion of special point in book etc.

ĕxcūse' (-z) *v.t.* (attempt to) lessen or remove blame attaching to; forgive; grant exemption to; dispense with. *n.* (-s), apology; exculpation. ~ me, polite formula of apology for interrupting, disagreeing, etc. excū'satorў *a.*

ex div. *abbr.* ex dividend.

ĕx'ĕăt *n.* leave of absence.

ĕx'ĕcrable *a.* abominable.

ĕx'ĕcrāte *v.* express or feel abhorrence for; utter curses. ~ā'tion *n.*

ĕxĕc'ūtant (-gz-) *n.* performer, esp. of music.

ĕx'ĕcūte *v.t.* carry out, perform; put to death.

ĕxĕcū'tion *n.* executing; skill in performing music; destructive work; seizure of goods for debt; capital punishment. ~er *n.* one who executes criminals.

ĕxĕc'ūtĭve (-gz-) *a.* concerned with execution of laws, policy, etc.; of an executive. *n.* executive branch of government or organization; person(s) having supreme executive authority, esp. President of U.S., Governor of State; holder of executive or managerial position in business etc.

ĕxĕc'ūtor (-gz-) *n.* person appointed by testator to execute his will.

èxĕcūtor'ial *a.* ~trix (pl. *-trĭcēs*) *n.* female executor.

ĕxėgē'sis *n.* exposition, esp. of Scripture. ĕxėgĕt'ĭc(al) *aa.*

èxĕm'plar (-gz-) *n.* model; type.

èxĕm'plarў (-gz-) *a.* fit to be imitated; serving as example.

èxĕm'plifȳ (-gz-) *v.t.* give or be example of. ~ficā'tion *n.*

èxĕmpt' (-gz-) *a.* not liable or exposed or subject to (duty, danger, etc.), free *from*. *v.t.* grant immunity or freedom (*from*). ~tion *n.*

ĕx'équies (-kwĭz) *n.pl.* funeral rites.

ĕx'ercīse (-z) *n.* employment (of faculties etc.); practice; use of muscles etc., esp. for health's sake; (task set for) bodily or mental or spiritual training; religious observance; (U.S.) ceremony on special occasion. *v.* use; give exercise to; take exercise; perplex, worry.

èxĕrt' (-gz-) *v.t.* exercise; bring to bear; put forth; ~ one*self*, use efforts or endeavours. èxĕr'tion *n.*

ĕxfō'liāte *v.i.* come off in scales or layers. ~ā'tion *n.*

ĕx grā'tia (-shĭa), (done, made) as favour, in absence of legal right. [L]

exhalā'tion (ĕksa-) *n.* evaporation; what is exhaled.

èxhāle' *v.* give off, be given off, in vapour; breathe out.

exhaust' (ĭgzaw-) *v.t.* draw off; consume, use up; empty of contents; deal with exhaustively; drain of energy, resources, etc.; tire out. *n.* expulsion or exit of spent steam, products of combustion, etc. from engine etc.; fluid, gases, etc. expelled. ~ible *a.*; ~ibil'itў *n.* exhaus'tion *n.* (esp.) total loss of strength.

exhau'stive (igzaw-) *a.* complete, comprehensive.

exhib'ĭt (ĭgzĭ-) *v.t.* display; manifest; show publicly. *n.* thing exhibited. exhib'ĭtor *n.*

exhibi'tion (ĕksĭ-) *n.* display; public show; sum allowed to student from funds of college etc. ~er *n.* student holding exhibition. ~ism *n.* tendency towards display or extravagant behaviour, esp. indecent exposure of person. ~ist *n.*

exhil'arāte (ĭgzĭ-) *v.t.* enliven, gladden. ~ā'tion *n.*

exhort (ĭgzort') *v.t.* admonish earnestly; urge (*to*). ~ā'tion *n.*; ~ative, ~atorў *aa.*

èxhūme' *v.t.* disinter. ~mā'tion *n.*

ĕx'ĭgence, ~encў *nn.* urgent need; emergency.

ĕx'ĭgent *a.* urgent; exacting.

ĕx'ĭgible *a.* that may be exacted.

èxĭg'ūous *a.* scanty, small, slender. èxĭgū'itў *n.*

ĕx'īle *n.* penal banishment; long absence from one's country etc.; person in exile. *v.t.* banish.

èxist' (-gz-) *v.i.* be, have being; live, sustain life. ~ent *a.*

èxis'tence (-gz-) *n.* fact, mode, of living; all that exists.

èxistĕn'tial (-gz-) *a.* of or relating to or predicating existence. ~ism *n.* anti-intellectualist philosophy assuming that reality as existence can only be lived by man as free and responsible being, but never become object of thought. ~ist *a.* & *n.*

ĕx'ĭt[1] *n.* going out; way out; departure; death.

ĕx'ĭt[2], (stage direction) goes off stage. [L]

Exod. *abbr.* Exodus.

ĕx'odus *n.* departure, esp. in considerable numbers; departure of Israelites from Egypt.

ĕx offĭ'cio (-shĭō) *adv.* & *a.* in virtue of one's office. [L]

èxŏg'amў *n.* custom compelling man to marry outside tribe or group. ~mous *a.*

Exon. *abbr.* (Bishop) of Exeter.

èxŏn'erāte (-gz-) free *from* (blame etc.); exculpate. ~ā'tion *n.*

èxŏphthăl'mĭc *a.* (med.) causing protrusion of eyeball.

exor(s). *abbr.* executor(s).

èxor'bĭtant (-gz-) *a.* grossly excessive; extravagant. ~ance *n.*

ĕx'orcīze *v.t.* expel (evil spirit) by invocation etc.; clear of spirits thus. ~cĭsm, ~cĭst *nn.*

èxor'dĭum *n.* (pl. *-iums*, *-ia*), introductory part of discourse or treatise. èxor'dĭal *a.*

èxotĕ'rĭc *a.* intelligible to outsiders; ordinary, popular.

ėxŏt'ĭc (-gz-) a. introduced from abroad; strange, bizarre. n. exotic plant etc.

ėxpănd' v. spread out; develop; increase; become genial. ~ėd a. (esp., of sheet metal) slit and stretched into lattice.

ėxpănse' n. wide area or extent of land, space, etc. expăn'sion n. expanding, increase, extension.

ėxpăn'sĭve a. able or tending to expand; extensive; genial.

ĕx păr'tė adv. & a. from or on behalf of one side only. [L]

ėxpā'tiāte (-shĭ-) v.i. speak or write copiously, ~ā'tion n.

ėxpā'triāte (or -pă-) v.t. banish, (refl.) withdraw, from one's native country. n. & a. (-at), expatriated (person).

ėxpĕct' v.t. reckon on; anticipate; look for; suppose.

ėxpĕc'tant a. expecting; expecting to become. ~ancў n.

ĕxpĕctā'tion n. anticipation; what one expects; probability; (pl.) prospects of inheritance.

ėxpĕc'torāte v. cough or spit out from chest or lungs; spit. ~ant a. & n. (medicine) promoting expectoration. ~ā'tion n.

ėxpē'dĭent a. suitable, advisable; more politic than just. n. contrivance, device. ~ence, ~encў nn.

ĕx'pėdīte v.t. help on, facilitate, progress of; dispatch.

ĕxpėdĭ'tion n. promptness, dispatch; (men, ships, etc. sent on) journey or voyage for some definite purpose. ~arў a. (to be) employed on expedition.

ĕxpėdĭ'tious a. done with or marked by expedition.

ėxpĕl' v.t. throw out; eject.

ėxpĕnd' v.t. spend (money, time, care, etc.); use up, consume. ~able a. (esp.) that can be spared, likely or meant to be sacrificed or destroyed.

ėxpĕn'dĭture n. expending; amount expended.

ėxpĕnse' n. cost, charge; (pl.) outlay in executing commission etc.

ėxpĕn'sĭve a. costly.

expēr'ience n. (knowledge based on) personal observation or contact; incident that affects one. v.t. suffer, feel, undergo. ~d a. (esp.) wise or skilful through experience.

ĕxpērĭĕn'tial a. (esp.) regarding all knowledge as derived from experience.

ėxpē'riment n. procedure adopted or operation carried out to make discovery, observation, test, etc. v.i. make experiment(s).

ėxpĕrĭmĕn'tal a. based on or done by way of experiment. ~ĭst n.

ĕx'pĕrt a. trained by practice, skilful, skilled. n. person having special skill or knowledge. ĕxpertise' (-ēz) n. expert opinion or skill or knowledge.

ĕx'pĭāte v.t. pay penalty of, make amends for (sin). ~ā'tion, ~ātor nn.; ~ā'torў a.

ėxpīre' v. breathe out; die; die out; come to end. ĕxpirā'tion n.; ėxpīr'atorў a.

ėxpīr'ў n. termination.

ėxplain' v.t. make known; make intelligible; account for.

ĕxplanā'tion n. statement or circumstance that explains.

ėxplăn'atorў a. serving to explain.

ėxplē'tĭve a. serving to fill out sentence etc. n. expletive word or phrase, esp. oath.

ĕx'plĭcable (or ĭksplĭk'-) a. explainable.

ĕx'plĭcatorў (or -ĭk'-) a. explanatory.

ėxplĭ'cĭt a. expressly stated; definite; outspoken.

ėxplōde' v. discredit; (cause to) expand violently with loud report.

ĕx'ploit n. heroic or spectacular feat. v.t. (ĭksploit'), work (mine etc.); utilize for one's own ends. ~ā'tion n.

ėxplōre' v.t. examine (country etc.) by going through it; examine by touch; inquire into. ĕxplorā'tion n.; ėxplor'atĭve, ~ratorў aa.

ėxplō'sion (-zhn) n. going off with loud noise; outbreak; sudden violent expansion.

ėxplō'sĭve a. tending to explode; of or like explosion; (of consonant) produced by stopping and release of breath. n. explosive agent or material or consonant; high ~, explosive with very violent and shattering effect.

expō′nent *n*. person or thing that explains or interprets; type, representative; (alg.) symbol indicating power of quantity etc. **~ĕn′tial** *a*. & *n*. (quantity etc.) involving unknown quantity or variable as (part of) exponent.

expōrt′ *v.t*. send (goods etc.) to another country. *n*. (ĕks′-), exported article; (usu. pl.) amount exported. **ĕxportā′tion** *n*.

expōse′ (-z) *v.t*. leave or place in unsheltered or unprotected position; subject (*to* risk etc.); exhibit *for* sale; disclose; unmask, show up; (photog.) subject (film, sensitized paper, etc.) to action of light. **~d** *a*. (esp.) unsheltered, not protected against wind, sea, etc.

exposé (ĕkspō′zā) *n*. disclosure (of discreditable thing). [F]

ĕxposi′tion (-z-) *n*. description, explanation; exhibition. **ĕxpŏs′itor** *n*.; **ĕxpŏs′itory** *a*.

ĕx pōst făc′to, acting retrospectively. [L]

ĕxpŏs′tūlāte *v.i*. make (esp. friendly) remonstrance. **~ā′tion** *n*.

expō′sure (-zher) *n*. exposing, being exposed; length of time photographic film etc. is exposed; unmasking or revealing of error, crime, etc.

expound′ *v.t*. set forth in detail; explain, interpret.

exprĕss′ *v.t*. represent by symbols etc. or in language; put into words; manifest, reveal; press etc. out; send by express messenger or company or train. *a*. definitely stated; done etc. for special purpose; travelling etc. at high speed; (of train etc.) with few intermediate stops. *n*. express train, messenger, etc.; (U.S.) company carrying parcels etc. *adv*. with speed; by express train etc. **~ agent**, (U.S.) agent of express company. **~ delivery**, by special postal messenger. **~ rifle**, discharging bullet with high initial velocity. **~ible** *a*.

exprĕ′ssion *n*. (mode or manner of) expressing; wording, word, phrase; expressive quality; aspect (of face), intonation (of voice); (alg.) symbols

expressing quantity. **~al** *a*. **~ism** *n*. movement in literature etc expressing emotional experience rather than depicting external world. **~ist** *n*. & *a*.; **~is′tic** *a*.

exprĕss′ive *a*. serving to express; significant.

exprĕss′ly *adv*. explicitly; on purpose.

exprō′priāte *v.t*. dispossess; take away (property). **~ā′tion**, **~ātor** *nn*.

expŭl′sion *n*. expelling, being expelled. **~sive** *a*.

expŭnge′ (-j) *v.t*. erase, strike out.

ĕx′purgāte (-per-) *v.t*. remove objectionable matter from (book etc.); clear away (such matter). **~ā′tion**, **~ātor** *nn*.

ĕx′quisite (-z-) *a*. of extreme beauty or delicacy; acute, keen. *n*. fop.

exrx. *abbr*. executrix.

ĕx-sĕr′vice *a*. formerly belonging to (fighting) service.

ĕx′tant (*or* -ănt′) *a*. still existing.

ĕxtĕm′porĕ *adv*. & *a*. without preparation; off-hand. **~rā′néous**, **~rary** *aa*.; **~rize** *v*. produce, speak, etc. extempore. **~rizā′tion** *n*.

extĕnd′ *v*. stretch out; reach; accord (*to*); prolong; enlarge; tax powers of. **~ible**, **extĕn′sible** *aa*.; **~ibil′ity** *n*.

extĕn′sile (*or* -il) *a*. that can be protruded or stretched out.

extĕn′sion *n*. extending; enlargement, additional part; (*University*) *E~*, extramural studies conducted by university etc.

extĕn′sive *a*. large, far-reaching.

extĕn′sor *n*. muscle extending part of body.

extĕnt′ *n*. space covered; width of application, scope.

extĕn′ūāte *v.t*. lessen seeming magnitude of (guilt etc.) by partial excuse. **~ā′tion** *n*.; **~atory** *a*.

extē̄r′ior *a*. outer, outward. *n*. exterior aspect or part.

extēr′mināte *v.t*. root out, destroy utterly. **~ā′tion**, **~ātor** *nn*.

extēr′nal *a*. outside; of, consisting in, belonging or referring to, etc., outward world or what is outside; (of evidence) derived from source independent of thing discussed. **~ăl′ity** *n*. **~īze** *v.t*. give or attribute

external existence to. **exter'nals**
n.pl. outward features or aspect;
external circumstances; non-
-essentials.

extinct' *a.* no longer burning; (of
volcano) that has ceased eruption;
quenched; that has died out.

extinc'tion *n.* extinguishing; making
or becoming extinct; destruction.

exting'uish (-nggw-) *v.t.* put out,
quench; eclipse; annihilate; wipe
out (debt). **~er** *n.* (esp.) cap for
extinguishing candle etc.

ex'tirpate *v.t.* root out, destroy
utterly. **~ā'tion** *n.*

extol' *v.t.* praise enthusiastically.

extort' *v.t.* get by force, threats, importunity, etc.

extor'tion *n.* extorting, esp. of
money; illegal exaction. **~ate** *a.*
(esp.) exorbitant. **~er** *n.*

ex'tra *a.* additional; larger, better.
adv. more than usually; addi-
tionally. *n.* extra thing; thing
charged extra; (crick.) run not
scored off bat; actor engaged for
small part or as one of crowd;
special edition of newspaper.
~-special, (colloq.) especially good
etc.

ex'tra- in comb., outside, not within
scope of. **extrajudi'cial** *a.* not
made in court; not legally authorized. **~mun'dane** *a.* outside of our
world or of universe. **~-offi'cial** *a.*
not pertaining to office. **~parō'-
chial** (-k-) *a.* outside, not concerned
with, parish. **~sen'sory** *a.* outside
scope of perception by senses.

extract' *v.t.* take out; draw forth;
deduce, derive (*from*); obtain
(juices etc.) by suction, distillation,
etc.; find (root of number); copy
out, quote. *n.* (ĕks'-) essence;
concentrated preparation; passage
from book etc. **extrac'tive** *a.* (of
industries) dependent on mining
and oil.

extrac'tion *n.* extracting; descent,
lineage.

ex'tradite *v.t.* deliver (fugitive criminal) to authorities of State where
crime was committed. **~i'table** *a.*
liable to or warranting extradition.
extradi'tion *n.*

extramūr'al *a.* outside walls of town

etc.; outside scope of ordinary
university teaching etc.

extrā'neous *a.* of external origin; not
naturally belonging; foreign.

extraor'dinary (-trŏr- *or* -traŏr-) *a.*
out of usual course; specially employed; exceptional, surprising.

extrăp'olate *v.* calculate or infer or
deduce from known data further
facts, terms, etc. lying outside
their range. **~ā'tion** *n.*

extraterritor'ial *a.* **~** *privilege, status,*
etc., of being free from jurisdiction
of State in which one is; **~** *rights,*
of State over its subjects abroad.

extrăv'agance *n.* extravagant expenditure; want of restraint.

extrăv'agant *a.* wild, absurd; exorbitant; profuse, wasteful.

extrăvagăn'za *n.* fantastic composition, language, or behaviour.

extravert : see **extrovert.**

extrēme' *a.* outermost; utmost;
going to great lengths, not moderate. *n.* thing at either end, esp.
(pl.) things as remote or different
as possible; extreme degree etc.
~ unction, (R.C. Ch.) anointing by
priest of dying person. **~ly** *adv.* in
extreme degree; very. **extrē'mism**
n. holding of extreme views, advocacy of extreme measures. **extrē'mist** *n. & a.*

extrěm'ity *n.* extreme point, end;
esp. (pl.) hands and feet; extreme
adversity, danger, etc.

ex'tricate *v.t.* disentangle, release.
~ā'tion *n.*

extrin'sic *a.* not inherent or intrinsic;
extraneous.

ex'trovert, extra- *n.* (psychol.)
person with thoughts and activities directed to things outside self.
~ver'sion *n.*

extrude' (-roo-) *v.t.* thrust or squeeze
out; shape by forcing through
mould. **extru'sion** *n.* **extru'sive** *a.*
(esp., of rocks) solidified after extrusion by volcanic action etc.

exū'berant (-gz-) *a.* luxuriant, prolific;
effusive, copious, lavish. **~ance** *n.*

exūde' (-gz-) *v.* ooze out or give off
like sweat. **exūdā'tion** *n.*

exult' (-gz-) *v.i.* rejoice, triumph
(*at, in, over*). **~ancy, exultā'tion**
nn.; **~ant** *a.*

éxū'viae *n.pl.* animal's cast skin, shell, etc. ~ial *a.*

eyas (ī'as) *n.* young hawk not yet fully trained.

eye (ī) *n.* organ of sight; iris of this; look, gaze; power of seeing, observation, perception; eye-like thing; spot, hole, loop, leaf-bud of potato, etc. *v.t.* observe, watch closely or suspiciously. ~ball, whole eye. ~brow, fringe of hair over eye. ~-glass, lens to assist sight, protect eye, etc.; (pl.) pair of these joined by bar over bridge of nose. ~lash, one of fringe of hairs on eyelid. ~lid, movable fold of skin covering eye. ~-opener, enlightening or surprising fact etc. ~piece, lens(es) at eye end of optical instrument. ~-shadow, cosmetic for eyelids. ~shot, distance one can see. ~sight, faculty or power of seeing. ~sore, thing that offends sight. ~-tooth, pointed tooth just under eye, canine. ~wash, (sl.) humbug, blarney. ~witness, one who can testify from his own observation. ~ful *n.* (esp., sl.) striking or attractive sight. ~less *a.*

eye'lét (īl-) *n.* small hole; loop-hole.

eyot, ait (āt) *n.* small island in river.

eyre (ār) *n.* (hist.) circuit (court).

eyrie (ār'ĭ) *n.* aerie.

Ezek. *abbr.* Ezekiel.

F

F (ĕf), (mus.) fourth note in scale of C major.

F. *abbr.* Fahrenheit.

f. *abbr.* feet; feminine; filly; foot; *forte*; franc(s); free; from.

fa (fah) *n.* (mus.) fourth note of major scale in tonic sol-fa.

F.A. *abbr.* Football Association.

făb *a.* (sl.) fabulous, marvellous.

fā'ble *n.* story not based on fact, myth, legend; short moral tale, esp. with animals for characters. ~d *a.* celebrated in fable, legendary.

făb'rĭc *n.* thing put together; build-ing; structure; construction; woven material.

făb'ricāte *v.t.* construct, manufac-ture; invent (fact), forge (docu-ment). ~ā'tion *n.*

făb'ūlous *a.* celebrated in fable, in-credible; (colloq.) marvellous.

façade' (-sahd) *n.* face, esp. principal front, of building; frontal or out-ward appearance.

fāce *n.* front of head; expression, grimace; effrontery; aspect; sur-face; front, right side; dial-plate of clock etc.; striking surface of bat, racket, golf-club, etc.; *lose* ~, be humiliated, lose credit or good name; *on the* ~ *of it*, to judge by appearance, obviously; *save one's* ~, save one's credit, good name, or reputation. *v.* meet firmly; be opposite to; look, (mil.) turn, in some direction; cover part of (garment) with other material, esp. at edge; cover surface of with other material. ~-ache, neuralgia. ~-card, king, queen, or knave. ~-lift, plastic operation for tighten-ing skin of face; improvement in appearance. ~ value, that stated on coin, note, etc.; apparent value. ~r *n.* blow in face; sudden diffi-culty or problem. ~less *a.* (esp.) unknown, unidentified or un-identifiable.

fă'cét *n.* one side of many-sided body, esp. cut gem.

facē'tiae (-shĭē) *n.pl.* pleasantries. facē'tious *a.* given to or marked by pleasantry, waggish.

fă'cia (*or* fā-; -sha) *n.* plate over shop-front with name etc.

fā'cial *a.* of face. *n.* (colloq.) face--massage etc.

fă'cīle *a.* easy; working easily; fluent; flexible.

făcĭl'ĭtāte *v.t.* make easy, promote. ~ā'tion *n.*

facĭl'ĭtȳ *n.* absence of difficulty; dexterity; (usu. pl.) opportunity.

fā'cĭng *n.* (esp.) what garment is faced with, esp. cuffs and collar of military jacket etc.; surface covering of different material.

făcsĭm'ĭlė *n.* exact copy, esp. of writing, picture, etc.

făct *n.* thing done; thing known to

be true; what is true or existent, reality; *in* ~, in reality, really, indeed.

făc'tion *n.* self-interested or unscrupulous party; prevalence of party spirit. **făc'tious** *a.*

făctĭ'tious *a.* artificial, got up.

făc'tĭtĭve *a.* ~ verb, expressing idea of making, calling, or thinking to be.

făc'tor *n.* commercial agent; (Sc.) land-steward; any of numbers etc. whose product is given number etc.; element in result; gene; ~ *of safety*, ratio between maximum possible load, stress, etc. on structure or material and what it is required to bear. ~**age** *n.* factor's commission. **factŏr'ial** *n.* product of integer multiplied by all lower integers; *a.* of factor or factorial. ~**ĭze** *v.t.* find factors of.

făc'torў *n.* building or range of buildings for manufacture of goods.

făctō'tum *n.* man of all work; servant managing master's affairs.

făc'tūal *a.* concerned with, of the nature of, fact.

făc'ultative *a.* permissive, optional.

făc'ultў *n.* aptitude for particular action; physical or mental power; (teaching staff of) department of learning at university etc.; members of profession, esp. medicine; (esp. eccl.) authorization.

făd *n.* pet notion, craze. **fădd'ist** *n.*; **fădd'ў** *a.*

fāde *v.* droop, wither; (cause to) lose freshness or colour; disappear gradually; (of sound) grow faint; (of brake) gradually lose power; ~ *in*, *out*, *up*, gradually increase or decrease brightness or intensity or distinctness of (cinema picture, sound, etc.). *n.* fading in or out. ~**lėss** *a.* unfading.

fae'cēs (-z) *n.pl.* sediment; excrement of bowels. **fae'cal** *a.*

fā'erĭe *n.* fairyland; the fairies.

făg *v.* toil, grow or make weary; (at schools) do service for seniors. *n.* drudgery; junior liable to fag; (sl.) cigarette. ~**-end**, inferior remnant; very end. **făgged** (-gd) *a.* tired (*out*).

făgg'ot *n.* bundle of sticks for fuel; bundle of steel rods; (pl.) dish of chopped liver, lights, etc. *v.* (esp.) ornament, join, with faggoting or faggot-stitch. ~**-stitch**, stitch used in faggoting. **făgg'oting** *n.* (needlework) drawn-thread or other openwork with cross-threads fastened together in middle like faggots.

Fahr. *abbr.* Fahrenheit.

Fahrenheit (fă'renhīt) *a.* (of scale, thermometer) with 32° and 212° for freezing- and boiling-points of water.

faience (fī'yahns) *n.* painted and glazed earthenware.

fail *v.* be missing; be deficient; break down; not succeed; go bankrupt; disappoint; neglect. *n.* failure; *without* ~, for certain, whatever happens. ~**ing** *n.* deficiency, failure; foible, fault, weakness.

faille (*or* fīl *or* fīy) *n.* soft corded fabric of silk etc.

fai'lure *n.* non-performance; ill success; bankruptcy; unsuccessful person, thing, or attempt.

fain[1] *pred. a.* (arch.) willing; glad. *adv.* gladly.

fain[2], **fains** (-z), **fēns** (-z), child's formula claiming exemption.

faint *a.* feeble; inclined to swoon; dim, pale; timid. *v.i.* & *n.* swoon. ~**-heart**, coward. ~**-hearted**, timid.

fair[1] *n.* periodical gathering for sale of goods, often with shows and entertainments; bazaar; trade exhibition. ~**-ground**, open space for fair etc. ~**ing**[1] *n.* present bought at fair.

fair[2] *a.* beautiful; blond, not dark; just, equitable; of moderate quality or amount; (of weather) favourable. *adv.* in fair manner; *bid* ~ *to do*, show promise of doing. *n.* (arch.) (pretty) woman. ~ **copy**, transcript free from corrections. ~ **play**, equal opportunities, just treatment. ~**-weather**, fit only for fine weather.

fair'ing[2] *n.* structure round part of aircraft etc. to improve streamlining, give protection, etc.

Fair'-Isle (-īl) *a.* knitted in characteristic coloured designs.

fair'lў *adv.* (esp.) utterly; rather.

fair'way n. navigable channel; part of golf-course running between hazards from tee to green.

fair'y n. small supernatural being with magical powers. a. of fairies; fairy-like. ~ **lamps**, ~ **lights**, small coloured lights for esp. outdoor decoration. ~**land**, home of fairies. ~ **ring**, ring of darker grass caused by fungi. ~**-tale**, tale of fairies; incredible story; falsehood.

fait accompli (fāt ahkawṅ'plē) n. thing done and past arguing about. [F]

faith n. trust; belief in religious doctrine or divine truth; religion; loyalty, fidelity, confidence. ~**-cure**, ~**-healer**, ~**-healing**, by power of faith, not medical skill.

faith'ful a. loyal, constant; true, accurate. ~**ly** adv. (esp., colloq.) with binding assurances; *yours* ~*ly*, formula at end of business letter.

faith'less a. (esp.) perfidious, false.

fāke v.t. do *up*, make specious; contrive or tamper with in order to deceive. n. piece of faking; faked thing.

fā'kir (-er; or fakēr') n. Moslem etc. religious mendicant or ascetic.

falchion (fawl'chon) n. broad curved convex-edged sword.

falcon (faw'kn) n. small diurnal bird of prey, esp. one trained to hawk for sport. ~**er**, trainer of hawks. ~**ry** n. hawking; breeding and training of hawks.

fǎl'derǎl n. gewgaw, trifle.

fald'stool (fawl-) n. bishop's armless chair; movable folding stool or desk for kneeling at.

fall (fawl) v.i. (fěll, fallen), descend freely, drop, come down, lose high position; abate, droop; collapse; sin, perish; lapse; occur; ~ *back on*, retreat or have recourse to; ~ *down on*, fail in; ~ *for*, be carried away or taken in by; ~ *foul of*, collide with; ~ *in*, (mil.) (cause to) take place(s) in line; ~ *off*, decrease, degenerate; ~ *out*, quarrel, (mil.) leave ranks; ~ *short*, not go far enough; ~ *short of*, fail to reach or obtain; ~ *through*, miscarry, fail; ~ *to*, begin eating or fighting. n. falling; amount that falls,

autumn; cataract (often pl.); descent; drop; downfall, ruin; kind of veil. ~**-out**, (esp.) radio-active dust settling after nuclear explosion etc. ~**-pipe**, carrying rainwater from roof etc. to ground.

fallā'cious a. containing fallacy; delusive.

fǎll'acy n. misleading argument; delusiveness; flaw in syllogism; error.

fǎl'-lǎl n. piece of finery.

fǎll'ĭble a. liable to err or be erroneous. ~**bil'ity** n.

fǎll'ow[1] (-ō) a. ploughed etc. but left uncropped (often fig.); uncultivated. n. fallow ground.

fǎll'ow[2] (-ō) a. of pale brownish yellow. ~ **deer**, kind smaller than red deer.

false (fŏls) a. erroneous, deceptive; deceitful, lying; spurious. ~ **bottom**, horizontal partition above true bottom of box etc. ~ **pretences**, misrepresentations meant to deceive. ~ **quantity**, blunder as to length of (Latin) vowel. ~ **step**, stumble; transgression. **fal'sity** n.

false'hood (fŏls-h-) n. falseness, lying, lie(s).

falsětt'ō (fŏl-) n. (pl. -os), voice above one's natural range.

fal'sify (fŏl-) v.t. fraudulently alter; misrepresent, pervert; disappoint. ~**fica'tion** n.

fal'ter (fŏl-) v. go unsteadily; say or speak hesitatingly; waver.

fāme n. public report, rumour; reputation; renown. **fāmed** (-md) p.p. & a. famous; currently reported.

famĭl'iar (-lyar) a. intimate; well known; common; unceremonious; amorously intimate (*with*). n. intimate friend; demon attending witch etc. **famĭliǎ'rity** n.

famĭl'iarīze (-lya-) v.t. make familiar; accustom. ~**zā'tion** n.

fǎm'ily n. household; set of parents and children or of relations; person's children; lineage; race; group of allied genera. ~ **allowance**, paid by State etc. in proportion to size of family. ~ **bible**, with fly-leaves for entering births etc. ~ **man**, man with family, domestic person. ~ **planning**, birth control. ~ **tree**, genealogical tree. **famil′ial** a.

făm′īne n. extreme scarcity of food etc.; starvation.

făm′ish v. reduce or be reduced to extreme hunger.

fā′mous a. celebrated; (colloq.) very good, excellent.

făn[1] n. winnowing-machine; instrument, usu. folding and sector-shaped, for agitating air to cool face etc.; anything spreading out in fan shape; rotating apparatus giving current of air. v.t. winnow; move (air), sweep *away*, (as) with fan; drive air (as) with fan upon; increase (flames etc.) (as) by fanning; spread (*out*) in fan shape. ~-**belt**, for driving rotating fan. ~**light**, fan-shaped window over door. ~**tail**, (pigeon) with fan-shaped tail. ~ **tracery**, elaborate tracery of fan-vaulting. ~-**vault(ing)**, English 15th-c. vault(ing) with ribs diverging like sticks of fan.

făn[2] n. (sl.) enthusiast, devotee. ~-**mail**, letters from fans.

fanăt′ic n. & a. (person) filled with excessive or mistaken enthusiasm, esp. in religion. ~**al** a.; ~**ism** n.

făn′cier n. connoisseur.

făn′ciful a. indulging in fancies; capricious; imaginary.

făn′cў n. faculty of imagination; delusion; supposition; caprice, whim; taste, liking. a. ornamental, not plain; of whimsical kind. v.t. conceive, imagine; (colloq.) have good conceit of (oneself); take fancy to, like. ~ **dress**, masquerade costume. ~-**free**, not in love. ~-**work**, ornamental needlework etc.

făndăng′ō (-ngg-) n. (pl. -*oes*), lively Spanish dance.

fāne n. (poet.) temple.

făn′fāre n. flourish of trumpets, bugles, etc.

fănfăronāde′ n. arrogant talk.

făng n. canine tooth; serpent's venom-tooth; prong of tooth.

făntā′sĭa (-z-; *or* -azē′a) n. musical etc. composition with form subordinated to fancy.

făntăs′tĭc a. extravagantly fanciful; grotesque, quaint. ~**ăl′itў** n.

făn′tasў, ph- n. faculty of imagination; fancy; fantastic concept, design, etc.

fār adv. at or to great distance; by much. n. great distance. a. distant, remote. ~-**away**, remote, long past; dreamy. **F~ East**, countries of eastern Asia. ~-**fetched**, not obvious, forced. ~-**flung**, widely extended. ~ **gone**, very ill, drunk, much in debt, etc. ~-**off**, remote. ~-**reaching**, widespread, reaching distant points in time, space, etc. ~-**seeing**, prescient, prudent. ~-**sighted**, far-seeing, seeing distant things more clearly than near ones.

fă′rad n. electromagnetic unit of capacity.

fārce n. dramatic work with sole object of exciting laughter; absurdly futile proceeding, pretence, mockery. **fār′cical** a.

fār′del n. (arch.) bundle, burden.

fāre n. cost of passenger's conveyance; passenger; food. v.i. (poet.) go, travel; get on; be fed.

fārewĕll′ (-rw-) int. & n. good-bye.

farī′na (*or* -rē-) n. flour or meal of corn, nuts, or starchy roots; (chem.) starch. **fărĭnā′ceous** a. starchy. **fă′rĭnōse** a. mealy.

fārm n. tract of land used for cultivation, or of water used for breeding oysters etc.; dwelling-place on farm. v. take proceeds of (tax, office) on payment of fixed sum; cultivate, till the soil. ~**stead**, farm with buildings. ~**yard**, yard of farm-house. **fār′mer** n.

fār′ō n. gambling card-game.

farrā′gō (*or* -rah-) n. (pl. -*os*), medley, hotchpotch.

fă′rrier n. shoeing-smith; horse-doctor. ~**ў** n.

fă′rrow (-ō) n. giving birth to, litter of, pigs. v. bear (pigs), bear pigs.

fār′ther (-dh-) adv. more far; (usu. *fur*-) also, in addition. a. more distant or advanced; (usu. *fur*-) additional, more. ~**most** a. farthest. **fār′thĕst** a. most distant; adv. to, at, greatest distance.

fār′thĭng (-dh-) n. quarter of penny.

fār′thingāle (-dhĭngg-) n. (hist.) hooped petticoat.

f.a.s. abbr. free alongside ship.

fă'scia (-shĭa) *n.* (archit.) long flat surface of wood or stone under eaves or cornice; facia.

făs'cicle, făs'cicūle *n.* bunch, bundle; instalment of book.

făs'cināte *v.t.* make (victim) powerless by one's presence or look; charm irresistibly. **~ā'tion** *n.*

Făsc'ism (-sh-) *n.* principles and organization of Italian nationalist anti-communist dictatorship (1922–43); system of extreme right-wing totalitarian racialist political beliefs and practices. **Făsc'ist** *n. & a.*

făsh *v.t.* (Sc.) trouble, bother.

făsh'ion (-shn) *n.* make, shape, style; way, manner; prevailing custom or style, esp. in dress; habit, thing, person, etc. temporarily admired, adopted, etc. in esp. high society. *v.t.* form, shape. **~-plate,** (picture showing) person wearing latest fashion. **~able** *a.* of or in (latest) fashion.

fast[1] (fah-) *v.i.* go without food or some kinds of food, esp. as religious observance. *n.* fasting; going without food.

fast[2] (fah-) *a.* firm, fixed, steady; rapid; pleasure-seeking. *adv.* firmly, tightly; quickly.

fasten (fah'sn) *v.* attach, fix, secure; become fast. **~er, ~ing** *nn.*

făstid'ious *a.* easily disgusted, hard to please.

fast'nėss (fah-) *n.* (esp.) stronghold, fortress.

făt *a.* well-fed, plump; greasy, oily; fertile, rich, rewarding; (colloq.) stupid; *a ~ lot,* very little. *n.* fat part of thing; oily substance composing fat parts of animal bodies.

fā'tal *a.* destructive, ruinous; deadly, ending in death.

fā'talism *n.* belief that all is predetermined; submission to all that happens as inevitable. **~ist** *n.*; **~is'tic** *a.*

fatăl'itỹ *n.* death by accident, in war, etc.

fāte *n.* power predetermining events from eternity; what is destined; death, destruction. *v.t.* preordain; (*p.p.*) doomed.

fāte'ful (-tf-) *a.* fraught with destiny; decisive; fatal.

fa'ther (fahdh-) *n.* male parent; forefather; originator; priest; superior of monastic house; oldest member; (pl.) elders; *F~s* (*of the Church*), Christian writers of first five centuries. *v.t.* beget; originate; pass as father or author of. **F~ Christmas,** Christmas personified as white-bearded old man with sack of Christmas presents. **~-in-law,** wife's or husband's father. **~land,** native country. **~hood** *n.*; **~lėss, ~lỹ** *aa.*

făth'om (-dh-) *n.* measure of 6 ft., esp. in soundings. *v.t.* sound (water); comprehend. **~lėss** *a.* that cannot be fathomed.

fatigue' (-ēg) *n.* weariness from exertion; wearying task. *v.t.* tire.

fătt'en *v.* make or grow fat; enrich (soil).

făttỹ *a.* of or like fat. *n.* (usu. voc.) fat person. **~ degeneration,** morbid condition with deposits of fat in tissues.

făt'ūous *a.* vacantly silly; purposeless. **fatū'itỹ** *n.*

fau'cet *n.* tap for barrel etc.

fault *n.* defect, blemish; culpability, responsibility for something wrong; offence, misdeed; (tennis etc.) ball wrongly served; (hunting) loss of scent, check; (geol.) break in continuity of strata etc.; *find ~ (with),* criticize unfavourably, complain (of); *to a ~,* excessively. *v.* cause fault in (strata etc.), show fault; find fault with. **~lėss, ~ỹ** *aa.*

faun *n.* Latin rural deity with goat's horns, legs, and tail.

fau'na *n.* (pl. -ae, -as), animals of region or epoch. **fau'nal** *a.*

fauteuil' (fōtēry) *n.* theatre stall. [F]

faux pas (fō pah) *n.* indiscreet speech or action, mistake. [F]

fā'vour (-vɛr) *n.* liking, goodwill, approval; partiality; aid; thing given or worn as mark of favour; (arch.) looks. *v.t.* regard, treat, with favour; oblige; resemble in features.

fā'vourable (-vɛr-) *a.* well disposed; commendatory; promising, auspicious, helpful, suitable.

fā'vourite (-vɛr-) *a. & n.* (person or thing) preferred above others;

(person) chosen as intimate and unduly favoured by superior; (competitor) generally thought most likely to win. **~tǐsm** *n.*

fawn¹ *n.* fallow deer in first year; light yellowish brown. *a.* fawn-coloured. *v.* bring forth fawn.

fawn² *v.i.* (of dog etc.) show affection by frisking, grovelling, etc.; lavish caresses *upon*; behave servilely.

fay *n.* (poet.) fairy.

F.B.I. *abbr.* Federal Bureau of Investigation (U.S.).

F.C. *abbr.* Football Club.

fcap, fcp *abbr.* foolscap.

F.D. *abbr., Fidei Defensor* [L], Defender of the Faith.

fē'altў *n.* duty of feudal vassal to lord; faithful adherence.

fear *n.* emotion caused by impending evil; alarm, dread. *v.* be afraid (of); revere (God); be anxious; hesitate; shrink from. **fear'ful** *a.* terrible; afraid; (colloq.) annoying etc. **fear'less** *a.* feeling no fear; brave. **fear'some** *a.* (usu. joc.) appalling.

fea'sible (-z-) *a.* practicable, possible; plausible. **~bǐl'itў** *n.*

feast *n.* religious anniversary; annual village festival; sumptuous meal; gratification, rich treat. *v.* (cause to) partake of feast; fare sumptuously; regale.

feat *n.* notable act, esp. of valour; surprising performance.

feath'er (fĕdh-) *n.* appendage of bird's skin with central shaft fringed with thin narrow barbs; plumage; feathered game; piece(s) of feathers attached to end of arrow or dart; plume worn in hat etc.; very light thing. *v.* furnish or line or coat with feather(s); turn oar so that it passes through air edgeways; manipulate (propeller etc.) to lessen air resistance etc.; **~ one's nest**, enrich oneself. **~ bed**, mattress stuffed with feathers. **~-bed**, make things easy for, pamper. **~-brain(ed), ~-head(ed)**, flighty or silly (person). **~-stitch**, zigzag embroidery stitch. **~weight**, light person or thing; boxing-weight (9 st.). **~ed, ~ў** *aa.*

fea'ture *n.* (usu. pl.) part(s) of the face, external appearance; characteristic or prominent part, article, etc.; (cine.) long film forming chief part of programme. *v.* make attraction or special feature of; exhibit as feature; take part (*in*). **~less** *a.*

Feb. *abbr.* February.

fĕb'rǐfūge *n.* medicine to reduce fever.

fē'brǐle (*or* fĕ-) *a.* of fever, feverish.

Fĕb'ruarў *n.* second month of year.

fec. *abbr., fecit, fecerunt* [L], made.

fĕck'lèss *a.* (Sc.) feeble, futile.

fĕc'ūlence *n.* dregs, scum; filth. **~ent** *a.*

fē'cŭnd (*or* fĕ-) *a.* fertile. **fĕcŭn'ditў** *n.*

fĕc'undāte (*or* fĕ-) *v.t.* make fruitful; impregnate. **~ā'tion** *n.*

fed, *p.t.* & *p.p.* of **feed**. **~ up**, (sl.) surfeited, disgusted, bored.

Fed. *abbr.* Federal; Federation.

fĕd'eral *a.* politically united, but independent in internal affairs; of central government in federation; (U.S. hist.) of Federal government or Union party in Civil War. **~ǐsm, ~ǐst** *nn.*; **~īze** *v.*

fĕd'erāte *v.* unite on federal basis or for common object. *a.* (-at), so united. **~ā'tion** *n.* federating; federal society. **~atǐve** *a.*

fĕdōr'a *n.* kind of soft felt hat.

fee *n.* sum payable to official, professional man, etc. for services; charge esp. for instruction at school, entrance for examination, etc.; inherited estate. *v.t.* pay fee to; engage for fee. **~-simple**, estate without limitation to any class of heirs; absolute possession.

fee'ble *a.* weak; deficient in character or intelligence; wanting in energy or force or effect.

feed *v.* (fĕd), supply with food; put food in mouth of; eat; graze; gratify or comfort (*with*); nourish; keep supplied, supply with, supply (*in*)*to*; (sl.) give (actor etc.) cues etc.; **~ on**, use as food, consume. *n.* feeding; pasturage; fodder; (colloq.) meal; (sl.) one who feeds actor etc. **~-back**, return to input of part of output of system or process. **~-pipe**, pipe conveying material etc. to machine. **~er** *n.*

(esp.) child's bib; tributary; feeding-apparatus in machine.

feel v. (*fĕlt*), explore or perceive by touch; be conscious of, be consciously; experience; be affected by; have pity *for*; have vague or emotional conviction; ~ *like*, (esp.) be inclined for. n. sense of touch; sensation characterizing something. **~er** n. (esp.) organ of touch in some animals; tentative suggestion.

fee'ling n. sense of touch; physical sensation; emotion; (pl.) susceptibilities; consideration for others; conviction or opinion. a. sensitive; sympathetic.

feet: see **foot**.

feign (fān) v. pretend; simulate.

feint[1] (fā-) n. sham attack, blow, etc., meant to deceive opponent; pretence. v.i. make feint.

feint[2] (fā-) a. & adv. (commerc., of lines etc.) faint(ly).

fĕld'spăr n. kinds of crystalline usu. white or flesh-red mineral.

fĕli'cĭtāte v.t. congratulate. **~ā'tion** n.

fĕli'cĭtous a. apt, well-chosen. **~cĭtў** n. happiness; happy faculty in expression.

fē'līne a. of cats or cat family; cat-like. n. feline animal.

fĕll[1] n. animal's hide or skin with hair; thick matted wool.

fĕll[2] n. wild high stretch of country in N. England etc.

fĕll[3] a. fierce; destructive.

fĕll[4] v.t. strike down; cut down (tree); stitch down (seam).

fell[5], p.t. of **fall**.

fĕll'ah (-a) n. (pl. -aheen, -ahs), Egyptian peasant.

fĕll'oe (-lǐ, -lō) n. (section of) outer rim of wheel.

fĕll'ow (-ō) n. comrade, associate; counterpart, equal; co-opted graduate member of college; member of some learned societies; (colloq.) man, boy. a. of same class; associated in joint action etc. **~-feeling**, sympathy. **~-traveller**, non-Communist sympathizer with Communism.

fĕll'owshĭp (-lō-) n. sharing; companionship; body of associates; status of college fellow.

fĕl'ō dė sē' n. self-murder.

fĕl'on n. one who has committed felony; whitlow. **fĕlō'nious** a. **fĕl'onў** n. crime graver than misdemeanour.

fĕl'spăr n. feldspar.

fĕlt[1] n. fabric of interlocked or matted fibres of wool, fur, etc. v. make into or form felt; mat together.

felt[2], p.t. of **feel**.

fĕlŭcc'a n. small Mediterranean coasting vessel with oars or lateen sails or both.

fem. abbr. feminine.

fē'māle a. of offspring-bearing sex; (of plants) fruit-bearing; of female animals or plants; fitted to receive corresponding or male part. n. female person or animal.

fĕm'ĭnine a. of women; womanly; (gram., of gender) proper to appellations of females. ~ **ending**, **rhyme**, of two syllables with second unstressed. **fĕmĭnin'itў** n.

fĕm'ĭnĭsm n. advocacy of women's rights. **~ĭst** n. & a.; **~ĭs'tic** a. **~īze** v. make or become feminine.

fĕm'oral a. of thigh.

fē'mur n. thigh-bone.

fĕn n. low marshy tract of land. **fĕnn'ў** a.

fĕnce n. enclosure or barrier along boundary of field etc.; guard in machine; receiver of stolen goods. v. practise sword play; surround (as) with fence; deal in stolen goods; ~ *with*, parry, try to evade.

fĕn'cĭble n. (hist.) soldier liable only for home service.

fĕn'cĭng n. art of sword-play; (material for) fences.

fĕnd v. ward or keep *off*; provide *for* (one*self* etc.).

fĕn'der n. thing used to keep something off, esp. frame round hearth to keep in falling coals, mat etc. hung over vessel's side, bumper or (U.S.) wing of motor-car.

fĕnėstrā'tion n. arrangement of windows in building; (surg.) perforation of medial wall of inner ear.

Fē'nian a. & n. (hist.) (member) of organization for overthrowing English government in Ireland.

fĕnn'ėc n. small N.-Afr. fox.

fĕnn'el *n.* fragrant yellow-flowered herb used for flavouring.

fens : see **fain²**.

fĕnt *n.* remnant, short end (of cloth).

fĕn'ūgreek *n.* leguminous plant with seeds used in farriery.

feoff (fĕf) *n.* fief.

fēr'al *a.* wild; savage.

fēr'ial *a.* (eccl.) not appointed for festival or fast.

fēr'ment *n.* leaven or other fermenting agent; fermentation; agitation, tumult. *v.* (-ĕnt') suffer or subject to fermentation; excite, stir up. **~ā'tion** *n.* process like that induced by leaven in dough, with effervescence, heat, and change of properties; excitement.

fēr'mium *n.* transuranic metallic element.

fĕrn *n.* kinds of vascular cryptogam freq. with feathery fronds. **~erў** *n.* place for growing ferns.

ferō'cious *a.* fierce, cruel. **ferō'cĭtў** *n.*

fĕ'rrĕt¹ *n.* kind of polecat used in catching rabbits, rats, etc. *v.* hunt with ferrets; clear out, drive out, with ferrets; rummage or search *about* (*for*), search *out*. **~ў** *a.*

fĕ'rrĕt² *n.* cotton or silk tape.

fĕ'rriage *n.* conveyance by, charge for using, ferry.

fĕ'rrĭc, fĕ'rrous *aa.* of or containing iron.

fĕrro- in comb., of or containing iron. **fĕrrō-cŏn'crēte** *n.* reinforced concrete. **~-mǎng'anēse** (-ngg-; -z) *n.* alloy of manganese and iron. **~tȳpe** *n.* (process producing) positive photograph on thin iron plate.

ferru'ginous (-rōō-) *a.* of iron-rust; rust-coloured, reddish-brown.

fĕ'rrule *n.* metal ring or cap at end of stick etc.

fĕ'rrў *v.* take or go in boat, work boat, over river, lake, etc.; fly (aircraft, passenger, etc.) from place to place, esp. on regular service or across ocean or continent. *n.* ferrying place or service; boat etc. for ferrying.

fēr'tĭle *a.* bearing abundantly; fruitful. **fertil'ĭtў** *n.*

fēr'tĭlīze *v.t.* make fertile, fecundate. **~zā'tion** *n.* **~zer** *n.* (esp.) manure.

fē'rule (-ōōl) *n.* cane or rod or esp. flat ruler for punishing children.

fēr'vent *a.* hot, glowing; ardent, intense. **fer'vencў** *n.*

fēr'vĭd *a.* glowing, impassioned.

fēr'vour (-er) *n.* vehemence, passion, zeal.

fĕs'cūe *n.* kinds of pasture grass.

fĕsse (-s) *n.* (her.) broad horizontal bar across middle of field.

fĕs'tal *a.* of feast; gay.

fĕs'ter *v.i.* generate matter; cause suppuration; rankle; rot. *n.* festering condition.

fĕs'tĭval *n.* festal day; celebration, merry-making; (periodic) series of musical etc. performances etc. of special importance.

fĕs'tĭve *a.* of feast; joyous.

fĕstĭv'ĭtў *n.* gaiety, festive celebration; (pl.) festive proceedings.

fĕstōōn' *n.* hanging chain of flowers, ribbons, etc. *v.t.* adorn with, form into, festoons.

fē'tal *a.* foetal.

fĕtch *v.* go for and bring back; draw forth; be sold for; deal (blow).

fĕtch'ing *a.* attractive.

fête (fāt) *n.* festival, entertainment. *v.t.* entertain; make much of.

fē'tĭd (*or* fĕ-), **foe'tĭd** (fē-) *a.* stinking.

fĕt'ish (*or* fē-) *n.* inanimate object worshipped by primitive peoples; anything irrationally reverenced, adored, etc. **~ism, ~ist** *nn.*

fĕt'lŏck *n.* part of horse's leg where tuft of hair grows behind pastern-joint.

fĕtt'er *n.* shackle for feet; bond; (pl.) captivity; restraint. *v.t.* bind (as) with fetters.

fĕtt'le *n.* condition, trim.

fetus : see **foetus**.

feu *n.* (Sc. law) (land held by) perpetual lease at fixed rent. **~ duty**, rent of feu.

feud¹ *n.* lasting mutual hostility esp. between two tribes or families.

feud² *n.* fief.

feu'dal *a.* of fief; of or like or according to feudal system. **~ system**, medieval European system by which land was held of superior in return for military service, homage, etc. **~ism, ~ist** *nn.*; **~is'tĭc** *a.*

feu'datory *a.* feudally subject *to.* *n.* feudal vassal.

fē'ver *n.* (disease with) bodily reaction characterized by raised temperature, restlessness, etc.; nervous excitement. **~ed** *a.* affected by fever; restless, agitated. **~ish** *a.* of or like, having symptoms of, fever; excited, fitful, restless.

fē'verfew *n.* herb formerly used as febrifuge.

few *a. & n.* not many; *not a ~,* many; *a good ~, quite a ~,* a fair number; *the ~,* the minority, the elect, etc. **~ness** *n.*

fey (fā) *a.* (Sc.) disordered in mind (freq. with over-confidence etc.) like one about to die.

fĕz *n.* red felt Turkish cap.

ff. *abbr.* folios; following (pages); *fortissimo* [It.], very loud.

F.F.I. *abbr.* free from infection.

Fg. Off. *abbr.* Flying Officer.

F.H. *abbr.* fire hydrant.

fiancé (fēahn'sā) *n.* (fem. *-ée*), one's betrothed.

fiăs'cō *n.* (pl. *-os*), failure, breakdown; ignominious result.

fi'at *n.* authorization; decree.

fib *n.* trivial lie. *v.i.* tell fib. **fĭbb'er** *n.*

fī'bre (-b*er*) *n.* thread-like filament; substance formed of fibres; structure, grain; small root or twig. **~-board,** stiff board of fibrous material. **~-glass,** glass in fibrous form for packing, insulation, etc. **fī'brous** *a.*

fī'brin *n.* insoluble protein present in clotted blood or plasma.

fī'broid *a.* like fibre or fibrous tissue. *n.* fibroid uterine tumour.

fibrosī'tis *n.* inflammation of fibrous tissue.

fĭb'ūla *n.* (pl. *-ae, -as*), bone on outer side of lower leg; (archaeol.) brooch.

fī'chu (-shoō) *n.* small triangular shawl for shoulders and neck.

fĭck'le *a.* inconstant, changeable.

fĭc'tion *n.* invention; invented statement or narrative; literature consisting of such narrative; conventionally accepted falsehood. **~al** *a.*

fĭcti'tious *a.* not genuine; assumed; imaginary.

Fid. Def. *abbr., Fidei Defensor* [L], Defender of the Faith.

fĭdd'le *n.* violin; (naut.) contrivance for stopping things from rolling off table; (sl.) artful trick or piece of cheating. *v.* play (on) fiddle; potter, move aimlessly; (sl.) falsify (accounts etc.), manipulate to one's own advantage. **~-de-dee**! nonsense! **~stick,** fiddle-bow; (usu. pl. as *int.*) nonsense. **fĭdd'ler** *n.* **fĭdd'ling** *a.* (esp.) petty, trifling.

fĭdĕl'ĭtў (*or* fī-) *n.* faithfulness, loyalty; accuracy.

fĭdg'ĕt *n.* restless state or mood; one who fidgets. *v.* move restlessly; be or make uneasy, worry. **fĭdg'ĕtў** *a.*

fĭdū'ciarў (-sha-) *a.* held or given in trust; of trust or trustee(ship); (of currency) depending on public confidence. *n.* trustee.

fie (fī) *int.* expressing sense of outraged propriety.

fief *n.* estate held on condition of homage and service to superior lord.

field *n.* (piece of) ground, esp. for pasture or tillage or playing game; tract rich in some product; scene of battle; expanse of sea, snow, etc.; area or sphere of action, operation, etc.; (her.) surface of (division of) escutcheon; all competitors or all except favourite; (crick. etc.) fieldsmen, fielders. *v.* act as fielder, stop and return (ball); put (team etc.) into field. **~-day,** (mil.) day of exercise in manœuvres etc., review; day of brilliant or exciting events. **~-dressing,** wound-dressing for use in field. **~ events,** athletic events other than races. **~fare,** kind of thrush. **~-glass(es),** binocular telescope for outdoor use. **~-gun,** light and mobile for use in field. **~-hand,** slave working on plantation; farm-labourer. **F~ Marshal,** general officer of highest rank. **~sman,** fielder at cricket etc. **~-sports,** (esp.) hunting, shooting, and fishing. **~er** *n.* one of side not batting; one who fields ball.

fiend *n.* devil; superhumanly wicked person; (sl.) person excessively addicted (esp. to something injurious). **~ish** *a.*

fierce *a.* violent in hostility; raging,

vehement; not smooth or easy in action; intense.

fiery (fīr'ĭ) *a*. consisting of fire, flaming; flashing; inflaming; irritable; spirited; (of cricket pitch) making ball rise dangerously.

fĭĕs'ta *n*. festival, holiday.

fīfe *n*. small shrill flute; fifer. *v.i.* play fife. **fī'fer** *n*.

fĭfteen' (*or* fĭf'-) *a. & n*. one more than fourteen (15, XV); Rugby football side of fifteen players. **~th** *a. & n*.

fĭfth *a. & n*. next after fourth. **~ column**, organized body working for enemy within country at war etc.

fĭf'tў *a. & n*. five times ten (50, L). **~-~**, half-and-half, equally. **~tĭeth** *a. & n*.

fĭg¹ *n*. (broad-leaved tree bearing) soft pear-shaped many-seeded fruit; valueless thing. **~leaf**, device tor concealing what is indecorous. **~wort**, brown-flowered herb.

fĭg² *v.t.* **~** *out* dress up, adorn. *n*. dress; condition.

fig. *abbr.* figurative(ly); figure.

fight *v.* (*fought*, pr. fawt), contend in battle or single combat or with fists; struggle (*for*), strive; maintain against opponent; **~** *shy of*, keep aloof from, avoid. *n*. fighting; battle; boxing-match; strife, conflict; *show* **~**, not yield tamely. **~er** *n*. (esp.) aircraft designed for combat rather than bombing etc.

fĭgh'ting *a.* (esp.) able and eager, bred or trained, to fight; engaged in fighting. **~ chance**, chance of succeeding by great effort. **~-cock**, game-cock trained to fight. **~ drunk**, pugnaciously drunk. **~ fish**, kind of Siamese fish. **~ fit**, extremely fit. **~-line**, part of armed force engaged in direct combat with enemy. **~ mad**, angry enough to fight. **~-man**, member of armed forces.

fĭg'ment *n*. invented statement; imaginary thing.

fĭg'ūrative *a.* metaphorical; emblematic; pictorial, plastic.

fĭg'ure (-ger) *n*. external form; bodily shape; image; emblem, type; diagram, illustration; evolution in dancing; character denoting

number (0, 1, 2, etc.); **~** (*of speech*) recognized abnormal form of expression giving variety, force, etc.; **~** *of speech*, metaphor etc.; piece of exaggeration. **~d** *a.* (esp., mus.) of bass, with harmonies indicated by figures under or over notes. *v.* represent in diagram or picture; imagine; calculate, estimate, be estimated; make appearance. **~head**, carved bust etc. over ship's cutwater; merely nominal leader etc.

fĭg'ūrine (-ēn) *n*. statuette.

filagree : see filigree.

fĭl'ament *n*. thread-like body, fibre; metal wire etc. inside electric lamp made incandescent by current. **~mĕn'tary**, **~mĕn'tous** *aa*.

fĭl'bert *n*. (nut of) cultivated hazel.

fĭlch *v.t.* steal, pilfer.

fīle¹ *n*. instrument for abrading or smoothing surfaces. *v.t.* smooth, reduce, remove, with file; elaborate, polish. **fī'lings** *n.pl.* particles rubbed off by file.

fīle² *n*. stiff pointed wire or other device for keeping papers for reference; papers so kept. *v.t.* place on or in file, put *away*, as record or for reference.

fīle³ *n*. (mil.) front-rank man and man or men directly behind him; (mil.) two men; row of persons or things one behind the other; (chess) line of squares across board from player to player. *v.i.* march or walk in file.

fĭl'et (-lā; *or* fē-) *n*. square-meshed net or lace.

fĭl'ĭal *a.* of or due from son or daughter.

fĭlĭā'tion *n*. parentage; descent; formation of branches, branch.

fĭl'ĭbĕg *n*. (Sc.) kilt.

fĭl'ĭbŭster *n*. person engaging in unauthorized warfare against foreign State; (U.S.) obstruction or obstructionist in legislative assembly. *v.i.* act as filibuster.

fĭl'igree, **fĭl'a-** *n*. fine ornamental tracery of gold or other wire; anything delicate and frail.

fĭll *v.* make or become full; block up (hole etc.); spread over, pervade; satisfy, satiate; occupy; adulterate;

~ *in*, complete; ~ *up*, fill completely, fill petrol-tank. *n.* full supply; enough to fill something. ~ing station, place where petrol may be bought. ~er *n.* (esp.) anything used to fill gap, increase bulk, etc.

fill'ĕt *n.* ribbon etc. for binding hair or worn round head; (pl.) animal's loins; slice or strip of boneless meat, esp. near loins or ribs, undercut of sirloin, boned and rolled middle cut of veal, etc.; (half of) one side of fish detached from backbone; (archit.) narrow flat band between mouldings. *v.t.* bind, encircle, with fillet; divide or cut into fillets.

fill'ip *n.* sudden release of bent finger or thumb from restraint of thumb or finger, slight smart stroke thus given; stimulus. *v.t.* propel with fillip; give fillip to.

fill'ỹ *n.* female foal; (sl.) girl.

film *n.* thin skin or layer; (piece or roll of) celluloid etc. coated with light-sensitive emulsion for exposure in camera; story etc. recorded on film in moving pictures; dimness over eyes; slight veil of haze etc. *v.* cover, become covered (as) with film; record with film camera. ~ camera, (esp.) camera for making motion pictures. ~-pack, photographic films arranged in pile. ~-setting, photographic composing of matter to be printed. ~-star, star actor in films. ~ỹ *a.*

fil'ter *n.* device for freeing liquid or gas from impurities by passing it through paper, charcoal, etc.; porous substance used for this; screen for absorbing light of certain colours, electrical device for suppressing certain frequencies, etc. *v.* pass through filter; (of traffic) be allowed to pass in certain direction when other traffic is held up; make way (*through, into*, etc.), leak *out*; obtain by filtering. ~-bed, tank or pond for filtering large quantities, esp. of sewage. ~-tip, (cigarette with) mouthpiece of porous material.

filth *n.* loathsome dirt; garbage; obscenity. fil'thỹ *a.*

fil'trāte *n.* filtered liquor. *v.* filter. ~ā'tion *n.*

fin *n.* organ for propelling and steering, projecting from body of fish etc.; fin-like projection on aircraft, rocket, etc.; (sl.) hand.

fin. *abbr., ad finem* [L], towards the end.

finā'gle *v.* (U.S. sl.) use, get by, trickery; wangle.

fī'nal *a.* at the end, coming last; conclusive, decisive; (gram.) expressing purpose or intention. *n.* last or deciding heat or game or competition; (also pl.) last of series of examinations; edition of newspaper published latest in day. ~ist *n.* competitor in final.

fina'lĕ (-nah-) *n.* last movement of instrumental composition; close of opera, drama, etc.

fīnăl'itỹ *n.* final act, state, or utterance; being final.

fī'nalize *v.t.* put in final form; approve final form of.

fīnănce' (*or* fī-) *n.* management of money; (pl.) pecuniary resources. *v.t.* furnish with finances or money, find capital for. fīnăn'cial (*or* fī-) *a.* fīnăn'cier (*or* fī-) *n.* one skilled in finance; capitalist.

finch *n.* kinds of small bird.

find *v.t.* (*found*), come across, meet with, obtain; discover; ascertain; determine; supply; ~ *out*, discover, detect. *n.* what is found, pleasing discovery. ~er *n.* ~ing *n.* (esp.) verdict, decision.

fin de siecle (făṅ de syākl') *a.* of end of 19th c., advanced, decadent. [F]

fine[1] *n.* sum fixed as penalty; sum paid for privilege. *v.* punish by fine.

fine[2] *a.* of high quality; pure, refined; thin, in small particles; excellent; handsome, imposing; bright, free from rain; smart, showy; fastidious. *n.* fine weather. *adv.* finely. *v.* make (beer) clear; (of liquid) become clear; (with *away, down, off*), make or become finer. ~ art, one of those appealing to sense of beauty, esp. painting, sculpture, architecture; anything requiring refined and subtle skill. ~-drawn, subtle, extremely thin. ~ gentleman, lady person of fashion; one who thinks himself above work. ~-spun, delicate, too subtle. **fi'nerў** *n.* showy dress or decoration.

finĕ**sse'** *n.* subtle management; artfulness; (whist etc.) attempt to win trick by playing lower card while holding higher. *v.* use finesse; manage by finesse; make finesse, play by way of finesse.

fing'er (-ngg-) *n.* one of terminal members of hand (usu. excluding thumb); corresponding part of glove; breadth of finger (¾ in.) as measure, small quantity of liquor; finger-like object. *v.t.* touch, turn about, with fingers; play upon (musical instrument) with fingers; mark (music) with signs showing which fingers are to be used. ~post, signpost at turning of road. ~print, impression of finger, esp. as used for identification. ~stall, cover to protect injured finger. ~ing[1] *n.* (marks indicating) proper use of fingers in playing music.

fing'ering[2] (-ngg-) *n.* kind of knitting-wool for stockings etc.

fin'ial *n.* ornamental top to gable, canopy, etc.

fin'ical, fin'icking *aa.* over-nice, fastidious; too much finished in details.

fin'is (*or* fī-) *n.* end.

fin'ish *v.* bring to end, come to end (of); perfect, put final touches to. *n.* last stage, decisive result; completed state. ~er *n.* (esp.) workman doing final operation; crushing blow etc.

fi'nite *a.* bounded, limited; (gram., of verb) limited by number and person.

finn'an (hădd'ock) *n.* smoke-cured haddock.

finn'ў *a.* like or having fins.

fiōrd, fjōrd (fy-) *n.* narrow arm of sea between cliffs.

fĭr *n.* (wood of) kinds of evergreen conifer with needles placed singly on shoots.

fīre *n.* state of combustion; flame, glow; burning fuel; conflagration; burning heat; fervour, spirit; discharge of fire-arms; *under* ~, being shot at. *v.* set fire to; catch fire;

bake, cure by artificial heat; expel, dismiss; supply with fuel; (cause to) become heated or excited; (cause to) explode; (of gun) go off; propel from gun. ~-arm, gun, pistol, etc. ~-bomb, incendiary. ~brand, piece of burning wood; kindler of strife. ~-break, area cleared of trees, buildings, etc. to stop advance of fire. ~brick, capable of withstanding great heat and used for grates etc. ~-brigade, organized body of firemen. ~-clay, used for fire-bricks etc. ~damp, (miner's name for) explosive mixture of methane and air. ~dog, andiron. ~-eater, pugnacious or quarrelsome person. ~-engine, for extinguishing fire. ~-escape, apparatus for escape from house on fire. ~fly, insect emitting phosphorescent light. ~-irons, tongs, poker, and shovel. ~man, man employed to extinguish fires; man who tends furnace etc. ~place, grate or hearth in room. ~-plug, connexion in water-main for fire-hose. ~side, space round fire-place; home life. ~-warden, officer protecting forests against fire. ~-water, alcoholic spirits. ~work, device giving spectacular effect by use of combustibles etc.; (pl.) pyrotechnic display.

fīr'ing *n.* (esp.) fuel; discharge of firearms. ~-line, front line of troops. ~-party, ~-squad, squad detailed to fire volleys at military funeral or shoot condemned man.

fĭr'kĭn *n.* small cask; half kilderkin.

fĭrm[1] *n.* partnership for carrying on business, commercial house.

fĭrm[2] *a.* of solid structure; fixed, steady; steadfast, resolute; (of offer etc.) not liable to cancellation after acceptance. *v.* solidify; fix firmly.

fĭr'mament *n.* vault of heaven. **fĭrmamĕn'tal** *a.*

fĭrst *a.* earliest in time or order; foremost in position or rank or importance. *n.* first day (*of* month); first edition; beginning; (holder of) place in first class in examination etc.; first place or prize in race etc.; best quality. *adv.* before all or something else; for the first time.

~ **aid**, given before doctor comes.
~**-fruits**, season's products as offered to God; first results. **first'ly** *adv.* first.

firth *n.* arm of sea, estuary.

fis'cal *a.* of public revenue.

fish[1] *n.* (pl. freq. same), vertebrate cold-blooded animal living in water; flesh of fish; (colloq.) person. *v.* (try to) catch fish (in); search *for*; draw *out*; seek by indirect means *for*. ~**-hook**, barbed hook for catching fish. ~**-kettle**, long oval vessel for boiling fish. ~**monger**, dealer in fish. ~**-slice**, cook's flat implement for turning or taking out fish. ~**wife**, woman selling fish.

fish[2] *n.* piece of wood for strengthening mast etc.; ~(-*plate*) flat plate of iron etc. strengthening joint etc. *v.t.* mend, join, etc. with fish.

fish[3] *n.* piece of ivory etc. used as counter in games.

fish'er *n.* animal or (arch.) person that fishes. ~**man**, one who lives by fishing; angler.

fish'ery *n.* business of fishing; fishing-ground.

fish'y *a.* of or like fish; (sl.) dubious, open to suspicion.

fiss'ile *a.* tending to split; capable of undergoing nuclear fission.

fi'ssion (-shn) *n.* (biol.) division of cell etc. as mode of reproduction; splitting of atomic nucleus. ~**able** *a.* capable of undergoing nuclear fission.

fi'ssure (-sher) *n.* cleft, split; narrow opening; cleavage. *v.* split.

fist *n.* clenched hand; (colloq.) hand, handwriting. *v.t.* strike with fist. **fis'tic(al)** *aa.* (joc.) pugilistic. **fis'ti-cuffs** *n.pl.* fighting with fists.

fis'tula *n.* pipe or spout; pipe-like ulcer.

fit[1], **fitt**, **fytte** *n.* (hist.) section of poem.

fit[2] *n.* sudden seizure of hysteria, fainting, epilepsy, etc.; violent access or outburst, capricious impulse.

fit[3] *a.* qualified, competent, worthy; becoming, proper; in good health or condition. *n.* way thing fits. *v.* be in harmony (with); be or make of or adjust to right size and shape;

join (*on*, *together*, *up*, etc.) parts that fit; adapt; make competent *for* or *to*; supply *with*; ~ *in*, make room, time, etc. for, adapt oneself, conform, be adapted; ~ *on*, try on; ~ *out*, *up*, equip. ~**ment** *n.* piece of fixed furniture. **fitt'er** *n.* (esp.) mechanic fitting together parts of engines etc.; one who makes garments etc. fit. **fitt'ing** *n.* (esp., usu. pl.) fixture, fitment; *a.* (esp.) becoming, proper.

fitch, **fitch'ew** *nn.* (fur or hair of) polecat.

fit'ful *a.* active by fits and starts; spasmodic, intermittent.

five *a.* & *n.* one more than four (5, V). ~**fold** *a.* & *adv.* ~**r** *n.* (colloq.) £5 note.

fives (-vz) *n.* game in which ball is struck with hands or bat against walls of court.

fix *v.* make firm or stable or permanent; fasten, secure; direct (eyes etc.) steadily *on*; attract and hold (attention etc.); identify, locate; settle, specify; mend, repair; arrange, make ready; do for, get even with; tamper with, arrange result of, etc., esp. by bribery. *n.* dilemma, difficult position; position determined by bearings etc.; (sl.) dose of drug.

fixa'tion *n.* fixing or being fixed; (psychol.) arrest of emotional development; obsession, obsessional attachment; conversion of atmospheric nitrogen into compounds. ~**āte'** *v.* **fix'ative** *n.* preparation for fixing esp. colours or pencil etc. drawings, or for keeping hair tidy.

fix'edly *adv.* intently. ~**edness** *n.*

fix'ings (-z) *n.pl.* (U.S.) equipment; trimmings of dress or dish.

fix'ity *n.* fixed state; stability, permanence.

fix'ture *n.* thing fixed in position; (pl.) articles annexed to land or house; (date fixed for) match, race, etc.

fizz *v.i.* hiss or splutter; effervesce. *n.* fizzing sound; effervescence; (colloq.) champagne. **fizz'y** *a.*

fizz'le *v.i.* hiss or splutter feebly; ~ *out*, come to lame conclusion. *n.* fizzling sound; fiasco.

fl. *abbr.* florin(s); *floruit* [L], flourished; fluid.

f.l. *abbr.*, *falsa lectio* [L], false reading.

Fla. *abbr.* Florida.

flăbb'ergast (-gah-) *v.t.* (colloq.) overwhelm with astonishment.

flăbb'ÿ *a.* limp, not firm; nerveless, feeble.

flăc'cĭd (-ks-) *a.* flabby. ~ĭd'ĭtÿ *n.*

flăg[1] *n.* kinds of plant with bladed or sword-shaped leaf.

flăg[2] *n.* flat slab of rock; (pl.) pavement of flags. *v.t.* pave with flags. ~-stone, flag.

flăg[3] *n.* piece of bunting etc. attached to staff or halyard as standard, ensign, or signal. *v.t.* place flag on or over, mark out with flags; signal to by waving flag etc.; ~ *down*, bring to stop thus. ~-day, on which money is raised by sale of small paper flags; (U.S.) June 14, anniversary of adoption of Stars and Stripes by Congress. ~-lieutenant, admiral's A.D.C. ~-officer, -rank, (rank of) admiral or vice- or rear-admiral. ~-ship, with admiral on board. ~-staff, pole on which flag is hung. ~-wagging, (sl.) signalling with flags held in hands.

flăg[4] *v.i.* hang down; droop; lag, lose vigour; fall off in interest.

flă'gĕllant (or flajĕl'-) *n.* and *a.* (one) who scourges himself, esp. as religious discipline. **flă'gĕllate** *v.t.* scourge. ~ā'tion *n.*

flăgeolĕt' (-jŏl-) *n.* small wind-instrument of recorder family.

flagĭ'tious *a.* deeply criminal, heinous.

flăg'on *n.* vessel to hold liquor.

flā'grant *a.* glaring, scandalous. ~ance, ~ancÿ *nn.*

flail *n.* hand threshing-implement. *v.* beat or strike (as) with flail; wave or swing wildly or erratically.

flair *n.* selective instinct for what is good, paying, etc.

flăk *n.* (German) anti-aircraft fire.

flāke *n.* light fleecy tuft or piece esp. of snow; thin broad piece; layer. *v.* fall in, sprinkle with, flakes; take, come (*off* etc.), in flakes. **flā'kÿ** *a.*

flăm'beau (-bō) *n.* (pl. *-s* or *-x*, pr. *-z*), torch.

flămboy'ant *a.* florid, gorgeous. ~ance *n.*

flăme *n.* (tongue-like portion of) ignited gas; visible combustion; bright light; passion esp. of love; sweetheart. *v.i.* emit flames; break *out*, blaze *up*, into anger; shine, gleam.

flā'men *n.* (Rom. ant.) priest of particular deity.

flamĕn'cō *n.* Spanish gipsy style of singing and dancing.

flā'ming *a.* very hot or bright; (colloq.) bloody, damned.

flamĭn'gō (-ngg-) *n.* (pl. *-oes*), tall long-necked wading-bird with slender legs and scarlet wing--coverts.

flămm'able *a.* inflammable.

flăn *n.* open tart.

flănge (-j) *n.* projecting flat rim, collar, or rib. *v.t.* provide with flange.

flănk *n.* side of body between ribs and hip; side of building, mountain, body of troops, etc. *v.t.* guard or strengthen or attack on flank; be posted or situated at side(s) of.

flănn'el *n.* (piece of) open woollen stuff, usu. napless; (pl.) (white) flannel trousers. *a.* made of flannel. **flănnelĕtte'** *n.* cotton fabric imitating flannel. **flănn'elled** (-ld) *a.* dressed in flannels.

flăp *v.* strike, drive (flies etc.), with broad thing; move (wing), be moved, up and down; beat wings; sway about, flutter. *n.* light stroke of broad thing; motion of wing etc.; broad hanging piece attached by one side only; hinged panel on trailing edge of aircraft wing; (colloq.) state of agitation or fuss. ~jack, flat round batter-cake baked on griddle; round flat powder-compact.

flăpp'er *n.* (esp.) young wild duck etc.; (sl.) girl in late teens.

flāre *v.* blaze with bright unsteady flame; (cause to) widen or spread (gradually) outwards; ~ *up*, burst into sudden blaze or anger, break out. *n.* bright unsteady light; unshaded flame in open air, esp. used as signal or guide; outburst of flame; flared shape. ~path, line of lights to guide aircraft landing or taking off. ~-up, sudden blaze or outburst.

flǎsh v. break into flame or sparks; gleam; appear or occur suddenly; move swiftly; fill or flood (stream etc.) with water. n. sudden short blaze; instant; sudden short access; emblem, usu. coloured patch or ribbon, worn esp. on shoulder of uniform; very brief news report; flash-bulb or other means of producing photographer's flashlight; ostentation. a. gaudy, showy; counterfeit; slang. ~-back, (cine. etc.) reversion, episode etc. reverting, to earlier period. ~-bulb, for producing photographer's flashlight. ~light, flashing light in lighthouse etc.; bright sudden light for photography indoors, at night, etc.; electric torch. ~point, temperature at which vapour from oil etc. will ignite.

flǎsh'ǐng n. strip of metal to obviate flooding or soaking at joint of roofing etc.

flǎsh'ў a. gaudy, tawdry.

flask (-ah-) n. pocket-bottle of metal or glass; narrow-necked bulbous bottle; vacuum flask.

flǎt¹ n. rooms usu. on one floor forming complete residence. ~let n. small flat, esp. of one room.

flǎt² a. horizontal, level; lying at full length; smooth, even; not curved or rounded or sharp; unqualified; dull; dejected; without effervescence, insipid, stale; below true pitch; fixed, unvarying. n. flat surface or part; level ground; low--lying marshy land; (pl.) level ground covered by tides or shallow water; shallow basket; section of scenery on frame; punctured tyre; (mus.) note lowered by semitone, sign (♭) indicating this. adv. downright, plainly; below true pitch; quite; ~ out, at top speed, all out. ~-fish, kinds including turbot, plaice, etc. ~foot, (U.S. sl.) policeman. ~-footed, having feet not normally arched; clumsy; determined. ~-iron, for smoothing linen. ~ race, without jumps or hurdles. ~ spin, aircraft's nearly horizontal spin (when controls are almost useless); panic, consternation. ~-top, (U.S.) air-

craft-carrier. **flǎtt'en** v. make or become flat; ~ten out, (esp.) crush, bring (aircraft) or be brought parallel with ground after dive or climb. ~tish a.

flǎtt'er v.t. fawn upon; over-praise; gratify self-esteem of; (of portrait) exaggerate good looks of. **flǎtt'erer**, ~ў nn.

flǎt'ūlent a. generating gas in alimentary canal; caused by, troubled with, accumulation of this; inflated, pretentious. ~ence, ~encў nn.

flaunt v. wave proudly; display oneself; show off, parade.

flau'tǐst n. flute-player.

flā'vour n. mixed sensation of smell and taste; distinctive taste, characteristic quality. v.t. give flavour to, season. ~ǐng n.; ~lèss a.

flaw¹ n. crack, rent; blemish; defect in document etc. v. crack, damage, mar. ~lèss a.

flaw² n. squall of wind, short storm.

flǎx n. blue-flowered plant cultivated for its seeds and for textile fibre obtained from stem; N.Z. plant with leaves yielding textile fibre. **flǎx'en** a. of flax; (of hair) very pale yellow.

flay v.t. strip off skin or hide of; peel off; criticize severely.

flea n. small wingless jumping insect feeding on human and other blood. ~-bane, kinds of plant. ~-bag, (joc.) sleeping-bag. ~-bite, bite of flea; (fig.) mere trifle. ~-bitten, (of horse) having bay or sorrel spots or flecks on lighter coat.

flěck n. spot in skin, freckle; patch of colour etc.; speck. v.t. mark with flecks.

fled, p.t. & p.p. of **flee**.

flědge v.t. provide with feathers or down. ~ling n. young bird just fledged; callow person.

flee (flē) v. (flěd), run away from; take to flight; shun.

fleece n. woolly covering, esp. of sheep; wool shorn from sheep. v.t. strip, plunder. **flee'cў** a.

fleer v.i. laugh mockingly, jeer. n. mocking look or speech.

fleet¹ n. naval armament; number of ships or boats under one commander or sailing in company;

number of vehicles or aircraft forming group or unit.

fleet² *a.* (poet.) swift, nimble.

fleet³ *v.i.* glide away, be transitory; pass or move swiftly. ~ing *a.*

Flĕm'ĭsh *a.* & *n.* (language) of Flanders.

flĕnse *v.t.* cut up and slice fat from (whale etc.); flay (seal).

flĕsh *n.* soft substance, esp. muscular parts, of animal body between skin and bones; meat; pulpy substance of fruit etc.; plumpness, fat; the body, man's physical nature. *v.t.* incite by taste of blood; initiate in bloodshed. ~ **and blood**, (material of) body; mankind; human nature; one's (*own*) near relations or descendants. ~-**and-blood**, real, living. ~-**colour**, yellowish-pink. ~**pots**, high living.

flĕsh'ings (-z) *n.pl.* close-fitting flesh-coloured garment.

flĕsh'lỹ *a.* carnal; worldly.

flĕsh'ỹ *a.* plump; of or like flesh.

fleur-de-lis (flĕr de lē') *n.* (pl. *fleurs-*, pr. as sing.), heraldic lily; royal arms of France.

flew, *p.t.* of **fly**.

flĕx¹ *v.t.* bend, esp. by action of flexors.

flĕx² *n.* flexible insulated wire for conveying electric current.

flĕx'ĭble *a.* easily bent; pliable; supple. ~**bĭl'itỹ** *n.*

flĕ'xion (-kshn) *n.* bending, bent state; bent part; inflexion. ~**al** *a.*

flĕx'or *n.* muscle that bends part of body.

flĕx'ūous, *a.* full of bends, winding. **flĕxūŏs'itỹ** *n.*

flĕ'xure (-ksher) *n.* bending, bent state; bend, curve.

flĭck *n.* light blow with whiplash, duster, etc.; jerk; slight turn of wrist; (pl., sl.) cinema. *v.t.* strike, dash *away* or *off*, deliver or play (ball), with flick; give flick with. ~-**knife**, weapon with blade held in handle by catch released with flick of finger.

flĭck'er *v.i.* shine or burn unsteadily; show fitful vibration. *n.* flickering light or motion.

flī'er, flỹ'er *n.* one that flees or flies; airman; fast animal, vehicle, etc.

flight¹ *n.* act, mode, of flying; swift movement, esp. through air; migrating body, flock, of birds or insects; swift passage of time; series (*of* stairs, hurdles for racing); volley (*of* arrows etc.); feather etc. on dart or arrow; air-force unit of about six machines; journey in aircraft. ~-**deck**, on aircraft--carrier, for taking off and landing. ~-**lieutenant**, officer of R.A.F. below squadron-leader.

flight² *n.* running away; hasty retreat.

fligh'tỹ *a.* fickle, changeable, fanciful.

flĭm'sỹ (-z-) *a.* slight, frail; paltry, shallow. *n.* thin kind of paper, reporters' copy; (sl.) banknote(s).

flĭnch *v.i.* draw back, shrink; wince.

flĭng *v.* (*flŭng*), rush, go violently; throw, hurl. *n.* throw, cast; vigorous dance; spell of indulgence in impulse.

flĭnt *n.* hard stone found in nodules; piece of flint used with steel to produce fire; flint nodule worked by prehistoric man as tool or weapon; piece of hard alloy used to produce spark in petrol lighter etc. ~-**glass**, pure lustrous kind. ~**lock**, (lock of) gun discharged by spark from flint. **flĭn'tỹ** *a.*

flĭp *n.* fillip, flick; hot sweetened mixture of spirits, eggs, etc. *v.* propel, strike, with flip; make, move with, flick.

flĭpp'ant *a.* treating serious things lightly; disrespectful. ~**ancỹ** *n.*

flĭpp'er *n.* limb used to swim with by turtle, walrus etc.; (sl.) hand.

flĭrt *v.* fillip, jerk; wave or move briskly; play at courtship (*with*). *n.* flirting movement; woman who encourages, man who pays, attentions for amusement. **flĭrtā'tion** *n.*; ~**ā'tious** *a.*

flĭt *v.i.* remove, change one's residence; pass lightly or rapidly (*about*); fly lightly and swiftly. *n.* (esp. stealthy) removal.

flĭtch *n.* side of bacon.

flĭv'ver *n.* (sl.) cheap motor-car.

float *v.* rest, drift, on surface of liquid; hover before eye or mind; (of water) support, bear along; circulate; launch (company, scheme). *n.* thing that floats or rests on surface of liquid; raft; low--bodied cart; platform on wheels; tool for smoothing plaster etc.; (pl.) footlights. **~er** *n.* (sl.) blunder, bloomer.

floatation : see flotation.

floa′ting *a.* (esp.) not settled in definite state or place; (of capital etc.) not fixed or permanently invested, not funded. **~ dock,** floating structure usable as dry dock. **~ light,** lightship. **~ rib,** not attached to breastbone in front. **~ vote,** that cannot be relied on by any party.

flŏcc′ūlent *a.* like tufts of wool.

flŏck[1] *n.* lock, tuft, of wool, etc.; powdered wool-refuse etc. **~-bed,** stuffed with flocks. **~-paper,** wall-paper sized and powdered with flock.

flŏck[2] *n.* large number of people; animals of one kind, esp. birds, feeding or travelling together; sheep or goats kept together; congregation in relation to its pastor. *v.i.* congregate, go in flocks.

flōe *n.* sheet of floating ice.

flŏg *v.t.* beat with whip, stick, etc.; cast fishing-line repeatedly over; (sl.) sell.

flood (flŭd) *n.* inflow of tide; inundation; downpour; *the F~,* great deluge recorded in Genesis. *v.* inundate; irrigate; come in great quantities. **~gate,** for admitting or excluding esp. flood-water. **~-tide,** advancing tide.

flood′-light (-ŭd-) *n. & v.t.* (illuminate with) copious artificial lighting directed on building etc.

floor (-ôr) *n.* lower surface of interior of room; rooms on one level in house; storey; level area; part of legislative chamber where members sit and speak; right of speaking; *take the ~,* speak. *v.t.* furnish with floor; knock down; confound, nonplus; overcome. **~-show,** entertainment presented on floor of night-club etc. **~-walker,** (U.S.) shop-walker.

flŏp *v.* sway about heavily and loosely; move, fall, sit, etc. *down,* awkwardly or negligently or with soft thud; (sl.) collapse, fail.

n. flopping motion and sound; (sl.) failure. *adv.* with a flop. **flŏpp′y** *a.*

flôr′a *n.* (pl. -*ae,* -*as*), (list of) plants of region.

flôr′al *a.* of flowers or floras.

florĕs′cence *n.* flowering time or state. **~ent** *a.*

flôr′ĕt *n.* any small flower of composite flower.

flôr′iāte *v.t.* decorate with floral ornament.

flôr′icŭlture *n.* cultivation of flowers. **~cŭl′tural** *a.;* **~ cŭl′turist** *n.*

flŏ′rĭd *a.* ornate, flowery; ruddy, high-coloured. **florĭd′itў** *n.*

flŏ′rĭn *n.* English two-shilling coin; (hist.) English gold coin of Ed. III.

flŏ′rĭst *n.* one who deals in, raises, or studies flowers.

flôr′uĭt (-ŏŏ-) *n.* period at which person was alive or worked.

flŏss *n.* rough silk enveloping silkworm's cocoon. **~ silk,** untwisted filaments of silk for embroidery etc. **flŏss′ў** *a.*

flotā′tion, float- *n.* floating, esp. of company or enterprise.

flotĭll′a *n.* small fleet.

flŏt′sam *n.* floating wreckage.

flounce[1] *v.i.* go with agitated or violent motion, throw body about. *n.* fling or jerk of body or limb.

flounce[2] *n.* gathered strip with lower edge hanging, esp. round woman's skirt etc.

floun′der[1] *n.* small flat-fish.

floun′der[2] *v.i.* struggle and plunge; proceed in bungling or struggling fashion.

flour (-owr) *n.* finer part of meal got by bolting. *v.t.* sprinkle with flour. **flour′ў** *a.*

flou′rish (flŭ-) *v.* grow vigorously; thrive, prosper; wave or throw about. *n.* flowing ornamental curve in writing; sweeping gesture with weapon, hand, etc.; florid passage; fanfare of horns etc.

flout *v.t.* express contempt for by word or act.

flow (-ō) *v.i.* glide along as stream; circulate; (of talk, style, etc.) move easily; (of dress etc.) hang easily; gush out; be in flood. *n.* flowing; rise of tide; copious supply.

flow′er *n.* part of plant (usu. not green) from which seed or fruit develops; (bot.) reproductive organ in plant; flowering plant; state of blooming; best part, pick *of*; prime *of*; ∼s *of speech*, ornamental phrases. *v.* produce flowers; ornament with floral design etc. **∼ĭng** *a.* (esp.) producing (conspicuous) flowers, grown chiefly for flowers.

flow′erў *a.* abounding in flowers; full of fine words.

flow′ing (-ōĭ-) *a.* (esp.) fluent, easy; (of line) smoothly continuous.

flown, *p.p.* of **fly**[2].

flu (floo) *n.* (colloq.) influenza.

flŭc′tūāte *v.i.* vary, rise and fall; be unstable. **∼ā′tion** *n.*

flue[1] (floo) *n.* fluff.

flue[2] (floo) *n.* smoke-duct in chimney; channel for conveying heat.

flu′ent (floo-) *a.* copious and ready, flowing. **flu′encў** *n.*

flŭff *n.* light feathery stuff separating from dressed wool etc.; soft fur; soft downy mass; (theatr.) fluffing. *v.* make into fluff; shake *up, out,* into fluffy mass; (sl.) blunder in theatrical part, forget or bungle (lines, cue, etc.); (sl.) bungle (stroke etc. in games). **flŭff′ў** *a.*

flu′ĭd (-oo-) *a.* moving readily, capable of flowing; not solid or rigid or stable. *n.* fluid substance; liquid, liquid secretion. **∼ ounce,** twentieth or (U.S.) sixteenth of pint. **fluĭd′ifў** *v.*; **fluĭd′itў** *n.*

fluke[1] (-oo-) *n.* parasitic flatworm in liver of sheep etc.; flat-fish, esp. common flounder.

fluke[2] (-oo-) *n.* triangular plate on arm of anchor; barbed head of lance etc.; (pl.) whale's tail.

fluke[3] (-oo-) *n.* lucky accidental stroke; stroke of (esp. good) luck. *v.* make fluke; get, hit, etc. by fluke. **flu′kў** *a.*

flume (-oo-) *n.* artificial channel for conveying water.

flŭmm′erў *n.* kinds of sweet dish; empty compliments; trifles.

flŭmm′ox *v.t.* (sl.) bewilder.

flŭmp *v.* fall or move heavily, throw *down,* with dull noise. *n.* action or sound of flumping.

flung, *p.t.* of **fling.**

flŭnk *v.* (sl.) (cause to) fail, esp. in examination.

flŭnk′ey *n.* liveried servant, footman; toady, snob.

fluorĕs′cence (floo-) *n.* coloured luminosity produced in some materials by direct action of light. **fluorĕsce′** *v.i.*; **∼ent** *a.*

flu′orīde (floo-) *n.* compound of fluorine. **fluŏ′rĭdāte** *v.t.* add fluoride to (public water-supply).

fluorine (floo′orēn) *n.* pungent corrosive gaseous element.

flu′orīte, flū′or-spăr (floo-) *nn.* translucent or transparent mineral, natural calcium fluoride.

flŭ′rrў *n.* nervous hurry, agitation; gust, squall. *v.t.* agitate, confuse.

flŭsh[1] *v.* spurt, rush out; cleanse (drain etc.) by flow of water; (cause to) glow or blush. *n.* rush of water; sudden abundance; rush of emotion, elation; (mechanism for) flushing of drain etc.; glow, blush; freshness, vigour. *a.* full, in flood; having plenty; (of money) abundant; level or even (*with*).

flŭsh[2] *n.* (cards) hand, regular sequence, of cards all of one suit.

flŭsh[3] *v.* (cause to) fly up suddenly.

flŭs′ter *v.* confuse, flurry; be in flurry. *n.* flurry, agitation.

flute (floot) *n.* (player of) wood-wind instrument, long pipe with holes stopped by keys and mouth-hole at side; flute-like organ stop; semi-cylindrical vertical groove in pillar etc. *v.* play (on) flute; whistle, sing, etc. in flute-like tones; make grooves in. **flu′ting** *n.*

flŭtt′er *v.* flap wings without flying or in short flights; descend etc. quiveringly; flit, hover; be agitated, agitate; move irregularly. *n.* fluttering; tremulous excitement; stir, sensation; (colloq.) speculation, gamble.

flu′tў (floo-) *a.* soft and clear in tone.

flu′vial (floo-) *a.* of or found in rivers.

flŭx *n.* (arch.) morbid discharge of blood, excrement, etc.; flowing; inflow of tide; continuous succession of changes; substance added, mixed with metal, etc., to assist fusion.

flŭxion (-kshn) *n.* (math.) **rate** of

change of continuously varying quantity. **~al**, **~arў** *aa*.

flȳ¹ *n*. two-winged insect; kinds of plant-disease caused by flies. **~-blown**, tainted. **~-catcher**, kinds of bird. **~-trap**, trap for flies; kinds of plant.

flȳ² *v*. (*flew*, pr. floō, *flown*, pr. -ōn), move through air with wings or in aircraft; jump clear over (fence etc.); flutter, wave, set or keep (flag) flying; travel swiftly; hasten, rush; flee; *let ~*, hurl (missile), shoot or hit or use strong language (*at*). *n*. flying; one-horse hackney-carriage; strip or lap on garment, to contain or cover button-holes; flap at entrance of tent; part of flag furthest from staff; (theatr. pl.) space over proscenium. **~-half**, (Rugby footb.) half-back who stands off from scrum-half. **~-leaf**, blank leaf at beginning or end of book. **~-over**, bridge carrying road etc. over another. **~-past**, ceremonial flight of aircraft past saluting-base etc. **~-wheel**, heavy-rimmed wheel regulating machinery. **~-weight**, boxing-weight (8 st.).

flȳ³ *a*. (sl.) knowing, wideawake.

flyer : see **flier**.

flȳ'ing *a*. & *n*. **~-boat**, seaplane with boat-like fuselage. **~ bomb**, crewless explosive-filled aircraft. **~ buttress**, slanting from pier etc. to wall and with open space below it. **~ column**, military etc. force equipped for rapid movement. **~ fish**, either of two kinds of fish which are able to rise in air. **~ fox**, kinds of fruit-eating bat found in tropical East and Australia. **~ jump**, **leap**, with running start. **~-machine**, heavier-than-air contrivance capable of being controlled in air. **~-man**, airman. **~-officer**, R.A.F. rank below flight-lieutenant. **~ saucer**, saucer-like object occas. reported as having been seen in air. **~ squad**, detachment of police organized for rapid movement. **~ start**, passing starting-point at full speed.

F.M. *abbr*. Field Marshal; frequency modulation.

F.O. *abbr*. Flying Officer; Foreign Office.

fo. *abbr*. folio.

foal *n*. young of horse, ass, etc. *v*. bear foal.

foam *n*. froth formed in liquid; froth of saliva or perspiration; (poet.) sea. *v.i.* emit foam; froth, gather foam. **foa'mў** *a*.

fŏb¹ *n*. (hist.) small pocket for watch etc. in men's breeches.

fŏb² *v.t.* palm *off*; put *off with* something inferior.

f.o.b. *abbr*. free on board.

fō'cal *a*. of, at, a focus. **~ length**, distance between centre of lens etc. and its focus.

fo'c's'le : see **forecastle**.

fō'cus *n*. (pl. -cī, -*uses*), point at which rays meet after reflection or refraction or from which rays appear to proceed; point at which object must be situated to give clearly defined image; *in ~*, situated at this point, sharply defined; focal length; adjustment of lens to produce clear image; central or originating point. *v*. (make) converge to focus; bring into focus; adjust focus of (lens, eye); concentrate (mind etc.).

fŏdd'er *n*. dried food, hay, etc. for cattle. *v.t.* give fodder to.

fōe *n*. enemy; opponent.

foe'tus (fē-) **fē'tus** *n*. developed embryo in womb or egg. **foe'tal** *a*.

foetid : see **fetid**.

fŏg¹ *n*. aftermath; rank grass.

fŏg² *n*. vapour suspended at or near earth's surface; thick mist; opaque cloudy patch on photographic negative. *v.t.* envelop (as) in fog; (photog.) cause fog on; perplex, bewilder. **~-horn**, sounding instrument for warning ships in fog. **~-signal**, detonator placed on railway-line etc. in fog as signal. **fŏgg'ў** (-g-) *a*.

fō'g(e)y (-g-) *n*. old-fashioned fellow (usu. *old ~*).

foi'ble *n*. weak point, fault; point half of sword or foil.

foie-gras (fwahgrah')*n*. = *pâté de foie gras*. [F]

foil¹ *n*. thin sheet or leaf of metal;

thing that sets another off by contrast.

foil[2] *v.* baffle, parry, frustrate.

foil[3] *n.* blunt-edged sword with button on point.

foist *v.t.* introduce surreptitiously or wrongfully; palm off *on*.

fol. *abbr.* folio.

fōld[1] *n.* enclosure for sheep; church, body of believers. *v.t.* enclose (sheep) in fold.

fōld[2] *v.* double (flexible thing) over upon itself; bend portion of; be (able to be) folded; clasp; envelop, wrap; ~ *up*, make more compact by folding, (colloq.) collapse, fail. *n.* folding; hollow between two thicknesses, among hills, etc.; coil; line made by folding. ~**ing doors**, door of two hinged parts with edges meeting. ~**er** *n.* cover for holding loose papers etc.

fōliā′ceous *a.* of or like leaves; laminated.

fō′liage *n.* leaves, leafage.

fō′liate *a.* leaf-like, having leaves. *v.*(-āt), split into laminae. ~**ā′tion** *n.*

fō′liō *n.* (pl. -*os*), leaf of paper etc. numbered only on front; page or two facing pages of ledger; sheet of paper folded once; largest-sized volume, made of such sheets; number of words (72 or 90 or (U.S.) 100) as unit in reckoning length of document. *a.* formed of sheet(s) folded once; folio-sized.

folk (fōk) *n.* nation, race; (pl.) people in general; people of specified class; relatives. ~**-custom**, ~**-dance**, ~**-song**, of the people. ~**-lore**, traditional beliefs etc.: study of these. ~**sy̆** *a.* (colloq.) of or like (customs etc. of) the people; sociable.

foll. *abbr.* following (words etc.).

fŏll′icle *n.* small sac or vesicle; cocoon. **fŏllĭc′ūlar** *a.*

fŏll′ow (-ō) *v.* go or come after; pursue; take as guide; be necessary inference; grasp meaning (of); ~ *on*, (crick., of side) be compelled by smallness of score to bat again immediately after first innings; ~ *suit*, play card of suit led, do same thing as somebody else; ~ *through*, carry stroke through

after striking ball; ~ *up*, pursue steadily or to conclusion; add to (action etc.) *with* or *by*. ~**-on**, following on.

fŏll′ower (-ōer) *n.* adherent, disciple; maidservant's admirer.

fŏll′owing (-ō-) *n.* body of adherents. *a.* now to be mentioned.

fŏll′y̆ *n.* foolishness; foolish act, conduct, idea, etc.; costly structure (considered) useless.

fomĕnt′ *v.t.* bathe with lotion, apply warmth to; foster. ~**ā′tion** *n.*

fŏnd *a.* tender, loving; doting; (arch.) foolishly credulous; ~ *of*, full of love for, much inclined to.

fŏn′dant *n.* kind of soft sweetmeat.

fŏn′dle *v.* caress.

fŏnt[1] *n.* receptacle for baptismal water; oil reservoir of lamp.

fŏnt[2] *n.* (U.S.) fount (of type).

fōod, *n.* victuals, nourishment; material for mind. ~**stuff**, material for food; (pl.) articles of food.

fōol[1] *n.* silly person, simpleton; unwise person; (hist.) jester, clown; dupe; *play the* ~, indulge in buffoonery. *v.* play the fool; trifle; cheat, dupe. ~**proof**, proof against, even fool's incompetence. ~**'s cap**, ancient jester's cap with bells; dunce's conical paper cap. ~**'s errand**, fruitless one. ~**'s paradise**, illusory happiness.

fōol[2] *n.* dish of stewed crushed fruit mixed with cream etc.

fōo′lery̆ *n.* fooling; foolish act or thing.

fōol′hardy̆ *a.* foolishly venturesome; needlessly daring.

fōo′lish *a.* void of understanding; indiscreet; stupid.

fōol′scăp *n.* long folio writing or printing paper (about $17 \times 13\frac{1}{2}$ in.).

fōot *n.* (pl. *feet*), termination of leg; *on* ~, walking, in motion; step, pace, tread; infantry; metrical unit with one syllable accented; linear measure (12 in.); lower part, base. *v.t.* add up (account); pay (bill); put (new) foot to (stocking); ~ *it*, go on foot. ~**-and-mouth (disease)**, contagious fever, esp. of horned cattle. ~**-candle**, illumination produced by standard candle at distance of one foot. ~**fall**

sound of footstep. ~-fault, (lawn-tennis) (make, declare guilty of) fault because of feet wrongly placed in serving. F~ Guards, Brigade of Guards. ~-hill, at base of mountain(s). ~hold, support for feet, surface for standing on. ~lights, along front of stage. ~-loose, unhampered by ties or obligations. ~man, liveried servant; infantryman. ~note, at foot of page. ~pad, unmounted highwayman. ~path, for pedestrians only. ~-plate, platform in locomotive for driver and fireman. ~-pound, energy needed to raise 1 lb. one foot. ~print, impression left by foot. ~rule, rigid measure one foot long. ~sore, with sore feet, esp. from walking. ~-stalk, stalk of leaf etc.; attachment of barnacle, etc. ~step, tread, footprint. ~stool, for feet of persons sitting.

foot'ball (-awl-) n. large round or elliptical inflated ball; games played with football. ~er n. foot'er n. (sl.) game of football.

foot'ing n. foothold; secure position; degree of intimacy, status, position; projecting course at foot of wall etc.

foo'tle v.i. (sl.) trifle, play the fool. foo'tling a. (esp.) trivial, insignificant.

foo'zle v.t. (sl.) bungle.

fŏp n. dandy, vain man. fŏpp'erў n. conduct etc. of fop. fŏpp'ish a.

for (fer; emphat, or at end of clause fôr; fŏr chiefly before it) prep. in place of; in defence or favour of; with view to; as regards, in direction of; because of, on account of. conj. seeing that, since. forasmŭch' as, (arch.) since, because.

f.o.r. abbr. free on rail.

fŏ'rage n. food for horses and cattle; foraging. v. collect forage (from); search for food; rummage. ~-cap, infantry undress cap.

forā'mĕn n. (pl. -mina), (anat., zool.) orifice, hole. forăm'ĭnate, ~āted aa. having foramina.

fŏ'ray n. & v.i. (make) incursion, raid.

forbade : see forbid.

fôr'bear[1] (-ār) n. (usu. pl.) ancestor(s).

forbear'[2] (-ār) v. (forbōre, -bōrne), abstain or refrain (from); be patient. ~ance n.; ~ing a.

forbid' v.t. (forbăd(e), forbidden), command not to do; not allow; prevent.

forbidd'ing a. repellent, uninviting.

fôrce[1] n. (north.) waterfall.

fôrce[2] n. strength, violence, intense effort; body of men; (pl.) troops; compulsion; influence, effectiveness. v.t. constrain, compel; strain, urge; break open by force; ravish; drive, propel; artificially hasten maturity of; impose or press (up)on (person); effect or produce by effort; ~ person's hand, compel him to act etc. prematurely or unwillingly; ~ the pace, adopt high speed in race. ~d landing, unpremeditated landing of aircraft in emergency. ~d march, requiring special effort. fôr'cĕdlў adv.

fôrce'ful (-sf-) a. forcible.

force majeure (fôrs mahzher') n. irresistible compulsion; circumstances beyond one's control. [F]

fôrce'-meat (-sm-) n. (meat chopped etc. for) stuffing.

fôr'cĕps n. (pl. same), surgical pincers; (zool.) forceps-like organ.

fôr'cible a. done by or involving force; telling, effective.

fôrd n. shallow place where river etc. may be crossed. v.t. wade across (river etc.).

fôre adv. in front. a. situated in front. n. fore part; bow of ship; to the ~, in front, conspicuous. int. (golf) warning person of ball's line of flight. ~-and-aft rigged, having ~-and-aft sails, set lengthwise, not to yards. ~-cabin, in fore part of ship.

fôre'ärm[1] n. arm from elbow to wrist.

fôreärm'[2] v.t. arm beforehand.

forebode (forbōd') v.t. betoken, portend.

forebō'ding (forb-) n. presentiment, omen.

fôrecast' (-ahst) v.t. (-cast or -ed), estimate or conjecture beforehand. n. (fôr'-) conjectural estimate, esp. of coming weather.

forecastle, fo'c's'le (fō'ksl) n. (hist.)

short raised deck at ship's bow; (crew's quarters in) forward part under deck in merchant-ship.

foreclose' (-z) v. bar (person entitled to redeem mortgage) on non-payment of money due; take away power of redeeming (mortgage). **foreclo'sure** (-zher) n.

fore'court (-kōrt) n. enclosed space before building, outer court.

foredoom' (fōrd-) v.t. doom beforehand; predestine.

forefather (fōr'fahdher) n. (pl.) ancestors, progenitors.

fore'finger (-ngg-) n. finger next thumb.

fore'foot n. front foot of beast; foremost piece of keel.

fore'front (-ŭnt) n. very front.

forego (fōrgō') v. (-wĕnt, -gŏne) precede. **fore'gŏne conclusion**, reached without necessary facts etc.; easily foreseeable result. **fore'gŏing** a. previously mentioned.

fore'ground n. part of view nearest observer.

fore'hănd n. part of horse in front of rider; forehand side or stroke. a. (tennis etc., of stroke) made with palm turned forwards; on side (usu. right) on which this is made.

fore'head (-ĕd; or fŏ'rĭd) n. part of face above eyebrows.

fŏ'reign (-rĭn) a. not of or in one's own country; of another district, parish, etc.; alien, dissimilar, irrelevant. **fŏ'reigner** n. alien, stranger; foreign ship etc.

forejŭdge' (fōrj-) v.t. judge before hearing evidence.

foreknow (fōrnō') v.t. (-knew, pr. -nū, -known), know beforehand. **foreknowledge** (fōrnŏl'ĭj) n.

fore'land n. promontory, cape.

fore'lĕg n. beast's front leg.

fore'lŏck n. lock of hair just above forehead.

fore'man n. president and spokesman of jury; workman superintending others.

fore'mast n. forward lower mast.

foremĕn'tioned (fōrm-) a. previously mentioned.

fore'mōst a. first in place or order; chief, best. adv. first.

fore'noon n. day till noon.

forĕn'sic a. of courts of law. ~ **medicine**, medical jurisprudence.

foreordain' (fōrōr-) v.t. appoint beforehand. **foreordĭnā'tion** n.

fore-rŭn' (fōr-r-) v.t. (-răn, -rŭn), be precursor of, foreshadow. ~**ner** n.

foresail (fōr'sl, -sāl) n. principal sail on foremast.

foresee (fōrsē') v.t. see beforehand.

foreshadow (fōrshăd'ō) v.t. prefigure, be type or presage of.

fore'shore n. shore between high and low water marks.

foreshor'ten (fōrsh-) v.t. (of visual perspective) cause apparent shortening in (object); represent thus in drawing.

foreshow (fōrshō') v.t. (p.p. -shown), foretell, foreshadow.

fore'sight n. foreseeing; provident care.

fore'skin n. prepuce.

fŏ'rĕst n. large tract covered chiefly with trees and undergrowth. v.t. plant with trees; make into forest. ~**er** n. officer in charge of forest; dweller in forest. ~**rў** n. science and art of managing forests.

forestall (fōrstawl') v.t. be beforehand with; anticipate.

fore'stay n. stay from foremast-head to ship's stem.

fore'tāste n. partial enjoyment or suffering in advance. v.t. (-āst') have foretaste of.

foretĕll' (fōrt-) v.t. (-tōld), predict, prophesy; be precursor of.

forethought (fōr'thawt), n. provident care; deliberate intention.

fore'tŏp n. top of foremast.

forĕv'er adv. always, constantly.

forewarn (fōrwōrn') v.t. warn beforehand.

forewent, p.t. of **forego**.

forewoman (fōr'wŏoman) n. (hist.) president of jury of matrons; workwoman supervising others.

foreword (fōr'werd), n. preface.

fŏr'feit (-fĭt) a. lost owing to crime or fault. n. forfeited thing; fine, penalty; (pl.) game in which player redeems forfeit by performing ludicrous task. v.t. pay or surrender as penalty.

fŏr'feiture (-fĭt-) n. forfeiting.

fŏrfĕnd' v.t. avert.

forgăth'er (-dh-) *v.i.* assemble, associate, converse.

forgave, *p.t.* of **forgive.**

forge[1] *v.i.* advance gradually; ~ *ahead,* take lead.

forge[2] *n.* smithy; furnace or hearth for melting or refining metal. *v.* shape by heating in fire and hammering; invent (tale, lie); counterfeit.

for'gery *n.* forging or falsifying of document; forged thing.

forgět' (-g-) *v.* (-*gŏt,* -*gŏtten*), lose remembrance of; neglect, overlook; ~ *oneself,* act presumptuously, unworthily, etc., lose consciousness. ~-**mė-nŏt,** plant with small blue flower.

forgět'ful (-g-) *a.* apt to forget.

forgive' (-g-) *v.t.* (-*gāve,* -*gĭven*), pardon; remit. ~**ness** *n.* pardon.

forgō' *v.t.* (-*wĕnt,* -*gŏne*), go without, relinquish.

fork *n.* pronged implement for digging etc.; pronged instrument used in eating, cooking, etc.; tuning fork; bifurcation, divergence into branches; forked part, esp. of bicycle frame. *v.* form fork; branch; dig with fork; ~ *out,* (sl.) hand over, pay. ~-**lift,** mechanical device for lifting and moving heavy objects.

forlŏrn' *a.* forsaken; in pitiful condition. ~ **hope,** storming-party; desperate enterprise.

fŏrm *n.* shape, arrangement of parts, visible aspect; class in school; set order of words; document with blanks to be filled up; formality; behaviour according to rule or custom; (of horse, athlete, etc.) good condition or style; bench; hare's lair. *v.* fashion, mould; take shape, become solid; make up, amount to; (mil.) draw up in order, assume (formation).

fŏr'mal *a.* of or concerned with form; according to recognized form(s) or rule(s); ceremonial, conventional; done as a matter of form, perfunctory; prim, stiff. ~**ism,** ~**ist** *nn.* strict observance, observer, of forms; criticism, critic, concerned with form rather than content.

formăl'dėhȳde *n.* colourless gas used in solution as preservative and disinfectant. **fŏr'malin** *n.* aqueous solution of this.

formăl'ity *n.* formal act or conduct; primness, precision.

fŏr'malize *v.t.* make formal; give definite form to.

fŏr'măt (*or* -mah) *n.* shape and size of book etc.

fŏrmā'tion *n.* forming; thing formed; parts or units formed into body or group; disposition of troops etc.

fŏr'mative *a.* serving to form; (of suffix etc.) used in forming words. *n.* formative element.

fŏrme *n.* body of type locked up in chase for printing.

fŏr'mer, *a.* of the past, earlier; first-named. *pron. the* first or first-named of two. ~**ly** *adv.*

fŏr'mic *a.* of ants. ~ **acid,** colourless irritant volatile acid used in tanning etc.

fŏr'midable *a.* to be dreaded; difficult to overcome, resist, etc.

fŏrm'less *a.* without distinct or regular form.

fŏr'mula *n.* (pl. -*ae,* -*as*), systematic or set form of words or symbols; recipe; rule, principle, constitution, etc., expressed in symbols and figures.

fŏr'mulary *a.* & *n.* (collection) of formulas or set forms.

fŏr'mulate *v.t.* reduce to or express in formula; set forth systematically. ~**ā'tion** *n.*

fŏr'nicate *v.i.* commit fornication, ~**ā'tion** *n.* sexual intercourse between man and unmarried woman. ~**ātor** *n.*

forsāke' *v.t.* (-*sŏŏk,* -*sāken*), give up, renounce; desert, abandon.

forsōōth' *adv.* (arch.) no doubt, indeed.

forswear' (-swār) *v.t.* (-*swōre,* -*swōrn*), abjure, renounce; perjure one*self*; (*p.p.*) perjured.

forsȳ'thia *n.* kinds of spring-flowering ornamental shrub with bright-yellow flowers.

fŏrt *n.* fortified place (usu. single building); trading-station.

fŏrte[1], *n.* one's strong point.

fŏr'tė[2] (mus. direction) loud; *double*

~, very loud. ~-*piano*, loud, then immediately soft. [It.]

forth *adv.* forward(s); out of doors; onwards in time. ~**coming**, about or likely to come forth; approaching; ready to make or meet advances. ~**right**, going straight, unswerving; outspoken; decisive. ~**with**, immediately, without delay.

fortieth : see **forty**.

fortifica′tion *n.* art of fortifying; (usu. pl.) defensive work(s).

for′tify *v.t.* strengthen; provide with defensive works; confirm (statement); strengthen (wine etc.) with spirits.

fortiss′imo, *adv.* (mus. direction) very loud. *a. & n.* very loud (passage). [It.]

for′titude *n.* courage in pain or adversity.

fort′night *n.* two weeks. ~**ly** *adv. & a.* (happening, appearing) once a fortnight.

for′tress *n.* military stronghold.

fortu′itous *a.* due to chance. **fortu′ity** *n.*

for′tunate *a.* lucky, prosperous, auspicious.

for′tune (*or* -choŏn) *n.* chance as power in men's affairs; luck; prosperity, wealth; large sum of money; coming lot. *v.i.* happen; come by chance *upon*. ~**-hunter**, man seeking rich wife. ~**-teller**, foreteller of future.

for′ty *a. & n.* four times ten (40, XL). ~ **winks**, short nap. **for′tieth** *a. & n.*; ~**fold** *a. & adv.*

for′um *n.* place of public discussion; court, tribunal.

for′ward *a.* in or of fore part of ship; in front; towards front; well--advanced; ready, prompt; pert. *n.* (footb. etc.) first-line player. *adv.* towards future; to front; progressively. *v.t.* help forward, promote; send (letter etc.) on; dispatch. ~**er** *n.* ~**s** *adv.* forward.

forwent, *p.t.* of **forgo.**

forworn′ *a.* (arch.) tired out.

fosse *n.* canal, ditch, trench.

foss′ick *v.i.* (Austral. sl.) rummage, search.

foss′il *n.* remains of plant or animal preserved in earth's crust; fossil person or thing. *a.* fossilized; belonging to past, esp. former geological period; antiquated. ~**ize** *v.* turn into, preserve as, fossil. ~**iza′tion** *n.*

fos′ter *v.t.* encourage, harbour (feeling); cherish. ~**-brother, -sister,** boy, girl, brought up with child of different parentage. ~**-child, -daughter, -son,** child as related to foster-parents. ~**-father, -mother, -parents,** person(s) raising child of other parents as their own.

fought, *p.t. & p.p.* of **fight.**

foul *a.* offensive, loathsome, stinking; dirty, soiled; charged with noxious matter; clogged, choked; morally polluted; obscene; unfair, against rules; (of weather) wet, rough; (naut.) in collision, entangled, etc.; *fall* ~ *of*, come into collision with. *n.* collision, entanglement, in riding, rowing, etc.; foul blow, stroke, etc. *adv.* unfairly. *v.* make or become foul; entangle; become entangled; collide with; block. ~**-mouthed**, given to foul language. ~ **play**, unfair play; treacherous dealing, violence, murder.

fou′lard (fōō-) *n.* thin soft smooth material of silk etc.

foul′ly (-l-li) *adv.* vilely, cruelly.

fou′mart (fōō-) *n.* polecat.

found[1] *v.t.* lay base of; establish, originate; base, build up. **foun′der**[1], ~**ress** *nn.* one who founds institution(s) etc.

found[2] *v.t.* melt and mould (metal), fuse (materials for glass); make thus. **foun′der**[2] *n.*

found[3], *p.t. & p.p.* of **find.**

founda′tion *n.* origination; endowed institution; solid ground or base; basis. ~ **garment**, woman's supporting undergarment. ~**-stone**, esp. one laid with ceremony. ~**er** *n.* participant in revenues of foundation.

founder[1,2]: see **found**[1,2].

foun′der[3] *v.* (of ship) fill with water and sink; fall down, give way; (of horse) collapse, fall lame; cause (horse, ship) to founder.

found′ling *n.* deserted infant of unknown parents.

foundress : see **found**[1].

foun'dry *n.* factory or workshop for founding metal, glass, etc.

fount[1] *n.* complete set of printing type of one size and face.

fount[2] *n.* spring, source, fountain.

foun'tain (-tǐn) *n.* spring; source; artificial jet of water. ~**-head**, chief or original source. ~**-pen**, with ink reservoir.

four (fōr) *a.* & *n.* one more than three (4, IV); four-oared boat or its crew; (pl.) military formation four deep. ~**-flusher**, (U.S.) pretender, humbug. ~**-in-hand**, vehicle with four horses and no outrider; kind of necktie. ~**-poster**, bed with four tall posts. ~**some**, game between two pairs, (colloq.) party of four; *a.* (of Scotch reel etc.) performed by four persons. ~**-square**, firmly placed, steady. ~**-wheeler**, four-wheeled horse-drawn cab. ~**fold**, *a.* & *adv.*

four'teen (fōr-; *or* -ēn') *a.* & *n.* one more than thirteen (14, XIV). ~**th** *a.* & *n.*

fourth (fōrth) *a.* & *n.* next after third; quarter, one of four equal parts. ~**ly** *adv.*

fowl *n.* kinds of bird kept to supply eggs and flesh for food; bird. *v.i.* hunt, shoot, or snare wildfowl. ~**ing-piece**, light gun used in fowling. ~**-pest**, infectious disease of fowls. ~**er** *n.*

fŏx *n.* red-furred quadruped preserved as beast of chase; crafty person. *v.* act craftily; deceive; discolour with brown spots. ~**glove**, tall plant with purple or white flowers. ~**-hole**, (mil.) hole in ground as shelter against missiles or as firing-point. ~**hound**, bred to hunt foxes. ~**-hunt**, ~**-hunting**, chasing of fox with hounds. ~**-tail**, kinds of grass. ~**-terrier**, small short-haired terrier bred for unearthing foxes. ~**-trot**, ballroom dance based on fast or slow walking-steps.

fŏx'glove (-ŭv) *n.* tall handsome plant with spikes of purple or white flowers.

fŏx'ў *a.* fox-like; crafty(-looking); reddish-brown; foxed.

foy'er (-ā; *or* fwah'yā) *n.* large room in theatre etc. for use in intervals.

F.P. *abbr.* field punishment; fire-plug.

fp. *abbr.*, *forte-piano* [It.], loud, then soft.

Fr. *abbr.* Father; French.

fr. *abbr.* franc(s).

frăb'jous *a.* (colloq.) joyful, glorious.

frā'cas (-kah) *n.* (pl. same), noisy quarrel.

frăc'tion *n.* numerical quantity that is not integer; small part, amount, etc. ~**al** *a.* of fraction(s), very small; ~**al distillation**, separation of mixture into fractions having different boiling-points. ~**āte** *v.t.* separate into fractions of differing properties. ~**ā'tion** *n.*

frăc'tious *a.* unruly, peevish.

frăc'ture *n.* breaking or breakage, esp. of bone. *v.* cause fracture in, be fractured.

frā'gǐle *a.* easily broken; of delicate constitution. **fragǐl'itў** *n.*

frăg'ment *n.* part broken off; isolated or incomplete part or piece. *v.t.* break into fragments. ~**arў** *a.*; ~**ā'tion** *n.*

frā'grance *n.* being fragrant; perfume.

frā'grant *a.* sweet-smelling.

frail[1] *n.* rush basket for figs, raisins, etc.

frail[2] *a.* fragile, delicate; morally weak, unchaste. ~**tў** *n.* liability to yield to temptation; weakness, foible.

frāme *v.t.* shape, direct, dispose; adapt, fit; construct; articulate (words); form in mind; set in frame; serve as frame for; concoct false accusation or contrive evidence against. *n.* construction, make, build; case, border, enclosing picture etc.; glazed structure to protect plants; skeleton, substructure; single picture on cinema film or transmitted by television. ~ **aerial**, of wires on wooden framework. ~**-house**, of wooden framework covered with boards etc. ~**-up**, (sl.) conspiracy. ~**work**, frame, substructure.

frănc *n.* French, Belgian, and Swiss monetary unit.

fran'chise (-z) *n*. right to vote; citizenship; (hist.) privilege.

Francis'can *a. & n.* (member) of order of St. Francis.

fran'cium *n*. (chem.) radioactive element of alkali-metal group.

franc'olin *n*. kinds of partridge.

fran'gipane, frangipan'i (-j-) *n*. perfume of red jasmine; kinds of pastry or sweetmeat of almonds, cream, etc.

frank[1] *a*. candid, open, sincere; undisguised.

frank[2] *v.t.* put mark or signature on (letter etc.) to ensure free delivery; stamp; facilitate passage etc. of. *n*. (hist.) franking signature, franked cover.

frank'furter *n*. highly seasoned smoked sausage.

frank'incense *n*. aromatic gum resin burnt as incense.

frank'lin *n*. (hist.) landowner of free but not noble birth.

fran'tic *a*. wildly excited by pain, joy, etc.; violent.

frater'nal *a*. of brothers, brotherly. **~nity** *n*. brotherliness; religious body; guild; (U.S.) college or school society. **frat'ernize** *v.i.* associate, make friends.

frat'ricide *n*. killing, killer, of brother or sister.

fraud *n*. criminal deception; dishonest trick; disappointing person etc. **~ulence** *n*.; **~ulent** *a*.

fraught (frawt) *a*. **~ with**, involving, threatening (disaster etc.), full of.

fray[1] *n*. fight, conflict; brawl.

fray[2] *v*. rub; make or become ragged at edge.

frazz'le *n*. worn or exhausted state.

F.R.C.M., F.R.C.O. *abbr.* Fellow of Royal College of Music, of Organists.

F.R.C.P.(E.), F.R.C.S.(E.) *abbr.* Fellow of Royal College of Physicians (of Edinburgh), of Surgeons (of Edinburgh).

freak *n*. caprice, vagary; monstrosity; eccentric person. *a*. that is a freak; abnormal, monstrous, freakish. **~ed** (-kt) *a*. oddly flecked or streaked. **~ish** *a*.

freck'le *n*. light brown spot on skin. *v*. spot, become spotted, with freckles.

free *a*. (*freer, freest*, pr. -eer, -eïst), not in bondage; at liberty; (of translation) not literal; clear of obstructions; disengaged, available; spontaneous; lavish, unreserved; not charged for. *adv*. freely; without cost or charge. *v.t.* (*freed*), make free, set at liberty; disentangle. **~-board**, part of ship's side between waterline and deck. **F~ Church**, Protestant church unconnected with State. **~ hand**, absolute discretion. **~-hand**, (of drawing) done without ruler, compasses, etc. **~lance**, unattached journalist etc.; person working for himself and not employer. **~man**, holder of freedom *of* city etc. **~ port**, open to all traders alike. **~stone**, fine-grained sandstone or limestone easily cut or sawn. **~-thinker**, rejector of authority in religious belief. **~ trade**, commerce left to its natural course without customs duties. **~-wheel**, (in bicycle) driving-wheel able to revolve while pedals are at rest; *v.i.* ride bicycle with pedals stationary, drive car with clutch disengaged. **~ will**, power of directing one's actions voluntarily.

free'booter *n*. pirate.

free'dom *n*. personal or civil liberty; liberty of action; undue familiarity; franchise; participation in privileges of citizenship *of* borough etc.

free'hold *n*. land etc. held by owner in absolute possession; this tenure. **~er** *n*.

free'martin *n*. hermaphrodite or imperfect female of ox kind.

Free'mason *n*. member of fraternity having elaborate ritual and secret signs. **freema'sonry** *n*. system and institutions of Freemasons; secret or tacit brotherhood, instinctive sympathy.

free'sia (-z-) *n*. fragrant flowering plant of iris kind.

freeze *v*. (*froze, frozen*), (cause to) become, be covered with, ice; be cold enough for water to become ice; become cold or rigid, congeal, chill or be chilled, by frost, cold, fear, etc.; feel extreme cold; preserve by refrigeration; make (assets etc.) unrealizable, stabilize (prices etc.); ~ **out**, exclude or eliminate by competition, coldness, etc.; ~ *up*, freeze hard, immobilize or make unusable etc. by freezing. *n.* state, coming, period, of frost or freezing or being frozen; *deep* ~, (part of) refrigerator kept at very low temperature. ~**-up** (period of) being frozen up. ~**zing** *a.* (esp.) very cold; chilling, distant; ~**zing- -point**, temperature at which water freezes.

freight (frāt) *n.* (charge for) hire of ship for transporting goods; ship- -load, load; transport of goods by water or (U.S.) land; (U.S.) freight train. *v.t.* load (ship etc.). ~ **train**, (U.S.) goods train. ~**age** *n.* hire or hiring of ship etc. for, cost of, con- veyance of goods. ~**er** *n.* (esp.) cargo ship.

French *a.* of France or its people or language; *take* ~ *leave*, act, go away, without permission or notice. *n.* French language. ~ **bean**, kidney or haricot bean. ~ **chalk**, finely powdered talc as lubricant etc. ~ **horn**, brass wind instrument with long tube coiled in circle. ~**-polish**, (polish with) solution of shellac and methylated spirit pro- ducing high gloss. ~ **window**, glazed folding door(s).

frĕnĕt'ĭc *a.* frantic, frenzied.

frĕn'zŷ *n.* delirious fury; wild folly. **frĕn'zied** *a.* driven to frenzy, in- furiated.

frē'quencŷ *n.* frequent occurrence; (phys.) rate of recurrence (of vibration etc.); (electr.) number of cycles per second of alternating current or potential.

frē'quent[1] *a.* often occurring, com- mon; numerous; habitual.

frĕquĕnt'[2] *v.t.* go often or habitually to. **frĕquentā'tion** *n.* ~**ative** *a.* expressing frequent repetition; *n.* such verb. ~**ĕd** *a.* much resorted to.

frĕs'cō *n.* (method of) painting in water-colour on fresh plaster. *v.t.* paint thus.

frĕsh *a.* new, novel; not stale or faded; vigorous; inexperienced; unsullied; refreshing; (U.S. sl.) pre-

sumptuous, forward. *adv.* freshly. ~**en** *v.*

frĕsh'ĕt *n.* river flood.

frĕsh'lŷ *adv.* recently; vigorously; with fresh appearance.

frĕsh'man (-an), **frĕsh'er** (sl.) *nn.* university student in first year.

frĕt[1] *n.* pattern of straight lines joined usu. at right angles. *v.t.* variegate, chequer; ornament. ~**saw**, very narrow saw stretched in frame for cutting thin wood in ornamental patterns etc. ~**work**, wood or stone cut in patterns.

frĕt[2] *v.* gnaw; wear by rubbing; chafe, worry; waste away. *n.* irritation, vexation. ~**ful** *a.* querulous.

frĕt[3] *n.* bar or ridge on fingerboard of guitar etc.

Freu'dian (-oid-) *a.* of Freud's system of psycho-analysis; (colloq.) sexual, sexy. *n.* disciple of Freud.

Fri. *abbr.* Friday.

frī'able *a.* easily crumbled. ~**bil'itŷ** *n.*

frī'ar *n.* brother or member of esp. mendicant religious order. ~**ŷ** *n.*

frĭbb'le *v.i.* trifle. *n.* trifler.

fricassee' *n.* dish of fried or stewed cut-up meat with sauce. *v.t.* make fricassee of.

frĭc'ative *a.* made by friction of breath in narrow opening. *n.* fricative consonant.

frĭc'tion *n.* rubbing of two bodies; (phys. etc.) resistance to relative motion of surfaces in contact; (fig.) disagreement; attrition; chaf- ing as medical treatment etc.

Frī'day *n.* sixth day of week; *Good* ~, Friday before Easter.

frĭdge, frĭg (-j) *nn.* (colloq.) refri- gerator.

friend (frĕnd) *n.* one joined to another in intimacy and affection; one who is on same side; (pl.) rela- tions; sympathizer, helper; *F*~, Quaker. ~**lĕss** *a.*

friend'lŷ (frĕ-) *a.* acting or disposed to act as friend; on amicable terms. ~ **society**, association assisting members in sickness, old age, etc.

friend'ship (frĕ-) *n.* friendly relation of feeling.

frieze[1] *n.* coarse woollen cloth with nap.

frieze² *n.* member of entablature between architrave and cornice; band of decoration.

frig : see **fridge**.

frig′ate *n.* (hist.) warship next in size to ships of line; cruiser; large corvette. **~-bird,** large tropical raptorial sea-bird.

fright *n.* sudden or violent fear; grotesque-looking person.

frigh′ten *v.t.* throw into fright; drive *away, into,* etc. by fright; (*p.p.*) affected with fright *at* or *of.*

fright′ful *a.* dreadful, shocking; ugly; (sl.) great, awful.

fri′gid *a.* intensely cold; lacking ardour; repellent. **frigid′itў** *n.*

frill *n.* fluted strip of woven material gathered at one edge; (pl., colloq.) airs, unnecessary elaboration. **~ed, ~ў** *aa.* **~ing** *n.* (material for) frills.

fringe (-j) *n.* bordering of loose threads, tassels, or twists; front hair cut short over forehead; border, outskirts, margin; (attrib.) extra, supplementary, secondary. *v.t.* adorn with fringe; serve as fringe to.

fripp′erў *n.* finery, needless or tawdry ornament; trifles.

frisk *v.* move sportively, gambol; search. *n.* gambol. **~ў** *a.* lively.

fritill′arў (*or* frit′-) *n.* meadow plant of lily kind; kinds of butterfly.

fritt′er¹ *n.* fried batter, often containing sliced fruit etc.

fritt′er² *v.t.* throw *away* in trifling and wasteful way.

friv′olous *a.* paltry, trifling; futile; silly. **frivŏl′itў** *n.*

frizz¹ *v.i.* sputter in frying. **frizz′le¹** *v.* fry, toast, grill, with sputtering noise.

frizz² *v.* crisp (hair), form into mass of small curls. *n.* frizzed hair or state. **frizz′le²** *v.* frizz (hair), curl (*up*) crisply; *n.* frizzled hair. **~ў** *a.*

Frl. *abbr., Fraülein* [G.], Miss.

frō *adv.* to and **~,** backwards and forwards.

frŏck *n.* monk's gown, (fig.) priestly character; woman's or esp. child's dress. **~-coat,** man's long-skirted coat.

frŏg¹ *n.* tailless amphibian with long web-footed hind legs. **~man,** underwater swimmer wearing long rubber shoes like frog's hind feet; **~-march,** carry (prisoner) face downwards with four men each holding a limb.

frŏg² *n.* elastic horny substance in middle of horse's sole.

frŏg³ *n.* attachment to waist-belt to support sword; military coat-fastening of spindle-shaped button and loop.

frŏl′ĭc *a.* (arch.) mirthful. *v.i.* play pranks, gambol. *n.* prank, merry-making. **~some** *a.* sportive.

from (from, *emphat. or at end of clause* frŏm) *prep.* out of; because of; at a distance; since, ever since.

frŏnd *n.* leaf-like organ of ferns etc. **~age** *n.;* **~ōse′** *a.* frond-like.

front (-ŭnt) *n.* face; fore part; forward position or situation; scene of actual fighting; combination of forces etc. to achieve end; (meteor.) boundary between warm-air and cold-air masses; part of seaside resort facing sea; part of theatre where audience sits; false hair over forehead; false shirt-front; disguise. *a.* of or at front. *v.* face, look; confront, oppose; furnish with front. **~ door,** principal entrance.

fron′tage (-ŭn-) *n.* land abutting on street or water; extent of front; front of building.

fron′tal (-ŭn-) *a.* of or on front; of forehead. *n.* covering for altar-front; façade.

fron′tier (-ŭn-) *n.* boundary between states; border of settled or inhabited part. *a.* of or on frontier. **~sman,** one living on frontier of civilization.

fron′tispiece (-ŭn-) *n.* illustration at beginning of book etc.

front′let (-ŭn-) *n.* band worn on forehead; phylactery.

front′ward (-ŭn-) *a.* looking to front. *adv.* towards front.

frŏst *n.* freezing; frozen dew or vapour; (sl.) failure, fiasco. *v.t.* injure with frost; cover (as) with frost; ice (cake etc.); roughen surface of (glass etc.), make opaque. **~bite,** inflammation of skin etc. from frost. **~ing** *n.* (esp.) icing for cakes. **~ў** *a.*

frŏth *n.* foam; scum; idle talk. *v.i.* emit or gather foam. ~ў *a.*

frown *v.* knit brows; express disapprobation. *n.* wrinkled brows; look of severity, deep thought, etc.

frowst *n.* (colloq.) close and fusty atmosphere. ~ў *a.*

frow'zў *a.* fusty; slatternly, dingy.

froze(n), *p.t.* & *p.p.* of freeze.

F.R.S. *abbr.* Fellow of Royal Society.

frŭc'tĭfў *v.* bear fruit; make fruitful. ~fĭcā'tion *n.* fructifying; reproductive parts of fern etc.

frŭc'tōse *n.* kind of sugar found in fruits and honey.

fru'gal (frōō-) *a.* sparing, economical. frugăl'itў *n.*

fruit (frōōt) *n.* (usu. pl.) vegetable products fit for food; (esp. edible and juicy or pulpy) seed of plant with its envelope; product, result. *v.i.* bear fruit. ~-cake, etc., containing currants, raisins, etc. ~ machine, kind of slot-machine for gambling. ~-sugar, fructose. ~ār'ian *a.* & *n.* (of) one who lives on fruit. ~erer *n.* dealer in fruit. ~ful *a.* fertile, prolific; remunerative. ~less *a.* not bearing fruit; useless, vain.

fruĭ'tion (frōō-) *n.* realization of hopes etc.

fruĭ'tў (-ōō-) *a.* of fruit; (of wine) tasting of grape; of strong or rich quality.

fru'mentў (frōō-) *n.* dish of hulled wheat boiled in milk and sweetened.

frŭmp *n.* old-fashioned dowdily-dressed woman. ~ish, ~ў *aa.*

frŭstrāte' *v.t.* baffle, counteract, foil. ~ā'tion *n.*

frŭs'tum *n.* (pl. -ta, -tums), part of regular solid cut off by plane parallel to base.

frӯ[1] *n.* young fishes fresh from spawn; *small* ~, young or insignificant beings.

frӯ[2] *v.* cook in boiling fat. *n.* fried fish etc.; internal parts of animals, usu. eaten fried. ~ing-pan, shallow long-handled pan for frying.

F.S. *abbr.* Fleet Surgeon.

F.S.R. *abbr.* Field Service Regulations.

ft. *abbr.* feet, foot.

fuchsia (fū'sha) *n.* drooping-flowered ornamental shrub.

fū'cus *n.* (pl. -ci, pr. -sī), kinds of seaweed with flat fronds.

fŭdd'le *v.t.* intoxicate; stupefy, confuse.

fŭdd'ў-dŭddў *n.* & *a.* fussy or old-fashioned (person).

fŭdge *v.t.* patch, make *up*, in makeshift way. *n.* nonsense; kind of soft toffee.

fū'el *n.* material for fire; thing that feeds passion etc.

fŭg *n.* stuffy atmosphere.

fūgā'cious *a.* fleeting, elusive. fūgă'citў *n.*

fū'gal *a.* of, like (that of), fugue.

fū'gĭtive *a.* fleeing; fleeting, transient. *n.* one who flees (*from*).

fugue (fūg) *n.* (mus.) polyphonic composition with theme taken up successively by different parts; (psychol.) period of disappearance or wandering, freq. with loss of memory.

führer (fūr'er) *n.* leader; despot, (petty) tyrant.

fŭl'crum *n.* (pl. -ra), point against or on which lever is placed to get purchase or support.

fulfĭl' (fōō-) *v.t.* bring to pass; carry out; satisfy; bring to end. ~ment *n.*

fŭl'gent *a.* shining.

fūlī'gĭnous *a.* sooty, dusky.

full[1] (fōōl) *a.* filled to capacity; replete; crowded; copious; complete, perfect, entirely visible; swelling. *adv.* quite, exactly. ~ back, (position of) football player placed behind half-backs. ~-blooded, vigorous, hearty, sensual. ~-blown, quite open. ~-bottomed, (of wig) long and full behind. ~ brother, etc., having same father and mother. ~-dress debate, formal prearranged (esp. parliamentary) debate. ~ stop, complete cessation; punctuation mark used at end of sentence.

full[2] (fōōl) *v.t.* clean and thicken (cloth). ~er *n.*; ~er's earth, kind of clay used in fulling.

full'ў (fōō-) *adv.* completely.

ful'mar (fōōl-) *n.* kind of petrel.

fŭl'mĭnant *a.* fulminating; (of disease) developing suddenly.

fŭl′mĭnāte *v.* flash, explode, detonate; (fig.) thunder forth, issue censures. *n.* (esp.) very sensitive explosive (~ *of mercury*) used in detonators. **~ā′tion** *n.*

ful′some (foŏ-) *a.* cloying, disgusting by excess.

fŭl′vous *a.* tawny.

fū′marōle *n.* smoke-hole in volcano.

fŭm′ble *v.* grope about; handle or deal with awkwardly.

fūme *n.* odorous smoke, vapour, or exhalation; fit of anger. *v.* subject to fumes; darken (oak etc.) thus; chafe, fret. **fū′mў** *a.*

fū′mĭgāte *v.t.* subject to fumes, disinfect or purify thus. **~ā′tion**, **~ātor** *nn.*

fū′mĭtorў *n.* herb formerly used in medicine.

fŭn *n.* sport, amusement; jocularity; *make ~ of, poke ~ at,* ridicule. **~-fair,** (part of) fair devoted to amusements and side-shows.

fūnăm′būlĭst *n.* rope-walker.

fŭnc′tion *n.* work thing is designed to do; official duty; formal or important social meeting; (math.) variable quantity in relation to other(s) in terms of which it may be expressed. *v.i.* fulfil function; operate. **~al** *a.* of function(s); shaped, designed, etc. with regard only to function. **~arў** *n.* official.

fŭnd *n.* permanently available stock; capital sum; (pl.) pecuniary resources; *the ~s,* stock of national debt. *v.t.* make debt permanent at fixed interest.

fŭn′dament *n.* buttocks.

fŭndamĕn′tal *a.* of or serving as base or foundation; essential, primary. *n.* fundamental rule, note, etc. **~ism** *n.* adherence to traditional beliefs etc.

fū′nerăl *n.* burial or cremation of dead; funeral procession or service. *a.* of, used at, funeral. **fūnēr′eal** *a.* fit for funeral; dismal, dark.

fū′nerarў *a.* of, used for, funeral or burial.

fŭn′gĭcīde (-j-) *n.* fungus-destroying substance.

fŭng′us (-ngg-) *n.* (pl. *-gi,* pr. *-jī,* *-uses*), mushroom, toadstool, or allied plant; spongy morbid growth. **fŭng′oid, fŭng′ous** *aa.*

fūnĭc′ūlar *a.* of rope or its tension. **~ railway,** one worked by cable and stationary engine.

fŭnk *n.* (sl.) fear, panic; coward. *v.* show funk; evade, shirk; be afraid of.

fŭnn′el *n.* tube with cone-shaped end for conducting liquids into small opening; chimney of steam-engine or ship.

fŭnn′ў *a.* comical, amusing; queer. *n.* narrow boat for one sculler. **~-bone,** part of elbow over which ulnar nerve passes.

fūr *n.* dressed coat of certain animals used as lining, trimming, etc.; (freq. pl.) garment of fur; short fine hair of some animals; (collect.) furred animals; coating, crust. *v.* trim, line, cover, coat, become coated, with fur. **fūrr′ў** *a.*

fur. *abbr.* furlong.

fūr′bĕlow (-ō) *n.* flounce; pleated border; (pl.) showy ornaments.

fūr′bĭsh *v.t.* polish *up;* renovate.

fūr′cāte (*or* -at) *a.* forked, branched. **fūrcā′tion** *n.*

fūr′ĭous *a.* raging, frantic, very angry, violent; uproarious.

fūrl *v.* roll up (sail); fold up, close; become furled.

fūr′lŏng *n.* measure of length (220 yds.).

fūr′lough (-ō) *n.* leave of absence.

fūr′nace (-ĭs) *n.* apparatus with chamber for applying intense heat; closed fireplace for heating building; hot place.

fūr′nish *v.t.* provide (*with*); fit up with furniture.

fūr′nĭture *n.* movable contents of house or room; rigging, stores, etc. of ship.

fūrōr′ė *n.* outburst of popular enthusiasm.

fŭ′rrĭer *n.* dealer in, dresser of, furs.

fŭ′rrow (-ō) *n.* narrow trench made by plough; rut; wrinkle. *v.t.* plough; make furrows in.

fŭr′ther (-dh-) *adv.* to greater distance; in addition. *a.* more remote; additional. *v.t.* promote, favour. **~ance** *n.* **~more** *adv.* moreover.

~**mōst** a. most distant. **fŭr′thĕst** a. & adv.

fŭr′tǐve a. sly, stealthy.

fŭr′y̆ n. fierce passion, wild anger; violence; angry woman; *like* ~, intensely, furiously, swiftly.

fŭrze n. spiny yellow-flowered shrub; gorse. **fŭr′zy̆** a.

fŭs′cous a. dark-coloured.

fūse[1] (-z) v. melt with intense heat; blend (as) by melting; be put out of action by blowing of fuse; cause fuse(s) of to blow; supply with fuse(s). n. easily-fusible wire in circuit, designed to melt when circuit is overloaded.

fūse[2] (-z) n. cord, casing, etc., filled or saturated with combustible matter for igniting explosive. v.t. fit fuse to.

fū′selage (-zelǐj; *or* -ahzh) n. body or framework of aircraft.

fū′sel oil (-z-) n. mixture of alcohols, by-product of production of industrial alcohol.

fū′sible (-z-) a. that may be fused. **fūsǐbil′ity̆** n.

fū′sǐl (-z-) n. obsolete light musket. **fūsǐlier′** (-z-) n. soldier of some regiments formerly armed with fusil. **fūsǐllāde′** (-z-) n. continuous discharge of firearms.

fū′sion (-zhn) n. fusing; fused mass; coalition; energy-releasing union of atomic nuclei to form heavier nucleus.

fŭss n. bustle; excessive commotion or concern; ostentatious activity; *make a* ~, (esp.) make a scene, complain; *make a* ~ *of*, lavish care, endearments, flattery, etc. on. v. make fuss; busy oneself restlessly, move fussily; worry; ~ *over*, make fuss of. ~**-pot**, (colloq.) fussy person. **fŭss′y̆** a. (given to) making a fuss; excessively ornate, full of petty or over-elaborate detail.

fŭstanĕll′a n. man's stiff full white skirt in modern Greece etc.

fŭs′tǐan n. twilled short-napped cotton cloth; bombast. a. made of fustian; bombastic, worthless.

fŭs′tǐc n. (wood yielding) yellow dye.

fŭs′ty̆ a. stale-smelling, musty, stuffy; antiquated.

fut. *abbr.* future.

fū′tǐle a. useless, frivolous, worthless. **fūtǐl′ity̆** n.

fū′ture a. about to happen or be or become. n. time to come; future condition, events, etc.

fū′turǐsm n. early 20th-c. artistic and literary movement departing violently from tradition. ~**ǐst** a. & n.; ~**ǐs′tǐc** a.

fūtūr′ity̆ n. future time, events, etc.

fŭzz n. fluff; fluffy or frizzy hair. **fŭzz′y̆** a. fluffy; blurred, indistinct.

fy̆l′fot n. swastika.

fytte : see **fit**[1].

F.Z.S. *abbr.* Fellow of Zoological Society.

G

G (jē), (mus.) 5th note in scale of C major.

g. *abbr.* guinea; gram(s).

Ga. *abbr.* Georgia.

găb n. (colloq.) talk, chatter.

găb′ardine, găb′erdine (-ēn) n. twilled cloth esp. of fine worsted.

găbb′le v. talk inarticulately or too fast. n. rapid talk.

gā′ble n. triangular part of wall at end of ridged roof.

gaboon′ n. fine-grained mahogany-like African wood.

gā′by̆ n. simpleton.

găd v.i. wander with no serious object. ~**about**, gadding person.

găd′fly̆ n. cattle-biting fly.

gădg′ĕt n. small fitting, contrivance, piece of mechanism, etc.

gā′doid a. & n. (fish) of cod kind.

Gael (gāl, *or* găl) n. Scottish or Irish Celt. ~**ǐc** a. & n. (language) of Gaels.

găff[1] n. barbed fishing-spear; stick with hook for landing fish. v.t. seize with gaff.

găff[2] n. (sl.) cheap place of amusement (*freq. penny* ~).

găff[3] n. (sl.) *blow the* ~, let out secret.

găffe n. blunder, indiscreet remark or act.

găff′er n. old man; foreman, boss.

găg *n.* thing thrust into mouth to prevent speech, hold it open, etc.; (parl.) closure; actor's interpolation; comic business, joke, etc. *v.* apply gag to, silence; make gags; choke, retch.

găg'a (*or* gah-) *a.* fatuous, senile.

gāge[1] *n.* pledge, security; challenge.

gāge[2] *n.* greengage.

găgg'le *n.* flock (of geese).

gai'ĕtў *n.* being gay, mirth; amusement, merry-making.

gai'lў *adv.* in gay manner.

gain *v.* obtain, secure; win; reach; persuade. *n.* increase of wealth, profit; money-making. ~ful *a.* lucrative; paid.

gainsay' *v.t.* (-*said*, pr. -ād, -ĕd) deny, contradict.

gait *n.* manner of or carriage in walking.

gai'ter *n.* covering of leather etc. for leg or ankle.

Gal. *abbr.* Galatians.

gal. *abbr.* gallon(s).

gā'la (*or* gah'-) *n.* festive occasion, fête.

galăc'tĭc *a.* of galaxy.

găl'antine (-ēn) *n.* white meat cut up, boiled, and served cold in jelly.

găl'axў *n.* irregular luminous band of stars encircling heavens; island universe; brilliant company.

gāle[1] *n.* bog-myrtle.

gāle[2] *n.* strong wind; storm; (meteor.) wind of velocity 39–54 m.p.h.

galē'na *n.* (min.) native lead sulphide.

găl'ilee *n.* porch, chapel, at entrance of church.

gall[1] (gawl) *n.* bile; asperity, rancour; (U.S.) assurance, impudence. ~-bladder, vessel near liver containing gall. ~-stone, calculus in gall-bladder.

gall[2] (gawl) *n.* painful swelling, blister, etc.; sore; (southern U.S.) patch of barren soil. *v.t.* rub sore; vex, humiliate.

gall[3] (gawl) *n.* excrescence on trees caused by insect.

găll'ant (*or* galănt') *a.* fine, stately; brave; attentive to women. *n.* man of fashion; ladies' man. găll'antrў *n.* bravery; courtliness; gallant act or speech.

găll'éon *n.* Spanish sailing-ship.

găll'erў *n.* covered walk, colonnade; (southern U.S.) veranda; raised floor or balcony over part of area of church etc.; highest of such balconies in theatre, with cheapest seats; passage, corridor; room for showing works of art.

găll'ey *n.* low flat one-decked vessel, usu. rowed; large row-boat of man--of-war; ship's kitchen; tray for set-up type. ~ proof, proof in slip form.

găll'iard *n.* (music for) quick and lively old dance in triple time.

Găll'ĭc *a.* of Gaul or Gauls; French. găll'ĭcĭsm *n.* French idiom. ~īze *v.t.*

găllĭnā'ceous *a.* of order including domestic poultry.

găll'ĭpŏt *n.* small earthen glazed pot.

găll'ĭum *n.* rare bluish-white metallic element.

găllĭvănt' *v.i.* gad about.

găll'on *n.* measure (four quarts) for liquids, corn, etc.

gallŌŌn' *n.* narrow close braid.

găll'op *n.* horse's fastest pace; track or ground for galloping horses. *v.* go at gallop; make (horse) gallop; talk etc. very fast. ~āde' *n.* lively dance.

găll'oway *n.* small breed of horse.

găll'ows (-ōz) *n.pl.* (usu. as sing.) structure for hanging criminals; any similar structure; punishment of hanging.

galōre' *adv.* in plenty.

galŏsh', go- *n.* overshoe.

galŭmph' *v.i.* go prancing exultantly.

gălvăn'ĭc *a.* of, produced by, suggesting, galvanism.

găl'vanĭsm *n.* electricity produced by chemical action. găl'vanīze *v.t.* apply galvanism to; rouse by shock or excitement. ~īzā'tion *n.*

gălvanŏm'éter *n.* instrument for measuring electric current.

găm'bĭt *n.* (chess) kinds of opening with sacrifice of piece.

găm'ble *v.i.* play games of chance for money, esp. for high stakes; take risks (*with*). *n.* act of gambling; risk, risky undertaking. ~r *n.*

gămboge' (-ōŌzh) *n.* gum-resin used as yellow pigment.

găm′bol *n*. & *v.i.* (give) frisky movement, leap.

gāme[1] *n*. spell of play, pastime, sporting contest; jest; dodge, trick; subdivision of tennis set, whist rubber, etc.; score that wins game; animals, birds, etc. hunted for sport or food. *a*. spirited; ready. *v.i.* gamble. **~-cock**, of kind bred for fighting. **~keeper**, man employed to breed game, prevent poaching, etc. **~smanship**, art or practice of winning unfairly without breaking rules. **~some** *a*. sportive. **~ster** *n*. gambler.

gāme[2] *a*. (of leg etc.) crippled.

gamēte′ (*or* găm′-) *n*. mature sexual cell.

găm′in (*or* -ăṅ) *n*. street urchin, impudent child.

gămm′a *n*. Greek letter; kind of moth. **~ rays**, very short X-rays.

gămm′er *n*. old woman.

gămm′on[1] *n*. bottom piece of flitch of bacon with hind leg.

gămm′on[2] *n*. complete victory at backgammon; humbug, deception. *v*. defeat at backgammon; talk plausibly, hoax, deceive.

gămm′y *a*. (sl., of limb) crippled.

gămp *n*. (colloq.) umbrella.

găm′ut *n*. whole series of recognized notes in music; compass of voice; entire range or scope.

gā′mў *a*. smelling or tasting like game kept until it is high.

găn′der *n*. male goose.

găng *n*. set of workmen, slaves, or prisoners; set of associates, esp. for criminal purposes. *v.i.* (colloq.) join *up*; **~ up on**, act in concert against. **~-plank**, plank for walking into or out of boat. **~er** *n*. foreman of gang of workmen.

găng′ling (-ngg-) *a*. loosely built, lanky.

găng′lion (-ngg-) *n*. (pl. -*ia*) knot on nerve from which nerve-fibres radiate; nerve-nucleus in central nervous system. **~ŏn′ic** *a*.

găng′rēne (-ngg-) *n*. mortification of part of body. **găng′rĕnous** *a*.

găng′ster *n*. member of gang of criminals. **~ism** *n*.

găngue (-ng) *n*. earth or matrix in which ore is found.

găng′way *n*. opening in ship's bulwarks; bridge; passage, esp. between rows of seats.

gănn′et *n*. kinds of large sea-bird.

găn′oid *a*. (of fish-scale) smooth and bright; with ganoid scales.

găn′try *n*. stand for barrels; structure supporting travelling crane, railway signals, etc.

gaol (jāl) *n*. prison. *v.t.* put in prison. **~bird**, habitual criminal. **~er** *n*.

găp *n*. breach in hedge or wall; interval; wide divergence.

gāpe *v.i.* open mouth wide; stare *at*; yawn. *n*. yawn; stare.

gă′rage (-ahzh *or* -ij; *or* -ahzh′) *n*. building or shed for storing, repairing, etc., motor-vehicles. *v.t.* put or keep in garage.

gärb *n*. (esp. distinctive) dress or costume. *v.t.* dress.

gär′bage *n*. offal used as food; refuse; filth.

gär′ble *v.t.* distort or confuse (facts, statements, etc.).

gär′board (-erd) *n*. planks or plates on ship's or boat's bottom next keel.

gär′den *n*. piece of ground for growing flowers, fruit, or vegetables; (pl.) pleasure-grounds. *v*. cultivate, work in, garden. **~er** *n*.

gärdē′nia *n*. (kinds of tree and shrub with) fragrant white or yellow flower.

gärgăn′tuan *a*. gigantic.

gär′gle *v*. wash throat or mouth, wash (throat etc.), with liquid. *n*. liquid so used, held in throat and kept in motion by breath.

gär′goyle *n*. grotesque spout projecting from gutter.

gär′ish *a*. obtrusively bright, gaudy.

gär′land *n*. wreath or chaplet. *v.t.* crown or deck with garland.

gär′lic *n*. plant with strong-smelling pungent bulbs.

gär′ment *n*. article of dress.

gär′ner *n*. storehouse for corn etc. *v.t.* store up (usu. fig.).

gär′net *n*. vitreous mineral, esp. red kind used as gem.

gär′nish *v.t.* decorate, esp. dish of food. *n*. materials for this.

gär′niture *n*. appurtenances.

gă′rret *n*. room on top floor.

găr'rison n. troops stationed in town. v.t. furnish with, occupy as, garrison.

garrŏtte' n. (apparatus for) Spanish capital punishment by strangulation; highway robbery by throttling victim. v.t. execute, throttle, thus.

găr'rulous (-ōōl-) a. talkative; chattering. **garru'lĭty** (-ōōl-) n.

găr'ter n. band to keep stocking up; the G~, (badge of) highest order of English knighthood. v.t. fasten (stocking), encircle (leg) with garter. ~-stitch, pattern made by knitting all rows plain.

gărth n. (arch.) close, garden, paddock.

găs¹ n. (pl. găses), any aeriform or completely elastic fluid, esp. one not becoming liquid or solid at ordinary temperatures; coal-gas etc. used for light or heat, nitrous oxide gas as anaesthetic, irritant or poisonous gas etc. used in warfare etc., explosive mixture of methane and air in coal-mine; empty talk, boasting. v. kill or injure with gas; talk emptily or vaguely. ~-chamber, in which prisoners are killed by poisonous gas. ~-fitter, workman installing and repairing gas-pipes etc. ~-holder, gasometer. ~-mask, respirator for protection against harmful gases. ~-meter, apparatus registering amount of gas consumed. ~-ring, hollow iron ring of gas-burners, used for cooking etc. ~-works, place for manufacture of coal-gas.

găs² n. (U.S.) petrol.

găsconāde' n. & v.i. boast, brag.

găs'eous (or gā-) a. of or in form of gas.

găsh n. long deep cut or wound, cleft. v.t. make gash in.

găs'ĭfȳ v. change into gas. ~-fĭcā'tion n.

găs'kėt n. small cord securing furled sail to yard; packing esp. for gas-tight joints in internal-combustion engine.

găs'olēne, -ine (-ēn) n. (U.S.) petrol.

gasŏm'ėter n. reservoir from which gas is distributed; (chem.) vessel for holding gas.

gasp (gahsp) v. catch breath with open mouth, strain for air or breath; utter with gasps. n. convulsive catching of breath; at one's last ~, at point of death. ~er n. cheap cigarette.

găss'ȳ a. of, full of, like, gas.

găs't(e)ropŏd n. mollusc with locomotive organ placed ventrally.

găs'trĭc a. of stomach.

găs'tronŏme n. connoisseur of cookery. **gastrŏn'omer, gastrŏn'omȳ** nn.; ~nŏm'ic(al) aa.

găt n. (sl.) revolver or other firearm.

gāte, n. opening in wall closable with barrier; barrier closing opening of wall, regulating passage of water, etc.; electronic device, signal, etc. controlling passage of current, selecting signals, etc.; H-shaped arrangement of slots through which gear-lever is moved; (money paid by) spectators at esp. sporting event. ~-crash, attend social gathering etc. uninvited. ~-house, lodge, building over gate. ~-way, opening closed by gate.

găth'er (-dh-) v. bring or come together; collect; pluck; draw together in folds or wrinkles; develop purulent swelling; pick up; infer. n. small fold or pucker made by running thread through part of dress etc. ~ĭng n. assembly; purulent swelling.

GATT abbr. General Agreement on Tariffs and Trade.

gauche (gōsh) a. without ease or grace, socially awkward. ~erie (-erē) n. [F]

gau'chō (gow-) n. mounted herdsman of pampas, of mixed Eur. and Amer.-Ind. descent.

gaud n. showy ornament, gewgaw, jewel.

gau'dȳ n. annual college dinner for old members etc. a. tastelessly showy.

gauge (gāj) n. standard measure; capacity, extent; kinds of instrument for measuring or testing; criterion, test. v.t. measure exactly, test dimensions of; measure contents of; estimate.

Gaul n. inhabitant of ancient Gaul; (joc.) Frenchman.

gault n. clay and marl beds lying between chalk and lower greensand.

gaunt *a.* lean, haggard, grim.

gaunt'lĕt[1] *n.* (hist.) armoured glove; glove with long loose wrist, esp. for driving etc.

gaunt'lĕt[2] *n. run the* ~, undergo punishment of passing between two rows of men etc. armed with sticks etc. (freq. fig.).

gauze *n.* thin transparent fabric of silk, wire, etc. gau'zў *a.*

gave, *p.t.* of give.

găv'el *n.* auctioneer's or chairman's hammer.

gavŏtte' *n.* (music for) lively 18th-c. dance.

gawk *n.* awkward or bashful person. gaw'kў *a.*

gay *a.* light-hearted, mirthful; showy; dissolute.

gāze *v.i.* look fixedly. *n.* intent look.

gazē'bo *n.* structure whence view may be had.

gazĕlle' *n.* small graceful soft-eyed kinds of antelope.

gazĕtte' *n.* newspaper, esp. official journal. *v.t.* publish in official gazette.

găzĕtteer' *n.* geographical dictionary.

G.B. *abbr.* Great Britain.

G.B.E. *abbr.* Dame *or* Knight Grand Cross (of Order) of British Empire.

G.C. *abbr.* George Cross.

G.C.B. *abbr.* Knight Grand Cross of the Bath.

G.C.E. *abbr.* General Certificate of Education.

G.C.F., G.C.M. *abbr.* greatest common factor, measure.

G.C.M.G. *abbr.* Dame *or* Knight Grand Cross of St. Michael and St. George.

G.C.V.O. Dame *or* Knight Grand Cross of Royal Victorian Order.

gear (gēr) *n.* apparatus, tackle, tools; system of cog-wheels etc. connecting motor with its work and usu. allowing change of speed ratio between driving and driven parts; harness; apparel, household utensils. *v.t.* harness; put in gear, provide with gear; adjust (*to*). ~-box, ~-case, enclosing gear-changing mechanism. ~-lever, for engaging gear.

gĕck'ō *n.* kinds of lizard found in warm climates.

gee *int.* (U.S.) of asseveration, discovery, etc.

geese : see goose.

gee'zer (g-) *n.* (sl.) old person.

Geiger counter (gī'ger) *n.* instrument used for measuring radioactivity.

gei'sha (gā-) *n.* Japanese professional hostess and entertainer.

gĕl *n.* semi-solid colloidal solution.

gĕl'atĭn(e) (*or* -ēn) *n.* transparent amorphous substance used in making jellies, soups, etc. gĕlăt'ĭnous *a.*

gĕld (g-) *v.t.* castrate. ~ing *n.* gelded horse etc.

gĕl'ĭd *a.* ice-cold; cool.

gĕl'ĭgnīte *n.* gelatine-like explosive with base of wood-pulp.

gĕm *n.* precious stone; thing of great beauty or worth; jewel. *v.t.* adorn (as) with gems.

gĕm'ĭnāte *v.t.* double; arrange in pairs. *a.* (-ĭt) arranged in pairs. ~ā'tion *n.*

Gĕm'ĭnī, Twins, third constellation and sign of zodiac.

gĕmmif'erous *a.* yielding gems.

gĕn *n.* (sl.) information.

Gen. *abbr.* General; Genesis.

gen. *abbr.* genitive.

gendarme (zhŏn'dărm) *n.* French soldier employed in police duties. ~rie (-erē) *n.* force of gendarmes; gendarmes' office.

gĕn'der *n.* grammatical classification or one of classes (*masculine, feminine, neuter*) roughly corresponding to two sexes and sexlessness.

gēne *n.* factor in germ-cell causing development of inherited characteristic.

gĕnĕăl'ogў *n.* pedigree; lineage; study of pedigrees. ~ŏ'gical *a.*; ~ogĭst *n.*

genera : see genus.

gĕn'eral *a.* applicable to all, not partial or particular; prevalent, usual; vague, lacking detail; (mil.) above rank of colonel; (in titles) chief, head. *n.* officer next below Field Marshal (also used of *lieutenant-*~, *major-*~); commander of army; (colloq.) general servant; (arch.) *the* public.

gĕneraliss'imō *n.* (pl. -*os*), commander of combined forces.

gĕnerăl′itў *n.* general statement; vagueness; majority *of*.

gĕn′eralīze *v.* reduce to general laws; form general notion(s); base general statement on; bring into general use; use generalities, speak vaguely, **∼zā′tion** *n.*

gĕn′erallў *adv.* in general sense; in most respects; usually.

gĕn′eralshĭp *n.* office of general; military skill; management.

gĕn′erāte *v.t.* bring into existence. **∼ative** *a.* **∼ātor** *n.* apparatus for producing steam, etc.; machine for converting mechanical into electrical energy, dynamo.

gĕnera′tion *n.* procreation, begetting; single step in descent or pedigree; all persons born about same time; period of about 30 years.

gĕnĕ′rĭc *a.* characteristic of genus or class; not specific.

gĕn′erous *a.* noble-minded; not mean; munificent; abundant. **∼ŏs′itў** *n.*

gĕn′ĕsĭs *n.* origin; mode of formation or generation.

gĕnĕt′ĭc *a.* of or in origin; of genetics. *n.pl.* study of heredity and variation of organisms.

gē′nĭal *a.* mild, warm; cheering; sociable. **gēnĭăl′itў** *n.*

gē′nĭe *n.* (pl. usu. *genĭī*), sprite or goblin of Arabian tales.

gĕn′ĭtal *a.* of generation. *n.pl.* external genital organs.

gĕn′itĭve *a.* & *n.* (case of nouns etc.) indicating source, origin, or possession. **gĕnitī′val** *a.*

gē′nĭus *n.* (pl. *-iuses*, *-ĭī*), tutelary spirit; exalted intellectual power; person having this.

gĕn′ocīde *n.* extermination of race, nation, etc.

genre (zhahṅr) *n.* kind, esp. of art or literature; **∼**(*-painting*), portrayal of scene(s) from ordinary life.

gĕnt *n.* (vulg.) gentleman.

gĕnteel′ *a.* (arch. or vulg.) elegant, stylish; well-bred.

gĕn′tian (-shn) *n.* kinds of usu. blue-flowered plant. **∼ violet**, dye used as antiseptic.

gĕn′tĭle *a.* not of Jewish race; heathen. *n.* gentile person.

gĕntĭl′itў *n.* gentle birth; social superiority; upper-class habits.

gĕn′tle *a.* well-born; mild, quiet; not rough or severe. *n.* maggot as bait. **∼folk**, people of good family.

gĕn′tleman (-tĕlm-) *n.* (pl. *-men*), chivalrous well-bred man; man of good social position; (pl.) male part of audience. **∼līke**, **∼lў** *aa.* behaving or looking like, befitting, a gentleman.

gĕn′tlenĕss (-tĕl-) *n.* kindliness, mildness; freedom from violence.

gĕn′tlewoman (-tĕlwŏŏman) *n.* (pl. *-en*, pr. *-wĭmĭn*), woman of good birth or breeding, lady.

gĕn′tlў *adv.* mildly, kindly; quietly, softly, slowly.

gĕn′trў *n.* people next below nobility in position and birth; (contempt.) people.

gĕn′ūflĕct *v.i.* bend knee esp. in worship. **gĕnūflĕ′xion** (-kshn) *n.*

gĕn′ūĭne *a.* pure-bred; not sham or counterfeit; authentic.

gē′nus *n.* (pl. *gĕn′era*), group of animals, plants, etc., containing several species; (loosely) kind, class.

Geo. *abbr.* George.

gēocĕn′trĭc *a.* considered as viewed from earth's centre; having earth as centre.

gē′ōde *n.* (stone with) cavity lined with crystals etc.

gĕŏd′esў *n.* branch of mathematics dealing with figure and area of earth or large portions of it. **gĕodĕs′ĭc**, **∼dĕt′ĭc** *aa.*; **∼detic line**, shortest line joining two points on (spherical) surface.

gĕŏg′raphў *n.* science of earth's form, physical features, etc.; features of place; manual of geography. **geŏg′rapher** *n.*; **∼grăph′ĭc(al)** *aa.*

gĕŏl′ogў *n.* science of earth's crust, its strata, and their relations. **∼ŏ′gical** *a.*; **∼ogĭst** *n.* **∼ogīze** *v.i.* practise geology.

gĕŏm′ĕtrў *n.* science of properties and relations of magnitudes in space. **gĕomĕt′rĭc(al)** *aa*; **gĕomĕtrĭ′cian** *n.*

gĕophўs′ĭcs (-z-) *n.* physics of earth. **∼ical** *a.*; **∼icĭst** *n.*

gĕopŏl′itĭcs *n.* study of politics as influenced by geography. **∼lĭt′ĭcal** *a.*

Georg. *abbr.* Georgics.

georgĕtte' (jŏrj-) *n.* thin crêpe of fine twisted yarn.

Geor'gĭan (jŏr-) *a.* of time of George I–IV or George V.

Ger. *abbr.* German.

gerā'nĭum *n.* kinds of wild plant with fruit like crane's bill; cultivated pelargonium.

gĕr'falcon (-awkn) *n.* Icelandic or any large northern falcon.

gĕrĭăt'rĭc *a.* of old age and its diseases. **~s** *n.pl.* branch of medicine or social science dealing with these.

gĕrm *n.* portion of organism capable of developing into new one; rudiment, elementary principle; microbe.

gĕr'man[1] *a.* in fullest sense of relationship.

Gĕr'man[2] *a. & n.* (native, language) of Germany. **~ measles**, disease like mild measles. **~ silver**, white alloy of nickel etc. **Germăn'ic** *a. & n.* Teutonic.

gĕrmăn'der *n.* kinds of plant, esp. speedwell.

gĕrmāne' *a.* relevant or pertinent (*to*).

gĕrmā'nĭum *n.* greyish-white rare metallic element.

gĕr'mĭcīde *n.* substance destructive of germs. **~cī'dal** *a.*

gĕr'mĭnal *a.* of germs; in earliest stage of development.

gĕr'mĭnāte *v.* sprout, bud; cause to shoot, produce. **~ā'tion** *n.*

gĕrontŏl'ogў *n.* study of ageing and the aged.

gĕ'rrўmănder *v.t.* manipulate (constituency etc.) to gain unfair electoral advantage.

gĕ'rund *n.* form of Latin verb constructed as noun; English verbal noun in *-ing*. **gerŭn'dĭve** *n.* Latin verbal adjective from gerund stem.

gĕss'ō *n.* gypsum used in painting and modelling.

gesta'pō (gestah-) *n.* Nazi secret police.

gĕstā'tion *n.* carrying in womb between conception and birth.

gĕstic'ūlāte *v.* use expressive motion of limbs etc. with or instead of speech. **~ā'tion** *n.*; **~ative**, **~atorў** *aa.*

gĕs'ture *n.* significant movement of limb or body; step or move calculated to evoke response from another.

gĕt (g-) *v.* (p.t. *gŏt*; p.p. *gŏt*, (U.S.) *gŏtten*), obtain, earn, gain, win, procure; fetch; learn; induce; beget; experience or suffer; catch or contract; have inflicted; (colloq.) puzzle, corner; (colloq.) understand; succeed in coming or going *to, away*, etc., succeed in bringing, placing, etc.; become; **~ in**, (esp.) be elected; **~ out of**, (esp.) escape from, evade; **~ through**, (esp.) pass examination, reach or bring to destination; **~ up**, (esp.) rise from bed, organize, set on foot, arrange appearance of, produce, (of wind etc.) begin to be violent. **~-ăt-able**, accessible. **~-away**, (esp.) escape. **~-together**, meeting, social gathering. **~-up**, style of costume, production, etc.

gē'um *n.* kinds of rosaceous plant.

gew'-gaw (g-) *n.* gaudy plaything or ornament.

gey'ser (gāz- *or* gēz- *or* gīz-) *n.* hot spring; apparatus for heating water.

ghast'lў (gah-) *a.* horrible, frightful; deathlike, pallid.

gha(u)t (gawt) *n.* (Anglo-Ind.) steps leading to river; landing-place; Hindu funeral pyre.

ghee (gē) *n.* Indian clarified buffalo-milk butter.

gher'kĭn (gĕr-) *n.* young or small cucumber for pickling.

ghett'ō (gĕ-) *n.* (pl. *-os*), Jews' quarter.

ghillie : see **gillie**.

ghost (gō-) *n.* dead person appearing to the living, spectre; emaciated or pale person; semblance; hack doing work for which another takes credit. *v.* act or write as ghost. **~ly** *a.* spiritual; as of ghost, spectral.

ghoul (gōol) *n.* spirit said to prey on corpses. **~ish** *a.*

G.H.Q. *abbr.* General Headquarters.

ghyll : see **gill**[2].

G.I. *abbr.* (U.S.) government issue; (colloq.) enlisted man.

gī'ant *n.* being of superhuman size; very tall or large person, animal, etc.; person of extraordinary ability. *a.* gigantic. ~('s)-stride, gymnastic apparatus enabling user to take huge strides round pole. ~ĕss *n.* ~ĭsm *n.* abnormal growth esp. of bones.

Gib. *abbr.* (colloq.) Gibraltar.

gĭbb'er (j-, g-) *v.i.* chatter inarticulately. *n.* such chatter. ~ĭsh (j-, g-) *n.* unintelligible speech.

gĭbb'ĕt *n.* post on which body of executed criminal was exposed. *v.t.* expose on gibbet; hold up to contempt.

gĭbb'on (g-) *n.* kinds of long-armed tailless ape.

gĭbb'ous (g-) *a.* convex, protuberant; (of moon etc.) with bright part greater than semicircle and less than circle. gĭbbŏs'ĭtў *n.*

gībe, jībe[1] *v. & n.* flout, jeer; mock, taunt.

gĭb'lĕts *n.pl.* parts of bird removed before cooking.

gī'bus *n.* opera-hat.

gĭdd'ў (g-) *a.* dizzy; disposed to fall or stagger or spin round; making dizzy; excitable, flighty.

gĭft (g-) *n.* thing given, present; natural endowment. *v.t.* endow with gifts; present.

gĭg (g-) *n.* light two-wheeled one-horse carriage; light ship's boat; rowing-boat, esp. for race.

gĭgăn'tĭc *a.* huge, giant-like. gīgăn't-ĭsm *n.* giantism.

gĭgg'le (g-) *v.i.* laugh continuously in foolish or affected or ill-bred way, titter. *n.* such laugh.

gĭg'olō *n.* male professional dancing-partner; man supported by mistress.

gigue (zhēg) *n.* music for jig, esp. as movement in suite.

gila (monster) (hē'la) *n.* large venomous lizard of New Mexico etc.

Gĭlbĕr'tian (g-) *a.* topsy-turvy in vein of Gilbert & Sullivan opera.

gĭld[1] (g-) *v.t.* (p.p. *gilded, gilt*), cover thinly with gold; tinge with golden colour; make specious.

gĭld[2] : see guild.

gĭll[1] (g-) *n.* (usu. pl.) respiratory organ(s) of fish etc.; flesh below person's jaws and ears.

gĭll[2], ghўll (g-) *n.* deep wooded ravine; narrow mountain torrent.

gĭll[3] *n.* quarter-pint measure.

gĭll'ĭe, gh- (g-) *n.* sportsman's or (hist.) Highland chief's attendant.

gĭll'ўflower *n.* clove-scented pink; wallflower.

gĭlt[1] (g-) *n.* gilding. *a.* overlaid with gold. ~-edged, (esp., of securities) of finest quality, bearing fixed interest, safe (not touched by market fluctuations).

gĭlt[2] *n.* young sow.

gĭm'bals (g- *or* j-) *n.pl.* contrivance of rings etc. for keeping things horizontal at sea.

gĭm'crăck *n.* trumpery ornament etc. *a.* flimsy, trumpery.

gĭm'lĕt (g-) *n.* small boring-tool.

gĭmm'ick (g-) *n.* (sl.) tricky or ingenious device, idea, etc.

gĭmp (g-) *n.* twist of silk etc. with cord or wire running through.

gĭn[1] *n.* snare, trap; kinds of crane and windlass; machine separating cotton from seeds. *v.t.* trap; treat (cotton) in gin.

gĭn[2] *n.* spirit distilled from grain or malt, flavoured with juniper etc.

gĭn'ger (-j-) *n.* (tropical plant with) hot spicy root; mettle, spirit; light reddish yellow. *v.t.* put mettle or spirit into, rouse *up*. ~ ale, ~ beer, ~ pop (colloq.), ~ wine, ginger-flavoured drinks. ~bread, ginger-flavoured treacle cake. ~-nut, small round ginger-flavoured biscuit. gĭn'gerў *a.*

gĭn'gerlў (-j-) *a.* with or showing extreme caution to avoid noise etc. *adv.* in gingerly manner.

gingham (gĭng'am) *n.* plain-woven freq. striped or checked cotton cloth.

gĭnk'gō (g-) *n.* yellow-flowered Chinese and Japanese tree.

gĭp'sў, gy- *n.* member of tawny-skinned black-haired wandering race.

gĭraffe' (-ahf) *n.* ruminant quadruped with long neck.

gĭ'randōle *n.* revolving firework or jet of water; branched candle bracket or candlestick.

gĭ'rasōl(e) (*or* -ŏl) *n.* opal with reddish glow in bright light.

gĭrd[1] (g-) *v.t.* (*girded or girt*), encircle or fasten (on) with waistbelt etc.;

~ one*self*, ~ (*up*) one's *loins*, prepare for action.

gĭrd² (g-) *v.i.* gibe (*at*).

gĭr'der (g-) *n.* beam supporting joists; iron or steel beam, lattice, etc., forming span of bridge etc.

gĭr'dle¹ (g-) *n.* cord, belt, used to gird waist; thing that surrounds; corset; (anat.) bony support for limbs. *v.t.* surround with girdle.

gĭr'dle² (g-) *n.* circular iron plate for baking scones etc.

gĭrl (g-) *n.* female child; young unmarried woman; maid-servant; man's sweetheart. **G~ Guide(s)**, (member of) organization parallel to boy scouts. **~hŏŏd** *n.*; **~ish** *a.*

giro (jīr'ō) *n.* simple banking and credit-transfer system.

girt, *p.t.* & *p.p.* of **gird**.

gĭrth (g-) *n.* band round body of horse securing saddle; measurement round more or less cylindrical thing. *v.t.* encircle (horse), secure (saddle), with girth.

gĭst (j-) *n.* substance, pith.

gĭve (g-) *v.* (*gāve, gĭven*), bestow gratuitously; grant, accord; deliver, administer; consign, put; pledge; devote; present, offer (one's hand, arm, etc.); impart, be source of; assume, grant, specify; collapse, yield, shrink; **~** *in*, yield; **~** *off*, emit; **~** *out*, (esp.) announce, distribute, break down or cease from exhaustion etc., run short; **~** *up*, (esp.) resign, surrender, abandon one*self* *to*, cease from effort, pronounce incurable or insoluble. *n.* yielding to pressure; elasticity. **~-and-take**, mutual concession, exchange of talk. **~-away**, unwitting disclosure. **gĭv'er** *n.*

gĭv'en (g-) *a.* (esp.) disposed, prone (*to*); granted as basis of reasoning etc.; fixed, specified. **~ name**, Christian name.

gĭzz'ard (g-) *n.* bird's second stomach for grinding food.

Gk. *abbr.* Greek.

glā'brous *a.* smooth-skinned.

glacé (glah'sā) *a.* (of cloth etc.) smooth, glossy; iced, sugared.

glā'cial (-sh(i)al; *or* -ā-) *a.* of ice, icy; (chem.) pure, crystalline.

glā'ciāted (-s- *or* -sh-) *a.* marked by

ice-action; covered with glaciers. **~ā'tion**, *n.*

glā'cier (*or* -ā-) *n.* slowly moving river or mass of ice.

glā'cis (*or* -ā- *or* -ah-) *n.* gentle slope; bank sloping down from fort.

glăd *a.* pleased; joyful, cheerful. **glădd'en** *v.t.* make glad.

glāde *n.* clear space in forest.

glăd'iātor *n.* trained fighter in ancient Roman shows. **~tōr'ial** *a.*

glădiō'lus *n.* (pl. -*lī*), plant of iris kind with bright flower-spikes.

glăd'some *a.* joyful, cheerful.

glăd'stone băg' *n.* light portmanteau with top fastening, opening out flat.

glair *n.* white of egg; similar viscous substance. *v.t.* smear with glair.

Glam. *abbr.* Glamorganshire.

glăm'our *n.* magic, enchantment; delusive or alluring beauty or charm. **glăm'orīze** *v.t.*; **glăm'orous** *a.*

glance (-ah-) *v.* glide *off*; give brief or momentary look; **~** *at*, make brief allusion to. *n.* swift oblique movement or impact; flash, gleam; brief look.

glănd *n.* organ secreting chemical compounds required for particular function of body; similar organ in plant. **glăn'dūlar** *a.*

glăn'ders (-z) *n.pl.* contagious horse-disease.

glāre *v.i.* shine oppressively; look fiercely. *n.* oppressive light; tawdry brilliance; fierce look.

glass (-ah-) *n.* siliceous substance, usu. transparent, lustrous, hard, and brittle; glass drinking-vessel; looking-glass; lens; (pl.) pair of spectacles; field-glass, telescope, barometer, etc. *v.t.* fit or cover with glass; reflect. **~-house**, greenhouse; (sl.) military prison. **~-paper**, paper covered with powdered glass, for polishing etc. **~ wool**, glass in fibre form, used esp. for heat insulation. **~ȳ** *a.* like glass; (of eye) fixed, dull.

glaucō'ma *n.* eye-disease with tension of eye-ball and gradual impairment of sight.

glau'cous *a.* of dull greyish green or blue.

glāze *v.* fit with glass or windows; cover (pottery etc.) with vitreous substance or (surface) with smooth lustrous coating; (of eye) become glassy. *n.* substance used for, surface produced by, glazing.

glā′zier (*or* -zher) *n.* one who glazes windows etc.

G.L.C. *abbr.* Greater London Council.

gleam *n.* subdued or transient light. *v.i.* emit gleam(s).

glean *v.* gather corn left by reapers; pick up (facts etc.). **~er** *n.*; **~ings** *n.pl.*

glēbe *n.* land going with benefice; earth, land, field.

glee *n.* musical composition for several voices; mirth, lively delight. **~ful** *a.*

gleet *n.* thin morbid discharge.

glĕn *n.* narrow valley.

glĕngă′rrў (-n-g-) *n.* kind of Highland cap.

glĭb *a.* fluent, voluble, plausible.

glīde *v.* pass, proceed, by smooth continuous movement; go stealthily; (of aircraft) fly without engines. *n.* gliding motion or flight. **glī′der** *n.* engineless aircraft.

glĭmm′er *v.i.* shine faintly or intermittently. *n.* faint light or gleam. **~ing** *n.* (esp.) faint idea, indication, etc.

glĭmpse *n.* faint transient appearance; brief view. *v.t.* see faintly or partly or momentarily.

glĭnt *v.i. & n.* flash; glitter.

glĭssāde′ (*or* -ahd) *n. & v.i.* slide down slope of ice etc.

glĭssăn′dō *adv.*, *n. & a.* (effect produced by) sliding finger along string of fiddle, piano-keys, etc.

glĭs′ten (-sn) *v.* shine as or like smooth lustrous surface; sparkle.

glĭtt′er *n. & v.i.* (shine with) brilliant tremulous light.

gloa′mĭng *n.* evening twilight.

gloat *v.i.* feast eyes or mind greedily, malignantly, etc. (*on* or *over*).

glō′bal *a.* of whole of group of items etc.; of or extending over whole world.

globe *n.* spherical body; *the* earth; spherical chart of earth or constellations; approximately spherical glass vessel or cover. **~-trotting,**

travelling as sightseer through (many) foreign countries. **glōbōse′** *a.*; **globŏs′itў** *n.*

glŏb′ūlar *a.* globe-shaped; composed of globules. **~ă′ritў** *n.*

glŏb′ūle *n.* small spherical body, esp. of liquid. **~lin** *n.* one of class of simple proteins.

glŏck′enspiel (-ēl) *n.* musical instrument of bells or tuned metal bars played with hammers.

gloom *n.* darkness; melancholy, depression. *v.i.* look or be sullen or depressed; be dull. **~ў** *a.* dark; dismal; sullen.

glôr′ia *n.* doxology beginning 'Glory be to the Father'; (music for) hymn forming part of Mass etc.

glôr′ifў *v.t.* make glorious or radiant; extol. **~ficā′tion** *n.*

glôr′ious *a.* possessing or conferring glory; splendid, excellent.

glôr′ў *n.* exalted renown, fame; resplendent majesty, beauty, etc.; halo of saint. *v.i.* exult *in.* **~-hole** place where things are heaped together haphazard.

Glos. *abbr.* Gloucestershire.

glŏss[1] *n.* superficial lustre; specious appearance. *v.t.* give gloss to; make specious. **~ў** *a.*

glŏss[2] *n.* marginal explanation; comment, interpretation. *v.t.* insert glosses in, make or write gloss on; explain.

glŏss′arў *n.* dictionary of technical or special words, partial dictionary. **~ār′ial** *a.*

glŏtt′is *n.* opening at upper part of windpipe and between vocal cords. **glŏtt′al** *a.*

glove (-ŭv) *n.* hand-covering of leather, wool, etc.; padded glove for boxing. *v.t.* provide with gloves.

glow (-ō) *v.* emit flameless light and heat; burn with bodily heat or emotion; show warm colour. *n.* glowing state; ardour. **~-worm,** beetle emitting green light from abdomen.

glow′er (*or* -owr) *v.i.* scowl (*at*).

glōze *v.* palliate, explain away.

glu′cōse (gloo-) *n.* kind of sugar found in blood, fruits, etc.

glue (gloo) *n.* (viscous solution of) hard gelatin used as cement; any similar substance. *v.t.* stick with glue. **gluey** (glōō'ĭ) *a.*

glŭm *a.* dejected, sullen.

glume (-ōōm) *n.* husk.

glŭt *v.t.* feed or indulge to the full, satiate; overstock. *n.* surfeit; excessive supply.

glu'tĕn (glōō-) *n.* viscid part of flour. **glu'tĭnous** *a.* viscous, sticky.

glŭtt'on *n.* excessive eater; person insatiably eager *for*; voracious animal of weasel kind but much larger. **~ous** *a.*; **~ў** *n.*

glў'cerĭn, -ine, (-ēn) *n.* colourless sweet viscous liquid got from oils or fats.

glŷp'tĭc *a.* of carving, esp. on gems.

G.M. *abbr.* George Medal.

gm. *abbr.* gram(s).

G-man *n.* (U.S.) Federal criminal investigation officer.

G.M.C. *abbr.* General Medical Council.

G.M.T. *abbr.* Greenwich mean time.

gn(s). *abbr.* guinea(s).

gnarled (nārld) *a.* knobby, rugged, twisted.

gnăsh (n-) *v.* (of teeth) strike together; grind (teeth).

gnăt (n-) *n.* small biting fly.

gnaw (n-) *v.* bite persistently, wear away thus; corrode, torture.

gneiss (gnīs; *or* n-) *n.* laminated rock of quartz, feldspar, and mica.

gnome (nōm) *n.* goblin, dwarf. **gnō'mish** *a.*

gnō'mĭc (n-) *a.* of maxims, sententious.

gnō'mon (n-) *n.* rod showing time by shadow on marked surface of sundial.

gnŏs'tĭc (n-) *a.* of knowledge; having esoteric spiritual knowledge. *n.* *G~*, early Christian heretic claiming knowledge of spiritual mysteries. **G~ism** *n.*

G.N.P. *abbr.* gross national product.

G.N.R. *abbr.* Great Northern Railway.

gnu (nōō) *n.* oxlike antelope.

gō¹ *v.i.* (went, gŏne) walk, travel, proceed; move, pass; become; (of money) be spent in or on; collapse, give way, fail; extend, reach; ~ *by*, be guided by, pass; ~ *in for*, enter as competitor, take as one's object, style, etc.; ~ *out*, be extinguished, become unfashionable, mix in

society; ~ *under*, fail, sink, succumb. *n.* (pl. *goes*), animation, dash; (sl.) state of affairs; success; turn, try (*at*); *on the* ~, in motion; *it's no* ~, nothing can be done. **~-ahead**, enterprising. **~-between**, intermediary. **~-cart**, kind of child's push-chair. **~-getter**, (sl.) active pushing person. **~-off**, start. **~-slow**, policy or action of working slowly to reduce output, obtain concessions, etc.

gō² *n.* Japanese game played on board marked with intersecting lines.

goad *n.* spiked stick for urging cattle; thing that incites or torments. *v.t.* urge with goad; drive by annoyance.

goal *n.* point where race ends; object of effort; destination; posts between which football etc. is to be driven, points won by doing this. **~-keeper**, player protecting goal. **~ie** *n.* (colloq.) goal-keeper.

goat *n.* horned ruminant quadruped; licentious person; fool; *get one's* ~ (sl.), irritate one. **~sucker**, nightjar. **~ee** *n.* chin-tuft like goat's beard. **~ish, ~y** *aa.*

gŏb *n.* (sl.) mouth; (vulg.) clot of spittle etc.

gōbăng' *n.* (simple) Japanese board-game.

gŏbb'ĕt *n.* lump, esp. of raw flesh or food.

gŏbb'le¹ *v.* eat hurriedly and noisily.

gŏbble² *v.i.* (of turkey-cock) make characteristic sound in throat; make similar sound when speaking etc. **~r** *n.* turkey-cock.

gŏb'lĕt *n.* (arch.) bowl-shaped drinking-cup; glass with foot and stem.

gŏb'lĭn *n.* mischievous demon.

gō'bў *n.* kinds of small fish.

G.O.C.(-in-C.) *abbr.* General Officer Commanding(-in-Chief).

gŏd *n.* (*God*) supreme being, creator and ruler of universe; superhuman being worshipped as possessing divine power; idol; adored person; (theatr., pl.) occupants of gallery. **~child**, baptized child in relation to godparent. **~-daughter**, female godchild. **~father**, **~mother**, male, female, godparent. **~fearing**, religious.

~forsaken, dismal, forlorn. ~-parent, sponsor at baptism. ~send, unexpected welcome event or acquisition. ~son, male godchild. ~less *a*. not recognizing God; impious, wicked. ~like *a*. ~ly *a*. pious, devout.

gŏdd'ĕss *n*. female deity; adored woman.

gō'det (-ā; *or* -ĕt') *n*. triangular piece inserted in seam of skirt, glove, etc.

godē'tia (-sha) *n*. free-flowering hardy annual.

gŏd'head (-ĕd) *n*. divine nature, deity.

gŏd'wĭt *n*. marsh bird like curlew.

gō'er *n*. person or thing that goes.

gō'ffer, gō'pher² *v.t.* flute or crimp with hot irons.

gŏgg'le *v.i.* roll eyes about; (of eyes) roll about, project. *a*. (of eyes) protuberant, rolling. *n.pl.* spectacles for protecting eyes from glare, dust, etc.

gō'ing *n*. (esp.) condition of ground for riding etc. *a*. in action, in operation; existing, to be had. ~s-on, behaviour.

goi'tre *n*. morbid enlargement of thyroid gland. goi'trous *a*.

Gŏlcŏn'da *n*. mine of wealth.

gōld *n*. precious yellow metal; coins of this; wealth; colour of gold. *a*. of or coloured like gold. ~-beater, one who beats gold into gold-leaf. ~finch, bright-coloured song-bird. ~fish, small golden-red Chinese carp. ~-leaf, gold beaten into thin sheet. ~smith, worker in gold. ~ standard, financial system in which paper etc. money is redeemable in gold.

gō'lden, *a*. of gold; coloured or shining like gold; precious. ~ mean, neither too much nor too little. ~-rod, plant with yellow flower-spikes. ~ syrup, pale treacle. ~ wedding, 50th wedding anniversary.

gŏlf (*or* gŏf) *n*. game in which small hard ball is struck with clubs over surface of course into series of small holes. *v.i.* play golf. ~er *n*.

gŏll'iwŏg *n*. quaint black doll with fuzzy hair.

golosh : see galosh.

golŭp'tious *a*. (joc.) delicious (esp. of food).

G.O.M. *abbr.* grand old man.

gŏmbeen' *n*. (Anglo-Ir.) usury. ~-man, money-lender.

gŏn'dola *n*. light Venetian canal--boat; car suspended from airship; (U.S.) flat roofless railway car. gŏndolier' *n*. rower of gondola.

gone, *p.p.* of go.

gŏn'er *n*. (sl.) person or thing in desperate case.

gŏn'falon *n*. banner, often with streamers, hung from cross-bar.

gŏng *n*. resonant metal disk; saucer--shaped bell; (sl.) medal. *v.t.* direct (motorist) to stop by sounding gong etc.

gŏnorrhoe'a (-rēa) *n*. inflammatory discharge from urethra or vagina.

gōō *n*. (sl.) anything viscous or sticky. gōō'y *a*.

gŏod, *a*. having right qualities, adequate; virtuous, morally excellent; worthy; proper; well-behaved; benevolent; agreeable; suitable; considerable. *n*. profit, well-being; (pl.) movable property, merchandise. ~ afternoon, ~ evening, ~ morning, ~ night, salutations at meeting or parting. ~-fellowship, sociability. ~-for-nothing, ne'er--do-well. ~-looking, handsome. ~-natured, of kindly disposition. ~ people, fairies. ~ly *a*. handsome; of imposing size etc. good'y (-goody) *a*. & *n*. obtrusively, feebly, or sentimentally virtuous (person).

gŏod-bye' *int.* expressing good wishes at parting. *n*. leave-taking, saying good-bye.

gŏod'nĕss *n*. virtue; excellence; kindness; essence or nutriment.

gŏodwill' *n*. kindly feeling; heartiness; established custom of business etc.

gōō'fy *a*. (sl.) silly, stupid.

gōō'gly *n*. (crick.) off-break ball with leg-break action.

gōōn *n*. (sl.) stupid oaf; wildly inconsequential clown.

gōōsăn'der *n*. kind of duck.

gōōse *n*. (pl. *geese*, pr. gēs), large webfooted bird; simpleton; tailor's smoothing-iron. ~flesh, bristling

state of skin due to cold or fright.
~-grass, bristly scrambling weed.
~-step, stiff-kneed balancing-drill,
esp. as parade step.

goose'berry (-zb-) n. (edible berry of)
thorny shrub.

go'pher[1] n. kinds of Amer. burrowing
rodent.

gopher[2] : see goffer.

Gor'dian a. cut the ~ knot, solve
problem by force or evasion.

gore[1] n. clotted blood.

gore[2] n. wedge-shaped piece in
garment; triangular or lune-
-shaped piece in umbrella, balloon,
etc. v.t. furnish or shape with
gore(s).

gore[3] v.t. pierce with horn.

gorge n. internal throat; contents of
stomach; surfeit; narrow opening
between hills; rocky ravine. v. feed
greedily; satiate.

gor'geous a. richly coloured; splendid,
dazzling.

gor'get n. armour for throat;
woman's wimple; necklace.

gor'gon n. terrible or repulsive
woman.

gorgonzo'la n. rich veined Italian
cheese.

gorill'a n. large powerful arboreal
anthropoid ape.

gor'mandize v.i. eat gluttonously.

gorse n. prickly yellow-flowered
shrub.

Gor'sedd (-dh) n. meeting of Welsh
bards and druids esp. at eisteddfod.

gor'y a. blood-stained; involving
(much) bloodshed.

gosh int. of surprise etc.

gos'hawk (-s-h-) n. large short-
-winged hawk.

gos'ling (-z-) n. young goose.

gos'pel n. Christian revelation; books
of four evangelists, any of these,
portion from one read at Communion service; thing to be believed, principle that one acts
upon or preaches. ~ler n. reader
of gospel in Communion service;
hot ~ler, revivalist.

goss'amer n. filmy substance of small
spiders' webs floating in calm air;
flimsy thing; delicate gauze. a.
light, flimsy, as gossamer.

goss'ip n. familiar acquaintance;

tattler, esp. woman; idle talk;
informal talk or writing esp. about
persons. v.i. talk or write gossip.
~ column, regular newspaper
column of gossip. ~y a.

gossoon' n. (Anglo-Ir.) lad.

got, p.t. & p.p. of get.

Goth n. one of Germanic invaders of
E. and W. Empires in 3rd–5th
cc.; uncivilized person, vandal.
~ic a. & n. (language) of Goths;
black-letter or sans-serif bold (type
etc.); (architecture etc.) of or in
style prevalent in W. Europe in
12th–16th cc. or revived in England
in 18th–19th cc.

gouache (goo'ahsh) n. (painting in)
opaque water-colour.

gouge n. concave-bladed chisel.
v.t. cut or force (out) with or as
with gouge.

gou'lash (goo-; or -ahsh) n. ragout of
steak and vegetables seasoned with
paprika.

gourd (gord or goord) n. (large fleshy
fruit of) kinds of trailing or climbing
plant; dried rind of fruit used as
bottle.

gour'mand (goor-) n. lover of good
fare; glutton.

gourmet (goor'mā) n. connoisseur
of table delicacies, esp. wine.

gout n. disease with painful inflammation of small joints; drop or
splash, esp. of blood. ~y a.

gov (guv) n. (sl.) governor, sir.

gov'ern (gu-) v. rule with authority;
conduct policy and affairs of State
etc.; curb, control; sway, influence.
~ance n. action, manner, power,
etc. of governing; sway, control.

gov'erness (gu-) n. female teacher,
esp. in private household. ~ car(t),
light two-wheeled vehicle with
inward-facing side seats.

gov'ernment (gu-) n. form of polity;
persons governing State; State as
agent; administration or ministry.
~men'tal a.

gov'ernor (gu-) n. ruler; official
governing province, town, etc.;
executive head of State of U.S.;
one of governing body of institution; (sl.) one's employer or father,
sir; (mech.) automatic regulator
ensuring even motion or constant

speed. ~ **general**, representative of Crown in dominion.

gow'an *n.* (Sc.) daisy.

gowk *n.* fool; (dial.) cuckoo.

gown *n.* woman's, esp. formal or elegant, dress; robe of alderman, judge, clergyman, member of university, etc. *v.t.* attire in gown.

goy *n.* (Yiddish for) gentile.

G.P. *abbr.* general practitioner.

G.P.I. *abbr.* general paralysis of the insane.

G.P.O. *abbr.* General Post Office.

G.R. *abbr.* general reserve; *Georgius Rex*, King George.

gr. *abbr.* grain(s); grammar.

grăb *v.* seize suddenly, snatch; appropriate greedily; capture. *n.* sudden clutch or attempt to seize; rapacious proceedings; (mech.) device, esp. hinged double bucket, for clutching or gripping.

grāce *n.* attractiveness, charm, esp. of elegant proportions or ease and refinement of movement, manner, etc.; (mus.) ~(-*note*) embellishment of extra note(s); favour; unconstrained goodwill; divine regenerating and inspiring influence; delay granted; mercy; thanksgiving at meals; *his, her, your, G~*, forms for addressing or referring to duke, duchess or archbishop. *v.t.* add grace to, adorn; honour. ~**ful** *a.* full of grace or charm. ~**less** *a.* shameless, depraved.

gră'cile *a.* slender. ~**cil' itў** *n.*

gră'cious *a.* condescending; kindly; merciful.

gradāte' *v.* (cause to) pass by gradations from one shade to another; arrange in gradations.

gradā'tion *n.* each stage in transition or advance; series of degrees in rank, intensity, etc.; arrangement in grades. ~**al** *a.*

grāde *n.* degree in rank, merit, etc.; gradient, slope; (U.S.) class or form in school; *make the* ~, succeed. *v.t.* arrange in grades; reduce to easy gradients.

grā'dely (-dlĭ) *a.* (dial.) excellent, thorough; handsome; real, true.

grā'dient *n.* (amount of) slope in road, railway, etc.

grăd'ūal *a.* happening by degrees;

not steep or abrupt. *n.* (music for) anthem sung between Epistle and Gospel in Mass.

grăd'ūāte *v.* take or admit to academic degree; (U.S.) pass examination on leaving high school etc.; arrange in gradations; mark in degrees or portions. *n.* (-ĭt), one who has graduated. ~**ā'tion** *n.*

grā'dus *n.* dictionary for use in writing Latin verse.

graffi'tō (-fē-) *n.* (pl. -*ti*, pr. -tē), drawing or writing on wall etc.

graft[1] (grahft) *n.* shoot, scion, planted in slit of another stock; piece of transplanted living tissue. *v.* insert as graft, insert graft(s); fix (*in, on*) in vital or indissoluble union.

graft[2] (grahft) *n.* (practices for securing) illicit political or business spoils. *v.i.* seek or make graft.

grail *n.* legendary platter used by Christ at Last Supper.

grain *n.* fruit or corn of cereal; (collect.) wheat or allied foodgrass; corn; (pl.) refuse malt after brewing; particle, least possible amount; smallest unit of troy etc. weight; texture in skin, wood, stone, etc.; arrangement of lines of fibre in wood; *in* ~, fast dyed, by nature. *v.* form into grains; paint in imitation of grain of wood.

grăllatōr'ial *a.* of long-legged wading birds.

grăm[1] *n.* chick-pea; any pulse used as horse-fodder.

grăm[2], **grămme** *n.* unit of weight in metric system.

gram. *abbr.* grammar.

gramēr'cў *int.* (arch.) thank you.

grămĭnā'ceous *a.* of or like grass.

grămĭnĭv'orous *a.* grass-eating.

grămm'alogue (-ŏg) *n.* (shorthand) word represented by single sign; such sign.

grămm'ar *n.* science of sounds, inflexions, and constructions used in language; book on grammar. ~**-school**, founded for teaching Latin, later often of public-school type; secondary school with academic curriculum. **grammār'ian** *n.* one versed in grammar. **grammăt'ical** *a.* according to grammar.

gramme : see **gram²**.

grăm'ophōne *n.* phonograph reproducing sound from flat discs.

grăm'pus *n.* kinds of blowing and spouting cetacean.

grăn'arỹ *n.* storehouse for grain; region producing grain.

grănd *a.* (in titles) chief, of highest rank; of chief importance; imposing, lofty, noble; (colloq.) excellent. *n.* grand piano; (U.S. sl.) 1,000 dollars. **grandad,** (fam. for) grandfather. **grandam(e),** (arch. for) grandmother. **~child,** one's child's child. **~-daughter,** one's child's daughter. **~father,** one's parent's father. **~father clock,** clock with tall wooden case and usu. weight- -and-pendulum movement. **~ma,** grandmother. **~mother,** one's parent's mother. **~pa,** grandfather. **~parent,** one's parent's parent. **~ piano,** one with strings horizontal. **~sire,** grandfather; method of ringing changes on bells. **~son,** one's child's son. **~-stand,** principal stand for spectators at races etc.

grăndee' *n.* Spanish or Portuguese nobleman of highest rank; great personage.

grăn'deur (-dy*er*) *n.* high rank, eminence; majesty, splendour.

grăndĭl'oquent *a.* pompous or inflated in language. **~ence** *n.*

grăn'diōse *a.* imposing; planned on large scale. **grăndiŏs'itỹ** *n.*

grānge (-j) *n.* country-house with farm buildings.

grā'ngerīze (-j-) *v.t.* illustrate (book etc.) with extra prints etc. esp. cut from other books.

grăn'īte *n.* hard granular crystalline rock of quartz, mica, etc.

grănn'ỹ *n.* (colloq.) grandmother; **~**(-*knot*), reef-knot crossed wrong way.

grant (-ah-) *v.t.* consent to give; concede, permit; transfer legally. *n.* granting; thing or sum granted. **grantee', gran'tŏr** *nn.* person to whom, by whom, property etc. is legally transferred.

grăn'ūlar *a.* of or like grains.

grăn'ūlāte *v.* form into grains; roughen surface of. **~ā'tion** *n.*

grăn'ūle *n.* small grain.

grāpe *n.* green or purple berry growing in clusters on vine; grape-shot; diseased growth on pastern. **~-fruit,** small acid juicy shaddock growing in clusters. **~-shot,** small balls as scattering charge for cannon. **~-vine,** (colloq.) channels by which rumours are carried.

grăph (*or* -ahf) *n.* symbolic diagram representing relation between two variables.

grăph'ic *a.* of drawing, painting, etching, etc.; vividly descriptive; of writing; of diagrams or symbolic curves.

grăph'īte *n.* crystalline form of carbon used in pencils, as lubricant, etc.

graphŏl'ogỹ *n.* study of handwriting. **~ogĭst** *n.*

grăp'nel *n.* grappling-iron; small many-fluked anchor.

grăpp'le *n.* clutching instrument; grip (as) of wrestler; close contest. *v.* seize; grip with hands; come to close quarters with; contend in close fight *with.* **grappling-iron,** iron- -clawed instrument thrown with rope to seize esp. enemy's ship.

grasp (-ah-) *v.* clutch, seize greedily; hold firmly; understand, realize. *n.* fast hold, grip; mental hold, mastery. **~ing** *a.* avaricious.

grass (-ah-) *n.* herbage, kinds of plant with blade-like leaves eaten by horses, cattle, etc.; any species of this; grazing; pasture land; grass- -covered ground, lawn. *v.t.* cover with turf; (sl.) knock down. **~-cloth,** fine light linen-like cloth made from vegetable fibres. **~hopper,** kinds of jumping chirping insect. **~-snake,** harmless common ringed snake. **~ widow,** (sl.) married woman whose husband is absent. **grass'ỹ** *a.*

grāte¹ *n.* frame of metal bars holding fuel in fireplace etc.

grāte² *v.* rub to small particles on rough surface; grind, creak; have irritating effect. **~r** *n.* utensil for grating.

grāte'ful *a.* thankful; feeling or showing gratitude.

grăt'icūle *n.* measuring scale incorporated in optical instrument.

grăt′ĭfȳ *v.t.* please, delight; indulge. **~fĭcā′tion** *n.*

grăt′in (-ăṅ) *n.* dish baked with crust of breadcrumbs, grated cheese, etc.; *au* **~**, so prepared.

grā′tĭng *n.* framework of parallel or crossed bars.

grā′tĭs *adv.* & *a.* (given, done) for nothing, free.

grăt′ĭtūde *n.* being thankful.

gratū′ĭtous, *a.* got or done gratis; uncalled for, motiveless.

gratū′ĭtȳ *n.* money present for services, tip; bounty to soldier.

gravā′mĕn *n.* essence, worst part, *of* accusation.

grave[1] *n.* hole dug for corpse; mound or monument over it; being dead, death. **~stone,** inscribed stone over grave. **~yard,** burial ground.

grāve[2] *v.t.* (p.p. *graved, graven*), engrave, carve; fix indelibly. **~n image,** idol.

grāve[3] *a.* serious, weighty; dignified, solemn; low-pitched. **~ accent,** the accent `.

grāve[4] *v.t.* clean (ship's wooden bottom) by burning and tarring. **~ving dock,** dry dock.

grăv′el *n.* coarse sand and small stones; disease with aggregations of urinary crystals. *v.t.* lay with gravel; puzzle, nonplus. **grăv′ellȳ** *a.* of or like gravel.

grăv′id *a.* pregnant.

graving dock : see **grave**[4].

grăv′ĭtāte *v.i.* move or tend by force of gravity; sink (as) by gravity; be attracted *to*(-*wards*).

gravĭtā′tion *n.* force manifested as mutual attraction between all particles in universe; gravitating. **~al** *a.*

grăv′ĭtȳ *n.* solemnity; importance; weight; attractive force by which bodies tend towards centre of earth.

grā′vȳ *n.* (sauce made from) juices exuding from meat in and after cooking.

gray : see **grey**.

gray′lĭng *n.* silver-grey freshwater fish.

grāze[1] *v.* touch lightly in passing; abrade (skin etc.) in rubbing past; go with passing contact *against, by,* etc. *n.* grazing; abrasion.

grāze[2] *v.* feed on growing grass; pasture cattle. **grā′zier** (-zher) *n.* one who feeds cattle for market.

grease *n.* melted fat of dead animal; fatty or oily matter, esp. as lubricant. *v.t.* lubricate or smear with grease; bribe. **~-gun,** kind of pump for lubricating with grease. **~-paint,** composition for painting actors' faces etc. **grea′ser** (-z-) *n.* (esp. ship's) fireman; (U.S. sl.) native Mexican or Spanish- -American. **grea′sȳ** (*or* -zĭ) *a.* of, like, or smeared with grease; slimy; disagreeably unctuous.

great (grāt) *a.* large in bulk or number; considerable in extent or time; important, pre-eminent; of great ability; familiar; pregnant; hard, difficult, grievous. *n.* what is great; great persons. **~-aunt,** one's parent's aunt. **~coat,** large heavy overcoat. **G~ Dane,** large smooth-haired mastiff-like dog. **~-nephew, ~-niece,** one's nephew's or niece's child. **~ primer,** size of printing-type (18-point). **~-uncle,** one's parent's uncle.

great′lȳ (grāt-) *adv.* much.

greave *n.* armour for shin.

grēbe *n.* kinds of almost tailless diving bird.

Grē′cian *a.* Greek.

greed *n.* insatiate desire for food or wealth. **gree′dȳ** *a.* gluttonous, avaricious.

Greek *n.* native of Greece; Greek language. *a.* of Greece or its people.

green *a.* of colour like grass; unripe, young; inexperienced; not seasoned or dried. *n.* green colour; green part of thing; (pl.) vegetables; piece of public or common grassy land; grass-plot for special purpose. **~back,** U.S. Treasury note. **~finch,** bird with gold and green plumage. **~fly,** aphis. **~gage,** roundish green plum. **~horn,** simpleton, novice. **~house,** glass-house for delicate plants. **~-room,** accommodating actors when off stage. **~sand,** (geological formation of) sand (-stone) containing dark-green hydrated iron silicate. **~stone,** kind of jade. **~stuff,** green vegetables.

~sward, turf. **~wood,** woodlands in summer. **~ish** *a.*

gree'nery *n.* vegetation.

green'grocer (*or* -grō'-) *n.* retailer of fruit and vegetables. **~y** *n.*

gree'ning *n.* kind of apple green when ripe.

greet[1] *v.t.* accost with salutation; salute, receive (*with* words etc.); meet (eye, ear, etc.). **~ing** *n.*

greet[2] *v.i.* (Sc.) weep.

grėgār'ious *a.* living in flocks or communities; fond of company.

Grégōr'ian *a.* of plainsong. **~ calendar,** reformed calendar of Pope Gregory XIII.

grĕg'ory-pow'der *n.* powder of rhubarb etc. used as aperient.

grĕm'lin *n.* (R.A.F. sl.) mischievous sprite said to cause mishaps to aircraft etc.

grėnāde' *n.* small explosive shell thrown by hand or shot from rifle--barrel; device for releasing gases etc. **grĕnadier'** *n.* soldier who threw grenades; (pl.) first regiment of household infantry.

grĕn'adine (-ēn) *n.* French cordial syrup of pomegranates.

grew, *p.t.* of **grow.**

grey, gray (grā) *a.* coloured like ashes or lead; clouded, dull; white or hoary with old age. *n.* grey colour, pigment, or clothes; grey horse; cold sunless light. *v.* make or become grey. **~beard,** old man. **~ friar,** Franciscan monk. **~ hen,** female of black grouse. **~ matter,** grey-looking parts of central nervous system; (joc.) intellectual power.

grey'hound (grā-) *n.* slender swift dog used in coursing hares etc.

grey'lăg (grā-) *n.* common European wild goose.

grid *n.* framework of parallel bars; system of numbered squares for map references; network of lines, electric-power connections, etc.; gridiron.

gridd'le *n.* girdle.

grid'iron (-īrn) *n.* metal cooking utensil supporting food for grilling or broiling; frame for supporting ship in dock; (U.S.) football field.

grief *n.* sorrow, deep trouble; *come to* **~,** meet with disaster, fail.

grie'vance *n.* real or fancied ground of complaint.

grieve *v.* give deep sorrow to; feel grief.

grie'vous *a.* oppressive, painful; flagrant, heinous.

griff'in, griff'on[1]**, grŷph'on** *n.* fabulous creature with eagle's head and wings and lion's body.

griff'on[2] *n.* small coarse-haired terrier-like dog of Belgian breed.

grig *n.* small eel; cricket.

grill[1] *n.* gridiron; grilled food; (also **~-room**) room where food is grilled and served. *v.* broil on grill; put (prisoner etc.) through severe questioning.

grill[2]**, grille** *n.* grating, latticed screen; (tennis) square opening in end wall of court.

grilse *n.* young salmon that has been only once to sea.

grim *a.* stern, merciless; of harsh aspect; ghastly, joyless.

grimāce' *n.* wry face made in disgust or jest; affected look. *v.i.* make grimace.

grimal'kin (-awl-) *n.* old she-cat; spiteful hag.

grime *n.* dirt deeply ingrained. *v.t.* blacken, befoul. **grī'my** *a.*

grĭn *v.i.* show teeth in pain or smile. *n.* act of grinning; broad or forced or mirthless smile.

grĭnd *v.* (*ground*), crush to small particles; harass with exactions; sharpen; study hard, toil; rub gratingly. *n.* grinding; hard dull work; walk etc. for exercise; steeple-chase; (U.S.) student who works hard. **~stone,** (stone used for) revolving disc for grinding, sharpening, etc. **~er** *n.* (esp.) molar tooth.

grĭp *n.* firm hold, grasp; way of holding; mastery, intellectual hold; (U.S.) gripsack. *v.* grasp tightly; take firm hold. **~sack,** (U.S.) traveller's handbag.

grīpe *v.* affect with colic pains; (sl.) complain. *n.* (pl.) colic pains; complaint.

grippe *n.* influenza.

grĭsaille' (-zāl *or* -zīy) *n.* painting in grey monochrome.

gris'kin *n.* lean part of loin of bacon pig.

gris'ly (-z-) *a.* causing terror or horror.

grist *n.* corn for grinding.

grist'le (-sl) *n.* tough flexible tissue; cartilage. **grist'ly** (-slĭ) *a.*

grit *n.* small particles of sand etc.; gritstone; (colloq.) pluck, endurance. *v.* make grating sound; grind or clench (teeth). **~stone,** coarse sandstone. **gritt'ÿ** *a.*

grits *n.pl.* oats husked but unground; coarse oatmeal.

grizz'le *v.i.* (colloq.) whimper, cry fretfully.

grizz'led (-zld) *a.* grizzly.

grizz'ly *a.* grey, grey-haired. **~ bear,** large fierce N.-Amer. bear.

grm. *abbr.* gram(s).

groan *v.* make deep sound expressing pain or grief or disapproval; be oppressed or loaded. *n.* groaning.

groat *n.* silver fourpenny piece.

groats *n.pl.* hulled (and crushed) grain, esp. oats.

gro'cer *n.* dealer in spices, tea, sugar, and domestic stores. **~ÿ** *n.* grocer's trade or goods or (U.S.) shop.

grog *n.* drink of spirit, esp. rum, and water. **grogg'ÿ** (-g-) *a.* drunk; unsteady, shaky.

grog'ram *n.* coarse fabric of silk, mohair, etc.

groin *n.* depression between belly and thigh; edge formed by intersecting vaults. *v.t.* build with groins.

groom *n.* servant who tends horses; bridegroom. *v.t.* tend (horse); give neat or attractive appearance to; prepare (person) for office, occasion, etc. **~sman,** friend attending bridegroom at wedding.

groove *n.* channel or hollow; routine. *v.t.* make groove(s) in.

grope *v.i.* feel about as in dark; search blindly; **~** (*one's way*), move cautiously.

gros'beak *n.* kinds of small bird with large beak.

gros'grain (grog-) *n.* corded fabric or ribbon of silk etc.

gross¹ *n.* twelve dozen.

gross² *a.* luxuriant, rank; flagrant; total, not net; coarse; indecent. *n.* bulk.

grot *n.* (poet.) grotto.

grotesque' (-sk) *n.* decorative style with fantastic interweaving of human and animal forms with foliage; (pop.) comically distorted figure etc. *a.* in grotesque style; bizarre, absurd.

grott'ō *n.* (pl. *-oes*), picturesque cave; structure imitating cave.

grouch *n.* (U.S.) complaint; sulky grumbling mood; grumbler. *v.i.* grumble. **~ÿ** *a.*

ground¹ *n.* surface of earth; bottom of sea or water; (pl.) dregs; land; (pl.) enclosed land attached to house; field or place of action; floor or level; (painting etc.) surface worked upon; foundation, motive. *v.* fix or place on ground; base upon cause or principle; instruct thoroughly; run ashore; keep on ground, prevent from taking off or flying. **~-bait,** bait thrown to bottom to attract fish. **~ bass,** (mus.) short bass phrase repeated with varied upper parts. **~-floor,** storey on level of outside ground. **~ nut,** peanut. **~sman,** man in charge of cricket-ground etc. **~-rent,** rent paid for ground leased for building. **~ speed,** aircraft's speed relative to ground. **~ staff,** non-flying personnel servicing aircraft etc. **~-swell,** heavy sea due to storm etc. **~work,** foundation, chief ingredient.

ground², *p.t.* & *p.p.* of grind.

groun'ding *n.* (esp.) instruction in elements of subject.

ground'less *a.* without motive or foundation.

ground'ling *n.* kinds of fish living at bottom; (arch.) frequenter of pit of theatre.

ground'sel *n.* kinds of weed.

group (-oop) *n.* number of persons or things near or belonging or classed together. *v.* form or fall into group; classify. **~-captain,** R.A.F. officer below air commodore.

grou'per (-oo-) *n.* kinds of sea-fish used for food.

grouse¹ *n.* gallinaceous bird with feathered feet, esp. reddish-coloured British game-bird.

grouse² *v.i.* & *n.* (sl.) grumble.

grout *n.* thin fluid mortar; (pl.) dregs. *v.t.* apply grout to.

grōve *n.* small wood; group of trees.

grŏv′el *v.i.* lie prone, abase oneself. **grŏv′eller** *n.*

grow (-ō) *v.* (*grew*, pr. grōō, p.p. *grown*, pr. -ō-), develop or exist as living plant; produce by cultivation; increase in size, height, amount, etc.; come by degrees; let grow; (pass.) be covered with growth. **～er** *n.*

growl *n.* guttural sound of anger; rumble; murmur, complaint. *v.* make growl. **～er** *n.* (esp., arch.) four-wheeled cab.

grown, *p.p.* of **grow.**

grown′-ŭp (-ō-) *a.* & *n.* adult.

growth (-ōth) *n.* increase; what has grown or is growing; (path.) morbid formation.

groyne *n.* structure run out into sea etc. to stop shifting of beach.

grŭb *v.* dig superficially; clear (ground) of roots etc.; dig *up*, *out*; plod, toil. *n.* larva of insect; (sl.) food. **grŭbb′y̆** *a.* (esp.) dirty, grimy.

grŭdge *v.t.* be unwilling to give or allow. *n.* resentment, ill-will.

gru′el (-ōō-) *n.* liquid food of oatmeal etc.; (sl.) severe punishment. **～ling** *a.* exhausting, punishing.

grue′some (-ōō-) *a.* grisly, disgusting.

grŭff *a.* surly; rough-voiced.

grŭm′ble *n.* faint growl; murmur; complaint. *v.* utter grumble; utter grumblingly; complain; murmur.

grŭm′py̆ *a.* ill-tempered.

grŭnt *n.* low gruff sound characteristic of hogs; any similar sound. *v.* utter (with) grunt.

gruyère (grōō′yār) *n.* Swiss or French pale cows′-milk cheese full of holes.

gryphon : see **griffin.**

gs. *abbr.* guineas.

G.S.O. *abbr.* General Staff Officer.

G-string (jē′-) *n.* cord round waist supporting narrow strip of cloth etc. between legs.

gua′nō (gwah-) *n.* excrement of sea-fowl used as manure.

guarantee′ (gă-) *n.* giver of guaranty or security; guaranty; recipient of guaranty. *v.t.* be guarantee for; answer for; engage, secure. **～tor′** *n.* **gua′ranty̆** *n.* written or other undertaking to answer for performance of obligation; ground of security.

guard (gärd) *n.* defensive posture; watch, vigilant state; protector; sentry; official in charge of train; soldiers etc. protecting place or person; (pl.) household troops; device to prevent injury or accident. *v.* protect, defend; take precautions *against*; keep in check. **～house,** place of detention for military etc. offenders. **～-room,** room for military guard or for keeping prisoners under guard. **～s′man,** soldier of guards.

guar′dian (gär-) *n.* keeper, protector; one having custody of person or property of minor etc.; (hist.) member of elected board administering poor laws. **～ship** *n.*

gua′va (gwah-) *n.* (tropical tree with) acid fruit used for jelly etc.

gūbernatōr′ial *a.* of governor.

gŭdg′eon[1] (-jon) *n.* small freshwater fish; credulous person.

gŭdg′eon[2] (-jon) *n.* kinds of pivot and metal pin. **～-pin,** (esp.) that holding piston and connecting-rod together.

guel′der rōse (gĕ-, -z) *n.* small tree with balls of white flowers.

guer′don (gêr-) *n.* (poet.) reward.

guernsey (gêrn′zĭ) *n.* thick knitted woollen jersey.

guer(r)ill′a (ger-) *n.* man engaged in **～** *war*(*fare*), irregular war waged independently by small bodies.

guess (gĕs) *v.* conjecture, think likely; conjecture rightly. *n.* rough estimate, conjecture. **～-work,** guessing.

guest (gĕst) *n.* person entertained at another's house or table, or lodging at hotel etc.

guffaw′ *n.* coarse or boisterous laugh. *v.* make or say with guffaw.

gui′dance (gī-) *n.* guiding; direction.

guide (gīd) *n.* one who shows way; professional conductor of traveller, climber, etc.; adviser; directing principle; guide-book. *v.t.* act as guide to; lead, direct. **～-book,** of information about place etc. **～-dog,** dog trained to lead blind person. **～-post,** finger-post. **～d** *a.* (esp., of missile etc.) of which course may be controlled during flight etc.

guild, gild² (gĭ-) *n.* society for mutual aid or with common object, esp. medieval trade- or craft-association. ~-hall, meeting-place of medieval guild; town hall.

guile (gīl) *n.* treachery, deceit. ~ful, ~less *aa.*

guill'emot (gĭ-) *n.* kinds of sea-bird.

guilloche (gĭlōsh') *n.* (archit.) ornament like braided ribbons.

guillotine (gĭl'otēn) *n.* beheading--machine; machine for cutting paper; (parl.) method of shortening discussion of bill by fixing voting times. *v.t.* use guillotine upon.

guilt (gĭ-) *n.* having committed offence; culpability. ~less *a.* innocent.

guil'ty (gĭ-) *a.* culpable, criminal; conscious of guilt.

guinea (gĭn'ĭ) *n.* sum of 21s. ~-fowl, gallinaceous bird with white--spotted slate plumage. ~-pig, small S.-Amer. rodent common as pet; person receiving guinea fees, esp. company director; person used as subject of scientific experiment.

guipure' (gĭ-; *or* gē'-) *n.* heavy lace of cut-out pieces of linen joined by openwork embroidery.

guise (gīz) *n.* external, esp. assumed, appearance; pretence.

guitar' (gĭ-) *n.* six-stringed musical instrument played with fingers or plectrum.

gulch *n.* (U.S.) ravine, gully.

gules (-lz) *n. & a.* (her.) red.

gulf *n.* portion of sea like bay but usu. narrower at mouth; deep hollow, chasm; impassable dividing line. G~ Stream, oceanic warm current from Gulf of Mexico.

gull¹ *n.* kinds of long-winged web--footed sea-bird.

gull² *n. & v.t.* dupe, fool. ~ible *a.*; ~bil'ity *n.*

gull'et *n.* food-passage from mouth to stomach; throat.

gull'y *n.* water-worn ravine; gutter, drain; (crick.) part of ground between point and slips.

gulp *v.* swallow hastily or with effort; gasp. *n.* act of gulping; effort to swallow; large mouthful.

gum¹ *n.* firm flesh in which teeth stand. ~boil, small abscess on gum.

gum² *n.* viscid secretion of some trees and shrubs, used as glue etc.; (pl.) kinds of sweetmeat; sticky secretion in inner corner of eye; gum-tree. *v.t.* apply gum to; stick with gum. ~ arabic, gum exuded from kinds of acacia. ~boot, rubber boot. ~-tree, gum-exuding tree. **gumm'y** *a.*

gum'bo *n.* (U.S.) soup thickened with okra pods.

gump'tion *n.* (colloq.) practical sense.

gun *n.* general name for firearms, e.g. cannon, shot-gun, rifle; revolver; member of shooting-party. ~boat, small warship with heavy guns. ~-carriage, support in which gun is mounted. ~-cotton, explosive of cotton steeped in nitric and sulphuric acids. ~man, armed law--breaker. ~-metal, alloy of copper and tin or zinc; dark brownish-grey colour. ~powder, explosive of saltpetre, sulphur, and charcoal. ~room, in warship, for junior officers or as lieutenants' mess--room. ~-running, smuggling of firearms. ~smith, maker of small firearms.

gunn'er *n.* officer, man, of artillery; (naut.) warrant officer in charge of battery, magazine, etc. **gunn'ery** *n.* management of large guns.

gunn'y *n.* coarse sacking or sack, usu. of jute fibre.

gun'ter *n.* flat 2-ft. rule with scales etc. for mechanical solution of surveying etc. problems.

gun'wale (-nal) *n.* upper edge of ship's or boat's side.

gupp'y *n.* very small bright-coloured tropical fresh water fish.

gur'gle *n.* bubbling sound. *v.* make, utter with, gurgle(s).

gur'nard *n.* sea-fish with large spiny head.

guru (gōō'rōō) *n.* Hindu spiritual teacher.

gush *n.* sudden or copious stream; effusiveness. *v.* flow with gush; emit gush of; speak or behave effusively. ~er *n.* (esp.) profusely--spouting oil-well.

guss'et *n.* triangle let in to strengthen or enlarge garment etc.

gust *n.* sudden violent rush of wind;

burst of rain, smoke, anger, etc. **∼ў** *a*.

gŭstā′tion *n*. tasting. **gŭs′tatorў** *a*.

gŭs′tō *n*. zest; enjoyment.

gŭt *n*. (pl.) bowels or entrails; intestine; (pl., sl.) pluck; material for violin strings or fishing-line; narrow water-passage. *v.t.* remove guts of; remove or destroy internal fittings of (house etc.).

gŭtt′a-pēr′cha (*or* -ka) *n*. rubber-like substance got from juice of some Malayan trees.

gŭtt′er *n*. shallow trough below eaves, channel in street, carrying off water; channel, groove. *v*. (of candle) melt away rapidly with wax etc. flowing down. **∼snipe**, street urchin.

gŭtt′ural *a*. of or produced in throat. *n*. guttural sound or letter.

guy[1] (gī) *n*. rope, chain, to steady crane-load etc. or secure tent. *v.t.* secure with guy(s).

guy[2] (gī) *n*. effigy of Guy Fawkes burnt on 5 Nov.; grotesquely dressed perscn; (U.S.) man, fellow. *v.t.* exhibit in effigy, ridicule by mimicry.

gŭzz′le *v*. drink, eat, greedily. **gŭzz′ler** *n*.

G.W.R. *abbr*. Great Western Railway.

gȳbe *v.i.* (of fore-and-aft sail or boom) swing to other side; (of boat etc.) change course thus.

gўm *n*. (sl.) gymnasium, gymnastics. **∼-tunic**, girl's or woman's short sleeveless belted garment for games etc., esp. as school uniform.

gўmkha′na (-kah-) *n*. meeting for competition and display esp. of riding.

gўmnā′sїum (-z-) *n*. (pl. -*ums*, -*a*), room etc. fitted up for gymnastics; highest-grade school in Germany etc.

gўm′năst *n*. expert in gymnastics.

gўmnăs′tĭc *a*. of gymnastics. **∼s** *n. pl*. muscular exercises, esp. as done in gymnasium.

gȳnaecŏl′ogў (g-) *n*. science of diseases of women. **∼lŏ′gĭcal** *a*.; **∼logĭst** *n*.

gўp *n*. male college servant at Cambridge and Durham.

gўpsŏph′ĭla *n*. kinds of plant with numerous small delicate flowers.

gўp′sum *n*. mineral from which plaster of Paris is made.

gypsy : see **gipsy**.

gyrāte′ *v.i.* move in circle or spiral. **∼ā′tion** *n*.; **gȳr′atorў** *a*.

gyr′ō *n*. gyroscope. **∼-compass**, gyroscope used as compass.

gȳr′oscōpe *n*. solid rotating wheel mounted in ring, with axis free to turn in any direction, used to maintain equilibrium, constant direction, etc. **∼scŏp′ic** *a*.

gȳve *n*. & *v.t.* fetter.

H

H *abbr*. hard (of pencil).

h. *abbr*. hot; hour(s).

ha *int*. expressing surprise, triumph, etc.

Hab. *abbr*. Habakkuk.

hā′bēăs cōr′pus *n*. writ requiring person to be brought before judge etc.

hăb′erdăsher *n*. dealer in small articles of dress etc. **∼ў** *n*.

hăb′ergeon (-jon) *n*. (hist.) sleeveless coat of mail.

habïl′ïments *n.pl*. dress.

hăb′ĭt *n*. settled tendency or practice; constitution (of body or mind); dress; lady's riding-dress. *v.t.* clothe.

hăb′ĭtable *a*. that can be inhabited. **∼bĭlĭtў** *n*.

habitant (ăbētahṅ′) *n*. (descendant of) French settler in Canada or Louisiana.

hăb′ĭtăt *n*. natural home of plant or animal.

hăbĭtā′tion *n*. inhabiting; place of abode.

habĭt′ūal *a*. customary; given to (specified) habit.

habĭt′ūāte *v.t.* accustom (*to*). **∼ā′tion** *n*.

hăb′ĭtūde *n*. constitution; custom, tendency.

habĭt′ūé (-ā) *n*. frequenter (*of*).

hăcĭĕn′da *n*. (Sp.-Amer.) estate, plantation.

hăck[1] *n*. wound, gash, esp. from kick. *v*. cut, mangle; kick. **∼-saw**, saw with narrow blade set in frame.

hǎck² *n.* hired horse; horse for ordinary riding; hired, esp. literary, drudge; scribbler; (U.S.) taxi. *v.i.* ride at ordinary pace or on road; (U.S.) operate taxi(s). **~work,** dull routine work, esp. of literary hack.

hǎck'ing *a.* (of cough) short, dry, and frequent.

hǎck'le *n.* steel flax-comb; long feathers on neck of domestic cock etc.; fishing-fly dressed with hackle--feather; *with* **~s** *up*, angry, ready to fight. *v.t.* dress with hackle.

hǎck'ney *n.* horse for ordinary riding. *v.t.* make common or trite by repetition. **~-cab, -carriage,** etc. vehicle plying for hire.

had, *p.t. & p.p.* of **have.**

hǎdd'ock *n.* common sea-fish used for food.

Hā'dēs (-z) *n.* (Gk. myth.) abode of departed spirits.

Hǎdj'ǐ, Hǎjj'ǐ *n.* Moslem pilgrim who has been to Mecca.

hae'matǐn *n.* bluish-black constituent of haemoglobin.

hae'matīte, hěm- (*or* hě-) *n.* red or brown or blackish iron ore.

haemoglō'bǐn *n.* oxygen-carrying pigment of red blood-cells.

haemophǐl'ǐa *n.* hereditary incapacity of blood to clot. **~ǐăc** *n. & a.*

haemorrhage, hem- (hěm'orǐj) *n.* escape of blood from blood-vessels, bleeding.

haemorrhoids, hem- (hěm'oroidz) *n.pl.* varicose veins of anus.

hǎf'nǐum *n.* rare metallic element.

haft (hah-) *n.* handle (of knife etc.). *v.t.* furnish with haft.

hǎg¹ *n.* ugly old woman. **~ridden,** afflicted by nightmare.

hǎg² *n.* (Sc.) soft place in moor; firm place in peat-bog.

Hag. *abbr.* Haggai.

hǎgg'ard *a.* wild-looking (esp. from fatigue, privation, etc.); (of hawk) untamed. *n.* haggard hawk.

hǎgg'is *n.* minced heart etc. of sheep boiled in maw with oatmeal etc.

hǎgg'le *v.i. & n.* dispute, esp. about price or terms.

hǎgiǒg'rapha (-gǐ-) *n.pl.* Hebrew Scriptures not included under Law and Prophets.

hǎgiǒg'raphў (-gǐ-) *n.* (writing of) life or lives of saint(s). **~grǎph'ic** *a.*

hǎgiǒl'atry *n.* worship of saints.

ha ha (hah hah) *int.* representing laughter.

ha=ha (hah'hah) *n.* sunk fence bounding park or garden.

hail¹ *n.* pellets of condensed and frozen vapour falling in shower; shower *of* questions etc. *v.* pour down as or like hail. **~-stone,** pellet of hail.

hail² *int.* of greeting. *v.* salute; greet (*as*); call to; be come *from*. *n.* hailing.

hair *n.* any or all of fine filaments growing from skin esp. of human head; hair-like thing. **~cloth,** cloth made of hair. **~-do,** (colloq.) (mode of) dressing of hair. **~line,** (esp.) very thin line. **~pin bend,** very sharp bend where road etc. doubles back. **~-raising,** full of excitement and terror. **~'s-breadth,** minute distance; very narrow (escape etc.). **~-shirt,** ascetic's or penitent's shirt of haircloth. **~-splitting,** over-subtle(ty). **~-spring,** fine spring regulating balance-wheel of watch. **~ trigger,** trigger acting on very slight pressure. **~lĕss, ~līke, ~ў** *aa.*

Hajji : see **Hadji.**

hāke *n.* cod-like sea-fish.

hakeem', -kim' (-ēm) *n.* Moslem physician.

halā'tion *n.* (phot.) spreading of light beyond its proper boundary in negative.

hǎl'berd *n.* (hist.) combined spear and battle-axe. **~ier'** *n.* man armed with halberd.

hǎl'cўon *n.* bird fabled to calm wind and sea; kingfisher. *a.* peaceful, quiet.

hāle¹ *a.* robust, vigorous.

hāle² *v.t.* drag forcibly.

half (hahf) *n.* (pl. *halves*), either of two (esp. equal) parts into which thing is divided; (colloq.) school term; (colloq.) half-back, half--holiday, etc. *a.* amounting to half. *adv.* in part; equally. **~-and-~,** (mixture of) half one thing and half another. **~-back,** position or player between forwards and backs.

~-**baked**, incomplete, half-witted.
~-**bound**, -**calf**, etc., with leather back and corners only. ~-**breed**, (person) of mixed race. ~-**brother**, -**sister**, related by one parent only. ~-**caste**, half-breed. ~-**crown**, coin worth 2s. 6d. ~-**deck**, (esp.) deck covering about half of partly open craft. ~-**hearted**, lacking courage or zeal. ~-**hitch**, one formed by passing end of rope round standing part and then through bight. ~-**holiday**, day of which (latter) half is holiday. ~-**life**, time required for half atoms of radioactive substance to disintegrate. ~-**mast**, half height of mast; at ~-*mast*, (of flag) lowered to this position as symbol of mourning. ~-**moon**, (shape of) moon with disc half illuminated. ~ **mourning**, black relieved by grey etc. ~ (-)**nelson**, wrestling hold. ~-**pay**, given to officer not in actual service or after retirement. ~-**seas-over**, half drunk. ~-**timber(ed)**, with spaces in timber frame filled with bricks or plaster. ~-**tone**, semitone; tone between extreme lights and shades; (photographic reproduction) representing tones by large or small dots. ~-**volley**, ball hit or returned as soon as it touches ground. ~-**wit(ted)**, imbecile.

halfpenny (hā'pnĭ) n. (pl. *halfpence*, pr. hā'pens, *halfpennies*), bronze coin worth half penny.

hăl'ĭbut n. large flat fish.

hălĭtō'sĭs n. (med.) foul breath.

hall (hawl) n. large public room; college dining-room; building for residence or instruction of students etc.; residence of landed proprietor; entrance-passage, (U.S.) any corridor or passage. ~**mark**, (stamp with) impression used for marking standard of gold, silver, etc. ~**way**, (U.S.) entrance-hall, passage.

hăllĕlu'jah (-lōōya) int. & n. alleluia.

halliard : see **halyard**.

hallō', -**loa'** int. & n. hello.

hallōō' int. & n. (cry) inciting dogs to chase etc. v. cry halloo; urge on (dogs) with shouts; shout.

hăll'ow (-ō) v.t. make or honour as holy. ~**e'en**, eve of All Hallows. **H~mas**, All Hallows.

hallū'cĭnāte (or -lōō-) v.t. produce hallucinations in. ~**ā'tion** n. illusion; apparent perception of object not present. ~**atorў**, ~**ative** aa.

hăl'ma n. game played on board of 256 squares.

hā'lō n. (pl. -*oes*), circle of light round sun, moon, etc.; disc of light round head of saint. v.t. surround with halo.

hăl'ogĕn n. any of group of elements fluorine, chlorine, bromine, iodine.

halt[1] (hawlt or hŏ-) n. stoppage on march or journey; small railway-station without usual staff etc. v. come or bring to stand.

halt[2] (hawlt or hŏ-) a. lame. v.i. hesitate; walk hesitatingly; limp.

hal'ter (hawl- or hŏ-) n. rope, strap, with noose or headstall for horses or cattle; rope for hanging person.

halve (hahv) v.t. divide into halves; reduce to half.

hăl'yard, **hăll'ĭard** n. rope or tackle for raising and lowering sail etc.

hăm[1] n. back of thigh; thigh and buttock; cured hog's thigh; (licensed) operator of amateur radio station; (sl.) (inexperienced or ineffective but) flamboyant performer. v. overact. ~-**fisted**, (sl.) large- or heavy-handed, clumsy. **hămm'ў** a.

hăm[2] n. (hist.) town, village.

hămadrȳ'ăd n. wood-nymph.

hăm'bŭrger (-ger) n. fried cake of chopped beef.

hăm'lĕt n. small village, esp. without church.

hămm'er n. instrument or contrivance or machine for beating, striking, breaking, driving nails, etc.; auctioneer's mallet. v. strike or drive (as) with hammer. ~-**cloth**, cloth covering driver's seat in coach. ~-**lock**, hold in which wrestler's arm is bent behind back.

hămm'ock n. bed of canvas or netting suspended by cords at ends.

hăm'per[1] n. basketwork packing-case.

hăm'per[2] v.t. obstruct movement of; impede, hinder.

hăm'ster n. small rat-like rodent.

hăm'string n. any of five tendons at back of human knee; tendon at back of hock. *v.t.* (*-inged* or *-ŭng*), cripple by cutting hamstring(s).

hand *n.* terminal part beyond wrist of human arm or monkey's limb; charge, disposal, agency, share (*in* doing); pledge of marriage; (right or left) side; source; skill, style, esp. of writing; person in reference to skill; manual worker in factory etc.; (pl.) ship's crew; hand-like thing, esp. pointer of clock etc., bunch of bananas; 4 in. as measure of horse's height; cards dealt to card-player, round or game of cards. *v.t.* help with hand (*into, out of,* etc.); deliver or transfer (as) with hand. ~**bag**, small bag for purse etc. carried by woman. ~**bill**, notice circulated by hand. ~**book**, short treatise, guide-book. ~**-cuff**, put handcuffs on. ~**-cuffs**, (pl.) pair of metal rings joined by short chain for securing prisoner's hands. ~**-gallop**, easy gallop. ~**-out**, (U.S.) alms etc. given (as) to beggar; information etc. distributed to press etc. ~ **over hand**, with each hand in turn passing over the other, as in rope-climbing; gaining rapidly in pursuit. ~**-picked**, carefully chosen. ~**rail**, rail along edge of stairs etc. ~**s down**, easily, without efforts. ~**s off**! do not touch. ~**spike**, lever for shifting heavy objects by hand. ~**s up**! order to lift hands in sign of surrender, assent, etc. ~**writing**, (style of) writing by hand.

h. & c. *abbr.* hot and cold (water).

hănd′ful (-ool) *n.* (pl. *-fuls*), enough to fill hand; small number or quantity; (colloq.) troublesome person or task.

hăn′dĭcăp *n.* disadvantage imposed on superior competitor to equalize chances; race etc. in which handicaps are imposed; disadvantage, disability. *v.t.* impose handicap on; place at disadvantage.

hăn′dicraft (-ahft) *n.* manual art, trade, or skill. ~**sman** *n.*

hăn′dĭwork (-wĕrk) *n.* thing done or made by hands or by personal agency.

handkerchief (hăng′kerchĭf) *n.* square of linen, silk, etc., used to wipe nose etc. or worn round neck.

hăn′dle *n.* part of thing by which it is held. *v.t.* touch or feel with hands; manage, deal with; treat in discourse. ~**bar(s)**, steering-bar of bicycle etc.

hănd′maid, -en *nn.* (arch.) female servant.

hănd′sel (-ns-) *n.* New-Year gift; earnest money; foretaste. *v.t.* give handsel to.

hănd′some (-ns-) *a.* of fine appearance; generous; considerable.

hăn′dy *a.* ready to hand; convenient to handle; clever with hands. ~**man**, man useful for all sorts of odd jobs.

hăng *v.* (*hŭng,* exc. as below), (cause to) be supported by hooks etc. from above; attach (wall-paper); cause to rest on hinges etc.; decorate (wall *with* drapery etc.); (*hanged*) suspend, be suspended, by neck, esp. as capital punishment; droop; hover; ~ *about,* wait idly, linger, stay about; remain or be suspended. *n.* way thing hangs; *get* ~ *of,* get knack of, understand. ~ **man**, executioner. ~**nail**, agnail. ~**er**[1] *n.* (esp.) loop etc. by which thing hangs; short sword; ~**er-on**, follower, dependent. ~**ings** *n.pl.* drapery for walls etc.

hăng′ar *n.* shed for housing aircraft etc.

hăng′dŏg *a.* base and sneaking.

hăng′er[2] *n.* wood on hill-side.

hăng′ōver *n.* aftermath of alcoholic excess.

hănk *n.* coil or length of wool, thread, etc.

hănk′er *v.i.* crave, long, *after* or *for.*

hănk′y *n.* (colloq.) handkerchief.

hănk′y-pănk′y *n.* underhand dealing.

hăn′som *n.* light two-wheeled cab with driver mounted behind.

Hants *abbr.* Hampshire.

hăp *n.* (arch.) chance, luck. *v.i.* happen.

hăphăz′ard (-p-h-) *n.* mere chance. *a.* casual. *adv.* casually.

hăp′less *a.* unlucky.

hăp′ly *adv.* (arch.) perhaps.

hā′′p′orth *n.* halfpennyworth.

hăpp′en *v.i.* come to pass, fall out, occur; come by chance.

hăpp'ў *a.* lucky, fortunate; content; glad; apt, felicitous. ~-go-lucky, haphazard; easy-going.

hă'ra-kĭ'rĭ *n.* Japanese suicide by disembowelment.

harăngue' (-ng) *n.* speech to assembly; vehement address. *v.* make harangue (to).

hă'rass *v.t.* worry, trouble; attack repeatedly. ~ment *n.*

hăr'bĭnger (-j-) *n.* one who announces another's approach, forerunner.

hăr'bour (-b*er*) *n.* place of shelter for ships; shelter. *v.* come to anchor in harbour; give shelter to; entertain. ~age *n.* shelter.

hărd *a.* firm, solid; stern, unyielding, cruel; difficult to bear or do; inclement, severe; strenuous; (U.S., of liquor) spirituous, strong. *adv.* strenuously, severely; with difficulty. *n.* firm beach or foreshore; roadway across foreshore. ~bake, almond toffee. ~board, compressed fibre-board. ~-boiled, (of eggs) boiled until white and yoke are solid; callous, hard-headed, sophisticated. ~ core, broken stones, clinker, etc. as road foundation. ~ court, lawn-tennis court · of asphalt etc. not grass. ~ currency, readily convertible into other currencies. ~-favoured, harsh-featured. ~-headed, practical, not sentimental. ~-hearted, unfeeling, merciless. ~-laid, tightly twisted or woven. ~ lines, ill luck, bad fortune. ~-pan, firm compacted subsoil of clay etc.; hard unbroken ground. ~ sell, aggressive salesmanship. ~ up, short of money. ~ware, ironmongery. ~ water, containing mineral salts which decompose soap, cause incrustations in boilers, etc. ~wood, of deciduous trees as opp. pines and firs. ~en *v.* make or grow hard, callous, or hardy. ~ness *n.*

hăr'dĭhŏŏd *n.* audacity.

hărd'lў *adv.* with difficulty; scarcely; harshly, severely.

hărd'shĭp *n.* hardness of fate or circumstance; severe suffering or privation.

hăr'dў *a.* bold; robust; capable of resisting exposure.

hāre *n.* speedy mammal with long ears, short tail, and divided upper lip. *v.i.* run very fast. ~ and hounds, paper-chase. ~-brained, rash, wild. ~-lip, fissure of upper lip.

hāre'bĕll *n.* round-leaved slender--stalked pale-blue flower.

hār'em *n.* women's part of Moslem dwelling; its occupants, esp. wives and concubines.

hă'rĭcot (-ō) *n.* ragout, usu. of mutton. ~ bean, dried French bean.

hărk *v.i.* listen; (as call to hounds) go (*forward* etc.); ~ back, retrace course to find scent; revert (*to* subject).

hăr'lĕquĭn *n.* (in pantomime) mute character in parti-coloured be-spangled tights. ~āde' *n.* part of pantomime.

hăr'lot *n.* prostitute. ~rў *n.*

hărm *n.* & *v.t.* damage, hurt. ~ful *a.* that does harm. ~less *a.* that does no harm.

hărmŏn'ĭc *a.* of or in harmony. *n.* secondary tone produced by vibration of aliquot parts of sonorous body; component frequency of wave etc. which is integral multiple of fundamental frequency. ~ minor, (mus.) scale with minor sixth and major seventh both ascending and descending.

hărmŏn'ĭca *n.* mouth-organ.

hărmō'nious *a.* in concord; free from dissent; tuneful.

hăr'monĭst *n.* one skilled in harmony.

hărmō'nium *n.* keyboard musical instrument with bellows and metal reeds.

hăr'monīze *v.* bring into, be in, harmony; add notes to (melody) to form chords. ~zā'tion *n.*

hăr'monў *n.* agreement, concord; combination of notes to form chords; melodious sound.

hăr'nĕss *n.* gear of draught horse etc.; (hist.) defensive armour. *v.t.* put harness on; utilize (waterfall etc.) for motive power.

hărp *n.* musical instrument with strings of graduated lengths played with fingers. *v.i.* play harp; dwell tediously *on*. ~ĭst *n.*

hărpōŏn' *n.* spear-like missile for

catching whales etc. *v.t.* strike with harpoon.

hǎrp'sǐchŏrd (-k-) *n.* keyboard musical instrument with strings plucked by quill or metal points.

hǎr'pў *n.* monster with woman's face and bird's wings and claws; rapacious and cruel woman.

hǎr'quèbus, ǎr- *n.* (hist.) portable gun supported on tripod.

hǎ'rrǐdan *n.* haggard old woman, vixen.

hǎ'rrǐer *n.* hound used in hunting hare; (pl.) pack of these; (pl.) hare-and-hounds club; kind of falcon.

Hǎ'rris tweed *n.* hand-woven tweed made in Harris in Hebrides.

hǎ'rrow (-ō) *n.* frame with tines or discs for breaking clods etc. *v.t.* draw harrow over; distress, wound (feelings etc.).

hǎ'rrў *v.t.* ravage, spoil (land, people); harass.

hǎrsh *a.* severe, unfeeling; rough to ear, taste, etc.

hǎrt *n.* male of (esp. red) deer.

hǎr'tèbeest *n.* large S.-Afr. antelope.

hǎrts'hŏrn (-s-h-) *n.* former source of ammonia got from hart's horns.

hǎrt's'-tongue (-tŭng) *n.* fern with long undivided fronds.

hār'um-scār'um *a.* reckless.

hǎr'vèst *n.* season for reaping and storing of grain etc.; season's yield. *v.t.* reap and gather in. ~**er** *n.* reaper; reaping-machine.

has : see **have.**

hǎsh *v.t.* cut (cooked meat etc.) in small pieces for warming up. *n.* dish of hashed meat; mess, botch; *settle* ~ *of*, make end of, do for.

hǎsh'ǐsh *n.* narcotic drug got from hemp.

hā'slèt (-z-) *n.* edible offal, esp. of pig.

hasp (hah-) *n.* clasp passing over staple and secured by pin etc.

hǎss'ock *n.* kneeling-cushion.

hāste *n.* urgency of movement; hurry; *make* ~, be quick. *v.i.* go in haste.

hā'sten (-sn) *v.* (cause to) proceed or go quickly.

hā'stў *a.* hurried; rash; quick-tempered. ~ **pudding,** pudding of oatmeal, cornmeal, etc. stirred in boiling milk or water.

hǎt *n.* outdoor head-covering, esp. with brim. ~**-trick,** (crick.) taking three wickets with successive balls. **hǎtt'èd** *a.* wearing a hat.

hǎtch[1] *n.* lower half of divided door; aperture in door, floor, etc.; hatchway, trap-door over it. ~**way,** opening in deck for lowering cargo.

hǎtch[2] *v.* bring or come forth from egg; incubate; form (plot). *n.* hatching; brood hatched.

hǎtch[3] *v.t.* engrave or draw (parallel) lines on.

hǎtch'erў *n.* place for hatching (esp. fish-) eggs.

hǎtch'èt *n.* light short axe.

hǎtch'ment *n.* armorial tablet of deceased person.

hāte *v.t.* dislike strongly; bear malice to. *n.* hatred.

hāte'ful (-tf-) *a.* exciting hatred.

hā'trèd *n.* active dislike; ill-will.

hatted : see **hat. hǎtt'er** *n.* hatmaker or dealer.

haugh'tў (haw-) *a.* proud, arrogant.

haul *v.* pull or drag forcibly; transport by cart etc.; turn ship's course; (of wind) shift, veer. *n.* hauling; distance hauled; catch (of fish etc.); amount or things acquired, booty. ~**age** *n.* conveyance of loads, charge for it. ~**ier** *n.* one who hauls, esp. tubs in coal-mine; jobbing carter; haulage contractor.

haulm (hawm) *n.* stalks of beans, peas, potatoes, etc.

haunch *n.* part of body between ribs and thigh; leg and loin of deer etc. as food.

haunt *v.t.* (of ghosts etc.) visit frequently with manifestations of their presence and influence; be persistently in or with; obsess. *n.* place of frequent resort.

haut'boy (hō- *or* ōb-) *n.* old name for oboe.

haute couture (ōt kōōtūr') *n.* (world of) high fashion. [F]

hauteur (ōter') *n.* haughtiness.

Havǎn'a *n.* cigar of Cuban tobacco.

have (hǎv, hav) *v.* (3rd sing. pres. *has*, pr. hǎz, haz; p.t. & p.p. *had*, pr. hǎd, had), hold in possession; possess, contain; enjoy, suffer; be burdened with; (sl.) *be had*, be taken in or cheated. *v. aux.* with p.p. of another vb. forming compound or perfect tenses of that vb. *n.* (sl.) swindle; (pl.) those who have, *the* wealthy etc. **~-nŏts** *n.pl.* those without wealth, privilege, etc.

hā'ven *n.* harbour; refuge.

hā'ver *v.i.* (Sc.) talk foolishly, babble. *n.* (usu. pl.) nonsense.

hăv'ersăck *n.* soldier's or traveller's canvas bag for provisions carried on back or over shoulder.

hăv'oc *n.* devastation.

haw *n.* hawthorn berry.

haw'finch *n.* common grosbeak.

hawk[1] *n.* bird of prey used in falconry; rapacious person. *v.* hunt with hawk. **~-moth**, large moth with hovering and darting flight. **~-nosed**, with aquiline nose.

hawk[2] *v.* clear throat noisily; bring (phlegm etc.) *up* from throat.

hawk[3] *v.t.* carry about for sale. **~er** *n.* itinerant vendor, street seller.

hawse (-z) *n.* part of ship's bows in which **~-holes** are cut for anchor cables. **haw'ser** *n.* large rope, small cable, freq. of steel.

haw'thorn *n.* thorny shrub or small tree bearing red berries.

hay *n.* grass mown and dried for fodder. **~cock**, conical heap of hay. **~ fever**, summer catarrh etc. caused by pollen etc. **~loft**, loft for hay in outbuilding. **~maker**, one employed in drying grass for hay; (sl.) swinging blow. **~stack**, regular pile of hay. **~wire**, tangled, in disorder, crazy.

hăz'ard *n.* dice-game; chance; danger, risk; winning opening in tennis-court; (golf) bunker, water, or other bad ground. *v.t.* expose to hazard; run hazard of; venture on (guess etc.). **~ous** *a.* risky.

hāze[1] *n.* (slight) mist; mental obscurity. *v.t.* make hazy.

hāze[2] *v.t.* (naut.) harass with overwork; (U.S.) subject to cruel horseplay.

hā'zel *n.* nut-bearing bush or small tree; light- or yellowish-brown colour of ripe hazel-nut.

hā'zy *a.* misty; vague.

HB *abbr.* hard black (of pencil).

H-bomb (āch-) *n.* hydrogen bomb.

H.C. *abbr.* House of Commons.

H.C.F. *abbr.* highest common factor.

hē *pron.* (obj. *him*, poss. *his*; pl. *they*, obj. *them*, poss. *their*), the male person or animal in question. *n.* (pl. *hes*) & *a.* male. **~-man**, masterful or virile man.

H.E. *abbr.* high explosive; His Excellency.

head (hĕd) *n.* upper part of man's, anterior part of animal's, body; ruler, chief, principal person, headmaster, headmistress; thing like head in form or position; source of stream; division in discourse etc.; culmination. *v.* lead, influence, direct; put oneself or be put at head of; get ahead of, turn *back* or *off* thus; strike (football) with head; make *for*. **~ache**, continuous pain in head; (colloq.) troublesome or annoying thing. **~-dress**, esp. ornamental covering for head. **~light**, powerful light at front of car etc. **~-line**, (line at top of page etc. with) title or summary esp. of important or sensational news item. **~master**, **~mistress**, principal master, mistress, of school. **~-on**, with front of vehicle etc. pointed towards or running into something. **~-phone**, telephone etc. receiver attachable to listener's ears. **~piece**, helmet; (colloq.) intellect. **~room**, overhead space. **~stall**, part of bridle or halter fitting round head. **~-stone**, grave-stone. **~way**, progress. **~ wind**, blowing from directly in front. **~er** *n.* (esp.) head-first plunge; (footb.) stroke made with head. **~ing** *n.* title etc. at head of page etc.; horizontal passage in mine etc.

head'land (hĕd-) *n.* promontory; unploughed strip at end of field.

head'lŏng (hĕd-) *a.* rash, precipitate. *adv.* rashly, precipitately.

head'quarters (hĕdkwor-) *n.pl.* centre of operations; commander-in-chief's residence.

heads'man (hĕd-) *n.* one who beheads.

head'strŏng (hĕd-) *a.* self-willed.

head'y (hĕd-) *a.* impetuous; (of liquor etc.) apt to intoxicate.

heal *v.* restore to health; cure; become sound. **~er** *n.*

health (hĕl-) *n.* soundness of body,

mind, etc.; condition of body; toast in person's honour. ~ful a. health-giving; conducive to moral etc. welfare.

health′ỹ (hĕl-) a. having or conducive to good health.

heap n. group of things lying one on another; (colloq.) large number or amount. v.t. pile in heap; load; accumulate.

hear v. (*heard*, pr. hĕrd), perceive with ear; listen, give audience, to; listen judicially to; be informed; entertain notion *of*; receive message etc. *from*. ~say, gossip, rumour. ~er n. ~ing n.; *hard of* ~*ing*, slightly deaf; ~ing-aid, device for improving hearing of partially deaf.

hear′ken (här-) v.i. listen (*to*).

hearse (hĕrs) n. vehicle for conveying coffin.

heart (härt) n. organ of circulation; seat of emotions or affections; soul, mind; courage; central or vital part, essence; (conventionally) heart- -shaped thing; (pl.) suit of playing- -cards marked with hearts; *at* ~, in inmost feelings; *by* ~, in or from memory; *with all one's* ~, sincerely, willingly; *take to* ~, be much affected by; *have the heart*, be hard-hearted enough (*to*). ~-breaking, ~-broken, causing, crushed by, great distress. ~burn, burning sensation in chest. ~burn- ing, jealousy, grudge. ~felt, sin- cere. ~-rending, distressing. ~sease, (esp. small wild) pansy. ~sick, despondent. ~-strings, one's deepest affections. ~-to-~, frank, sincere (talk). ~-whole, not in love.

hear′ten (här-) v. inspirit, cheer.

hearth (härth) n. floor of fireplace. ~-rug, rug laid before hearth. ~-stone, slab forming hearth; stone for whitening hearth.

hear′tilỹ (här-) adv. in hearty manner; very.

heart′less (härt-) a. unfeeling, pitiless.

hearty (här′tĭ) a. vigorous; genial; sincere; (of meals) copious.

heat n. hotness; hot weather; in- flamed state of body; warmth of feeling; anger; preliminary contest

winner(s) of which compete in final. v. make or become hot; inflame. ~-stroke, affection of nervous system due to exposure to excessive heat. ~-wave, period of very hot weather. ~èdly adv. vehemently, angrily.

heath n. flat waste tract of land, esp. covered with low shrubs; under- -shrub of heather kind. ~-cock, blackcock. ~ỹ a.

hea′then (-dh-) a. not Christian, Jewish, Moslem, or Buddhist. n. heathen person; unenlightened person. ~dom, ~ism nn.; ~ish a.

heather (hĕdh′er) n. (esp.) purple- -flowered plant of moors and heaths. ~ mixture, (fabric, esp. tweed) of mixed or speckled hues. ~ỹ a.

heave v. (*heaved*, naut. also *hŏve*), lift, raise; utter (sigh, groan) with effort; (naut.) haul; (colloq.) throw; pull (*at* rope etc.); swell, rise; dis- place; ~ *in sight*, become visible; ~ *to*, bring vessel to standstill with head to wind. n. heaving.

heav′en (hĕ-) n. sky; regions above; abode of God; place of bliss. ~lỹ a. of heaven, divine; of sky; of divine or (colloq.) great excellence.

heav′ilỹ (hĕ-) adv. ponderously; sorrowfully, dejectedly.

Heav′isīde layer (hĕ-; lār) n. part of ionosphere reflecting back longer radio waves.

heav′ỹ (hĕ-) a. of great weight; of great specific gravity; compact, dense; laden; abundant; striking or falling with force; hard to digest; (of ground) difficult to travel over; dull, tedious, oppressive, sad. ~-handed, clumsy. ~ hydrogen, deuterium. ~ spar, barytes. ~ water, deuterium oxide, with same chemical properties as water but greater density. ~-weight, boxing- -weight (over 12 st. 7 lb.).

Heb. *abbr.* Hebrews.

hĕbdŏm′adal a. weekly.

Hēbrā′ic a. of Hebrews or Hebrew. **Hē′brāism, Hē′brāist** nn.; **Hēbrā- is′tic** a.

Hē′brew (-rōō) n. & a. (person, Semi- tic language) of tribe or nation descended from Abraham, Isaac, and Jacob; Jew, Jewish.

hĕc'atomb (-ōm *or* -ōōm) *n.* great public sacrifice.

hĕck'le *v.t.* hackle (flax etc.); interrupt or harass (speaker, esp. election candidate) with questions etc.

hĕc'tĭc *a.* consumptive; (sl.) excited, wild.

hĕc'togrăm, hĕc'tolitre (-lēt*er*), **hĕc'tomĕtre** *nn.* 100 grams, litres, metres.

hĕc'tograph (-grahf) *n.* apparatus for multiplying copies of writing. *v.t.* multiply with this.

hĕc'tor *v.* bluster, bully.

hĕdge *n.* fence of bushes or low trees; barrier of turf, stone, etc. *v.* surround with hedge; make or trim hedges; secure oneself against loss on (bet etc.); avoid committing oneself. **~-hopping,** aircraft's low flight, rising and falling over ground obstacles. **~row,** row of bushes forming hedge. **~-sparrow,** common European warbler. **~er** *n.*

hĕdge'hŏg *n.* small spiny nocturnal insectivorous quadruped.

hē'donĭsm *n.* doctrine that pleasure is chief good. **~ist** *n.*; **~ist'ic** *a.*

heed *v.t.* attend to; take notice (of). *n.* care, attention. **~ful, ~less** *aa.*

hee'-haw *n. & v.i.* bray.

heel[1] *n.* hinder part of human foot; (pop.) quadruped's hind foot, hinder part of hoof; part of sock etc. that covers, or of boot etc. that supports, heel; (U.S.) contemptible person, cad. *v.* (Rugby footb.) pass (ball) backward (*out* of scrum) with heel. **~ball,** shoemaker's polishing mixture of wax and lamp black. **~tap,** liquor left at bottom of glass. **~ed** *a.* (U.S.) armed, esp. with revolver; supplied with money etc. **~er** *n.* (esp. U.S.) local worker for professional politician.

heel[2] *v.* (of ship etc.) lean over; make heel. *n.* heeling.

hĕft *n.* weight. *v.t.* lift, esp. to judge weight. **hĕf'tў** *a.* heavy; sturdy; stalwart.

hĕgĕm'onў (-g-; *or* hē'jĭ-; *or* hĕ-) *n.* leadership.

heif'er (hĕf-) *n.* young cow that has not had calf.

heigh (hā) *int.* expr. encouragement

or inquiry. **~-hō,** expr. boredom etc.

height (hīt) *n.* measure from base to top; elevation above ground or sea level; high point; top; utmost degree.

heigh'ten (hī-) *v.t.* raise higher; intensify; exaggerate.

hei'nous (hān-) *a.* atrocious.

heir (ār) *n.* person entitled to property or rank as legal representative of former holder. **~ apparent, presumptive,** whose claim cannot, may, be superseded by birth of nearer heir. **~loom,** piece of property that has been in family for generations. **~èss** *n.*

held, *p.t. & p.p.* of **hold.**

hĕl'ical *a.* spiral.

helices : see **helix.**

hĕl'icŏpter *n.* aircraft with horizontal air-screws.

hē'liograph *n.* signalling apparatus reflecting flashes of sunlight. *v.t.* send (message) by this.

hē'liotrōpe (*or* hĕl'-) *n.* plant with small clustered purple flowers: colour or scent of these.

hēlĭotrŏp'ĭc *a.* (of plant) turning under influence of light.

hĕl'ĭpŏrt *n.* station for helicopter passenger services.

hē'lĭum *n.* light almost inert gaseous atmospheric element.

hē'lĭx (*or* hĕ-) *n.* (pl. -*icēs*), spiral; rim of external ear.

hĕll *n.* abode of dead or damned; state of misery; gaming-house. **~ĭsh** *a.*

hĕll'ebŏre *n.* kinds of ranunculaceous plant including Christmas rose.

Hĕll'ēne *n.* Greek. **~ē'nic** *a.*; **~ēnĭsm, ~ēnĭst** *nn.*

hĕllō' *int. & n.* calling attention or expr. surprise or greeting.

hĕlm[1] *n.* tiller or wheel for managing rudder; space through which helm is turned. **~sman,** steersman.

hĕlm[2] *n.* (arch.) helmet.

hĕl'mĕt *n.* defensive or protective head-cover of soldiers, firemen, etc

hĕl'ot *n.* Spartan slave; serf.

hĕlp *v.t.* (*helped*; arch. p.t. *hōlp,* p.p. *hōlpen*), aid, assist; remedy, prevent, avoid. *n.* assistance; domestic servant; (U.S.) farm or household servants; remedy; helper.

hĕlp'ful *a*. useful, serviceable.

hĕl'ping *n*. (esp.) portion of food.

hĕlp'lĕss *a*. unable to help oneself; without help or power.

hĕlp'māte, -meet *nn*. helpful companion, esp. husband or wife.

hĕl'ter-skĕl'ter *adv*. in disordered haste.

hĕlve *n*. handle of weapon or tool.

Hĕlvē'tian *n*. & *a*. Swiss.

hĕm[1] *n*. border, esp. made by turning in and sewing down edge of cloth. *v.t.* sew edge thus; ~ *about, in, round,* enclose, confine, encircle. ~**stitch,** (hem with) ornamental open-work stitch.

hĕm[2] *int*. expr. hesitation or calling attention.

hematite : see **haematite**.

hĕmĭplē'gĭa *n*. paralysis of one side of body.

hĕm'ĭsphēre *n*. half sphere; half celestial sphere; half earth, esp. as divided by equator or by line dividing Europe, Asia and Africa from America. ~**ĕ'rĭc(al)** *aa*.

hĕm'ĭstĭch (-k) *n*. half line of verse.

hĕm'lŏck *n*. (poisonous potion got from) umbelliferous plant.

hemorrhage etc.: see **haemorrhage** etc.

hĕmp *n*. Asiatic annual herbaceous plant; its fibre used for rope etc.; kinds of narcotic drug got from it. ~**en** *a*.

hĕn *n*. female of birds, esp. of common domestic fowl. ~**-harrier,** kind of hawk. ~**pecked,** domineered over by wife.

hĕn'bāne *n*. narcotic and poisonous plant; drug from this.

hĕnce *adv*. from here; from now; as result of or inference from this. ~**forth,** ~**forward,** from this time forward.

hĕnch'man *n*. (hist.) squire, page; follower; political supporter.

hĕndĕc'agon *n*. plane figure of eleven sides or angles.

hĕndĕcasўll'able *n*. verse or line of eleven syllables. ~**ăb'ic** *a*. & *n*.

hĕndī'adўs *n*. expression of single idea by two words coupled with *and*.

hĕnn'a *n*. (yellowish-red dye from) Egyptian privet.

hĕn'rў *n*. electro-magnetic unit of inductance.

hĕpăt'ic *a*. of liver.

hĕp'ta- in comb., seven. **hĕp'tagon** *n*. plane rectilineal figure of seven sides; ~**ăg'onal** *a*. ~**hĕd'ron** *n*. solid of seven faces. **hĕp'tarchў** (-k-) *n*. (esp.) seven kingdoms of Angles and Saxons in Britain. ~**sўll'able** *n*. verse of seven syllables; ~**syllăb'ĭc** *a*. ~**teuch** (-ūk) *n*. first seven books of O.T.

her *pron*. & *a*., obj. (and colloq. subj.) and poss. case of *she*, and corresponding adj., with abs. form *hers*.

hĕ'rald *n*. officer who made State proclamations etc.; messenger; forerunner. *v.t.* proclaim approach of; usher in. **H~s College,** corporation recording pedigrees and granting armorial bearings. **hĕrăl'dĭc** *a*. ~**rў** *n*. science of herald; armorial bearings, heraldic pomp.

hĕrb *n*. soft-stemmed plant dying down to ground after flowering; plant used for food, medicine, etc. ~**ā'ceous** *a*. of or like herbs. ~**ў** *a*.

hĕr'bage *n*. herbs; pasturage.

hĕr'bal *a*. of herbs. *n*. book about herbs. ~**ĭst** *n*. writer on herbs; dealer in medicinal herbs.

hĕrbār'ĭum *n*. collection of dried herbs.

hĕrbĭv'orous *a*. herb-eating.

hĕrcūlē'an (*or* -kū'-) *a*. strong as Hercules; (of task) of great difficulty.

hĕrd *n*. number of cattle feeding or travelling together; (contempt.) common people; herdsman. *v*. go in herd; tend; drive or crowd. ~**sman,** keeper of herds.

here *adv*. in or to this place; at this point. *n*. this place or point. ~**about(s),** somewhere near here. ~**after,** (in) future, (in) next world. ~**at,** at this. ~**by,** by this means. ~**in,** in this book, place, etc. ~**inafter,** below (in document). ~**of,** of this. ~**to,** to this. ~**tofore,** formerly. ~**upon,** after or in consequence of this. ~**with,** with this.

hĕrĕd′ĭtable *a*. that can be inherited. ~bĭl′ĭtў *n*.

hĕrĕdĭt′ament (*or* hĕrĕd′-) *n*. hereditable property; inheritance.

hĕrĕd′ĭtarў *a*. descending by inheritance; transmitted from one generation to another; holding position by inheritance.

hĕrĕd′ĭtў *n*. tendency of like to beget like; property by which off-spring inherit characteristics of parents etc.; germinal constitution.

hĕrĕs′ĭarch (-k; *or* -rē-) *n*. leader or founder of heresy.

hĕ′rĕsў *n*. opinion contrary to ortho-dox (Christian) belief or to accepted doctrine.

hĕ′rĕtĭc *n*. holder of heresy. hĕrĕt′ĭcal *a*.

hĕ′rĭtable *a*. that can be inherited.

hĕ′rĭtage *n*. what is or may be inherited; one's portion or lot.

hĕrmăph′rodīte *n*. & *a*. (person, animal, etc.) with characteristics or organs of both sexes. ~ĭt′ic *a*.; ~ītĭsm *n*.

hĕrmĕt′ĭc *a*. of alchemy. ~ seal, air-tight closure of vessel. ~allў *adv*.

hĕr′mĭt *n*. person living in solitude. ~age *n*. hermit's abode.

hĕr′nĭa *n*. (path.) tumour resulting from protrusion of internal part through walls of cavity containing it.

hēr′ō *n*. demigod; man admired for great or noble deeds; person of extreme courage; chief man in poem, play, etc.

Herod. *abbr*. Herodotus.

hĕrō′ĭc *a*. of, fit for, worthy of, or having qualities of hero; epic; (of metre) used in heroic poetry. *n*. (pl.) heroic verse; high-flown language or sentiments.

hĕ′rōĭn *n*. analgesic and hypnotic drug prepared from morphine.

hĕ′rōĭne *n*. female hero.

hĕ′rōĭsm *n*. heroic conduct.

hĕ′ron *n*. long-necked long-legged wading bird. ~rў *n*.

hĕr′pēs (-z) *n*. shingles; painless form of it. herpĕt′ĭc *a*.

hĕ′rrĭng *n*. N.-Atlantic edible fish. ~bone, (pattern) of lines etc. set obliquely in alternate rows; (fabric,

stitch, brickwork, etc.) having this pattern; work or mark with this pattern.

hers : see her.

hĕrsĕlf′ *pron*., emphat. & refl. form of she.

Herts. *abbr*. Hertfordshire.

Hĕr′tzian waves (-ts-) *n.pl*. electro--magnetic waves.

Hes. *abbr*. Hesiod.

hĕs′ĭtant (-z-) *a*. hesitating. ~ancў *n*.

hĕs′ĭtāte (-z-) *v.i*. feel or show in-decision; scruple. ~ā′tion *n*.

Hĕspēr′ĭan *a*. western.

Hĕs′perus *n*. evening star, Venus.

hĕss′ĭan (*or* -shn) *n*. strong coarse cloth of mixed hemp and jute. H~ boots, high tasselled boots.

hĕtero- in comb., other, different. hĕt′erodўne *n*. & *a*. (apparatus for) producing audible frequency from combination of two high-frequency (radio) waves; *v.i*. produce this effect. ~genĕt′ic *a*. descended from different ancestral stock. ~mōr′-phic, existing or occurring in dif-ferent forms. ~sĕx′ual *a*. of normal relation of sexes; of opposite sex.

hĕt′erodŏx *a*. not orthodox. ~ў *n*.

hĕterogē′néous *a*. diverse; composed of diverse elements. ~genē′itў *n*.

hĕt′man *n*. Polish or Cossack com-mander.

heuris′tĭc *a*. of or concerned with finding out (for oneself).

hew *v*. chop, cut, with axe, sword, etc.; cut into shape; cut (coal) from seam. hew′er *n*. hewn *a*. made or shaped by hewing.

hĕx′a- in comb., six. hĕx′achord *n*. (mus.) series of six consecutive notes with semitone between third and fourth. ~gon, six-sided figure; hexăg′onal *a*. ~grám *n*. starshaped figure formed by two intersecting equilateral triangles. ~hĕd′ron *n*. solid having six faces; ~hĕd′ral *a*. hĕxăm′éter *n*. line of six metrical feet; ~mĕt′ric(al) *aa*. ~teuch (-ūk) *n*. first six books of O.T.

hey (hā) *int*. calling attention or expr. joy, surprise or question.

hey′day (hā-) *n*. bloom, prime.

H.F. *abbr*. high frequency.

hf bd, hf cf *abbr*. half-bound; half--calf.

H.G. *abbr.* High German; His (Her) Grace; Holy Ghost; Horse Guards.

hg. *abbr.* hectogram.

HH *abbr.* double-hard (of pencil).

H.H. *abbr.* His (Her) Highness; His Holiness.

hhd *abbr.* hogshead.

hī *int.* calling attention.

hīā′tus *n.* (pl. *-uses*), gap in series etc.; break between two vowels not in same syllable.

hī′bĕrnāte *r.i.* spend winter (of animals) in torpid state or (of persons) in mild climate. **~ā′tion** *n.*

Hībĕr′nian *a. & n.* (native) of Ireland.

hĭbĭs′cus *n.* kinds of tropical plant with large bright-coloured flowers.

hĭcc′up, hĭcc′ough (-kup) *n.* involuntary audible spasm of respiratory organs. *r.* make, utter with, hiccup.

hĭc jā′cĕt n. epitaph. [L]

hĭck *n.* (colloq.) bumpkin, provincial.

hĭck′orў *n.* N.-Amer. tree allied to walnut; its wood.

hid, hidden : see **hide²**.

hĭdăl′gō *n.* (pl. *-os*), Spanish gentleman.

hīde¹ *n.* animal's skin, raw or dressed; (joc.) human skin. **~-bound**, bigoted, rigidly conventional.

hīde² *v.* (p.t. *hĭd*, p.p. *hĭdden* and *hĭd*), put or keep out of sight; conceal oneself; keep (fact) secret (*from*); obstruct view of. **~-out**, hiding--place.

hīde³ *n.* medieval measure of land.

hĭd′ĕous *a.* repulsive, revolting.

hī′dĭng *n.* thrashing.

hīe *r.i. & refl.* (poet.) go quickly.

hī′erărch (-k) *n.* chief priest.

hī′erărchў (-k-) *n.* each of three divisions of angels; priestly government; organized priesthood in successive grades; any graded organization. **~ăr′chĭc(al)** *aa.*

hĭerăt′ĭc *a.* of priests (esp. of abridged form of ancient Egyptian hieroglyphs); of style of (esp. Greek or Egyptian) art using traditional conventions.

hī′eroglўph *n.* figure of object standing for word or syllable, esp. in ancient Egyptian writing. **~glў′phĭc** *a.*; **~glўph′ics** *n.pl.*

hī′-fī (*or* -fī′) *n. & a.* (colloq.) (repro-duction of sound, apparatus reproducing sound) with high degree of fidelity to original.

hĭgg′le *r.i.* dispute about terms.

hĭgg′ledў-pĭgg′ledў (-geld-) *adv. & a.* in utter confusion.

high (hī) *a.* of great or specified upward extent; of exalted rank, position, or quality; (of meat etc.) slightly tainted; (of sound) acute in pitch; great; intense; expensive; (sl.) drunk. *n.* high degree or place or level; high gear; area of high barometric pressure. *adv.* far up, aloft; in or to high degree; at high rate. **~ball**, (U.S.) whisky etc. and (usu. aerated) water in tall glass. **~boy**, (U.S.) tallboy. **~brow**, intellectual (person). **H~ Church**, (party, principles, etc.) giving high place to ritual, sacraments, etc. **H~ Court**, supreme court of justice. **~ explosive**, powerful and rapidly detonated. **~flown**, extravagant, bombastic. **~ frequency**, (having frequency of) 3–30 megacycles per sec. **~-handed**, overbearing. **~-light(s)**, brightest or brightly lighted part(s) of picture etc. **~light**, emphasize, make prominent. **H~ Mass**, with incense, music, etc. **~-minded**, morally elevated. **~-pressure**, (fig.) intense, urgent. **~ priest**, (esp. Jewish) chief priest. **~ road**, main road. **~ school**, secondary school, esp. one preparing for university. **~ sea(s)**, outside territorial waters. **~-spirited**, of courageous spirit. **~ tea**, at which meat is served. **~-toned**, lofty, noble. **~ water**, time, state, of tide at full. **~-water mark**, (esp.) highest point of intensity, excellence, etc.

high′land *a.* of highlands, **~er** *n.* inhabitant of highlands, esp. of Scotland. **~s** *n.pl.* mountainous or elevated country, esp. (*H~s*) northern part of Scotland.

high′lў *adv.* in high degree, at high rate; favourably, honourably.

High′ness *n.* title of princes.

high′way *n.* public road, main route. **~man**, (hist.) (usu. mounted) man robbing passengers on highway.

H.I.H. *abbr.* His (Her) Imperial Highness.

hi′jăck *v.t.* (sl.) steal (esp. contraband or stolen goods) in transit.

hīke *n.* & *v.i.* walk, tramp.

hilăr′ious *a.* cheerful, merry.

hilă′rĭtў *n.* merriment.

hĭll *n.* small mountain; rising ground, (upward) slope; heap, mound. **~billy**, (U.S. colloq.) rustic mountaineer, esp. of southern U.S. **~ock** *n.* small hill; mound. **~ў** *a.*

hĭlt *n.* handle of sword, knife, etc. *v.t.* furnish with hilt.

hĭm *pron.*, obj. (& colloq. subj.) case of *he*.

H.I.M. *abbr.* His (Her) Imperial Majesty.

hĭmsĕlf′ *pron.*, emphat. & refl. form of *he*.

hīnd¹ *n.* female (esp. red) deer.

hīnd² *n.* farm worker; rustic.

hīnd³ *a.* at back, posterior. **~quarter**, leg and loin of beef, mutton, etc.; (pl.) rump and hind legs. **~sight**, (esp.) perception after event. **~er¹** *a.* hind. **~mōst** *a.*

hĭn′der² *v.t.* impede; prevent.

Hĭn′di (-ē) *n.* vernacular language of N. part of Indian peninsula.

hĭn′drance *n.* obstruction.

Hĭndū′ (-dōō; *or* hĭn′-) *a.* of Hindus or Hinduism. *n.* one who professes Hinduism. **~ism** *n.* religion of majority of Indian people.

Hĭndusta′ni (-ahnē) *a.* & *n.* (language) of Hindustan.

hĭnge (-j) *n.* movable joint like that by which door is hung on post; piece of gummed paper for mounting postage-stamp. *v.* attach (as) with hinge; turn *on*.

hĭnn′ў *n.* offspring of she-ass by stallion.

hĭnt *n.* covert or indirect suggestion; slight indication. *v.* suggest covertly; **~ at**, give hint of.

hĭn′terlănd *n.* district behind that lying along coast etc.

hĭp¹ *n.* projection of pelvis and upper part of thigh-bone at side of body.

hĭp² *n.* fruit of wild rose.

hip³ *int.* used to introduce cheer.

hipped (hĭpt) *a.* low-spirited.

hĭpp′ō *n.* (colloq.) hippopotamus.

hĭppocăm′pus *n.* (pl. -*pī*), kinds of small fish with forepart of body like horse's head.

hĭpp′ocrăs *n.* spiced wine.

Hĭppocrăt′ic oath *n.* oath embodying code of medical ethics.

hĭpp′odrōme *n.* course for chariot races etc.

hĭpp′ogriff, -gryph *n.* fabulous griffin-like creature with horse's body.

hĭppopŏt′amus *n.* (pl. -*muses*, -*mī*), large tusked heavy-bodied short-legged African quadruped inhabiting rivers etc.

hĭp′ster *a.* (of garment) hanging from belt etc. round hips.

hīre *n.* payment for use of thing, labour, etc.; hiring, being hired. *v.t.* employ, engage, for wages; procure or grant use of for payment. **~ purchase**, system by which hired thing becomes hirer's property after number of payments. **~ling** *n.* (contempt.) one who works for hire.

hīr′sūte *a.* hairy.

his (hĭz) *pron.* & *a.*, poss. case of *he*.

hĭss *n.* sharp sound of *s* esp. as sign of disapproval etc. *v.* make hiss; express disapproval of thus; utter with angry hiss.

hĭst *int.* used to call attention.

hĭst′amine (*or* -ēn) *n.* substance occurring in animal tissues and concerned in allergic reactions etc.

hĭstŏl′ogў *n.* study of structure of organic tissues.

hĭstôr′ian *n.* writer of history.

hĭstŏ′ric *a.* noted in history; not fictional or legendary. **~ present**, present tense used instead of past in narration. **hĭstŏ′rical** *a.* of or belonging to or connected with history or past; not legendary; dealing with historical events. **~ĭ′cĭtў** *n.* historic quality or character.

hĭstôriŏg′rapher, -phў *nn.* writer, writing, of esp. official history.

hĭs′torў *n.* continuous methodical record of important or public events; past events, study of these; (eventful) career; story.

hĭstriŏn′ic *a.* of acting; stagy. **~s** *n.pl.* theatricals; stagy language; play-acting for effect.

hĭt *v.* strike with blow or missile; aim blow; light upon, find; suit. *n.* blow; stroke of satire etc.; successful attempt; success. **~-or-miss**, (colloq.) casual, careless.

hĭtch v. move with jerk; fasten with loop etc.; become so fastened; hitch-hike. n. jerk; kinds of noose or knot; impediment, temporary stoppage. **~-hike**, travel by means of lifts in vehicles.

hĭth′er (-dh-) adv. to this place. a. situated on this side; the nearer. **hĭtherto′** (-ōō) adv. up to this time.

hīve n. artificial home for bees; busy swarming place. v. place, live, store, etc. (as) in hive.

hīves (-vz) n.pl. various physical disorders, as skin eruptions, laryngitis, etc.

H.L. abbr. House of Lords.

hl. abbr. hectolitre.

h'm : see **hum²**.

H.M. abbr. His (or Her) Majesty('s).

H.M.I.(S.) abbr. His (or Her) Majesty's Inspector (of Schools).

H.M.S., H.M.S.O. abbr. His (or Her) Majesty's Ship, Stationery Office.

hō int. expr. triumph, derision, etc., calling attention, etc.

H.O. abbr. Home Office.

ho. abbr. house.

hoar (hōr) a. grey with age; white. **~-frost**, white frost.

hoard (hōrd) n. store (esp. of money or treasure) laid by; amassed stock. v. amass and put away, store up; treasure up.

hoar′ding (hōr-) n. temporary board fence round building etc.; boarding for posting bills.

hoarse (hōrs) a. (of voice) rough, husky; having hoarse voice.

hoary (hōr′ĭ) a. white or grey with age; venerable.

hoax v.t. deceive esp. by way of joke. n. such deception.

hŏb n. flat iron shelf at side of grate. **~-nail**, heavy-headed nail for boot-sole.

hŏbb′le v. walk lamely, limp; tie together legs of (horse etc.) to keep it from straying. n. limping gait; rope etc. used to hobble horse.

hŏbb′ledėhoy n. awkward youth.

hŏbb′y¹ n. favourite pursuit outside one's main occupation. **~-horse**, wicker figure of horse fastened about waist of morris-dancer etc.;

child's toy of horse-headed stick; rocking-horse; horse on merry-go-round; favourite theme, obsession.

hŏbb′y² n. small falcon.

hŏb′gŏblĭn n. mischievous imp; bogy.

hŏb′-nŏb v.i. drink together; hold familiar intercourse (with).

hō′bō n. (pl. -os), (U.S.) wandering workman or tramp.

hŏck¹ n. joint of quadruped's hind leg between true knee and fetlock.

hŏck² n. white Rhine wine.

hŏck³ n. (U.S. sl.) in ~, in prison, in pawn, in debt, v.t. pawn.

hŏck′ey n. team-game played with ball and curved sticks between goals.

hō′cus v.t. hoax; drug.

hō′cus-pō′cus n. jugglery, deception.

hŏd n. trough on staff for carrying mortar etc. **~man**, bricklayer's labourer.

hŏdd′en n. (Sc.) coarse woollen cloth.

Hŏdge n. typical English agricultural labourer.

hodge-podge : see **hotch-potch**.

hŏdŏm′ėter n. instrument for measuring distance travelled by wheeled vehicle etc.; surveyor's wheel for measuring distances.

hōe n. tool for scraping up weeds etc. v. use hoe; weed (crops), loosen (soil), dig out, up, etc., with hoe. **~-down**, (U.S.) (music for) lively square dance; informal dance.

hŏg n. swine, esp. castrated boar; hogget; greedy person. v.t. cut (mane) short; take all or unfair share of. **~like**, greedy. **~-mane**, horse's mane clipped short. **~-plum**, kinds of plum-like fruit used as food for hogs. **~'s-back**, sharply crested steep-sided hill-ridge. **~-tie**, (U.S.) secure by tying together animal's four feet or person's hands and feet. **~wash**, swill given to pigs. **hŏgg′ish** a. greedy.

hŏgg′ėt (-g-) n. yearling sheep.

hŏgg′ĭn n. mixture of gravel, clay, etc. for paths etc.

hŏg′manay (-anā) n. (Sc.) last day of year.

hŏgs′head (-z-hĕd) n. large cask; liquid measure (52½ gals.).

hoick v.t. (sl.) lift or jerk (out etc.).

hoi pŏlloi' (*or* pŏl'-), the masses. [Gk.]

hoist, *v.t.* raise (esp. flag) aloft; raise with tackle etc. *n.* shove up; goods lift; fixed crane.

hoi'tȳ-toi'tȳ *a.* haughty, petulant. *int.* expr. surprised protest etc.

hō'key-pō'key *n.* cheap ice-cream sold in street.

hō'kum *n.* (sl.) false sentiment, sentimental or melodramatic nonsense.

hōld[1] *v.* (*hĕld*), keep fast, grasp; possess; contain, have room for; observe, celebrate; restrain; think, believe; not give way; keep going; be valid; ~*down*, (U.S.) keep (job etc.); ~ *forth*, speak publicly or at length; ~ *hard!* (colloq.) stop!; ~ *in*, keep in check; ~ *out*, offer, endure, persist; ~ *out for*, refuse to accept anything but; ~ *over*, postpone; ~ *up*, delay, rob with gun or (threat of) violence; ~ *water*, bear examination; ~ *with*, approve of. *n.* grasp; means of holding; means of exerting influence *on* or *over*. ~-**all**, portable case for clothes etc. ~-**up**, delay, stoppage; robbery by holding up. ~**er** *n.* (esp.) device for holding. ~**ing** *n.* (esp.) land or stocks held. ~**ing company,** one formed to hold shares of other companies.

hōld[2] *n.* cavity below deck for cargo.

hōle *n.* hollow place; gap; burrow; perforation; cavity into which ball must be got in some games, (golf) point scored by doing this in fewest strokes; distance, part of golf-course, between tee and hole; (colloq.) wretched place; dilemma, fix. *v.* make hole(s) in; hit golf-ball into hole. ~-**and-corner**, secret, underhand.

hŏl'iday (-dǐ) *n.* day of cessation from work or of recreation; (freq. pl.) period of this, vacation.

hō'liness *n.* sanctity; *H~*, title of Pope.

hŏll'and *n.* linen fabric, freq. unbleached.

hŏll'andaise (-z) **(sauce)** *n.* creamy sauce of butter, egg-yolks, vinegar, etc.

hŏll'ands (-z) *n.* Dutch gin.

hŏll'ō, holloa' (-ō) *v.* shout, call out; call to hounds. *n.* shout, cry.

hŏll'ow (-ō) *a.* having hole, cavity, or depression; not solid; empty; not full-toned; false, unreal. *n.* hollow place; hole; valley. *adv.* completely. *v.t.* make hollow in.

hŏll'ȳ *n.* evergreen prickly-leaved shrub with red berries.

hŏll'ȳhŏck *n.* tall plant with large showy flowers.

holm[1] (hōm) *n.* islet, esp. in river; flat ground by river.

holm[2] (hōm) *n.* (usu.~-*oak*),evergreen oak, ilex.

hō'lmium *n.* metallic element of rare--earth group.

hŏl'ocaust *n.* whole burnt-offering; wholesale sacrifice or destruction.

hŏl'ograph (-ahf) *a.* & *n.* (document) wholly in handwriting of person in whose name it appears.

hōl'ster *n.* leather pistol-case.

hōlt[1] *n.* copse; wooded hill.

hōlt[2] *n.* (esp. otter's or badger's) lair.

hō'lȳ *a.* belonging or devoted to God; of high moral or spiritual excellence. ~ **day**, religious festival. **H~ Ghost, H~ Spirit**, third person of Trinity. ~ **orders**, those of bishop, priest, deacon, and (R.C. Ch.) subdeacon. **H~ Thursday,** Thursday in Holy Week; Ascension Day. ~ **water**, water blessed by priest. **H~ Week**, that preceding Easter Sunday. **H~ Writ**, Bible.

hō'lȳstōne *n.* sandstone for scouring. *v.t.* scour with holystone.

Hom. *abbr.* Homer.

hŏm'age *n.* formal acknowledgement of allegiance; tribute paid to person or merit.

hŏm'būrg *n.* man's soft felt hat.

hōme *n.* dwelling-place, residence; (U.S.) private house; native land; institution of refuge or rest; (in games) goal; home match, win, etc. *a.* pertaining to home; not foreign; played etc. on team's own ground. *adv.* to or at home; to point aimed at. *v.i.* go home (esp. of pigeons). **H~ Counties**, those lying round London. ~ **farm**, farm attached to residence of occupier of estate. ~**land**, native land. **H~ Office,**

(building of) department of Secretary of State for Home Affairs. -~ **Rule**, self-government. ~**sick**, depressed by absence from home. ~**spun**, (cloth) of yarn spun at home. ~**stead**, house with outbuildings; farm. ~**work**, (esp.) lessons etc. to be done by schoolchild at home. ~**r** *n.* homing pigeon. ~**ward** *a. & adv.* (going, leading) towards home. ~**wards** *adv.* hō'mĭng *a.* (esp. of pigeon) trained to fly home from distance.

hōme'lў (-ml-) *a.* plain; unpretending; not beautiful.

Homĕ'rĭc *a.* of or in style of Homer; heroic.

hŏm'ĭcīde *n.* killing, killer, of human being. ~cī'dal *a.*

hŏmĭlĕt'ĭc *a.* of homilies. ~s *n.pl.* art of preaching.

hŏm'ĭlў *n.* sermon; discourse.

hŏm'ĭnў *n.* ground maize boiled in water or milk.

hōmoeŏp'athў (-mĭ-) *n.* treatment of disease by drugs that in healthy person would produce similar symptoms. hō'moeopath, ~pathist *nn.* ~păth'ic *a.* (esp., joc.) minute.

hŏmogĕnē'ĭtў *n.* uniformity.

hŏmogē'nĕous *a.* of same kind or nature; uniform.

homŏ'gĕnīze *v.t.* treat (milk) so that fat globules emulsify and cream does not separate.

homŏl'ogous *a.* having same relation or value; corresponding. hŏm'ologue (-g) *n.* homologous thing.

homŏl'ogў *n.* homologous relation, correspondence.

hŏm'onўm *n.* word of same form as another but different sense. homŏn'ўmous *a.*

hŏm'ophōne *n.* word or symbol having same sound as another.

hŏmōsĕx'ūal *a.* of or having sexual propensity for one's own sex. *n.* homosexual person.

homŭnc'ūlus *n.* little man, manikin.

hō'mў *a.* suggesting or like home.

Hon. *abbr.* honorary; Honourable.

hōne *n.* whetstone, esp. for razors. *v.t.* whet on hone.

hon'ĕst (ŏ-) *a.* upright; not lying or cheating or stealing; chaste.

hon'ĕstў (ŏ-) *n.* uprightness, truthfulness; plant with purple flowers and flat round fruits.

hon'ey (hŭ-) *n.* (pl. -eys), (sweet viscid fluid worked up by bees etc. from) nectar of flowers; sweetness; darling. ~**dew melon**, smoothskinned melon with very sweet greenish flesh. ~**moon**, (spend) newly married couple's holiday together. ~**suckle**, climbing shrub with fragrant flowers. **honeyed** (-nĭd) *a.* sweet, sweet-sounding.

hon'eycōmb (hŭ-; -m) *n.* bees' wax structure of hexagonal cells for honey and eggs; pattern etc. resembling this. *v.t.* fill with cavities; undermine.

hŏnk *n. & v.i.* (make) cry of wild goose or sound of motor horn.

honorār'ĭum (ŏ-) *n.* (pl. -ums, -a), (voluntary) fee for nominally unpaid esp. professional services.

hon'orarў (ŏn-) *a.* conferred as honour; holding honorary title or position; unpaid.

hŏnorĭf'ĭc *a. & n.* (expression) implying respect.

hŏnōr'ĭs cau'sa (-zā), as mark of esteem. [L]

honour (ŏn'er) *n.* glory, high reputation; chastity; mark of respect; (pl.) civilities to guests etc.; (pl.) distinction for proficiency in examination; (golf) right of driving off first; (pl., cards) four (or five) top cards in (esp. trump-) suit. *v.t.* respect highly; confer honour on; accept or pay (bill) when due.

hon'ourable (ŏner-) *a.* deserving or bringing honour; generous, not base; **H~**, official or courtesy title of High-Court justices, younger sons of earls, etc.

hōoch *n.* (U.S. sl.) alcoholic spirits, esp. inferior or illicit.

hŏod[1] *n.* covering for head and neck; badge worn over gown to show university degree; thing like hood in shape or use, esp. waterproof (folding) top or cover of motor-car etc.; (U.S.) bonnet of car. *v.t.* cover with hood.

hŏod[2], hōo'dlum *nn.* (U.S. sl.) ruffian, rowdy, esp. gangster, gunman, violent criminal.

hōo'dōo *n.* (U.S.) malignant spell;

(person or thing bringing) bad luck. *v.t.* bring bad luck to.

hŏŏd′wĭnk *v.t.* deceive, humbug.

hoo′ey *n.* (U.S. sl.) nonsense.

hoof *n.* (pl. *-fs, -ves*), horny casing of foot of horse etc.; (joc.) human foot. *v.* strike with hoof; (sl.) kick; (sl.) go on foot. **~er** *n.* (U.S. sl.) dancer.

hook *n.* bent piece of wire etc. for catching hold or for hanging things on; curved cutting instrument; hooked stroke; (boxing) short swinging blow with elbow bent. *v.* grasp, secure, fasten, catch, with hook; (golf) drive ball far to left; (crick.) play ball round from off to on without hitting it at pitch; (Rugby footb.) secure (ball) in scrum with foot; ~ *it*, (sl.) make off, run away; ~ *up*, connect or link together (esp. radio etc. stations). **~ and eye**, small hook and loop as dress-fastener. **~-up**, interconnexion of parts etc.; parts etc. so linked together. **~worm**, (disease caused by) kinds of worm infesting man and some beasts. **~ed** (-kt) *a.* bent like hook. **~er**[1] *n.* (esp., Rugby footb.) player in front row of scrum who hooks ball.

hook′ah (-*a*) *n.* tobacco pipe with long flexible tube and vase of water through which smoke is drawn.

hook′er[2] *v.* kinds of small Dutch etc. coasting or fishing vessel.

hoo′lĭgan *n.* young street rough, rowdy; member of street gang. **~ism** *n.*

hoop *n.* circular band of metal, wood, etc. esp. for binding cask etc.; wooden or iron circle trundled by child; iron arch through which balls are driven in croquet. *v.t.* bind with hoops.

hoo′poe (-oo) *n.* bird with gay plumage and erectile crest.

hooray : see **hurrah.**

hoot *v.* make loud sounds, esp. of disapproval; assail with hoots; utter hoot; (cause to) make hoot. *n.* inarticulate shout of derision etc.; sound of steam-whistle, motor-car horn, etc.; owl's cry. **~er** *n.* (esp.) siren etc., esp. as signal for work to begin or cease.

Hoo′ver *n.* make of vacuum cleaner. *v.t.* clean with Hoover. **P.**

hŏp[1] *n.* plant with bitter cones used to flavour beer etc.; (pl.) ripened cones of this plant. *v.i.* bear, gather, hops. **~head**, (U.S. sl.) drug addict.

hŏp[2] *v.* spring on one foot; (of birds etc.) jump; hop over; move or go quickly or with leaping motion; go or transport by air; (U.S.) jump on (train etc.); ~ *it*, (sl.) go away. *n.* hopping; spring; (colloq.) dance; distance travelled by air in one stage. **~scotch**, child's game of hopping over lines marked on ground.

hope *n.* expectation and desire; trust; ground of hope; person or thing that hope centres in. *v.* expect and desire; feel hope. **~ful** *a.* feeling hope; promising. **~less** *a.*

hŏpp′er[1] *n.* (esp.) funnel-like device for feeding grain into mill etc.; barge discharging mud through collapsible bottom.

hŏpp′er[2] *n.* hop-picker.

hŏp′săck *n.* woollen dress-fabric of coarse weave.

Hor. *abbr.* Horace.

hŏrde *n.* troop of Tartar or other nomads; large crowd or troop.

hore′hound (hŏr-) *n.* herb with aromatic bitter juice.

horī′zon *n.* line at which earth and sky appear to meet; limit of mental perception, interest, etc.

hŏrĭzŏn′tal *a.* parallel to plane of horizon; level, flat; of or at horizon. *n.* horizontal line, bar, etc.

hŏr′mōne *n.* product of living cells carried by blood-stream to other cells. **~ŏn′ic** *a.*

hŏrn *n.* excrescence, often curved and pointed, on head of cattle etc.; horn-like projection; emblem of cuckold; substance of horns, article made of this; more or less horn--shaped wind instrument; funnel--shaped part of gramophone etc., amplifying sound. *v.t.* furnish with horns. **~beam**, tough-wooded hedgerow tree. **~bill**, bird with horn-like excrescence on bill. **~book**, (hist.) child's alphabet etc. on framed paper covered with thin horn. **~-rimmed**, (of spectacles) rimmed with horn or tortoiseshell. **~ed** *a.* having horn(s); **~ed toad**, small spiny-scaled lizard of U.S. and Mexico.

hŏrn'blĕnde *n.* dark-brown or (greenish-) black mineral constituent of granite etc.

hŏr'nėt *n.* large species of wasp.

hŏrn'pīpe *n.* (music for) lively dance associated esp. with sailors.

hŏr'nў *a.* of or like horn; hard.

horŏl'ogў *n.* clock-making. **horo-lŏ'gical** *a.*

hŏ'roscōpe *n.* astrologer's chart of sky and planets at given time, supposed to reveal influence of stars on destiny.

hŏ'rrible *a.* exciting horror; hideous, shocking; unpleasant.

hŏ'rrĭd *a.* horrible; unpleasing.

horrĭf'ĭc *a.* horrifying.

hŏ'rrĭfў *v.t.* excite horror in; shock.

hŏ'rror *n.* terrified shuddering; terror; intense dislike or fear; horrifying thing.

hors de combat (ōrdekawm'bah), disabled. [F]

hors-d'œuvre (ōrder'vr) *n.* (pl. usu. -*s*), extra dish as relish, esp. at beginning of meal.

hŏrse *n.* solid-hoofed quadruped used as beast of burden and draught and for riding on; (collect.) cavalry; vaulting-block in gymnasium; frame for supporting things. *v.t.* provide with horse(s); carry (person) on one's back. **~-box**, stall for taking horses by rail etc. **~-chest-nut**, (fruit of) large ornamental tree with conical clusters of white or pink flowers. **~-coper**, horse-dealer. **H~ Guards**, cavalry brigade of British Household troops. **~hair**, from mane or tail of horse, esp. as used in upholstery. **~-laugh**, loud coarse laugh. **~-leech**, large kind of leech; insatiable person. **~man**, (skilled) rider on horseback. **~man-ship**, skill in riding. **~-play**, rough or boisterous play. **~power**, unit for measuring rate of doing work. **~-radish**, plant with pungent root used as condiment. **~-sense**, (colloq.) strong common sense. **~shoe**, iron shoe for horse; thing of

this shape. **~whip**, whip for horse; *v.t.* chastise (person) with this. **~woman**, (skilled) woman rider on horseback. **~lėss** *a.*

hŏr'sў *a.* addicted to horses or horse-racing; affecting dress and language of groom or jockey.

hŏr'tatĭve *a.* of exhortation.

hŏr'tatorў *a.* exhorting.

hŏr'tĭcŭlture *n.* art of gardening. **~cŭl'tural** *a.*; **~cŭl'turĭst** *n.*

Hos. *abbr.* Hosea.

hōsănn'a (-z-) *n.* cry of adoration.

hose (hōz) *n.* stockings; (hist.) breeches; flexible tube for convey-ing liquids. *v.* provide with hose; water or wash *down* (as) with hose.

hō'sier (-zher) *n.* dealer in hose, men's underwear, etc. **~ў** *n.*

hŏs'pĭce *n.* travellers' house of rest kept by religious order etc.; home for destitute or sick.

hŏs'pĭtable *a.* given to hospitality.

hŏs'pĭtal *n.* institution for care of sick; charitable institution. **~īze** *v.t.* send to, admit into, hospital.

hŏspĭtăl'itў *n.* friendly and liberal reception of guests or strangers.

hŏs'pĭtaller *n.* member of charitable religious order.

hōst[1] *n.* large number; army.

hōst[2] *n.* one who entertains another; landlord of inn; animal having parasite.

hōst[3] *n.* bread, wafer, consecrated in Eucharist.

hŏs'tage *n.* person handed over or seized as pledge.

hŏs'tel *n.* house of residence for students etc.

hŏs'telrў *n.* (arch.) inn.

hō'stėss *n.* woman who entertains guests; mistress of inn.

hŏs'tīle *a.* of enemy; opposed.

hŏstĭl'itў *n.* enmity; warfare; (pl.) acts of war; opposition.

hŏt *a.* of high temperature, very warm; giving or feeling heat; pungent; ardent; excited; (of news) fresh; (sl.) easily identifiable as stolen. *v.t.* (colloq.) heat *up*. *adv.* hotly, eagerly, angrily. **~ air**, (sl.) excited or boastful talk. **~bed**, bed of earth heated by fermenting manure; place that promotes growth. **~ dog**, hot sausage sandwiched in roll of bread. **~foot**, in hot haste. **~head**, hasty person. **~house**, heated building with glass roof and sides for growing plants. **~-plate**, (esp.) heated metal plate, portable heater, for cooking etc. **~pot**, dish of stewed meat and vegetables. **~-press**, (press or glaze in) kinds of press heated by electricity, steam, etc. **~ water**, (esp.) trouble, scrape.

hŏtch′pŏtch, hŏdge′-pŏdge *nn.* confused assemblage, jumble, medley.

hŏtĕl′ *n.* house for entertainment of travellers etc.; (large) inn. **~ier** *n.* hotel-keeper.

Hŏtt′entŏt *n.* one of short stocky people of S-W. Africa etc.

hough (hŏk) *n.* hock of horse etc.

hound *n.* dog for chase; runner following scent in paper-chase; despicable man. *v.t.* hunt, drive, (as) with hounds; urge *on*.

hour (owr) *n.* 60 minutes; (pl.) fixed habitual time for work etc.; short time; (pl.) (prayers or offices for) seven times of day appointed for prayers; *small* **~s**, early hours after midnight. **~glass**, sand-glass running an hour.

houri (hoor′ĭ, howr′ĭ) *n.* nymph of Moslem paradise.

hour′lў (owr-) *a. & adv.* (occurring etc.) every hour.

house *n.* (pl. pr. -zĭz), building for habitation or specified purpose; (boys etc. in) boarding-house or other division of school etc.; (building of) legislative etc. assembly; (audience in, performance at) theatre etc.; mercantile firm; family, dynasty; workhouse; (astrol.) sign of zodiac as seat of planet's influence. *v.t.* receive, store, etc. (as) in house; provide house(s) for; (naut.) place in secure position. **~boat**, fitted up for living in. **~breaker**, burglar; demolition worker. **~keeper**, woman managing affairs of house. **~leek**, pink-flowered succulent herb growing on walls and roofs. **~maid**, female servant in charge of reception and bedrooms. **~-martin**, common martin. **~master**, keeper of school boarding-house. **~-physi-**

cian, **~-surgeon**, resident doctor of hospital or institution. **~-proud**, preoccupied with care etc. of home. **~-warming**, party etc. celebrating entry into new house. **~wife**, mistress of house; domestic manager; (pr. hŭz′ĭf) case for sewing requisites. **~work**, cleaning, cooking, etc. **~y** (-**~y**) *n.* (mil. sl.) variant of lotto.

house′hōld (-s-h-) *n.* inmates of house; domestic establishment; royal or imperial household. **~ gods**, (Rom. ant.) divinities presiding over household; (fig.) essentials of home life. **~ troops**, those guarding sovereign's person. **~ word**, familiar saying or name.

hou′sing[1] (-z-) *n.* horse's trappings.

hou′sing[2] *n.* (esp.) provision of houses; (protective) covering. **~ estate**, residential estate planned as whole.

hove *p.t. & p.p.* of **heave**.

hŏv′el (*or* hŭ-) *n* shed, outhouse; mean dwelling.

hŏv′er (*or* hŭ-) *v.i.* (of bird etc.) hang in air; loiter *about*. **~craft**, vehicle supported just above surface of ground etc. on cushion of air.

how *adv.* in what way; by what means; to what extent. *n.* way thing is done. **~bē′it** *adv.* nevertheless. **~ĕv′er** *adv.* nevertheless; in or to whatever way or degree. **~sōĕv′er** *adv.* in or to whatever manner or degree.

how′dah (-*a*) *n.* seat, usu. with canopy, on elephant's back.

how′itzer *n.* short gun firing shell at high elevation.

howl *v.* (of animal) utter long loud doleful cry; (of person) utter long cry of pain, derision, etc.; utter words thus. *n.* such cry. **~er** *n.* kinds of S. Amer. monkey; glaring blunder. **~ing** *a.* (esp.) dreary; (sl.) extreme, glaring.

hoy[1] *n.* small coasting vessel, usu. rigged as sloop.

hoy[2] *int.* used to call attention.

hoy′den *n.* boisterous girl.

h.p. *abbr.* hire purchase; horse-power.

H.Q. *abbr.* headquarters.

hr *abbr.* hour.

H.R.H., H.S.H. *abbr.* His (Her) Royal, Serene, Highness.

H.T. *abbr.* high tension.

ht wkt *abbr.* hit wicket.

hŭb *n.* central part of wheel, from which spokes radiate; centre of interest etc.

hŭbb'le-bŭbb'le *n.* form of hookah.

hŭbb'ŭb *n.* din; tumult.

hŭck'abăck *n.* rough-surfaced linen or cotton fabric for towels etc.

hŭck'leberrў *n.* (fruit of) kinds of N.-Amer. berry-bearing shrub.

hŭck'ster *n.* hawker; mercenary person. *v.* haggle; hawk.

hŭdd'le *v.* heap, crowd, or nestle promiscuously. *n.* confused heap etc.; confusion.

hūe[1] *n.* colour, tint.

hūe[2] *n.* ~ *and cry*, clamour of pursuit; outcry.

hŭff *v.* bully; offend; take offence; (draughts) remove (opponent's man) as forfeit. *n.* fit of petulance. ~**ĭsh**, ~**ў** *aa.*

hŭg *v.t.* squeeze tightly in one's arms; keep close to (shore etc.); cling to. *n.* close or rough clasp.

hūge *a.* very large or great. ~**ly** *adv.* enormously.

hŭgg'er-mŭgger *a. & adv.* secret(ly); confused(ly), in a muddle.

Hū'guenot (-genō; *or* -ŏt) *n.* (hist.) French Protestant.

hu'la (-hula) (hoo-) *n.* Hawaiian women's dance.

hŭlk *n.* body of dismantled ship; unwieldy vessel; big person or mass. ~**ing** *a.* bulky; clumsy.

hŭll[1] *n.* outer covering or pod of beans etc. *v.t.* remove hull of.

hŭll[2] *n.* frame of ship. ~ **down**, far away, so that hull is invisible.

hŭllabaloō' *n.* uproar.

hŭllō' *int. & n.* hello.

hŭm[1] *v.* murmur continuously like bee or top; sing with closed lips. *n.* humming sound.

hŭm[2], **h'm** *int.* expr. hesitation, doubt, etc. *n. & v.i.* (make) this interjection.

hū'man *a.* having or showing qualities distinctive of man; that is a man or consists of men; not divine or animal or mechanical. *n.* (joc.) human being. ~**kīnd** *n.* mankind.

~**ly** *adv.* (esp.) by, for, as, etc. (mere) man.

hūmāne' *a.* benevolent, compassionate; (of studies) tending to refinement.

hū'manĭsm *n.* system of thought etc. concerned with human rather than supernatural values etc., or with humanity rather than individuals; literary culture, esp. study of classical languages, antiquities, etc. ~**ĭst** *n.*; ~**ĭs'tic** *a.*

hūmănĭtār'ian *n.* one who devotes himself to welfare of mankind at large; philanthropist. *a.* of or holding views of humanitarians. ~**ĭsm** *n.*

hūmăn'ĭtў *n.* human nature; human race; humaneness; (pl.) polite scholarship.

hū'manīze *v.* make or become human or humane.

hŭm'ble *a.* having or showing low estimate of one's own importance; lowly, modest; *eat* ~ *pie*, make humble apology, submit humbly. *v.t.* abase, lower.

hŭm'ble-bee *n.* bumble-bee.

hŭm'bŭg *n.* sham, deception; impostor; kind of usu. peppermint-flavoured boiled sweet. *v.t.* delude, cheat.

hŭm'drŭm *a.* dull, commonplace.

hū'meral *a.* of shoulder.

hū'merus *n.* bone of upper arm.

hū'mĭd *a.* damp. **hūmĭd'itў** *n.*

hū'mĭdŏr *n.* box etc. for keeping cigars or tobacco moist.

hūmĭl'iāte *v.t.* humble, abase; mortify. ~**ā'tion** *n.*

hūmĭl'itў *n.* humbleness; meekness.

hŭmm'ing-bird *n.* kinds of very small brilliantly coloured Amer. tropical bird making humming sound with vibrating wings.

hŭmm'ock *n.* hillock.

hūmorĕsque' (-sk) *n.* (mus.) lively instrumental composition.

hū'morist *n.* humorous talker, writer, etc. **hū'morous** *a.* full of humour; funny.

hū'mour (*or* ū-) *n.* state of mind, mood, inclination; faculty of perceiving ludicrous; comicality, jocose imagination; (hist.) one of four chief fluids of body supposed to determine physical and mental qualities. *v.t.* comply with humour of, indulge.

hŭmp *n.* protuberance esp. on back; (sl.) depression. *v.* make hump--shaped; (Austral.) hoist or carry (pack etc.); (sl.) exert one*self*. **~back**, (person having) back with hump.

humph (hmf) *int.* expr. dissatisfaction etc.

hŭmp'tў *n.* large firm cushion as seat.

hū'mus *n.* vegetable mould.

Hŭn *n.* one of Asiatic race ravaging Europe in 4th & 5th centuries; (contempt.) German.

hŭnch *n.* thick piece, hunk; (sl.) presentiment, intuition. *v.t.* bend convexly; thrust *up* to form hump. **~back**, humpback.

hŭn'dred *n.* & *a.* ten times ten (100, C); subdivision of county. **~weight**, 112 lb.; (U.S.) 100 lb. **~fold** *a.* & *adv.* **hŭn'dredth** *a.* & *n.*; *Old H~*, (tune of) metrical version of Ps. 100.

hung, *p.t.* & *p.p.* of **hang**.

hŭng'er (-ngg-) *n.* uneasy sensation or exhausted condition caused by want of food; strong desire. *v.i.* feel hunger; crave *for*. **~-strike**, refusal to take food.

hŭng'rў (-ngg-) *a.* feeling or showing hunger; eager; (of soil) poor, barren.

hŭnk *n.* large or clumsy piece, lump.

hŭnt *v.* pursue wild animals for food or sport; search *for*; drive *out*; **~** *down*, hunt, pursue, until caught and killed etc. *n.* hunting; persons hunting with pack; hunting district **~ball**, ball given by members of hunt. **~ing-box**, small house used during hunting season. **~ing--ground**, place where one hunts (freq. fig.). **~sman**, hunter; man in charge of pack of hounds.

hŭn'ter *n.* one who hunts; horse for hunting; watch with cover protecting glass. **hŭn'tress** *n.*

Hunts. *abbr.* Huntingdonshire.

hūr'dle *n.* portable frame with bars etc. for temporary fence etc.; frame to be jumped over in **~-race**; (pl.) hurdle-race. *v.i.* run in hurdle-race. **~r** *n.* hurdle-maker; hurdle-racer.

hūr'dy-gūrdў *n.* musical instrument with droning sound, played by turning handle; barrel-organ.

hūrl *v.t.* throw violently. *n.* violent throw.

hūr'ley *n.* Irish game resembling hockey.

hūr'lў-būr'lў *n.* commotion.

hurrah', hurray', hooray' (hoŏ-) *int.* & *n.* (shout) expr. joy or approval. *v.i.* shout hurrah.

hŭ'rrĭcāne (*or* -an) *n.* violent storm, esp. destructive cyclone in W. Indies etc. **~-deck**, light upper deck on river steamer. **~-lamp**, designed not to be extinguished by high wind.

hŭ'rrў *n.* undue haste; eagerness; need for haste. *v.* (cause to) move or act with haste. **~-scurry**, (in) disorderly haste. **hŭ'rried** (-ĭd) *a.*: **hŭ'rriedlў** *adv.*

hūrst *n.* wood, wooded eminence.

hūrt *v.* injure, damage, pain; distress, wound; (colloq.) suffer pain. *n.* wound, injury; harm. **~ful** *a.*

hūr'tle *v.i.* move swiftly esp. with clattering sound, come with crash.

hŭs'band (-z-) *n.* man joined to woman by marriage. *v.t.* manage thriftily; (arch.) till, cultivate. **~man**, farmer. **~rў** *n.* farming; economy.

hŭsh *v.* silence; be silent; **~** *up*, suppress. *n.* silence. **~-~**, (colloq.) highly confidential, very secret. **~-money**, sum paid to avoid exposure. **~abў** *int.* used to lull child.

hŭsk *n.* dry outer covering of fruit or seed. *v.t.* remove husk from.

hŭs'kў[1] *a.* full of, dry as, husks; hoarse; (colloq.) tough, strong and vigorous. *n.* husky person.

hŭs'kў[2] *n.* Eskimo dog.

hussăr' (hoŏz-) *n.* light cavalry soldier.

hŭss'ў (*or* -zĭ) *n.* pert girl; worthless woman.

hŭs'tĭngs (-z) *n.* (hist.) platform for nomination of candidates for Parliament; election proceedings.

hŭs'tle (-sl) *v.* push roughly, jostle; hurry; push one's way, bustle. *n.* hustling.

hŭt *n.* small mean house; shed; temporary wooden etc. building.

~ment *n.* (usu. pl.) accommodation in huts. **hǔtt′ěd** *a.* consisting of or supplied with huts.

hǔtch *n.* box-like pen for rabbits etc.

huzza′ (-ah) *int., n.,* & *v.i.* (arch.) hurrah.

H.W.M. *abbr.* high-water mark.

Hy *abbr.* Henry.

hȳ′acinth *n.* kinds of bulbous plant with bell-shaped flowers; reddish--orange variety of zircon.

hyaena : see **hyena**.

hȳ′alīne (*or* -ǐn) *a.* crystal-clear; vitreous, transparent.

hȳ′aloid *a.* glass-like.

hȳ′brid *n.* offspring of two animals or plants of different species etc.; cross-breed. *a.* cross-bred, mongrel; heterogeneous. ~**ism**, ~**īzā′-tion** *nn.*; ~**īze** *v.*

hȳ′dra *n.* (Gk. myth.) snake whose many heads grew again when cut off; fresh-water polyp.

hȳdrā′ngea (*or* -ăn-; -ja) *n.* kinds of shrub with globular clusters· of white, blue, or pink flowers.

hȳ′drant *n.* water-pipe with nozzle for hose.

hȳ′drāte *n.* chemical compound of water with element etc. *v.* (cause to) take up or combine with water. **hȳdrā′tion** *n.*

hȳdrau′lic *a.* of water conveyed through pipes etc.; operated by resistance offered when liquid is forced through tube etc.; (of cement) hardening under water. *n.pl.* science of conveyance of liquids through pipes etc., esp. as motive power.

hȳ′drō *n.* (colloq.) hydropathic hotel.

hȳ′dro-, in *comb.* water-; of or combined with hydrogen. **hȳdrocȧr′bon** *n.* compound of hydrogen and carbon. ~**cěph′alus** *n.* brain--disease, esp. of children, with accumulation of fluid in cranial cavity; ~**cěphǎl′ǐc**, ~**cěph′alous** *aa.* ~**cȳǎn′ǐc acid** *n.* solution of hydrogen cyanide in water. ~**dȳnǎm′ǐcs** *n.pl.* science of forces exerted by liquids. ~**ělěc′tric** *a.* using water-power to produce electricity. **hȳdrǒg′raphȳ** *n.* description of waters of earth. **hȳdrǒl′ysis** *n.*

decomposition by reaction with water; ~**lȳt′ǐc** *a.* **hȳdrǒm′eter** *n.* instrument for finding densities of liquids. **hȳdrǒp′athȳ** *n.* medical treatment by external and internal application of water; ~**păth′ǐc** *a.* ~**phō′bǐa** *n.* aversion to water, esp. as symptom of rabies in man; rabies. ~**phōne** *n.* kinds of instrument for detecting sound in or through or by aid of water. ~**plāne** *n.* fin-like device enabling submarine to rise etc. ~**pǒn′ǐcs** *n.pl.* cultivation of plants in water containing dissolved nutrients. ~**quǐnōne′** *n.* phenolic substance used as photographic developer etc. ~**stǎt′ǐcs** *n.* branch of mechanics concerned with pressure and equilibrium of liquids at rest; ~**stǎt′ǐc** *a.* ~**thě′rapȳ** *n.* hydropathy. **hȳdrǒx′ȳl** *n.* radical consisting of one atom of hydrogen and one atom of oxygen.

hȳ′drogȧn *n.* light colourless odourless gaseous element combining with oxygen to form water. ~ **bomb**, immensely powerful bomb in which hydrogen atoms are condensed to form helium. ~ **cyanide**, highly poisonous volatile gas or liquid. **hȳdrǒ′gėnāte, -īze** *vv.t.* charge, cause to combine, with hydrogen. ~**ā′tion** *n.* **hȳdrǒ′gėnous** *a.*

hȳ′drous *a.* containing water.

hȳē′na, hȳae′na *n.* carnivorous quadruped allied to dog; cruel, treacherous or rapacious person.

hȳ′giene (-jēn) *n.* principles of health; sanitary science. **hȳgie′nǐc** *a.*

hȳgrǒm′eter *n.* instrument measuring humidity of air etc.

hȳgroscǒp′ǐc *a.* tending to absorb water, esp. from air.

Hȳ′men[1] *n.* god of marriage. **hȳmenē′al** *a.*

hȳ′men[2] *n.* (anat.) fold of mucous membrane partially closing vagina of virgin female.

hȳmenǒp′tera *n.pl.* order of insects with four membranous wings. ~**terous** *a.*

hymn (hǐm) *n.* song of praise esp. to God or other divine being. *v.t.* praise in hymns, express (as) in hymn. ~**ǒl′ogȳ** *n.* study of composition of hymns; hymns collectively. **~ŏl'ogĭst** *n.*

hўm'nal *a.* of hymns. *n.* hymn-book.

hўm'nodў *n.* singing or composition of hymns; hymns collectively.

hў'oscīne (*or* -sēn) *n.* alkaloid used as sedative etc.

hўper-, in comb., over-, excessive. **hўperaesthē'sĭa** (-z-) *n.* (path.) morbid sensitivity of nerves; excessive sensibility; **~aesthĕt'ic** *a.* **~crĭt'ical** *a.* too critical. **~sŏn'ĭc** *a.* (of speed) greatly exceeding that of sound. **~tĕn'sion** *n.* abnormally high blood-pressure; extreme tension.

hўpēr'bola *n.* curve produced when cone is cut by plane making larger angle with base than side of cone makes. **~bŏl'ĭc** *a.*

hўpēr'bolė *n.* rhetorical exaggeration. **hўperbŏl'ical** *a.*

hўperbōr'ėan *a. & n.* (inhabitant) of extreme north.

hўpēr'trophў excessive development, morbid enlargement, of gland etc. **~phied** (-fíd) *a.*

hў'phen *n.* sign (-) used to join or divide words. *v.t.* join, divide, with hyphen. **~āte** *v.t.* hyphen.

hўpnō'sĭs *n.* (pl. *-osēs*), (artificial production of) state like deep sleep in which subject is responsive to suggestion.

hўpnŏt'ĭc *a.* of hypnosis. *n.* thing that produces sleep; person under hypnosis.

hўp'notĭsm *n.* (production of) hypnosis. **~ĭst** *n.*; **~īze** *v.t.*

hў'pō *n.* (photog.) sodium thiosulphate, used in fixing.

hў'pocaust (*or* hĭ-) *n.* (Rom. ant.) hollow space under floor for heating house or bath from furnace.

hўpochŏn'dria (-k-) *n.* state of causeless depression; excessive anxiety about one's health. **~driăc** *a.* of hypochondria; *n.* sufferer from hypochondria.

hўpŏc'rĭsў *n.* simulation of virtue; dissimulation, pretence.

hўp'ocrĭte, *n.* person guilty of hypocrisy; dissembler. **hўpocrĭt'ical** *a.*

hўpodēr'mĭc *a.* introduced beneath skin. *n.* hypodermic injection or

syringe. **~ needle, syringe,** used in hypodermic injection.

hўpŏs'tasĭs *n.* (pl. *-sēs*), (metaphys.) underlying substance; (theol.) personality (of Christ), person (of Godhead). **~stăt'ic(al)** *aa.* **hўpŏ'statīze** *v.t.* make into or treat as substance.

hўpŏt'ėnūse *n.* side opposite right angle of triangle.

hўpŏth'ėcāte *v.t.* pledge, mortgage.

hўpŏth'ėsĭs *n.* (pl. *-sēs*), supposition made as basis for reasoning etc. **hўpothĕt'ĭc(al)** *a.* of or resting on hypothesis.

hўr'ăx *n.* kinds of small pachydermatous hoofed quadruped.

hў'son *n.* kind of green tea from China.

hўss'op *n.* small bushy aromatic herb.

hўsterĕc'tomў *n.* surgical removal of uterus.

hўstēr'ĭa *n.* functional disturbance of nervous system; morbid excitement. **hўstė'rĭcal** *a.* **hўstė'rĭcs** *n.pl.* fit of hysteria.

I

I[1], **i**, as Roman numeral, 1.

I[2] (ī) *pron.* (obj. *me*, poss. *my*; pl. *we*, obj. *us*, poss. *our*), subj. case of 1st pers. pron. *n.* ego; subject or object of self-consciousness.

I. *abbr.* Idaho; Island(s); Isle.

i. *abbr.* intransitive.

Ia. *abbr.* Iowa.

iăm'bus (pl. *-buses*), **ī'ămb** *nn.* metrical foot of one short and one long syllable. **iăm'bic** *a.* of or based on iambs. **~bics** *n.pl.* iambic verse.

I.A.T.A., I.A.W. *abbr.* International Air Transport Association, Alliance of Women.

ib., ibid. *abbr.*, *ibidem*.

ī'bĕx *n.* (pl. *ibex* or *ibexes*), kinds of wild goat with scimitar-like horns.

ĭbī'dĕm, in same book, passage, etc. [L]

ī′bĭs *n.* (pl. *ibis* or *ibises*), stork-like bird with long curved bill.

I.C.B.M. *abbr.* inter-continental ballistic missile.

ice *n.* frozen water; (with pl.) frozen confection; *dry* ~, solid carbon dioxide. *v.t.* cover (as) with ice; freeze; cool (wine) in ice; cool by adding ice to; cover with icing. ~ **age,** period when ice covered large parts of earth. ~**berg,** mass of floating ice at sea. ~**-box,** refrigerator. ~**-breaker,** boat with reinforced bow for breaking channel through ice. ~**-cap,** mass of thick ice covering polar region etc. ~ **cream,** frozen cream, custard, etc. ~**-fall,** steep part of glacier like frozen waterfall. ~**-field,** extensive sheet of floating ice. ~**-floe,** flattish free mass of floating ice. ~**-hockey,** form of hockey played on ice with flat disc instead of ball. ~**-plant,** with leaves covered with pellucid watery vesicles. ~**-water,** iced water. ~**-wool,** kind of glossy two-ply wool for knitting etc.

Ice′land spar (īsl-) *n.* particularly transparent kind of spar.

ĭchneu′mon (-k-) *n.* small brown weasel-like quadruped allied to mongoose. ~**(fly),** kinds of small hymenopterous insect parasitic on other insects.

ī′chŏr (-k-) *n.* (Gk. myth.) ethereal fluid flowing like blood in veins of gods.

ĭchthȳŏl′ogȳ (-k-) *n.* study of fishes. ~**lŏ′gĭcal** *a.*; ~**logĭst** *n.*

ī′cicle *n.* tapering spike of ice hanging from eaves etc.

ī′cing *n.* (esp.) coating of sugar and water etc. for cakes etc.; formation of ice on aircraft. ~ **sugar,** finely powdered sugar.

ī′con *n.* image, statue; sacred painting, mosaic, etc. **īcŏn′ĭc** *a.* ~**ŏl′ogy** *n.* study of icons; symbolism. ~**ŏs′tasĭs** *n.* screen with icons, separating sanctuary from main body of Orthodox church.

īcŏn′oclăsm *n.* breaking of images.

īcŏn′oclăst *n.* breaker of images; one who assails cherished beliefs. **īcŏnoclăs′tic** *a.*

I.C.S. *abbr.* Indian Civil Service.

ĭc′tus *n.* rhythmical or metrical stress.

ī′cȳ *a.* abounding in ice; very cold; (of manner) chilling.

ĭd *n.* part of mind comprising instinctive impulses of individual etc.

Id. *abbr.* Idaho.

I.D. *abbr.* Intelligence Department.

id. *abbr., idem.*

I.D.B. *abbr.* illicit diamond-buying.

īdė′a *n.* notion conceived by mind; vague belief, fancy; plan, intention, aim. **īdėā′tion** *n.* formation or relation of ideas.

īdė′al (*or* -dē-) *a.* perfect; existing only in idea; visionary. ′*n.* perfect type; actual thing as standard for imitation. ~**ĭsm** *n.* system of thought holding object of external perception to consist of ideas; representation in ideal form. ~**ĭst** *n.*; ~**ĭs′tic** *a.*

īdė′alīze *v.* make or treat as ideal. ~**zā′tion** *n.*

ī′dem, (in) the same (author etc.). [L]

īdĕn′tĭcal *a.* same; agreeing in all details (*with*).

īdĕn′tĭfȳ *v.t.* treat as identical; associate inseparably *with*; establish identity of. ~**fĭcā′tion** *n.*

īdĕn′tĭtȳ *n.* absolute sameness; being specified person or thing; individuality.

ĭd′ėogrăm, -graph (*or* ī-; -ahf) *nn.* character in pictorial writing indicating idea, not name, of thing.

īdėŏl′ogȳ *n.* scheme of ideas at basis of political etc. theory or system; characteristic way of thinking. ~**lŏ′gĭcal** *a.*

ides (īdz) *n.pl.* (Rom. ant.) 15th (or 13th) of month.

ĭd ĕst, that is. [L]

ĭd′iocȳ *n.* mental condition of idiot; utter foolishness.

ĭd′iom *n.* language; form of expression peculiar to language. **ĭdiomăt′ic** *a.*

ĭdiosȳn′crasȳ *n.* constitution or view or feeling peculiar ′to person. **ĭdiosȳncrăt′ic** *a.*

ĭd′iot *n.* person too deficient in mind to be capable of rational conduct; utter fool. **ĭdiŏt′ic** *a.*

ī′dle *a.* lazy, indolent; unoccupied;

useless, purposeless. *v.* be idle;
pass (time) thus; (of engine) run
slowly without doing any work.
~r *n.*; ĭ'dly *adv.*

ĭ'dol *n.* image as object of worship;
false god; object of devotion.

ĭdŏl'ater *n.* worshipper of idols;
devout admirer. ~tress, ~trў *nn.*;
~trous *a.*

ĭ'dolīze *v.t.* make idol of; venerate or
love to excess. ~zā'tion *n.*

ĭ'dyll (*or* ĭ-) *n.* (account of) peace-
fully or romantically blissful scene,
incident, etc. idўll'ĭc *a.*

i.e. *abbr.*, *id est* [L], that is.

ĭf *conj.* on condition or supposition
that; whenever; whether.

ĭg'lōō *n.* Eskimo dome-shaped snow
house.

ĭg'nēous *a.* of fire; produced by
volcanic action.

ĭg'nĭs făt'ūus *n.* will-o'-the-wisp.

ĭgnīte' *v.* set fire to; take fire.
ĭgnī'tion *n.* (esp.) (mechanism for)
starting combustion in cylinder of
motor engine.

ĭgnō'ble *a.* of low birth or position;
mean, base.

ĭgnomĭn'ĭous *a.* mean, shameful;
humiliating.

ĭg'nomĭnў *n.* dishonour, infamy.

ĭgnorā'mus *n.* (pl. *-muses*), ignorant
person.

ĭg'norance *n.* want of knowledge.

ĭg'norant *a.* lacking knowledge;
uninformed (*of*).

ĭgnōre' *v.t.* refuse to take notice of.

ĭgua'na (-gwah-) *n.* large S.-Amer.
tree lizard.

ĭguăn'odon (-gw-) *n.* huge fossil
saurian.

i.h.p. *abbr.* indicated horse-power.

IHS *abbr.* Jesus.

ī'kŏn *n.* icon.

Il. *abbr.* Iliad.

ī'lĕx *n.* (pl. *-exes*), evergreen oak;
(bot.) genus including holly.

ĭl'ĭac *a.* of flank or hip-bone.

ĭlk *a.* (Sc.) same; *of that* ~, of place,
estate, etc., of same name; (vulg.)
of that family, class, etc.

ĭll *a.* in bad health, sick; bad; evil;
faulty, deficient. *n.* evil; harm;
(pl.) misfortunes. *adv.* badly,
unfavourably; scarcely. ~-advised,
injudicious. ~-bred, rude. ~-

-favoured, uncomely. ~-gotten,
gained by evil means. ~-judged,
unwise. ~-omened, attended by
bad omens. ~-starred, unlucky.
~-tempered, morose. ~-timed,
unseasonable. ~-treat, ~-use,
treat badly.

Ill. *abbr.* Illinois.

ĭllā'tion *n.* deduction, conclusion.

ĭllā'tive *a.* inferential.

ĭllē'gal *a.* contrary to law. ĭllē-
găl'itў *n.*

ĭllĕ'gĭble *a.* not legible, unreadable.
~bĭl'itў *n.*

ĭllĕgĭt'ĭmacў *n.* bastardy.

ĭllĕgĭt'ĭmate *a.* not legitimate, bastard. *v.t.* (-āt), declare illegitimate.

ĭllĭb'eral *a.* narrow-minded; sordid;
stingy. ĭllĭberăl'itў *n.*

ĭllĭ'cĭt *a.* unlawful.

ĭllĭm'ĭtable *a.* boundless.

ĭllĭt'eracў *n.* being illiterate.

ĭllĭt'erate *a.* unlearned; unable to
read. *n.* illiterate person.

ĭll'nĕss *n.* ill health, sickness; disease.

ĭllŏ'gĭcal *a.* devoid of, contrary to,
logic. ĭllŏgĭcăl'itў *n.*

ĭllū'mĭnant (*or* -ōō-) *a.* serving to
illuminate. *n.* source or agent of
illumination.

ĭllū'mĭnāte (*or* -ōō-) *v.t.* light up;
throw light on; decorate with lights
as sign of festivity; decorate (MS.
etc.) with gold etc. ~ā'tion,
~ātor *nn.*; ~ative *a.*

ĭllū'mĭne, (poet.) ĭllūme' (*or* -ōō-) *vv.t.*
light up; enlighten.

ĭllū'sion (*or* -ōō-) *n.* deceptive appearance or belief. ~ĭst *n.* (esp.)
conjuror. ĭllū'sĭve (*or* -ōō-) *a.*

ĭllū'sorў (*or* -ōō-) *a.* deceptive.

ĭll'ustrāte *v.t.* make clear, esp. by
examples or drawings; adorn with
pictures. ĭllustrā'tion *n.* illustrating; example; drawing etc. in book
etc. ĭll'ustrative *a.*; ~ātor *n.*

ĭllŭs'trĭous *a.* distinguished.

I.L.O. *abbr.* International Labour
Organization.

I.L.P. *abbr.* Independent Labour
Party.

ĭm'age *n.* imitation of object's external form, esp. figure of saint or
divinity, idol; optical appearance
produced by rays of light reflected
from mirror or refracted through

transparent medium; mental picture, idea, conception. *v.t.* make image of; mirror; picture.

ĭm' agerÿ (-ĭj-) *n.* statuary; images; figurative illustration.

imă'gĭnable *a.* that can be imagined.

ĭmă'gĭnarÿ *a.* existing only in, due to, imagination.

ĭmăgĭnā'tion *n.* mental faculty forming images of objects not present to senses; fancy; creative faculty of mind. **ĭmă'gĭnatĭve** *a.*

ĭmă'gĭne *v.t.* form mental image of, conceive; suppose, think; fancy.

ĭm'agĭsm *n.* movement in poetry etc. aiming at exact use of visual images. ~**ĭst** *n.* & *a.*

ĭmā'gō *n.* (pl. *-gos* or *-gĭnēs*), final and perfect stage of insect.

ĭmam' (-ah-) *n.* prayer-leader of mosque; Moslem spiritual leader.

ĭmbăl'ance *n.* disturbance of mental or physical equilibrium.

ĭm'bĕcīle (*or* -ēl) *a.* mentally weak; idiotic. *n.* imbecile person; person with mental age of 3–7. ~**cĭl'ĭc** *a.*; ~**cĭl'ĭtÿ** *n.*

imbed : see **embed.**

ĭmbībe' *v.t.* drink in; drink; inhale; absorb.

ĭm'brĭcāte *v.* arrange, be arranged, so as to overlap like tiles. ~**ā'tion** *n.*

ĭmbro'glio (-ōlyō) *n.* confused or complicated situation.

ĭmbrue' (-ōō) *v.t.* stain.

ĭmbūe' *v.t.* saturate, dye; inspire.

ĭm'ĭtable *a.* that can be imitated. **ĭmĭtabĭl'ĭtÿ** *n.*

ĭm'ĭtāte *v.t.* follow example of; mimic; be like. ~**ā'tion**, ~**ātor** *nn.*; ~**atĭve** *a.*

ĭmmăc'ūlate *a.* pure, spotless.

ĭmm'anent *a.* inherent; (of God) pervading universe. ~**ence** *n.*

ĭmmatēr'ĭal *a.* incorporeal; unimportant. ~**ăl'ĭtÿ** *n.*

ĭmmatūre' *a.* not mature. ~**rĭtÿ** *n.*

ĭmmea'surable (-mĕzher-) *a.* not measurable, immense. ~**bĭl'ĭtÿ** *n.*

ĭmmē'dĭate *a.* without intervening medium, direct; occurring at once. ~**ly** *adv.* without delay.

ĭmmĕmōr'ĭal *a.* ancient beyond memory.

ĭmmĕnse' *a.* vast, huge. ~**ly** *adv.* vastly; very much.

ĭmmĕn'sitÿ *n.* vastness; infinity.

ĭmmĕrse' *v.t.* (-*sible*), dip, plunge; put under water; involve deeply, absorb. **ĭmmĕr'sion** *n.* (esp.) baptism by plunging whole person in water; ~**sion heater**, electrical heating element immersed in water.

ĭmm'ĭgrant *n.* & *a.* (person) immigrating.

ĭmm'ĭgrāte *v.i.* come as settler (*into* country). ~**ā'tion** *n.*

ĭmm'ĭnent *a.* impending, soon to happen. ~**ence** *n.*

ĭmmō'bīle *a.* immovable; motionless. ~**bĭl'ĭtÿ** *n.* **ĭmmō'bĭlīze** *v.t.* make or keep immobile or stationary.

ĭmmŏd'erate *a.* excessive.

ĭmmŏd'ĕst *a.* indecent, indelicate; impudent. **ĭmmŏd'ĕstÿ** *n.*

ĭmm'olāte *v.t.* sacrifice; kill as sacrifice. **ĭmmolā'tion** *n.*

ĭmmŏ'ral *a.* morally wrong or evil; dissolute. **ĭmmorăl'ĭtÿ** *n.*

ĭmmōr'tal *a.* undying; famous for all time. *n.* immortal being, esp. (pl.) gods of antiquity; (pl.) members of Fr. Academy. ~**ăl'ĭtÿ** *n.*; ~**alīze** *v.t.*

ĭmmōr'tĕlle' *n.* flower retaining colour when dried.

ĭmmo'vable (-mōō-) *a.* not movable; unyielding. ~**bĭl'ĭtÿ** *n.*

ĭmmūne' *a.* having immunity.

ĭmmū'nitÿ *n.* exemption (*from*); living organism's power of resisting and overcoming infection.

ĭmm'ūnīze *v.t.* make immune (*against*). ~**zā'tion** *n.*

ĭmmūre' *v.t.* imprison, shut up.

ĭmmū'table *a.* unchangeable; unalterable. ~**bĭl'ĭtÿ** *n.*

imp *n.* little devil; mischievous child.

ĭm'păct *n.* collision, striking; (immediate) effect, influence. *v.t.* (-ăkt'), drive or wedge together. ~**ĕd** *a.* (of tooth) remaining within jaw; (of fracture) with broken parts locked together. **impăc'tion** *n.*

impair' *v.t.* damage, weaken. ~**ment** *n.* deterioration; injury.

ĭmpāle' *v.t.* transfix on stake; (her.) combine (two coats of arms) by placing one on each side of central line of shield. ~**ment** *n.*

ĭmpăl'pable *a.* imperceptible to touch; not easily grasped.

impărt' v.t. give, give share of; communicate (to).

impăr'tial a. not partial, fair. **impărtiăl'itў** (-shĭ-) n.

impass'able (-pah-) a. that cannot be traversed. **~bĭl'itў** n.

im'passe (-ahs; or -ahs') n. deadlock; fix.

impăss'ĭble a. incapable of feeling or emotion; not subject to suffering. **~bĭl'itў** n.

impă'ssioned (-shŏnd) a. deeply moved; ardent.

impăss'ĭve a. void of feeling or emotion. **impassĭv'itў** n.

impăs'tō n. laying on of paint thickly.

impā'tient (-shĕnt) a. not patient; intolerant. **impā'tience** n.

impeach' v.t. call in question; disparage; accuse, esp. of treason etc. **~ment** n.

impĕcc'able a. not liable to sin; faultless. **~bĭl'itў** n.

impĕcū'nĭous a. having little or no money. **impĕcūnĭŏs'itў** n.

impē'dance n. (electr.) ratio of electromotive force to current it produces in circuit.

impēde' v.t. retard; hinder.

impĕd'iment n. hindrance, obstruction; esp. stammer etc. in speech.

impĕdĭmĕn'ta n.pl. baggage esp. of army.

impĕl' v.t. drive, force; propel.

impĕnd' v.i. hang (over); be imminent. **~ence** n.; **~ent** a.

impĕn'ĕtrable, a. not penetrable; impervious; inscrutable. **~bĭl'itў** n.

impĕn'itent a. not penitent. **~ence** n.

impĕ'rative a. (gram.) expressing command; peremptory; urgent, obligatory. n. (gram.) imperative mood.

impercĕp'tible a. not perceptible; very slight or gradual.

impercĕp'tĭve, impercĭp'ient aa. lacking perception.

impĕr'fĕct a. not perfect; incomplete; faulty; (gram.) implying action going on but not completed.

imperfĕc'tion n. faultiness; fault, blemish.

impĕr'ial a. of empire or sovereign State ranking with this; of emperor; supreme; majestic. n. small tuft of beard beneath lower lip, **~ism** n. rule of emperor; principle or spirit of empire. **~ist** n. & a.; **~is'tic** a.

impĕ'ril v.t. endanger.

impēr'ĭous a. domineering; commanding; urgent.

impē'rishable a. not perishable; that cannot perish.

impĕr'mĕable a. impervious.

impĕr'sonal a. having no personality or personal reference; (gram., of verb) having no subject or purely formal one.

impĕr'sonāte v.t. play part of, pretend to be. **~ā'tion, ~ātor** nn.

impĕr'tinent a. insolent, saucy; irrelevant. **~ence** n.

impertŭr'bable a. not excitable; calm. **~bĭl'itў** n.

impĕr'vĭous a. impenetrable, inaccessible (to).

impĕt'ūous a. moving violently or fast; acting rashly. **~ŏs'itў** n.

im'pĕtus n. (pl. -uses), moving force; momentum; impulse.

im'pī n. body of Zulu etc. warriors.

impī'ĕtў n. lack of piety.

impinge' (-j) v.i. make impact (on). **~ment** n.

im'pĭous a. not pious; wicked, profane.

imp'ish a. of or like imp.

implăc'able a. not appeasable; inexorable. **~bĭl'itў** n.

implant' (-ahnt) v.t. insert, fix; instil; plant. **implantā'tion** n.

im'plĕment[1] n. tool, utensil.

im'plĕmĕnt[2] v.t. carry into effect. **~ā'tion** n.

im'plĭcāte v.t. entwine, entangle; involve; imply. **~ā'tion** n.

impli'cĭt a. involved though not expressed; unquestioning.

implōde' v. (cause to) burst inwards.

implōre' v.t. beg earnestly.

implў' v.t. involve truth of; mean; insinuate, hint.

impolīte' a. uncivil, rude.

impŏl'itĭc a. injudicious.

impŏn'derable a. very light; that cannot be weighed or estimated. n. imponderable thing.

impōrt' v.t. bring in (esp. foreign goods) from abroad; imply, mean. n. (ĭm'-), meaning, implication;

importance; imported commodity. ~ā'tion, ~er *nn.*

impŏr'tance *n.* being important.

impŏr'tant *a.* of great consequence; momentous; pompous.

impŏr'tūnate *a.* persistent in solicitation. importū'nity *n.*

impŏr'tūne (*or* -ūn') *v.t.* solicit pressingly and repeatedly.

impōse' (-z) *v.* place (thing) on; lay (tax etc.) on; palm off (*on*); exert influence *on* by striking appearance etc.; ~ *on,* take advantage of, deceive.

impō'sing (-z-) *a.* impressive, esp. in appearance.

imposi'tion (-z-) *n.* imposing, imposing on; laying on *of hands* (in ordination etc.); thing imposed, esp. work set as punishment at school.

imposs'ible *a.* not possible; not easy or convenient; (colloq.) outrageous, intolerable. ~bil'ity *n.*

im'pŏst *n.* (hist.) tax, duty.

impŏs'tor *n.* one who assumes false character; swindler.

impŏs'ture *n.* fraudulent deception.

im'potent *a.* powerless; decrepit; (of males) without sexual power. ~ence *n.*

impound' *v.t.* shut up in pound; confiscate.

impŏv'erish *v.t.* make poor; exhaust strength of. ~ment *n.*

imprăc'ticable *a.* impossible in practice; impassable. ~bil'ity *n.*

imprēcā'tion *n.* cursing; curse. im'prĕcātory *a.*

imprĕg'nable *a.* proof against attack. ~bil'ity *n.*

im'prĕgnāte *v.t.* make pregnant; fill, saturate. ~ā'tion *n.*

imprĕsăr'iō *n.* (pl. -os), organizer of esp. musical public entertainments.

imprēscript'ible *a.* that cannot be legally taken away.

imprĕss'[1] *v.t.* force into service. ~ment *n.*

imprĕss'[2] *v.t.* imprint, stamp, by pressure; enforce, fix; affect deeply. *n.* (im'-), mark impressed; characteristic mark. ~ible *a.*; ~ibil'ity *n.*

imprĕ'ssion *n.* impressing, mark impressed; print from type or engraving; issue, unaltered reprint of book etc.; effect produced on mind; belief. ~able *a.* easily impressed or influenced. ~abil'ity *n.*

imprĕ'ssionism (-shon-) *n.* method of painting or writing so as to give general effect without detail. ~ist *n.* & *a.*; ~is'tic *a.*

imprĕss'ive *a.* making deep impression on mind or senses, exciting deep feelings.

imprimā'tūr *n.* licence to print.

imprī'mis, in the first place. [L].

imprint' *v.t.* impress mark on. *n.* (im'-), impression; printer's or publisher's name in book etc.

impris'on (-z-) *v.t.* put into prison; confine. ~ment *n.*

improb'able *a.* not likely; incredible. ~bil'ity *n.*

imprō'bity *n.* wickedness.

imprŏmp'tū *adv.* & *a.* extempore. *n.* improvised or extempore performance, composition, etc.

improp'er *a.* inaccurate, wrong; unseemly, indecent.

imprō'priate *v.t.* place (tithes, benefice, etc.) in lay hands. ~ā'tion *n.*

improve' (-ōōv) *v.* make or become better; make good use of (occasion, opportunity). ~ment *n.* ~r *n.* (esp.) one working at trade for low wage to improve skill.

improv'ident *a.* heedless, thriftless. ~ence *n.*

im'provīse *v.t.* compose, utter, provide, etc., extempore. ~sā'tion *n.*; improvī'satory *a.*

impru'dent (-rōō-) *a.* rash, indiscreet. ~ence *n.*

im'pūdent *a.* shameless; pert, insolent. im'pūdence *n.*

impugn' (-ūn) *v.t.* call in question, challenge.

im'pulse *n.* impelling; impetus; sudden tendency to act without reflection. impŭl'sive *a.* apt to be moved, prompted, by impulse.

impū'nity *n.* exemption from loss or punishment.

impūre' *a.* dirty; unchaste; adulterated, mixed. impūr'ity *n.*

impūte' *v.t.* attribute (*to*); ascribe. impūtā'tion *n.*

in *prep.* expr. inclusion or position within limits of space, time, circumstance, etc. *adv.* expr. position bounded by certain limits, or movement to point enclosed by them; (of fire etc.) burning; (of player etc.) having turn or right to play; in fashion or season or office; ~ *for*, committed to. *adj.* internal, living etc. inside; (sl.) fashionable. *n.* (esp.) ~*s and outs*, turnings to and fro, details. ~-patient, one remaining in hospital for treatment etc.

in. *abbr.* inch(es).

ĭnăbĭl'ĭtў *n.* being unable.

ĭnăccĕss'ĭble (-ks-) *a.* not to be reached; unapproachable. ~-bĭl'ĭtў *n.*

ĭnăcc'ūrate *a.* not exact. ~acў *n.*

ĭnăc'tion *n.* absence of action; sluggishness, inertness. **ĭnăc'tĭve** *a.*; **ĭnactĭv'ĭtў** *n.*

ĭnăd'ĕquate *a.* insufficient. ~acў *n.*

ĭnadmĭss'ĭble *a.* not allowable. ~bĭl'ĭtў *n.*

ĭnadvĕr'tent *a.* inattentive; unintentional. ~ence, ~encў *nn.*

ĭnā'lĭenable *a.* not alienable.

ĭnămora'tō (-rah-) *n.* (fem. -*ta*), lover; loved one.

ĭnāne' *a.* empty; silly, senseless. **ĭnăn'ĭtў** *n.*

ĭnăn'ĭmate *a.* void of life; spiritless, dull.

ĭnanĭ'tion *n.* exhaustion from lack of nourishment.

ĭnăpp'lĭcable *a.* irrelevant; unsuitable. ~bĭl'ĭtў *n.*

ĭnăpp'osĭte (-z-) *a.* not apposite.

ĭnapprē'cĭable (-sha-) *a.* not appreciable; not worth reckoning.

ĭnapprō'prĭate *a.* not appropriate.

ĭnăpt' *a.* unskilful. ~ĭtūde *n.*

ĭnărtĭc'ūlate *a.* not jointed; not articulate, indistinct; dumb; unable to express one's ideas.

ĭnărtĭs'tĭc *a.* not following principles of, unskilled in, art.

ĭnasmŭch' as *adv.* seeing that.

ĭnattĕn'tion *n.* lack of attention; negligence. **ĭnattĕn'tĭve** *a.*

ĭnau'dĭble *a.* that cannot be heard. ~bĭl'ĭtў *n.*

ĭnau'gūral *a. & n.* (ceremony, speech, etc.) of or at inauguration. **ĭnau'gūrate** *v.t.* admit to, enter upon, with ceremony; begin. ~ā'tion *n.*

ĭnauspĭ'cious *a.* not of good omen; unlucky.

ĭn'bôrn *a.* implanted by nature.

ĭn'brĕd (*or* -ĕd') *a.* innate; born of closely related parents. **ĭn'-breedĭng** *n.* breeding from closely related individuals.

Inc. *abbr.* Incorporated.

ĭncăl'cūlable *a.* beyond calculation; uncertain. ~bĭl'ĭtў *n.*

ĭn căm'era, in judge's private room, not in open court. [L]

ĭncăndĕsce' *v.* glow, cause to glow, with heat. **ĭncăndĕs'cent** *a.* glowing with heat; shining; (of artificial light) produced by glowing filament. ~ence *n.*

ĭncăntā'tion *n.* spell, charm.

ĭncā'pable *a.* not capable; disqualified; lacking in ordinary powers. ~bĭl'ĭtў *n.*

ĭncapă'cĭtāte *v.t.* make incapable or unfit. ~ĭtā'tion *n.*

ĭncapă'cĭtў *n.* inability; legal disqualification.

ĭncăr'cerāte *v.t.* imprison, ~ā'tion *n.*

ĭncăr'nadīne *a.* flesh-coloured; crimson. *v.t.* dye crimson.

ĭncăr'nate *a.* embodied in flesh, esp. in human form. *v.t.* (-āt), embody. ~ā'tion *n.* (esp., *I*~, of Christ).

ĭncau'tious *a.* rash.

ĭncĕn'dĭarў, *a.* of, guilty of, malicious setting on fire of property etc.; intended to cause fires; (fig.) inflammatory. *n.* incendiary person or bomb. ~rĭsm *n.*

ĭncĕnse'[1] *v.t.* make angry.

ĭn'cĕnse[2] *n.* gum, spice, giving sweet smell when burned; smoke of this, esp. in religious ceremonial.

ĭncĕn'tĭve *n.* something inciting or encouraging to action; stimulus, inducement, esp. to increase output. *a.* inciting.

ĭncĕp'tion *n.* beginning. ~ĭve *a.* beginning; initial; (of verb) expressing beginning of action.

ĭncĕr'tĭtūde *n.* uncertainty.

ĭncĕss'ant *a.* continual; repeated.

ĭn'cĕst *n.* sexual intercourse of near kindred. **ĭncĕs'tūous** *a.*

ĭnch *n.* measure of length, twelfth part of foot; amount (of rainfall) that would cover surface to depth of 1 in., (of pressure) that balances weight of column of mercury 1 in. high; small amount. *v.* move by inches, edge *forward* etc.

ĭn'choate (-kōat) *a.* just begun; undeveloped. *v.t.* (-āt), begin. **ĭn'-chōative** (*or* ĭnkō'-) *a.* (of verbs) inceptive.

ĭn'cidence *n.* falling on, contact with, thing; range, scope, extent.

ĭn'cident *a.* apt to occur, naturally attaching (*to*). *n.* event, occurrence; episode.

ĭncĭden'tal *a.* casual; not essential; (of music) interpolated in play etc. **~ally** *adv.* (esp.) by the way.

ĭncin'erāte *v.t.* consume by fire. **~ā'tion, ~ātor** *nn.*

ĭncĭp'ient *a.* beginning.

ĭncĭse (-z) *v.t.* make cut in; engrave. **ĭncĭ'sion** *n.*

ĭncĭ'sive *a.* sharp; trenchant.

ĭncĭ'sor (-z-) *n.* any of front teeth between canines.

ĭncīte' *v.t.* urge on, stir up. **~ment** *n.*

ĭncĭvĭl'ĭty *n.* rudeness.

incl. *abbr.* inclusive.

ĭnclĕm'ent *a.* (of weather) severe, esp. cold or stormy. **~ency** *n.*

ĭnclīnā'tion *n.* slope, slant; propensity; liking, affection.

ĭnclīne' *v.* lean, cause to lean; bend forward or downward; dispose, be disposed; tend. *n.* (ĭn'-), inclined plane; slope.

ĭnclūde' (-ōod) *v.t.* comprise, regard, treat, as part of whole. **ĭnclū'sion** *n.*

ĭnclū'sive (-ōo-) *a.* including; comprehensive; including all accessory payments; (quasi-*adv.*) the term(s) named being included.

incog. *abbr.* incognito.

ĭncŏgni'to (-ētō; *or* ĭnkŏg'nĭtō) *a. & n.* (person) unknown or concealed under false name etc. *adv.* with one's identity concealed.

ĭncōhēr'ent *a.* not coherent; inconsequential. **~ence** *n.*

ĭncombŭs'tĭble *a.* not consumable by fire. **~bĭl'ĭty** *n.*

ĭn'come (-ŭm) *n.* periodical (esp. annual) receipts from work, investments, etc.

ĭn'comĭng (-kŭ-) *n.* entrance, arrival. *a.* coming in, succeeding, accruing.

ĭncommĕn'surable (-sher-) *a.* having

no common measure; not comparable in size, value, etc. **~bĭl'ĭty** *n.*

ĭncommĕn'surate (-sher-) *a.* out of proportion; inadequate.

ĭncommōde' *v.t.* trouble, annoy; inconvenience.

ĭncommō'dious *a.* not commodious, inconvenient.

ĭncommū'nicable *a.* that cannot be shared or told. **~bĭl'ĭty** *n.*

ĭncommūnica'dō (-ah-) *a.* without means of communication, in solitary confinement.

ĭncŏm'parable *a.* matchless.

ĭncompăt'ĭble *a.* opposed; discordant; inconsistent. **~bĭl'ĭty** *n.*

ĭncŏm'pétent *a.* not competent; not legally qualified. **~ence** *n.*

ĭncomplēte' *a.* not finished.

ĭncŏmprĕhĕn'sĭble *a.* that cannot be understood. **~bĭl'ĭty** *n.*

ĭnconceiv'able (-sēv-) *a.* that cannot be imagined. **~bĭl'ĭty** *n.*

ĭnconclū'sive (-lōo-) *a.* not convincing or decisive.

ĭncŏng'ruous (-nggrōo-) *a.* out of keeping; absurd. **ĭncongru'ĭty** (-grōo-) *n.*

ĭncŏn'séquent *a.* wanting in logical sequence; irrelevant, illogical. **~ence** *n.*

ĭncŏnséquĕn'tial *a.* inconsequent; of no consequence.

ĭnconsĭd'erable *a.* not worth considering; of small size, value, etc.

ĭnconsĭd'erate *a.* thoughtless, rash; not considerate of others.

ĭnconsĭs'tent *a.* not consistent; incompatible. **ĭnconsĭs'tency** *n.*

ĭnconsō'lable *a.* not to be comforted.

ĭncŏn'sonant *a.* not harmonizing (*with*). **ĭncŏn'sonance** *n.*

ĭnconspĭc'ūous *a.* not readily seen or noticed.

ĭncŏn'stant *a.* fickle; variable; irregular. **ĭncŏn'stancy** *n.*

ĭncontĕs'table *a.* past dispute.

ĭncŏn'tinent *a.* lacking self-restraint; unable to control urine etc. **~ence** *n.*

ĭncŏntrover'tĭble *a.* indisputable.

ĭnconvē'nience *n.* (instance of) want of adaptation to personal requirement or ease. *v.t.* put to incon-

venience, be troublesome to.
~ient *a.*

inconver'tible *a.* not convertible
(esp. of currency). ~bil'ity *n.*

incor'porate *v.t.* combine into one
substance or whole (*with, in, into*);
constitute as legal corporation.
a. (-at), incorporated. ~ā'tion *n.*

incorpor'eal *a.* not composed of
matter; of immaterial beings.

incorrect' *a.* improper; inaccurate.

inco'rrigible *a.* past correction.

incorrup'tible *a.* that cannot decay;
that cannot be bribed. ~bil'ity,
(arch.) **incorrup'tion** *nn.*

increase' *v.* become, make, greater or
more numerous; intensify. *n.*
(in'-), growth, enlargement; increased amount; *on the* ~, increasing.

incred'ible *a.* that cannot be believed;
surprising. ~bil'ity *n.*

incred'ulous *a.* unbelieving. **incre-
dū'lity** *n.*

in'crement *n.* (amount of) increase;
profit.

incrim'ināte *v.t.* charge with crime;
involve in accusation. ~ā'tion *n.*;
~atory *a.*

incrustā'tion *n.* encrusting, being
encrusted; crust, hard coating.

in'cūbāte *v.* hatch, sit on (eggs);
subject (micro-organisms) to
warmth; undergo incubation.
~ā'tion *n.* (esp.) early phase of
disease between infection and
appearance of symptoms. ~ātor
n. apparatus for hatching birds,
rearing premature infants or developing micro-organisms.

in'cūbus *n.* evil spirit supposed to
descend on sleeping persons;
person or thing that oppresses like
nightmare.

in'culcāte *v.t.* urge, impress persistently (*in* etc.). ~ā'tion *n.*

in'culpāte *v.t.* accuse, blame; involve
in charge. ~ā'tion *n.*

incum'bent *a.* resting as duty (*up*)*on.
n.* holder of benefice. ~ency *n.*

incunăb'ūla *n.pl.* early printed
books, esp. before 1500.

incur' *v.t.* fall into, bring on oneself.

incūr'able *a. & n.* (person) that
cannot be cured. ~bil'ity *n.*

incūr'ious *a.* indifferent.

incūr'sion *n.* invasion; sudden
attack.

Ind. *abbr.* Independent; India(n);
Indiana.

indebt'ed (-dĕt-) *a.* owing money or
gratitude (*to*).

indē'cent *a.* unbecoming; immodest,
obscene. ~ency *n.*

indeci'pherable *a.* that cannot be
deciphered.

indeci'sion *n.* want of decision,
hesitation.

indeci'sive *a.* not decisive; irresolute.

indeclī'nable *a.* not inflected.

indecor'ous (*or* indĕk'-) *a.* unbecoming.

indecor'um *n.* lack of decorum.

indeed' *adv.* in truth; really.

indefăt'igable *a.* unwearying.

indefea'sible (-z-) *a.* that cannot be
forfeited or annulled. ~bil'ity *n.*

indefen'sible *a.* admitting of no
defence. ~bil'ity *n.*

indefi'nable *a.* that cannot be defined.

indef'inite *a.* vague, undefined.

indel'ible *a.* that cannot be deleted or
effaced, permanent. ~bil'ity *n.*

indel'icate *a.* coarse, immodest.
indel'icacy *n.*

indem'nify *v.t.* secure against loss or
legal responsibility; compensate
(*for* loss etc.). ~fica'tion *n.*

indem'nity *n.* security against
damage or loss; exemption from
penalties etc.; compensation, esp.
exacted from defeated belligerent.

indent' *v.* make notches, dents, or
recesses in; (print.) set back
(beginning of line) further from
margin; make requisition or
written order *for. n.* (in'-), official
requisition, order; indentation;
indenture. ~ā'tion *n.*

inden'ture *n.* document drawn up in
duplicate and divided into two with
zigzag line; sealed agreement, esp.
binding apprentice to master. *v.t.*
bind by indenture.

indepen'dence *n.* being independent;
independent income. **I~ Day,** U.S.
holiday (4 July), anniversary of
Declaration of Independence.
~ency *n.* independent State;
(hist.) Congregationalism.

indepen'dent *a.* not depending on
authority (*of*); not depending on

something else for validity, efficiency etc.; not needing to earn livelihood; (of income etc.) making one independent; unwilling to be under obligation to others. *n.* politician etc. independent of any party.

indĕscrī'bable *a.* vague; beyond description. ~bil'itў *n.*

indĕstrŭc'tible *a.* that cannot be destroyed. ~bil'itў *n.*

indĕtĕr'minable *a.* that cannot be ascertained or settled.

indĕtĕr'minate *a.* not fixed in extent, character, etc.; vague.

in'dĕx *n.* (pl. -*exes*, -*ĭcēs*), forefinger; hand, pointer, on instruments; (alg.) symbol indicating what power of factor is to be taken; list of names, prices, subjects, etc. esp. alphabetical list with references. *v.t.* furnish (book) with index; enter in index.

In'dia (Ĭ-). ~man, (hist.) ship engaged in East Indian trade. ~ paper, soft absorbent kind from China used for proofs or first impressions of engravings; (*Oxford*) ~ *paper* very thin tough opaque printing-paper. i~rubber, rubber, esp. piece of rubber for rubbing out pencil-marks etc.

In'dian (Ĭ-) *a.* & *n.* (native) of peninsula or (since 1950) of predominantly Hindu Republic of India; (one of original inhabitants) of America and W. Indies. ~club, heavy bottle-shaped club for gymnastic exercises. ~ corn, maize. ~ file, single file. ~ ink, black pigment. ~ summer, period of calm dry hazy weather in late autumn, esp. in northern U.S.

in'dicāte *v.t.* point out, make known, show; be sign of, betoken. ~ā'tion *n.* ~ātor *n.* (esp.) board etc. in railway station etc. showing times etc. of trains etc.

indic'ative *a.* suggestive, giving indications, *of*; (gram., of verbal mood) stating thing as fact, not conditional or subjunctive. *n.* indicative mood.

indict' (-īt) *v.t.* accuse, esp. by legal process. ~able *a.* (rendering one) liable to be indicted. ~ment *n.*

formal accusation; document containing charge.

indiff'erence *n.* absence of interest or attention; neutrality; unimportance.

indiff'erent *a.* impartial; unconcerned; neither good nor bad; rather bad.

indi'gĕnous *a.* native, belonging naturally (*to* soil etc.).

in'digent, *a.* needy, poor. ~ence *n.*

indigĕs'tible *a.* not (easily) digestible. indigĕs'tion *n.* difficulty in digesting food.

indig'nant *a.* moved by anger and scorn or sense of injury. indignā'tion *n.*

indig'nitў *n.* unworthy treatment, insult, slight.

in'digō *n.* (pl. -*os*), (blue dye obtained from) kinds of plant; colour between blue and violet in spectrum.

indirĕct' (*or* -īr-) *a.* not direct. ~ object, (gram.) person, thing, affected by action of verb but not acted on. ~ speech, reported speech. ~ tax, not levied on persons but (esp.) on importation or production of goods etc.

indis'cipline *n.* want of discipline.

indiscreet' *a.* injudicious, unwary.

indiscrĕ'tion *n.* imprudence; rashness; social transgression.

indiscrim'inate *a.* confused; undiscriminating. ~ā'tion *n.*

indispĕn'sable *a.* not to be dispensed with; necessary; that cannot be set aside. ~bil'itў *n.*

indispōse' (-z) *v.t.* make unfit or unable; make averse. ~d *a.* (esp.) out of health.

indisposi'tion (-zĭ-) *n.* ill-health; disinclination, aversion.

indis'pūtable *a.* beyond dispute.

indissŏl'ūble (*or* indis'-) *a.* not dissoluble.

indistĭnct' *a.* not distinct; confused, obscure.

indisting'uishable (-nggw-) *a.* not distinguishable.

indīte' *v.t.* put into words, compose; (joc.) write (letter etc.).

in'dĭum *n.* rare silver-white soft metallic element.

indivĭd'ūal *a.* single; particular;

of or for single person or thing; characteristic of particular person etc. *n.* single member of class, group, etc.; single human being; (vulg.) person. ~**ăl'itў** *n.*; ~**alīze** *v.t.*

ĭndĭvĭd'ūalĭsm *n.* egoism; social theory favouring free action of individuals. ~**ĭst** *n.* & *a.*; ~**ĭs'tĭc** *a.*

ĭndĭvĭs'ĭble (-z-) *a.* not divisible.

ĭndŏc'trĭnāte *v.t.* teach; imbue *with* doctrine etc. ~**ā'tĭon** *n.*

Ĭndō-Eurŏpē'an (ĭ-) *a.* & *n.* (of, of people speaking one of) family of languages spoken over most of Europe and in Asia as far as N. India.

ĭn'dŏlent *a.* lazy, slothful. ~**ence** *n.*

ĭndŏm'ĭtable *a.* unyielding.

ĭn'door (-dôr) *a.* done etc. within house or under cover.

ĭndoors' (-ôrz) *adv.* within house, under cover.

indorse etc.: see **endorse** etc.

ĭndū'bĭtable *a.* beyond doubt.

ĭndūce' *v.t.* (-*cible*), prevail on, persuade; bring about; produce by induction; infer. ~**ment** *n.* (esp.) attraction that leads one on.

ĭndŭct' *v.t.* install.

ĭndŭc'tance *n.* (electr.) coefficient of self-induction.

ĭndŭc'tĭon, *n.* inducting; general inference from particular instances; (med.) inducing (of labour); (electr.) production of (changes in) electric current etc. by proximity of neighbouring circuit etc.; *self-*~, reaction of current in circuit upon itself.

ĭndŭlge' (-j) *v.* gratify; give free course to; take one's pleasure freely *in*; (colloq.) drink (too much). ~**ent** *a.* (esp.) too lenient or forbearing.

ĭndŭl'gence *n.* indulging; privilege granted; (R.C. Ch.) remission of punishment still due for sin after sacramental absolution.

ĭn'dūrāte *v.* make or become hard. ~**ā'tĭon** *n.*

ĭndŭs'trĭal *a.* of industries; engaged in, connected with, industry; having highly developed industries. ~**ĭsm**, ~**ĭst** *nn.*; ~**īze** *v.t.*

ĭndŭs'trĭous *a.* diligent, hard-working.

ĭn'dŭstrў *n.* diligence; branch of

trade or manufacture; manufacturing.

ĭnē'brĭate *a.* drunken. *n.* drunkard. *v.t.* (-āt), make drunk. ~**ā'tĭon** *n.*

ĭnēbrī'ĕtў *n.* drunkenness.

ĭnĕd'ĭble *a.* not edible.

ĭnĕff'able *a.* unutterable.

ĭnĕffĕc'tĭve *a.* not producing desired effect; inefficient.

ĭnĕffĕc'tūal *a.* not producing (intended, expected, etc.) effect.

ĭnĕffĭ'cient (-shnt) *a.* not fully capable; ineffective. ~**encў** *a.*

ĭnĕlăs'tĭc *a.* not elastic or adaptable; rigid. **ĭnĕlăstĭ'cĭtў** *n.*

ĭnĕl'ĕgant *a.* ungraceful, unrefined; unpolished. ~**ance** *n.*

ĭnĕl'ĭgĭble *a.* not eligible, not qualified *for*.

ĭnĕlŭc'table *a.* not to be escaped from.

ĭnĕpt' *a.* out of place; absurd, silly. ~**ĭtūde** *n.*

ĭnēqual'ĭtў (-ŏl-) *n.* want of equality; variableness; unevenness.

ĭnē'quĭtable *a.* unfair, unjust.

ĭnĕrăd'ĭcable *a.* that cannot be rooted out.

ĭnĕrt' *a.* without inherent power of action; sluggish, slow; chemically inactive.

ĭnĕr'tĭa (-sha) *n.* inertness, sloth; property of matter by which it continues in existing state of rest or motion unless acted on by external force.

ĭnĕscā'pable *a.* not to be escaped.

ĭnĕs'tĭmable *a.* too great etc. to be estimated.

ĭnĕv'ĭtable *a.* unavoidable; bound to happen or appear. ~**bĭl'ĭtў** *n.*

ĭnĕxăct' (-gz-) *a.* not exact. ~**ĭtūde** *n.*

ĭnĕxcū'sable (-z-) *a.* that cannot be justified.

ĭnĕxhau'stĭble (-ĭgzaw-) *a.* that cannot be exhausted.

ĭnĕx'orable *a.* relentless. ~**bĭl'ĭtў** *n.*

ĭnĕxpē'dĭent *a.* ~**encў** *n.*

ĭnĕxpĕn'sĭve *a.* cheap.

ĭnĕxpēr'ĭence *n.* want of experience.

ĭnĕx'pert (*or* -ẽrt') *a.* unskilled.

ĭnĕx'pĭable *a.* not to be expiated.

ĭnĕx'plĭcable (*or* -plĭk'-) *a.* that cannot be explained. ~**bĭl'ĭtў** *n.*

ĭnĕxprĕss'ĭble *a.* not to be expressed in words.

ĭnĕxtĭng'uĭshable (-nggw-) *a.* unquenchable.

ĭn ĕxtrē'mĭs, at point of death. [L]

ĭnĕx'trĭcable *a.* that cannot be loosed, solved, or escaped from.

inf. *abbr.* infinitive; *infra* [L], below.

ĭnfăll'ĭble *a.* not liable to err; unfailing, sure. **~bĭl'ĭtў** *n.*

ĭn'famous *a.* of ill fame; vile.

ĭn'famў *n.* ill fame; vileness.

ĭn'fancў *n.* babyhood; minority; early stage of development.

ĭn'fant *n.* baby; child under 7; person under 18.

ĭnfăn'ta *n.* (usu. eldest) daughter of king and queen of Spain or Portugal.

ĭnfăn'tĭcīde *n.* murder of newborn child; person guilty of this.

ĭn'fantīle *a.* (as) of infants; childish. **ĭnfăn'tĭlĭsm** *n.* mentally or physically undeveloped state.

ĭn'fantrў *n.* foot-soldiers.

ĭnfăt'ūāte *v.t.* inspire with extravagant passion. **~ā'tion** *n.*

ĭnfĕct' *v.t.* contaminate; implant disease-forming micro-organisms in; (of micro-organisms etc.) invade; imbue (*with*).

ĭnfĕc'tion *n.* communication of disease; diffusive influence.

ĭnfĕc'tious *a.* transmissible by infection; apt to spread.

ĭnfĕlĭ'cĭtous *a.* not felicitous.

ĭnfĕlĭ'cĭtў *n.* unhappiness.

ĭnfĕr' *v.t.* deduce, conclude; imply. **ĭn'ference** *n.*; **ĭnferĕn'tial** *a.*

ĭnfēr'ĭor *a.* situated below; lower in rank etc.; of poor quality. *n.* inferior person. **ĭnfērĭŏ'rĭtў** *n.*

ĭnfĕr'nal *a.* of hell; hellish.

ĭnfĕr'nō *n.* (pl. -*os*), hell.

ĭnfĕr'tīle *a.* not fertile. **~tĭl'ĭtў** *n.*

ĭnfĕst' *v.t.* haunt, swarm in or about. **~ā'tion** *n.*

ĭn'fĭdel *n.* disbeliever in (true) religion. *a.* unbelieving; of infidels.

ĭnfĭdĕl'ĭtў *n.* unfaithfulness.

ĭn'-fighting *n.* boxing at closer quarters than arm's length.

ĭn'fĭltrāte *v.* introduce or permeate (as) by filtration; penetrate (*into*) by infiltration. **~ā'tion** *n.* (esp.) gradual penetration by small groups etc.

infin. *abbr.* infinitive.

ĭn'fīnĭte *a.* boundless; endless; very great or many. **ĭnfĭn'ĭtūde** *n.*

ĭnfĭnĭtĕs'ĭmal *a.* infinitely or very small. **~ calculus,** differential and integral calculuses conceived as one.

ĭnfĭn'ĭtĭve *a.* & *n.* (verb-form) expressing verbal notion without predicating it of subject.

ĭnfĭn'ĭtў *n.* immensity; infinite number or extent.

ĭnfĭrm' *a.* weak; irresolute. **~ĭtў** *n.*

ĭnfĭr'marў *n.* hospital; sick-quarters in school etc.

ĭn flagrăn'tĕ dĕlĭc'tō, in act of committing offence. [L]

ĭnflāme' *v.t.* set on fire with passion etc.; add heat or fuel to; cause inflammation in.

ĭnflămm'able[1] *a.* easily set on fire or excited. **~bĭl'ĭtў** *n.*

ĭnflămm'able[2] *n.* (U.S.) inflammable substance.

ĭnflammā'tion *n.* condition of living tissue marked by heat, swelling, redness and usu. pain.

ĭnflămm'atorў *a.* tending to inflame with passion etc.

ĭnflāte' *v.t.* distend with air or gas; puff up; raise (price) artificially; resort to inflation of (currency). **ĭnflā'tĕd** *a.* (esp., of language) bombastic. **~ā'tion** *n.* (esp.) fall in value of money due to increase of purchasing power in relation to goods available for purchase. **~ā'tionarў** *a.*

ĭnflĕct' *v.t.* modify (word) to express grammatical relation; change or vary pitch of. **~tion** *n.* inflexion.

ĭnflĕx'ĭble *a.* unbendable; unbending; unyielding. **~bĭl'ĭtў** *n.*

ĭnflĕ'xion (-kshn) *n.* inflecting; inflected form; inflecting suffix etc.; modulation of voice etc. **~al** *a.*

ĭnflĭct' *v.t.* lay on (blow etc.); impose (*upon*). **~tion** *n.* (esp.) troublesome or boring experience.

ĭnflorĕs'cence *n.* arrangement of flowers, collective flower, of plant.

ĭn'flow (-ō) *n.* flowing in.

ĭn'fluence (-lōō-) *n.* action insensibly exercised; ascendancy, moral power; thing or person exercising this. *v.t.* exert influence upon; affect. **~ĕn'tial** *a.* having great influence.

ĭnfluĕn′za (-lōō-) *n.* infectious febrile disorder.

ĭn′flŭx *n.* flowing in.

ĭnfōrm′ *v.* tell; inspire; bring charge (*against*). **~ed** *a.* (esp.) enlightened. **~er** *n.* one who informs against another.

ĭnfōr′mal *a.* not observing forms; without formality. **~ăl′ĭtў** *n.*

ĭnfōr′mant *n.* giver of information.

ĭnformā′tion *n.* telling; what is told; knowledge; news; charge or accusation. **ĭnfōr′mative** *a.* giving information; instructĭve. **ĭnfōr′matorў** *a.* giving information.

ĭn′fra *adv.* below or further on in book etc. [L]

ĭn′fra dig. *abbr.* beneath one's dignity.

ĭnfrăc′tion *n.* infringement.

ĭn′fra-rĕd′ *a.* situated below or beyond red in spectrum.

ĭnfrē′quent *a.* not frequent. **~encў** *n.*

ĭnfringe′ (-j) *v.t.* transgress, violate. **~ment** *n.*

ĭnfūr′ĭāte *v.t.* enrage.

ĭnfūse′ (-z) *v.* (*-sible*), instil; steep. be steeped, in liquid to extract properties.

ĭnfū′sion *n.* (liquid extract obtained by) infusing; admixture.

ĭnfūsōr′ĭa *n.pl.* class of protozoa.

ĭngē′nĭous (-j-) *a.* clever at contriving; cleverly contrived.

ingénue (ăn′zhānū) *n.* artless girl, esp. as stage type. [F]

ĭngĕnū′ĭtў (-j-) *n.* ingeniousness.

ĭngĕn′ūous (-j-) *a.* frank; artless.

ĭngĕst′ (-j-) *v.t.* take in (food etc). **ĭngĕs′tion** *n.*

ingle (ĭng′gl) *n.* (Sc.) fire on hearth. **~-nook**, chimney-corner.

ĭnglōr′ĭous (ĭn-g-) *a.* ignominious; obscure.

ĭng′ot (-ngg-) *n.* mass of cast metal, esp. gold, silver, or steel.

ingrained′ (ĭn-g-; *or* ĭn′-g-) *a.* deeply rooted, inveterate.

ĭn′grāte (ĭn-g-) *n.* ungrateful person.

ingratiāte (ĭn-grā′shĭ-) *v.refl.* get into favour *with*.

ĭngrăt′ĭtūde (ĭn-g-) *n.* want of gratitude.

ĭngrē′dĭent (ĭn-g-) *n.* component part in mixture.

ĭn′grĕss (ĭn-g-) *n.* (right of) entrance.

ĭngūr′gĭtāte (ĭn-g-) *v.t.* swallow greedily.

ĭnhăb′ĭt *v.t.* dwell in, occupy. **~ant** *n.*

ĭnhāle′ *v.t.* take into lungs; breathe in. **ĭnhā′lant** *n.* (esp.) medicinal substance for inhaling. **~lā′tion** *n.* **ĭnhā′ler** *n.* apparatus for introducing liquid or vapour into breathing passages.

ĭnharmō′nĭous *a.* not harmonious.

ĭnhēre′ *v.i.* exist, abide, *in*; be vested *in*. **ĭnhēr′ence** *n.*; **ĭnhĕr′ent** *a.*

ĭnhĕ′rĭt *v.* receive, succeed, as heir; derive from parents etc. **~ance** *n.* inheriting; what is inherited. **~or** *n.*; **~rĕss, ~trĭx** *nn. fem.*

ĭnhĕ′sion *n.* inhering.

ĭnhĭb′ĭt *v.t.* prohibit; hinder, restrain. **ĭnhĭbĭ′tion** *n.* (esp.) blocking of thought or action by emotional resistance. **~orў** *a.*

ĭnhŏs′pĭtable *a.* not hospitable; affording no shelter.

ĭnhū′man *a.* brutal, unfeeling, barbarous. **ĭnhūmăn′ĭtў** *n.*

ĭnhūme′ *v.t.* bury.

ĭnĭm′ĭcal *a.* hostile; harmful.

ĭnĭm′ĭtable *a.* defying imitation.

ĭnĭ′quĭtous *a.* unjust; wicked.

ĭnĭ′quĭtў *n.* wickedness.

ĭnĭ′tial *a.* of, existing or occurring at, beginning. *n.* (esp.) first letter of name. *v.t.* mark, sign, with initials.

ĭnĭ′tiāte (-shĭ-) *v.t.* originate, set on foot; admit, introduce (*into*). *n.* (-at), initiated person. **~ā′tion** *n.*; **~atorў** *a.*

ĭnĭ′tiative (-shya-) *n.* first step; lead; ability to initiate, enterprise.

ĭnjĕct′ *v.t.* force (fluid *into*) as by syringe. **ĭnjĕc′tion** *n.* injecting; liquid etc. injected.

ĭnjudĭ′cious (-jōō-) *a.* unwise, ill-judged.

ĭnjŭnc′tion *n.* authoritative order; judicial process restraining from wrongful act or compelling restitution etc.

ĭn′jure (-jer) *v.t.* do wrong to; hurt, harm, impair. **~d** *a.* (esp.) showing sense of wrong, offended.

ĭnjur′ĭous (-joor-) *a.* wrongful; harmful; calumnious.

ĭn′jurў *n.* wrong; damage.

ĭnjŭs′tĭce *n.* want of equity, unfairness.

ĭnk *n.* coloured (usu. black) fluid for writing or printing; black liquid ejected for protection by cuttle--fish etc. *v.t.* mark, cover, or smear with ink. **ĭnk'y̆** *a.*

ĭnk'lĭng *n.* hint, slight knowledge or suspicion (*of*).

ĭn'land *n.* interior of country. *a.* within country; remote from sea or border. *adv.* in, towards, interior.

ĭn'-law (*or* -aw') *n.* (colloq., usu. pl.) relative by marriage.

ĭnlay' *v.t.* (*inlaid*), embed (thing *in* groundwork of another); ornament thus. *n.* (ĭn'-) inlaid ornament.

ĭn'lĕt *n.* small arm of sea.

ĭn'ly̆ *adv.* inwardly.

ĭn'māte *n.* occupant (*of* house, etc.).

ĭn mēmōr'ĭăm, in memory of. [L]

ĭn'mōst *a.* most inward.

ĭnn *n.* public house for lodging etc. of travellers; *I~s of Court*, four legal societies having exclusive right of admitting to practise at English bar. **~keeper**, keeper of inn.

ĭnn'ards (-dz) *n.pl.* (colloq.) entrails.

ĭnnāte' (*or* ĭn'-) *a.* inborn.

ĭnn'er *a.* further inward; interior, internal. *n.* circle next bull's eye of target. **~most** *a.*

ĭnn'ĭngs (-z) *n.* (pl. same), (crick. etc., freq. fig.) batsman's or side's turn at batting.

ĭnn'ocent *a.* sinless; not guilty; simple, guileless; harmless. *n.* innocent person, esp. young child. **~ence** *n.*

ĭnnŏc'ūous *a.* harmless.

ĭnn'ovāte *v.i.* bring in novelties; make changes. **~ā'tion, ~ātor** *nn.*

ĭnnūĕn'dō *n.* (pl. -oes), allusive (usu. depreciatory) remark.

ĭnnū'merable *a.* countless.

ĭnobsĕr'vance (-z-) *n.* non-observance; inattention. **~ant** *a.*

ĭnŏc'ūlate *v.t.* impregnate *with* disease etc., esp. as protective measure. **~ā'tion** *n.*

ĭnō'dorous *a.* odourless.

ĭnoffĕn'sĭve *a.* unoffending; not objectionable.

ĭnŏp'erable *a.* that cannot be cured by operation.

ĭnŏp'erative *a.* not working or taking effect.

ĭnŏpp'ortūne *a.* unseasonable.

ĭnōr'dĭnate *a.* immoderate, excessive.

ĭnōrgăn'ĭc *a.* without organized physical structure; (chem.) not organic.

ĭn'put (-ŏot) *n.* putting in; what is put in, esp. power or energy put into electric circuit etc., information put into computer etc. for storage etc.

ĭn'quĕst *n.* legal or judicial inquiry into matter of fact, esp. by coroner into cause of death.

ĭnquī'ĕtūde *n.* restlessness.

ĭnquīre', en- *v.* make search (*into*); seek information; ask.

ĭnquīr'y̆, en- *n.* asking; question; investigation.

ĭnquĭsĭ'tion (-z-) *n.* investigation; official inquiry; (hist., R. C. Ch.) ecclesiastical tribunal for suppression of heresy. **~al** *a.*

ĭnquĭs'ĭtĭve (-z-) *a.* curious, prying.

ĭnquĭs'ĭtor (-z-) *n.* investigator; officer of Inquisition. **~ōr'ĭal** *a.* (esp.) offensively prying.

I.N.R.I. *abbr., Iesus Nazarenus Rex Iudaeorum* [L], Jesus of Nazareth King of the Jews.

ĭn'road *n.* hostile incursion; encroachment.

ĭn'rŭsh *n.* violent influx.

ĭnsalū'brĭous (*or* -ŏo-) *a.* unhealthy.

ĭnsāne' *a.* mad; senseless.

ĭnsăn'ĭtary̆ *a.* not sanitary.

ĭnsăn'ĭty̆ *n.* madness.

ĭnsā'tiable (-sha-) *a.* that cannot be satisfied; greedy. **~bĭl'ĭty̆** *n.*

ĭnsā'tiate (-shyat) *a.* never satisfied.

ĭnscrībe' *v.t.* write (*in, on*); enter on list; mark with characters; (geom.) trace (figure) within another so that some points of their boundaries coincide.

ĭnscrĭp'tion *n.* words inscribed on monument, coin, etc.

ĭnscru'table (-ŏo-) *a.* mysterious, impenetrable. **~bĭl'ĭty̆** *n.*

ĭn'sĕct *n.* small invertebrate animal with segmented body and six legs.

ĭnsĕc'tĭcīde *n.* preparation for killing insects. **~ĭv'orous** *a.* insect-eating; (of plant) trapping and digesting insects.

ĭnsĕcūre' *a.* not secure or safe; not feeling safe.

insĕm'ināte *v.t.* fertilize, make pregnant. **~ā'tion** *n.*

insĕn'sate *a.* unfeeling; stupid; mad.

insĕn'sible *a.* imperceptible; unconscious; void of feeling; unaware. **~bil'itў** *n.*

insĕn'sitive *a.* not sensitive.

insĕn'tient (-shĭ-) *a.* inanimate.

insĕp'arable *a.* that cannot be separated. **~bil'itў** *n.*

insĕrt' *v.t.* place or fit or thrust (*in, into*); introduce. *n.* (in'-), thing (to be) inserted. **insĕr'tion** *n.* inserting; thing inserted; (narrow band of) trimming inserted or for inserting into textile fabric.

in'sĕt *n.* (esp.) extra page(s) inserted in book etc.; small map etc. inserted within border of larger. *v.t.* put in as inset.

in'shōre *adv. & a.* close to shore.

in'sīde (*or* īd') *n.* inner side or part; interior; (-īd'), (colloq.) stomach, entrails. *a.* (in'-), situated on or in, coming or derived from, inside; indoor; (of information etc.) not accessible to outsiders; (footb. etc., of players or position) between outside left or right and centre forward. *adv.* (-īd'), on or in or to inside. *prep.* (-īd'; *or* in'-), on or to inside of; within. **~ out**, so that inner becomes outer side; thoroughly. **~r** *n.* accepted member of group, society, etc.; one in secret or 'know'.

insid'ious *a.* treacherous; proceeding secretly or subtly.

in'sight (-īt) *n.* mental penetration.

insig'nia *n.pl.* badges or marks (*of* office etc.).

insignif'icant *a.* unimportant; meaningless. **insignif'icance** *n.*

insincēre' *a.* not sincere, disingenuous. **insincĕ'ritў** *n.*

insin'ūāte *v.t.* introduce gradually or subtly; convey indirectly. **~ā'tion** *n.*

insip'id *a.* flavourless; dull, lifeless. **insipid'itў** *n.*

insist' *v.* dwell emphatically (*on*); maintain positively; **~** (*up*)*on*, demand urgently or persistently. **~ence**, **~encў** *nn.*; **~ent** *a.*

in sī'tū, in its (original) place. [L]

insobri'etў *n.* intemperance.

in so fār' *adv.* to such extent or degree (*as*).

in'sōle *n.* inner sole.

in'solent *a.* offensively contemptuous; insulting. **in'solence** *n.*

insŏl'ūble *a.* not to be solved; not to be dissolved. **~bil'itў** *n.*

insŏl'vent *a. & n.* (debtor) unable to pay debts. **insŏl'vencў** *n.*

insŏm'nia *n.* sleeplessness. **~ăc** *a. & n.* (of) person suffering from insomnia.

insomŭch' *adv.* to such an extent.

insou'ciant (-sōō-) *a.* unconcerned. **~ance** *n.*

inspăn' *v.* (S. Afr.) yoke team to vehicle.

inspĕct' *v.t.* look closely into; examine officially. **inspĕc'tion** *n.*

inspĕc'tor *n.* (esp.) police-officer ranking next below superintendent. **~toral**, **~tŏr'ial** *aa.* **~torate** *n.* office of inspector, body of inspectors.

inspīre' *v.* breathe in; infuse thought or feeling into; animate; create (feeling *in*); suggest or prompt (expression of opinion etc.). **inspīrā'tion** *n.* (esp.) divine influence supposed to have inspired Scriptures etc.; inspiring principle; sudden happy idea.

inspi'rit *v.t.* put life into, animate; encourage.

inspiss'āte (*or* in'-) *v.t.* thicken, condense.

inst. *abbr.* instant, of current month.

instabil'itў *n.* lack of stability.

install' (-awl) *v.t.* place in office with ceremony; establish (*in* place etc.); place in position. **~ā'tion** *n.* (ceremony of) installing; apparatus etc. installed.

instal'ment (-awl-) *n.* any of several successive parts of sum payable, serial story, etc.

in'stance *n.* example; particular case; request. *v.t.* cite as instance; (usu. pass.) exemplify.

in'stant *a.* urgent, pressing; immediate; of current calendar month. *n.* precise (esp. present) point of time; short time. **~lў** *adv.* at once.

instantā'neous *a.* occurring, done, etc. in an instant.

ĭn stā'tū quō (ăn'tė), in same state as formerly. [L]

ĭnstead' (-ĕd) *adv.* as substitute or alternative; in place *of*.

ĭn'stĕp *n.* top of foot between toes and ankle; part of shoe etc. fitting this.

ĭn'stĭgāte *v.t.* incite (*to*); bring about by persuasion. **~ā'tion, ~ātor** *nn.*

ĭnstĭl' *v.t.* put in by drops; infuse (feeling, idea, etc.) gradually. **ĭnstĭllā'tion** *n.*

ĭn'stĭnct *n.* innate impulse; intuition; inborn and usu. rigid pattern of behaviour. *a.* (-ĭnkt'), filled or charged (*with*). **ĭnstĭnc'tĭve** *a.*

ĭn'stĭtūte *v.t.* establish; set on foot; appoint. *n.* organized body for promotion of scientific or other object; its building.

ĭnstĭtū'tion *n.* instituting; established law or custom; (colloq.) familiar object; (building of) organization for promoting public object. **~al** *a.* of (esp. charitable) institution(s); organized into institutions.

ĭnstrŭct' *v.t.* teach; inform; give information to; direct. **ĭnstrŭc'tor, ~trèss** *nn.*

ĭnstrŭc'tion *n.* teaching; information; (esp. pl.) directions, orders. **~al** *a.*

ĭnstrŭc'tĭve *a.* enlightening.

ĭn'strument (-rōō-) *n.* tool, implement; contrivance for producing musical sounds; legal document.

ĭnstrŭmĕn'tal (-rōō-) *a.* serving as instrument or means (*to, in*); (gram., of case) denoting instrument or means. *n.* instrumental case. **~alĭst** *n.* performer on musical instrument. **~ăl'ĭtў** *n.* agency, means.

ĭnstrŭmĕntā'tion (-rōō-) *n.* arrangement of music for instruments.

ĭnsubŏr'dĭnate *a.* disobedient; unruly. **ĭnsubŏrdĭnā'tion** *n.*

ĭnsubstăn'tial *a.* lacking solidity or substance; not real. **~tĭăl'ĭtў** (-shĭ-) *n.*

ĭnsŭff'erable *a.* unbearable.

ĭnsuffĭ'cient (-shĕnt) *a.* not enough, inadequate. **~encў** *n.*

ĭn'sūlar *a.* belonging to an island; of or like islanders, esp. narrow-minded. **~ĭsm, ĭnsūlă'rĭtў** *nn.*

ĭn'sūlāte *v.t.* isolate, esp. by nonconductors to prevent passage of electricity etc. **~ā'tion** *n.* **ĭn'sūlātor** *n.* (esp.) non-conducting substance or device.

ĭn'sūlĭn *n.* pancreatic hormone controlling amount of glucose in blood.

ĭn'sŭlt *n.* scornful abuse; indignity; affront. *v.t.* (-ŭlt'), treat with insult.

ĭnsū'perable *a.* that cannot be got over. **~bĭl'ĭtў** *n.*

ĭnsuppŏr'table *a.* unbearable.

ĭnsur'ance (-shoor-) *n.* contract to indemnify insured against loss of or damage to property etc., to pay fixed sum(s) on person's death, etc., in return for payment of premium etc.; sum paid for this, premium.

ĭnsure' (-shoor) *v.* issue, take out, insurance policy.

ĭnsŭr'gent *a.* in revolt; rebellious. *n.* rebel.

ĭnsurmoun'table *a.* insuperable.

ĭnsurrĕc'tion *n.* incipient rebellion; rising. **~arў** *a.*; **~ĭst** *n.*

ĭnsuscĕp'tĭble *a.* not susceptible. **~bĭl'ĭtў** *n.*

ĭntăct' *a.* untouched; unimpaired; entire.

ĭntaglio (-tah'lĭō) *n.* (pl. *-os*), (gem with) incised or engraved design.

ĭn'tāke *n.* (place of) taking in; amount taken in.

ĭntăn'gĭble (-j-) *a. & n.* that cannot be touched or mentally grasped. **~bĭl'ĭtў** *n.*

ĭn'tĕger *n.* whole number; thing complete in itself.

ĭn'tĕgral *a.* of or essential to a whole; complete; of, denoted by, involving, integer(s); *~ calculus*, branch of calculus dealing with integrals of functions etc. *n.* quantity of which given function is differential or differential coefficient.

ĭn'tĕgrāte *v.t.* complete, form into whole; indicate average or sum of; find integral of. *a.* (-at), made up of parts; whole, complete. **~ā'tion** *n.*

ĭntĕg'rĭtў *n.* wholeness; soundness; uprightness.

ĭntĕg'ūment *n.* skin, husk, or other (natural) covering.

ĭn'tĕllĕct *n.* faculty of knowing and reasoning; understanding.

ĭntĕllĕc'tion *n.* action or process of understanding. **ĭntĕllĕc'tĭve** *a.*

ĭntĕllĕc'tūal *a.* of, appealing to, requiring use of, intellect; enlightened; given to mental pursuits, of superior intelligence. *n.* intellectual person. ~**alĭsm**, ~**alĭst**, ~**ăl'ĭtў** *nn.*

ĭntĕll'ĭgence *n.* intellect; quickness of understanding; news; (persons engaged in) obtaining of esp. secret information; secret service. ~ **quotient**, ratio of mental to chronological age. ~ **test**, designed to ascertain mental age.

ĭntĕll'ĭgent *a.* having or showing (high degree of) understanding.

ĭntĕllĭgĕnt'sĭa *n.* class of intellectuals, esp. in pre-revolutionary Russia.

ĭntĕll'ĭgĭble, *a.* that can be understood; comprehensible. ~**bĭl'ĭtў** *n.*

ĭntĕm'perate *a.* immoderate; excessively indulgent of appetite; addicted to drinking. ~**ance** *n.*

ĭntĕnd' *v.t.* purpose; design. ~**ĕd** *n.* (colloq.) person one intends to marry.

ĭntĕnse' *a.* existing in high degree; vehement; strenuous; strained. **ĭntĕn'sĭtў** *n.*

ĭntĕn'sĭfў *v.* make or become intense; increase opacity of (photographic negative etc.).

ĭntĕn'sĭon *n.* intensity of quality.

ĭntĕn'sĭve *a.* of or relating to or expressing intensity; concentrated; increasing production of limited area etc.; emphasizing. *n.* intensive word or prefix.

ĭntĕnt'¹ *n.* intention; *to all* ~*s* (*and purposes*), practically.

ĭntĕnt'² *a.* resolved, bent (*on*); absorbed; eager.

ĭntĕn'tion *n.* intending; purpose, aim. ~**al** *a.* done on purpose.

ĭntĕr' *v.t.* place (corpse etc.) in earth or tomb; bury.

ĭn'ter- in comb., among, between; mutual(ly), reciprocal(ly).

ĭntĕrăct' *v.i.* act reciprocally or on each other. **ĭntĕrăc'tion** *n.*

ĭnter ā'lĭa, among other things. [L]

ĭnterbreed' *v.* cross-breed; breed with each other.

ĭntĕr'calarў (*or* -căl'-) *a.* inserted to harmonize calendar with solar year; having such additions; interpolated, intervening.

ĭntĕr'calāte *v.t.* insert; interpose. ~**ā'tion** *n.*

ĭntercēde' *v.i.* plead (*for* another); mediate.

ĭntercĕpt' *v.t.* seize, catch, stop, etc. in transit; cut off. **ĭntercĕp'tion** *n.* ~**or** *n.* (esp.) aircraft designed to intercept enemy raiders.

ĭntercĕ'ssion *n.* interceding. **ĭn'tercĕssor** (*or* -sĕs'-) *n.* ; ~**cĕss'orў** *a.*

ĭnterchānge' (-j) *v.* put in each other's place; make exchange of; alternate. *n.* (ĭn'-) reciprocal exchange; alternation; road junction so arranged that paths of vehicles do not cross.

ĭn'tercŏm *n.* system of internal communication, esp. in aircraft.

ĭntercommū'nĭcāte *v.i.* have communication with each other. ~**ā'tion** *n.*

ĭntercommū'nion (-yon) *n.* communion or fellowship esp. between religious bodies.

ĭn'tercourse (-ōrs) *n.* social communication, dealings; sexual connexion.

ĭnterdĕpĕn'dent *a.* mutually dependent.

ĭnterdĭct' *v.t.* forbid; prohibit; restrain. *n.* (ĭn'-), authoritative prohibition. ~**dĭc'tion** *n.*

ĭn'terĕst *n.* legal concern, title, right; advantage; personal influence; money paid for use of money lent etc.; (quality etc. exciting) concern or curiosity or attention. *v.t.* excite curiosity or attention of; cause to take interest (*in*); (*p.p.*) having private interest, not impartial. **ĭn'terĕstĭng** *a.* exciting interest.

ĭnterfēre' *v.i.* come into collision or opposition (*with*); meddle; intervene. **ĭnterfēr'ence** *n.* (esp.) effect produced by meeting of light etc. waves; (radio etc.) disturbance of desired signals.

ĭnterfēr'on *n.* protein preventing development of virus in cell.

ĭnterfūse' (-z) *v.* mix; blend. **ĭnterfū'sion** *n.*

ĭn'terim *n.* meantime. *a.* intervening; provisional, temporary.

intēr′ior *a.* situated within; inland; internal, domestic. *n.* interior part, region, etc.; inside; (department of) home affairs.

intĕrjĕct′ *v.t.* say abruptly or parenthetically; interpose.

interjĕc′tion *n.* exclamation, ejaculation. ~al *a.*

interlāce′ *v.* bind intricately together; interweave.

interlārd′ *v.t.* mix (speech etc.) *with.*

interleave′ *v.t.* insert leaves between leaves of (book).

interlịne′ *v.* insert words between lines of; insert thus; make such insertions. ~lin′ear *a.* written etc. between lines.

interlŏck′ *v.* engage, connect, join, etc. by overlapping etc.; lock together; connect (switches, levers, etc.) so that they cannot be operated independently.

interlŏc′ūtor *n.* one who takes part in conversation. ~ū′tion *n.* ~ūtorў *a.*

interlōpe′ *v.i.* intrude, thrust oneself into others′ affairs. **in′terlōper** *n.*

in′terlūde (*or* -ōōd) *n.* (performance filling) interval between parts of play etc.; intervening time, event, etc. of different kind.

intermă′rriage (-ĭj) *n.* marriage between members of different families, races, etc. **intermă′rrў** *v.i.*

intermĕdd′le *v.i.* meddle (*with, in*).

intermē′diarў *a.* acting between parties; intermediate. *n.* (esp.) mediator.

intermē′diate *a. & n.* (thing) coming *between* in time, place or order.

intĕr′ment *n.* burial.

intermĕzz′o (-tsō *or* -dzō) *n.* (pl. -*zzi* pr. -ē, -*ōs*), (mus.) instrumental passage in opera; short connecting movement or composition.

intĕr′minable *a.* endless; tediously protracted.

interming′le (-nggl) *v.* mix together, mingle (*with*).

intermi′ssion *n.* pause, cessation; interval in theatre etc.

intermit′ *v.* suspend; stop for a time. ~mitt′ent *a.*

intermix′ *v.* mix together. ~ture *n.*

intĕrn′ *v.t.* confine within prescribed limits. ~ee′, ~ment *nn.*

intĕr′nal *a.* of, in, inside of thing; of inner nature of thing; of domestic affairs of country; subjective; (of student etc.) working etc. inside examining university. ~-combustion engine, in which motive-power is derived from combustion of fuel inside engine.

internă′tional (-shon-) *a.* existing, carried on, etc. between nations. *n.* (one who takes part in) international match etc.; *I*~, international association for promoting esp. joint political action of working classes. ~ĭsm *n.* ~ĭst *n.* (esp.) advocate of community of interests between nations.

Internătionale′ (I-; -shonahl) *n.* revolutionary socialist hymn.

internă′tionalīze *v.t.* make international; bring under joint protection etc. of different nations. ~īzā′tion *n.*

in′tĕrne *n.* (U.S.) resident medical assistant in hospital.

internē′cine *a.* mutually destructive; deadly.

intĕr′pĕllāte (*or* -ĕl′-) *v.t.* interrupt to demand explanation. ~ā′tion *n.*

interpĕn′ĕtrāte, *v.* pervade; penetrate mutually. ~ā′tion *n.*

interplăn′ĕtarў *a.* between planets.

in′terplay *n.* reciprocal play.

In′terpŏl (I-) *n.* International Criminal Police Commission.

intĕr′polāte *v.t.* make (esp. misleading) insertions in; insert or introduce between other things. ~ā′tion *n.*

interpōse′ (-z) *v.* insert, make intervene; introduce, use, say, etc., as interruption or interference; intervene; interrupt. **intĕrposi′tion** *n.*

intĕr′pret *v.* explain; render, represent; act as interpreter. ~ā′tion *n.*

intĕr′prĕter *n.* (esp.) one who translates orally.

interrĕg′num *n.* (pl. -*na,* -*nums*), interval between successive reigns; interval, pause.

intĕ′rrogāte *v.t.* question closely or formally. ~ā′tion, ~ātor *nn.*

interrŏg′ative *a.* of, suited to, used in asking, questions. *n.* interrogative pronoun etc.

interrŏg′atorў *a.* of inquiry. *n.*

question, set of questions, esp. put formally to accused person etc.

interrŭpt' *v.t.* break in upon; break continuity of; obstruct (view etc.). **interrŭp'tion** *n.*

intersĕct' *v.* divide by passing or lying across; cross or cut each other. **intersĕc'tion** *n.* point, line, where lines or planes intersect; place where roads etc. cross.

interspĕrse' *v.t.* scatter, place here and there (*between*); diversify (*with* things so placed).

in'terstāte *a.* existing etc. between States.

intĕr'stice *n.* chink, crevice, gap. **interstĭ'tial** *a.* of or forming or occupying interstice(s).

intertwīne' *v.* entwine, be entwined.

in'terval *n.* intervening time or space; pause; break; (mus.) difference of pitch between two sounds; at ~s, here and there, now and then.

intervēne' *v.i.* occur in meantime; come between persons or things; interfere, mediate. **intervĕn'tion** *n.* interference, mediation.

in'terview (-vū) *n.* meeting face to face, esp. for purpose of obtaining statement, assessing qualities of candidate, etc. *v.t.* have interview with.

interweave' *v.t.* weave together; blend intimately.

interzō'nal *a.* between zones.

intĕs'tate *a.* not having made will. *n.* intestate person. **intĕs'tacÿ** *n.*

intĕs'tine *n.* (either part of) alimentary canal between stomach and anus. **intĕs'tinal** (*or* -ī'nal) *a.*

in'tĭmate[1] *a.* closely acquainted; familiar; close. *n.* intimate friend. **in'timacÿ** *n.*

in'tĭmāte[2] *v.t.* make known, state; imply. ~ā'tion *n.*

intĭm'ĭdāte *v.t.* frighten, cow. ~ā'tion *n.*

in'to (-tōō) *prep.* expr. motion or direction to point within, or change, condition, result.

intŏl'erable *a.* not to be endured.

intŏl'erant *a.* not tolerant (*of*). ~ance *n.*

intonā'tion *n.* (esp.) intoning; production of musical tones; modulation of voice in speaking.

intōne' *v.t.* recite in singing voice.

in tō'tō, entirely. [L]

intŏx'ĭcant *a.* intoxicating. *n.* intoxicating (esp. alcoholic) substance.

intŏx'ĭcāte *v.t.* make drunk; excite, elate, beyond self-control. **intŏxĭcā'tion** *n.*

intrăc'table *a.* not docile; not easily dealt with. ~bĭl'itÿ *n.*

intramūr'al *a.* situated, done, within walls of city, house, etc.

intrăn'sĭgent (-z-) *a.* uncompromising, esp. in politics. *n.* uncompromising republican.

intrăn'sĭtive (*or* -ahns-) *a.* not taking direct object. *n.* intransitive verb.

intravē'nous *a.* in(to) vein(s).

intrĕp'ĭd *a.* fearless; brave. **intrĕ-pĭd'itÿ** *n.*

in'tricate *a.* entangled; involved; complicated. **in'tricacÿ** *n.*

in'trigue (-ēg; *or* -ēg') *n.* underhand plotting or plot; secret amour. *v.* (-ēg'), carry on intrigue; employ secret influence; rouse interest or curiosity of.

intrĭn'sic *a.* inherent; essential.

introdūce' *v.t.* (-*cible*), usher in, bring forward; make (person) known to another; bring into use, draw attention to; bring before Parliament.

introdŭc'tion *n.* introducing; preliminary matter in book; introductory treatise etc.; formal presentation. **introdŭc'torÿ** *a.*

intrō'ĭt *n.* psalm etc. sung while priest approaches altar.

introspĕc'tion *n.* examination of one's own thoughts or feelings. ~tive *a.*

introvĕrt' *v.t.* turn (mind etc.) inwards upon itself. *n.* (in'-), person given to introversion. **introvĕr'sion** *n.*

intrude' (-ōōd) *v.* thrust (*into*), force (*upon*); come uninvited, thrust oneself in. **intru'sion** *n.* **intru'sive** *a.* intruding, tending to intrude; (of rock) forced while molten into cavities etc. of other rocks.

intuī'tion *n.* immediate apprehension by mind without reasoning; immediate insight. **intuī'tional** *a.*

intū'ĭtive *a.* of, possessing, or perceived by intuition.

ĭn'undāte *v.t.* flood, submerge. inundā'tion *n.*

ĭnūre' *v.t.* habituate, accustom. ~ment *n.*

inv. *abbr.*, *invenit* (L), designed this.

ĭnvāde' *v.t.* make hostile inroad into; encroach on.

ĭn'valĭd¹ *a.* & *n.* (person) enfeebled or disabled by illness or injury. *v.t.* (-ēd; *or* -ēd') remove from active service, send *home* etc. as invalid. ~ĭsm *n.*

ĭnvăl'ĭd² *a.* not valid. ~āte *v.t.* make invalid. ~ā'tion, invalĭd'ĭtў *nn.*

ĭnvăl'ūable *a.* above price.

ĭnvār'ĭable *a.* always the same; (math.) constant. *n.* constant. ~bĭl'ĭtў *n.*

ĭnvā'sion (-zhn) *n.* invading; encroachment.

ĭnvĕc'tĭve *n.* violent attack in words.

ĭnveigh' (-vā) *v.i.* speak violently, rail *against.*

ĭnvei'gle (-vā-; *or* -vē-) *v.t.* entice, seduce (*into*). ~ment *n.*

ĭnvĕnt' *v.t.* devise, originate; fabricate. ĭnvĕn'tion *n.* inventing; thing invented; inventiveness. ~ĭve *a.*; ~or *n.*

ĭn'ventorў *n.* list of goods etc. *v.t.* enter in inventory.

ĭnvernĕss' (cloak) *n.* man's cloak with removable cape.

ĭnvēŕse' (*or* ĭn'-) *a.* inverted in position, order, or relation; (of ratio etc.) between two quantities one of which increases as other decreases. *n.* (ĭn'-) inverted state; direct opposition. ĭnvēŕ'sion *n.* (esp.) reversal of natural order of words.

ĭnvēŕt' *v.t.* reverse position, order, relation, etc. of. *n.* (ĭn'-) homosexual. ~ed **commas**, commas raised above line (' ' or " ") at beginning and end of quotation etc. ~ **sugar**, kind not readily crystallizing, used in foods etc.

ĭnvēŕ'tĕbrate *a.* without backbone or spinal column; weak-willed. *n.* invertebrate animal.

ĭnvĕst' *v.* clothe, dress; endue (*with* qualities etc.); lay siege to; employ (money *in* stocks etc.), lay out money (*in*). ~or *n.*

ĭnvĕs'tigāte *v.t.* examine, inquire into. ~ā'tion, ~ātor *nn.*

ĭnvĕs'titure *n.* formal investing of person (*with* office, etc.) esp. ceremony of conferment of honours by sovereign etc.

ĭnvĕst'ment *n.* investing; money invested; property in which money is invested.

ĭnvĕt'erate *a.* deep-rooted, confirmed. ĭnvĕt'eracў *n.*

ĭnvĭd'ĭous *a.* giving offence, esp. by injustice etc.

ĭnvĭ'gĭlāte *v.i.* maintain surveillance over examinees. ~tor *n.*

ĭnvĭg'orāte *v.t.* make vigorous; animate. ~ā'tion *n.*; ~ative *a.*

ĭnvĭn'cĭble *a.* unconquerable; not to be subdued. ~bĭl'ĭtў *n.*

ĭnvĭ'olable *a.* not to be violated. ~abĭl'ĭtў, ~acў *nn.* ĭnvĭ'olate *a.* not violated; unbroken, unprofaned.

ĭnvĭs'ĭble (-z-) *a.* that cannot be seen. ~ **exports**, shipping services, foreign investments, etc. ~ **ink, writing**, not visible until treated by heat etc.

ĭnvīte' *v.t.* request courteously to come, *to* do, etc.; solicit courteously; attract. *n.* (colloq.) invitation. ĭnvĭtā'tion *n.* ĭnvī'tĭng *a.* (esp.) attractive, tempting.

ĭnvocā'tion *n.* invoking; calling upon in prayer. ĭnvŏc'atorў *a.*

ĭn'voice *n.* list of goods sent, with prices etc. *v.t.* make invoice of.

ĭnvōke' *v.t.* call on in prayer; appeal to; ask earnestly for; summon (spirit) by charms.

ĭn'volūcre (*or* -ōō-) *n.* (bot.) whorl or rosette of bracts round inflorescence.

ĭnvŏl'untarў *a.* done etc. without exercise of will.

ĭn'volūte (*or* -ōōt) *a.* intricate; curled spirally. ~u'tion *n.* involving; intricacy; curling inwards, part so curled.

ĭnvŏlve' *v.t.* entangle or implicate or include (*in*); entail. ĭnvŏlved' (-vd) *a.* (esp.) complicated, tangled. ~ment *n.*

ĭnvŭl'nerable *a.* not vulnerable. ~bĭl'ĭtў *n.*

ĭn'ward *a.* situated within; directed towards inside; mental, spiritual. *adv.* inwards. ~lў *adv.* internally; not aloud; in mind or spirit. ~ness *n.* (esp.) inner nature. **~s** *adv.* towards inside; within mind or soul.

inwrought' (-rawt; *or* in'-) *a.* decorated (*with*); wrought (*in, on*).

i'odine (*or* -ēn) *n.* volatile greyish--black crystalline non-metallic element; tincture of this as antiseptic. **i'odize** *v.t.* treat with iodine. **iō'doform** (*or* -ŏd-) *n.* compound of iodine used as antiseptic etc.

I.O.M. *abbr.* Isle of Man.

i'on *n.* electrically charged atom or group of atoms; free electron or positron. **iŏn'ic**[1] *a.* **~ize** *v.* convert or be converted (wholly or partially) into ions. **~izā'tion** *n.*

Iŏn'ic[2] (ī-) *n.* of Ionia; (archit.) of one of five classical orders.

iŏn'osphēre *n.* ionized region in upper atmosphere.

iō'ta *n.* Greek letter i; jot.

I O U (ī ō ū') *n.* signed document acknowledging debt.

I.O.W. *abbr.* Isle of Wight.

ipécăcüăn'ha (-na) *n.* root of S.Amer. plant used as emetic etc.

ip'sé dĭx'ĭt *n,* (pl. *-ts*), dogmatic statement; dictum. [L]

ip'sō făc'tō *adv.* by that very fact. [L]

I.Q. *abbr.* intelligence quotient.

i.q. *abbr., idem quod* [L], the same as.

Ir. *abbr.* Ireland; Irish.

I.R.A., I.R.B. *abbr.* Irish Republican Army, Brotherhood.

irăs'cible (*or* īr-) *a.* irritable; hot--tempered. **~bil'itў** *n.*

irāte' *a.* angry. **īre** *n.* (poet.) anger.

īridā'ceous *a.* (of plants) of iris kind.

iridĕs'cent *a.* showing rainbow-like colours. **~ence** *n.*

irĭd'ium (*or* ī-) *n.* hard white brittle metallic element of platinum group.

ī'ris *n.* pigmented diaphragm surrounding pupil of eye; kinds of bulbous or tuberous plant with sword-shaped leaves and showy flowers.

Ir'ish (īr-) *a.* of Ireland. *n.* Irish language; (pl.) Irish people. **~ stew,** dish of stewed mutton, onions, and potatoes. **~ terrier,** breed with rough wiry reddish--brown coat. **~ wolfhound,** very large hound.

irk *v.t.* tire, bore. **~some** *a.* tedious, tiresome.

iron (ī'ern) *n.* abundant metallic element used for tools etc.; tool etc. of iron, esp. one heated to smooth linen etc.; type of hardness; preparation of iron as tonic; (pl.) fetters. *a.* of iron; robust; unyielding. *v.t.* smooth with heated iron; **~ out,** get rid of (as) by ironing. **~ age,** period characterized by use of iron weapons etc. **~ curtain,** barrier to passage of persons and information at limit of Soviet sphere of influence. **~ lung,** rigid case over body of paralytic patient for prolonged artificial respiration. **~master,** manufacturer of iron. **~monger,** dealer in iron goods. **~mongery,** iron goods. **~-mould,** spot caused by iron-rust or ink-stain. **~stone,** kinds of hard iron-ore.

irŏn'ic, ~al *aa.* of, using, said in, addicted to, irony.

īr'onist *n.* one who uses irony.

īr'onў *n.* expression of meaning by use of words normally conveying opposite meaning; apparent perversity of fate or circumstances.

irrā'diāte *v.t.* shine upon; throw light on; light up (face etc.); subject to radiation. **~ā'tion** *n.*

irrā'tional *a.* unreasonable, illogical; not endowed with reason; (math., of number etc.) not rational, not expressible as finite fraction. **~ăl'itў** *n.*

irreclai'mable *a.* not to be reclaimed or reformed.

irrec'oncilable *a.* implacably hostile; incompatible. **~bil'itў** *n.*

irrecov'erable (-kŭ-) *a.* that cannot be recovered or remedied.

irredee'mable *a.* irreclaimable, hopeless; not to be redeemed.

irredū'cible *a.* not reducible.

irref'ragable *a.* indisputable, unanswerable.

irrefrăn'gible (-j-) *a.* inviolable.

irref'ūtable (*or* irrefū'-) *a.* not to be refuted. **~bil'itў** *n.*

irreg'ūlar *a.* contrary to rule; uneven, varying; not in regular service. *n.* member of irregular military force. **irregūlă'ritў** *n.*

irrĕl'evant *a.* not relevant. **~ance** *n.*

irrĕli'gion (-jn) *n.* hostility or indifference to religion; impiety. ĭrrĕlĭ'gious *a.*

ĭrrĕmē'dĭable *a.* past remedy.

ĭrrĕmo'vable (-mōō-) *a.* not removable. ~bĭl'ĭtў *n.*

ĭrrĕp'arable *a.* that cannot be made good.

ĭrrĕplā'ceable (-sa-) *a.* of which loss cannot be supplied.

ĭrrĕprĕss'ĭble *a.* that cannot be repressed.

ĭrrĕproa'chable *a.* faultless, blameless. ~bĭl'ĭtў *n.*

ĭrrĕsĭs'tĭble (-zĭs-) *a.* too strong, convincing, charming, etc. to be resisted. ~bĭl'ĭtў *n.*

ĭrrĕs'olūte (-zol-; *or* -ōōt) *a.* hesitating; wanting in resolution. ~u'tion *n.*

ĭrrĕspĕc'tĭve *a.* ~ of, not taking into account, without reference to.

ĭrrĕspŏn'sĭble *a.* not responsible; acting, done, without due sense of responsibility. ~bĭl'ĭtў *n.*

ĭrrĕtrie'vable *a.* not retrievable.

ĭrrĕv'erent *a.* wanting in reverence. ~ence *n.*

ĭrrĕvēr'sĭble *a.* that cannot be reversed. ~bĭl'ĭtў *n.*

ĭrrĕv'ocable *a.* unalterable; gone beyond recall. ~bĭl'ĭtў *n.*

ĭ'rrĭgāte *v.t.* supply (land) with water; water (land) by system of artificial channels; (med.) moisten (wound etc.) with constant flow of liquid. ĭrrĭgā'tion *n.*

ĭ'rrĭtable *a.* quick to anger; sensitive to stimuli; inflamed, sore. ~abĭl'ĭtў *n.*

ĭ'rrĭtant *a. & n.* (substance or agency) causing irritation.

ĭ'rrĭtāte *v.t.* excite to anger, annoy; inflame. ~ā'tion *n.*

ĭrrŭp'tion *n.* invasion; violent entry.

ĭs, 3rd pers. sing. pres. of **be.**

Is. *abbr.* Island(s).

Isa. *abbr.* Isaiah.

ĭsagŏ'gĭc *a.* introductory. ~s *n.pl.* study of literary etc. history of Bible.

 īsinglass (ī'zĭngglahs) *n.* kind of gelatin got from sturgeon etc.

Is'lam (ĭs- *or* ĭz-; *or* -ahm) *n.* religion revealed through Prophet Mohammed; Moslem world. **Islăm'ic** *a.*; ~ĭsm *n.*

island (ī'l-) *n.* piece of land surrounded by water; detached or isolated thing. *v.* make into island; isolate; dot as with islands. ~ universe, galaxy, gigantic system of stars etc. separated from other galaxies by vast stretches of space. ~er *n.*

isle (īl) *n.* (usu. small) island.

ĭs'lĕt (ī'l-) *n.* small island.

ī'sobār *n.* line on map etc. connecting places with same barometric pressure. ~ă'rĭc *a.*

ī'solāte *v.t.* place apart or alone; separate (esp. infectious patient from others). ~ā'tion *n.* ~ā'tionĭsm *n.* policy of keeping aloof from affairs of other States.

ī'somēr *n.* one of two or more compounds with same elementary composition but different properties. īsomĕ'rĭc *a.* īsŏm'erĭsm *n.*

īsŏs'celes (-selēz) *a.* (of triangle) having two sides equal.

ī'sothērm *n.* line on map etc. connecting places with same mean temperature. īsothēr'mal *a.*

ī'sotōpe, *n.* one of two or more forms of chemical element with different atomic weight and nuclear properties. ~ŏp'ic *a.*

Isrā'elĭ (ĭz-) *a. & n.* (inhabitant) of modern Israel.

ĭss'ūe *n.* outgoing, outflow; result, outcome; children; question, dispute; issuing; copies of journal etc. issued at one time. *v.* go or come out, emerge; be derived, result; give or send out; publish, circulate; supply *with* equipment etc.

ĭs'thmus (*or* ĭs'mus) *n.* (pl. -*muses*), neck of land; narrow connecting part.

ĭt[1] *pron.* (poss. *its*; pl. *they*, obj. *them*, poss. *their*), thing named or in question; indefinite or undefined or impersonal action, condition, object, etc.; (sl.) the very person or thing, perfection; (sl.) sexual attraction.

ĭt[2] *n.* (colloq.) Italian vermouth.

I.T.A. *abbr.* Independent Television Authority.

i.t.a. *abbr.* initial teaching alphabet.

ital. *abbr.* italics.

Ităl'ĭan (ĭ-) *a. & n.* (native, language) of Italy.

ităl'ĭc *a.* (of type etc.) sloping; *I~*, of ancient Italy. *~s n. pl.* italic type. *~ĭze v.t.* print in italics; underline, emphasize.

itch *n.* irritation in skin; disease with itch; restless desire. *v.i.* feel itch; crave uneasily, long.

ĭ'tĕm *n.* any one of enumerated things; detail of news etc. in newspaper etc. *adv.* also, likewise. *~ĭze v.t.* state in items.

ĭt'erāte *v.t.* repeat; state repeatedly. *~ā'tion n. ~ative a.* (esp., gram.) frequentative.

ĭtĭn'erant (*or* ĭ-) *a.* travelling from place to place, esp. on circuit. *n.* itinerant person. *~ancy̆ n.; ~āte v.i.*

ĭtĭn'erary̆ (*or* ĭ-) *n.* record of travel; guide-book; route. *a.* of roads or travelling.

its *pron. & a.*, poss. case of *it.*

ĭtsĕlf' *pron.*, emphat. and refl. form of *it.*

I.T.V. *abbr.* Independent Television.

ĭ'vory̆ *n.* white substance of tusks of elephant etc.; (sl., pl.) dice, piano-keys, teeth, etc. *~ tower*, (esp. artist's) seclusion from world.

ĭ'vy̆ *n.* climbing evergreen with shining leaves. **ĭ'vied** (-ĭd) *a.* overgrown with ivy.

I.W. *abbr.* Isle of Wight.

I.W.W. *abbr.* Industrial Workers of the World.

ĭx'ĭa *n.* kinds of S.-Afr. iridaceous plant with showy flowers.

J

J (jā), broad-pointed (pen-nib).

J. *abbr.* Judge; Justice.

jăb *v.t.* poke roughly; stab; thrust abruptly. *n.* abrupt stabbing blow.

jăbb'er *v.* chatter volubly; utter fast and indistinctly. *n.* chatter, gabble.

jabot (zhăb'ō) *n.* frill at neck or down front opening of shirt, blouse, etc.

jă'cĭnth *n.* reddish-orange gem, kind of zircon.

jăck *n.* kinds of machine for turning spit, lifting weights from below, etc.; (esp. young or small) pike; ship's flag, esp. one flown from bow and showing nationality; knave in cards; figure striking bell on outside of clock; small ball aimed at in bowls; (U.S.) money. *v.t.* hoist (*up*) with jack. *~boot*, large boot coming above knee. **J~-in-office**, fussy official. **J~-in--the-green**, man in framework covered with leaves in May-day sports. **J~ Ketch**, common hangman. *~-of-all-trades*, one who can turn his hand to anything. *~-o'-lantern*, will-o'-the-wisp; (U.S.) pumpkin lantern. *~pot*, (esp. cumulative) prize in lottery etc. *~ tar*, common sailor. *~-towel*, roller-towel.

jăck'al (-awl) *n.* kinds of carrion--eating Afr. and Asian animal of dog kind; one who does preparatory drudgery.

jăck'anāpes *n.* pert fellow; coxcomb.

jăck'ăss *n.* male ass; blockhead.

jăck'daw *n.* daw.

jăck'ĕt *n.* coat-like garment for upper part of body; animal's coat; skin of potato; outside wrapper of book. *v.t.* cover with jacket.

jăck'-knīfe *n.* large pocket clasp--knife; dive in which diver touches feet or ankles with hands. *v.i.* double or rise up like (blades of) jack-knife (esp. of two vehicles coupled together).

Jăcobē'an *a.* of reign of James I of England.

Jăc'obĭn *n.* Dominican friar; member of extreme democratic club established 1789 in Paris.

Jăc'obīte *n.* adherent of exiled Stuarts.

jăc'onĕt *n.* kinds of esp. glazed or waterproofed cotton cloth.

jāde¹ *n.* poor or worn-out horse. **jā'dĕd** *a.* worn out, weary, esp. with hard work; sated.

jāde² *n.* hard translucent light-green, bluish, or whitish stone used for ornaments etc.; carved piece of this; light green. **jā'deite** (-dīt) *n*. jade-like stone.

Jăff'a (orange) *n*. large oval seedless orange.

jăg[1] *n*. sharp projection. *v.t.* cut, tear, break, unevenly. **jăgg'ĕd** *a*.

jăg[2] *n*. (U.S. colloq.) drinking-bout, spree.

jăg'ūar (or -gw-) *n*. large Amer. carnivorous spotted quadruped of cat kind.

jail etc.: see **gaol** etc.

jăl'ap *n*. purgative drug.

jalŏp'ў *n*. battered old motor-car.

jalousie (zhăl'ōōzē) *n*. blind, shutter, with slats sloping upwards from without.

jăm[1] *v*. squeeze; (cause to) get wedged; block (passage); (radio etc.) cause interference with (programme etc.). *n*. squeeze; stoppage; crowded mass, esp. of logs in river or traffic on road etc.

jăm[2] *n*. conserve of fruit boiled with sugar. *v.t.* make into jam. **jămm'ў** *a*.

Jam. *abbr*. Jamaica; James (N.T.)

jămb (-m) *n*. side post, side, of doorway, window, etc.

jămboree' *n*. (sl.) celebration; merry-making; large rally of Boy Scouts.

Jan. *abbr*. January.

jangle (jăng'gl) *n*. harsh discordant metallic noise. *v*. (cause to) make jangle; wrangle.

jăn'issarў, -zarў *n*. (hist.) one of body of Turkish infantry.

jăn'ĭtor *n*. doorkeeper; (U.S.) caretaker of building.

Jăn'ūarў *n*. first month of year.

japăn' *n*. hard usu. black glossy varnish. *v.t.* make black and glossy (as) with japan.

Jăpanēse' (-z) *a. & n*. (native, language) of Japan.

jāpe *v.i. & n*. jest.

japŏn'ĭca *n*. kinds of ornamental plant, esp. Japanese quince.

jăr[1] *v*. strike discordantly, grate; wrangle. *n*. jarring sound; shock or thrill; quarrel. **jărr'ĭng** *a*.

jăr[2] *n*. pottery or glass vessel, usu. cylindrical.

jardinière (zhărdĭnyār') *n*. ornamental stand or pot for plants or flowers. [F]

jăr'gon *n*. debased or unintelligible language, gibberish; language peculiar to class, profession, etc.

jărgonĕlle' *n*. kind of pear.

jăr'vey *n*. driver of Irish jaunting--car.

Jas. *abbr*. James.

jăs'mĭn(e) (-z- *or* -s-), **jĕss'amĭn(e)** *n*. kinds of shrub with white or yellow flowers.

jăs'per *n*. red, yellow, or brown opaque quartz.

jaun'dĭce *n*. (yellow discoloration of skin etc. due to) excess of bile pigment in blood. **jaun'diced** (-ĭst) *a*. affected with jaundice; coloured by envy, jealousy, spleen, etc.

jaunt *n*. pleasure excursion. *v.i.* take jaunt. **~ing-car**, light two-wheeled vehicle with seats back to back.

jaun'tў *a*. airily self-satisfied; sprightly.

ja'va (jah-) *n*. (U.S. sl.) coffee.

jăv'elin (-vl-) *n*. light spear.

jaw *n*. (esp. lower) bone containing teeth; (pl.) mouth; (pl.) gripping members of machine etc.; (colloq.) talk, lecture. *v*. (sl.) talk tediously; lecture, scold.

jay *n*. noisy chattering bird of brilliant plumage; silly chatterer. **~-walker**, pedestrian carelessly walking in or crossing roadway.

jăzz *n*. Amer. popular syncopated music with marked rhythm, much improvisation, etc.; dance music imitating this. *a*. of or in jazz; discordant; loud or fantastic. *v*. play, dance to, arrange as, jazz; brighten, liven (*up*). **jăzz'ў** *a*.

jeal'ous (jĕl-) *a*. watchfully tenacious; suspicious, resentful, of rivalry in affections; envious (*of*). **jeal'ousў** *n*.

jean *n*. heavy twilled cotton fabric; (pl.) garment, esp. overalls or trousers, of this.

jeep *n*. small short powerful motor vehicle with four-wheel drive.

jeer *v*. scoff derisively (*at*); deride. *n*. gibe, taunt.

jehad : see **jihad**.

Jĕhō'vah (-a) *n*. O.T. name of God.

jĕjune' (-ōōn) *a*. poor, barren.

jĕll *v.i.* (colloq.) set as jelly; take shape, crystallize.

jĕll'y *n.* soft stiffish usu. semi-transparent substance made with gelatin etc., esp. as food; anything of similar consistency; (sl.) gelignite. *v.* turn into, set in or as, jelly. **~-bag**, muslin etc. bag for straining juice from fruit-pulp for jelly. **~-fish**, kinds of marine animal with jelly-like body and stinging tentacles. **jĕll'ied** (-ĭd) *a.*

jĕmm'y *n.* burglar's crowbar.

jĕnn'ĕt *n.* small Spanish horse.

jĕnn'y wrĕn *n.* (pop.) wren.

jeop'ardīze (jĕp-) *v.t.* endanger. **jeop'ardỹ** *n.* danger.

Jer. *abbr.* Jeremiah.

jĕrbō'a *n.* small African jumping rodent with long hind legs.

jĕrĕmī'ad *n.* complaining tirade.

jĕrk[1] *n.* sharp sudden pull, twist, etc.; spasmodic twitch of muscle; jerking throw. *v.* pull, thrust, throw, etc. with jerk; move with jerk(s). **jĕr'kỹ** *a.*

jĕrk[2] *v.t.* cure (esp. beef) by drying in long slices in sun.

jĕr'kĭn *n.* (hist.) man's close-fitting jacket, often of leather; sleeveless jacket.

jĕ'rrĭcăn, jĕ'rrỹ-căn *n.* five-gal. container for liquids.

jĕ'rrỹ *n.* (sl.) chamber-pot.

jĕ'rrỹ-builder (-bĭl-) *n.* builder of unsubstantial houses with bad materials. **~-building** *n.*; **~-built** *a.*

jĕr'sey (-zĭ) *n.* knitted fabric; close-fitting knitted upper garment.

Jeru'salem ăr'tĭchōke (-rōō-) *n.* kind of sunflower with edible tubers.

jĕss *n.* short strap round leg of hawk.

jessamine : see **jasmine**.

jĕst *n.* joke; fun; object of derision. *v.i.* joke, make jests. **~er** *n.* (esp., hist.) professional entertainer in court etc.

Jĕs'ūĭt (-z-) *n.* & *a.* (member) of Society of Jesus, R.C. priestly order. **Jĕsūĭt'ĭcal** *a.* (hist.) crafty, casuistical. **~ĭsm, ~rỹ** *nn.*

jĕt[1] *n.* hard black lignite taking brilliant polish. **~-black**, deep glossy black.

jĕt[2] *n.* stream or shoot of water, gas, etc., esp. used to propel aircraft etc.; spout, nozzle, for emitting jet; jet-propelled aircraft etc. *v.* spurt or spout forth in jet(s).

jĕt'sam *n.* goods jettisoned and washed ashore.

jĕtt'ĭson *v.t.* throw (goods) overboard, esp. to lighten ship in distress.

jĕtt'ỹ[1] *a.* jet-black.

jĕtt'ỹ[2] *n.* mole; landing-pier.

jeu d'esprit (zhĕr dĕsprē'), witty or humorous trifle. [F]

Jew (jōō) *n.* person of Hebrew race or religion. **jews' harp**, musical instrument of vibrating metal strip in small iron frame held between teeth. **Jew'ĕss** *n.*; **~ĭsh** *a.* **~rỹ** *n.* Jews collectively; Jewish quarter.

jew'él (jōō-) *n.* precious stone; jewelled ornament; precious thing. **jew'elled** *a.* adorned with jewels; (of watch) fitted with jewels in pivot-holes. **jew'éller, jew'ellerỹ, jew'elrỹ** *nn.*

Jĕz'ébel *n.* shameless woman.

jĭb[1] *n.* triangular stay-sail from outer end of jibboom to fore-topmast head or from bowsprit to masthead; *cut of one's* **~**, one's personal appearance. **~boom**, spar from end of bowsprit.

jĭb[2] *v.i.* (of horse etc.) stop and refuse to go on; **~** *at*, show repugnance at, raise objections to.

jibe[1] : see **gibe**. **jĭbe**[2] *n.* & *v.* gybe.

jĭbe[3] *v.i.* (U.S.) chime *in* or agree (*with*).

jĭff'(ỹ) *n.* (colloq.) very short time.

jĭg *n.* lively dance, music for it. *v.* dance jig; move up and down rapidly and jerkily. **~saw**, (U.S.) machine fretsaw. **~saw puzzle**, picture etc. cut in irregular pieces to be fitted together.

jĭgg'er[1], **chĭg'ōe** *n.* small flea burrowing into skin of human foot.

jĭgg'er[2] *v.t.* (colloq. in mild oaths) damn.

jĭgg'er[3] *n.* small glass or measure, esp. for spirits.

jĭgg'erỹ-pō'kerỹ *n.* (sl.) trickery, underhand dealing.

jĭgg'le *v.t.* rock or jerk lightly.

jĭhad', jĕ- (-ahd) *n.* religious war of Moslems against unbelievers.

jĭlt *n.* woman who capriciously discards lover. *v.t.* treat thus.

jingle (jĭng′gl) *n.* mixed noise as of small bells, links of chain, etc.; repetition of same or similar sound in words; verse etc. full of jingles etc. *v.* (cause to) make jingle.

jing′ō (-ngg-) *n.* (pl. *-oes*) bellicose patriot. ~**ism** *n.*; ~**is′tic** *a.*

jink *v.* move with sudden quick turn(s), dodge. *n.* jinking movement; *high* ~*s,* frolic, boisterous fun.

jinn *n.* genie.

jinrick′sha *n.* rickshaw.

jinx *n.* (U.S. colloq.) person or thing bringing bad luck; malignant spell.

jitt′er *v.i.* be nervous, act nervously. ~**s** *n.pl.* extreme nervousness; *have the* ~*s,* be jittery. ~**bug,** jive, jiver; jittery person. **jitt′erў** *a.* jumpy, nervy.

jiu-jitsu : see ju-jitsu.

jīve *n.* & *v.i.* (dance to) hot jazz.

Jn. *abbr.* Junction.

Jno. *abbr.* John.

jŏb *n.* (esp. small) piece of work done for hire etc.; what one has to do; business, affair, state of things; post, situation. *v.* do jobs; hire, let out, for time or job; buy and sell as broker; handle corruptly. ~ **lot,** miscellaneous lot. **jŏbb′er** *n.* **jŏbb′erў** *n.* corrupt dealing. **jŏbb′ing** *a.* employed in odd occasional jobs. ~**less** *a.* out of work.

jŏck′ey *n.* rider in horse-races. *v.* cheat, trick; manœuvre *for* advantageous position.

jocōse′ *a.* playful, waggish. **jocŏs′itў** *n.*

jŏc′ūlar *a.* humorous, joking. **jŏcūlă′ritў** *n.*

jŏc′und *a.* merry, sprightly. **jocŭn′ditў** *n.*

jŏdh′purs (-perz; *or* jō-) *n.pl.* riding-breeches reaching to ankle and tight below knee.

jō′ey *n.* (Austral.) young kangaroo; young animal.

jŏg *v.* shake with push or jerk; nudge; stimulate (memory); walk, trot, at slow pace. *n.* push, nudge; slow walk or trot. ~**trot,** slow regular trot.

jŏgg′le¹ *v.* shake, move (as) by repeated jerks. *n.* slight shake.

jŏgg′le² *n.* (joint with) key let into two stones etc. to prevent their sliding on one another. *v.t.* join by joggle.

John (jŏn) *n.* ~ **Barleycorn,** malt liquor. ~ **Bull,** personification of English people; typical Englishman. ~ **Dory,** edible sea-fish.

johnny (jŏn′I) *n.* (colloq.) fellow, esp. fashionable idler. ~**-cake,** cake of (U.S.) maize-meal or (Austral.) wheatmeal.

join *v.* put together, fasten, unite; unite, be united, in friendship etc.; take part with others (in), become member etc. (of); ~ *up,* enlist. *n.* point, line, plane, of junction.

joi′ner *n.* (esp.) maker of furniture and light woodwork. ~**ў** *n.* joiner's work.

joint *a.* combined; shared by two or more in common. *n.* point at which two things join; structure by which two bones fit together; leg, loin, etc. of carcass as used for food. *v.t.* connect by joint(s); fill up joints of (wall etc.), point; divide at joint or into joints. ~ **stock,** common fund, share capital.

join′tréss *n.* widow holding jointure.

join′ture *n.* provision made by husband for wife's support after his death.

joist *n.* one of parallel timbers stretched from wall to wall to take ceiling laths or floor boards. **jois′tĕd** *a.*

jōke *n.* thing said or done to excite laughter. *v.i.* make jokes; banter. **jō′ker** *n.* one who jokes; extra card as highest trump in some games; (U.S.) clause inserted in document etc. to nullify or modify its effect.

jŏll′ifў *v.* make merry; tipple; make jolly. ~**ficā′tion** *n.*

jŏll′itў *n.* merrymaking.

jŏll′ў *a.* joyful; festive, jovial; (colloq.) pleasant, delightful. *n.* (nav. sl.) Royal Marine. *v.t.* banter, talk into good humour, flatter. *adv.* (colloq.) very. ~**(-boat),** clinker-built ship's boat smaller than cutter.

jōlt *v.* jerk from seat etc.; move along with jerks. *n.* such jerk; surprise, shock. ~**ў** *a.*

Jon. *abbr.* Jonathan.

Jŏn'athan *n.* (*Brother*) ~, personified people, typical citizen, of U.S.

jŏn'quil *n.* kind of narcissus with clusters of fragrant flowers.

Jŏr'dan almond (ah'm-) *n.* fine almond, esp. from Malaga.

jŏr'um *n.* large drinking-bowl.

Jos. *abbr.* Joseph.

Joseph. *abbr.* Josephus.

jŏsh *v.* (U.S. sl.) banter, tease.

Josh. *abbr.* Joshua.

jŏss *n.* Chinese idol. **~-house,** Chinese temple. **~-stick,** incense--stick of fragrant gum mixed with clay.

jŏss'er *n.* (sl.) fool; fellow.

jŏ'stle (-sl) *v.* knock or push (*against* etc.); elbow. *n.* jostling.

jŏt *n.* small amount, whit. *v.t.* write (*down*) briefly or hastily.

joule (*or* jōōl) *n.* (electr.) unit of work.

jounce *v.* bump, bounce, jolt.

jour'nal (jĕr-) *n.* diary; log-book; daily record, newspaper or other periodical; part of shaft or axle resting on bearings. **~ēse'** (-z) *n.* journalists' English. **~ism** *n.* **jour'nalist** *n.* editor of or writer for newspaper etc. **~is'tic** *a.*

jour'ney (jĕr-) *n.* distance travelled; expedition to some distance, round of travel. *v.i.* make journey. **jour'neyman** *n.* qualified mechanic or artisan working for another.

joust (*or* jōōst) *n.* combat with lances between two mounted knights. *v.i.* engage in joust.

Jōve *n.* (myth.) Jupiter.

jō'vial *a.* merry; convivial. **jōviǎl'ity** *n.*

jowl *n.* jaw, jaw-bone, cheek; prominent throat or neck.

joy *n.* gladness, pleasure. *v.i.* rejoice. **~-ride,** (sl.) stolen or other pleasure--ride in car etc. **~stick,** (sl.) control lever of aircraft. **joy'ful, joy'less, joy'ous** *aa.*

J.P. *abbr.* Justice of the Peace.

jr. *abbr.* junior.

ju'bilant (jōō-) *a.* exultant.

ju'bilāte (jōō-) *v.i.* exult, manifest joy. **~ā'tion** *n.*

ju'bilee (jōō-) *n.* fiftieth anniversary; time of rejoicing.

Jud. *abbr.* Judith.

Judā'ic (jōō-) *a.* Jewish.

Ju'dāism (jōō-) *n.* being Jewish; Jewish religion, culture, community, etc.

jŭdd'er *v.i.* shake, shudder violently. *n.* (sound of) juddering.

Judg. *abbr.* Judges.

judge *n.* public officer appointed to try causes in court of justice; (of God) supreme arbiter; one appointed to decide dispute or contest; person qualified to decide on merits of thing or question. *v.* pass sentence upon; try (cause); decide (question); decide; act as judge, form judgement (*of*).

jŭdg(e)'ment (-jm-) *n.* sentence of court of justice etc.; misfortune as sign of divine displeasure; opinion, estimate; critical faculty; good sense; *Last J~,* God's trial of souls at end of world. **J~ day,** day of Last Judgement. **~ debtor,** one against whom judgement for payment has been given. **~ summons,** against defaulting judgement debtor.

ju'dicature (jōō-) *n.* administration of justice; body of judges.

judi'cial (jōō-) *a.* of or by court of law; of or proper to judge; impartial.

judiciary (jōōdǐsh'arǐ) *n.* judges collectively.

judi'cious (jōō-) *a.* sensible, prudent; skilful.

ju'dō (jōō-) *n.* modern development of ju-jitsu.

jŭg *n.* deep vessel for liquids with handle and usu. spout; (sl.) prison. *v.t.* stew (hare etc.) in jug or jar; (sl.) imprison.

Jŭgg'ernaut (-g-) *n.* idol of Krishna dragged yearly in procession on car under whose wheels devotees formerly threw themselves.

jŭgg'ins (-gǐnz) *n.* (sl.) simpleton.

jŭgg'le *v.* perform feats of dexterity (*with* balls etc. tossed up); play juggling tricks with; ~ *with,* manipulate deceitfully. **jŭgg'ler, jŭgg'lery** *nn.*

Jugoslav : see **Yugoslav.**

jŭg'ūlar *a.* of neck or throat. *n.* one of four great veins of neck.

juice (jōōs) *n.* liquid part of vegetable or fruit; fluid part of animal body; (sl.) petrol, electricity. jui'cў *a.* full of juice, succulent (freq. fig.).

ju-jit'su, jiu- (jōō-, -sōō) *n.* Japanese art of wrestling etc.

ju-ju (jōō'jōō) *n.* (W.-Afr.) charm or fetish; magic power of this.

jujube (jōō'jōōb) *n.* jelly- or gum-like sweetmeat.

juke'-bŏx (jōō-) *n.* slot-machine record-player.

ju'lĕp (jōō-) *n.* drink of spirit and water iced and flavoured esp. with mint.

Ju'lian căl'ĕndar (jōō-) *n.* reformed calendar introduced by Julius Caesar.

juliĕnne' (zhōō-) *n.* soup of finely chopped vegetables in meat broth.

Julў' (jōō-) *n.* seventh month of year.

jŭm'ble *v.t.* mix (*up*) in confusion. *n.* confused heap etc.; muddle. ~ sale, of miscellaneous second-hand goods.

jŭm'bō *n.* (pl. *-os*) big clumsy person, animal, or thing. ~-size(d), very large.

jŭmp *v.* leap, spring from ground etc.; rise or move with sudden start; leap over; leave (rails); (U.S.) get on (train etc.); seize (abandoned or forfeited claim); (sl.) attack suddenly; ~ *at*, accept eagerly; ~ *the gun*, make premature start; ~ *the queue*, take precedence of others waiting, get preferential treatment; ~ *to*, arrive at (conclusion) hastily or rashly; ~ *to it*, act smartly or promptly. *n.* leap; start caused by shock etc.; sudden rise or transition; *the* ~*s*, state of nervous excitement. ~ bid, (bridge) bid of more tricks than necessary in suit already bid. ~ed-up, upstart. ~ing-off place, point of departure. ~-off, final round between tied horses or riders in jumping competition. ~ seat, (U.S.) folding seat in car etc. ~ing *pred. a.* (esp., sl.) crowded, lively and noisy.

jŭm'per *n.* hip-length loose outer garment; upper part of naval rating's uniform; knitted upper garment not opening in front.

jŭm'pў *a.* nervous, panicky.

jun., junr. *abbr.* junior.

jŭnc'tion *n.* joining-point, esp. place where roads, railway lines, etc. meet (and unite).

jŭnc'ture *n.* concurrence of events, state of affairs.

June (jōōn) *n.* sixth month of year.

jŭng'le (-ngg-) *n.* land overgrown with tangled vegetation, esp. as home of wild beasts; thick tangled mass; scene of savage or ruthless struggle etc.

ju'nĭor (jōō-) *a.* (the) younger; of less standing. *n.* junior person, esp. barrister who has not taken silk, (U.S.) student in last year but one before graduating.

ju'nĭper (jōō-) *n.* kinds of evergreen shrub with prickly leaves and dark purplish berries.

jŭnk[1] *n.* (naut.) salt meat; old cable cut up for oakum etc.; discarded material, scrap; worthless rubbish. ~-shop, (esp.) second-hand dealer's shop.

jŭnk[2] *n.* flat-bottomed sailing-vessel of China seas.

jŭnk'ĕt *n.* dish of milk curdled by rennet; feast. *v.i.* feast, picnic.

Junōĕsque' (jōō-, -k) *a.* resembling Roman goddess Juno in stately beauty.

jŭn'ta *n.* deliberative or administrative council in Spain or Italy; clique, faction.

Ju'pĭter (jōō-) *n.* (myth.) chief Roman god; largest planet in solar system.

Jurăss'ĭc (joor-) *a.* of rock system marked by prevalence of oolitic limestone.

jurĭd'ical (joor-) *a.* of judicial proceedings; legal.

jurisconsŭlt' (joor-) *n.* one learned in law.

jurĭsdic'tion (joor-) *n.* administration of justice; (extent or area of) legal or other authority.

jurĭspru'dence (joorĭsprōō-) *n.* science of, skill in, law.

jur'ĭst (joor-) *n.* one versed in law; writer on law. jurĭs'tic(al) *aa.*

jur'or (joor-) *n.* member of jury.

jury (joor'ĭ) *n.* body of persons sworn to render verdict in court of justice; judges in competition. **~-box,** enclosure in court for jury. **~man, ~woman,** juror.

jury-mast (joor'ĭmahst) *n.* temporary mast.

jŭss'ĭve *a.* (gram.) expressing command.

jŭst *a.* upright, fair; correct, due, proper, right. *adv.* exactly; barely; not long before; (colloq.) quite, positively; **~** *now,* at this moment, a little time ago.

jŭs'tĭce *n.* justness, fairness; judicial proceedings; judge; magistrate.

jŭstĭ'cĭarў (-sh-) *n.* administration, administrator, of justice. *a.* of administration of justice.

jŭs'tĭfў *v.t.* show justice or rightness of; vindicate, make good; (theol.) declare free from penalty of sin; (print.) adjust (line of type) to fill space neatly. **~fĭable, ~fĭcātĭve, ~fĭcātory** *aa*; **~fĭcā'tion** *n.*

jŭt *v.i.* project. *n.* projection.

jute (jōot) *n.* fibre from bark of some plants, used for sacking etc.

Juv. *abbr.* Juvenal.

ju'vĕnīle (jōo-) *a.* youthful; of or for the young. *n.* young person. **~ lead,** (actor playing) part of youthful hero. **~ĭl'ĭtў** *n.*

juvĕnĭl'ĭa (jōo-) *n.pl.* works produced in youth.

jŭxtapōse' (-z; *or* jŭks'-) *v.t.* put side by side. **jŭxtaposĭ'tion** *n.*

K

Kăff'ir (-fer) *n.* member of S.-Afr. Bantu race. **~ lily,** showy-flowered S.-Afr. herbaceous plant.

kail : see **kale.**

kai'ser (kīz-) *n.* (hist.) German emperor.

ka'ka, ka'kapō (kah-) *nn.* kinds of New Zealand parrot.

kăkėmō'nō *n.* Japanese usu. silk wall-picture mounted on rollers.

kāle, kail *n.* cabbage, esp. curly-leaved kind not forming compact head; (Sc.) vegetable broth. **~yard,** (Sc.) kitchen garden.

kalei'doscōpe (-lĭ-) *n.* tube producing endless variety of bright-coloured symmetrical patterns; (fig.) constantly changing scene etc. **~scŏp'ĭc** *a.* (esp.) constantly shifting, infinitely varied.

kalends : see **calends.**

Kan. *abbr.* Kansas.

kana'ka (-ah-; *or* -ă-) *n.* South Sea Islander.

kăngarōō' (-ngg-) *n.* Austral. marsupial with strongly developed hindquarters and great leaping-power. **~ closure,** form of closure in which only certain amendments may be discussed. **~ court,** self-constituted court, esp. one held by prisoners, vagabonds, etc. **~-rat,** small Austral. marsupial.

kā'olĭn *n.* fine white clay used for porcelain etc.

kā'pŏk (*or* kah-) *n.* fine silky fibres round seed of **~-tree,** used to stuff cushions etc.

kăr'ma *n.* (Buddhism) sum of person's actions in one state of existence viewed as deciding his fate in next; destiny.

kă'rrĭ *n.* (hard red timber of) Austral. tree.

kā'tўdĭd *n.* (U.S.) large green American grasshopper.

kau'rĭ (kow-) *n.* (wood of) N.-Z. coniferous tree. **~-gum,** its resin.

kay'ak (kī-) *n.* Eskimo one-man canoe.

K.B. *abbr.* King's Bench.

K.B.E. *abbr.* Knight Commander of (Order of) British Empire.

K.C. *abbr.* King's Counsel; King's College (London).

kc. *abbr.* kilocycles.

K.C.B., K.C.M.G., K.C.V.O. *abbr.* Knight Commander of (Order of) the Bath, of (Order of) St. Michael and St. George, of Royal Victorian Order.

kea (kā'a) *n.* green Alpine parrot of New Zealand.

kĕbabs' (-ahbz) *n.pl.* dish of small pieces of meat etc., esp. cooked on skewers.

kĕdge *v.* warp ship, move, by

winding in hawser attached to small anchor. *n.* this anchor.

kĕdg'eree *n.* dish of fish, rice, eggs, etc.

keel[1] *n.* lowest longitudinal timber etc. on which ship's framework is built up. *v.* turn (ship) keel upwards; ~ *over*, (U.S.) (cause to) fall or collapse (as if) in faint.

keel[2] *n.* flat-bottomed boat on Tyne etc. for loading colliers.

keel'son, kĕl- *n.* set of timbers or plates fastening floor-timbers to keel.

keen[1] *a.* sharp; strong, acute, penetrating; eager, ardent.

keen[2] *n.* Irish funeral song accompanied with wailing. *v.* utter keen; utter in wailing tone.

keep *v.* (*kĕpt*), pay due regard to, observe; protect, have charge of; retain possession of; maintain; maintain (woman) as mistress; reserve for future use; maintain, remain, in good or specified condition; continue, remain, remain in; conduct, maintain, for profit; (colloq., esp. Camb. Univ.) reside, lodge; ~ *goal*, *wicket*, be goal-keeper, wicket-keeper. *n.* maintenance, food; (hist.) tower, citadel; *for* ~*s*, for good, permanently. ~**er** *n.* (esp.) gamekeeper; custodian of museum etc.; ring that keeps another on finger. ~**ing** *n.* (esp.) custody, charge; agreement, harmony.

keep'sāke *n.* thing treasured for sake of giver.

kĕg *n.* small barrel.

kĕlp *n.* kinds of large seaweed; (calcined ashes of) mass of large seaweeds.

kĕl'pĭe *n.* (Sc.) malevolent water-spirit.

kelson : see **keelson**.

kĕlt[1] *n.* salmon that has spawned.

Kelt[2] etc.: see **Celt**[2] etc.

kĕn *n.* range of knowledge or sight. *v.* (Sc.) know.

kĕnn'el[1] *n.* house for shelter of house-dog or hounds. *v.* go to or put into kennel; live or keep in kennel.

kĕnn'el[2] *n.* gutter.

kept *p.t.* & *p.p.* of **keep**.

kĕrb *n.* stone edging to pavement etc.

kĕr'chief (-ĭf) *n.* cloth used to cover head.

kĕrf *n.* slit made by cutting, esp. with saw; cut end of felled tree.

kĕr'mĕs (-z) *n.* (red dye-stuff made from dried bodies of) female of S.-Eur. and N.-Afr. insect.

kĕrn *n.* (hist.) light-armed Irish foot-soldier; peasant.

kĕr'nel *n.* part within hard shell of nut or stone fruit; body of seed within husk etc.; central or essential part.

kĕ'rosēne *n.* mixture of liquid hydrocarbons as fuel-oil etc.; paraffin.

kĕr'sey (-zĭ) *n.* coarse usu. ribbed woollen cloth.

kĕs'trel *n.* kind of small hawk.

kĕtch *n.* small two-masted or cutter-rigged coasting vessel.

kĕtch'up *n.* sauce of mushrooms, tomatoes, etc.

kĕtt'le *n.* metal vessel with spout and handle for boiling water; *pretty* ~ *of fish*, awkward state of affairs. ~**-drum**, drum with parchment stretched over hollow brass or copper hemisphere.

key[1] (kē) *n.* instrument for turning bolt of lock; solution; code, crib, manual; (mus.) system of definitely related notes based on particular note; lever for finger in piano, typewriter, etc.; instrument for winding clock etc.; roughness, projection, etc. assisting adhesion, part of first coat of plaster securing rest. *v.t.* fasten with wedge, bolt, etc.; ~ *up*, stimulate, increase nervous tension in. *a.* essential, of vital importance. ~**board**, set of keys on piano etc. ~**hole**, that by which key enters lock. ~**note**, note on which key is based; (fig.) dominant idea etc. ~ **signature**, sharps or flats at beginning of (section of) composition to indicate key. ~**stone**, central stone of arch; (fig.) central principle etc. ~**less** *a.* (esp. of watch) not requiring key for winding.

key[2] (kē) *n.* reef, low island, in Florida, W. Indies, etc.

K.G. *abbr.* Knight of (Order of) the Garter.

kg. *abbr.* kilogram.

kha′ki (kah-) *a.* dull brownish yellow. *n.* khaki cloth, esp. as used for service uniforms.

khan[1] (kahn) *n.* ruler, official, in Central Asia etc. **~ate** *n.* khan's rule or district.

khan[2] (kahn) *n.* caravanserai.

kib′butz′ (-ōōts) *n.* (pl. -*zim*), collective farm in Israel.

kibe *n.* ulcerated chilblain.

kib′itzer *n.* (U.S.) (esp. meddling) onlooker.

ki′bosh *n.* (sl.) *put the ~ on*, do for, dispose of.

kick *v.* strike out with foot; strike or move with foot; score (goal) by kicking ball; drive *out* etc. forcibly and contemptuously; (of gun) recoil; ~ *up*, raise (dust), create (fuss, noise). *n.* kicking; blow with foot; recoil of gun; resilience; (sl.) stimulating effect, thrill; (sl.) protest, complaint; *the ~*, (sl.) summary dismissal. **~-off**, (footb.) kick with which game is started. **~-start(er)**, foot-operated lever to start esp. motor-cycle engine. **~er** *n.* (esp.) horse given to kicking.

kick′shaw *n.* fancy dish; toy, trifle.

kid *n.* young goat; kid-skin leather; (sl.) child. *v.* give birth to kid; (sl.) hoax, humbug. **kidd′y** *n.* child.

kid′nap *v.t.* steal (child); carry off (person) illegally.

kid′ney *n.* either of pair of glandular organs serving to excrete urine; kidney of sheep etc. as food; nature, kind. **~-bean**, scarlet runner or dwarf French bean.

kie-kie (kē′kē) *n.* N.Z. climbing plant with leaves used for baskets etc.

kil′derkin *n.* (cask holding) 16 or 18 gallons.

kill *v.* put to death, slay; cause death of; destroy, make useless; perform killing. *n.* killing; animal(s) killed esp. by sportsman. **~-joy**, depressing person. **~er** *n.* (esp.) murderous ruffian. **~ing** *a.* (esp.) exhausting; (colloq.) overwhelmingly funny.

kiln (*or* kil) *n.* furnace, oven, esp. for calcining lime or baking bricks, pottery, etc.

kil′ō (*or* kē-) *n.* kilogram; kilometre.

kil′o- in comb. = 1,000. **kil′ocycle** *n.* 1,000 cycles per second as unit of wave-frequency. **~gram** *n.* weight of 1,000 grams (2·205 lb. avoird.). **~litre** (-lēter) *n.* measure of 1,000 litres (35·31 cu. ft.). **~mētre** *n.* measure of 1,000 metres (3280·89 ft.). **~ton** (-ŭn) *n.* 1,000 tons; explosive force of kiloton of TNT. **~watt** (-wŏt) *n.* 1,000 watts.

kilt *n.* pleated skirt from waist to knee, esp. as part of Highland male dress. *v.t.* tuck up (skirts) round body; gather in vertical pleats.

kimō′nō *n.* long Japanese robe with wide sleeves; dressing-gown like this.

kin *n.* ancestral stock, family; one's relatives. *pred. a.* related.

kind *n.* race of animals etc.; class, sort; *in ~*, in goods etc., not money, (of repayment) in something of same kind as that received; *~ of*, (colloq.) rather, as it were, in some degree. *a.* gentle, benevolent, friendly, considerate.

kin′dergarten *n.* school for young children not yet receiving formal education.

kin′dle, *v.* set on fire, light; inspire; become kindled; glow. **kind′ling** *n.* (esp.) small wood etc. for lighting fires.

kind′ly *a.* kind, sympathetic. *adv.* in kind manner.

kin′dred *n.* blood relationship; one's relations. *a.* related by blood; similar.

kine : see **cow**.

kin′ema *n.* cinema.

kinet′ic (*or* kī-) *a.* of or due to motion. ~ **energy**, energy possessed by moving body by virtue of its motion.

king *n.* male sovereign ruler of independent State; (chess) principal piece, mating of which is object of game; (draughts) piece that has reached opponent's base-line; playing-card bearing representation of king. **K~ Charles spaniel**, black-and-tan silky-coated toy spaniel. **~-crab**, large marine arachnid with horseshoe-shaped carapace. **~cup**, marsh marigold. ~ **penguin**, large species of penguin. **~pin**, most important person in organization etc. ~post, upright post from tie-beam to rafter-top. ~'s Bench, division of High Court of Justice. ~'s Counsel, practising barrister appointed as counsel to Crown. ~'s evil, scrofula, formerly held curable by king's touch. ~-size(d), large. ~lў *a.* belonging or appropriate to king; kinglike, majestic.

king'dom *n.* State, territory, ruled by king; domain; province of nature; ~ *come,* (sl.) next world.

king'fisher *n.* small brilliant--plumaged bird diving for fish.

kink *n.* back-twist in wire, chain, or rope; tight twist or curl; (fig.) mental or moral twist. *v.* form, cause (wire etc.) to form, kink. ~ў *a.* (esp., colloq.) eccentric; perverted.

kink'ajou (-ōō) *n.* nocturnal raccoon--like animal.

kins'folk (-zfōk) *n.pl.* relations by blood. kin'sman, -woman *nn.*

kin'ship *n.* relationship; similarity.

ki'ŏsk (kē-) *n.* light open structure for sale of newspapers etc.; structure for public telephone in street etc.

kip *n.* (sl.) sleep; bed. *v.i.* sleep; ~ *down,* go to bed.

kipp'er *v.t.* cure (herring etc.) by splitting open, salting, drying, and smoking. *n.* kippered fish, esp. herring; male salmon in spawning season.

kirk *n.* (Sc.) church. ~ session, minister and elders of congregation as lowest court of Church of Scotland.

kirsch (kērsh) *n.* spirit distilled from wild cherries.

kir'tle *n.* (arch.) woman's gown or outer petticoat.

kis'mĕt (-z-) *n.* destiny, fate.

kiss *n.* caress given with lips. *v.t.* touch with lips as sign of affection, reverence, etc.; touch lightly; ~ *hands,* kiss sovereign's hand on appointment to office. ~-curl, small curl on forehead, at nape of neck, etc. ~ing-gate, gate hung in U- or V-shaped enclosure.

kit[1] *n.* wooden tub; contents of soldier's valise or knapsack; personal equipment; outfit. *v.t.* supply with kit. ~-bag, for soldier's or traveller's kit.

kit[2] *n.* (now rare) small fiddle.

kit'-căt *n.* portrait less than half-length but including hands.

kitch'ĕn *n.* room used for cooking. ~ garden, for fruit and vegetables. ~er *n.* cooking-range. ~ĕtte' *n.* very small room, alcove, etc., fitted up as kitchen.

kīte *n.* bird of prey of falcon family; rapacious person; light freq. paper--covered framework flown in wind by string etc., esp. as toy; (sl.) aircraft.

kĭth *n.* ~ *and kin,* friends and relations; kinsfolk.

kitt'en *n.* young of cat; playful girl. *v.i.* bring forth kittens. ~ish *a.*

kitt'iwāke *n.* kind of seagull.

kitt'ў[1] *n.* pet name for kitten.

kitt'ў[2] *n.* pool in some card games; joint or accumulated fund.

ki'wĭ (kē-) *n.* N.Z. bird with rudimentary wings and no tail.

kl. *abbr.* kilolitre.

klăx'on *n.* powerful electric car-horn. P.

klĕptomā'nĭa *n.* morbid tendency to theft. klĕptomā'nĭăc *n.*

Klieg (-ēg) light *n.* very bright arc--light.

km. *abbr.* kilometre.

knăck *n.* acquired dexterity; trick, habit.

knăck'er *n.* buyer of useless horses for slaughter.

knăg *n.* knot in wood.

knăp *v.t.* break (flints) with hammer etc.; break, snap.

knăp'săck *n.* soldier's or traveller's bag strapped to back.

knăp'weed *n.* weed with purple flowers on globular head.

knăr *n.* knot in wood.

knāve *n.* unprincipled man, rogue; lowest court card of suit. knā'verў *n.*; knā'vĭsh *a.*

knead *v.t.* work up into dough or paste; make (bread, pottery) thus; massage.

In words beginning kn-, k is silent.

knee *n.* joint between thigh and lower leg; part of garment covering this; angular piece of iron etc. **~-cap**, bone in front of knee-joint. **~-hole**, (of table etc.) with space for knees between drawer-pedestals.

kneel *v.i.* (*knĕlt*), fall or rest on knees, esp. in prayer or reverence.

knĕll *n.* sound of bell, esp. at funeral or after death; omen of death or extinction.

knelt, *p.t. & p.p.* of **kneel**.

knew, *p.t.* of **know**.

knĭck'erbŏckers *n.pl.* loose-fitting breeches gathered in at knee.

knĭck'ers *n.pl.* (colloq.) knicker-bockers; woman's drawers.

knĭck'-knăck *n.* light dainty article of furniture, dress, or food; trinket.

knīfe *n.* (pl. *-ives*), blade with sharpened longitudinal edge fixed in handle; blade in cutting-machine; *the* **~**, (colloq.) surgery. *v.t.* cut or stab with knife. **~-edge**, sharp edge of knife; narrow ridge of rock etc.; steel wedge on which pendulum etc. oscillates. **~-pleats**, narrow overlapping pleats.

knight (nīt) *n.* person raised to rank below baronetcy; (hist.) person raised to honourable military rank; piece in game of chess. *v.t.* make (person) knight. **~ bachelor**, not belonging to special order. **~-errant**, medieval knight wandering in search of chivalrous adventures; chivalrous or quixotic person. **~-errantry**, practice or conduct of knight-errant. **~ Templar**, Templar. **~age** *n.* (list of) knights. **~hood** *n.*; **~lȳ** *a.*

knĭt *v.* (*knĭtted* or *knĭt*), form (texture, garment) of interlooping yarn or thread; make, form (wool, etc.) into, knitted fabric; wrinkle (brow); make or become compact; unite (*together*, *up*). **~wear**, knitted garments.

knĭtt'ing *n.* (esp.) work in process of knitting. **~-needle, -pin**, slender pointed rod of metal etc. used in knitting.

knŏb *n.* rounded protuberance; handle of door etc.; small lump of coal etc. **~kĕ'rrie**, short knob-headed stick of S.-Afr. tribes.

knŏbb'lȳ, knŏbb'ȳ *aa.* (esp.) covered with (small) knobs.

knŏck *v.* strike, esp. with hard blow; drive with knock; make knocking noise; collide with or be driven against; (U.S. sl.) depreciate, disparage; **~** *about*, treat roughly, wander, lead irregular life; **~** *back*, down (drink); **~** *down*, fell with blow, dispose of at auction; **~** *off*, stop work, stop (work), (colloq.) do or make rapidly, esp. without effort; **~** *out*, make (opponent in boxing) unable to rise or continue in specified time, make unconscious; **~** *up*, make etc. hastily, score (runs) at cricket, awaken by knocking at door, exhaust. *n.* blow, rap, esp. at door; (crick. sl.) innings. **~-about**, boisterous, noisy; suitable for rough use. **~-down**, (of price) minimum. **~-knees**, that knock together in walking. **~-out**, (blow) knocking boxer out; (competition) in which defeated competitors are eliminated. **~-up**, practice or casual game at tennis etc. **~er** *n.* (esp.) metal appendage hung on door for knocking with.

knōll *n.* small hill, mound.

knŏp *n.* small decorative knob; ornamental loop or tuft in yarn etc.

knŏt *n.* intertwining of parts of one or more strings etc. to fasten them together; tangled mass, cluster; hard mass esp. in trunk at insertion of branch; (naut.) division marked by knots in log-line; nautical mile per hour as unit of speed; (loosely) nautical mile; difficulty. *v.* tie knot in (string, etc.); form knot(s); entangle. **~-grass**, weed with intricate stems and pink flowers. **knŏtt'ȳ** *a.* full of knots; puzzling.

knout *n.* scourge formerly used in Russia. *v.t.* flog with knout.

know (nō) *v.* (*knew*, pr. nū, *known*), be aware (of); perceive with certainty; be acquainted with; recognize. *n.* (colloq.) *in the* **~**,

In words beginning kn-, k is silent.

having confidential or exclusive information. ~-**how**, practical knowledge of methods, expertness. **know'ing** a. (esp.) cunning, wide awake. **know'ingly** adv. in knowing manner; consciously, intentionally.

knowl'edge (nŏl-) n. knowing; what one knows; all that is or may be known. ~**able** a. intelligent or well-informed.

Knt. abbr. Knight.

knuck'le n. bone at finger-joint; projection of knee- or ankle-joint of quadruped; this as joint of meat. v. strike, rub, etc. with knuckles; ~ under, give in, submit. ~**bones**, game played with sheep's knuckle-bones. ~**duster**, metal instrument to protect knuckles and increase effect of blow.

knur n. knot on tree-trunk; hard concretion; wooden ball struck with club-ended stick in game of ~ and spell.

k.o. abbr. knock-out.

kōa'la (bear) (-ahla) n. Austral. tailless arboreal marsupial with thick grey fur.

kō'dăk n. kind of camera. **P.**

kohl (kōl) n. powder used in East to darken eyelids etc.

kohlra'bǐ (kōlrah-) n. cabbage with turnip-like stem.

kolin'skÿ n. fur of Siberian mink.

koodoo, kudu (kōō'dōō) n. large white-striped S.-Afr. antelope.

kǒp'je (-pǐ) n. (S.-Afr.) small hill.

Koran (kōr'an, korahn') n. sacred book of Moslems.

kō'sher a. (of food etc.) fulfilling requirements of Jewish law.

kou'miss (kōō-) n. fermented liquor of mare's milk.

kowtow' n. Chinese custom of touching ground with forehead as sign of submission etc. v.i. make kowtow; be obsequious.

kraal (krahl) n. S.-Afr. hut-village within fence; cattle enclosure.

kraft (-ah-) n. kind of strong packing-paper.

kra'ken (-ah-) n. mythical Norwegian sea-monster.

krĕm'lǐn n. citadel of Russian town,

esp. Moscow; the K~, (used for) Russian government.

kris (-ēs) n. Malay or Indonesian wavy-bladed dagger.

krŏmĕs'kÿ n. small fried roll of minced chicken etc.

krÿp'ton n. (chem.) rare almost inert gaseous element.

Kt abbr. Knight.

kū'dŏs n. (sl.) glory, renown.

kudu : see **koodoo**.

kuk'rĭ (kōō-) n. heavy curved knife as Gurkha weapon.

ku'lăk (kōō-) n. prosperous, esp. landowning, Russian peasant.

kümm'el (kōō- or kǐ-) n. liqueur flavoured with cumin seed.

kursaal (koor'zahl) n. building for visitors at health resort.

Ky abbr. Kentucky.

kÿ'lōe n. one of breed of small long-horned Scotch cattle.

kÿ'mograph n. instrument recording variations of pressure etc.

kyr'ǐĕ (ele'ison) (kēr-, -lā-; or kīr'ǐ) n. (musical setting of) Gk. words used esp. at beginning of mass.

L

L, l (ĕl), as Roman numeral, 50.

L., L abbr. Latin; learner; Linnaeus; Liberal.

l. abbr. left; libra(e) (L), pound(s); line; lira, lire (It.); litre(s).

la (lah) n. (mus.) sixth note of major scale in tonic sol-fa.

La abbr. Louisiana.

L.A. abbr. Los Angeles.

laa'ger (lahg-) n. encampment, esp. in circle of wagons. v. form into, place in, laager; encamp.

lăb n. (colloq.) laboratory.

Lab. abbr. Labour; Labrador.

lā'bel n. slip attached to object to give some information about it; classifying phrase etc. v.t. attach label to.

lā'bial a. of lips; (phonet.) formed by

In words beginning kn-, k is silent.

complete or partial closure of lips. *n.* labial sound.

lā'bĭle *a.* (chem. etc.) unstable.

lăb'oratorў (*or* labŏ'-) *n.* place used for scientific experiments etc.

labōr'ious *a.* hard-working, toilsome; (of style) laboured.

lā'bour (-b*er*) *n.* exertion of body or mind; task; pains of childbirth; workers; *L~,* Labour Party. *v.* exert oneself; work hard; be troubled or impeded; treat laboriously. **Labor Day,** U.S. public holiday on first Monday· in September. **~ exchange,** State office for finding employment for unemployed. **~ force,** body of workers employed or available. **L~ Party,** party supporting interests of labour. **~er** *n.* (esp.) man doing unskilled work. **~īte** *n.* member or adherent of Labour Party.

Lăb'rador (retriever) *n.* kind of black or golden retriever.

labūr'num *n.* leguminous tree with yellow hanging flowers.

lăb'ўrinth *n.* network of winding passages; maze; intricate arrangement. **lăbўrĭn'thĭne** *a.*

lăc¹ *n.* resinous secretion of E.-Ind. insect.

lac² : see lakh.

L.A.C. *abbr.* Leading Aircraftman.

lāce *n.* cord etc. passed through eyelets or hooks to fasten or tighten boots, stays, etc.; trimming-braid; kinds of fine open-work patterned fabric. *v.* fasten, tighten, compress, trim, with lace; flavour (beverage) *with* spirit. **lā'cў** *a.*

lă'cerāte *v.t.* tear, rend; wound (feelings etc.) **~ā'tion** *n.*

lăch'rўmal (-k-) *a.* of tears.

lăch'rўmātorў (-k-) *a.* of or causing tears.

lăch'rўmōse (-k-) *a.* tearful.

lăck *n.* deficiency or want. *v.t.* need, be without. **~-lustre,** (of eye etc.) dull. **~ing** *a.* wanting, deficient.

lăckadai'sĭcal (-z-) *a.* languishing, affected; listless.

lăck'ey *n.* footman; obsequious person.

lacŏn'ĭc *a.* using, expressed in, few words. **~ism** *n.*

lăc'quer (-k*er*) *n.* (Japanese etc. ware coated with) hard decorative varnish taking high polish; kinds of varnish used as protective coating etc.

lacrŏsse *n.* orig. N.-Amer. game with ball carried in net at end of stick.

lăctā'tion *n.* suckling; secretion of milk. **lăc'tèal** *a.* of milk; conveying chyle. **lăc'tĭc** *a.* of milk. **lăc'tōse** *n.* milk sugar.

lacū'na *n.* (pl. *-ae*), hiatus, blank, esp. in MS. etc.

lacŭs'trĭne (*or* -ĭn) *a.* of lakes.

lăd *n.* boy, young fellow. **lădd'ў** *n.*

lădd'er *n.* set of cross-bars (rungs) between two uprights of wood etc., used as means of ascent; vertical flaw in stocking etc.; (fig.) means of rising. *v.i.* develop ladder(s).

lāde *v.t.* (p.p. *lā'den*), load (ship); ship (goods); (*p.p.*) loaded or burdened (*with*). **lā'dĭng** *n.* (esp.) *bill of lading,* receipt to consignor for goods shipped.

la-di-da (lahdĭdah') *a.* pretentious or affected, esp. in pronunciation.

lā'dle *n.* long-handled large-bowled spoon for transferring liquids; vessel for pouring molten metal. *v.t.* transfer with ladle; **~ out,** distribute esp. in large quantities.

lā'dў *n.* gentlewoman, woman of good birth or breeding; (prefixed to name) woman of title below duchess; mistress *of* house; (courteously for) woman; (pl.) women's lavatory. **~bird,** kinds of small beetle, usu. reddish-brown with black spots. **L~-chapel,** chapel in large church dedicated to Virgin. **L~ Day,** Annunciation, 25 Mar., a quarter-day. **~'s-maid,** in charge of lady's toilet. **~smock,** cuckoo--flower.

lā'dўlike *a.* behaving etc. like, befitting, lady.

lā'dўshĭp *n.* (esp.) used as substitute for titled lady's name.

lăg¹ *v.i.* go too slow, hang back, fall *behind. n.* (amount of) retardation or delay. **lăgg'ard** *n.* & *a.* lagging (person).

lăg² *n.* (sl.) convict.

lăg³ *v.t.* encase (boiler etc.) with insulating material. **lăgg'ing** *n.*

lăg'an *n.* goods or wreckage on bed of sea.

la'ger (beer) (lahg-) *n.* light orig. German beer.

lagōōn' *n.* shallow salt-water lake parted from sea by sand-bank, coral reef, etc.

la'hăr (lah-) *n.* avalanche of volcanic mud.

lā'ĭc *a.* non-clerical. *n.* layman. ~al *a.*; ~īze *v.t.*

laid, *p.t. & p.p.* of **lay.** ~ **paper,** watermarked with close parallel lines.

lain, *p.p.* of **lie.**

lair *n.* wild beast's lying-place.

laird *n.* (Sc.) landowner.

laissez-faire (lay'say făr') *n.* freedom from government interference with industrial etc. affairs. [F]

lā'ĭtў *n.* laymen.

lāke[1] *n.* large body of water surrounded by land.

lāke[2] *n.* kind of (esp. crimson) pigment or dye.

lăkh (-k), **lăc**[2] *n.* (Anglo-Ind.) 100,000 (usu. *of rupees*).

Lăll'ans *n. & a.* (of or in) Lowland Sc. vernacular, esp. as literary language.

lăm *v.* (sl.) hit hard, thrash.

Lam. *abbr.* Lamentations.

la'ma[1] (lah-) *n.* Tibetan or Mongolian Buddhist monk. ~serў (*or* lamah'-) *n.* monastery of lamas.

lama[2] : see **llama.**

lămb (-m) *n.* young sheep, its meat; innocent, weak, or dear person. *v.i.* bring forth lamb. ~swool, fine soft wool of lambs.

lămbāst(e)' *v.t.* (colloq.) beat, thrash.

lăm'bent *a.* (of flame etc.) playing about surface; gently brilliant. **lăm'bencў** *n.*

lāme *a.* crippled by injury or defect esp. in foot or leg; limping or unable to walk; (of metre) halting; (of story etc.) unsatisfactory. *v.t.* make lame, cripple. ~ **duck,** disabled or weak person; defaulter on Stock Exchange.

lamé (lah'mā) *n. & a.* (material) with metal thread inwoven.

lamĕnt' *n.* passionate expression of grief; elegy. *v.* utter lament; express or feel grief for; (*p.p.*)

mourned for. **lăm'ĕntable** *a.* deplorable, regrettable. ~ā'tion *n.* lament, lamenting.

lăm'ĭna *n.* (pl. -ae), thin plate or flake or layer. **lăm'ĭnar, ~ate** *aa.* ~āte *v.* beat or roll (metal) into laminae; split into layers; manufacture by placing layer on layer. ~ā'tion *n.*

Lămm'as *n.* 1 August, old harvest festival, Sc. quarter-day.

lămp *n.* vessel with oil and wick for giving light; glass vessel enclosing candle or other illuminant; (fig.) source of spiritual etc. light. ~-**black** pigment made from soot. ~-**lighter,** of street-lamps. ~-**post,** supporting street-lamp.

lăm'pĭon *n.* glass pot holding light for illuminations.

lămpōōn' *n.* virulent satire. *v.t.* write lampoon(s) against.

lăm'prey *n.* eel-like fish with sucker mouth.

Lăncăs'trĭan *a. & n.* (native) of Lancashire; (hist.) (adherent) of House of Lancaster.

lance (-ah-) *n.* horseman's long spear; similar implement for spearing fish etc. *v.t.* prick or open with lancet. ~-**corporal,** N.C.O. below corporal.

lance'lĕt (lahnsl-) *n.* small fish-like marine animal.

lăn'cĕolate *a.* shaped like spearhead, tapering to each end.

la'ncer (-ah-) *n.* soldier of cavalry regiment; (pl.) kind of square dance.

lan'cĕt (-ah-) *n.* pointed two-edged surgical knife; high narrow pointed arch or window.

lăn'cĭnāting *a.* (of pain) shooting.

Lancs. *abbr.* Lancashire.

lănd *n.* solid part of earth's surface; ground, soil, expanse of country; country, State; landed property, (pl.) estates. *v.* disembark, go or put ashore; bring to or reach place, stage, or position; bring (aircraft), come, to earth from air; deal (blow etc.); alight after jump etc.; bring (fish) to land; win (prize etc.). ~-**bank,** bank issuing notes on security of landed property. ~**fall,** approach to land esp. for first time in voyage or flight. **~holder,** proprietor or (usu.) tenant of land. **~lady,** woman keeping inn or lodgings; woman having tenants. **~locked,** almost or quite enclosed by land. **~lord,** person of whom another holds any tenement; keeper of inn or lodgings. **~-lubber,** person ignorant of sea and ships. **~mark,** boundary mark; conspicuous object; notable event. **~mine,** explosive mine laid in or dropped on ground. **~rail,** harsh-voiced bird. **~slide,** sliding down of mass of land, land fallen, from cliff or mountain; overwhelming majority of votes. **~slip,** landslide. **~less** *a.*; **~ward** *a., adv.,* & *n.*; **~wards** *adv.*

lăn'dau *n.* four-wheeled carriage with top whose back and front can be raised and lowered. **lăndaulĕt(te)'** *n.* car with movable hood over rear seats.

lăn'dĕd *a.* possessing, consisting of, land.

lănd'grāve *n.* (hist.) title of some German potentates.

lăn'dĭng *n.* (esp.) landing-place; platform, floor, passage, at head of stairs. **~-craft,** for putting ashore troops and equipment, esp. on beach. **~-net,** net for landing hooked fish. **~-place,** place for disembarking. **~-stage,** (usu. floating) platform for landing passengers and goods. **~-strip,** airstrip.

lănd'scāpe *n.* piece of inland scenery; picture of it. *v.t.* improve by landscape gardening or architecture. **~ architecture, gardening,** design and lay-out of parks, large spaces, etc., esp. to produce natural--seeming pictorial effects.

lāne *n.* narrow road between hedges; narrow street; passage or strip between rows of persons etc., or marked out for runners in race, streams of traffic, etc.; prescribed route for ships, aircraft, etc.

lăng sÿne *adv.* & *n.* (Sc.) (in) the old days.

lăng'uage (-nggw-) *n.* words and their use; speech; form of speech used by people etc.; style; vocabulary; wording.

lăng'uĭd (-nggw-) *a.* inert, lacking vigour; spiritless; sluggish, slow; faint, weak.

lăng'uĭsh (-nggw-) *v.i.* lose or lack vitality; lose intensity; droop, pine (*for*); affect languor.

lăng'uor (-ngg*er*) *n.* faintness; lassitude; soft or tender mood. **~ous** *a.*

langur (l*a*nggoor') *n.* kinds of long--tailed monkey.

lănk *a.* lean and tall; long; (of grass, hair, etc.) long and limp. **lănk'ÿ** *a.* tall, long.

lăn'olĭn *n.* fatty matter got from sheep's wool.

lăn'tern *n.* transparent case protecting flame of candle etc.; light--chamber of lighthouse; apparatus for projecting image on screen; superstructure on roof etc. admitting light at sides. **~ jaws,** long thin jaws giving hollow look to face. **~-slide,** piece of glass bearing image etc. for projection on screen.

lăn'yard *n.* short cord for fastening or holding something.

Lāodĭcē'an *a.* & *n.* (person) lacking zeal, esp. in religion or politics.

lăp[1] *v.* drink by scooping with tongue; drink (*up*) greedily; (of waves etc.) move with lapping sound (against). *n.* act or sound of lapping.

lăp[2] *n.* tail or skirt of coat; front of woman's skirt held up as receptacle; thighs of sitting person; one circuit of course in race; overlapping part or amount; one turn of rope etc. round drum, roller, etc. *v.* swathe, enfold, wrap; (make) overlap; (racing etc.) pass (competitor) by lap; travel over lap (of). **~dog,** small enough to be held in lap. **~-joint,** made by overlapping. **~ robe,** (U.S.) rug covering knees of seated person in vehicle.

lapĕl' (*or* lăp'-) *n.* part of coat-breast folded back. **lapĕlled'** (-ld) *a.*

lăp'ĭdarÿ *a.* of stones; engraved on stone; (of style) suitable for inscriptions. *n.* cutter etc. of stones.

lăp'ĭs lăz'ūlĭ *n.* (pigment from or colour of) bright blue semi-precious stone.

lăpp'ĕt n. flap or fold of garment, flesh, etc.

lăpse n. slip of memory etc.; slight mistake; backsliding; termination through disuse etc.; elapsing. v.i. fall back or away; become void, fall in; elapse.

lăp'sus lĭng'uae (-nggwē), slip of the tongue. [L]

lăp'wing n. bird of plover family, peewit.

lǎr n. (pl. lǎr'ēs), ancient Rom. household deity; ~es and penā'tēs (-z), household gods, home.

lǎr'board (-berd) n. & a. (naut.) port.

lǎr'cĕnў n. theft. **lǎr'cĕnous** a.

lǎrch n. bright-foliaged deciduous coniferous tree; its timber.

lǎrd n. pig fat prepared for cooking etc. v.t. insert strips of bacon in (meat etc.) before cooking; garnish (talk etc.) with particular words etc. ~ў a.

lǎr'der n. room or cupboard for storing provisions.

lares : see lar.

lǎrge a. of considerable or relatively great magnitude; of wide range, comprehensive. n. at ~, at liberty, free, at full length, as whole, broadcast, without definite aim. ~ly adv. (esp.) to great or preponderating extent.

lǎr'gĕsse n. money or gifts scattered esp. on occasions of rejoicing; generous or plentiful bestowal.

lar'gō, (mus.) (passage etc. to be rendered) slowly and in broad dignified style. [It.]

lă'riat n. rope with running noose; lasso.

lǎrk[1] n. kinds of small bird including skylark. ~spur, plant with irregular-shaped blue or pink flowers.

lǎrk[2] n. frolic, spree; amusing incident. v.i. play tricks, frolic about.

lă'rrikin n. (Austral.) hooligan.

lǎr'va n. (pl. -ae), immature insect after leaving egg, grub. **lǎr'val** a.

larўng'oscōpe (-ngg-) n. instrument for inspecting larynx.

lărўngŏt'omў (-ngg-) n. cutting into larynx.

lă'rўnx n. cavity in throat holding vocal chords. **larўn'gĕal** (-j-) a.

lărўngī'tĭs (-j-) n. inflammation of larynx.

Lăs'cǎr n. E.-Indian seaman.

lascĭv'ĭous a. lustful.

lā'ser (-z-) n. device producing intense narrow orderly beam of light.

lăsh v. make sudden movement of tail, limb, etc.; pour, rush; beat with thong etc.; urge as with whip; castigate; tie tightly. n. stroke with thong etc.; flexible part of whip; eyelash. **lăsh'ings** n.pl. (sl.) plenty.

lăsh'er n. weir; pool below it.

lăss n. girl. ~ie n.

lăss'ĭtūde n. languor; disinclination to exert or interest oneself.

lăss'ō, lăssoo' n. rope etc. with running noose used esp. for catching cattle. v.t. catch with lasso.

last[1] (-ah-) n. shoemaker's model for shaping shoe etc. on.

last[2] (-ah-) a. after all others; coming at end; most recent; utmost. adv. (esp.) on last occasion before present. n. last-mentioned person or thing; last performance of certain acts; end; at (long) ~, in the end, after much delay.

last[3] (-ah-) v.i. go on; remain unexhausted or adequate or alive. **la'sting** a. permanent; durable; n. kind of hard cloth used for boot-tops etc.

last'lў (-ah-) adv. finally.

Lat. abbr. Latin.

lat. abbr. latitude.

lătch n. bar with catch as fastening of gate etc.; small spring lock as fastening of outer door. v.t. fasten with latch.

lătch'ĕt n. (arch.) thong for fastening shoe.

lāte a. after right time; far on in day or night or period; backward; now dead; that occurred lately. adv. after right time; far on in time. n. of ~, recently.

lateen' sail n. triangular sail on long yard at angle of 45° to mast.

lāte'lў (-tl-) adv. not long ago; in recent times.

lā'tent a. concealed; dormant; existing but not developed or manifest. **lā'tencў** n.

lăt′eral *a.* of, at, toward, or from side(s). *n.* lateral shoot or branch.

lā′těx *n.* milky fluid exuding from cut surfaces of some plants, esp. as raw material of rubber.

lath (-ah-) *n.* (pl. pr. -dhz), thin strip of wood.

lāthe (-dh) *n.* machine for turning wood, metal, etc. or with revolving disc for throwing and turning pottery.

lăth′er (-dh-) *n.* froth of soap or other detergent and water; frothy sweat of horse. *v.* form lather; cover (esp. chin etc. for shaving) with lather; (sl.) thrash.

Lăt′ĭn, *n.* language of ancient Rome; inhabitant of ancient Latium; member of mod. Latin people. *a.* of or in Latin; of Latium or ancient Rome; of Latin church; of peoples speaking languages descended from Latin. ∼ **America,** all Spanish-, French-, or Portuguese-speaking parts of America. ∼ **Church,** branch of Christian Church acknowledging Pope. ∼**ism** *n.* idiom characteristic of Latin. ∼**ist** *n.* Latin scholar. **lăt′ĭnīze** *v.t.*; ∼**īzā′tion** *n.*

lăt′ĭtūde *n.* scope, full extent; freedom from restriction in action or opinion; angular distance N. or S. of equator; (usu. pl.) regions, climes.

lătĭtūdĭnār′ĭan *a. & n.* (person) claiming or allowing latitude of opinion, esp. in religion.

latrine′ (-ēn) *n.* place for evacuation of bowels or bladder.

lătt′er *a.* recent; second-mentioned; belonging to end of period, world, etc. *n.* second-mentioned thing or person. ∼**-day,** modern. ∼ **end,** death. ∼**lў** *adv.* of late; towards end of period etc.

lătt′ĭce *n.* structure of laths or bars crossing each other with interstices; arrangement resembling this; lattice window. ∼ **window,** window so made, with small panes set in lead. **lătt′ĭced** (-st) *a.*

laud *v.t.* praise, extol. **lau′dable** *a.* commendable. ∼**abĭl′ĭtў,** ∼**ā′tion** *nn.*; ∼**atorў** *a.* ∼**s** *n.pl.* first of day-hours of Church.

laudanum (lŏd′nŭm) *n.* tincture of opium.

laugh (lahf) *v.* make sounds etc. usual in expressing amusement, exultation, and scorn; utter with laugh; pass *off* with jest; ∼ *at,* make fun of, ridicule; ∼ *out of court,* deprive of hearing by ridicule. *n.* sound or act of laughing. ∼**able** *a.* amusing; ridiculous.

laugh′ĭng (-ahf-) *a.* indulging in laughter. *n.* (esp.) laughter. ∼**-gas,** nitrous oxide as anaesthetic. ∼ **hyena,** kinds of hyena with howl like fiendish laughter. ∼ **jackass,** Austral. giant kingfisher. ∼**-stock,** object of general derision.

laugh′ter (-ahf-) *n.* act or sound of laughing.

launch[1] (law- *or* lah-) *v.* hurl, discharge, send forth; start, send off, (on career etc., *into* expense, abuse, etc.); set (vessel) afloat; ∼ *out* (esp.) spend money freely. *n.* launching of ship.

launch[2] (law- *or* lah-) *n.* man-of-war's largest boat; large mechanically propelled boat.

laun′der, *v.* wash and get up (linen etc.); bear laundering (*well* etc.). ∼**ětte′** *n.* establishment where automatic washing-machines may be used (**P**). **laun′drėss** *n.* woman who launders.

laun′drў *n.* room or establishment for laundering linen; clothes etc. for washing; laundering.

laur′ėate *a.* wreathed with laurel; *poet* ∼, poet receiving stipend as officer of British Royal Household.

lau′rel (lŏ-) *n.* kinds of glossy-leaved shrub; (sing. or pl.) wreath of bay-leaves as emblem of victory or poetic merit. **lau′relled** (-ėld) *a.* wreathed with laurel.

laurustĭ′nus (lŏ-) *n.* evergreen flowering shrub.

la′va (lah-) *n.* matter discharged in fluid form by volcano.

lăv′atorў *n.* room etc. for washing hands and face; water-closet, urinal.

lāve *v.t.* wash, bathe; wash against, flow along.

lăv′ėnder *n.* fragrant-flowered shrub, its flowers and stalks used to perfume linen etc.; pale purplish colour of its flower. ~-water, perfume of distilled lavender etc.

lā′ver[1] n. kinds of edible seaweed.

lā′ver[2] n. (bibl.) vessel for ablutions.

lăv′erock (-vr-) n. lark.

lăv′ish a. profuse, prodigal; (too) abundant. v.t. bestow or spend lavishly.

law n. rule established among community and enjoining or prohibiting certain action; system made up of such rules; rule of action or procedure; legal profession or knowledge; law-courts, litigation; correct statement of invariable sequence between specified conditions and specified phenomenon. ~-abiding, obedient to law. ~-court, court of law. ~giver, maker of (esp. code of) laws. ~ merchant, laws regulating trade and commerce. ~-officer, (esp.) Attorney- or Solicitor-General. ~ of nations, international law, law regulating relation between states. ~suit, prosecution of claim in lawcourt.

law′ful a. permitted or appointed by law; not illegal.

law′less a. having no laws; disobedient to law; unbridled.

lawn[1] n. kind of fine linen or (now usu.) cotton.

lawn[2] n. close-mown turf in gardens etc. ~ tennis, modification of tennis played with rackets on court without walls.

law′yer n. member of legal profession; one versed in law.

lăx[1] a. negligent; not strict; loose; vague. lăx′ity n.

lăx[2] n. Swedish or Norwegian salmon.

lăx′ative a. & n. (medicine) tending to loosen bowels.

lay[1], p.t. of lie.

lay[2] n. minstrel's song, ballad.

lay[3] a. non-clerical; non-professional; amateur. ~ brother, sister, member of religious order employed in manual labour. ~man, person not in orders; person without professional or special knowledge of subject. ~ reader, layman licensed to conduct religious services.

lay[4] v.t. (laid), deposit on surface; put in specified position; put or bring into specified state; impose, enjoin; bury; calm, allay; make subside; beat down (crop); set (trap) in readiness; set on table; wager; produce (egg); ~ by, store; ~ down, relinquish (office etc.), formulate (principle), sacrifice (life), (begin to) construct, store (wine) in cellar; ~ off, discharge (temporarily), (colloq.) desist; ~ on, provide for supply of, (sl.) arrange, organize; ~ out, prepare (corpse) for burial, arrange, plan arrangement of, spend (money), (refl.) take pains to do; ~ up, store, save, (pass.) be confined to bed. n. way, position or direction in which something lies; (sl.) line of business etc. ~about, habitual loafer or tramp. ~-by, part of road extended to allow vehicle to stop without interfering with traffic. ~-out, (plan or drawing of) arrangement of printed page, site, etc.

lay′er n. person etc. that lays; (usu. lār) thickness of matter spread over surface; shoot fastened down to take root. v.t. propagate by layers; arrange in layers.

layĕtte′ n. clothes etc. needed for new-born child.

lay fig′ure (-ger) n. artist's jointed wooden model of human figure; nonentity; unreal character in novel, etc.

lā′zar (or lă-) n. (hist.) poor and diseased person, esp. leper. ~-house, leper-house.

lăzarĕt′ n. ship's storage-space, esp. between decks.

lāze v. (colloq.) idle, pass (time) away in idleness. n. (time spent in) lazing.

lā′zy a. averse to work; indolent; inducing indolence. ~-bones, lazy person.

l.b. abbr. leg-bye.

lb. abbr., libra(e) [L], pound(s).

l.b.w. abbr. leg before wicket.

L.C. abbr. left centre (of stage); Lord Chancellor.

l.c. abbr., loco citato [L.], in the place quoted; lower case.

L.C.C. abbr. London County Council.

L.C.J. abbr. Lord Chief Justice.

L.C.M. abbr. lowest common multiple.

L.-Cpl *abbr.* Lance-corporal.

L.D.S. *abbr.* Licentiate in Dental Surgery.

lea *n.* piece of meadow or arable or pasture land.

L.E.A. *abbr.* Local Education Authority.

lead[1] *v.* (*lĕd*), conduct, guide, esp. by going in front; direct movements of; guide by persuasion; guide actions or opinions of, induce *to*; spend (life etc.); have first place (in), go or be first; be leader, leading counsel or actor, etc.; (of road etc.) go *to*; play as first card, be first player; ask leading questions (of); ~ *on*, entice into going further than was intended; ~ *to*, have as result; ~ *up to*, serve to introduce, direct conversation towards. *n.* example; leading place, leadership; (player of) chief part; (cards) act or right of playing first, card or suit led; artificial watercourse; (electr.) connecting-wire to or from electrical device; channel in ice-field; strap etc. for leading dog.

lead[2] (*lĕd*) *n.* heavy soft grey metallic element; stick of graphite in pencil; bullets; lump of lead used in sounding; (print.) metal strip for spacing out letters or lines of type; (pl.) piece of usu. flat roof covered with lead. *v.t.* cover, weight, frame, separate, etc. with lead.

lead'en (*lĕd-*) *a.* (as) of lead; heavy, slow; inert; lead-coloured.

lea'der *n.* (esp.) leading article; leading counsel; chief violin--player in orchestra etc.; front horse in team, front runner etc. in race; shoot at apex of stem or principal branch. **~ětte'** *n.* short leading article.

lea'ding *a.* (esp.) chief; of most importance; giving guidance. *n.* guidance. **~ article**, expression of editorial opinion in newspaper etc. **~ case**, (law) case serving as precedent. **~ counsel**, senior of two or more counsel acting for one party in law case. **~ edge**, forward edge of wing etc. of aircraft. **~ lady, man**, actress, actor, of chief part in play etc. **~ note**, seventh note of ascending scale. **~ question**,

one framed to prompt desired answer. **~-rein**, to lead horse with. **~-strings**, with which children are taught to walk.

leaf *n.* (pl. *leaves*), expanded organ (usu. green) of plant springing from stem or branch, or directly from root; (pop.) petal; foliage; single thickness of folded paper, esp. in book; very thin sheet of metal etc.; hinged part or flap of door, table, etc.; movable part used to extend table-top. *v.i.* ~ *through*, turn over pages of book etc. **~-lard**, made from layers of fat round pig's kidneys. **~-mould**, soil composed chiefly of decaying leaves. **~age** *n.* **~let** *n.* (esp.) printed paper, single or folded, for distribution. **~ў** *a.*

league[1] (-g) *n.* (arch.) measure of distance, usu. about 3 miles.

league[2] (-g) *n.* (parties to) compact for mutual help or association for common interests; group of football etc. clubs playing each other in championship; *in* ~, allied (*with* etc.). *v.* combine in league.

leak *n.* flaw in vessel etc. allowing passage of liquid etc.; liquid etc. escaping through flaw; escape or loss of electric current etc., device for securing this; divulging of esp. secret information etc., information etc. divulged. *v.* escape, allow escape of, through leak; divulge (secret etc.), be divulged; ~ *out*, become known improperly. **~age** *n.*; **~ў** *a.*

leal *a.* (Sc.) loyal; honest.

lean[1] *a.* thin, not plump; meagre, poor; (of meat) not fat; ~ *years*, years of scarcity. *n.* lean part of meat.

lean[2] *v.* (*leant*, pr. *lĕnt*, or *leaned*), be or put in sloping position; be inclined or partial *to*; rely or depend *on*. *n.* inclination, slope. **~-to**, shed etc. with roof leaning against wall of larger building. **~ing** *n.* tendency or inclination.

leap *n.* & *v.* (*leapt* pr. *lĕpt*, or *leaped*), jump. **~frog**, game in which players vault over others bending down. **~-year**, with 29 Feb. as intercalary day.

learn (*lĕrn*) *v.* (*learnt* or *learned*, pr. -nd), get knowledge of or skill in by study, experience, or being

taught; find out; (vulg.) teach
lear′nèd (lĕr-) *a.* deeply read,
erudite. **~er** *n.* person learning,
esp. tyro. **~ing** *n.* knowledge got
by study; erudition.

lease *n.* contract by which land or
tenement is conveyed for term by
owner (*lessor*) to tenant (*lessee*), usu.
for rent. *v.t.* grant or take on lease.
~hold, tenure or tenement on
lease. **~holder,** tenant on lease.

leash *n.* thong for holding dogs; set
of three hounds, hares, etc. *v.t.* put
leash on; hold in leash.

lea′sing (-z-) *n.* (bibl.) lying, lie.

least *a.* smallest. *n.* least amount.
adv. in least degree.

leath′er (lĕdh-) *n.* material made by
tanning or otherwise dressing hides;
article or piece of leather; stirrup
strap; (pl.) leggings; (sl.) cricket-
-ball or football. *v.t.* cover or
furnish or polish with leather; flog.
~-jacket, larval stage of crane-fly.
~ing *n.* flogging. **~n** *a.* made of
leather. **~ў** *a.* (esp.) tough as
leather.

leave[1] *n.* permission; **~** (*of absence*),
permission to be absent from duty,
period for which this lasts; *on* **~**,
absent thus; *take* **~** (*of*), bid farewell (to).

leave[2] *v.* (*lĕft*), let remain; bequeath;
not consume or deal with; go away
(from); cease to reside at or belong
to; trust or commit to another;
abandon.

leav′en (lĕ-) *n.* substance used to
make dough ferment and rise;
tinge or admixture *of.* *v.t.* ferment
with leaven; permeate, transform,
modify (*with* tempering element).

lea′vings (-z) *n.pl.* what is left.

lĕch′er *n.* (arch.) fornicator,
debauchee. **~ous** *a.* lustful.
lĕch′erў *n.*

lĕc′tern *n.* reading- or singing-desk
in church.

lĕc′ture *n.* discourse delivered to
class or other audience; piece of
admonition. *v.* deliver lecture (to);
admonish. **~r** *n.* (esp.) university
professor's assistant. **~ship** *n.*

led, *p.t.* & *p.p.* of **lead**[1].

lĕdge *n.* narrow shelf or projection;
rock-ridge below sea-level.

lĕdg′er *n.* book in which debtor-and-
-creditor accounts are kept. **~-line,**
(mus.) short line added above or
below stave.

lee *n.* shelter given by neighbouring
object; side of something away
from wind. **~-shore,** to leeward of
ship. **~way,** drift to leeward; lost
time. **leeward** (lū′*a*rd) *a.* & *adv.* on
or towards side turned from wind;
n. leeward direction or region.

leech[1] *n.* (arch.) physician.

leech[2] *n.* kinds of usu. aquatic
blood-sucking worm; person sucking profit out of others.

leech[3] *n.* free edge of sail.

leek *n.* onion-like culinary herb.

leer *n.* & *v.i.* glance with lascivious or
malign expression. **~ў** *a.* knowing;
sly; wary.

lees (-z) *n.pl.* sediment of wine etc.;
worst part after best is gone.

left[1] *p.t.* & *p.p.* of **leave**[2].

lĕft[2] *a.* of or situated on side opposite
right; of left in politics. *n.* left
side; (pol. etc.) more advanced
or radical party, group, etc. *adv.*
on or to left side. **~-wing,**
-winger, (politician etc.) of extreme left. **~ward** *a.* & *adv.*;
~wards *adv.*

lĕft-hăn′dèd *a.* using left hand in
preference to right; awkward,
clumsy; ambiguous; (of marriage)
morganatic; adapted for, delivered
with, left hand; rotated, directed,
etc. to left. **lĕft-hăn′der** *n.* left-
-handed person, blow, etc.

lĕg *n.* one of limbs on which person or
animal walks and stands; leg of
animal as food; artificial leg;
support of chair or other piece of
furniture; (colloq.) section of
journey etc.; (crick.) part of field
to left of right-handed or right of
left-handed batsman, esp. rear
part of this; *long, short, square,* **~**,
(position of) fielders on leg side;
pull person's **~**, hoax or befool him.
v.i. **~** *it,* walk or run hard. **~ be-**
fore (wicket), illegal stopping by
batsman's leg of ball which would
have bowled him. **~-pull,** instance
of pulling person's leg, hoax.

lĕg′acў *n.* thing or sum left by will;
anything handed down.

lē'gal *a*. of or based on law; appointed or required or permitted by law. ~ism *n*. exaltation of law or formula. ~ist *n*. lĕgăl'itў *n*. lawfulness. ~īze *v.t*. make lawful; bring into harmony with law; ~īzā'-tion *n*.

lĕg'ate *n*. papal ambassador.

lĕgatee' *n*. recipient of legacy.

lĕgā'tion *n*. diplomatic minister and his suite; his official residence.

lĕga'tō (-ah-) *adv., a.,* & *n*. (passage to be performed, skill in performing) smooth(ly) and connected(ly). [It.]

lĕ'gend *n*. traditional story, myth; inscription or motto on coin etc. lĕ'gendarў *a*. famous, existing only, in legend.

lĕ'gerdĕmain *n*. sleight of hand, conjuring; hocus-pocus.

lĕgg'ing (-g-) *n*. (usu. pl.) outer covering of leather etc. for lower leg.

lĕgg'ў(-g-) *a*. disproportionately long--legged.

lĕghorn' (-gŏrn); *or* lĕg'h-) *n*. (hat of) kind of plaited straw; breed of fowls.

lĕ'gible *a*. easily read, clear. ~bĭl'itў *n*.

lē'gion (-jn) *n*. division of 3,000–6,000 men in ancient Roman army; great number; *British L*~, national association of ex-service men; *Foreign L*~, body of foreign volunteers in esp. French army. ~arў *a*. of legion or legions; *n*. soldier of legion. lēgionnaire' (-jon-) *n*. member of esp. French Foreign Legion.

lĕ'gislāte *v.i.* make laws. ~ā'tion *n*. (enacting of) laws. ~atĭve *a.*; ~ātor *n*. ~ature *n*. law-making body of State.

lĕgĭt'imate *a*. born in lawful wedlock; lawful; regular, proper; (of plays, theatre, etc.) of or in or belonging to body of plays not including revues, farces, etc. *v.t.* (-āt), make legitimate; justify. ~macў, ~mā'-tion, ~mīzā'tion *nn.*; ~mīze *v.t*.

lĕgĭt'imism *n*. adherence to sovereign or pretender with claim based on direct descent. ~ist *n*.

lĕgū'minous *a*. bearing seed in valved pods (as beans, peas, etc.).

lei (lā *or* lā'ē) *n*. Polynesian garland of flowers etc. worn round neck.

Leics. *abbr*. Leicestershire.

leisure (lĕzh'er) *n*. spare time; freedom from pressing business; *at* ~, not occupied, without hurry; *at* one's ~, when one has time. ~d, ~lў *aa*. deliberate, not hurried; *adv*. without hurry.

leit-motiv (lī'tmōtēf) *n*. (mus.) theme associated throughout work with some person, situation, or sentiment. [G]

lĕm'an *n*. (arch.) sweetheart, paramour.

lĕmm'ing *n*. small arctic and sub--arctic rodent.

lĕm'on[1] *n*. pale-yellow acid fruit; its colour; tree bearing it. ~-grass, grass yielding fragrant oil. ~ squash, drink of lemon-juice and (soda-)water. ~-wood, small N.Z. evergreen tree. ~āde' *n*. drink made from or flavoured like lemons.

lĕm'on[2] sōle *n*. kind of plaice.

lē'mūr *n*. kind of nocturnal mammal allied to monkeys.

lĕnd *v.t.* (*lent*), grant temporary use of (thing); let out at interest or for hire; bestow, contribute; accommodate (one*self*) *to*.

lĕngth *n*. measurement from end to end in space or time; (pros.) quantity of vowel or syllable; long stretch or extent; piece of cloth etc. of certain length; *at* ~, in detail, at last. ~en *v*. make or become longer. ~ways (-z) *adv.*; ~wīse (-z) *adv*. & *a*. ~ў *a*. of unusual or undue length.

lē'nĭent *a*. indisposed to severity; mild. ~ence, ~encў *nn*.

lĕn'ĭtĭve *a*. & *n*. soothing (drug etc.).

lĕn'itў *n*. mercifulness.

lĕns (-z) *n*. piece of glass etc. spherically curved on one or both sides, used in spectacles etc.; transparent body behind iris of eye.

lent[1] *p.t.* & *p.p.* of **lend**.

Lĕnt[2] *n*. period of fasting and penitence from Ash Wednesday to Easter Eve. ~ lily, daffodil. ~en *a*. of or in or suited to Lent.

lĕntic'ūlar *a*. shaped like lentil or lens; of lens of eye.

lĕn′til *n.* (seed of) leguminous plant grown for food.

lĕn′tĭsk *n.* mastic tree.

lĕn′tō *a.* & *adv.* (mus.) slow(ly). [It.]

Lē′ō, Lion, fifth constellation and sign of zodiac.

lē′onīne *a.* lionlike.

leop′ard (lĕp-) *n.* large feline carnivore with dark-spotted fawn coat; panther. **~ĕss** *n.*

lē′otard *n.* close-fitting body-garment worn by dancers, acrobats, etc.

lĕp′er *n.* person with leprosy.

lĕpĭdŏp′terous *a.* of or belonging to order of insects (moths and butterflies) with four scale-covered wings.

lĕp′rechaun (-k-) *n.* Irish sprite like little old man.

lĕp′rosў *n.* endemic chronic disease affecting skin, nerves, etc. and freq. producing deformities.

lĕs′bĭan (-z-) *a.* of homosexuality in women; (of woman) homosexual. *n.* homosexual woman. **~ism** *n.*

lèse maj′esté (lāz mǎzh′ĕstā) *n.* affront to sovereign or ruler; presumption. [F].

lē′sion (-zhn) *n.* injury, esp. (path.) morbid change in functioning or texture of organ.

lĕss *a.* smaller; of lower rank or degree; of smaller quantity, not so much (of). *n.* smaller amount or quantity or number. *adv.* to smaller degree or extent or amount. *prep.* minus, not including.

lessee : see **lease.**

lĕss′en *v.* diminish, decrease.

lĕss′er *a.* not so great as other or rest, minor, smaller.

lĕss′on *n.* portion of Scripture etc. read at divine service; thing to be learnt by pupil; spell of teaching; warning experience; example.

lessor : see **lease.**

lĕst *conj.* in order that . . . not; for fear that.

lĕt[1] *v.t.* (*lĕtted* or *lĕt*), (arch.) hinder, obstruct. *n.* (lawn tennis etc.) obstruction of ball or player after which ball must be served again.

lĕt[2] *v.* (*lĕt*), allow or enable or cause to; grant use of for rent or hire; **~ alone,** not interfere with or do, not to mention; **~ down,** lower,

fail at need, disappoint; **~ in(to),** admit (to), insert in surface (of); **~ in for,** involve in; **~ loose,** release; **~ off,** fire (gun etc.), allow to go or escape, lease in portions; **~ on,** (sl.) reveal secret; **~ out,** open door for exit to, allow to escape, slacken; **~ slip,** release, divulge, miss (opportunity); **~ up,** cease, slacken, relax. *n.* letting, lease.

lē′thal *a.* causing or sufficient or designed to cause death.

lĕth′argў *n.* torpid or apathetic state. **lĕthǎr′gĭc** *a.*

Lē′thè *n.* river in Hades producing forgetfulness of past.

lĕtt′er *n.* any of symbols of which written words are composed; written message, epistle; literal meaning; (pl.) kinds of legal or formal letter; type used in printing; (pl.) literature, authorship as profession. *v.t.* impress title etc. on (book-cover); classify with letters. **~press,** matter printed from type. **~ed** *a.* (esp.) literate, well-read. **~ing** *n.* (esp.) (style of) letters drawn, inscribed, etc.

lĕtt′uce (-tĭs) *n.* crisp-leaved garden herb much used as salad.

leu′cocÿte *n.* colourless blood-corpuscle.

leucŏt′omў *n.* incision into brain to relieve some forms of mental disorder.

leukae′mĭa *n.* blood disease with excess of white corpuscles.

Lev. *abbr.* Leviticus.

lĕvǎnt′[1] *v.i.* abscond, bolt.

Lĕvǎnt′[2] *n.* E. Mediterranean region. **~īne** *n.* inhabitant of Levant; *a.* of, trading to, Levant.

lĕv′ee[1] (-vĭ) *n.* sovereign's reception for men only; assembly of visitors.

lĕv′ee[2] (-vĭ; *or* -vē′) *n.* embankment against river floods.

lĕv′el *n.* (instrument for giving or testing) horizontal line or plane; social or intellectual standard; plane of rank or authority; more or less flat surface or country; *on the* **~,** (colloq.) honest(ly), truthful(ly). *a.* horizontal; on equality (*with*); even; in same line or plane (*with*). *v.* make level, even, or uniform;

place on same level; lay low, raze, abolish; take aim *at*. ~ **crossing**, intersection of road and railway etc. at same level. ~-**headed**, mentally well-balanced. **lĕv'elled** (-*eld*) *a*.; **lĕv'eller**, ~**ling** *nn*.; ~**ly** *adv*.

lē'ver *n*. bar or other rigid structure used as mechanical aid to raise weight; tool used in prising. *v*. use lever; move, act upon, (as) with lever. ~**age** *n*. power, advantage gained by use, of lever; influence.

lĕv'erèt *n*. young hare.

lĕvī'athan *n*. (bibl.) sea monster; huge ship; anything large of its kind.

lĕv'ĭtāte *v*. (make) rise and float in air. ~**tā'tion** *n*.

Lē'vīte *n*. one of tribe of Levi, esp. assisting priests in care of (Jewish) temple etc. **Lĕvĭt'ical** *a*. of Levites or their duties.

lĕv'ĭtў *n*. want of thought, unseasonable jocularity, frivolity.

lĕv'ў *n*. collecting of tax or compulsory payment; enrolling of soldiers etc.; amount or number levied. *v.t*. raise or impose compulsorily; extort; enlist, enrol (soldiers etc.).

lewd *a*. lustful, indecent.

Lew'is gŭn (lōō-) *n*. kind of light machine-gun.

lĕxĭcŏg'rapher, **lĕxĭcŏg'raphў** *nn*. maker, making, of dictionaries.

lĕx'ĭcon *n*. dictionary.

ley (lā) *n*. land temporarily under grass.

Ley'den jär (lī-) *n*. kind of electrical condenser.

L.F. *abbr*. low frequency.

L.G. *abbr*. Life Guards; Low German.

L.I. *abbr*. Light Infantry; Long Island.

līabil'itў *n*. being liable; (pl.) debts etc. for which one is liable.

lī'able *a*. legally bound, subject *to*, answerable *for*; exposed or apt *to*.

līai'son (-zn) *n*. illicit amour; connection, touch, intercommunication (*between*, *with*). **liaise'** (-z) *v.i*. (colloq.) establish or maintain liaison (*with*).

līa'na (-ah-) *n*. kinds of twining plant in tropical forests.

lī'ar *n*. (esp. habitual) teller of lie(s).

lī'as *n*. blue limestone rich in fossils.

Lib. *abbr*., *Liber* [L], Book; Liberal.

lībā'tion (*or* lĭ-) *n*. drink-offering; (joc.) potation.

lī'bel *n*. (publishing of) written etc. statement damaging to person's reputation; false defamatory statement. *v.t*. defame falsely, misrepresent maliciously. **lī'bellous** *a*.

lĭb'eral *a*. open-handed, generous; abundant; open-minded, unprejudiced; (pol. etc.) of Liberal party, (moderately) progressive, favouring individual liberty, democratic reform, etc. *n*. holder of liberal views, member of Liberal party. ~**ĭsm** *n*. **lĭberăl'ĭtў** *n*. (esp.) munificence; freedom from prejudice. ~**īze** *v.t*.

lĭb'erāte *v.t*. set at liberty, release. ~**ā'tion**, ~**ātor** *nn*.

lĭbertār'ĭan *n*. & *a*. (person) advocating or permitting (extreme) liberty of thought and action.

lĭb'ertĭne (*or* -ēn) *n*. licentious or dissolute man. ~**nĭsm** *n*.

lĭb'ertў *n*. being free, freedom; right or power to do as one pleases; piece of presumption; (pl.) privileges enjoyed by prescription or grant. ~-**man**, sailor ashore on leave.

lĭbĭd'ĭnous *a*. lustful.

lĭbī'dō (*or* -bē-) *n*. sexual drive, esp. as motive force of human activity.

Lī'bra, Scales, seventh constellation and sign of zodiac.

lī'brarў *n*. collection of books or place in which it is kept; reading- and writing-room in house. **lībrār'ĭan** *n*. custodian of library.

lĭbrĕtt'ō *n*. (pl. -*ti*, pr. -tē, -*os*), text of opera etc. **lĭbrĕtt'ist** *n*.

lice : see **louse**.

lī'cence *n*. formal authority to marry, carry on some trade, etc.; document conveying it; (excessive) liberty of action; licentiousness. **lī'cense** *v.t*. authorize; grant licence to or for; authorize use of, esp. for sale of alcoholic drinks. ~**d victualler**, innkeeper with licence to sell alcohol. **līcensee'** *n*. holder of licence.

līcĕn'tiate (-shĭ-) *n*. holder of certificate from collegiate or examining body.

licĕn'tious *a.* lascivious, lewd.

li'chen (-k-; *or* lich'-) *n.* plant organism composed of fungus associated with alga growing on rocks, trees, etc.

li'chi (-chē; *or* lē-) *n.* (sweetish pulpy fruit of) Chinese tree.

lick *v.t.* pass tongue over; take *off* or *up* by licking; play lightly over; (sl.) thrash, defeat. *n.* act of licking; smart blow; small quantity. **~spittle,** toady. **~ing** *n.* thrashing, defeat.

lic'tor *n.* Roman official bearing axe and rods before magistrate.

lid *n.* cover for aperture, esp. at top of vessel; eye-lid.

li'dō (lē-) *n.* public open-air swimming-pool or pleasure-beach.

lie[1] *n.* intentional false statement; imposture; false belief. *v.i.* (pres. p. *lȳing*), tell lie(s); be deceptive.

lie[2] *v.i.* (pres. p. *lȳing*; p.t. *lay*, p.p. *lain*), be in or assume horizontal position on supporting surface; be at rest on something; be situated, spread out to view, etc.; remain, be; be comprised; (law) be sustainable or admissible. *n.* way thing lies; **~** *of the land,* posture of affairs. **~-in,** (colloq.) lying in bed late in morning.

lief *adv.* (arch.) willingly.

liege *a.* (arch.) entitled to receive or bound to give feudal service or allegiance. *n.* liege lord; vassal, subject.

lien (lē'*en*) *n.* right to hold property till debt on it is paid.

lieu (lū) *n.* *in* **~,** instead (*of*).

Lieut., Lieut.-Col., Lieut.-Gen. *abbr.* Lieutenant; Lieutenant-Colonel, -General.

lieutĕn'ant (lĕft-; nav. let-; U.S. loōt-) *n.* vicegerent or deputy or subordinate commander; officer next in rank below captain; (nav.) junior officer. **~-colonel,** mil. officer next in rank below colonel. **~-commander,** nav. officer between commander and lieutenant in rank. **~-general,** mil. officer between general and major-general in rank. **~ancȳ** *n.*

life *n.* (pl. *lives*), active principle peculiar to animals and plants; living state; living things and their movements; energy or vivacity; events of individual's existence or written story of them; business and pleasures of world. **~belt,** belt of buoyant material to support body in water. **~-blood,** blood necessary to life; (fig.) vitalizing influence. **~boat,** boat for saving life in storms. **~buoy,** appliance for keeping person afloat. **~-guard,** bodyguard of soldiers; person watching against accidents to bathers. **L~ Guards,** regiment of household cavalry. **~-preserver,** short stick with loaded end. **~-size,** of same size as object represented. **~time,** duration of life. **~less** *a.* dead; lacking animation etc. **~like** *a.* exactly like real person or thing. **li'fer** *n.* (sl.) sentence of, one sentenced to, life imprisonment.

lift *v.* raise to higher level; take up, hoist; elevate; steal, plagiarize; (of cloud etc.) rise, disperse. *n.* lifting; layer of leather in heel; help, esp. given to walker by taking him some distance in vehicle; apparatus for hoisting or lifting, esp. for taking people or goods from one floor or level to another; lifting power.

lig'ament *n.* tough fibrous tissue binding bones together.

lig'ature *n.* tie or bandage; (mus.) slur or tie; (print.) two or more letters joined (æ, fl, ffl, etc.). *v.t.* bind or connect with or in ligature.

li'ger (-g-) *n.* offspring of lion and tigress.

light[1] (līt) *n.* natural agent that makes things visible; presence or effect of this; source of light; (pl.) traffic lights; means of procuring fire; brightness of eyes or aspect; mental illumination; way thing presents itself to mind. *a.* (of place) having plenty of light; (of colours) pale, not deep. *v.* (*lĭt* or *lighted*), set burning begin burning; give light to; show way with light; brighten with animation. **~house,** structure with beacon light for guiding or warning ships. **~ship,** anchored ship with beacon light. **~-year,** distance light travels in one year as unit of measurement. **ligh'ter**[1] *n.* (esp.) device for producing light.

light[2] (līt) *a.* not heavy; of little weight or low specific gravity; deficient in weight; easy to wield or digest or do; not ponderous; elegant; not grave or important; trivial; inconstant; loose; not dense or tenacious. *adv.* lightly. *v.i.* (lĭt or *lighted*), come by chance (*upon*); (arch.) alight. **~ engine,** railway engine with no train attached. **~-fingered,** thievish. **~-headed,** delirious. **~-hearted,** gay, untroubled. **~-heavy weight,** boxing weight (12 st. 7 lb.). **~ horse,** light-armed cavalry. **~ infantry,** light-armed foot-soldiers. **~-minded,** flighty, frivolous, irresponsible. **~weight,** person or thing under average weight; boxing weight (9 st. 9 lb.).

ligh'ten[1] *v.* make or grow lighter; reduce weight or load of; relieve of care; mitigate.

ligh'ten[2] *v.* make or grow bright; flash; emit lightning.

lighter[1] : see **light**[1].

ligh'ter[2] *n.* boat for loading and unloading ships not brought to wharf etc. **~age, ~man** *nn.*

light'ning *n.* visible electric discharge between clouds or cloud and ground. **~-conductor, ~-rod,** metal rod or wire fixed to building etc. to divert lightning to earth.

lights *n.pl.* lungs of sheep, pigs, etc. as food.

light'some *a.* gracefully light; merry, agile.

lig'neous *a.* woody.

lig'nīte *n.* brown coal of woody texture.

lig'num vī'tae *n.* kinds of hard--wooded tree of W. Indies etc.

līke *a.* similar, resembling; such as, characteristic of; in promising state or right mood for. *prep.* in manner of; to same degree as. *adv.* probably; (vulg.) so to speak. *n.* counterpart, equal; like thing or person; (pl.) likings. *v.* find agreeable or satisfactory; feel attracted by; wish for. **lī'k(e)able** *a.*

līke'lihŏŏd (-kl-) *n.* probability.

līke'lў (-kl-) *a.* probable; such as may well happen or be or prove true; to be expected *to*; promising, apparently suitable. *adv.* probably.

lī'ken *v.t.* represent as similar *to.*

līke'nèss (-kn-) *n.* resemblance; semblance; portrait.

līke'wise (-kwīz) *adv.* & *conj.* (bibl.) similarly; also, moreover.

lī'kĭng *n.* one's taste; regard or taste or predilection *for.*

lī'lac *n.* kinds of shrub with fragrant usu. pale pinkish-violet blossoms; colour of these. *a.* lilac-coloured.

lĭlĭā'ceous *a.* of lily kind.

Lĭllĭpū'tian *a.* diminutive.

lĭlt *v.* sing rhythmically or melodiously. *n.* (song with) marked rhythmical cadence.

lĭl'ў *n.* kinds of bulbous plant with large showy flowers; heraldic fleur--de-lis. **~ of the valley,** spring flower with small fragrant white bells.

lĭmb[1] (-m) *n.* edge of surface; edge of sun, moon, etc.

lĭmb[2] (-m) *n.* leg, arm, or wing; main branch of tree; branch of cross; spur of mountain.

lĭm'ber[1] *n.* detachable front of gun--carriage. *v.t.* attach limber to (gun).

lĭm'ber[2] *a.* flexible; lithe, agile. *v.* make limber or supple, esp. by exercise; **~ up,** exercise in preparation for athletic etc. exertion.

lĭm'bō *n.* (pl. *-os*), region on border of hell, supposed abode of just who died before Christ's coming and of unbaptized infants; condition of neglect or oblivion.

līme[1] *n.* white caustic substance got by burning kinds of rock. *v.t.* smear (twigs), catch (bird), with bird-lime; treat with lime. **~kiln,** furnace for making lime. **~light,** intense white light formerly used as spotlight etc. in theatre; (fig.) glare of publicity. **~stone,** rock consisting chiefly of calcium carbonate.

līme[2] *n.* round acid fruit of lemon kind; (drink made from) juice of this.

līme[3] (-tree) *n.* ornamental tree with heart-shaped leaves.

lĭm'erĭck *n*. kind of five-line jingle or nonsense verse.

lī'mey *n*. (U.S. sl.) English sailor, Englishman.

lĭm'ĭt *n*. bounding line, terminal point, bound that may not or cannot be passed. *v.t.* set limits to; serve as limit to; restrict; (*p.p.*) scanty. ~arў *a*. restrictive. ~ā'- tion *n*. limiting; limited condition, disability; limiting rule or circumstance.

lĭmn (-m) *v.t.* (arch.) paint (picture); portray. **lĭm'ner** *n*.

lĭm'ousine (-ōōzēn) *n*. motor-car with closed body and partition behind driver.

lĭmp¹ *v.i.* go with lame gait; (of verse) halt. *n*. limping gait.

lĭmp² *a*. not stiff or springy; without energy.

lĭm'pėt *n*. mollusc with low conical shell adhering tightly to rocks.

lĭm'pĭd *a*. transparently clear. **lĭmpĭd'itў** *n*.

lī'nage *n*. (payment according to) number of lines in printed matter.

lĭnch'pĭn *n*. pin passed through axle- -end to keep wheel on.

Lincs. *abbr*. Lincolnshire.

lĭnc'tus *n*. syrupy etc. preparation for soothing throat etc.

lĭn'den *n*. lime-tree.

līne¹ *n*. piece of cord serving some purpose; wire over which telegraphic etc. messages travel; long narrow mark; row of persons or things; one of very narrow horizontal strips in which televised scenes are photographed etc.; single verse of poetry; lineage; series of things, esp. ships etc. following same route; track or course or direction; limit or boundary; contour or outline; equator; measure of one-twelfth of inch; (pl., mil.) set of field-works or boundaries of encampment; regular regiments, esp. infantry. *v*. mark with lines; post men or take post or stand at intervals along (road etc.). ~s'man, soldier of line regiment; umpire's or referee's assistant deciding where or whether ball touches or crosses line.

līne² *v.t.* apply layer of usu. different material to inside of; fill (purse etc.); serve as lining for. **lī'ning** *n*.

lĭn'ėage *n*. lineal descent, ancestry.

lĭn'ėal *a*. in direct line of descent or ancestry.

lĭn'ėament *n*. (usu. pl.) distinctive feature(s) or characteristic(s), esp. of face.

lĭn'ėar *a*. of or in lines; long and narrow and of uniform breadth.

lĭn'ėn *a*. made of flax. *n*. linen cloth; articles made of this, cotton, etc.; undergarments, bed-linen. ~fold, (of panelling) with carved decoration representing folded or pleated linen.

lī'ner *n*. one of line of passenger- -ships, aircraft, etc.

lĭng¹ *n*. long slender sea-fish.

lĭng² *n*. kinds of heather.

lĭng'er (-ngg-) *v.i.* be slow to depart; seem long; stay about, dally; be protracted.

lingerie (lă'nzherē) *n*. women's underclothes.

lĭng'ō (-ngg-) *n*. (pl. -*oes*), foreign language; queer way of talking.

lĭng'ual (-nggw-) *a*. of tongue; of speech or languages.

lĭn'guĭst (-nggw-) *n*. person skilled in (foreign) languages. **lĭnguĭs'tĭc** *a*. of study of languages; of language. **lĭnguĭs'tĭcs** *n.pl.* study of language.

lĭn'ĭment *n*. (oily) liquid for rubbing bruised etc. part.

lĭnk¹ *n*. one loop or ring of chain etc.; thing or person that unites; member of series; measure of 7·92 in. *v*. connect, join *to*, *together*, etc.; clasp or intertwine.

lĭnk² *n*. (hist.) torch of pitch and tow for lighting people along streets.

lĭnks *n.pl.* ground on which golf is played.

Linn. *abbr*. Linnaeus.

Lĭnnae'an *a*. of Linnaeus or his classification of plants.

lĭnn'ėt *n*. song-bird.

lī'nō *n*. linoleum. ~cut, (print from) design cut on block of linoleum.

lĭnō'lėum *n*. floor-covering of canvas thickly coated with oxidized linseed-oil.

lī'notўpe *n*. machine casting line of type at single operation of casting.

lĭn'seed *n*. seed of flax.

lĭnsey-wŏŏl'sey (-zĭ, -zĭ) *n*. dress--fabric of cotton warp and wool weft.

lĭn'stŏck *n*. (hist.) staff holding match for firing gun.

lĭnt *n*. soft material for dressing wounds etc.; fluff.

lĭn'tel *n*. horizontal timber or stone over door or window.

lī'on *n*. large powerful carnivorous beast of cat family; courageous person; celebrity. lī'onĕss *n*. lī'onīze *v.t.* treat as celebrity.

lĭp *n*. either edge of opening of mouth; edge of vessel, cavity, etc.; (sl.) impudence. ~stick, stick of cosmetic for colouring lips.

lĭ'quefȳ *v*. make or become liquid. ~făc'tion *n*.

lĭquĕs'cent *a*. becoming liquid.

liqueur' (-kūr; *or* -kēr) *n*. kinds of strong alcoholic sweet liquor with aromatic flavouring.

lĭ'quĭd *a*. having consistence like that of water or oil; neither solid nor gaseous; having clearness of water; (of sounds) flowing, clear, pure; (of assets etc.) easily convertible into cash. *n*. liquid substance; sound of *l* or *r*. lĭquĭd'ĭtȳ *n*.; lĭ'quĭdīze *v.t.*

lĭ'quĭdāte *v.t.* pay off (debt), wind up affairs of (company etc.); put an end to, get rid of (freq. by violent means). ~ā'tion *n*. (esp.) *go into* ~, have affairs wound up, become bankrupt. ~ātor *n*.

lĭ'quor (-ker) *n*. alcoholic or other drink; liquid used in or resulting from some process.

lĭ'quorĭce (-ker-) *n*. black substance used in medicine and as sweetmeat; plant from whose root it is obtained.

lisle thread (līl) *n*. fine hard-twisted kind of thread.

lĭsp *v*. pronounce sibilants with sound like *th*; say lispingly. *n*. lisping pronunciation.

lĭss'om *a*. lithe, agile.

lĭst[1] *n*. (pl.) palisades enclosing tilting-ground; scene of contest.

lĭst[2] *n*. roll or catalogue or inventory. *v.t.* enter in list.

lĭst[3] *v*. (3 sing. pres. *list* or *listeth*; past *list* or *listed*), (arch.) desire, choose (*to do*).

lĭst[4] *n*. inclination of ship etc. to one side. *v.i.* lean over to one side.

lĭ'sten (-sn) *v.i.* make effort to hear something, hear with attention; give ear *to*; ~ *in*, listen to radio transmission, tap telephone communication, etc.

lĭst'lĕss *a*. without inclination or energy; languid.

lit, *p.t.* & *p.p.* of light[1],[2].

lĭt'anȳ *n*. series of petitions for use in church services.

lĭt'eracȳ *n*. ability to read and write.

lĭt'eral *a*. of letters of alphabet; exactly corresponding to original; giving words their ordinary sense.

lĭt'erarȳ *a*. of or constituting or concerned with literature.

lĭt'erate *a*. able to read and write. *n*. literate person.

lĭterā'tī (*or* -ahtĭ) *n.pl.* lettered or learned persons.

lĭterā'tĭm *adv*. letter for letter.

lĭt'erature *n*. books and written composition valued for form and style; writings of period, country, etc.; (colloq.) printed matter.

līthe (-dh) *a*. pliant, supple; easily bent.

lĭth'ia water *n*. mineral water containing lithium salts.

lĭth'ium *n*. soft silver-white metallic element.

lĭth'ograph (-ah-) *v.t.* engrave or draw on stone and print impressions from it. *n*. such impression. lĭthŏg'rapher, lĭthŏg'raphy *nn*.; lĭthŏgrăph'ĭc *a*.

lĭthŏt'omy *n*. operation of cutting for stone in bladder.

Lit. Hum. *abbr.*, *Literae Humaniores* [L], the more humane studies.

lĭt'igant *a*. engaged in lawsuit. *n*. party to lawsuit.

lĭt'igāte *v*. go to law; contest at law. ~ā'tion *n*.

lĭtī'gious *a*. fond of litigation; contentious.

lĭt'mus *n*. blue colouring-matter turned red by acids.

lī'tre (lē-) *n*. unit of capacity in metric system (about 1¾ pints).

Litt.D. *abbr*. Doctor of Letters.

lĭtt'er *n*. carrying-couch formerly

used as carriage; kind of stretcher for wounded; bedding for beasts; odds and ends, rubbish, lying about; young brought forth at one birth. *v.* provide (horse etc.) with litter; make (place) untidy; bring forth young.

littérateur (lēterahter') *n.* man of letters. [F]

litt'le *a.* not great or big or much; small in quantity; short in stature or distance or time; unimportant; paltry or mean. *n.* not much, only a small amount; (for a) short time or distance; ~ **by** ~, by degrees. *adv.* to a small extent only; not at all. ~ **people,** fairies.

litt'oral *a.* of or on or near shore. *n.* region lying along shore.

lit'urgy (-ter-) *n.* Church's formularies for public worship. **litūr'gical** *a.*

live[1] *a.* that is alive or real or active; not dead or fictitious or exhausted or recorded; capable of being exploded, kindled, etc.; charged with electricity. ~**-oak,** Amer. evergreen tree. ~**stock,** domestic animals kept or dealt in for use or profit. ~ **weight,** weight of animal etc. before it is killed. ~ **wire,** (fig.) forceful and energetic person.

live[2] *v.* have life; be or continue alive; subsist; conduct oneself in specified way; enjoy life to full; pass or spend; dwell.

live'lihood (-vl-) *n.* means of living, sustenance.

live'long (-vl-) *a.* whole (tedious or delightful) length of.

live'ly (-vl-) *a.* lifelike or realistic; full of life or energy; gay; (joc.) exciting or dangerous.

li'ven *v.* brighten (*up*).

liv'er[1] *n.* one who lives in specified way.

liv'er[2] *n.* organ secreting bile and purifying blood; dark reddish-brown colour; flesh of animal's liver as food; diseased or disordered liver. ~**ish,** ~**y**[2] *aa.* having symptoms of disordered liver.

liv'erwort (-wert) *n.* kinds of primitive plant allied to mosses.

liv'ery[1] *n.* allowance of provender for horses; distinctive clothes worn by member of City Company or person's servant. ~ **company,** one of London City Companies that formerly wore livery. ~**man,** member of livery company or keeper of livery stables. ~ **stables,** stables where horses are kept for owner at fixed charge or let out for hire.

liv'id *a.* of bluish leaden colour.

liv'ing *n.* (esp.) livelihood; benefice. *a.* (esp.) now alive; (of likeness) exact; (of rock) in native condition and site; *within* ~ *memory,* within memory of people still living. ~**-room,** room for general day use. ~ **wage,** on which it is possible to live.

liz'ard *n.* kinds of (usu.) four-legged reptile.

L.J. *abbr.* Lord Justice.

ll. *abbr.* lines.

lla'ma, la'ma[2] (lah-) *n.* woolly-haired ruminant used in S. America as beast of burden.

LL.B., LL.D. *abbr.* Bachelor, Doctor, of Laws.

Lloyd's (loidz) *n.* incorporated society of marine underwriters. ~ **register,** annual classified list of ships.

L.M.S.(R.) *abbr.* London Midland and Scottish (Railway).

L.N.E.(R.), L.N.W.(R.) *abbr.* London and North Eastern, North Western, (Railway).

lō *int.* (arch.) look! behold!

loach *n.* small fresh-water fish.

load *n.* what is carried or borne; amount that cart etc. can carry; material object or force acting as weight or clog; pressure of superstructure on arch etc.; total amount of electric current supplied at given time; (pl., colloq.) heaps, lots, plenty. *v.* put load on; put (goods etc.) aboard or on vehicle etc.; burden; charge (gun etc.); supply in abundance or excess *with*; adulterate to increase weight, strength, etc. of; add extra charge to (insurance premium); charge (question) with hidden implication. ~**line,** ship's waterline when laden. ~**-shedding,** cutting-off of electricity supply to area to avoid overloading of generators.

load'stŏne, lōde- *n.* magnetic oxide of iron; piece of it used as magnet; thing that attracts.

loaf¹ *n.* (pl. *-ves*), piece of bread baked alone or as part of batch. **~ sugar,** sugar cut into lumps.

loaf² *v.i.* spend time idly; hang about; saunter. **~er** *n.*

loam *n.* rich soil of clay, sand, and decayed vegetable matter; clay paste for brickmaking etc. **loa'mў** *a.*

loan *n.* thing lent; sum to be returned with or without interest. *v.t.* grant loan of. **~-word,** word adopted in one language from another.

loath, lōth *pred. a.* disinclined, reluctant, unwilling.

loathe (-dh) *v.t.* regard with disgust, detest. **loa'thing** (-dh-) *n.* **loath'-some** *a.* repulsive, odious.

lŏb *v.t.* toss, bowl, or send (ball) with slow or high-pitched motion. *n.* ball bowled underhand at cricket or sent high in air at lawn-tennis.

lō'bar *a.* of lobe, esp. of lung.

lŏbb'ў *n.* porch, entrance-hall; ante--room or corridor; (in legislative buildings) hall open to public; (in House of Commons etc.) one of two corridors to which members retire to vote; (U.S.) group of lobbyists representing particular interest. *v.* interview (members of legislature) in lobby, try to influence legislation by this and other personal contacts. **~ist** *n.*

lōbe *n.* roundish and flattish projecting or pendulous part of organ, freq. one of two or more divided by fissure; lower pendulous external part of ear.

lobē'lĭa *n.* garden flower used esp. as edging.

lobŏt'omў *n.* leucotomy.

lŏb'ster *n.* long-tailed clawed shellfish; its flesh as food. **~-pot,** basket for trapping lobsters.

lŏb'worm (-wẽrm) *n.* large earthworm as fishing-bait.

lō'cal *a.* of place; belonging or peculiar to some place or places. *n.* (colloq.) near-by public house; (U.S.) branch of trade union.

~ colour, (esp.) details characteristic of place or time inserted in literary work to give actuality. **~ option,** right given to district to prohibit local sale of alcoholic liquor. **~ism** *n.* attachment to place; local idiom etc. **~īze** *v.t.* invest with characteristics of place; restrict to particular place.

locale' (-ahl) *n.* scene or locality of operations or events.

locăl'itў *n.* thing's position; site or scene of something.

locăte' *v.* state locality of; discover exact place of; establish in place; (pass.) be situated; (U.S. colloq.) take up residence. **locā'tion** *n.* (esp.) place other than studio where (part of) film is photographed.

lŏc'ative *a. & n.* (case) denoting place where.

loc. cit. *abbr., loco citato* [L], in passage already quoted.

lŏch (-ch) *n.* Scottish lake or arm of sea.

lŏck¹ *n.* tuft of hair or wool; (pl.) hair of head.

lŏck² *n.* fastening for door etc.; appliance to keep wheel from revolving etc.; mechanism by which gun is fired; section of river or canal confined within sluiced gates; extent to which plane of fore wheels of car etc. can be made to cross that of rear wheels. *v.* fasten with lock; bring or come into rigidly fixed position; jam or catch or make catch; store *up* inaccessibly; go, convey (boat) through lock. **~jaw,** kind of tetanus in which jaws are rigidly closed. **~-keeper,** custodian of river or canal lock. **~out,** exclusion of workmen by employer. **~smith,** maker and mender of locks. **~-up,** (time of) locking up school etc. for night; room etc. for detention of prisoners.

lŏck'er *n.* (esp.) small cupboard, esp. one reserved for individual in public room.

lŏck'ét *n.* small case for portrait etc. usu. hung from neck.

lōcomō'tion *n.* going from one place to another; power of accomplishing this.

lōcomō'tĭve *a.* of or effecting locomotion; not stationary. *n.* (esp. steam-) engine that goes from place to place by its own power.

lō'cum *n.* deputy acting for clergyman, doctor, etc. in his absence.

lō'cus *n.* (pl. -*ci*, pr. -*si*), exact place of something; (math.) curve etc. made by all points satisfying certain conditions, or by defined motion of point or line or surface.

lō'cust *n.* destructive winged insect migrating in swarms; kinds of tree and their fruit.

locū'tion *n.* style of speech; word etc. considered in regard to style.

lōde *n.* vein of metal ore. ~**star**, star that is steered by, esp. pole-star. ~**stone** : see **load-stone**.

lŏdge *n.* (arch.) small house; gate--keeper's cottage or porter's room; (of freemasons etc.) members of branch, place where they meet. *v.* provide with sleeping-quarters; reside as lodger; deposit for security or attention; fix in; settle; place. **lŏdg'er** *n.* person paying for accommodation in another's house. **lŏdg'ing** *n.* place where one lodges. **lŏdge'ment** (-jm-) *n.* stable position gained, foothold; accumulation of intercepted matter.

lŏft *n.* attic; room over stable; pigeon-house; gallery in church or hall. *v.t.* send (golf-ball) high; slope (face of club) backward from vertical.

lŏf'tў *a.* of imposing height; haughty; exalted, high-flown, sublime.

lŏg[1] *n.* unhewn piece of felled tree; any large rough piece of wood; apparatus for gauging ship's speed; detailed record of ship's voyage, aircraft's flight, performance of machine, etc. ~**-rolling**, (esp. unprincipled) combination for mutual help. ~**wood**, (wood of) Amer. tree used in dyeing. *v.t.* (esp.) enter in log; (of ship etc.) make (distance). **lŏgg'ing** (-g-) *n.* (esp.) felling, cutting, and transporting timber.

lō'g[2] *abbr.* logarithm.

lō'ganbĕrrў *n.* hybrid between raspberry and Amer. blackberry.

lŏg'an(-stōne) *n.* poised heavy stone rocking at touch.

lŏg'arĭthm *n.* one of class of arithmetical functions tabulated for simplifying computation. **lŏgarĭth'mĭc** *a.*

lŏgg'erhead *n.* at ~*s*, disagreeing or disputing (*with*).

lŏgg'ia (-jya) *n.* open-sided gallery or arcade, esp. looking on open court; roofed but open-sided extension to house etc.

logging : see **log**[1].

lŏ'gĭc *n.* (scheme of or treatise on) science of reasoning; chain of reasoning, arguments. **lŏ'gĭcal** *a.* of logic; in conformity with principles of logic; capable of correct reasoning. **logĭ'cian** *n.*

logĭs'tĭcs *n.pl.* (esp. arithmetical) calculation; art of moving, quartering, and supplying troops etc. **logĭs'tĭc** *a.*

lŏg'os *n.* (theol.) Word, second person of Trinity.

loin *n.* (pl.) part of back between hip bone and false ribs; (sing.) joint of meat cut from loins. ~-**cloth**, worn round loins.

loi'ter *v.i.* linger on way, hang about; be dilatory.

lŏll *v.* recline or stand in lazy attitude; hang *out*.

Lŏll'ard *n.* English 14th cent. heretic holding views like those of Wyclif. ~**ism**, ~**ry** *nn.*

lŏll'ĭpŏp *n.* large boiled sweet on stick.

lŏll'op *v.i.* move in clumsy bounds.

lŏlly *n.* lollipop; water ice etc. on stick; (sl.) money.

Londin., London. *abbr.* (Bishop) of London.

Lon'don (lŭ-). ~ **particular**, (arch.) thick London fog. ~ **pride**, kind of pink-flowered saxifrage. ~**er** *n.*

lōne *a.* (usu. poet. or rhet.) solitary, single; lonely. ~ **hand**, hand played, person playing, against rest at euchre etc.; *play* ~ *hand*, act alone. ~ **wolf**, person acting, living, etc. alone. **lō'ner** *n.* (U.S. etc.) lone wolf. ~**some** *a.* lonely; *by, on, one's* ~*some*, all alone.

lōne'lў (-nl-) *a.* solitary, isolated; unfrequented; dejected by feeling alone.

lŏng[1] *a.* measuring much from end

to end in space or time; (colloq.) tall; protracted; dilatory; of specified length. *n.* long interval or period; long vowel or syllable. *adv.* for or by long time; throughout specified time; (comp.) after implied point of time. **~boat,** sailing-ship's largest boat. **~-bow,** bow drawn by hand and discharging long arrow; *draw the ~-bow,* exaggerate or invent. **~ chance,** involving great uncertainty. **~-cloth,** kind of calico. **~ drink,** one large in quantity or served in tall glass. **~hand,** ordinary writing. **~-headed,** sagacious. **~ hop,** short-pitched ball in cricket. **~-jump,** jump measured along ground. **~ odds,** very uneven chances. **~ primer,** size of printing type (10 point). **~ run:** *in the ~ run,* ultimately. **~shanks,** kind of plover. **~ ship,** ancient ship of war for large number of rowers. **~shore,** found or employed on or frequenting the shore. **~ sight,** vision that sees (only) distant objects clearly. **~-sighted,** having long sight; having prevision, sagacious. **~stop,** man fielding straight behind wicket-keeper. **~-suffering,** bearing provocation patiently. **~-term,** involving, lasting, designed for, etc. a long time. **~-winded,** tedious, prolix. **~ways, ~wise** *advv.* in direction parallel with thing's length.

lŏng² *v.i.* yearn, wish vehemently (*for*). **~ing** *n. & a.;* **~ingly** *adv.*

long.³ *abbr.* longitude.

lŏngĕv'ĭtў (-j-) *n.* long life.

longing : see **long²**.

lŏn'gĭtūde (-j-) *n.* angular distance east or west along equator from meridian. **~tū'dĭnal** *a.* of or in length; lying longways; of longitude.

lōō¹ *n.* round card game. **~ table,** kind of round or oval table.

loo² *n.* (colloq.) lavatory.

lōō'bў *n.* silly fellow.

lōō'fah *n.* fibrous pod of plant used as flesh-brush.

lŏŏk *v.* use or direct one's eyes; make effort to see; make search; express by eyes; have specified appearance or aspect; face or be turned in specified direction; **~ down on,** consider oneself superior to; **~ forward to,** anticipate (with pleasure); **~ in,** make short visit; **~ out,** (esp.) be vigilant, be prepared *for;* **~ up,** (esp.) improve; **~ up to,** respect. *n.* act of looking; gaze or glance; expression of eyes; appearance or aspect; (pl.) personal appearance. **~-in,** (esp.) chance of success. **~ing-glass,** mirror, quick-silvered glass. **~-out,** watch; post of observation; man etc. stationed to watch; view; prospect of luck; person's own concern.

lŏŏk'er-on *n.* onlooker.

lōŏm¹ *n.* apparatus for weaving fabrics; (inboard part of) shaft of oar.

lōŏm² *v.i.* appear dimly; be seen in vague magnified or threatening shape.

lōōn¹ *n.* (Sc.) scamp; fellow.

lōōn² *n.* kinds of water bird.

lōō'ny *n. & a.* (sl.) lunatic.

lōŏp *n.* figure made by curve crossing itself; similarly shaped part of cord etc. so crossing or meeting; knitting stitch; **~ the ~,** (cause aircraft to) describe vertical loop in air. *v.* make loop or loops in; form loop; fasten with loop or loops. **~-line,** railway or telegraph line that leaves main line and joins it again. **~er** *n.* (esp.) kinds of caterpillar.

lōŏp'-hōle *n.* narrow vertical slit in wall; (fig.) means of evasion or escape.

lōō'pў *a.* (sl.) crazy.

lōōse *a.* released from bonds or restraint; not compact or fixed or tight; not close-fitting; not exact or literal; careless; wanton, incontinent; *at a ~ end,* without definite occupation. *n.* vent; (Rugby) open forward play; *on the ~,* without restrictions or restraint. *adv.* loosely, with loose hold. *v.t.* let loose, untie; free from constraint; detach from moorings etc. **~ box,** stall in which horse can move about. **~-leaf,** (of notebook etc.) with leaves separate and detachable.

lōō'sen v. make or become loose or looser; ~ *up*, relax, limber up.

loose'strīfe (-s-s-) n. kinds of flowering plant.

lōōt n. booty, spoil. v. take loot from; carry off loot.

lŏp[1] v.t. cut away branches or twigs of (tree); cut off.

lŏp[2] v.i. hang limply. ~-**ear**, drooping ear; rabbit with lop-ears. ~-**sided**, with one side lower, smaller, heavier, etc.

lōpe n. & v.i. (run with) long smooth bounds.

loq. abbr., *loquitur* [L], speaks.

loquā'cious a. talkative, babbling. **loquă'citў** n.

lō'quat (-ŏt) n. (small reddish fruit of) Chinese and Japanese tree.

lōrd n. feudal superior, master, ruler, chief, owner, husband; God or Christ; nobleman; first word of personal style of marquis, earl, viscount, or baron; title prefixed to Christian name of younger son of duke or marquis; honorary title of e.g. bishops, Lord Mayors, judges of supreme court. int. expressing wonder etc. v. play lord *over*. ~**s and ladies**, wild arum. **L~'s day**, Sunday. **L~'s prayer**, that beginning 'Our father'. **L~'s supper**, Eucharist. ~**lў** a. haughty, imperious, lofty; of or fit for lord. ~**ship** n. rule, ownership *of*, *over*; estate, domain; *your* ~**ship**, respectful form of address to noblemen, bishops, judges.

lōre n. body of tradition and facts on subject.

lorgnette (lōrnyĕt') n. eyeglasses held in hand, usu. by long handle.

lōrn a. (arch.) desolate, forlorn.

lŏ'rrў n. strong usu. flat open truck for carrying heavy goods by road.

lōr'ў n. kinds of parrot.

lose (lōōz) v. (lŏst), be deprived of; cease to have; let pass from one's control; get rid of; forfeit; be worsted in; suffer loss or detriment, be worse off (*by*); cause loss of to; (*p.p.*) vanished, not to be found, deprived of help or salvation, astray. **lo'ser** n.

lŏss n. losing; what is lost; detriment resulting from losing; *at a* ~, (esp.)

puzzled, at fault. ~ **leader**, article sold at loss to attract custom.

lost : see **lose**.

lŏt n. one of set of objects used to secure chance selection; this method, share or office given by it; share, fortune, destiny; appointed task; piece of land allotted to person, offered for sale, etc.; article or set of articles put up for sale at auction etc.; (colloq.) considerable number or amount; *the* ~, whole number or quantity; *bad* ~, worthless or disreputable person.

loth : see **loath**.

Lothār'iō n. (pl. -*os*), libertine.

lō'tion n. liquid preparation used externally to heal wound etc.

lŏtt'erў n. arrangement for distributing prizes by chance among holders of tickets.

lŏtt'ō n. game of chance with numbers drawn at random.

lō'tus n. legendary plant inducing blissful languor; kinds of water-lily etc.

loud a. strongly audible, sonorous; noisy; (of colour etc.) obtrusive, flashy. adv. loudly. ~-**speaker**, (esp. radio) device for converting electrical impulses into sounds loud enough to be heard at distance.

lough (lŏch) n. (Irish) loch.

lounge (-j) v.i. loll, recline; go lazily; idle. n. spell of, place for, lounging; sofa or deep chair; sitting room in hotel etc. ~-**suit**, man's suit for informal day wear.

lour, lower[2] (lowr) v.i. frown, look sullen; (of sky etc.) look dark and threatening. n. scowl.

louse n. (pl. *līce*), kinds of blood-sucking insect parasitic on mammals; (pl. -*es*), low contemptible person. **lou'sў** (-z-) a. infested with lice; (sl.) very bad; (sl.) abundantly supplied, swarming, *with*.

lout n. hulking or rough mannered fellow. ~**ish** a.

lou'ver, -vre (lōō-) n. erection on roof with unglazed side-openings for ventilation etc.; arrangement of overlapping boards etc. to admit air but exclude rain.

lov'able (lŭ-) a. inspiring affection.

lŏv'age (lŭ-) *n.* kinds of herb used for flavouring etc.

love (lŭv) *n.* fondness, warm affection; sexual passion; sweetheart or loved object; (tennis etc.) no score, nil; *in ~ (with)*, enamoured (of); *make ~*, pay amorous attentions (*to*), engage in sexual intercourse. *v.* be in love (with); feel affection for; delight in; admire; like to see. **~ affair**, temporary or illicit relationship between people in love. **~ all**, state of game before either side has scored. **~-bird**, kinds of small parrot. **~-child**, illegitimate child. **~-in-a-mist**, blue-flowered garden plant. **~-lies-bleeding**, garden plant with drooping red spike. **~-lorn**, pining with love; jilted. **~sick**, languishing with love.

love'less (lŭvl-) *a.* unloving; unloved.

lovely (lŭv'lĭ) *a.* exquisitely beautiful; (colloq.) delightful.

lov'er (lŭ-) *n.* suitor or sweetheart; partner in illicit sexual relations; (pl.) pair in love; admirer or devotee (*of*).

lov'ing (lŭ-) *a.* kind, affectionate. **~-cup**, large drinking-vessel passed round at banquet etc.

low[1] (lō) *n.* moo, sound made by cows. *v.i.* utter low.

low[2] (lō) *a.* not placed high or reaching far up; not attaining high degree; of humble rank; no longer full or abundant; lacking in vigour; degraded or vulgar or rascally. *adv.* in or to low place; on low diet; for low stakes; in low voice; *lie ~*, (esp., sl.) keep quiet or out of way. **~boy**, (U.S.) low chest of drawers. **~brow**, (person) not highly intellectual or cultured. **L~ Church**, Evangelical party in Church of England. **~er case**, (of letters) not capital; (in) small letters. **~er class**, (of) lower orders. **~er deck**, petty officers and men of Navy or ship. **~er orders**, people of inferior social status. **~ pressure**, atmospheric condition sending barometer down. **~ relief**, bas-relief. **L~ Sunday**, Sunday after Easter. **~ tide**, level of ebbed sea; time of

extreme ebb. **~ water**, low tide; *in ~ water*, out of funds.

lower[1] (lō'er) *v.* let or haul down; make or become lower; be degrading to; reduce bodily condition of.

lower[2] : see **lour**.

low'land (lō-) *n.* low-lying country. *a.* of or in such country or Lowlands. **Low'lander**, inhabitant of Lowlands. **Low'lands** (-z), less mountainous part of Scotland.

low'lĭ (lō-) *a.* humble; unpretending.

loy'al *a.* faithful; true to allegiance; devoted to sovereign, mother country, etc. **loy'alĭst** *a.* & *n* (person) remaining loyal to ruler, government etc. **loy'altĭ** *n.*

lŏz'enge (-j) *n.* rhombus or diamond figure, esp. as heraldic bearing; lozenge-shaped thing; small tablet of medicine, flavoured sugar, etc. to be dissolved in mouth.

l.p. *abbr.* large-paper; long-playing record; long primer; low pressure.

L.R.A.M., L.R.C.P., L.R.C.S., L.R.S.M. *abbr.* Licentiate of Royal Academy of Music, College of Physicians, College of Surgeons, Schools of Music.

LSD *abbr.* lysergic acid diethylamide, drug producing schizophrenic symptoms.

L.(£)S.D., l.s.d. *abbr.* pounds, shillings and pence.

L.S.E., L.S.O. *abbr.* London School of Economics, Symphony Orchestra.

L.T. *abbr.* low tension.

Lt., Lt.-Cdr., Lt.-Col., Lt.-Gen. *abbr.* Lieutenant, Lieutenant-Commander, -Colonel, -Generel.

Ltd. *abbr.* Limited.

lŭbb'er *n.* clumsy fellow, lout. **~lĭ** *a.* awkward, unskilful.

lū'brĭcāte (*or* lŏŏ-) *v.t.* oil or grease (machinery); make slippery or smooth with fluid etc. **~cant** *a.* & *n.* lubricating (substance). **~cā'tion** *n.*

lūbrĭ'cĭtĭ (*or* lŏŏ-) *n.* lewdness, wantonness.

lūcerne' (*or* lŏŏ-) *n.* clover-like fodder-plant.

lū'cĭd (*or* lŏŏ-) *a.* free from obscurity; clearly expressed or arranged; bright. **lucĭd'itĭ** *n.*

Lū'cĭfer (*or* lōō-) *n.* morning star; Satan; (*l*~) match.

lŭck *n.* good or ill fortune; chance. **~lèss** *a.* unfortunate; unhappy.

lŭck'ў *a.* favoured by fortune; enjoying good luck; due to luck rather than skill or merit; bringing etc. good luck. **~ dip**, receptacle at bazaars etc. containing small articles, into which each comer dips.

Lucr. *abbr.* Lucretius.

lū'crative (*or* lōō-) *a.* yielding gain, profitable.

lū'cre (*or* lōō-) *n.* pecuniary gain as motive; *filthy* ~, (joc.) money.

lucūbrā'tion (lōō-) *n.* (usu. pl.) esp. pedantic or elaborate literary work.

lū'dĭcrous (*or* lōō-) *a.* absurd, ridiculous; laughable.

lū'dō (*or* lōō-) *n.* game played on board with dice and counters.

lŭff *v.i.* bring ship's head nearer wind.

lŭg¹ *v.* drag with effort or violence; pull hard *at*. *n.* hard or rough pull.

lŭg² *n.* (dial.) ear; projection from casting etc. by which it may be fixed in place.

lŭgg'age *n.* (bags etc. for) traveller's baggage. **~-rack**, shelf for luggage in train etc.

lŭgg'er (-g-) *n.* small ship with four-cornered sails set fore-and-aft. **lŭg'sail** (-sl) *n.* four-cornered sail bent on unequally slung yard.

lugū'brious (lōō-) *a.* doleful.

lŭg'worm (-ērm) *n.* large marine worm used for bait.

lūke'warm (-kw-; *or* lōō-) *a.* neither hot nor cold; half-hearted.

lŭll *v.* send to sleep; soothe; hoodwink; allay; (of storm or noise) lessen, fall quiet. *n.* intermission in storm etc., interval of quiet.

lŭll'abў *n.* soothing refrain or song to put child to sleep.

lŭmbā'gō *n.* painful usu. inflammatory affection of muscles of loins.

lŭm'bar *a.* of loins.

lŭm'ber¹ *n.* disused articles of furniture etc.; useless or cumbrous material; roughly prepared timber. *v.* cumber or obstruct; cut and prepare forest timber. **~jack**, **~man**, feller, dresser, or conveyer of lumber. **~-room**, room for lumber.

lŭm'ber² *v.i.* move in blundering noisy way.

lū'mĭnarў (*or* lōō-) *n.* shedder of light, esp. sun or moon; person noted for learning etc.

lūmĭnĕs'cent (*or* lōō-) *a.* emitting light not due to incandescence. **~ence** *n.*

lū'mĭnous (*or* lōō-) *a.* emitting or full of light, shining; glowing in dark. **lūmĭnŏs'itў** *n.*

lŭmp¹ *n.* compact shapeless mass; whole taken together; protuberance or swelling; heavy ungainly person. *v.* class or mass *together*. **~ sugar**, sugar cut into cubes. **~ sum**, sum including number of items or paid down all at once.

lŭmp² *v.t.* (only in contrast with *like*), put up with ungraciously.

lŭm'pish *a.* heavy; clumsy; dull.

lŭm'pў *a.* full of or covered with lumps; (of water) choppy.

lū'nacў (*or* lōō-) *n.* insanity; folly.

lū'nar (*or* lōō-) *a.* of, in, depending on, or caused by moon. **~ month**, interval between new moons, about 29½ days; (pop.) four weeks.

lū'nāte (*or* lōō-) *a.* crescent-shaped.

lū'natĭc (*or* lōō-) *a.* insane; outrageously foolish. *n.* lunatic person.

lūnā'tion (*or* lōō-) *n.* time from one new moon to next.

lŭnch *n.* midday meal; light refreshment esp. between breakfast and midday dinner. *v.* take lunch; provide lunch for.

lŭn'cheon (-shn) *n.* formal midday meal; lunch.

lūne (*or* lōōn) *n.* figure formed by two arcs enclosing space.

lūnĕtte' (*or* lōō-) *n.* arched aperture in concave ceiling to admit light; semicircular space decorated with painting etc.

lŭng *n.* either of pair of breathing-organs in man and many vertebrates.

lŭnge (-j) *n.* thrust with sword etc.; sudden forward movement, plunge. *v.* make lunge; drive (weapon etc.) violently.

lū'pĭn (*or* lōō-) *n.* kinds of leguminous garden and fodder plant with long tapering flower spikes.

lū′pīne (*or* lōo-) *a.* of or like wolves.

lū′pus (*or* lōo-) *n.* ulcerous disease of skin.

lūrch[1] *n.* *leave in the ~,* desert in difficulties.

lūrch[2] *n.* sudden lean to one side, stagger. *v.i.* make lurch(es), stagger.

lūr′cher *n.* cross-bred dog between collie and greyhound.

lūre *n.* bunch of feathers used to recall hawk; something used to entice; enticing quality. *v.t.* recall with lure; entice.

lūr′id *a.* ghastly, glaring, unnatural, or terrible in colour etc.; sensational.

lūrk *v.i.* keep out of sight; be hidden; be latent or elusive.

lū′scious (-sh*us*) *a.* richly sweet in taste or smell; appealing to senses; cloying.

lŭsh *a.* luxuriant, succulent.

lŭst *n.* passionate enjoyment or desire; lascivious passion. *v.i.* have strong or excessive desire. **~ful** *a.* lascivious.

lŭs′tral *a.* used in lustration.

lŭstrā′tion *n.* ceremonial washing or other rite of purification.

lŭs′tre *n.* quality of shining by reflected light, shining surface; brilliance, splendour; (prismatic glass pendant of) chandelier; (pottery, porcelain, with) iridescent glaze.

lŭs′trous *a.* shining; luminous.

lŭs′trum *n.* (pl. *-tra, -trums*), period of five years.

lŭs′tŷ *a.* healthy and strong; vigorous, lively.

lūte[1] (*or* lōot) *n.* guitar-like musical instrument. **lu′tanist** *n.* lute-player.

lūte[2] (*or* lōot) *n.* composition for making joints airtight etc.

lūtē′tium (-shi*um*; *or* lōo-) *n.* metallic element of rare-earth group.

Lu′theran (lōo-) *a.* of Protestant reformer Martin Luther or Lutheran Church. *n.* member of Lutheran Church. **~ism** *n.*

lŭxūr′iant *a.* profuse, exuberant; florid. **~ance** *n.*

lŭxūr′iāte *v.i.* revel, feel keen delight *in.*

lŭxūr′ious *a.* fond of luxury; self-indulgent; very comfortable.

lŭx′ury (-ksh*eri*) *n.* use of or indulgence in what is choice or costly; refined and intense enjoyment; thing desirable but not essential.

L.W.M. *abbr.* low water mark.

LXX *abbr.* Septuagint.

lycée (lē′sā) *n.* French State secondary school. [F]

lŷch′gāte *n.* roofed gateway of churchyard.

lŷe *n.* water made alkaline with wood ashes etc.; any strong alkaline solution, esp. for washing.

lying : see **lie**[1],[2].

lŷke′-wāke *n.* watch kept at night over dead body.

lŷmph *n.* colourless fluid from tissues or organs of body; matter from cowpox vesicles used in vaccination. **~ăt′ic** *a.* of or secreting lymph; *n.* veinlike vessel conveying lymph.

lŷnch *v.t.* execute by mob action without due process of law.

lŷnx *n.* feline wild beast noted for keen sight.

lyre *n.* obsolete ∪-shaped stringed instrument. **~-bird,** Austral. bird with lyre-shaped tail.

lŷ′ric *a.* of or for lyre; of nature of song; (of poem etc.) directly expressing poet's own sentiments etc. and usu. short; writing lyric poetry. *n.* lyric poem; (freq. pl.) words of song. **~al** *a.* resembling, using language appropriate to, lyric poetry. **~ism** *n.*

M

M, m (ĕm), as Roman numeral, 1,000.

M., M *abbr.* Monsieur; motorway.

m. *abbr.* maiden over; male; married; masculine; metre(s); mile(s); million(s); minute(s).

ma (mah) *n.* (vulg.) mother.

M.A. *abbr.* Master of Arts.

ma'am (mahm, măm, m) *n.* madam (esp. in addressing queen or royal princess or officer in women's services).

măc *n.* (colloq.) mackintosh.

maca'bre (-ahbr) *a.* gruesome, grim.

macăd'am *n. & a.* road-surface got by compacting stone broken small. **~īze** *v.t.*

macaque' (-ahk) *n.* kind of monkey.

măcarō'nǐ *n.* pasta in long tubes; 18th-cent. dandy.

măcarŏn'ic *a.* (of verse) containing Latin etc. words, native words with Latin endings, etc. **~s** *n.pl.* macaronic verse.

măcaroōn' *n.* biscuit or small cake of ground almonds etc.

macaw' *n.* kinds of parrot.

Macc. *abbr.* Maccabees.

māce[1] *n.* (hist.) heavy usu. spiked club; staff of office, esp. that symbolizing Speaker's authority in House of Commons.

māce[2] *n.* nutmeg-husks dried and used as spice.

mǎ'cédoine (-dwahn) *n.* mixture of fruits or vegetables.

mǎ'cerāte *v.* make or become soft by soaking. **~ā'tion** *n.*

Măch (nŭm'ber) (-k; *or* -ahk) *n.* ratio of velocity of body to velocity of sound in same fluid medium.

mǎch'ete (-et; *or* machā'tǐ) *n.* C.--Amer. and W.-Ind. broad heavy knife.

Măchiavĕll'ian (-kǐ-) *a.* unscrupulous, crafty; deep-laid.

machǐc'olāte *v.t.* furnish (parapet etc.) with openings for dropping stones etc. on assailants. **~ā'tion** *n.*

măchinā'tion (-kǐ-) *n.* (usu. pl.) intrigue; scheme, plot.

machine' (-shēn) *n.* apparatus in which action of several parts is combined for applying mechanical force to purpose; controlling organization in politics etc.; bicycle, motor-car etc. *v.t.* print, sew, etc. with machine. **~-gun**, continuous-firing mounted gun mechanically loaded and fired. **~ tool**, mechanically operated cutting or shaping tool. **machi'nǐst** *n.* operator of machine.

machi'nerӯ (-shē-) *n.* machines; mechanism; organization.

măck'erel *n.* edible sea-fish. **~ sky**,

sky dappled with small white fleecy clouds.

măck'inaw (blanket) *n.* (U.S. & Canada) heavy blanket. **~ coat**, short usu. double-breasted heavy woollen coat.

măc(k)'intŏsh *n.* cloth waterproofed with rubber; coat or sheet of this.

macra'mé (-ahmǐ) *n.* fringe etc. of knotted thread or cord.

măcrocéphăl'ic *a.* large-headed.

măc'rocŏsm *n.* universe; any great whole.

măd *a.* of disordered mind, insane; rabid; wildly foolish; (colloq.) annoyed. **~cap**, reckless person. **~house**, lunatic asylum. **mad'man**, **mad'woman** *nn.* lunatic. **măd'nèss** *n.*

măd'am *n.* polite formal address to woman; (colloq.) woman in charge of brothel.

mădame' (-ahm) *n.* (pl. *mesdames*, pr. măd-) Fr. form of **madam**; as title, prefixed like *Mrs.* to foreign woman's name.

mădd'en *v.t.* make mad; irritate.

mădd'er *n.* (dye got from root of) herbaceous climbing plant.

made : see **make**.

Madeir'a (-ēra) *n.* kinds of fortified wine from Madeira. **~ cake**, kind of rich sweet cake without fruit.

mademoiselle (mădmwăzĕl') *n.* (pl. *mesdemoiselles*, pr. măd-), unmarried Frenchwoman; French governess etc.; as title, prefixed like *Miss* to foreign woman's name.

madŏnn'a *n.* (picture or statue of) Virgin Mary. **~ lily**, tall white lily.

măd'répôre, *n.* kinds of coral.

măd'rigal *n.* usu. unaccompanied contrapuntal part-song.

mae'lstrom (māl-) *n.* great whirlpool.

mae'nad *n.* bacchante; wild fury or shrew.

mae'strō (mī-) *n.* eminent musical teacher or conductor.

ma'fïa (mah-; *or* mafē'a) *n.* (persons sharing) Sicilian hostility to law, police, etc.; secret international criminal organization.

măgazine' (-zēn) *n.* store for explosives, arms, or military provisions; periodical publication containing articles etc. by different writers.

magĕn'ta *n*. (colour of) brilliant crimson aniline dye.

măgg'ot *n*. grub or larva, esp. of blue-bottle or cheese-fly. **~ў** *a*.

Mā'gī *n.pl.* ancient Persian priestly caste; 'wise men from the east'.

mă'gĭc *n*. art of influencing events by occult control of nature or spirits; mysterious agency or power; conjuring tricks; *black, white, ~,* performed by aid of demons, benevolent spirits. **~ lantern,** apparatus for projecting pictures on screen. **mă'gĭcal** *a*. of, like, produced by, magic. **magĭ'cian** *n*. one skilled in magic; wizard.

măgĭstēr'ĭal *a*. of magistrate; authoritative; dictatorial.

mă'gĭstracў *n*. magistrates; magisterial office.

mă'gĭstrate *n*. civil officer administering law, esp. one trying minor offences etc. **~ature** *n*.

măg'ma *n*. molten rocks below earth's crust.

măgnā'lĭum *n*. light tough alloy of aluminium and magnesium.

măgnăn'ĭmous *a*. high-souled, above petty feelings. **măgnanim'itў** *n*.

măg'nāte *n*. man of wealth, authority, etc.

măgnē'sia (-sha) *n*. magnesium oxide; (*milk of*) **~,** magnesium hydroxide used as antacid etc. **~n** *a*. of or containing magnesia.

măgnē'sĭum (-z- *or* -sh-) *n*. silvery-white metallic element burning with bright white light.

măg'nĕt *n*. piece of iron having property of attracting iron and of pointing north; thing that attracts.

măgnĕt'ĭc *a*. of or like or acting as magnet; exercising attraction; mesmeric. **~ic equator,** imaginary line round earth through points where angle between horizontal and direction of earth's magnetic field is zero. **~ic north,** pole towards which compass needle points (about 6° W. of true N.). **~ic storm,** erratic disturbance of earth's magnetism.

măg'nĕtĭsm *n*. magnetic phenomena; science of these; personal charm.

măg'nĕtīze *v.t.* make into magnet; attract like magnet. **~zā'tion** *n*.

măgnē'tō *n*. (pl. -*os*), (esp.) ignition apparatus of petrol engine.

măg'nĕtrŏn *n*. (phys.) thermionic tube for generating very-high-frequency oscillations.

măgnĭf'ĭcent *a*. splendid; imposing; excellent. **~ence** *n*.

măg'nĭfў *v.t.* increase apparent size of with lens etc.; exaggerate; (arch.) extol. **~fĭcā'tion** *n*.

măgnĭl'oquence *n*. high flown words or style. **măgnĭl'oquent** *a*.

măg'nĭtūde *n*. size, bulk; importance.

măgnō'lĭa *n*. flowering tree.

măg'num *n*. two-quart bottle.

măg'pīe *n*. black and white chattering bird; (shot hitting) circle on target between inner and outer circles.

Măg'yar (*or* mŏd'yar) *n*. & *a*. (member, language) of race predominant in Hungary. **~ blouse** etc., with sleeves cut in one piece with bodice.

maharaja(h) (mah-harah'ja) *n*. title of some Indian princes. **mahara'nee** (-nī) *n*. maharajah's wife.

mahăt'ma (ma-h-) *n*. person of preternatural powers in esoteric Buddhism.

mah-jŏngg' *n*. Chinese game played with pieces called tiles.

mahŏg'anў (ma-h-) *n*. (tropical Amer. tree with) reddish-brown wood used for furniture etc.; colour of this.

mahout' (ma-h-) *n*. elephant-driver.

maid *n*. virgin; spinster; young girl; female servant.

maidan (mīdahn') *n*. (Anglo-Ind.) open space, parade-ground.

mai'den *n*. virgin; spinster (usu. joc.); (hist.) kind of guillotine; (crick.) maiden over. *a*. unmarried; untried; with blank record. **~hair,** kinds of delicate fern. **~head, ~hood,** virginity. **~ name,** woman's surname before marriage. **~ over,** one in which no runs are scored. **~ speech,** M.P.'s first speech in Parliament. **~lў** *a*.

mail[1] *n*. armour of metal rings or plates. **~ed fist,** physical force.

mail[2] *n*. letters etc. conveyed by post; the post; train or other vehicle carrying mail. *v.t.* send by mail. **~ order,** order for goods to be sent by post.

maim *v.t.* cripple, mutilate.

main[1] *a.* chief, principal. *n.* high sea; main pipe or channel for water, gas, etc.; *in the ~*, for the most part; *with might and ~*, with all one's might. **~land**, country or continent without adjacent islands. **~mast**, principal mast. **~sail** (-sl), lowest sail, sail set on after part, of main-mast. **~spring**, chief spring of watch or clock (also fig.). **~stay**, from main-top to foot of foremast, (fig.) chief support. **~-top**, platform at head of lower mainmast.

main[2] *n.* number called in hazard before dice are thrown; match between fighting-cocks.

main'ly *adv.* in the main.

maintain' *v.t.* keep up; keep going; keep in repair; support; assert as true. **main'tenance** *n.* maintaining; subsistence; (law) offence of aiding party in litigation without lawful cause.

maison(n)ette' (-z-) *n.* small house; part of house let or used separately.

maize *n.* (edible seed of) Amer. cereal plant.

Maj., Maj.-Gen. *abbr.* Major, Major--General.

maj'esty *n.* stateliness of aspect, language, etc.; sovereign power; title used in speaking to or of sovereign. **majes'tic** *a.*

majol'ica *n.* kind of ornamented Italian earthenware.

ma'jor[1] *n.* army officer next in rank above captain; (mil. sl.) sergeant--major.

ma'jor[2] *a.* greater of two things, classes, etc.; senior; (mus., of interval) greater by chromatic semitone than minor; (of key, scale) having major third. *n.* person of full age; major premiss; major key; major suit; (U.S.) university etc. subject to which special attention is given. *v.i.* (U.S.) take course, qualify, *in* major. **~do'mo** (pl. *-os*), house--steward. **~-general**, army officer ranking next below lieutenant--general. **~ premiss**, (log.) first premiss of syllogism, containing general rule. **~ suit**, (bridge) spades or hearts.

majo'rity *n.* greater number or part (*of*); number by which winning vote exceeds next; full age; rank of major.

make *v.* (*made*), create, manufacture; cause to exist, bring about; amount to, constitute; bring total up to; represent as being or doing; acquire by effort, earn; win (trick); score (runs); produce by cookery; perform or execute; utter or record; *~ believe*, pretend; *~ do*, manage (*with* substitute etc.); *~ for*, take direction of; *~ good*, fulfil (promise etc.), pay for or repair (damage etc.), succeed in undertaking; *~ out*, draw up or write out (list etc.), represent as, understand; *~ shift with*, use as temporary expedient; *~ up*, supply deficiency, complete, compensate for, arrange (type) in pages, concoct, adapt (actor's face etc.) for part, apply cosmetics (to). *n.* way thing is made; figure or shape; brand, sort; *on the ~*, intent on gain. **~-believe**, pretence. **~shift**, method, tool, etc. used for want of better. **~-up**, way actor etc. is made up; way type is made up into pages; materials used for making up, cosmetics; fundamental qualities of character. **~weight**, small quantity added to make up weight.

ma'ker *n.* one who makes, esp. Creator.

ma'king *n.* (esp. pl.) essential qualities; (U.S., pl.) tobacco and paper for making cigarette; *be the ~ of*, ensure success etc. of.

Mal. *abbr.* Malachi.

Malacc'a cāne *n.* rich-brown walking--cane from stem of palm.

mal'achite (-kīt) *n.* green mineral taking high polish.

maladjust'ment *n.* faulty adjustment.

maladministra'tion *n.* faulty administration.

mal'adroit *a.* bungling, tactless.

mal'ady *n.* ailment, disease.

Malagăs'y *a. & n.* (native, language) of Madagascar.

malaise' (-z) *n.* feeling of illness or uneasiness.

mal'amūte *n.* Eskimo dog.

mal'apert *a.* (arch.) saucy; forward.

măl'aprŏpĭsm *n.* ludicrous confusion between words.

mălăpropos' (-pō) *adv.* & *a.* (done, said, etc.) inopportunely.

malār'ĭa *n.* intermittent and remittent fever transmitted by mosquitoes. **malār'ial**, **~ĭous** *aa.*

măl'contĕnt *n.* disaffected person.

māle *a.* of sex that begets offspring by fecundating female; (of parts of machinery) designed to enter or fill corresponding female part. *n.* male person or animal or plant.

mălĕdĭc'tion *n.* curse. **mălĕdĭc'torў** *a.*

măl'ĕfăctor *n.* criminal, evil-doer.

malĕf'ĭc *a.* harmful.

malĕf'ĭcent *a.* hurtful; doing wrong. **~ence** *n.*

malĕv'olent *a.* wishing ill to others. **malĕv'olence** *n.*

mălfea'sance (-z-) *n.* official misconduct.

mălfŏrmā'tion *n.* faulty formation. **mălfŏrmed'** (-md) *a.*

măl'ĭce *n.* ill-will; desire to do harm. **malĭ'cious** *a.*

malign' (-īn) *a.* injurious. *v.t.* slander, misrepresent.

malĭg'nant *a.* feeling or showing intense ill-will; (path., of disease) of form that kills, (of tumour) cancerous. **~nancў** *n.*

malĭg'nitў *n.* malignant character or feeling.

maling'er (-ngg-) *v.i.* pretend illness to escape duty.

măl'ĭson (-zn) *n.* (arch.) curse.

măll'ard *n.* wild duck.

măll'ėable *a.* that can be shaped by hammering; pliable. **~bil'itў** *n.*

măll'ėt *n.* hammer, usu. of wood; implement for striking croquet or polo ball.

măll'ow (-ō) *n.* kinds of plant.

mălmai'son (-z-) *n.* variety of large-flowered usu. pink carnation.

malmsey (mahm'zĭ) *n.* strong sweet wine from Greece, Madeira, etc.

mălnūtrĭ'tion *n.* insufficient nutrition.

mălō'dorous *a.* stinking.

mălprăc'tĭce *n.* wrongdoing, esp. by one in position of trust; doctor's improper treatment of patient.

malt (-ŏ- *or* -aw-) *n.* barley or other grain prepared for brewing etc. *v.t.* convert grain into malt.

Maltese (mawltēz') *a.* & *n.* (native, language) of Malta. **~ cross**, badge of Order of St. John, with four equal limbs broadened at ends.

măltreat' *v.t.* ill-treat. **~ment** *n.*

malt'ster (-ŏ- *or* -aw-) *n.* one who makes malt.

mălvā'ceous *a.* of mallow genus.

mălversā'tion *n.* corrupt handling of public or trust money.

măm'ba[1] *n.* kinds of venomous African snake.

măm'ba[2], **măm'bō** *n.* (music for) dance of W. Indian origin.

mam(m)a' (-ah) *n.* mother.

mămm'al *n.* member of class of animals that give suck. **mammā'lian** *a.*

mămm'arў *a.* of breasts. **~ gland**, milk-secreting gland.

mămm'on *n.* wealth as idol or evil influence.

mămm'oth *n.* large extinct elephant. *a.* huge.

mămm'ў *n.* child's word for mother; (U.S.) white children's coloured nurse.

măn *n.* (pl. *mĕn*), human being; human race; male and usu. adult person; husband; male servant, workman, ordinary soldier or sailor; piece in chess, draughts, etc. *v.t.* supply with men; guard, fortify. **~-at-arms**, soldier, esp. medieval. **~hole**, aperture in floor, sewer, etc., for man to pass through. **~-hour**, one hour's work by one man. **~-of-war**, warship. **~-power**, amount of men available for State or other service. **~trap**, trap set to catch esp. trespassers.

Man. *abbr.* Manitoba.

ma'na (mah-) *n.* impersonal supernatural power or force.

măn'acle *n.* (usu. pl.) fetter(s). *v.t.* put manacles on.

măn'age *v.* conduct working of; have effective control of; bend to one's will; cajole; contrive. **~able** *a.*

măn'agement (-ĭjm-) *n.* managing or being managed; administration; manager(s).

măn'ager (-nĭj-) *n.* person conducting business etc.; one skilled in managing money etc. **~ess** *n.*; **mănagēr'ĭal** *a.*

mănatee' *n.* large aquatic herbivorous mammal.

Mancun. *abbr.* (Bishop) of Manchester.

măndā'mus *n.* superior court's writ conveying command to lower one.

măn'darĭn *n.* high Chinese official; (esp. reactionary) person of influence and standing; small flattened orig. Chinese orange.

măn'date *n.* authoritative command; commission to act for another, esp. from League of Nations to administer territory; political instructions from electorate. *v.t.* commit (territory etc.) *to* mandatary authority. **măn'datarў** *n.* receiver of mandate. **măn'datorў** *a.* (esp.) obligatory.

măn'dĭble *n.* lower jaw-bone; either part of bird's beak; either half of crushing organ in mouth-parts of insects etc.

măn'dolĭn(e) *n.* stringed musical instrument of guitar kind played with plectrum.

măndrăg'ora, măn'drāke *nn.* narcotic plant with forked root.

măn'drel *n.* rod or spindle supporting work to be turned, shaped, etc.

măn'drĭll *n.* large baboon.

māne *n.* long hair of horse's or lion's neck; person's long thick hair.

mănège' (-āzh) *n.* training of horses; movements of trained horse.

mā'nēs (-z) *n.pl.* deified souls of ancestors; shade of dead person.

măn'ful *n.* brave, resolute.

măng'anese (-ngganēz) *n.* grey brittle metallic element; black dioxide of this.

mănge (-j) *n.* skin-disease of dogs etc.

măng'el-wûr'zel, măng'old(-wûr'zel) (-ngg-) *n.* large kind of beet used as cattle-food.

mā'nger (-j-) *n.* eating-trough in stable.

măng'le¹ (-nggl) *n.* machine for rolling and pressing washed clothes. *v.t.* put through mangle.

măng'le² (-nggl) *v.t.* hack, cut about, mutilate; spoil.

măng'o (-nggō) *n.* (pl. *-oes*), (fleshy fruit of) Indian tree.

măng'ōsteen (-ngg-) *n.* (juicy fruit with red rind of) E.-Ind. tree.

măng'rōve (-ngg-) *n.* tropical sea--shore tree with interlacing roots above ground.

mā'ngў (-j-) *a.* having mange; squalid, shabby.

mănhăn'dle *v.t.* move by men's strength alone, handle roughly.

măn'hŏŏd *n.* men of country; adult age in males; manliness.

mā'nĭa *n.* mental derangement marked by great excitement and (freq.) violence; craze, passion (*for*).

mā'nĭăc *n.* & *a.* (person) affected with mania. **manī'acal** *a.*

măn'ĭc (*or* mā-) *a.* of or affected with mania. **~-depressive**, of, (person) affected with, mental disorder esp. with alternating mania and depression.

măn'ĭcūre *n.* cosmetic care and treatment of hands. *v.t.* apply manicure to. **~rĭst** *n.*

măn'ĭfĕst *a.* clear to sight or mind; indubitable. *v.t.* make manifest; reveal *itself*; appear. *n.* list of ship's cargo for customs officials. **~ā'tion** *n.*

mănĭfĕs'tō *n.* (pl. *-os*) public declaration of policy or principles.

măn'ĭfōld *a.* of various forms, origins, functions, etc.; many and diverse. *n.* pipe etc. with several outlets.

măn'ĭkĭn *n.* little man; lay figure.

manĭll'a *n.* fibre used for ropes etc. **~ paper**, stout brown wrapping--paper.

măn'ĭŏc *n.* cassava.

manĭp'ūlāte *v.t.* handle; deal skilfully with; manage craftily. **~ā'tion, ~ātor** *nn.*

mănkīnd' *n.* human species.

măn'līke *a.* like man, mannish.

măn'lў *a.* having qualities or bearing of, befitting, man.

mănn'a *n.* food miraculously supplied to Israelites in wilderness.

mănn'equĭn (*or* -kĭn) *n.* woman employed to wear and show off clothes; lay-figure for shop windows etc.

mănn'er *n.* way thing is done or happens; sort or kind; style; (pl.) social bearing. **~ed** *a.* (esp.) showing mannerisms. **~ĭsm** *n.* excessive addiction to distinctive literary or artistic manner; trick of style or behaviour. ~less *a.* ~ly *a.* well--mannered, polite.

mann'ish *a.* characteristic of man as opp. to woman.

manœu'vre (-ōōv*er*) *n.* strategical or tactical movement; agile or skilful movement; skilful or crafty plan. *v.* perform, make perform, manœuvre(s); force or work *into*, *out*, etc.; manipulate adroitly. **manœu'vrable** *a.* capable of being (easily) manœuvred. ~**vrabil'ity** *n.*

manŏm'eter *n.* instrument for measuring gas- or vapour- or blood-pressure.

măn'or *n.* territorial unit of feudal period; (country estate with) substantial house. **manōr'ial** *a.*

măn'sard (roof) *n.* roof with two slopes, the steeper below, usu. broken by projecting windows.

mănse *n.* (esp. Sc. Presbyterian) minister's house.

măn'sion (-shn) *n.* large dwelling--house; (pl.) block of flats.

man'slaughter (-awt*er*) *n.* criminal homicide without malice aforethought.

măn'tel *n.* structure above and around fireplace. ~**piece**, mantel. ~**-shelf**, shelf above fireplace.

măntill'a *n.* Spanish woman's lace veil worn over head and shoulders.

măn'tis *n.* kinds of insect.

măn'tle *n.* loose sleeveless cloak; fragile hood round gas-jet to give incandescent light; region lying below earth's crust; fold of skin protecting mollusc's viscera etc. *v.* envelop, cover (as) with mantle; (of liquids) form scum; (of blood) suffuse cheeks.

măn'ūal *a.* of or done with hands. *n.* handbook, primer, textbook; organ keyboard.

mănūfăc'ture *n.* making of articles or material, esp. in large quantities. *v.t.* produce by labour, esp. on large scale; invent, fabricate.

mănūmit' *v.t.* give freedom to (slave). **mănūmi'ssion** *n.*

manūre' *n.* dung or other substance used for fertilizing soil. *v.t.* treat with manure.

măn'ūscript *a.* & *n.* (book, document) written by hand, not printed; (of) author's copy for printer.

Mănx *a.* & *n.* (Celtic language) of Isle of Man.

man'y̆ (mĕ-) *a.* numerous, much more than one. *n.* many people or things; *the* multitude.

Maori (mowr'i) *n.* & *a.* (member, language) of aboriginal N.Z. race.

măp *n.* flat representation of earth or part of it, or of (part of) heavens. *v.t.* make map of; ~ *out*, plan out, arrange in detail.

ma'ple *n.* kinds of tree. ~**-leaf**, emblem of Canada. ~ **sugar**, sugar got from kind of maple.

maquette' (-kĕt) *n.* small preliminary model for sculpture.

maquis (măk'ē) *n.* secret force of French patriots during German occupation (1940–5); dense scrubby forest in Corsica etc.

mar *v.t.* impair, spoil.

Mar. *abbr.* March.

ma'rabou (-bōō) *n.* large W.-Afr. stork; its down as trimming etc.

mără̆c(c)'a *n.* dried gourd etc. with stones or seeds inside used as percussion instrument.

măraschi'no (-skē-) *n.* liqueur made from small black cherry.

Mă'rathon *n.* road foot-race of great length; test of endurance.

maraud' *v.i.* make raid, pillage. **marau'der** *n.*

mar'ble *n.* kinds of limestone used in sculpture and architecture; (pl.) collection of sculpture; small ball of marble etc. used in child's game; (pl.) game played with marbles. *v.t.* give veined or mottled appearance to (esp. paper).

mar'casite *n.* (piece of) crystalline iron pyrites used as ornament.

March[1] *n.* third month of year. ~ **hare**, hare in breeding season.

march[2] *v.* (cause to) walk in military manner or with regular paces; progress steadily. *n.* action or piece of marching; distance covered in marching; progress; piece of music suitable for marching to. ~**-past**, ceremonial march past saluting-point.

march[3] *n.* (usu. pl.) boundary or

debatable strip between countries etc. *v.i.* have common boundary (*with*).

mär'chioness (-sh*o*-) *n.* wife of marquis.

märe *n.* female of horse or other equine animal. **~'s-nest**, illusory discovery.

mär'garine (-g- *or* -j-) *n.* edible fat resembling butter.

märge *n.* (colloq.) margarine.

mär'gin *n.* border; strip near edge of something; plain space round printed page etc.; extra amount over what is necessary; difference between cost and selling-price; sum deposited with stockbroker to cover risk of loss.

mär'ginal *a.* of or written in margin; of or at edge; close to limit; close to (esp. lower) limit of profitability, success, desirability, etc. **~ constituency**, one in which majority is too small for seat to be regarded as safe. **~ā'lia** *n.pl.* marginal notes.

mär'gräve *n.* title of some princes of Holy Roman Empire. **~vine** (-*a*vēn) *n.* margrave's wife.

märguerite' (-gerēt; *or* mär'-) *n.* kinds of large daisy.

Mär'ian *a.* of Virgin Mary or Mary, Queen of England or Mary, Queen of Scots.

mä'rigōld *n.* kinds of yellow-flowered plant.

märijua'na (-hwahn*a*) *n.* dried leaves of common hemp smoked as narcotic.

marim'ba *n.* (musical instrument developed from) primitive Afr. and C.-Amer. xylophone.

märinäde' *n.* mixture of wine or vinegar with herbs and spices in which fish or meat is steeped before cooking. *v.t.* steep in marinade.

mä'rināte *v.t.* marinade.

marine' (-ēn) *a.* of, from, or beside sea; for use at sea; of shipping. *n.* shipping; soldier serving on board ship. **~ stores**, (shop selling) old ships' materials. **mä'riner** *n.* sailor; *master mariner*, captain of merchant ship.

märionětte' *n.* puppet worked with strings.

mä'rital *a.* of husband; of marriage.

mä'ritime *a.* situated. dwelling, or found near sea; connected with seafaring.

mär'joram *n.* kinds of aromatic culinary herb.

mark[1] *n.* principal German monetary unit.

mark[2] *n.* target; thing aimed at; normal standard; indication of or trace left by something; visible sign, stain, spot, or dent on something; line etc. indicating position; unit in appraising merit of work; heel-mark for fair catch in Rugby football. *v.* make mark on; distinguish with mark; characterize or serve as mark of; assign marks of merit to; notice, observe, watch; record as score or act as scorer in games; keep close to (opposing player) in games; **~ down**, reduce price of; **~ off**, separate by boundary; **~ out**, trace out boundary of, plan (course), destine; **~ time**, lift feet as though marching while halted, fail to advance or make progress; **~ up**, increase price of. **~-up**, amount of increase in price of goods to cover overhead expenses and profit.

märked (-kt) *a.* (esp.) noticeable, conspicuous. **mär'kėdly** *adv.*

mär'ker *n.* (esp.) scorer at billiards; bookmark; anything used to indicate position on ground to aircraft, course at sea to boats, etc.

mär'kėt *n.* gathering for sale of commodities or live-stock; space or building used for it; seat of or facilities for trade; (prices in) stock-market; *Common M~*, association of countries as unit with common external tariffs and internal free trade. *v.* bring or send to or sell in market; buy goods in market. **~ cross**, cross in market-place. **~ garden(er)**, growing vegetables for sale. **~-place**, open space where market is held. **~-price**, prevailing price in ordinary conditions. **~ town**, town with market on fixed day(s). **~able** *a.* fit for sale; in demand.

mär'king *n.* (esp.) colouring of feathers, skin, etc. **~-ink**, indelible ink for marking linen.

marks'man *n.* (pl. -*men*), skilled shot, esp. with rifle. **~ship** *n.*

marl *n.* kind of rich soil often used as fertilizer.

mar'line-spike *n.* pointed tool for unravelling rope to be spliced.

mar'malade *n.* preserve of pulp and peel of oranges etc. in sugar.

marmor'eal *a.* of marble; white or cold or polished as marble.

mar'moset (-z-; *or* -s-) *n.* small bushy--tailed monkey.

mar'mot *n.* burrowing rodent of squirrel family.

ma'rocain *n.* thin fine dress-fabric with wavy texture.

maroon'[1] *n.* brownish-crimson colour; firework exploding with loud report. *a.* maroon-coloured.

maroon'[2] *v.t.* put and leave ashore on desolate island or coast; cut off, leave stranded.

marque (-k) *n.*: *letters of* **~**, (hist.) licence to act as privateer.

marquee' (-kē) *n.* large tent.

mar'quetry (-kǐ-) *n.* inlaid work.

mar'quis, -quess *n.* peer ranking between duke and earl or count. **~ate** *n.*

marquise' (-kēz) *n.* Fr. marchioness; finger-ring with gem(s) in pointed oval.

ma'rriage (-rǐj) *n.* act, ceremony, or state of being married; union. **~ lines**, certificate of marriage. **~able** *a.* old enough or fit for marriage.

ma'rrow (-ō) *n.* fatty substance in cavity of bones; (*vegetable*) **~**, kind of gourd. **~bone**, bone with edible marrow; (pl., joc.) knees. **~fat**, kind of large pea.

ma'rry *v.* unite, give, or take in wedlock; take wife or husband; unite intimately.

Mars (-z) *n.* Roman god of war; fourth planet from sun.

marsa'la (-sah-) *n.* sweet Sicilian sherry-like wine.

Marseillaise' (-selāz) *n.* national anthem of France.

marsh *n.* low-lying watery ground. **~-gas**, light inflammable gas found in coal-mines etc. **~mallow**, shrubby herb; sweetmeat made from its root. **~y** *a.*

mar'shal *n.* official of royal household etc. directing ceremonies; officer of high or (*field* **~**) highest rank. *v.t.* arrange in due order; conduct with ceremony. **~lling yard**, railway yard in which goods trains etc. are assembled.

marsu'pial *a.* of class of mammals carrying young in pouch. *n.* marsupial animal.

mart *n.* market.

martell'ō tower *n.* small circular fort for coast defence.

mar'ten *n.* weasel-like animal with valuable fur.

mar'tial *a.* warlike; suited to or loving war. **~ law**, military government suspending ordinary law.

mar'tin *n.* kinds of bird of swallow family.

martinet' *n.* strict disciplinarian.

mar'tingale (-ngg- *n.* check-strap preventing horse from rearing etc.; gambling system of doubling stakes at each venture.

marti'ni[1] (-ēnǐ) *n.* kind of rifle.

marti'ni[2] (-ēnǐ) *n.* cocktail of gin and vermouth.

Mar'tinmas *n.* St. Martin's day, 11 November.

mart'let *n.* (her.) footless bird.

mar'tyr (-er) *n.* person undergoing death or suffering for great cause, esp. adherence to Christian faith; **~ to**, constant sufferer from. *v.t.* put to death as martyr; torment. **~dom** *n.* **~ŏl'ogў** *n.* list, history, of (esp. Christian) martyrs.

mar'vel *n.* wonderful thing; wonderful example *of. v.i.* feel surprise, wonder. **mar'vellous** *a.* astonishing, extraordinary, preternatural.

Marx'ian, Marx'ist *aa.* & *nn.* (adherent) of Karl Marx's philosophy of history or belief in necessity of abolishing private property. **Marx'ism** *n.*

marzipan' (*or* mar'-) *n.* sweet confection of ground almonds.

masc. *abbr.* masculine.

mascar'a *n.* coloured gum for making up eyelashes etc.

mas'cot *n.* luck-bringer.

mas'culine *a.* (gram.) of gender to which names of males normally belong; male, manly; vigorous;

mannish. *n.* masculine gender, noun, etc. ~**lin'itў** *n.*

mā'ser (-z-) *n.* device for producing or amplifying microwaves.

măsh *n.* malt, bran, etc. mixed with water into thick liquid; (sl.) mashed potatoes. *v.t.* make into mash; crush or pound to pulp.

măsh'ie *n.* metal-headed golf-club with lofted face (no. 5 iron).

mask (mah-) *n.* hollow figure of face or head; covering for concealing or protecting face or part of it; gas- -mask; clay, wax, etc. likeness of face, esp. made by taking mould from face; face or head of fox; disguise. *v.t.* cover with mask; disguise, hide, or screen as with mask. ~**ed ball**, at which masks are worn.

măs'ochĭsm (-k-) *n.* pleasure in suffering physical or mental pain, esp. as form of sexual perversion. ~**chĭst** *n.*; ~**chĭs'tic** *a.*

mā'son *n.* worker in stone; free-mason. **masŏn'ĭc** *a.* of freemasons. ~**rў** *n.* stonework; freemasonry.

masque (mahsk) *n.* kind of poetic drama with pageantry. **ma'squer** *n.* person taking part in masque or masquerade.

masquerāde' (mahske-) *n.* masked ball; false show, pretence. *v.i.* appear in disguise; ~ *as*, pretend to be.

Măss¹ *n.* (celebration of) Eucharist; (musical setting of) liturgy used in this.

măss² *n.* large body of matter; dense aggregation, large number, un-broken expanse, (*of*); quantity of matter body contains; *the* majority or main part (*of*); (pl.) *the* lower classes. *v.* gather into mass; concentrate (troops etc.). ~ **communication**, directed to or reaching majority of people. ~ **meeting**, large usu. political assembly of people. ~**-produce**, produce (standardized articles) in large quantities by standardized means; ~ **production**.

Mass. *abbr.* Massachusetts.

măss'acre *n.* general slaughter. *v.t.* make massacre of.

măss'age (-ahzh; *or* -ahzh') *n.* kneading and rubbing of muscles etc., usu. with hands. *v.t.* treat thus. **măsseur'** (-ēr), (fem.) **-euse** (-ērz) *nn.* one who practises massage.

măssif' (-ēf) *n.* mountain heights forming compact group.

măss'ĭve *a.* large and heavy or solid; substantial.

mast¹ (mahst) *n.* fruit of beech, oak, etc., esp. as food for pigs.

mast² (mahst) *n.* upright to which ship's yards and sails are attached; long pole etc. supporting flag, aerial, etc.; *before the* ~, as ordinary seaman.

ma'ster (mah-) *n.* person having control; ship's captain; male head of household; teacher; head of some colleges; employer; skilled work-man; great artist; holder of university degree above bachelor's; title of heir of some Sc. baronies etc. *v.t.* acquire complete knowledge of; worst or reduce to sub-jection. ~**-key**, opening many different locks. ~**piece**, consummate piece of workmanship, best work. ~**ful**, *a.* imperious. ~**lў** *a.* worthy of master. ~**ў** *n.* masterly skill; dominion; superiority.

măs'tĭc *n.* (kinds of tree yielding) gum or resin used for varnish etc.; pale brownish-yellow colour of this; kinds of waterproof cement.

măs'tĭcāte *v.t.* chew. ~**ā'tion** *n.*

măs'tĭff (*or* mah-) *n.* dog of large strong breed.

măs'todŏn *n.* large extinct elephant--like mammal.

măs'toid *a.* shaped like female breast. *n.* conical prominence in temporal bone: (colloq.) mastoidi-tis. ~**ī'tis** *n.* inflammation of mastoid.

măs'turbāte *v.* practise masturbation (on). ~**ā'tion** *n.* sexual stimulation esp. by manipulation of one's own genitals.

măt¹ *n.* coarse fabric of plaited fibre etc.; piece of material laid on floor, table, etc. to protect surface; tangled mass; *on the* ~, (colloq.) in trouble. *v.* bring or come into thickly tangled state.

mat²: see **matt**.

măt′adŏr *n.* man whose task is to kill bull in bull-fight.

mătch¹ *n.* slip of wood, wax, etc. with head that ignites when rubbed; fuse. **~lock,** obsolete musket fired with fuse. **~wood,** splinters.

mătch² *n.* person or thing equal to or nearly resembling or corresponding to another; marriage; person in respect of eligibility for marriage; contest, game. *v.* find or be match for; place in competition *with* or contest *against*; be equal, correspond. **~board,** board fitting into others by tongue along one edge and groove along other. **~maker,** one given to scheming to arrange marriages. **~ point,** state of game when one side needs only one point to win match. **~less** *a.* without equal, peerless.

māte¹ *n. & v.t.* checkmate.

māte² *n.* one of pair of birds, lovers, or married people; fellow workman, assistant; (colloq.) friend; (colloq.) as form of address among equals; subordinate officer of merchant ship. *v.* pair; marry. **mā′tey** *a.* maty.

măt′é (-ā) *n.* (tea made by infusing) dried leaves etc. of S.-Amer. shrub.

mā′ter *n.* (sl.) mother.

matēr′ial *a.* composed of or connected with matter; unspiritual; important, essential. *n.* that from which thing is made; elements; stuff, fabric.

matēr′ialism *n.* belief that only matter is real or important; rejection of spiritual values etc. **~list** *n. & a.*; **~lis′tic** *a.*

matēr′ialize *v.* (cause to) appear in bodily form; become fact. **~zā′tion** *n.*

matēr′nal *a.* of mothers; motherly; related on mother's side.

matēr′nity *n.* motherhood; (attrib.) of, suitable or caring for, etc., women in childbirth or pregnancy.

măthĕmăt′ics *n.* science of space and number. **măthĕmăt′ical** *a.* of mathematics; rigorously precise. **măthĕmati′cian** *n.* **măths,** (U.S.) **măth** *n.* (colloq.) mathematics.

măt′inée (-nā) *n.* theatrical etc. performance in afternoon. **~ coat,**

~ jacket, baby's short coat. **~ idol,** handsome actor.

măt′ins *n.* (R.C. Ch.) first canonical hour, prop. said at midnight; Anglican morning prayer.

mā′tri- (*or* mă-) in comb., mother-, of women. **mā′triărch** (-k) *n.* woman corresponding in status to patriarch; **~ărchal** *a.* **~ărchy** (-ki) *n.* social organization in which woman is head of family. **~cīde** *n.* (person guilty of) killing own mother; **~cīdal** *a.* **~lĭn′eal, ~lĭn′ear** *aa.* of or based on (kinship with) mother or female line.

matric′ *n.* (colloq.) matriculation.

matric′ūlāte *v.* admit, be admitted, as student in university. **matrĭcūlā′tion** *n.*

măt′rimony *n.* marriage. **~ō′nial** *a.*

mā′trix (*or* mă-) *n.* (pl. *-ĭcēs, -ixes*), womb; mass of rock etc. enclosing gems etc.; mould in which type etc. is cast or shaped.

mā′tron *n.* married woman; woman in charge of nursing in hospital; housekeeper in school or institution. **~ly** *a.* like esp. elderly married woman; staid; portly.

mătt, măt² *a.* dull, without lustre.

Matt. *abbr.* Matthew.

măt′er *n.* physical substance; thing(s), material; content as dist. from form, substance; affair, concern; purulent discharge. *v.i.* be of importance; make difference (*to*); secrete or discharge pus. **~-of-fact,** prosaic, ordinary, unimaginative.

mătt′ing *n.* fabric of hemp, bast, etc. as covering etc.

mătt′ock *n.* tool like pick with adze and chisel-edge ends.

mătt′ress *n.* case stuffed with hair, straw, etc. as bed; springs etc. stretched in frame as support for mattress.

măt′ūrāte *v.i.* (med.) attain full development, ripen. **~ā′tion** *n.*

matūre′ *a.* fully developed; ripe; adult. *v.* bring to or reach mature state. **matūr′ity** *n.*

mătūtī′nal *a.* of or in morning.

mā′ty *a.* (colloq.) sociable, friendly.

maud′lin *a.* weakly sentimental.

maul *n.* heavy hammer, usu. of

wood. *v.t.* beat and bruise; handle roughly, savage.

maul'stick *n.* stick used to steady hand in painting.

maun'der *v.i.* talk ramblingly.

maun'dy *n.* Maundy-Thursday ceremony of washing feet of poor etc. **~ money**, silver coins minted for English sovereign's almsgiving on Maundy Thursday. **M~ Thursday**, Thursday before Easter.

mauser (mow'zer) *n.* kind of magazine rifle or pistol.

mausole'um *n.* building erected as tomb and monument.

mauve (mōv) *n. & a.* pale purple.

măv'erick *n.* (U.S.) unbranded calf etc.; unorthodox or undisciplined person.

mā'vis *n.* song-thrush.

maw *n.* stomach of animal.

maw'kish *a.* of faint sickly flavour; feebly sentimental.

măxill'ary *a.* of esp. upper jaw.

măx'im[1] *n.* general truth of science or experience; principle or rule of conduct.

măx'im[2] *n.* kind of machine-gun.

măx'imal *a.* greatest possible in size, duration, etc.

măx'imum *n.* (pl. usu. *-ima*), highest or greatest degree or magnitude or quantity. *a.* greatest.

măx'imus *a.* eldest of the name.

may[1] *v.aux.* (3rd sing. *may*; p.t. *might*), expressing possibility, permission, request, wish, etc.

May[2] *n.* fifth month of year; bloom, prime; hawthorn blossom. **~-day**[1], 1 May, esp. as country festival. **~-fly**, ephemeral insect. **~pole**, flower-decked pole danced round on May-day. **~ queen**, girl chosen as queen of May-day festivities. **~-tree**, hawthorn. **may'ing** *n.* celebration of May-day festival.

ma'ya (mah-) *n.* illusion. [Skr.]

may'bė *adv.* perhaps.

May-day[1]: see **May**[2].

may'day[2], standard vocal distress signal of maximum urgency.

may'hĕm *n.* crime of maiming.

mayonnaise' (-z) *n.* (dish with) creamy dressing of oil, egg-yolk, vinegar, etc.

mayor (mār) *n.* head of town corporation. **~al** *a.*; **~alty** *n.* **~ess** *n.* mayor's wife or lady fulfilling her ceremonial duties.

măzarine' (-ēn; *or* măz'-) *n. & a.* deep rich blue.

māze *n.* complex and baffling network of paths, lines, etc.; tangle, confusion. **mā'zy** *a.*

mā'zer *n.* (hist.) hardwood drinking bowl.

mazūr'ka *n.* (music for) lively Polish dance in triple time.

M.B. *abbr.* Bachelor of Medicine.

M.B.E. *abbr.* Member of Order of British Empire.

m/c *abbr.* megacycle.

M.C. *abbr.* Master of Ceremonies; Member of Congress; Military Cross.

M.C.C. *abbr.* Marylebone Cricket Club.

Md. *abbr.* Maryland.

M.D. *abbr.* Doctor of Medicine; mentally deficient.

me[1] (mē, mĭ) *pron.*, obj. case of *I.*

mē[2], **mi** (mē) *n.* (mus.) third note of major scale in tonic sol-fa.

Me. *abbr.* Maine.

M.E. *abbr.* Middle English.

mead[1] *n.* alcoholic liquor of fermented honey and water.

mead[2] *n.* (poet.) meadow.

meadow (mĕd'ō) *n.* piece of grassland, esp. used for hay; low-lying ground, esp. near river. **~sweet**, meadow plant with fragrant flowers.

mea'gre *a.* lean, scanty.

meal[1] *n.* coarsely ground edible part of grain or pulse.

meal[2] *n.* (taking of) food, esp. at table at customary time.

mea'lie *n.* (S.-Afr.) maize; corn-cob.

mea'ly *a.* of, like, or containing meal; (of boiled potatoes) dry and powdery. **~-mouthed**, not outspoken.

mean[1] *a.* of low degree or poor quality; ignoble; ungenerous; stingy.

mean[2] *v.* (*meant*, pr. mĕnt), purpose, design; be resolved; intend; signify.

mean[3] *a.* equidistant from two extremes; intermediate; average. *n.* mean degree or state or course; (pl.) intermediate steps to result;

resources; money. ~s test, inquiry into financial resources of applicant for assistance etc. ~time, ~while nn. & advv. (in) intervening time.

mëǎn'der v.i. wind about; go deviously. n. (usu. pl.) sinuous winding; winding path, course, etc.

mea'ning n. what is meant; significance. a. expressive, significant. ~ful, ~less aa.

mea'sles (-zlz) n.pl. acute infectious disease with red rash. mea'slў a. of, like, having, measles; (sl.) scanty, worthless.

measure (mēzh'er) n. size or quantity found by measuring; vessel, rod, tape, etc. for measuring; (prescribed) extent or amount; rhythm, metre, musical time; suitable action; legislative enactment. v. ascertain size, quantity, etc. of with measure; be of specified length etc.; deal out; bring into competition with. ~urable a. (esp.) not too small or great to be measured; within ~urable distance of, getting near. meas'urement n.

meat n. flesh of beasts as food. mea'tў a. (esp., fig.) full of substance.

mëchǎn'ĭc (-k-) n. skilled workman, esp. one making or repairing or using machinery.

mëchǎn'ĭcal (-k-) a. of, working or produced by, machines or mechanism; automatic; of mechanics.

mëchanĭ'cian (-k-) n. one skilled in construction, care, etc. of machines.

mëchǎn'ĭcs (-k-) n. branch of applied mathematics treating of motion; mechanism, functioning; science of machinery.

mëch'anĭsm (-k-) n. way machine works; structure or parts of machine; piece of machinery; framework, structure, technique. ~ĭst n. one holding that organic life admits of mechanico-chemical explanation. ~ĭs'tic a.

mëch'anīze (-k-) v.t. make mechanical; substitute mechanical power for man-power or horse-power in (army etc.) ~īzā'tion n.

mëd'al n. usu. coin-shaped piece of metal commemorating event etc.

or awarded as distinction. ~play, (golf) in which scoring is by strokes, not holes. mëd'allĭst n. winner of prize medal.

mëdǎll'ion (-yon) n. large medal; circular picture etc.

mëdd'le v.i. busy oneself unduly with; interfere in. ~some a. given to meddling.

mediaeval : see medieval.

mē'dĭal a. situated or occurring in middle.

mē'dĭan a. in middle. n. line from angle of triangle to middle point of opposite side.

mē'dĭate a. involving intermediate agency or action. v.i. (-āt), act as go-between or peace-maker. mēdĭā'tion n.

mëd'ĭcal a. of medicine; requiring or supplying medical not surgical treatment. n. (colloq.) medical student, medical examination. ~ jurisprudence, medicine used or required in law.

mëd'ĭcament (or mĭdĭc'-) n. substance used in curative treatment.

mëd'ĭcāte v.t. impregnate with medicinal substance.

mëdĭ'cinal a. healing or curative.

medicine (mëd'sn) n. art of preserving and restoring health, esp. by other means than surgery; drugs, potions, etc., used in this. ~-man, witch-doctor.

mëdĭē'val, -ĭae'val a. of Middle Ages. ~ĭsm, ~ĭst nn.

mē'dĭōcre a. middling, second-rate. mēdĭŏc'rĭtў (or më-) n. mediocre quality or person.

mëd'ĭtāte v. plan mentally; ponder over. ~tā'tion n.; ~tatĭve a.

Mëdĭterrā'nëan a. & n. (of, living near) inland sea between S. Europe and N. Africa.

mē'dĭum n. (pl. -s, -ĭa), middle quality, degree, etc.; means or agency; liquid vehicle with which pigments are mixed; person claiming ability to communicate with spirits etc.; channel for communication of information, propaganda, etc. ~ĭs'tic a. of spiritualist mediums.

mëd'lar n. (tree with) fruit eaten when decayed.

mĕd'ley _n._ heterogeneous mixture.

mĕdŭll'a _n._ marrow of bones; spinal marrow; hindmost segment of brain. **~rў** _a._

meed _n._ (poet.) reward; merĭted portion _of._

meek _a._ submissive; gentle.

meer'schaum (-shm) _n._ creamy clay used esp. for pipe-bowls; tobacco--pipe with meerschaum bowl.

meet[1] _a._ (arch.) fitting, proper.

meet[2] _v._ (_mĕt_), come into contact or company (with); confront; become perceptible to; satisfy (need etc.); experience. _n._ assembly for hunting etc.

mee'tĭng _n._ (esp.) assembly for entertainment, (Quaker) worship, etc., persons assembled; duel; race--meeting. **~-house,** Nonconformist place of worship.

mĕg'a- in comb., great, large; a million (times). **mĕg'acўcle** _n._ (in measuring electromagnetic frequencies) million cycles. **~death** _n._ (in measuring mortality in war) death of million people. **~lĭth** _n._ huge esp. prehistoric stone, esp. as monument. **~phōne** _n._ speaking--trumpet. **~ton** _n._ explosive force equivalent to million tons of T.N.T. **~vōlt, ~watt** _nn._ million volts, watts.

mĕgalomā'nĭa _n._ insane self-exaltation; mania for big things.

mĕgalosaur'us _n._ huge extinct carnivorous reptile.

mĕg'ohm (-ōm) _n._ million ohms.

mē'grĭms _n.pl._ low spirits.

meio'sĭs (mīō-) _n._ (pl. -_sēs_), understatement.

mĕlanchō'lĭa (-k-) _n._ mental illness marked by depression.

mĕlanchŏl'ĭc (-k-) _a._ (liable to) melancholy.

mĕl'ancholў (-k-) _n._ (tendency to) sadness and depression. _a._ sad; depressing.

mĕld _v._ (cards) declare (card(s)) for score; make meld. _n._ melding; card(s) melded.

mĕlée (mĕl'ā) _n._ confused fight or struggle.

mĕllif'luous (-loo-) _a._ sweet-sounding.

mĕll'ow (-ō) _a._ soft and rich in flavour, colour, or sound; softened by age etc.; genial; partly drunk. _v._ make or grow mellow; ripen.

mĕlŏd'ic _a._ of melody; (of minor scale) with major sixth and seventh when ascending and minor sixth and seventh when descending.

mĕlō'dĭous _a._ full of melody.

mĕl'odist _n._ composer of melodies.

mĕl'odrama (-rah-) _n._ drama marked by crude appeals to emotion. **~dramăt'ĭc** _a._

mĕl'odў _n._ sweet music; arrangement of notes in musically expressive succession; principal part in harmonized music.

mĕl'on _n._ kinds of sweet-fruited gourd.

mĕlt _v._ (cause to) become liquefied by heat; soften, be softened; dissolve, vanish (_away_); **~ down,** reduce to molten metal.

mĕl'ton _n._ kind of heavy woollen cloth.

mem. _abbr._, _memento_ [L], remember.

mĕm'ber _n._ limb or other bodily organ; distinct part of complex structure; person belonging to society, order, etc. **M~ of Parliament,** person elected to House of Commons. **~ship** _n._ being member; (number of) members.

mĕm'brāne _n._ layer of connective tissue round organ, lining cavity, etc., in living organism. **~ā'nĕous, ~anous** _aa._

mĕmĕn'tō _n._ (pl. -_os_), object serving as reminder or kept as memorial.

mĕm'ō _n._ (colloq.) memorandum.

mĕm'oir (-wăr) _n._ record written from personal knowledge etc.; (auto-) biography; essay on learned subject.

mĕm'orable _a._ likely or worthy to be remembered.

mĕmorăn'dum _n._ (pl. -_da_), note or record for future use; informal letter without signature etc.

mĕmōr'ĭal _a._ commemorative. _n._ memorial object, custom, etc.; (usu. pl.) chronicle; written representation to authorities. **M~ Day,** U.S. holiday (usu. 30 May) commemorating dead of armed forces. **~īze** _v.t._ commemorate; address memorial to.

mĕm'orize _v.t._ learn by heart.

měm′orў *n.* faculty by which things are recalled to or kept in mind; what is remembered; posthumous repute; part of computer in which information etc. may be stored.

měm′-sah′ĭb *n.* (Anglo-Ind., hist.) European married woman.

měn′ace *n.* threat. *v.t.* threaten.

ménage (mā′nahzh) *n.* household.

měnă′gerĭe *n.* collection of wild animals in captivity.

měnd *v.* repair, patch; put right; improve; rectify. *n.* repaired place; *on the ~,* improving.

měndā′cious *a.* lying. **měndă′citў** *n.*

měndelē′vĭum *n.* transuranic element.

Měndē′lĭan *a.* of genetic principles formulated by G. J. Mendel. **Měn′delĭsm** *n.*

měn′dĭcant *n.* beggar. *a.* begging. **~ancў** *n.*

měnhā′den *n.* fish of herring family of Atlantic coast of N. America.

měn′hir (-ēr) *n.* prehistoric monumental monolith.

mē′nĭal *n.* household servant. *a.* servile, degrading.

měnĭngī′tĭs (-j-) *n.* inflammation of membranes enveloping brain and spinal cord.

měnĭs′cus *n.* lens convex on one side and concave on other.

měn′opause *n.* period of life when menstruation ceases.

měn′sēs (-z) *n.pl.* monthly discharge of blood etc. from uterus of primates.

měn′strual (-ŏŏ-) *a.* of menses. **měn′struāte** *v.i.* discharge menses. **měnstruā′tion** *n.*

měn′struŭm (-ŏŏ-) *n.* (pl. -*ua*), solvent

měn′sūrable *a.* measurable.

měnsūrā′tion *n.* measuring; mathematical rules for computing length, area, etc.

měn′tal *a.* of or in mind; (sl.) feeble-minded. **~ age,** stage of development normally reached at specified age. **~ arithmetic,** performed without use of written figures. **~ defective,** person not an idiot or insane but unequal to conduct of ordinary affairs. **~ home, hospital, institution,** etc., for care of mentally disordered persons. **měntăl′itў** *n.*

(esp.) (degree of) intellectual power; (loosely) mind, character.

měn′thŏl *n.* camphor-like substance used in relieving pain etc.

měn′tion *v.t.* speak of, refer to. *n.* mentioning.

měn′tŏr *n.* adviser, counsellor.

měn′ū *n.* list of dishes to be served or available.

méphĭt′ic *a.* pestilential, noxious.

měr′cantīle *a.* trading; of trade or merchants. **~ marine,** shipping employed in commerce.

měr′cēnarў *a.* working for money or reward; not disinterested; (of soldiers in foreign service) hired. *n.* mercenary soldier.

měr′cer *n.* dealer in textile fabrics, esp. silks etc. **měr′cerў** *n.*

měr′cerīzed *a.* (of cotton) having silky lustre given by treatment with caustic alkali.

měr′chandīse (-z; *or* -s) *n.* mercantile commodities; goods for sale. *v.* (-z), buy and sell; promote sales of.

měr′chant *n.* wholesale trader, esp. with foreign countries; dealer; (U.S.) retail trader. **~man, ~ ship,** ship of merchant navy. **~ marine, ~ navy,** commercial shipping. **~able** *a.* saleable, marketable.

měr′cĭful *a.* having or feeling or showing mercy.

měr′cĭless *a.* cruel, pitiless.

mercūr′ĭal *a.* of lively temperament; of or containing mercury.

Měr′cūrў¹ *n.* (myth.) Roman god of eloquence etc. and messenger of gods; planet nearest sun.

měr′cūrў² *n.* heavy lustrous silver-white normally liquid metallic element; column of this in thermometer etc. **mercūr′ic, měr′curous** *aa.*

měr′cў *n.* abstention from infliction of suffering or punishment; disposition to forgive; act of mercy; blessing; *at the ~ of,* wholly in power of or subject to.

mēre¹ *n.* (poet.) lake.

mēre² *a.* barely or only what it is said to be, nothing more than. **~lў** *adv.* only.

měrétrĭ′cious *a.* showily attractive, flashy.

mergăn′ser *n.* kinds of diving fish-eating duck.

mērge v. lose or cause to lose character or identity in something else; join or blend gradually (*into, with*). **mēr'ger** n. (esp.) combination of firms etc. into one.

mērid'ian n. sun's position at noon; star's highest altitude; circle passing through place and N. & S. poles.

mērid'ional a. of south of France or Europe; southern.

meringue' (-răng) n. confection of sugar and beaten egg-white baked crisp.

meri'nō (-rē-) n. (pl. -os), kind of sheep; fine yarn or soft fabric of its wool; fine woollen yarn.

mě'rit n. commendable quality; goodness; (pl.) deserts; intrinsic rights and wrongs (*of* case etc.). v.t. deserve. ~ŏc'racy n. aristocracy of merit. ~ōr'ious a. praiseworthy.

mēr'le n. (arch.) blackbird.

mēr'lin n. small European falcon.

mēr'maid, mēr'man nn. fabled woman, man, of sea with fish-tail.

mě'rriment n. hilarious enjoyment; mirth.

mě'rrў a. laughing, given to laughter; full of fun; slightly tipsy. ~-go-round, revolving machine carrying wooden horses, cars, etc., for riding on or in. ~making, festivity. ~thought, wish-bone.

me'sa (mā-) n. high rocky precipitous-sided tableland.

mésalliance (mězăl'iahns) n. marriage with social inferior.

měscăl' n. (strong intoxicant made from) agave; small cactus with button-like tops chewed as intoxicant. **měs'caline** (*or* -ēn) n. hallucinative narcotic drug.

mesdames, mesdemoiselles : see madame, mademoiselle.

měsh n. one of spaces between threads of net; net, network; woven etc. openwork fabric. v. catch in net; (of toothed wheel etc.) engage, interlock.

měs'merĭsm (-z-) n. (arch.) hypnotism. **měsmě'rĭc** a.; **měs'merīze** v.t.

měs'ō- (*or* -z-) in comb., middle. **měsolĭth'ĭc** a. of Stone Age between palaeolithic and neolithic. **M~zō'ĭc**

a. of (period of) rocks above Palaeozoic.

mē'sŏn (-z-; *or* mě-) n. particle intermediate in mass between proton and electron.

měss n. (arch.) portion of food; spilt liquid etc.; dirty or untidy state; difficult situation, trouble; company, esp. in army or navy, feeding together; its meal or mess-room; *make a* ~ *of,* bungle. v. make dirty or untidy; take meals; potter *about;* ~ *up,* bungle. ~mate, member of same mess, esp. on ship. **měss'ў** a. untidy, dirty.

měss'age n. communication sent from one person to another; inspired communication of prophet, writer, etc.

měss'enger (-j-) n. bearer of message.

Messi'ah (-a) n. deliverer expected by Jews; Christ as this. **Messĭăn'ĭc** a.

messieurs (māsyēr'), pl. of monsieur.

Měss'rs. (-erz) abbr. prefixed as title to name of firm etc. or introducing list of gentlemen.

měss'uage (-wĭj) n. dwelling-house with outbuildings and land.

met : see meet.

met. abbr. meteorology etc.

mětăb'olĭsm n. process of building up and breaking down protoplasm. **mětabŏl'ĭc** a.

mětacăr'pus n. part of hand between wrist and fingers. ~căr'pal a.

mět'al n. any of class of substances represented by gold, silver, iron, etc.; broken stone for roads or railway ballast; (pl.) rails of railway. v.t. furnish or supply with metal; make or mend (road) with metal. **mětăll'ĭc** a. of or like or yielding metal.

mět'allŭrgў (*or* mĭtăl'-) n. science of extraction, working, and properties of metals and alloys. ~ŭr'gĭcal a.; ~urgĭst n.

mětamŏr'phĭc a. (of rocks) changed after formation by heat or pressure. ~phĭsm n. this process.

mětamŏr'phōse (-z) v. subject to or undergo metamorphosis or metamorphism.

mětamŏr'phosĭs n. (pl. -osēs), change of form, esp. magic transformation; change of character, circumstances.

etc.; (biol. etc.) change between immature form and adult.

mĕt'aphor n. application of name or descriptive term to object to which it is not literally applicable. **mĕtaphŏ'rĭc(al)** aa.

mĕtaphȳs'ĭcs (-z-) n. branch of philosophy concerned with nature of being, truth, etc. **~ical** a.; **mĕtaphȳsĭ'cian** n.

mĕtatăr'sus n. part of foot between ankle and toes. **~tăr'sal** a.

mĕtăth'ĕsĭs n. (pl. -esēs), transposition of letters or sounds.

mēte v.t. portion out.

mĕtĕmpsȳchō'sĭs (-k-) n. (pl. -osēs), migration of soul at death into another body.

mē'tĕor n. meteoroid made luminous by entering earth's atmosphere. **mĕtĕŏ'rĭc** a. of meteors; (fig.) dazzling, rapid. **~īte** n. (fragment of) fallen meteor. **~oid** n. small solid body moving through space.

mĕtĕorŏl'ogȳ n. study of atmospheric phenomena, esp. as determining weather. **~lŏ'gĭcal** a.; **~logĭst** n.

mē'ter n. apparatus registering amount of water, electricity, etc. passing through, time elapsed, etc. v. count or measure by meter. **~age** n.

mē'thāne n. marsh-gas.

mĕthĭnks' v.impers. (arch.) it seems to me.

mĕth'od n. way of doing something; orderliness. **mĕthŏd'ĭcal** a. orderly, systematic.

Mĕth'odĭsm n. evangelistic religious movement founded by Charles & John Wesley & George Whitefield. **~ĭst** n. & a.

mĕth'ȳl (or mē'thĭl) **alcohol** n. wood alcohol. **mĕth'ȳlāte** v.t. mix this with (alcohol), usu. to make it unfit for drinking.

mĕtic'ūlous a. slavishly accurate or correct or proper.

métier (mā'tyā) n. trade or profession or 'line'. [F]

mĕtŏn'ȳmȳ n. substitution of name of attribute for that of thing.

mē'tre¹ n. any form of poetic rhythm.

mē'tre² n. unit of length (39·37 in.) in metric system. **mĕt'rĭc** a. of **metric system**, decimal measuring system.

mĕt'rĭcal a. of or in metre; involving measurement.

mĕtrŏl'ogȳ n. science or system of measures.

mĕt'ronōme n. instrument marking time by pendulum etc. **~nŏm'ĭc** a.

mĕtrŏp'olĭs n. chief city.

mĕtropŏl'ĭtan a. of metropolis; having authority over bishops of province. n. metropolitan bishop.

mĕtt'le n. disposition, natural vigour and ardour esp. of horse. **~some** a. spirited.

mew¹ n. sea-gull.

mew² v. (of hawk) moult; shut up, confine.

mew³ n. & v.i. (utter) cat's cry.

mews (-z) n. series of private stables (now usu. as garages, flats, etc.) round yard or along sides of lane.

mĕzz'anine (-ēn) a. & n. (low storey) between two others, esp. ground and first floors.

mĕzz'o (-tsō or -dzō) adv. (mus.) moderately, half. [It.] **~ fŏr'tė** moderately loud. **~-soprano**, (person with) voice between contralto and soprano. **~ vō'ce** (-chĭ), (in) tone of medium loudness.

mĕ'zzotint (-dz-) n. kind of copper or steel engraving.

m.f. abbr., mezzo forte.

M.F.H. abbr. Master of Fox-hounds.

mg. abbr. milligram(s).

m.g.d. abbr. million gallons per day.

Mgr. abbr. Monseigneur; Monsignor.

mi : see **me²**.

M.I. abbr. Military Intelligence; Mounted Infantry.

miaow (mĭow') n. & v.i. mew.

mĭăs'ma (-z-; or mī-) n. noxious exhalation from marshes, putrid matter, etc. **~mĭc** a.

Mic. abbr. Micah.

mĭ'ca n. kinds of mineral found as small glittering scales or crystals separable into thin plates.

mice, pl. of **mouse**.

Mich. abbr. Michigan.

Mĭch'aelmas (-kel-) n. feast of St. Michael, 29 Sept. **~ daisy**, kinds of hybrid perennial aster.

mĭck'ey n. take the **~**, try to get a 'rise' (out of).

mĭ'cro- in comb., small, minute; millionth part of. **mĭcrobĭŏl'ogȳ** n.

study of micro-organisms. ~**cŏsm** *n*. little world, epitome (*of*). ~**dŏt** *n*. photograph reduced to mere dot. ~**film** *n*. (photographic reproduction on) very small film. **micrŏm'ĕter** *n*. instrument for measuring minute distances. ~**-or'ganĭsm** *n*. organism not visible to unaided eye. ~**phōne** *n*. device converting sound waves into (changes in) electrical energy. ~**wave** *n*. electro-magnetic wave (less than 30 cm.).

mī'crōbe *n*. micro-organism, esp. one causing disease or fermentation.

mī'cron *n*. millionth of metre.

mī'croscōpe *n*. lens or combination of lenses making minute objects visible. **microscŏp'ĭc** *a*. of, with, like, microscope; too small to be seen clearly without microscope. **micrŏs'copy** *n*.

mictūrī'tion *n*. urination.

mĭd *a*. middle of; intermediate. ~**day**, noon. ~**-off**, ~**-on**, fielders nearer batsman than long-off and long-on.

mĭdd'en *n*. dung-hill; refuse-heap.

mĭdd'le *a*. equidistant from extremities; intermediate in rank, quality, etc. *n*. middle point or position; waist. **M~ Ages**, about A.D. 600–1450. ~**man**, trader intermediate between producer and consumer. ~**-weight**, boxing-weight (11 st. 6 lb.).

mĭdd'lĭng *a*. moderately good; fairly well in health. *adv*. fairly or moderately.

mĭdd'y *n*. (colloq.) midshipman.

mĭdge *n*. gnat; small insect.

mĭdg'ĕt *n*. diminutive person; dwarf. *a*. extremely small.

mĭd'land *a*. & *n*. (part of country) remote from sea or borders. **M~s**, midland counties of England.

mĭd'night *n*. twelve o'clock at night. *a*. of or at or dark as midnight.

mĭd'rĭff *n*. diaphragm.

mĭd'shipman *n*. (hist.) junior naval officer between cadet and sub-lieutenant.

mĭdst *n*. middle.

mĭd'summer *n*. period of summer solstice, about 21 June. **M~ Day**, 24 June. ~ **madness**, extreme folly.

mĭd'wīfe *n*. (pl. -*ives*), woman who assists others in childbirth. **mĭd'-wifery** (-frĭ) *n*.

mien (mēn) *n*. bearing or look.

might[1], *p.t.* of **may**.

might[2] *n*. great power or strength or resources.

migh'ty *a*. powerful, great. *adv*. (colloq.) very.

mignonĕtte' (mĭnyo-) *n*. plant with fragrant greyish-green flowers.

mi'graine (mē- or mī-; *or* -ān') *n*. recurrent paroxysmal headache.

mī'grant *a*. that migrates. *n*. migrant bird etc.

migrāte' *v.i.* move from one place, esp. one country, to another; (of birds etc.) come and go with seasons. ~**ā'tion** *n*.; **mī'gratory** *a*.

mĭka'dō (-kah-) *n*. (pl. -*os*), Emperor of Japan.

mīke *n*. (colloq.) microphone.

milch *a*. giving, kept for, milk.

mīld *a*. gentle; not severe or harsh or drastic; not bitter. ~ **steel**, tough and malleable steel with low percentage of carbon.

mil'dew *n*. growth of minute fungi on plants or on leather etc. exposed to damp. *v*. taint, be tainted, with mildew.

mīle *n*. linear measure (1,760 yds.); race over one mile. ~**stone**, roadside pillar marking miles; stage (*in* career etc.). **mī'l(e)age** *n*. distance in miles; travelling allowance at fixed rate per mile. **mī'ler** *n*. (colloq.) man, horse, trained to run mile.

mĭl'foil *n*. common yarrow.

mĭl'ĭtant *a*. engaged in warfare; combative. *n*. militant person. ~ **suffragette**, suffragette employing or advocating violent measures. ~**ancy** *n*.

mĭl'ĭtarĭsm *n*. exaltation of or reliance on military force and methods. ~**ĭst** *n*.

mĭl'ĭtary *a*. pertaining to soldiers or army or land warfare. *n*. soldiery. ~ **band**, combination of wood-wind, brass, and percussion.

mĭl'ĭtāte *v.i.* serve as argument or influence *against*.

milĭ'tia *n*. (-sha) military force, esp. citizen army; (hist.) auxiliary branch of British military service. ~**man**, member of militia.

milk *n.* opaque white fluid secreted by female mammals for feeding young; cow's milk as article of food; milk-like liquid. *v.t.* draw milk from; get money out of, exploit. ~**maid**, woman milking cows or working in dairy. ~**man**, seller of milk. ~ **shake**, milk flavoured and shaken up. ~**sop**, unmanly fellow. ~-**teeth**, temporary first teeth in young mammals. ~y̆ *a.* of or like or mixed with milk; M~y Way, galaxy.

mill *n.* building or apparatus for grinding corn; grinding-machine; machine or building for manufacturing processes etc. *v.* grind or treat in mill; produce grooves etc. in (metal, edge of coin, etc.); (of cattle etc.) move round and round in mass. ~**board**, stout pasteboard. ~**hand**, factory worker. ~-**race**, current of water driving mill-wheel. ~**stone**, circular stone for grinding corn; ~**stone grit**, hard siliceous carboniferous rock. ~-**wheel**, turning machinery of water-mill.

millénár'ian *a.* of or expecting millennium. *n.* believer in millennium.

millénn'ium *n.* thousand-year period; coming time of happiness on earth. **millĕnn'ial** *a.*

millepede : see **millipede**.

mill'er *n.* one whose business is to grind corn. ~'**s thumb**, small freshwater fish.

millĕs'imal *a.* thousandth.

mill'ĕt *n.* (minute seed of) kinds of cereal plant.

mill'i- in comb., one-thousandth of. **mill'ibǎr** *n.* thousandth of bar². ~**grǎm** *n.* thousandth of gram. ~**sĕcond** *n.* thousandth of second. ~**mētre** *n.* thousandth of metre.

mill'iard *n.* thousand millions.

mill'iner *n.* maker or seller of women's hats, ribbons, etc. **mill'-inery** *n.*

mill'ion (-yon) *n.* ten hundred thousand; million pounds, dollars, etc. ~**aire'** *n.* person possessing million; person of great wealth. ~**th** *a. & n.*

mill'ipēde, millé- *n.* kinds of many--legged creature.

milt *n.* roe of male fish.

mīme *n.* (Gr. & Rom. ant.) kind of simple farcical drama; play etc. with mimic gestures and action usu. without words; actor in mime. *v.* act in mime.

mim'éograph *n.* apparatus for making copies from stencils. *v.t.* reproduce with mimeograph.

mimē'sis *n.* protective mimicry.

mimĕt'ic *a.* of or showing imitation, mimicry, or mimesis.

mim'ic *a.* feigned, esp. to amuse; sham; imitative. *n.* person who mimics. *v.t.* copy speech or gestures of, esp. to amuse others, imitate or resemble closely. ~**ry̆** *n.* mimicking; resemblance of animal etc. in colour, markings, etc. to environment or other animal.

mimō'sa (*or* -z-) *n.* kinds of leguminous plant, esp. wattle and sensitive plant.

mina : see **mynah**.

min'arĕt *n.* tall slender tower of mosque.

min'atory̆ (*or* mī-) *a.* threatening.

mince *v.* cut (meat etc.) very small; walk with affected delicacy. *n.* minced meat. ~**meat**, mixture of minced apples, currants, spices, suet, etc. ~-**pie**, patty of mincemeat.

mīnd *n.* seat of consciousness, thought, volition, and feeling; intellectual powers; memory; opinion. *v.* bear in mind; heed; have charge of; object (to); take care or heed (of). ~**ed** *a.* disposed, inclined. ~**ful** *a.* taking thought or care (*of*).

mīne[1] *pron. & a.* the one(s) belonging to me.

mīne[2] *n.* excavation from which minerals are extracted; explosive charge placed ready to go off when required. *v.* dig for minerals; burrow or make subterranean passage(s) in. ~**field**, sea or land area sown with mines. ~-**layer**, vessel for laying mines. ~-**sweeper**, ship for clearing away floating or submarine mines. **mī'ner** *n.* worker in mine; soldier who lays mines.

mĭn'eral *n.* substance got by mining; inorganic natural substance; (pop.) substance neither animal nor vegetable; mineral water. *a.* of or belonging to minerals. ~ **water,** water naturally impregnated with esp. medicinal mineral(s); effervescent drink.

mĭnerăl'ogў *n.* science of minerals. ~lŏ'gical *a.*; ~logĭst *n.*

mĭnéstrō'né *n.* Italian mixed--vegetable soup with pasta.

ming'le (-nggl) *v.* (cause to) mix; blend; unite *with.*

min'gy (-jĭ) *a.* (colloq.) stingy.

mĭn'ĭ *n.* (colloq.) small car etc.

mini- in comb., miniature, (very) small. min'ibŭs *n.* car carrying many passengers. ~cab *n.* small taxi. ~car *n.* small car. ~skirt *n.* extremely short skirt.

min'ĭature *n.* painted portrait on small scale; small-scale representation. *a.* small-scale, diminutive. ~tūrĭst *n.* painter of miniatures.

mĭn'ĭm *n.* (mus.) open-headed note with stem, equal to half semibreve; 1/60 fluid drachm. ~al *a.* very minute, least possible.

mĭn'ĭmīze *v.t.* reduce to or estimate at minimum.

mĭn'ĭmum *n.* (pl. *-ima*), least amount attainable, usual, etc.

mĭn'ion (-yon) *n.* spoilt darling, favourite; servile agent; size of printing-type (7-point).

min'ĭster *n.* executive agent; person in charge of department of State; diplomatic representative, esp. ranking below ambassador; (esp. Nonconformist) clergyman.

mĭnistēr'ĭal *a.* of minister or his office; of government. ~ist *n.* supporter of government.

min'ĭstrant *a.* & *n.* ministering (person).

mĭnistrā'tion *n.* (act of) ministering.

mĭn'ĭstrў *n.* priestly office; ministers of church; office or building or department of minister of State; ministers forming government.

mĭn'ĭver *n.* plain white fur in ceremonial costume.

mĭnk *n.* small semi-aquatic stoat-like animal; its fur.

Minn. *abbr.* Minnesota.

minn'ésĭnger *n.* medieval German lyrical poet and singer.

minn'ow (-ō) *n.* small freshwater fish of carp family.

Mĭnō'an (*or* mī-) *a.* & *n.* (language, inhabitant) of ancient Crete or its Bronze-Age culture.

mī'nor *a.* lesser of two units or sets; of lesser kind, importance, etc.; (mus.) less by semitone than corresponding major interval, (of key, scale, etc.) containing minor third. *n.* person under age; minor key, interval, etc.

mĭnŏ'rĭtў (*or* mī-) *n.* (period of) being under age; smaller number or part, esp. in voting.

mĭn'ster *n.* large church.

mĭn'strel *n.* medieval singer or musician; poet; (pl.) band of entertainers with blacked faces etc. mĭn'strelsў *n.* minstrel's art; poetry.

mint[1] *n.* aromatic culinary herb; peppermint.

mint[2] *n.* place where money is coined. *v.t.* coin (money); invent.

mĭnūĕt' *n.* slow stately dance in triple time; music for this or (part of) movement of suite etc. in same style.

mī'nus *prep.* less, with deduction of; (colloq.) deprived of. *n.* minus sign (−); negative quantity.

mĭn'uscūle (*or* -ŭs'-) *a.* (of letter etc.) small, not capital; (colloq.) small, diminutive. *n.* lower-case letter.

mĭn'ute[1] (-ĭt) *n.* sixtieth part of hour or degree; short time; memorandum, summary, (pl.) official record of proceedings. *v.t.* draft; make minute of.

mĭnūte'[2] *a.* very small; precise, going into details.

mĭnū'tia (-shĭa) *n.* (pl. *-ae*) trivial point, small detail.

mĭnx *n.* sly girl, hussy.

Mī'ocēne *a.* (geol.) of middle division of tertiary strata.

mĭ'racle *n.* event due to supernatural agency; remarkable event or object. mĭrăc'ūlous *a.* supernatural; wonderful.

mirage' (-ahzh) *n.* illusion produced by atmospheric conditions.

mīre *n.* swampy ground; mud. *v.* sink in, bespatter with, mud.

mĭ′rror *n.* smooth surface, esp. of glass backed with mercury etc., reflecting images; model, faithful reflection. *v.t.* reflect as in mirror. ~ image, image (as) reflected in mirror, with right and left sides transposed.

mĭrth *n.* being merry, laughter. ~ful, ~less *aa.*

mĭr′y̆ *a.* muddy.

mĭsadvĕn′ture *n.* (piece of) bad luck; *by* ~, by accident.

mĭsallī′ance *n.* unsuitable marriage.

mĭs′anthrōpe *n.* hater of mankind. mĭsanthrŏp′ĭc *a.*; mĭsăn′thropy̆ *n.*

mĭsapplȳ′ *v.t.* apply or use wrongly. mĭsăpplĭcā′tion *n.*

mĭsăpprėhĕnd′ *v.t.* misunderstand. ~hĕn′sion *n.*

mĭsapprō′prĭāte *v.t.* apply dishonestly to one's own use. ~ā′tion *n.*

mĭsbėgŏtt′en *a.* illegitimate.

mĭsbėhāve′ *v.i.* & *refl.* behave improperly. mĭsbėhā′viour *n.*

misc. *abbr.* miscellaneous; miscellany.

mĭscăl′cūlāte *v.* calculate wrongly. ~ā′tion *n.*

mĭscall′ (-awl) *v.t.* call by wrong name.

mĭscă′rriage (-rĭj) *n.* miscarrying.

mĭscă′rry̆ *v.i.* fail of success; go astray; be delivered prematurely of child.

mĭscast′ (-ahst) *v.t.* cast wrongly or unsuitably. ~ing *n.*

mĭscėgėnā′tion *n.* interbreeding between races.

mĭscellā′nea *n.pl.* (collection of) miscellaneous items.

mĭscellā′néous *a.* of mixed composition or character; of various kinds. mĭscĕll′any̆ (*or* mĭs′-) *n.* miscellaneous collection.

mĭschance′ (-ahns) *n.* unlucky accident.

mĭs′chief (-chĭf) *n.* harm, injury, wrought by person or other agent; discord; childish scrapes; playful malice. mĭs′chievous *a.*

mĭsconceive′ *v.* have wrong idea of; misunderstand. mĭsconcĕp′tion *n.*

mĭscŏn′duct *n.* improper conduct, esp. adultery. ~dŭct′ *v.t.* & *refl.*

mĭsconstrue′ (-ōō) *v.t.* put wrong construction on. ~strŭc′tion *n.*

mĭs′count *n.* wrong count, esp. of votes. *v.t.* (-ownt′), count wrongly.

mĭs′crėant *n.* villain.

mĭsdāte′ *v.t.* date wrongly.

mĭsdeal′ *v.* make mistake in dealing. *n.* wrong deal.

mĭsdeed′ *n.* wrong deed.

mĭsdėmea′nour (-or) *n.* indictable but not felonious offence; misdeed.

mĭsdĭrĕct′ *v.t.* direct wrongly. mĭsdirec′tion *n.*

mĭsdo′ĭng (-dōō-) *n.* misdeed.

mĭsdoubt′ (-owt) *v.t.* (arch.) have misgivings about.

mise-en-scène (mēz ahṅ sän′) *n.* setting. [F]

mī′ser (-z-) *n.* one living miserably to hoard wealth. ~ly̆ *a.*

mĭs′erable (-z-) *a.* wretchedly unhappy or poor or uncomfortable; pitiable; mean.

mĭsĕ′rĭcŏrd (-z-) *n.* projection under hinged seat in choir stall to support person standing.

mĭs′ery̆ (-z-) *n.* acute unhappiness; distressing poverty.

mĭsfea′sance (-z-) *n.* wrongful exercise of lawful authority.

mĭsfīre′ *v.* fail to fire correctly. mĭs′fīre *n.*

mĭs′fĭt *n.* garment etc. that does not fit; person ill-adapted to surroundings etc.

mĭsfŏr′tūne *n.* calamity; bad luck.

mĭsgive′ *v.t.* (-gāve, -gĭven), (of mind etc.) suggest misgivings to. mĭsgĭv′ĭng *n.* apprehension, uneasy doubt.

mĭsgŏv′ern (-gŭ-) *v.t.* govern badly. ~ment *n.*

mĭsguī′ded (-gī-) *a.* misdirected, erring.

mĭshăn′dle *v.t.* handle roughly or improperly.

mĭshăp′ (-s-h-) *n.* unlucky accident.

mĭsinfŏrm′ *v.t.* give wrong information to. mĭsĭnformā′tion *n.*

mĭsĭntĕr′prĕt *v.t.* interpret wrongly. ~ā′tion *n.*

mĭsjŭdge′ *v.t.* judge wrongly. ~ment *n.*

mĭslay′ *v.t.* so place (thing) as to be unable to find it.

mĭslead′ (-lēd) *v.t.* lead astray; give wrong impression to.

mĭsmăn′age v.t. manage badly or wrongly. **~ment** n.

mĭsnāme′ v.t. call by wrong name.

mĭsnō′mer n. (use of) wrongly applied name.

mĭsŏg′amў n. hatred of marriage. **~mĭst** n.

mĭsŏ′gўnў (-j- or -g-) n. hatred of women. **mĭsŏ′gўnĭst** n.

mĭsplāce′ v.t. put in wrong place; bestow on ill-chosen object. **~ment** n.

mĭs′prĭnt n. error in printing. v.t. (-ĭnt′), print wrongly.

mĭsprī′sion n. (esp.) concealment of one's knowledge (of offence).

mĭspronounce′ v.t. pronounce wrongly. **mĭspronŭnciā′tion** n.

mĭsquōte′ v.t. quote wrongly. **mĭsquotā′tion** n.

mĭsread′ v.t. (past -read, pr. -rĕd), read or interpret wrongly.

mĭsrĕprĕsĕnt′ (-z-) v.t. represent wrongly. **~ā′tion** n.

mĭsrule′ (-ōō) v.t. rule badly. n. bad government.

miss[1] v. fail to hit, reach, meet, find, catch, or perceive; pass over; regret absence of; fail. n. failure; give (thing) a **~**, avoid, leave alone.

miss[2] n. (title of) unmarried woman or girl.

Miss. abbr. Mississippi.

miss′al n. R.C. Mass-book.

miss′el(-thrŭsh) n. large thrush.

mĭs-shā′pen a. deformed.

miss′īle n. object or weapon capable of being thrown or projected.

miss′ĭng a. not present, not found.

mi′ssion n. persons sent out as envoys or evangelists; missionary post, organization, etc.; errand of mission; vocation.

mi′ssionarў a. of religious missions. n. person doing missionary work.

miss′ĭs n. (vulg.) mistress; (joc.) wife.

miss′ĭve n. letter.

mĭs-spĕll′ v.t. spell wrongly.

mĭs-spĕnd′ v.t. (-spĕnt), spend amiss or wastefully.

mĭs-stāte′ v.t. state wrongly. **~ment** n.

mĭst n. water-vapour in drops smaller than rain; dimness, blurring, caused by tears in eyes etc.

mĭstāke′ v. (-tōōk, -tāken), come to wrong conclusion about, misinterpret; erroneously take (person or thing) for another; (p.p.) due to error, ill-judged. n. error, blunder; mistaken opinion or act.

mĭstīme′ v.t. time wrongly.

mĭst′letōe (-zltō; or -s-) n. parasitic white-berried plant.

mĭstrănslāte′ v.t. translate incorrectly. **~ā′tion** n.

mĭs′trĕss n. woman in relation to servants; woman having control; female teacher; man's paramour; (arch.) Mrs.

mĭstrŭst′ v.t. feel no confidence in. n. lack of confidence; uneasy doubts. **~ful** a.

mĭs′tў a. of, in, or like mist; of dim outline; obscure.

mĭsŭnderstănd′ v. (-stōōd), not understand rightly. **~ing** n.

mĭsūse′ (-z) v.t. use wrongly; ill-treat. n. (-s), wrong use.

mīte[1] n. anything very small; small child or person.

mīte[2] n. small arachnid found in cheese etc.

Mĭth′ras n. Persian god identified with sun. **~aĭsm** n.

mĭt′ĭgāte v.t. appease, alleviate; reduce severity of. **~ā′tion** n.; **~ātorў** a.

mī′tral a. of **~** valve, between left atrium and ventricle of human heart.

mī′tre[1] n. bishop's tall pointed head-dress. v.t. put or bestow mitre on.

mī′tre[2] n. joint in which line of junction bisects angle between joined pieces. v.t. join thus; shape to make mitred corner.

mĭtt n. mitten; (sl.) hand; (pl., sl.) boxing-gloves.

mĭtt′en n. glove leaving fingers and thumb-tip bare or with no partition between fingers.

mix v. unite or blend into one mass; compound together; become united, mingle (with); **~** up, confuse.

mixed (-kst) a. of diverse qualities or elements; of or for both sexes; **~ed** up, confused. **~ed marriage**, between persons of different races, religions, etc. **~er** n. (esp.) apparatus for mixing or beating food in cookery; *good, bad,* ~*er,* one who gets on well, badly, with others.

mix'ture *n.* mixing; what is mixed, esp. medicinal preparation; vaporized fuel mixed with air in internal combustion engine.

miz(z)'en-mast *n.* aftermost mast of three-masted ship.

mizz'le *v.i.* (sl.) decamp, make off.

ml. *abbr.* millilitre(s).

M.L.F. *abbr.* Multilateral (Nuclear) Force.

Mlle(s) *abbr.* Mademoiselle, Mesdemoiselles.

MM. *abbr., Messieurs.*

M.M. *abbr.* Military Medal.

mm. *abbr.* millimetre(s).

Mme. *abbr., Madame.*

Mmes. *abbr., Mesdames;* freq. prefixed to list of names as pl. of **Mrs.**

mnemon'ic (n-) *a.* of, designed to aid, memory. ~**s** *n.pl.* mnemonic art or system.

Mo. *abbr.* Missouri.

M.O. *abbr.* Medical Officer; money order.

mo *abbr.* (sl.) moment.

mo'a *n.* large extinct flightless N.-Z. bird.

moan *n.* low inarticulate sound expressing pain or grief. *v.* utter moan; lament, complain.

moat *n.* wide usu. water-filled ditch round castle, town, etc. ~**ed** *a.*

mob *n.* riotous crowd; rabble; gang; promiscuous gathering. *v.t.* attack in mob; crowd round and molest. **mob'ster** *n.* gangster.

mob-cap' *n.* (hist.) woman's indoor cap covering whole head.

mo'bile *a.* (readily or freely) movable; (of troops etc.) easily moved from place to place; of changing expression. *n.* sculpture etc. with parts moving easily in currents of air. **mobil'ity** *n.*

mo'bilize *v.* call up, assemble, prepare, for warfare etc.

mocc'asin *n.* Amer.-Ind. soft shoe of deerskin etc.; venomous snake of southern U.S.

mo'cha (-ka) *n.* coffee of fine quality.

mock *v.* scoff at, ridicule, mimic; jeer, scoff. *n.* object of mockery. *a.* sham, mimic, counterfeit. ~**-heroic,** burlesquing, burlesque

imitation of, heroic style. ~**ing--bird,** kinds imitating other birds' notes. ~ **orange,** syringa. ~**-turtle (soup),** made of calf's head to imitate turtle soup. ~**-up,** full--sized scale model. **mock'ery** *n.* derision; laughing-stock; travesty.

mod. *abbr.* modern.

mo'dal *a.* of mode or form as opp. to substance; (mus.) of modes; (gram.) of or expressing mood or manner. **modal'ity** *n.*

mode *n.* way in which thing is done; current fashion; (mus.) scale (-system) with fixed characteristic arrangement of intervals.

mod'el *n.* representation of designed or actual object; design, pattern; object of imitation; (copy of) garment etc. by recognized designer; person employed to pose for artist etc., show off clothes, etc. *a.* that is a model; exemplary, excellent of its kind. *v.* fashion, shape; manipulate, produce by manipulating, clay, wax, etc.; act as model, wear for display. **mod'elling** *n.* (esp.) representation of form in sculpture or of relief and solidity in painting etc.

mod'erate *a.* avoiding extremes, temperate; not excessive; middling in quantity or quality. *n.* person of moderate views. *v.* (-āt), make or become less violent or excessive; act as moderator. ~**ā'tion** *n.* ~**ātor** *n.* mediator; president of Presbyterian assembly; substance used in controlling nuclear reaction.

mod'ern *a.* of present and recent times; new-fashioned; not concerned with classics. *n.* (esp. in pl.) person living in modern times. **moder'nity** *n.*

mod'ernism *n.* modern view(s), artistic fashion(s), etc., esp. tendency to modify traditional religious doctrines etc. in light of recent research etc. ~**ist** *n.;* ~**is'tic** *a.*

mod'ernize *v.t.* make modern; adapt to modern ideas, taste, etc. ~**īzā'tion** *n.*

mod'est *a.* not overrating one's own merit; unassuming; not excessive; pure-minded, decorous. **mod'esty** *n.*

mod'icum *n.* small quantity.

mŏd′ĭfȳ v.t. tone down, qualify; make less severe; make partial changes in. ~ĭcā′tion n.

mō′dĭsh a. fashionable.

mŏd′ūlar a. based on module(s).

mŏd′ūlāte v. vary or regulate tone or pitch (of); (mus.) pass (from one key to another); (radio etc.) vary frequency etc. of (wave) by effect of another. ~ā′tion n. mŏd′ūlātor n. (esp.) chart used for tonic sol-fa exercises.

mŏd′ūle n. unit or standard of measurement, esp. as determining proportions of building etc.

mō′dus ŏperăn′dī n. method of working. [L]

mō′dus vĭvĕn′dī n. compromise pending settlement of dispute. [L]

mō′gul n. great or important personage.

M.O.H. abbr. Medical Officer, Ministry, of Health.

mō′hair n. (yarn or fabric made from) hair of Angora goat; imitation of this.

Mohămm′ĕdan, Mahŏm′ĕtan a. & n. Moslem. ~ism n.

mō′hō n. discontinuity between earth's crust and mantle. mō′hōle n. hole drilled through sea-bed to mantle.

moi′dōre (or -ōr′) n. former Portuguese gold coin.

moi′ĕtȳ n. half.

moil v.i. drudge.

moiré (mwär′ā) a. watered; like watered silk in appearance.

moist a. slightly wet, damp; rainy. moi′sten (-sn) v. make or become moist. moi′sture n. liquid diffused through air etc. or condensed on surface.

mōke n. (sl.) donkey.

mōl, mōle⁴ n. (chem.) equivalent in grams of molecular weight of substance.

mō′lar¹ a. & n. grinding (tooth).

mō′lar² a. (phys.) of, acting on or by, masses.

molăss′ĕs (-z) n. treacle-like syrup drained from raw sugar.

mōle¹ n. abnormal pigmented prominence on skin.

mōle² n. small burrowing animal with short soft fur. ~hill, mound thrown up by mole. ~skin, mole's fur; kind of strong soft fustian.

mōle³ n. massive stone etc. structure as pier or breakwater.

mole⁴: see mol.

mŏl′ĕcūle n. smallest particle (usu. group of atoms) of substance that can exist without losing chemical identity. molĕc′ūlar a.

molĕst′ v.t. subject to intentional annoyance. mŏlĕstā′tion n.

mŏll n. (sl.) gangster's mistress; woman.

mŏll′ĭfȳ v.t. soften, appease. ~ĭcā′tion n.

mŏll′usc n. animal of phylum of soft-bodied unsegmented usu. hard-shelled invertebrates.

mŏll′ȳcŏddle n. milksop. v.t. coddle.

Mō′loch (-k) n. Canaanite idol to which children were sacrificed.

mō′ltĕn a. liquefied by great heat.

mŏl′tō adv. (mus.) very. [It.]

mō′lȳ n. fabulous magic herb.

molȳb′dĕnum n. greyish-white metallic element.

mō′ment n. point or brief space of time; importance, weight; (mech.) measure of power of force to cause rotation. ~arȳ a. lasting only moment. momĕn′tous a. of great importance.

momĕn′tum n. (pl. -ta), quantity of motion of moving body; (pop.) force of motion gained by moving body.

Mon. abbr. Monday; Monmouthshire.

mŏn′achal (-k-) a. monastic. mŏn′achism (-k-) n.

mŏn′ad n. (philos. etc.) ultimate or primary unit; univalent element. monăd′ĭc a.; ~ism n.

mŏn′arch (-k) n. sovereign with title of king, emperor, etc.; supreme ruler. monăr′chĭc(al) aa.; ~ism, ~ist nn. mŏn′archȳ n. (state under) monarchical government.

mŏn′asterȳ n. residence of community, usu. of monks. monăs′tic a. of monks or monasteries. ~ticism n.

Monday (mŭn′dĭ; or -ā) n. second day of week.

mon′ĕtarȳ (mŭn-) a. of coinage or money.

mon′etīze (mŭn-) *v.t.* make into or recognize or put into circulation as money. **~zā′tion** *n.*

mon′ey (mŭ-) *n.* current coin; banknotes or other documents representing it; wealth. **~-changer**, person changing money at fixed rate. **~-lender**, one lending money at interest. **~-market**, sphere of operations of dealers in stocks and bills. **~-order**, post-office order for payment of money. **~-spinner**, kind of small spider. **mon′eyed** (-ĭd) *a.* wealthy.

Mŏng′ol, Mŏngō′lĭan (-ngg-) *aa. & nn.* (member) of race now inhabiting Mongolia or of yellow-skinned straight-haired type of mankind; *m~*, (mental defective) of type physically resembling Mongols. **~ism** *n.* this type of mental deficiency. **~oid** *n. & a.* (defective) of this type.

mŏng′ōōse (-ngg-) *n.* small carnivorous tropical mammal.

mong′rĕl (mŭngg-) *a. & n.* (animal, esp. dog) of no definable breed or type, resulting from various crossings; hybrid.

mŏn′ism *n.* any theory denying duality of matter and mind.

mŏn′ĭtor *n.* pupil in school with disciplinary etc. duties; one who listens to and reports on foreign broadcasts, telephone conversations, etc.; detector for induced radio-activity; shallow-draught armoured ship of heavy gunpower; kind of lizard. *v.t.* act as monitor of (broadcast etc.).

monk (mŭ-) *n.* member of male community living apart under religious vows. **~s(-)hood**, plant with blue hood-like flowers. **~ish** *a.*

monk′ey (mŭ-) *n.* kinds of mammal closely allied to man; (sl.) temper; (sl.) £500. *v.i.* play tricks (*with*). **~-jacket**, sailor's short close-fitting jacket. **~-nut**, peanut. **~-puzzle**, kind of prickly tree.

mono *abbr.* monophonic (sound etc.)

mŏn′(o)- in comb., alone, sole, single. **mŏn′ochrōme** (-k-) *n. & a.* (picture etc.) having only one colour; **~chromăt′ic** *a.* **monŏc′ūlar** *a.* one--eyed; adapted for one eye.

monŏg′amў *n.* condition, rule, or custom of being married to only one person at a time; **~gamous** *a.* **~lĭth** *n.* single block of stone as pillar, monument, etc. **~lĭth′ĭc** *a.* of or like monolith; unified and homogeneous; massive. **~mā′nĭa** *n.* obsession of mind by single idea or intent; **~-mā′nĭăc** *n.* **~phŏn′ĭc** *a.* (of sound) not stereophonic, transmitted etc. on single channel. **~plāne** *n.* aircraft with one pair of wings. **~rail** *n.* railway with cars running on single rail. **~sўll′able** *n.* word of one syllable; **~sўllăb′ĭc** *a.* **~thēĭsm** *n.* doctrine that there is only one God; **~thēĭst** *n.*, **~thēĭs′tĭc** *a.* **~tўpe** *n.* printing apparatus casting and setting up type in single letters. **P. ~vā′lent** *a.* univalent.

monŏx′īde *n.* oxide containing one oxygen atom.

mŏn′ocle *n.* single eye-glass.

mŏn′odў *n.* dirge or elegy.

mŏn′ogrăm *n.* two or more letters, esp. initials, interwoven.

mŏn′ograph (-ahf) *n.* treatise on single object or class of objects.

mŏn′olŏgue (-g) *n.* soliloquy; long speech by one person; dramatic composition for one speaker.

monŏp′olĭst *n.* holder or supporter of monopoly.

monŏp′olīze *v.t.* secure monopoly of. **~zā′tion** *n.*

mŏnŏp′olў *n.* exclusive trading privilege; sole possession or control.

mŏn′otōne *n.* sound continuing or repeated on one note or without change of tone. **monŏt′onous** *a.* unvarying in tone; always the same, without variety. **monŏt′onў** *n.*

mŏnseigneur′ (-sānyê̄r) *n.* French title of princes, cardinals, etc.

monsieur (mosyê̄r′) *n.* (pl. *messieurs*), French title prefixed to man's name; sir; Frenchman; (hist.) second son or next younger brother of French king.

mŏnsi′gnor (-sēnyê̄r) *n.* title of some R.-C. prelates etc.

mŏnsōōn′ *n.* seasonal wind prevailing in S. Asia; rainy season accompanying SW. monsoon.

mŏn'ster n. misshapen creature; person or thing of portentous appearance or size; inhumanly cruel or wicked person.

mŏn'strance n. vessel in which consecrated Host is exposed.

mŏnstrŏs'itў n. monstrousness; misshapen or outrageous thing.

mŏn'strous a. like monster; huge; outrageous.

Mont. abbr. Montana; Montgomeryshire.

mŏn'tage (-ahzh) n. selection, cutting, and arrangement of shots in cinema film; (picture etc. produced by) juxtaposition of (parts of) photographs etc.

month (-ŭ-) n. period of moon's revolution; any of twelve divisions of calendar year. **month'lў** a. recurring, payable, etc. once a month; n. monthly magazine etc.; adv. once a month.

mŏn'ūment n. anything designed or serving to commemorate something. **mŏnūmĕn'tal** a. of or serving as monument; colossal or stupendous.

moo v.i. & n. (make) lowing sound.

mooch v.i. (colloq.) loiter about; slouch along.

mood[1] n. (gram.) group of forms in conjugation of verb serving to indicate function in which it is used.

mood[2] n. state of mind or feeling. **moo'dў** a. subject to changes of mood; depressed, sullen.

moon n. satellite revolving round earth in lunar month and reflecting light from sun; (poet.) month. v.i. go dreamily or listlessly. ~calf, born fool. ~light, light of moon. ~lighting, activities by night; holding of two jobs at same time. ~shine, moonlight; visionary stuff; (sl.) illicitly distilled spirits. ~-stone, felspar with pearly lustre used as gem. ~-struck, lunatic. **moo'nў** a. (esp.) listless, stupidly dreamy

moor[1] n. tract of uncultivated and often heather-clad ground. ~cock, male red grouse. ~hen, water-hen. ~land, (of) moors.

moor[2] v.t. attach (boat etc.) by rope to shore or something fixed. ~age n. place, charge, for mooring. ~ings n.pl. place, anchors and chains, etc. for mooring.

Moor[3] n. one of Moslem people of NW. Africa. ~ish a.

moose n. (pl. same) N.-Amer. elk.

moot n. (hist.) meeting, esp, legislative or judicial. a. that can be argued, debatable. v.t. raise (question etc.) for discussion.

mŏp[1] n. bundle of yarn etc. fixed to stick for use in cleaning; thick untidy head of hair. v. clean or wipe (as) with mop; wipe up (as) with mop; ~ up, absorb, dispose of, (mil.) complete subjugation of area etc. by capturing or killing remaining troops etc.

mŏp[2] v.i. ~ and mow, grimace.

mōpe v.i. be dull, dejected, and spiritless.

mō'pĕd n. motorized bicycle.

moquĕtte' (-k-) n. piled fabric used for upholstery etc.

moraine' n. debris deposited by glacier.

mŏr'al a. concerned with character etc. or with right and wrong; good, virtuous. n. moral teaching; (pl.) habits or conduct from moral point of view. ~ certainty, probability too great to admit of reasonable doubt.

morale' (-ahl) n. discipline and spirit pervading army etc.

mŏr'alist n. one who teaches morality. **moralis'tic** a.

morăl'itў n. moral principles or rules; moral conduct; kind of moralizing drama.

mŏr'alīze v.i. indulge in moral reflection. ~zā'tion n.

morăss' n. wet swampy tract, bog.

mŏrator'ium n. legal authorization to debtor to postpone payment; agreed or authorized delay or postponement.

Morā'vian a. & n. (native) of Moravia; (member) of Hussite Protestant sect.

mŏr'bĭd a. not natural and healthy; indicative etc. of disease. **morbid'itў** n.

mŏr'dant a. caustic, biting; (of acids

etc.) corrosive. *n.* acid used in etching; substance used for fixing dyes etc.

mŏre *a.* & *pron.* greater or additional quantity or number or degree (of). *adv.* to greater degree or extent or amount.

morĕl' *n.* kinds of edible fungus.

morĕll'ō *n.* dark-coloured bitter cherry.

moreo'ver (mŏrō-) *adv.* besides, further.

mŏr'ēs (-z) *n.pl.* social customs, moral principles, etc. of class, group, etc.

mŏrganăt'ic *a.* (of marriage) between man of exalted rank and woman of lower rank who remains in her former station.

mŏrgue (-g) *n.* place where bodies are kept for identification etc.; materials kept for reference by newspaper etc.

mŏ'ribŭnd *a.* in dying state.

Mŏr'mon *n.* & *a.* (member) of U.-S. Christian sect. ~ism *n.*

mŏrn *n.* (poet.) morning.

mŏr'ning *n.* day from dawn till noon or midday meal. ~ coat, tail-coat with front sloped away. ~ dress, men's formal daytime wear. ~-glory, Amer. climbing plant with showy flowers. ~ star, Venus etc. seen to east before sunrise.

morŏcc'ō *n.* (pl. *-os*), fine flexible leather of goatskin tanned with sumac; imitation of this.

mŏr'on *n.* adult with mental development of child of about nine or ten. **morŏn'ic** *a.*

morōse' *a.* of bitter unsociable temper; sullen.

mŏr'phēme *n.* elementary significant linguistic unit.

Mŏr'pheus (-fūs) *n.* (Rom. myth.) god of dreams.

mŏr'phia, mŏr'phine (-ēn) *nn.* narcotic principle of opium.

mŏrphŏl'ogȳ *n.* study of form of animals and plants; branch of philology dealing with inflexion and word-formation. ~lŏ'gical *a.*

mŏ'rris (dance) *n.* English traditional dance in fancy costume.

mŏ'rrow (-ō) *n.* next day.

mŏrse[1] *n.* walrus.

Mŏrse[2] **(cōde)** *n.* telegraphic alphabet with letters represented by combinations of long and short signals.

mŏr'sel *n.* mouthful, bit; small quantity.

mŏr'tal *a.* subject to or causing death; (of sin) deadly. *n.* human being.

mŏrtăl'itȳ *n.* being mortal; loss of life on large scale; death-rate.

mŏr'tar *n.* vessel in which drugs, food, etc. are pounded with pestle; short gun throwing shells etc. at high angles; mixture of lime, sand, and water used to make joints between stones etc. ~board, on which building mortar is held for use; college cap with flat stiff square top.

mortgage (mŏr'gĭj) *n.* conveyance of property as security for debt until money is repaid. *v.t.* make over by mortgage; pledge in advance. **mortgagee'** *n.* holder of mortgage. ~**gagor'** (-jŏr) *n.* person who pledges property in mortgage.

mŏrti'cian *n.* (U.S.) undertaker.

mŏr'tifȳ *v.* chasten (flesh etc.) by repression; humiliate, chagrin; be affected with gangrene. ~**ficā'tion** *n.*

mŏr'tise *n.* hole into which end of another part of framework etc. is fitted. *v.t.* make mortise in; join by mortise. ~ lock, one fitting into mortise in edge of door.

mŏrt'main *n.* condition of land etc. held inalienably by corporation.

mŏr'tūarȳ *a.* of or for burial. *n.* place for temporary reception of corpses.

mosā'ic[1] (-z-) *n.* picture or pattern made with small coloured pieces of stone, glass, etc. *a.* of or like such work.

Mosā'ic[2] (-z-) *a.* of Moses.

mosĕlle' (-z-) *n.* dry white wine from Moselle valley.

Mŏs'lėm, Mŭs'lĭm (*or* -z-) *n.* one who professes Islam. *a.* of Moslems.

mŏsque (-k) *n.* Moslem place of worship.

mosqui'tō (-kē-) *n.* (pl. *-oes*), kinds of gnat, esp. with long blood-sucking proboscis. ~-curtain, ~-net, fine-meshed net for keeping mosquitoes from bed etc.

mŏss *n.* swamp, peat-bog; kinds of small cryptogamous plant growing on moist surfaces. ~-rose, with moss-like growth on calyx and stalk. ~-trooper, 17th-c. free-booter on Scottish border. **mŏss'ў** *a.* moss-grown.

mōst *a. & pron.* greatest number, quantity, or degree (of). *adv.* in great or greatest degree. **mōst'ly** *adv.* predominantly, in the main.

mot (mō) *n.* ₁witty saying. ~ *juste*, (zhōōst), *the* most precisely right expression. [F]

mōte *n.* particle of dust, esp. speck seen floating in sunbeam.

mōtĕl' *n.* roadside hotel or group of cabins for motorists.

mōtĕt' *n.* (mus.) usu. unaccompanied anthem in R.C. or Lutheran Church.

mŏth *n.* kinds of usu. nocturnal lepidopterous insect; clothes-moth or other insect with larvae feeding on wool, fur, etc. ~-eaten, injured by moths; antiquated. **mŏth'ў** *a.* infested with moths.

moth'er (mŭdh-) *n.* female parent; head of nunnery etc.; old woman. *v.t.* (esp.) act like mother to. ~ country, native land; country in relation to its colonies. ~-in-law, wife's or husband's mother. ~ of pearl, iridescent lining of oyster and other shells. ~ tongue, native language. ~hōōd *n.*; ~lèss, ~lў *aa.*

mōtif' (-ēf) *n.* distinctive feature or dominant idea of design, composition, etc.

mō'tion *n.* moving; gesture; proposition formally made in deliberative assembly; application to judge or court for order etc.; evacuation of bowels. *v.* make motion esp. to direct or guide person. ~-picture, cinematograph film. ~lèss *a.*

mō'tivāte *v.t.* supply motive or inducement to, be motive of. ~ā'tion *n.*; ~ā'tional *a.*

mō'tive *n.* what induces person to act. *a.* productive of motion or action.

mŏt'ley *a.* parti-coloured; heterogeneous. *n.* fool's motley garb.

mō'tor *n.* motive agent or force; apparatus, esp. internal combustion engine, supplying motive power for vehicle or machinery; motor-car. *a.* giving, imparting, or producing motion; driven by motor. *v.i.* go or convey by car. ~-bike (colloq.), ~-cycle, two-wheeled motor-driven road vehicle. ~-car, motor-driven usu. four-wheeled passenger road vehicle. ~way, fast highway for motor vehicles. ~ĭst *n.* driver of car. ~īze *v.t.* equip or supply with motor transport or engine.

mŏtt'le *v.t.* mark or cover with spots or blotches.

mŏtt'ō *n.* (pl. -oes), saying or esp. heraldic inscription expressing appropriate sentiment or aspiration.

mou'jĭk (mōōzh-) *n.* Russian peasant.

mould[1] (mōld) *n.* loose earth; soil rich in organic matter.

mould[2] (mōld) *n.* fungous growth on damp surface.

mould[3] (mōld) *n.* hollow vessel in which fluid or plastic material is shaped or cast; pudding etc. shaped in mould; form or character. *v.t.* shape (as) in mould; model.

moul'der (mōl-) *v.i.* decay to dust; crumble away.

moul'ding (mōl-) *n.* (esp.) ornamental strip applied to building etc.; material, esp. of wood, for this.

moul'dў (mōl-) *a.* covered with mould; decaying; 'rotten'.

moult (mōlt) *v.* shed feathers in changing plumage. *n.* moulting.

mound *n.* heap or bank of earth.

mount[1] *n.* mountain or hill.

mount[2] *v.* ascend, go upwards; climb on to; put upon or provide with animal for riding; provide with or fix on or in support(s) or· setting; organize, arrange; ~ *guards*, post, be posted, to keep watch (*over*); ~ *up*, increase in amount. *n.* margin round picture etc., card etc. on which drawing etc. is mounted; setting; horse etc. for riding.

moun'tain (-tĭn) *n.* hill of impressive height; large heap or pile. ~ ash, scarlet-berried tree. **mountaineer'** *n.* mountain-climber; *v.i.* climb mountains. **moun'tainous** *a.* abounding in mountains; huge.

moun'tėbănk *n.* impudent trickster, buffoon.

Moun'tў *n.* (colloq.) member of Royal Canadian Mounted Police.

mourn (-ōrn) *v.* be sorrowful or distressed; grieve for loss of. **~er** *n.* one who mourns; person attending funeral. **mourn'ful** *a.* **mour'ning** *n.* lamentation; (wearing of) black clothes as sign of bereavement.

mouse *n.* (pl. *mīce*), kinds of small rodent; shy or timid person; (sl.) black eye. *v.i.* (-z), hunt for or catch mice.

mousse (mōōs) *n.* dish of flavoured and freq. frozen whipped cream etc.

moustache (mʌstahsh') *n.* hair on upper lip.

Mouster'ian (-ōō-) *a.* of middle Palaeolithic culture associated with *Le Moustier*, France.

mou'sў *a.* quiet or timid as mouse; insignificant; dull greyish-brown.

mouth *n.* (pl. pr. -dhz), cavity of head used in eating and speaking; opening at which anything enters; outfall of river. *v.* speak pompously or with exaggerated distinctness, declaim; grimace. **~-organ**, kinds of small reed instrument played by sucking or blowing. **~piece**, part of musical instrument etc. placed before or between lips; part of telephone etc. spoken into; person speaking for others. **mouth'ful** *n.*

move (mōōv) *v.* change position, posture, place, or abode (of); stir or rouse; affect with emotion; propose as resolution. *n.* moving, esp. of piece at chess etc.; step or proceeding. **mo'vable** *a.* that can be moved or removed; (of property) personal. **mo'ver** *n.* (esp.) one who moves proposal. **mo'vie** *n.* motion picture. **mo'ving** *a.* (esp.) touching, affecting; rousing; **moving staircase,** escalator.

move'ment (-ōōvm-) *n.* moving; moving mechanism, esp. of watch; principal division of musical work; (group organized for) combined action or endeavour *for* some end.

mow[1] (mō) *n.* stack of hay, corn, etc.

mow[2] (mō) *v.* (p.p. *mown*, pr. mōn), cut grass etc. with scythe or machine.

mow[3] : see **mop**[2].

M.P. *abbr.* Member of Parliament; Military Police.

m.p. *abbr.* melting-point.

mp. *abbr.*, *mezzo piano* [It.], moderately soft.

m.p.g., m.p.h. *abbr.* miles per gallon, hour.

Mr. (mĭs'ter), **Mrs.** (mĭs'ĭz), titles prefixed to name of man or of married woman.

M.R. *abbr.* Master of the Rolls; Midland Railway.

M.R.B.M. *abbr.* medium range ballistic missile.

M.R.C.P., M.R.C.S., *abbr.* Member of Royal College of Physicians, of Surgeons.

MS. (ĕm'ĕs'), *abbr.* manuscript.

M.Sc. *abbr.* Master of Science.

M.S.L. *abbr.* mean sea level.

MSS. *abbr.* manuscripts.

M.T. *abbr.* Motor Transport.

Mt. *abbr.* Mount.

M.T.B. *abbr.* motor torpedo-boat.

much *a. & pron.* great quantity or amount (of). *adv.* in great degree; by great deal. **~ of a ~ness,** very much alike.

mū'cilage *n.* viscous substance got from plants; adhesive substance. **mūcilă'ginous** *a.*

muck *n.* manure; dirt, filth; rubbish. *v.* manure; clean *out*; fool or mess *about*; **~ in,** share esp. rations or quarters (*with*); **~ up,** bungle, make mess of. **~-raking,** seeking out and publishing of scandals etc. **muck'ў** *a.*

mū'cous *a.* secreting or covered by mucus. **~ membrane,** inner surface-lining of hollow organs of body.

mū'cus *n.* sticky secretion usu. forming protective covering for mucous membrane.

mud *n.* wet soft soil or earthy matter. **~guard,** guard over wheel as protection against mud. **~-slinging,** esp. reckless or violent abuse, invective. **mudd'ў** *a.* like or covered with mud, thick, turbid; *v.t.* make muddy.

mudd'le *v.* bewilder, confuse; bungle, mix *up*; act in confused ineffective manner. *n.* muddled condition.

muezz'in (mōō-) *n.* official of Moslem mosque proclaiming hours of prayer from minaret.

muff[1] *n.* cover of fur etc. for hands.

muff[2] *n.* duffer, bungler. *v.t.* fail in, bungle; miss (catch etc.).

mŭff′ĭn n. light flat spongy cake eaten hot with butter. **~eer′** n. castor for sprinkling muffins with salt or sugar.

mŭff′le v.t. wrap *up* for warmth; wrap up to deaden sound. **mŭff′ler** n. warm scarf; motor-car etc. silencer.

mŭf′tĭ n. plain clothes as opp. uniform.

mŭg n. usu. cylindrical drinking--vessel; (sl.) mouth, face;](sl.) fool, dupe. v. (sl.) study hard; get *up* by hard study. **mŭgg′ĭns** (-z) n. simpleton.

mŭgg′ў (-g-) a. warm, damp, and oppressive.

mŭg′wŭmp n. (U.S.) great man; political independent.

mūlătt′ō n. (pl. *-os*), person of mixed Negro and white blood.

mŭl′berrў n. (tree bearing) dark-red oval compound fruit.

mŭlch n. wet straw, leaves, etc. put round plant's roots. v.t. cover or spread with mulch.

mŭlct v.t. punish by fine; deprive *of*. n. fine.

mūle n. offspring of mare and he-ass; obstinate person; kind of spinning--machine. **mūlĕteer′** n. mule-driver. **mū′lish** a. obstinate, intractable.

mŭll v.t. heat and spice (wine, beer).

mŭll′ah n. Moslem theologian.

mŭll′ein (-lĭn) n. kinds of woolly--leaved herb.

mŭll′ĕt n. kinds of edible sea--fish.

mŭllĭgataw′nў n. highly seasoned curry-flavoured soup.

mŭll′ion n. upright separating lights of divided window.

mŭl′tĭ- in comb., many. **mŭltĭfār′ious** a. of many kinds. **~form** a. having many forms. **~lăt′eral** a. many--sided; (of treaty etc.) in which more than two parties participate. **~-millionaire′** (-lyon-) n. person with fortune of several millions. **~pār′tĭte** a. divided into many parts. **~plĕx** a. manifold.

mŭl′tĭple a. of many parts, components, branches, kinds, etc. n. quantity exactly divisible by another.

mŭltĭplĭcănd′ n. quantity to be multiplied.

mŭltĭplĭcā′tion n. multiplying.

mŭltĭplĭ′cĭtў n. manifold variety, great number (*of*).

mŭl′tĭplĭer n. (esp.) number by which another is multiplied.

mŭl′tĭplў v. make or become many; find quantity produced by taking given quantity given number of times.

mŭl′tĭtūde n. great number; throng; *the* many. **mŭltĭtū′dĭnous** a.

mŭm[1] int. enjoining silence or secrecy. a. silent.

mŭm[2] n. (colloq.) mother.

mŭm′ble v. speak indistinctly; chew or bite as with toothless gums. n. indistinct talk.

mŭmbō-jŭm′bō n. meaningless ritual; mystification, obscurity of language etc.

mŭmm′er n. actor in traditional popular performance; play-actor. **mŭmm′erў** n. ridiculous ceremonial.

mŭmm′ifў v. turn into mummy or mummy-like thing. **~fĭcā′tion** n.

mŭmm′ў[1] n. dead body preserved by embalming, esp. by ancient Egyptians; dried-up body.

mŭmm′ў[2] n. (colloq.) mother.

mŭmps n.pl. contagious disease with swollen neck and face.

mŭnch v. chew steadily.

mŭn′dāne a. of this world.

mūnĭ′cĭpal a. of municipality. **~īze** v.t.

mūnĭcĭpăl′itў n. town or district with local self-government; its governing body.

mūnĭf′ĭcent a. splendidly generous. **mūnĭf′ĭcence** n.

mū′nĭments n.pl. title-deeds and similar records.

mūnĭ′tions n.pl. military weapons, ammunition, equipment, and stores.

mŭnt′jăk n. small Asian deer.

mūr′al a. of or in or on wall. n. mural painting etc.

mūr′der n. unlawful and intentional killing of human being. v.t. kill (human being) unlawfully; spoil by bad execution etc. **mur′derer**, **~ĕss** nn.; **~ous** a.

mūr′ĕx n. shell-fish from which Tyrian purple was obtained.

mŭr'kў a. dark, gloomy.

mŭr'mur (-er) n. subdued continuous sound; subdued expression of discontent; hushed speech. v. produce, say or speak in, murmur. **~ous** a.

mŭ'rrain (-rĭn) n. infectious disease in cattle; (arch.) plague.

mŭs'căt n. kinds of grape. **muscatĕl'** n. muscat; raisin or strong sweet wine made from muscats.

mŭs'cle (-sl) n. contractile fibrous band or bundle producing motion in animal body; lean flesh or meat; muscular strength. v.i. (sl.) force one's way in.

Mŭs'covite n. & a. Russian; (native) of Moscow.

mŭs'cūlar a. of or in muscles; with well-developed muscles. **~ă'ritў** n.

mūse¹ (-z) v.i. ponder, meditate.

mūse² n. M~, (Gk. myth.) one of nine sister goddesses presiding over arts and sciences; poet's inspiration or genius.

mūse'um (-zĭ-) n. place where objects illustrating art, science, etc. are exhibited, studied, etc. **~-piece**, object fit for museum; antiquated person.

mŭsh n. soft pulp; (U.S.) maize porridge. **mŭsh'ў** a. soft; (sl.) weakly sentimental.

mŭsh'rōōm n. kinds of edible fungus noted for rapidity of growth; upstart person or thing. v.i. gather mushrooms; expand rapidly; take mushroom shape. **~ cloud**, characteristic cloud produced by nuclear explosion.

mū'sĭc (-z-) n. art of combining sounds for reproduction by voice or instrument(s) in rhythmic, melodic, and harmonic form; sounds so produced; record or score of these for reproduction; any pleasant sound. **~-hall**, variety theatre. **mū'sical** a. of, fond of, skilled in, set to, music; sweet-sounding; n. play, film, etc. of which (esp. light) music is essential part. **mūsĭ'cian, ~ianship** nn.; **mūsĭ'cianlў** a.

mŭsk n. substance secreted by male musk-deer used as basis of perfumes; kinds of plant with musky smell. **~-deer**, small hornless ruminant of Central Asia. **~-melon**, common melon. **~-rat**, large N. Amer. aquatic rodent; its fur. **~-rose**, climbing rose with fragrant white flowers. **mŭs'kў** a.

mŭs'kĕt n. (hist.) infantryman's esp. unrifled gun. **mŭskĕteer'** n. (hist.) soldier with musket. **mŭs'kĕtrў** n. (instruction in) rifle-shooting.

Muslim : see **Moslem**.

mŭs'lĭn (-z-) n. fine gauzy cotton fabric.

mŭs'quash (-ŏsh) n. (fur of) musk-rat.

mŭss'el n. kinds of bivalve mollusc.

Mŭss'ulman a. & n. Moslem.

mŭst¹ n. grape-juice before or during fermentation; new wine.

mŭst² v. aux. be obliged to; be certain to. n. something imperative.

mŭs'tăng n. wild or half-wild horse.

mŭs'tard n. (hot pungent seeds of) yellow-flowered plant; condiment etc. made from its ground seeds. **~ gas**, colourless oily liquid used as irritant gas.

mŭs'ter n. assembling of men for inspection etc.; pass ~, bear inspection, come up to standard. v. bring or come together, collect; summon up (courage etc.).

mŭs'tў a. mouldy; antiquated, stale.

mū'table a. liable to change; fickle. **~bĭl'itў** n.

mū'tant a. & n. (individual) differing from parents as result of mutation.

mūtā'tion n. change; (organism arising from) change in gene structure of reproductive cell.

mūtā'tĭs mūtăn'dĭs, with necessary changes. [L]

mūte¹ a. silent; without speech, dumb; soundless. n. clip, pad, etc. to deaden sound of musical instrument. v.t. muffle or deaden sound of. **mū'tĭsm** n. dumbness.

mūte² v.i. (of birds) void dung.

mū'tĭlāte v.t. injure, make imperfect, by depriving of part. **mūtĭlā'tion** n.

mūtĭneer' n. one who mutinies.

mū'tĭnous a. rebellious.

mū'tĭnў n. open revolt against authority, esp. refusal of members of armed forces to obey orders. v.i. engage in mutiny.

mŭtt *n.* (sl.) stupid person.

mŭtt′er *v.* speak, utter, in low tone; grumble. *n.* muttering.

mŭtt′on *n.* sheep's meat.

mū′tūal *a.* felt or done by each to other; bearing same relation to each other; (improperly) common to two or more.

mŭzz′le *n.* beast's snout; open end of gun-barrel; cage etc. put on animal's muzzle. *v.t.* put muzzle on; silence.

mŭzz′ỹ *a.* dazed, hazy; stupid with drink.

M.V. *abbr.* motor vessel; muzzle velocity.

M.V.O. *abbr.* Member of (Royal) Victorian Order.

Mw *abbr.* megawatt(s).

Mx. *abbr.* Middlesex.

my (mī, mi) *a.* of, belonging to, affecting, me.

M.Y. *abbr.* Motor Yacht.

mўcŏl′ogỹ *n.* study of fungi.

mўelī′tis *n.* inflammation of spinal cord.

mỹ′na(h), mi′na *n.* kinds of starling of SE. Asia.

mўō′pia *n.* short sight. **mўŏp′ic** *a.*

mў′riad *n.* & *a.* vast number (of).

myr′midon (mẽr-) *n.* unscrupulously faithful follower or attendant, hired ruffian.

myrrh (mẽr) *n.* gum-resin used in perfumes, medicine, etc.

myr′tle (mẽr-) *n.* kinds of plant, esp. European evergreen shrub with fragrant white flowers.

mўsĕlf′ (*or* mi-) *pron.*, emphat. and refl. form of *I*.

mўstēr′ious *a.* full of, wrapped in, or affecting mystery.

mўs′terỹ *n.* revealed religious truth, esp. one beyond human intelligence; (pl.) secret religious rites; miracle-play; secrecy; obscurity.

mўs′tic *a.* spiritually symbolic; esoteric; enigmatical. *n.* one who seeks union with deity through contemplation etc. or believes in spiritual apprehension of truths beyond understanding. ~al *a.*; ~ism *n.*

mўs′tifỹ *v.t.* bewilder; humbug. ~ficā′tion *n.*

mўstique′ (-tẽk) *n.* atmosphere of mystery investing some doctrines, arts, etc.

mўth *n.* (primitive) tale embodying esp. ancient popular belief or idea; fictitious person or thing. **mўth′ic(al)** *aa.*

mўthŏl′ogỹ (*or* mi-) *n.* body, study, of myths. ~lŏ′gical *a.*; ~logist *n.*

mўxomatō′sis *n.* contagious fatal virus disease of rabbits.

N

n (ĕn) *n.* (math.) indefinite quantity or power.

N. *abbr.* North.

n. *abbr.* neuter; nominative; noon; noun.

N.A.A.F.I., Naafi (năf′ĭ) *abbr.* Navy, Army, and Air Force Institutes.

năb *v.t.* (sl.) catch, arrest.

nā′bŏb *n.* ostentatiously wealthy person.

nā′cre (-ker) *n.* mother-of-pearl. **nā′creous** *a.*

nā′dir *n.* point opposite zenith; lowest point.

năg[1] *n.* horse, esp. saddle-horse.

năg[2] *v.* find fault (with) or scold persistently (*at*). **năgg′ing** *a.* (esp. of pain etc.) gnawing, persistent.

Nah. *abbr.* Nahum.

nai′ăd (nī-) *n.* (pl. *-ds* or *-dēs*), water nymph.

nail *n.* horny growth covering outer tip of human finger or toe; bird's or beast's claw; small, usu. pointed and broad-headed metal spike. *v.t.* fasten with nail(s); fix or hold tight; secure, catch.

nain′sŏok *n.* fine soft cotton fabric.

naïve (nah-ēv′), *a.* artless, unaffected; amusingly simple. **naïve′té** (-vtā), -tỹ *n.*

nā′kĕd *a.* unclothed, nude; defenceless; bare, uncovered; plain; unprotected; barren; (of eye) unassisted.

năm′bỹ-păm′bỹ *a.* insipidly pretty; mildly sentimental.

nāme *n.* word by which individual person, animal, place, or thing is spoken of or to; family, clan; reputation, fame. *v.t.* give name to; speak of or to by name; nominate, appoint; identify; (of Speaker) mention (M.P.) as disobedient to Chair. ~-day, day of saint whose name one bears. ~sake, person or thing of same name. ~less *a.* obscure; left unnamed; unmentionable. ~ly *adv.* that is to say, viz.

năn'cў(-boy) *n.* effeminate or homosexual young man.

nănkeen' *n.* yellowish-buff cotton cloth.

nănn'ў *n.* child's nurse.

nănn'ў-goat *n.* she-goat.

nā'no-sĕcond *n.* thousand millionth of second.

năp[1] *v.i.* & *n.* (take) short sleep, esp. by day.

năp[2] *n.* soft or downy surface of cloth. *v.t.* give nap to.

năp[3] *n.* card-game; tip that horse etc. is certain to win; *go* ~, stake everything or all one can. *v.t.* tip as certain winner.

nā'palm (-ahm) *n.* jellied petrol for use as incendiary.

nāpe *n.* back of neck.

nā'perў *n.* table-linen.

năph'tha *n.* inflammable oil distilled from coal etc. ~lēne, white crystalline compound used for dyes, to protect clothes against moth, etc.

năp'kĭn *n.* piece of linen etc. for wiping lips etc. at table; triangle or folded square of absorbent material wrapped round waist and between legs of baby.

Napōlĕŏn'ĭc *a.* of, like (that of), Napoleon Bonaparte.

năpp'ў *n.* (colloq.) baby's napkin.

narciss'ism *n.* morbid self-love or self-admiration. ~ist *n.*; ~is'tĭc *a.*

narciss'us *n.* (pl. -ssuses, -ssī), kinds of flowering bulb.

narcō'sĭs *n.* unconsciousness induced by narcotics.

narcŏt'ĭc *a.* inducing drowsiness, sleep, or insensibility. *n.* narcotic drug or influence.

nard *n.* spikenard.

nar'ghilĕ (-gĭ-) *n.* hookah.

nark *n.* (sl.) police spy, informer.

narrāte' *v.t.* recount, relate, give con-

tinuous account of. ~tion, ~tor, *nn.* nă'rrative *n.* spoken or written recital of connected events; *a.* of, in, by, etc. narration.

nă'rrow (-ō) *a.* of small width in proportion to length; restricted; with little margin; illiberal, prejudiced, exclusive. *n.* (usu. pl.) narrow part of sound, strait, river, or pass. *v.* make or become narrower; lessen, contract. ~ly *adv.* (esp.) closely; only just.

nar'whal (-wal) *n.* Arctic whale with tusk developed into long straight spirally-twisted horn.

nā'sal (-z-) *a.* of nose; (of sounds) produced with nose passages open; (of voice etc.) having unusual or disagreeable number of nasal sounds. *n.* nasal letter or sound.

năs'cent *a.* in process of birth; just beginning to be.

nastūr'tium (-shm) *n.* trailing red- or yellow-flowered garden plant.

nas'tў (nah-) *a.* repulsively dirty; obscene; ill-natured, spiteful; unpleasant; disagreeable.

Nat. *abbr.* Nathaniel; National(ist).

nā'tal *a.* of or from birth.

natā'tion *n.* swimming. nātatōr'ĭal, nā'tatorў *aa.*

nā'tion *n.* people having common descent, language, history, etc.; society united under one government in political State.

nă'tional *a.* of nation; common to or characteristic of whole nation. *n.* member of specified State. ~ism, ~ist *nn.*; ~is'tĭc *a.* nătionăl'itў *n.* (esp.) status as member of nation.

nă'tionalīze *v.t.* (esp.) transfer (land, industry, etc.) from private ownership and control to that of State. ~īzā'tion *n.*

nā'tive *a.* inborn; by virtue or reason of (place of) one's birth; occurring naturally; born in place, indigenous; of natives. *n.* one (esp. non-European) born in place; indigenous animal or plant; oyster reared wholly or partly in British waters.

nativ'itў *n.* birth, esp. of Christ; horoscope.

N.A.T.O., Nā'tō *abbr.* North Atlantic Treaty Organization.

nătt'er *v.i.* (colloq.) chat, gossip; chatter, esp. trivially or fretfully. *n.* chat.

nătt'ў *a.* spruce, trim.

nă'tural (-ch*er*-) *a.* of, according to, provided by, nature; physically existing; not artificial or conventional; (mus.) not flat or sharp; illegitimate. *n.* half-witted person; person etc. naturally endowed, easy or obvious choice (*for*); (sign, ♮, indicating) natural note. ~ **history**, (esp. popular or unscientific) study of natural objects. ~ **selection**, process by which groups etc. of organisms most suited to environment tend to survive. ~**ly** *adv.* (esp.) as might be expected, of course.

nă'turalism (-ch*er*-) *n.* morality, philosophy, etc., excluding supernatural or spiritual; realism. ~**ist** *n.* (esp.) student of animals or plants. ~**is'tic** *a.*

nă'turalize (-ch*er*-) *v.t.* admit (alien) to citizenship; adopt (foreign word etc.), introduce (plant etc.) into new environment. ~**izā'tion** *n.*

nā'ture *n.* thing's essential qualities; innate character; general characteristics and feelings of mankind; kind, sort, class; physical power causing phenomena of material world; *state of* ~, unregenerate condition, uncultured or uncultivated or undomesticated state, nakedness.

naught (nawt) *n.* nothing. *pred. a.* worthless.

naughty (naw'tĭ) *a.* badly behaved; disobedient; wicked.

nau'sėa *n.* feeling of sickness; loathing. **nau'sėāte** *v.t.* affect with nausea. **nau'sėous** *a* causing nausea; nasty; disgusting, loathsome.

nautch'-girl *n.* E.-Ind. professional dancing-girl.

nau'tical *a.* of sailors or navigation; maritime. ~ **mile**, 6080 ft.

nau'tilus *n.* kinds of cephalopod mollusc.

nā'val *a.* of navy; of warships; of ships.

nāve[1] *n.* body of church apart from chancel and aisles.

nāve[2] *n.* hub of wheel.

nā'vel *n.* pit on belly left by severance of umbilical cord; central point of anything. ~ **orange**, large orange with navel-like formation at top.

năv'ĭgable *a.* affording passage for ships; that can be steered. ~**bĭl'itў** *n.*

năv'ĭgāte *v.* voyage, sail ship; sail or steam on or through (sea, river, air); manage, direct course of. ~**ā'tion** *n.* (esp.) methods of determining position and course of ship etc. ~**ātor** *n.* (esp.) sea explorer.

năvv'ў *n.* labourer excavating for canals, roads, etc.; mechanical excavator.

nā'vў *n.* warships with their crews and organization; officers and men of navy; fleet. ~(-)**blue**, (of) very dark blue.

nay *adv.* no; or rather, and even. *n.* refusal.

Năzarēne *a. & n.* (native) of Nazareth.

Năz'arīte *n. & a.* (member) of ascetic Hebrew sect.

nāze *n.* headland.

Nazi (nah'tsĭ, -zĭ) *n. & a.* (member) of German National Socialist party or (person) holding similar views.

N.B. *abbr.* New Brunswick; North Britain; *nota bene* [L], note well.

n.b. *abbr.* no ball.

n.b.g. *abbr.* no bloody good.

N.C. *abbr.* North Carolina.

N.C.B. *abbr.* National Coal Board.

N.C.O. *abbr.* non-commissioned officer.

n.d. *abbr.* no date.

N.D., N.Dak. *abbr.* North Dakota.

NE. *abbr.* north-east.

Nėăn'dėrthal (-tahl) *a.* ~ *man*, of type inhabiting Europe in late Pleistocene period.

neap (-tide) *n.* tide with high-water level at its lowest.

Nėapŏl'itan *a. & n.* (inhabitant) of Naples. ~ **ice**, ice-cream in layers of various colours and flavours.

near *adv.* in(to) proximity in space or time; nearly; closely. *prep.* near to in space, time, condition, or semblance. *a.* closely related; close (to); (of way) direct, short; with little difference; parsimonious; left-hand. *v.* draw near (to).

~-sighted, short-sighted. **near'lў**
adv. almost; closely; *not* ~*ly*,
nothing like.

neat[1] *n.* ox, cow; cattle. ~**herd,**
cowherd.

neat[2] *a.* undiluted; nicely made or
proportioned; tidy, methodical;
cleverly done, phrased, etc.; deft,
dextrous.

nĕb *n.* (Sc.) beak, nose; tip.

Neb. *abbr.* Nebraska.

nĕb'ūla *n.* (pl. -ae), cloudy luminous
patch in sky consisting of stars,
dust, etc. **nĕb'ular** *a.*

nĕb'ūlous *a.* cloud-like; hazy, vague.
nebulŏs'itў *n.*

nĕ'cĕssarў *a.* indispensable; that
must be done; inevitable. *n.* thing
without which life cannot be
maintained; desirable thing not
regarded as luxury.

nĕcĕssĭtār'ĭan *a.* & *n.* (person) maintaining doctrine of determinism.
~**ĭsm** *n.*

nĕcĕss'ĭtāte *v.t.* render necessary;
involve as condition, result, etc.

nĕcĕss'ĭtous *a.* poor, needy.

nĕcĕss'ĭtў *n.* constraint or compulsion regarded as law governing (all)
human action; imperative need;
indispensable thing; (usu. pl.) pressing need.

nĕck *n.* part of body connecting head
with shoulders; contracted or
narrow part of anything between
wider parts. *v.i.* (sl.) exchange
caresses. ~**lace,** ornament round
neck. ~**tie,** band of silk etc. worn
with shirt-collar. ~**let** *n.* ornament, small fur, etc. worn round
neck.

nĕc'romăncў *n.* dealings with dead
as means of divination; magic,
sorcery. ~**măncer** *n.*; ~**măn'tĭc** *a.*

nĕcrŏp'olĭs *n.* cemetery.

nĕcrō'sĭs *n.* (pl. -osēs), mortification of piece of bone or tissue.
nĕcrŏt'ĭc *a.*

nĕc'tar *n.* (myth.) drink of gods;
sweet fluid yielded by plants.
nĕc'tarў *n.* plant's nectar-secreting
organ.

nĕc'tarĭne (*or* -ēn) *n.* kind of peach
with thin downless skin.

née (nā), (before married woman's
maiden name) born. [F]

need *n.* want, requirement; necessity
(*of*); time of difficulty; destitution,
poverty. *v.* stand in need of,
require; be under necessity to do.
~**ful** *a.* requisite; *the* money required. ~**lĕss** *a.*

nee'dle *n.* pointed slender instrument
pierced with eye for thread etc.;
knitting-pin; bar of mariner's compass; indicator on dial etc.; pointed
instrument in etching, surgery, etc.;
obelisk; sharp rock, peak; slender
crystal; leaf of fir or pine. *a.* (of
game etc.) crucial, arousing tense
excitement. *v.t.* goad, irritate.
~**woman,** woman skilled in needlework. ~**work,** sewing, embroidery,
etc.

needs (-z) *adv.* of necessity.

nee'dў *a.* necessitous.

ne'er (nār) *adv.* (poet.) never. ~**-do-
-well,** -weel, good-for-nothing person.

nĕfār'ĭous *a.* wicked.

nĕgā'tion *n.* denying; negative statement etc.; negative or unreal thing.

nĕg'ative *a.* expressing or implying
denial, prohĭbition, or refusal;
wanting positive attributes; opposite to positive; denoting quantity
etc. to be subtracted. *n.* negative
statement, word, quality, quantity,
etc.; print in which lights and
shadows of nature are reversed,
made by direct action of light on
emulsion. *v.t.* veto; serve to disprove; contradict; neutralize.

nĕglĕct' *v.t.* slight, disregard; leave
uncared for; leave undone. *n.*
neglecting or being neglected; careless treatment; negligence. ~**ful** *a.*

nĕgligé (nĕg'lĭzhā) *n.* free-and-easy
attire; woman's loose ornamental
dressing-gown.

nĕg'lĭgence *n.* want of proper care
or attention; carelessness. **nĕg'lĭ-
gent** *a.*

nĕg'lĭgĭble *a.* that may be neglected.

nĕgō'tiāte (-shĭ-) *v.* confer with view
to compromise or agreement; get
or give money value for (bill,
cheque); transfer (bill etc.) to
another; deal successfully with.
nĕgō'tiable *a.*; **nĕgōtiā'tion,**
~**ātor** *nn.*

Nĕ'grĕss *n.* female Negro

Nĕ'grō *n*. (pl. -*oes*), member of black-
-skinned African race. *a*. of this
race. **nē'groid** *a*. & *n*. (person) with
some Negro characteristics.

nĕ'gus *n*. hot wine and water.

Neh. *abbr*. Nehemiah.

neigh (nā) *v.i.* & *n*. (utter) cry of
horse.

neighbour (nā'ber) *n*. dweller next
door, near, in same district, or in
adjacent country; person or thing
near or next another. **~hood** *n*.
district; people of district; vicinity.
~ing *a*. near or next. **~lў** *a*. like
good neighbour, friendly, helpful.

nei'ther (nīdh-; *or* nēdh-) *adv*. not
either. *conj*. nor; nor yet. *a*. & *pron*.
not the one or the other.

nĕl'son *n*. class of wrestling holds
with arm passed under opponent's
from behind and hand applied to
his neck.

nem. con. *abbr*., *nemine contradicente*
[L], with no dissentients.

nĕm'ĕsis *n*. retributive justice.

nē'ō- in comb., new. **nēolith'ĭc** *a*. of
later stone age, with polished stone
implements. **~-pā'ganism** *n*. reversion to pagan ideas. **~plăsm** *n*.
autonomous new growth of body
tissue, tumour. **~plā'tonism** *n*. 3rd-
-century mixture of Platonic ideas
with Oriental mysticism; **~platŏn'ĭc**
a. **~zō'ĭc** *a*. of geological period
after palaeozoic.

neŏl'ogism *n*. coining or use of new
words; new word, meaning, etc.

nē'on *n*. colourless almost inert
atmospheric gaseous element. *a*. of
or using or characterized by bright
coloured light from tube containing
neon.

nē'ophўte *n*. new convert; religious
novice; beginner, tyro.

nĕ'phew (-v- *or* -f-) *n*. brother's or
sister's son.

nĕphrĭt'ĭc *a*. of kidneys; suffering
from nephritis. **nĕphrī'tĭs** *n*. inflammation of kidneys.

nĕp'otĭsm *n*. favouritism to relatives
esp. in conferring offices etc.

Nĕp'tūne *n*. (Rom. myth.) god of sea:
sea; third largest planet.

nĕptū'nĭum *n*. transuranic element.

nēr'ēĭd *n*. (Gk. myth.) sea-nymph;
(zool.) kind of marine worm.

nĕrve *n*. sinew, tendon; (bot.) rib of
leaf; (anat.) fibrous connection conveying impulses of sensation or
motion between brain and other
parts; (pl.) (esp. disordered) bodily
state in regard to interaction
between brain and other parts,
exaggerated sensitiveness, nervousness; presence of mind; coolness in
danger; assurance. *v.t.* give
strength, vigour, or courage to.

nĕrve'lĕss (-vl-) *a*. wanting in vigour
or spirit.

nĕr'vous *a*. sinewy, muscular; of
nerves; excitable, highly strung;
agitated, tense; timid. **~ break-
down**, (colloq.) loss of emotional
and mental stability.

nĕr'vў *a*. (colloq.) impudent; nervous,
apprehensive.

nĕs'cient *a*. ignorant; agnostic.
~ence *n*.

nĕss *n*. headland.

nĕst *n*. structure or place in which
bird lays eggs and shelters young;
breeding-place or lair; snug retreat,
shelter, bed, haunt; brood, swarm;
small chest *of drawers*, set *of* (small)
tables fitting together. *v.i.* make
or have nest. **~-egg**, money saved
up as reserve or nucleus. **nĕs'tling**
(-sl-) *n*. bird too young to leave
nest.

nĕs'tle (-sl) *v*. settle oneself, be
settled, comfortably; press close
(*to*); lie half-hidden or sheltered.

Nĕs'tŏr *n*. wise old man.

nĕt[1] *n*. meshed fabric of cord, thread,
hair, etc.; piece of this used for
catching fish, covering, protecting,
dividing tennis-court, etc. *v*. cover,
confine, catch, with net; send (ball)
into net; make net; make by
netting. **~-cord**, cord supporting
top of tennis net. **~work**, arrangement or pattern of intersecting
lines; complex system *of*; system of
interlinked radio etc. stations.

nĕt[2], **nĕtt** *a*. left after all deductions;
free from deduction; (of weight) not
including wrappings etc. *v.t.* yield
(sum) as true profit.

nĕt'ball *n*. team game in which ball is
thrown through net hanging from
ring on post.

nĕth'er (-dh-) *a*. lower. **~mōst** *a*.

nĕt'suke (-ōōkā) *n.* Japanese carved buttonlike girdle ornament.

nett : see net[2].

nĕtt'ĭng *n.* (esp.) fabric of netted string etc.

nĕtt'le *n.* plant with stinging hairs on leaves etc. *v.t.* irritate, provoke. ~-rash, skin eruption like those produced by nettle-stings.

neur'al *a.* of nerves. **neurăl'gia** (-ja) *n.* intermittent neural pain, esp. in face and head. **neurăl'gĭc** *a.*

neurăsthē'nĭa *n.* nervous debility. ~thĕn'ĭc *a.*

neurī'tĭs *n.* inflammation of nerve(s).

neurŏl'ogў *n.* scientific study of (esp. diseases of) nervous system. ~lŏ'gĭcal *a.*; ~logĭst *n.*

neur'on *n.* nerve-cell with appendages.

neurō'sĭs *n.* (pl. *-osēs*), derangement of normal function due to disorders of nervous system. **neurŏt'ĭc** *a.* & *n.* (person) suffering from neurosis.

neu'ter *a.* neither male nor female; neither masculine nor feminine; intransitive. *n.* neuter word etc.; neutered animal. *v.t.* castrate.

neu'tral *a.* taking neither side; impartial; neither acid nor alkaline; neither positive nor negative; vague, indeterminate. *n.* neutral State or person; position of gear mechanism in which no power is transmitted. **neutrăl'itў** *n.* **neu'tralīze** *v.t.* make neutral; counterbalance; render ineffective. ~īzā'tion *n.*

neutri'no (-ē-) *n.* neutral elementary particle of negligible mass.

neu'trŏn *n.* neutral elementary particle of almost same mass as proton.

Nev. *abbr.* Nevada.

nĕv'er *adv.* at no time, not ever; not at all; (colloq.) surely not; ~ *mind*, do not be troubled, it does not matter; (*on*) *the* ~-~, (by) hire-purchase. ~**more**, never again. ~**theless**, for all that; notwithstanding.

new *a.* now first introduced or discovered; fresh, additional; different, changed; recent; not worn. ~**comer**, newly arrived person. ~**fangled**, different from good old fashion. ~**moon**, moon when first visible as crescent. **N~ Style**, (according to) Gregorian calendar. **N~ Testament**, part of Bible dealing with Christ and his followers. **N~ World**, the Americas. **N~ Year's Day**, 1 Jan.

new'el *n.* centre pillar of winding stair; corner- or end-post of stair-rail.

New'foundland (-*fun*-; *or* -fown'-) *n.* large thick-coated breed of dog.

new'lў *adv.* recently, afresh.

New'markĕt *n.* card-game.

news (-z) *n.* tidings; fresh event reported. ~**agent**, dealer in newspapers etc. ~**-letter**, periodical sent by post to subscribers, members of group, etc. ~**monger**, gossip. ~**paper**, periodical publication with news etc. ~**print**, paper for newspapers. ~**-reel**, cinema film of recent news. ~**-theatre**, cinema showing news-reels etc. ~**ў** *a.* (colloq.) full of news; inquisitive.

newt *n.* small tailed amphibian allied to salamander.

Newtō'nĭan *a.* & *n.* (follower) of Sir Isaac Newton or his theory of universe.

nĕxt *a.* nearest; immediately following or preceding. *adv.* in next place or degree, on next occasion. *prep.* in or into next place or degree to. *n.* next person or thing. ~**-of-kin**, nearest relative.

nĕx'us *n.* bond, link; connected group or series.

N.F. *abbr.* Newfoundland; Norman French.

N.H. *abbr.* New Hampshire.

N.H.S. *abbr.* National Health Service.

N.I. *abbr.* National Insurance.

nĭb *n.* pen-point; (pl.) crushed cocoa-beans.

nĭbb'le *v.* take small bites at; bite gently or cautiously. *n.* nibbling, esp. at bait.

nĭb'lĭck *n.* golf-club (no. 8 iron) with heavy lofted head.

nīce *a.* fastidious; punctilious, subtle, fine; agreeable; kind, friendly, considerate.

nī'cetў *n.* precision; minute distinction, unimportant detail; *to a* ~, as precisely as possible.

niche *n.* shallow recess in wall for statue or other ornament; suitable place or position.

nick[1] *n.* notch or groove serving as catch, guide, mark, etc.; critical or opportune moment *of time. v.t.* indent; make nick in; just catch in time; nab.

Nick[2] *n. Old* ~, the devil.

nick'el *n.* silver-white metallic element used esp. in alloys and as plating; (U.S.) five-cent piece. *v.t.* coat with nickel. ~ **silver**, alloy of nickel, zinc, and copper.

nick'name *n.* name added to or substituted for regular name. *v.t.* give nickname to.

nic'otine (-ēn) *n.* poisonous alkaloid found in tobacco. ~**tin'ic ă'cid** *n.* member of vitamin-B group.

nic'titāte *v.i.* blink, wink. ~**ā'tion** *n.*

niece *n.* brother's or sister's daughter.

niĕll'ō *n.* (work inlaid with) black alloy for filling lines engraved on silver etc.

nif'tў *a.* (sl.) neat, smart, clever.

nigg'ard *n.* stingy person. ~**lў** *a.* stingy; meanly small.

nigg'er (-g-) *n.* (offensive term for) Negro or other dark-skinned person; dark shade of brown.

nigg'le *v.i.* spend time, be over-elaborate, on petty details. **nigg'ling** *a.*

nigh *adv. & prep.* near.

night *n.* time from sunset to sunrise; (period of) darkness. ~**-bird**, person who goes about; by night. ~**-cap**, drink before going to bed. ~**-club**, club open late at night. ~**dress**, ~**gown**, loose garment worn in bed. ~**fall**, end of daylight. ~**jar**, nocturnal bird with harsh cry. ~**mare**, horrible dream; any haunting fear, horrible experience. ~**shade**, kinds of poisonous plant. **night'lў** *a.* happening etc. in night, recurring every night; *adv.* every night.

night'ingāle (-ngg-) *n.* small migratory bird with melodious song often heard at night.

ni'hilism (*or* nīĭ-) *n.* views of Tsarist--Russian extremist revolutionaries. **ni'hilist** *n.*; ~**is'tic** *a.*

nǐl *n.* nothing.

nil'gai (-gī) *n.* large short-horned Indian antelope.

Nīlŏt'ĭc *a.* of (region of) river Nile.

nǐm'ble *a.* agile, swift; (of mind etc.) quick, clever.

nǐm'bus *n.* (pl. -bī, -buses), halo, aureole; (meteor.) rain-cloud.

nǐn'compōōp *n.* feeble person.

nīne *a. & n.* one more than eight (9, IX). ~**pins**, kind of skittles. ~**fold** *a. & adv.* **nīnth** *a. & n.* next after eighth; (that is) one of nine equal parts.

nīne'teen' *a. & n.* one more than eighteen (19, XIX). ~**th** *a. & n.*

nīne'tў *a. & n.* nine times ten (90, XC). ~**tieth** *a. & n.*

nǐnn'ў *n.* weak foolish person.

niō'bium *n.* rare metallic element.

nǐp[1] *v.* pinch, squeeze sharply, bite; check growth of; (sl.) go nimbly; ~ *in the bud*, stop at very beginning. *n.* pinch, sharp squeeze, bite; biting cold.

nǐp[2] *n.* small quantity of spirits etc. *v.i.* take (frequent) nips.

Nǐp[3] *n. & a.* (sl.) Japanese.

nǐpp'er *n.* (sl.) boy; great claw of crustacean; (pl.) implement with jaws for gripping or cutting.

nǐpp'le *n.* point of mammal's breast; teat of baby's bottle; nipple-like protuberance or projection.

nǐpp'ў *a.* cold; (sl.) nimble.

nîrva'na (-ah-) *n.* extinction of individuality and absorption into supreme spirit as Buddhist highest good.

nisi : see **decree**.

nǐt *n.* egg of louse or other parasite.

nī'trāte *n.* salt of nitric acid.

nī'tre *n.* saltpetre. **nī'tric** *a.*

nī'trogėn *n.* colourless tasteless odourless gaseous element forming largest part of atmosphere. ~ **fixation**, process of combining atmospheric nitrogen with other elements. **nītrŏ'gėnous** *a.* of or containing nitrogen.

nī'trō- in comb., containing nitrogen. **nītrocĕll'ūlōse** *n.* solid high explosive; constituent of some plastics etc. ~**-glў'cerin(e)** (*or* -ēn) *n.* violently explosive oily liquid.

nī'trous *a.* of, like, or impregnated

with nitre; of or containing nitrogen.

nĭt'wĭt *n.* (sl.) fool, idiot.

nĭx *n.* (sl.) nothing.

N.J. *abbr.* New Jersey.

N. lat. *abbr.* north latitude.

N. Mex. *abbr.* New Mexico.

NNE., NNW. *abbr.* north north-east, -west.

nō, particle used to express negative reply to question, request, etc. *a.* not any, not one; not a. *adv.* not; by no amount, not at all. *n.* (pl. *noes*), word *no*, denial or refusal; (pl.) voters against motion. **~ ball,** unlawfully delivered ball in cricket. **~-ball,** pronounce (bowler) to have delivered no ball. **~body,** no person; person of no importance. **~how,** in no way. **~wise,** in no manner or degree.

N.O. *abbr.* natural order.

N°, No. *abbr.* number.

n.o. *abbr.* natural order; not out.

Nō'ah (-a). **~'s ark,** child's toy model of ark containing animals etc.

nŏb[1] *n.* head; (cribbage) knave of same suit as turn-up card.

nŏb[2] *n.* (sl.) member of upper classes. **nŏbb'ŷ** *a.* smart, fine.

nŏbb'le *v.t.* (sl.) tamper with (racehorse etc.); get hold of dishonestly; catch.

nobē'lium *n.* transuranic element.

nobĭl'ĭarŷ *a.* of nobility.

nobĭl'ĭtŷ *n.* class of nobles; noble character or rank.

nō'ble *a.* illustrious by rank, title, or birth; of lofty character; magnanimous; of imposing appearance. *n.* nobleman; obsolete gold coin. **~man,** peer.

noblĕsse' *n.* nobility of foreign country. **~ oblige'** (-ēzh), privilege entails responsibility. [F]

nobody : see **no.**

nŏck *n.* notch at end of bow for holding string or in arrow to receive bowstring. *v.t.* set (arrow) on bowstring.

nŏctûr'nal *a.* of, active in, night.

nŏc'tûrne *n.* pensive melancholy musical composition; (paint. etc.) night-piece.

nŏd *v.* incline head slightly and quickly; let head droop, be drowsy; make slip or mistake; (of plumes) dance. *n.* nodding of head esp. in assent; this as sign of absolute power.

nŏdd'le *n.* (colloq.) head.

nŏdd'ŷ *n.* tern-like tropical sea-bird.

nōde *n.* knob on root or branch; hard tumour on joint; intersecting point of planet's orbit and ecliptic; point at which curve crosses itself; point or line of rest in vibrating body. **nō'dal** *a.* **nodōse'** *a.* knotty, knobbed; **nodŏs'ĭtŷ** *n.*

nŏd'ūle *n.* small rounded lump of anything; small knotty tumour, ganglion. **~lar, ~lōse, ~lous** *aa.*

nŏgg'ĭn (-g-) *n.* small mug; small measure of liquor.

nŏgg'ĭng (-g-) *n.* brickwork etc. in timber framing.

noise (-z) *n.* clamour, din; any sound. *v.t.* make public, spread *abroad*. **~lĕss** *a.*

noi'some *a.* noxious, disgusting.

noi'sy (-zĭ) *a.* loud; full of or making much noise; rowdy.

nō'lĕns vō'lĕns (-z) *adv.* willy-nilly. [L]

nom. *abbr.* nominal; nominative.

nō'mad *a.* & *n.* (member of tribe) roaming from place to place for pasture. **nomăd'ĭc** *a.*

nŏm de guerre' (gār) *n.* assumed name under which person fights, writes, etc. **nom de plume** (plōōm') *n.* pen-name. [F]

nō'menclātor *n.* giver of names, esp. in classification.

nomĕn'clature (*or* nō'-) *n.* system of names or naming; terminology.

nŏm'ĭnal *a.* of or like noun; in name or word only; not real or substantial. **~ĭsm** *n.* doctrine that abstract concepts are mere names. **~ĭst** *n.*; **~ĭs'tic** *a.*

nŏm'ĭnāte *v.t.* appoint, propose for election, to office. **~ā'tion, ~ātor** *nn.* **nŏmĭnee'** *n.* one who is nominated.

nŏm'ĭnative *a.* & *n.* (gram.) (case) used as subject; (word) in this case. **~tī'val** *a.*

nŏn- in comb., not. For the meanings of combinations not given below the main word should be consulted.

nŏn-appear'ance *n*. failure to appear, esp. in court of law. **~-belli'gerent** *a*. & *n*. (State) not taking active or open part in war; **~-belli'gerency** *n*. **~-colle'giate** *a*. not belonging to college; not having collegiate system. **~-commi'ssioned** *a*. not holding commission (esp. of Army officers below lieutenant). **~-cŏm'batant** *a*. not fighting; *n*. civilian in time of war, non-combatant member of army etc. **~-committ'al** *a*. refusing to commit oneself to view, course of action, etc. **~-condŭct'ing**, **~-condŭc'tive** *aa*. not conducting heat or electricity; **~-condŭc'tor** *n*. **~-essĕn'tial** *a*. & *n*. (thing) that is not essential. **~-flăm**, **~-flămm'able** *aa*. not inflammable. **~-intervĕn'tion** *n*. (esp.) policy of not interfering in affairs of other State(s). **~-jur'or** (joor-) *n*. (hist.) beneficed clergyman who refused oath of allegiance to William and Mary. **~-rèsis'tance** (-zĭs-) *n*. (policy of) not resisting even wrongly exercised authority etc. **~-skĭd** *a*. (of tyres) designed not to skid. **~-smō'ker** *n*. person who does not smoke; railway carriage etc. where smoking is not permitted. **~-stŏp** *a*. not stopping, esp. at intermediate stations etc.; *adv*. without a stop. **nŏn'suit** (-ūt) *n*. stoppage of lawsuit when plaintiff fails to make out case; *v.t*. subject to nonsuit. **~-ū'nion** *a*. not belonging to trade union, not made etc. by union labour. **~-ū'ser** (-z-) *n*. neglect to use right, by which it may become void.

nō'nage *n*. being under age.

nōnagĕnār'ian (*or* nŏ-) *n*. person between 90 and 100 years old.

nŏnce *n*. time being, present. **~-word**, one coined for occasion.

nŏn'chalant (-sh-) *a*. unmoved, indifferent, cool. **~ance** *n*.

nŏn cŏm'pŏs (*mĕn'tĭs*), insane. [L]

nŏnconfŏr'mĭst *n*. & *a*. (person) dissenting from esp. Anglican Church or refusing to conform to accepted practices etc. **nŏnconfŏr'mĭty** *n*.

nŏn'dĕscript *a*. hard to classify; indeterminate. *n*. nondescript person or thing.

none (nŭn) *pron*. not any *of*; no person(s). *a*. no, not any. *adv*. by no amount, not at all.

nŏnĕn'tĭtў *n*. non-existence; person of no account.

nōnes (-nz) *n.pl*. (Rom. ant.) ninth day before ides; (eccl.) office orig. said at ninth hour.

nonesuch : see **nonsuch**.

nŏnpareil' (-rĕl) *a*. unrivalled, unique. *n*. person or thing that is unrivalled; size of printing-type (6-point).

nŏnplŭs' *v.t*. reduce to hopeless perplexity.

nŏn'sense *n*. absurd or meaningless words or ideas; foolish conduct. *int*. rubbish! **nŏnsĕn'sical** *a*.

nŏn sĕq'uĭtur *n*. illogical inference. [L]

non(e)'sŭch (nŭns-) *n*. unrivalled person or thing; paragon.

noo'dle[1] *n*. simpleton.

noo'dle[2] *n*. strip or ball of cooked dough served esp. in soup.

noŏk *n*. secluded corner, recess.

noon *n*. twelve o'clock in day. **~day**, **~tide**, midday.

noose *n*. loop with running knot; snare. *v.t*. catch with or enclose in noose.

nŏr *conj*. and not, neither, and no more.

nor' *abbr*. north.

Nŏr'dĭc *a*. of tall blond dolichocephalic racial type of N. Europe, esp. Scandinavia.

nŏrm *n*. standard, type.

nŏr'mal *a*. conforming to standard, usual, regular, ordinary. *n*. usual state, level, etc. **nŏr'malcў, nŏrmăl'itў** *n*.; **~ize** *v.t*.

Nŏr'man *n*. native of Normandy. *a*. of Normans or Normandy.

Nŏrse *a*. of (language of) ancient Scandinavia, esp. Norway.

north *n*. point opposite sun at noon; northern part of country etc. *adv*. towards or in north. *a*. situated etc. in or towards north; facing north; coming from north. **~-east**, **~-west**, regions half-way between north and east, north and west. **~-easter**, **~-wester**, north-east, north-west, wind. **~-easterly**, **~-**

-westerly, towards or coming from north-east, north-west. ~-eastern, ~-eastward(s), ~-eastwardly, ~-western, ~-westward(s), ~-westwardly, in or towards north-east, north-west. ~ star, pole-star. ~-west etc., see *north-east* etc. nŏr'therlў (-dh-) *a.* & *adv.* towards, blowing from, north or thereabouts. ~ward *a. adv.* & *n.*; ~wards *adv.*

Northants. *abbr.* Northamptonshire.

nŏr'thern *a.* living or situated in, coming from, characteristic of, north, esp. of England, Europe, or U.S. ~ lights, aurora borealis. ~er *n.* native of north.

Northumb. *abbr.* Northumberland.

Norvic. *abbr.* (Bishop) of Norwich.

Nŏrwē'gian (-jn) *a.* & *n.* (native, language) of Norway.

Nos. *abbr.* numbers.

nōse (-z) *n.* member of face or head above mouth; sense of smell; open end of nozzle of pipe, etc.; prow; projecting part. *v.* perceive smell of, discover by smell; smell *out*; thrust nose against or into; pry or search; push one's way with nose (esp. of ship). ~-bag, fodder-bag hung to horse's head. ~-dive, (make) air-craft's steep downward plunge. ~-gay, bunch of flowers. ~-ring, ring fixed in nose of bull etc. for leading, or worn in nose as orna-ment.

nō's(e)y (-z-) *a.* (sl.) inquisitive.

nō'sing (-z-) *n.* rounded edge of step etc., or shield for it.

nosŏl'ogў *n.* classification of diseases.

nŏstăl'gia *n.* home-sickness; senti-mental yearning for, wistful or regretful remembrance of, what is past. nŏstăl'gic *a.*

nŏs'tril *n.* either opening in nose admitting air to lungs etc.

nŏs'trum *n.* quack remedy, patent medicine; pet scheme.

nosy : see nosey.

nŏt *adv.* expressing negation, refusal, or denial. ~ half, (sl.) very, very much.

nō'ta bē'nė, mark well, note this. [L]

nŏtabil'itў *n.* prominent person; being notable.

nō'table *a.* worthy of note, striking, eminent. *n.* eminent person.

nō'tarў *n.* person publicly authorized to draw up deeds and perform other formal duties. notār'ial *a.*

notā'tion *n.* representing of num-bers, quantities, etc. by symbols; set of symbols used for this.

nŏtch *n.* V-shaped indentation on edge or across surface. *v.t.* make notches in; make (specified score) at cricket; mark, record, etc. by notches.

nōte *n.* written sign representing pitch and duration of musical sound; single tone of definite pitch made by instrument, voice, etc.; sign, characteristic; brief record of facts etc. for speech etc.; comment on passage in book; short letter; formal diplomatic communication; banknote; distinction, eminence. *v.t.* observe, notice; set down as thing to be remembered; (*p.p.*) cele-brated, well known *for*. ~book, book for memoranda etc. ~paper, letter-paper.

nōte'worthy (-twẽrdhi) *a.* worthy of note or attention; remarkable.

no'thing (nŭ-) *n.* no thing, not any-thing, nought; no amount; thing of no importance; (with pl.) trifling thing, remark, etc. *adv.* not at all; in no way. ~nėss *n.* (esp.) non-existence; what does not exist.

nō'tice *n.* intimation, warning, an-nouncement; heed, attention; re-view or comment in newspaper etc. *v.t.* perceive, take notice of; remark upon. nō'ticeable (-sa-) *a.*

nō'tifў *v.t.* report, give notice of; inform. ~fiable *a.* that must be notified. ~ficā'tion *n.*

nō'tion *n.* concept; idea, concep-tion; view, opinion. ~al *a.*

notōr'ious *a.* known and talked of; known to deserve (ill) name. nōtori'etў *n.*

Notts. *abbr.* Nottinghamshire.

nŏtwithstănd'ing *prep.* in spite of. *adv.* nevertheless.

nougat (noō'gah) *n.* sweetmeat of sugar, egg-white, nuts, etc.

nought (nawt) *n.* figure 0; nothing.

noun *n.* word used as name of person or thing, substantive.

nou'rish (nŭ-) *v.t.* sustain with food; foster, cherish, nurse. ~ing *a.* containing nourishment. **~ment** *n.* sustenance, food, nutrition.

nous *n.* common sense, gumption.

Nov. *abbr.* November.

nō'va *n.* (pl. *-vae*), star showing sudden and great increase of light and energy for short period.

nŏv'el[1] *n.* fictitious prose tale of considerable length. **nŏvelĕtte'** *n.* short romantic novel without literary merit; **~ĕtt'ish** *a.* **nŏv'elĭst** *n.* novel-writer.

nŏv'el[2] *a.* of new kind, strange, hitherto unknown. **nŏv'eltÿ** *n.*

Novĕm'ber *n.* eleventh month of year.

novē'na *n.* (R.C. Ch.) special prayers or services on nine successive days.

nŏv'ĭce *n.* probationary member of religious order; beginner, tyro. **novĭ'tiate, -ciate** (-shĭ-) *n.* period of being novice; novice; novices' quarters.

now *adv.* at present time; in immediate past. *n.* this time; present. **~adays** *adv.* & *n.* (at) present day.

nō'where (-ār) *adv.* in, at, to, no place.

nŏ'xious (-kshŭs) *a.* harmful, unwholesome.

nŏzz'le *n.* vent or spout of hose-pipe etc.

n.p. *abbr.* net personalty; new paragraph.

N.R. *abbr.* North Riding.

nr. *abbr.* near.

N.S. *abbr.* New Style; Nova Scotia.

N.S.P.C.C. *abbr.* National Society for Prevention of Cruelty to Children.

N.S.W. *abbr.* New South Wales.

N.T. *abbr.* New Testament; Northern Territory.

N.T.P. *abbr.* normal temperature and pressure.

nū'ance (-ahńs) *n.* delicate difference in or shade of meaning, colour, etc.

nū'bīle *a.* marriageable (esp. of women). **nūbil'itÿ** *n.*

nū'clĕar *a.* (esp.) of atomic nuclei, atomic. **~ fission,** splitting of certain large nuclei into parts, with enormous release of energy. **~ fuel,** source of atomic energy. **~ reactor,** atomic pile.

nū'clĕus *n.* (pl. *-eī*), central part or thing round which others collect; kernel of aggregate or mass; central

part of cell; positively charged internal core of atom. **nūclē'ĭc** *a.*

nūde *a.* naked, unclothed. *n.* nude figure in painting etc.; (representation of) *the* undraped human figure.

nū'dist *n.* one who advocates or practises going unclothed; *a.* of nudists. **nū'dĭtÿ** *n.*

nŭdge *v.t.* & *n.* push esp. with elbow to draw attention privately.

nū'gatorÿ *a.* futile, trifling; inoperative, not valid.

nŭgg'ĕt (-g-) *n.* rough lump of gold etc.

nui'sance (nū-) *n.* source of annoyance; obnoxious act, circumstance, thing, or person.

nŭll *pred. a.* void, not valid; expressionless.

nŭll'ĭfÿ *v.t.* neutralize; make invalid. **~ficā'tion** *n.*

nŭll'ĭtÿ *n.* lack of force or efficacy; document etc. that is null.

Num. *abbr.* Numbers.

nŭmb (-m) *a.* torpid; deprived of sensation. *v.t.* make numb.

nŭm'ber *n.* aggregate of units, sum, company; word or symbol stating how many; numbered person or thing, esp. single issue of periodical etc.; item; (pl.) metrical feet, verses. *v.t.* count; mark or distinguish with number; include *in, with,* etc.; have or amount to specified number. **~ one,** oneself; (nav. sl.) first lieutenant. **~-plate,** plate bearing motor vehicle's index-mark and number. **~ed** *a.* (esp.) restricted or few in number. **~less** *a.* innumerable.

nū'meral, *a.* of number; denoting number. *n.* word or figure(s) denoting number.

nū'merate *a.* & *n.* (person) familiar with basic elements of mathematics or science. **~acÿ** *n.*

nūmerā'tion *n.* numbering.

nū'merātor *n.* one who counts; number above line in vulgar fraction.

nūmĕ'rĭcal *a.* of, in, denoting, etc. number.

nūmerŏl'ogÿ *n.* study of occult significance of numbers.

nū'merous *a.* comprising many units; many.

nū′minous *a*. divine; suggesting or revealing presence or influence of a god.

nūmismăt′ic (-z-) *a*. of coins or medals. ~s, nūmis′matist *nn*.

nŭm′skŭll *n*. blockhead.

nŭu *n*. woman living in convent under religious vow. ~'s veiling, thin woollen fabric.

nŭn′ciō (-shĭ-) *n*. (pl. *-os*), Pope's diplomatic representative.

nŭnn′erў *n*. house or community of nuns.

nŭp′tial *a*. of marriage or wedding. *n.pl.* wedding.

nūrse *n*. woman who suckles another's child or has charge of child; person trained for care of sick. *v*. suckle, give suck; act as nurse to, be nurse; cherish; clasp, hold, manage, etc. carefully; (of candidate) work in (constituency) in anticipation of election. nūrs(e)′ling *n*. infant, esp. in relation to its nurse. nūr′sing *a*. & *n*.; nursing home (usu. privately run) house for reception of surgical cases, invalids, etc.

nūr′serў *n*. room(s) assigned to children; *day* ~, institution taking charge of young children during day; place, sphere, etc. by or in which qualities, classes of people, etc. are fostered or bred; plot of ground where young plants, vegetables, etc., are reared esp. for sale. ~ garden, plant nursery. ~ governess, governess of young children. ~man, grower of plants etc. for sale. ~ rhyme, traditional verses for young children. ~ school, for young children under school age.

nūr′ture *n*. bringing up, rostering, care; nourishment. *v.t.* bring up, rear.

N.U.S. *abbr*. National Union of Students.

nŭt *n*. (kernel of) fruit consisting of hard shell enclosing edible kernel; (sl.) head; (sl.) lunatic; female screw in small metal block for securing bolt; (pl.) small lumps of coal; *off one's* ~, out of one's mind. *v.i.* seek or gather nuts. ~brown, brown as ripe hazel-nut. ~-case, (sl.) lunatic. ~crackers, instrument for cracking nuts. ~-gall, gall of dyer's oak used in dyeing. ~hatch, small creeping bird. ~-tree, esp. hazel.

nūtā′tion *n*. nodding; oscillation of earth's axis.

nŭt′měg *n*. hard aromatic seed of E.-Ind. tree used as spice etc.

nū′tria *a*. fur of coypu.

nū′trient *a*. & *n*. (thing) serving as or providing nourishment. nū′triment *n*. nourishing food. nūtri′tion *n*. food; nourishing. nūtri′tious *a*. efficient as food, nourishing. nū′tritive *a*. serving as food; concerned in nutrition.

nŭts *a*. (sl.) crazy, mad. *int*. expr. contempt etc.

nŭtt′ў *a*. (esp.) of rich mellow flavour.

nŭx yŏm′ica *n*. seed yielding strychnine.

nŭzz′le *v*. nose; burrow, press, rub, or sniff with nose; nestle, lie snug.

NW. *abbr*. north-west.

N.W.T. *abbr*. North-west Territories.

N.Y. *abbr*. New York.

nȳ′lon *n*. synthetic plastic material of great tensile strength and elasticity; (pl.) nylon garments, esp. stockings.

nўmph *n*. mythological semi-divine maiden of sea, mountain, wood, etc.; immature form of some insects.

nўmphomā′nia *n*. morbid and uncontrollable sexual desire in women. ~iăc *n*.

nўstăg′mŭs *n*. rapid involuntary oscillation of eyeball.

N.Z. *abbr*. New Zealand.

O

O¹, oh (ō) *int*. prefixed to vocative name or expressing various emotions.

O.² *abbr*. Ohio.

oaf *n*. awkward lout. oa′fish *a*.

oak *n*. forest tree with hard wood, acorns and lobed leaves; its wood. *a*. made of oak. ~-apple, ~-gall, ~-wart, kinds of excrescence pro-

duced on oak by gall-flies. **oa'ken**
a. made of oak.

oa'kum *n.* caulking-fibre got by
picking old rope to pieces.

oar *n.* long stout bladed shaft used
to propel boat, esp. one pulled with
both hands; oarsman. *v.* row.
~**sman**, rower.

ŏā'sĭs *n.* (pl. *oasēs*), fertile spot in
desert.

oast *n.* hop-drying kiln. ~**-house**,
building containing this.

oat *n.* (pl.) (grain of) cereal grown as
food for man and horses; oat-stem
used as shepherd's pipe. ~**cake**,
thin unleavened cake of oatmeal.
oa'ten *a.*

oath *n.* (pl. pr. ōdhz), appeal to God
etc. in witness of truth of statement, binding character of promise, etc.; profanity.

O.B. *abbr.* old boy.

ob. *abbr.*, *obiit* [L], died.

Obad. *abbr.* Obadiah.

ŏbblĭga'tō (-ah-) *a. & n.* (part, accompaniment) forming integral part of
musical composition.

ŏb'dūrate *a.* hardened; stubborn.
ob'dūracȳ *n.*

O.B.E. *abbr.* Officer of (Order of)
British Empire.

ō'bĕah (-*a*), **ō'bĭ²** *nn.* sorcery of
W.-Afr. origin.

obē'dience *n.* obeying; submission;
complying; (sphere of) authority.

obē'dient *a.* submissive to superior's
will; dutiful.

obei'sance (-bā-) *n.* gesture expressing
submission, respect, etc.; homage.

ŏb'ĕlĭsk *n.* tapering stone shaft of
rectangular section; mark (†) of
reference.

ŏb'ĕlus *n.* (pl. -*lī*), mark (-, ÷)
placed against spurious word etc.
in ancient MS.; mark (†) of
reference.

obēse' *a.* corpulent. **obē'sĭtȳ** *n.*

obey' (-bā) *v.* perform bidding of; be
obedient (to).

ŏb'fuscāte *v.t.* darken; stupefy, bewilder. ~**ā'tion** *n.*

ō'bĭ¹ *n.* Japanese woman's wide sash.

obi² : see **obeah**.

ō'bĭter dĭc'tum *n.* (pl. -*ta*), casual
remark, esp. judge's opinion expressed incidentally.

obĭt'ūarȳ *n.* record of death(s); brief
biography of deceased. *a.* recording
death; concerning deceased person.

ŏb'jĕct *n.* material thing; person or
thing to which action or feeling is
directed; end, purpose; (gram.)
word governed by transitive verb
or preposition; *expense no* ~, no
expense spared. *v.* (-ĕkt'), state
reason against; announce opposition or feel dislike or reluctance (to).
~ **glass, lens**, lens in telescope etc.
nearest object. **objĕc'tĭfȳ** *v.t.* present
as object of sense; make objective.
objĕc'tor *n.* one who objects, esp. to
military etc. service.

objĕc'tion *n.* objecting; adverse reason or statement; expression of
disapproval or dislike. ~**able** *a.*
(esp.) undesirable, offensive.

objĕc'tĭve *a.* external to the mind;
actually existing; dealing with etc.
outward things not thoughts or
feelings; (gram.) constructed as or
appropriate to object. *n.* object
lens; objective case; object or
purpose aimed at. ~**tĭvĭsm**, ~-
tĭv'ĭtȳ *nn.*

ŏb'jūrgāte *v.t.* chide, scold. ~**ā'tion** *n.*

ŏb'lāte¹ *n.* dedicated person.

oblāte'² *a.* (of sphere) flattened at
poles.

oblā'tion *n.* thing offered to God;
pious donation. ~**al** *a.*

ŏb'lĭgāte *v.t.* bind *to* do; oblige.

ŏblĭgā'tion *n.* binding agreement, esp.
written contract or bond; duty;
(indebtedness for) service or benefit.
oblĭg'atorȳ *a.* binding; not optional.

oblĭge' *v.t.* constrain, compel, require;
be binding on; confer favour on;
(pass.) be bound (*to*) by gratitude.
oblī'gĭng *a.* ready to serve others;
accommodating.

oblique' (-ēk) *a.* slanting; diverging
from straight line or course; inclined at other than right angle,
greater or less than right angle;
indirect. ~ **case**, any case other
than nominative or vocative.
oblī'quĭtȳ *n.*

oblĭt'erāte *v.t.* blot out, erase, efface.
~**ā'tion** *n.*

oblĭv'ion *n.* having or being for-
gotten. **oblĭv'ious** *a.*

ŏb'lŏng *a. & n.* (figure, object) elongated in one direction; (rectangle) with adjacent sides unequal.

ŏb′loquў *n.* abuse, detraction.

obnŏ′xious (-kshŭs) *a.* offensive, objectionable; disliked.

ō′boe (-ō) *n.* double-reeded wood--wind musical instrument.

ō′bol (*or* ŏ-) *n.* ancient Gk. silver coin.

obscēne′ *a.* indecent, lewd; repulsive. **obscĕn′itў** *n.*

obscūrăn′tism *n.* opposition to inquiry, enlightenment, and reform. **~tist** *a.* & *n.*

obscūrā′tion *n.* darkening, being darkened; eclipse.

obscūre′ *a.* dark, indistinct; hidden, undistinguished; not clear. *v.t.* make obscure or invisible. **obscūr′itў** *n.*

ŏb′sĕquies (-ĭz) *n.* funeral rites.

obsē′quĭous *a.* fawning, servile.

obsĕr′vance (-z-) *n.* keeping or performance (of law, occasion, etc.); rite, ceremonial act.

obsĕr′vant (-z-) *a.* good at observing.

ŏbservā′tion (-z-) *n.* observing or being observed; comment, remark, statement.

obsĕr′vatorў (-z-) *n.* building for astronomical observation.

obsĕrve′ (-z-) *v.* keep, follow, adhere to; perceive, watch, take notice of; say esp. by way of comment. *n.* one who observes; one who keeps watch.

obsĕss′ *v.t.* haunt, fill mind of. **obsĕ′ssion** *n.*; **obsĕ′ssional, obsĕss′ive** *aa.*

obsĭd′ĭan *n.* dark vitreous volcanic rock.

ŏbsolĕs′cent *a.* becoming obsolete. **~ence** *n.*

ŏb′solēte *a.* disused, discarded.

ŏb′stacle *n.* hindrance, impediment.

obstĕt′rĭc(al) *aa.* of child-birth or midwifery. **obstĕt′rics, ŏbstĕtrĭ′cian** *nn.*

ŏb′stĭnate *a.* stubborn, intractable. **ŏb′stĭnacў** *n.*

obstrĕp′erous *a.* noisy, wild.

obstrŭct′ *v.* block up; make impassable or difficult of passage; retard or prevent progress of.

obstrŭc′tion *n.* obstructing, being obstructed; hindering esp. of Parliamentary business by talking against

time; obstacle. **~ism** *n.*; **~ist** *n.* & *a.*

obstrŭc′tive *a.* causing, designed to cause, obstruction.

obtain′ *v.* acquire; get; have granted; be prevalent or established.

obtrude′ (-ōōd) *v.t.* thrust importunately forward. **obtru′sion** *n.*; **obtru′sive** *a.*

obtūse′ *a.* blunt, not sharp or pointed; greater than one right angle and less than two; dull, slow of perception.

ŏb′vĕrse *n.* side of coin or medal that bears head or principal design; front or top side; counterpart or complement of statement etc.

ŏb′vĭāte *v.t.* clear away, get rid of; prevent.

ŏb′vĭous *a.* seen or realized at first glance; evident.

O.C. *abbr.* Officer Commanding.

ŏcari′na (-rē-) *n.* egg-shaped musical wind instrument.

occā′sion *n.* suitable juncture, opportunity; reason; (time marked by) special occurrence. *v.t.* be occasion or cause of.

occā′sional *a.* made or meant for, acting on, etc. special occasion(s); not regular or frequent; incidental. **~ly** *adv.* sometimes.

Oc′cident (ŏks-) *n. the* West, esp. opp. Orient. **ŏccidĕn′tal** *a.*

ŏc′cĭput (-ks-) *n.* back of head. **ŏccĭp′ital** *a.*

occlude′ (-ōōd) *v.t.* close, obstruct; (chem.) absorb (gases). **occlu′sion** *n.* (esp.) overlapping position of teeth when jaws are brought together. **occlu′sive** *a.*

occŭlt′ *a.* esoteric; recondite; involving the supernatural, mystical, magical; hidden. *v.t.* hide by passing in front of. **ŏccultā′tion, ŏcc′ultism, ŏcc′ultist** *nn.*

ŏcc′ŭpant *n.* person holding property or office; one who resides or is in place. **ŏcc′ŭpancў** *n.*

ŏccŭpā′tion *n.* (period of) occupying or being occupied; calling or employment. **~al** *a.* (esp.) incidental to or caused by one's occupation; **~al therapy**, use of handicrafts etc. in treatment of disease etc.

ŏcc′ŭpier *n.* person in (esp. temporary

or subordinate) possession of land, house, etc.

ŏcc'ūpȳ *v.t.* take military possession of; reside in; hold (office); take up, fill, be in; busy, keep engaged.

occūr' *v.i.* be met with or found in some place or conditions; come into one's mind; take place, happen. **occŭ'rrence** *n.* happening; incident.

ocean (ō'shn) *n.* (one of main divisions of) great body of water surrounding land of globe; *the* sea; immense expanse or quantity. **ŏcĕăn'ĭc** (*or* -shĭ-) *a.*; **~ŏg'rapher. ~ŏg'raphȳ** *nn.*

ŏ'cĕlot *n.* S.-Amer. feline animal resembling leopard.

ochre (ō'ker) *n.* kinds of earth used as pigment; pale brownish-yellow colour. **ō'chrĕous, ō'chrous** *aa.*

o'clŏck' *adv.* by the clock.

Oct. *abbr.* October.

oct. *abbr.* octavo.

ŏc'tagon *n.* plane figure with eight angles and sides; octagonal building. **octăg'onal** *a.* eight-sided.

ŏctahĕd'ron (*or* -hē-) *n.* solid figure contained by eight plane faces. **~ral** *a.*

ŏc'tāne *n.* hydrocarbon of paraffin series. **~ number,** percentage of octane in fuel as measure of its anti-knock properties.

ŏc'tave (-ĭv) *n.* eighth day after festival, eight days beginning with festival; (mus.) note eight diatonic degrees above or below another, interval between them.

ŏctā'vō *n.* (*abbr.* 8vo), (size of) book with sheets folded into 8 leaves or 16 pages.

ŏctĕnn'ĭal *a.* lasting, recurring every, eight years.

ŏctĕt' *n.* (composition for) eight singers or players; group of eight.

Octō'ber (ŏ-) *n.* tenth month of year.

ŏctodĕ'cĭmō *n.* (*abbr.* 18mo), (size of) book with sheets folded into 18 leaves or 36 pages.

ŏctogénār'Ian *a.* & *n.* eighty-year-old (person).

ŏc'topus *n.* (pl. *-uses*), mollusc with eight suckered arms round mouth.

ŏctosȳll'able *n.* & *a.* (word, verse) of eight syllables. **ŏctosȳllăb'ĭc** *a.*

O.C.T.U., Octu *abbr.* Officer Cadets Training Unit.

ŏc'ūlar *a.* of, for, by, with, etc. eyes or sight, visual. **ŏc'ūlist** *n.* eye--specialist.

ō'dalĭsque (-k) *n.* Eastern female slave or concubine.

ŏdd *a.* not even, not divisible by two; additional; casual; extraordinary, strange. *n.pl.* (often treated as sing.) inequalities; difference; variance, strife; ratio between amounts staked by parties to bet; chances in favour of some result. **~ job,** casual disconnected piece of work. **~s and ends,** remnants, stray articles. **~s on,** with chances, betting, in favour. **~ly** *adv.* **~ment** *n.* remnant, stray fragment.

ŏdd'itȳ *n.* strangeness; peculiar trait; queer person.

ōde *n.* lyric poem of exalted style and tone.

ō'dĭous *a.* hateful, repulsive.

ō'dĭum *n.* general dislike or reprobation.

ŏdontŏl'ogȳ *n.* scientific study of teeth.

ōdorĭf'erous *a.* diffusing (usu. pleasant) odours.

ō'dour (-der) *n.* pleasant or unpleasant smell; fragrance. **~lĕss, ō'dorous** *aa.*

ŏd'ȳssey *n.* (account of) long adventurous journey.

oecumenic : see **ecumenic.**

O.E.D. *abbr.* Oxford English Dictionary.

Oe'dĭpus complex *n.* infantile fixation on parent of opposite sex.

oesŏph'agus *n.* canal from mouth to stomach, gullet.

of (ov, ŏv) *prep.* from; concerning; out of; among; relating to.

ŏff *adv.* away, at or to distance; out of position; loose, separate, gone; discontinued, stopped. *prep.* from; no longer upon. *a.* further; far; (of horses, vehicles, etc.) on right; (crick.) towards or from or in side of field which batsman faces when playing. *n.* off side. **~ and on,** occasionally, intermittently. **~--beat,** (sl.) unconventional, unusual. **~-hand,** extempore, without preparation; casual, curt. **~-licence,**

(shop etc. holding) licence to sell beer etc. for consumption off premises. ~-**print**, reprint of part of publication. ~**scourings**, worthless part, dregs. ~**side**, (footb. etc., of player) in position where he may not kick, handle, or hit ball. ~-**white**, not quite pure white.

ŏff′al *n*. refuse, waste stuff; edible organs of animal; bran or other by-product of grain; carrion.

offĕnce′ *n*. transgression, misdemeanour; illegal act; aggressive action; wounded feeling, resentment; wounding of feelings.

offĕnd′ *v*. transgress; hurt feelings of; outrage. **offĕn′der** *n*.

offĕn′sĭve *a*. aggressive; insulting; disgusting, nauseous. *n*. attack, offensive campaign or stroke.

ŏff′er *v*. present by way of sacrifice; tender for acceptance or refusal; express readiness or show intention (*to* do); attempt. *n*. expression of readiness to do or give or sell; proposal, esp. of marriage; bid. **ŏff′erĭng** *n*. thing offered. **ŏff′ertŏrў** *n*. collection of money at religious service.

ŏff′ĭce *n*. duty, task, function; position with duties attached to it; tenure of official position, esp. that of Minister of State; authorized form of worship; place for transacting business; room etc. for clerks; department, local branch, company etc. for specified purpose; (pl.) parts of house devoted to household work etc.

ŏff′ĭcer *n*. holder of public, civil, or ecclesiastical office; holder of authority in armed services, mercantile marine, etc., esp. one with commission in armed forces; president, treasurer, etc. of society etc. *v.t.* provide with officers.

offĭ′cial *a*. of office or its tenure; holding office; usual with persons in office; properly authorized. *n*. person holding public office or engaged in official duties. ~**dom**, ~**ism** *nn*. ~**ēse′** *n*. language of official documents.

offĭ′ciāte (-shĭ-) *v.i.* perform divine service; act in official capacity. **offĭ′ciant** *n*.

offĭ′cinal *a*. (of herb or drug) used in medicine.

offĭ′cious *a*. intrusive, meddlesome.

ŏff′ĭng *n*. part of visible sea distant from shore; position at distance from shore; *in the* ~, at hand, ready or likely to happen etc.

ŏff′sĕt *n*. lateral branch, esp. as used for propagation; sloping ledge; set-off; (print. etc.) transfer of ink from newly-printed surface to another surface; method of printing by transferring ink from plate etc. to rubber roller and thence to paper.

ŏff′shōot *n*. side shoot or branch.

ŏff′spring *n*. progeny, issue.

O.F.S. *abbr*. Orange Free State.

ŏft, ŏft′tīmes *advv*. (arch.) often.

often (ŏf′n) *adv*. frequently, many times, at short intervals.

ōgēē′ (*or* ō′-) *n*. & *a*. (moulding) showing S-shaped curve in section; S-shaped (line etc.).

og(h)am (ŏg′am) *n*. ancient British and Irish alphabet; inscription in, letter of, this.

ō′gīve (*or* -īv′) *n*. diagonal rib of vault; pointed arch.

ō′gle *v*. make eyes (at). *n*. amorous glance.

ō′gre (-ger) *n*. man-eating giant. **ō′gress** *n*.; **ō′greĭsh** *a*.

oh : see **O¹**.

O.H.G. *abbr*. Old High German.

ohm (ōm) *n*. unit of electrical resistance.

O.H.M.S. *abbr*. On His (Her) Majesty's Service.

ohō′ *int*. expressing surprise or exultation.

oil *n*. liquid viscid substance with smooth and sticky feel; oil-colour (usu. pl.). *v.t.* apply oil to, lubricate; treat with oil. ~**cake**, compressed linseed etc. as cattle-food or manure. ~**cloth**, kind of thin linoleum. ~-**colour**, paint or pigment ground in oil. ~-**field**, tract of oil-bearing strata. ~**man**, maker or seller of oils. ~-**painting**, use of, picture in, oil-colours. ~**skin**, cloth waterproofed with oil; garment or (pl.) suit of it. ~-**well**, well yielding mineral oil. **oiled** *a*. (sl.) drunk. **oi′lў** *a*. of, like, covered or soaked with, oil; unctuous.

oint′ment *n.* unctuous healing or beautifying preparation for skin.

O.K. (ō kā) *a.* & *adv.* all right. *n.* approval, sanction. *v.t.* sanction.

oka′pi (-ah-) *n.* rare African ruminant mammal.

ŏkay′ *a., adv., n.* & *v.t.* O.K.

Okla. *abbr.* Oklahoma.

ŏ′kra (*or* ŏ-) *n.* African plant with fibrous stem and fruits used as vegetable etc.

ŏld *a.* advanced in age; not young or near its beginning; dating from far back; long established; former. *n.* old time. **~ country**, mother country. **O~ English**, language spoken in England from 5th to 11th cc. **~ face**, style of printing type. **~-fashioned**, antiquated; not new-fangled. **O~ Glory**, Stars and Stripes. **~ hand**, experienced or practised person. **O~ Harry**, the devil. **~ maid**, elderly spinster. **~ man**, southernwood; (colloq.) husband. **~-man′s beard**, kinds of clematis. **~ master**, great painter of past. **O~ Nick**, Devil. **~ school tie**, used as symbol of loyalty to tradition, esp of public schools. **O~ Style**, (by) Julian calendar. **O~ Testament**, part of bible treating of pre-Christian times etc. **~-time**, of the past. **~ wives′ tale**, foolish story. **~ woman**, fussy or timid man; (colloq.) wife.

ŏ′lden *a.* (arch.) old-time.

ŏld′ster *n.* one no longer young.

ŏlĕă′ginous *a.* having properties of or producing oil; oily, greasy.

ŏlĕăn′der *n.* evergreen poisonous flowering shrub.

ŏlĕăs′ter *n.* wild olive.

ŏ′lĕograph (-ahf) *n.* picture printed in oils.

ŏlfăc′torў *a.* concerned with smelling.

ŏl′ĭgărchy (-kĭ) *n.* government, State governed, by few; members of such government. **ŏl′ĭgărch** *n.* member of oligarchy **ŏlĭgăr′chĭc(al)** *aa.*

ŏlĭvā′ceous *a.* olive-green.

ŏl′ĭve *n.* oval hard-stoned fruit yielding oil; tree bearing it; olive-colour. *a.* dull yellowish green; brownish-yellow. **~-branch**, branch of olive-tree as emblem of peace; (usu. pl.) children. **~-oil**, clear

pale-yellow non-drying oil got from olives.

olўm′pĭăd *n.* period of four years between Olympic games.

Olўm′pĭan *a.* of Olympus; magnificent, condescending; aloof.

Olўm′pĭc *a.* **~ Games**, ancient-Greek athletic contest; quadrennial international athletic meeting.

O.M. *abbr.* Order of Merit.

ŏm′bre (-er) *n.* 17th & 18th-c. card-game for three.

ŏm′budsman *n.* person appointed to investigate private individuals′ grievances against governmental or local authorities.

ō′mĕga *n.* last letter of Greek alphabet; last of series etc.

ŏm′elĕt, -ĕtte (-ml-) *n.* dish of beaten eggs fried in butter.

ō′mĕn *n.* sign portending good or evil, presage. **ŏm′ĭnous** *a.* of evil′ omen, inauspicious.

omĭ′ssion *n.* (instance of) omitting or being omitted.

omĭt′ *v.t.* leave out, not include; leave undone, neglect.

ŏm′nĭbus *n.* (pl. -uses), road vehicle plying on fixed route or in service of hotels etc. *a.* serving several objects at once; comprising several items.

ŏmnĭp′otent *a.* all-powerful. **~ence** *n.*

ŏmnĭprĕs′ent (-z-) *a.* present everywhere. **~ence** *n.*

ŏmnĭ′scient (*or* -shent) *a.* knowing everything. **~ence** *n.*

ŏm′nĭum găth′erum (-dh-) *n.* miscellaneous assemblage.

ŏmnĭv′orous *a.* feeding on anything that offers (esp. of reading).

ŏm′phalŏs *n.* centre, hub.

O.N. *abbr.* Old Norse.

on *prep.* (ŏn, on) (so as to be) supported by, covering, attached to, etc.; (so as to be) close to, in direction of; at, near; concerning, about; added to. *adv.* (ŏn), (so as to be) on something; in some direction, forward; in advance; in(to) movement or operation or activity. *a.* & *n.* (crick.) (in, towards, from) side of field behind batsman as he plays.

ŏn′ager *n.* wild ass.

once (wŭns) *adv.* for one time, on one occasion, only; at some time in past; *at* ~ without delay. *conj.* as soon as; when once. *n.* one time, performance, etc. ~**-over,** (colloq.) single and rapid survey etc.

ŏn′coming (-n-kŭ-) *n.* approach. *a.* approaching.

one (wŭn) *a.* lowest cardinal number; single and integral; only, without others; identical, same. *n.* number or figure 1, unit, unity; single thing, person, or example. *pron.* any person; the speaker. ~**-horse,** petty, poorly equipped. ~**-man,** requiring, concerning, consisting of, etc. one person only. ~**-sided,** lopsided; partial, unfair, prejudiced. ~**-track,** (of mind) fixed on one line of thought or action. ~**-way,** along which traffic is permitted in one direction only. ~**ness** *n.* singleness; singularity; unity, agreement; sameness. **on′er** *n.* (sl.) remarkable person or thing.

oneir′omăncy (-nīr-) *n.* divination by dreams.

ŏn′erous *a.* burdensome.

onesĕlf′ (wŭ-) *pron.* emphatic & refl. form of *one.*

onion (ŭn′yon) *n.* edible bulb of pungent smell and flavour.

ŏn′loŏker *n.* one who looks on.

ō′nlў *a.* that is, are, the one or all the specimen(s) of the class, sole. *adv.* solely, merely, exclusively. *conj.* but then; with this restriction, drawback, or exception only.

ŏnomatopoe′ia (-pēa) *n.* formation of names or words suggestive by their sound of object or action to be named.

ŏn′sĕt *n.* attack, assault, beginning.

ŏn′slaught (-awt) *n.* fierce attack.

Ont. *abbr.* Ontario.

ŏn to, ŏn′to *prep.* to position on.

ŏntŏl′ogў *n.* department of metaphysics concerned with nature of being. ~**ŏ′gĭcal** *a.*; ~**gĭst** *n.*

ō′nus *n.* responsibility for or burden of doing something.

ŏn′ward *a.* directed onward.

ŏn′ward(s) (-z) *adv.* further on; towards front; progressively.

ŏn′ўx (*or* ō-) *n.* kinds of quartz with different colours in layers.

ō′olīte *n.* granular limestone. **ōolĭt′ĭc** *a.*

ōō′mĭăk *n.* large open Eskimo boat.

ōōze *n.* wet mud, slime; sluggish flow, exudation. *v.* pass slowly through pores etc.; exude; leak *out* or *away.* **ōō′zў** *a.*

ŏp *a.* using patterns etc. of kinds that produce optical illusions.

O.P. *abbr.* observation post; opposite prompter.

op. *abbr.* operation; operator; opus.

o.p. *abbr.* out of print; over proof.

opă′citў *n.* opaqueness.

ō′pal *n.* milk-white or bluish stone with iridescent reflections. ~**ĕs′cence** *n.* changing of colour as in opal. ~**ĕs′cent** *a.* ~**īne** *a.* like opal.

opāque′ (-k) *a.* not transmitting light, not transparent; not lucid, obscure; dull-witted.

op. cit. *abbr., opere citato* [L], in the work quoted.

ōpe *v.* (poet.) open.

ō′pen *a.* not closed or blocked up; unlocked; unconfined, uncovered; exposed, manifest; public; not exclusive or limited; clear; expanded, spread out; not close, unfolded; communicative, frank. *v.* make or become open or more open; unclose, unlock; declare open; begin, make start. *n.* open space, air, competition, etc. ~ **air,** outdoors. ~ **boat,** undecked boat. ~**-cast,** (of mining) on surface. ~**-eyed,** vigilant, watchful. ~**-faced,** ingenuous-looking. ~**-handed,** generous, liberal. ~**-hearted,** frank, generous. ~ **letter,** letter printed in newspaper etc. but addressing individual. ~ **mind,** accessibility to new ideas; unprejudiced or undecided state. ~ **mouth,** mouth open esp. in gaping surprise. ~ **order,** formation with wide spaces between units. ~ **question,** matter on which opinions differ. ~**-work,** (pattern) with interstices in material. ~**er** *n.* (esp.) implement for opening bottles, tins, etc.

ō′pening (-pn-) *n.* (esp.) gap, aperture; commencement; preliminary statement; opportunity. *a.* (esp.) initial, first.

ō′penlў *adv.* publicly, frankly.

ŏp′era *n.* (branch of art concerned

with) dramatic composition or performance of which music is essential part. ~-glass(es), small binoculars used in theatres etc. ~-hat, man's collapsible tall hat. ~-house, theatre for operas.

ŏp'erāte v. be in action, produce effect; perform or carry on operation(s); work (machine, etc.); direct working of. ŏp'erable a. (med.) that can be treated by operation. ~ātor n.

ŏperăt'ĭc a. of or like opera.

ŏperā'tion n. action, working; financial transaction; piece of surgery; military action. ~al a. (esp.) engaged on, used for, warlike operations.

ŏp'erative a. in operation; practical; of surgical operations. n. worker, esp. in factory; private detective.

ŏperĕtt'a n. short light opera.

ophĭd'ian a. & n. (reptile) of suborder including snakes.

ŏphthăl'mĭa n. inflammation of eye. ophthăl'mic a. of or for eye; affected with ophthalmia. ~mŏl'ogў n. study of (diseases of) eye. ~moscōpe n. instrument for examining eye.

ō'pĭate n. drug for easing pain or inducing sleep. a. inducing drowsiness.

opīne' v.t. express or hold opinion (that).

opĭn'ion (-yon) n. belief based on grounds short of proof; view; professional advice. ~ātĕd a. unduly confident in one's opinions; stubborn.

ō'pĭum n. drug made from poppy and used as narcotic, intoxicant, etc.

opŏss'um n. kinds of small Amer. and Austral. marsupial.

opp. abbr. opposite.

ŏpp'ĭdan n. boy at Eton not on foundation.

oppō'nent n. adversary, antagonist.

ŏpp'ortūne a. (of time) suitable, favourable, well-selected; done etc. at opportune time. ~nism n. adaptation of policy or method to circumstances; time-serving. ~nist n. & a.

ŏpportū'nĭtў n. favourable juncture, good chance, opening.

oppōse' (-z) v.t. place in opposition or contrast (to); set oneself against; resist. oppō'sable a. (of digit, esp. thumb) that can be applied so as to meet another. oppōsed' a. contrary, contrasted; hostile, adverse.

ŏpp'osite (-z-) a. contrary in position or kind; facing; diametrically different; the other (of contrasted pair). n. opposite thing or term. adv. in opposite position or direction. prep. opposite to. ~ number, person in corresponding position in another set etc. ~ prompter, to actors' right.

ŏpposi'tion (-z-) n. antagonism, resistance; (chief) party opposed to that in office; contrast; diametrically opposite position. a. (esp.) of Parliamentary opposition.

oppress' v.t. govern tyrannically; treat with gross harshness or injustice; weigh down. oppre'ssion, oppress'or nn. ~ĭve a. (esp. of weather etc.) sultry, close.

opprō'brious a. vituperative, abusive; infamous, disgraceful.

opprō'brium n. disgrace, infamy; expression of this.

oppugn' (-ūn) v.t. controvert, call in question.

ŏp'sonin n. substance, present in blood-serum, promoting destruction of bacteria by white corpuscles. opsŏn'ic a.

ŏpt v.i. exercise option, choose; ~ out (of), choose not to take part etc. (in).

opt. abbr. optative.

ŏp'tative a. & n. (gram.) (mood) expressing wish.

ŏp'tic a. of eye or sight. n. (now joc.) eye. ŏp'tical a. visual; aiding sight; of or according to optics. ŏptĭ'cian (-shn) n. maker or seller of optical instruments. ŏp'tics n. science of sight and of properties of light.

ŏp'timism n. view that good must ultimately prevail; sanguine disposition. ~ĭst n.; ~ĭs'tĭc a.

ŏp'tĭmum n. most favourable conditions; best amount. a. best.

ŏp'tion n. choice, choosing; right to choose; purchased right to buy, sell, etc. on specified conditions at specified time; alternative (esp. *of a fine*). ~**al** *a*. not obligatory.

ŏp′ŭlent *a*. rich, wealthy; well stored; abundant. ~**ence** *n*.

ō′pus (*or* ŏ-) *n*. musical composition(s) as separately numbered part of composer's work.

ŏr[1] *n*. (her.) gold or yellow.

ŏr[2] *prep. & conj.* (arch.) before.

or[3] (ŏr, er) *conj.* introducing second of two alternatives.

ŏracle *n*. place at which ancient Greeks consulted gods for advice or prophecy; response received there; divine revelation; person or thing serving as infallible guide. **ŏrăc′ūlar** *a*. (esp.) dogmatic; of doubtful meaning.

ŏr′al *a*. spoken, verbal; of mouth. *n*. oral examination. **ŏr′allў** *adv*.

ŏ′range[1] (-ĭnj) *n*. globular reddish-yellow fruit; tree bearing it; its colour. *a*. orange-coloured. ~**stick**, stick of orange-wood for manicuring nails. ~**āde′** *n*. drink made from orange-juice etc. **ŏ′rangerў** *n*. (part of) building for protection of orange-trees.

Orange[2] (ŏ′rĭnj) *n*. (attrib. & in comb.) of Irish ultra-Protestant party.

ŏrăng′-outăng′ (-o͞o-), **-u′tan** (-o͞o-) *n*. large anthropoid ape.

ŏrāte′ *v.i.* (joc.) make speech.

ŏrā′tion *n*. speech, esp. of ceremonial kind.

ŏ′rator *n*. maker of speech; eloquent public speaker.

ŏratŏr′ĭō *n*. (pl. -*os*), semi-dramatic musical composition usu. on sacred theme.

ŏ′ratorў[1] *n*. small chapel; place for private worship. **O~**, (branch or house of) R.C. society of simple priests without vows.

ŏ′ratorў[2] *n*. rhetoric; speeches; eloquent language. ~**ŏ′rĭcal** *a*.

ŏrb *n*. sphere, globe; globe surmounted by cross as part of regalia; (poet.) eye. **ŏrbĭc′ūlar** *a*. spherical or circular.

ŏr′bĭt *n*. eye-socket; curved course of planet, comet, satellite, etc., complete circuit of this; range, sphere; *in* ~, travelling in orbit round esp.

earth. *v*. (cause to) travel in orbit (round). ~**al** *a*.

ŏrc *n*. kinds of cetacean, esp. killer whale.

Orcā′dĭan (ŏr-) *a & n*. (inhabitant) of Orkney.

ŏr′chard *n*. enclosure with fruit-trees.

ŏr′chĕstra (-k-) *n*. place occupied by band or chorus in theatre or concert-room; body of instrumental performers, combination of instruments. **ŏrchĕs′tral** *a*. **ŏr′chĕstrāte** *v.t.* arrange or score for orchestra. ~**ā′tion** *n*.

ŏr′chĭd (-k-) *n*. (flower of) kinds of plant, freq. with brilliantly coloured or grotesquely shaped flowers. ~**ā′ceous** *a*.

ŏr′chĭs (-k-) *n*. (esp. wild) orchid.

ord. *abbr*. ordained; order; ordinary.

ŏrdain′ *v.t.* confer holy orders on; destine; decree.

ŏrdé′al (*or* -ēl′) *n*. experience that tests character or endurance.

ŏr′der *n*. social class or rank; grade of Christian ministry; religious fraternity; company to which distinguished persons are admitted as honour or reward, insignia worn by its members; friendly society; (biol.) classificatory subdivision of class; (archit.) mode of treatment, esp. (*five* ~*s*) of column and entablature; sequence, succession; method; tidiness; efficient state; stated form of divine service; (accepted) rules of procedure; law-abiding state; injunction; authoritative direction or instruction. *v.t.* put in order; ordain; command, prescribe; direct tradesman etc. to supply.

ŏr′derlў *a*. methodically arranged; tidy; not unruly; (mil.) of or for orders or administrative business. *n*. soldier in attendance on officer; hospital attendant.

ŏr′dĭnal *a*. of or defining place in series. *n*. ordinal number; (book containing) prescribed form of ceremony at ordinations etc.

ŏr′dĭnance *n*. authoritative direction; religious rite; (U.S.) by-law.

ŏr′dĭnand *n*. candidate for ordination.

ŏr′dĭnarў *a*. normal; not exceptional; commonplace. *n*. ordinary condition, course, etc.; (eccl.) O~, bishop in his diocese, archbishop in his province; *in* ~, by permanent appointment, not temporary or extraordinary.

ŏrdĭnā′tion *n.* ordaining; conferring of holy orders.

ŏr′dnance *n.* mounted guns; department for military stores etc. ~ **survey,** official survey of Great Britain.

ŏr′dūre (*or* -dy*er*) *n.* dung; filth.

ŏre *n.* native mineral yielding metal.

Ore(g). *abbr.* Oregon.

ŏr′eăd *n.* mountain nymph.

ŏr′gan, *n.* musical instrument of pipes supplied with wind by bellows and sounded by keys; part of body serving some vital function; voice; medium of opinion, esp. newspaper. ~-**builder,** maker of organs. ~-**grinder,** player of barrel-organ. ~-**stop,** (handle bringing into action) set of organ-pipes of similar tone-quality.

ŏr′gandĭe *n.* fine stiffish muslin.

ŏrgăn′ĭc *a.* of bodily organs; (of disease) affecting structure of. organ; structural; organized; (chem.) (formed from compounds) occurring naturally as constituent of organisms. ~ **chemistry,** chemistry of hydrocarbons and their derivatives.

ŏr′ganĭsm *n.* living animal or plant; anything capable of growth and reproduction; whole with interdependent parts.

ŏr′ganĭst *n.* player of organ.

ŏr′ganīze *v.* furnish with vital organs; form into organic whole; give orderly structure to; bring into working order; make arrangements for. ŏrganĭzā′tion *n.* (esp.) organized body or system.

ŏr′gasm *n.* climax of sexual excitement.

ŏr′gў *n.* drunken or licentious revel; (pl.) revelry, debauchery. ŏrgĭăs′tĭc *a.*

ŏr′ĭel *n.* projecting part of upper room containing window; such window.

ŏr′ĭent *n.* eastward part of sky or earth; countries east of Mediterranean and S. Europe. *a.* (of sun etc.) rising, nascent; oriental. *v.t.* (-ĕnt′), orientate.

ŏrĭĕn′tal *a.* of Eastern or Asian world or its civilization. *n.* native of East. ~ĭst *n.* expert in oriental languages, cultures, etc. ~īze *v.*

ŏr′ĭentāte *v.t.* build (church) with chancel end to east; settle or find (compass) bearings of; arrange (map) on same bearings as oneself etc.; (*refl.*) take one's bearings, become accustomed to new situation etc. ~ā′tion *n.*

ŏ′rĭfĭce *n.* mouth of cavity, aperture.

ŏ′rĭflămme *n.* sacred red banner of old French kings; bright conspicuous object.

orig. *abbr.* original(ly).

ŏ′rĭgĭn *n.* source; extraction; starting-point.

ŏrĭ′gĭnal *a.* existent from first; primitive; earliest; not imitative or derived; creative. *n.* pattern, archetype; thing from which another is copied; eccentric person. ŏrĭgĭnăl′ĭtў *n.*

ŏrĭ′gĭnāte *v.* initiate or give origin to, be origin of; have origin; take rise. ~ā′tion, ~ātor *nn.*

ŏr′ĭōle *n.* kinds of bird with black and yellow plumage.

ŏ′rĭson (-zn) *n.* (arch.) prayer.

ŏr′lop *n.* lowest deck of ship with three or more decks.

ŏr′molu (-ōō) *n.* gilded bronze; gold-coloured alloy; articles made of or decorated with these.

ŏr′nament *n.* thing that adorns; person whose presence confers grace or honour; decorative work. *v.t.* (-ĕnt′), adorn, beautify. ŏrnamĕn′tal *a.*; ~ā′tion *n.*

ŏrnāte′ *a.* much adorned.

ŏrnĭthŏl′ogў *n.* study of birds. ~lŏ′gĭcal *a.*; ~logĭst *n.*

ŏrnĭthorhyn′chus (-rĭngk-) *n.* Austral. aquatic furred egg-laying mammal with duck's bill and webbed feet.

ŏ′rotŭnd (*or* ŏr-) *a.* magniloquent.

ŏr′phan *n.* & *a.* (child) bereaved of parent(s). *v.t.* bereave of parent(s). ~age *n.* institution for orphans.

ŏr′pĭment *n.* bright-yellow mineral used as pigment.

ŏ′rrerў *n.* clockwork model of planetary system.

ŏ'rrĭs-root n. violet-scented root of kinds of iris.

ŏr'tho- in comb., straight, right. orthochrŏmăt'ĭc a. (photog.) reproducing colours in correct relative intensities. ~clāse n. common felspar. ŏrthō'ĕpў n. science of correct pronunciation. ŏrthŏp'terous a. (of insects) of order with straight narrow fore wings and broad hind wings folded down back.

ŏr'thodŏx a. holding correct or accepted views; not heretical; O~, of Eastern or Greek branch of Christian Church. ŏr'thodoxў n.

ŏrthŏg'raphў n. (correct or conventional) spelling. ŏrthogrăph'ĭc(al) áa.

ŏrthopae'dĭc a. curing or treating deformity. ~s n. orthopaedic surgery.

ŏr'tolan n. garden bunting.

ŏ'rўx n. large long-horned antelope.

O.S. abbr. Old Style; Ordinary Seaman; Ordnance Survey; outsize.

Os'car (ŏ-) n. gold-plated statuette awarded annually for film production etc.

os'cillāte (ŏsĭ-) v. swing like pendulum, move to and fro; vacillate; (of radio receiver, etc.) radiate electro-magnetic waves. ~ā'tion, ~ātor nn.; ~ātorў a.

ŏs'cūlāte v. kiss; have three or more points of contact (with). ~ā'tion n.; ~ātorў a.

ŏ'sier (-zher) n. (shoot of) willow used in basketwork.

ŏs'mĭum (-z-) n. metallic element.

ŏsmō'sĭs (-zm-) n. tendency of solvent separated from solution by membrane to pass through and dilute the solution. ŏsmŏt'ĭc a.

ŏs'prey n. large sea-shore bird preying on fish; egret plume.

ŏss'ĕous a. bony; having bones.

ŏss'ĭcle n. small bone.

ŏss'ĭfў v.t. turn into bone; harden; make or become rigid. ~fĭcā'tion n.

ŏss'ūarў n. charnel-house; bone-urn.

ŏstĕn'sĭble a. professed; used as blind. ~bĭl'itў n.

ŏstĕn'sorў n. monstrance.

ŏstentā'tion n. pretentious display; showing off. ~tious a.

ŏstĕŏl'ogў n. study of bones.

ŏstĕŏp'athў n. treatment of disease by manipulation of bones. ŏs'tĕopăth n.; ~păth'ĭc a.

ŏs'tler (-sl-) n. stableman at inn.

ŏs'tracīze v.t. exclude from society, refuse to associate with. ŏs'tracĭsm n.

ŏs'trich n. large flightless swift-running bird valued for its feathers.

O.T. abbr. Old Testament.

oth'er (ŭdh-) a. not same; separate in identity, distinct in kind; alternative, additional; every second; some . . . or ~ some unknown; the ~ day, a few days ago. pron. other person, thing, specimen, etc. adv. otherwise. ~ world, world beyond grave. ~-worldly, not concerned with this world. ~nèss n. being other, difference. ~wīse (-z) adv. in different way, state, circumstances, or respects; or else.

ō'tĭc a. of ear.

ō'tiōse (-shĭ-) a. not required, serving no practical purpose.

ŏtt'er n. (fur of) aquatic fish-eating mammal.

ŏtt'ō n. attar.

ŏtt'oman[1] n. cushioned seat like sofa without arms or back.

Ott'oman[2] (ŏ-) a. of Turkish Empire. n. (pl. -ans), Turk.

O.U. abbr. Oxford University.

oublĭëtte' (ōō-) n. secret dungeon with trapdoor entrance.

ouch[1] n. (arch.) clasp or buckle.

ouch[2] int. expressing annoyance or pain.

ought (awt) v. aux. expr. duty, rightness, probability, etc.

ounce[1] n. unit of weight, $\frac{1}{16}$ lb. avoirdupois, $\frac{1}{12}$ lb. troy; fluid ~, $\frac{1}{20}$ (U.S. $\frac{1}{16}$) pint.

ounce[2] n. snow-leopard; (poet.) lynx.

O.U.P. abbr. Oxford University Press.

our (owr) pron. & a., poss. case of we, with abs. form ours.

oursĕlf' (owr-) pron., emphat. and refl. form of we = I.

oursĕlves' (owr-) pron., emphat. and refl. form of we.

ousel, ouzel (ōō'zl) n. blackbird; kinds of thrush.

oust v.t. put out of possession, eject; seize place of.

out *adv.* away from or not in place, (normal) state, fashion, etc.; not at home; (crick.) having finished innings; on strike; not burning; to or at an end; in(to) open, sight, notice, etc.; ~ *of date*, obsolete, antiquated; ~ *of doors*, in(to) open air; ~ *of the way*, inaccessible; unusual.

out- in comb., out of, external, not at centre, to excess, so as to defeat or excel, etc. **outbăl'ance** *v.t.* outweigh. **~board** *a.* (esp., of motor--boat) with engine etc. attached outside boat at stern; (of motor) so attached. **~fāce'** *v.t.* stare down; brave, defy. **~fall** (-awl) *n.* mouth of river etc. **~field** *n.* (crick.) part of field remote from pitch. **~flow** (-ō) *n.* what flows out, amount flowing out. **~gĕn'eral** *v.t.* defeat by superior generalship. **~gō'** *v.t.* surpass, excel. **~gōings** *n.pl.* outlay, expenditure. **~growth** (-ōth) *n.* offshoot. **~jŏck'ey** *v.t.* overreach. **~manœu'vre** (-ōōver) *v.t.* get better of by superior strategy. **~march'** *v.t.* march faster or further than. **~mătch'** *v.t.* be more than match for. **~mō'dĕd** *a.* out of date. **~pāce'** *v.t.* move faster than. **~pātient** (-shnt) *n.* patient not lodged in hospital etc. **~pouring** (-pōr-) *n.* effusion; expression of emotion. **~rānge'** (-j) *v.t.* have longer range than. **~rīde'** *v.t.* ride faster or further than. **~rīder** *n.* mounted attendant, motor-cyclist, riding before, behind, or beside carriage, procession, etc. **~rī'val** *v.t.* surpass. **~sail'** *v.t.* sail faster than. **~sĭt'** *v.t.* stay longer than. **~sīze** *n. & a.* (person or thing) larger than normal or than standard size. **~smărt'** *v.t.* (colloq.) outwit. **~văl'ūe** *v.t.* surpass in value.

out'băck *a. & n.* (of) remoter areas of Australia.

outbĭd' *v.t.* bid higher than.

out'break (-āk) *n.* breaking out of emotion, war, disease, fire, etc.

out'building (-bĭ-) *n.* outhouse.

out'bŭrst *n.* bursting out, esp. of emotion in vehement words.

out'cast (-ah-) *a. & n.* (person) cast out from home and friends.

outclass' (-ah-) *v.t.* surpass by wide difference.

out'come (-kŭm) *n.* result, issue.

out'crŏp *n.* rock etc. emerging at surface; breaking out.

out'crȳ *n.* clamour; uproar.

out-dĭs'tance *v.t.* get far ahead of.

outdo' (-ōō) *v.t.* surpass, excel.

out'door (-ōr) *a.* existing, done, etc. out of doors. **~doors'** (-z) *adv.* out of doors.

ou'ter *a.* further from centre or inside; on outside. *n.* (hit on) outer circle of target. **~mōst** *a.*

out'fĭt *n.* complete equipment; (organized) group or company. *v.t.* provide with outfit; supply *with*. **out'fĭtter** *n.* (esp.) seller of men's clothes.

outflănk' *v.t.* get round flank of.

outgrŏw' (-ō) *v.t.* grow faster or get taller than; get rid of with advancing age; get too big for (clothes, etc.).

out'house *n.* shed etc. adjoining main house.

ou'ting *n.* pleasure-trip.

outlănd'ish *a.* foreign looking or sounding; unfamiliar, bizarre.

outlast' (-ah-) *v.t.* last longer than.

out'law, *n.* person deprived of protection of law. *v.t.* proscribe, declare outlaw. **~rȳ** *n.*

out'lay *n.* expenses.

out'lĕt *n.* means of exit; vent; market.

out'lĭer *n.* outlying or detached part.

out'līne *n.* external boundary; line(s) enclosing visible object; contour; rough draft, summary; (pl.) main features. *v.t.* draw or describe in outline; mark outline of.

outlive' *v.t.* live longer than; live beyond; get over effect of.

out'lŏŏk *n.* view, prospect; what seems likely to happen; general view of life.

out'lȳing *a.* far from centre; detached; remote.

outnŭm'ber *v.t.* exceed in number.

outpoint' *v.t.* score more points than, defeat on points.

out'pōst *n.* detachment on guard at some distance from army; outlying settlement etc.

out'put (-ŏŏt) *n.* amount produced.

out'rāge n. forcible violation of others' rights, sentiments, etc.; gross offence or indignity. v.t. subject to outrage; insult; infringe violently.

outrā'geous a. immoderate, extravagant; violent, furious; grossly cruel, offensive, etc.

outré (oo'trā) a. eccentric, outraging decorum. [F]

out'rigger n. spar or framework projecting from or over ship's side; (boat with) rowlock(s) on projecting bracket(s) or long parallel float(s) attached by beams etc.

out'right adv. altogether, entirely; once for all; without reservation. a. not qualified or limited, thorough-going.

outrun' v.t. outstrip; pass limit of.

out'sĕt n. start.

outshīne' v.t. be more brilliant than.

out'sīde (or -īd') n. external surface, outer parts; external appearance; position without; highest computation. a. of, on, or nearer outside; greatest existent or possible. adv. (-īd'), on or to outside; not within. prep. (-īd'), external to; beyond limits of; without.

outsī'der n. non-member of circle, party, etc.; horse etc. or person not known to have chance in race or competition.

out'skĭrts n.pl. outer border, fringe.

out'spăn v. (S.-Afr.) unyoke, unharness.

outspō'ken a. frank, unreserved.

out'spread (-ĕd) a. spread out.

outstăn'dĭng a. prominent, conspicuous; still unsettled.

outstay' v.t. stay longer than; stay beyond limits of.

out'strĕtched a. stretched out.

outstrĭp' v.t. pass in running etc.; surpass in progress, competition, etc.

outvōte' v.t. outnumber in voting.

out'ward, a. directed towards outside; physical; external, superficial. adv. outwards. ~lў adv. in outward appearance; on surface. **out'-wards** (-z) adv. in outward direction.

outweigh' (-wā) v.t. exceed in weight, value, influence, etc.

outwĭt' v.t. prove too clever for; overreach.

out'work (-ẽrk) n. advanced or detached part of fortress etc.; work done outside shop, factory, etc.

outwôrn' a. worn out.

ouzel : see **ousel.**

Ov. abbr. Ovid.

ova : see **ovum.**

ō'val a. shaped like egg. n. elliptical closed curve; thing with oval outline.

ō'varў n. ovum-producing organ in female; seed-vessel in plant. **ovār'ĭan** a.

ō'vāte a. egg-shaped.

ovā'tion n. enthusiastic reception, general applause.

ov'en (ŭ-) n. receptacle for baking or cooking in; small furnace or kiln.

ō'ver adv. outward and downward from brink, erect position, etc.; above in place or position; more than; covering whole surface; from one side, end, etc. to other; from beginning to end; at end; done with. n. (crick.) number of balls bowled from one end before change is made to other; play during this time. prep. above; concerning; across; on or to other side, end, etc. of. ~lў adv. (U.S.) over, excessively. ~mŭch a., n. & adv. too much.

ō'ver- in comb. **ōverăct'** v. act (part etc.), act part, with exaggeration. ~ärm a. & adv. overhand. ~awe' v.t. restrain or repress by awe. ~băl'ance v. (cause to) lose balance and fall; outweigh. ~blown' (-ōn) a. too full-blown, past its prime. ~board adv. from within ship into water; throw ~board, abandon, discard. ~bûr'den v.t. burden too much. ~call' (-awl), v. bid more (on) than hand is worth, bid higher (than); **ō'vercall** n. ~căp'italīze v. fix or estimate capital (of) too high. ~chĕck n. (cloth with) larger check pattern over smaller. ~cloud' v.t. cloud over. ~dōse n. excessive dose. ~drĕss' v. dress with too much display and ornament. ~drīve n. gear that increases ratio of car-speed to that of engine. ~drīve' v.t. drive too hard; drive or work to exhaustion. ~ĕs'tĭmāte v.t. estimate too highly; n. too high an estimate. ~grow' (-ō) v. cover with growth; grow too large; out-grow. ~hǎnd *a*. & *adv*. with hand above object held, above shoulder in bowling etc.; with arm out of water in swimming. ~hǎng' *v*. jut out (over); impend (over). ~hǎng *n*. (amount of) overhanging; over-hanging part. ~hear' *v.t*. hear as unperceived or unintended listener. ~joyed' *a*. transported with joy. ~kill *n*. amount by which capacity to kill exceeds numbers aimed at. ~lā'den *a*. overloaded, overbur-dened. ~lǎnd *adv*. (partly) by, on, or over land (and not water). ~leaf' *adv*. on other side of leaf (of book etc.). ~lie' *v.t*. lie on top of, smother (child) thus; ~lŏrd *n*. supreme lord; feudal superior. ~mǎntel *n*. orna-mental carving, mirror, etc. over mantelpiece. ~ma'ster (-mah-) *v.t*. get complete victory or control over. ~mǎtch' *v.t*. be too strong for. ~-nīce' *a*. too fastidious. ~pass (-ahs) *n*. bridge etc. carrying traffic over road etc., esp. motorway. ~plǔs *n*. surplus. ~-prodūce' *v.t*. produce in excess of demand or of defined amount; ~-prodǔc'tion *n*. ~-prōōf' *a*. containing more alcohol than proof spirit. ~rīde' *v.t*. ex-haust (horse) by riding; trample under horse's hoofs; ride over with armed force; slip or lie over; have or claim superior authority to, disregard, set aside. ~rǔff' *v.t*. overtrump. ~rule' (-ōōl) *v.t*. set aside by superior authority; annul, reject. ~sea(s) *adv*. & *a*. across or beyond sea. ~sew (-sō) *v.t*. sew together (two edges) so that thread between stitches lies over edges. ~shǎd'ow (-ō) *v.t*. cast shadow over; outshine. ~shoot' *v.t*. go, send missile, beyond (mark etc.); ~ *the mark*, go too far, exaggerate. ~shŏt *a*. (of wheel) turned by water flowing over it. ~sleep' *v. refl*. & *i*. miss in-tended time of rising by sleeping too long. ~spill *n*. (esp.) surplus popula-tion of town etc. accommodated elsewhere. ~spread' (-ĕd) *v.t*. cover surface of; become diffused over. ~stāte' *v.t*. state too strongly, exaggerate; ~stātement *n*. ~stĕp' *v.t*. pass over (boundary). ~strǔng'

a. intensely or too highly strung; (of piano) with strings in sets cross-ing each other obliquely. ~sǔb-scrībe' *v.t*. subscribe more than amount of. ~task' (-tah-) *v.t*. burden too heavily. ~tǎx' *v.t*. make excessive demand on; burden with excessive taxes. ~tŏp' *v.t*. be or become higher than; surpass. ~train' *v*. (cause to) lose condition by too much training. ~trǔmp' *v*. play higher trump (than), take by overtrumping. ~wīnd' *v.t*. damage (watch etc.) by winding too far.

ō'verall (-awl) *n*. garment worn over others as protection against dirt etc.; (pl.) protective trousers or suit; (mil., pl.) officer's full-dress tight trousers. *a*. taking every-thing into account, inclusive, total.

overbear' (-ār) *v.t*. bear down by weight or force; repress; out-weigh. ~ing *a*. domineering, masterful.

ō'vercast (-ah-) *a*. covered with cloud; dark, gloomy. *v.t*. (-ahst'), sew over raw edges of.

ōverchǎrge' *v*. charge too highly with explosive, electricity, etc.; use exaggeration or too much detail in; charge too much. *n*. (ō'-), excessive or extra charge.

ō'vercoat *n*. large coat worn over ordinary clothing.

overcome' (-ǔm) *v.t*. prevail over, get the better of; be victorious. *a*. exhausted, made helpless, deprived of self-possession.

ōvercrowd' *v.t*. (esp.) crowd more people into space than there is proper accommodation for. ~ing *n*.

ōverdo' (-dōō) *v.t*. carry to excess; cook too long; overtax strength of.

ō'verdraft (-ah-) *n*. overdrawing of bank account; amount by which balance is overdrawn.

ōverdraw' *v*. draw cheque in excess of (one's account); make overdraft; exaggerate in describing.

ōverdūe' *a*. more than due; late, in arrear.

ōverflow' (-ō) *v*. flow over, flood; extend beyond limits or capacity of; be so full that contents over-flow; be very abundant. *n*. (ō'-), what overflows or is superfluous. **~ meeting**, for those for whom there is no room at meeting etc.

ōverhaul' *v.t.* pull to pieces for inspection, examine condition of; catch up, overtake.

ōverhead' (-ĕd) *adv.* on high; in sky; in storey above. *a.* (ō'-), placed overhead; (of charges, etc.) due to office expenses, management, etc. **~s** *n.pl.* overhead charges.

ōverlăp' *v.* partly cover; cover and extend beyond; partly coincide.

ōverlay' *v.t.* cover surface of *with* coating, etc. *n.* (ō'-), thing laid over something.

ōverlook' *v.t.* have prospect of from above; take no notice of, condone; superintend; bewitch with evil eye.

ōver-night' *adv.* on preceding evening; through night (until next morning); during night, suddenly. *a.* (ō'-) done etc. overnight; (of luggage) holding (only) what is required for night.

ōverpow'er *v.t.* reduce to submission, subdue; overwhelm, be too intense or violent for.

ōverrāte' *v.t.* esteem or assess too high.

ōverreach' *v.* circumvent, outwit; (of horse) strike forefoot with hind hoof; strain (one*self*) by reaching too far.

ōverrŭn' *v.* harry and spoil; swarm or spread over; go beyond or exceed; exceed time etc. allowed; (print.) carry over words or lines of type to another line or page.

ōversee' *v.t.* superintend. **ō'verseer** *n.*

ō'vershoe (-ōō) *n.* shoe of rubber, felt, etc. worn outside another.

ō'versight *n.* omission to notice; mistake of inadvertence; supervision.

ōverstrain' *v.t.* damage by exertion; stretch too far. *n.* (ō'-), overstraining, being overstrained.

ō'vert (*or* -ĕrt') *a.* openly done, unconcealed.

ōvertāke' *v.t.* come up with, catch up (and pass); come suddenly upon.

ōverthrow' (-ō) *v.t.* knock down; cast out from power; put an end to; vanquish. *n.* (ō'-), defeat, subversion; (crick. etc.) fielder's return not

stopped near wicket, etc. and so allowing further run(s).

ō'vertīme *adv.* beyond regular hours of work. *n.* (payment for) extra time worked.

ō'vertone *n.* (mus.) harmonic; (subtle or elusive) secondary quality, colour, etc.; implication.

ō'verture *n.* opening of negotiations; formal proposal or offer; (mus.) orchestral prelude.

ōvertŭrn' *v.* upset, overthrow; (cause to) fall down or over. *n.* (ō'-), upsetting, revolution.

ōverwee'ning *a.* arrogant.

ō'verweight (-wāt) *n.* excessive weight. *a.* beyond weight allowed or desirable. *v.t.* (-āt'), overburden, overload.

ōverwhĕlm' *v.t.* bury, submerge utterly; crush; overpower with emotion etc.; deluge *with*. **~ing** *a.* irresistible by numbers, weight, etc.

ōverwork' (-ĕrk) *v.* work too hard; weary or exhaust with work. *n.* excessive work.

ōverwrought' (-rawt) *a.* suffering reaction from excitement; too elaborate.

ō'vidŭct *n.* tube conducting egg from ovary to uterus.

ō'vifŏrm *a.* egg-shaped.

ō'vīne *a.* of or like sheep.

ovip'arous *a.* egg-laying.

ō'vipŏs'itor (-z-) *n.* tube with which insect deposits eggs.

ō'void *a.* egg-shaped.

ō'vum *n.* (pl. -a), female germ-cell capable when fertilized of developing into new individual; egg.

owe (ō) *v.* be under obligation to (re)pay or render; be in debt (*for*); be indebted for (*to*). **ow'ing** *pred. a.* yet to be paid, due. **owing to**, caused by; in consequence of, on account of, because of.

owl *n.* night bird of prey; solemn person, wise-looking dullard. **ow'lĕt** *n.* young owl. **ow'lĭsh** *a.*

own (ōn) *a.* (after poss.), and not another's; (abs.) own property, kindred, etc.; *of one's ~*, belonging to one; *hold one's ~*, maintain one's position, not be defeated; *on one's ~*, (sl.) independently, unaided, on one's own account, responsibility, etc. *v.* have as property, possess; acknowledge authorship or paternity of; admit as valid, true, etc.; ~ *up,* (colloq.) confess.

ow′ner (ōn-) *n.* possessor, proprietor. ~-**driver,** ~-**occupier,** one who owns car he drives, house he lives in. ~**ship** *n.;* ~**less** *a.*

ŏx *n.* (pl. *oxen),* kinds of large horned ruminant quadruped; castrated male of domestic species. ~-**bow,** U-shaped collar of ox-yoke; (U.S.) (land inside) horse-shoe bend in river. ~-**eye (daisy),** kinds of plant with large white or yellow flowers. ~**lip,** hybrid between primrose and cowslip.

ŏxăl′ĭc ă′cĭd *n.* intensely sour poisonous acid used in inks, polishes, etc.

Oxf. *abbr.* Oxford.

ox′ford *n.* low shoe laced over instep.

oxidā′tion *n.* oxidization.

ŏx′īde *n.* compound of oxygen with another element or with radical.

ŏx′ĭdīze *v.* (cause to) combine with oxygen; rust; cover with coating of oxide. ~**īzā′tion** *n.*

Oxon. *abbr.* (Bishop) of Oxford; Oxfordshire; Oxford University.

Oxō′nian (ĕ-) *n. & a.* (member) of University of Oxford; (inhabitant) of Oxford.

ŏxў-acĕt′ўlēne *a.* of, using, welding etc. with, mixture of oxygen and acetylene.

ŏx′ўgen *n.* colourless odourless tasteless gaseous element essential to life and to combustion. ~**āte,** ~**īze** *vv.t.* supply or treat or mix with oxygen; oxidize. ~**ā′tion** *n.*

ŏxўmŏr′on *n.* figure of speech with pointed conjunction of seeming contradictories.

ŏyĕz′ *int.* of public crier or court officer bespeaking silence and attention.

oy′ster *n.* kinds of bivalve mollusc usually eaten alive; silent or extremely discreet person.

oz. *abbr.* ounce(s).

ō′zōne *n.* form of oxygen with pungent odour, used as bleaching agent etc.; (pop.) invigorating seaside air.

P

P. *abbr.* (car) park; pawn.

p. *abbr.* page; participle; past; pence, penny; perch(es).

p. *abbr., piano* [It.], soft.

Pa. *abbr.* Pennsylvania.

p.a. *abbr.* per annum.

păb′ūlum *n.* food.

pāce[1] *n.* (space covered by) single step in walking or running; gait; speed, rate of progression. *v.* walk (over, about) esp. with slow or regular step; measure (distance) by pacing; test speed of; set pace for. ~-**maker,** one who sets pace.

pā′cĕ[2] *prep.* by leave of; with all due deference to. [L]

păch′ўdĕrm (-k-) *n.* large thick-skinned mammal, esp. elephant or rhinoceros. ~**dĕr′matous** *a.*

pacĭf′ĭc *a.* tending to peace, of peaceful disposition. **pă′cĭfĭsm** *n.* advocacy of avoiding or abolishing war. **pă′cĭfĭst** *a. & n.*

pă′cĭfў *v.t.* appease; reduce to state of peace. ~**fĭcā′tion** *n.*

păck *n.* bundle of things wrapped or tied together for carrying, esp. pedlar's bundle or soldier's knapsack; method of packing for market; lot, set; hounds of hunt; forwards of Rugby-football team; set of playing-cards; large area of floating ice driven or packed together; (application of) wet sheet etc. for swathing round (part of) body, cold compress, kinds of cosmetic paste, etc. *v.* put (things) together into bundle, box, etc., fill (bag etc.) with clothes etc., for transport or storing; put closely together, cram, crowd together, form into pack; wrap tightly, wedge; put up (meat, fruit, etc.) in tins etc. for preservation; fill (jury, meeting, etc.) with partisans; ~ *off,* send away; *send* ~*ing,* dismiss summarily. ~-**horse,** horse used for carrying packs. ~-**ice,** ice pack. ~**ing-case,** case or framework for packing goods. ~**ing needle,** large curved needle for sewing up packages. ~**man,** pedlar. ~-**thread,** stout thread.

păck′age *n.* parcel; box etc. in which

goods are packed, esp. for sale. *v.t.* make up into, enclose in, package. ~ **deal**, (colloq.) inclusive bargain or transaction.

păck'ĕt *n.* small package; (colloq.) large sum of money; mail-boat.

păct *n.* covenant; compact.

păd[1] *n.* soft saddle; piece of soft stuff used to raise surface, improve shape, etc.; leg-guard in games; sheets of blotting or writing paper in block; (fleshy cushion forming sole of) paw of some animals; water- -lily leaf; (sl.) bed, lodging. *v.t.* make soft; improve shape of, fill out, protect, with pads or padding. **păddʹĭng** *n.* (esp.) superfluous words etc. to fill out space etc.

păd[2] *v.* travel (along) on foot; walk softly.

păddʹle *n.* short oar with broad blade at one or each end; striking-board in paddle-wheel; (zool.) fin or flipper; action or spell of paddling. *v.* propel with paddle(s); row gently; walk with bare feet in shallow water. ~**-wheel**, wheel with boards at right angles to circumference for propelling ship.

păddʹock[1] *n.* small field; enclosure where horses are assembled before race; (Austral. etc.) field.

păddʹock[2] (arch., dial.) frog or toad.

păddʹў[1] *n.* (colloq.) rage, temper.

păddʹў[2] *n.* growing rice. ~**-field**, rice-field.

pădʹlŏck *n.* detachable lock hanging by hinged or pivoted hoop. *v.t.* secure with padlock.

padre (pahʹdrā) *n.* (colloq.) chaplain, clergyman.

paeʹan *n.* song or shout of triumph, thanksgiving, joy, etc.

paeʹderast, pĕd- (*or* pē-) *n.* sodomite. ~**ў** *n.*

paediătʹrĭc, pĕd- *a.* of or dealing with children's diseases. ~**s, p(a)ediatrĭʹcian** *nn.*

pāʹgan *n.* & *a.* heathen. ~**ĭsm** *n.*

pāge[1] *n.* boy employed as liveried servant or personal attendant. *v.t.* call name of (person sought) in public rooms of hotel etc.

pāge[2] *n.* one side of leaf of book etc. *v.t.* number pages of.

păʹgeant (-jnt) *n.* spectacular per-

formance, usu. illustrative of historical events; any brilliant show. **păʹgeantrў** *n.* splendid display; empty show.

păʹgĭnāte *v.t.* number pages of (book etc.). ~**āʹtion** *n.*

pagōʹda *n.* temple, sacred tower, in China etc.

pah *int.* expr. disgust.

paid *a.* remunerated with money; given in discharge of obligation; (of debt etc.) discharged; *put ~ to*, (colloq.) finish off.

pail *n.* bucket; (U.S.) vessel used to carry meal etc.

paillette (pălyĕtʹ, pīyĕtʹ) *n.* spangle.

pain *n.* bodily or mental suffering; (pl.) throes of childbirth; (pl.) trouble taken. *v.t.* inflict pain on. **painstaking**, careful, industrious, ~**ful, ~lĕss** *aa.*

paint *n.* colouring-matter prepared for application to surface. *v.* portray or make pictures in colours; coat or adorn with paint; apply rouge etc. to (face etc.); depict in words. ~**ed lady**, butterfly with spotted orange-red wings. ~**er**[1], ~**ing** *nn.*

painʹter[2] *n.* rope at bow of boat for making it fast.

pair *n.* set of two; thing with two corresponding parts not used separately; engaged or married or mated couple; (Parl.) (either of) two voters on opposite sides arranging both to be absent from division etc. *v.* arrange or unite as pair or in pairs; mate; ~ *off*, form into pairs.

Paiʹsley (-zlĭ) *a.* of characteristic pattern or soft bright colours of kind of woollen shawl.

pajamas : see **pyjamas**.

paʹkėha (pah-) *n.* (N.Z.) white man.

Pakistaʹnĭ (pah-, -tah-) *n.* & *a.* (inhabitant, native) of Pakistan.

păl *n.* (sl.) comrade. *v.i.* (usu. ~ *up*), make friends.

pălʹace *n.* official residence of sovereign, archbishop, or bishop; stately mansion or building.

pălʹadĭn *n.* peer of Charlemagne's court; knight errant.

pāʹlaeo-, pāʹleo- (*or* pă-) in comb., ancient. **palaeŏgʹraphў** *n.* study of

ancient writing and inscriptions.
~lith'ĭc *a.* of earlier Stone Age.
palaeontŏl'ogў *n.* study of extinct
animals and plants. **~zō'ĭc** *a.* of or
containing ancient forms of life.

păl'ais (-ay; *or* -ĭ) *n.* dance hall.

pălanquin', -keen (-kēn) *n.* Eastern
covered litter.

păl'atable *a.* pleasant to taste; agreeable to mind.

păl'ate *n.* roof of mouth; front
(*hard* ~) or back (*soft* ~) part of
this; (sense of) taste, liking.
păl'atal *a.* of palate; (of sound)
made with tongue against or near
palate; *n.* palatal sound. **~talīze**
v.t. make palatal.

palā'tial *a.* like palace, splendid.

păl'atīne *a.* having local jurisdiction
exclusive of royal or imperial
courts; *count* ~, (German) count
having supreme jurisdiction in his
fief; *county* ~, county where earl
orig. had royal privileges. **palăt'ĭ-
nate** *n.* count palatine's territory.

pala'ver (-lah-) *n.* conference; empty
words. *v.* talk profusely; cajole.

pāle¹ *n.* stake etc. as part of fence;
boundary.

pāle² *a.* (of complexion etc.) whitish,
not ruddy; faintly coloured; (of
colour) faint, (of light) dim. *v.* grow
or make pale. **~face,** supposed N.
Amer. Ind. name for white man.

păl'ĕtte *n.* artist's flat tablet for
mixing colours on; range or choice
of colours. **~-knife,** knife with
long round-ended flexible blade.

pal'frey (paw-) *n.* (arch.) saddle-
-horse.

păl'ĭmpsĕst *n.* parchment, etc. used
for second time after original
writing has been erased.

păl'ĭndrōme *n.* word etc. that reads
same backwards as forwards.
pălindrŏm'ĭc *a.*

pā'ling *n.* (usu. pl.) fence of pales.

pălĭsāde' *n.* fence of pointed stakes.
v.t. enclose with palisade.

pā'lish *a.* somewhat pale.

pall¹ (pawl) *n.* cloth spread over
coffin etc.; ecclesiastical vestment;
(fig.) cloak (of darkness). **~-bearer,**
mourner holding edge of pall at
funeral.

pall² (pawl) *v.i.* become tiresome.

Pallā'dĭan *a.* in pseudo-classical style
of 16th-c. Italian architect Palladio.

pallā'dĭum *n.* hard silvery-white
metallic element.

păll'ĕt¹ *n.* straw bed, mattress.

păll'ĕt² *n.* projection on part of
machine engaging with teeth of
wheel; organ-valve.

păll'ĭasse *n.* straw mattress.

păll'ĭāte *v.t.* alleviate without curing;
excuse, extenuate. **~ā'tion** *n.*
păll'ĭatĭve *a. & n.* (thing) serving to
palliate.

păll'ĭd *a.* pale, sickly-looking.

păll'or *n.* paleness.

palm (pahm) *n.* inner surface of hand
between wrist and fingers; kinds of
tree with unbranched stem and
crown of large esp. fan-shaped
leaves; various trees substituted
for this on Palm Sunday; (prize for)
supreme excellence. *v.* conceal in
hand in sleight-of-hand etc.; ~ *off,*
impose fraudulently, pass off.
P~ Sunday, Sunday before Easter.

păl'mar *a.* of or in palm of hand.

păl'marў *a.* pre-eminent. **păl'mate**
a. shaped like open palm or hand.
palm'er *n.* pilgrim returned from
Holy Land.

pălmĕtt'ō *n.* (pl. -*os*), kinds of small
palm.

palm'ĭst (pahm-) *n.* teller of character
or fortune from lines etc. in palm
of hand. **~rў** *n.*

palm'ў (pahm-) *a.* (esp.) flourishing.

pălmўr'a *n.* kind of palm with fan-
-shaped leaves used for matting etc.

păl'pable *a.* that can be touched or
felt; readily perceived. **~bĭl'ĭtў** *n.*

păl'pāte *v.t.* (med.) examine by
touch. **~ā'tion** *n.*

păl'pĭtāte *v.i.* pulsate, throb; tremble.
~ā'tion *n.*

palsy (pawl'zĭ) *n.* paralysis; paralytic
trembling. **pal'sied** (-zĭd) *a.* paralytic; trembling.

pal'ter (pawl-) *v.i.* equivocate. shuffle.

pal'trў (pawl-) *a.* petty, contemptible,
trifling.

păm'pas *n. pl.* vast treeless S.-Amer.
plains. **~-grass,** gigantic ornamental grass.

păm'per *v.t.* over-indulge.

păm'phlĕt *n.* small unbound esp. controversial treatise. **~eer'** *n.* writer of pamphlets; *v.i.* write pamphlets.

păn¹ *n.* shallow vessel used in cooking etc.; shallow receptacle or tray; hollow or depression in ground; (*hard*) **~**, hard substratum of soil. *v.* wash (gold-bearing gravel) in pan; criticize harshly, disparage; **~** *out*, yield gold, succeed, turn out (*well* etc.).

păn² *v.* (cause film-camera to) turn horizontally to follow movement etc. *n.* (sequence made by) panning.

Păn³ *n.* Gk. god of flocks and shepherds, represented with goat's horns, ears, and legs. **pan-pipe(s)**, musical instrument of graduated series of reeds or pipes.

păn⁴ *a. & n.* panchromatic (film).

păn- in comb., of or for all. **~-African** *a.* of or for all Africans. **~-American** *a.* of all States of N. & S. America; of all Americans. **~-Hellenism** *n.* political union of all Greeks.

pănacè'a *n.* universal remedy.

panáche' (-sh; *or* -ahsh) *n.* display, swagger.

pănama' (-ah) *n.* light fine soft plaited hat.

păn'cāke *n.* thin flat usu. fried batter-cake. *v.i.* make pancake landing. **~** landing, landing of aircraft without use of undercarriage.

pănchromăt'ic (-k-) *a.* (phot.) equally sensitive to all colours of spectrum.

păn'crèas *n.* gland near stomach supplying digestive secretion. **păncrèăt'ic** *a.*

păn'da *n.* raccoon-like Himalayan animal; large rare bear-like black-and-white animal of Tibet etc.

păndĕm'ic *a. & n.* (usu. infectious disease) of world-wide distribution.

păndėmō'nium *n.* scene of anarchy; confusion and din.

păn'der *n.* go-between in clandestine amours; procurer. *v.i.* act as pander; **~** *to*, encourage, minister to, cater for (base passions, weaknesses, etc. or person in respect of these).

pāne *n.* single sheet of glass in window.

pănégy'ric *n.* laudatory discourse;

eulogy. **~ical** *a.*; **păn'ėgyrist** *n.*; **păn'ėgyrize** *v.t.*

păn'el *n.* distinct or separate part of surface, esp. of door, wainscot, etc.; usu. long narrow rectangular board etc.; surface holding or displaying controls, switches, recording dials, etc.; list of jurors, jury; group of people for special purpose. **~-game,** quiz-game played esp. in public by panel of entertainers etc. **~ist** *n.* member of panel. **păn'elled** *a.*; **păn'elling** *n.*

păng *n.* sudden sharp pain.

păng'a (-ngg-) *n.* large broad-bladed African knife.

păngō'lin (-ngg-) *n.* scaly ant-eater.

păn'hăndle *n.* handle of pan; (U.S.) narrow strip of territory. *v.i.* (U.S.) beg in street.

păn'ic *a.* (of fear etc.) unreasoning, excessive. *n.* wild infectious fright; sudden general alarm. *v.* affect, be affected, with panic. **~-stricken, -struck,** stricken with panic. **păn'icky** *a.*

păn'icle *n.* (bot.) branched inflorescence forming loose irregular cluster.

pănjăn'drum *n.* (mock title for) great personage.

pănn'ier *n.* one of pair of baskets carried by beast of burden; part of skirt looped up round hips.

pănn'ikin *n.* small metal drinking-vessel.

păn'oply *n.* full armour (now usu. fig.). **păn'oplied** (-lid) *a.*

pănora'ma (-ah-) *n.* (representation of) landscape, prospect, continuous series of scenes, etc. esp. spread out before or (partly) surrounding spectator. **pănorăm'ic** *a.*

păn'sy (-z-) *n.* kinds of flowering plant of violet family; (colloq.) effeminate man, male homosexual.

pănt *v.* gasp for breath; throb; yearn. *n.* gasp; throb.

păntalĕttes' (-ts) *n.pl.* (hist.) young girl's long loose frilled drawers.

păntaloon' *n.* foolish old man, esp. clown's butt in pantomime etc.; (hist.) tight trousers strapped under instep.

păntĕch'nicon (-kn-) *n.* furniture van.

păn'thĕïsm *n.* identification of God with universe; worship of all gods. **~ĭst** *n.*; **~ĭs'tic(al)** *aa.*

păn'thĕon *n.* temple of all gods; building with memorials of illustrious dead.

păn'ther *n.* leopard; (U.S.) puma.

păn'ties (-ĭz) *n.pl.* (colloq.) short--legged knickers.

păn'tĭle *n.* curved roof-tile.

păn'tograph (-ahf) *n.* instrument for copying on any scale.

păn'tomĭme *n.* dumb show; dramatic usu. Christmas entertainment based on traditional fairy-tale.

păn'trў *n.* room in which provisions, plate, etc. are kept.

pănts *n.pl.* trousers; drawers.

păp[1] *n.* (arch.) nipple of breast.

păp[2] *n.* soft or semi-liquid food; mash, pulp. **păpp'ў** *a.*

papa' (-ah) *n.* father.

pā'pacў *n.* Pope's (tenure of) office; papal system. **pā'pal** *a.* of Pope or his office.

papaw' *n.* (S. Amer. tree with) pulpy edible fruit; pawpaw.

pā'per *n.* substance made of interlaced fibres of linen rags, wood, etc. in thin flexible sheets, used for writing, printing, wrapping, etc.; bank-notes; documents; set of examination questions; newspaper; essay, memorandum. *v.t.* paste paper on, *over*, etc.; (sl.) fill (theatre etc.) by issuing free tickets. *a.* of or for paper(s). **~back**, book bound in paper. **~-boy**, boy who delivers or sells newspapers. **~-chase**, cross-country run following trail of torn-up paper. **~-hanger**, one who decorates walls etc. with wallpaper. **~-knife**, blunt knife for cutting leaves of book etc. **~mill**, paper-making mill. **~ money**, bank-notes etc. **~weight**, small heavy object to hold papers down.

papier-mâché (păp'yā mah'shā) *n.* moulded paper pulp made into solid objects.

papĭll'a *n.* (pl. -*ae*), small nipple-like protuberance. **păp'illarў** *a.*

pā'pĭst *n.* (derog.) Roman Catholic. **papĭs'tĭcal** *a.*; **pā'pĭstrў** *n.*

papōōse' *n.* Red-Indian young child.

păp'rĭka (*or* -rē'ka) *n.* (red condiment made from) dried pods of kinds of pepper.

papŷr'us *n.* (writing-material made esp. by ancient Egyptians from stem of) kind of sedge; MS. written on this.

păr[1] *n.* equality, equal footing; average or normal value or degree; face value; (golf) number of strokes needed by scratch player for hole or course.

păr[2] *n.* (colloq.) paragraph.

pă'ra- in comb., beside, beyond, wrong, irregular. **parăm'ĕter** *n.* variable, esp. one that is constant in given case. **~mĭl'itarў** *a.* ancillary to or assisting armed forces. **~nŏr'mal** *a.* lying outside range of normal scientific experience etc. **~psychŏl'ogў** (-sĭk-) *n.* study of phenomena lying outside sphere of ordinary psychology. **~tŷ'phoid** *n.* kind of enteric fever resembling mild typhoid.

pă'rable *n.* narrative used to typify moral or spiritual truth.

parăb'ola *n.* plane curve formed by intersection of cone with plane parallel to its side.

părabŏl'ĭc(al) *aa.* of or like parable or parabola.

pă'rachute (-shōōt) *n.* umbrella-like apparatus designed to reduce speed of fall from height. **~** *v.* convey or descend by parachute. **~tĭst** *n.*

parāde' *n.* display, ostentation; muster of troops etc. for inspection, ground used for this; public promenade. *v.* assemble for parade; display ostentatiously; march with display (through).

pă'radigm (-īm) *n.* example, pattern, esp. of inflexion of word.

pă'radĭse *n.* garden of Eden; heaven; region or state of supreme bliss. **paradī'sal**, **~dĭs'ĭac(al)** *aa.*

pă'radŏs *n.* earthwork, esp. along back of trench, against attack from rear.

pă'radŏx *n.* seemingly absurd or self--contradictory though possibly true statement etc. **păradŏx'ical** *a.*

pă'raffĭn *n.* waxy or oily mixture of hydrocarbons got by distillation of petroleum etc.

pă′ragon *n.* model of excellence; excellent person or thing.

pă′ragraph (-ahf) *n.* distinct passage in book etc. usually marked by indentation of first line; mark of reference (¶); detached item of news etc. in newspaper.

pă′rakeet, pă′roquet (-kĕt) *n.* small long-tailed parrot.

pă′rallăx *n.* (angular amount of) apparent displacement of object caused by change of observation point. **părallăc′tic** *a.*

pă′rallĕl *a.* (of lines) continuously equidistant; precisely similar, analogous, or corresponding. *n.* imaginary line on earth's surface, line on map, marking degree of latitude; comparison, analogy; mark of reference (‖). *v.t.* represent as similar; compare; be parallel or correspond to. **~ĭsm** *n.*

părallĕlĕp′ĭpĕd *n.* solid contained by parallelograms.

părallĕl′ŏgrăm *n.* four-sided rectilinear figure whose opposite sides are parallel.

pă′ralȳse (-z) *v.t.* affect with paralysis; make helpless or ineffectual; cripple.

parăl′ȳsĭs *n.* (partial) incapacity to move or feel; powerless or immobile state. **păralȳt′ĭc** *a. & n.* (person) affected with paralysis or rendered helpless; causing paralysis.

pă′ramount *a.* supreme. **~cȳ** *n.*

pă′ramour (-oor) *n.* illicit lover.

păranoi′a *n.* mental illness with delusions of grandeur etc. **păranoi′ăc** *a. & n.*; **pă′ranoid** *a.*

pă′rapĕt *n.* low wall at edge of roof, balcony, bridge, etc.; mound along front of trench.

păr</ă>phĕrnā′lĭa *n.pl.* personal belongings; accessories, odds and ends.

pă′raphrāse (-z) *n.* restatement of sense of passage etc. in other words. *v.t.* express meaning of in other words. **păraphrăs′tĭc** *a.*

păraplē′gĭa *n.* paralysis of lower part of body. **păraplē′gic** *a. & n.*

pă′rasīte *n.* interested hanger-on; sycophant; animal or plant living in or on another. **părasĭt′ĭc** *a.*; **pă′rasītĭsm** *n.*

părasŏl′ *n.* sunshade.

pă′ratroōps *n. pl.* airborne troops landing by parachute.

păr′boil *v.t.* boil partially; overheat.

păr′bŭckle *n.* rope for raising or lowering casks etc.

păr′cel *n.* package of goods etc.; piece of land; *part and* **~**, essential part. *v.t.* divide (*out*) into portions; make (*up*) into parcels. **~-gilt**, partly gilded, esp. (of cup etc.) gilt inside.

părch *v.* slightly roast; make hot and dry.

părch′ment *n.* skin prepared for writing etc.; MS. on this.

părd *n.* (arch.) leopard.

păr′don *n.* forgiveness; remission of punishment; courteous forbearance; (eccl.) indulgence, Breton festival of patron saint. *v.t.* forgive; excuse. **~able** *a.* **~er** *n.* (hist.) licensed seller of indulgences.

pāre *v.t.* trim or reduce by cutting away edge or surface of; whittle away. **pār′ĭng** *n.* (esp.) strip of rind.

părĕgŏ′rĭc *n.* camphorated tincture of opium.

pār′ent *n.* father or mother; forefather; source, origin. **~age** *n.*; **parĕn′tal** *a.*

parĕn′thĕsĭs *n.* (pl. *-thesēs*), word, clause, or sentence inserted into passage independently of grammatical sequence; (sing. or pl.) round brackets used for this; (fig.) interlude. **parĕn′thĕsīze** *v.t.*; **părĕnthĕt′ĭc** *a.*

păr ĕx′cellence (-ahṅs), above all others so called. [F]

păr′gĕt *v.t. & n.* roughcast; (cover or adorn with) plaster or pargeting. **~ing** *n.* ornamental plaster relief work.

părhē′lion *n.* (pl. *-ia*), bright spot in solar halo, mock sun.

păr′iah (*or* -ī′a) *n.* Indian of low or no caste; social outcast.

Pār′ian *a.* from Paros.

parī′etal *a.* of wall of body or any of its cavities. **~ bones**, pair forming part of sides and top of skull.

păr′ī păss′ū, simultaneously and equally. [L]

pă′rish *n.* division of diocese having its own church and clergyman;

local-government district, esp. (hist.) for poor-law administration; inhabitants of parish. **parish'ioner** (-sh*o*-) *n.* inhabitant of parish.

pă'rită *n.* being on a par or at par; equivalence.

pârk *n.* large enclosed piece of ground attached to country house or laid out or preserved for public use; artillery, space in camp occupied by it; place where vehicles may be left. *v.t.* leave in park or other place until required. ~**ing-meter**, mechanical device for collecting parking-fee esp. in street. ~**way**, (U.S.) wide landscaped road.

pâr'kin *n.* oatmeal gingerbread.

pâr'lance *n.* way of speaking.

pâr'ley *n.* meeting between representatives of opposed forces to discuss terms. *v.i.* hold discussion on terms.

pâr'liament (-la-) *n.* deliberative body consisting of House of Commons and House of Lords and forming (with sovereign) legislature of U.K.; legislative assembly in other countries. ~**âr'ian** *n.* skilled parliamentary debater. **pârliamĕn'tară** *a.* of, in, concerned with, enacted by, parliament.

pâr'lour *n.* sitting-room in small house; private room in inn. ~**-games**, esp. round games of kind played at parties. ~**maid**, maid waiting at table.

pâr'lous *a.* (arch.) perilous; hard to deal with.

Pârmĕsăn' (-z-) *n.* hard cheese of kind made at Parma.

Pârnăss'us *n.* Gk. mountain associated with worship of Apollo and the Muses.

parō'chĭal (-k-) *a.* of parish; of narrow range, merely local. ~**ĭsm** *n.*

pă'rodă *n.* composition in which author's characteristics are ridiculed by imitation; travesty. *v.t.* write parody of; caricature.

parōle' *n.* word of honour, esp. prisoner's promise not to attempt escape.

păronomā'sĭa (-z-) *n.* play on words; pun.

paroquet : see **parakeet**.

parŏt'ĭd *a. & n.* (gland) near ear.

pă'roxăsm *n.* fit (*of* pain, rage, etc.).

pâr'quet (-kĭ *or* -kā) *n.* flooring of wooden blocks arranged in a pattern. *v.t.* lay with parquet.

pârr *n.* young salmon.

pă'rricĭde *n.* murder, murderer, of father. **părricĭ'dal** *a.*

pă'rrot *n.* kinds of mainly tropical bird with hooked bill, some of which can imitate speech; unintelligent imitator or chatterer. *v.t.* repeat or imitate mechanically. ~**-fish**, kinds of fish with brilliant colouring or mouth like parrot's bill.

pă'rră *v.t.* ward off, avert. *n.* parrying.

pârse (-z) *v.t.* describe (word), analyse (sentence), in terms of grammar.

pâr'sĕc *n.* unit of stellar distance, distance at which annual parallax of star would be one second of arc.

pâr'sĭmoną *n.* carefulness in employment of money etc.; stinginess. **pârsĭmō'nĭous** *a.*

pâr'sley *n.* culinary herb used for seasoning and garnishing.

pâr'snip *n.* (plant with) sweet fleshy root used as vegetable.

pâr'son *n.* parish clergyman; (colloq.) any clergyman. ~**'s nose**, rump of cooked table bird. ~**age** *n.* parson's house. **parsŏn'ic(al)** *aa.*

pârt *n.* some but not all; share, allotted portion; assigned character or role; one of melodies making up harmony of concerted music; region, direction, way; side in dispute or dealing; (pl.) ability. *adv.* partly, in part. *v.* divide into parts; separate; make parting in (hair); ~ *company* (*with*), separate (from); (sl.) part with one's money; ~ *from*, (make) leave or separate, say good-bye to; ~ *with*, give up, surrender, say good-bye to. ~**-owner**, sharer of ownership. ~**-song**, song for two or more voice-parts. ~**-time**, employed for, taking up, only part of working-day etc. ~**-timer**, part-time worker. **pâr'tĭng** *n.* leave-taking; dividing line of combed hair; ~ *of the ways*, place where road etc. forks.

pârtāke' *v.i.* (-tŏŏk, -tāken), take

share (*in, of, with*); eat or drink some *of*; have something of character *of*.

pàrterre' (-tār) *n.* level garden space filled with flower-beds etc.; part of ground floor of theatre behind orchestra.

pàr'tial *a.* biased, unfair; not total or complete; *be ~ to*, like. **pàrtiăl'itў** (-shĭ-) *n.*

pàrti'cĭpāte *v.i.* have share, take part, (*in*). **~pant, ~pā'tion** *nn.*

pàr'tĭcĭple *n.* adjective formed by inflexion from verb. **pàrtĭcĭp'ĭal** *a.*

pàr'tĭcle *n.* minute portion of matter; smallest possible amount; minor esp. indeclinable part of speech; prefix or suffix with distinct meaning.

pàr'tĭcoloured (-kŭl-) *a.* partly of one colour, partly of another.

partĭc'ūlar *a.* relating to one as distinguished from others; special; scrupulously exact; fastidious. *n.* detail, item; (pl.) detailed account. **partĭcŭlă'ritў** *n.* **~lў** *adv.* very; to special extent; in detail.

partĭc'ūlarīze *v.* mention one by one; go into particulars. **~zā'tion** *n.*

pàr'tĭsan¹ (-zn) *n.* (hist.) kind of halberd.

pàrtĭsăn'² (-z-) *n.* adherent of party or side or cause; guerrilla. **~ship** *n.* strong party spirit.

pàrti'tion *n.* division into parts; structure effecting division; compartment. *v.t.* divide into parts; divide *off* by partition.

pàr'titive *a. & n.* (word) denoting part of collective whole.

pàrt'lў *adv.* with respect to a part; in some degree; not wholly.

pàrt'ner *n.* sharer; one associated with others in business; either of pair in marriage or dancing or game. *v.t.* make partner(s); be partner of. **~ship** *n.*

pàr'tridge *n.* kinds of game-bird.

pàrtūr'ient *a.* about to give birth.

pàrtūri'tion *n.* childbirth.

pàr'tў *n.* body of persons united in cause or in opposition to another body; body of persons travelling or engaged together; social reception; person consenting or contributing to affair; either side in lawsuit, con-

tract, or other transaction. **~ line,** shared telephone line; set policy of political party. **~ wall,** wall separating and shared by two adjoining buildings etc.

pàr'venū *n.* person who has risen from obscurity; upstart.

pàs'chal (-k-) *a.* of Passover; of Easter.

pàsh'a (*or* pah-) *n.* Turkish or Egyptian officer of high rank.

pàsque'-flower (-skf-) *n.* kind of anemone.

pass (-ah-) *v.* (p.p. *passed*, or as adj. *past*), move onward, proceed; cause to go; be current; change; die; go by; come to end; percolate; be accepted as adequate; be sanctioned; satisfy examiner; happen; go across; outstrip; surpass; spend; hand round; give currency to; utter; ~ *away*, die; ~ *for*, be accepted as; ~ *off*, fade away, be carried through, palm off, distract attention from; ~ *out*, (colloq.) become unconscious; ~ *over*, omit, make no remark upon. *n.* passing, esp. of examination; standard that satisfies examiners without entitling to honours; state, critical position; written permission or ticket or order; thrust in fencing; (footb. etc.) passing of ball from one player to another; narrow passage through mountains etc. **~-book,** book recording customer's transactions with bank. **~-key,** master-key. **~word,** selected word etc. distinguishing friend from enemy.

pa'ssable *a.* that can bear examination or inspection; fairly good.

pass. *abbr.* passive.

pàss'age *n.* passing, transit; crossing, being conveyed, from port to port; corridor; (pl.) what passes between two persons; part of speech or literary work.

pàss'ant *a.* (her.) shown as walking with dexter fore-paw raised.

passé (pă'sā) *a.* (fem. -*ée*), past the prime; out of date. [F]

pàss'ènger (-j-) *n.* traveller by public conveyance; traveller in car etc. who is not driving; ineffective member of team etc.

passe-partout (pahspàrtōō') *n.* kind

of adhesive tape or paper used for framing pictures etc.

passer-bȳ' (pah-) *n.* one who passes, esp. casually.

pǎss'erīne *a.* of sparrow kind.

pǎss'im adv. here and there, throughout. [L]

pa'ssǐng (-ah-) *a.* (esp.) transient, fleeting. *adv.* (arch.) very. **~-bell,** bell rung immediately after death.

pǎ'ssion *n.* strong emotion; anger; sexual love; *P~*, sufferings of Christ on cross; (musical setting of) Gospel narrative of this. **~-flower** kinds of usu. climbing plant with flower suggesting instruments of the Passion. **P~ week,** Holy Week or preceding week. **~lĕss** *a.*

pǎ'ssionate *a.* prone or due to, showing, passion; lacking self-control.

pǎss'ǐve *a.* acted upon, not acting; inert; submissive; of or in passive voice. *n.* passive voice or form. **~ voice,** of verb, indicating that subject suffers action of the verb. **passǐv'itў** *n.*

Pa'ssōver (pah-) *n.* Jewish spring festival commemorating deliverance from bondage in Egypt.

pass'pōrt (-ah-) *n.* official document showing identity, nationality, etc. of traveller abroad.

past (-ah-) *a.* gone by; just over. *n.* past time; person's past life or career. *prep.* beyond. *adv.* by. **~ master,** thorough master, expert.

pǎs'ta (*or* -ah-) *n.* (dish of) kind of Italian food-paste used to make macaroni etc.

pāste *n.* flour kneaded with water, suet, butter, etc. as material for pastry; flour and water or similar mixture as adhesive; relish of pounded fish, meat, etc.; material of imitation gems. *v.t.* fasten with paste; cover (as) by pasting; (sl.) beat, thrash. **~board,** cardboard; (sl.) visiting or playing card.

pǎs'tel *n.* (crayon made of) dry pigment-paste; drawing in pastel. *a.* of or in pastel; (of colour) soft and pale. **pǎs'tel(l)ǐst** *n.* artist using pastels.

pǎs'tern *n.* part of horse's foot between fetlock and hoof.

pǎs'teurīze (-ter-) *v.t.* partially sterilize (milk etc.) by keeping for some time at high temperature. **~zā'tion** *n.*

pǎstiche' (-ēsh) *n.* musical or other medley of borrowings; literary or other work imitating style of author, period, etc.

pǎs'tǐlle (*or* -ēl') *n.* kinds of small sweet, esp. medicated.

pa'stǐme (-ah-) *n.* recreation; sport or game.

pa'stor (-ah-) *n.* minister of congregation; spiritual adviser. **pa'storate** *n.* pastor's (tenure of) office; body of pastors.

pa'storal (-ah-) *a.* of shepherds; of rural life; of pastor. *n.* pastoral poem or picture; letter from bishop or other pastor to clergy or people.

pā'strў *n.* baked flour-paste; food made of or with it.

pa'sture (-ah-) *n.* herbage for cattle; land or field under such crop. *v.* put (cattle) to pasture; graze. **pa'sturage** *n.* pasturing; pasture, pasture-land.

pǎs'tў[1] *n.* pie of meat etc. enclosed in pastry crust and baked without dish.

pā'stў[2] *a.* of or like paste; pallid.

pǎt *v.t.* strike gently with open hand or other flat surface. *n.* patting touch or sound; small mass, esp. of butter, made (as) by patting. *adv. & a.* apposite(ly), opportune(ly).

pǎtch *n.* piece put on in mending; piece of plaster over wound; cover protecting injured eye; (hist.) small piece of black silk etc. worn to show off complexion; large or irregular spot on surface, distinct area or period; small plot of ground; *not a ~ on,* not to be compared with. *v.t.* mend with patch(es); piece *together*; appear as patches on (surface); *~ up,* repair, set to rights, esp. hastily or temporarily. **~ pocket,** pocket sewn on like patch. **~work,** work made of small pieces of different colours etc. sewn together (freq. fig.). **pǎtch'ў** *a.* (esp.) irregular, uneven.

pāte *n.* (colloq.) head.

pâté (pah'tā) *n.* smooth paste of meat etc.; patty. **~ de foie gras** (fwah grah), pâté made from livers of fatted geese. [F]

patěll'a n. knee-cap.

pǎt'en n. plate for bread at Eucharist.

pā'tent (or -ǎ-) a. obvious, unconcealed; patented; *letters* ~, open letter from sovereign etc. conferring right, title, etc., esp. sole right to make, use, or sell invention. n. letters patent; grant of sole right to make or sell, invention or process protected by this. v.t. obtain patent for (invention). ~ **leather,** leather with fine black varnished surface. ~ **medicine,** proprietary medicine. ~ee' n. holder of patent.

pā'ter n. (sl.) father. **pāter-famǐl'iǎs** n. head of family.

patēr'nal a. of father, fatherly; related through father, on father's side. ~ism n. (esp.) government etc. (as) by father. ~is'tǐc a.; **patēr'nitȳ** n.

pǎt'ernǒster n. Lord's prayer, esp. in Latin; weighted fishing-line with hooks at intervals.

path (pahth, pl. pahdhz) n. foot-way; track; line along which person or thing moves. ~lěss a.

pathět'ǐc a. exciting or appealing to compassion; of emotions.

pǎthogěn'ic a. capable of producing disease.

pathǒl'ogȳ n. study of disease. ~lǒ'gical a.; ~logǐst n.

pā'thǒs n. pathetic quality.

pā'tience (-shns) n. endurance of pain or provocation; forbearance; calm and quiet waiting; perseverance; card-game, usu. for one.

pā'tient (-shnt) a. having or showing patience. n. person under medical treatment.

pǎt'ina n. incrustation, usu. green, on surface of old bronze; gloss produced by long use on woodwork etc.

pǎt'iō (or pah-) n. roofless inner courtyard; paved usu. roofless area near house.

pǎt'ois (-twah) n. regional dialect of common people.

pā'triǎrch (-k) n. father and ruler of family or tribe; bishop of certain sees in Eastern and R.-C. Churches; venerable old man. **pātriǎr'chal** a.; ~ate n. **pā'triǎrchȳ** n. government

by father or eldest male of tribe etc.; community so ruled.

patri'cian n. person of noble birth. a. of nobility; aristocratic.

pǎt'rǐcīde n. parricide. ~cī'dal a.

pǎt'rǐmonȳ n. property inherited from father or ancestors.

pā'trǐot (or pǎ-) n. champion or lover of his country. ~ǒt'ǐc a.; ~otǐsm n.

patrǐs'tǐc a. of Fathers of Church.

patrōl' n. going rounds, perambulating, to see that all is well; man or party or ship(s) charged with this; routine operational flight; detachment of troops sent to reconnoitre; unit of six Boy Scouts. v. act as patrol; go rounds of as patrol. ~man, (U.S.) police constable. ~-wagon, (U.S.) police van for prisoners.

pā'tron (or pǎ-) n. one who countenances, protects, or gives influential support to; tutelary saint; person having right of presentation to benefice. **patrō'nal** a. of patron saint. ~ess n.

pǎt'ronage (or pā-) n. patron's help; customer's support; dispensing of appointments; patronizing airs.

pǎt'ronize v.t. act as patron to; support, encourage; treat condescendingly.

pǎtronȳm'ǐc a. & n. (name) derived from that of father or ancestor.

pǎt'ten n. wooden sole mounted on iron ring for raising wearer's shoe above mud etc.

pǎtt'er[1] v. say, talk, with rapid utterance. n. rapid talk, esp. introduced into (comic) song; (sl.) lingo of class etc.

pǎtt'er[2] v.i. (of rain etc.) make tapping sound; run with quick short steps. n. sound of pattering.

pǎtt'ern n. excellent example; model; sample, esp. of cloth; design, esp. on surface; distribution of shots etc. v.t. decorate with pattern.

pǎtt'ȳ n. small pie or pasty.

pau'citȳ n. smallness of number or quantity.

paunch n. belly, stomach.

pau'per n. very poor person; recipient of poor-law relief, charity, etc. ~ǐsm, ~izā'tion nn.; ~īze v.t.

Paus. *abbr.* Pausanias.

pause (-z) *n.* interval of inaction or silence; break made in speech or reading; (mus.) mark (⌒) denoting lengthening of note or rest. *v.i.* make a pause; wait.

pavane' (-ahn) *a.* (music for) stately dance in slow duple time.

pāve *v.t.* cover (as) with pavement; (fig.) prepare *the way for*. **pā'vement** (-vm-) *n.* layer of flat stones, tiles, asphalt, etc., as surface of road or floor; paved footway.

pavil'ion (-ly*o*n) *n.* large tent; building for spectators or players of outdoor game; projecting subdivision of building. *v.t.* enclose like, furnish with, pavilion.

paw *n.* foot of beast with claws; (sl.) hand. *v.* touch with paw; (sl.) handle with dirty or clumsy hands; (of horse) strike ground with hoof.

paw'kў *a.* (of humour, esp. when Scottish) sly, quiet, dry.

pawl *n.* lever with catch for teeth of wheel or bar; bar to prevent capstan etc. from recoiling.

pawn[1] *n.* piece of least value in chess; (fig.) mere tool.

pawn[2] *n.* thing handed over as pledge or security; state of being pledged. *v.t.* deposit as security for money lent; pledge. **~broker**, keeper of shop where money is lent on security of pawned goods. **~ticket**, receipt for object pawned.

paw'paw *n.* (N.-Amer. tree with) sweet pulpy edible fruit.

păx *int.* used by schoolboys in demanding truce.

pay *v.* give as due; discharge debt to; bear cost; suffer penalty *for*; render, bestow (attention etc.); yield adequate return; let *out* (rope) by slackening it; *~ out*, take revenge on. *n.* amount paid; wages, salary; *in the ~ of*, employed by. **~-as-you-earn**, collection of income-tax by deduction from earnings. **~-load**, weight of goods, passengers, etc. carried by aircraft etc. **Paymaster-General**, head of Treasury department through which payments are made. **~-off**, (esp.) climax, denouement. **~roll**, list of employees receiving regular pay. **~able** *a.* (esp.) that must be paid, due. **~ee** *n.* person to whom payment is (to be) made. **~ment** *n.* paying; amount paid.

P.A.Y.E. *abbr.* pay-as-you-earn.

pay'nim *n.* (arch.) pagan.

P.C. *abbr.* Police Constable; postcard; Privy Council(lor).

p.c. *abbr.* per cent; postcard.

p.c.u. *abbr.* passenger car unit (in measuring capacity of road).

P.D. *abbr.* potential difference.

pd. *abbr.* paid.

p.e. *abbr.* personal estate.

pea *n.* kinds of plant bearing round seeds in pods and cultivated for food; one of the seeds. **~-soup**, (of fog) thick and yellow. **~-souper**, thick yellow fog.

peace *n.* freedom from or cessation of war; treaty securing this; civil order; quiet, calm; harmonious relations. **~maker**, reconciler. **~-offering**, propitiatory gift. **peace'able** (-sa-) *a.* disposed or leading to peace; peaceful. **~ful** (-sf-) *a.*

peach[1] *v.i.* (sl.) turn informer; inform.

peach[2] *n.* (tree bearing) large roundish stone-fruit with downy delicately coloured skin; (sl.) attractive young woman, thing of superlative merit. **~-colour(ed)**, (of) soft yellowish-pink colour of ripe peach. **~ melba**, *pêche melba*. **pea'chў** *a.*

pea'cŏck *n.* male bird with splendid plumage and fanlike tail; vain person. **~ blue**, bright lustrous blue of peacock's neck. **pea'fowl** *n.* peacock or peahen. **pea'hĕn** *n.* female of peacock.

pea'-jăcket *n.* sailor's short thick double-breasted overcoat.

peak[1] *v.i.* waste away. **~ed**[1] *a.* sharp-featured, pinched. **~ў** *a.* sickly, puny.

peak[2] *n.* pointed top, esp. of mountain; highest point in curve or record of fluctuations; projecting part of cap; narrow part of ship's hold. **~-hour, time**, time when peak-load occurs. **~-load**, maximum intensity of traffic, consumption of electricity, etc. **peaked** (-kt) *a.*[2] having peak.

peal *n.* loud ringing of bell(s); set of

bells; outburst of sound. *v.* sound forth, ring (bells), in peal.

pea′nut *n.* (fruit of) plant with pod ripening underground, containing two seeds valued as food and for their oil. **~ butter,** paste of ground peanuts.

pear (pār) *n.* (kinds of tree with) fleshy fruit tapering towards stalk. **~-shaped** *a.*

pearl (pêrl) *n.* lustrous usu. white concretion found in oyster and other shells and prized as gem; size of printing-type (5-point). *v.* fish for pearls; (of moisture) form drops, form drops on. **~ barley,** barley reduced by attrition to small rounded grains. **~ button,** button of (imitation) mother-of-pearl. **pearl′ies** (-z) *n.pl.* (costermongers wearing) dress decorated with many pearl buttons. **pearl′y** *a.* like pearl; wearing pearlies.

pear′main (pār-) *n.* kind of apple.

peas′ant (pĕz-) *n.* countryman, rustic, worker on land. **~ry** *n.* peasants collectively.

pease (-z) **pu′dding** (pŏŏ-) *n.* pudding of split dried peas boiled in cloth etc.

peat *n.* vegetable matter decomposed by water and partly carbonized; piece of this as fuel. **~-bog, -moss,** bog where peat is dug. **pea′ty** *a.*

pĕbb′le *n.* small water-rounded stone; rock-crystal used for spectacles, lens of this; kinds of agate. **~-dash,** (coat wall with) plaster with small stones embedded in it. **pĕbb′ly** *a.*

pĕcăn′ (*or* pē′-) *n.* (olive-shaped finely flavoured nut of) kind of hickory.

pĕccadĭll′ō *n.* (pl. -oes), trivial offence.

pĕcc′ant *a.* offending, sinning. **pĕcc′ancy** *n.*

pĕcc′ary *n.* small gregarious pig of S. and Central America.

pĕccā′vī, I have sinned; confession of guilt. [L]

pêche mĕl′ba (pāsh) *n.* confection of ice-cream and peaches. [F]

pĕck[1] *n.* measure of capacity (one-fourth of bushel) for dry goods.

pĕck[2] *v.* strike, pick up, pluck *out,* make (hole), with beak; make dab(s) *at;* eat fastidiously. *n.* stroke with beak; (joc.) kiss like bird's peck. **~er** *n.* (esp., sl.) courage, spirits. **~ish** *a.* (colloq.) somewhat hungry.

pĕc′tin *n.* gelatinous substance in ripe fruits etc., causing jam etc. to set.

pĕc′toral *a.* of or for breast or chest. *n.* ornamental breastplate.

pĕc′ūlāte *v.* embezzle. **~ā′tion, ~ātor** *nn.*

pĕcū′liar *a.* belonging to the individual; exclusive *to;* particular, special; odd. **pĕcūlĭă′rity** *n.* being peculiar; characteristic; oddity.

pĕcū′niary *a.* of or in money.

pĕd′agŏgue (-g) *n.* schoolmaster; pedant. **~gŏ′gical** *a.* **pĕd′agogy, pedagŏ′gics** *nn.* science of teaching.

pĕd′al *a.* of foot or feet. *n.* (wooden) key of organ played with feet; foot-lever in piano, cycle, etc. *v.* work pedals (of).

pĕd′ant *n.* one who overrates or parades learning or knowledge, or insists on strict adherence to formal rules. **pĕdăn′tic** *a.*; **~ry** *n.*

pĕdd′le *v.* be pedlar; trade or deal in as pedlar.

pederast etc.: see **paederast.**

pĕd′estal *n.* base of column; block on which something stands; either support of knee-hole table.

pĕdĕs′trian *a.* going or performed on foot; of walking; for those on foot; prosaic, dull. *n.* walker, traveller on foot. **~ism** *n.*

pediatric etc.: see **paediatric.**

pĕd′icel, pĕd′icle *nn.* stalk-like structure in plant or animal.

pĕd′icūre *n.* care or treatment of feet, toes, and esp. toe-nails.

pĕd′igree *n.* genealogical table; ancestral line; ancient descent. *a.* having known line of descent.

pĕd′iment *n.* triangular part crowning front of building.

pĕd′lar *n.* travelling vendor of small wares.

pĕdŏl′ogy *n.* science of soils.

pĕdŏm′eter *n.* instrument for estimating distance walked.

pĕdŭnc′le *n.* stalk of flower or fruit or cluster; stalk-like process.

peek *n.* & *v.i.* peep, glance.

peel[1] *n.* rind of fruit, thin soft bark

of young shoots, etc.; *candied* ~, candied rind of citrous fruits. *v.* strip of peel; take off (skin, bark, etc.); shed bark or skin or paper or paint; (sl.) strip for exercise etc.

peel[2] *n.* small square defensible tower near Scottish border.

pee'ling *n.* piece peeled off.

peen *n.* wedge-shaped end of hammer--head.

peep[1] *v.i.* look through narrow aperture; look quickly or furtively; come cautiously or partly into view; begin to appear. *n.* (esp. surreptitious) glance; first light (*of dawn, day*). ~-hole, small hole to peep through. ~show, exhibition of pictures etc. in lighted box viewed through lens in peep-hole. ~-toe(d), (of shoe etc.) allowing toes to be seen.

peep[2] *n.* & *v.i.* cheep, squeak.

peer[1] *v.i.* look narrowly; peep out.

peer[2] *n.* equal in rank or merit; duke, earl, marquis, viscount, or baron. ~ess *n.* peer's wife or female holder of peerage. **peer'age** *n.* peers; rank of peer. **peer'less** *a.* unequalled.

peeved (-vd) *a.* (sl.) irritated.

pee'vish *a.* querulous, irritable.

peewit : see **pewit**.

pĕg *n.* wooden, metal, etc., bolt or pin for holding together parts of framework, hanging things on, stopping cask-vent, marking cribbage-score, etc.; forked wooden peg or similar device for hanging washing on line; drink, esp. of spirits; *off the peg*, ready-made. *v.* fix, mark or hang *out*, (as) with peg(s); keep (prices etc.) stable; ~ *away*, work persistently (*at*); ~ *out*, (croquet) hit peg as final stroke in game, (sl.) die. ~-top, pear-shaped spinning top with metal peg; ~-*top trousers*, wide at hips, narrow at ankles.

pĕj'orative (*or* pē-) *a.* & *n.* depreciatory (word).

pēke *n.* Pekinese.

Pēkĭnēse' (-z) *n.* small breed of dog with long silky coat and flat face.

pĕk'ōe (*or* pē-) *n.* kind of black tea.

pĕlă'gĭc *a.* of or in or on open sea.

pĕlăȑgō'nium *n.* kinds of plant with showy flowers.

pĕlf *n.* money, wealth.

pĕl'ĭcan *n.* kinds of large bird with long hooked bill and pouch for storing fish.

pĕlisse' (-ēs) *n.* (hist.) woman's long cloak; child's outdoor garment; military cape or cloak.

pĕllā'gra (*or* -ă-) *n.* deficiency disease with dermatitis etc.

pĕll'ĕt *n.* small ball of paper etc.; pill; small shot.

pĕll'ĭcle *n.* thin skin or membrane or film. **pĕllĭc'ūlar** *a.*

pĕll'ĭtory *n.* bushy plant growing on walls.

pĕll-mĕll' *adv.* in disorder; headlong.

pĕllū'cĭd *a.* transparent, clear; free from obscurity.

pĕl'mĕt *n.* pendent border concealing curtain-rods etc.

pĕlō'ta *n.* Basque ball-game resembling tennis or rackets.

pĕlt[1] *v.* assail with missiles, abuse, etc.; (of rain) come down hard; run at full speed. *n.* pelting; speed.

pĕlt[2] *n.* undressed skin of sheep, goat, or fur-bearing animal; (joc.) human skin.

pĕl'vĭs *n.* lower abdominal cavity formed by haunch bones etc. **pĕl'vĭc** *a.*

pĕmm'ĭcan *n.* preparation of dried and pounded meat etc.

pĕn[1] *n.* implement of quill, metal, etc., for writing with ink; writing or literary style. *v.t.* compose and write (letter etc.). ~-friend, correspondent one has not met. ~knife, small pocket-knife. ~manship, skill in, style of, handwriting. ~-name, literary pseudonym.

pĕn[2] *n.* small enclosure for cows, sheep, poultry, etc. *v.t.* enclose; put or keep in confined space.

pĕn[3] *n.* female swan.

pĕn[4] *n.* (U.S. sl.) penitentiary.

P.E.N. *abbr.* (International Association of) Poets, Playwrights, Editors, Essayists, and Novelists.

Pen., Penin. *abbr.* Peninsula.

pē'nal *a.* of or involving punishment; punishable; punitive. ~ **servitude**, imprisonment with hard labour. ~ize *v.t.* make punishable; subject to penalty or comparative disadvantage.

pĕn'altў *n.* fine or other punishment; disadvantage imposed for breaking rule, failing to fulfil condition, etc.; (goal scored by) penalty kick. ~ **area,** (footb.) area in front of goal within which breach of rules involves penalty kick. ~ **kick,** free kick (at goal).

pĕn'ance *n.* sacrament of confession etc.; act, esp. one imposed by priest, performed as expression of penitence.

pence : see **penny.**

penchant (pahṅ'shahṅ) *n.* inclination or liking (*for*).

pĕn'cil *n.* instrument for drawing or writing, esp. of graphite enclosed in wooden cylinder or metal case with tapering end; artist's style; set of rays or lines meeting at point. *v.t.* draw or mark or write with lead pencil.

pĕn'dant, -dent *a.* (usu. -*ent*), hanging, overhanging. *n.* (usu. -*ant*), ornament hung from necklace etc.; thing serving as complement to something else.

pĕn'ding *a.* awaiting decision or settlement. *prep.* during; until.

pĕn'dūlous *a.* hanging, swinging.

pĕn'dūlum *n.* body suspended so as to be free to swing, esp. in clock.

pĕn'ėtrāte *v.* find access or pass into or through; make a way; permeate; find out, discern. pĕn'ėtrable *a.* pĕn'ėtrāting *a.* discerning, gifted with insight; (of voice etc.) piercing, easily heard. pĕnėtrā'tion *n.* (esp.) acute insight. pĕn'ėtrātive *a.*

pĕng'uïn (-nggw-) *n.* kinds of flightless sea-bird of southern hemisphere.

pĕnïcill'ïn *n.* antibiotic obtained from mould.

pėnïn'sūla *n.* piece of land almost surrounded by water or projecting far into sea etc.

pē'nïs *n.* male copulatory organ.

pĕn'ïtent *a.* repenting, contrite. *n.* penitent person; person doing penance. pĕn'ïtence *n.*

pĕnïtĕn'tial *a.* of penitence or penance.

pĕnïtĕn'tiarў (-sha-) *n.* reformatory; (U.S.) prison. *a.* of penance or reformatory treatment.

Penn. *abbr.* Pennsylvania.

pĕnn'ant *n.* tapering flag, esp. that at mast-head of ship in commission.

pĕnn'ïléss *a.* destitute.

pĕnn'on *n.* long narrow triangular or swallow-tailed flag; long pointed streamer of ship.

pĕnn'ў *n.* (pl. *pence, pennies*), bronze coin worth one-twelfth of shilling; *a pretty* ~, a good sum of money. ~-**farthing,** early kind of bicycle with large front wheel and small rear one.

pĕnnўroy'al *n.* kind of mint formerly used in medicine.

pĕnn'ўweight (-wāt) *n.* 20th part of 1 oz. Troy.

pēnŏl'ogў *n.* study of punishment and prison management.

pĕn'sïle *a.* hanging down.

pĕn'sion *n.* periodical payment made in consideration of past service, old age, widowhood, etc. *v.t.* grant pension to; ~ *off*, dismiss with pension. ~**able** *a.* (esp.) entitling to pension. ~**arў** *a.* of pension; *n.* recipient of pension. ~**er** *n.*

pĕn'sïve *a.* plunged in thought; melancholy.

pĕnt *a.* closely confined, shut *in* or *up.*

pĕn'ta- in comb., five. pĕn'tachŏrd (-k-) *n.* series of five notes. pĕn'tacle *n.* figure of five-pointed star used as symbol, esp. in magic. pĕn'tad *n.* number 5; group of five. ~**gon** *n.* five-sided (usu. plane rectilinear) figure; **P~gon,** U.S. Dept. of Defence; pentăg'onal *a.* ~**hĕd'ron** *n.* solid figure of five faces; ~**hĕd'ral** *a.* pentăm'ėter *n.* verse-line of five feet. ~**teuch** (-ūk) *n.* first five books of O.T. ~**tŏn'ic** *a. & n.* (scale) of five notes.

Pĕn'tėcŏst *n.* Jewish harvest festival fifty days after Passover; Whit Sunday. pĕntėcŏs'tal *a.*

pĕnt'house (-t-h-) *n.* sloping roof supported against wall of building; separate flat, house, etc. on roof of tall building.

pĕntstē'mon *n.* kinds of bright--flowered Amer. herbaceous plant allied to foxglove.

pėnŭl'tïmate *a.* last but one. *n.* penultimate syllable.

pėnŭm'bra *n.* partly lighted shadow

on skirts of total shadow; partial shadow. **pĕnŭm'bral** *a.*

pĕnūr'ious *a.* poor; stingy.

pĕn'ūrў *n.* destitution, poverty.

pē'on *n.* Sp.-Amer. day-labourer; enslaved debtor in Mexico etc. **~age** *n.* employment, service, of peons.

pē'onў *n.* garden plant with large handsome globular flowers.

people (pē'pl) *n.* race or nation; persons in general; subjects; parents or other relatives; commonalty. *v.t.* fill with people; populate; inhabit.

pĕp *n.* vigour, go, spirit. *v.t.* fill *up*, inspire, with energy and vigour. **~-pill,** pill containing stimulant drug. **~-talk,** talk meant to inspire hearers to exceptional effort etc.

P.E.P. *abbr.* Political and Economic Planning.

pĕpp'er *n.* pungent aromatic condiment from dried berries of some plants; (fruit of) kinds of capsicum. *v.t.* sprinkle or flavour with pepper; besprinkle; pelt with missiles. **~-and-salt,** of closely mingled dark and light. **~corn,** dried pepper berry, esp. as nominal rent. **~mint,** (kind of mint grown for) essential oil with pungent aromatic flavour; sweet flavoured with it. **pĕpp'erў** *a.* like pepper; hot-tempered.

pĕp'sĭn *n.* constituent of gastric juice. **pĕp'tĭc** *a.* digestive; of digestive system.

pĕr *prep.* by, by means or instrumentality of; for each. **~ annum** (ăn'um), (so much) by the year, yearly. **~ cent,** in every hundred.

pĕradvĕn'ture *adv.* (arch.) perhaps, perchance; by chance.

pĕrăm'būlāte *v.* walk through, over, or about. **~ā'tion** *n.* **~ātor** *n.* (esp.) pram.

perceive' (-sēv) *v.t.* become aware of by one of senses; apprehend; understand.

percĕn'tage *n.* rate or proportion per cent; proportion; share.

pĕr'cĕpt *n.* (philos.) object or product of perception.

percĕp'tĭble *a.* that can be perceived. **~bĭl'itў** *n.*

percĕp'tion *n.* act or faculty of perceiving. **~al** *a.*

percĕp'tĭve *a.* having or concerned in perception. **pĕrcĕptĭv'itў** *n.*

pĕrch[1] *n.* bird's resting place; elevated position; measure of length (5½ yds.). *v.* alight or rest on perch; put (as) on perch.

pĕrch[2] *n.* fresh-water fish.

perchance' (-ah-) *adv.* maybe.

pĕr'cheron (-she-) *n.* strong swift draught-horse.

percĭp'ient *a.* having perception. *n.* one who perceives, esp. thing outside range of senses.

pĕr'colāte *v.* filter, esp. through pores or perforations. **~ā'tion** *n.* **~ātor** *n.* (esp.) apparatus for making coffee by percolation.

percŭss' *v.t.* tap gently.

percŭ'ssion *n.* forcible striking of body against another; sound so made; (mus.) instruments struck with stick or hand or struck together in pairs. **~ cap,** in firearm, small cap or cylinder exploded by percussion of hammer. **percŭss'ĭve** *a.*

perdĭ'tion *n.* damnation.

pĕrdū(e)' *pred.a.* in ambush; hidden.

perdūr'able *a.* eternal; durable.

pĕ'régrĭnāte *v.* travel, journey. **~ā'tion** *n.*

pĕ'régrĭne (*or* -ēn) *n.* kind of falcon.

pĕ'rĕmptorў (-mt-; *or* perĕm'-) *a.* imperious; urgent.

perĕnn'ĭal *a.* not coming to an end; (of plant) coming up year after year. *n.* perennial plant.

pĕr'fĕct *a.* complete, not deficient; faultless; thoroughly learned or skilled or trained; exact, precise; entire, unqualified; (of tense) expressing completed action. *n.* perfect tense. *v.t.* (-ĕkt'), make perfect. **perfĕc'tĭble** *a.*; **~ĭbĭl'itў** *n.*

perfĕc'tion *n.* being or making perfect; perfect state; perfect person, specimen, etc.; highest pitch, extreme.

pĕr'fĕctlў *adv.* quite, quite well.

perfĕr'vĭd *a.* very fervid.

pĕr'fĭdў *n.* breach of faith, treachery. **perfĭd'ious** *a.*

pĕr'forāte *v.* pierce, make hole(s), esp. row(s) of holes, through. **~ā'tion** *n.*

perfôrce' *adv.* of necessity.

perform' v. carry into effect; accomplish; go through, execute; act, sing, etc. esp. in public; (of animals) do tricks etc. **~er** n.; **~ing** a.

perfor'mance n. execution; carrying out, doing; notable feat; performing of play etc., public exhibition.

per'fume n. (sweet) smell; scent; fragrance. v.t. (-ūm'), impart fragrance to. **perfu'mer** n. maker or seller of perfumes. **perfu'mery** n.

perfunc'tory a. done merely to pass muster; superficial.

per'gola n. arbour or garden-walk arched with climbing plants.

perhaps' (colloq. praps) adv. it may be, possibly.

per'i n. fairy of Persian mythology.

pe'rianth n. outer part of flower, calyx and corolla.

pericar'dium n. (pl. -ia), membranous sac enclosing heart. **~diac** a. **~di'tis** n. inflammation of pericardium.

pe'ricarp n. seed-vessel of plant.

pericra'nium n. membrane enclosing skull.

pe'rigee n. point in planet's orbit nearest earth.

perihe'lion n. point in planet's orbit nearest sun.

pe'ril n. danger, risk. **~ous** a.

perim'eter n. line or set of lines bounding closed figure; boundary, outer edge or limits.

per'iod n. amount of time during which something runs its course; menses; indefinite portion of history, life, etc.; complete sentence; full stop (.); (pl.) rhetorical language. a. of or characteristic of (past) period. **period'ic** a. of revolution of heavenly body; recurring at (regular) intervals; **~ic table**, table of chemical elements in order of atomic weights. **~i'city** n.

period'ical a. periodic; published at regular intervals. n. periodical publication.

peripatet'ic a. & sb. itinerant, going from place to place; Aristotelian.

periph'ery n. bounding line, esp. of closed curvilinear figure; boundary, surrounding surface, area, etc. **periph'eral** a.

periph'rasis n. (pl. -asēs), roundabout speech or phrase, circumlocution. **periphras'tic** a.

pe'riscope n. arrangement of tube and mirrors for viewing objects above surface or eye-level, beyond obstruction, etc.

pe'rish v. suffer destruction, lose life; come to untimely end; (cause to) lose natural qualities; (of cold etc.) reduce to distress. **~able** a. that will not last long. **~ables** n.pl. perishable goods, esp. in transit. **~er** n. (sl.) blighter. **~ing** a. troublesome, annoying.

peristal'sis n. wave of contractions propelling contents of alimentary canal etc. along it. **~al'tic** a.

pe'ristyle n. row of columns round temple, cloister, etc.; space so surrounded.

peritone'um n. membrane lining abdominal cavity. **peritoni'tis** n. inflammation of peritoneum.

pe'riwig n. wig.

pe'riwinkle[1] n. evergreen trailing plant with light-blue flower.

pe'riwinkle[2] n. edible shell-fish like small snail.

per'jure (-jer) v. refl. forswear oneself. **per'jured** a. guilty of perjury. **per'jury** n. swearing to statement known to be false; false evidence given under oath; breach of oath.

perk[1] n. (sl.) perquisite.

perk[2] v. lift or prick up self-assertively or jauntily; cheer or brighten or smarten up. **~y** a. self-assertive, jaunty.

perm[1] n. (colloq.) permanent wave. v.t. give permanent wave to.

perm[2] v.t. (colloq.) permutate. n. system of permutations.

per'mafrost n. permanently frozen layer of soil etc. below earth's surface in arctic etc. regions.

per'manent a. lasting or meant to last indefinitely; **~ wave**, artificial wave in hair lasting until hair grows out. **~ence** n. being permanent. **~ency** n. permanence; permanent thing, employment, etc.

per'meable a. admitting passage of fluid etc. **~bil'ity** n.

per'meate v. penetrate, saturate, pervade; be diffused. **permea'tion** n.

Per'mian a. & n. (of) Palaeozoic geological system abcve Carboniferous.

permiss'ible a. allowable, that may be permitted. **~bil'ity** n.

permi'ssion n. leave, licence. **permiss'ive** a. giving permission; licensing but not enjoining something.

permit' v. give leave or consent or opportunity (for or to); admit doing or occurrence (of). n. (per'-), written order giving permission.

per'mūtāte v.t. change, arrange in different order or combination.

permūtā'tion n. (math.) variation of lineal order of set of things, each of different arrrangements of which such set is capable; change, changed order or arrangement.

permūte' v.t change arrangement of, esp. in all possible ways.

perni'cious a. destructive, injurious.

pernick'ety a. (colloq.) fastidious, (over-)precise.

pe'rorāte v.i. speak at length; sum up and conclude speech etc. **~ā'tion** n.

perox'ide n. compound of oxygen containing maximum proportion of oxygen; peroxide of hydrogen used as bleach, antiseptic, etc. v.t. bleach with peroxide of hydrogen.

perpend' v. (arch.) consider.

perpendic'ular a. at right angles to plane of horizon or to given line etc.; erect, upright; very steep; P~, of or in style of English Gothic architecture of late 14–16 cc. n. perpendicular line etc. **~lă'rity** n.

per'pétrāte v.t. be guilty of; commit. **~ā'tion, ~ātor** nn.

perpet'ūal a. eternal; held or holding for life; continuous; (colloq.) frequent, repeated.

perpet'ūāte v.t. make perpetual; not allow to go out of use or memory. **~ā'tion** n.

perpétū'ity n. perpetual continuance or possession; in ~, for ever.

perplex' v.t. bewilder, puzzle; complicate, tangle. **perplex'ity** n.

per pro. abbr., per procurationem [L], by proxy.

per'quisite (-z-) n. casual emolument etc. attached to employment beyond salary or wages.

pe'rry n. fermented drink made from pears.

per sē, by or in itself, intrinsically. [L]

per'sécūte v.t. pursue (esp. heretic) with enmity and injury; harass, worry. **~ū'tion, ~ūtor** nn.

persévēre' v.i. continue steadfastly, persist. **persévēr'ance** n.

Per'sian a. & n. (native, language) of Persia. ~ blind, Venetian blind; shutter with similar horizontal slats or louvres. ~ lamb, (silky tightly curled black fur of) young of Asian breed of sheep.

per'siflage (-ahzh) n. light raillery, banter.

persimm'on n. yellowish-orange plum-like astringent fruit of Amer. tree.

persist' v.i. continue to exist or do something in spite of obstacles. **~ence, ~ency** nn.; **~ent** a.

per'son n. individual human or divine being; one's body or bodily presence; character in play; (gram.) one of three classes of pronouns and verb forms appropriated to person speaking, spoken to, or spcken of. **~able** a. good-looking. **per'sonage** n. person of rank or importance; character in play etc.

persō'na n. (pl. -ae, -as), (psychol.) aspect of personality corresponding to attitude cf the moment.

persō'na grā'ta n. acceptable person, esp. diplomat. [L]

per'sonal a. one's own; individual, private; done etc. in person; directed against or referring to individual; (law) of or comprising all property except land; (gram.) of or denoting one of the three persons. **~īze** v.t. (esp.) identify as belonging to particular person. **~ly** adv. in person, in one's own person; for one's own part.

personăl'ity n. personal existence or identity; distinctive personal character; (esp. well-known) person; (pl.) personal remarks.

per'sonalty n. personal property.

persō'na nŏn grā'ta n. unacceptable person. [L]

per'sonāte v.t. play part of; pretend to be. **~ā'tion** n.

persŏn'ĭfȳ _v.t._ attribute personal nature to; symbolize by human figure; embody, exemplify typically. **~fĭcā'tion** _n._

pĕrsonnĕl' _n._ body of employees; persons engaged in particular service, profession, etc.

perspĕc'tĭve _n._ art of drawing so as to give effect of solidity and relative position and size; relation or proportion between visible objects, parts of subject, etc.; view, prospect; _in ~_, according to rules of perspective, in proportion. _a._ of or in perspective.

pĕr'spĕx _n._ light transparent plastic substitute for glass. **P.**

pĕrspĭcā'cious _a._ having mental penetration or discernment. **pĕrspĭcă'cĭty** _n._

perspĭc'ūous _a._ expressed with clearness; lucid. **pĕrspĭcū'ĭty** _n._

perspīre' _v._ sweat. **pĕrspĭrā'tion** _n._ sweat, sweating.

persuāde' (-sw-) _v.t._ convince; impel by argument, expostulation, etc.

persuā'sion (-sw-) _n._ persuading; conviction; religious belief or sect; (joc.) sort or class.

persuā'sĭve (-sw-) _a._ able to persuade, winning.

pĕrt _a._ forward, saucy.

pertain' _v.i._ belong, relate.

pĕrtĭnā'cious _n._ persistent, obstinate. **pĕrtĭnă'cĭty** _n._

pĕr'tĭnent _a._ to the point; pertaining, relevant. **~ence** _n._

pertûrb' _v.t._ disquiet; throw into agitation. **pĕrturbā'tion** _n._

peruke' (-ōōk) _n._ wig.

peruse' (-ōōz) _v.t._ read; scan. **peru'sal** _n._

Peru'vĭan (-ōō-) _a. & n._ (native) of Peru.

pervāde' _v.t._ spread through, permeate, saturate. **pervā'sĭve** _a._

pervĕrse' _a._ obstinately or wilfully in the wrong; wayward; peevish; wicked. **perver'sĭty** _n._

pervĕrt' _v.t._ turn or lead aside from proper or normal use, practice, religious belief, etc.; interpret wrongly; lead astray. _n._ (pĕr'-) perverted, esp. sexually abnormal, person.

pĕr'vĭous _a._ allowing passage or access; not impervious.

pĕse'ta (-sā-) _n._ Spanish monetary unit (100 centimos).

peso (pā'sō) _n._ S.-Amer. monetary unit (100 centavos).

pĕss'arȳ _n._ instrument, medicated plug, inserted into or worn in vagina.

pĕss'ĭmĭsm _n._ tendency to look at worst aspect of things. **~ĭst** _n._; **~ĭs'tĭc** _a._

pĕst _n._ troublesome or destructive person, animal, or thing.

pĕs'ter _v.t._ plague, importune.

pĕs'tĭcīde _n._ substance destroying esp. insect pests. **~cīdal** _a._

pĕstĭf'erous _a._ noxious; spreading infection; foul.

pĕs'tĭlence _n._ fatal epidemic disease, esp. bubonic plague.

pĕs'tĭlent _a._ deadly or pestiferous; troublesome; obnoxious. **pĕstĭlĕn'tial** _a._ pestilent; pernicious; annoying.

pĕ'stle (-sl) _n._ instrument for pounding substances in mortar.

pĕt[1] _n._ animal or person that affection is lavished on; favourite. _v.t._ make pet of; fondle, indulge in petting.

pĕt[2] _n._ ill-humour, fit of peevishness.

Pet. _abbr._ Peter.

pĕt'al _n._ each division of flower corolla, esp. when separate.

pĕtărd' _n._ (hist.) small explosive device for blowing in door etc.

pē'ter[1] _v.i._ ~ _out_, give out, come to an end.

pē'ter[2] _n. & v.i._ (whist etc.) signal or call for trumps.

pē'tersham _n._ thick ribbed or corded ribbon used for waist-bands, hat--bands etc.

pĕt'ĭōle _n._ leaf-stalk.

petite (petēt') _a._ (fem.) of small dainty build.

pĕtĭ'tion _n._ request, supplication, esp. written. _v._ make petition (to); ask humbly. **~er** _n._ (esp.) plaintiff in divorce suit.

petit point (petē'pwăn) _n._ (embroidery) series of small parallel diagonal stitches.

pĕt'rel _n._ small sea-bird with black--and-white plumage.

Petriburg. _abbr._ (Bishop) of Peterborough.

pĕtrĭfăc'tion *n.* petrifying, being petrified; petrified mass.

pĕt'rĭfȳ *v.* turn into stone; paralyse or stupefy with terror, astonishment, etc., become or make rigid.

pĕt'ro- in comb., rock. **pĕtrochĕm'ĭcal** (-k-) *a.* of petrochemistry or petrochemicals; *n.* substance obtained from petroleum or natural gas. ~chĕm'istrȳ *n.* chemistry of rocks or of petroleum. **pĕtrŏl'ogȳ** *n.* study of origin, structure, etc. of rocks.

pĕt'rol *n.* refined petroleum used as fuel in internal combustion engines, gasolene. ~ **station**, place where petrol may be bought.

pĕtrō'lĕum *n.* mineral oil.

pĕtrŏl'ĭc *a.* of petrol or petroleum.

pĕtt'ĭcoat *n.* woman's garment worn immediately beneath dress.

pĕtt'ĭfŏgger (-g-) *n.* inferior or rascally lawyer; petty practitioner. **pĕtt'ĭfŏgging** *a.* dishonest, quibbling; petty.

pĕtt'ĭng *n.* indulgence in kissing, fondling, etc.

pĕtt'ĭsh *a.* fretful, peevish.

pĕtt'ȳ *a.* unimportant, trivial; little--minded; minor, inferior. ~ **cash**, (cash kept for) small items of expenditure. ~ **officer**, non-commissioned officer in navy.

pĕt'ūlant *a.* peevishly impatient or irritable. ~ance *n.*

pĕtū'nĭa *n.* plant with vivid funnel--shaped flowers.

pew *n.* enclosure for family etc., fixed bench with back, in church; (sl.) seat.

pē'wĭt, pee- *n.* kind of plover named from its cry, lapwing.

pew'ter *n.* grey alloy of tin and lead etc.; utensils of this.

pf. abbr., piano forte [It.], soft, then loud.

P.G. *abbr.* paying guest.

phā'ĕton (*or* fāt-) *n.* light four--wheeled open carriage.

phăg'ocȳte *n.* leucocyte capable of destroying dead or foreign material.

phăl'ănx *n.* (pl. -*xes* or -*ges*, pr. -jĕz) body of infantry in close formation; united or organized party or company; bone of finger or toe.

phăl'arōpe *n.* kinds of small wading and swimming bird.

phăll'us *n.* image of penis. **phăll'ĭc** *a.*

phăn'tăsm *n.* illusion, phantom vision of absent person.

phăntăsmagōr'ĭa (-z-) *n.* crowd or succession of dim or doubtfully real persons. ~gŏ'ric *a.*

phantasy : see fantasy.

phăn'tom *n.* spectre, apparition; dim image; (attrib.) unreal.

Phār'aoh (-rō), *n.* title of ruler of ancient Egypt.

phă'risee *n.* formalist; self-righteous person; hypocrite. ~sā'ĭc(al) *aa.*; ~sāism *n.*

phārmaceu'tical *a.* of pharmacy; of use or sale of medicinal drugs. ~ĭcs, ~ĭst *nn.*

phār'macĭst *n.* one qualified to practise pharmacy.

phārmacŏl'ogȳ *n.* science of nature and action of drugs. ~ogĭst *n.*

phārmacopoe'ĭa (-pĭa) *n.* book with list etc. of drugs; stock of drugs.

phār'macȳ *n.* (shop etc. for) preparation and dispensing of drugs.

phār'ŏs *n.* lighthouse; beacon.

phă'rȳnx *n.* cavity behind mouth and nose. **pharȳn'gĕal** (-j-) *a.*

phāse (-z) *n.* aspect of moon or planet; stage of development or process or recurring sequence; each of different physical states in which substance can exist. *v.t.* divide into or carry out by phases.

Ph.B., Ph.D. *abbr.* Bachelor, Doctor, of Philosophy.

phea'sant (fĕz-) *n.* long-tailed bright--plumaged game-bird.

phĕnă'cĕtin *n.* antipyretic drug.

phĕnobār'bĭtōne *n.* hypnotic and sedative drug.

phĕnŏm'ĕnal *a.* of or concerned with phenomena; remarkable, prodigious.

phĕnŏm'ĕnon *n.* (pl. -*ena*), observed or apparent object or fact or occurrence; remarkable person or thing, wonder.

phew *int.* expressing disgust, relief, etc.

phĭ'al *n.* small bottle.

Phil. *abbr.* Philippians.

phĭlăn'der *v.i.* make love esp. in trifling manner. ~derer *n.*

phĭl'anthrōpe *n.* lover of mankind.

phĭlăn'thropȳ *n.* love, practical

benevolence, towards mankind. **phĭlanthrŏp′ĭc** *a.* loving one's fellow men; of, engaged in, promotion of human well-being. **~pĭst** *n.*; **~īze** *v.*

phĭlăt′ĕlў *n.* stamp-collecting. **phĭla-tĕl′ĭc** *a.*; **~list** *n.*

phĭlharmŏn′ĭc (-lãr-) *a.* (in names of orchestras etc.) devoted to music.

phĭl′hellēne (-lel-) *n.* lover of Greece; supporter of cause of Greek independence. **~hellĕn′ĭc** (*or* -ēn-) *a.*; **~hĕll′ĕnĭsm, ~hĕll′ĕnĭst** *nn.*

phĭlĭpp′ĭc *n.* invective, tirade.

phĭl′ippine (-ēn) *n.* almond or other nut with double kernel.

Phĭl′ĭstīne (*or* -ĭn) *n. & a.* uncultured (person). **~ĭnĭsm** *n.*

phĭlŏl′ogў, *n.* science of language. **phĭlolō′gian, phĭlŏl′ogĭst** *nn.*; **phĭlo-lŏ′gĭcal** *a.*

phĭloprogĕn′ĭtĭve *a.* prolific; loving one's offspring.

phĭlŏs′opher *n.* student or possessor of philosophy.

phĭlŏsŏph′ĭc(al) *aa.* of, consonant with, showing, philosophy.

phĭlŏs′ophīze *v.i.* theorize; moralize.

phĭlŏs′ophў *n.* pursuit of wisdom or knowledge, esp. of ultimate reality or of general causes and principles; philosophical system; system for conduct of life; serenity, resignation.

phĭl′tre *n.* love-potion.

phlĕbī′tis *n.* inflammation of walls of vein. **~ĭt′ĭc** *a.*

phlĕbŏt′omў *n.* blood-letting as medical treatment.

phlegm (flĕm) *n.* bronchial mucus ejected by coughing; coolness of character or temper; impassiveness. **phlĕgmăt′ĭc** *a.* not easily agitated; sluggish.

phlŏx *n.* kinds of plant with clusters of white or coloured flowers.

phō′bĭa *n.* (esp. morbid) fear or aversion.

Phoe′bus (fē-) *n.* Greek sun-god; (poet.) sun.

phoe′nix (fē-) *n.* bird fabled to burn itself and rise renewed from its ashes; paragon.

phŏn *n.* unit in measuring loudness of sound.

phōne *n. & v.* (colloq.) telephone.

phō′nēme *n.* (phonet.) group of variants regarded as essentially same speech-sound.

phonĕt′ĭc *a.* of or representing vocal sound; of sounds of spoken language. **phōnĕtĭ′cian, phonĕt′ĭcs** *nn.*

phō′n(e)y *a.* (sl.) false, sham, counterfeit.

phŏn′ĭc (*or* -ō-) *a.* acoustic, phonetic.

phō′nogrăm *n.* sound-record made by phonograph; symbol representing spoken sound.

phō′nograph (-ahf) *n.* instrument automatically recording and reproducing sounds. **~grăph′ĭc** *a.*

phonŏl′ogў *n.* science of vocal sounds; system of sounds in language. **phōnolŏ′gĭcal** *a.*

phŏs′phāte *n.* salt of phosphoric acid. **phŏs′phīte** *n.* salt of phosphorous acid.

phŏsphorĕsce′ *v.i.* show phosphorescence. **phŏsphorĕs′cence** *n.* faint luminosity without (perceptible) heat. **phŏsphorĕs′cent** *a.*

phŏsphŏr′ĭc, phŏs′phorous *aa.* containing phosphorus in lower, higher, valency.

phŏs′phorus *n.* non-metallic wax-like element appearing luminous in dark.

phō′tō *n.* (pl. -*os*), (colloq.) photograph. **~-finish,** close finish of race in which winner is identified by photography.

phō′to- in comb., light. **phōto-chĕm′ĭcal** *a.* of chemical action of light. **~-ĕlĕc′trĭc** *a.* of or utilizing emission of electrons from bodies exposed to light; **~-electric cell,** device for detection and measurement of light. **~-ĕlĕc′tron** *n.* electron liberated from substance irradiated by light of suitable frequency. **photŏm′ĕter** *n.* instrument for measuring intensity of light; **~mĕt′rĭc** *a.*; **photŏ′mĕtrў** *n.* **~phō′bĭa** *n.* dread of light. **~sphēre** *n.* luminous envelope of sun or star from which its light and heat radiate. **~sўn′thĕsĭs** *n.* (bot.) process by which carbon dioxide is converted into carbohydrates by chlorophyll under influence of light. **~thĕ′rapў** *n.* treatment of skin affections etc. by influence of light.

phōtogē′nĭc (*or* -ĕ-) *a.* producing light; photographing well.

phō'tograph (-ahf) *n.* picture taken by means of chemical action of light on sensitive film. *v.* take photograph of; admit of being photographed. **photŏg'rapher, ~graphў** *nn.*; **~grăph'ĭc** *a.*

phō'togrāvure (*or* -avūr) *n.* (print.) process of reproduction from photographically etched metal plate; print so produced.

phōtolĭthŏg'raphў *n.* lithographic process in which plates are made photographically.

phō'ton *n.* quantum unit of light or other radiant energy.

phō'tostăt *n.* (copy made by) apparatus for making photographic copies of documents etc. **~stăt'ĭc** *a.* **P.**

phrā'sal (-z-) *a.* **~** *verb*, (gram.) verb and adverb forming idiomatic phrase.

phrāse (-z) *n.* mode of expression, diction; small group of words, usu. without predicate; short pithy expression; (pl.) mere words; (mus.) short sequence of notes. *v.t.* express in words; group in phrases.

phrāsĕŏl'ogў (-z-) *n.* choice or arrangement of words. **~lŏ'gĭcal** *a.*

phrĕnĕt'ĭc *a.* frenetic.

phrĕnŏl'ogў *n.* study of external cranium as indicative of mental faculties etc. **~gĭst** *n.*

phthī'sĭs (th- *or* fth-) *n.* pulmonary tuberculosis. **phthis'ĭcal** (tĭz-, fthĭz-) *a.*

phŭt *adv.* go **~**, collapse, come to grief.

phўlăc'terў *n.* small leather box containing Hebrew texts on vellum, worn by Jews; amulet.

phўlloxēr'a *n.* plant-louse injurious to vines.

phў'lum *n.* (pl. -*la*), major classificatory division of plant and animal kingdoms, comprising organisms of same general form.

phўs'ĭc (-z-) *n.* medical art or profession; (colloq.) medicine. *v.t.* dose with physic.

phўs'ĭcal (-z-) *a.* of matter; of the body; of nature or according to its laws; of physics.

phўsĭ'cian (-z-) *n.* one legally qualified in medicine as well as surgery; one who practises medicine.

phўs'ĭcĭst (-z-) *n.* person learned in physics.

phўs'ĭcs (-z-) *n.pl.* science of properties, nature, and interaction of matter and energy.

physiogn'omў (-zĭŏn-) *n.* face as index of character; art of judging character from face and form; characteristic aspect. **~omĭst** *n.*

phўsĭŏg'raphў (-z-) *n.* description of natural phenomena; physical geography. **phўsĭogrăph'ĭcal** *a.*

phўsĭŏl'ogў (-z-) *n.* science of functioning of living organisms. **~lŏ'gĭcal** *a.*; **~logĭst** *n.*

physiothĕ'rapў *n.* treatment of disease by exercise, heat, or other physical agencies. **~pĭst** *n.*

phўsique' (-zēk) *n.* bodily structure and development.

pī *n.* (math.) Gk. letter π as symbol of ratio of circumference to diameter of circle (3·14159).

pī'a mā'ter *n.* inner membrane enveloping brain and spinal cord.

pĭaniss'imo *adv. & n.* (mus.) (passage to be played) very softly. [It.]

pī'anĭst *n.* player of piano.

pĭa'nō[1] (-ah-) *adv. & n.* (mus.) (passage to be played) softly. [It.]

pĭăn'ŏ[2] (pl. -*os*), **pĭănofŏr'tĕ** *nn.* musical instrument played by keys which cause hammers to strike metal strings. **~-organ**, mechanical piano constructed like barrel-organ.

pĭăzz'a (-tsa), *n.* square or market-place in Italian town.

pibroch (pē'brŏ*ch*) *n.* series of variations for bagpipe.

pī'ca *n.* size of type (12-point).

pĭc'adŏr *n.* mounted man with lance in bull-fight.

pĭcarĕsque' (-k) *a.* (of fiction) relating to rogues.

pĭcayūne' *a.* (U.S.) mean, paltry.

pĭccalĭll'ĭ *n.* pickle of chopped vegetables, mustard, and spices.

pĭcc'anĭnnў *n.* Negro child.

pĭcc'olō *n.* (pl. -*os*), small high-pitched flute.

pĭck[1] *n.* tool with sharp-pointed iron cross-bar for breaking up ground etc.

pĭck[2] *v.* break (ground etc.), make (hole), (as) with pick; probe (teeth etc.) with pointed instrument; open (lock) with skeleton key etc.; clear (bone etc.) of adherent flesh; pluck, gather (flower, fruit, etc.); pull asunder; select carefully; ~ *up*, take hold of and lift, raise, gain, acquire, take along with one, give lift to, regain, recover health, make acquaintance of casually, (of engine) accelerate, select (teams) by alternate choosing. *n*. picking; selection; *the* best. **~pocket,** one who steals from pockets. **~-up,** esp. picking up; person 'picked up'; game between sides chosen by picking up; device for converting vibrations from gramophone needle into electrical impulses; **~-up (truck),** small light motor-truck.

pick′-a-bǎck *adv., a. & n.* (ride) on shoulders or back like a bundle.

pick′ǎxe *n*. pick. *v*. break, work, with pickaxe.

pick′erel *n*. young pike.

pick′et *n*. peg or pointed stake driven into ground; small body of men on military police duty; man or party stationed to deter would--be workers during strike etc. *v.t.* set with stakes; post or act as picket; beset with pickets.

pick′ings (-z) *n.pl.* gleanings, perquisites.

pick′le *n*. brine or other liquor for preserving food etc.; plight, predicament; (usu. pl.) vegetables etc. preserved in vinegar etc.; young rascal. *v.t.* preserve in or treat with pickle. **pick′led** (-ld) *a*. drunk.

pic′nic *n*. pleasure party including outdoor meal. *v.i.* take part in picnic. **pic′nicker** *n*.

pi′cō- (pē-) in comb., one million--millionth. **pi′cocūrie** *n*. million--millionth of curie.

picot (pē′kō) *n*. one of series of small loops forming edging to frill, lace, etc. *v.t.* edge with picots.

picotee′ *n*. carnation etc. with dark-edged petals.

pictōr′ial *a*. of, in, by, or with painting or pictures.

pic′ture *n*. painting or drawing of objects, esp. as work of art; portrait; beautiful object; scene; mental image; photograph; cinema film. *v.t.* represent in picture; describe graphically; imagine. **~-gallery,** (hall etc. containing) collection of pictures. **~ postcard,** postcard with picture on back.

picturesque′ (-kcherěsk) *a*. like, fit to be subject of, picture; (of language etc.) strikingly graphic.

pidg′in, pi′geon² (-jn) *n*. (colloq.) business, concern. **~ English,** jargon used esp. in dealings with Chinese.

pie¹ *n*. magpie.

pie² *n*. dish of meat or fruit encased in or covered with paste. **~crust,** baked paste of pie. **~man,** seller of pies.

piebald (pī′bawld) *a*. having light and dark colour in irregular patches; motley, heterogeneous. *n*. piebald horse etc.

piece *n*. distinct part of composite whole; fragment; specimen; example; man at chess etc.; coin; picture, drama, or literary or musical composition; *by the* ~, according to amount done; *in* ~*s*, broken; *break to* ~*s*. break into fragments; *go to* ~*s*, collapse. *v.t.* make of pieces; put together or mend; make out. **~-goods,** textile fabrics woven in recognized lengths. **~-work,** work paid for by the piece.

pièce de résistance (pyās de rāzē′-stahns), most substantial dish; most important item. [F]

piece′meal (-sm-) *adv. & a.* (done) piece by piece, part at a time.

pied (pīd) *a*. of black and white or of mixed colours.

pier *n*. support of spans of bridge; pillar; solid part of wall between windows etc.; structure running out into sea; breakwater. **~-glass,** large tall mirror.

pierce *v*. go through or into like spear or needle; penetrate; bore.

pierrot (pēr′ō) *n*. entertainer with whitened face and loose white dress.

pietà (pyātah′) *n*. picture or sculpture of Virgin with Christ's body. [It.]

pi′ětism *n*. movement begun in 17 c. for revival of piety in Lutheran Church; extreme or affected piety. **~ist** *n*.; **pietis′tic** *a*.

pī′etȳ *n.* piousness.

piff′le *n.* (sl.) silly stuff. **piff′ling** *a.* trivial, worthless.

pig *n.* swine, hog; greedy, dirty, obstinate, or annoying person; oblong mass of smelted iron or other metal. *v.i.* (of sow) produce litter; live in dirty untidy way. **~-headed,** obstinate. **~-iron,** iron in pigs or rough bars. **~nut,** kind of edible tuber. **~skin,** leather made of pig's skin. **~-sticking,** hunting of wild boar with spear. **~-sty,** sty for pigs; dirty hovel. **~tail,** plait of hair hanging from back of head. **pigg′erȳ** *n.* pig-breeding establishment; pig-sty. **pigg′ish** *a.*; **pig′lėt, pig′ling** *nn.*

pi′geon[1] (-jn) *n.* bird with many varieties, wild and domesticated; dove; person who is rooked or plucked. **~-hole,** *n.* compartment in cabinet etc. for papers etc. *v.t.* deposit in pigeon-hole; put aside for future consideration, neglect; store tidily, esp. in mind.

pigeon[2] : see **pidgin.**

pig′ment *n.* colouring-matter. *v.t.* colour (tissue) with natural pigment. **~ā′tion** *n.* natural coloration.

pigmy : see **pygmy.**

pīke[1] *n.* spear formerly used by infantry; peaked top of hill; large voracious freshwater fish. **~staff,** wooden shaft of pike; *plain as a ~-staff,* quite plain.

pīke[2] *n.* toll-bar; turnpike road.

pī′kelėt (-kl-) *n.* crumpet.

pilǎff′, pilau′ (-ow), **-aw** *n.* Oriental dish of rice with meat, spices, etc.

pilǎs′ter *n.* rectangular pillar projecting from wall.

pilch *n.* infant's triangular wrapper worn over diaper.

pil′chard *n.* small sea-fish allied to herring.

pīle[1] *n.* heap, esp. of flat things laid on one another; plates of dissimilar metals laid alternately for producing electric current; (*atomic*) **~,** apparatus for initiating and controlling chain reaction; pyre; building of imposing height; (sl.) fortune. *v.t.* lay or throw in pile; load; **~** *up,* run (ship) on rocks etc., wreck, crash.

pīle[2] *n.* vertically-sunk piece of heavy timber etc. for support of building etc.

pīle[3] *n.* nap of velvet, carpet, etc.

pīle[4] *n.* (pl.) haemorrhoids.

pil′fer *v.* steal or thieve in petty way.

pil′grim *n.* person who journeys to sacred place; traveller. **P~ Fathers,** earliest English Puritan settlers of colony of Plymouth, Mass. **~age** *n.* pilgrim's journey; mortal life.

pill *n.* small ball of medicine to be swallowed whole; *the ~,* oral contraceptive; (sl.) ball. **~-box,** small round shallow box for pills; hat shaped like this; (mil.) small round concrete emplacement.

pill′age *n.* & *v.* plunder.

pill′ar *n.* slender upright structure serving to support arch or other architectural weight; column. *v.t.* support (as) with pillars. **~-box,** hollow pillar for posting letters in.

pill′ion (-lyon) *n.* (hist.) cushion attached to hinder part of saddle for second rider; seat for passenger behind saddle of motor-cycle etc.

pill′orȳ *n.* frame with holes for head and hands in which offender was placed. *v.t.* set in pillory; expose to ridicule.

pill′ow (-ō) *n.* cushion as support for head, esp. in bed; pillow-shaped thing. *v.t.* rest, prop up, (as) on pillow. **~-case,** **~-slip,** washable cover for pillow. **~ lace,** lace made with bobbins on pillow.

pil(l)′ūle *n.* small pill.

pī′lōse, pī′lous *aa.* hairy. **pīlǒs′itȳ** *n.*

pī′lot *n.* person in charge of ships entering or leaving harbour etc.; person operating flying controls of aircraft; guide. *v.t.* act as pilot to; guide course of. *a.* preliminary, experimental, small-scale. **~ balloon,** small meteorological balloon. **~-cloth,** blue woollen greatcoat cloth. **~age** *n.* pilot's function or fee. **~lėss** *a.*

piměn′tō *n.* allspice; sweet pepper.

pimp *n.* & *v.i.* pander.

pim′perněl *n.* plant with small scarlet or blue or white flower, closing in dull weather.

pim′ple *n.* small solid round tumour of skin. **pim′pled** (-ld), **~lȳ** *aa.*

pin *n.* piece of thin stiff wire with point and head used as fastening; wooden or metal peg, rivet, etc.; skittle; (pl., sl.) legs. *v.t.* fasten with pin(s); transfix with pin, lance, etc.; seize and hold fast; bind *down* (*to* statement, promise, etc.). ~-**feather**, ungrown feather. ~-**money**, allowance to woman for dress expenses, etc.; very small sum. ~-**point**, locate or define (target etc.) with minute precision. ~**prick**, petty irritation. ~**s and needles**, tingling sensation in limb recovering from numbness. ~-**stripe**, very narrow stripe. ~-**table**, table for game resembling bagatelle. ~**tail**, kinds of duck and grouse with pointed tail. ~-**tuck**, narrow ornamental tuck. ~-**up**, (picture pinned up on wall etc. of) glamorous girl, famous person, etc.

pin'afore *n.* child's or woman's washable sleeveless covering worn over dress etc.

pince-nez (păns'nā) *n.* pair of eye-glasses with spring to clip nose.

pin'cers (-z) *n.pl.* gripping tool forming pair of jaws; pincer-shaped claw in crustaceans etc. **pin'cer** *a.* (of attacking movement etc.) converging.

pinch *v.* nip, esp. with finger and thumb; pain or injure by squeezing; (of cold etc.) nip, shrivel; stint, be niggardly; (sl.) steal, arrest. *n.* nip, squeeze; stress of want etc.; small amount; *at a* ~, in a strait or emergency.

pinch'beck *n.* gold-like copper and zinc alloy used in cheap jewellery etc. *a.* made of pinchbeck; spurious, sham.

pine[1] *v.i.* waste away with grief, want, etc.; long (*for*).

pine[2] *n.* kinds of evergreen needle-leaved coniferous tree; pineapple. ~**apple**, large exotic fruit resembling pine-cone in shape. ~-**cone**, fruit of pine. ~-**kernel**, edible seed of some pine-trees. ~-**marten**, kinds of marten.

pin'eal *a.* shaped like pine-cone. ~ **body**, small cone-shaped body in brain.

ping *n.* sound as of bullet's flight,

v.i. emit ping. ~-**pong**, table-tennis.

pin'ion[1] (-nyon) *n.* outer joint of bird's wing; (poet.) wing; flight-feather. *v.t.* cut off pinion to prevent flight; restrain by binding arms to side.

pin'ion[2] (-nyon) *n.* small cog-wheel engaging with larger.

pink[1] *v.t.* run through with sword; ornament with perforations.

pink[2] *n.* garden plant with clove-scented flowers; pale-red colour; fox-hunter's red coat; point of perfection or excellence. *a.* pink-coloured; mildly socialist. ~-**eye**, kind of contagious conjunctivitis.

pink[3] *v.i. & n.* (make) slight dull metallic sound esp. of imperfectly running motor engine.

pinn'ace *n.* man-of-war's double-banked boat; ship's boat.

pinn'acle *n.* small pointed turret crowning buttress, roof, etc.; culmination or climax. *v.t.* set (as) on pinnacle; furnish with pinnacles.

pinn'ate *a.* with leaflets, tentacles, etc., on each side of stalk or axis.

pinn'y *n.* (colloq.) pinafore.

pin'oc(h)le (-okl; *or* pē-) *n.* (U.S.) game like bezique.

pint *n.* measure of capacity ($\frac{1}{8}$ gal.); (colloq.) pint of beer.

pin'ta *n.* (colloq.) pint of milk.

pin'tle *n.* bolt or pin, esp. that on which rudder hangs.

pin'to *a. & n.* piebald (horse).

pinx. *abbr., pinxit* [L], painted (this).

pi'ny *a.* of, abounding in, smelling like, pines.

pioneer' *n.* one of advance corps preparing road for troops; explorer; beginner of any enterprise etc. *v.* act as pioneer (in).

pi'ous *a.* devout, religious; (arch.) dutiful. ~ **fraud**, deception for good object.

pip[1] *n.* seed of apple, pear, orange, etc.

pip[2] *n.* spot on domino, die, or playing-card; star on army officer's shoulder. *v.t.* (colloq.) blackball; defeat, beat; fail in examination.

pip[3] *n.* disease of poultry etc.; *the* ~, (sl.) (fit of) depression or boredom or bad temper.

pip[4] *n.* high-pitched momentary sound, esp. as time-signal.

pipe *n.* tube of earthenware, metal, etc., esp. for conveying gas, water, etc.; musical wind-instrument; organ-tube; boatswain's whistle; (pl.) bagpipes; bird's note; tubular organ etc. in body; (tobacco held by) narrow tube with bowl at one end for smoking tobacco; (cask holding) measure of capacity for wine (105 gals.). *v.* play on pipe; summon, lead, etc. by sound of pipe or whistle; utter shrilly; (of birds) sing; trim with piping; convey (as) through pipes; furnish with pipe(s); force icing etc. through aperture to make ornamental shapes; ~ *down*, be quiet. ~**clay**, (whiten with) fine white clay used for tobacco-pipes and cleaning esp. military equipment. ~**-dream**, extravagant fancy, impossible wish, etc., like opium-smoker's dream. ~**-line**, line of pipes for conveying petrol, etc. across country; channel of supply, communication, etc. ~ **major**, N.C.O. commanding regimental pipers. **pi'per** *n.* (esp. strolling) player of pipe; bagpiper; *pay the* ~*r*, defray cost, bear expense. **pi'ping** *n.* cord enclosed in pipe-like fold along seam etc. as trimming on dress etc.; cord-like line of icing etc.; *a.* shrill; *adv.* sizzling, extremely (hot).

pipette' *n.* slender tube used for transferring or measuring small quantities of liquid.

pip'it *n.* kinds of small bird.

pip'kin *n.* small earthenware pot.

pipp'in *n.* kinds of apple.

piquant (pē'kant) *a.* pungent, sharp, appetizing, stimulating. ~**ancy** *n.*

pique (pēk) *v.t.* wound pride or stir curiosity of; plume one*self* (*on*). *n.* pettishness, resentment.

piqué (pē'kā) *n.* stiff ribbed cotton fabric.

piquet' (-kĕt) *n.* card-game for two players.

piran'ha (-ahny*a*) *n.* voracious tropical Amer. freshwater fish.

pir'ate (-at) *n.* (ship used by) sea-robber; one who infringes copyright or regulations, encroaches on rights of others, etc. *v.t.* publish regardless of copyright. **pir'acy** *n.*; **pirat'ic(al)** *aa.*

pirouette' (-rōō-) *n. & v.i.* (ballet-dancer's) spin round on toe.

pis'catory, piscator'ial *aa.* of fishing.

Pis'ces (-z; *or* pī-), Fishes, twelfth constellation and sign of zodiac.

pis'ciculture *n.* fish-rearing.

pisci'na (-sē-) *n.* (pl. -*ae*, -*as*), stone basin in niche on south side of altar.

pisciv'orous *a.* fish-eating.

pish *int.* expressing contempt or impatience.

piss *v.* (now vulg.) make water; discharge with urine. *n.* urine.

pista'chio (-shĭō; *or* -tah- *or* -tā-) *n.* (pl. -*os*) kind of nut with green kernel.

pis'til *n.* seed-bearing organ in flowers. **pis'tillate** *a.*

pis'tol *n.* small fire-arm used with one hand. *v.t.* shoot with pistol.

pistole' *n.* (hist.) esp. Spanish gold coin.

pis'ton *n.* plug fitting bore of hollow cylinder in which it moves to and fro; sliding valve in cornet etc. ~**-ring**, packing-ring on piston. ~**-rod**, rod connecting piston to other parts of machine.

pit[1] *n.* natural hole in ground; hole made in digging for minerals etc.; covered hole as trap; depression in skin or any surface; (back part of) floor of theatre auditorium; hollow in floor etc. for inspection or repair of underside of vehicle etc.; sunken enclosure for animals etc.; (U.S.) part of floor of exchange used for special branch of business; ~ *of the stomach*, depression between cartilages of false ribs. *v.t.* make pit(s) in; store in pit; match *against*. ~**fall**, covered pit as trap; unsuspected snare or danger. ~**-head**, (ground round) top of shaft of coal-mine. ~**man**, coal-miner; (U.S.; pl. -*s*), connecting-rod.

pit[2] *n. & v.t.* (remove) stone of stone-fruit.

pit'-(a-)pat *adv. & n.* (with) sound as of light quick steps.

pitch[1] *n.* dark resinous tarry substance. *v.t.* coat, smear, etc. with pitch. ~ **black, dark,** etc., intensely dark. ~**blende,** mineral containing uranium oxide, important source of radium etc. ~**pine,** resinous kinds of pine. **pitch′y** *a.* (esp.) dark as pitch.

pitch² *v.* set up in chosen position; encamp; give chosen altitude, gradient, intensity, etc. to; throw, fling, fall; (of ship etc.) plunge in longitudinal direction; incline, dip; (sl.) tell (yarn etc.); ~ *in,* (colloq.) set to work vigorously; ~ *into,* attack vigorously, esp. with words; ~ *on,* choose. *n.* act or process of pitching; height, degree, intensity, gradient; acuteness of tone; place, esp. in street or market, where one is stationed; (crick.) part of ground between and about wickets; (mech.) distance between successive points etc. (as teeth of cog-wheel, turns of screw-thread). ~**-and-toss,** game in which coins are pitched at mark and then tossed up. ~**fork,** long-handled two-pronged fork for tossing hay etc.; *v.t.* (esp.) thrust forcibly or hastily *into* (office, position, etc.). ~**-pipe,** small musical pipe used to set pitch for tuning or singing. **pitched** (-cht) *a.* (of battle) set, not casual. **pitch′er¹** *n.* (esp.) player delivering ball in baseball.

pitch′er² *n.* large jug, ewer. ~**-plant,** plant with pitcher-shaped leaves.

pit′eous *a.* deplorable; stirring or claiming pity.

pith *n.* spongy cellular tissue in stems of plants or lining rind of orange etc.; chief part; vigour, energy. *v.t.* remove pith from. **pith′y** *a.* of, like, full of, pith; condensed and forcible, terse.

pithecăn′thropus *n.* extinct primitive ape-like man.

pit′iable *a.* deserving of pity or contempt.

pit′iful *a.* compassionate; stirring pity; contemptible.

pit′iless *a.* showing no pity.

pi′ton (pē-) *n.* peg, spike, etc. driven into rock, crevice, etc. as support for climber etc.

pitt′ance *n.* scanty allowance, small amount.

pitū′itary *a.* of or secreting phlegm or mucus. ~ **gland,** small ductless gland at base of brain. **pitū′itrin** *n.* hormone produced by pituitary gland.

pit′y *n.* sorrow for another's suffering; regrettable fact, ground for pity. *v.t.* feel pity for.

piv′ot *n.* shaft or pin on which something turns; man on whom body of marchers wheels; cardinal or central point. *v.* turn (as) on pivot; wheel, hinge (*on*); provide with pivot. ~**al** *a.*

pix′ie, pix′y *n.* fairy, sprite. ~ **hood,** child's or woman's pointed hood.

pizzica′tō (-tsĭkah-) *a. & adv.* (played) by plucking string of violin etc. with finger. *n.* pizzicato note or passage. [It.]

pl. *abbr.* Place; plate(s); plural.

P.L.A. *abbr.* Port of London Authority.

plăc′able *a.* easily appeased; mild-tempered. ~**bil′ity** *n.*

plăc′ard *n.* paper with announcement for posting up. *v.t.* post placards on; advertise by placards.

placāte′ *v.t.* conciliate, propitiate. ~**ā′tion** *n.*; ~**ā′tory** *a.*

plāce *n.* particular part of space; space or room of or for person etc.; city, town, village, residence, building; (duties of) esp. public office or employment; rank, station, position; building or spot devoted to specified purpose; place-kick; *in* ~ *of,* instead of; *in, out of,* ~, (un)suitable, (in)appropriate; *take* ~, happen; *take the* ~ *of,* be substituted for. *v.t.* put or dispose in place; assign rank or order or class to; invest (money), dispose of (goods etc.), put (order for goods etc.) into hands of firm etc.; get (goal) by place-kick. ~**-kick,** (Rugby footb.) kick at ball placed on ground esp. by another player after try. **plāce′ment** (-sm-) *n.*

placĕn′ta *n.* (pl. -*ae*), spongy organ nourishing foetus in mammals. **placĕn′tal** *a.*

plā′cer *n.* deposit of gravel, sand, etc. on bed of stream containing minerals, esp. gold.

plă′cĭd *a.* calm, unruffled; not easily disturbed. **placĭd′ity** *n.*

plăck'ĕt *n.* (pocket esp. in) opening or slit at top of skirt.

plā'gĭarīze *v.* take and use another's (writings etc.) as one's own. **~ism, ~ist** *nn.*

plāgue (-g) *n.* fatal epidemic disease, esp. bubonic plague in London in 1665; infestation *of* pest; (colloq.) nuisance. *v.t.* pester, worry. **~-spot**, locality infested with plague; source or centre of moral corruption. **plā'guy** (-gĭ) *a.* annoying.

plaice *n.* kind of flat-fish.

plaid (plăd) *n.* long piece of woollen cloth as part of Highland costume; tartan cloth.

plain *a.* clear, evident; straightforward; ordinary, homely; not decorated or embellished or luxurious; not good-looking. *adv.* intelligibly, clearly. *n.* level tract of country. **~ sailing**, simple and straightforward course of action etc. **~song**, traditional church music sung in unison in medieval modes and free rhythm. **~-spoken**, outspoken.

plaint *n.* accusation, charge; (poet.) lamentation.

plain'tiff *n.* party bringing suit into court of law.

plain'tive *a.* mournful-sounding.

plait (plăt) *n.* tress of hair or band of straw etc. made by interlacing. *v.t.* form into plait.

plăn *n.* drawing exhibiting relative position and size of parts of building etc., diagram, map; project, design. *v.* make plan of; design; arrange beforehand, scheme.

plănchĕtte' (-sh-) *n.* small board on castors, with pencil for automatic writing etc.

plāne[1] *n.* tall spreading broad-leaved tree.

plāne[2] *n.* level surface; (supporting-surface of) aircraft; level (*of* attainment etc.). *a.* forming or lying in plane; smooth or level as plane. *v.i.* travel, glide, in aircraft. **~-table**, surveying instrument of drawing-table mounted on tripod.

plāne[3] *n.* tool for smoothing esp. wooden surface by paring shavings from it. *v.t.* smooth, pare (*away* etc.), with plane.

plăn'ĕt *n.* heavenly body revolving round sun or planet. **~ār'ĭum** *n.* model or structure representing solar system etc. **~arȳ** *a.*

plăn'gent (-j-) *a.* (of sound) thrilling, vibrating, moaning. **~encȳ** *n.*

plănk *n.* long flat piece of smoothed timber; item of party or other programme. *v.t.* lay etc. with planks; (sl.) put *down* (esp. money). **~-bed**, bed of boards without mattress. **plănk'ing** *n.* structure, floor, etc. of planks.

plănk'tŏn *n.* drifting or floating organisms found in sea or fresh water.

plāno-cŏn'cāve, -cŏn'vĕx *aa.* (of lens etc.) with one surface plane and other concave, convex.

plant (-ah-) *n.* living organism without power of locomotion or special organs of digestion etc.; kinds of this excluding trees and shrubs; equipment for industrial process; (sl.) hoax, trap. *v.t.* place (seed etc.) in ground to grow; furnish (land etc.) *with* plants, settlers, etc.; fix firmly, establish; deliver (blow etc.); (sl.) conceal (stolen goods, evidence of complicity, etc.) on person etc.

plăn'tain[1] (-tĭn) *n.* herb yielding seed used as food for cage-birds.

plăn'tain[2] (-tĭn) *n.* tropical tree and fruit like banana.

plăntā'tion *n.* number of trees etc. planted together; estate for cultivation of cotton, tobacco, etc.; (hist.) colony.

plan'ter (-ah-) *n.* (esp.) occupier of esp. (sub-)tropical plantation.

plăn'tigrāde *a. & n.* (animal) walking on soles of feet.

plaque (plahk) *n.* ornamental tablet of metal, porcelain, etc.

plăsh[1] *n. & v.* splash.

plăsh[2], **pleach** *vv.t.* bend down and interweave hedge-growth.

plăsm, plăs'ma (-z-) *nn.* protoplasm; coagulable solution of salts and protein in which blood-corpuscles are suspended; (-*a*, phys.) ionized gas in which numbers of electrons and positive ions are approximately equal. **plăs'mic** *a.*

pla'ster (-ah-) *n.* fabric spread with

medicinal substance etc. for application to body; (smooth surface of) mixture esp. of lime, sand, and hair spread on walls etc.; preparation of gypsum used to make moulds, immobilize limb, etc. *v.t.* cover with or like plaster; apply, stick, etc. like plaster to; coat, bedaub; (sl.) bomb heavily. ~ **of Paris**, fine white powder of calcined gypsum setting hard when mixed with water. **pla′stered** *a.* (sl.) drunk. **pla′sterer** *n.*; **pla′stery** *a.*

plăs′tic *a.* moulding; giving form to clay, wax, etc.; easily moulded; made of (synthetic) plastic. *n.* natural or synthetic substance that can be moulded by heat or pressure. ~ **arts**, those concerned with modelling. ~ **bomb**, plastic explosive. ~ **surgery**, repair or restoration of lost, damaged, etc. tissue. ~**ize** *v.t.* make plastic.

plăs′ticine (-ēn) *n.* composition used as substitute for modelling clay. **P.**

plăs′tron *n.* fencer's breast-plate; Lancers' breast-cloth; woman's ornamental bodice-front.

plăt *n.* patch of ground.

plāte *n.* flat thin sheet of metal, glass, etc.; engraved piece of metal; illustration printed from engraved plate etc.; stereotype etc. cast for printing from; table-utensils of gold, silver, or other metal; shallow usu. circular vessel from which food is eaten etc.; part of denture fitting to mouth and holding teeth; cup as prize for (horse-)race, race for this; *selling-*~, (horse-)race of which winner must be sold at fixed price. *v.* cover with plates of metal; cover with thin coating of silver, gold, etc. ~ **glass**, thick fine-quality glass for mirrors, windows, etc. ~**-layer**, workman laying and repairing railway lines. ~**-powder**, for cleaning silver etc. **plā′ter** *n.* (esp.) inferior race-horse.

plă′teau (-tō) *n.* (pl. -s, -x, pr. -z), tract of high comparatively level ground.

plăt′en *n.* plate in printing-press by which paper is pressed against type; corresponding part in typewriter etc.

plăt′fŏrm *n.* level surface raised above surrounding ground or floor esp. one from which speaker addresses audience; area, esp. raised surface, along side of line at railway station on which passengers alight, wait for train, etc.; party etc. policy or programme.

plăt′inum *n.* white heavy ductile malleable metallic element.

plăt′itūde *n.* commonplace remark. **plătitū′dinous** *a.*

Platŏn′ic *a.* of Plato or his doctrines; (of love etc.) free from sensual desire. **Plā′tonism, Plā′tonist** *nn.*

platōōn′ *n.* subdivision of infantry company.

plătt′er *n.* (esp. wooden) plate or dish.

plăt′ypus *n.* ornithorhynchus.

plau′dit *n.* (usu. pl.) round of applause; commendation.

plau′sible (-z-) *a.* (deceptively) seeming reasonable or probable, apparently honest, true, etc. ~**bil′ity** *n.*

play *v.* move about in lively or capricious manner; pass or strike lightly or gently; have free movement; sport, trifle, amuse oneself; engage in games, gambling, acting, or make-believe; perform on musical instrument; take part in (game); have as opponent in game; move piece in game, put card on table, strike ball, etc.; act in drama etc., perform; keep (fish, dupe) lightly in hand till secure; ~ *at*, engage in in trivial or light-hearted way; ~ *back*, reproduce (newly recorded music etc.); ~ *ball*, (U.S.) co-operate (*with*); ~ *down*, minimize; ~ *fair*, play or act fairly; ~ *false*, deceive, betray; ~ *the game*, play fair; ~ *the market*, speculate in stock market; ~ *off*, oppose (person *against* another) for one's own advantage. ~ *on*, (crick.) play ball on to one's own wicket, make use of (person's credulity etc.); ~ *up*, play vigorously, be mischievous or unruly, exasperate by such behaviour; ~ *up to*, act in support of (another actor), flatter, toady to; ~ *with*, amuse oneself with, trifle with, treat lightly. *n.* fitful or light movement; freedom of movement; recreation; trifling; playing of game, ball, etc.; dramatic piece; gambling. ~-**acting**, playing a part; posing. ~-**actor**, actor. ~-**back**, (device for) playing back recorded music etc. ~-**bill**, theatre programme or poster. ~**boy**, man devoted to (irresponsible) pleasure and gaiety. ~**fellow**, companion in childhood. ~**ground**, school recreation-ground. ~**house**, theatre. ~**mate**, playfellow. ~**thing**, toy. ~**wright**, dramatist. **played out** a. exhausted of energy, vitality, or usefulness; out of date. **play'er** n. (esp.) actor; professional player at cricket etc. **play'ful** a. frolicsome, sportive. **play'ing-card** n. one of pack or set of cards used for games.

pla'za (-ah-) n. square, open space.

plea n. pleading, earnest request; excuse; defence; defendant's or prisoner's statement.

pleach : see **plash²**.

plead v. address court as advocate or party; allege as plea; ~ *guilty*, *not guilty*, admit, deny, liability or guilt; ~ (*with*), make earnest appeal (to). ~**ing** n. formal statement of charge or defence.

plea'sance (-lĕz-) n. (arch.) pleasure--ground.

plea'sant (-lĕz-) a. agreeable; giving pleasure. ~**rỹ** n. jest.

please (-z) v. be agreeable, give joy or gratification, (to); choose, be willing, like. *imper.* as *int.* or *adv.* as courteous qualification to request etc.

pleasure (plĕzh'er) n. satisfaction, delight; sensuous enjoyment; will, discretion, choice. a. used, meant, etc. for pleasure or recreation. ~**rable** a. affording pleasure.

pleat n. flattened fold in cloth. *v.t.* make pleat(s) in.

plĕb n. & a. (colloq.) plebeian.

plĕbei'an (-bĭan) a. of common people; of low birth. n. plebeian person.

plĕb'iscïte (*or* -ĭt) n. decision of whole people by direct voting.

plĕc'trum n. (pl. -ra), small implement of ivory etc. for plucking strings of musical instrument.

plĕdge n. thing deposited as security or pawned; token, earnest, proof; toast; solemn promise. *v.t.* deposit as pledge; pawn; bind (one*self*); drink to health of.

plĕdg'ĕt n. small wad of lint etc.

Pleiads (plī'adz), **Plei'adĕs** (-z) n.pl. cluster of stars in Taurus.

Plei'stocēne (plī- *or* plē-) a. & n. (of) system of rocks immediately overlying Pliocene.

plē'narỹ a. not subject to limitation or exceptions; fully attended, representing all sections etc.

plĕnïpotĕn'tiarỹ (-sha-) n. & a. (envoy etc.) having full powers.

plĕn'ïtūde n. abundance; fullness; completeness.

plĕn'tēous, plĕn'tïful aa. copious, abundant.

plĕn'tỹ n. abundance; quite enough. *adv.* (colloq.) quite.

plē'num n. full assembly.

plē'onăsm n. use of more words than are needed to express meaning. **plēonăs'tïc** a.

plĕth'ora n. excess of red corpuscles in blood; over-supply, glut. **plĕthŏ'rïc** a.

pleur'isỹ (ploor-) n. inflammation of membrane enclosing lungs. **pleurĭt'ïc** a.

plĕx'us n. network, esp. of nerve fibres etc.

plī'able, plī'ant aa. easily bent or influenced; supple, yielding; accommodating. **plīabïl'itỹ, plī'ancỹ** nn.

plī'ers (-z) n.pl. pincers with flat grip for bending wire etc.

plight¹ (plīt) *v.t.* (arch.) pledge; engage one*self*.

plight² (plīt) n. condition, state; predicament.

Plĭm'soll. ~ **line, mark**, statutory load-line on hull of ship.

plĭm'sŏlls n.pl. rubber-soled canvas shoes.

Plin. *abbr.* Pliny.

plĭnth n. slab or course between ground or floor and pedestal, pillar, wall, etc.

Plī'ocēne a. & n. (of) period or system of rocks at top of Tertiary.

plŏd *v.i.* walk or work laboriously. **plŏdd'er** n.; **plŏdd'ing** a.

plŏt *n.* small piece of land; plan or essential facts of tale, play, etc.; conspiracy. *v.* devise secretly; hatch secret plans; make chart, diagram, graph, etc. of. **plŏtt'er** *n.*

plough (plow) *n.* implement for furrowing and turning up soil; similar instruments for clearing away snow etc. *v.* turn up with plough; furrow, make (furrow); advance laboriously *through*; cut or force way; (sl.) reject (candidate) in examination; ~ *back*, plough (crop) into soil to enrich it, reinvest (profits etc.) in business etc. ~**man**, guider of plough. ~**share**, blade of plough.

plo'ver (-ŭv-) *n.* kinds of wading bird; (pop.) lapwing.

ploy *n.* (colloq.) manœuvre, move; (north.) undertaking, occupation.

plŭck *v.* strip (bird) of feathers; plunder or swindle; summon *up*; pick or gather; pull at, twitch; tug or snatch *at*; (sl.) reject (candidate) in examination. *n.* beast's heart, liver, and lungs; courage. **plŭck'y̆** *a.* brave, spirited.

plŭg *n.* something fitting into and stopping or filling hole or cavity; pin etc. for making electrical contacts; (piece of) tobacco pressed into cake or stick. *v* stop with plug; put plug into; (sl.) work hard; (sl.) shoot; (sl.) make known or popular by frequent repetition, commendation, etc.; ~ *in*, connect with switch-board, electric current, etc. by using plug.

plŭm *n.* kinds of stone-fruit and tree; currant or raisin; good thing, best thing, prize. ~ **cake**, ~ **duff**, ~ **pudding**, cake or pudding containing raisins, currants, etc. **plŭmm'y̆** *a.* (esp., of voice etc.) (too) rich and mellow.

plu'mage (-ōō-) *n.* bird's feathers.

plŭmb (-m) *n.* ball of lead attached to line for testing perpendicularity of walls etc.; perpendicularity; sounding-lead. *a.* vertical; level, true. *adv.* vertically; exactly; (U.S., sl.) quite, utterly. *v.* sound (water); measure (depth); ascertain depth or get to bottom of; make vertical; work as plumber. ~-**line**, string with plumb attached.

plŭmbā'gō *n.* graphite; kinds of herbaceous plant with spikes of tubular flowers.

plŭmb'er (-m*er*) *n.* artisan who fits and repairs pipes, tanks, etc. **plŭmb'ing** *n.* (esp.) water- and drainage-pipes of building etc.

plume (-ōō-) *n.* feather, esp. large and showy; feathery ornament in hat, hair, etc.; feather-like formation, esp. of smoke. *v.t.* furnish with plume; pride one*self* (*on*); preen (feathers). **plumōse'**, **plu'my̆** *aa.* feathery.

plŭmm'ĕt *n.* plumb or plumb-line; sounding-lead. *v.i.* plunge.

plŭmp¹ *a.* full, rounded, fleshy, filled out. *v.* make or become plump.

plŭmp² *v.* drop or plunge abruptly; ~ *for*, vote for, choose, have strong preference for. *adv.* with sudden or heavy fall; flatly. *a.* direct, unqualified.

plŭn'der *v.* rob forcibly, esp. as in war; rob, steal, embezzle. *n.* plundering; pillage, spoils.

plŭnge (-j) *v.* immerse completely; put suddenly, throw oneself, dive, (*into*); (of horse) start violently forward; (sl.) gamble deeply, run into debt. *n.* plunging, dive. **plŭn'ger** *n.* (esp.) pump-piston; (sl.) gambler, speculator.

plupĕr'fect (-ōō-) *a.* & *n.* (tense) expressing action completed before past point of time.

plur'al (-oor-) *a.* more than one in number. *n.* plural number, word, or form. ~**ĭsm** *n.* holding of plural offices or votes. **plurăl'ĭty̆** *n.* being plural; pluralism; majority (*of*). ~**īze** *v.* make, express in, plural.

plŭs *prep.* with the addition of; or more. *a.* additional, extra; having plus sign prefixed; positive. *n.* symbol (+) of addition or positive quantity or charge; additional or positive quantity.

plŭsh *n.* cloth of silk, cotton, etc. with long soft pile. ~**y̆** *a.*

Plut. *abbr.* Plutarch.

Plu'tō (-ōō-) *n.* small planet in orbit beyond Neptune's.

plutŏc'racy̆ (-ōō-) *n.* State in which

power belongs to rich; wealthy class. **plu'tocrăt** *n.*; **plutocrăt'ĭc** *a.*

plutō'nium (-ōō-) *n.* transuranic element.

plu'vial (-ōō-) *a.* of or caused by rain.

pluvĭŏm'ĕter (-ōō-) *n.* rain gauge.

plȳ[1] *n.* fold, thickness, strand. ~-**wood**, strong board made of layers with grains crosswise.

plȳ[2] *v.* wield vigorously; work at; supply persistently, assail vigorously (*with*); (of ship, vehicle, etc.) go to and fro (*between*).

P.M. *abbr.* Police Magistrate; Prime Minister; Provost Marshal.

p.m. *abbr.*, *post meridiem* [L], after noon; post mortem.

P.M.G. *abbr.* Paymaster-General; Postmaster-General.

P.N.E.U. *abbr.* Parents' National Educational Union.

pneumăt'ĭc (n-) *a.* of, acting by, containing, filled with, (compressed) air.

pneumō'nĭa (n-) *n.* acute inflammation of lungs. **pneumŏn'ĭc** *a.*

pnxt abbr., *pinxit* [L], painted this.

P.O. *abbr.* Petty Officer; Pilot Officer; postal order; Post Office.

pō'a *n.* kinds of meadow-grass.

poach[1] *v.t.* cook (esp. egg without shell) by simmering or steaming.

poach[2] *v.* take (game, fish) illegally; encroach or trespass (*on*), esp. for this purpose. **poa'cher** *n.*

pō'chard *n.* kinds of diving duck.

pŏchĕtte' (-sh-) *n.* woman's envelope--shaped handbag.

pŏck *n.* eruptive spot in small-pox etc. ~-**marked** *a.*

pŏck'ĕt *n.* small bag inserted in garment for carrying money etc.; pecuniary resources; pouch at corner or on side of billiard-table into which balls are driven; cavity in earth, rock, etc., esp. filled with ore etc.; local condition of atmosphere affecting flight of aircraft; (enemy forces occupying) isolated area; *in* ~, having profit (of so much); *out of* ~, a loser (*by*). *a.* of suitable size or shape for carrying in pocket; small, diminutive. *v.* put into pocket; appropriate; submit to (affront etc.), conceal (feelings). ~-**book**, small book-like case for

bank-notes, papers, etc.; (U.S.) woman's handbag. ~-**knife**, small folding knife. ~-**money**, money for occasional expenses.

pŏd *n.* long seed-vessel of pea, bean, etc. *v.* form pods; take from pods, shell.

pŏdg'ȳ *a.* short and fat.

pō'dium *n.* continuous projecting base or pedestal; raised platform round arena of amphitheatre; dais.

pō'ĕm *n.* metrical composition; elevated composition in prose or verse; something compared to poem.

pō'ĕsȳ *n.* (arch.) poems or poetry.

pō'ĕt *n.* writer of poems. ~ **laureate** : see **laureate**. **poetăs'ter** *n.* inferior poet. **pō'ĕtess** *n.*; **pō'ĕtīze** *v.*

pŏĕt'ĭc(al) *aa.* of poets or poetry; suitable to or having qualities of poetry. **pŏĕt'ĭcs** *n.* literary criticism of or treatise on poetry. **pŏĕt'ĭcīze** *v.t.* make poetic.

pō'ĕtrȳ *n.* poet's art or work; expression, esp. in metrical form, of elevated thought or feeling; poems; quality calling for poetical expression.

pogrŏm' *n.* organized massacre, esp. of Jews in Russia.

poi'gnant (-nant *or* -nyant) *a.* pungent; keen, penetrating; moving, vivid. ~**ancȳ** *n.*

poinsĕtt'ĭa *n.* plant with large scarlet leaves surrounding small yellowish flowers.

point *n.* dot; particular place or spot; exact moment; unit of measurement, value, scoring, etc.; stage, degree; item, detail; salient feature; effectiveness; sharp end, tip; projection, promontory; (pl.) tapering movable rails for directing train etc. from one line to another; (position of) fielder at cricket near batsman on off side; cord on sail for tying up reef; electrical outlet; (hist.) tagged lace. *v.* sharpen, furnish with point; give point to; fill joints of (brickwork etc.) with mortar or cement; direct attention (as) by extending finger; direct (finger, weapon, etc. *at*); (of dog) indicate presence of game by standing rigid, looking towards it; ~ *out*, indicate, show, call attention to; ~ *to*, indicate (as) by pointing; ~ *up*, emphasize. **~-blank**, with aim or weapon level, at short range; directly, flatly. **~-duty**, of constable etc. stationed at particular point to regulate traffic etc. **~ of view**, position from which thing is seen or viewed. **~-to-~**, (race) over course defined only by landmarks. **poin'tėd** *a*. (esp.) cutting, emphatic; made evident; **~ėdly** *adv*. **~lėss** *a*. (esp.) without point, meaningless; in which no point is scored.

poin'ter *n*. (esp.) rod used to point to words etc. on screen, blackboard, etc.; breed of dog trained to point at game; (colloq.) hint, indication.

poise (-z) *v*. hold in balanced or steady position; be balanced; hover, hang suspended. *n*. equilibrium; way thing hangs or balances; ease of manner, assurance.

poi'son (-zn) *n*. substance that when absorbed by living organism kills or injures it; harmful principle, influence, etc. *v.t.* administer poison to; fill with prejudice; spoil, corrupt, pervert. **~ gas**, noxious gas used in war etc. **~ ivy**, trailing or climbing plant producing poisonous effects when touched. **~ pen**, anonymous writer of scurrilous or libellous letters.

pōke *v*. push with (end of) finger, stick, etc.; stir (fire), make thrusts (*at* etc.) with stick etc.; thrust forward. *n*. poking; thrust, nudge. **~-bonnet**, bonnet with projecting brim or front.

pō'ker[1] *n*. metal rod for poking fire.

pō'ker[2] *n*. card-game in which players bet on value of hand held. **~-face**, (person with) face that does not reveal thoughts or feelings.

pō'kў *a*. (of room etc.) confined, mean, shabby.

pō'lar *a*. of or near either pole of earth; having polarity; like pole or pole-star; magnetic; directly opposite. **polā'ritў** *n*. tendency to point to magnetic poles or to place axis in particular direction; possession of negative and positive poles; direction towards single point.

pō'larīze *v.t.* confine vibrations of (esp. light-waves) to single direction or plane; give polarity to; **~īzā'tion** *n*.

pōl'der *n*. low-lying land reclaimed from sea etc.

pōle[1] *n*. long slender rounded piece of wood or metal esp. as support for scaffolding, tent, etc.; measure of (length (5½ yds.). *v.t.* push, move, with pole. **~-jump**, jump with aid of pole held in hands.

pōle[2] *n*. either of two points in celestial sphere about which stars appear to revolve; either extremity of earth's axis; each of two opposite points on surface of magnet at which magnetic forces are manifested; positive or negative terminal point of electric cell etc.; each of two opposed principles etc. **~-star**, star near N. pole of heavens; guide, lodestar.

Pōle[3] *n*. native of Poland.

pōle'-ăxe *n*. battle-axe; butcher's slaughtering axe. *v.t.* kill or strike with pole-axe.

pōle'căt *n*. small fetid weasel-like animal.

polĕm'ĭc *a*. controversial, disputatious. *n*. controversy. **~al** *a*.

police' (-ēs) *n*. (members of) organized body responsible for maintaining public order or employed to enforce regulations etc. *v.t.* control or furnish with police; act as police in. **~-court**, court of summary jurisdiction. **~-dog**, dog trained to attack or track criminals etc. **~man**, **~woman**, member of police force. **~ state**, State regulated by secret police. **~-station**, office of local police force.

pŏl'ĭcў[1] *n*. statecraft; course of action adopted by government, party, etc.; sagacious procedure.

pŏl'ĭcў[2] *n*. document containing contract of insurance.

pō'lĭō (colloq.), **pōlĭomўĕlī'tĭs** (*or* pŏ-) *nn*. infectious disease of central nervous system with temporary or permanent paralysis.

pŏl'ĭsh[1] *v*. make or become smooth or glossy by friction; make elegant or cultured; smarten *up*; finish *off* quickly. *n*. smoothness, glossiness;

substance used to produce polished surface; refinement.

Pō'lish² *a.* & *n.* (language) of Poland or Poles.

polite' *a.* cultivated, well-bred; refined, elegant; courteous.

pŏl'itĭc *a.* judicious, expedient; sagacious, prudent.

polit'ical *a.* of State or its government; of public affairs; of or taking part in politics. ~ **economy,** theory of production and distribution of wealth. ~ **geography,** that dealing with boundaries etc. of States.

pŏlĭti'cian (-shn) *n.* person engaged or interested in politics.

pŏl'itĭcs *n.* science and art of government; political affairs, life, principles, etc.

pŏl'ĭtў *n.* form of civil administration; organized society, State.

pŏl'ka *n.* (music for) lively dance in duple time. ~-**dot(s),** pattern of uniformly arranged dots.

pōll¹ *n.* head; counting of voters, voting, number of votes; questioning of sample of population to estimate trend of public opinion. *v.* crop hair of; cut off top of (tree etc.) or horns of (beast); take votes of, vote, receive votes of. ~-**tax,** tax levied on every person. **pōll'ster** *n.* conductor of public-opinion poll.

Pŏll² *n.* parrot. ~-**parrot,** parrot.

pŏll'ack, -ock *n.* sea-fish allied to cod.

pŏll'ard *n.* tree made by polling to produce close head of young shoots; hornless animal. *v.t.* make pollard of (tree).

pŏll'ĕn *n.* fertilizing powder discharged from flower's anther.

pŏll'ināte *v.t.* fertilize with pollen. **pŏllĭnā'tion** *n.*

pō'llĭng-bōōth *n.* place, esp. temporary structure, where vote is recorded at election.

pollūte' (*or* -ōōt) *v.t.* destroy purity of. **pollū'tion** *n.*

pō'lō *n.* game like hockey played by teams of mounted players. ~-**neck, -necked,** (having) close-fitting rolled collar.

pŏlonaise' (-z) *n.* (hist.) form of woman's dress; (music for) kind of dance.

polō'nĭum *n.* radioactive metallic element.

polō'nў *n.* kind of sausage.

pŏl'tergeist (-gīst) *n.* spirit announcing its presence by noise, mischievous behaviour, etc.

pŏltrōōn' *n.* coward. ~**erў** *n.*

pŏl'ў- in comb., many. **pŏlyăn'drous** *a.* of or practising polyandry. ~**ăn'drў** *n.* plurality of husbands. ~**chromăt'ic** (-kr-) *a.* many--coloured. ~**chrōme** (-kr-) *n.* & *a.* (work of art, esp. statue) painted etc. in many colours. ~**clĭn'ĭc** *n.* general clinic or hospital. ~**glŏt** *a.* & *n.* (person) speaking or writing several languages; of, written in, several languages. ~**gon** *n.* figure with many angles or sides; **polў'-gonal** *a.* ~**hē'dron** *n.* many-sided solid; ~**hē'dral** *a.* ~**măth** *n.* person of varied learning, great scholar. ~**sўllăb'ĭc** *a.* having many syllables; using polysyllables; ~**sўll'able** *n.* ~**thĕĭsm** *n.* belief in more than one god; ~**thĕĭst** *n.*; ~**thĕĭs'tĭc** *a.*

pŏlўăn'thus *n.* kinds of cultivated primula.

polўg'amў *n.* having more than one wife or husband at once. ~**mĭst** *n.*; ~**mous** *a.*

pŏl'ymer *n.* compound, complex molecule, formed by combination of identical molecules. **polўm'erīze** *v.* combine to form polymer. ~**īzā'tion** *n.*

pŏl'ўp *n.* kinds of animal of low organization, as sea-anemones.

polўph'onў *n.* (style of composition with) combination of individual melodies harmonizing together. ~**phŏn'ĭc** *a.*

pŏl'ўpodў *n.* kinds of fern growing on rocks, walls, etc.

pŏl'ўpus *n.* (pl. -pī, -puses), kinds of tumour, esp. of nose.

pŏlўstȳr'ēne, pŏl'ўthēne *nn.* kinds of thermoplastic material.

pŏlўtĕch'nĭc (-k-) *a.* dealing with, devoted to, various arts. *n.* technical school or college.

pŏm *n.* Pomeranian.

pomace (pŭm'ĭs) *n.* mass of crushed apples in cider-making.

pomade' (-ahd *or* -ād) *n.* scented

ointment for hair. *v.t.* apply pomade to.

pŏme'grănate (-mg-) *n.* large tough--rinded many-seeded fruit.

Pŏmerā'nĭan *n.* breed of small silky--haired dogs.

pomm'el (pŭ-) *n.* knob of sword--hilt; projecting front part of saddle.

pŏmm'ў *n.* (Austral., N.Z.) immigrant from Britain.

pŏmp *n.* splendid display; splendour, grandeur.

pŏm'pŏm[1], **-ŏn** *nn.* tuft of silk threads etc. on shoe etc.; small-flowered kinds of chrysanthemum and dahlia.

pŏm'pŏm[2] *n.* automatic quick-firing gun.

pŏm'pous *a.* magnificent, splendid; showing self-importance; (of language) inflated. **pŏmpŏs'itў** *n.*

pŏn'chō *n.* (pl. *-os*), S.-Amer. cloak of rectangular piece of material with slit in middle for head.

pŏnd *n.* small body of still water artificially formed; natural pool or small lake.

pŏn'der *v.* think (over), muse.

pŏn'derable *a.* & *n.* (thing) of appreciable weight. **~bĭl'itў** *n.*

pŏn'derous *a.* heavy; unwieldy; laborious; laboured.

pōne *n.* (in southern U.S.) maize bread.

pŏn'gee (-jē) *n.* soft unbleached Chinese or Japanese silk.

pŏn'iard (-yard) *n.* dagger. *v.t.* stab with poniard.

pŏn'tiff *n.* Pope; bishop; chief priest.

pŏntif'ical *a.* of or befitting pontiff; solemnly dogmatic. *n.* office-book with forms for rites performed by bishop; (pl.) bishop's vestments and insignia.

pŏntif'icate *n.* (period of) office of bishop or Pope. *v.i.* (-āt), officiate as bishop; speak or act pompously or dogmatically.

pŏntōon'[1] *n.* flat-bottomed boat etc. as one of supports of temporary bridge.

pŏntōon'[2] *n.* kind of card-game.

pō'nў *n.* horse of any small breed; small glass of liquor; (sl.) £25. **~-tail**, hair worn hanging from back of head like horse's tail.

pōo'dle *n.* kinds of dog with long curling hair.

pooh (pōō, pŏō) *int.* of contempt. **pooh-pooh'** *v.t.* express contempt for.

pōol[1] *n.* small body of still water; puddle; deep still place in river.

pōol[2] *n.* collective stakes in cards or betting; (usu. pl.) organized gambling, esp. by post, on football--match results; game for several players on billiard-table; combination of manufacturers etc.; common fund or supply. **~** *v.t.* place in common fund; merge; share.

pōop *n.* stern of ship; aftermost and highest deck. *v.t.* (of wave) break over poop of (ship).

poor *a.* having little money or means; deficient (*in*); (of soil) unproductive; inadequate; despicable, insignificant; deserving pity. **~-box**, alms-box esp. in church. **~-law**, **~-rate**, (hist.) providing for support of paupers. **~-spirited**, meek, cowardly. **~lў** *adv.* scantily, defectively; with no great success; *pred. a.* unwell. **~nèss** *n.* defectiveness; deficiency; poverty.

pŏp[1] *n.* small abrupt explosive sound; (colloq.) champagne, ginger-beer. *v.* make pop; (colloq.) let off (pistol etc.); go or come unexpectedly or suddenly; put quickly (*in, down,* etc.); (sl.) pawn; (U.S.) parch (maize) until it bursts open. *adv.* with sound of pop; suddenly. **~corn**, sweetened popped maize. **~ gun**, toy gun shooting pellets by compressed air or spring.

pŏp[2] *n.* (colloq.) father.

pŏp[3] *a.* (of music etc.) popular. *n.* pop record or music.

pop. *abbr.* population.

pŏp'-eyed (-īd) *a.* bulging-eyed.

pōpe *n.* bishop of Rome as head of R.C.Ch. **pō'perў** *n.* (derog.) papal system.

pŏp'injay *n.* fop, coxcomb.

pō'pish *a.* of popery; papistical.

pŏp'lar *n.* kinds of tall slender tree freq. with tremulous leaves.

pŏp'lin *n.* closely-woven corded fabric.

pŏpp'a *n.* (U.S.) papa.

pŏpp'ét *n.* darling; lathe-head.

~-valve, quick-acting mushroom-
-shaped valve.

pŏpp'ĭng-crease n. (crick.) line in
front of and parallel to wicket.

pŏpp'ў n. kinds of plant with bright
flowers and milky narcotic juice;
~(-red), bright scarlet.

pŏpp'ўcŏck n. (sl.) nonsense.

pŏp'ūlace n. common people.

pŏp'ūlar a. of the people; generally
liked or admired. n. **pŏpūlă'rĭtў**,
~ĭzā'tion nn.; ~ĭze v.t.

pŏp'ūlāte v.t. form population of;
supply with inhabitants. **pŏpūlā'-
tion** n. (number of) inhabitants;
people of country etc. **pŏp'ūlous** a.
thickly populated.

pŏr'celain (-sl- or -sel-) n. finest kind
of earthenware, china. a. of porcelain; delicate, fragile.

pŏrch n. covered approach to entrance of building; (U.S.) veranda.

pŏr'cĭne a. of or like pigs.

pŏr'cūpĭne n. rodent armed with
pointed quills.

pŏre[1] n. minute opening in skin,
membrane, etc. for transpiration
etc.

pŏre[2] v.i. ~ over, have eyes or mind
intent upon.

pŏrk n. pigs' flesh as food. ~er n.
young fattened hog.

pŏrnŏg'raphў, n. treatment of,
literature etc. treating, obscene
subjects. ~grăph'ĭc a.

pŏr'ous a. having pores; permeable.
pŏrŏs'ĭtў n.

pŏr'phyrў n. kinds of rock with large
crystals in fine-grained ground
mass.

pŏr'poise (-pus) n. kinds of small
whale.

pŏ'rrĭdge n. oatmeal or other meal
boiled in water or milk.

pŏ'rrĭnger (-j-) n. small bowl from
which porridge etc. is eaten.

pŏrt[1] n. harbour; town or place
possessing harbour.

pŏrt[2] n. opening in ship's side for
entrance etc.; ~(-hole), aperture
in ship's side to admit light and air.

pŏrt[3] v.t. hold (rifle, sword) diagonally
in front of body. n. bearing, deportment.

pŏrt[4] n. left-hand side of ship etc.
looking forward. v. turn to port.

pŏrt[5] n. strong sweet red wine.

pŏr'table a. that can be carried about,
movable. ~bĭl'ĭtў n.

pŏr'tage n. transport of goods or its
cost; carrying necessary between
two navigable waters.

pŏr'tal n. door(way), gate(way).

pŏrtcŭll'ĭs n. grating raised and
lowered in grooves as defence of
gateway. ~ed a.

pŏrtend' v.t. foreshadow; be omen or
presage of.

pŏr'tĕnt n. omen, significant sign;
prodigy. **pŏrtĕn'tous** a. of or like
portent; solemn, pompous.

pŏr'ter[1] n. gate-keeper, door-keeper,
esp. of large building.

pŏr'ter[2] n. person employed to carry
burdens, esp. passengers' luggage at
railway-station; (U.S.) attendant in
sleeping-car etc. ~age n. (charge
for) work of porters.

pŏr'ter[3] n. dark-brown bitter beer.
~-house steak, (U.S.) choice cut of
beef between sirloin and tenderloin.

pŏrtfō'lĭō n. (pl. -os), case for loose
drawings, sheets of paper, etc.;
securities held by investor etc.;
office of minister of State; minister
without ~, one not in charge of
department of State.

pŏr'tĭcō n. (pl. -os) colonnade serving
as porch to building.

pŏr'tion n. part allotted, share; helping; dowry; destiny or lot; part,
some (of). v.t. divide into portions,
share out; give dowry to. ~less a.
without dowry.

Pŏrt'land cĕmĕnt' n. cement resembling in colour ~ stone, limestone
from Portland.

pŏrt'lў a. bulky, corpulent; of stately
appearance.

pŏrtmăn'teau (-tō) n. (pl. -s, -x, pr.
-z), case for clothes etc. opening
like book. ~ word, invented word
combining sounds and meanings of
two others.

pŏr'trait (-rĭt) n. likeness of person
or animal; description. ~ure n.
portraying; portrait(s).

pŏrtray' v.t. make likeness of;
describe. ~al n.

pŏr'trĕss n. female porter.

Pŏrtūguese' (-gēz) n. & a. (native,
language) of Portugal.

pōse (-z) *v.* propound for solution; arrange in required attitude; set up, give oneself out, *as. n.* attitude of body or mind, esp. one assumed for effect.

pō'ser *n.* puzzling question or problem.

pŏsh *a.* (sl.) smart, stylish; high-class. *v. refl. & i.* smarten oneself *up*.

pŏs'ĭt (-z-) *v.t.* lay down as basis of argument or inference.

posi'tion (-z-) *n.* way thing is placed; state of affairs; mental attitude; situation; rank or status; office; strategic point; *in, out of,* ~, in, out of, proper place. *v.t.* place in position; find position of. ~al *a.*

pŏs'ĭtĭve (-z-) *a.* formally or explicitly laid down; definite; unquestionable; absolute; confident in opinion, cocksure; not negative; greater than zero; (gram., of degree of adj. etc.) expressing simple quality without qualification or comparison; (photog.) showing lights and shades as seen in nature. *n.* positive degree, adjective, quantity, photograph, etc.

pŏs'ĭtĭvĭsm (-z-) *n.* philosophy of Comte recognizing only positive facts and observable phenomena; religion founded on this. ~ist *n. & a.;* ~ĭs'tĭc *a.*

pŏs'ĭtrŏn (-z-) *n.* positive counterpart of electron.

pŏss'ė *n.* body *of* police or of men summoned to aid sheriff.

possĕss' (-z-) *v.t.* hold as property; own, have; (of demon etc.) occupy, dominate; have mastery of; infatuate; seize. **possĕss'or** *n.;* ~ory *a.*

posse'ssion (-zĕshn) *n.* possessing or being possessed; occupancy; thing possessed; (pl.) property.

possĕss'ĭve (poz-) *a.* of or indicating possession; desirous of possessing or keeping as one's own. *n.* possessive case or word.

pŏss'ĕt *n.* hot drink of milk with wine, spices, etc.

pŏssĭbĭl'ĭtў *n.* state or fact of being possible; thing that may exist or happen.

pŏss'ĭble *a.* that can exist, be done, or happen; that may be or become; tolerable, reasonable, intelligible. *n.* highest possible score; possible candidate, member of team, etc.

pŏss'ĭblў *adv.* (esp.) perhaps.

pŏss'um *n.* (colloq.) opossum; *play* ~, feign illness or death.

pōst[1] *n.* upright of timber or metal fixed in ground etc.; *the* ~, winning--post. *v.t.* display (notice etc.) on post, notice-board, wall, etc.

pōst[2] *n.* official conveying of letters and parcels; single collection, delivery, etc. of letters etc.; post office, letter-box; size of writing--paper (about 20×16 in.). *v.* put (letter etc.) into official receptacle for transmission by post; travel with relays of horses; hurry; enter in ledger; supply with latest information. *adv.* with post-horses; express, in haste. ~-**boy**, postilion. ~**card**, card conveying message by post. ~-**chaise**, (hist.) travelling carriage (with horses) hired from stage to stage. ~-**haste**, with all speed. ~-**horses**, formerly kept at inns etc. for travellers etc. ~**man**, man who collects or delivers post. ~**mark**, official mark stamped on letters. ~**master**, ~**mistress**, official in charge of post office. **P~master General**, administrative head of postal service. ~ **office**, building in which postal business is carried on.

pōst[3] *n.* place where soldier etc. is stationed; place of duty; fort, outpost; trading-post; situation, employment; *last* ~, last bugle-call before *lights out. v.t.* assign post or duty to; send or appoint to office, command, etc.

pōst- in comb., after, behind. **pōst-clăss'ĭcal** *a.* of period later than classical. ~-**dāte'** *v.t.* affix or assign later than actual date to (cheque, event, etc.). ~-**dĭlū'vĭan** (*or* -dĭ-; *or* -ōō-) *a.* after Flood. ~-**grăd'ūate** *a. & n.* (student) continuing studies after graduation; of such studies. **Pōst-Imprĕ'ssionĭsm** *n.* developments in painting following Impressionism; **Pōst-Imprĕ'ssionist** *n. & a.;* -ĭs'tĭc *a.* ~**lūde** *n.* (mus.) concluding piece or movement. ~-**nā'tal** *a.* occurring etc. after birth. ~-**nŭp'tial** *a.* subsequént to marriage. ~-ō'bǐt a. & n. (bond) taking effect after death of specified person. ~-prǎn'dǐal a. after--dinner. ~-war a. of period after war, esp. of 1914–18 or 1939–45.

pō'stage n. charge for carriage by post. ~-stamp, adhesive label of specified value to be affixed to envelope etc. by sender.

pō'stal a. of, carried by, etc. post. ~ order, kind of money-order.

pō'ster n. placard for posting in public place.

pōste rěs'tante (-tahnt), n. post-office department where letters are kept till applied for.

pǒstēr'ior a. hinder; later in time or order. n. buttocks. ~ǐǒ'rǐtў n.

pǒstě'rǐtў n. descendants; later generations.

pǒs'tern (or pō-) n. back or side entrance; private door.

pǒs'thumous (-tū-) a. born or published after father's or author's death; occurring after death.

postǐl(l)'ion (-lyon) n. man riding one of horses drawing carriage.

pōst merǐd'iem, after noon. [L] pōst-merǐd'ian a.

pōst-mǒr'těm a. after death. n. examination of body after death; discussion of game etc. after its end.

postpōne' v.t. defer, put off. ~ment n.

post'script (pōsk-) n. addition at end of letter etc.

pǒs'tūlant n. candidate esp. for admission to religious order.

pǒs'tūlate n. thing claimed or assumed as basis of reasoning etc.; prerequisite. v.t. (-āt), demand, require, claim, take for granted.

pǒs'ture n. carriage; attitude of body or mind; condition, state. v.i. take up posture for effect; pose.

pō'sў (-z-) n. bunch of flowers; inscribed motto inside ring.

pǒt[1] n. vessel of earthenware, metal, glass, etc.; chamber-pot; contents of pot; large sum; cup etc. won as prize; pot-belly; (sl.) marijuana. v.t. put into pot for preservation; plant in flower-pot; (billiards) pocket; bag (game etc.); shoot. ~-belly, (person with) protuberant belly. ~-boiler, work written merely

to earn money. ~herb, herb used in cooking. ~-hook, hook for hanging pots over fire etc.; curved stroke in handwriting. ~ luck, whatever is to be had for a meal. ~-roast, braise; braised meat. ~sherd, piece of broken earthenware. ~-shot, random shot.

pǒtt'ěd a. preserved in pot or jar; abridged, condensed, brief.

pǒt[2] n. pot-hole.

pō'table a. drinkable.

pǒt'ǎsh n. crude potassium carbonate.

potǎss'ium n. light soft silvery-white metallic element.

potā'tion n. drinking; draught.

potā'tō n. (pl. -oes), plant with tubers used as food; its tuber.

poteen', potheen' (-t-h-) n. Irish whisky from illicit still.

pō'tent a. powerful; cogent; strong; influential. ~encў n. pō'tentāte n. monarch, ruler.

potěn'tial a. capable of coming into being, latent; (gram., of mood etc.) expressing possibility. n. potential mood; potential electric energy. ~tǐǎl'itў (-shǐ-) n. ~tiǒm'ěter (-shǐ-) n. instrument for measuring differences of potential.

pǒth'er (-dh-) n. fuss; din.

pǒt'-hōle n. deep hole or pit in ground etc.; depression in road surface. pǒt'-hōler, -hōling nn. explorer, exploring, of pot-holes.

pō'tion n. draught of medicine or poison.

pot-pourri (pō'pōorē; or -ē') n. scented mixture of dried petals and spices; musical or literary medley.

pǒtt n. writing- or printing-paper (usu. $15\frac{1}{2} \times 12\frac{1}{2}$ in.).

pǒtt'age n. (arch.) soup or stew.

pǒtt'er[1] v.i. move (about etc.), work, etc. in feeble or aimless or desultory manner.

pǒtt'er[2] n. maker of earthenware vessels. pǒtt'erў n. earthenware; potter's work or workshop.

pǒtt'ў a. (sl.) insignificant; crazy.

pouch n. small bag; detachable pocket; bag-like receptacle in which marsupials carry undeveloped young, other bag-like natural receptacle. v. put into pouch; take shape of or hang like pouch.

pouffe (pōof) *n.* low stuffed seat or cushion.

poult (pōlt) *n.* young fowl, turkey, or game-bird. **poul'terer** *n.* dealer in poultry.

poul'tice (pōl-) *n.* soft usu. hot dressing applied to sore or inflamed part. *v.t.* apply poultice to.

poul'try (pōl-) *n.* domestic fowls.

pounce[1] *v.i.* swoop, come suddenly down (*on*). *n.* pouncing; sudden swoop.

pounce[2] *n.* fine powder used to prevent ink from spreading, transfer design, etc.

pound[1] *v.* crush, bruise, (as) with pestle; thump, pummel; walk, run, etc. heavily.

pound[2] *n.* enclosure for detention of stray cattle etc.

pound[3] *n.* measure of weight (16 oz. avdp., 12 oz. troy); monetary unit (20 shillings). **poun'dage** *n.* commission or fee on transaction involving money payment; charge for postal order etc.; payment by weight.

pour (pōr) *v.* (cause to) flow in stream or shower; discharge copiously; (of rain) descend heavily.

pout[1] *v.* protrude lips, (of lips etc.) protrude, esp. pettishly, sullenly, etc. *n.* pouting. ～**er** *n.* & *a.* (esp.) (pigeon) with great power of inflating crop.

pout[2] *n.* sea-fish allied to cod.

pŏv'ertў *n.* want, indigence; deficiency (*in*, *of*); inferiority, poorness. ～**-stricken**, poor.

P.O.W. *abbr.* prisoner of war.

pow'der *n.* mass of fine dry particles; cosmetic or medicine in this form; gunpowder. *v.* reduce to powder; sprinkle with powder. ～**-blue**, soft pale blue. ～**-flask**, ～**-horn**, ～**-magazine**, for carrying or storing gunpowder. ～**-monkey**, (hist.) boy carrying gunpowder on ship during fight. **pow'derў** *a.*

pow'er *n.* ability to do or act; vigour, energy; control, influence, ascendancy; authority; influential person etc.; State with international influence; mechanical energy applicable to work; magnifying power of lens; (math., of number) product

of specified number of factors each of which is the number itself. ～**-house**, ～**-station**, house or station for generating and distributing electric power. **pow'ered** (-*erd*) *a.* equipped with mechanical or electrical power.

pow'erful *a.* having great power.

pow'erless *a.* without power; wholly unable (*to*).

pow'-wow *n.* N.-Amer. Indian conference or council; (colloq.) conference, palaver.

pŏx *n.* syphilis.

P.P. *abbr.* parcel post; parish priest.

pp. *abbr.* pages.

pp *abbr.*, *pianissimo* [It.], very soft.

p.p. *abbr.* past participle; *per pro*.

ppm. *abbr.* parts per million.

P.P.S. *abbr.* Parliamentary Private Secretary; *post postscriptum* [L], further postscript.

P.P.U. *abbr.* Peace Pledge Union.

P.R. *abbr.* proportional representation.

P.R.A. *abbr.* President of Royal Academy.

prăc'ticable *a.* that can be done, used, etc. ～**bil'itў** *n.*

prăc'tical *a.* of, concerned with, shown in, etc. practice; inclined to action rather than speculation; such in effect though not in name, virtual.

prăc'ticallў *adv.* (esp.) virtually.

prăc'tice *n.* action as opposed to theory; habitual action; established method; exercise to improve skill; lawyer's or doctor's professional business; *general* ～, practice of doctor who is not specialist; *in* ～, (esp.) actually, lately practised in skill etc., in good training; *out of* ～, not in practice. **prăctĭ'cian** *n.* practitioner; practical person.

prăc'tise *v.* carry out in action; pursue profession; exercise oneself in; impose *on*. ～**d** (-st) *a.* experienced, expert.

prăctĭ'tioner *n.* professional worker, esp. in medicine; *general* ～, doctor in general practice.

prae'tor *n.* ancient-Roman magistrate of lower rank than consul. **praetŏr'ian** *a.* of praetor; of bodyguard of Roman emperor or general.

prăgmăt'ĭc(al) *aa*. (usu. -*al*) meddlesome; positive, dictatorial; (usu. -*ic*) treating facts of history with reference to their practical lessons; of State affairs. **prăg'matĭsm** *n*. philosophical doctrine appraising ideas etc. by practical considerations. **prăg'matĭst** *n*.

prair'ĭe *n*. large treeless tract of esp. N.-Amer. grass-land.

praise (-z) *v.t.* express approbation of; commend; glorify. *n*. commendation, praising. **~worthy** (-zwĕrdhĭ) *a*. commendable, worthy of praise.

praline (prah'lĕn) *n*. sweetmeat of almonds etc. browned in sugar.

prăm *n*. carriage for child, esp. baby, pushed by hand.

prance (-ah-) *v.i.* (of horse) spring from hind legs; walk, move, in elated or arrogant manner. *n*. spring, caper.

prăn'dĭal *a*. of or at dinner.

prănk[1] *n*. frolic, practical joke.

prănk[2] *v.t.* deck (*out*); adorn.

prăsĕōdўm'ĭum (-z-) *n*. metallic element of rare-earth group.

prāte *v.i.* discourse foolishly; talk solemn nonsense.

prăt'-fall (-awl) *n*. fall on buttocks.

prătt'le *v.i.* talk in childish or artless way. *n*. prattling talk.

prawn *n*. kinds of crustacean like large shrimp. *v.i.* fish for prawns.

pray *v*. offer prayers, make supplication; ask earnestly; beg for.

prayer (prār) *n*. (form of words used in) address of thanksgiving, entreaty, etc. to God; praying; entreaty. **~-book**, book of forms of prayer, esp. public liturgy of Church of England. **~ful** *a*.

P.R.B. *abbr*. Pre-Raphaelite Brotherhood.

pre- *pref*. before (in time, place, order, or importance), freely used with Eng. words, only the more important of which are given below.

preach *v*. deliver sermon; talk like preacher of sermon; give obtrusive moral advice. **~er** *n*. **~ĭfў** *v.i.* preach tediously.

prĕăm'ble *n*. part of document etc. serving as introduction.

prĕ-arrănge' *v*. arrange beforehand. **~ment** *n*.

Preb. *abbr*. Prebendary.

prĕb'end *n*. (land etc. yielding) stipend of canon or member of chapter. **prĕbĕn'dal** *a*. **prĕb'endarў** *n*. holder of prebend.

prĕcār'ĭous *a*. dependent on chance; uncertain; perilous.

prĕcast' (-ahst) *v.t.* cast (concrete) in blocks before use in construction. *a*. (prē'-), so cast.

prĕcau'tion *n*. prudent foresight; thing done beforehand to avoid apprehended evil. **~arў** *a*.

prĕcēde' *v*. come or go before in place or time; cause to be preceded *by*.

prĕ'cedence (*or* prĭsē'-) *n*. priority; right of preceding others; superiority, higher position.

prĕ'cedent *n*. previous case, decision, etc. taken as example, rule, etc.

prĕcĕn'tor *n*. leader of choir's or congregation's singing.

prĕ'cĕpt *n*. rule for action or conduct; kinds of writ or warrant.

prĕcĕp'tor *n*. teacher, instructor. **~tōr'ĭal** *a*.; **~trĕss** *n*.

prĕcĕ'ssion *n*. change by which equinoxes occur earlier in each successive sidereal year.

prē'cĭnct *n*. space within boundaries of place or building; (pl.) *the* environs *of*; area from which main-road (or all) traffic is excluded; subdivision of city or ward.

prĕcĭŏs'ĭtў (-shĭ-) *n*. affectation of refinement.

prĕ'cious *a*. of great value, valuable, highly valued; affectedly refined; (colloq.) out-and-out. *adv*. extremely, very.

prĕ'cipice *n*. vertical steep face of rock, cliff, mountain, etc.

prĕcĭp'ĭtāte *v.t.* throw headlong down; cause to go hurriedly or violently; cause (solid matter in solution) to be deposited; condense (vapour) into drops. *a*. (-ĭt), headlong; rash; done too soon. *n*. (-ĭt), solid matter precipitated. **prĕcĭp'ĭtance**, **~ancў**, **prĕcĭpĭtā'tion** *nn*.

prĕcĭp'ĭtous *a*. of or like precipice; steep.

prĕcis (prā'sē) *n*. summary, abstract.

prĕcĭse' *a*. strictly worded; definite,

exact; particular. ~lỹ *adv.* (esp.) exactly; just so.

prĕcī'sian *n.* punctilious or formal person.

prĕcī'sion *n.* accuracy. *a.* designed for exact work.

prĕclude' (-ōōd) *v.t.* prevent; make impracticable.

prĕcō'cious *a.* remarkable for early development; too forward. **prĕcŏ'citỹ** *n.*

prĕcŏgnī'tion *n.* foreknowledge; preliminary examination.

prĕconceive' *v.t.* form (opinion etc.) beforehand. ~cĕp'tion *n.* (esp.) prejudice.

prĕconcĕrt' *v.t.* agree upon beforehand.

prĕ-condī'tion *n.* prior condition. *v.t.* condition beforehand.

prĕcŭr'sor *n.* forerunner, harbinger. ~ỹ *a.* preliminary.

prĕdā'cious *a.* predatory; of predatory animals.

prĕ-dāte' *v.t.* antedate.

prĕd'ator *n.* predatory animal.

prĕd'atorỹ *a.* of, addicted to, plunder or robbery; (of animal) preying on others.

prĕdĕcease' *v.t.* die before (another). *n.* death before another's.

prĕ'dĕcĕssor *n.* former holder of office or position.

prĕdĕs'tine *v.t.* appoint or ordain beforehand. ~nā'tion *n.* (esp.) God's appointment from eternity of some of mankind to salvation.

prĕdĕtĕr'mine *v.t.* determine beforehand, predestine. ~nate *a.*; ~nā'tion *n.*

prĕd'icable *a.* that can be predicated or affirmed. *n.* predicable thing. ~bĭl'itỹ *n.*

prĕdĭc'ament *n.* unpleasant, trying, or dangerous situation.

prĕd'icate *n.* what is predicated; (gram.) what is said of subject, including copula. *v.t.* (-āt), assert, affirm, as true or existent. ~ā'tion *n.* **prĕdĭc'ative** *a.* making predication; (gram.) forming (part of) predicate.

prĕdict' *v.* forecast; prophesy. ~abĭl'itỹ, **prĕdĭc'tion** *nn.*; ~able, ~ive *aa.*

prĕdigĕst' (*or* -dĭ-) *v.t.* make (food) easy to digest.

prĕdilĕc'tion *n.* mental preference, partiality (*for*).

prĕdispōse' (-z) *v.t.* render liable, subject, or inclined (*to*) beforehand. **prĕdisposī'tion** *n.* state favourable *to*.

prĕdŏm'ināte *v.i.* have chief power or influence; prevail; preponderate. ~ance *n.*; ~ant *a.*

prĕ-ĕm'inent *a.* excelling all others. ~ence *n.*

prĕ-ĕmp'tion *n.* purchase of thing before it is offered to others; right to first refusal. **prĕ-ĕmpt'** *v.* **prĕ-ĕmp'tive** *a.* (esp., of bid in bridge) intended to prevent opponents from bidding.

preen *v.t.* trim (feathers) with beak; smooth and adorn, show pride in, one*self.*

prĕ-exist' *v.i.* exist earlier, esp. in previous life. ~ence *n.*

Pref. *abbr.* Preface.

pref. *abbr.* preference etc.; preferred; prefix.

prē'făb (*or* -ăb') *n.* prefabricated house. **prēfăb'ricāte** *v.t.* make in sections for assembly on site. ~ricā'tion *n.*

prĕf'ace *n.* introductory remarks prefixed to book, etc; preamble of speech etc. *v.t.* introduce or begin (as) with preface. **prĕf'atorỹ** *a.*

prē'fĕct *n.* various civil and military officers in ancient Rome; senior pupil maintaining discipline in school; chief administrative officer of French department; head of Paris police. ~ŏr'ial *a.* ~ure *n.* prefect's office, residence, etc.

prĕfĕr' *v.t.* choose rather, like better; bring forward (claim etc.); promote *to* office. **prĕf'erable** *a.*; **prĕf'erablỹ** *adv.* **prĕfĕr'ment** *n.* advancement, promotion; (esp. ecclesiastical) appointment. **prĕferred'** (-ĕrd) *a.* (of stock) preference.

prĕf'erence *n.* preferring, thing preferred; prior right; favouring, esp. by lower import duty. *a.* (of stock etc.) on which dividend is paid before any on ordinary shares. **prĕferĕn'tial** *a.* of, giving, receiving, preference.

prēfig'ure (-ger) *v.t.* be type of, imagine, beforehand. **prefigurā'-tion, ~ment** *nn.*

prē′fīx n. preposition or particle prefixed to word; title or particle prefixed to name. v.t. (ĭks′ or -ĭks) add or join at beginning.

prĕg′nant a. with child, with young; fruitful in results; big *with* (consequences etc.); suggestive. **prĕg′-nancȳ** n.

prēhĕn′sīle (or -ĭl) a. (of tail, foot, etc.) capable of grasping. ⁓**sion** n. power of grasping.

prēhĭstŏ′rĭc a. before period recorded in history. **prēhĭs′torȳ** n.

prē-ĭgnĭ′tion n. too-early ignition in internal combustion engine.

prējŭdge′ v.t. pass judgement on before trial or proper inquiry. ⁓**ment** n.

prĕj′udĭce (-jŏŏ-) n. preconceived opinion, bias; injury or detriment resulting from action or judgement. v.t. impair validity or prospects of; inspire with prejudice. **prĕjudĭ′-cial** a.

prĕl′acȳ n. (Church government by) prelates; dignity of prelate. **prĕl′ate** n. bishop or ecclesiastic of equal or higher rank. **prĕlăt′ical** a.

prēlĭm′ n. (colloq.) preliminary examination; (print., pl.) matter preceding text.

prēlĭm′ĭnarȳ a. preceding and leading up to main business etc., introductory. n. preliminary step or arrangement.

prĕl′ūde n. performance, event, etc. serving as introduction (*to*); (mus.) introductory movement, esp. before fugue. v.t. serve as prelude to, introduce with prelude.

prē-mă′rĭtal a. occurring etc. before marriage.

prĕm′atūre (or -ūr′) a. occurring, done, before right or usual time; hasty. ⁓**tūritȳ** n.

prĕmĕd′itāte (or prē-) v.t. think out or design beforehand. ⁓**ā′tion** n.

prĕm′ĭer (or prē-) a. foremost, leading; having precedence of all others. n. prime minister. ⁓**ship** n.

prĕmière′ (-myār) n. first performance.

prĕm′ĭse n. (freq. **prĕm′ĭss**), proposition from which inference is drawn; (pl.) beginning of a deed specifying names of parties, property, etc.;

(pl.) house or building with grounds etc. v.t. (prĭmīz′) say or write by way of introduction.

prē′mĭum n. amount or instalment payable for insurance policy; fee for instruction in profession etc.; bonus; *at a* ⁓, at more than nominal value; *put a* ⁓ *on*, provide incentive to. **P⁓ Bond**, government bond not bearing interest but with periodical chance of prize.

premiss : see **premise**.

prēmonĭ′tion n. forewarning; presentiment. **prēmŏn′ĭtorȳ** a.

prē-nā′tal a. existing, occurring, before birth.

prĕn′tĭce n. & a. (arch.) apprentice. ⁓ **hand**, inexpert hand.

prēŏccūpā′tion n. occupying beforehand; mental absorption.

prēŏcc′ūpȳ v.t. occupy beforehand; prevent from attending to other things.

prēôrdain′ v.t. ordain beforehand, predestine.

prĕp n. (colloq.) (period of) school preparation, homework.

prep. *abbr.* preparation; preparatory; preposition.

prepaid : see **prepay**.

prĕparā′tion n. preparing; (usu. pl.) thing(s) done to make ready; (time spent in) preparation of lessons as part of school routine; substance prepared for particular use etc.

prĕpă′ratĭve a. & n. preparatory (act).

prĕpă′ratorȳ a. & n. serving to prepare; introductory (*to*); (school) preparing for higher, esp. public, school or (U.S.) for college.

prĕpāre′ v. make ready; put or get in train or proper state; make preparations (*for* etc.).

prĕpay′ v. (-*paid*), pay beforehand; pay postage of. **prē′paid** a. (esp., of envelope) stamped. ⁓**ment** n.

prĕpĕnse′ a. deliberate, intentional; *malice* ⁓, intention to injure.

prĕpŏn′derant a. superior in number, weight, etc. ⁓**ance** n. superiority or excess in number, influence, etc.

prĕpŏn′derāte v.i. be heavier; be superior in influence, quantity, or number.

prĕposĭ′tion (-z-) n. indeclinable word

serving to mark relation between noun or pronoun it governs and another word. ~al *a.*

prĕpossĕss' *v.t.* imbue (*with*); take possession of; prejudice, usu. favourably. ~ing *a.*; **prĕpossĕ's- sion** *n.*

prĕpŏs'terous *a.* utterly absurd; perverse; contrary to reason.

prĕpō'tent *a.* very powerful; more powerful than others. ~ence, ~encў *nn.*

prē'pūce *n.* foreskin, loose integument covering end of penis.

Prē-Răph'āelīte *a.* & *n.* (member, follower) of ~ *Brotherhood*, 19th-c. group of English artists and men of letters.

prē-rélease' *a.* & *n.* (film) exhibited before date of release.

prĕrĕ'quisite (-z-) *a.* & *n.* (thing) required as previous condition.

prĕrŏg'ative *n.* (theoretically unrestricted) right of sovereign; peculiar right or privilege.

Pres. *abbr.* President.

pres. *abbr.* present.

prĕs'age *n.* omen; presentiment. *v.t.* (prĭsāj') foreshadow, foretell, foresee.

prĕsbўō'pia (-z-) *n.* long-sightedness incident to old age. ~ŏp'ic *a.*

prĕs'bўter (-z-) *n.* local officer of early Christian Church; priest of Episcopal Church; elder of Presbyterian Church. **prĕs'bўterў** (-z-) *n.* body of presbyters, esp. court above kirk-session; eastern part of chancel beyond choir; (R. C. Ch.) priest's house.

Prĕsbўtēr'ian (-z-) *a.* & *n.* (member) of Protestant national church of Scotland, recognizing no higher office than presbyter's. ~ism *n.*

prē'scient (-shĭ-) *a.* having foreknowledge or foresight. ~ence *n.*

prĕscrībe' *v.* lay down authoritatively; (med.) advise use of; suggest remedy (*for*). **prĕscrĭp'tion** *n.* prescribing; physician's (usu. written) direction for composition and use of medicine; uninterrupted use as basis of right. **prĕscrĭp'tive** *a.* prescribing; based on prescription; prescribed by custom.

prē'script *n.* ordinance, law.

prĕs'ence (-z-) *n.* being present; place where person is; personal appearance; readiness at need.

prĕs'ent[1] (-z-) *a.* in place in question, here; now existing, occurring, being dealt with, etc.; (gram.) denoting present action etc. *n.* present tense; *the* present time; *at* ~, now; *for the* ~, for this time, just now.

prĕs'ent[2] (-z-) *n.* gift.

prĕsĕnt'[3] (-z-) *v.t.* set in conspicuous position; introduce; exhibit; hold out; offer, deliver, give; ~ *arms*, hold rifle etc. in saluting position. *n.* position of weapon in presenting arms. ~able *a.* of decent appearance; fit to be shown. ~abil'itў *n.*

prĕsentā'tion *n.* presenting, esp. formal; gift; formal introduction esp. at court.

prĕsĕn'timent (-z-) *n.* vague expectation, foreboding.

prĕs'entlў (-z-) *adv.* before long; (U.S.) at present.

prĕservā'tion (-z-) *n.* preserving; being preserved.

prĕsĕr'vative (-z-) *a.* & *n.* (substance etc.) tending to preserve.

prĕsĕrve' (-z-) *v.t.* keep safe; keep alive; maintain, retain; keep from decay; treat (food etc.) to prevent decomposition or fermentation; keep (game etc.) undisturbed for private use. *n.* jam; place where game etc. is preserved (freq. fig.).

prĕsīde' (-z-) *v.i.* be chairman or president. **presiding officer**, person in charge of polling-booth.

prĕs'idencў (-z-) *n.* (period of) office of president.

prĕs'ident (-z-) *n.* person presiding over meetings and proceedings of society etc.; head of college, council, company, etc.; elected head of republic. **prĕsidĕn'tial** *a.*

prĕsĭd'ium *n.* presiding body or standing committee esp. in Communist organization.

prĕss[1] *v.* subject to steady push or squeeze; flatten, shape, take *out* (crease etc.), smooth (esp. clothes), etc. thus; exert pressure (on); be urgent, urge; crowd; hasten, urge one's way, *on* etc.; force (offer etc.) *on*. *n.* crowding, crowd; pressure, hurry, of affairs etc.; kinds of instrument for compressing, flattening, extracting juice, etc.; machine for printing, printing-house; *the* newspapers; large usu. shelved cupboard for clothes, books, etc. **~ conference,** meeting with journalists. **~-clipping, ~cutting,** article, review, etc. cut from newspaper etc. **~-gallery,** gallery for reporters, esp. in House of Commons. **~man,** journalist. **~-mark,** library shelf-mark. **~-stud,** fastener of which the two parts engage by pressure. **press'ing** *n.* gramophone record; series of records made at one time or from one mould. **~ing** *a.* (esp.) urgent; persistent.

press² *v.t.* force to serve in army or navy; **~** *into service,* requisition, make use of. **~-gang,** body employed to press men for navy.

pre'ssure (-sh*er*) *n.* exertion of continuous force, (amount of) force so exerted; urgency; constraining or compelling influence. **~-cooker,** vessel for cooking in steam at high pressure. **~ group,** group of persons exerting political pressure. **pre's-surized** *a.* designed for maintenance of normal air-pressure at high altitudes etc.

prestidigita'tion *n.* conjuring. **prestidi'gitator** *n.*

prestige' (-ēzh) *n.* influence or reputation.

prestiss'imo *adv., a. & n.* (mus.) very quick (passage etc.). [It.]

pres'tō *adv., a. & n.* rapid(ly), quick (movement, piece of music). [It.]

pre-stressed' (-ĕst) *a.* (of concrete) compressed before loading by use of steel wires etc. under tension.

presume' (-z-) *v.* take for granted; venture (*to*); be presumptuous, take liberties. **presu'mably** *adv.* as may be presumed, probably.

presump'tion (-z-) *n.* supposition; balance of probability; arrogance, assurance.

presump'tive (-z-) *a.* giving ground for presumption; *heir* **~,** one who may be displaced by birth of nearer heir.

presump'tuous (-z-) *a.* unduly confident, arrogant, forward.

presuppose' (-z) *v.t.* assume beforehand; involve, imply. **presuppos'tion** *n.*

pretĕnce' *n.* pretending, make-believe; pretext; claim.

pretĕnd' *v.* give oneself out (*to* be or do), make believe; profess or allege falsely; presume (*to*), lay claim. **pretĕn'der** *n.* claimant (*to* title etc.).

pretĕn'sion *n.* (assertion of) claim; pretentiousness.

pretĕn'tious *a.* making claim to great merit or importance, esp. when unwarranted; ostentatious.

prĕt'erite *a. & n.* past (tense).

pretermit' *v.t.* omit to mention, do, or perform; leave off for a time.

preternă'tural (-ch*er*-) *a.* outside ordinary course of nature, supernatural.

prē'tĕxt *n.* ostensible reason; excuse. *v.t.* (-ĕkst'), allege as pretext.

pretŏn'ic *a.* immediately before stressed syllable.

prett'y (-i-) *a.* attractive to eye, ear, or aesthetic sense, esp. in diminutive or trivial way; fine, good; *a* **~** *penny,* a lot of money. *n.* pretty thing or person; (golf) fairway. *adv.* fairly, moderately; *sitting* **~,** (sl.) in position of advantage, safety, etc. **prett'y-pretty,** overdoing the prettiness. **prett'ify** *v.t.* make pretty. **prett'ily** *adv.;* **pret'tiness** *n.*

prĕt'zel *n.* crisp salted biscuit.

prevail' *v.i.* be victorious (*against* etc.); attain one's object; predominate; be usual or current; **~** *on,* persuade.

prĕv'alent *a.* prevailing, in general use, experience, etc. **~ence** *n.*

prevă'ricate *v.i.* make evasive or misleading statements. **~ā'tion, ~ātor** *nn.*

prevē'nient *a.* (esp., of grace) preceding repentance.

prevĕnt' *v.t.* hinder, stop. **prevĕn'tion** *n.* **prevĕn'tative, prevĕn'tive** *aa. & nn.* (agent, drug, etc.) serving to prevent (esp. disease).

prē'view (-vū) *n.* view, esp. of film, before public showing.

prē'vious *a.* coming before in time or order; prior *to;* (sl.) done or acting hastily. *adv.* previously *to.*

prévi'sion *n.* foresight; foreknowledge.

prē'-war (-ôr) *a.* & *adv.* before war
(esp. of 1914–18 or 1939–45).

prey (prā) *n.* animal hunted or killed
by carnivorous animal for food;
victim. *v.i.* ~ (*up*)*on*, seek or take
as prey; exert baneful influence on.

pri'apism *n.* persistent erection of
penis; indecency.

price *n.* money for which thing is
bought or sold; odds; what must
be given, done, etc. to obtain thing;
at any ~, whatever the cost, on
any terms; *at a* ~, at high cost.
v.t. fix or inquire price of; estimate
value of. ~**less** *a.* invaluable; (sl.)
ineffably amusing, absurd, etc.

prick *v.* pierce slightly, make minute
hole in; pain sharply, feel sharp
pain; spur, goad; erect (ears)
alertly; ~ *up one's ears*, listen
intently. *n.* pricking, mark of it;
(arch.) goad. ~**-eared**, ~**-ears**,
(having) erect pointed ears. **prick'er**
n. (esp.) pricking instrument.

prick'le *n.* thorn-like process; small
thorn; hard-pointed spine. *v.* feel
sensation as of prick(s).

prick'ly *a.* having prickles; extremely
irritable or touchy; tingling. ~
heat, inflammation of sweat glands
with prickly sensation. ~ **pear**,
(kinds of cactus with) pear-shaped
fleshy edible fruit.

pride *n.* unduly high opinion of oneself; arrogance; (proper) sense of
one's own worth, position, etc.;
feeling of elation and pleasure;
group (*of lions, peacocks*, etc.); *take*
~ *in*, be proud of. *v. refl.* ~ one*self*
(*up*)*on*, be proud of.

prie-dieu (prēdyê̂r') *n.* kneeling-desk
or -chair. [F]

priest, *n.* minister of religious worship; clergyman, esp. above deacon
and below bishop. ~**craft**, ambitious or worldly policy of priests.
~**'s hole**, secret chamber in house
where R.-C. priests hid from persecution. ~**-ridden**, held in subjection by priests. ~**ess**, ~**hood** *nn.*
~**ly** *a.* of or like or befitting priest.

prig *n.* boringly or affectedly or
primly moral, cultured, learned,
etc., person. **prigg'ish** *a.*

prim *a.* consciously precise, formal;
prudish.

pri'macy *n.* office of primate; pre-
eminence.

pri'ma dŏnn'a (prē-) *n.* principal
female singer in opera.

pri'ma fā'cie (-shĭē) *adv.* & *a.*
(arising) at first sight, (based) on
first impression. [L]

pri'mal *a.* primitive, primeval; fundamental.

pri'mary *a.* original; holding or
sharing first place in time or importance or development. *n.*
primary colour, assembly, election,
feather, etc. ~ **assembly**, meeting
for selection of candidates for
election. ~ **colour**, one not obtained
by mixing others. ~ **education**,
~ **school**, (school for) first stage
of education. ~ **election**, election
of candidate(s) for election. ~
feather, large flight feather of
bird's wing. ~ **planet**, one revolving directly round sun.

pri'mate *n.* archbishop; member of
highest order of mammals (-ā'tēz),
including man, apes, etc.

prime *a.* chief, most important;
primary, fundamental; of highest
quality. *n.* first of divine offices;
first or best part of something;
state of highest perfection; prime
number. *v.t.* (hist.) supply (firearm)
with gunpowder for firing charge;
put water into (pump), petrol into
carburettor of (engine), etc., to
make it start working; equip (*with*
information etc.); ply *with* liquor;
cover (wood etc.) with size, under-
-coating, etc. before painting.
~ **minister**, head of Government.
~ **number**, integer with no integral
factors. **pri'ming** *n.* (esp.) gunpowder etc. for exploding charge;
preparation for priming wood etc.
for painting.

pri'mer (*or* prī-) *n.* elementary school-
book; manual; sizes of printing-
-type.

primē'val *a.* of first age of world;
primitive, ancient.

prim'itive *a.* ancient; of early, simple,
or old-fashioned kind; original. *n.*
one of primitive society etc.; painter
or picture of pre-Renaissance period

or using unsophisticated techniques.

primogĕn'iture *n.* principle by which property descends to eldest son.

primôr'dial *a.* existing at or from beginning.

prim'rōse (-z) *n.* (plant bearing) pale-yellow early spring flower; cultivated kinds of this; pale yellow. ~**path**, pursuit of pleasure.

prim'ūla *n.* kinds of flowering plant including primrose.

pri'mus[1] *a.* first, eldest, of the name.

pri'mus[2] (**stove**) *n.* stove burning vaporized oil. **P.**

prince *n.* sovereign; ruler of small State; male member of royal family; (in some foreign titles) noble of high rank. ~**lȳ** *a.* (worthy) of a prince; sumptuous, splendid.

prin'cèss *n.* prince's wife; female member of royal family.

prin'cipal *a.* first in importance; chief, leading. *n.* head of some institutions; principal actor, singer, etc.; person for whom another acts as agent etc.; original sum lent or invested. ~**boy**, actress playing leading male part in pantomime. **prin'cipallȳ** *adv.* for the most part, chiefly.

principál'itȳ *n.* rule of, State ruled by, prince; (pl.) one of nine orders of angels; *the P~*, Wales.

prin'ciple *n.* primary source or element; fundamental truth; rule by which conduct may be guided.

prink *v.* smarten, dress up.

print *n.* mark left on surface by pressure; impression left on paper by inked type or photography; reading-matter produced from type etc.; engraving, newspaper, photograph; printed fabric; *in, out of, ~*, on sale, sold out. *v.t.* stamp or impress; produce by means of printing-types etc.; express, publish, in print; write in imitation of printing; stamp (fabric) in colours. **prin'ter** *n.* (esp.) one who prints books etc.

pri'or *n.* superior of religious house; (in abbey) officer next under abbot. *a.* earlier; antecedent. *adv.* ~ *to*, before. ~**èss** *n.*

priŏ'ritȳ *n.* precedence in time, order, rank, etc.; (thing having) claim to early or earliest consideration, action, etc.

pri'orȳ *n.* religious house governed by prior or prioress.

prise : see **prize**[3].

pri'sm *n.* solid figure whose two ends are similar, equal, and parallel rectilineal figures, and whose sides are parallelograms; transparent body of this form with refracting surfaces; anything refracting light etc. **prismăt'ic** (-z-) *a.* of or like prism; (of colour) such as is produced by refraction through prism; rainbow-like.

pris'on (-zn) *n.* place of captivity or confinement, esp. for law-breakers. ~-**camp**, camp for prisoners of war, political offenders, etc.

pris'oner (-zn-) *n.* person kept in prison; member of enemy's forces captured in war; captive.

pris'tine (*or* -ēn) *a.* ancient, unspoilt.

prith'ee (-dhǐ) *int.* (arch.) accompanying request or question.

pri'vacȳ (*or* prǐ-) *n.* being private, freedom from publicity or observation.

pri'vate *a.* not public or official; not affecting or concerning community; individual, personal; secret, confidential; secluded. *n.* private soldier; *in ~*, privately, in private life. ~ **member**, M.P. who is not member of Government. ~ **parts**, genitals. ~ **soldier**, ordinary soldier not holding commissioned or non-commissioned rank. ~ **view**, view of exhibition etc. before it is open to public.

privateer' *n.* (hist.) armed privately-owned vessel authorized by government to attack (esp. merchant shipping of) hostile State. ~**ing** *a.* acting etc. like privateer.

privā'tion *n.* want of necessaries or comforts; hardship.

priv'ative *a.* (gram.) denoting loss, absence, want, etc.

priv'èt *n.* white-flowered evergreen shrub.

priv'ilége *n.* right, advantage, or immunity belonging to person, class, or office; monopoly, patent.

v.t. invest with privilege; allow (*to* do) as privilege. **priv'ileged** (-ljd) *a.*

priv'ity *n.* being privy (*to*); (law) any legally recognized relation between two parties.

priv'y *a.* hidden, secret, private, confidential; ~ *to*, in the secret of. *n.* place for evacuation of bowels or bladder. **P~ Council**, body of advisers chosen by sovereign. ~ **purse**, allowance from public revenue for monarch's private expenses. ~ **seal**, State seal affixed to documents of minor importance.

prize[1] *n.* reward given as symbol of victory or superiority; thing (to be) striven for; reward in lottery, competition, etc. *v.t.* value highly. ~-**fight**, boxing-match for money. ~-**fighter**, professional pugilist.

prize[2] *n.* ship or property captured in naval warfare. ~ **money**, money realized by sale of prize(s).

prize[3], **prise** *v.t.* force (*open, up,* etc.) by leverage.

prō *n.* (colloq.) professional.

P.R.O. *abbr.* Public Records Office; Public Relations Officer.

prō'a *n.* kinds of Malay boat, esp. fast sailing-boat with small canoe etc. rigged parallel to it.

prō and cŏn *adv.* for and against. **prōs and cŏns** *n.pl.* reasons for and against.

prŏbabil'ity *n.* being probable; (most) probable event; likelihood measured by ratio of favourable cases to all cases possible; *in all* ~, most likely.

prŏb'able *a.* that may be expected to happen or prove true or correct; likely. *n.* probable candidate, member of team, etc. **prŏb'ably** *adv.* most likely.

prō'bate (*or* -āt) *n.* official proving of will. *v.t.* (-āt), (U.S.) prove (will).

probā'tion *n.* testing of person's conduct or character; moral trial or discipline; system of suspending sentence during good behaviour. ~ **officer**, official supervising offender on probation. ~**ary** *a.* **probā'tioner** *n.* person on probation, esp. novice in religious house, nurse in training

prōbe *n.* blunt-ended surgical instrument for exploring wound etc.; probing, investigation; device for exploring otherwise inaccessible place, object, etc. *v.* explore with probe; examine closely.

prō'bity (*or* -ŏ-) *n.* uprightness, integrity.

prŏb'lém *n.* doubtful or difficult question; thing hard to understand or deal with. **prŏblémǎt'ic(al)** *aa.* doubtful, questionable.

probŏs'cis *n.* elephant's trunk; long flexible snout; insect's sucking--tube; (joc.) long nose.

prō-cathē'dral *a.* & *n.* (church) used as cathedral.

procē'dure (-dy*er*) *n.* mode of conducting business. **procē'dural** *a.*

proceed' *v.i.* go on; make one's way; adopt course of action; continue or resume; issue, originate; take legal proceedings. ~**ing** *n.* (esp.) piece of conduct; (pl.) business done at meeting; (pl.) legal steps or action.

prō'ceeds *n.pl.* produce of sale etc.

prō'cĕss[1] *n.* state of going or being carried on; method of operation in manufacture etc.; (print.) method of reproduction other than simple engraving; action at law; summons or writ; outgrowth, protuberance. *v.t.* subject to legal or manufacturing process.

procĕss'[2] *v.i.* (colloq.) go in procession.

procĕ'ssion *n.* array of persons etc. going along in fixed order. ~**al** *a.* of, in, for, processions; *n.* processional hymn. ~**ary** *a.* going in procession (esp. of kind of caterpillar).

proclaim' *v.t.* announce publicly and officially; tell or declare openly. **prŏclamā'tion** *n.* proclaiming; formula or document that proclaims.

procliv'ity *n.* natural leaning or tendency (*to*).

prōcŏn'sul *n.* ancient-Roman provincial governor; (rhet.) modern colonial governor; deputy consul. **prōcŏn'sūlar** *a.*; ~**ate**, ~**ship** *nn.*

procrǎs'tǐnāte *v.i.* defer action, be dilatory. ~**ā'tion** *n.*

prō'crēāte *v.* beget offspring, beget. ~**ā'tion** *n.*; ~**ative** *a.*

prŏc'tor *n.* university official with disciplinary powers; person managing causes in esp. ecclesiastical court; *King's, Queen's, P~,* official with power to intervene in cases of divorce etc. **prŏctōr'ial** *a.*

procūr'able *a.* that can be procured.

prŏcūrā'tion *n.* procuring, bringing about; action as another's agent. **prŏc'ūrātor** *n.* proxy, agent; holder of power of attorney.

procūre' *v.t.* succeed in getting; bring about or cause by others' agency. **~ment** *n.* **~er, ~ess** *nn.* (esp.) pimp.

prŏd *v.t.* poke with stick etc., esp. to arouse or urge on, goad. *n.* prodding touch; pointed instrument.

prŏd'igal *a.* wasteful; lavish *(of). n.* spendthrift. **prŏdigăl'itў** *n.*

prŏd'igў *n.* marvellous thing; wonderful person, esp. precocious child. **prodi'gious** *a.* marvellous; enormous.

produce' *v.t.* bring forward for inspection etc.; bring (play etc.) before public; yield, give birth to; cause or bring about; make or manufacture. *n.* (prŏd'ūs) yield, amount produced; agricultural or natural products. **produ'cer** *n.* (esp.) person producing articles of consumption or manufacture; one who directs production of play etc.; **~r gas,** inflammable gas made by passing air through red-hot coke. **produ'cible** *a.*

prŏd'uct *n.* thing produced by natural process or manufacture; (math.) quantity obtained by multiplying quantities together.

produc'tion *n.* producing; thing(s) produced; literary or artistic work; style etc. of producing play etc.

produc'tive *a.* producing, esp. abundantly. **prŏductiv'itў** *n.* (esp.) efficiency in industrial production.

prō'em *n.* prefatory discourse.

Prof. *abbr.* Professor.

prŏfanā'tion *n.* profaning.

profāne' *a.* secular; heathen, unhallowed; irreverent, blasphemous. *v.t.* pollute, violate; treat with irreverence. **profăn'itў** *n.* blasphemy; profane swearing; irreverent speech or behaviour.

profĕss' *v.* represent oneself to feel or believe in; declare oneself to be or do; have as one's trade or art or profession; teach as professor; take vows of, receive into, religious order. **profĕss'ĕdlў** *adv.* (esp.) by one's own account.

profĕ'ssion *n.* declaration, avowal; vow made on entering, being in, religious order; vocation or calling, esp. of learned or scientific or artistic kind. **profĕ'ssional** *a.* of or belonging to a profession, following occupation as means of livelihood; maintaining proper standard, not amateurish; played etc. by professionals; *n.* professional worker, player, etc. **~alism** *n.*; **~alize** *v.t.*

profĕss'or *n.* person who makes profession *(of* religion etc.); holder of university chair or other teacher of high rank. **~ate, ~ship** *nn.*; **profĕssōr'ial** *a.* **profĕssōr'iate** *n.* professorship; body of professors.

prŏff'er *v.t. & n.* offer.

profi'cient (-shnt) *a. & n.* expert, adept. **profi'ciencў** *n.*

prō'file *(or* -ēl) *n.* side view, side outline, esp. of human face; journalistic biographical sketch. *v.t.* represent in profile, give profile to.

prŏf'it *n.* advantage, benefit; (freq. pl.) pecuniary gain, excess of returns over outlay. *v.* be of advantage (to); be benefited or assisted. **~able** *a.* useful; yielding profit, lucrative. **~eer'** *v.i.* make inordinate profits on scarce or necessary goods, esp. in war-time; *n.* one who profiteers. **~less** *a.*

prŏf'ligate *a. & n.* licentious, dissolute, or recklessly extravagant (person). **prŏf'ligacў** *n.*

prō fōr'ma, for form's sake; (of invoice) sent to purchaser before goods are despatched. [L]

profound' *a.* deep; of great insight or knowledge; hard to penetrate or unravel; intense, unqualified. **profŭn'ditў** *n.*

profūse' *a.* lavish, extravagant, copious, excessive. **profū'sion** *n.*

progĕn'itive *a.* of, capable of, production of offspring. **progĕn'itor** *n.* ancestor. **prŏ'genў** *n.* offspring, descendants.

prŏg'nathous, *a.* with projecting jaws; (of jaws) projecting.

prŏgnō'sis *n.* (pl. *-osēs*), forecast of course of disease.

prognŏs'tic *n.* pre-indication (*of*); prediction. *a.* foretelling, predictive (*of*). ~āte *v.t.* foretell. ~ā'tion *n.*

prō'grămme, prō'grăm *n.* plan of intended proceedings; descriptive notice, list, of series of events, items, etc.; entertainment etc., esp. of several items or forming part of series; series of coded instructions for computer etc. *v.t.* work out programme for, instruct (computer etc.) by means of programme.

prō'grĕss (*or* -ŏ-) *n.* forward movement; advance; development; (arch.) State journey, official tour. *v.i.* (-ĕs'), move forward or onward; advance, develop.

progrĕ'ssion *n.* progress; advance from stage to stage; (mus.) passing from one note etc. to another; (math.) series of quantities each in same relation to preceding one. ~al *a.*

progrĕss'ive *a.* moving forward; proceeding step by step; advancing in social conditions, character, etc.; favouring progress or reform; (of disease etc.) continuously increasing. *n.* advocate of progressive policy.

prohĭb'it *v.t.* forbid, debar, prevent. **prohibi'tion** (-ŏĭ-) *n.* forbidding; order that forbids something; forbidding by law of making or sale of intoxicants. **prohibi'tionist** *n. & a.*

prohĭb'itive *a.* prohibiting; serving to prevent use etc. of something; (of price) so high as to preclude purchase.

projĕct' *v.* make plans for; cast, throw, impel; cause (light, image) to fall on surface; represent by drawing straight lines from centre through points of (figure etc.); protrude, jut out. *n.* (prŏj'-; *or* prō-), plan, scheme.

projĕc'tile (*or* -ĭl) *a.* impelling; that can be projected by force, esp. from gun etc. *n.* projectile body or missile.

projĕc'tion *n.* projecting; part that protrudes; display of film in cinema etc.; orderly system of representing earth etc. on plane surface; map etc. made by projecting. ~ist *n.* person operating film projector.

projĕc'tor *n.* (esp.) apparatus for projecting rays of light, throwing picture on screen, etc.

Prol. *abbr.* Prologue.

prolăpse' *v.i.* slip forward or down out of place. *n.* (prō'-) prolapsing, esp. of uterus or rectum.

prō'lāte *a.* (of sphere) lengthened in direction of polar diameter.

prōlĕgŏm'ĕna *n.pl.* preliminary remarks or dissertation.

prōle *n.* (colloq.) proletarian.

prōlĕtār'ian *a. & n.* (member) of proletariat. ~īze *v.t.*; ~īzā'tion *n.*

prōlĕtār'iat *n.* lowest class of community in ancient Rome; class of wage-earners or of those dependent on daily labour for subsistence; lowest class, common people.

prolĭf'erāte *v.* reproduce itself, grow, by multiplication of elementary parts; increase rapidly, multiply. ~ā'tion *n.*

prolĭf'ic *a.* producing (much) offspring; fruitful, abundantly productive.

prō'lĭx (*or* -ĭks') *a.* lengthy; long-winded; tedious. **prolĭx'itў** *n.*

prō'lŏgue (-g) *n.* preliminary discourse etc. esp. introducing play; act, event, serving as introduction (*to*). *v.t.* introduce, furnish, with prologue.

prolŏng' *v.t.* make longer; cause to continue; (*p.p.*) long. **prōlongā'tion** (-ngg-) *n.*

prŏm *n.* (colloq.) promenade concert; promenade.

prŏmĕnade' (-ahd) *n.* walk, drive, etc., for exercise, display, etc.; place for this; (U.S.) school or college dance. *v.* make promenade (on, through, etc.); lead about, esp. for display. ~ concert, one at which (part of) audience is not provided with seats. ~ deck, upper deck on liner.

promē'thĭum *n.* radioactive metallic element of rare-earth group.

prŏm'inence *n.* being prominent; protuberance; *solar* ~, cloud of incandescent hydrogen projecting from sun.

prŏm'ĭnent *a.* projecting; conspicuous; distinguished.

promĭs'cūous *a.* of mixed and disorderly composition; indiscriminate esp. of or in sexual intercourse. **prŏmĭscū'ĭtў** *n.*

prŏm'ĭse *n.* explicit undertaking to do or not to do something; thing promised; favourable indications. *v.* make promise (to) to give, do, etc.; seem likely (*to*), hold out good etc. prospect. **prŏm'ĭsĭng** *a.* likely to turn out well, hopeful, full of promise.

prŏm'ĭssory *a.* conveying or implying promise. **~ note**, signed document containing promise to pay stated sum.

prŏm'ontorў *n.* point of high land jutting out into sea etc.; protuberance.

promōte' *v.t.* move up to higher office or position; help forward or initiate process or formation of; promote sales of, esp. by advertising. **promō'ter** *n.* (esp.) one who promotes formation of joint-stock companies. **promō'tion** *n.*; **promō'tional** *a.*

prŏmpt *a.* done, made, etc. at once or without delay; ready in action. *v.t.* incite, prime, inspire; help out (actor, speaker) by suggesting words etc. *n.* thing said to help memory esp. of actor. **~-box**, prompter's box on stage. **~-side**, side of stage to actor's left. **prŏmp'ter** *n.* (esp.) person prompting actors. **~ing** *n.* (esp.) incitement. **~ĭtūde** *n.* promptness.

prŏm'ulgāte *v.t.* publish as coming into force or having authority. **~ā'tion** *n.*

prōne *a.* lying face or front downwards; (loosely) lying flat, prostrate; inclined, disposed (*to*).

prŏng *n.* spike of fork. *v.t.* pierce, turn up, etc. with prong. **~ed** *a.* having prongs.

pronŏm'ĭnal *a.* of (nature of) pronoun.

prō'noun *n.* word serving as substitute for noun.

pronounce' *v.* utter formally; pass judgement, give (as) one's opinion; articulate, esp. with ref. to mode of

pronouncing. **pronounced'** (-st) *a.* (esp.) strongly marked; decided. **~ment** *n.* authoritative or formal declaration of opinion etc.

pronŭncĭamĕn'tō *n.* manifesto, esp. of insurgents.

pronŭncĭā'tion *n.* mode of pronouncing.

prōōf *n.* fact, evidence, or reasoning that proves truth or existence of something; test or trial; impression from type subject to correction before final printing; careful impression of engraved plate before printing of ordinary issue; standard of strength of alcoholic spirit. *a.* (of armour) of proved strength; impenetrable; **~ against**, impenetrable by; not to be overcome or shaken by. *v.t.* make proof, esp. against water or bullets. **~-reader**, person employed in correcting printers' proofs. **~ spirit**, standard mixture of alcohol and water used in computing alcoholic strength.

prŏp[1] *n.* thing used to support something or keep it upright; supporter of cause etc. *v.t.* support (as) by prop, hold *up* thus.

prŏp[2] *n.* (colloq.) aircraft propeller.

prŏp[3] *n.* (theatr.) stage property.

prop. *abbr.* proposition.

prŏpagăn'da *n.* (means of) disseminating doctrine, information, etc. in order to promote or injure cause etc.; (esp. misleading) information etc. so disseminated.

prŏp'agāte *v.* multiply or reproduce by sowing, grafting, breeding, etc.; spread or disseminate. **~ā'tion** *n.*

propĕl' *v.t.* drive or push forward; give onward motion to. **propĕll'ant** *a.* & *n.* (thing, esp. explosive) that propels. **propĕll'er** *n.* revolving shaft with blades for propelling ship, aircraft, etc.

propĕn'sĭtў *n.* inclination, tendency.

prŏp'er *a.* (arch.) own; suitable, appropriate; right; decent, decorous; (arch.) handsome; (colloq.) thorough. **~ly** *adv.* fittingly, suitably; rightly, duly; with good manners; (colloq.) thoroughly.

prŏp'ertў *n.* owning; thing owned; landed estate; attribute or quality; portable thing used on stage.

prŏph'ĕcў̆ *n.* prophesying; prophetic utterance; prediction.

prŏph'ĕsў̄ *v.* speak as prophet; predict.

prŏph'ĕt *n.* inspired teacher; revealer or interpreter of God's will; one who predicts. ~ĕss *n.* prophĕt'ĭc(al) *aa.* of prophet; predicting, containing prediction (*of*).

prŏphў̆lăc'tĭc *a.* & *n.* (medicine, measure) tending to prevent disease. prŏphў̆lăx'ĭs *n.*

propĭn'quĭtў̆ *n.* nearness in place; close kinship.

propĭ'tiāte (-shĭ-) *v.t.* appease; gain forgiveness or favour of. ~ā'tion *n.*; ~ā'torў̆ *a.*

propĭ'tious *a.* well-disposed, favourable (*to*); suitable *for*.

propô̄r'tion *n.* comparative part; part bearing definite relation to whole; comparative relation, ratio; symmetry; due relation between things or parts of thing. *v.t.* make proportionate. propô̄r'tional *a.* in 'due proportion, corresponding in degree or amount; ~al **representation**, representation of parties etc. in parliament in proportion to total support in election. propô̄r'tionate *a.* that is in proportion (*to*).

propō'sal (-z-) *n.* proposing; scheme etc. proposed; offer of marriage.

propōse' (-z) *v.* put forward as problem, object, plan, intention, candidate, or toast; offer marriage (*to*); intend.

prŏposi'tion (-z-) *n.* statement, assertion; predication; (math.) formal statement of theorem or problem; proposal; offer of terms; (sl.) task, problem, opponent, *v.t.* make proposal to.

propound' *v.t.* offer for consideration or solution.

proprī'ĕtarў̆ *a.* of proprietor; holding property; held in private ownership; of which manufacture or sale is restricted by patent etc.

proprī'ĕtor *n.* owner. ~tô̄r'ial *a.*; ~trĕss *n.*

proprī'ĕtў̆ *n.* fitness, rightness; correctness of behaviour or morals; (pl.) *the* conventions of polite behaviour.

propŭl'sion *n.* (means of) propelling; impelling influence. ~ĭve *a.*

prorōgue' (-g) *v.* discontinue meetings of (parliament) without dissolving it; be prorogued. prōrogā'tion *n.*

prōsā'ĭc (-z-) *a.* like prose; unpoetical; commonplace.

proscē'nĭum *n.* part of theatre stage in front of curtain, esp. with enclosing arch.

proscrībe' *v.t.* put out of protection of law; banish, exile; forbid by law. proscrĭp'tion *n.*; proscrĭp'tĭve *a.*

prōse (-z) *n.* ordinary non-metrical form of language; plain speech. *v.i.* talk tediously.

prŏs'ĕcūte *v.t.* pursue or carry on; institute legal proceedings against. prŏsĕcū'tion *n.* prosecuting; prosecuting party. prŏs'ĕcūtor *n.* one who prosecutes, esp. in criminal court; *public prosecutor*, law officer conducting criminal proceedings in public interest.

prŏs'ĕlў̄te *n.* Gentile convert to Jewish faith; any convert. ~tĭsm *n.* practice of proselytizing. ~tīze *v.* seek proselytes; make proselyte of.

prŏs'odў̆ *n.* science of versification. ~dĭst *n.*

prŏs'pĕct *n.* extensive view; mental scene; expectation; (colloq.) possible or likely purchaser, subscriber, etc. *v.* (-ĕkt') explore (*for* gold etc.). ~or *n.*

prospĕc'tĭve *a.* concerned with, applying to, future; expected, future.

prospĕc'tus *n.* (pamphlet etc. containing) description of chief features of school, commercial company, etc.

prŏs'per *v.* succeed, thrive; make successful. prospĕ'ritў̆ *n.* prospering; wealth. prŏs'perous *a.* flourishing, successful; auspicious.

prŏs'tāte *n.* large gland accessory to male generative organs. ~tăt'ĭc *a.*

prŏs'tĭtūte *n.* woman offering her body for sexual intercourse for payment. *v.t.* make prostitute of; sell for base gain, put to ignoble use. prŏstĭtū'tion *n.*

prŏs'trāte *a.* lying with face to ground, esp. in submission or humility; lying horizontally; over-thrown; exhausted. *v.t.* throw or lay flat on ground; overcome; reduce to extreme physical weakness. **prostrā'tion** *n.*

prō'sȳ (-z-) *a.* tedious, commonplace, dull.

prōtăctin'ium *n.* radioactive metallic element.

protăg'onist *n.* chief person in drama etc.; champion.

prō'tēan *a.* of or like Proteus; versatile, variable.

protĕct' *v.t.* keep safe; shield; secure.

protĕc'tion *n.* protecting, defence; patronage; protecting person or thing; system or policy of protecting home industries by tariffs etc. **~ism** *n.*; **~ist** *n. & a.*

protĕc'tive *a.* serving, showing desire, to protect. **~ coloration, ~ colouring**, colouring making animals difficult to see in their natural surroundings. **~ custody**, detention of person by police etc. to protect him from harm.

protĕc'tor *n.* person who, thing or device that, protects; regent in charge of kingdom during minority, absence, etc. of sovereign. **~orate** *n.* (period of) office of protector of State; protectorship or control of State by stronger one, territory as protected. **~orship, ~rèss** *nn.*

prŏt'égé (-āzhā) *n.* (fem. *-gée*), person under protection or patronage of another.

prō'tēin (*or* -tēn) *n.* kinds of organic compound forming important part of all living organisms and essential constituents of food of animals.

pro tem. *abbr., pro tempore* [L], for the time, temporarily.

protĕst' *v.* affirm solemnly; make protest (*against*); (U.S.) protest against. *n.* (prō'-) expression of dissent or disapproval; remonstrance.

Prŏt'estant *n.* member, adherent, of any of western Christian Churches repudiating papal authority and separated from Roman communion. *a.* of Protestants or Protestantism. **~ism** *n.*

prŏtestā'tion *n.* solemn affirmation.

prō'tocŏl *n.* draft of diplomatic document, esp. of agreed terms of treaty; (rigid observance of) **rules** of diplomatic etiquette.

prō'tomărtyr (-ter) *n.* first martyr.

prō'ton *n.* positively charged particle forming part (or in hydrogen whole) of nucleus of atom.

prō'toplăsm *n.* essential matter of living organisms, viscid translucent substance of which cells principally consist. **~plăs'mic** *a.*

prō'totȳpe *n.* original thing or person in relation to any copy, improved form, etc. **~tȳpal, ~tȳp'ical** *aa.*

prōtozō'a *n.pl.* division of animal kingdom comprising animals essentially consisting of simple cell. **prōtozō'on** *n.* member of protozoa. **~zō'ic** *a.* (of strata) containing earliest traces of living beings.

protrăct' *v.t.* prolong, lengthen out; draw to scale. **protrăc'tile** *a.* that can be extended. **protrăc'tion** *n.* **protrăc'tor** *n.* instrument for measuring angles; muscle serving to extend limb etc.

protrude' (-ōōd) *v.* stick out; thrust out. **protru'sion** *n.*; **protru'sive** *a.*

protū'berant *a.* bulging out; prominent. **~ance** *n.*

proud *a.* valuing oneself (too) highly; haughty, arrogant; feeling or showing (proper) pride; feeling greatly honoured; imposing, splendid. **~ flesh**, overgrown flesh round healing wound.

Prov. *abbr.* Proverbs; Province.

prove (prōov) *v.* (p.p. *proved*, arch. *proven*), give proof of; demonstrate; ascertain by experience; establish validity of (will); turn out (*to* be); test. **prō'vable** *a.* **prō'ven** (*or* -ōō-) *a.* proved.

prŏv'enance *n.* (place of) origin.

prŏv'ender *n.* fodder; (joc.) food.

prŏv'erb, *n.* short pithy saying in general use; adage, saw; byword. **prover'bial** *a.* of proverbs; notorious or constantly spoken of.

provīde' *v.* make due preparation; stipulate; take precautions; equip, supply; **~ for**, secure maintenance of. **provī'ded, provī'ding** *conjj.* on condition or understanding (*that*).

prŏv'idence *n.* timely care; thrift; beneficent care of God or nature; *P~*, God. **prŏv'ident** *a.* having or showing foresight, thrifty. **provi-děn'tial** *a.* of or by divine foresight or interposition; extremely lucky.

prŏv'ĭnce *n.* (esp. principal) administrative division of country; (pl.) whole of country outside capital; archbishop's or metropolitan's district; sphere of action; concern.

provĭn'cial *a.* of province; (having speech, manners, etc.) of provinces. *n.* inhabitant of province(s); head of religious order in province; archbishop, metropolitan. **~ism** *n.*

provi'sion *n.* providing; what is provided; provided amount *of*; (pl.) eatables and drinkables; proviso. **~al** *a.* for the time being, temporary, subject to revision.

provī'so (-zō) *n.* (pl. *-os*), stipulation; limiting or stipulating clause. **provī'sory** *a.* conditional; making provision.

prŏvocā'tion *n.* provoking; what provokes, esp. what arouses anger, lust, etc. **provŏc'ative** *a.* tending to provocation (*of*); intentionally arousing sexual desire, anger, etc.

provōke' *v.t.* rouse, incite, (*to*); irritate; call forth. **provō'king** *a.*(esp., colloq.) annoying.

prŏv'ost *n.* head of some colleges; head of Sc. municipal corporation or burgh; (*usu.* provō'), officer of military police. **~-marshal**, commander of military police.

prow *n.* fore-part immediately about stem of boat or ship.

prow'ĕss *n.* valour; gallantry.

prowl *v.* go about in search of prey or plunder; pace restlessly; wander through.

prox. *abbr.* proximo.

prŏx'ĭmate *a.* nearest, next before or after.

prŏxim'ĭtў *n.* nearness; neighbourhood.

prŏx'ĭmō *a.* of next month.

prŏx'ў *n.* agency of substitute; authorized agent; document authorizing one to vote on another's behalf; vote so given. *a.* done, given, etc. by proxy.

prude (prōōd) *n.* woman of squeamish propriety.

pru'dent (-ōō-) *a.* avoiding rashness; discreet. **~ence** *n.* **prudĕn'tial** *a.* of, involving, etc. prudence.

pru'derў (-ōō-) *n.* conduct or notions of prudes. **pru'dĭsh** *a.*

prune[1] (prōōn) *n.* dried plum; plum suitable for drying; dark reddish purple.

prune[2] (prōōn) *v.t.* rid of dead or overgrown parts; remove (superfluities); clear of superfluities.

pru'nus (-rōō-) *n.* kinds of tree bearing stone-fruit.

prur'ĭent (-oor-) *a.* given to or springing from lascivious thoughts. **prur'ience, ~encў** *nn.*

Prŭ'ssian *a. & n.* (native) of Prussia. **~ blue**, deep greenish-blue pigment.

prŭss'ĭc ă'cĭd *n.* hydrocyanic acid.

prў *v.i.* look, inquire, etc. inquisitively.

P.S. *abbr.* Police Sergeant; postscript; prompt side; (U.S.) Public School.

Ps. *abbr.* Psalm(s).

psalm (sahm) *n.* one of the songs in Book of Psalms; sacred song, hymn. **~ist** *n.* author of psalms. **~odў** *n.* practice or art of singing psalms etc.; arrangement of psalms for singing.

psal'ter (sawl-) *n.* (version, copy, of) Book of Psalms.

psal'terў (sawl-) *n.* ancient plucked stringed instrument.

psephŏl'ogў (sĕf-) *n.* statistical analysis of elections. **~gĭst** *n.*

pseudo- (*or* s-) in comb., false(ly), spurious(ly), seeming(ly).

pseud'onўm (sū-) *n.* fictitious name, esp. assumed by author. **pseudŏ'nўmous** *a.*

pshaw (shaw, -ah) *int.* expressing contempt or impatience.

psĭttacō'sĭs (s-) *n.* contagious disease of parrots etc. communicable to man.

P.S.V. *abbr.* Public Service Vehicle.

psyche (sī'kĭ) *n.* soul, spirit, mind.

psychĕdĕl'ĭc (sĭk-; *or* -dē-) *a.* (of drug) hallucinatory, giving illusion of freedom from limitations of reality; suggesting experience or effect of such drugs.

psychī'atrў (sĭk-) *n.* study and treatment of mental disease. **psўchĭăt'rĭc(al)** *aa.*; **~trĭst** *n.*

psy'chic (sīk-) *a. & n.* psychical; (person) susceptible to psychical or occult influences. **psȳ'chical** *a.* of soul or mind; of phenomena etc. apparently outside domain of physical law.

psycho (sī'kō) *n.* (sl.) psychopath. *v.t.* (sl.) psycho-analyse.

psy'cho- (sī'kō) in comb., soul, mind, mental(ly). **psycho-anăl'ўsĭs** *n.* psychology of unconscious mind; therapeutic method employing this; **~-ăn'alȳse** *v.t.*; **~-ăn'alȳst** *n.*; **~-ănalȳt'ĭc(al)** *aa.* **~mō'tor** *a.* of motion resulting from mental activity. **~neurō'sĭs** *n.* functional nervous or mental disorder; **~-neurŏt'ĭc** *a. & n.* **~path** *n.* mentally deranged or emotionally unstable person; **~păth'ĭc** *a* **~-somăt'ĭc** *a.* of or resulting from (interaction of) mind and body, or influence of one on the other. **~thě'rapў** *n.* therapy by psychological means.

psychŏl'ogў (sīk-) *n.* (treatise on, system of) science of nature, functions, and phenomena of mind; mind, psychological characteristics. **~lŏ'gĭcal** *a.* of psychology or mind; **~logical moment**, psychologically appropriate moment, nick of time. **~logĭst** *n.*

psychō'sĭs (sīk-) *n.* severe mental illness. **psychŏt'ĭc** *a. & n.* (person) suffering from or liable to psychosis.

P.T. *abbr.* physical training.

Pt. *abbr.* Part; Point; Port.

pt. *abbr.* pint.

ptär'mĭgan (t-) *n.* kinds of bird of grouse family.

Pte *abbr.* Private.

ptěrodăc'tўl (t-) *n.* extinct winged reptile.

P.T.O. *abbr.* please turn over.

Ptŏlĕmā'ĭc (t-) *a.* of Egyptian dynasty of Ptolemies.

ptō'maine (t-) *n.* kinds of poisonous organic compound.

pŭb *n.* (colloq.) public-house.

pū'bertў *n.* sexual maturity.

pū'bēs (-z) *n.* region of lower abdomen covered with hair in adult; pubic hair. **pū'bĭc** *a.*

pūbĕs'cence *n.* arrival at puberty; downiness, soft down. **~ent** *a.*

pŭb'lĭc *a.* of, concerning, community as a whole; open to, shared by, people in general; open to general observation, done etc. in public. *n.* (members, section, of) community as a whole; *in ~*, publicly, openly. **~-house**, house licensed to sell alcoholic liquor. **~ relations**, relations of department, organization, etc., with general public. **~ relations officer**, person charged with maintaining good public relations. **~ school**, large usu. endowed private secondary boarding- or day-school; school provided at public expense as part of system of public education. **~-spirited**, animated or prompted by zeal for common good. **~ utilities**, services or supplies commonly available in large towns.

pŭb'lĭcan *n.* keeper of public-house; (bibl.) tax-gatherer.

pŭblĭcā'tion *n.* publishing; published book, periodical, etc.

pŭb'lĭcĭst *n.* writer on public concerns, esp. political journalist; publicizer.

pŭblĭ'cĭtў *n.* being or making public, esp. (business of) advertising or making publicly known. **~ agent**, person employed for publicity.

pŭb'lĭcīze *v.t.* bring to public notice, esp. by advertisement etc.

pŭb'lĭclў *adv.* in public; without concealment; openly.

pŭb'lĭsh *v.t.* make generally known; formally announce; prepare and issue copies of (book etc.) for sale to public. **~er** *n.* person whose trade is publishing books etc.

pūce *a. & n.* brownish purple.

Pŭck[1] *n.* mischievous goblin.

pŭck[2] *n.* rubber disk used in ice-hockey.

pucka : see **pukka**.

pŭck'er *v.* contract or gather (*up*) into wrinkles or folds. *n.* wrinkle, fold, bulge.

pu'dding (pŏŏ-) *n.* kinds of food made of ingredients mixed in soft mass; sweet course of meal. **~-cloth**, cloth in which pudding is boiled. **~-stone**, conglomerate rock of rounded pebbles in brown matrix.

pŭdd'le *n.* small dirty pool; kind of rough cement of kneaded clay. *v.* work (clay) into puddle; stir (molten iron); dabble in water or mud.

pū'dency *n.* modesty.

pŭdĕn'da *n.pl.* external genital organs.

pŭdg'y *a.* podgy.

pueb'lō (pwĕ-) *n.* (pl. -s), communal Indian village or settlement in New Mexico etc.

pū'erīle *a.* childish; trivial. **pŭerĭl'-ity** *n.*

pŭĕr'peral *a.* of or due to childbirth.

pŭff *n.* short quick blast of breath or wind; smoke or vapour sent out by it; pad of down etc. for applying powder to skin; cake etc. of light pastry; laudatory notice. *v.* emit puff or puffs; smoke in puffs; pant; advertise in laudatory manner; inflate, become inflated; swell *up, out.* **~-adder**, large very venomous African viper. **~-ball**, ball-shaped fungus emitting spores in cloud of fine powder. **~ paste, ~ pastry,** light flaky pastry. **~ sleeve,** short full sleeve gathered into band. **pŭffed** (-ft) *a.* (esp.) **~** *up,* elated, proud. **pŭff'y** *a.* short-winded; puffed out, swollen.

pŭff'ĭn *n.* large-billed sea-bird.

pŭg[1] *n.* small snub-nosed breed of dog; **~-nose**, short snub or flat nose.

pŭg[2] *n.* loam or clay mixed and kneaded for brickmaking etc. *v.t.* make into pug; pack (esp. space under floor) with pug etc. to deaden sound.

pŭg[3] *n.* (Anglo-Ind.) footprint of wild animal.

pŭg[4] *n.* (sl.) pugilist.

pū'gĭlĭsm *n.* boxing. **~ĭst** *n.* boxer, prize-fighter. **~ĭs'tĭc** *a.*

pŭgnā'cĭous *a.* disposed to fight. **pŭgnă'cĭty** *n.*

puisne (pū'nĭ) *a.* (law) later; (of judge) inferior, junior.

pū'ĭssant (*or* pwĭ-) *a.* wielding great power; potent. **~ance** *n.*

pūke *v.* vomit.

pŭkk'a, pŭck'a *a.* (Anglo-Ind.) real, genuine. **~ sahib,** real gentleman.

pŭl'chrĭtūde (-k-) *n.* beauty.

pūle *v.i.* whine; be querulous.

pull (pŏŏl) *v.* draw forcibly towards one; exert pulling force; pluck, gather; propel boat by pulling oar(s); check (horse); (crick.) strike ball from off to leg; (golf) hit ball widely to left; **~** *face,* distort features into grimace; **~** *about,* treat roughly; **~** *down,* demolish, lower in health etc.; **~** *in,* move towards near side, into parking--place, etc. **~** *off,* win, manage successfully; **~** *out,* move away, move towards off side; **~** *round,* (cause to) recover; **~** *through,* get safely through; **~** one*self together,* rally, recover oneself; **~** *up,* (cause to) stop, reprimand, improve one's relative position, uproot. *n.* pulling, wrench, tug; means of exerting influence; (esp. unfair) advantage; rough proof; spell of rowing; pulled stroke; deep draught of liquor; draw at pipe etc.; handle for pulling. **~-in**, place for pulling in, esp. at roadside. **~-on**, (garment) pulled on and without fastenings. **~over**, garment pulled on over head. **~-through**, cord for drawing cleaning-pad etc. through rifle. **~-up**, place for pulling up vehicles etc., esp. for refreshment.

pŭll'ĕt (pŏŏ-) *n.* young domestic fowl before moulting.

pū'lley (pŏŏ-) *n.* grooved wheel(s) for cord etc. to run over, mounted in block and used to lift weight etc.; wheel or drum mounted on shaft and turned by belt, used to increase speed or power.

Pull'man (coach) (-ŏŏ-) *n.* railway--coach etc. arranged as comfortable saloon, sleeping-car, etc.

pŭll'ūlāte *v.* grow or multiply rapidly. **~ā'tion** *n.*

pŭl'monarў *a.* of lungs; affected with or subject to lung-disease.

pŭlp *n.* fleshy part of fruit, animal body, etc.; soft formless mass, esp. of materials for paper-making. *v.* reduce to pulp; become pulpy. **pŭl'pў** *a.*

pul'pĭt (-ŏŏ-) *n.* erection for preaching from; preaching.

pulque (pŏŏl'kā; *or* -ē) *n.* Mexican fermented drink of sap of agave etc.

pŭlsāte' (or pŭl'-) *v.i.* expand and contract rhythmically; throb, vibrate, quiver. **~ā'tion** *n.*

pŭlse¹ *n.* rhythmical throbbing of arteries; point where this can be felt externally; throb, thrill, of life or emotion; beat. *v.i.* pulsate.

pŭlse² *n.* edible seeds of peas, beans, lentils, etc.

pŭl'verīze *v.* reduce, crumble, to powder or dust; demolish, crush, smash. **~īzā'tion** *n.*

pū'ma *n.* large tawny American feline quadruped.

pŭm'īce(-stone) *n.* light kind of porous lava used for rubbing off stains, polishing, etc.

pŭmm'el *v.t.* strike repeatedly, esp. with fists.

pŭmp¹ *n.* machine used for raising water; kinds of machine for raising or moving liquids, compressing gas, etc. *v.* work pump; remove, raise, compress, inflate, etc. (as) by pumping; elicit information (from) by persistent or artful questions; make *dry* by pumping; **~ out**, empty by pumping; **~ up**, inflate (tyre etc.). **~-room**, room at spa where medicinal water is sold.

pŭmp² *n.* light shoe for dancing etc.

pum'pernickel (pŏŏ-) *n.* wholemeal rye bread.

pŭmp'kin *n.* (large globular or oval fruit of) trailing plant.

pŭn *n.* humorous use of word to suggest different meanings, of different words of same sound, etc. *v.i.* make pun(s).

pŭnch¹ *v.* strike with fist; bore or perforate (as) with punch; drive (nail etc. *in*, *out*) with punch; drive (cattle etc.). *n.* blow with fist; tool hammered or pressed against surface to be pierced or stamped, or bolt or nail to be driven in or out; (sl.) vigour, effective force, momentum; *pull* one's **~es**, refrain from using one's full forces, be soft or lenient. **~-ball**, inflated or stuffed ball used for practice in punching. **~-drunk**, stupefied with repeated punches. **~-up**, (sl.) fight with fists, brawl.

pŭnch² *n.* mixture of spirit or wine with (hot) water or milk, lemon, spice, etc. **~-bowl**, bowl in which punch is mixed; round deep hollow in hill(s).

pŭnch³ *n.* short-legged thickset draught horse.

Pŭnch⁴ *n.* humpbacked buffoon in puppet-show called **~ and *Judy*.**

pŭn'cheon (-chn) *n.* large cask.

Pŭnchǐněll'ō *n.* (pl. *-os*), chief character in Italian puppet-show; fat person of comical appearance.

pŭnc'tāte *a.* marked with dots, holes, etc.

pŭnctǐl'io *n.* (pl. *-os*), nice point of ceremony or honour; petty formality. **pŭnctǐl'ious** *a.* attentive to punctilios; careful about detail.

pŭnc'tūal *a.* observant of appointed time; not late. **~ăl'itў** *n.*

pŭnc'tūāte *v.t.* mark or divide with stops, commas, etc.; interrupt (*with*). **~ā'tion** *n.* practice or art of punctuating.

pŭnc'ture *n.* pricking; hole made by it. *v.* make puncture in; suffer puncture.

pŭn'dǐt *n.* learned Hindu; learned person, expert.

pŭn'gent (-j-) *a.* having strong sharp taste or smell; stinging, caustic, biting. **~encў** *n.*

pŭn'ish *v.t.* subject to retributive or disciplinary suffering; inflict penalty on; (colloq.) handle or test severely. **~able** *a.*; **~ment** *n.*

pū'nĭtĭve *a.* inflicting punishment, retributive.

pŭnk¹ *n.* (arch.) prostitute.

pŭnk² *n.* rotten wood etc. used as tinder; worthless or inferior person or thing. *a.* worthless, bad.

pŭnk'a(h) (-ka) *n.* (E.-Ind.) large swinging cloth fan on frame.

pŭnn'ět *n.* small chip basket for fruit etc.

pŭn'ster *n.* maker of puns.

pŭnt¹ *n.* flat-bottomed boat propelled by pole. *v.* propel with or use punt-pole; convey, go, in punt.

pŭnt² *v.* kick football dropped from hands before it reaches ground. *n.* such kick.

pŭnt³ *v.i.* lay stake against bank in some card-games; (colloq.) bet. **pŭn'ter** *n.*

pŭ′nў *a*. undersized, feeble.

pŭp *n*. puppy. *v*. bring forth pups; give birth to.

pū′pa *n*. (pl. -*ae*), chrysalis.

pū′pil *n*. person being taught; child under guardianship; opening in centre of iris of eye. pū′pillage *n*. nonage, minority; being a pupil. pū′pillarў *a*. under guardianship; of pupil(s); of pupil of eye.

pŭpp′ét *n*. figure of person etc. worked by strings etc.; person controlled by another. ~ govern-ment, ~ State, etc., one seeming independent but really controlled by another.

pŭpp′ў *n*. young dog; conceited young man. ~hood *n*.; ~ish *a*.

pūr′blīnd *a*. dim-sighted; lacking discernment; obtuse, dull.

pŭr′chase *n*. buying; thing bought; leverage, fulcrum; grip or hold. *v.t.* buy.

pūr′dah (-d*a*) *n*. (E. Ind.) curtain screening women from strangers; system of secluding women.

pūre *a*. without admixture; un-adulterated; chaste, innocent; mere. ~lў *adv*. solely, entirely.

pūr′ée (-ā) *n*. thin pulp of vegetables etc. (boiled and) passed through sieve.

pūrgā′tion *n*. purification, purging. pūr′gatĭve *a*. aperient; purifying; *n*. purgative medicine.

pūr′gatorў *n*. condition or place of spiritual purging; place of tem-porary suffering or expiation. ~tōr′ial *a*.

pūrge *v.t.* make physically or spiri-tually clean; clear (bowels) by evacuation; clear *of* charge etc.; expiate; rid of objectionable or alien elements, members, etc. *n*. purging; purgative.

pūrĭfīcā′tion *n*. purifying; ritual cleansing.

pūr′itў *v.t.* make pure, cleanse; clear of foreign elements.

pūr′ist *n*. stickler for correctness esp. in language. pūr′ism *n*.

pūr′itan *n*. (hist., *P*~), member of extreme English Protestant party regarding Reformation as incom-plete; person of extreme strictness in religion or morals. *a*. puritanical. pūrĭtăn′ical *a*.; ~ism *n*.

pūr′itў *n*. freedom from physical or moral pollution.

pūrl[1] *v.i.* flow with babbling sound.

pūrl[2] *n*. edging of twisted gold or silver wire or of small loops; in-verted stitch in knitting. *v*. invert knitting stitch(es).

pūr′ler *n*. heavy fall.

pūr′lieu (-lū) *n*. (usu. pl.) outskirts, outlying region.

pūr′lin *n*. horizontal beam running along length of roof.

purloin′ (p*er*-) *v.t.* steal, pilfer.

pūr′ple *n*. colour mixed of red and blue; (hist.) crimson; cardinal's scarlet official dress; *the* ~, im-perial, royal, etc. rank, power, or office. *a*. of purple. *v*. make or grow purple.

pūr′port *n*. meaning, tenor, of docu-ment or speech. *v.t.* (-ōr′) have as its purport; profess, be intended to seem (*to* do).

pūr′pose *n*. object, thing intended; fact or faculty of resolving on something; *on* ~, in order (*to* etc.) designedly, not by accident; *to the* ~, relevant; *to good, little, no*, etc. ~, with good, little, etc. effect or result. *v.t.* design, intend. ~ful, ~less *aa*. ~ly *adv*. on purpose. pūr′posĭve *a*. having, serving, done with, etc. purpose.

pūrr *n*. low continuous vibratory sound with which cat etc. expresses pleasure; similar sound, esp. made by motor-engine etc. *v*. make, express or utter with, purr.

pūrse *n*. small pouch for carrying money in; funds; sum given as present or prize. *v*. contract (esp. lips), be contracted, in wrinkles. ~-proud, puffed up by wealth. ~-strings, control of expenditure.

pūr′ser *n*. ship's officer keeping accounts and superintending com-fort etc. of passengers.

pūrs′lane (-ĭn) *n*. succulent herb used in salads etc.

pursū′ance (p*er*-) *n*. carrying out, pursuing (*of* object etc.).

pursū′ant (p*er*-) *adv*. conformably *to*.

pursūe′ (p*er*-) *v*. follow with intent to kill, capture, or overtake; per-

sistently assail; proceed along; continue; follow (profession etc.).
pursuit' (-ūt) *n*. pursuing; profession, employment, recreation; **pursuit plane**, fighter aircraft.

pūr'suivant (-sĭv-) *n*. officer of College of Arms below herald.

pūr'sў *a*. corpulent.

pūr'ulent *a*. of, containing, or discharging pus. **~ence** *n*.

purvey (pervā') *v*. procure and supply (provisions); act as purveyor. **~or** *n*. one whose business it is to supply provisions etc. esp. on large scale.

pūr'view (-vū) *n*. range of physical or mental vision.

pŭs *n*. matter produced by festering or inflammation.

push (poŏsh) *v*. move (away) by exertion of force; (cause to) thrust *out* etc.; make one's way forcibly or persistently; propel, impel, urge; carry (matter etc.) to further or furthest point; **~** *off*, push against bank etc. with oar etc. to get boat into stream etc., (colloq.) leave, go away. *n*. act of pushing; application of propelling force; shove; vigorous effort; enterprise, self-assertion. **~-bike**, (sl.) bicycle worked by pedalling. **~-cart**, hand barrow. **~-chair**, child's carriage like chair on wheels. **~over**, (colloq.) thing very easy to do etc., person very easily convinced, charmed, etc. **~ful, pu'shing** *aa*. (esp.) thrusting, self-assertive.

pūsĭllăn'ĭmous (-z-) *a*. faint-hearted; mean-spirited. **pūsĭllanĭm'itў** *n*.

puss (poŏs) *n*. cat; hare; playful or coquettish girl. **~-moth**, large downy-looking moth.

pu'ssy (poŏ-) *n*. (colloq.) cat. **~foot**, prohibitionist; *v.i.* tread softly or lightly, move warily. **~-willow**, kinds of willow with silky catkins.

pŭs'tūle *n*. pimple. **~lar, ~lous** *aa*. **pŭs'tulāte** *v.i.* form pimples.

put (poŏt) *v*. (p.t. & p.p. *put*) transfer to specified place; set in specified position; cause to be in specified state; express in words; hurl (*weight* etc.) from hand placed close to shoulder; **~** *about*, (cause to) turn round, trouble, annoy; **~** *across*, impose on, succeed in de-

ceiving, explaining, etc.; **~** *away*, (sl.) imprison; **~** *down*, suppress, have (pet etc.) destroyed, account *to*; **~** *in*, spend (time), make (*an appearance*); **~** *off*, postpone, evade (*with* excuse etc.), dissuade, (of boat etc.) leave shore; **~** *on*, increase (*weight, speed*, etc.), put (clock) forward, produce on stage etc., bet, set *to* bowl, work, etc., put upon; **~** *out*, extinguish, dislocate, disconcert, confuse, irritate, inconvenience, turn out, cause to be out; **~** *through*, connect by telephone, cause to undergo or experience, complete; **~** *up*, propose, publish (banns), offer for sale etc., pack for sale etc., lodge and entertain, build; **~** *up to*, inform of, instruct in, instigate; **~** *up with*, submit to, tolerate; **~** *upon*, oppress, take advantage of. *n*. throw, cast. **~-up**, fraudulently concocted.

pū'tatĭve *a*. supposed, reputed.

pū'trĕfў *v*. become putrid, go bad, rot; fester. **~făc'tion** *n*.; **~făctive** *a*.

pūtrĕs'cent *a*. of or in process of rotting. **~ence** *n*.

pū'trĭd *a*. decomposed, rotten; stinking. **pūtrĭd'itў** *n*.

putsch (poŏch) *n*. revolutionary attempt. [Swiss G.]

pŭtt *v*. strike golf-ball gently to roll it into hole. *n*. putting stroke. **pŭtt'er** *n*. straight-faced club for putting. **pŭtt'ing-green** *n*. smooth turf round hole.

pŭtt'ee (-ĭ) *n*. long strip of cloth wound spirally round leg and serving as gaiter.

pŭtt'ў *n*. cement of whiting, linseed oil, etc. for fixing panes of glass etc.; polishing powder used by jewellers. *v.t.* fix, fill, etc. with putty.

pŭzz'le *n*. perplexing question; problem or toy designed to test ingenuity. *v*. perplex, be perplexed; make *out* by exercising ingenuity etc. **~ment** *n*.; **pŭz'zling** *a*.

pxt. *abbr.*, *pinxit* [L], painted this.

pўae'mĭa *n*. severe bacterial infection of blood.

pўg'mў, pĭg'mў *n*. member of dwarf race; very small person or thing. *a*. of pygmies; dwarf; stunted.

pўja′mas, paja′mas (-ahmaz) *n.pl.*
loose silk or cotton trousers tied
round waist; sleeping-suit of loose
trousers and jacket.

pỹ′lon *n.* gateway esp. of Egyptian
temple; tall lattice-work structure,
esp. carrying overhead electric
cables.

pỹorrhoe′a (-rǐa) *n.* (disease of tooth-
-sockets with) discharge of pus.

pỹr′acǎnth, pỹracǎn′thus *n.* evergreen scarlet-berried thorny shrub.

pў′ramǐd *n.* solid figure with triangular or square or polygonal base and
sloping sides meeting at apex;
monumental (esp. ancient Egyptian) stone structure of this shape.
pўrǎm′ǐdal *a.* shaped or arranged
like pyramid.

pỹre *n.* pile of combustibles esp. for
burning corpse.

pỹrī′tēs (-z) *n.* native sulphide of
iron, copper, etc.

pỹr′ō *n.* white crystalline substance
used as photographic developer etc.

pỹromā′nia *n.* incendiary mania.
~mā′niǎc *n. & a.*

pỹrǒm′ěter *n.* instrument for measuring high temperatures.

pỹrotěch′nic(al) (-ěk-) *aa.* of or like
fireworks. ~těch′nics *n.* art of
making, display of, fireworks.

Pў′rrhic (-rǐk) *a. & n.* (of) metrical
foot of two short syllables (◡◡).
~ dance, ancient-Greek war-dance.
~ victory, victory achieved at tco
great cost.

Pўth′ian (-dh-) *a.* of Delphi or
Delphic oracle or priestess of
Apollo.

pỹ′thon *n.* large non-venomous snake
that crushes its prey.

Pў′thonèss *n.* Pythian priestess.

pўx *n.* vessel in which Host is reserved; box in which specimen coins
are deposited at mint. *v.t.* test
(coin) by weight and assay.

Q

Q. *abbr.* Queen.
q. *abbr.* query.
Q.B., Q.C. *abbr.* Queen's Bench,
Counsel.

Q.E.D. *abbr., quod erat demonstrandum*
[L], which was to be proved.

Q.M., Q.M.G., Q.M.S., Quartermaster,
Quartermaster General, Quartermaster Sergeant.

qr. *abbr.* quarter.

Q.S. *abbr.* Quarter Sessions.

q.s. *abbr., quantum sufficit* [L], as
much as suffices.

qt. *abbr.* quart(s).

q.t. *abbr.* (sl.) quiet.

qu. *abbr.* quasi; query.

quā conj. as, in the capacity of. [L]

quǎck[1] *n.* harsh cry of ducks. *v.i.*
utter quack(s); talk loudly and
foolishly.

quǎck[2] *n.* ignorant pretender to skill
esp. in medicine etc.; charlatan.
quǎck′erў *n.*

quad (-ǒd) *abbr.* quadrangle; quadrat;
quadruplet.

Quadragěs′ima (-ǒd-) *n.* first Sunday
in Lent. quadragěs′imal (-ǒd-) *a.*
lasting 40 days; Lenten.

quadrangle (kwǒd′rǎnggl) *n.* four-
-sided figure, esp. square or rectangle; four-sided court (partly)
enclosed by parts of college etc.
building(s). quadrǎng′ūlar *a.*

quad′rant (-ǒd-) *n.* (thing shaped like)
quarter of circle or sphere; instrument for taking angular measurements etc.

quad′rat (-ǒd-) *n.* small metal block
used by printers in spacing. quad′-
rate *a. & n.* square, squarish.

quadrǎt′ic (-ǒd-) *a.* involving second
and no higher power of unknown
quantity or variable. *n.* quadratic
equation; (pl.) algebra dealing with
these.

quad′rature (-ǒd-) *n.* expression of
area bounded by curve by equivalent square; position of heavenly
body in relation to another 90°
away.

quadrěnn′ial (-ǒd-) *a.* occurring
every, lasting, four years.

quadrilǎt′eral (-ǒd-) *a.* four-sided. *n.*
quadrilateral figure or area.

quadrille′ *n.* square dance, music for
it; card-game for four persons,
played with 40 cards.

quadrillion (kwǒdril′yon) *n.* fourth
power of million; (U.S.) fifth
power of thousand.

quadrĭnō'mĭal (-ŏd-) *a.* consisting of four algebraic terms.

quadrĭpăr'tīte (-ŏd-) *a.* consisting of four parts; shared by or involving four parties.

quadrōōn' (-ŏd-) *n.* offspring of white and mulatto.

quad'rupĕd (-ŏdrōō-) *n. & a.* four--footed (animal).

quad'ruple (-ŏdrōō-) *a.* fourfold; of four parts or parties; four times greater than. *n.* number or amount four times greater than another. *v.* multiply by four. quadru'plicāte (-ōō-) *v.t.* multiply by four; make in quadruplicate; *a.* (-ĭt), four times repeated or copied; *in ~plicate,* in four exactly similar examples or copies.

quad'ruplĕt (-ŏdrōō-) *n.* one of four children born at one birth.

quae'stor *n.* ancient-Roman official with financial duties. *~ship n.*

quaff (-ŏf) *v.* drink in copious draughts.

quăg *n.* marshy or boggy spot.

quăgg'a *n.* S.-Afr. animal related to ass and zebra.

quăg'mīre (*or* -ŏ-) *n.* quaking bog, marsh, slough.

quail¹ *n.* bird allied to partridge.

quail² *v.i.* flinch, show-fear.

quaint *a.* unfamiliar or old-fashioned; daintily odd.

quāke *v.i.* tremble; rock to and fro. *n.* quaking; earthquake. quā'kў *a.*

Quā'ker *n.* member of Society of Friends. *~ĕss, ~ĭsm nn.; ~ĭsh a.*

qualĭfĭcā'tion (-ŏl-) *n.* qualifying; thing that qualifies; modification. qualĭfĭcā'torў *a.*

qua'lĭfў (-ŏl-) *v.* attribute quality to, describe *as;* make or become competent, fit, entitled, eligible, etc. (*for, to*); modify, limit; moderate, mitigate.

qua'lĭtative (-ŏl-; -ta- *or* -tā-) *a.* concerned with or depending on quality.

qua'lĭtў (-ŏl-) *n.* degree of excellence, relative nature or kind or character; (characteristic) trait; attribute; timbre.

qualm (-ahm) *n.* momentary faint or sick feeling; misgiving; scruple of conscience.

quan'darў (-ŏn-) *n.* perplexed state; dilemma.

quant (-ŏ-) *n.* kind of punting-pole. *v.* propel boat with quant.

quan'tĭfў (-ŏn-) *v.t.* express as quantity.

quan'tĭtative (-ŏn-; -ta- *or* -tā-) *a.* of or measured or measurable by quantity; based on vowel quantity.

quan'tĭtў (-ŏn-) *n.* amount, sum; specified or considerable amount; (figure or symbol representing) thing having quantity; (pl.) large amounts or numbers; length or shortness of sound or syllable.

quant. suff. abbr., quantum sufficit [L], as much as suffices.

quan'tum (-ŏn-) *n.* required or desired or allowed amount; discrete unit quantity of energy.

quarantine (kwŏ'rantēn) *n.* (period of) isolation imposed on ship, person, etc. that may carry infection. *v.t.* put in quarantine.

quark (*or* -ōrk) *n.* supposed sub--nuclear particle.

qua'rrel¹ (kwŏ-) *n.* (hist.) cross-bow bolt.

qua'rrel² (kwŏ-) *n.* occasion of complaint; violent contention or altercation (*between*); rupture of friendly relations (*with*). *v.i.* find fault *with;* contend violently, fall out, have dispute (*with*). *~some a.*

qua'rrў¹ (kwŏ-) *n.* intended prey; object of pursuit.

qua'rrў² (kwŏ-) *n.* excavation, place from which stone is extracted for building etc. *v.* extract from quarry; form, cut or dig (as) in, quarry; search laboriously.

qua'rrў³ (-ŏ-) *n.* diamond-shaped pane of glass; square tile.

quart (kwŏrt) *n.* quarter of gallon, two pints; pot or bottle (usu. *~-bottle*) containing it.

quar'tan (-ōr-) *n. & a.* (arch.) (ague or fever) with paroxysm every third day.

quar'ter (kwōr-) *n.* fourth part; one of four equal or corresponding parts; grain-measure (8 bushels); quarter of cwt (28 lb., U.S. 25 lb.); period ending at each quarter-day; point of time 15 min. before or after hour; quarter of dollar (25 cents); quarter-mile race; point of compass, direction; district, locality; source of supply, help, or information; (pl.) lodgings, abode, station; mercy shown to enemy in battle. *v.t.* divide into quarters; divide by 4; put (troops, etc.) into quarters; provide with lodgings; (her.) bear quarterly or among quarterings on shield. **~-day**, day on which quarterly payments are due. **~deck**, part of upper deck between stern and after--mast. **~master**, (naut.) rating in charge of steering, signals, hold--stowing, etc.; (mil.) regimental officer in charge of quartering, rations, ammunition, etc. **~ sessions**, court held quarterly by justices of peace in counties or recorder in boroughs. **~-staff**, long stout iron-tipped pole as weapon.

quar'tering (-ŏr-) *n.* division into quarters; (her., pl.) coats marshalled on shield to denote alliances of family with others.

quar'terly (-ŏr-) *a.* occurring, due, every quarter of year. *n.* quarterly magazine. *adv.* once every quarter; (her.) in four, or in two diagonally opposite, quarters of shield.

quar'tern (-ŏr-) *n.* quarter of pint or peck; **~** (*loaf*), four-pound loaf.

quartĕt(te)' (-ŏr-) *n.* musical composition for four voices or instruments; players or singers rendering this; set of four.

quar'to (-ŏr-) *n.* (abbr. *4to*; pl. *-os*), (size of) book with sheets folded into four leaves or eight pages. **~ paper**, paper of size or shape of quarter-sheet.

quartz (-ŏr-) *n.* kinds of siliceous mineral. **quar'tzite** (-ts-) *n.* hard sandstone containing quartz grains.

quā'sar (-s- *or* -z-) *n.* quasi-star, source in space of intense electromagnetic radiation.

quash (kwŏsh) *v.t.* annul; reject as not valid.

quā'si- in comb., seeming(ly), not really, half-, almost.

quassia (kwŏsh'a) *n.* S.-Amer. tree; (bitter decoction made from) wood or bark or root of this.

quăt'er-cĕntē'nary (*or* -ŏt-) *n.* four hundredth anniversary.

quater'nary *a.* having four parts; (geol., *Q~*) belonging to period subsequent to Tertiary. *n.* set of four things; number four.

quater'nion *n.* set of four; (pl.) kind of calculus.

quatrain (kwŏt'rĭn) *n.* four-line stanza.

quat'refoil (kă-) *n.* four-cusped figure resembling symmetrical four-lobed leaf or flower.

quā'ver *v.* vibrate, shake, tremble (esp. of voice or musical sound); say in trembling tones. *n.* trill; tremulousness in speech; (mus.) note equal to half crotchet.

quay (kē) *n.* artificial landing-place for loading or unloading ships.

Que. *abbr.* Quebec.

quea'sy (-z-) *a.* inclined to sickness or nausea; liable to qualms or scruples.

queen *n.* king's wife; female sovereign of kingdom; woman, country, etc. supreme in specified sphere; perfect female of bee, wasp, ant, etc.; court-card between king and knave; chess-piece with greatest freedom of movement. *v.* make queen; **~ it**, play the queen; advance (pawn), be advanced, to opponent's end of board, where it is replaced by queen etc. **~-dowager**, late king's wife. **~-mother**, queen-dowager who is mother of king or queen. **queen'ly** *a.*

queer *a.* strange, odd, eccentric; of questionable character; out of sorts. *n.* (sl.) homosexual. *v.t.* (sl.) spoil, put out of order esp. by unfair means.

quĕll *v.t.* suppress, crush.

quĕnch *v.t.* slake (thirst); extinguish (fire); cool; stifle or suppress. **~less** *a.* unquenchable.

quĕrn *n.* hand-mill for grinding corn etc.

quĕ'rulous (-rŏŏ-) *a.* complaining; peevish.

quēr'y *n.* question, question-mark, esp. indicating doubt of correctness of statement etc. *v.t.* call in question, question accuracy of.

quĕst *n.* seeking; thing sought;

inquiry or search. *v.i.* go *about* in search, search *about*.

ques'tion (-chn) *n.* sentence put in interrogative form; problem, concern, matter; subject of discussion or voting; doubt; *call in ~*, question, throw doubt on; *in ~*, under consideration; *out of the ~*, not to be considered or thought of. *v.t.* ask questions of, interrogate; throw doubt upon. **~-mark**, punctuation mark (?) placed at end of written question. **~-time**, time allowed for putting questions, esp. to minister in House of Commons. **~able** *a.* doubtfully true; not clearly consistent with honesty or wisdom. **~less** *adv.* indubitably.

ques'tionnaire' (*or* kĕ-) *n.* series of questions for obtaining information on special points.

queue (kū) *n.* hanging plaited tail of hair or wig, pigtail; line of persons etc. awaiting turn to buy, proceed, etc. *v.i.* form *up*, take one's place, stand, in queue.

quibb'le *n.* play on words; equivocation, evasion. *v.i.* use quibbles.

quick *a.* living; lively, prompt; sensitive, intelligent; rapid, swift. *n.* sensitive flesh below nails or skin; seat of feeling or emotion. *adv.* quickly. **~lime**, unslaked lime. **~sand**, loose wet sand readily swallowing up heavy objects. **~set**, (hedge) formed of living plants, esp. hawthorn. **~silver**, mercury; coat back of (mirror-glass) with amalgam of tin. **~ trick**, (bridge) card that should take trick in first or second round of suit. **quick'ly** *adv.*; **~ness** *n.*

quick'en *v.* give life to; come to life; (of foetus) make perceptible movements; animate, inspire, kindle; accelerate; make or become quicker

quid[1] *n.* (sl.) sovereign, pound.

quid[2] *n.* lump of tobacco for chewing.

quidd'ity *n.* essence, real nature.

quid prō quō *n.* compensation, tit for tat. [L]

quies'cent (*or* -ī-) *a.* inert, dormant; silent. **~ence** *n.*

qui'et *n.* undisturbed state; tranquillity, repose; calm, silence. *a.*

with little or no sound or motion; of gentle disposition; (of colour etc.) unobtrusive; tranquil. *v.* soothe, calm, reduce to quiet; become quiet. **qui'eten** *v.*; **qui'etūde** *n.*

qui'etism *n.* passive attitude towards life, esp. as form of religious mysticism. **~ist** *n. & a.*

quiē'tus *n.* death; finishing stroke.

quiff *n.* lock of hair brushed upwards in front.

quill *n.* large feather of wing or tail; hollow stem of feather; pen, fishing-float, plectrum, etc. made of quill; porcupine's spine; hollow reed used as bobbin or musical pipe. *v.t.* goffer; wind on bobbin.

quilt *n.* bed-cover, esp. of quilted material. *v.t.* cover, line, etc. with padding; make of padding kept in place between two layers of material by lines of stitching.

quin *n.* (colloq.) quintuplet.

qui'nary *a.* of the number 5; of five things.

quince *n.* (tree bearing) hard acid pear-shaped fruit used as preserve etc.

quincentē'nary *n.* 500th anniversary.

quinc'unx *n.* (arrangement of) four objects at corners and one in centre of rectangle.

quin'ine (-ēn; *or* -ēn') *n.* bitter drug used as febrifuge etc.

Quinquagĕs'ima (Sunday) *n.* Sunday before Lent.

quinquĕnn'ial *a.* five-year-long; five-yearly.

quin'quĕrēme *n.* ancient galley with five banks of oars.

quin'sў (-z-) *n.* abscess forming round tonsil.

quin'tain (-tǐn) *n.* (hist.) mark set up to be tilted at, with sandbag on pivoted bar.

quin'tal *n.* 100 lb.; hundredweight; 100 kilograms.

quintĕss'ence *n.* purest form or manifestation *of* some quality etc.; highly refined extract.

quintĕt(te)' *n.* (performers of) musical composition for five voices or instruments; set of five.

quintill'ion (-yon) *n.* fifth power, (U.S.) cube, of million.

quĭn'tūple *a.* fivefold. *v.* multiply, increase, fivefold.

quĭn'tūplĕt *n.* set of five; one of five children born at a birth.

quĭp *n.* witty and sarcastic or taunting remark.

quīre[1] *n.* 24 sheets of writing-paper; collection of leaves one within another in MS. or book; folded sheet of book.

quīre[2] *n. & v.* (arch.) choir.

quĭrk *n.* trick of action or behaviour.

quĭrt *n.* short-handled riding-whip with braided-leather lash.

quĭs'lĭng (-z-) *n.* collaborator with invading enemy.

quĭt *v.* (*quitted*, rarely *quit*), give up, abandon; leave; (U.S.) stop. *pred.a.* rid *of*; absolved. **~-rent,** rent paid by freeholder or copyholder in lieu of service.

quĭtch *n.* couch-grass.

quīte *adv.* completely, altogether, absolutely; rather, to some extent.

quĭts *pred. a.* on even terms by retaliation or repayment.

quĭtt'ance *n.* release from obligation; receipt for payment.

quĭv'er[1] *n.* case for arrows.

quĭv'er[2] *v.i.* tremble or vibrate with slight rapid motion. *n.* quivering motion or sound.

qui vive (kē'vēv'). *on the* ~, on the alert. [Fr.]

quĭxŏt'ĭc *a.* idealistic but impracticable, foolishly or absurdly generous, chivalrous, etc. **quĭx'otrў** *n.*

quĭz *v.t.* examine, put series of questions to; survey through eye--glass. *n.* questioning, series of questions, esp. as entertainment or competition.

quĭzz'ĭcal *a.* mocking, bantering, gently amused.

quŏd *n.* (sl.) prison.

quoin (koin) *n.* external angle of building, corner-stone; wedge used in printing or gunnery.

quoit (k- *or* kw-) *n.* heavy flat iron or rope ring thrown to encircle peg etc.; (pl.) game played with quoits.

quŏn'dam *a.* that was; former.

quōr'um *n.* number that must be present to constitute valid meeting.

quot. *abbr.* quotation etc.

quō'ta *n.* share to be contributed to or received from total by one of parties concerned.

quō'table *a.* worth quoting from or quoting. **~bĭl'itў** *n.*

quotā'tion *n.* quoting; passage or price quoted. **~-marks** (' ' or " "), used at beginning and end of quoted words.

quōte *v.* cite as example, authority, etc.; repeat or copy out passage(s), statement(s), etc. (of); state price (of). *n.* (colloq.) passage quoted; (usu. pl.) quotation-mark(s).

quŏth *v.t.* p.t. 1st & 3rd pers. (arch.) said.

quotĭd'ĭan *a.* daily, of every day; commonplace.

quō'tient (-shnt) *n.* result given by dividing one quantity by another.

q.v. *abbr., quod vide* [L], which see.

qy. *abbr.* query.

R

R. *abbr.* Réaumur; *Regina* [L] Queen; *retarder* [F], to retard (watch etc.); *Rex* [L], King; right; River.

r. *abbr.* right; röntgen(s); runs.

R.A. *abbr.* Royal Academician, Academy; Royal Artillery.

răbb'ĕt *n.* groove or notch cut along edge or face of wood etc. to receive edge or tongue of another piece. *v.t.* cut rabbet in; join with rabbet.

răbb'ī *n.* Jewish doctor of law, esp. ordained leader of congregation. **răbb'ĭn** *n.* rabbi. **răbb'ĭnate** *n.*; **rabbĭn'ĭc(al)** *aa.*

răbb'ĭt *n.* gregarious burrowing mammal of hare family; (sl.) feeble player or person. *v.i.* hunt rabbits. **~-punch,** punch on back of neck. **~-warren,** warren; overcrowded maze of streets, rooms, etc. **răbb'itў** *a.*

răbb'le *n.* disorderly crowd, mob; contemptible or inferior people; *the* lowest classes. **~-rousing,** appealing to or stirring up the rabble.

Răbĕlai'sĭan (-z-) *a.* exuberantly and coarsely humorous.

răb'ĭd *a.* furious, unreasoning; affected with rabies, mad. **rabĭd'ĭtў** *n.*

rā'bĭĕs (-z) *n.* canine madness, acute virus disease of dogs etc.

R.A.C. *abbr.* Royal Armoured Corps; Royal Automobile Club.

rac(c)ōōn' *n.* bushy-tailed Amer. nocturnal carnivore.

rāce¹ *n.* contest of speed, (pl.) series of these for horses etc.; course of life; strong current in sea etc.; channel of stream; track or channel in which something moves or slides. *v.* (make) go at full speed, esp. out of gear or when resistance is diminished; compete in speed (with); enter (horse etc.) for race; attend races. **~-card**, programme of races. **~-course**, ground for horse-racing. **~-horse**, horse bred or kept for racing. **~-meeting**, horse--racing fixture.

rāce² *n.* group of persons etc. (regarded as) of common stock; posterity *of*; great division of living creatures; descent, kindred; distinct ethnical stock. **~ riot**, outbreak of violence and disorder due to racial antagonism. **rā'cĭsm** *n.* belief in unchanging fundamental differences between races of men; racialism. **rā'cĭst** *n. & a.*

rāce³ *n.* root (of ginger).

racēme' *n.* inflorescence with flowers attached by short stalks along central stem. **ră'cėmōse** *a.*

răchĕl' (-sh-) *a.* (of face-powder) of yellowish-brown shade.

rachĭt'ĭc (-k-) *a.* of, affected with, rickets.

rā'cial *a.* of race; concerning, caused by, etc. differences, relationship, etc. between races of men. **~ĭsm** *n.* (encouragement of) racial antagonism. **~ĭst** *n. & a.*

răck¹ *n.* kinds of framework with bars, pegs, shelves, etc. for holding fodder or keeping articles on or in; cogged or indented rail or bar gearing with wheel, pinion, etc.; instrument of torture for stretching victim's joints. *v.t.* torture on rack; inflict torture or strain on. **~-rent**, (exact) extortionate rent (from or for).

răck² *n.* driving clouds; destruction (usu. **~** *and ruin*).

răck³ *v.t.* draw off (wine, cider, etc.) from lees.

răck'ĕt¹ *n.* network of cord, catgut, etc. stretched across elliptical frame with handle, used as bat in tennis etc.; (pl.) game with ball rebounding from end wall of court.

răck'ĕt² *n.* uproar, din; game, line of business; way of making money etc. by dubious or illegal means. *v.i.* live gay life; move about noisily. **răckėteer'** *n.* (esp.) member of criminal gang practising extortion, intimidation, etc.; *v.i.* act as racketeer, conduct racket. **răck'ĕtў** *a.* noisy; dissipated.

rā'cў *a.* of distinctive quality or vigour; lively, spirited, piquant.

R.A.D.A. *abbr.* Royal Academy of Dramatic Art.

rā'dȧr *n.* (apparatus for) determination of direction and range of objects by radio devices.

răd'd'le *n.* red ochre. *v.t.* paint with raddle; plaster with rouge.

rā'dĭal *a.* of, in, or like rays or radii; having, lying or moving along, etc., spokes or radiating lines; of radius of forearm.

rā'dĭan *n.* angle at centre of circle subtending arc whose length is equal to radius.

rā'dĭance *n.* brilliant light; dazzling looks or beauty.

rā'dĭant *a.* emitting rays; issuing or operating radially; beaming with joy etc.; bright or dazzling. *n.* point or object from which heat or light radiates.

rā'dĭȧte *v.* diverge or emit from centre; emit rays of light, heat, etc.; transmit by wireless; be arranged like spokes; disseminate. **rādĭā'tion** *n.* (esp.) (emission of) rays and particles characteristic of radioactive substances; **~ation sickness**, effects of exposure to radioactivity. **rā'dĭātor** *n.* arrangement or apparatus for radiating warmth, cooling motor-engine, etc.

răd'ical *a.* of, from, or going to root(s); fundamental, inherent, essential; primary; thorough; desiring or advocating fundamental reforms. *n.* person holding radical political opinions; quantity forming or expressed as root of another; atom or group of atoms forming base of compound and remaining unchanged during reactions. ~ **sign,** sign (√, ∛, etc.) indicating square, cube, etc. root of number to which it is prefixed.

răd′ĭcle *n.* part of seed that develops into root; root-like subdivision of nerve or vein; chemical radical.

rā′dĭō *n.* wireless telegraphy and telephony; wireless receiving set; wireless programmes. *v.* transmit by radio. **~grăm¹,** combined wireless receiver and electric gramophone.

rā′dĭō- in comb., of rays or radiation; of radium or radioactivity; radio-active. **rādĭoăctĭv′ĭtў** *n.* emission of, property of emitting by dis-integration of atomic nuclei, rays capable of penetrating opaque bodies etc.; **~ăc′tĭve** *a.* **~-astrŏ′-nomў** *n.* branch of astronomy dealing with investigation of celes-tial bodies by radar, or with electromagnetic radiations from outside earth's atmosphere. **~-cār′bon** *n.* radioactive isotope of carbon used in dating organic materials from ancient deposits etc. **~grăm²** *n.* X-ray photograph; message sent by radio-telegraphy. **~graph** (-ahf) *n.* X-ray photograph. **rādĭŏg′raphў** *n.* photography or examination by means of X-rays; **rādĭŏg′rapher** *n.*; **rādĭogrăph′ĭc** *a.* **~locā′tion** *n.* radar. **rādĭŏl′ogў** *n.* scientific study of X-rays, radio-activity, etc. **rādĭŏs′copў** *n.* examination by X-rays; **~scŏp′ĭc** *a.* **~telĕg′raphy,** **~ telĕph′onў** *nn.* wireless telegraphy, telephony. **~-tĕl′escōpe** *n.* instrument or appara-tus used to detect electro-magnetic radiations in radio-astronomy. **~-thĕ′rapў** *n.* treatment of disease by X-rays or other forms of radiation.

răd′ĭsh *n.* (plant with) fleshy pun-gent root eaten raw.

rā′dĭum *n.* radioactive metallic element.

rā′dĭus *n.* (pl. -ĭī), straight line from centre to circumference of circle or sphere; any of set ρf spokes or other objects diverging from point like radii of circle; circular area as measured by its radius; thicker and shorter bone of forearm.

rā′dĭx *n.* (pl. -ĭcēs) number or symbol used as basis of numeration scale.

rā′dŏn *n.* heavy almost inert radio-active gaseous element.

R.A.F. *abbr.* Royal Air Force.

răff′ĭa *n.* (soft fibre from leaves of) kinds of palm.

răff′ĭsh *a.* of dissipated appearance; disreputable.

răff′le *n.* lottery in which article is assigned by drawing lots etc. *v.* sell by raffle; take part in raffle (*for*).

raft (-ah-) *n.* flat floating structure of timber etc., esp. as substitute for boat in emergencies; collection of logs etc. fastened together for transportation by water. *v.t.* trans-port (as) on raft.

raf′ter (-ah-) *n.* one of sloping beams forming framework of roof.

răg¹ *n.* torn or frayed piece of woven material; remnant; (contempt.) flag, handkerchief, newspaper, etc.; (pl.) tattered clothes; *glad* **~s,** fine clothes. **~ doll,** stuffed doll with body etc. made of cloth. **~time,** music with much syncopation. **~ trade,** (colloq.) business of making, selling, etc. women's clothes. **~wort,** yellow-flowered wild plant.

răg² *n.* kinds of hard coarse stone breaking up in thick slabs.

răg³ *v.* (sl.) torment, tease; play rough jokes on; engage in rag. *n.* (sl.) noisy disorderly conduct or scene; spree, lark; practical joke; students' procession etc. with much horse-play.

răg′amŭffĭn *n.* ragged dirty fellow.

rāge *n.* (fit of) violent anger; object of widespread temporary popu-larity. *v.i.* rave, storm; be violent, be at the height.

răgg′ĕd (-g-) *a.* shaggy, hanging in tufts; full of rough or sharp pro-jections; not smooth or uniform or polished; torn or frayed; wearing rags. **~ robin,** crimson-flowered wild plant.

răg′lan *n.* overcoat without shoulder--seams, with top of sleeve carried up to neck. *a.* (having sleeves) of this kind.

ragout' (-o͞o) *n.* dish of meat in small pieces stewed with vegetables and highly seasoned.

raid *n.* sudden incursion to secure military advantage, booty, etc.; air-raid; surprise visit by police. *v.* make raid (upon).

rail[1] *n.* level or sloping bar as part of fence, gate, etc.; iron bar making part of track of railway or tramway. *v.t.* furnish or enclose with rails. ~**head**, furthest point reached by railway, point where rail transport ends; ~**road**, (esp. U.S.) railway; *v.t.* rush *into, through* etc. ~**way**, road laid with rails for passage of trains; company, organization, etc. required for working of this.

rail[2] *n.* kinds of small bird.

rail[3] *v.i.* use abusive language. **rai'llery** *n.* banter.

rai'ling *n.* fence or barrier of rails etc.

rai'ment *n.* clothing, apparel.

rain *n.* condensed moisture of atmosphere falling visibly in separate drops; fall of these; (rain-like descent of) falling particles, objects, etc., continuous succession; *the ~s,* tropical rainy season. *v.* send down rain; fall or send down like rain; *it ~s,* rain falls, there is a rain of. ~**bow,** arch of prismatic colours formed in rain or spray by sun's rays. ~**coat,** waterproof coat. ~**fall,** total amount of rain falling within given area in given time. ~**-gauge,** instrument for measuring rainfall. **rai'ny** *a.* in or on which (much) rain falls; ~**y day,** (fig.) time of (esp. pecuniary) need.

raise (-z) *v.t.* set upright; make stand up; rouse; build up; breed; rear, bring up; utter; put or take into higher position; extract from earth; increase amount or heighten level of; levy, collect, procure; ~ *Cain, hell,* create trouble or uproar; ~ one's *eyebrows,* look supercilious or surprised or shocked; ~ *a laugh,* cause others to laugh; ~ *the wind,* procure money for some purpose. *n.* increase in amount; (U.S.) rise (in salary etc.).

rai'sin (-zn) *n.* dried grape.

raison d'être (rā'zawṅ dā'tr) *n.* what accounts for or justifies or has caused thing's existence. [F]

raj (rahj) *n.* rule, sovereignty. **rajah** (rah'ja) *n.* Indian king or prince or noble.

rāke[1] *n.* pole with comb-like cross--bar for drawing hay etc. together, smoothing loose soil, etc.; various implements resembling rake or used for similar purposes; dissipated or immoral man. *v.* use rake; collect, draw together, (as) with rake; ransack, search (*through* etc.); sweep with eyes, shot, etc. ~**-off,** (share of) profit, commission, etc. in esp. illegitimate transaction.

rāke[2] *v.* (of ship) project beyond keel at upper part of bow or stern; (of mast, funnel, etc.) incline towards stern or rear; give backward inclination to. *n.* amount to which thing rakes; raking position or build.

rā'kish *a.* of dissolute appearance or manners; (of ship) smart, seeming built for speed.

rall. *abbr., rallentando* [It.], gradually slower.

rǎll'y[1] *v.* bring or come together for united effort; revive by effort of will; throw off illness; (of prices etc.) recover from depression. *n.* act of rallying; recovery of energy or spirit; mass meeting; (tennis etc.) interchange of strokes between service and winning of point; motorists' or motor-cyclists' competitive event, esp. over public roads.

rǎll'y[2] *v.t.* banter, chaff.

rǎm *n.* uncastrated male sheep; swinging beam for breaching walls, battering-ram; pile-driving or hydraulic or pumping-machine or parts of them. *v.* beat firm; force home; pack closely; butt; collide violently with, charge or crash *into*; impress by repetition. ~**rod,** (hist.) rod for ramming home charge of muzzle-loader.

R.A.M. *abbr.* Royal Academy of Music.

Rǎmadǎn' (*or* -ahn) *n.* ninth month

of Moslem year, with rigid fast during daylight hours.

răm'ble *v.i.* walk without definite route; talk in desultory or irrelevant way. *n.* rambling walk. **răm'bler** *n.* (esp.) kinds of freely climbing rose. **răm'bling** *a.* (esp.) disconnected, desultory; irregularly planned or arranged.

R.A.M.C. *abbr.* Royal Army Medical Corps.

răm'ĕkĭn -quin (-kĭn) *n.* (dish of cheese etc. baked in) small mould.

răm'ĭfȳ *v.* form branches or subdivisions; develop into complicated system. **rămĭfĭcā'tion** *n.*

ramōse' *a.* branched, branching.

rămp[1] *n.* slope, inclined plane, etc. joining two levels; sloping floor, roadway, (end of) railway platform, etc.; stairway for entering or leaving aircraft. *v.* be rampant; furnish or construct with ramp.

rămp[2] *n.* (sl.) swindle; charging of extortionate prices.

rămpāge' *v.i.* (joc.) rage, storm, rush about. *n.* (răm'-), outbreak of violent behaviour; *on the* ~, rampaging. **rămpā'geous** *a.*

răm'pant *a.* (her., of lion etc.) standing on hind legs with fore-paws in air; extravagant, unrestrained, rank, luxuriant. ~**ancȳ** *n.*

răm'părt *n.* defensive mound of earth; defence, protection.

răm'shăckle *a.* rickety, tumbledown.

ran, *p.t.* of **run**.

rănch *n.* Amer. cattle- or horse-breeding establishment. *v.i.* conduct ranch.

răn'cĭd *a.* smelling or tasting like rank stale fat. **răncĭd'itȳ** *n.*

rănc'our *n.* malignant hate; bitterness. **rănc'orous** *a.*

rănd *n.* (S.-Afr.) highlands on either side of river valley; monetary unit (100 cents).

răndăn' *n.* boat for one sculler and two oarsmen.

răn'dom *n. at* ~, haphazard; without aim or purpose. *a.* made, done, etc. at random.

răn'dȳ *a.* lustful.

ranee (rah'nĭ) *n.* Indian queen or princess.

rang, *p.t.* of **ring**[2].

rănge (-j) *n.* row, line, tier, or series of things, esp. buildings or mountains; freedom or opportunity to range; (U.S.) stretch of grazing or hunting ground; piece of ground with targets for shooting; sphere; scope; compass; register; distance attainable by gun or projectile; distance between gun etc. and objective; cooking fireplace. *v.* place or arrange in row or ranks or in specified situation or order; extend, reach; vary between limits; rove, wander, go all about. ~**-finder,** instrument for estimating range.

rā'nger (-j-) *n.* (esp.) keeper of royal or other park; (pl.) mounted force; senior Girl Guide.

rā'ngȳ (-j-) *a.* (chiefly U.S.) of long slender form.

rănk[1] *n.* row, queue; soldiers in single line abreast; (pl.) common soldiers; distinct social class, grade of dignity, station; high station; place in scale; ~ *and file,* common soldiers, ordinary or undistinguished people. *v.* arrange in rank; assign rank to; have rank or place. **rănk'er** *n.* (commissioned officer who has been) soldier in the ranks.

rănk[2] *a.* too luxuriant; coarse; offensive, loathsome; flagrant; gross.

rănk'le *v.i.* fester, give intermittent or constant pain.

răn'săck *v.t.* search recesses of; pillage.

răn'som *n.* redeeming of captive; money or other consideration paid for it. *v.t.* buy freedom or restoration of; set free on payment of ransom.

rănt *v.* use bombastic language; preach noisily. *n.* tirade; noisy empty talk.

ranŭn'cŭlus *n.* (pl. -*luses,* -*li*), kinds of plant including buttercup. **ranŭncŭlā'ceous** *a.*

răp[1] *n.* smart slight blow; sound (as) of this, esp. on door. *v.* strike smartly; make sound of rap; ~*out,* utter abruptly.

răp[2] *n.* (*not*) the least bit.

rapā'cious *a.* grasping, greedy, extortionate, predatory. **rapă'citȳ** *n.*

răpe[1] *v.t.* carry off by force; violate chastity of, ravish, force sexual intercourse on. *n.* raping. **rā'pĭst** *n.*

răpe[2] *n.* plant grown as food for sheep and for its oil-yielding seed.

răp'ĭd *a.* speedy, swift. *n.* (freq. pl.) steep descent in river-bed with swift current. **rapĭd'ĭtў** *n.*

rā'pĭer *n.* light slender sword for thrusting only.

răp'ĭne *n.* plundering.

rappŏrt' (*or* -pōr) *n.* communication, (sympathetic) relationship.

răpprŏche'ment (-shmahn) *n.* restoration of harmonious relations esp. between States. [F.]

răpscăll'ĭon *n.* rascal.

răpt *a.* carried away in spirit; absorbed; enraptured.

răptŏr'ĭal *a.* of or like birds of prey, predatory.

răp'ture *n.* (expression of) ecstatic delight. **răp'turous** *a.*

rāre[1] *a.* thin, not dense; scarce, uncommon; of uncommon excellence, remarkably good. **~lў** *adv.* seldom, not often; uncommonly.

rāre[2] *a.* (esp. of steak) underdone.

rarebit : see **Welsh rabbit.**

rār'efў *v.* lessen density or solidity of; refine; become less dense. **rārefăc'tion** *n.*

rār'ĭtў *n.* rareness; rare thing.

R.A.S.C. *abbr.* Royal Army Service Corps.

ra'scal (rah-) *n.* rogue, knave, scamp. **rascăl'ĭtў** *n.*; **ra'scallў** *a.*

rāse (-z), **rāze** *v.t.* completely destroy, level with the ground.

răsh[1] *n.* skin eruption in spots or patches.

răsh[2] *a.* hasty, impetuous; over-bold, reckless.

răsh'er *n.* thin slice of bacon or ham.

rasp (-ah-) *n.* coarse file; grating sound or effect. *v.* scrape with rasp; scrape roughly; grate upon; make grating sound.

ra'spberrў (rahzb-) *n.* (garden shrub with) usu. red juicy fruit; (sl.) sound expressing derision; expression of severe disapproval.

răt *n.* kinds of rodent resembling but larger than mouse; person who deserts his party or union. *v.i.* hunt or kill rats; play the rat, desert or betray one's friends. **~-race**, ruthless competitive struggle.

rā't(e)able *a.* liable to, assessed for, payment of local rates. **~abĭl'ĭtў** *n.*

rătafĭ'a (-fĭa) *n.* liqueur flavoured with almonds, fruit-kernels, etc.; biscuit similarly flavoured.

rătch'ĕt *n.* set of teeth in edge of bar or wheel into which cog etc. may catch, allowing motion in one direction only; ratchet-wheel. **~-wheel**, wheel with rim so toothed.

rāte[1] *n.* statement of numerical proportion between two sets of things; standard or way of reckoning; (measure of) value, tariff charge, cost, (relative) speed; assessment on property levied by local authorities; class. *v.* estimate worth or value of; consider, regard as; subject to payment of local rate; rank or be rated *as.* **~payer**, person liable to pay local rates.

rāte[2] *v.t.* scold angrily.

ra'tel (rah-) *n.* carnivorous mammal allied to weasel.

rāthe (-dh) *a.* (arch.) coming or blooming early.

ra'ther (-ahdh-) *adv.* more truly or properly; to a greater extent; somewhat; for choice, sooner (*than*); (colloq.) most emphatically, assuredly.

răt'ĭfў *v.t.* confirm or accept by signature or other formality. **rătĭfĭcā'tion** *n.*

rā'tĭng *n.* (esp.) position or class in warship's crew; non-commissioned member of ship's company.

rā'tĭō (-shĭ-) *n.* (pl. -*os*), quantitative relation between similar magnitudes; proportion.

rătĭŏ'cĭnāte *v.i.* reason, esp. formally. **rătĭocĭnā'tion** *n.*

rā'tion *n.* fixed allowance or individual share of provisions etc. *v.t.* put on ration; share (*out*) in fixed quantities.

ră'tional *a.* able to reason; sensible; sane; moderate; of or based on reasoning; (math.) expressible without radical signs. **ră'tionalĭsm** *n.* rejection of doctrines not consonant with reason. ~ist *n.* & *a.*; ~is'tic *a.*; rational'ity *n.*

rationa'le (-ah-) *n.* fundamental reason or logical basis.

ra'tionalize *v.* bring into conformity with reason; reorganize on scientific lines; find plausible or reasonable motive(s), reason(s), etc. (for). ~iza'tion *n.*

rat'lin(e) *n.* (usu. pl.) small line(s) fastened across ship's shrouds like ladder-rungs.

rattan' *n.* palm with long thin many-jointed stems; cane of this.

rat'tle *v.* give out rapid succession of short sharp sounds; cause such sounds by shaking something; move or fall with rattling noise; say or recite rapidly; (make) move quickly; (sl.) shake nerves of, fluster, frighten. *n.* instrument or plaything made to rattle; horny rings at end of rattlesnake's tail; rattling sound; incessant talker. ~snake, kinds of venomous snake making rattling noise with tail. ~-trap, rickety or shaky thing, esp. vehicle. rat'tler *n.* (esp.) rattlesnake. rat'tling *a.* & *adv.* (sl.) remarkably (good, fast, etc.).

rau'cous *a.* hoarse; harsh-sounding.

rav'age *v.* lay waste, plunder; make havoc. *n.* (esp., pl.) destructive effects *of.*

rave *v.* talk or say wildly or deliriously; (of sea, wind, etc.) howl, roar; speak with rapturous admiration (*about, of*).

rav'el *v.* entangle or disentangle; separate into strands, fray.

rave'lin (-vl-) *n.* outwork of two faces forming salient angle outside main ditch of fortification.

ra'ven[1] *n.* kinds of large black hoarse-voiced bird of crow kind. *a.* of glossy black.

rav'en[2] *v.i.* seek prey or plunder; feed voraciously. rav'enous *a.* voracious; famished, very hungry.

ravine' (-ēn) *n.* deep narrow gorge; mountain-cleft.

ravio'li *n.* (Italian dish of) small pasta cases containing meat etc.

rav'ish *v.t.* commit rape upon; enrapture, fill with delight.

raw *a.* uncooked; in natural or unwrought state; crude, inexperienced, unskilled; stripped of skin; sore, sensitive to touch; (of weather) damp and chilly. *n.* raw place on skin; sensitive spot; raw state. ~-boned, gaunt. ~ deal, unfair treatment. ~hide, (whip of) untanned leather.

ray[1] *n.* single line or narrow beam of light or other radiant energy; remnant or beginning of enlightening influence; any of set of radiating lines, parts, or things; marginal part of daisy etc. *v.* issue, come *out* etc., in rays.

ray[2] *n.* kinds of flat-fish allied to skate.

ray[3] : see re[1].

ray'on *n.* (cellulose) artificial silk.

raze : see rase.

ra'zor *n.* instrument for shaving. ~-back, sharp ridge; kind of whale. ~-bill, kinds of bird. ~-edge, keen edge; sharp mountain ridge; critical situation; sharp line of division. ~-fish, ~-shell, bivalve with long narrow shell.

razz'le(-dazzle) *n.* (sl.) excitement, bustle; spree.

R.B.A. *abbr.* Royal (Society of) British Artists.

R.C. *abbr.* Red Cross; right centre (of stage); Roman Catholic.

R.C.M. *abbr.* Royal College of Music.

R.C.M.P. *abbr.* Royal Canadian Mounted Police.

R.C.N., R.C.O., R.C.P., R.C.S. *abbr.* Royal College of Nursing, of Organists, of Physicians, of Surgeons.

R.D. *abbr.* refer to drawer; Royal (Naval Reserve) Decoration; Rural Dean.

Rd., rd. *abbr.* Road.

R.D.C. *abbr.* Rural District Council.

re[1] (rā), ray[3] *n.* (mus.) second note of major scale in tonic sol-fa.

re[2] *prep.* in the matter of.

re-, pref. attachable to any verb or verbal derivative with the senses *once more, again, anew, afresh, repeated, back.* For words with this prefix, if not found below, the root-words should be consulted.

R.E. *abbr.* Royal Engineers.

reach *v.* stretch *out*, extend; stretch out hand etc.; get as far as, attain to, arrive at; amount to; pass or take with outstretched hand etc.; (naut.) sail with wind abeam. *n.* act of reaching; range of hand etc.; compass, scope; continuous extent, esp. stretch of river etc.; (naut.) tack. **~-me-down**, (sl.) ready-made (garment).

rĕăct' *v.i.* produce reciprocal or responsive effect; respond to stimulus; undergo (esp. chemical) change under some influence. **~ĭve** *a.* tending to react. **rĕăc'tor** *n.* (esp.) atomic pile.

rĕăc'tion *n.* return of previous condition after interval of opposite; response to stimulus; retrograde tendency in politics etc.; (chem.) interaction of substances resulting in chemical change. **~arў** *a. & n.* (person) inclined or favourable to reaction.

read *v.* (*read*, pr. rĕd), (be able to) convert into intended or appropriate words or meaning (written or printed words, figures, markings, etc.); follow with eyes and reproduce mentally or vocally (written or printed words etc.); study by reading; convey when read, record, indicate; find written or printed; interpret in certain sense; read and mark for correction (printer's *proof*); divine, foretell, expound significance of. **~able** *a.* (esp.) pleasant and easy to read; interestingly written. **~abĭl'itў** *n.*

read'er *n.* (esp.) person employed by publisher to read and report on MSS.; printer's proof-corrector; senior university lecturer; book containing passages for instruction, exercise, etc. **~ship** *n.* office of university reader.

read'ilў (rĕd-) *adv.* without reluctance; willingly; easily.

read'ĭnėss (rĕd-) *n.* prompt compliance; quickness in argument or action; prepared state.

rea'ding *n.* (esp.) literary knowledge, scholarship; entertainment at which something is read; interpretation, view taken, rendering; variation found in another MS. etc.; figure etc. shown by instrument, dial, etc.; presentation of bill to legislative assembly. **~-desk**, desk for supporting book etc., lectern.

read'ў (rĕ-) *a.* with preparations complete; in fit state; willing; quick; facile; within reach; unreluctant; fit for immediate use or action. *adv.* beforehand; in readiness. *n.* position in which rifle is held before the present; (sl.) ready money. *v.t.* prepare. **~-made**, (of clothes) made in standard shapes and sizes; not new or original, trite. **~ money**, cash, actual coin. **~ reckoner**, (collection of) table(s) showing results of arithmetical calculations.

rēā'gent *n.* substance used to produce chemical reaction.

rė'al *a.* actually existing or occurring; objective; genuine; consisting of immovable property. *n.* what actually exists, esp. opp. *ideal. adv.* (U.S.) really, very.

rė'alĭsm *n.* fidelity of representation; truth to nature; doctrine that general ideas have objective existence; belief that matter has real existence. **~ĭst** *n. & a.*; **~ĭs'tĭc** *a.*

rĕăl'itў *n.* being real; likeness to original; existent thing; real existence; what is real; real nature *of.*

rė'alīze *v.t.* convert (hope, plan, etc.) into fact; make realistic; apprehend clearly; convert into money; fetch as price. **~zā'tion** *n.*

rė'allў *adv.* in fact; positively; **~?** is that so?

realm (rĕlm) *n.* kingdom; sphere, domain.

rė'altor (*or* -ăl'-) *n.* (U.S.) real-estate agent (member of Nat. Assoc. of Real Estate Boards).

rė'altў *n.* real estate.

ream[1] *n.* twenty quires or 480-500 sheets of paper.

ream[2] *v.t.* widen, shape, bevel out (hole). **rea'mer** *n.* tool for reaming.

reap *v.* cut grain etc. with sickle or machine; harvest. **rea'per** *n.* (esp.) mechanical device for reaping.

rear[1] *v.* raise; build; bring up, breed, cultivate; (of horse etc.) rise on hind feet.

rear[2] *n.* back part of esp. army or

fleet; space or position at back; (attrib.) hinder, back; *bring up the* ~, come last. ~-admiral, flag officer below vice-admiral. ~-guard, troops etc. detached to protect rear, esp. in retreat. ~guard action, engagement between rear-guard and enemy. ~-view mirror, one enabling driver of vehicle to see traffic behind. ~most *a.* furthest back. ~ward *a., adv. & n.*; ~wards *adv.*

rearm' *v.* arm again, esp. with more modern weapons or after disarming. rear'mament *n.*

rea'son (-z-) *n.* (fact adduced or serving as) argument, motive, cause, or justification; intellectual faculty by which conclusions are drawn from premises; sense, sanity; sensible conduct; moderation. *v.* use argument *with* by way of persuasion; form or try to reach conclusions by connected thought; think *out.* ~able *a.* sound of judgement; moderate, tolerable, sensible; inexpensive, not extortionate.

reassure' (-shoor) *v.t.* restore to confidence; confirm again in opinion etc.; reinsure.

Réaumur (rā'ō-) *a.* (of or in thermometric scale) with freezing-point of water at 0° and boiling-point at 80°.

rebar'bative *a.* forbidding, repellent.

re'bate *n.* deduction from sum to be paid, discount. *v.t.* (-āt'), reduce, deduct.

re'beck *n.* early form of fiddle with three strings.

reb'el *n.* person who rises in arms against or refuses allegiance to established government; person who resists authority or control. *v.i.* (ribel'), act as rebel (*against*); feel or show opposition, repugnance, etc. (*against*).

rebell'ion (-lyon) *n.* open esp. armed resistance to established government or any authority.

rebell'ious *a.* in rebellion; disposed to rebel, insubordinate, refractory.

rebound' *v.i.* spring back after impact; recoil. *n.* (rē'-), rebounding, recoil; reaction after emotion.

rebuff' *n. & v.t.* check, snub, repulse.

rebuke' *v.t.* reprove, reprimand, censure authoritatively. *n.* rebuking, being rebuked; reproof.

re'bus *n.* enigmatic representation of name, word, etc. by pictures etc. suggesting its syllables.

rebut' *v.t.* force back; refute, disprove. rebutt'al *n.*

recal'citrant *a. & n.* obstinately disobedient or refractory (person). ~ance *n.*

recall' (-awl) *v.t.* summon back; cancel appointment of; bring back *to* memory; (cause to) remember; revive, resuscitate; revoke, annul. *n.* recalling, being recalled.

recant' *v.* withdraw and renounce as erroneous or heretical; disavow former opinion etc. recanta'tion *n.*

re'cap *v.* (colloq.) recapitulate. *n.* recapitulation.

recapit'ulate *v.* summarize, restate briefly. ~ā'tion *n.*

recast' (-ah-) *v.t.* (esp.) remodel, reconstruct; give new form or character to.

recce (-k-) *n.* (mil. etc. sl.) reconnaissance.

recd. *abbr.* received.

recede' *v.i.* go or shrink back; slope backwards; withdraw, retreat; decline in value etc.

receipt' (-sēt) *n.* receiving or being received, (usu. pl.) amount of money received; written acknowledgement of receipt of payment etc.; (arch.) place where money is officially received. *v.t.* write or give receipt on or for.

receive' (-sēv) *v.* accept delivery of; take into one's hands or possession; acquire, get; have sent to or conferred etc. on one; be affected or operated on by wireless etc. transmission, convert electro-magnetic waves into perceptible signals; allow, admit; entertain as guest; welcome; accept as true. recei'ver *n.* (esp.) person appointed to administer debtor's or disputed property; one who receives stolen goods; apparatus for receiving transmitted signals etc.

recen'sion (-shn) *n.* revision of text; revised text.

re'cent *a.* not long past, that happened or existed lately; not long established, modern. ~ly *adv.*; rē'cencў *n.*

rěcěp'tacle *n.* vessel, space, or place for receiving or holding.

rěcěp'tion *n.* receiving or being received into place or company; esp. formal or ceremonious (assembly of) welcome; occasion of receiving guests; welcome of specified kind; receiving of wireless etc. signals, efficiency with which they are received. ~-room, room available or suitable for receiving guests. ~ist *n.* person employed to receive clients, patients, etc.

rěcěp'tive *a.* able or quick to receive ideas etc. ~tiv'itў *n.*

rěcěss' *n.* temporary cessation of work etc.; (esp. Parliamentary) vacation; niche or alcove; retired or secret place. *v.* set back; provide with recess(es); take recess.

rěcě'ssion *n.* receding, withdrawal; receding part; temporary decline in activity or prosperity. ~al *a.* & *n.* of recess; (hymn) sung while clergy and choir withdraw after service.

rěcěss'ive *a.* tending to recede; (of inherited character) latent when dominant contrary character is present.

recherché (reshār'shā) *a.* choice; carefully thought out. [F]

rěcid'ivism *n.* habitual relapse into crime. ~ist *n.*

rě'cipē (*or* -ĭ) *n.* statement of ingredients and procedure for preparing dish etc.

rěcip'ient *n.* one who receives.

rěcip'rocal *a.* in return; mutual; expressing mutual relation; inversely correspondent. *n.* (math.) function or expression so related to another that their product is unity.

rěcip'rocāte *v.* interchange; requite, make return (*with*); go with alternate backward and forward motion. ~ā'tion *n.*

rěciprŏ'citў *n.* reciprocal condition, mutual action; principle or practice of give-and-take, esp. between States.

rěci'tal *n.* detailed account or narration *of* facts etc.; programme of music performed by one or two persons.

rěcitā'tion *n.* (esp.) reciting as entertainment; piece recited.

rěcitative' (-ēv) *n.* (words, part, given in) musical declamation between song and ordinary speech.

rěcite' *v.* repeat aloud, declaim, from memory, esp. before audience; rehearse (facts), mention in order, enumerate.

rěck'less *a.* regardless of consequences, rash, heedless.

rěck'on *v.* ascertain number or amount (of) by counting or calculation; count; settle accounts *with*; rely or base plans (*up*)*on*; (colloq.) conclude, suppose, be supposed. ~er *n.* (esp.) aid to reckoning. ~ing *n.* (esp.) tavern bill; *day of* ~*ing*, time of atonement, punishment, etc.

rěclaim' *v.t.* win back from vice or error; reform; civilize; bring (land) under cultivation from sea or from waste state. rěclamā'tion *n.*

rěcline' *v.* assume or be in recumbent position; lie or lean back or on one side.

rěcluse' (-ōōs; *or* rě'-) *n.* person living in retirement or isolation.

rěcogni'tion *n.* recognizing, being recognized; acknowledgement.

rěcŏg'nizance (*or* -kŏn-) *n.* bond by which person engages before court or magistrate to observe some condition; sum pledged as surety for such observance.

rěc'ognize *v.t.* know again, identify as known before; accord notice or consideration to; acknowledge or realize validity, quality, character, claims, etc. of. rěcogni'zable *a.*; ~zabil'itў *n.*

rěcoil' *v.i.* start back, shrink, in horror or disgust or fear; rebound; (of fire-arms) kick. *n.* act or fact or sensation of recoiling.

rěcollěct' *v.t.* succeed in remembering, call to mind. rěcollěc'tion *n.* (esp.) person's memory or time over which it extends; thing remembered, reminiscence.

rěcomměnd' *v.t.* commit *to* care of; speak or write of, suggest, as fit for employment etc.; advise; be recom-

mendation of. **rĕcommĕndā'tion** n.
(esp.) letter etc. recommending
person; quality etc. recommending
thing; advice.

rĕc'ompĕnse v.t. requite; make
amends to; compensate. n. reward;
requital; compensation.

rĕc'oncīle v.t. make friendly after
estrangement; make resigned;
harmonize; make compatible; show
compatibility of. **rĕc'oncīlable** a.;
rĕconcīliā'tion n.

rĕc'ondīte (or rĭkŏn'-) a. abstruse;
obscure.

rĕcondī'tion v.t. restore to proper,
habitable, or usable condition.

rĕcŏnn'aissance (-nĭs-) n. reconnoitring survey or party.

rĕconnoi'tre v. (pres. p. -tring), approach and try to learn position
and condition or strategic features
of (enemy, district, etc.).

rĕcŏn'stītūte v.t. restore former constitution to; constitute again.
rĕcŏnstītū'tion n.

rĕconstrŭct' v.t. construct again,
repair, restore to former condition
or appearance; construct anew in
the mind. **rĕconstrŭc'tion** n. (esp.)
model etc. of something lost or
damaged.

rĕcōrd' v. register, set down for
remembrance or reference; represent in permanent form, esp. for
reproduction. n. (rĕ'-), being recorded, recorded state; (document, monument, etc. preserving)
recorded evidence, information,
etc.; (disc, tape, etc. bearing) trace
from which sounds etc. can be
reproduced; facts known about
person's past, esp. list of previous
crimes, convictions, etc. known to
police; best performance or most
remarkable event of its kind; off
the ∼, unofficial; on ∼, legally or
otherwise recorded. a. best etc.
recorded. ∼-**breaking**, outdoing all
predecessors. ∼-**player**, apparatus
for reproducing sound of record.
recōr'ding n. (esp.) (process of
making) record of performance etc.;
recorded programme, performance,
etc.

recōr'der n. (esp.) city or borough
magistrate holding court of quarter

sessions; recording apparatus;
wood-wind musical instrument
with mouthpiece at end.

rĕcount'[1] v.t. narrate; tell in detail.

rĕcount'[2] v.t. count again. n. (rē'-),
recounting, esp. of votes.

recoup' (-ōōp) v.t. compensate for
(loss); reimburse; ∼ oneself, recover what one has expended or
lost. ∼**ment** n.

recourse' (-ōrs) n. resorting to possible
source of help; thing resorted to.

recov'er (-kŭ-) v. regain possession
or use or control of; reclaim; secure
restitution (of) or compensation
(for) by legal process; bring or come
back to life, health, or normal state
or position; get over, cease to feel
effects of; retrieve. **recov'erў** n.

rĕc'rĕant a. & n. craven, cowardly,
apostate (person). ∼**ancў.**n.

rĕc'rĕāte[1] v.t. refresh, entertain. **rĕ-
crĕā'tion** n. pastime; relaxation;
amusement. ∼**tive** a.

rē-crĕāte'[2] v.t. create anew.

recrim'ināte v.i. retort accusation,
indulge in mutual or counter
charges. **recrimīnā'tion** n.; ∼**ā'-
torў** a.

rĕcrudĕsce' (-ōō-; or rē-) v.i. break out
again. ∼**ĕs'cence** n.; ∼**ĕs'cent** a.

recruit' (-ōōt) n. newly enlisted
soldier; person who joins society
etc. v. enlist recruits (for), enlist
(person); replenish, reɪnvigorate.
∼**ment** n.

rĕc'tal a. of rectum.

rĕc'tăngle (-nggl) n. plane rectilinear
four-sided figure with four right
angles. **rĕctăng'ūlar** a.

rĕc'tīfў v.t. put right, correct; exchange for what is right; (chem.)
purify, esp. by redistilling; change
(electric current) from alternating
to direct. **rĕctīfīcā'tion** n.

rĕctilin'ear, **-ĕal** aa. in or forming
straight line; bounded or characterized by straight lines.

rĕc'tītūde n. moral uprightness.

rĕc'tō n. right-hand page of open
book; front of leaf.

rĕc'tor n. parson of parish retaining
tithe; head parish priest; Episcopal
clergyman having charge of congregation; head of some educational
or religious institutions. **rĕctōr'ial** a.;

~ship *n*. **rĕc'torў** *n*. rector's benefice or house.

rĕc'tum *n*. final section of large intestine.

rĕcŭm'bent *a*. lying, reclining.

rĕcū'perāte *v*. restore, be restored, recover, from exhaustion, illness, loss, etc. ~ā'tion *n*.; ~ative *a*.

rĕcūr' *v.i.* go back in thought or speech; return *to* mind etc.; occur again; (math., of decimal figure etc.) be repeated indefinitely. **rĕcŭ'rrence** *n*. **rĕcŭ'rrent** *a*. occurring again, often, or periodically.

rĕcūrve' *v*. bend backwards.

rĕc'ūsant (-z-; *or* rĭkū'-) *n*. & *a*. (hist.) (person) refusing to attend Ch. of England services; (person) refusing submission or compliance. ~ancў *n*.

rĕd *a*. of colour varying from crimson to orange; having to do with bloodshed, burning, violence, or revolution; communist. *n*. red colour; red cloth or clothes; red ball at billiards; debtor side of account; radical, republican or (esp.) communist; *in the* ~, insolvent, in debt; *see* ~, be so angry as to lose self-control. ~ **admiral**, kind of butterfly. **R~ Army**, Soviet-Russian army. ~ **biddy**, mixture of cheap red wine and methylated spirit. ~-**blooded**, full of vigour and zest. ~**breast**, robin. ~-**brick**, of modern English university or universities. ~**cap**, military policeman. ~**coat**, (hist.) British soldier. ~ **cross**, St. George's cross, emblem of England; (emblem of) international societies for care of wounded etc. in war. ~ **ensign**, flag of British merchant-ships. ~ **flag**, symbol of revolution or socialism; danger signal. ~-**handed**, in act of crime. ~ **herring**, smoked herring; subject, fact, etc. introduced to distract attention from point in hand. ~-**hot**, heated to redness; furious, excited. **R~ Indian**, Amer. Indian. ~ **lead**, red oxide of lead as pigment etc. ~-**letter day**, joyfully memorable day. ~ **light**, danger signal. ~**poll**, kinds of bird. ~ **rag**, thing that excites rage. ~**shank**, kind of snipe. ~**skin**, American Indian. ~**start**, red-tailed European song-

bird. ~ **tape**, excessive adherence to forms in official transactions. ~**wing**, kinds of bird. ~**wood**. (esp.) tall Californian timber-tree.

rĕdd'en *v*.; **rĕdd'ĭsh** *a*.

rĕdăn' *n*. field-work with two faces forming salient angle.

rĕdeem' *v.t.* buy back; recover by expenditure of effort; compound for by payment; perform (promise); save, rescue, reclaim; deliver from sin; make amends, compensate, for. **rĕdee'mer**, *n*. one who ransoms or redeems, esp. Christ. **rĕdĕmp'tion** *n*.; **rĕdĕmp'tive** *a*.

rĕdĕploy'ment *n*. transfer, re-allocation (*of* troops, labour, etc.).

rĕdĭn'tĕgrāte *v.t.* restore to wholeness or unity. **rĕdĭntĕgrā'tion** *n*.

rĕd'olent *a*. smelling strongly, strongly suggestive *of*. ~**ence** *n*.

rĕdoub'le[1] (-ŭbl) *v*. intensify; increase, multiply.

rĕdoub'le[2] (-ŭbl) *v.t.* double again. *n*. instance of redoubling.

rĕdoubt' (-owt) *n*. detached out-work without flanking defences.

rĕdoubt'able (-owt-) *a*. formidable.

rĕdound' *v.i.* result in, have effect of, contributing *to* advantage, credit, etc.

rĕdress' *v.t.* put right again; remedy, make up for. *n*. redressing; compensation, reparation.

rĕduce' *v*. bring down; lower; weaken; impoverish; diminish; subdue; bring, come, convert, etc. *to* other form etc.; restore to proper position parts displaced by (fracture etc.); reduce one's weight. **rĕdū'cer** *n*. (esp.) agent for reducing density of photographic negatives. **rĕdū'cible** *a*.

rĕdŭc'tion *n*. reducing or being reduced; reduced copy.

rĕdŭn'dant *a*. superfluous, excessive; pleonastic; copious, luxuriant; dispensed with as no longer needed. ~**ance**, ~**ancў** *nn*.

rĕdū'plĭcāte *v.t.* make double; repeat. ~ā'tion *n*. (esp., gram.) repetition of syllable or letter in word-formation.

rē-ĕch'ō (-k-) *v*. echo; go on echoing, resound.

reed *n*. (tall straight stalk of) kinds of

firm-stemmed water or marsh plant; (growth of) reeds; vibrating part of some musical instruments; (pl.) reed instruments; weaver's instrument for separating warp--threads and beating up weft; small semi-cylindrical moulding. *v.t.* thatch with reed; make into, fit with, reed. **ree′dy̆** *a.* (esp.) like reed-instrument in tone.

rē-ĕd′ĭt *v.t.* edit again, make new edition of.

reef[1] *n.* one of several strips along top or bottom of sail that can be taken in or rolled up. *v.* take in reef(s) of sail. **~-knot,** symmetrical double knot. **ree′fer**[1] *n.* (esp.) close double-breasted stout jacket.

reef[2] *n.* ridge of rock, sand, etc., about level with water's surface; lode or vein cf auriferous quartz, bed rock.

ree′fer[2] *n.* marijuana cigarette.

reek *n.* foul or stale smell; smoke, vapour, exhalation. *v.i.* smell unpleasantly (*of*); emit vapour, steam; emit smoke.

reel[1] *n.* kinds of winding-apparatus; cylinder for holding wound cotton, wire, etc.; quantity of cinema film etc. wound on one reel; (*straight*) *off the* **~,** without stopping. *v.* wind on, take *off*, reel; draw *in*, *up*, etc. by use of reel; rattle *off* without pause or apparent effort.

reel[2] *v.i.* be in a whirl, be dizzy; sway, stagger; be shaken. *n.* reeling motion or sensation.

reel[3] *n.* (music for) lively esp. Sc. dance, usu. of two or four couples.

rē-ĕn′trant *a. & n.* (angle) that points inward.

rē-ĕn′try̆ *n.* (esp., bridge etc.) *card of* **~,** high card that can be relied on to give holder lead.

reeve[1] *n.* (hist.) chief magistrate of town or district; (Canada) president of village or town council.

reeve[2] *v.t.* (naut.) pass rope etc. *through* ring etc.; thread or fasten with rope etc.

reeve[3] *n.* female of ruff.

ref. *abbr.* (sl.) referee; reference.

rĕfĕc′tion *n.* slight meal; refreshment by food or drink.

rĕfĕc′tory̆ (*or* rĕf′ĭ-) *n.* room for meals

in monastery etc. **~ table,** long narrow table.

rĕfĕr′ *v.* trace or ascribe *to*; assign *to*; send on or direct *to* some authority or source of information; have relation, make allusion, *to*; **~ back,** postpone consideration of by referring *to* committee etc. **rĕf′erable** *a.*

referee′ *n.* arbitrator, person chosen to decide between opposing parties; umpire, esp. in football. *v.* act as referee (in).

rĕf′erence *n.* referring (*back*) to some authority; scope given to such authority; relation, respect, allusion, etc. *to*; direction *to* page, book, etc. where information may be found; person vouching for another; testimonial. **~ book,** book not for continuous reading but to consult on occasion. **~ library,** library of books that can be consulted but not taken away. **rĕferĕn′tial** *a.*

rĕferĕn′dum *n.* referring of question to electorate for direct decision.

rē′fĭll *n.* what serves to refill anything. *v.t.* (-ĭl′), fill again.

rĕfīne′ *v.* free from impurities or defects; purify, clarify; make elegant or cultured; employ subtlety of thought or language; improve (*up*)*on* by introducing refinements. **~ment** *n.* (esp.) fineness of feeling or taste; subtle or ingenious manifestation *of*, piece of elaborate arrangement. **refi′ner** *n.* **refi′nery̆** *n.* place where raw material is refined.

rĕfĭt′ *v.* restore (ship etc.) to serviceable condition; fit again; undergo refitting. *n.* (rē′-), process of refitting. **~ment** *n.*

rĕflā′tion *n.* restoration of currency to previous condition after deflation.

rĕflĕct′ *v.* throw back (light, heat, sound); (of mirror etc.) show image (of); reproduce to eye or mind; bring credit, discredit, etc. *on*; meditate, consider; make disparaging remarks *on*. **rĕflĕc′tion,** **-ĕxion** (-kshn) *n.* reflected light, heat, colour, or image; thing bringing discredit *on*; thought; reconsideration. **~ive** *a.* (esp.) thoughtful, given to meditation. **~or** *n.*

body or surface reflecting rays, esp. in required direction.

rē′flĕx *n*. reflected light or image; reproduction; reflex action. *a*. recurved; reflected; of, connected with, etc., reflex action. **~ action**, involuntary action of muscle etc. as automatic response to stimulus of sensory nerve. **~ angle**, angle larger than 180°. **~ camera**, photographic camera in which reflected image can be seen up to moment of exposure. **rēflĕxed′** (-kst) *a*. bent or folded back.

reflexion : see **reflection**.

rėflĕx′ĭve *a*. & *n*. (word, form) implying agent's action on himself; (verb) indicating identity of subject and object; (pronoun etc.) referring to subject.

rĕf′luent (-ŏŏ-) *a*. flowing back. *n*. condensed vapour flowing back into still etc. **~ence** *n*.

rē′flŭx *n*. flowing back; ebb.

rėfōrm′ *v*. make or become better; abolish or cure abuses etc. *n*. removal of abuse(s) esp. in politics; amendment; improvement. **~ative** *a*.

rĕformā′tion *n*. reforming, being reformed, esp. radical change for the better in political or religious or social affairs; *the R~*, 16th-c. movement for reform of Church of Rome ending in establishment of Reformed or Protestant Churches.

rėfōr′matorў *a*. tending or intended to produce reform. *n*. reformatory institution, esp. for juvenile offenders.

rėfōr′mer *n*. (esp.) advocate or supporter of parliamentary reform; leader in Reformation.

rėfrăct′ *v.t.* deflect (light) at certain angle at point of passage from medium of different density. **rėfrăc′tion, rėfrăc′tor** *nn*.; **rėfrăc′tive** *a*.

rėfrăc′torў *a*. stubborn, unmanageable; rebellious; resistant to heat, treatment, etc.

rėfrain′[1] *n*. recurring phrase or line, esp. at end of stanzas.

rėfrain′[2] *v*. hold back, keep oneself from some act etc. or *from* indulgence, action, etc.

rėfrĕsh′ *v.t.* make feel fresher; provide with refreshment; freshen up (memory). **~er** *n*. (esp.) extra fee to counsel in prolonged case. **rėfrĕsh′ment** *n*. (esp., usu. pl.) light repast, food and drink.

rėfrĭ′gerant *a*. & *n*. (substance) serving to refrigerate.

rėfrĭ′gerāte *v.t.* make cool or cold; expose (food etc.) to low temperature, esp. to preserve it. **~ā′tion** *n*. **rėfrĭ′gerātor** *n*. cabinet or room or apparatus for refrigerating.

rĕft *p.p.* & *pred. a*. taken or torn (*away*, *from*).

rĕf′ūge *n*. shelter from pursuit or danger or trouble; person, course, etc. giving shelter or resorted to in difficulties. **rĕfūgee′** *n*. person escaped, esp. abroad, from persecution, war, etc.

rėfŭl′gent *a*. shining, gloriously bright. **~ence** *n*.

rėfŭnd′ *v*. pay back; reimburse. *n*. (rē′-), repayment, money etc. repaid.

rėfū′sal (-z-) *n*. refusing; chance of taking thing before it is offered to others.

rėfūse′[1] (-z) *v*. reject; deny what is solicited or required; not accept; (of horse) fail to take jump (at).

rĕf′ūse[2] *n*. & *a*. (what is) rejected as worthless or left over after use etc.

rėfūte′ *v.t.* prove falsity or error of; rebut by argument. **rĕfūtā′tion** *n*.

rėgain′ *v.t.* recover possession of; reach (place) again; recover (*footing* etc.).

rē′gal *a*. of or by kings; magnificent. **rėgăl′itў** *n*.

rėgāle′ *v.t.* entertain choicely (*with*); give delight to.

rėgā′lĭa *n.pl.* insignia of royalty used at coronation etc.; insignia of order.

rėgārd′ *v*. gaze upon; give heed to, take into account; have respect or reverence for; look on *as*, consider; concern, have relation to; *as ~s*, so far as relates to. *n*. look; attention, heed, care, concern; esteem; (pl.) friendly feelings. **rėgārd′ful** *a*. **rėgār′ding** *prep*. concerning, relating to. **rėgārd′less** *o*. (freq. sl. as *adv*., taking no account of expense, consequences, etc.).

rėgár′dant *a.* (her.) looking backward.

rėgátt′a *n.* meeting for boat or yacht races.

rē′gencў *n.* (period of) office of regent or commission acting as regent; *R~*, period (1810–20) when George, Prince of Wales, was regent. *a.* of or in style of Régency.

rėgĕn′erāte *v.t.* invest with new and higher spiritual nature; improve moral condition of; breathe more vigorous life into. *a.* (-at), spiritually born again; reformed. **rėgĕnerā′tion** *n.*

rē′gent *n.* person administering kingdom during minority, absence, or incapacity of monarch; member of governing board in some universities. *a.* (placed after *n.*) acting as, having position of, regent.

rė′gĭcīde *n.* killer or participator in killing of king; killing of king. **rė′gĭcīdal** *a.*

régime, re- (rāzhēm′) *n.* method of government; prevailing system of things; regimen.

rė′gĭmen *n.* prescribed course of treatment, way of life, or esp. diet.

rė′gĭment *n.* permanent unit of army consisting of several battalions or troops or companies; large array or number. *v.t.* form into regiment(s), organize in groups or according to system. **rėgĭmĕn′tal** *a.* **rėgĭmĕn′tals** *n.pl.* military uniform, regimental dress. **~ā′tion** *n.*

rē′gion (-jn) *n.* tract of country; district etc. of more or less definitely marked boundaries or characteristics; separate part of world etc.; sphere or realm *of*; part round some bodily organ. **rē′gional** *a.*

rė′gĭster *n.* book in which items are recorded for reference; official list; compass of voice or instrument; recording indicator of speed etc.; adjustable plate for regulating draught etc.; exact correspondence in position etc., esp. of successive impressions in colour--printing. *v.* record; enter or cause to be entered in register; enter name in register; make mental note of; make impression; (make) correspond exactly; record automatic-

ally, indicate; show (emotion etc.) in face etc. **rėgĭstrā′tion** *n.*

rėgĭstrar′ *n.* person charged with keeping register.

rė′gĭstrў *n.* place where registers are kept. **~ office,** (esp.) place where registers of births etc. are kept and marriages are performed without religious ceremony; employment agency for domestic servants.

Rē′gĭus *a.* of, holding, certain chairs at some British universities.

rėg′nant *a.* reigning.

rē′grĕss *n.* going back; backward tendency. *v.i.* (rĭgrĕs′), move backwards. **rėgrĕ′ssion** *n.* backward movement; relapse, reversion. **rėgrĕss′ĭve** *a.*

rėgrĕt′ *v.t.* be sorry for loss of; be sorry for something past; grieve at; deplore, express regret at. *n.* sorrow for loss; repentance or sorrow for something done or left undone; (intimation of) disappointment at inability to do something. **~ful, rėgrĕtt′able** *aa.*

rėgroup′ (-ōop) *v.* form, form into, new group(s).

regt. *abbr.* regiment.

rĕg′ūlar *a.* following or exhibiting a principle; consistent; systematic; habitual; not capricious or casual; not defective or amateur; acting or done uniformly; correct; (eccl.) bound by religious rule, belonging to monastic order. *n.* one of regular clergy; soldier of regular or standing army (usu. in pl.). **~ army,** of professional soldiers. **rĕgūlă′ritў** *n.*; **~īze** *v.t.*; **~īzā′tion** *n.*

rĕg′ūlāte *v.t.* control by rule, subject to restrictions; adapt to requirements; adjust (watch etc.) to work accurately. **~ātor** *n.* (esp.) device for regulating watch etc., or passage of steam, air, etc.

rĕgūlā′tion *n.* regulating or being regulated; prescribed rule, authoritative direction; (attrib.) ordinary, usual, formal.

rėgŭr′gĭtāte *v.* gush back; pour or cast out again. **~ā′tion** *n.*

rēhabĭl′ĭtāte *v.t.* restore to rights, reputation, etc.; restore to previous condition, normal health or capacity, etc. **~tā′tion** *n.*

rēhăsh′ *v.t.* put into new form without real change or improvement. *n.* presentation of same material in new form.

rèhearse′ (-hêrs) *v.* recite, say over; give list of, enumerate; practise before performing in public. **rèhear′sal** *n.*

Reich (rīch) *n.* German State; *Third* ~, Nazi régime.

reign (rān) *n.* sovereignty, rule; sway; sovereign's period of rule. *v.i.* be king or queen, rule; prevail.

rēĭmbûrse′ *v.t.* repay (person); refund. ~**ment** *n.*

rein (rān) *n.* long narrow strap used to guide horse; means of control. *v.t.* check, pull *back* or *up*, hold *in*, with reins; govern, control.

rēĭncârnā′tion *n.* renewed or repeated incarnation, esp. successive incarnations in new bodies of soul after death. **rēĭncâr′nate** *a.* & *v.t.*

rein′deer (rān-) *n.* deer of cold climates used for drawing sledges etc.

rēĭnfôrce′ *v.t.* support or strengthen by additional men or material. **reinforced concrete**, with metal bars, gratings, or wire embedded in it. ~**ment** *n.* (esp., freq. pl.) additional men, ships, etc.

reins (rānz) *n.pl.* (arch.) kidneys; loins.

rēĭnstāte′ *v.t.* re-establish *in*, restore to, lost position, privileges, etc.; restore to health or proper order. ~**ment** *n.*

rēĭnsure′ (-shoor) *v.* insure again, esp. against loss that one has underwritten. **rēĭnsur′ance** *n.*

rēĭt′erāte *v.t.* repeat over again or several times. ~**ā′tion** *n.*; ~**ative** *a.*

rei′ver (rē-) *n.* (arch.) marauder, raider.

rèjĕct′ *v.t.* put aside or discard as not to be accepted, believed, used, etc.; cast up again. *n.* (rē′-), rejected thing or person.

rèjoice′ *v.* cause joy to, make glad; feel joy, be glad; make merry, celebrate event. **rèjoi′cing** *n.* (esp., pl.) festivities.

rèjoin′ *v.* say in answer; retort; join again. **rèjoin′der** *n.* what is rejoined or said in reply.

rèju′venāte (-ōō-) *v.* make or grow young again. ~**ā′tion** *n.*

rèlăpse′ *v.i.* fall back into worse state after improvement. *n.* relapsing, esp. deterioration in patient's condition after partial recovery.

rèlāte′ *v.* narrate, recount; bring into relation; have reference or stand in some relation *to*. **rèlā′tĕd** *a.* connected, allied, akin by blood or marriage.

rèlā′tion *n.* narration, narrative; connexion between persons or things; kinsman, kinswoman, relative. ~**al** *a.*; ~**ship** *n.*

rĕl′ative *a.* in relation or proportion to something else; involving or implying comparison or relation; having application or reference *to*; (gram.) referring to expressed or implied antecedent, attached to antecedent by relative word. *n.* one related by blood or marriage; relative thing or term or word, esp. pronoun.

rĕlativ′itў *n.* (esp.) theory of universe, showing that all motion is relative and treating space and time as four related dimensions.

rèlăx′ *v.* (cause or allow to) become loose or slack or limp; abate, mitigate; grow less tense, rigid, etc. **rèlaxā′tion** *n.* partial remission *of* penalty etc.; cessation from work, recreation, amusement; diminution of tension, pressure, etc. **rèlăx′ing** *a.* (esp.) enervating.

rèlay′ (*or* rē′-) *n.* set of fresh horses to replace tired ones; gang of men, supply of materials, etc. similarly used; switch etc. by which one electric current is made to control another; relaying, programme etc. relayed. *v.t.* provide with, replace by, etc., relays; pass on or re-broadcast (message, radio programme, etc.) received from another source. ~ **race**, between teams of which each person does part of distance.

rèlease′ *v.t.* set free, liberate, deliver; unfasten; remit, make over to another; exhibit etc. (film etc.) generally or for first time; make (information) public. *n.* liberation from confinement, fixed position, trouble, etc.; written discharge, receipt; conveyance of right or estate; first or general exhibition, offering for sale, etc. of film, book, etc., film etc. so shown, offered, etc.

rĕl'ĕgāte v.t. consign or dismiss to usu. inferior position, sphere, etc., esp. transfer (football team) to lower division of league. **rĕlĕgā'tion** n.

rĕlĕnt' v.i. relax severity; give way to compassion. **rĕlĕnt'less** a.

rĕl'ĕvant a. bearing upon, pertinent to, matter in hand. **~ance, ~ancy** nn.

rĕlī'able a. that may be relied upon. **~bĭl'ĭtў** n.

rĕlī'ance n. trust, confidence; thing depended on. **rĕlī'ant** a.

rĕl'ĭc n. part of holy person's body or belongings kept as object of reverence; (pl.) dead body, remains, of person; what has survived destruction or wasting; surviving trace or memorial of.

rĕl'ĭct n. widow.

rĕlief'[1] n. alleviation of or deliverance from pain, distress, etc.; assistance given to poor, esp. formerly under Poor Law, or to victims of disaster etc.; delivery of place from siege; (replacing by) person(s) appointed to take turn of duty.

rĕlief'[2] n. method of carving, moulding, etc., in which design projects from surface; piece of sculpture etc. in relief; effect of relief given by colour, shading, etc.; distinctness of outline.

rĕlieve' v.t. bring, give, be, relief to; bring into relief, make stand out.

rĕlī'gion (-jn) n. system of faith and worship; human recognition of personal God or gods entitled to obedience; monastic state. **rĕlī'gious** a. imbued with religion; devout; n. person bound by monastic vows.

rĕlĭn'quĭsh v.t. give up, let go, resign, surrender. **~ment** n.

rĕl'ĭquarў n. receptacle for relic(s).

rĕl'ĭsh n. distinctive flavour or taste of; enjoyment of food or other things; zest; liking for; thing eaten with plainer food to add flavour. v. get pleasure out of, be pleased with; smack of.

rĕlŭc'tant a. unwilling, disinclined. **~ance** n.

rĕlў' v.i. put one's trust, depend with confidence, (up)on.

rĕmain' v.i. be left over; abide, stay in same place or condition; be left behind; continue to be. **rĕmain'der** n. residue; remaining persons or things; unsold stock, esp. of books; residual interest; v.t. dispose of remaining stock of (book) at reduced price. **rĕmains'** (-z) n.pl. what remains over; surviving parts or amount; relic(s) of antiquity etc.; dead body.

rĕmand' (-ah-) v.t. send back (prisoner) into custody to allow of further inquiry. n. recommittal to custody. **~ home**, place of detention for juvenile offenders.

rĕmărk' v. take notice of, perceive; observe; say by way of comment; make comment (up)on. n. noticing; comment; thing said. **~able** a. worth notice; exceptional; striking.

R.E.M.E. abbr. Royal Electrical and Mechanical Engineers.

rĕm'ĕdў n. cure for disease or any evil; healing medicine or treatment; redress. v.t. rectify, make good. **rĕmē'diable, rĕmē'dial** aa.

rĕmĕm'ber v.t. retain in, recall to, memory; not forget; make present to, tip; convey greetings from. **~brance** n. memory, recollection; keepsake; (pl.) greetings conveyed through third person. **~brancer** n. title of certain officials.

rĕmind' v.t. put in mind of, to do, etc.; cause to remember. **rĕmin'der** n. thing that reminds or is meant to remind.

rĕmĭnĭsce' v.i. (colloq.) indulge in reminiscence(s). **rĕminĭs'cence** n. remembering; something recalling something else; remembered fact or incident; (pl.) collection of memories etc. in literary form. **rĕminĭs'cent** a. recalling past things, given to or concerned with remembering; reminding or suggestive of.

rĕmiss' a. careless of duty; negligent; lacking energy.

rĕmĭ'ssion n. forgiveness of sins etc.; remittance of debt etc.; diminution of force etc. **rĕmĭss'ible** *a.* that may be remitted.

rĕmĭt' *v.* pardon (sins, etc.); refrain from exacting or inflicting (debt, punishment, etc.); abate, slacken; refer *to* some authority, send back to lower court; send (esp. money). **rĕmĭtt'ance** *n.* sending of money, money sent. **rĕmĭtt'ent** *a.* & *n.* (fever) that abates at intervals.

rĕm'nant *n.* small remaining quantity or piece or number.

rĕmŏn'strance *n.* remonstrating; protest.

rĕm'onstrāte (*or* rĭmŏn'-) *v.* make protest; urge in remonstrance; ~ *with*, expostulate with, reprove.

rĕmŏrse' *n.* bitter repentance; compunction. ~**ful**, ~**less** *aa.*

rĕmōte' *a.* far apart; far away in place or time; not closely related; distant *from*; out-of-the-way, secluded. ~ **control**, control from a distance.

rēmount' *v.* mount again; provide with fresh horse(s). *n.* horse to replace one killed or worn out.

rĕmo'vable (-mōō-) *a.* that can be removed. ~**bĭl'ĭtȳ** *n.*

rĕmo'val (-ōō-) *n.* removing, being removed.

rĕmove' (-ōōv) *v.* take off or away from place occupied; convey to another place; dismiss; change one's residence, go away *from*. *n.* stage in gradation; promotion to higher form at school; form in some schools. **removed'** *a.* distant or remote *from*; (of cousins) *once*, *twice*, etc. ~*d*, with difference of one, two, etc. generations.

rĕmū'nerāte *v.t.* pay for service rendered. ~**ā'tion** *n.* pay. ~**ative** *a.* profitable.

Rĕnaiss'ance *n.* revival of arts and letters in 14–16 cc.; style of art and architecture developed by it; (r~), any similar revival.

rē'nal *a.* of kidneys.

rĕnăs'cence *n.* rebirth; renaissance. **rĕnăs'cent** *a.* springing up anew; being reborn.

rĕnd *v.* (*rĕnt*), tear or wrench; split or divide.

rĕn'der *v.t.* give in return; pay as due; present, submit; reproduce, por-

tray; execute, translate; melt (fat) *down*; give (first) coat of plaster etc. to. ~**ing** *n.* (esp.) version; interpretation, performance.

rendezvous (rŏn'dāvōō) *n.* (pl. same, pr. -ōōz), place appointed for assembling or meeting; meeting by appointment. *v.i.* meet at rendezvous.

rĕndĭ'tion *n.* (esp.) rendering, performance.

rĕn'egāde *n.* deserter of party or principles; apostate.

rĕnēge' (-g; *or* -ĭg) *v.i.* go back on promise, back out.

rĕnew' *v.* make (as good as) new; patch, fill up, replace; begin, make, say, etc. anew. **rĕnew'al** *n.*

rĕnn'ĕt[1] *n.* curdled milk from calf's stomach, artificial preparation, used in curdling milk for cheese etc.

rĕnn'ĕt[2] *n.* kinds of dessert apple.

rĕnounce' *v.t.* consent formally to abandon; surrender, give up; repudiate; withdraw from, discontinue; forsake.

rĕn'ovāte *v.t.* restore to good condition or vigour; repair. **rĕnovā'tion** *n.*

rĕnown' *n.* fame, high distinction; being celebrated. ~**ed** *a.* famous.

rĕnt[1], *p.t.* & *p.p.* of **rend**.

rĕnt[2] *n.* tear in garment etc.; gap, cleft, fissure.

rĕnt[3] *n.* periodical payment for use of land, house, room; payment for hire of machinery etc. *v.* take, occupy, or use at rent; let or hire for rent; be let (at). **rĕn'tal** *n.* sum payable as rent; income from rents.

rentier (rahṅ'tyā) *n.* person deriving income from property, investments, etc. [F]

rĕnŭncĭā'tion *n.* renouncing, document expressing this; self-denial, giving up of things.

rĕp[1], **rĕpp** *n.* corded upholstery fabric.

rĕp[2] *n.* (colloq.) repertory (theatre).

rĕpaint' *v.t.* paint again. *n.* (rē'-), repainted golf-ball.

rĕpair'[1] *v.i.* resort; go (*to*).

rĕpair'[2] *v.t.* restore to good condition, renovate, mend; remedy; make amends for. *n.* restoring to sound condition; condition for working or using.

rĕp'arable *a.* that can be repaired or made good.

rĕparā'tion *n.* recompense for injury; compensation, esp. (pl.) that paid by defeated country for damage done in war.

rĕpartee' *n.* witty retort; (making of) witty retorts.

rĕpast' (-ah-) *n.* meal.

rĕpā'triăte (*or* -pă-) *v.t.* restore or return to native land. **~ā'tion** *n.*

rĕpay' *v.* (*repaid*), pay back; return, retaliate; requite, recompense. **~ment** *n.*

rĕpeal' *v.t.* annul, revoke. *n.* repealing, revocation.

rĕpeat' *v.* say or do over again; recite, rehearse; reproduce; recur. *n.* (mus.) passage to be repeated; repeating, thing repeated. **rĕpea'tĕdly** *adv.* **rĕpea'ter** *n.* (esp.) watch etc. striking hours etc. when required; fire-arm firing several shots without reloading.

rĕpĕl' *v.t.* drive back, repulse; ward off; be repulsive or distasteful to. **rĕpĕll'ent** *a.*

rĕpĕnt' *v.* feel regret, contrition, etc. for what one has done or left undone; think with regret or contrition *of.* **rĕpĕn'tance** *n.*; **~ant** *a.*

rĕpercŭ'ssion *n.* recoil after impact; indirect effect or reaction (*of*).

rĕp'ertoire (-twar) *n.* stock of pieces etc. that performer or company is accustomed or prepared to give.

rĕp'ertorў *n.* repertoire. **~ company, theatre,** etc., one having stock of plays ready for performance, or presenting different play each week etc.

rĕpĕti'tion *n.* repeating or being repeated; copy, replica; saying by heart, piece to be so said. **~ti'tious, rĕpĕt'ĭtĭve** *aa.*

rĕpine' *v.i.* fret, be discontented.

rĕplāce' *v.t.* put back in place; take or fill up place of, provide substitute for; (pass.) be succeeded or superseded (*by*). **~ment** *n.*

rĕplay' *v.t.* play (match) again after abandonment or draw. *n.* (rē'-), replayed match.

rĕplĕn'ish *v.t.* fill up again (*with*). **~ment** *n.*

rĕplēte' *a.* filled, well stocked, stuffed, sated. **rĕplē'tion** *n.*

rĕp'lĭca *n.* duplicate made by original artist; exact copy, facsimile.

rĕplŷ' *v.* make answer, respond. *n.* replying; what is replied.

rĕpôrt' *v.* bring back account of; tell as news; make official or formal statement; inform against; take down, write description of, etc. for publication; give account of. *n.* common talk, rumour; repute; account given or opinion formally expressed after investigation; account by teacher of pupil's conduct and progress; description, reproduction, or epitome of speech, law case, scene, etc., esp. for newspaper publication; sound of explosion. **rĕpôr'tage** (-ahzh) *n.* (style of) reporting for press. **rĕpôr'ter** *n.* (esp.) person reporting for newspaper.

rĕpōse'[1] (-z) *v.t.* place (trust etc.) *in.*

rĕpōse'[2] (-z) *v.* rest, lay to rest, give rest to; be lying or laid; be supported or based *on.* *n.* rest; sleep; peaceful state, tranquillity; restful effect. **~ful** *a.*

rĕpŏs'ĭtorў (-z-) *n.* receptacle; place where things are stored or may be found; recipient of secrets etc.

rĕpou'ssé (-oosā) *a.* & *n.* (ornamental metal work) hammered into relief from reverse side.

repp : see **rep**[1].

repr. *abbr.* represent etc.; reprinted.

rĕprĕhĕnd' *v.t.* rebuke, censure. **~hĕn'sible** *a.*; **~hĕn'sion** *n.*

rĕprĕsĕnt' (-z-) *v.t.* place likeness of before mind or senses; make out to be; allege that; describe or depict as; reproduce in action or show, perform, play; symbolize, stand for, correspond to; be substitute or deputy for, esp. be accredited deputy for in legislative assembly etc. **rĕprĕsĕntā'tion** *n.*; **~ā'tional** *a.*

rĕprĕsĕn'tatĭve (-z-) *a.* serving to represent; esp. typical of class, containing typical specimens; of or based on representation of body of persons, esp. whole people, in government or legislation. *n.* sample, specimen; typical embodiment *of*; agent; person representing another, section of community, etc.

rĕprĕss' v.t. keep under; put down; suppress. **~ĭble, ~ĭve** aa.; **reprĕ's-sion** n.

rĕprieve' v.t. suspend or cancel execution of. n. remission or commutation of capital sentence.

rĕp'rĭmand (-ah-) n. official rebuke. v.t. rebuke officially.

rĕprĭnt' v.t. print again. n. (rē'-), new impression, esp. without alterations.

rĕprī'sal (-z-) n. retaliation.

rĕproach' v.t. upbraid, scold; convey reproach to. n. upbraiding, censure; thing that brings discredit. **~ful** a.

rĕp'robāte v.t. express or feel disapproval of; (of God) cast off. a. & n. (-āt or -ĭt), (person) cast off by God, hardened in sin, of abandoned character, etc. **~ā'tion** n.

rĕprodūce' v. produce again; produce copy or representation of; carry on (species etc.) by breeding or propagation. **~cible** a. **rĕprodŭc'tion** n. (esp.) breeding or propagation; copy. **rĕprodŭc'tive** a.

rĕproŏf' n. (expression of) blame. **rĕprove'** (-ōŏv) v.t. rebuke, blame.

rĕp'tĭle n. crawling animal; member of cold-blooded lung-breathing class of vertebrates including snakes; mean grovelling person. **rĕptĭl'ĭan** a.

rĕpŭb'lĭc n. State in which supreme power rests in people and their elected representatives.

rĕpŭb'lĭcan a. of, characterizing, etc. republic(s); advocating or supporting republican government; R~, of U.S. political party opposed to Democrats. n. supporter or advocate of republican government; R~, member or supporter of Republican party.

rĕpū'dĭāte v. disown, disavow, deny; refuse to recognize or obey (authority) or discharge (obligation). **~ā'tion** n.

rĕpŭg'nance n. aversion, disinclination; inconsistency or incompatibility of ideas, tempers, etc. **rĕpŭg'nant** a. distasteful; contradictory, incompatible.

rĕpŭlse' v.t. drive back; rebuff, reject. n. defeat, rebuff. **rĕpŭl'sion** n. tendency of bodies to repel each other; aversion. **rĕpŭl'sive** a. exciting repulsion; loathsome, disgusting.

rĕp'ūtable a. of good repute.

rĕpūtā'tion n. what is generally said or believed about character of person or thing; credit, respectability, good fame; the credit or distinction of.

rĕpūte' n. what is generally thought or supposed; reputation. **rĕpū'tĕd** p.p. & a. generally considered, reckoned, spoken, or reported of; supposed, accounted, reckoned.

rĕquĕst' n. asking for something, thing asked for; being sought after, demand. v.t. seek permission to do; ask to be given, favoured with, etc.; ask.

rĕ'quĭĕm n. mass for dead; musical setting for this.

rĕquīre' v.t. demand, order; ask as of right; lay down as imperative; need, call for. **~ment** n.

rĕ'quĭsĭte (-z-) a. needed, required. n. what is required or necessary.

rĕquĭsĭ'tion (-z-) n. formal demand, usu. in writing; order to furnish supplies for army etc. v.t. demand supply or use of; press into service.

rĕquīte' v.t. make return for; reward or avenge; give in return. **rĕquī'tal** n.

rere'dŏs (rēr̄d-) n. ornamental screen covering wall at back of altar.

rĕscĭnd' v.t. abrogate, revoke, cancel. **rĕscĭ'ssion** (-zhn) n.

rĕ'scrĭpt n. edict or official pronouncement.

rĕs'cūe v.t. deliver from attack, custody, danger, or harm. n. rescuing, being rescued.

rĕsearch' (-sĕr̄-) n. careful search or inquiry; endeavour to discover facts by study or investigation; course of critical investigation. v.i. engage in research(es).

rĕs'ĕda (-z-) n. dull greyish-green colour.

rĕsĕm'ble (-z-) v.t. be like; have similarity to. **rĕsĕm'blance** n.

rĕsĕnt' (-z-) v.t. show or feel indignation at; feel injured or insulted by. **~ful** a.; **~ment** n.

rĕservā'tion (-z-) n. (esp.) express or tacit limitation or exception; tract of land reserved esp. for exclusive occupation of group, tribe, etc.; practice of retaining portion of Eucharistic elements after celebration; engaging of seats etc. in advance, seats etc. so engaged.

rĕsẽrve' (-z-) v.t. postpone use or enjoyment or treatment of; hold over; retain possession or control of; set apart (for); engage (seat etc.) in advance. n. something reserved for future use; part of assets held in cash etc., of profits not distributed, etc.; tract reserved for native tribe, wild animals, etc.; troops held in reserve; forces outside regular army and navy liable to be called out in emergencies; (in games) extra player chosen in case substitute should be needed; limitation or qualification; self-restraint; reticence, lack of cordiality; intentional suppression of truth. **rĕsẽrved'** a, reticent, uncommunicative. **rĕsẽr'vĕdlў** adv. guardedly; without openness. **rĕsẽr'vist** n. member of military etc. reserve.

rĕs'ervoir (-zervwär) n. place where anything is kept in store; (reserve) store of information etc.; receptacle for fluid, esp. one for storing large quantity of water.

rēshŭff'le v.t. shuffle again; rearrange (posts in Cabinet etc.) without altering membership etc. n. instance of reshuffling.

rĕsīde' (-z-) v.i. have one's home; be in residence; (of rights etc.) be vested in. **rĕs'idence** n. residing; place where one resides; abode; in ~ence, living or staying regularly at or in some place. **rĕs'idencў** n. (hist.) residence of British political agent at Indian native court. **rĕs'ident** a. residing; located; n. permanent inhabitant; diplomatic representative in protectorate etc. **rĕsidĕn'tial** a. suitable for or occupied by private houses; requiring, connected with, residence. **rĕsidĕn'tiarў** a. bound to, of or for, official residence; n. ecclesiastic bound to residence.

rĕs'idūe (-z-) n. remainder, what is left over; rest of estate when liabilities have been discharged. **rĕsid'ūal**

a. remaining, left over. **rĕsid'ūarў** a. of residue of estate; residual. **rĕsid'ūum** n. (pl. -dua), what remains, esp. after combustion or evaporation.

rĕsign' (-z-) v. relinquish, surrender; reconcile (oneself) to; give up office, retire. **rĕsignā'tion** (-zĭg-) n. resigning of office; uncomplaining endurance. **rĕsigned'** a. having resigned oneself; content to endure; submissive.

rĕsil'ience (-z-) n. power of resuming original form after compression etc.; elasticity; buoyancy, power of recovery. ~ent a.

rĕs'in (-z-) n. adhesive secretion of trees and plants. v.t. rub or treat with resin. ~if'erous a. yielding resin. **rĕs'inous** a.

rĕsist' (-z-) v. stop course, withstand action or effect, of; strive against, oppose; offer resistance. **resis'tance** n. resisting; power of resisting; (esp. underground) civilian movement or organization resisting occupying power; (elect.) capacity in conducting body to resist flow of current, anything offering such resistance. **resis'tant, resis'tible** aa. ~lĕss a. that cannot be resisted.

rĕs'olūble (-z-) a. resolvable.

rĕs'olūte (-z-; or -ōōt) a. firm of purpose; determined; constant.

rĕsolū'tion (-z-; or -ōō-) n. resolute temper or character or conduct; thing resolved on; formal expression of opinion of meeting; solving of question etc.; resolving or being resolved.

rĕsolve' (-z-) v. disintegrate, analyse, break up into parts; convert or be converted into; (mus.) convert (discord), be converted, into concord; solve, settle; (cause to) decide upon; pass resolution by vote. n. resolution come to in mind; steadfastness. **rĕsōlved'** a. resolute.

rĕs'onant (-z-) a. echoing, resounding; continuing to sound; causing reinforcement or prolongation of sound, esp. by vibration. ~ance n.

rĕs'onāte (-z-) v.i. produce or show resonance. ~ātor n. (esp.) appliance for increasing sound by resonance.

rèsŏrt' (-z-) *v.i.* turn for aid etc. *to*; go often or in numbers *to*. *n.* thing to which recourse is had, recourse; frequenting, being frequented; place frequented for holidays etc.; *in the last* ~, as a last expedient.

rèsound' (-z-) *v.i.* ring or echo; produce echoes, go on sounding, fill place with sound; be much mentioned or repeated.

rèsource' (-sōrs) *n.* (pl.) means of supplying want, stock that can be drawn on; expedient, device; means of passing time. ~**ful** *a.* good at devising expedients.

rèspèct' *n.* deferential esteem; (pl.) message or attention conveying this; heed or regard *to*; reference or relation (*to*); particular, point, aspect. *v.* treat or regard with deference, esteem, or honour; treat with consideration, spare. ~**ing** *prep.* with regard or relation to.

rèspèc'table *a.* deserving respect; of fair social standing, honest and decent; of some amount or size or merit. ~**bil'itÿ** *n.*

rèspèct'ful *a.* showing deference.

rèspèc'tive *a.* of or connected with each individual, group, etc., of those in question; several, particular.

respīre' *v.* breathe; take breath. **rès'pirable, rès'pirātorÿ** *aa.* **rèspirā'tion** *n.* breathing; single inspiration and expiration; process by which organism utilizes oxygen from its environment. **rès'pirātor** *n.* apparatus worn over mouth and nose to filter etc. inhaled air; gas-mask.

rès'pite (*or* -īt) *n.* delay permitted in discharge of obligation or suffering of penalty; interval of rest or relief. *v.t.* grant or bring respite to.

rèsplèn'dent *a.* brilliant, glittering. ~**ence**, ~**encÿ** *nn.*

rèspŏnd' *v.i.* make answer; act etc. in response (*to*). **rèspŏn'dent** *a.* making answer; in position of defendant; *n.* defendant in divorce suit; one who answers.

rèspŏnse' *n.* answer; action, feeling, etc. aroused by stimulus etc.; part of liturgy said or sung by congregation in reply to priest.

rèspŏnsibil'itÿ *n.* being responsible; charge, trust.

rèspŏn'sible *a.* liable to be called to account; morally accountable for actions; of good credit and repute; trustworthy; involving responsibility.

rèspŏn'sions *n.pl.* first examination for Oxford B.A. degree.

rèspŏn'sive *a.* answering; by way of answer; responding readily to some influence.

rèst[1] *v.* be still; cease from exertion or action; lie in sleep or death; be tranquil; give relief or repose to; place, lie, lean, rely, base, depend, etc., (*up*)*on*. *n.* repose or sleep; resting; prop or support or steadying-piece; pause in music, elocution, metre, etc.; *at* ~, tranquil, quiet, inert, settled; *set at* ~, satisfy, assure; *come to* ~, stop; *lay to* ~, bury. ~**ing-place**, place where thing lies or rests; grave.

rèst[2] *v.i.* remain in specified state; ~ *with*, be in hands or charge or choice of. *n. the* remainder or remaining parts or individuals (*of*); *for the* ~, as regards anything beyond what has been mentioned.

rès'taurant (-tor-; *or* -ahn̄) *n.* place where meals may be had. **rèstaurateur'** (-orahtēr) *n.* restaurant-keeper.

rèst'ful *a.* quiet, soothing.

rèstitū'tion *n.* restoring of property etc. to its owner; reparation.

rès'tive *a.* intractable, resisting control, fidgety.

rèst'less *a.* finding or affording no rest; uneasy, agitated, fidgeting.

rèstorā'tion *n.* action or process of restoring; representation of original form of ruined building, extinct animal, etc.; *R*~, (period of) re-establishment of monarchy in England in 1660.

rèstŏr'ative *a. & n.* (medicine or food or agency) tending to restore health or strength.

rèstore' *v.t.* give back, make restitution of; replace, put back; repair, alter, so as to bring back as nearly as possible to original form, state, etc.; bring back *to* dignity etc., to health, into use, etc. **rèstŏr'able** *a.*; **rèstŏr'er** *n.*

rèstrain' *v.t.* check or hold in (from); keep under control; repress;

confine. ~ĕdly *adv.* with restraint; without exuberance or exaggeration.

rĕstraint' *n.* restraining or being restrained; ·check; confinement; self-control; avoidance of exaggeration; reserve.

rĕstrict' *v.t.* confine, bound, limit. rĕstric'tion *n.*; rĕstric'tĭve *a.*

rĕsŭlt' (-z-) *v.i.* arise as consequence, effect, or conclusion (*from*); end *in*. *n.* what results; consequence; issue; product of calculation. rĕsŭl'tant *a.* resulting; *n.* product, outcome, esp. of action of two or more forces, agents, etc.

rĕsūme' (-z-) *v.* take again or back; reoccupy; begin again; recommence; make résumé of. rĕsŭmp'tion *n.*; rĕsŭmp'tĭve *a.*

résumé (rā'zūmā) *n.* summary, abstract.

rĕsūr'gent *a.* rising again after subsidence or defeat or disappearance. ~ence *n.*

rĕsurrĕct' (-z-) *v.t.* bring back to life; (colloq.) exhume; revive practice or memory of.

rĕsurrĕc'tion (-z-) *n.* rising or being raised from the dead or the grave; revival from disuse, decay, etc. ~-man, ~ĭst *nn.* (hist.) one who exhumed corpses for dissection.

rĕsŭs'cĭtāte *v.* revive, return or restore to life, vogue, vigour, etc. ~ā'tion *n.*

rē'tail *n.* sale of goods in small quantities. *adv.* by retail. *v.* (-āl'), sell by retail; be retailed; recount. rĕtai'ler (*or* rē'-) *n.*

rĕtain' *v.t.* keep in place, hold fixed; keep possession of, continue to have, use, recognize, etc; keep in mind; secure services of, esp. by preliminary fee. ~ing fee, retainer. ~ing wall, wall supporting and confining mass of earth or water.

rĕtai'ner *n.* retaining, being retained; fee paid to secure services of barrister etc.; (hist.) dependent or follower; (joc.) servant.

rĕtăl'iāte *v.* repay in kind; retort *upon* person; make return or requital (esp. of injury). ~ā'tion *n.*; ~ative, ~ā'torў *aa.*

rĕtärd' *v.t.* make slow or late; delay progress, accomplishment, etc. of. ~ā'tion *n.*; ~atĭve, ~atorў *aa.*

rĕtär'dĕd *a.* (esp., of child) behind what is normal in mental or physical development.

rĕtch (*or* -ĕ-) *v.i.* make motion of vomiting. *n.* such motion, sound of it.

rĕtĕn'tion *n.* retaining. rĕtĕn'tĭve *a.* serving, tending, apt, etc. to retain, esp. not forgetful.

R. (et) I. *abbr.,* *Regina et Imperatrix* [L], Queen and Empress; *Rex et Imperator* [L], King and Emperor.

rēthĭnk' *v.t.* think out or over again (and alter).

rĕt'ĭcence *n.* reserve in speech; uncommunicativeness. ~ent *a.*

rĕtic'ūlar *a.* net-like.

rĕtic'ulāte *v.* divide, arrange, be divided or marked or arranged, in(to) network. *a.* (-at), reticulated. ~ā'tion *n.*

rĕt'ĭcūle *n.* (arch.) woman's handbag.

rĕt'ĭna *n.* (pl. -as, -ae), layer at back of eyeball sensitive to light. rĕt'ĭnal *a.*

rĕt'ĭnūe *n.* great person's suite of attendants.

rĕtīre' *v.* withdraw from place or company or occupation; retreat; recede; go to bed; cause or compel to retire from office. rĕtīred' *a.* that has retired from office etc.; secluded. rĕtire'ment (-īrm-) *n.* seclusion; condition of having retired from work. rĕtīr'ing *a.* shy; fond of seclusion.

rĕtŏrt'[1] *v.* repay in kind, cast back (*up*)*on*; make, say by way of, repartee, countercharge, or counter-argument. *n.* incisive reply; turning of argument or charge against its author; piece of retaliation.

rĕtŏrt'[2] *n.* distilling-vessel usu. of glass with long downward-bent neck; cylinder in which coal is heated to produce gas; furnace in which iron is heated to produce steel.

rētouch' (-ŭch) *v.t.* amend or improve (esp. photograph) by new touches.

rĕtrāce' *v.t.* trace back to source or beginning; go back over.

rĕtrăct' v. withdraw or pull back; be retracted or retractable; withdraw (promise etc.); recant. **rētrăctā'tion, rĕtrăc'tion** nn.; ~**able,** ~**īle,** ~**īve** aa.

rētread' (-ĕd) v.t. put new tread on (tyre). n. (rē'-), retreaded tyre.

rĕtreat' v.i. go back, retire; recede, slope away. n. act of or military signal for retreating; withdrawing into seclusion; place of seclusion or shelter; temporary retirement for religious exercises.

rĕtrĕnch' v. reduce amount of, cut down; economize. ~**ment** n.

rĕtrĭbū'tion n. recompense, usu. for evil, vengeance. **rĕtrĭb'ūtĭve** a.

rĕtrieve' v. regain possession of; rescue from bad state etc., restore to good state; repair; find and bring in game. **rĕtrie'val** n. **rĕtrie'ver** n. dog of breed specially adapted for retrieving game.

rĕt'rō- (or rē-) in comb., backwards, back. **retroăc'tĭve** a. (esp.) having retrospective effect. ~**cĕ'ssion** n. ceding back of territory. ~**choir** (-kwīr) n. part of cathedral or large church behind altar. ~**-rŏckĕt** n. rocket fired in opposite direction or at oblique angle to course of spacecraft etc. ~**vĕrtĕd** a. turned backwards.

rĕt'rogrāde a. directed backwards; reversing progress; reverting, esp. to inferior state; declining. v.i. move backwards; decline, revert.

rĕtrogrĕss' v.i. move backwards; deteriorate. **rĕtrogrĕ'ssion** n.; ~**ĭve** a.

rĕt'rospĕct n. view or survey of past time or events. **rĕtrospĕc'tion** n. looking back; indulgence or engagement in retrospect. **retrospĕc'tĭve** a. of, in, etc., retrospection; applying to or affecting past actions etc.

retrou'ssé (-ōōsā) a. (of nose) turned up.

rĕtūrn' v. come or go back; revert; give, send, pay, lead, etc. back; say in reply; respond to (play of partner or opponent in games); report in answer to official demand, state by way of report or verdict; elect as member of Parliament. n. returning or being returned; coming round again; return ticket; side or part falling away from front or direct line; what is returned; (coming in of) proceeds or profit; report. ~**ing officer,** official conducting election and announcing result. ~ **match,** between same sides as before. ~ **ticket,** ticket for journey to place and back again.

rēū'nion n. reuniting, being re-united; social gathering.

rēūnīte' v. bring or come together, join, again.

rĕv n. (colloq.) revolution (of internal-combustion engine). v. increase speed of revolutions (of), speed up.

Rev. abbr Revelation; Reverend.

Revd. abbr. Reverend.

rĕvămp' v.t. patch up again, revise.

rĕveal'[1] v.t. make known by super-natural means; disclose, betray; show, let appear.

rĕveal'[2] n. internal side surface of opening or recess.

rĕveill'e (-vĕlĭ or -vălĭ) n. military waking-signal.

rĕv'el v.i. make merry, be riotously festive; take keen delight in. n a merry-making.

rĕvĕlā'tion n. revealing; striking disclosure; knowledge disclosed by divine or supernatural agency, esp. (the R~, R~s) last book of N.T.

rĕv'elrў n. revelling.

rĕvĕnge' (-j) v.t. inflict punishment, exact retribution, for; avenge. n. desire for vengeance; act that satisfies this. ~**ful** a.

rĕv'ĕnūe n. annual income, esp. of State; department collecting State revenue.

rĕvĕr'berāte v. echo or throw back or reflect sound, light, or heat. ~**ā'tion** n. (esp.) echo, rolling sound. ~**ātor** n.; ~**ātorў** a.

rĕvēre' v.t. regard with deep and affectionate or religious respect.

rĕv'erence n. revering or being revered; deep respect. v.t. revere.

rĕv'erend a. deserving reverence by age, character, or associations; esp. as prefix to clergyman's name etc.

rĕv'erent a. feeling or showing reverence. **rĕverĕn'tial** a. of or showing reverence.

rĕv'erie n. (fit of) musing, day-dream.

revers' (-vēr) *n.* turned-back front edge of garment.

rever'sal *n.* reversing or being reversed.

reverse' *a.* contrary, inverted, upside down. *v.* turn the other way round or up, or inside out; invert; transpose; revoke, annul; (cause to) move or turn in opposite direction. *n. the* contrary (*of*); (device etc. on) back of coin etc.; piece of misfortune, disaster; *in* ~, with position reversed, the other way round, in reverse gear. ~ **gear**, gear permitting vehicle to be driven backward. ~**sible** *a.*; ~**sibil'ity** *n.*

rever'sion *n.* reverting, return to former state or habit; passing of estate or office at appointed time back to grantor or his heirs; right of succession to such estate etc. ~**ary** *a.*

revert' *v.i.* return *to* former condition, primitive state, etc.; recur in thought or talk; fall in by reversion. ~**ible** *a.* (of property) subject to reversion.

revêt'ment *n.* facing of masonry etc. on rampart or embankment.

review' (-vū) *n.* revision; survey, inspection; retrospect; published account or criticism of book etc.; periodical in which events, books, etc. are reviewed. *v.* view again; survey, look back on; hold review of (troops, etc.); write review of (book). **review'er** *n.* writer of review(s).

revile' *v.t.* call by ill names; abuse, rail at.

revise' (-z) *v.t.* examine and amend faults in. *n.* proof-sheet embodying corrections made in earlier proof. **revi'sion** (-zhn) *n.* revising; revised edition or form. ~**sory** *a.*

revi'val *n.* reviving or being revived; (campaign to promote) reawakening of religious fervour. ~**ism**, ~**ist** *nn.*

revive' *v.* come or bring back to consciousness, life, vigour, notice, or vogue.

reviv'ify *v.t.* restore to animation, activity, vigour, or life. ~**fica'tion** *n.*

rev'ocable *a.* that may be revoked. **revoca'tion** *n.*

revoke' *v.* rescind, withdraw, cancel; (cards) fail to follow suit though able to. *n.* revoking at cards.

revolt' *v.* cast off allegiance, make rising or rebellion (*against*); feel revulsion; affect with disgust. *n.* insurrection; rebellious mood; sense of loathing. ~**ing** *a.* disgusting, horrible.

revolu'tion (*or* -ōō-) *n.* revolving; single completion of orbit or rotation; fundamental change; forcible substitution of new government or ruler for old. ~**ary** *a.* involving great change; of political revolution; *n.* instigator etc. of political revolution. ~**ize** *v.t.*

revolve' *v.* turn round; rotate; go rolling along. **revol'ver** *n.* (esp.) pistol that will fire several shots without reloading.

revue' *n.* loosely constructed entertainment reviewing or satirizing current events etc.

revul'sion (-shn) *n.* sudden violent change of feeling.

reward (-ôrd) *n.* return or recompense for service or merit; requital for good or evil; sum offered for detection of criminal, restoration of lost thing, etc. *v.t.* give or serve as reward to.

Rex *n.* reigning king. [L]

R.F.C. *abbr.* Rugby Football Club.

R.G.S. *abbr.* Royal Geographical Society.

R.H. *abbr.* Royal Highness.

Rh *abbr.* rhesus (factor).

R.H.A. *abbr.* Royal Horse Artillery.

Rhadaman'thine (*or* -in) *a.* sternly and incorruptibly just.

rhap'sody *n.* enthusiastic highflown utterance or composition. **rhapso'dical** *a.*; ~**odist** *n.*; ~**odize** *v.t.*

Rhe'nish *a.* of (regions near) Rhine.

rhe'nium *n.* rare very hard heavy metallic element.

rhe'ostat *n.* device for varying resistance of electric current.

rhe'sus *n.* small Indian monkey. ~ **factor**, complex substance or antigen normally present in human red blood cells. ~**-positive**, ~**-negative**, having, without, rhesus factor.

rhet'oric *n.* art of speaking or writing effectively; inflated or exaggerated language. **rhĕtŏ'rĭcal** *a.* (esp., of question) asked not for information but to produce effect. **~ĭ'cian** *n.*

rheum (-ōō-) *n.* watery secretion or discharge of mucous membrane etc.

rheumăt'ĭc (-ōō-) *a.* of, suffering from, subject to, causing, or caused by rheumatism. *n.* rheumatic patient; (pl., colloq.) rheumatism. **rheu'mat-ĭsm** *n.* disease marked by inflammation and pain in joints, esp. rheumatoid arthritis. **rheu'matoid** *a.* of or like rheumatism; **~toid arthritis,** chronic progressive disease with inflammatory changes in joints etc.

rheu'mў (-ōō-) *a.* affected with rheum; (of air) damp, raw.

R.H.G. *abbr.* Royal Horse Guards.

rhine'stōne (rīns-) *n.* kind of rock crystal; paste diamond.

rhī'nō[1] *n.* (pl. *-os*), (sl.) rhinoceros.

rhī'nō[2] *n.* (sl.) money.

rhĭnŏ'ceros *n.* large animal with horn or two horns on nose.

rhī'zōme *n.* prostrate or subterranean stem sending out roots from lower and shoots from upper surface.

rhō'dĭum *n.* hard white metallic element of platinum group.

rhōdŏdĕn'dron *n.* kinds of evergreen shrub with large flowers.

rhŏmb, rhŏm'bus *nn.* plane equilateral figure with opposite angles equal and acute or obtuse; lozenge- or diamond-shaped object, marking, etc. **~ĭc** *a.* **~oid** *a.* (nearly) rhomb-shaped; *n.* quadrilateral figure with opposite sides and angles equal.

R.H.S. *abbr.* Royal Horticultural, Humane, Society.

rhu'bărb (-ōō-) *n.* plant with fleshy leaf-stalks cooked and eaten as fruit; (purgative from root of) Chinese plant of same genus.

rhўme, rīme[1] *n.* identity between terminal sounds of words or verse-lines; word providing rhyme; rhymed verse; poem, poetry. *v.* (of words etc.) end in rhymes; be, use as, rhyme (*to, with*); versify, write rhymes.

rhўth'm (-dh-) *n.* measured flow of words in verse or prose; movement

or pattern with regulated succession of strong and weak elements, opposite or different conditions, etc. **rhўth'mĭc(al)** *aa.*

R.I. *abbr.* R. et I.; Rhode Island; Royal Institution.

rĭb *n.* one of curved bones round upper part of body; denser, firmer, or stronger part, esp. ridge along surface, serving to support, strengthen, etc.; spur of mountain, wave-mark on sand, hinged rod of umbrella frame, ridged effect in knitting. *v.t.* provide with ribs, act as ribs of; mark with ridges, esp. (knitting) by combination of plain and purl stitches; (sl.) tease. **rĭbb'ĭng** *n.* (esp.) knitted ribs.

R.I.B.A. *abbr.* Royal Institute of British Architects.

rĭb'ald *a.* scurrilous, irreverent, indecent. *n.* ribald person. **~rў** *n.*

rĭb'and *n.* (arch.) ribbon.

rĭbb'on *n.* (piece or length of) silk or other fine material woven into narrow band; ribbon of special colour worn to indicate membership or possession of knightly order, medal, etc.; long narrow strip; (pl.) driving-reins. **~ building, development,** of houses etc. in narrow strips along main roads.

R.I.C. *abbr.* Royal Institute of Chemistry, Irish Constabulary.

rīce *n.* (pearl-white seeds, used as food, of) annual cereal grass of marshy ground in warm climates. **~-paper,** edible paper used in baking etc.; thin paper made from rice-straw; Chinese painting-paper.

rĭch *a.* wealthy, having riches; fertile, abounding *in;* valuable; (of dress, etc.) splendid, costly; (of food) containing large proportion of fat, butter, eggs, sugar, etc.; highly amusing; abundant. **rĭch'es** (-ĭz) *n.* wealth; valuable possessions. **rĭch'lў** *adv.* (esp.) fully.

rĭck[1] *n.* stack of hay, corn, peas, etc. *v.t.* form into rick(s).

rĭck[2] *n. & v.t.* wrench, sprain.

rĭck'ĕts *n.* children's disease with softening of bones, bow-legs, etc. **rĭck'ĕtў** *a.* of, like, or having rickets; shaky, insecure.

rĭck'shaw *n.* light two-wheeled

hooded vehicle drawn by man or men.

ric′ochet (-shā) *n*. rebounding of projectile etc. from object it strikes; hit made after this. *v.i.* (*-cheted -cheting*, pr. -shād, -shāïng), glance or skip with rebound(s).

rid *v.t.* (p.t. *ridded, rid*; p.p. *rid*), disencumber or relieve (*of*); *get ∼ of*, get free of, throw away, discard. **ridd′ance** *n*.

ridd′le[1] *n*. question designed to test ingenuity in divining answer or meaning; puzzling fact, thing, or person. *v.i.* speak in, propound, riddles.

ridd′le[2] *n*. coarse sieve. *v.t.* sift; fill with holes, esp. of gunshot (also fig.).

ride *v*. (*rōde, ridden*), sit on and be carried by horse etc.; go on horseback, bicycle, train, or other conveyance; manage horse; lie at anchor; float buoyantly; oppress, tyrannize over; *∼ up*, (of garment etc.) work upwards when worn, *n*. journey in vehicle; spell of riding; road esp. through wood for riding on; *take for a ∼*, (sl.) kidnap and murder, make fool of. **ri′der** *n*. (esp.) additional clause amending or supplementing document; expression of opinion etc. added to verdict; corollary. **ri′derless** *a*.

ridge *n*. line of junction in which two sloping surfaces meet; long narrow hill-top; mountain range; any narrow elevation along surface. *v*. form or break up into ridges, mark with ridges; earth *up*. *∼-pole*, horizontal pole of long tent; horizontal timber supporting tops of roof-rafters. *∼-tile*, tile used for ridge of roof. *∼way*, road along ridge.

rid′icule *n*. derision, mockery. *v.t.* make laughing-stock of; deride, mock at. **ridic′ulous** *a*. deserving to be laughed at, absurd.

ri′ding[1] *n*. (esp.) green track through or beside wood. *∼-habit*, woman's long-skirted costume for riding side-saddle. *∼-light*, light shown by ship riding at anchor.

ri′ding *n*. administrative division of Yorkshire, N.Z., etc.

rife *pred. a*. of common occurrence; prevailing, current, numerous.

riff′le *v*. flick (*through*), ruffle; shuffle playing-cards rapidly, esp. with pack divided into two halves. *n*. riffling.

riff′-raff *n*. rabble; disreputable people.

ri′fle *v.t.* search and rob; make spiral grooves in (gun, etc.). *n*. gun with rifled barrel; (pl.) troops armed with these.

rift *n*. fissure, chasm, crack, split. *∼ valley*, valley formed by sinking of earth's crust between two (parallel) faults.

rig[1] *v.t.* provide ship with spars, ropes, etc.; fit (*out, up*) with clothes or equipment; set *up* hastily or as makeshift. *n*. way ship's masts, sails, etc. are arranged; person's look as determined by clothes etc.; *∼(-out)*, outfit, costume.

rig[2] *v.t.* manipulate (esp. *the market*) fraudulently.

rigg′ing *n*. (esp.) ropes etc. used to support masts and work or set sails etc.

right (rīt) *a*. morally good, just; proper, correct, true; on or to right hand; in good or normal condition; not mistaken. *v.t.* restore to proper, straight, or vertical position; make reparation for; avenge, vindicate, rehabilitate; correct, set in order. *n*. what is just; fair treatment; justification; fair claim; being entitled to privilege or immunity; what one is entitled to; (pl.) right condition, true state; right-hand region or part or direction; more conservative or reactionary or traditional political group, wing, party, etc.; *by ∼s*, if right were done; *in the ∼*, having justice or truth on one's side; *set to ∼s*, arrange properly, tidy up. *adv*. straight; all the way (*round, to*, etc.), completely; quite, very; justly, properly, correctly, truly; to right hand; *serve* (person) *∼*, (impers.) be no worse than he deserves. *int*. expr. agreement or consent. *∼ angle*, angle of 90°; *at ∼ angles*, turning through, placed at, etc., right angle, perpendicular(ly). *∼*

bank, that on right hand of person looking downstream. **~-down,** thorough(ly). **~ hand,** hand having same relation to front of body as east has to north; region or direction or position on this side; chief or indispensable assistant. **~-handed,** using right hand more than left; struck, made, etc. with right hand. **~ mind,** sane or normal state of mind. **~-minded,** disposed or inclined towards what is right. **~ of way,** (path subject to) right to pass over another's ground. **~ side,** right-hand side; side (of fabric etc.) meant for use or show; *on the ~ side of,* younger than, in person's good books or favour. **~ whale,** whalebone whale. **~-wing,** (of or belonging to) political right. **~ist** *a.* & *n.* right-wing (person).

righteous (rī'chŭs) *a.* virtuous, upright, just, honest.

right'ful *a.* legitimately entitled to position etc.; that one is entitled to.

right'lў *adv.* justly, correctly, properly, justifiably.

rī'gĭd *a.* stiff, unyielding, not flexible; inflexible, harsh. **rĭgĭd'ĭtў** *n.*

rĭg'marōle *n.* rambling or meaningless talk.

rĭg'ŏr mŏr'tĭs n. stiffening of body after death. [L]

rĭg'our *n.* severity, strictness, harshness; cruel extremity *of* cold etc.; strict application, observance, etc. (*of*). **rĭg'orous** *a.*

rīle *v.t.* (sl.) anger, irritate.

rĭll *n.* tiny stream.

rĭm *n.* outer ring of wheel (not including tyre); outer frame; (esp. raised) edge or border. *v.t.* furnish with rim, serve as rim to; edge. **~less** *a.*

rīme[1] : see **rhyme.**

rīme[2] *n.* hoar-frost. *v.t.* cover with rime. **rī'mў** *a.*

rīnd *n.* bark; peel; skin of bacon etc.; outer crust of cheese etc.

rĭng[1] *n.* circlet of gold etc. worn esp. on finger; circular object, appliance, arrangement, etc.; enclosure for circus-riding, boxing, betting, etc.; combination of persons acting together for control of market or policy. *v.t.* encompass; hem in; fit

with ring; put ring in nose of (pig, bull). **~-bolt,** bolt with ring attached for fastening rope to etc. **~dove,** wood-pigeon. **~-fence,** fence all round estate etc. **~-finger,** third finger esp. of left hand. **~leader,** instigator in mutiny, riot, etc. **~ main,** electric wiring in circular form for power points. **~-master,** manager of circus performance. **~ road,** road passing round town. **~tail,** kinds of hawk, eagle, and opossum. **~worm,** skin--disease in circular patches.

rĭng[2] *v.* (*răng,* rarely *rŭng;* p.p. *rŭng*), give forth clear resonant sound; (of place) resound, re-echo; (of ears) be filled with sensation as of bell-ringing; make ring; ring bell; announce or signal or summon by sound of bell; **~ off,** end telephone call; **~ up,** make telephone call to. *n.* ringing sound, resonance; act of ringing bell; set of (church) bells. **rĭng'er** *n.* (esp., sl.) *a* (*dead*) **~** *for,* the image of.

rĭng'lĕt *n.* curly lock of hair; hanging curl. **rĭng'lĕtĕd** *a.*

rĭnk *n.* stretch or sheet of ice used for curling or skating; floor for roller-skating; bowling-green.

rĭnse *v.t.* pour water into and out of to remove dirt etc.; wash lightly, pour liquid over; put through clean water to remove soap; remove by rinsing. *n.* rinsing; (application of) liquid for rinsing, esp. for tinting hair.

rī'ot *n.* tumult, disorder; disturbance of peace by crowd; loud revelry; loose living; unrestrained indulgence or display. *v.i.* make or engage in riot; revel. **rī'otous** *a.*

rĭp[1] *v.* cut or tear or split, esp. with single quick motion; strip *off* or *away* or open *up* thus; (of material) be ripped; rush along; *let* (thing) **~,** do not check speed or interfere. *n.* act of ripping; long tear or cut. **~-cord,** cord for releasing parachute, opening balloon gas-bag, etc. **~-tide,** fast-flowing tide or current; rough water where tides meet. **rĭpp'er** *n.* one who rips; (sl.) first--rate person or thing. **rĭpp'ing** *a.* (sl.) splendid, first-rate.

rĭp² *n.* dissolute person, rake.

rĭp³ *n.* stretch of broken water in sea or river.

R.I.P. *abbr.*, *requiesca(n)t in pace* [L], may he, they, etc. rest in peace.

rĭpār'ĭan *a.* of or on river-bank. *n.* riparian proprietor.

rīpe *a.* ready to be reaped, gathered, eaten, used, or dealt with; mature, fully developed; prepared, in fit state, *for*. **rī'pen** *v.* mature, make or grow ripe.

rĭpōste' *n.* quick return thrust in fencing; counter-stroke, retort. *v.i.* deliver riposte.

rĭpp'le *n.* ruffling of water's surface; small wave(s); gentle lively sound rising and falling. *v.* form or flow in ripples; sound like ripples; make ripples in.

rīse (-z) *v.i.* (*rose*, pr. rōz; *risen*, pr. rĭ'zn), get up from lying or sitting or kneeling; get out of bed; cease to sit for business; make revolt; ascend, soar; project or swell upwards; come to surface; have origin, begin to flow. *n.* upward incline; social advancement; increase in rank, price, amount, wages, etc.; origin; *take a* ∼ *out of*, draw into display of temper etc. **rī'ser** *n.* (esp.) vertical piece connecting two treads of staircase. **rī'sĭng** *n.* (esp.) insurrection.

rĭs'ĭble (-z-) *a.* inclined to laugh; of laughter. ∼**bĭl'ĭtў** *n.*

rĭsk *n.* hazard; chance of bad consequences; exposure to mischance. *v.t.* expose to chance of injury or loss; venture on, take chances of. **rĭs'kў** *a.* full of risk; risqué.

rĭs'qué (-kā) *a.* suggestive of or bordering on indecency.

rĭss'ōle *n.* fried ball or cake of minced meat or fish.

rīte *n.* religious or solemn ceremony or observance.

rĭt'ūal *a.* of or with rites. *n.* performance of ritual acts; prescribed order for performing religious service. ∼**ĭsm** *n.* (excessive) performance of ritual. ∼**ĭst** *n.*; ∼**ĭs'tĭc** *a.*

rī'val *n.* person or thing that competes with another. *v.t.* vie with, be comparable to. ∼**rў** *n.*

rīve *v.* (*rived*, *riven*), strike or rend asunder; wrench; split; be split.

rĭv'er *n.* large natural stream of water flowing in channel.

rĭv'erīne *a.* of, situated or dwelling on banks of, river.

rĭv'ĕt *n.* nail or bolt for holding together metal plates etc. *v.t.* clinch; join or fasten with rivets; concentrate, direct intently (*upon*); engross attention (of). **rĭv'ĕter** *n.*

rĭv'ūlĕt *n.* small stream.

R.M. *abbr.* Resident Magistrate; Royal Mail; Royal Marines.

R.M.S., R.M.S.P. *abbr.* Royal Mail Steamer, Steam Packet (Co.).

R.N. *abbr.* Royal Navy.

RNA *abbr.* ribonucleic acid.

R.N.L.I. *abbr.* Royal National Lifeboat Institution.

R.N.(V.)R. *abbr.* Royal Naval (Volunteer) Reserve.

roach *n.* small freshwater fish.

road *n.* way, esp. with prepared surface, for foot passengers, riders, and vehicles; way of getting *to*; route; (usu. pl.) piece of water near shore in which ships can ride at anchor; *on the* ∼, travelling; *royal* ∼, smooth or easy way (*to* success etc.). ∼ **fund**, fund for maintenance of roads etc. ∼**-hog**, reckless, dangerous, or bad-mannered driver of car etc. ∼**-house**, inn or restaurant on main road in country district. ∼**man**, man employed in repairing roads. ∼**-sense**, capacity for intelligent behaviour on roads. ∼**stead**, sea-roads. ∼**way**, (esp.) part of road, bridge, etc. used by vehicles. ∼**worthy**, (of vehicle) fit to be used on road. **road'ster** *n.* (esp.) sturdy bicycle for ordinary use on roads; open car.

roam *v.* ramble, wander or travel unsystematically (about). ∼**er** *n.*

roan¹ *a.* (of animal) with coat of which prevailing colour is thickly interspersed with another. *n.* roan horse or cow.

roan² *n.* soft sheepskin leather used in bookbinding.

roar (rōr) *n.* loud deep hoarse sound (as) of lion, thunder, voice(s) in rage or pain or loud laughter, etc. *v.* utter, send forth, roar; say, sing,

etc. in or with roar; be full of din.
~ing *a.* (esp.) riotous, noisy,
boisterous; stormy; brisk.

roast *v.* cook or heat by exposure to
open fire or in oven, furnace, sun,
etc.; undergo roasting; (sl.) banter.
a. roasted. *n.* (dish of) roast meat.
~ing *a.* very hot.

rŏb *v.* despoil of property by violence;
feloniously plunder; deprive (*of*);
commit robbery. **rŏbb'erў** *n.*

rōbe *n.* long loose garment, esp. as
indication of rank, office, etc.;
dressing-gown, bath-wrap; (U.S.
etc.) dressed skin of animal used
as garment or rug. *v.* invest in,
assume, robe or vestments; dress.

rŏb'ĭn *n.* small brown red-breasted
bird; (U.S.) red-breasted thrush.

rō'bŏt *n.* apparently human automaton; machine-like person. *a.*
automatically controlled.

Robt. *abbr.* Robert.

robŭst' *a.* of strong health and phy-
sique; not slender or weakly;
vigorous; sensible, straightforward.

rŏc *n.* gigantic bird of Eastern legend.

R.O.C. *abbr.* Royal Observer Corps.

rŏch'ĕt *n.* surplice-like vestment of
bishop or abbot.

rŏck¹ *n.* solid part of earth's crust;
mass of this; large detached stone
or boulder; (U.S.) stone of any
size; *on the* ~*s*, in financial straits.
~-bottom, (sl.) very lowest. ~
crystal, crystallized quartz. ~-
-garden, rockery. ~-plant, plant
growing among rocks or suitable
for rock-garden. ~-rose, cistus.
~-salmon, dogfish. ~-salt, common
salt occurring as massive deposit in
earth's crust. **rŏck'erў** *n.* artificial
heap of rough stones etc. for
growing rock-plants.

rŏck² *v.* (make) oscillate; move to
and fro (as) in cradle or in arms;
sway from side to side; shake,
reel, dance violently. *n.* rocking
motion, spell of rocking. ~er *n.*
(esp.) one of curved bars on which
cradle, chair, etc. rocks; rocking-
-chair; goldminer's cradle. **rŏck'ing**
a. that rocks; swaying, oscillating;
~ing-chair, chair mounted on
rockers. ~ing-horse, child's wood-
en horse on rockers. ~ing-stone,

large boulder so poised that it
rocks easily.

rŏck'ĕt¹ *n.* kinds of flowering plant.

rŏck'ĕt² *n.* cylindrical case that can
be projected to distance or height
by reaction of gases when contents
are ignited; shell or bomb projected
by rocket propulsion; projectile
driven by rocket propulsion for
exploration of space etc. *v.t.* rise or
fly straight and fast like rocket;
(of prices) rise rapidly. ~ propulsion, propulsion by reaction of
gases expelled backward at high
velocity. ~eer' *n.* expert on rocket
missiles. ~rў *n.* science or practice
of rocket propulsion.

rŏck'ў¹ *a.* of rock; full of rocks;
rugged, hard, as rock.

rŏck'ў² *a.* unsteady, tottering.

rocō'cō *a. & n.* (of) style of decoration
with much scroll-work, shell motifs,
asymmetrical effects, etc.

rŏd *n.* slender straight round stick or
metal bar; wand, switch; cane or
birch for flogging; fishing-rod;
measure of length, pole (5½ yds.).

rode, *p.t.* of **ride.**

rō'dent *n. & a.* (mammal) of order
including rats, voles, beavers, etc.

rōde'ō (-dā-) *n.* round-up of cattle for
branding etc.; exhibition of cowboys' skill.

rŏdomontāde' *n.* boastful talk, brag.
v.i. talk boastfully.

rōe¹ *n.* (collect. sing.) small kind of
deer. ~buck, male roe.

rōe² *n.* mass of eggs (*hard* ~) in
female fish; *soft* ~, male fish's milt.

roentgen: see **röntgen.**

rogā'tion *n.* (usu. pl.) special sup-
plications chanted on three days
before Ascension Day. **R~ days,**
Monday, Tuesday and Wednesday
preceding Ascension Day. **R~
Sunday,** Sunday before Ascension
Day.

rŏ'ger *int.* used to indicate that
message has been received and
understood; (sl.) right! very well.

rōgue (-g) *n.* rascal, swindler, knave;
mischief-loving child; arch or sly
person; wild beast, esp. elephant,
living apart from herd and of
savage temper. **rō'guerў** (-ge-) *n.*
rō'guĭsh *a.* (esp.) arch.

roi′ster *v.i.* revel noisily, be uproarious. **roi′sterer** *n.*; ~**ing** *n.* & *a.*

role (rōl) *n.* actor's part; one's task or function.

rōll *n.* cylinder formed by turning paper, cloth, etc. over and over on itself without folding; document in this form; register, list; more or less cylindrical mass of something; small loaf of bread for one person; rolling motion or gait; continuous sound of thunder or drum or shouting; *struck off the* ~*s*, disqualified from practising as solicitor. *v.* move or send or go in some direction by turning over and over on axis; wallow; sway or rock; undulate, show undulating motion or surface; sound with vibration; flatten with roller; make into or form roll; make by rolling. ~**-call**, calling over of list of persons. ~**ed gold**, thin coating of gold applied by rolling. ~**-top desk**, desk with flexible cover sliding in curved grooves. **rō′ller** *n.* (esp.) cylinder used alone or as part of machine for smoothing, crushing, spreading printer's ink, etc.; long swelling wave; breed of canary with trilling song; ~**er skate**, skate mounted on small wheels or rollers; ~**er-towel**, with ends joined, running on roller. **rō′lling** *n.* & *a.*; ~**ing-mill**, mill which rolls steel into thin sheets; ~**ing-pin**, roller for pastry etc.; ~**ing-stock**, railway locomotives, wagons, etc.

rōll′icking *a.* exuberantly gay, boisterous.

rō′lȳ-pō′lȳ *n.* pudding of paste covered with jam and rolled up; (attrib.) podgy, plump.

Rom. *abbr.* Romans (N.T.).

rom. *abbr.* roman (type).

Rō′man *a.* of ancient or modern city of Rome; of people or State or Christian Church of Rome. *n.* member of ancient Roman State; inhabitant of Rome; Roman Catholic; roman type. ~ **candle**, tube discharging coloured balls in fireworks. ~ **Catholic**, (member) of Church of Rome. ~ **nose**, nose with prominent bridge. ~ **numerals**, numerals expressed in letters of

Roman alphabet. **r~ type**, upright type in ordinary use in W. Europe etc. (opp. *italic*). **Rō′manize** *v.*; ~**izā′tion** *n.*

romance′ *n.* **R~**, vernacular language of old France developed from Latin; (collect., *R~*) languages so developed; medieval tale of chivalry; tale with scenes and incidents remote from everyday life; episode or love affair suggesting such tale; romantic character or quality; exaggeration, picturesque falsehood. *a.* (*R~*), derived or descended from Latin. *v.i.* exaggerate, invent or tell fantastic stories, lie.

Rōmanĕsque′ (-k) *a.* & *n.* (of or in) style in architecture etc. prevalent between classical and Gothic periods.

romăn′tic *a.* marked by or suggestive of or given to romance; imaginative, remote from experience, visionary; (of literary or artistic method etc.) preferring grandeur or passion or irregular beauty to finish and proportion. *n.* romantic person, esp. writer, painter, or musician. ~**ism**, ~**ist** *nn.*

Rŏm′any *n.* gipsy; Indo-European language of gipsies.

Rō′mish *a.* papistical.

rŏmp *v.i.* play in lively and boisterous manner; (colloq.) move etc. easily and quickly; ~ *home*, win with great ease. *n.* piece of romping, frolic; play-loving lively merry girl or woman. ~**er(s)** *n.* young child's overall.

rŏn′deau (-ō), **rŏn′del** *nn.* kinds of poem with 10 or 13, 13 or 14, lines, two rhymes only, and opening words or lines used as refrains.

rŏn′dō *n.* (mus.) movement, composition, in which principal theme recurs twice or oftener.

röntgen, roentgen (rĕrn′tyen; *or* rĕnt′g-) *n.* unit of exposure to X-rays.

rōod *n.* crucifix, esp. on rood-screen; measure of land (usu. quarter acre). ~**-loft**, gallery above rood-screen. ~**-screen**, carved screen separating nave and choir.

rōof *n.* upper covering of house or

building; top of covered vehicle, tent, etc.; ~ *of the mouth*, palate. *v.t.* cover with roof; be roof of. ~-**tree**, ridge-pole of roof. **rōō'fing** *n.*; **rōō'flėss** *a.*

rŏŏk[1] *n.* chess-piece with power of moving in straight line.

rŏŏk[2] *n.* black hoarse-voiced gregarious bird of crow kind. *v.t.* swindle, cheat, esp. at cards etc.; charge extortionately. ~**erў** *n.* colony of rooks, seals, etc.; crowded cluster of mean houses.

rŏŏk'ie *n.* (sl.) recruit.

rŏōm *n.* space occupied or that might be occupied by something; capaciousness, ability to accommodate contents; opportunity, scope; part of house etc. enclosed by walls or partitions; (pl.) apartments or lodgings. *v.i.* share room(s) *with*; (U.S.) lodge. ~**ful** *n.* **rōō'mў** *a.* capacious, large.

rŏŏst *n.* bird's resting-place. *v.i.* settle for sleep; be perched or lodged for night. ~**er** *n.* domestic cock.

rŏŏt *n.* part of plant that fixes it to earth etc. and conveys nourishment to it from soil; (pl.) fibres or branches of this; (usu. pl.) plant(s) with edible roots; imbedded part of bodily organ or structure; source, means of growth, basis; (math.) factor of quantity which multiplied by itself gives that quantity; ultimate unanalysable element of word; (mus.) fundamental note of chord. *v.* (cause to) take root; fix or establish firmly; pull *up* by root; turn up ground in search of food; rout (*out*). ~-**stock**, rhizome. **rŏŏt'lėt** *n.*

rōpe *n.* stout line made by twisting together strands of hemp, flax, hide, or wire; string *of* pearls etc.; stringy formation in beer or other liquid; (pl.) ropes enclosing boxing--ring etc.; *know the* ~*s*, be familiar with conditions in some sphere of action. *v.t.* fasten or secure or connect with rope, put rope on; enclose or mark *off* with rope. ~-**dancer**, performer on tightrope. ~-**walk**, long shed etc. for rope--making. **rō'pў** *a.* rope-like; forming

or developing viscid glutinous or slimy threads; (sl.) extremely poor or inferior.

rôr'qual *n.* whale with dorsal fin.

rosa'ceous (-zāshus) *a.* of the order of plants including the rose.

rō'sarў (-z-) *n.* rose garden; prayer made up of Aves, Glorias, and Paternosters; string of beads for keeping count of these.

rōse[1] (-z) *n.* (prickly shrub bearing) beautiful and usu. fragrant red, yellow, or white flower; representation of flower; rose-shaped design or object; nozzle of watering-pot etc.; rose-colour. *a.* coloured like rose, of warm pink. ~**bud**, bud of rose; young girl. ~-**colour**, rosy red, pink; (fig.) pleasant state or outlook. ~-**water**, perfume distilled from roses. ~ **window**, circular window, usu. with spoke-like tracery. ~**wood**, close-grained fragrant kinds used in cabinet-making.

rose[2], *p.t.* of **rise**.

rō'sėate (-z-) *a.* rose-coloured.

rōse'marў (-zm-) *n.* evergreen fragrant shrub.

rōsē'ola (-z-) *n.* (disease with) rose--coloured skin-rash.

rosĕtte' (-z-) *n.* rose-shaped ornament made of ribbons etc., or carved in stone etc.

Rōsicru'cian (-zĭkrōō-) *a.* & *n.* (member) of secret society devoted to occult lore.

rŏs'in (-z-) *n.* resin, esp. in solid form. *v.t.* rub with rosin.

rŏs'ter (*or* rō-) *n.* list or plan showing turns of duty etc.

rŏs'tral *a.* (of column etc.) adorned with beaks of ancient war-galleys.

rŏs'trĭfórm *a.* beak-like.

rŏs'trum *n.* (pl. *-ra*, *-s*), platform for public speaking; pulpit; office etc. that enables one to gain the public ear; (Rom. ant.) beak of war-galley.

rō'sў (-z-) *a.* rose-coloured, warmly pink; promising, hopeful.

rŏt *v.* undergo decay by putrefaction or from want of use; cause to rot, make rotten; (sl.) chaff, tease. *n.* decay, rottenness; liver-disease of sheep; (sl.) nonsense, undesirable state of things; (sl.) sudden series of unaccountable failures. ~-gut, (liquor) injurious to stomach.

rō′ta *n.* list of persons acting, or duties to be done, in rotation.

rō′tarў *a.* rotating, acting by rotation.

rotāte′ *v.* move round axis or centre, revolve; arrange or take in rotation. **rotā′tion** *n.* rotating; recurrent series or period; regular succession. **rō′tative, rō′tatorў, rotā′tional** *aa.*

rōte *n.* mere habituation, unintelligent memory.

rō′tifer *n.* kinds of minute usu. microscopic aquatic animal.

rō′tograph (-ahf) *n.* photographic print, esp. of MS. or book.

rō′tor *n.* rotary part of machine; rotating system of helicopter.

rŏtt′en *a.* affected with rot; perishing of decay; morally, socially, or politically corrupt; worthless; (sl.) beastly.

rŏtt′er *n.* (sl.) person objectionable on moral or other grounds.

rotŭnd′ *a.* rounded, plump; sonorous, grandiloquent. **rotŭn′da** *n.* circular building or hall or room, esp. with dome. **rotŭn′ditў** *n.*

rou′ble (roo-) *n.* Russian monetary unit (100 copecks).

roué (roo′ā) *n.* debauchee, rake.

rouge (roozh) *n.* red powder or other cosmetic used to colour cheeks and lips; red plate powder of iron oxide. *v.* colour, adorn oneself, with rouge. ~-et-noir (-ā-nwahr′), card-game on table with red and black diamond-shaped marks on which stakes are placed.

rough (rŭf) *a.* of uneven or irregular surface; not smooth or level; hairy, shaggy; coarse in texture; violent; stormy, boisterous; riotous; harsh, unfeeling; deficient in finish; incomplete; approximate. *adv.* in rough manner. *n.* rough ground, esp. bordering fairway of golf-course; hardship, hard part of life; rowdy, hooligan, person ready for lawless violence; *the* unfinished or natural state; rough drawing etc. *v.t.* make rough; shape or plan *out*, sketch *in*, roughly; ~ *it*, do without ordinary conveniences of life. ~-and-ready, not elaborate, precise, over-particular, etc.; roughly efficient or effec-

tive. ~-and-tumble, irregular, scrambling, disorderly (scuffle etc.). ~cast, (coat, coated, with) plaster of lime and gravel. ~-dry, dry (laundry) without ironing. ~-hew, shape out roughly. ~-house, disturbance, row, rough fight. ~ luck, (colloq.) worse fortune than one deserves. ~-neck, (sl., U.S.) rowdy fellow, hooligan. ~shod, (of horse) having shoes with nail--heads projecting; *ride* ~-*shod*, domineer *over*. **rough′age** *n.* indigestible fibrous matter or cellulose in food-stuffs. **rough′en** *v.*

roulade (roolahd′) *n.* (mus.) florid vocal passage of runs etc.

rouleau (roolō′) *n.* (pl. -*s* or -*x*, pr. -z), cylindrical packet of coins; coil or roll.

roulette′ (roo-) *n.* gambling game played on table with revolving centre over which ball runs.

round *a.* spherical or circular or cylindrical; entire, continuous, all together; candid, outspoken; (of voice etc.) full and mellow. *n.* round object; rung of ladder; slice of bread; revolving motion; circuit, cycle, series, esp. of drinks served to all members of group at one time; (mil.) officer's inspection of guards and sentries; (golf) playing of all holes in course once; (mus.) kind of canon for three or more equal voices; one bout or spell; one stage in competition; *in the* ~, (that may be) seen from all sides, (of theatre) with seats for audience all round stage. *adv.* circularly; with rotation; with return to starting-point; by circuitous way; to, at, etc. all points, sides, members, etc. of area, company, etc. *prep.* so as to encircle or enclose; to or on further side of; to, at, etc. all or many points, sides, etc. of; about. *v.* invest with or assume round shape; pass round; make complete, symmetrical, etc. (freq. ~ *off*); turn *on* with retort etc.; ~ *up* (cattle) by riding round (freq. transf.). ~about *a.* circuitous, circumlocutory; *n.* merry-go-round; place where traffic must follow circuitous course. ~ dance, one in which dancers form ring. ~**game,** one in which each player plays on his own account. **R~head,** member of the Parliament party in 17th-c. civil war. ~ **numbers,** numbers stated without odd units etc. ~**robin,** written petition with signatures in circle to conceal order in which they were written. ~**s'man,** tradesman's employee going round for orders and with goods. ~ **sum,** considerable sum of money. ~**-table conference,** one at which parties present are all on equal footing. ~ **trip** etc., circular tour, outward and return journey. ~**-up,** act or occasion of rounding up.

roun'del n. small disc; rondeau.

roun'delay n. short simple song with refrain.

roun'ders n.pl. team-game with bat and ball in which unit of scoring is player's run round all bases.

round'ly adv. bluntly, plainly; in thoroughgoing way.

roup (rōōp) n. & v.t. (Sc.) (sell by) auction.

rouse (-z) v. stir up from sleep or quiescence; cease to sleep; become active.

rout[1] n. disorderly retreat of defeated troops; utter defeat; party of revellers or rioters; (arch.) large evening party. v.t. defeat utterly.

rout[2] v.t. search out, force or fetch out, rummage among etc.

route (rōōt, mil. rowt) n. way taken in getting from starting-point to destination. v.t. send etc. along particular route. ~**-march,** training march of soldiers etc.

routine (rōōtēn') n. regular course of procedure, unvarying performance of certain acts; set form, fixed arrangement. a. performed by rule or habitually.

rōve v. wander (over or through) without settled destination; move from place to place; (of eyes) look in changing directions. **rō'ver**[1] n. wanderer; R~, senior Boy Scout.

rō'ver[2] n. (arch.) sea-robber, pirate.

row[1] (rō) n. more or less straight line; number of objects or persons in row; line of seats.

row[2] (rō) v. propel boat with oars; convey in boat; row race with; be member of boat's crew. n. spell of rowing, boat-excursion. ~**ing--boat,** boat propelled with oars.

row[3] n. (colloq.) disturbance, noise, dispute; free fight; being reprimanded. v.t. reprimand, rate.

rowan (rō'an, row'an) n. (scarlet berry of) mountain ash.

row'dy a. rough, noisy, and disorderly. n. rowdy person. ~**ism** n.

row'el n. spiked revolving disc at end of spur.

rowlock (rŭl'ok) n. appliance serving as point of support for oar.

roy'al a. of, from, suited to, worthy of, king; belonging to family of, in service or under patronage of, king or queen; splendid, first-rate. n. royal stag, mast, or sail; size of paper (24 × 19, 25 × 20 in.); (colloq.) member of royal family. ~ **mast,** ~ **sail,** above topgallant mast and sail. ~ **stag,** stag with head of 12 or more tines. ~ **standard,** square banner with royal arms. **roy'alist** n. supporter of monarchy. **roy'alty** n. being royal; royal person(s); royal licence to work minerals; payment by lessee of mine to landowner; payment to patentee for use of patent or to author etc. for each copy sold, performance given, etc.

R.S. abbr. Royal Society.

R.S.A. abbr. Royal Scottish Academy, Society of Arts.

R.S.F.S.R. abbr. Russian Soviet Federal Socialist Republic.

R.S.M. abbr. Regimental Sergeant--Major.

R.S.P.C.A. abbr. Royal Society for Prevention of Cruelty to Animals.

R.S.V.P. abbr., répondez s'il vous plaît [F], please answer.

R.T., R/T abbr. radio telegraphy, telephony.

Rt. Hon., Rt. Rev. abbr. Right Honourable, Reverend.

R.T.O. abbr. Railway Transport Officer.

R.T.R. abbr. Royal Tank Regiment.

R.U. abbr. Rugby Union.

rŭb v. subject to friction; slide hand or object along or over surface of; polish, clean, abrade, chafe. make dry, make sore, by rubbing; take (stain etc.) *out*; freshen or brush *up*; come into, be in, sliding contact, exercise friction *against* etc.; get frayed or worn by friction; get *along* etc. with more or less restraint or difficulty; ~ *up the wrong way*, irritate or repel as by stroking cat against lie of fur. *n.* spell of rubbing; impediment or difficulty. **rubb'ing** *n.* (esp.) impression on paper of sepulchral brass etc. made by rubbing.

ruba'tō (rōōbah-) *n.* (mus.) slackening or hastening of note(s) without disturbance of general rhythm.

rubb'er[1] *n.* tough elastic substance made from coagulated juice of certain plants; indiarubber; person or appliance employed to rub; (pl.) galoshes, rubber boots. ~**neck** *n.* (U.S. sl.) sight-seeing tourist, inquisitive person; *v.i.* act as rubberneck, stare inquisitively. **rubb'erize** *v.t.* treat or coat with rubber. **rubb'ery** *a.*

rubb'er[2] *n.* three successive games between same sides or persons at bridge, whist, etc.; winning of two games in rubber.

rubb'ish *n.* waste or worthless matter; litter; trash, nonsense. **rubb'ishy** *a.*

rubb'le *n.* waste or rough fragments of stone, brick, etc.

ru'bicund (rōō-) *a.* ruddy, red-faced.

rubid'ium (ōō-) *n.* soft silvery metallic element.

ru'bric (rōō-) *n.* heading or passage in red or in special lettering; direction for conduct of divine service inserted in liturgical book.

ru'by (rōō-) *n.* crimson or rose-coloured precious stone; glowing red colour; size of printing-type (5½ point). *a.* ruby-coloured.

ruche (rōōsh) *n.* frill or quilling of gauze, lace, etc. *v.t.* gather into, trim with, ruche(s).

ruck[1] *n.* main body of competitors left out of the running; undistinguished crowd or general run.

ruck[2] *v. & n.* crease, wrinkle.

ruck'sack *n.* kind of knapsack slung from shoulders.

ruc'tion *n.* (sl.) dispute, row.

rudd'er *n.* flat piece hinged to stern of ship or boat for steering with;

similar device on aircraft. ~**less** *a.*

rudd'le *n. & v.t.* (mark or colour with) red ochre.

rudd'y *a.* freshly or healthily red; reddish; (sl.) bloody, damnable.

rude (rōōd) *a.* primitive, simple; in natural state; uncivilized, uneducated; roughly made; coarse; violent; vigorous, hearty; insolent, offensive.

ru'diment (rōō-) *n.* (pl.) elements or first principles (*of*); (pl.) germ of something undeveloped; (sing.) part or organ imperfectly developed as having no function. **rudimen'tary** *a.*

rue[1] (rōō) *n.* evergreen shrub with bitter strong-scented leaves.

rue[2] (rōō) *v.t.* repent of; wish undone or unbefallen. ~**ful** *a.* dejected, downcast.

ruff[1] *n.* projecting starched and goffered neck-frill; band of feathers, hair, or colour round bird's or beast's neck; kind of pigeon.

ruff[2] *n.* bird of sandpiper kind.

ruff[3] *n. & v.* trump(ing) at whist etc.

ruff'ian *n.* brutal violent lawless person. ~**ism** *n.*; ~**ly** *a.*

ruff'le *v.t.* disturb smoothness or tranquillity of. *n.* frill of lace etc.; ripple.

ru'fous (rōō-) *a.* reddish-brown.

rug *n.* thick woollen wrap or coverlet; floor-mat.

Rug'by (football) *n.* form of football in which ball may be carried.

rugg'ed (-g-) *a.* of rough uneven surface; harsh; austere.

rugg'er *n.* (colloq.) Rugby football.

rugōse' (rōō-) *a.* wrinkled, corrugated. **rugos'ity** *n.*

ru'in (rōō-) *n.* downfall; fallen or wrecked state; loss of means, moral character, etc.; (often pl.) remains of building etc. that has suffered ruin; cause or agent of ruin. *v.t.* reduce to ruins; bring to ruin; damage irrecoverably, destroy, bankrupt. ~**ā'tion** *n.* **ru'inous** *a.* in ruins, dilapidated; bringing ruin, disastrous.

rule (rōōl) *n.* principle or formula to which action or procedure conforms or is bound or intended to conform; canon, test, standard; normal state of things; sway, government, dominion; code of discipline of religious order; graduated, freq. jointed, strip used for measuring; (print.) thin slip of metal for separating headings, columns, etc.; *as a* ~, usually, more often than not; *work to* ~, slow down rate of working by strictly observing every rule. *v.* exercise sway or decisive influence over; keep under control; (pass.) be guided *by*; be ruler(s) of or *over*, bear rule; give judicial or authoritative decision; (of prices etc.) have specified general level; make parallel lines across (paper), make (line) with ruler etc.; ~ *out*, exclude. ~ **of thumb**, (method or procedure) based on experience or practice, not theory. **ru'ler** *n.* person or thing bearing (esp. sovereign) rule; straight strip or cylinder of wood etc. used for drawing lines. **ru'ling** *n.* (esp.) authoritative pronouncement, judicial decision.

rŭm[1] *n.* spirit distilled from products of sugar-cane; (U.S.) alcoholic liquor.

rŭm[2] *a.* (sl.) queer, strange.

rŭm'ba *n.* (ballroom dance imitating) Cuban Negro dance.

rŭm'ble *v.* make sound as of distant thunder, heavy cart, etc.; utter etc. with such sound; (sl.) grasp, detect, see through. *n.* rumbling sound; hind part of carriage or (U.S.) car arranged as extra seat or for luggage; (sl.) (esp. prearranged) gang-fight. ~-**seat**, (U.S.) dickey--seat.

ru'mĭnant (rōō-) *n.* animal that chews cud. *a.* of ruminants; ruminating.

ru'mĭnāte (rōō-) *v.i.* chew the cud; meditate, ponder. ~**ā'tion** *n.*; ~**ative** *a.*

rŭmm'age *v.* ransack, make search (in); fish *out*. *n.* rummaging search. ~-**sale**, sale of unclaimed articles at docks etc., or of odds and ends at bazaar etc.

rŭmm'er *n.* large drinking-glass.

rŭmm'ў[1] *a.* (sl.) queer, strange. *n.* kinds of card-game with object of collecting sets or groups of cards.

rŭmm'ў[2] *a.* of or like rum. *n.* (U.S.) drunkard.

ru'mour (rōō-) *n.* general talk, report, or hearsay, current statement, of doubtful accuracy. *v.t.* give currency to as rumour.

rŭmp *n.* tail-end of beast or bird; person's posterior; small or contemptible remnant. ~ **steak**, steak cut from ox-rump.

rŭm'ple *v.t.* crease, tousle.

rŭm'pus *n.* (sl.) row, uproar.

rŭn *v.* (p.t. *răn*, p.p. *run*), go or pass with speed, smooth motion, or regularity; compete in race etc.; spread rapidly; flow or emit contents; work or be in action; (of bus etc.) ply; be current, operative, or valid; be worded; enter for race or contest; set or keep going, control operations of; get (contraband) past coastguard, smuggle in; sew or make (*up*) loosely or hastily or with running-stitches; seek election; ~ *across*, *against*, fall in with; ~ *after*, pursue with attentions, seek society of; ~ *away*, flee, elope, bolt; ~ *away with*, carry off, accept (idea etc.) hastily, consume (money etc.); ~ *down*, (of clockwork) stop for want of winding, (of health etc.) become enfeebled, knock down, collide with, discover after search, disparage; ~ *in*, (colloq.) arrest, drive (new machinery) at moderate speed; ~ *into*, incur (debt), have collision with, reach (amount); ~ *off*, write or recite fluently, produce on machine, decide (race) after tie etc.; ~ *on*, be joined together, continue in same line, talk volubly or incessantly; ~ *out*, come to an end, exhaust stock *of*, put down wicket of (running batsman); ~ *over*, review, glance over, recapitulate, (of vehicle) pass over; ~ *through*, pierce, glance through, deal successively with, pervade, consume wastefully; ~ *to*, reach (amount etc.), have money etc. or be enough for, deteriorate by developing (seed); ~ *up*, accumulate quickly, force to bid higher, force up (price etc.). *n.* act or spell of running; (crick.) point scored by running between wickets etc.; way things tend to move; direction; (mus.) rapid scale-passage; continuous stretch, spell or course; journey, distance travelled; series or succession; common, general, or average type or class or line; general demand; enclosure for fowls etc.; range of pasture; licence to make free use of; ladder in stocking etc. **~-back**, space behind base-line of tennis-court. **~-down**, progressive reduction in amount, numbers, etc. **~way**, track or gangway; specially prepared surface for taking off and landing aircraft.

rŭn'away n. fugitive; bolting horse. a. fugitive; bolting; (of marriage) after elopement; out of control.

rune (rōōn) n. letter of earliest Germanic alphabet; similar character of mysterious or magic significance. **ru'nic** a.

rŭng[1] n. short stick fixed as cross-bar, esp. in ladder.

rung[2], p.t. & p.p. of **ring**[2].

rŭnn'el n. brook; gutter.

rŭnn'er n. racer; messenger; kinds of twining bean; creeping stem issuing from base of plant-stem and capable of rooting itself; sliding ring on rod etc.; long piece of wood etc. supporting body of sledge etc.; blade of skate; groove or rod for thing to slide along; long narrow strip of carpet, cloth, etc. **~ bean**, runner. **~-up**, competitor taking second place.

rŭnn'ing a. (esp.) consecutive; successive; flowing; cursive; discharging; (of loop etc.) made with knot that slides along rope etc. n. (esp.) act or manner of running; management; *in the* **~**, with chance of winning or success; *make the* **~**, set the pace. **~-board**, footboard of locomotive, car, etc. **~ commentary**, continuous commentary accompanying text or describing events that are taking place. **~ fight**, one kept up between pursuer(s) and pursued. **~ fire**, continuous firing, successive shots from different points. **~ jump**, one in which jumper runs to take-off. **~ title**, title printed at head of all (left-hand) pages of book etc.

rŭnn'ў a. (colloq.) tending to run or flow; running, (too) liquid.

rŭnt n. ox or cow of small breed; smallest animal of litter; dwarfish or undersized person.

rupee' (rōō-) n. monetary unit of India and Pakistan.

rŭp'ture n. breaking, breach; breach of harmonious relations; abdominal hernia. v. burst (cell, membrane, etc.); sever (connexion); affect with hernia; suffer rupture.

rur'al (roor-) a. in or of or suggesting country. **~ dean**, clergyman with precedence or jurisdiction over division of archdeaconry. **rurăl'itў** n.; **~ īze** v.t.

ruridĕcā'nal (roor-) a. of rural dean or deanery.

Rurītā'nian (roor-) a. romantically and picturesquely adventurous.

ruse (rōōz) n. stratagem, trick.

rŭsh[1] n. marsh plant with slender pithy stem; its stem; rushes as material; a thing of no value. **~light**, candle made by dipping pith of rush in tallow. **rŭsh'ў** a.

rŭsh[2] v. impel or carry along violently and rapidly; take by sudden assault; run precipitately or with great speed; go or act or do without proper consideration. n. act of rushing; violent or tumultuous advance; spurt, charge, onslaught; sudden migration of large numbers; strong run *on* or *for*; (pl., cinema) preliminary showings of film before cutting. a. (colloq.) urgent, (to be) done in haste. **~-hour**, time when traffic etc. is heaviest.

rŭsk n. piece of bread pulled or cut from loaf and rebaked; kinds of light biscuit.

rŭss'ĕt a. of soft reddish-brown. n. russet colour; rough-skinned russet-coloured apple.

Rŭ'ssia (-sha) **leather** n. fine soft leather tanned with birch-bark and rubbed with birch-oil.

Rŭ'ssian (-shn) n. & a. (native, language) of Russia. **~ boots**, high boots with cuffed tops. **~īze** v.t.; **~īzā'tion** n.

rŭst n. yellowish-brown coating

formed on iron by oxidation, and corroding it; colour of this; plant--disease with rust-coloured spots. *v.* contract, affect with, rust; lose quality or efficiency by disuse or inactivity. ~lèss *a.*

rŭs'tĭc *a.* rural; of or like country people or peasants; uncouth; of rude workmanship; of untrimmed branches or rough timber, with rough surface. *n.* countryman. rŭs'tĭcāte *v.* retire to or live in country; send down temporarily from university; mark (masonry) with sunk joint or roughened surface. ~ā'tion, rŭstĭ'cĭtў *nn.*

rŭs'tle (-sl) *n.* sound as of blown leaves or pattering rain. *v.* (cause to) make rustle; go with rustle; (U.S.) get or procure by one's own exertions; steal (cattle, horses). rŭs'tler *n.*

rŭs'tў[1] *a.* rusted, affected with rust; rust-coloured; discoloured by age; impaired by age or disuse.

rŭs'tў[2] *a.* rancid.

rŭt[1] *n.* track sunk by passage of wheels; beaten track, groove. rŭtt'ĕd, rŭtt'ў *aa.*

rŭt[2] *n.* periodic sexual excitement of male deer etc. rŭtt'ĭsh *a.*

ruth (roo-) *n.* (arch.) pity, compassion. ruth'lèss *a.*

ruthē'nĭum (roo-) *n.* hard greyish--white brittle metallic element.

R.V. *abbr.* Revised Version.

R.W.S. *abbr.* Royal Society of Painters in Watercolours.

Ry *abbr.* Railway.

rўe *n.* (grain of) cereal used as fodder etc.; rye whisky. ~-grass, kinds of fodder grass.

rў'ot *n.* Indian peasant.

R.Y.S. *abbr.* Royal Yacht Squadron.

S

S. *abbr.* Saint; Signor; soprano; South(ern);

s. *abbr.* second; shilling; singular; son.

S.A. *abbr.* Salvation Army; sex appeal; South Africa; *Sturm Abtei-*

lung [Ger.], (Nazi) Storm Detachment.

săbbatār'ĭan *a.* Sabbath-keeping; keeping Sunday as Sabbath. *n.* sabbatarian person. ~ĭsm *n.*

săbb'ath *n.* rest-day appointed for Jews on last day of week (Saturday); Sunday, esp. as day of obligatory abstinence from work and play.

sabbăt'ĭcal *a.* of or appropriate to Sabbath. ~ year, year of absence from esp. university duty for purposes of study and travel.

sā'ble *n.* small dark-furred arctic and subarctic carnivore; its skin or fur; black, esp. in heraldry; (pl.) mourning garments. *a.* black; gloomy.

săb'ot (-ō) *n.* shoe hollowed out from one piece of wood; wooden-soled shoe.

săb'otage (-ahzh) *n.* deliberate destruction of or damage to machinery, plant, etc. esp. by dissatisfied workmen, enemy agents, etc. *v.t.* commit sabotage on; wilfully damage or destroy. săboteur' (-ēr) *n.* one who commits sabotage.

sā'bre *n.* cavalry sword with curved blade. *v.t.* cut down or wound with sabre. ~-rattling, war-like, militaristic, threatening war. ~-toothed tiger, large extinct feline mammal with long sabre-shaped upper canines.

săc *n.* bag-like membrane enclosing cavity, cyst, etc.

săcch'arĭn(e) (-k-; *or* -ēn) *n.* & *a.* (of) white intensely sweet crystalline substance used as sugar-substitute. sacch'arĭne (*or* -ĭn *or* -ēn) *a.* sugary; of or containing or like sugar.

săcerdō'tal *a.* priestly; ascribing mysterious powers to or claiming excessive authority for priesthood. ~ĭsm, ~ĭst *nn.*

să'chet (-shā) *n.* small perfumed bag, esp. bag of lavender etc. for laying among clothes etc.

săck[1] *n.* large bag of coarse flax, hemp, etc., or paper etc.; amount held by sack; kinds of loose gown or coat; *the* ~, dismissal. *v.t.* put in sack(s); (colloq.) dismiss from employment. ~cloth, coarse stuff

such as sacks are made of. **sǎck'ful**
n. **~ing** *n*. material used for sacks
etc.

sǎck² *n*. (hist.) kinds of white wine
from Spain etc.

sǎck³ *v.t.* plunder (captured town
etc.). *n*. sacking.

sǎck'but *n*. (mus.) obsolete bass
trumpet with slide like trombone's.

sā'cral *a*. of sacrum.

sǎc'rament *n*. symbolic religious
ceremony, esp. one of seven rites of
Christian Church; *the* Eucharist,
(pl.) *the* consecrated elements;
thing of mysterious and sacred
significance. **sǎcramĕn'tal** *a*. of or
attaching great importance to
sacrament(s); *n*. observance analogous to but not reckoned among
sacraments.

sā'crėd *a*. consecrated or esteemed
dear *to* deity; dedicated or appropriated *to* some person or purpose;
hallowed by religious association;
inviolable, sacrosanct.

sǎc'rifice *n*. slaughter of victim, presenting of gift, or doing of act, to
propitiate god; such victim or gift
or act; giving up of thing for sake
of higher or more urgent one. *v*.
offer (as) sacrifice (*to*); give up as of
inferior importance (*to*); resign oneself to parting with. **sǎcrifi'cial** *a*.

sǎc'rilège *n*. violation of what is
sacred. **sǎcrilē'gious** (*or* -lǐ-) *a*.

sā'cring *n*. (arch.) consecration of
elements in Mass; ordination of
bishop, sovereign, etc. **~-bell**, bell
rung at elevation of Host.

sā'crist *n*. official in charge of sacred
vessels etc. of church or religious
house. **sǎc'ristan** *n*. sexton: sacrist.
sǎc'risty *n*. repository for church
vestments, vessels, etc.

sǎc'rosǎnct *a*. secured by religious
sanction against outrage; inviolable. **~sǎnc'tity** *n*.

sā'crum *n*. compound bone forming
back of pelvis.

sǎd *a*. sorrowful; showing or causing
sorrow; incorrigible; (of bread etc.)
heavy, doughy. **sǎdd'en** *v*.

sǎdd'le *n*. rider's seat on back of
horse etc. or on bicycle etc.; saddle-
-shaped thing, esp. ridge between
two summits; both loins of mutton

or venison as joint. *v.t.* put saddle
on; burden *with* task etc. **~-bag**,
one of a pair of bags laid across
horse etc. behind saddle. **sǎdd'ler**
n. maker of or dealer in saddles and
harness. **sǎdd'lery** *n*.

sā'dism (*or* -ǎ- *or* -ah-) *n*. sexual
delight in cruelty. **~ist** *n*.;
~is'tic *a*.

safǎr'i *n*. (E.-Afr. etc.) hunting or
other expedition esp. on foot.

sāfe¹ *a*. uninjured; out of or not
exposed to danger; affording
security or not involving danger;
cautious; reliable; sure. **~-conduct**,
immunity from arrest or harm on
particular occasion etc.

sāfe² *n*. ventilated cupboard for
provisions; fireproof and burglar-
-proof receptacle for valuables. **~-
-deposit**, building containing safes
or strong-rooms for hire.

sāfe'guard (-fgárd) *n*. proviso, quality,
circumstance, etc. tending to
prevent some evil or protect.
v.t. guard, protect, by precaution
or stipulation; protect (native
industries etc.) against foreign
imports.

sāfe'ty (-ft-) *n*. being safe; freedom
from danger or risks. **~ belt**, strap
etc. securing occupant to seat of
aircraft, motor vehicle, etc. **~
catch**, contrivance for locking gun-
-trigger. **~ curtain**, fireproof curtain
cutting off theatre stage from
auditorium. **~ fuse**, one that can
be ignited at safe distance from
charge. **~-glass**, glass so made as
to prevent splintering. **~-lamp**,
miner's lamp so protected as not to
ignite fire-damp. **~-match**, match
igniting only on specially prepared
surface. **~-pin**, brooch-like pin
with guard or sheath to protect
point. **~-razor**, razor with guard
protecting skin from cuts. **~-valve**,
automatic vent relieving excessive
pressure of steam; harmless outlet
for excitement etc.

sǎff'ron *n*. (orange-yellow stigmas of)
autumn crocus; colour of these.
a. saffron-coloured.

sǎg *v.i.* sink or subside under weight
or pressure; hang sideways or with
downward bulge or curve in middle.

n. sagging; amount that rope etc. sags.

sa'ga (sah-) *n.* medieval Icelandic or Norwegian prose tale; story of heroic achievement or adventure; long family chronicle.

sagā'cious *a.* having or showing insight and practical wisdom; (of animals) exceptionally intelligent, seeming to reason. **sagă'city** *n.*

sāge[1] *n.* aromatic herb with dull greyish-green leaves.

sāge[2] *a.* wise, judicious, experienced. *n.* person credited with profound wisdom.

săgg'ar *n.* fireproof clay case in which pottery is enclosed for baking.

Săgittār'ius, Archer, ninth constellation and sign of zodiac.

sā'gō *n.* starch prepared from palm-pith and used for puddings etc.

sah'ib *n.* former title of address to Europeans in India; (colloq.) gentleman.

said, *p.t.* & *p.p.* of **say.**

sail *n.* piece of canvas etc. extended on rigging to catch wind and propel vessel; (collect.) ship's sails; (collect., with number) ships; wind--catching apparatus attached to arm of windmill; spell of sailing. *v.* progress on water by use of sails or engine-power; start on voyage; navigate ship; traverse sea; glide; move smoothly or easily. ~-cloth, canvas for sails; kind of coarse linen. ~-plane, kind of glider.

sai'lor *n.* seaman, mariner, esp. below officer's rank; *bad, good,* ~, person very, not, liable to seasickness; ~(-hat), straw hat with flat or turned-up brim and flat top. ~ly *a.*

sain'foin *n.* kind of fodder-plant.

saint *n.* canonized person; one of blessed dead or other member of company of heaven; saint-like person. **sain'tĕd** *a.* that is a saint. **saint'hŏŏd** (-t-h-) *n.*; **saint'līke,** ~ly *aa.*

sāke *n.* used chiefly in phr. *for the* ~ *of, for* —'s or *my* etc. ~, out of consideration for; in the interest of; in order to please, get, etc.

salaam' (-ahm) *n.* Oriental salutation; low bow. *v.i.* make salaam.

sā'l(e)able *a.* fit for sale; finding purchasers. ~bĭl'ity *n.*

salā'cious *a.* lustful, lecherous; dealing with or suggestive of lewdness. **salăcity** *n.*

săl'ad *n.* cold dish of usu. uncooked vegetables; vegetable, esp. lettuce, used for salads. ~ **days,** inexperienced youth. ~-**dressing,** mixture of oil, vinegar, etc. used to season salad.

săl'amănder *n.* lizard-like animal supposed to live in fire; elemental spirit of fire; lizard-like amphibian related to newts.

sala'mi, sala'mē (-lah-) *n.* kinds of esp. Italian highly-seasoned sausage.

săl-ammō'niăc *n.* ammonium chloride.

săl'ary *n.* fixed periodical payment for other than manual or mechanical work. **salār'iat** *n.* salaried class. **săl'aried** (-id) *a.* paid by salary.

sāle *n.* selling; amount sold; public auction; disposal of stock at low prices; *for* ~, offered for purchase. ~**room,** room where goods are sold or public auctions are held. ~**sman,** person employed to sell goods or services. ~**smanship,** skill in selling.

saleable : see **salable.**

Săl'ic *a.* ~ *law,* law excluding females from dynastic succession.

sā'lient *a.* prominent, conspicuous; standing out; (of angle) pointing outwards. *n.* salient angle; projecting section of front etc. ~**ence** *n.*

sā'line *a.* impregnated with salt(s); of or like salt. **salin'ity** *n.*

sali'va *n.* mixed secretion of salivary glands and mucous glands of mouth. **săl'ivary** *a.* of, secreting, etc. saliva. **săl'ivāte** *v.i.* secrete or discharge (excessive amount of) saliva.

Sall. *abbr.* Sallust.

săll'ow[1] (-ō) *n.* (shoot or wood of) low-growing kinds of willow.

săll'ow[2] (-ō) *a.* (having complexion) of sickly yellow or yellowish brown.

săll'y *n.* rush from besieged place on

enemy; witticism, piece of banter. *v.i.* make sally; go *forth* or *out* for walk etc.

sălmagŭn'dĭ *n.* highly seasoned dish of chopped meat, anchovies, eggs, etc.; medley.

săl'mĭ *n.* dish of game etc. stewed with wine or sauce after partial roasting.

salmon (săm'on) *n.* large silver-scaled fish with orange-pink flesh. *a.* of colour of salmon. ~ **trout,** sea-trout.

salon (săl'awṅ) *n.* (gathering of esp. literary or artistic notabilities in) great lady's reception-room; (annual or other exhibition in) gallery etc. for showing works of art, photographs, etc.; hairdresser's establishment.

saloon' *n.* large room, esp. in hotel etc., fit for assemblies etc.; large cabin for first-class or all passengers in ship etc.; luxurious railway carriage without compartments; public room(s) for billiards etc.; (U.S.) drinking-bar; ~ (*car*), motor-car with closed body and no partition behind driver. ~ **bar,** first-class bar in English public-house. ~ **deck,** deck reserved for first-class passengers. ~**-keeper,** (U.S.) keeper of saloon.

Salop. *abbr.* Shropshire.

săl'sĭfy *n.* plant with fleshy root cooked as vegetable.

salt (sŏlt *or* sawlt) *n.* sodium chloride, substance obtained from sea-water by evaporation or from earth by mining or pumping, and used as seasoning or preservative of food; substance formed when (part of) hydrogen of acid is replaced by metal or metallic radical; (pl.) smelling-salts, aperient; salt-cellar; piquancy, pungency, wit; experienced sailor; ~ *of the earth,* people for whose existence world is better; *not worth one's* ~, useless, worthless; *take with a grain, pinch, of* ~, accept with reserve or scepticism. *a.* containing, tasting of, or treated with salt; bitter, pungent. *v.t.* preserve or season or treat with salt; make (mine etc.) appear rich by fraudulently introducing ore etc.; store *away* (money etc.); ~ *down,* preserve by salting, store away. ~**-cellar,** vessel holding salt for table use. ~**-marsh,** marsh overflowed by sea. ~**-mine,** mine yielding rock-salt. ~**-pan,** hollow near sea, vessel, used in getting salt by evaporation.

sălta'tion *n.* leaping, dancing; sudden transition. **sălta'torў** *a.*

sal'tĭngs (sŏ- *or* saw-) *n.pl.* salt marshes.

săl'tīre *n.* St. Andrew's cross (X) dividing shield etc. into four compartments.

saltpē'tre (sŏ- *or* saw-) *n.* white crystalline salty substance used in gunpowder etc.

sal'tў (sŏ-, saw-) *a.* of, like, tasting of, salt; pungent, witty.

salū'brĭous (*or* -ōō-) *a.* healthy. **salu'brĭtў** *n.*

salu'ki (-ōōgĭ) *n.* breed of large swift slender silky-coated hunting-dogs.

săl'ūtarў *a.* wholesome in operation; resulting in good.

sălūtā'tion *n.* (use of) words spoken or written in saluting; greeting.

salute' (-ōōt) *n.* gesture expressing respect, courteous recognition, etc. esp. at meeting or parting; (mil., nav., etc.) prescribed movement, use of flags, or discharge of gun(s) in sign of respect; (joc.) kiss. *v.* make salute or salutation (to); greet; kiss.

săl'vage *n.* (payment made or due for) rescue of property from loss at sea or by fire; saving and utilization of waste material; property etc. salvaged. *v.t.* make salvage of, save from wreck, fire, etc.

sălvā'tion *n.* fact or state of being saved from sin and its consequences; preservation from loss, calamity, etc.; thing that preserves from these. **S~ Army,** religious missionary body organized on quasi-military lines. **Salvā'tionist** *n.* member of Salvation Army.

sălve[1] (*or* sahv) *n.* healing ointment; something that soothes. *v.t.* anoint; soothe (pride, conscience, etc.).

sălve[2] *v.t.* salvage.

sǎl'ver *n.* tray for handing refreshments etc.

sǎl'vō *n.* (pl. *-oes*), simultaneous discharge of artillery, rockets, etc.; round or volley of applause.

sǎl volǎt'ĭlĕ *n.* solution of ammonium carbonate, used as restorative in faintness etc.

Sam. *abbr.* Samuel.

Samǎ'rĭtan *n.* inhabitant of ancient Samaria; *good* ~, one who helps the unfortunate.

sǎm'ba *n.* (ballroom dance imitating) Brazilian dance.

sǎm'būr *n.* Indian elk.

sāme *a.* uniform; unvarying; unchanged; identical; aforesaid; previously referred to; *the* ~, the same thing, (adv.) in the same manner; *just the* ~, in spite of that.

sǎm'īte *n.* rich medieval dress-fabric of silk.

sǎm'ovăr *n.* Russian urn for making tea.

Sǎm'oyĕd, -ēde (*-o-*y) *n.* white Arctic breed of dog.

sǎm'păn *n.* small river or coastal boat of China, Japan, etc.

sǎm'phīre *n.* cliff plant with aromatic saline fleshy leaves.

sa'mple (sah-) *n.* small part taken from quantity to give idea of whole; specimen or pattern. *v.t.* take samples of; try qualities of.

sam'pler (sah-) *n.* piece of embroidery worked to show proficiency.

sǎm'urai (*-ŏŏrī*) *n.* member of military caste in feudal Japan.

sǎnatōr'ĭum *n.* (pl. *-ia*, *-iums*), establishment for treatment of invalids, esp. convalescents and consumptives; room or building for sick in school or college.

sǎnc'tĭfȳ *v.t.* consecrate. make holy; purify from sin. ~fĭcā'tion *n.*

sǎnctĭmō'nious *a.* making show of sanctity or piety. ~monȳ *n.*

sǎnc'tion *n.* (clause containing) penalty or reward attached to law; penalty imposed for non-compliance with international law; consideration causing any rule to be obeyed; authoritative permission. *v.t.* authorize, countenance, permit.

sǎnc'tĭtȳ *n.* saintliness; sacredness, inviolability.

sǎnc'tūarȳ *n.* place recognized as holy or inviolable; church or holiest part of it; private retreat; place of refuge, esp. (hist.) place where debtor or fugitive from justice was immune from arrest or violence.

sǎnc'tum *n.* holy place; person's private room.

sǎnc'tus *n.* (music for) hymn beginning 'Holy, holy, holy' in Eucharist. ~ **bell**, bell rung at this.

sǎnd *n.* minute fragments resulting from wearing down of esp. siliceous rocks; (usu. pl.) grain of sand; (pl.) expanse of sand; (usu. pl.) sand-bank. *v.t.* sprinkle or mix or polish with sand. ~**bag**, bag filled with sand for use in fortification, as weapon, etc.; *v.t.* protect with sandbags; stun or fell with blow from sandbag. ~-**bank**, shoal or submarine bank of sand. ~-**blast**, (roughen, engrave, etc. with) jet of sand impelled by compressed air or steam. ~-**dune**, ~-**hill**, hill or ridge of drifted sand. ~**martin**, kind nesting in sandy banks. ~**paper**, (polish or smooth with) paper with layer of sand on surface. ~-**piper**, kinds of bird haunting open wet sandy places. ~-**shoes**, usu. of canvas with rubber or rope soles. ~**stone**, sedimentary rock of usu. quartz grains cemented together. ~**storm**, desert storm of wind with clouds of sand.

sǎn'dal *n.* sole without uppers attached to foot by thongs or straps; kinds of light open shoe. **sǎn'dalled** (-ld) *a.*

sǎn'dalwŏŏd *n.* kinds of scented wood.

S. & M. *abbr.* (Bishop) of Sodor and Man.

sǎnd'wǐch *n.* two or more slices of bread, toast, etc. with meat or other relish between; cake of two layers with jam etc. between; *open* ~, one with top layer of bread etc. omitted. *v.t.* insert between or among other things etc. esp. of different kind; put *together*, make into sandwich, *with*. ~-**board**, board carried by sandwich-man. ~ **course**, course of study in which periods of theoretical and practical work alternate. ~-man, man walking street with advertisement boards hung one before and one behind.

sănd'y̆ a. covered with sand; sand-coloured, yellowish-red; having sandy hair.

sāne a. of sound mind, not mad; sensible, rational.

sang, p.t. of sing.

sang-froid (sahnfrwah') n. coolness in danger or difficulty.

săng'uinary̆ (-nggwĭ-) a. attended by or delighting in bloodshed; bloodthirsty; bloody.

săng'uine (-nggwĭn) a. habitually hopeful, confident; expecting things to go well; blood-red; ruddy, florid.

sănguin'ĕous (-nggwĭ-) a. of blood; blood-coloured.

săn'hĕdrĭn (-nĭ-) n. supreme council and court of justice in ancient Jerusalem.

sănitār'ĭum n. sanatorium.

săn'ĭtary̆ a. of conditions that affect health, esp. with regard to dirt and infection; free from or designed to obviate influences deleterious to health; of sanitation; used during menstruation.

sănĭtā'tion n. measures conducing to preservation of public health; drainage and disposal of sewage.

săn'ity̆ n. saneness.

sank, p.t. of sink.

săns (-z) prep. (arch.) without. ~-cŭlŏtte' (sahn-) n. republican of Parisian lower classes in French Revolution; extreme republican or revolutionary.

sănsĕ'rĭf n. & a. (form of type or lettering) without serifs.

Săn'skrĭt n. & a. (of) ancient, classical, and sacred Indo-European language of Hindus in India.

Săn'ta Claus (-z) n. legendary personage supposed to fill children's stockings with presents at Christmas.

săp¹ n. vital juice of plants; vitality. v.t. drain of sap; exhaust vigour of. săp'lĕss, săpp'y̆ aa.

săp² n. digging of siege-trenches; covered siege-trench. v. approach (place) by sap; dig siege-trenches;

undermine (wall etc.); destroy (faith etc.) insidiously. săpp'er n. (esp.) private of Royal Engineers.

săp'ĭd a. savoury; not tasteless; not insipid. sapĭd'ity̆ n.

sā'pĭence n. wisdom; knowledge. sā'pĭent a. aping wisdom; would-be wise.

săp'lĭng n. young tree.

săponā'ceous a. soapy.

sapŏn'ĭfy̆ v. convert, be converted, into soap. ~fĭcā'tion n.

Sapphic (săf'ĭk) a. of Sappho. ~ stanza, ~ verse, in Greek metre used by Sappho. ~s n. Sapphic verse.

sapphire (săf'īr) n. transparent blue precious stone; its colour, azure. a. of sapphire blue.

sapph'ĭsm (săf-) n. lesbianism.

săp'rophȳte n. vegetable organism living on decayed organic matter.

să'răbănd n. (music for) slow Spanish dance in triple time.

Să'racen n. Arab or Moslem of time of crusades. Săracĕn'ĭc a. (esp.) of Moslem architecture.

săr'căsm n. bitter or wounding, esp. ironic, remark; use of, faculty of uttering, sarcasms. sarcăs'tĭc a.

sărcō'ma n. malignant tumour of connective tissue.

sărcŏph'agus n. (pl. -gī), stone coffin.

sărd n. yellow or orange cornelian.

sărdine' (-ēn) n. small fish of herring kind usu. tinned in oil.

sărdŏn'ĭc a. grimly jocular; full of bitter scorn; cynical.

săr'donyx n. onyx in which white layers alternate with sard.

sărgăss'ō n. (pl. -os), kinds of sea-weed floating in island-like masses in Gulf Stream.

sa'rī (sah-) n. length of material wrapped round body, worn as main garment by Hindu women.

sarŏng' n. long piece of cloth worn by Malays etc. tucked round waist or under armpits as skirt.

sărsaparĭll'a n. (tonic made from roots of) kinds of tropical Amer. smilax.

săr'sen(-stone) n. one of large sandstone boulders found scattered on esp. Wiltshire chalk downs.

săr'senėt, -cenėt (-sn-) n. soft silk fabric used for linings etc.

sártŏr'ial *a*. of tailors or clothes.

Sarum, (Bishop) of Salisbury.

sǎsh[1] *n*. scarf worn over one shoulder or round waist esp. as part of uniform or insignia.

sǎsh[2] *n*. frame holding window-glass, usu. made to slide up and down in grooves.

Sask. *abbr.* Saskatchewan.

sǎss'afrǎs *n*. (tonic made from) small N.-Amer. tree of laurel kind.

Sǎssenach (*-ch*) *n*. (Sc. and Ir. for) Englishman.

sat, *p.t.* of **sit.**

Sat. *abbr.* Saturday.

Sā'tan, the Devil. **satǎn'ic** *a*. of or like Satan; diabolical.

S.A.T.B. *abbr.* soprano, alto, tenor, bass.

sǎtch'el *n*. small bag, esp. for carrying school-books.

sāte *v.t.* gratify to the full; cloy, surfeit.

sateen' *n*. glossy cotton fabric woven like satin.

sǎt'ellīte *n*. hanger-on, dependant; small or secondary planet revolving round another; artificial body in orbital motion round earth etc.; State nominally independent but dominated by another. **~ town,** small town built to house excess population of another.

sā'tiāte (*-shǐ-*) *v.t.* sate.

satī'etў *n*. state of being glutted or satiated; feeling of disgust or surfeit caused by excess.

sǎt'in *n*. silk fabric with glossy surface on one side. **~-stitch,** long embroidery stitches laid close together. **~wood,** (hard light--coloured satiny wood of) kinds of tree. **sǎtǐnět(te)'** *n*. satin-like fabric partly or wholly of cotton or wool.

sǎt'īre *n*. composition in which vice or folly is held up to ridicule; use of ridicule, sarcasm, or irony to expose folly. **satī'ric** *a*. of or containing satire. **satī'rical** *a*.; **sǎt'irist** *n*.; **sǎt'irīze** *v.t.*

sǎtǐsfǎc'tion *n*. satisfying or being satisfied; thing that satisfies desire or gratifies feeling; payment of debt; atonement; amends for injury. **sǎtǐsfǎc'tory** *a*. causing satisfaction; adequate.

sǎt'isfў *v.t.* meet expectations or wishes of; content; be accepted by (person etc.) as adequate; pay, fulfil, comply with; still cravings of; convince; be sufficient for. **sǎt'isfied** (*-īd*), **~ing** *aa*.

sǎt'rǎp *n*. ancient-Persian provincial governor; subordinate ruler (esp. with implication of tyranny or luxury).

sǎ'turāte (*-cher-*) *v.t.* fill with moisture, soak, steep; imbue with or steep in learning, traditions, etc.; bomb so thoroughly that defences are powerless, destroy by bombing. **~d** *a*. (of solution) containing maximum possible quantity of dissolved substance. **saturā'tion** *n*.

Sǎt'urday (*or* -dǐ) *n*. seventh day of week.

Sǎt'ŭrn *n*. Roman god of agriculture; large planet with orbit outside Jupiter's.

sǎturnā'lia *n.pl.* S~, Roman festival of Saturn; scene or time of wild revelry. **~n** *a*.

sǎt'urnīne *a*. morose, cold and gloomy.

sǎt'yr (*-er*) *n*. one of class of woodland gods in train of Bacchus, freq. represented with ears, legs, etc. of goat, and budding horns; type of gross lustfulness.

sauce *n*. usu. liquid or soft preparation taken as relish with food; something that adds piquancy; (colloq.) sauciness. *v.t.* add sauce to; make piquant; (colloq.) be impudent to. **~-boat,** vessel in which sauce is served. **~pan,** usu. metal kitchen utensil with long handle, for boiling etc.

sau'cer *n*. small shallow vessel, esp. placed under cup, flower-pot, etc. to catch liquid spilled etc.; round shallow depression in ground.

sau'cў *a*. impudent, cheeky; (sl.) smart-looking.

sauerkraut (sowr'krowt) *n*. (German dish of) pickled cabbage.

sau'na (sow-) *n*. Finnish steam-bath or bath-house.

saun'ter *v.i.* walk in leisurely way. *n*. leisurely ramble or gait.

saur'ian *a*. & *n*. (of or like) lizard, crocodile, etc.

saus'age (sŏs-) *n.* minced meat enclosed in long cylindrical case of animal tissue etc.; (colloq.) sausage--shaped object, esp. observation balloon.

sauté (sō'tā) *a.* & *n.* (dish of vegetables etc.) quickly and lightly fried by tossing in fat. *v.t.* cook thus.

săv'age *a.* uncivilized, in primitive state; fierce, cruel; (colloq.) angry. *n.* member of savage tribe; brutal or barbarous person. *v.t.* attack and bite or trample; attack furiously. **săv'agerў** *n.* savage conduct or state.

savănn'a(h) *n.* wide treeless grassy plain esp. in tropical America.

săv'ant (-ahṅ) *n.* man of learning, scholar.

savate' (-aht) *n.* kind of French boxing with blows given by feet as well as hands.

săve *v.* rescue or preserve from danger or harm; effect spiritual salvation of; keep for future use; lay money etc. by; economize (in); prevent loss of; relieve from need of expending or from exposure to (annoyance etc.); (games) prevent opponent from scoring; ~ *up*, accumulate by economy. *n.* act of saving in football etc. *prep.* except, but. **sā'vĭng** *a.* (esp.) making reservation or exception; redeeming; *n.* (esp.) something saved; (pl.) amount of money put by; **savings--bank**, bank receiving small deposits.

săv'eloy *n.* highly seasoned dried sausage.

sā'viour (-vyer) *n.* deliverer, redeemer; saver from ruin etc.

săv'oir faire' (-vwâr) *n.* quickness to see and do right thing; address, tact.

sā'vorў *n.* aromatic kitchen herb.

sā'vour *n.* characteristic taste, flavour; essential virtue or property; tinge or hint *of.* *v.* appreciate flavour of, enjoy; smack or suggest presence *of.* **sā'vourў** *a.* with appetizing taste or smell; of stimulating or piquant flavour, not sweet; *n.* savoury dish, esp. at end of dinner.

savoy' *n.* rough-leaved winter cabbage.

săvv'ў *v.* (sl.) know. *n.* (sl.) knowingness; common sense.

saw[1], *p.t.* of **see**[2].

saw[2] *n.* old saying, maxim.

saw[3] *n.* implement with toothed edge for cutting wood etc. *v.* (p.p. *sawn, sawed*), cut or make with, use, saw; make to-and-fro motion as of saw or sawing. ~**bones**, (sl.) surgeon. ~**dust**, fine wood-fragments produced in sawing. ~--**edged**, with serrated edge. ~**fish**, kind armed with toothed snout. ~--**fly**, insect destructive to vegetation. ~**mill**, mill for mechanical sawing of wood into planks etc. ~--**pit**, pit in which lower of two men working two-handed saw stands. **saw'yer** *n.* workman who saws timber.

săx *n.* (colloq.) saxophone.

săxe (blue) *n.* slightly greenish blue.

săx'horn *n.* kinds of brass wind instrument of trumpet kind.

săx'ifrage *n.* kinds of Alpine or rock plant.

Săx'on *n.* & *a.* (member, language) of Germanic people by whom parts of England were occupied in 5th–6th cc.; (native) of Saxony; Anglo--Saxon.

săx'onў *n.* fine kind of wool; kinds of cloth made from it.

săx'ophōne *n.* powerful keyed brass reed instrument with conical tube.

say *v.* (*said,* pr. sĕd), utter or recite in speaking voice; state; speak, tell, express; adduce or allege in argument or excuse; repeat, rehearse. *n.* (opportunity of saying) what one has to say; share in decision. ~--**so**, (colloq.) unsupported assertion; authority. **say'ĭng** *n.* (esp.) common remark, maxim.

S.C. *abbr.* South Carolina; Special Constable.

sc. *abbr., scilicet* [L], to wit; *sculpsit* [L], carved or sculptured or engraved this.

scăb *n.* crust formed over sore in healing; kinds of skin- and plant--disease; blackleg. **scăbb'ў** *a.*

scăbb'ard *n.* sheath of sword, bayonet, dagger, etc.

scā'bĭes (-z) *n.* contagious parasitic skin-disease, itch.

scā'bious *n.* kinds of herbaceous plant with pincushion-shaped flowers.

scā'brous *a.* rough-surfaced; (of subject, situation, etc.) hard to handle with decency.

scāff'old *n.* temporary platform supported on poles for use of builders etc.; platform on which criminal is executed. **~ing** *n.* temporary structure of poles and planks providing builders etc. with platform(s); materials for this.

scald (-aw-) *v.t.* injure or pain with hot liquid or vapour; cleanse with boiling water; heat (liquid, esp. milk) to near boiling-point. *n.* injury to skin by scalding.

scāle[1] *n.* one of thin membranous horny or bony overlapping plates protecting skin of fishes, reptiles, etc.; thin plate or flake or film; scab; incrustation or deposit of rust, lime, etc.; tartar on teeth. *v.* remove scales or scale from; form or come off in scales. **scā'lȳ** *a.*

scāle[2] *n.* pan of balance; (pl.) balance or weighing instrument. *v.t.* weigh (specified amount).

scāle[3] *n.* series of degrees; graduated arrangement, classification, or system; (mus.) definite series of sounds ascending or descending by fixed intervals; relative dimensions (of plan, map, etc.); instrument or apparatus for use in measuring etc.; system of numeration or numerical notation in which value of figure depends on its place in order. *v.* climb up; represent in true relative proportions; ~ *down*, *up*, make smaller, larger, in due proportion, diminish or increase. **scaling-ladder**, ladder for climbing high walls.

scā'lēne *a.* unequal-sided.

scăll'ion *n.* kinds of onion.

scăll'op (*or* skŏ-) *n.* bivalve mollusc with shallow shell edged with small semicircular lobes; one valve of this esp. used for cooking and serving various dishes; one of series of convex rounded projections at edge of garment etc. *v.t.* bake (as) in scallop-shell; ornament with scallops.

scăll'ywăg *n.* (sl.) scamp, scapegrace.

scălp *n.* skin and hair of upper part of head; this cut or torn off as trophy by Amer. Indians (freq. fig.). *v.t.* take scalp of.

scăl'pel *n.* small surgical knife.

scămp[1] *n.* rascal, rogue.

scămp[2] *v.t.* do (work etc.) in perfunctory or inadequate way.

scăm'per *v.i.* run like frightened animal or playing child. *n.* scampering run.

scăm'pi *n.pl.* (dish of) kind of prawn.

scăn *v.* analyse metre (of line etc.) by examining feet, etc.; be metrically correct; look at all parts successively of; (television) resolve (picture) into elements of light and shade for transmission; traverse systematically with radar beam etc.

scăn'dal *n.* (thing occasioning) general feeling of outrage or indignation, esp. as expressed in talk; malicious gossip. **~īze** *v.t.* horrify, shock. **~monger** (-ŭngg-) *n.* one who invents or spreads scandals. **scăn'dalous** *a.*

Scăndinā'vian *a. & n.* (native) of Scandinavia.

scăn'dium *n.* rare metallic element.

scăn'sion *n.* metrical scanning, way verse scans.

scănt *a.* barely or not sufficient.

scănt'ling *n.* small beam, esp. one under 5 in. square; size to which stone or timber is to be cut.

scăn'tȳ *a.* barely sufficient; of small amount or extent.

scāpe *n.* shaft of column; long leafless flower-stalk springing from root.

scāpe'goat *n.* person blamed or punished for faults of others.

scāpe'grāce *n.* rascal, ne'er-do-well.

scăp'ūla *n.* (pl. -*lae*), shoulder-blade.

scăp'ūlar *a.* of scapula; *n.* kinds of monastic vestment; bandage for shoulder-blade.

scār[1] *n.* mark left on skin etc. by wound etc. *v.* mark with, form, scar(s).

scār[2] *n.* precipitous craggy part of mountain-side.

scă'rab *n.* ancient gem cut in form of beetle.

scārce *a.* not plentiful; rare; *make*

oneself ~, go away. *adv.* (arch.) scarcely.

scarce'ly (-slǐ) *adv.* hardly, only just; surely not.

scar'cǐtў *n.* being scarce; dearth (*of*).

scāre *v.t.* strike with sudden terror, frighten (*away, off,* etc.). *n.* sudden fright or alarm, esp. general alarm caused by baseless or exaggerated rumours. ~**crow,** device for frightening birds away from crops; badly dressed or grotesque person. ~**monger,** alarmist.

scarf[1] *n.* joint uniting two pieces of timber etc. endwise. *v.t.* join with scarf.

scarf[2] *n.* (pl. *-ves, -fs*), long strip of material worn round neck, over shoulders, or from shoulder to opposite hip; necktie with wide flowing ends. ~**-pin,** ~**-ring,** ornamental fastenings for necktie.

scǎ'rǐfў *v.t.* (surg.) make slight incisions in; scratch; criticize mercilessly. ~**fǐcā'tion** *n.*

scarlati'na (-tē-) *n.* scarlet fever.

scar'lĕt *n.* & *a.* (of) brilliant red colour inclining to orange. ~ **fever,** infectious fever with scarlet rash. ~ **runner,** scarlet-flowered climbing bean.

scarp *n.* steep slope, esp. inner side of ditch in fortification. *v.t.* make steep or perpendicular.

scar'per *v.i.* (sl.) go, make off.

scăt *n.* (jazz) singing of meaningless syllables.

scā'thing (-dh-) *a.* (of criticism etc.) withering, blasting.

scatŏl'ogў *n.* filthy or obscene literature. **scătolŏ'gical** *a.*

scătt'er *v.* throw or put here and there; sprinkle; distribute (shot); diffuse by reflection from particles; separate and disperse in flight etc. *n.* scattering; extent of distribution. ~**-brain,** thoughtless, flighty, or desultory person. ~**ed** *a.* (esp.) not situated together, wide apart; sporadic.

scătt'ў *a.* (sl.) scatter-brained, crazy.

scaup(-dŭck) *n.* kinds of duck of northern coasts.

scăv'ėnger (-j-) *n.* person employed to remove refuse from streets etc.; animal feeding on carrion etc.

scăv'enge *v.i.* be or act as scavenger.

scėnăr'ĭō (*or* -ār-) *n.* (pl. *-os*), outline or detailed plot of opera, film, etc.

scēne *n.* place of actual or fictitious occurrence; piece of continuous action that forms part of play; action, episode, situation; stormy action or encounter or outburst, esp. with display of temper; painted canvas, properties, etc. representing scene of action, stage set with these; *behind the* ~s, out of view of audience; out of sight, hearing, or knowledge of general public. ~**-painter,** painter of scenery. ~**-shifter,** one who changes scenes in theatre.

scē'nerў *n.* painted canvas, woodwork, etc. of stage setting; (general appearance of) natural features etc. of place or district.

scē'nǐc *a.* of or on stage; of scenery. ~ **railway,** miniature railway running through artificial scenery.

scĕnt *v.t.* discern (as if) by smell; make fragrant, perfume. *n.* characteristic odour of something; fragrance; trail, odour of animal etc. as means of pursuit by hound etc.; liquid perfume. ~**ėd** *a.* (esp.) fragrant, sweet-smelling. ~**less** *a.*

scĕp'tǐc (sk-) *n.* person who questions truth of religious doctrines; sceptical person. **scĕp'tǐcal** *a.* of sceptic(s); critical, doubtful, incredulous, hard to convince. ~**ǐsm** *n.*

scĕp'tre *n.* staff borne in hand as symbol of regal or imperial authority; sovereignty.

Sch. *abbr.* Scholar; School.

schĕd'ūle (sh-, U.S. sk-) *n.* tabulated statement of details, list, etc., esp. as appendix to principal document; time-table; *on* ~, at time appointed, provided for, etc. *v.t.* make schedule of, include in schedule; appoint time for, plan for fixed time.

schėmăt'ǐc *a.* of or like scheme or diagram; systematic, formalized.

schēme (sk-) *n.* systematic arrangement; outline, syllabus; plan of action; artful or underhand design. *v.i.* make plans, plan esp. in secret or underhand way. **schē'mer** *n.*; **schē'ming** *a.*

scherzo (skār'tsō) *n.* (mus.) vigorous and lively movement or composition. [It.]

schipp'erkė (sk- *or* sh-) *n.* small black smooth-haired dog of Belgian breed.

schism (sĭzm) *n.* separation or division in Church; offence of promoting schism. **schismăt'ĭc** *a.* & *n.* (person) tending to or guilty of schism; (member) of seceded branch of Church.

schist (sh-) *n.* fine-grained rock with components arranged in layers, splitting in thin irregular plates. **~ōse, ~ous** *aa.*

schiz'oid (skĭdz-; *or* -ts-) *a.* of, tending to, having, etc. schizophrenia. **schizophrē'nĭa** *n.* mental disorder marked by disconnexion between intellect and emotions etc. **schizophrĕn'ĭc** *a.*

schmal(t)z (shmawlts; *or* -ă-) *n.* sickly sentimentality.

schnăpps (shn-) *n.* strong hollands gin.

schnauzer (shnow'ts*er*) *n.* wire--coated German terrier.

schnĭt'zel (shn-) *n.* veal cutlet, esp. breadcrumbed and fried in butter.

schnōr'kel (shn-) *n.* tube supplying submerged submarine or diver with air.

schŏl'ar (sk-) *n.* (arch.) pupil; learned person; holder of scholarship. **~lў** *a.* erudite; (as) of, befitting, learned person. **~ship** *n.* learning, erudition; (right to) emoluments paid for fixed period from funds of school, university, State, etc. for defraying cost of education or studies.

scholăs'tĭc (sk-) *a.* of schools or education; academic, pedantic; (as) of schoolmen; dealing in logical subtleties. **scholăs'tĭcism** (sk-) *n.*

schōōl[1] (sk-) *n.* shoal of fish, whales, etc.

schōōl[2] (sk-) *n.* institution for educating children or giving instruction; its buildings; its pupils; time given to teaching; being educated in school; circumstances etc. serving to discipline or instruct; organized body of teachers and scholars in higher branch of study in Middle Ages, esp. as part of university; branch of study with separate examinations at university; (pl.) Oxford degree examination; (group or succession of) artists, disciples, etc. following or holding similar principles, opinions, etc. *v.t.* discipline, bring under control, train or accustom *to.* **~-ma'am, -marm,** (colloq.) schoolmistress. **~man,** teacher in medieval university; writer treating of logic, metaphysics, and theology as taught in medieval universities. **~master, ~mis⁺ress,** teacher in school. **~room,** room used for lessons, esp. in private house. **schōō'ling** *n.*

schōō'ner (sk-) *n.* small esp. two--masted fore-and-aft rigged ship; (U.S.) large tall beer-glass; *prairie* **~,** (U.S.) large covered wagon.

schottische (shŏtēsh') *n.* (music for) dance like slow polka.

sciăt'ĭc *a.* of hip or sciatic nerve; of or having sciatica. **~ nerve,** largest nerve in human body, passing down back of thigh to foot. **sciăt'ĭca** *n.* neuritis or neuralgia of sciatic nerve.

sci'ence *n.* (pursuit of) systematic and formulated knowledge; branch of knowledge, esp. (*natural* or *physical* **~**) one dealing with material phenomena and based on observation, experiment, and induction; such sciences as whole; trained skill in boxing, games, etc. **~ fiction,** fantasy dealing with future, imaginary pseudo-scientific achievements, etc. **scientif'ĭc** *a.* according to principles of science; of or concerned with science or natural sciences; having or requiring trained skill. **sci'entĭst** *n.* person learned in natural science(s).

sci'lĭcĕt *adv.* that is to say, namely. [L]

scĭll'a *n.* (plant or flower of) kinds of bulbous plant.

scĭm'ĭtar *n.* short curved Oriental sword.

scĭntĭll'a *n.* shred or atom.

scĭn'tĭllăte *v.i.* sparkle, twinkle; emit sparks. **scĭntĭllā'tion** *n.*

scĭ'on *n.* shoot cut for grafting; young member of family.

scĭ'ssion *n.* cutting, being cut; division, split.

sciss'ors (-zerz) *n.pl.* cutting implement of pair of blades pivoted together.

sclerō'sis *n.* (pl. -*sēs*), hardening of tissue esp. of arteries. **sclerŏt'ic** *a.* of or affected with sclerosis; of sclerotic; *n.* opaque white outer coat of eyeball forming white of eye.

S.C.M. *abbr.* State Certified Midwife; Student Christian Movement.

scŏff[1] *v.i.* speak derisively; mock or jeer *at.* *n.* mocking words; taunt.

scŏff[2] *v.t.* (sl.) eat; eat greedily.

scŏld *v.* find fault noisily; rail, rate, rebuke. *n.* railing or nagging woman.

scŏnce[1] *n.* bracket candlestick; socket holding candle.

scŏnce[2] *n.* (arch.) head.

scŏnce[3] *v.t.* inflict forfeit of beer upon for offence against table etiquette. *n.* such forfeit.

scŏne (*or* -ōn) *n.* soft flat cake of flour, orig. baked on girdle.

scōōp *n.* short-handled deep shovel for grain, flour, specie, etc.; long--handled ladle; gouge-like instrument; coal-scuttle; scooping; (colloq.) obtaining of news etc., news obtained, before or to exclusion of competitors. *v.* lift (*up*), hollow (*out*), (as) with scoop; slide from one note to another in music, esp. with voice; secure by sudden action or stroke of luck; gain advantage over by obtaining scoop.

scōōt *v.i.* (sl.) dart, shoot along; make off. **scōō'ter** *n.* child's toy vehicle of narrow foot-board on wheels propelled by pushes of one foot on ground; light motor-cycle.

scōpe *n.* outlook; sweep or reach of observation or action, range; opportunity, outlet.

scopŏl'amine (-ēn *or* -ĭn) *n.* drug used as sedative etc.

scŏrbū'tic *a.* of or affected with scurvy. *n.* scorbutic person.

scŏrch *v.* burn surface of so as to discolour, shrivel, pain, etc.; become discoloured, slightly burnt, etc. with heat; be very hot; (sl.) go at very high or excessive speed. *n.* mark of scorching. **~ed earth,** applied to policy of destroying everything that might be of use to invading enemy. **~er** *n.*, **~ing** *a.* (esp.) extremely hot (day, sun, etc.).

scŏre *n.*, notch cut; line cut or scratched or drawn; reckoning; number of points made by player or side in game; detailed table of these; copy of music showing parts etc.; (set of) twenty; weight of 20 lb. in weighing pigs etc.; category, head; (advantage etc. gained by) scoring off. *v.* mark with, make, notches or incisions or lines; slash, furrow; mark *up*, enter, record (*against*); record or keep score; win, make points in game etc.; secure advantage, have good luck; orchestrate, arrange (*for* instrument etc.); **~** *off*, (sl.) worst in argument etc., inflict humiliation on. **scŏr'er** *n.* (esp.) one who keeps score at cricket etc.

scŏr'ia *n.* (pl. -*iae*), slag; (pl.) (fragments of) cellular lava.

scŏrn *n.* disdain, contempt, derision; object of contempt. *v.t.* hold in contempt; abstain from, refuse *to* do, as unworthy. **~ful** *a.*

Scŏr'piŏ, Scorpion, eighth constellation and sign of zodiac.

scŏr'pion *n.* lobster-like arachnid with jointed stinging tail.

scŏt[1] *n.* (hist.) tax or rate. **~-free,** unharmed, unpunished, safe.

Scŏt[2] *n.* native of Scotland.

scŏtch[1] *v.t.* wound without killing; crush, stamp out.

Scŏtch[2] *a.* of Scotland or its inhabitants; in dialect(s) of English spoken in Scottish Lowlands. *n.* Scottish dialect; (colloq.) Scotch whisky. (Modern Scots usu. prefer the forms *Scots, Scottish,* exc. in **~** whisky etc.). **~ broth,** mutton broth thickened with pearl barley and vegetables. **~ fir,** common N. Eur. pine. **~ mist,** thick wet mist. **~ terrier,** small rough--coated short-legged terrier.

scŏ'ter *n.* large duck of northern coasts.

Scŏt'land Yǎrd *n.* headquarters of London metropolitan police; C.I.D. of Metropolitan Police Force.

Scŏts *a.* Scottish. *n.* Scottish Lowland dialect. **~man, ~woman,**

native of Scotland. **Scŏtt'ish** a. of Scotland or its people, dialect, etc.

scoun'drel n. wicked unscrupulous person; villain. **scoun'drelly** a.

scour[1] (-owr) v.t. rub bright or clean; clean out; clear off, out, etc.; purge drastically. n. act or process of scouring.

scour[2] (-owr) v. rove, range; go along hastily, esp. in search or pursuit.

scourge (skêrj) n. (arch.) whip for chastising persons; person or thing regarded as instrument of divine or other vengeance etc. v.t. chastise; afflict; use scourge on.

scout[1] n. man sent out to reconnoitre; Boy Scout; ship, aircraft, etc. for reconnoitring; male college servant at Oxford. v.i. act as scout. ~-master, officer in charge of Boy Scouts.

scout[2] v.t. reject with scorn.

scow n. large flat-bottomed boat.

scowl v.i. wear sullen look; frown. n. scowling aspect.

S.C.R. abbr. Senior Combination, Common, Room.

scrăbb'le v.i. scratch or grope busily (about).

scrăg n. skinny person or animal; bony part esp. of neck of mutton; (sl.) neck. v.t. garotte, throttle. **scrăgg'y** a. thin and bony.

scrăm v.i. (sl.) go away, get out.

scrăm'ble v. make way by clambering etc.; struggle with competitors to secure share of something; cook (eggs) by stirring in heated pan with butter etc.; alter frequency of sound etc. in telephoning etc. to make message unintelligible without special receiver; go rapidly or hastily. n. climb or rough walk; motor-cycle race or competition over rough ground; eager struggle or competition (for).

scrăp[1] n. small detached piece; shred or fragment; (pl.) odds and ends, leavings; waste material, esp. old iron etc., collected for re-working; picture or passage cut from newspaper etc. v.t. consign to scrap--heap; discard, destroy; condemn as past use. ~-book, book in which cuttings, etc. are kept. ~-iron, ~-metal, scrap. ~-heap,

collection of scrap metal or waste material (freq. fig.).

scrăp[2] n. & v.i. (engage in) scrimmage or fight or quarrel.

scrāpe v. clean, abrade, etc. with sharp or angular or rough edge etc. drawn over; take off, out, put on, etc. by scraping; drawn along with, produce from, emit, scraping sound; pass along so as (almost) to graze or be grazed; amass by scraping, with difficulty, etc.; practise economy; make awkward bow; bow and ~, be obsequious, stand on ceremony; ~ through, get through with squeeze or narrow shave. n. act or sound of scraping; awkward or difficult position, esp. as result of escapade etc. **scrā'per** n. (esp.) scraping instrument or appliance; (archaeol.) primitive wedge-shaped flint implement.

scrăpp'y a. fragmentary, disconnected.

scrătch v. score or wound superficially with claw or nail or something pointed; rub with the nails to relieve itching; make hole, strike out, mark through, etc. by scratching; erase name of, withdraw, from list of competitors etc. n. wound or mark or sound made by scratching; slight wound or cut; act of scratching oneself; starting--line for race etc.; zero, par, position of those receiving no handicap; come up to ~, be ready to start, embark on something, fulfil obligations, etc.; start from ~, have no handicap, start without any advantages, preparations, etc. a. collected haphazardly, heterogeneous; improvised; without handicap. **scrătch'y** a. (esp.) done in, making, scratches; grating; careless, unskilful, irregular; causing itch.

scrawl v. write or draw in hurried sprawling untidy way; cover with scrawls. n. something scrawled; hasty or illegible handwriting.

scraw'ny a. lean, scraggy.

scream v. utter piercing cry of terror, pain, uncontrollable mirth, etc.; make noise like this; utter in or with scream. n. screaming cry or sound;

(sl.) irresistibly comic thing, affair, etc. **screa'ming** a.; ~**ingly** adv.

scree n. (mountain slope covered with) loose stones sliding when trodden on.

screech n. loud shrill harsh cry or sound. v. make, utter with, screech. ~**-owl**, barn owl.

screed n. long tiresome letter or passage or harangue.

screen n. partition partly shutting off part of room etc., esp. that between nave and choir of church; movable piece of furniture designed to shelter from observation, draughts, excess of heat, etc.; anything used for or serving as shelter or concealment; smoke-screen, windscreen; upright surface on which images are projected, objects displayed, etc.; moving pictures, films; body, part of instrument, etc. intercepting light, electricity, etc.; large sieve or riddle; grid or mesh. v.t. shelter; hide partly or completely; protect from detection, penalties, interference, etc.; prevent from causing electrical interference; show on screen; sift, grade, by passing through screen etc.; scrutinize (persons), esp. to prevent espionage, political subversion, etc.; ~ off, shut off with, conceal behind, screen. ~**play**, (script of) film.

screw (-ōō) n. cylinder with spiral ridge called thread running round outside (male ~) or inside (female ~); metal male screw with slotted head for holding pieces of wood, etc. together; wooden or other screw as part of appliance for exerting pressure; revolving shaft with spiral blades for propelling ship, aircraft, etc.; one turn of screw; oblique curling motion; miser or extortioner; small twisted-up paper (of); (sl.) salary; unsound horse. v. fasten or tighten (as) with screw; press hard on, oppress; be miserly; extort out of; contort, distort; ~ up, contract, tighten by screwing, strain, make tense, intensify, twist up. ~**ball**, (U.S. sl.) mad, crazy (person). ~**driver**, tool for turning screws by slot.

screw'y a. (sl.) mad, crazy; suspicious, fishy.

scribb'le[1] v. write hurriedly or carelessly, scrawl; be author or writer. n. careless writing, thing carelessly written; scrawl. **scribb'ler**[1] n.

scribb'le[2] v.t. card (wool etc.) coarsely. **scribb'ler**[2] n.

scribe n. copyist, transcriber; writer; (hist.) clerk, secretary; (bibl.) ancient-Jewish keeper of records and interpreter of Law. v.t. mark for cutting etc. with tool called **scri'ber**.

scrim n. kind of thin canvas.

scrimm'age n. tussle, confused struggle, brawl. v.i. engage in scrimmage.

scrimp v. skimp.

scrim'shank v.i. (sl.) shirk duty, malinger. ~**er** n.

scrip[1] n. (arch.) wallet, satchel.

scrip[2] n. provisional certificate of money subscribed to company etc.; (collect.) such certificates.

script n. handwriting; type imitating handwriting; handwriting resembling printing; written examination answers; MS., typescript, text, of play, film, broadcast, etc.

scriptor'ium n. (pl. -ia), writing-room, esp. in monastery.

scrip'ture n. sacred book or writings, Bible; (attrib.) taken from or relating to Bible. **scrip'tural** a.

scriv'ener n. (hist.) drafter of documents; notary.

scrof'ula n. tuberculosis of lymphatic glands, esp. of neck. ~**lous** a.

scroll n. roll of parchment or paper; book of ancient roll form; ornament etc. more or less resembling roll of parchment; flowing or curling lines etc. ~**work**, ornament of spiral or curving lines.

scro'tum n. (pl. -ta), pouch or bag enclosing testicles. **scro'tal** a.

scrounge (-j) v. (colloq.) appropriate without leave; cadge, sponge; pry or search about.

scrub[1] v. rub hard with something coarse or bristly, esp. hard-bristled brush; pass (coal-gas etc.) through scrubber. n. scrubbing. **scrubb'er** n. (esp.) scrubbing-brush; pad for cleaning blackboard etc.; apparatus for removing impurities.

scrub² *n.* (ground covered with) shrubs, brushwood, or stunted trees etc.; stunted or insignificant person, animal, etc. ~ **oak, pine,** Amer. kinds of stunted oak, pine. **scrubb'ў** *a.*

scruff *n.* nape *of the neck.*

scruff'ў *a.* unkempt.

scrum *n.* scrummage; (colloq.) milling crowd. ~-**half,** half-back who puts ball into scrum.

scrumm'age *n.* (Rugby footb.) formation of forwards of both teams packed together with heads down and ball on ground between them; confused struggle or scuffle. *v.i.* form scrum; scrimmage.

scrump'tious *a.* (sl.) delicious.

scrunch *n.* & *v.* crunch.

scru'ple (-ōō-) *n.* unit of apothecaries' weight (20 grains); very small quantity; doubt or hesitation in regard to right and wrong, duty, etc. *v.t.* hesitate owing to scruples *to* do. **scru'pulous** *a.* conscientious even in small matters, not neglectful of details; having scruples, (over-)attentive to small points of conscience. **scrupulŏs'itў** *n.*

scrutineer' (-ōō-) *n.* official conducting scrutiny of votes.

scru'tinīze (-ōō-) *v.t.* look closely at; examine critically or in detail.

scru'tinў (-ōō-) *n.* critical gaze; close or detailed examination; official examination of votes at election to eliminate irregularities etc.

scrȳ *v.i.* practise crystal-gazing.

scud *v.i.* run, fly, straight and fast; skim along; (naut.) run before wind.

scuff *v.t.* wear, rub, scratch (shoes etc.), esp. with feet.

scuff'le *v.i.* & *n.* (engage in) confused struggle or scrambling fight.

scull *n.* one of pair of small light oars used by single rower; oar used to propel boat by working over stern. *v.* row, propel, with scull(s).

scull'erў *n.* back kitchen for washing dishes etc.

scull'ion *n.* (arch.) menial servant.

sculp'sit, carved or sculptured or engraved (this work). [L]

sculpt *v.* (usu. joc.) sculpture.

sculp'tor *n.* one who practises sculpture.

sculp'ture *n.* art of forming representations by chiselling, carving, casting, or modelling; work(s) of sculpture. *v.* represent in, form by, adorn with, practise, sculpture. **sculp'tural** *a.*

scum *n.* impurities that rise to surface of liquid; the worst part, refuse, offscouring (*of*). *v.* skim; be or form scum on; develop scum. **scumm'ў** *a.*

scum'ble *v.t.* soften, blend (oil-colour etc.) by overlaying with thin nearly dry coat of opaque colour, or by rubbing etc. *n.* scumbled effect or part.

scupp'er¹ *n.* hole in ship's side draining water from deck.

scupp'er² *v.t.* (sl.) sink (ship, crew); do for.

scurf *n.* flakes of dead skin, esp. in hair; scaly matter on surface. **scur'fў** *a.*

scu'rrilous *a.* grossly or obscenely abusive; given to, expressed with, coarse buffoonery. **scurril'itў** *n.*

scu'rrў *v.i.* run hurriedly, scamper. *n.* scurrying, bustle, rush; flurry (*of* snow etc.).

scur'vў *n.* disease resulting from deficiency of vitamin C. *a.* (arch.) paltry, contemptible, low, mean.

scut *n.* short tail, esp. of rabbit, hare, or deer.

scutch'eon (-chon) *n.* escutcheon.

scutt'er *v.i.* scurry.

scutt'le¹ *n.* receptacle for carrying and holding small supply of coal.

scutt'le² *n.* lidded opening in ship's deck or side or in roof or wall; part of car connecting bonnet with body. *v.t.* cut hole(s) in (ship etc.), sink thus.

scutt'le³ *v.i.* scurry; make off; retreat in undignified way. *n.* hurried gait; precipitate flight or departure.

scythe (-dh) *n.* mowing and reaping implement with long thin slightly curved blade, wielded with long sweeping stroke. *v.t.* cut with scythe.

s.d. *abbr.* several dates.

S.D., S. Dak. *abbr.* South Dakota.

SE., S.E. *abbr.* south-east; south-
-eastern.

sea *n.* expanse of salt water; ocean;
swell of sea, great billow; vast
quantity or expanse *of.* ~-anchor,
floating anchor used to keep vessel
from drifting or with head to wind.
~-anemone, kinds of bright-
-coloured polyp with petal-like
tentacles round mouth. ~board,
coastal region. ~ breeze, breeze at
sea; breeze on land from direction
of sea. ~-dog, old sailor. ~-eagle,
kinds of eagle feeding largely on
fish. ~-elephant, large seal with
proboscis. ~faring, *a.* occupied in
sea voyages; *n.* such occupation.
~ front, part of town facing sea.
~-going, designed for open sea,
not rivers etc. ~-gull, gull. ~-
-horse, steed of sea-god's chariot;
walrus; kinds of small fish with
prehensile tail, and forepart of body
resembling horse's head and neck.
~-kale, table vegetable. ~-level,
mean level of sea as used in reckoning heights of hills etc. and as
barometric standard. ~-lion, kinds
of large eared seal. ~man, sailor;
navigator; sailor below rank of
officer. ~mew, gull. ~-pink, thrift
(plant). ~plane, aircraft able to
alight on or take off from water.
~port, town with harbour. ~ rover,
pirate. ~scape, picture of scene at
sea. ~-serpent, snake-like monster
reported to have been seen at sea.
~-shell, shell of salt-water mollusc.
~-shanty, chanty. ~sick, suffering
sickness caused by motion of ship
etc. ~side, place(s) close to sea as
residence or resort. ~-trout, sea-
-fish of salmon kind. ~-urchin,
marine animal covered with spines.
~weed, plant growing in sea.
~-worthy, in fit state to put to sea.

seal[1] *n.* piece of wax etc. impressed
with device and attached to document as evidence of authenticity
etc., or to envelope or receptacle or
door so that it cannot be opened
without breaking seal; gem or metal
stamp used in making seal; this as
mark of office; substance used to
close aperture etc. *v.t.* affix seal to;
stamp or fasten or certify as correct
with seal; ratify; close securely or
hermetically; stop or shut *up*; set
significant mark on. sealing-wax,
composition for sealing letters etc.

seal[2] *n.* kinds of amphibious marine
animal of which some have valuable
fur. *v.i.* hunt seals. ~skin, skin of
fur-seals as material for garments
etc. sea'ler *n.* ship or man engaged
in seal-hunting.

Sea'lyham (-lǐam) *n.* wiry-haired
long-bodied short-legged terrier.

seam *n.* line of junction between two
edges, esp. those of two pieces of
cloth etc. sewn together; line,
groove, etc. formed by abutting
edges, mark resembling this; scar;
line of separation between strata;
thin stratum separating thicker
ones. *v.t.* join, mark, score, with
seam(s); furrow, ridge; (knitting)
purl. seam'less *a.* ~stress (sěm-),
sěmp'stress *nn.* sewing-woman.
sea'mȳ *a.* showing seams; ~y side,
wrong side of garment etc., worst,
roughest, or least presentable
aspect, esp. of life.

seance (sā'ahṅs; *or* -ans) *n.* sitting of
society etc.; meeting for exhibition
or investigation of spiritualistic
phenomena.

sear *v.t.* scorch, esp. with hot iron;
make callous.

search (sẽr-) *v.* examine thoroughly,
esp. to find something; make
search or investigation. *n.* act of
searching, investigation, quest. ~-
light, (light from) lamp designed to
throw strong beam of light in any
desired direction (freq. fig.). ~-
-party, party going out to look for
lost or concealed person or thing.
~-warrant, legal warrant to search
premises. sear'ching *a.* (esp.)
thoroughgoing, leaving no loopholes; probing, penetrating.

sea'son (-zn) *n.* each of four divisions
of year; period defined by earth's
changing position in regard to sun;
proper or fit time; period of indefinite or various length; season-
-ticket. *v.* bring or come into
efficient or sound condition by exposure, use, lapse of time, etc.;
flavour or make piquant. ~-ticket,
ticket valid for any number of

journeys, performances, etc. during specified length of time. ~able *a.* suitable to season; opportune. ~al *a.* depending on or varying with seasons. ~ing *n.* (esp.) condiments.

seat *n.* thing made or used for sitting on; chair etc. on which sitter rests, occupation of this as member of council, committee, etc.; buttocks, rump; part of garment covering this; site, location; country-house; manner of sitting horse etc. *v.t.* make sit; provide sitting accommodation for; place (one*self*) in sitting posture; put new seat to; establish in position. **sea'ting** *n.* (esp.) (arrangement or provision of) seats.

S.E.A.T.O., SEATO *abbr.* South East Asia Treaty Organization.

sèbā'ceous *a.* fatty; secreting or conveying oily matter.

sěc *a.* (of wine) dry.

Sec. *abbr.* Secretary.

sec. *abbr.* secant; second.

sē'cant (*or* sĕ-) *a.* cutting, intersecting. *n.* secant line, esp. radius of circle produced through end of arc to meet tangent to other end; ratio of this line to radius.

secateurs (sĕk'*at*ērz) *n.pl.* pruning-shears.

sècēde' *v.i.* withdraw formally from membership of Church or other body.

sècě'ssion *n.* seceding; body of seceders. ~al *a.*; ~ism *n.*; ~ist *n.* & *a.*

sèclude' (-ōōd) *v.t.* keep retired or away from company or resort. **sèclu'sion** (-ōōzhn) *n.* secluding, being secluded; retirement, privacy; secluded place.

sěc'ond *a.* next after first in time, position, rank, etc. (*to*); other, another; of subordinate importance or value; inferior. *n.* second person, class, etc.; (mus.) next to highest part, interval between succeeding degrees of scale; supporter, helper, esp. of boxer or duellist; sixtieth part of minute of time or angular degree; (pl.) goods of second quality, esp. coarse flour. *v.t.* back up, give one's support to; (sĭkŏnd'), remove (officer) temporarily from regiment etc. with view to staff or other extra-regimental employ-

ment; transfer (official etc.) temporarily to another department etc. ~-**best,** (what is) next in quality, inferior, to first. ~-**class,** inferior in quality, second-rate. ~ **cousin,** child of parent's first cousin. ~ **division,** prison treatment less rigorous than that of ordinary offenders. **S~ Empire,** Fr. Empire of Napoleon III. ~ **fiddle,** (esp.) inferior or less important part. ~-**hand,** not new, not original; (bought) after use etc. by another. ~-**rate,** of inferior quality. ~ **sight,** faculty of seeing future or distant occurrences as if present. ~ **string,** person or thing kept in reserve. ~ **thoughts,** (decision etc. after) reconsideration. ~ **wind,** recovered breath after exhaustion during exertion (freq. fig.). **sec'onder** *n.* (esp.) person speaking in support of resolution etc. **sěc'ondlў** *adv.* in the second place. **sécŏnd'ment** *n.* seconding, being seconded.

sěc'ondarў *a.* of minor importance, subordinate, subsidiary, auxiliary; of second rank or kind or period; not original or primary. ~ **education,** school, between primary and higher or university.

sē'crécў *n.* being secret.

sē'crĕt *a.* kept from general knowledge or view; not (to be) made known; confidential; working etc. in secret. *n.* thing (to be) kept secret; in ~, secretly. ~ **service,** service to government of undisclosed nature; (pop.) espionage and counter-espionage.

sěc'rétaire *n.* escritoire.

sěcrétār'ĭat *n.* body of secretaries; (premises of) department headed by Secretary(-General).

sěc'rétarў *n.* person employed to deal with correspondence, collect information, prepare business, etc. minister in charge of State department; principal assistant of Minister, ambassador, etc. ~ **bird,** long-legged long-tailed Afr. bird with crest of long feathers. **S~-General,** principal administrative officer of organization etc. **S~ of State,** Minister; U.S. Minister of Foreign Affairs. **sěcrétār'ial** *a.*

sĕcrēte' v.t. put into place of concealment; produce by secretion. **secrē'tion** n. concealing, concealment; action of gland etc. in extracting from blood etc. and elaborating substance(s) to fulfil function in body etc.; substance so produced. **sĕcrē'tory** a.

sē'crĕtive (or sĭkrē'-) a. given to making secrets, uncommunicative, needlessly reserved.

sĕct n. body of persons holding religious doctrines different from those of established or orthodox Church; religious denomination. **sĕctār'ian** a. & n.; ~**ār'ianism, sĕc'tary** nn.

sect. abbr. section.

sĕc'tion n. cutting; part cut off; one of parts into which something is divided; minor subdivision of book etc.; subdivision of platoon; part of community with separate interests or characteristics; (U.S.) area of one square mile into which public lands are divided; thin slice cut off for microscopic examination; (figure resulting from) cutting of solid by plane, representation of something supposed to be cut thus; section-mark. v.t. arrange in, divide into, sections. ~**-mark**, mark (§) indicating beginning of section etc. ~**al** a. (esp.) made up of sections that may be fitted together.

sĕc'tor n. plane figure contained by two radii and arc of circle, ellipse, etc., anything of this shape; subdivision of defensive position or system under one commander. **sĕctōr'ial** a.

sĕc'ular a. concerned with affairs of this world; not monastic or ecclesiastical; not religious; not sacred; occurring once in, lasting for, age or century. n. secular priest. ~ **clergy, priests**, those not belonging to monastic orders. ~**ism** n. (esp.) doctrine that morality should be based only on secular considerations. ~**īze** v.t.

sĕcūre' a. untroubled by danger or fear; impregnable; safe, reliable, firmly fixed, fastened, established, etc. v.t. fortify; confine, fasten, or close securely; obtain; guarantee; make safe.

sĕcūr'ity n. secure state or feeling; thing that serves as guarantee or pledge; guarantor, surety; certificate of stock etc.; safety of State from foreign interference or espionage. **S~ Council**, Council of Gen. Assembly of U.N. dealing with disputes threatening peace of world. ~ **risk**, person regarded as capable of becoming or liable to become dangerous to security of State.

sĕdăn' n. sedan-chair; (U.S.) saloon-car. ~**-chair**, 17th–18th-c. portable covered-in chair for one person, usu. carried on poles by two men.

sĕdāte' a. collected, composed; not impulsive or lively.

sĕdā'tion n. treatment by sedatives. **sĕd'ative** a. & n. (drug etc.) tending to soothe, allay anxiety or excitement, etc.

sĕd'entary a. sitting; requiring etc. continuance in sitting posture; accustomed or addicted to sitting still.

sĕdge n. grass-like plant growing in marshes or by water; bed of such plants. ~**-warbler**, small brown migratory bird with loud sweet song. **sĕdg'y** a.

sĕdil'ia n.pl. recessed usu. canopied seats in S. wall of chancel.

sĕd'iment n. matter that settles to bottom of liquid, dregs; material carried by water or wind which settles and consolidates to make rock. **sĕdimĕn'tary** a.; ~**ā'tion** n.

sĕdi'tion n. conduct or language inciting to rebellion. **sĕdi'tious** a.

sĕdūce' v.t. lead astray, tempt into sin or crime; induce to surrender chastity. ~**r** n.; **sĕdū'cible** a. **sĕdūc'tion** n. seducing, being seduced; thing that seduces. **sĕdŭc'tive** a. (esp.) alluring, enticing, winning.

sĕd'ulous a. persevering, diligent, assiduous, painstaking. **sĕdū'lity** n.

see[1] n. office, position, jurisdiction, of bishop.

see[2] v. (p.t. saw, p.p. seen), have or use power of perceiving with eye; descry, observe, look at; discern mentally; be passive spectator of; grant interview to; escort home, to the door, etc.; ~ about, attend to; ~ *over*, go over and inspect; ~ *through*, see real character of through disguise or false appearance, penetrate, continue to watch or take care of until end; ~ *to*, attend to; take care of or about.

seed *n*. (one of) germs of plants, esp. as used for sowing; seed-like fruit; semen; offspring; germ or latent beginning *of*; thing like seed in shape or size; thing introduced or implanted as nucleus etc.; seeded player; *go*, *run*, *to* ~, cease flowering etc. as seed develops; become shabby, worn-out, etc., deteriorate. *a*. grown, selected, kept, etc. for seed. *v*. produce or let fall seed; sprinkle (as) with seed; remove seeds from; introduce crystals, solid particles, etc. into to induce crystallization, condensation, etc.; arrange (draw, players in draw) so that certain players do not meet in early rounds of tournament etc. ~-**cake**, cake flavoured with caraway seeds. ~-**corn**, grain preserved to sow for new crop. ~-**pearl**, very small pearl. ~**sman**, dealer in seeds. ~-**vessel**, pod or capsule containing seeds. ~**ling** *n*. young plant raised from seed. **see'dy** *a*. full of seed; shabby; unwell.

see'ing *quasi-conj*. considering *that*; since, because.

seek *v*. (*sought*, pr. sawt), go in search of, look for; make search; try to obtain or bring about, try *to* do; ask for, request.

seem *v.i*. have air of appearance of; appear to be, exist, be true, etc. or *to* be or do. **see'ming** *a*. apparent; apparent only. ~**ingly** *adv*. **seem'ly** *a*. decent, decorous, becoming.

seen, *p.p.* of **see**[2].

seep *v.i*. ooze, percolate. ~**age** *n*.

seer *n*. one who sees visions; inspired person; prophet.

seer'sucker *n*. thin cotton etc. fabric with puckered surface.

see'-saw *a. & adv*. with backward--and-forward or up-and-down motion. *n*. (game on) long board supported in middle so that ends on which children etc. sit move alternately up and down. *v.i*. play

at, move up and down as in, see--saw; vacillate.

seethe (-dh) *v*. boil, bubble, be agitated.

seg'ment *n*. part cut off or separable from other parts; part of circle or sphere cut off by straight line or plane intersecting it. *v*. divide into segments; undergo cleavage. **segmen'tal** *a*. shaped like segment of circle. **segmentā'tion** *n*.

seg'regāte *v*. set apart, isolate; separate from general mass and collect together. **segregā'tion** *n*.

seigneur (sānyēr'), **seignior** (sā'ny*or*) *n*. feudal lord; lord of manor. **seigniôr'ial** *a*. **sei'gniorȳ** *n*. feudal lordship; feudal domain.

seine (sān) *n*. large vertical fishing--net with ends drawn together to enclose fish.

sei'sin, **-zin** (sēz-) *n*. (act of taking) possession of land by freehold.

seis'mic (sīz-) *a*. of earthquake(s). **seis'mograph** (-ahf) *n*. instrument for recording earthquake tremors. **seismŏg'raphȳ**, ~**mŏl'ogist**, ~**mŏl'ogy** *nn*.; **seismolŏ'gical** *a*.

seize (sēz) *v*. (law) put in possession *of*; take possession of by warrant or legal right; take or lay hold of forcibly or suddenly or eagerly; snatch; comprehend quickly or clearly; (of moving part of machinery) become stuck, jam, from undue heat or friction. **sei'zure** (-zh*er*) *n*. (esp.) sudden attack of apoplexy etc., stroke.

seizin : see **seisin**.

sel'dom *adv*. rarely; not often.

select' *a*. chosen for excellence; picked, choice; exclusive. *v.t*. pick out as best or most suitable. **selec'tion** *n*. selecting; what is selected; sorting out as factor in evolution of types of animal or plant better fitted to survive. **selec'tive** *a*.; ~**iv'itȳ**, ~**or** *nn*.

selē'nium *n*. non-metallic element whose electrical conductivity increases with intensity of light falling on it. ~ **cell**, kind of photo--electric device.

self *n*. (pl. *selves*), person's or thing's own individuality or essence;

(concentration on) one's own nature or state or interests or pleasure; (commerc., vulg., joc.) myself, yourself, himself, etc. a. (of colour) uniform, same throughout; (of material) same.

self- in comb., expressing reflexive action, automatic or independent action, or sameness. In the list which follows only such words are given as seem to require further explanation. **self-abuse'** n. masturbation. **~-ac'ting** a. automatic. **~-asser'tion** n. insistence on one's own claims, individuality, etc. **~-cen'tred** a. pre-occupied with one's own personality or affairs. **~-command'** n. power of controlling one's emotions. **~-con'scious** a. (esp.) embarrassed or unnatural in behaviour from inability to forget oneself. **~-contained'** a. complete in itself; uncommunicative. **~-defence'** n. (esp.) in phr. in ~-defence, not by way of aggression; art of ~-defence, boxing. **~-deni'al** n. voluntary abstention from pleasurable things. **~-deny'ing** a. sacrificing one's personal desires. **~-determina'tion** n. free will; choice of polity or allegiance exercised by nation. **~-deter'mined** a. exercising or effected by free will. **~-esteem'** n. favourable opinion of oneself. **~-ev'ident** a. needing no demonstration. **~-forget'ful** a. unselfish. **~-gov'erning** a. (of colony, territory, etc.) governing itself, autonomous; **~-gov'ernment** n. **~-help'** n. practice of fending for oneself. **~-impor'tant** a. having exaggerated idea of one's own importance; **~-impor'tance** n. **~-indul'gent** a. indulging one's own desires for ease, pleasure, etc.; **~-indul'gence** n. **~-in'terest** n. what one conceives to be for one's own interests or advantage; **~-in'terested** a. **~-made** a. (esp.) having risen from obscurity or poverty by one's own exertions. **~-opin'ionated** a. obstinate in one's own opinion. **~-por'trait** n. artist's portrait of himself. **~-possessed'** a. unperturbed, cool; **~-posse'ssion** n. **~-preserva'tion** n. instinct

impelling living things to go on living and avoid injury. **~-rai'sing** a. (of flour) not needing addition of baking-powder etc. **~-reli'ant** a. relying on one's own energies; ready to take responsibility; **~-reli'ance** n. **~-respect'** n. proper regard for one's dignity, standard of conduct, etc. **~-righ'teous** a. laying stress on one's own virtue. **~-sac'rifice** n. postponing of one's interest and desires to others'. **~-same** a. (the) very same. **~-sat'isfied** a. conceited; **~-satisfac'tion** n. **~-see'king** a. & n. seeking one's own advantage only. **~-ser'vice** a. in or at which customers help themselves and pay cashier afterwards. **~-sown'** a. sprung from chance-dropped seed. **~-star'ter** n. electrical appliance for starting motor without turning crank-handle. **~-styled** a. having taken name or description without justification. **~-suffi'cient** a. requiring nothing from outside; sufficient in one's own opinion, presumptuous; **~ suffi'ciency** n. **~-willed'** a. wilful, obstinate.

sel'fish a. deficient in consideration for others; actuated by or appealing to self-interest. **self'less** a. oblivious of self, incapable of selfishness.

sell v. (sold), make over or dispose of in exchange for money; deal in, keep stock of for sale; find purchasers; betray for money or other reward; promote sales (of); persuade or convince of value or importance of something; gain acceptance of, advertise or publish merits of; (sl.) trick, take in; ~ off, sell remainder of at reduced prices; ~ out, sell (all) one's shares in company, whole stock-in-trade, etc.; ~ short, (U.S.) sell stock etc. one does not possess, undervalue; ~ up, sell goods of by distress or legal process. n. hoax, take-in, swindle; disappointment. **~-out,** betrayal; selling of all copies, seats, etc., commercial success. **sell'er** n.; **~er's market,** market where supplies are short and prices high. **sell'ing** n.; **~ing-plate, ~ing-race,**

race in which winning horse must
be sold.

sĕl'vage, -vĕdge *n*. edge of cloth so
woven that it cannot unravel.

sĕmăn'tĭc *a*. of meaning; of semantics.
sĕmăn'tics *n*. branch of philology
concerned with, study of, meaning.

sĕm'aphōre *n*. post with movable arms
as signalling apparatus; signal(ling)
by person holding flag in each hand.
v. signal, send, by semaphore.

sĕm'blance *n*. outward appearance,
show.

sē'mĕn *n*. viscous whitish fluid secretion of male animal, containing
spermatozoa.

sĕmĕs'ter *n*. half-year term in esp.
Amer. universities etc.

sĕm'ĭ- in comb., half-, partly-, to
some extent, partial(ly), imper-
fect(ly). **sĕmi-ănn'ūal** *a*. half-
yearly. **~brēve** *n*. (mus.) longest
note in general use (○), equal to
half breve. **~cĭr̆cle** *n*. half of circle
or its circumference; **~cĭr̆'cūlar** *a*.
~cō'lon *n*. punctuation mark (;)
indicating more marked separation
than comma and less than full
stop. **~-condŭc'tor** *n*. electrical
conductor with resistance less than
that of insulator but greater than
that of metal etc. **~-dĕtăched'**
(-cht) *a*. (of house) joined to another
on one side only. **~-fĭ'nal** *n*. match
or round preceding final. **~-offĭ'cial**
(-shl) *a*. coming, but not formally
owned as coming, from official
source. **~-prĕ'cious** *a*. (of gem) of
less value than those called precious.
~quăver *n*. (mus.) black-headed
note with double-hooked stem (♪)
equal to half quaver. **~tōne** *n*.
(mus.) interval of (approximately)
half tone. **~vowel** *n*. sound or letter
representing it that is partly vowel
and partly consonant.

sĕm'ĭnal (*or* sē-) *a*. of seed or semen;
germinal, reproductive; pregnant
with consequences.

sĕm'ĭnăr *n*. (meeting of) group of
persons engaged in special study,
research, etc., esp. at university.

sĕm'ĭnarў *n*. place of education (esp.
fig.); school (or college) for training
esp. R.-C. priests. **~arĭst** *n*. student in seminary.

Sē'mīte (*or* sĕ-) *n*. member of any
of races supposed to be descended
from Shem. **Sĕmĭt'ĭc** *a*. & *n*.
(language) of Semites; (of) family
of languages including Hebrew etc.

sĕmolī'na (-lē-) *n*. hard round grains
of wheat used for puddings etc.

sĕmpĭtĕr̆n'al *a*. (rhet.) eternal.

sempstress : see **seamstress**.

Sen. *abbr*. Senate; Senator; Seneca;
Senior.

sē'narў *a*. of six. **~ scale,** (math.)
using six, not ten, as basis of
notation.

sĕn'ate *n*. legislative and administrative council of ancient Rome;
upper house of legislature in some
countries; governing body of some
universities. **sĕn'ator** *n*. member
of senate. **sĕnatōr̆'ial** *a*.

sĕnd *v*. (*sĕnt*) have conveyed, cause to
go, to destination; drive, cause to
go (*to* etc.); send message or letter;
grant, inflict; **~ *down*,** send away
from university; **~ *for*,** summon
(esp. politician to invite him to
form government), have brought;
~ *off*, send away, witness departure
of; **~ *on*,** forward; **~ *out*,** (esp.)
broadcast; **~ *up*,** (esp., colloq.)
satirize, (U.S.) send to prison.
~-off, friendly demonstration at
person's departure. **~-up,** (colloq.)
satire, showing *up* as ridiculous etc.
sĕn'der *n*.

sĕnĕs'cent *a*. growing old.

sĕn'eschal (-shl) *n*. steward of
medieval great house.

sē'nīle *a*. of, incident to or characteristic of, old age; having esp.
mental feebleness of (extreme) old
age. **sĕnĭl'itў** *n*.

sē'nĭor *a*. older in age or standing;
of higher degree. *n*. person of
advanced age or long service; one's
elder or superior in standing.
sēnĭŏ'ritў *n*.

sĕnn'a *n*. purgative prepared from
dried pods or leaves of cassia.

sĕnn'ĕt *n*. (hist.) signal call on trumpet.

sĕñor' (-ny-), **sĕñor'a, sĕñori'ta**
(-rē-) *nn*. (titles of respect for)
Spanish man, woman, young unmarried woman. [Sp.]

sĕnsā'tion *n*. consciousness of perceiving or seeming to perceive state etc. of body, senses, mind, etc.; (event, person, arousing) excited or violent feeling esp. *in* community, strong emotional impression. ~al *a.* causing, aiming at, etc. violently exciting effects. ~alism, ~alist *nn.*

sĕnse *n.* any of special bodily faculties (*of* sight, hearing, smell, taste, touch) by which sensation is roused; ability to perceive; (usu. pl.) senses as channels for gratifying desire for pleasure; (pl.) sanity regarded as attested by possession of senses; ability to perceive or feel; practical wisdom, judgment; prevailing sentiment; meaning. *v.t.* perceive by sense; be vaguely aware of. ~less *a.* wildly foolish; unconscious; meaningless, purposeless.

sĕnsĭbĭl'ĭtў *n.* capacity to feel; sensitiveness (*to*); delicacy of feeling.

sĕn'sĭble *a.* having or showing good sense; judicious; not unaware or unmindful *of*; perceptible by senses.

sĕn'sĭtĭve *a.* very open *to* or acutely affected by external impressions; touchy or quick to take offence; responsive to or recording slight changes of condition, readily affected by or susceptible *to* (light, agency, etc.). ~ plant, kind of mimosa with leaflets folding at a touch. sĕnsĭtĭv'ĭtў *n.*

sĕn'sĭtize *v.t.* make or render sensitive.

sĕnsōr'ĭal *a.* of senses or sensation or sensorium. sĕnsōr'ĭum *n.* brain as seat of sensation; sensory apparatus.

sĕn'sōrў *a.* of sensation or senses; receiving or transmitting sensation.

sĕn'sūal (*or* -shoo-) *a.* dependent on senses only; voluptuous, self-indulgent, carnal, licentious. ~ĭsm, ~ĭst, sĕnsūăl'ĭtў *nn.*

sĕn'sūous *a.* of or derived from or affecting senses.

sent, *p.t. & p.p.* of send.

sĕn'tence *n.* series of words grammatically complete in itself; (judicial declaration of) punishment allotted. *v.t.* pronounce judicial sentence on, condemn *to*.

sĕntĕn'tious *a.* aphoristic, pithy; affectedly or pompously moralizing.

sĕn'tient (-shĭ-) *a.* that feels or is capable of feeling. ~ence *n.*

sĕn'tĭment *n.* mental attitude, view; emotional thought expressed in words etc.; tendency to be swayed by feeling; mawkish tenderness. sĕntĭmĕn'tal *a.* swayed or dictated by shallow emotion; designed to excite or gratify the softer emotions. ~alĭsm, ~alĭst, ~ăl'ĭtў *nn.*

sĕn'tĭnel, sĕn'trў *nn.* soldier etc. posted to keep guard. sentry-box, hut large enough to hold sentry standing. sentry-go, duty of pacing up and down as sentry.

sĕp'al *n.* leaf or division of calyx.

sĕp'arable *a.* that can be separated. ~abĭl'ĭtў *n.*

sĕp'arate *a.* divided or withdrawn from others; independent, distinct, individual, of individuals. *v.* (-āt) make separate, sever; keep from union or contact; part, secede *from*, go different ways; remove (*from* mixture etc.). ~s *n.pl.* separate articles of dress suitable for wearing together in various combinations. sĕparā'tion *n.* (esp.) divorce from bed and board without dissolution of marriage. ~atĭsm, ~atĭst *nn.* (esp.) favouring of, one who favours, secession or withdrawal from political or religious union etc. sĕp'arātor *n.* (esp.) machine or appliance for separating, esp. cream from milk.

Sĕphar'dĭm *n. pl.* Jews of Spanish or Portuguese descent. ~dĭc *a.*

sē'pĭa *n.* (rich brown colour of) pigment made from inky secretion of cuttle-fish; sepia drawing. *a.* of colour of, drawn in, sepia.

sē'poy *n.* (hist.) Indian soldier in British-Indian army.

sĕp'sĭs *n.* state of bacterial poisoning of tissues or blood-stream.

sĕpt *n.* clan, esp. in Ireland.

Sept. *abbr.* September.

Sĕptĕm'ber *n.* ninth month of year.

sĕptē'narў *a.* of or involving the number seven, on basis of seven, by sevens. *n.* set of seven. sĕptĕnn'ĭal *a.* of, for, (recurring) every, seven years. sĕptĕt' *n.* (musical work for) seven voices, instruments, etc.

sĕp′tĭc *a*. causing or caused by putrefaction. **~ tank**, tank for rapid decomposition of organic matter in sewage.

sĕptĭcae′mĭa (-sē-) *n*. blood-poisoning.

sĕptūagénār′ĭan *n*. & *a*. (person) aged between 70 and 80.

Sĕptūagĕs′ĭma (Sunday) *n*. third Sunday before Lent.

Sĕp′tūagĭnt *n*. Greek version of Old Testament.

sĕpŭl′chral (-k-) *a*. of sepulchre(s); suggestive of tomb, gloomy, dismal.

sĕp′ulchre (-ker) *n*. tomb, burial vault or cave. *v.t*. lay in sepulchre.

seq. *abbr*. et seq.

sē′quel *n*. what follows after; continuation or resumption of story, process, etc.; after-effects, upshot.

sē′quence *n*. (order of) succession; coming after or next; unbroken series; set of things belonging next each other; episode or incident in film etc. **~ of tenses**, grammatical rule or practice by which tense of subordinate verb depends on that of main verb. **sē′quent** *a*. following; successive; consecutive. **sēquĕn′tial** *a*.

sēquĕs′ter *v.t*. seclude, isolate, set apart; confiscate, appropriate; seize temporary possession of. **sēquĕs′trāte** *v.t*. sequester, divert (income etc.) temporarily into other hands. **sēquĕstrā′tion** *n*.

sē′quĭn *n*. small coin-like glittering disc of metal etc. sewn to dress etc.

sēquoi′a *n*. kinds of Californian coniferous tree of immense height.

serăc′ *n*. castellated mass formed in glacier ice by intersection of crevasses.

sera′glio (-ahlyō) *n*. (pl. *-os*), harem; (hist.) sultan's walled palace at Constantinople.

serai (serī′) *n*. caravanserai.

sera′pĕ (-ah-) *n*. Spanish-Amer. blanket worn as cloak.

sĕ′raph *n*. (pl. *-ĭm*, *-s*) one of highest of nine orders of angels. **serăph′ĭc** *a*. of or like seraphim; angelic.

sēre *a*. dry, withered.

sĕrēnāde′ *n*. (music suitable for) performance of music at night in open, esp. by lover under lady's window.

v. entertain with, perform, serenade.

sĕrendĭp′ĭtў *n*. faculty of making happy discoveries by accident.

sĕrēne′ *a*. clear and calm; placid, unperturbed. **sĕrĕn′ĭtў** *n*.

sĕrf *n*. (hist.) one of class of labourers bound to and transferred with soil; oppressed person, drudge. **~age, ~dom, ~hood** *nn*.

sĕrge *n*. durable twilled worsted fabric.

sergeant (sar′jant) *n*. non-commissioned officer above corporal; police officer between inspector and constable. **~-at-arms**, serjeant-at-arms. **~-major**, non-commissioned officer of highest grade.

Sergt. *abbr*. Sergeant.

sĕr′ĭal *a*. of, in, forming, series; (of story etc.) issued, broadcast, etc. in instalments. *n*. serial story.

sĕrĭa′tĭm (*or* sēr-) *adv*. one by one.

sĕr′ies (-ēz *or* -ĭēz) *n*. succession or sequence or set of similar or similarly related things etc.; (math.) set of terms having common relation between successive terms; (electr.) set of circuits so arranged that same current traverses all; *in* **~**, so arranged.

sĕr′ĭf *n*. fine cross-line finishing off stroke of letter.

sĕrĭo-cŏm′ĭc *a*. partly serious and partly comic.

sĕr′ĭous *a*. thoughtful, earnest; important; requiring earnest thought or application; not frivolous or playful or slight or negligible etc.

serjeant (sar′jant) *n*. (hist.) member of superior order of barristers. **~-at-arms**, various officials of court, parliament, etc. with esp. ceremonial duties.

sĕr′mon *n*. discourse on religious or moral subject, esp. delivered from pulpit and usu. based on text of Scripture; admonition. **~īze** *v*.

sĕr′ous *a*. of or like serum.

sĕr′pent *n*. snake, esp. of large kinds; treacherous or cunning person; obsolete bass wind-instrument.

sĕr′pentīne *a*. of or like serpent; writhing, coiling, sinuous. *n*. kinds of mineral with markings like those of snake-skin.

sĕr'rate, sĕrrā'tĕd *aa.* having, forming, row of small projections like teeth of saw. **serrā'tion** *n.*

sĕr'ried (-rĭd) *a.* pressed close together, in close order, crowded.

sēr'um *n.* liquid separating from clot when blood coagulates; this as antitoxin etc.; watery animal fluid.

sĕr'vant *n.* person who has undertaken to carry out orders of employer, esp. one engaged in household work; person willing to serve another; *public* ~, State official; *civil* ~, member of civil service.

sĕrve *v.t.* be servant (to); do service or be useful (to); be employed (*in* army etc.), be soldier, sailor. etc.; meet needs (of), perform function, be suitable, suffice; set food on table; distribute, hand food or goods; make legal delivery of writ etc. (to); set ball in play at tennis etc.; (of male animal) copulate with (female); treat; ~, *it* ~*s*, *him* etc. *right*, he etc. has got his etc. deserts. *n.* (turn for) setting ball in play; ~ (one's) *time*, go through apprenticeship, prison sentence. **sĕr'ver** *n.* (esp.) celebrant's assistant, arranging altar etc.

sĕr'vice *n.* being servant; servants' status; master's or mistress's employ; department of royal or public employ, persons engaged in it, esp. (pl.) armed forces; set of vehicles etc. plying at stated times; work done for another; maintenance and repair work, esp. by vendor or manufacturer after sale; supply or laying-on of gas, water, etc. to house etc.; benefit conferred on, exertion made for, another; use, assistance; liturgical form for use on some occasion; meeting of congregation for worship; legal serving of writ etc.; set of dishes etc. for serving meal; (tennis etc.) act or manner or turn of serving. *v.t.* provide service for, do routine maintenance work on. ~ **dress**, ordinary uniform. ~ **flat**, one in which domestic service etc. is provided by management. ~ **road**, road giving access to houses etc. lying off main road.

sĕr'viceable *a.* useful; durable, hard-wearing.

sĕrviĕtte' *n.* table-napkin.

sĕr'vīle *a.* of slaves; like or as of slave; cringing, mean-spirited, slavish.

sĕr'vitor *n.* (arch.) attendant, servant.

sĕr'vitūde *n.* slavery, subjection, bondage.

sĕr'vō-mĕch'anĭsm (-k-) *n.* power-assisted device for controlling brake etc. **sĕr'vō-assĭs'tĕd** *a.*

sĕs'amė *n.* (seeds of) E.-Ind. herbaceous plant yielding oil and used as food.

sĕs'qui- in comb., one and a half. **sĕsquicĕntĕnn'ial** *a. & n.* (of) 150th anniversary. ~**pĕdā'lian** *a.* (of word) a foot and a half long.

sĕss'īle (*or*-ĭl) *a.* attached directly by base without stalk, peduncle, etc.

sĕ'ssion *n.* sitting, series of sittings, term of such sittings, for deliberative or judicial business; period between opening and prorogation of Parliament; academic year in some universities etc.; *petty* ~*s*, meeting of justices of peace for summary trial of certain offences; *Court of S*~, supreme civil court of Scotland. **sĕ'ssional** *a.*

sĕs'tĕrce *n.* ancient Roman coin, ¼ of denarius.

sĕt¹ *v.* (**set**), put, lay; cause to stand; station; place ready; dispose suitably; fix in position; cause to work; apply oneself *to* work etc.; impose or propound for solution or answer; give edge to (razor, saw); unite and secure in place after fracture; sow or plant or imbed; arrange (type) ready for printing; arrange setting or scenery for, place in setting or scene; provide (song, words) with music; insert (gem etc.) in gold etc. as frame or foil; curdle, solidify, harden; take shape; develop into maturity; (of sun etc.) sink below horizon; (of tide, current of feeling, etc.) have motion, gather force, show or feel tendency; fix (hair) when damp so that it dries in desired style; (of dog) take rigid attitude showing presence of game; affix (one's seal, signature, name, etc.)

to; adjust hands or mechanism of (clock, trap); fix or lay (eyes) *on*; direct and keep (hopes) *on*; clench (teeth); ~ *about*, begin, take steps toward; ~ *back*, impede or reverse progress of, (U.S.) cost (person) specified amount; ~ *in*, arise, get vogue, be established, fit (part of garment) into rest; ~ *off*, be adornment or foil to, enhance, start (person) talking, laughing, etc., begin journey; ~ *on*, urge to attack, attack; ~ *out*, (esp.) begin journey; ~ *to*, begin doing something vigorously; ~ *up*, start, cause, establish in some capacity, raise, begin to utter, prepare (machine) for operation. *n.* setting of sun; direction of current or wind; attack directed *at*; configuration; hang or fit; setting of hair; slip or shoot for planting; scene, scenery and props, (cinema etc.) stage with scenery etc.; granite paving-block; badger's burrow. ~-**back**, check or relapse. ~-**off**, thing set off against another; counterpoise, compensation. ~-**piece**, fireworks built up on scaffolding; elaborate display etc. prepared in advance or led up to. ~ **square**, draughtsman's appliance for drawing lines at certain angles. ~-**to**, bout of fighting or argument. ~-**up**, (colloq.) structure or arrangement (of organization etc.); situation.

sĕt² *n.* number of things or persons that belong or consort together; series, collection, group, clique; group of games in tennis etc. counting as unit to side winning more than half of them; radio etc. receiving-apparatus.

sĕtt *n.* (esp.) paving-block.

sĕttee' *n.* long seat with back and usu. arms for more than one person.

sĕtt'er *n.* (esp.) worker who prepares machine for operation; kinds of sporting dog trained to stand rigid on scenting game.

sĕtt'ing *n.* (esp.) music to which words are set; frame in which jewel etc. is set; surroundings, environment, scene; mounting or scenery etc. of (scene in) play, film, etc.

sĕtt'le¹ *n.* bench with high back and arms.

sĕtt'le² *v.* establish or become established in abode or place or way of life; sit or make sit down for stay; cease from wandering, change, disturbance, etc.; determine, agree upon, decide, appoint; colonize (country); subside, sink; deal effectually with; dispose of; pay bill; dispose legally for life *on*. ~**ment** *n.* (esp.) conveyance of, creation of estate(s) in, property esp. on marriage; company of social workers in poor or crowded district; newly settled tract of country. **sĕtt'ler** *n.* (esp.) one who settles in newly developed (tract of) country. **sĕtt'lor** *n.* (esp.) one who makes settlement of property.

sĕv'en *a. & n.* one more than six (7, VII). **sĕv'enth** *a. & n.*

sĕventeen' *a. & n.* one more than sixteen (17, XVII). ~**th** *a. & n.*

sĕv'entў *a. & n.* seven times ten (70, LXX). ~**tieth** *a. & n.*

sĕv'er *v.* disjoin, separate, divide; cut or break off. ~**ance** *n.*

sĕv'eral *a. & n.* a few, more than two; separate, diverse, distinct, individual, respective. **sĕv'erallў** *adv.*

sĕvēre' *a.* austere, strict; unsparing; vehement; arduous, exacting; unadorned, concise, not luxuriant. **sĕvĕ'ritў** *n.*

sew (sō) *v.* (p.p. *sewn*, *sewed*), use needle and thread or sewing--machine; fasten, join, make, etc. by sewing. **sewing-machine** machine for sewing or stitching.

sew'age *n.* spent water supply of community etc. including waste from domestic etc. premises. ~ **farm**, place for treatment and disposal of sewage. **sew'er** *n.* (usu. underground) pipe or conduit for conveying sewage. **sew'erage** *n.* (drainage by) sewers.

sewn, *p.p.* of **sew**.

sĕx *n.* being male or female; males or females collectively; sexual instincts, desires, activity, etc.; copulation. *v.t.* determine sex of. ~-**appeal**, sexual attractiveness. ~-**linked**, genetically dependent on sex-chromosome. **sĕx'lĕss** *a.*

sĕxagėnār'ĭan *a. & n.* (person) between 60 and 70.

Sĕxagĕs'ĭma (Sunday) *n.* second Sunday before Lent.

sĕxcĕntē'narў *a. & n.* (of) 600 or 600th anniversary.

sĕxĕnn'ĭal *a.* lasting six years; occurring once in six years.

sĕx'tant *n.* instrument including graduated arc of sixth of circle for measuring angular distances, esp. for observing altitude of sun etc.

sĕxtĕt' *n.* (musical work for) six voices or instruments.

sĕxtodĕ'cĭmō (*abbr.* 16mo) *n.* (size of) book with sheets folded into 16 leaves or 32 pages.

sĕx'ton *n.* officer charged with care of fabric and contents of church and freq. with duties of grave--digger etc.

sĕx'tŭple *a.* sixfold. *v.* multiply by six.

sĕx'ūal *a.* of or connected with sex or sexes. **sĕxŭăl'itў** *n.*; **sĕx'ūallў** *adv.*

sĕx'ў *a.* (colloq.) sexually attractive or provocative; engrossed with sex.

SF, sf *abbr.* science fiction.

sf. *abbr.*, *sforzando* [It.], with sudden emphasis.

s.f. *abbr.*, *sub finem* [L], towards the end.

s.g. *abbr.* specific gravity.

Sgt. *abbr.* Sergeant.

sh *int.* hush.

sh. *abbr.* shilling.

shăbb'ў *a.* dingy and faded from wear or exposure; worn, dilapidated; shabbily dressed; contemptible, paltry.

shăck *n.* roughly built hut or shanty.

shăck'le *n.* metal loop or staple, link closed by bolt, coupling link; (pl.) fetters, restraints. *v.t.* fetter, impede, trammel; fasten or couple with shackle.

shăd *n.* kinds of fish.

shădd'ock *n.* (tree bearing) largest kinds of citrous fruit.

shāde *n.* comparative darkness or obscurity; darker part of picture; (usu. pl.) cool retreat; (gradation of) colour; slight difference, small amount; unreal thing; ghost; screen excluding or moderating light, heat, etc.; eye-shield; glass cover. *v.* screen from light; make dark; darken (parts of drawing etc.); (make) pass by degrees into another shade of colour, opinion, etc. **shā'ding** *n.* **shā'dў** *a.* giving or situated in shade; of doubtful honesty, disreputable.

shăd'ow (-ō) *n.* (patch of) shade; dark figure projected by body intercepting rays of light; person etc. attending another like such shadow; unsubstantial or unreal thing; phantom, ghost; dark part of room etc.; obscurity; shelter or protection. *v.t.* cast shadow over; indicate obscurely; follow closely, persistently, and usu. secretly. **~-boxing**, boxing against imaginary opponent. **~ cabinet**, prospective or possible cabinet ministers of Opposition. **shăd'owlĕss, shăd'owў** *aa.*

shaft (-ah-) *n.* rod of spear, arrow, etc., more or less long and straight part connecting or supporting other parts etc.; long cylindrical rotating rod for transmission of motive power; stem, stalk; column between base and capital; arrow; streak or ray *of* light etc.; missile, arrow (*of* wit etc.); one of bars between which horse etc. is harnessed to vehicle; excavation giving access to mine, tunnel, etc.; well--like excavation or passage.

shăg *n.* rough mass of hair; strong coarse kinds of cut tobacco; sea--bird, kind of cormorant. **shăgg'ў** *a.* hairy, rough-haired; rough, coarse, tangled.

shagreen' *n.* kinds of untanned leather with rough granular surface; hard rough skin of some sharks etc.

shah *n.* king of Perṣia.

shāke *v.* (*shŏŏk, shāken*), move violently or quickly up and down or to and fro; (cause to) tremble or rock or vibrate; jolt or jar; brandish; weaken or make less stable; agitate, shock, disturb; **~ down**, bring or send down by shaking, (colloq.) settle down, (colloq.) make or occupy improvised bed, (U.S. sl) extort money from; **~ off**, get rid of by shaking, free oneself from, recover from; **~ up**, mix or loosen by shaking, stir or rouse (as) with shaking. *n.* shaking, jolt, jerk, shock; crack in growing timber; (mus.) rapid alternation of note with note above; milk shake. ~-down, makeshift bed; (U.S.) extortion of money. ~-up, shaking up; upheaval, thorough rearrangement or reorganization. shā'ker *n.* (esp.) vessel for shaking together ingredients of cocktails etc.

Shākespear'ian (-pēr-) *a.* of, as of, Shakespeare.

shăkō' *n.* (pl. -os) military cap with peak and upright plume or tuft.

shā'kў *a.* unsteady, trembling, infirm, tottering, wavering.

shāle *n.* fine-grained laminated sedimentary rock. ~-oil, oil obtained from bituminous shale. shā'lў *a.*

shall (-ăl, -al) *v.aux.* (pres. *I* etc. *shall, thou shalt*; past & cond. *I* etc. *should, thou shouldst*; neg. forms *shall not* or *shan't, should not* or *shouldn't*), forming compound tenses or moods expressing futurity, command, obligation, intention, etc.

shăll'op *n.* light open boat.

shallŏt' *n.* kind of small onion.

shăll'ow (-ō) *a.* of little depth; superficial, trivial. *n.* shallow place; shoal. *v.* make or become shallow(er).

shalt : see shall.

shăm *n.* imposture, pretence; person pretending to be what he is not; counterfeit thing. *a.* pretended, counterfeit. *v.* feign; pretend to be.

shăm'ble *v.i.* walk or run in shuffling or ungainly way. *n.* shambling gait.

shăm'bles (-lz) *n.* butchers' slaughter--house; scene of carnage or chaotic confusion.

shāme *n.* feeling of humiliation excited by consciousness of guilt, being ridiculous, offending against modesty, etc.; fear of this as restraint on behaviour; state of disgrace or ignominy or discredit; person or thing that brings disgrace; (colloq.) regrettable or unlucky thing. *v.t.* make ashamed, bring disgrace on; force by shame *into, out of,* etc. ~-fāced (-st) *a.*

bashful; ashamed, abashed. ~-ful, ~-lèss *aa.*

shămm'ў *n.* chamois-leather.

shămpōō' *v.t.* wash (hair); wash or clean (carpet, upholstery, etc.) without removing from position. *n.* shampooing; shampooing agent.

shăm'rŏck *n.* kind of trefoil, national emblem of Ireland.

shăn'dў *n.* mixture of beer and ginger beer or lemonade.

shănghai' (-hī) *v.t.* make unconscious with drug etc. and ship as sailor.

shănk *n.* leg, lower part of leg from knee to ankle; stem or shaft of nail, key, anchor, etc.

shan't : see shall.

shăntŭng' *n.* soft undressed Chinese silk, usu. undyed.

shăn'tў[1] *n.* hut, cabin; mean roughly constructed dwelling. ~-town, town, suburb, etc. of shanties.

shăn'tў[2], chan'tў (-ah-) *n.* sailors' song, with chorus, sung esp. while doing heavy work.

shāpe *n.* configuration, form; external appearance, guise; orderly arrangement, proper condition; pattern or mould. *v.* fashion into desired or definite shape; form, devise, plan; direct (one's course etc.); develop (*into*). ~-lèss *a.* ~-lў *a.* well-formed; of pleasing shape.

S.H.A.P.E. *abbr.* Supreme Headquarters of Allied Powers in Europe.

shărd, shĕrd *n.* potsherd; fragment, remnant.

shāre[1] *n.* part that falls to individual out of common stock or burden or achievement; one of equal parts into which company's capital is divided. *v.* apportion; give, get, have, share of; possess, use, endure, etc. jointly with others; ~ out, distribute. ~-holder, owner of shares in joint-stock company. ~-out, distribution.

shāre[2] *n.* plough-share.

shărk *n.* large voracious sea-fish; extortioner, swindler. ~-skin, skin of shark, shagreen; heavy smooth fabric with dull surface.

shărp *a.* with fine edge or point, not blunt; peaked or pointed; abrupt or angular or steep; keen, pungent;

shrill, piercing; biting, harsh; severe, painful; acute, sensitive; vigilant, clever; unscrupulous; speedy; (mus.) above true pitch, too high; a semitone higher than note named; (of key) having sharp(s) in signature. *n.* sewing--needle with sharp point; (mus.) note raised by semitone, sign (♯) indicating this. *adv.* sharply, abruptly; punctually; (mus.) above true pitch. *v.i.* cheat, swindle, esp. at cards. ~-set, hungry. ~-shooter, skilled shot. shar′pen *v.* make or become sharp. shar′per *n.*

shătt′er *v.* break suddenly and violently in pieces; wreck, utterly destroy.

shāve *v.* remove (hair), free chin etc. of hair, with razor; cut or pare away surface of (wood etc.) with sharp tool; pass close to without touching, miss narrowly. *n.* shaving, being shaved; narrow miss, escape, or failure; knife-blade with handle at each end for shaving wood etc. shā′ven *a.* shaved; closely clipped. shā′ver *n.* (esp.) electrical appliance for shaving face etc.; (colloq.) youngster. shā′ving *n.* (esp.) thin slice taken from surface with sharp tool, esp. plane. shaving-brush, brush for applying lather before shaving.

shawl *n.* rectangular piece of fabric freq. folded into triangle, worn over shoulders or head, round neck, etc., or wrapped round baby. shawled *a.* wearing shawl.

shē *pron.* (obj. *her*, poss. *her* and *hers*, pl. *they*, etc.), fem. pronoun of third pers. sing. *n.* female; woman. *a.* female.

sheaf *n.* (pl. -*ves*), bundle of cereal plants tied together after reaping; bundle of arrows, papers, or other things laid lengthwise together. *v.t.* bind into sheaf or sheaves.

shear *v.* (*sheared*; p.p. *shorn*, *sheared*), cut with sharp instrument; clip, take off, with shears; clip wool from; fleece, strip bare; distort or rupture by strain called shear. *n.* (pl.) cutting-instrument with two meeting blades pivoted or connected by spring and with

edges passing close over each other; kind of stress acting parallel to one face of object etc., and causing successive layers to shift laterally over each other. ~-legs, sheers. ~ling *n.* sheep once shorn. ~water *n.* long-winged sea-bird skimming close to water in flight.

sheath *n.* (pl. pr. -dhz), close-fitting cover, esp. for blade or tool; investing membrane, tissue, etc. sheathe (-dh) *v.t.* put into sheath; encase, protect with casing etc. shea′thing *n.* protective layer of boards, metal plates, etc. on machinery, wall, outside of wooden ship, etc.

sheave *n.* grooved wheel or pulley of pulley-block etc.

shĕbăng′ *n.* (U.S. sl.) house, shop, saloon; thing, business.

shĕbeen′ *n.* (Irish) pot-house or unlicensed public-house.

shĕd[1] *v.t.* (*shed*), let or have fall off; let or make flow (tears, blood); diffuse or radiate.

shĕd[2] *n.* roofed structure for shelter, storage, etc., freq. built as lean-to and occas. with open front or sides.

sheen *n.* brightness, lustre. ~y̆ *a.*

sheep *n.* (pl. same), timid gregarious woolly ruminant mammal bred for flesh and wool; (pl.) pastor's flock; person as stupid, timid, unoriginal, etc. as sheep. ~-dip, preparation for cleansing sheep of vermin or preserving their wool; place where sheep are dipped in this. ~-dog, collie; large shaggy-coated bob--tailed breed of dog. ~fold, enclosure for penning sheep. ~shank, pair of hitches shortening a rope without cutting it. ~skin, garment or rug of sheep's skin with wool on; leather or parchment of sheep's skin; deed or diploma on sheepskin. ~walk, tract of land as sheep--pasture. ~ish *a.* (esp.) bashful or embarrassed in manner.

sheer[1] *a.* mere, unqualified, absolute; thin, diaphanous; very steep and without a break. *adv.* perpendicularly; directly; clean.

sheer[2] *v.i.* deviate from course; ~ off, swerve away, make off. *n.* deviation of ship from course;

upward slope of ship's lines towards bow and stern.

sheer³ *n.* (pl.) hoisting apparatus of two or more poles attached at or near top. ~ **hulk**, dismasted ship fitted with sheers.

sheet *n.* rectangular piece of linen etc. as part of bedclothes; broad thin flat piece of glass, paper, etc.; complete piece of paper as made; wide expanse of water, flame, etc; rope or chain at lower corner of sail to extend it or alter its direction; *in ~s*, (of book etc.) printed but not bound. *v.t.* cover with sheet; secure (sail) with sheet. ~ **anchor**, large anchor used only in emergencies; best or only refuge. ~ **lightning**, lightning diffused or reflected by clouds. ~ **music**, music published in sheets, not in book form.

sheik(h) (-āk, -ēk) *n.* chief or head of Arab tribe, family, etc.

shei'la (-ē-) *n.* (Austral.) girl.

shĕk'el *n.* ancient Hebrew etc. weight and coin; (pl., sl.) money.

shĕl'drāke *n.* bright-plumaged wild duck. **shĕl'dŭck** *n.* female sheldrake.

shĕlf *n.* (pl. -ves), horizontal slab or board projecting from wall or forming one tier of bookcase or cupboard; ledge on cliff-face etc.; reef or sandbank; *on the ~*, put aside, done with.

shĕll *n.* hard outer case enclosing birds' eggs, nuts, some seeds and fruits, some molluscs and crustaceans, etc.; walls of unfinished or gutted building; explosive artillery projectile; light coffin. *v.* take out of shell; remove shell or pod from; bombard, fire at, with shells; (sl.) pay *out*. ~**-fish**, aquatic shelled mollusc or crustacean. ~**-pink**, delicate pale shade of pink.

shĕllăc' (*or* shĕ'-) *n.* purified lac esp. in thin plates. *v.t.* varnish, coat, with shellac.

shĕl'ter *n.* shield or barrier against exposure to harm; screen or cabin affording shelter; place of safety or immunity; sheltered state. *v.* act or serve as shelter to; shield; take shelter.

shĕlve¹ *v.* put on shelf; provide with

shelves; defer consideration of; remove from employment etc. **shĕl'vĭng** *n.* (esp.) (material for) shelves.

shĕlve² *v.i.* slope gently.

shĕp'herd (-perd) *n.* man who tends sheep; pastor. *v.t.* tend or drive sheep; marshal, guide, like sheep. ~**ess** *n.*

shĕr'bet *n.* Eastern cooling drink of fruit-juice etc.; effervescing drink, powder from which it is made.

sherd : see **shard**.

shĕ'rĭff *n.* chief executive officer of shire, charged with keeping peace etc.; (U.S.) elective officer responsible for law and order.

shĕ'rrў *n.* Spanish usu. fortified wine; similar wine made elsewhere.

Shĕt'land (pony) *n.* pony of small hardy breed orig. from Shetland Isles.

shew etc., var. of **show** etc.

shĭbb'olĕth *n.* catchword, (esp. outworn or empty) formula, etc. insisted on by group etc.

shield *n.* piece of defensive armour usu. carried in hand or on arm to ward off cuts and thrusts; (her.) escutcheon; protective plate etc. in machinery etc.; person or thing serving as protection or defence; shield-shaped thing, esp. sports trophy. *v.t.* protect, screen, esp. from censure or punishment.

shie'lĭng *n.* (Sc.) small hut used by shepherds, sportsmen, etc.

shĭft *v.* change or move from one position to another; change form or character; use expedients; manage, get along. *n.* change of place, character, etc.; expedient, device, trick; (arch.) chemise; relay or change of workman, length of time shift works. ~**-key**, key for adjusting typewriter to type capitals etc. ~**lĕss** *a.* lacking in resource; lazy, inefficient. **shĭf'tў** *a.* not straightforward, evasive, deceitful.

shĭlle'lagh (-ā'la) *n.* Irish cudgel.

shĭll'ĭng *n.* silver or cupro-nickel coin worth $\frac{1}{20}$ of pound.

shĭll'ў-shăllў *n.* vacillation, irresolution. *v.i.* vacillate.

shĭmm'er *n.* & *v.i.* (shine with)

tremulous or faint diffused light. **shimm'erў** a.

shin n. bony front of lower leg. v.i. climb (up) by using arms and legs. **~-bone,** tibia.

shin'dў n. brawl; row.

shine v. (shōne), emit or reflect light, be bright, glow; be brilliant, excel, in some respect or sphere; (colloq., p.t. and p.p. shined) polish (boots etc.). n. light, brightness; sunshine; lustre, sheen; polishing; (U.S. colloq.) liking, fancy. **shi'ner** n. (esp., sl.) black eye.

shing'le[1] (-nggl) n. slip of wood used as roof-tile etc.; (U.S.) small signboard; shingled hair. v.t. cover, roof, with shingles; cut (woman's hair) short and tapering from back of head to nape of neck.

shing'le[2] (-nggl) n. small rounded pebbles on sea-shore. **shing'lў** a.

shing'les (-ngglz) n.pl. painful virus infection of nerves with outbreaks of small blisters.

shin'tў n. game resembling hockey.

shi'nў a. shining, polished, rubbed bright.

ship n. large sea-going vessel; sailing--vessel with bowsprit and three square-rigged masts; (large) aircraft; space-ship. v. put, take, send away, etc. on ship; take ship, embark; take service on ship; consign (goods); fix (mast, rudder, etc.) in place; lay (sculls, oars) inside boat. **~-money,** (hist.) tax for providing navy. **~shape,** in good order, well arranged. **~wreck,** (cause, suffer) sinking or destruction of ship; ruin. **~-wright,** ship-builder. **~yard,** shipbuilding establishment. **ship'ment** n. putting of goods etc. on board; goods shipped. **shipp'er** n. (esp.) importer or exporter. **shipp'ing** n. (esp.) ships (of country, port, etc.).

shire n. county. **~ horse,** breed of heavy powerful draught-horses.

shirk v. evade, meanly avoid, duty etc. **shir'ker** n.

shirr v.t. gather with several parallel threads. **shirr'ing** n.

shirt n. man's loose sleeved garment for upper part of body; in **~-sleeves,** without coat or coat and waistcoat.

~-front, (stiffened or starched) breast of shirt; dicky. **shir'ting** n. **shir'tў** a. (sl.) annoyed.

shiv'er[1] v.i. tremble, shake, quiver, esp. with cold or fear. n. quivering or trembling, tremor. **shiv'erў** a.

shiv'er[2] n. one of many small pieces into which thing is shattered. v. break into shivers.

shoal[1] n. crowd, great number, esp. of fish swimming together. v.i. form shoals.

shoal[2] a. (of water) shallow. n. shallow place; submerged sand-bank. v.i. grow shallow(er).

shock[1] n. group of corn-sheaves propped together in field. v.t. arrange in shocks.

shock[2] n. unkempt or shaggy mass of hair.

shock[3] n. violent concussion or impact; violent shake or tremor of earth's crust as part of earthquake; sudden and disturbing physical or mental impression; stimulation of nerve(s) by passage of electric current through body; acute state of prostration following accidents, wound, etc. v.t. affect with horror or disgust; appear scandalous or improper or outrageous to; cause to suffer shock; give electric shock to. **~-absorber,** device to mitigate violence of impact, recoil of spring, etc. **~ tactics,** sudden and violent action. **~ troops,** picked troops for offensive action. **~er** n. (esp.) very bad specimen of anything. **~ing** a. (esp.) scandalous; improper; very bad.

shod a. wearing shoes; tipped, edged, etc. with metal.

shodd'ў n. (cloth of) woollen yarn made from shreds of old knitted or woven fabric. a. counterfeit, pretentious, trashy.

shoe (-ōō) n. outer covering of leather etc. for foot, esp. not reaching above ankle; plate of metal nailed to underside of hoof; thing like shoe in shape or use. v. (shod; pres. p. shoeing), fit with shoe(s). **~black,** boy or man who cleans shoes of passers-by. **~ horn,** curved piece of metal etc. for easing heel into back of shoe. **~-**

-string, string for lacing shoe; inadequate or very small sum of money. ~-tree, shaped block for keeping shoe in shape.

shone, *p.t.* & *p.p.* of shine.

shoo *int.* used to frighten birds etc. away. *v.* utter shoo; drive *away* etc. thus.

shook, *p.t.* of shake.

shoot *v.* (*shŏt*), come or go swiftly or suddenly; discharge or propel quickly (gun, bullet, etc.); wound or kill with missile from gun etc.; shoot game or fire at target; (of bud etc.) issue; (of plant) put forth buds; jut *out* or rise sharply *up*; (footb.) take shot at goal; photograph with cine-camera. *n.* bud or young branch; shooting--party; land where game is shot. shoo'ting *n.* (esp.) right of shooting over estate etc.; ~ing-box, sports-man's lodge for use in shooting season; ~ing-brake, (esp.) car with capacious box-like body; ~ing--gallery, place for indoor shooting at targets; ~ing-stick, spiked walking-stick with handle that can be used as seat.

shop *n.* building or room for retail sale of goods; workshop or place of manufacture; (talk dealing with) one's profession, trade, or business. *v.* go to shop(s) to make purchases; (sl.) inform against. ~keeper, keeper of retail shop. ~lifter, pre-tended customer who steals goods from shop. ~-soiled, soiled or faded by being shown in shop. ~-steward, person elected by fellow workmen as their spokesman. ~walker, attendant in large shop directing customers, supervising assistants, etc. shopp'ing *n.* (esp.) goods purchased in shop(s).

shore[1] *n.* land that skirts sea or large body of water; *in* ~, near(er) to shore. ~less *a.*; ~ward *a.* & *adv.*

shore[2] *n.* prop, beam set obliquely against wall etc. as support. *v.t.* support, prop *up*, with shores.

shorn, *p.p.* of shear.

short *a.* not long in space or time; not tall; soon traversed or finished; of less than the named amount etc.; failing to reach the measure or quality *of*; soon over; concise; angrily curt; (of pastry, clay, etc.) crumbling or breaking easily. *adv.* abruptly; before or without reach-ing end; without going to length of. *n.* short vowel or syllable; mark (˘) indicating that vowel is short; (colloq.) short circuit; short cinema etc. film; (pl.) trousers reaching to point above knee. *v.t.* (colloq.) short-circuit. ~bread, ~cake, rich dry cake of flour, butter, and sugar. ~ circuit, (esp. accidental) electric circuit through smaller resistance than in normal circuit; anything causing this. ~-circuit, cause short circuit in; shorten (process, passage, etc.) by avoiding or removing obstacle(s) etc.; by-pass, avoid. ~coming, failure to reach standard or perform duty; defect. ~ commons, scanty al-lowance of food. ~ cut, path or course shorter than usual or normal. ~hand, kinds of writing enabling reporter to keep pace with speaker. ~-handed, not having full number of workers required. ~horn, breed of cattle. ~(-)list, (enter in) list of candidates from whom final selec-tion will be made. ~-lived, having short life; ephemeral, brief. ~ sight, ability to see clearly only at short distance. ~-sighted, having short sight; deficient in foresight. ~-tempered, easily angered. ~ time, less than usual number of working hours or days. ~ wave, radio wavelength between 10 and 100 metres. ~-winded, easily becoming out of breath. shor'tage *n.* (amount of) deficiency. shor'ten *v.* become or make actually or apparently short(er); reduce amount of (sail) spread. short'ly *adv.* (esp.) before long; a short time *before* or *after*.

shot[1] *p.t.* & *p.p.* of shoot. *a.* woven with different-coloured warp and weft so that colour changes with point of view.

shot[2] *n.* attempt to hit something by shooting, throwing, or striking, or to attain end or solve question; discharging of gun etc.; person of specified skill in shooting; single missile for cannon etc.; small lead pellet(s), esp. in quantity used for single charge or cartridge; injection or dose of drug etc.; (sl.) dram of spirits; scene etc. photographed, photograph, photographing. ~-gun, smooth-bore gun for firing small shot. ~-tower, tower for making shot by pouring molten lead through sieves at top.

shŏt[3] *n.* share of reckoning or expenses.

should (-ŏŏd), *p.t.* & cond. of **shall**.

shoul'der (-ōl-) *n.* part of body at which arm or foreleg or wing is attached; projection or expansion comparable to human shoulder; (pl.) upper part of back; beast's foreleg as joint of meat. *v.* push with shoulder, jostle; hoist on to or lay across one's shoulders; assume (responsibility etc.). ~-blade, either flat bone of back jointed with arm-bone. ~-strap, band over shoulder connecting front and back of garment; band at shoulder of uniform etc.

shout *n.* loud cry calling attention or expressing joy, defiance, approval, etc. *v.* utter shout; speak or say loudly, call out.

shove (-ŭv) *n.* (strong) push. *v.* push, esp. vigorously or roughly; jostle; (colloq.) put. ~-halfpenny, game in which coin etc. is driven along polished table or board by blow with hand.

shov'el (-ŭv-) *n.* spade-like scoop for shifting earth, coal, etc. *v.t.* shift with shovel or spade.

shov'eller (-ŭv-) *n.* brightly coloured river-duck with large broad bill.

show (-ō) *v.* (p.p. *shown*, rarely *showed*), allow or cause to be seen; disclose, manifest; offer for inspection; exhibit; demonstrate, make understand; ~ *off*, display to advantage, act or talk for show, make ostentatious display of skill etc.; ~ *out*, accompany to door etc.; ~ *up*, make or be conspicuous or clearly visible, expose (fraud, imposter), appear, turn up. *n.* showing; outward appearance; ostentation, pomp; display, exhibition; spectacle, entertainment;

performance; (sl.) concern or undertaking; ~ *of hands*, voting by raising of hands. ~-boat, passenger-boat, esp. on Mississippi, used as theatre. ~-case, glazed case for exhibiting goods, curiosities, etc. ~-down, final test or reckoning or settlement; disclosure, revelation. ~-girl, girl employed to display her attractions in entertainment etc. ~-jumping, competitive display of horse-jumping. ~-man, exhibitor or proprietor of show. ~-manship, (esp.) capacity for exhibiting wares, capabilities, etc. to best advantage. ~-room, room in which goods are exhibited for sale. **show'ing** *n.* (esp.) presentation of film.

show'er *n.* brief fall of or *of* rain, hail, sleet; great number of missiles, gifts, questions, kisses, etc.; shower-bath. *v.* descend or send or give in shower; bestow lavishly upon; take shower-bath. ~-bath, bath in which water is sprayed from above. ~-ў *a.* rainy.

show'ў (-ōi) *a.* striking, making good display; brilliant; gaudy.

s.h.p. *abbr.* shaft horse-power.

shrank, *p.t.* of **shrink**.

shrăp'nel *n.* (pieces scattered by) shell scattering bullets, pieces of metal, etc., on explosion.

shrĕd *n.* small torn, broken, or cut piece; scrap, fragment; least amount. *v.* cut, tear, fray, etc. to shreds.

shrew (-ōō) *n.* small long-snouted mouse-like insectivorous mammal; scolding woman. ~-ish *a.* ill-tempered and scolding.

shrewd (-ōōd) *a.* sagacious, penetrating, astute; (of blow etc.) severe, sharp.

shriek *v.* & *n.* (utter, make) loud shrill piercing cry or sound.

shrie'valtў *n.* (tenure of) sheriff's office or jurisdiction.

shrĭft *n.* (arch.) shriving; *short* ~, summary treatment, short work, no mercy.

shrīke *n.* kinds of bird with strong hooked beak.

shrill *a.* piercing and high-pitched. *v.* sound, utter, shrilly.

shrimp *n.* small marine decapod crustacean; diminutive person.

shrine *n.* casket or tomb holding relics; sacred or revered place.

shrink *v.* (*shrănk*; *shrŭnk*). become or make smaller; (cause to) contract when wetted; cower, huddle together; recoil or flinch (*from*). ~**age** *n.* (amount of) shrinking of textile fabric.

shrive *v.t.* (*shrŏve*; *shriven*), (arch.) give absolution to, confess.

shriv'el *v.* contract into wrinkled, contorted, dried-up, etc. state.

shroud *n.* winding-sheet; concealing agency; (pl.) set of ropes supporting mast or topmast. *v.t.* clothe for burial; cover or disguise.

Shrōve'tide (-vt-), **Shrōve Tuesday** *nn.* three days, day, before Ash Wednesday.

shrŭb[1] *n.* drink of rum and lemon--juice etc.

shrŭb[2] *n.* woody plant of less size than tree and usu. branching from near ground. **shrŭbb'erў** *n.* (plantation of) shrubs. **shrŭbb'ў** *a.*

shrŭg *v.* draw up shoulders momentarily as gesture of indifference etc. *n.* shrugging.

shrunk, *p.p.* of **shrink**.

shrŭnk'en *a.* shrunk.

shŭck *n.* (U.S.) husk, pod. *v.t.* remove shucks of. ~**s** *int.* of contempt, indifference, or annoyance.

shŭdd'er *v.i.* (experience) sudden shivering due to horror, cold, etc.

shŭff'le *v.* move with scraping, sliding, or dragging motion; manipulate (cards in pack etc.) so that relative positions are changed; rearrange (posts in Cabinet etc.); put or push *in, off, together*, etc. by shuffling or in awkward or disorderly fashion; prevaricate, be evasive; get *out of* shiftily or evasively; ~ *off*, get out of, get rid of. *n.* shuffling; general change of relative positions; quick scraping movement of feet in dancing; piece of equivocation or sharp practice. ~**board**, shove-halfpenny.

shŭn *v.t.* avoid, keep clear of.

'shŭn ! *abbr.* (stand to) attention!

shŭnt *v.* divert (train etc.) or diverge on to side track. *n.* turning or being turned on to side track; conductor joining two points in electric circuit to form parallel circuit. **shŭn'ter** *n.* railwayman shunting trains.

shŭsh *v.* & *int.* (colloq.) hush.

shŭt *v.* (*shut*), close, close door etc. of; become, admit of being, shut; keep *in, out*, etc. by shutting door etc.; ~ *down*, close, cease working; ~ *in*, encircle, prevent free prospect or egress from or access to; ~ *off*, check flow of (water etc.) by shutting valve, separate, cut off; ~ *up*, (esp.) close securely, decisively, or permanently, put away in box etc., imprison, (colloq.) reduce to silence, shut one's mouth, stop talking. *a.* closed. ~**-down**, shutting down. ~**-eye**, (sl.) sleep.

shŭtt'er *n.* (esp.) movable wooden, iron, etc. screen inside or outside window; device for opening and closing aperture of camera; *put up the* ~*s*, close business, esp. permanently. *v.t.* provide or close with shutter(s).

shŭtt'le *n.* boat-shaped weaving--implement carrying weft-thread; thread-holder in sewing-machine carrying lower thread through loop of upper one. *v.* (cause to) move to and fro, esp. regularly, frequently, or rapidly. ~ **service**, of vehicles etc. to and fro over comparatively short distance.

shŭtt'lecock *n.* small piece of weighted cork etc. with ring of feathers projecting from one side, struck to and fro with battledore or badminton racket.

shȳ[1] *v.* & *n.* (colloq.) throw, fling.

shȳ[2] *a.* avoiding observation, timid, uneasy in company, bashful; wary, elusive; in comb., frightened of, averse to, avoiding; *fight* ~ *of*, avoid. *v.i.* start aside in alarm (*at*). *n.* shying. ~**lў** *adv.*; ~**nèss** *n.*

shȳ'ster *n.* (U.S. sl.) tricky unscrupulous lawyer etc.

si (sē) *n.* (mus.) te.

sī'al *n.* lighter outer crust of earth's surface.

Sīamēse' (-z) *a.* & *n.* (native, language) of Siam. ~ **cat**, short-haired kind, cream-coloured with chocolate-brown mask and points. ~ **twins,** twins congenitally united by common tissues.

sĭb′ĭlant *a.* hissing, sounding like hiss. *n.* sibilant speech sound. **~ance** *n.*

sĭb′lĭng *n.* (usu. pl.) any of two or more children with one or both parents in common.

sĭb′ўl *n.* woman uttering prophecies and oracles as mouthpiece of god; fortune-teller, witch. **sĭb′ўllīne** (*or* -ĭl′-) *a.* of sibyl; oracular, mysteriously prophetic.

sĭc, so, thus (spelt, used, etc.). [L]

sĭcc′ative *a.* & *n.* (substance etc.) of drying properties.

sick *a.* vomiting or disposed to vomit; ill, unwell; surfeited and tired *of;* disordered, perturbed; disgusted; pining *for.* **~-bay,** part of ship etc. used as hospital. **~-bed,** invalid's bed. **~ headache,** bilious headache. **~-list,** list of sick; *on the* **~-list,** ill. **sick′en** *v.* grow ill or show signs of illness; (cause to) feel nausea or loathing. **sick′ening** *a.* (esp.) annoying, disgusting.

sick′le *n.* short-handled implement with semicircular blade for reaping, lopping, etc. *a.* sickle-shaped, crescent.

sick′lў *a.* apt to be ill, chronically ailing; causing or suggesting sickness; languid, pale; mawkish, weakly sentimental.

sick′nèss *n.* being ill; disease; vomiting, nausea.

side *n.* one of more or less flat inner or outer surfaces of object, esp. as dist. from top and bottom, front and back, or ends; either surface of thing regarded as having only two; one of lines bounding superficial figure; lateral surface or part of trunk, esp. from armpit to hip or from fore to hind leg; part, position, region, aspect, etc., to right or left, turned in specified direction, remote from centre or axis, etc.; subordinate or less essential part etc.; (cause represented by, position in company with) one of sets of opponents in war, game, etc.;

team; line of descent through father or mother; spinning motion given to ball by striking it on side; (sl.) swagger, assumption of superiority; **~** *by* **~,** standing close together, esp. for mutual support. *a.* of, on, from, to, side; oblique, indirect; subordinate, subsidiary, not main. *v.i.* take part, be on same side, with. **~-arms,** weapons worn at side. **~board,** piece of dining-room furniture for holding dishes, wine, plate, etc.; (pl., sl.) side-whiskers. **~car,** jaunting-car; car for passenger(s) attachable to side of motor-cycle. **~-drum,** small double-headed drum. **~light,** light at side of vehicle etc.; small or narrow window at side of door, larger window, etc.; incidental light *on* subject etc.; light coming from side; *v.t.* illuminate from side. **~-line,** (esp.) boundary along side of field of play; subsidiary or secondary or additional business, pursuit, etc.; *on the* **~-lines,** merely looking on. **~-road,** minor or subsidiary road; road joining or diverging from main road. **~-saddle,** saddle for rider with both legs on same side of horse. **~-show,** minor show attached to principal one (freq. fig.). **~slip,** skid; (of aircraft) move, motion, sideways. **~sman,** assistant churchwarden. **~-step,** step taken sideways; *v.t.* avoid, evade, (as) by stepping sideways. **~-street,** street lying aside from main streets or roads, or through-traffic routes. **~-stroke,** swimming stroke made lying on side. **~-track,** siding, bypath; *v.t.* shunt; divert from course, purpose, etc. **~-view,** view from side, profile. **~-walk,** path for foot-passengers at side of road. **~-whiskers,** hair left unshaven on cheeks. **~lŏng** *a.* & *adv.* inclining to one side, oblique(ly). **~ways** *adv.* & *a.* to or from or on side.

sīdēr′éal *a.* of, measured or determined by, stars.

sī′dĭng *n.* short track by side of railway for shunting etc.

sī′dle *v.i.* walk obliquely, esp. in furtive or unobtrusive manner.

siege *n.* operations of encamped

force for gaining possession of fortified place; besieging or being besieged.

sĭenn'a *n.* (brownish-yellow or reddish-brown colour of) ferruginous earth used as pigment.

sĭe'rra *n.* Sp. or Sp.-Amer. mountain--range with serrated outline.

sĭes'ta *n.* midday rest in hot countries.

sieve (sĭv) *n.* utensil with meshed or perforated bottom through which liquids or fine particles can pass. *v.t.* put through, sift with, sieve.

sift *v.* put through, separate or get *out* with, use, sieve; closely examine details of, analyse; fall (as) from or through sieve; sprinkle. **sif'ter** *n.*

sig. *abbr.* signature.

sigh *n.* prolonged deep audible respiration expressive of dejection, weariness, longing, relief, etc. *v.* give sigh or sound resembling it; utter or express with sighs; yearn or long *for.*

sight *n.* faculty of vision; seeing or being seen; view; range or field of vision; scene or spectacle; ridiculous, repulsive, etc. sight; precise aim with gun or observing instrument, appliance attached to gun etc. for assisting this; (colloq.) large quantity; *at* (*first*) ∼, on first seeing. *v.t.* get sight of, esp by coming near; adjust sights of (gun etc.). ∼-**reading**, reading music at sight. ∼**seer**, ∼**seeing**, (person) going to see places or objects of special interest, beauty, etc. ∼**less** *a.* blind.

sign (sīn) *n.* significant gesture; mark or device with special meaning, symbol; token, indication, trace (*of*); omen, portent; (board bearing) name, description, device, etc. displayed in front of shop, inn, etc.; any of twelve equal divisions of zodiac; ∼ *of the cross,* gesture tracing shape of cross. *v.* mark *with* sign; affix one's name or initials to; write signature, write (one's name) as signature, give *away,* make *over,* etc. by signing one's name; make sign *to;* ∼ *off, on,* end, begin, occupation, broadcast, etc., esp. by writing or announcing one's name.

∼**board**, board with inscription etc. on or in front of inn, shop, etc. ∼**post**, post at crossroads etc. with arm(s) indicating direction of place(s); *v.t.* provide, indicate, point out, with signpost(s).

sig'nal[1] *n.* preconcerted or intelligible sign, device, conveying information or direction, esp. from a distance; message made up of signals; message etc. sent out or transmitted by radio etc. *v.* make signal(s) (to); transmit, announce, direct (*to* do), by signal. ∼-**book**, book containing code of signals. ∼-**box**, cabin on railway from which signals are given or worked. ∼**man** *n.* one who works railway signals. **sig'naller** *n.*

sig'nal[2] *a.* remarkable, conspicuous, striking.

sig'nalīze *v.t.* distinguish, make conspicuous or remarkable.

sig'natory̆ *n.* (party) whose signature is attached to document, esp. treaty.

sig'nature *n.* name, initials, or mark written with person's own hand as authentication of document etc.; stamp, impression; printer's letter(s) etc. on each sheet of book as guide in making up and binding; sheet as distinguished by signature; (mus.) sign(s) indicating key and time of composition, movement, etc. ∼ **tune**, tune used to identify performer, broadcast series, station, etc.

sig'nĕt *n.* small seal, esp. one set in finger-ring.

signif'icance *n.* being significant; meaning, import; consequence, importance.

signif'icant *a.* having or conveying meaning; full of meaning, highly expressive; important.

signĭficā'tion *n.* (esp.) exact meaning or sense.

sig'nifȳ *v.* be sign or symbol of; represent, mean, denote; intimate or announce; be of importance, matter.

signor (sē'nyōr), *signor'a, signori'na* (-ēna) *nn.* (titles of respect for) Italian man, woman, young unmarried woman. [It.]

sī'lage *n.* preservation of green fodder, fodder preserved, in silo or pit without drying.

sī'lence *n.* being silent; abstinence from speech or noise; reticence; neglect or omission to mention, write, etc.; absence of sound. *v.t.* make silent, reduce to silence; put down, repress; compel (gun, ship, etc.) to cease firing. **sī'lencer** *n.* (esp.) device for rendering gun, internal-combustion engine, etc. (comparatively) silent.

sī'lent *a.* not speaking; not uttering, making, or accompanied by, sound; (of letter) not pronounced; speaking little; not mentioning or referring to, passing over, something.

sī'lĕx *n.* flint, silica; kind of glass made of fused quartz.

silhouĕtte' (-loo-; *or* sī'-) *n.* portrait in profile cut from paper or done in solid black on white; dark outline, shadow in profile, against lighter background; contour, outline, profile. *v.t.* represent, exhibit, in silhouette.

sīl'ica *n.* hard mineral occurring as quartz, sand, etc. **sīlī'ceous, sīlī'cious** *aa.*

sīl'icon *n.* non-metallic element. **sīl'icōne** *n.* any of group of silicon compounds used in polishes, lubricants, insulators, etc.

sīlicō'sīs *n.* chronic lung disease caused by inhaling stone-dust.

silk *n.* strong soft lustrous fibre produced by some insect larvae etc., esp. silkworms; thread or textile fabric made from this; silk gown of King's or Queen's Counsel; silky styles of female maize-flower; (attrib.) made of silk; *take* ~, become Q.C. or K.C. ~ **hat,** tall stiff cylindrical hat covered with silk plush. ~**-screen,** of or made by stencil printing process in which ink is rolled through screen of silk etc. ~**worm,** mulberry--feeding moth caterpillar spinning cocoon of silk. **sīl'ken** *a.* made of, clad in, silk; soft or lustrous as silk. **sīl'ky** *a.* like silk in smoothness, softness, fineness, or lustre.

sill *n.* shelf or slab of wood or stone at base of window or doorway; layer or sheet of intrusive volcanic rock.

sīll'abŭb *n.* dish of cream or milk curdled with wine etc.

sīll'ў *a.* foolish, imprudent, thoughtless; weak of intellect; (arch.) harmless, innocent. *n.* (colloq.) silly person. ~ **point** etc. (crick.) fielder placed close up to batsman.

sī'lō *n.* (pl. *-os*), pit or airtight structure for preserving fodder for winter feed.

sīlt *n.* sediment deposited by water in channel, harbour, etc. *v.* choke, be choked, (*up*) with silt.

Sīlūr'ian *a. & n.* (of) series of Palaeozoic rocks below Devonian.

silvan : see **sylvan.**

sīl'ver *n.* one of precious metals, white lustrous ductile malleable metallic element; coins made of it or a substitute; money; vessels or implements made of it. *a.* of or producing or resembling silver; containing threads of silver; having clear ringing sound; eloquent; (of coinage) cupro-nickel. *v.* coat or plate with silver; make or become silvery; coat (mirror-glass) with tin and quicksilver amalgam. ~**-fish,** small silvery wingless insect found in damp places; white variety of goldfish. ~ **fox,** black fox fur with long hairs banded with white near tips. ~**-gilt,** (of) silver gilded over. ~ **paper,** tinfoil. ~ **plate,** silver or silver-plated domestic utensils etc. ~**-plate,** plate with silver. ~ **point,** drawing done with silver pencil on prepared paper. ~ **sand,** fine white pure quartz sand. ~ **screen,** cinema screen. ~**side,** upper side of round of beef. ~**-smith,** worker in silver. ~**-tongued,** eloquent. ~**-weed,** silvery-leaved wayside plant. ~**ў** *a.* like silver in whiteness and lustre; having clear soft ringing sound.

sī'ma *n.* part of earth's crust immediately below sial.

sīm'ian *a.* monkey-like. *n.* ape or monkey.

sīm'ilar *a.* like, alike, having resemblance (*to*), of same kind; (geom.) having same shape. **sīmilă'rity** *n.*

sim′ilė *n.* comparison of two things for purpose of illustration or ornament.

simil′itūde *n.* guise or outward appearance; simile.

simm′er *v.* be or keep just below boiling-point; be in state of suppressed anger or laughter. *n.* simmering state.

sim′nel-cāke *n.* rich decorated fruit--cake, usu. with almond paste.

sī′monў *n.* buying or selling of ecclesiastical preferment.

simoōm′, -ōon *n.* hot dry dust-laden desert wind.

sim′per *v.* smile in silly affected way; utter with simper. *n.* affected and self-conscious smile.

sim′ple *a.* of one element, kind, etc.; not complicated or elaborate or adorned; unsophisticated, artless, natural; inexperienced; humble; foolish, half-witted; easily solved or understood or done. *n.* (arch.) herb used in medicine. **∼-hearted, ∼-minded,** ingenuous.

sim′pleton (-plt-) *n.* foolish, gullible, or half-witted person.

simpli′citў *n.* simpleness.

sim′plifў *v.t.* make simple, make easy to do or understand. **∼ficā′tion** *n.*

simūlā′crum *n.* (pl. *-ra*), shadowy likeness, deceptive substitute, mere pretence.

sim′ūlāte *v.t.* feign; pretend to have or feel; counterfeit. **∼ā′tion** *n.*

simultā′néous *a.* existing, occurring, operating, at same time (*with*). **simultanē′itў** *n.*

sin[1] *n.* transgression against divine law; offence against good taste etc.; *live in ∼*, cohabit without being married. *v.i.* commit sin; offend *against*. **sin′ful, ∼lėss** *aa.*; **sinn′er** *n.*

sin[2] *abbr.* sine.

since *prep.* from (specified time) till now, within period between (specified past time) and now. *conj.* from time that; seeing that, because. *adv.* from that time till now; subsequently, later; before now.

sincēre′ *a.* free from pretence or deceit, genuine, frank, not assumed or put on. **∼lў** *adv.*; *yours ∼ly*, polite formula at end of letter. **sincē′ritў** *n.*

sin′ciput *n.* front of head or skull.

sīne *n.* (of angle) ratio between hypotenuse of right-angled triangle and side opposite angle concerned.

sī′nécūre (*or* sī-) *n.* office of honour or profit without duties attached.

sī′nė dī′ē, (adjourned) indefinitely. [L]

sī′nė quā nŏn, indispensable condition or qualification. [L]

sin′ew *n.* (piece of) tough fibrous animal tissue uniting muscle to bone; (pl.) muscles, strength; **∼s of war,** money. **sin′ewy** (-ūi) *a.*

sĭng *v.* (*săng, sŭng*), utter words or sounds in tuneful succession, esp. in set tune; produce vocal melody, utter (song, tune); make melodious, humming, whistling, etc. sounds; celebrate in verse; **∼ out** (colloq.) call out loudly; **∼ small,** adopt humble tone or manner. **∼song,** (in, recited with) monotonous rhythm or cadence; (colloq.) impromptu vocal concert. **sĭng′er** *n.*

sĭnge (-j) *v.* burn superficially or slightly, burn ends or edges (of); suffer singeing. *n.* superficial burn; singeing.

Sĭn(g)halēse′ (-nggalēz *or* -nal-) *n.* (member, Indo-European language, of) majority community in Ceylon. *a.* of Ceylon or Singhalese.

sĭng′le (-nggl) *a.* one only, not double or multiple; individual; of or for one person or thing; solitary, unaided; unmarried; (of game) with one person on each side; (of journey etc.) not return. *n.* single ticket; single game; hit etc. that counts one. *v.t.* choose *out* for attention or treatment of some kind. **∼ file,** line of persons etc. going one behind another. **∼-handed,** without assistance from others. **∼-hearted,** sincere, honest. **∼-minded,** single-hearted; keeping one purpose in view. **∼stick,** (fencing with) basket-hilted stick.

sĭng′lėt (-ngg-) *n.* undershirt, vest; athlete's garment like vest.

sĭng′leton (-ngglt-) *n.* player's only card of suit.

sĭng′ūlar (-ngg-) *a.* extraordinary, uncommon, surprising; strange, peculiar; (gram.) denoting or expressing one person or thing.

n. singular number; word in singular form. **sǐngūlǎ′rǐtў** *n.* (esp.) eccentricity, peculiarity. **~īze** *v.t.* (esp.) distinguish.

sǐn′ister *a.* of evil omen; harmful; wicked, corrupt, evil; villainous; (her.) on left side of shield etc.

sǐnk *v.* (*sǎnk*, *sǔnk*), become wholly or partly submerged in water etc.; fall or move slowly downwards; pass out of sight or below horizon; pass, lapse, degenerate (*into*); decline, droop, subside; gradually lose value, strength, etc.; penetrate, make way, *in*(*to*); cause or allow to sink; send below surface of liquid or ground; excavate, make by excavating; invest (money), lose esp. by investment; set aside, leave out of consideration; ruin, finish, do for. *n.* large fixed basin with pipe for escape of water to drain and usu. with supply of water connected; (usu. fig.) place in which foul water collects. **sǐnk′er** *n.* (esp.) weight used to sink fishing or sounding line. **sǐnk′ǐng** *n.* (esp.) internal sensation of collapse caused by hunger or apprehension; **~ing-fund**, fund set aside for gradual extinction of debt.

sǐnǒl′ogў (*or* sī-) *n.* study of China, its language, history, etc. **~gǐst** *n.*

sǐn′ter *n.* hard incrustation or deposit from mineral springs. *v.* (cause to) become solid mass by heating without melting.

sǐn′ūous *a.* with many curves, tortuous, undulating. **sǐnūǒs′itў** *n.* sinuousness; curve or bend.

sī′nus *n.* cavity, esp. one of cavities in bone of skull communicating with nostrils. **~ī′tǐs** *n.* inflammation of sinus.

sǐp *n.* sipping; small mouthful of liquid. *v.* drink in sips, take sip (of).

sīpe *n.* one of small grooves or channels in tyre-tread.

sī′phon *n.* pipe or tube bent so that one leg is longer than other, used for drawing off liquids by atmospheric pressure; aerated-water bottle with inserted tube through which liquid is forced by pressure of gas. *v.* (cause to) flow (as) through siphon.

sǐpp′ėt *n.* small piece of (fried) bread or toast served with soup etc.

sǐr *n.* title of honour placed before Christian name of knight or baronet; used (without name) in addressing master, superior in rank, age, etc., or equal. *v.t.* address as *sir*.

sǐr′dar *n.* commander-in-chief of Egyptian etc. army.

sīre *n.* father or male ancestor; male parent of beast, (esp.) stallion; (arch.) title of address to king etc. *v.t.* beget.

sǐr′ėn *n.* (Gk. myth., pl.) fabulous creatures living on rocky isle and luring seafarers by their singing; dangerously fascinating woman etc.; apparatus producing loud esp. wailing or ululating sound used as warning or signal.

sǐr′loin *n.* best part of loin of beef.

sǐrǒcc′ō *n.* (pl. *-os*), hot moist oppressive wind reaching Italy etc. from Africa.

sǐ′rrah *n.* (arch.) sir (used in anger, contempt, etc.).

sī′sal *n.* strong durable white fibre of agave etc. used for ropes etc.

sǐs′kǐn *n.* small migratory songbird.

sǐs′ter *n.* daughter of same parents as another person; female fellow-member of class or sect or human race; member of religious sisterhood; head nurse of ward in hospital etc. **~-in-law**, husband's or wife's sister, brother's wife. **~hood** *n.* (esp.) society of women bound by monastic vows or devoting themselves to religious or charitable work. **S~ of Mercy**, member of religious organization devoted to educational and charitable work. **~lў** *a.*

sǐt *v.* (*sǎt*), take, be in, position in which weight of body rests on buttocks; occupy seat as judge, member of legislative assembly, etc.; pose (*for* portrait etc. *to* painter etc.); take examination; (of Parliament etc.) hold session, transact business; (of animal, bird, etc.) rest with legs bent and body close to ground, remain on nest to hatch eggs; be in more or less permanent position; seat one*self*; cause to sit;

sit on (horse, eggs, etc.); ~ *down*, sit, esp. in public place as form of demonstration; ~ *down under*, submit tamely to; ~ *on* (esp., sl.) repress, snub; ~ *out*, remain to end of, outstay, take no part in dance etc.; ~ *up*, rise from lying to sitting posture, sit erect, (of animal) sit on hind-legs with forelegs straight or lifted in begging posture, remain out of bed. *n.* (esp.) set (of garment etc.); spell of sitting. **~-down,** (strike) in which strikers refuse to leave place of work. **sitt'er** *n.* (esp.) one who sits for portrait etc.; easy catch, stroke, shot, etc. **sitt'ing** *n.* (esp.) time during which person, assembly, etc. sits; occasion of sitting to artist etc.; clutch of eggs; **~ting-room,** room used for sitting in. **sitt'ing** *a.* (esp.) holding office, position, etc.; holding seat in Parliament etc.; in possession or occupancy.

sit'ar *n.* long-necked seven-stringed lute-like Indian musical instrument.

site *n.* ground on which town, building, etc. stands, stood, or is to stand; ground set apart for some purpose. *v.t.* locate, place, provide with site.

sit'uate *v.t.* place or put in position, situation, etc. *a.* (-at), in specified situation. **situa'tion** *n.* place, with its surroundings, occupied by something; set of circumstances, position of affairs, critical point or complication; place or paid office, esp. as domestic servant.

six *a. & n.* one more than five (6, VI). **~-foot,** measuring six feet. **~-foot way,** (on railway) space between two parallel pairs of rails. **~pence,** (silver or cupro-nickel coin worth) six pence. **~penny,** costing or worth sixpence. **~-shooter,** revolver firing six shots without reloading. **~er** *n.* (colloq.) (crick.) hit for six runs. **~fold** *a. & adv.*

six'teen' *a. & n.* one more than fifteen (16, XVI). **~-mo,** sexto-decimo. **~th** *a. & n.*

sixth *a.* next after fifth. *n.* sixth part; sixth (top) form in school; interval of five steps in diatonic scale.

six'ty *a. & n.* six times ten (60, LX). **~tieth** *a. & n.*

si'zar *n.* undergraduate at Cambridge etc. receiving allowance from college.

size[1] *n.* dimensions, magnitude; one of usu. numbered classes into which things are divided by size. *v.t.* group or sort in sizes or by size; ~ *up*, (esp., colloq.) form judgement of.

size[2] *n.* glutinous substance used for glazing paper, stiffening textiles, etc. *v.t.* treat with size.

si'z(e)able *a.* of fairly large size.

sizz'le *n. & v.i.* (make) sputtering or hissing noise, esp. in cooking.

S.J. *abbr.* Society of Jesus.

S.J.A.B. *abbr.* St. John Ambulance Brigade.

sjam'bok (sh-) *n.* rhinoceros-hide whip.

skate[1] *n.* large flat cartilaginous food-fish.

skate[2], *n.* one of pair of steel blades attached beneath boot-soles and enabling wearer to glide over ice; roller-skate. *v.* move, glide, perform, (as) on skates; pass lightly *over*.

skedadd'le *v.i.* (sl.) run away, retreat hastily.

skein (-ān) *n.* quantity of yarn etc. coiled and usu. loosely twisted; flight of wild geese etc.

skel'eton *n.* hard framework of bones, shell, woody fibre etc. supporting or containing animal or vegetable body; dried bones of body fastened together in same relative position as in life; emaciated person; (mere) outlines, elements, etc. *of. a.* of minimum size, forming nucleus etc. that can be added to if occasion arises. ~ **key,** key fitting many locks by having parts filed away. ~ **leaf,** leaf of which only network of veins remains. **skel'etal** *a.* **~ize** *v.t.* make skeleton of, reduce to skeleton.

skep *n.* wooden or wicker basket or hamper; straw or wicker bee-hive.

ske'rry *n.* rocky reef or islet.

sketch *n.* preliminary, rough, merely outlined, or unfinished drawing or painting; rough draft, general out-line; short slight play, usu. of single scene. *v.* make or give sketch of; make sketches. **skětch'ỹ** *a.* giving only slight or rough outline; light, flimsy, hurried, rough.

skew *a.* oblique, slanting, squint, not symmetrical.

skew'bald (-awld) *a.* with irregular patches of white and some colour.

skew'er *n.* wooden or metal pin for holding meat together etc. *v.t.* run skewer or other point through.

ski (skē, shē) *n.* one of pair of long slender pieces of wood etc. curved at front and strapped to foot, enabling wearer to glide over snow etc. *v.i.* travel on skis. **ski'er** *n.*

skid *n.* act of skidding; braking--device, esp. iron shoe, on wheel of vehicle; log, rail, etc. used esp. to make track over which heavy objects may be dragged or slid; runner used as part of landing--gear of aircraft. *v.i.* (of wheel etc.) slide without revolving, fail to grip ground, side-slip; (of vehicle etc.) slide sideways towards outside of curve when turning; slip, slide, esp. with (partial) loss of balance. **~-lid,** (sl.) crash-helmet. **~-pan,** surface artificially prepared to induce skidding, used for practice in controlling skidding vehicles.

skiff *n.* small light boat, esp. for rowing or sculling.

skil'ful *a.* having or showing skill, expert, adroit.

skill *n.* practised ability, expertness, facility; craft, art, etc. requiring skill. **skilled** *a.* (esp.) properly trained or experienced; requiring skill and experience.

skill'ét *n.* metal cooking utensil, usu. with feet and long handle; (U.S.) frying-pan.

skim *v.* take scum, cream, etc. from surface of liquid; read superficially; pass over surface, along, etc., rapidly and lightly with close approach or very slight contact. **~ milk,** milk with cream removed. **skimm'er** *n.* (esp.) perforated ladle etc. for skimming liquids.

skimp *v.* supply meagrely, use too little of; be parsimonious. **skim'pỹ**

a. meagre, inadequate, too small or tight.

skin *n.* tough flexible continuous integument of animal body; either layer of this; peel or rind; thin film or pellicle; outer covering of frame of ship, aircraft, etc.; complexion; hide cf flayed animal; animal's skin as wine- or water-vessel. *v.t.* strip skin from; flay, peel; heal over with new skin; (sl.) fleece, take all money of. **~-deep,** merely super-ficial. **~-dive,** dive without diving--suit. **~flint,** niggard, miser. **~ful,** as much liquor as one can hold. **~ game,** (U.S. sl.) swindle. **~-tight,** very close-fitting.

skink *n.* kinds of lizard.

skinn'y *a.* (esp.) lean, emaciated; mean, miserly.

skint *a.* (sl.) out of funds, penniless.

skip[1] *v.* caper, frisk; jump about, from ground, etc. lightly and easily; spring or leap over rope revolved over head and under feet; move boundingly; shift quickly from one subject etc. to another; omit, make omissions, in reading; (colloq.) pass over, leave out, ignore, omit; (sl.) decamp, bolt. *n.* skipping; skipping movement, esp. quick shift from one foot to other.

skip[2] *n.* captain of side at bowls, curling, etc.

skip[3] *n.* cage, bucket, etc., in which men or materials are lowered or raised in mines or quarries.

skipp'er *n.* captain of ship, aircraft, team, etc.

skirl *n.* & *v.i.* (make) shrill sound of bagpipes.

skir'mish *n.* & *v.i.* (engage in) irregular or desultory or unimpor-tant fighting or contest, esp. between detached or outlying bodies of troops etc.

skirt *n.* woman's outer garment hanging from waist, or this part of complete dress; part of coat etc. that hangs below waist; border or outlying part; flank of beef etc.; (sl.) woman. *v.* go or lie along or round edge or border of.

skir'ting-board *n.* narrow board round wall of room etc. close to floor.

skit *n.* light piece of satire, burlesque.

skitt′er *v.i.* skim or skip along surface esp. of water.

skitt′ish *a.* (of horse etc.) playful, fidgety, excitable; frivolous; lively, spirited.

skitt′le *n.* (pl.) game in which number of wooden pins are set up to be bowled or thrown down; one of pins used in this game. *v.* play skittles, knock down skittles; (crick.) get (batsmen) *out* easily and rapidly.

skū′a *n.* kinds of large rapacious predatory gull.

skulk *v.i.* lurk, conceal oneself, move stealthily, esp. in cowardly or sinister way.

skull *n.* bony case of brain; bony framework of head. **~-cap**, close-fitting brimless cap for top of head.

skunk *n.* N-Amer. animal of weasel kind; its fur; low contemptible person.

skȳ *n.* vault or arch of heaven; heaven; climate, clime. *v.t.* hit or throw (ball) very high; hang (picture) high on wall. **~-blue**, colour of clear summer sky. **~lark**, common lark; (*v.i.*) indulge in horseplay, play tricks or practical jokes. **~-line**, silhouette of buildings etc. against sky; visible horizon. **~light**, window in roof or ceiling. **~rocket**, rocket exploding high in air; *v.i.* ascend, shoot up, like sky-rocket. **~scraper**, very high building of many storeys.

Skȳe (terrier) *n.* small long-bodied short-legged long-haired Scotch terrier.

slab *n.* flat broad thickish piece of solid material; large flat piece of cake, chocolate etc.

slack[1] *a.* sluggish; not busy; remiss; relaxed; loose. *n.* slack part of rope; (pl.) trousers for casual etc. wear. *v.* slacken; idle or be remiss; slake; fall off in vigour, speed, etc. **~ water**, water, esp. tidal water about turn of tide, without apparent motion. **slack′en** *v.* make or become slack. **slack′er** *n.* shirker; idler.

slack[2] *n.* very small coal; coal-dust.

slag *n.* dross separated in fused state in smelting; volcanic lava.

slain, *p.p.* of **slay.**

slake *v.t.* assuage or satisfy (thirst, etc.); cause (lime) to heat and crumble by action of water.

sla′lŏm (-ah-) *n.* downhill ski-race on zigzag course between artificial obstacles.

slam[1] *v.* shut, throw or put *down* violently, with bang. *n.* sound (as) of slammed door.

slam[2] *n.* winning of all tricks (*grand* ~) or all but one (*little* ~) at whist, bridge, etc.

sla′nder (-ah-) *n.* false report maliciously uttered to person's injury; defamation, calumny. *v.t.* utter slander about, defame falsely. **~ous** *a.*

slang *n.* language in common colloquial use but not regarded as standard English; words or uses of them peculiar to class etc. *a.* of, expressed in, slang. *v.t.* (sl.) use abusive language to. **slang′ȳ** *a.* of nature of, given to use of, slang.

slant (-ah-) *v.* be or put in oblique position; slope; present (news etc.) in biased or unfair way. *n.* slope, oblique position; point of view, way of regarding something; slanted presentation etc., bias. **~wise** *adv.* & *a.* oblique(ly).

slap *v.t.* strike with palm of hand; smack. *n.* smart blow esp. with palm of hand or something flat. **~dash**, hasty, careless, happy-go-lucky; *adv.* in slapdash manner. **~stick**, flexible lath of pantomime harlequin; (of) boisterous knockabout type of comedy. **~-up**, (vulg.) first-rate, splendid, with no expense spared.

slash *v.* cut (at) with sweep of sharp weapon or implement; make gashes in, slit; lash with whip; cut, reduce, (prices etc.) drastically; criticize harshly. *n.* (wound or slit made by) slashing cut.

slat *n.* long narrow strip of wood, metal, etc. *v.i.* (esp. of sail) flap, slap, noisily.

S. lat. *abbr.* South latitude.

slate *n.* fine-grained grey rock easily split into thin smooth plates;

trimmed plate of this used esp. in roofing or for writing on; (U.S.) list of candidates etc. *v.t.* cover, roof, with slates; criticize severely; scold; (U.S.) designate, destine (*for*), appoint. **~-pencil**, stick of soft slate for writing on slate. **slā′tў** *a.*

slätt′ern *n.* untidy or slovenly woman. **~lў** *a.*

slaught′er (-awt-) *n.* killing of animal(s) for food; slaying, esp. of many persons or animals at once. *v.t.* kill ruthlessly or in great numbers, butcher. **~-house**, place for killing animals for food. **~ous** *a.* murderous.

Slav (-ahv) *a.* & *n.* (member) of any of peoples of East & Central Europe belonging to Slavonic linguistic group.

slāve *n.* one who is another's property; human chattel; helpless victim *to* or *of* some influence; submissive or devoted servant; drudge. *v.i.* work like slave, drudge. **~-driver**, overseer of slaves at work; hard taskmaster. **~ labour**, work of slaves; forced labour. **~-trade**, traffic in slaves, esp. former transportation of African Negroes to America. **slā′ver**[1] *n.* ship or person engaged in slave trade. **slā′verў**[1] *n.* condition of slave; slave-holding; drudgery.

slăv′er[2] *n.* saliva flowing or falling from mouth. *v.* let saliva run from mouth; drool; wet with saliva. **slăv′erў**[2] *a.*

slā′vish *a.* abject, servile; servilely imitative, without originality or independence.

Slavŏn′ic *a.* & *n.* (of) group of Indo-European languages including Russian, Polish, etc.

slay *v.t.* (*slew* pr. -ōō; *slain*), kill.

slea′zў *a.* flimsy, loosely-woven; shoddy, shabby, cheap.

slĕd *n.* & *v.* sledge.

slĕdge[1] *n.* vehicle on runners instead of wheels, for use esp. on snow. *v.* travel, go, convey, in sledge.

slĕdge[2], **~-hammer** *nn.* large heavy hammer usu. wielded with both hands.

sleek *a.* soft, smooth, and glossy; sleek-haired or -skinned; of well-fed comfortable appearance. *v.t.* make sleek.

sleep *n.* condition in which eyes are closed and nervous system inactive; spell of this; inert condition of some hibernating animals. *v.* (*slĕpt*), be or fall asleep; be dormant or inactive; rest in death; spend in sleeping; stay for night; provide sleeping-accommodation for. **~ing-bag**, lined and padded bag for sleeping in. **~ing-car, -carriage**, railway carriage with berths or beds. **~ing partner**, partner taking no share in actual working of business. **~-walker**, somnambulist. **slee′per** *n.* sleeping person; one of logs on which rails of railway etc. rest. **sleep′lĕss** *a.* **slee′pў** *a.* drowsy, feeling need of sleep; habitually indolent; without stir or bustle; (of pears etc.) beginning to rot.

sleet *n.* snow or hail falling in half-melted state. **slee′tў** *a.*

sleeve *n.* part of garment covering arm; tube or hollow shaft fitting over rod, spindle, etc.; cover for gramophone record. **~-valve**, valve in internal-combustion engine with sleeve(s) fitting interior of cylinder and sliding with piston. **sleeved, ~less** *aa.*

sleigh (slā) *n.* sledge, esp. as passenger-vehicle drawn by horses. *v.i.* drive, travel in, sleigh.

sleight (slīt) *n.* (arch.) dexterity; artifice. **~-of-hand**, conjuring, trick(s) displaying great dexterity; clever deception.

slĕn′der *a.* of small girth or breadth; slim; scanty, slight, meagre.

slept, *p.t.* & *p.p.* of **sleep**.

sleuth(-hound) (slōō-) *n.* bloodhound; detective. *v.i.* play the detective.

slew[1], **slue** (slōō) *v.* turn or swing round on axis.

slew[2], *p.t.* of **slay**.

slīce *n.* thin broad piece or wedge cut from esp. meat, bread, or cake; portion, share; slicing stroke; kinds of cooking or serving implement with thin broad blade. *v.* cut into slices, cut *off*; cut cleanly or easily; strike ball so that it flies or curves to right (or, with left-handed player, left).

slick *a.* sleek; adroit, quick, cunning; smooth, plausible. *v.t.* smooth, sleek. *n.* patch or film of oil on water.

slide *v.* (*slid*), (make) progress smoothly over surface; glide more or less erect over ice without skates; (cause to) glide or go smoothly or imperceptibly. *n.* act of sliding; track, slope, etc. for people or toboggans or goods or part of machine to slide on; part of machine etc. that slides; slip of glass with object or picture sliding into microscope or projector; kind of clasp for hair. ～-**fastener**, zip--fastener. ～-**rule**, graduated rule with similarly graduated sliding piece along centre, for performing mathematical calculations. ～--**valve**, valve with sliding plate for opening and closing orifice. **sli′ding** *a.* that slides; **sliding scale**, scale of payments etc. rising or falling in accordance with rise or fall of some standard.

slight (-īt) *a.* slender, slim; not good or substantial, rather flimsy or weak; small in amount, degree, etc.; unimportant, trifling. *v.t.* treat with indifference or disrespect, disdain, ignore. *n.* instance of slighting or being slighted. ～**lỹ** *adv.* in (only) slight degree etc.

slim *a.* slender; not stout or thick-set. *v.* make or become slim, esp. by dieting etc.

slime *n.* soft viscous or glutinous substance. **sli′mỹ** *a.* of, like, covered or smeared with, slime; vile, disgusting; repulsively meek or flattering.

sling[1] *n.* weapon of strap attached to staff or cords for hurling stones etc.; looped rope, belt, net, etc. for securing or supporting esp. bulky or heavy articles while being hoisted; bandage etc. looped round neck to support injured arm. *v.t.* (*slung*), throw, hurl; suspend, hoist, etc. with sling; suspend esp. between two points.

sling[2] *n.* spirit, esp. gin, with water, sugar, etc.

slink *v.i.* (*slŭnk*), go stealthily or with sneaking air.

slink′ỹ *a.* slinking; smooth and sinuous; (of garment) clinging.

slip[1] *n.* thin paste of finely ground clay etc. used for making or decorating pottery etc. ～-**ware**, pottery coated with slip.

slip[2] *n.* cutting from tree etc.; slim girl or boy; strip, relatively narrow piece (*of* paper etc.).

slip[3] *v.* slide momentarily by accident; lose footing or balance thus; make casual mistake; make way unobserved or quietly; (make) go easily, esp. with sliding motion; put *on, off*, get *into*, etc. easily or casually; let go or cease to check or hold; escape from, give slip to. *n.* act of slipping; sliding motion or movement; accidental or casual mistake, piece of misconduct, etc.; leash for slipping dogs; petticoat; bathing-drawers; pillow-case; inclined plane on which ships are built or repaired; fielder behind wicket on off side, (pl.) this part of field; *give* (person) *the* ～, evade or escape from, steal off from unperceived. ～-**coach** etc., coach that can be detached from train while running. ～-**knot**, knot that can be undone by pull; knot of running noose. ～-**on**, garment easy to put on. ～-**over**, (esp. sleeveless) pullover. ～-**stream**, current of air driven astern by propulsion unit of aircraft. ～**way**, inclined way leading into water in dock or shipyard. **slipp′ỹ** *a.* slippery; *look* ～*py*, make haste.

slipp′er *n.* light loose comfortable indoor shoe.

slipp′erỹ *a.* with smooth, polished, oily, etc. surface making foothold etc. insecure or object etc. difficult to grasp or hold; elusive, unreliable, shifty.

slip′shŏd *a.* with shoes down at heel; slovenly, careless, unsystematic.

slit *v.* cut or tear lengthwise; make slit in; cut in strips. *n.* long cut; long narrow opening like cut.

slith′er (-dh-) *v.i.* (colloq.) slide unsteadily, go with irregular slipping motion.

sliv'er (*or* -ī-) *n*. splinter; small narrow slice or piece. *v*. cut or split into slivers.

slŏbb'er *v*. & *n*. slaver, drivel. **slŏb'berў** *a*.

slōe *n*. (small ovate bluish-black fruit of) blackthorn.

slŏg *v*. hit hard and usu. unskilfully, esp. with bat or fist; work or walk doggedly. *n*. heavy random hit.

slō'gan *n*. catchword, rallying-cry, motto.

slōōp *n*. small one-masted fore-and--aft rigged ship.

slŏp *v*. spill; (allow to) flow over edge of vessel; spill or splash liquid on. *n*. (pl.) dirty or waste water of kitchen etc.; liquid or semi-liquid food. **~-basin, -bowl,** basin for receiving rinsings of tea-cups. **~--pail,** pail for removing bedroom slops.

slōpe *n*. stretch of rising or falling ground; inclined surface or way; inclination, deviation from horizontal or perpendicular. *v*. have or show slope; slant; (sl.) make *off*, go away.

slŏpp'ў *a*. wet, splashed, full of puddles; messy with liquid; watery; feeble, slovenly, maudlin.

slŏsh *v.t*. (sl.) splash, pour, swill; slog, punch. *n*. (sl.) heavy blow; slush. **slŏshed** *a*. (sl.) drunk.

slŏt[1] *n*. groove, channel, slit, etc. provided in machine etc. to admit some other part, coin, etc. *v.t*. provide with slot(s). **~-machine,** machine, esp. automatic retailer of small wares, operated by coin placed in slot.

slŏt[2] *n*. track of deer etc.

slōth *n*. laziness, indolence; kinds of long-haired slow-moving arboreal mammal of tropical America. **slōth'ful** *a*. indolent, lazy.

slouch *n*. loose ungainly carriage of body; downward droop of hat--brim. *v*. go, sit, etc. with slouch; droop. **~ hat,** soft hat with wide flexible brim.

slough[1] (-ow) *n*. swamp, miry place; *S~ of Despond,* state of hopeless depression.

slough[2] (slŭf) *n*. cast skin of snake etc.; dead tissue from surface of wound etc. *v*. drop off as, cast, slough.

slov'en (-ŭv-) *n*. person of careless, untidy, or dirty habits. **~lў** *a*. untidy or negligent in person or methods of work.

slow (-ō) *a*. not quick or fast; taking relatively long time to do, traverse distance, etc.; dull-witted, stupid; tedious; gradual, lingering; (of surface) tending to cause slowness; reluctant *to* do; (of clock etc.) behind correct time. *adv*. slowly. *v*. (usu. ~ *down*), reduce speed (of). **~-coach,** slow or indolent person. **~-motion,** (of film etc.) exposed at high speed, so that in projection at normal speed movements appear slow.

slow-worm (slō'-wẽrm) *n*. small European legless lizard.

slŭb *n*. thick place, lump, in yarn or thread; (attrib.) with irregular effect given by warp of uneven thickness.

slŭdge *n*. thick greasy mud; sewage; muddy or slushy sediment or deposit. **slŭdg'ў** *a*.

slue : see **slew**[1].

slŭg[1] *n*. kinds of slimy gastropod mollusc without shell; roughly or irregularly shaped bullet etc.; line of type in linotype printing.

slŭg[2] *n*. & *v.t*. (colloq.) (strike with) hard heavy blow.

slŭgg'ard *n*. lazy sluggish person. **slŭgg'ish** *a*. inert, inactive, slow--moving.

sluice (-ōōs) *n*. (sliding gate in) dam etc. with contrivance for controlling volume or flow of water; channel carrying off surplus water. *v*. let water off with sluice; flood or scour with flow of water.

slŭm *n*. dirty squalid overcrowded street, district, etc. *v.i*. go about in slums for charitable etc. purposes or out of curiosity.

slŭm'ber *n*. & *v.i*. sleep. **~ous, slŭm'brous** *a*.

slŭmp *n*. heavy, sudden, or continued fall in prices, demand, etc. *v.i*. undergo slump, fall in price; sit or flop down heavily and slackly.

slung, *p.t*. & *p.p*. of **sling**.

slunk, *p.t*. & *p.p*. of **slink**.

slŭr v. smudge, blur; pronounce indistinctly with sounds running into one another; sing or play smoothly and without break; mark with slur; pass *over* lightly. n. slight, discredit, stain; slurred sound or utterance; (mus.) curved line (⌒, ‿) over or under notes to be slurred.

slŭ′rrȳ n. thin sloppy cement, mud, etc.

slŭsh n. thawing snow; mud; silly sentiment. **slŭsh′ȳ** a.

slŭt n. slovenly woman, slattern. **slŭtt′ish** a.

slȳ a. crafty, wily; secretive; underhand; knowing, insinuating.

S.M. *abbr.* Sergeant-Major; short metre.

smăck[1] n. flavour; trace, suggestion, *of.* v.i. taste *of*; sugggest presence *of*.

smăck[2] n. single-masted sailing-vessel for coasting or fishing.

smăck[3] n. sharp slight sound as of surface struck with palm; slap, sounding blow, loud kiss. v. strike with palm or something flat; part (lips), be parted, audibly in eager anticipation or enjoyment. *adv.* (colloq.) (as) with smack, slap. **~er** n. (sl.) loud kiss; sounding blow; (U.S., sl.) dollar.

small (-awl) a. not large or big; comparatively little in size, importance, number, etc.; petty, mean, paltry. n. *the* small, slender, or narrow part (esp. *of back*); (pl., colloq.) small articles of laundry. *adv.* into small pieces, on small scale, etc. **~ fry**, young fish; youngsters; humble or unimportant people. **~-holding**, agricultural holding smaller than farm. **~ hours**, night-time after midnight. **~pox**, contagious disease, often fatal or disfiguring. **~-sword**, light tapering thrusting-sword. **~ talk**, ordinary talk on social occasions.

smalt (-awlt) n. (pigment made by pulverizing) glass coloured deep blue with cobalt.

smăr′mȳ a. (colloq.) unctuously ingratiating, fulsome.

smărt a. of some severity, sharp; brisk; clever, ingenious, quick at looking after one's own interests; quick in movement; of fresh or well-dressed or fashionable appearance. v.i. feel smart; be felt as painful. n. stinging pain. **smăr′ten** v.

smăsh v. break to pieces; bring or come to disaster; utterly defeat; bring or drive violently *down*, *into*, etc.; (tennis) hit (ball) hard downwards over net. n. (sound of) breaking to pieces; violent fall or collision; sudden disaster or bankruptcy; smashing stroke in lawn tennis. *adv.* with smash. **~-and--grab**, (colloq.) of robbery, with goods snatched from broken shop--window etc. **smăsh′ing** a. (sl.) very fine, wonderful.

smătt′ering n. slight knowledge (*of*).

smear v. daub with greasy, sticky, etc. substance; blur, smudge, blot; blacken character of, discredit publicly. n. (mark, stain, made by) smearing. **smear′ȳ** a.

smĕll n. sense by which odours are perceived, property perceived by this; smelling, sniff; bad odour, stench. v. (*smĕlt*), possess or exercise sense of smell; perceive or detect by smell; have or emit smell; be redolent *of*; stink. **~ing-salts**, preparation of ammonium carbonate and scent sniffed as cure for faintness etc. **smĕll′ȳ** a. evil-smelling, stinking.

smĕlt[1] n. small edible fish with delicate tender oily flesh.

smĕlt[2] v.t. fuse or melt (ore) to extract metal; obtain (metal) thus.

smelt[3], p.t. & p.p. of **smell**.

smew n. kind of small duck.

smī′lăx n. kinds of liliaceous climbing plant.

smile v. express pleasure, amusement, indulgent scorn, etc. with slight movement of features, upward curving of corners of mouth, etc.; express by smiling; be or appear propitious; look pleasant, have bright aspect. n. act of smiling; smiling expression or aspect.

smīrch v.t. & n. stain, soil, smear.

smīrk n. & v. (put on) conceited or inane smile, simper.

smite *v.* (*smōte, smitten*), strike, hit. chastise; defeat; strike, infect, possess, *with* disease, love, etc.

smith *n.* worker in metal, esp. iron. smith'y̆ (-dh-) *n.* blacksmith's workshop, forge.

smithereens' (-dh-) *n. pl.* (colloq.) small fragments.

smitten, *p.p.* of smite.

smŏck *n.* (arch.) chemise; loose--fitting short shirt-like outer garment, freq. with gathers or smocking at yoke. *v.t.* adorn with smocking. smŏck'ing *n.* kind of honeycomb needlework holding close gathers in place.

smŏg *n.* dense smoky fog.

smōke *n.* visible volatile product given off by burning substance; fumes, vapour; cigar, cigarette; spell of smoking tobacco etc. *v.* emit smoke or visible vapour; (of ·chimney, lamp, etc.) be smoky, discharge smoke into room; stain, dim, fumigate, preserve, drive *out*, etc. with smoke; inhale and exhale smoke of (tobacco, opium, etc.); smoke tobacco. smoking-carriage, concert, etc. in or at which smoking is allowed. ~-screen, dense volume of smoke to conceal military or naval operations etc. ~-stack, chimney, chimney-pipe. smō'ker *n.* (esp.) one who (habitually) smokes tobacco; smoking-carriage; smoking-concert. smō'ky̆ *a.* emitting, veiled with, obscure (as) with, coloured like, suggesting, etc. smoke.

smōōth (-dh) *a.* of even surface; free from projections and roughness; not harsh in sound, taste, etc.; (of progress, passage, etc.) not interrupted or disturbed by obstacles, storms, etc.; not hairy; conciliatory or plausible or flattering. *v.* make or become smooth; free from impediments etc. *n.* smoothing touch or stroke. ~-bore, unrifled gun. ~-spoken, ~-tongued, plausible, flattering.

smote, *p.t.* of smite.

smoth'er (-ŭdh-) *v.t.* suffocate, stifle, esp. with smoke; deaden (fire) with ashes etc.; suppress, cover (*up*); cover thickly (*with, in*). *n.* dense or suffocating smoke, dust, etc.

smoul'der (-ōl-) *v.i.* burn and smoke without flame (freq. fig.).

s.m.p. *abbr., sine mascula prole* [L], without male issue.

smŭdge[1] *n.* dirty mark, blur, smear. *v.* make smudge on or with; smear, blur; become blurred or smeared. smŭdg'y̆ *a.*

smŭdge[2] *n.* (fire producing) dense smoke, esp. to protect crops.

smŭg *a.* complacent, self-satisfied; consciously virtuous, respectable, etc.

smŭgg'le *v.* convey goods by stealth, esp. to evade payment of customs duties. smŭgg'ler *n.*

smŭt *n.* (black mark made by) flake of soot; obscene or indecent language; (fungus causing) plant--disease with blackening of grain etc. *v.t.* mark or infect with smut(s). smŭtt'y̆ *a.*

snăck *n.* slight, casual, or hasty meal. ~-bar, counter, bar, where sandwiches and other snacks may be obtained.

snàff'le *n.* simple bridle-bit without curb. *v.t.* put snaffle on; (sl.) appropriate.

snăg *n.* jagged projecting stump or point; obstacle, (unexpected) drawback.

snail *n.* aquatic or terrestrial mollusc with spiral or whorled shell capable of covering whole body; ~(-*wheel*) spiral cam.

snāke *n.* kinds of scaly limbless freq. poisonous reptile; treacherous or ungrateful person; ~ *in the grass*, secret enemy. *v.* (cause to) move in zigzag, sinuous, or winding course. ~-root, (root of) kinds of Amer. plant reputed to be antidotes to snake poison. snā'ky̆ *a.* of or infested with snakes; snake-like; treacherous-looking.

snăp *v.* make quick or sudden bite; speak with sudden irritation; break sharply; produce from or emit sudden sharp sound; close with snapping sound; take snapshot (of); pick *up* (esp. bargain) eagerly; ~ *one's fingers*, make audible fillip (*at*), esp. in contempt. *n.* act, fact, sound, of snapping; spring-catch; small crisp gingerbread biscuit;

sudden usu. brief spell of cold or frost; snapshot; kind of simple round card-game. *a.* taken or made suddenly or without notice, warning, preparation, etc. *adv.* with a snap. **~dragon**, kinds of plant with flowers that can be made to gape; Christmas game of snatching raisins from burning brandy. **~-fastener**, press-stud. **~ping turtle**, kinds of large ferocious Amer. freshwater turtle. **~ shot**, quick shot without deliberate aim. **~shot**, instantaneous photograph, esp. with hand-camera. **snăpp'er** *n.* (esp.) snap-fastener; snapping turtle. **snăpp'ish**, *a.* peevish, testy, malicious. **snăpp'y** *a.* snappish; quick, lively, full of vigour or spring.

snāre *n.* trap, esp. of running-noose kind (freq. fig.); gut or rawhide string stretched across lower head of side-drum. *v.t.* catch with snare. **~-drum**, side-drum.

snārl[1] *v.* (of dog etc.) make angry or quarrelsome sound with bared teeth; use ill-tempered or surly language; express by snarling. *n.* act or sound of snarling.

snārl[2] *n.* tangle, tangled condition, esp. of wool, hair, traffic, etc. *v.* tangle (*up*), mix together confusedly.

snătch *v.* seize, catch *at*, quickly, eagerly, or unexpectedly; take suddenly *away*, *from*, etc.; rescue narrowly *from*. *n.* hasty or sudden catch, grasp, snap, etc. *at*; short burst or spell (*of*); brief view, glimpse. **snătch'y** *a.* in short spells, disconnected.

sneak *n.* mean-spirited or underhand person; telltale; (crick.) ball bowled along ground. *v.* go furtively; (sl.) tell tales; (sl.) make off with furtively, steal. **~-thief**, one who steals what is in reach without breaking into buildings. **~ers** *n.pl.* (sl.) soft-soled shoes or slippers. **~ing** *a.* (esp.) furtive, unavowed.

sneer *n.* derisive smile or remark. *v.* smile derisively (*at*); express or suggest derision or disparagement.

sneeze *n.* act or sound of sneezing. *v.i.* make sudden involuntary convulsive expiration through nose;

~ at, despise, disregard, underrate.

snick *v.t.* make slight notch or cut in; (crick.) deflect (ball) with snick. *n.* slight notch or cut; batsman's light glancing blow.

snick'er *v.i.* & *n.* neigh, whinny; snigger.

snīde *a.* (sl.) counterfeit, bogus; slyly disparaging, sneering.

sniff *v.* draw up air audibly through nose; draw (*up*), take (*in*), etc. by sniffing. *n.* act or sound of sniffing; amount sniffed up.

sniff'le *v.i.* run at the nose; draw up mucus audibly; make sniffing or snuffling sound; be tearful. *n.* act or sound of sniffling; running mucus.

snif'ter *n.* (sl.) small amount of spirits etc.

snigg'er (-g-) *n.* & *v.i.* (utter) half-suppressed secretive laugh.

snip *v.* cut with scissors etc., esp. in small quick strokes. *n.* act of snipping; piece snipped off; (sporting sl.) certainty; (sl.) good bargain.

snīpe *n.* marsh game-bird with long straight bill. *v.* shoot snipe; shoot at men one at a time, usu. from cover and at long range. **snī'per** *n.*

snipp'et *n.* small piece cut off; scrap, fragment, (pl.) odds and ends.

snitch *v.* (sl.) inform, sneak; steal.

snīv'el *v.i.* sniffle; be lachrymose; show maudlin emotion. *n.* act of snivelling.

snŏb *n.* person who meanly or vulgarly admires, imitates, etc. those of superior social position, wealth, etc. or attaches great importance to differences of social position etc. **snŏbb'erў** *n.*; **snŏb'bish** *a.*

snōod *n.* fillet or band for woman's hair; net etc. loosely confining hair at back.

snŏok (*or* -ŏŏ-) *n.* (sl.) contemptuous gesture with thumb to nose and fingers spread; *cock a* **~**, make snook.

snōo'ker *n.* variety of (billiard-table) pool. **~ed** *a.* with balls in such position that direct play is impossible; (sl.) defeated, baffled.

snoop *v.i.* (colloq.) pry inquisitively. ~**er** *n.*

snoo'ty *a.* (sl.) supercilious.

snooze *v.* & *n.* (take) short sleep, esp. in day-time.

snore *n.* & *v.* (make) harsh or noisy respiration through mouth (and nose) during sleep.

snor'kel *n.* schnorkel.

snort *n.* loud or harsh sound made by driving breath violently through nose, noise resembling this. *v.* make snorting sound; express by snorting, utter with snorts. ~**er** *n.* (esp.) anything remarkable for size, violence, etc.

snott'y *a.* (sl.) running or foul with mucus. *n.* (sl.) midshipman.

snout[1] *n.* projecting part, including nose and mouth, of animal's head; (contempt.) person's nose; part, structure, etc. resembling snout.

snout[2] *n.* (prison sl.) tobacco.

snow (-ō) *n.* atmospheric vapour condensed, frozen into crystals, and falling in flakes; fall of these, layer of them on ground; something resembling snow, esp. in whiteness; (sl.) cocaine. *v.* let fall as or like snow, cover, strew, (as) with snow; *it ~s*, snow falls; ~ *under*, bury in snow, submerge, overwhelm; ~ *up*, block, imprison, with fallen snow. ~**-ball**, *n.* snow pressed or rolled into hard ball, esp. as missile; guelder-rose; anything growing or increasing rapidly; *v.* pelt with or throw snowballs, increase rapidly. ~**-blind**, with vision affected by glare of sun on snow. ~**-bunting**, small finch breeding in Arctic regions. ~**-drift**, snow piled up by wind. ~**-drop**, (white pendent flower of) small early-flowering bulbous plant; ~**-flake**, one of small crystalline masses in which snow falls; (white flower of) kinds of bulbous plant. ~**-goose**, white goose breeding in Arctic regions. ~**-line**, level above which snow never completely disappears. ~**-plough**, device for clearing snow from railway-line, road, etc. ~**-shoe**, one of pair of light racket-shaped strung frames enabling wearer to walk on surface of snow. ~**-white**, pure white. **snow'y** *a.*

snub[1] *v.t.* rebuff, humiliate, in sharp or cutting manner. *n.* snubbing, rebuff.

snub[2] *a.* (of nose) short and turned up.

snuff[1] *n.* black excrescence on wick of lighted candle. *v.* rid (candle) of snuff; put out or trim with scissors, fingers, etc.; ~ *it*, ~ *out*, (sl.) die.

snuff[2] *n.* powdered tobacco for sniffing up into nostrils. *v.* sniff.

snuff'le *v.* sniff, esp. audibly or noisily; speak like one with a cold. *n.* sniff; snuffling sound or speech.

snug *a.* sheltered, well-enclosed; comfortable; (of income etc.) sufficing for comfort. **snugg'ery** (-g-) *n.* snug place, esp. private room or den.

snugg'le *v.* move, lie, close *up to* for warmth etc.; hug, cuddle.

so *adv.* & *conj.* to extent, in manner, with result, described or indicated; of kind, in condition, etc. indicated; by that name or designation; on condition set forth or implied; for that reason, consequently, accordingly; indeed, in fact, also, as well. ~**-and-so**, substituted for name or expression not exactly remembered or not needing to be specified. ~**-called**, called by but doubtfully deserving that name. ~ *far as*, to extent to which. ~ *long*, farewell till our next meeting. ~ *long as*, provided that. ~**-so**, (colloq.) not very well or good; fair(ly).

S.O. *abbr.* Section Officer; Staff Office; Stationery Office; sub-office.

soak *v.* place or leave or lie in liquid for saturation; make or be saturated; take *up*, suck *in*; (of liquid etc.) make way *in(to)* etc. by saturation; booze. *n.* soaking; drinking-bout; hard drinker.

soap *n.* solid or semi-fluid cleansing agent, consisting of fat or oil combined with alkali. *v.* rub, smear, lather, etc. with soap. ~**-bubble**, iridescent bubble made usu. by blowing from thin film of soap and water. ~**-box**, box or rough platform of street orators; *a.* of or like street oratory. **~stone**, kind of massive talc with greasy feel. **~suds**, froth of soapy water. **~y** *a.* like, impregnated with, suggesting, etc. soap; ingratiating, unctuous, flattering.

soar (sōr) *v.i.* fly at, mount to, great height; hover or sail in air without flapping of wings or use of motor power.

sŏb *n.* convulsive catching of breath, esp. in weeping. *v.* weep or breathe or speak with sobs. **~-stuff**, exaggerated pathos, sentimentality.

sō'ber *a.* not drunk; not given to drink; moderate, sane, tranquil; (of colour) quiet. *v.* make or become sober. **sobrī'ĕtў** *n.*

sō'brĭquet (-kā), **sou-** (soō-) *n.* nickname.

Soc. *abbr.* Socialist; Society.

sŏcc'er (-k-) *n.* (colloq.) Association football.

sō'ciable (-sha-) *a.* fitted for or disposed to companionship or conversation; of, characterized by, friendly or pleasant companionship. **sociabĭl'itў** *n.*

sō'cial (-shl) *a.* living in communities; unfitted for solitary life; concerned with (constitution of) society or mutual relations of men or classes; relating to society. *n.* social gathering.

sō'cialĭsm (-sha-) *n.* political and economic principle that community as whole should have ownership and control of all means of production and distribution; policy aiming at this; state of society in which this principle is accepted. **~ĭst** *n. & a.*; **~ĭs'tĭc** *a.* **~īze** *v.t.* make socialistic; govern, organize, etc. on socialist principles.

sō'cialīte (-sha-) *n.* (U.S.) person prominent in fashionable society.

socī'ĕtў *n.* state of living in association with other individuals; (customs and organization of) social community; upper classes, people of fashion; company or companionship; association of persons with common interest, purpose, principle, etc.

sōcĭŏl'ogў *n.* study of human, esp.

civilized, society or of social problems. **sōcĭolŏ'gĭcal** *a.*; **~gĭst** *n.*

sŏck[1] *n.* short stocking not reaching knee; removable inner shoe-sole; light shoe of ancient comic actors.

sŏck[2] *n.* (sl.) hard or violent blow. *v.t.* hit hard; **~** (person) *one*, give him hard blow.

sŏck'ĕt *n.* hollow part or piece for thing to fit into etc.; hollow or cavity holding eye, tooth, etc.

sŏck'eye (-kī) *n.* kind of salmon.

sŏc'le *n.* plain rectangular plinth.

Socrăt'ĭc *a.* of or like Socrates.

sŏd[1] *n.* (piece of) turf; (poet.) surface of ground.

sŏd[2] (vulg.) *n.* sodomite.

sō'da *n.* compound of sodium in common use, esp. sodium carbonate or bicarbonate; soda-water. **~-fountain**, apparatus for drawing soda-water kept under pressure; shop, counter, etc. for making and serving ice-cream, soft drinks, etc. **~-water**, effervescent water charged under pressure with carbon dioxide.

sodăl'itў *n.* confraternity, esp. R.C. religious guild.

sŏdd'en *a.* saturated with liquid; heavy, doughy; stupid with drink.

sō'dĭum *n.* soft silver-white lustrous metallic element oxidizing rapidly in air. **~ carbonate**, common washing soda. **~ chloride**, common salt.

sŏd'omў *n.* unnatural sexual intercourse, esp. between males. **sŏd'o-mīte** *n.*; **~mĭt'ĭc** *a.*

sō'fa *n.* long seat with raised end(s) and back.

sŏff'it *n.* under-surface of lintel, arch, etc.

sŏft *a.* not hard; yielding to pressure; malleable, plastic, easily cut; smooth or fine textured; mild; moist or rainy; not loud or strident, low-toned; gentle, quiet, conciliatory; easily touched, compassionate; flabby, feeble; luxurious; silly; (sl.) easy; (of water) not containing calcium etc. salts which prevent lathering; (of drink) non-alcoholic. *adv.* softly. **~ goods**, textiles. **~ palate**, membranous back part of palate. **~-pedal**, 'play down', tone down. **~ soap**, semifluid soap; flattery; *v.t.* flatter.

~ **sugar**, granulated or powdered sugar. **~ware**, (in computer) programmes etc. not forming part of machine. **~wood**, (wood of) coniferous tree(s). **soften** (sŏfn) v. make or become soft(er); ~ *up*, reduce strength, resistance, etc. of; **~ing of the brain**, morbid esp. senile degeneration of brain. **sŏf'tў** n. soft, weak, silly, etc. person.

sŏgg'ў (-g-) a. sodden, waterlogged.

sōh n. (mus.) fifth note of major scale in tonic sol-fa.

soil[1] v. smear or stain with dirt etc.; tarnish, defile; admit of being soiled. n. dirty mark; defilement. **~-pipe**, sewage or waste-water pipe.

soil[2] n. ground, upper layer of earth in which plants grow.

soirée (swah'ra) n. evening party.

sŏj'ourn (-*ern*) n. & v.i. (make) temporary stay.

sōke n. (hist.) (district with) right of local jurisdiction.

sŏl n. (mus.) fifth note of major scale in some sol-fa systems.

sŏl'ace n. & v.t. comfort in distress or disappointment.

sō'lan (goose) n. gannet.

sō'lar a. of or reckoned by sun. n. solarium. ~ **plexus**, complex of nerves in abdomen behind stomach. ~ **system**, sun with planets, asteroids, etc. revolving round it.

solā̄r'ium n. (pl. *-ia*), room, balcony, etc. exposed to rays of sun.

sold, p.t. & p.p. of **sell**.

sōl'der (or sōd- or sŏd-) n. fusible metal or alloy used for joining metal surfaces or parts. v.t. join with solder.

sōl'dier (-jer) n. member of army, esp. private or N.C.O.; man of military skill and experience. v.i. serve as soldier. ~ **līke**, **~lў** aa. **sōl'dierў** n. soldiers as a class.

sōle[1] n. under surface of foot (freq. excluding heel), part of shoe or stocking below this; lower surface or base of plough, golf-club, etc. v.t. provide with (new) sole.

sōle[2] n. kinds of flat-fish esteemed as food.

sōle[3] a. one and only; exclusive. **sōle'lў** (-l-l-) adv.

sŏl'ēcĭsm n. offence against grammar, idiom, etiquette, etc.

sŏl'emn (-m) a. accompanied, performed, with ceremony; impressive; grave or deliberate; pompous. **sŏlĕm'nĭtў** n. **sŏl'emnīze** v.t. celebrate (festival); duly perform (esp. marriage ceremony); make solemn. **~īzā'tion** n.

sŏl'ēnoid n. (electr.) cylindrical coil of wire acting as bar magnet when current is passed through.

sŏl-fa' (-ah) n. (mus.) kinds of system of sight-singing and notation with syllabic names for notes.

solī'cĭt v.t. ask repeatedly or urgently; importune; request or invite; (of woman) accost and importune (man) for immoral purposes. **~ā'tion** n.

solī'cĭtor n. member of legal profession qualified to advise clients and instruct barristers but not to appear as advocate in higher courts; (chiefly U.S.) canvasser.

solī'cĭtous a. troubled, concerned; anxious, eager (*to* do). **solī'cĭtūde** n. being solicitous, anxiety, concern.

sŏl'ĭd a. of stable shape, not liquid or fluid; rigid, hard and compact; of three dimensions; of solid substance throughout, not hollow etc.; alike all through; substantial, well-grounded, sober, real; concerned with solids. n. solid substance or body; body or magnitude of three dimensions. **solĭd'ĭtў** n.; **solĭd'ĭfў** v.

sŏlĭdă'rĭtў n. community of interests, sympathies, and action.

solĭl'oquў n. (instance of) talking to oneself or without addressing any person. **solĭl'oquīze** v.i.

sŏlĭtaire' (or sŏl'-) n. diamond etc. set by itself; card-game for one person; game for one person of removing all pegs or marbles from board.

sŏl'ĭtarў a. alone, living alone; without companions; single; secluded, lonely. n. recluse; (colloq.) solitary confinement. **sŏl'ĭtūde** n. being solitary; solitary place.

sŏlmĭzā'tion n. expression in terms of sol-fa.

sō'lō n. (pl. *-os*), music, dance, etc.

performed by single player, singer, etc.; solo flight; kinds of card-game in which one player plays or may play alone against others. *a. & adv.* alone, without companion or partner. ~ **flight**, flight made without companion or instructor. **so'loïst** *n.*

sŏl'stice *n.* time, point in ecliptic, at which sun is farthest north or south of equator.

sŏl'üble *a.* that can be dissolved or solved. ~**bil'itў** *n.*

solü'tion (*or* -ōō-) *n.* dissolving or being dissolved, conversion of solid or gas into liquid form by mixture with solvent; solving or being solved, instance or method of solving, answer.

sŏlve *v.t.* explain, resolve; find answer to.

sŏl'vent *a.* able to pay all debts or liabilities; that dissolves or can dissolve. *n.* liquid capable of or used for dissolving something; dissolving, harmonizing, etc. influence or agent. **sŏl'vencў** *n.* being financially solvent.

Som. *abbr.* Somerset.

sōmăt'ic *a.* of body or its framework as dist. from internal organs.

sŏm'bre *a.* dark, gloomy, dismal.

sŏmbrer'o (-ārō) *n.* (pl. -*os*), broad--brimmed usu. felt hat.

some (sŭm, s*u*m) *a. & pron.* particular but unknown or unspecified (person or thing); certain quantity or number of (something); appreciable or considerable quantity (of); (colloq., emphat.) such in the fullest sense, something like. *adv.* (sl.) in some degree. ~**body**, some person; person of some note or consequence. ~**how**, in some indefinite or unspecified way, by some means or other. ~**one**, somebody. ~**thing**, some thing (esp. as vague substitute for n., a., etc.); ~*thing like*, rather like, vaguely resembling, (colloq.) highly satisfactory or superlative example or state of affairs,. ~**time**, (arch.) former(ly). ~**times**, at some times. ~**what**, in some degree. ~**where**, in, at, to, some place.

so'mersault *n. & v.i.* (make) leap or

spring in which person turns heels over head in air and lands on feet.

sŏmnăm'bülism *n.* (state characterized by) walking or performing other action during sleep. ~**ïst** *n.*; ~**ïs'tic** *a.*

sŏm'nolent *a.* sleepy, drowsy; inducing drowsiness. ~**ence** *n.*

son (sŭn) *n.* male child in relation to parent; male descendant; offspring, product, native, follower. ~**-in--law**, daughter's husband.

sō'nant *a. & n.* voiced (sound, letter).

sō'nar *n.* device for detecting and locating submerged objects by reflection of sonic and ultrasonic waves.

sona'ta (-ah-) *n.* musical composition for one or two instruments in several contrasted and related movements. ~ **form**, form of composition in which two subjects are successively stated, developed, and restated. **sŏnati'na** (-tē-) *n.* shorter or simpler form of sonata.

sŏng *n.* singing, vocal music; set of words for singing; poetry, poem. ~**-bird**, bird with musical song. ~**-thrush**, common thrush. ~**ster** *n.* singer; song-bird; poet. ~**stress** *n.*

sŏn'ic *a.* of, using, etc. sound or sound-waves. ~ **boom**, explosive noise produced by aircraft flying faster than speed of sound.

sŏnn'et *n.* poem of 14 lines arranged in one of certain definite rhyme--schemes. ~**eer'** *n. & v.i.* writer of, write, sonnet(s).

sonn'ў (sŭ-) *n.* familiar form of address to boy.

sonōr'ous (*or* sŏn'-) *a.* resonant, (capable of) giving out esp. rich or powerful sound. **sonŏ'ritў** *n.*

soͦon *adv.* not long after present or time in question; early; readily, willingly. **sooner or later**, at some time or other.

soͦot *n.* black powdery substance rising in smoke of coal, wood, etc., and adhering to sides of chimneys, etc. *v.t.* smudge, cover, choke (*up*), etc. with soot.

soͦoth *n.* (arch.) truth. ~**sayer**, one who foretells future events.

soͦothe (-dh) *v.t.* calm, tranquillize; reduce force or intensity of.

soot'y̆ *a.* of or like, as black as, black with, soot.

sŏp *n.* piece of bread etc. dipped or steeped in liquid before eating or cooking; something given to pacify or bribe. *v.* soak, steep; take *up* by absorption; be drenched. **sŏpp'y** *a.* soaked, wet; mawkish, foolishly sentimental.

Soph. *abbr.* Sophocles.

sŏph'ism *n.* specious but fallacious argument, esp. one meant to deceive. **sŏph'ist, sŏph'istry** *nn.*

sophis'ticāte *v.* make artificial, deprive of simplicity; make worldly-wise. **~ā'tion** *n.*

sŏph'omŏre *n.* second-year student in Amer. colleges and universities. **~mŏr'ic** *a.*

sōporif'ic (*or* sŏ-) *a. & n.* (drug etc.) tending to produce sleep.

soppy : see **sop.**

sopra'nō (-ah-) *n.* (pl. *-os*), (music for, singer with) highest singing voice in women and boys.

sŏr'cerer *n.* user of magic arts, wizard. **~ess, sŏr'cery** *nn.*

sŏr'did *a.* squalid, mean; ignoble, base; avaricious, mercenary.

sŏre *n.* place where skin or flesh is diseased or injured so as to be painfully tender or raw. *a.* painful, causing or suffering pain; irritable, sensitive; irritated, annoyed. *adv.* (arch.) grievously, severely.

sŏr'ghum (-gum) *n.* kinds of tropical grass.

sorŏ'rity *n.* (U.S.) women's college or university society.

sŏ'rrel[1] *n.* kinds of sour-leaved herb.

sŏ'rrel[2] *a. & n.* (horse) of bright chestnut or reddish-brown colour.

sŏ'rrow (-ō) *n.* (occasion or cause of) grief, sadness. *v.i.* feel sorrow; mourn. **~ful** *a.*

sŏ'rry *a.* pained at or regretful over something; feeling pity (*for*); wretched, paltry, shabby, mean.

sŏrt *n.* kind, variety; *of* **~s**, (colloq.) of not very satisfactory kind; *out of* **~s**, out of health, spirits or temper. *v.t.* separate into sorts or classes; take *out* (certain sorts from others). **~er** *n.* (esp.) letter-sorter at post-office.

sŏr'tie (-ē *or* -ĭ) *n.* sally, esp. of besieged party; operational flight by aircraft.

S.O.S. (ĕs'ōĕs'), international Morse-code signal of extreme distress; (colloq.) urgent appeal for help.

so-so : see **so.**

sŏt *n.* person stupefied by habitual drunkenness. **sŏtt'ish** *a.*

sŏtt'ō vō'ce (-chĭ) *adv.* in an undertone. [It.]

sou (sōō) *n.* (French coin worth) five centimes; (colloq.) halfpenny.

sou'chŏng (sōōsh-) *n.* choice China tea.

soufflé (sōō'flā) *n.* spongy dish made light with beaten white of egg.

sough (sōō*ch*, sow, sŭf) *n. & v.i.* (make) rushing, sighing, or rustling sound, as of wind in trees.

sought, *p.t. & p.p.* of **seek.** **~-after**, looked for, wanted, courted, pursued.

soul (sōl) *n.* spiritual or immaterial part of man; moral and emotional part, vital principle and mental powers, of man etc.; animating or essential part, personification or pattern *of*; departed or disembodied spirit; person. **soul'ful** *a.* having, expressing, appealing to, (higher) emotional or intellectual qualities; (colloq.) excessively emotional. **soul'less** *a.* (esp.) inhuman, inhumane.

sound[1] *n.* sensation produced in organs of hearing when surrounding air etc. vibrates; vibrations causing this; what is or may be heard. *v.* (cause to) emit sound; convey specified impression; utter, pronounce; give notice of by sound; declare, make known. **~-barrier**, excessive resistance of air to object moving at speed near that of sound. **~-board**, thin resonant board reinforcing tones in musical instrument. **~-box**, part of mechanical gramophone holding diaphragm and needle. **~-effects**, sounds other than speech or music in film, broadcast, etc. **~-post**, small wooden post beneath bridge of violin etc. supporting belly and connecting it with back. **~-proof,**

preventing passage of sound; *v.t.* make sound-proof. ~-**track**, part of film etc. carrying sound record. ~-**wave**, one of series of progressive longitudinal vibratory disturbances in air etc. stimulating auditory nerves. **soun'dĭng**[1] *a.* resonant, sonorous; high-sounding, imposing; ~**ing-board**, board or screen to reflect sound towards audience.

sound[2] *a.* healthy, free from disease or defects or corruption or heresy; financially solid or safe; correct, valid; thorough; (of sleep) unbroken. *adv.* soundly (*asleep*).

sound[3] *n.* strait; swimming-bladder of some fishes.

sound[4] *n.* surgeon's probe. *v.* investigate, test depth or quality of bottom of water, esp. with line and lead etc.; examine with sound; plunge or dive to bottom (of); inquire into person's views etc. esp. in cautious or indirect manner. **soun'dĭng**[2] *n.* (esp., pl.) measurement of depth of water; places where such soundings are taken.

soup (soōp) *n.* liquid food made by stewing bones, meat, vegetables, etc.; *in the* ~, (sl.) in difficulties, in trouble.

soupçon (soō'psawn) *n.* dash or trace (*of*).

sour (-owr) *a.* tasting tart or acid like unripe fruit or vinegar; (of smell) suggesting fermentation; (of soil) cold and wet; peevish, morose. *v.* turn sour. *n.* (U.S.) acid drink, usu. of whisky etc. with lemon- or lime-juice.

source (sōrs) *n.* place from which stream issues; origin, cause, (*of*); document etc. giving (original or primary) evidence as to fact etc.

souse *v.* put in pickle; plunge (*into* liquid), soak (*in*), drench. *n.* pickle made with salt; food in pickle. **soused** *a.* (sl.) very drunk.

soutane (soōtahn') *n.* cassock of R.-C. priests.

south *n.* point of horizon or compass opposite north; southern part of country etc.; southern States of U.S. *a.* & *adv.* towards, at, near, of, from, looking towards, etc. south. ~**down**, (one) of small

hornless breed of sheep with short fine wool. ~-**east**, ~-**west**, (of, in, to, from) direction or compass-point between south and east, west. ~-**easter**, ~-**wester**, south-east, south-west, wind. ~**paw**, left-handed (person). **south'erlў** (sŭdh-) *a.* & *adv.* towards, blowing from, south. ~**ward** *a.*, *adv.* & *n.*; ~**wards** *adv.*

south'ern (sŭdh-) *a.* of, in, looking, south. **S**~ **States**, States of U.S.A. lying south of Pennsylvania, Ohio River and Missouri. ~-**wood**, shrubby southern-European fragrant wormwood. ~**er** *n.* inhabitant of south, esp. of U.S.

souvenir (soō'vener) *n.* thing given or kept in memory of person, place, etc.

sou'-wĕs'ter *n.* south-west wind; waterproof hat with broad flap behind to protect neck.

sov., sovs. *abbr.* sovereign(s).

sŏv'ereign (-vrĭn) *a.* supreme; (of remedies etc.) very good. *n.* supreme ruler, esp. monarch; (hist.) English gold coin worth ·£1. ~**tў** *n.*

Sŏv'iĕt (*or* sō-) *n.* council, esp. elected organ of government of district, republic, etc., or (*Supreme* ~) whole, of U.S.S.R.; system of government by soviets; *the* U.S.S.R. *a.* of Soviets or Soviet Union. **S**~ **Union**, U.S.S.R. ~**ize** *v.* change or convert to Soviet form of government.

sow[1] (sō) *v.* (p.p. *sowed* or *sown*), scatter seed on or in earth, plant *with* seed; cover thickly *with*. ~**er** *n.*

sow[2] *n.* adult female pig. ~-**thistle**, kinds of common European weed with thistle-like leaves.

soy *n.* (sauce prepared from) soya-beans.

soy'a(-bean) *n.* (seed of) Asian leguminous plant yielding valuable meal, oil, etc.

sŏzz'led (-ld) *a.* (sl.) very drunk.

S.P. *abbr.* Service Police; sparking plug; starting price.

s.p. abbr., sine prole [L], without issue.

spa (-ah) *n.* watering-place, (place with) mineral spring.

spāce *n.* continuous extension; immeasurable expanse in which solar and stellar systems etc. are situated; region beyond earth's atmosphere; interval between points or objects; (sufficient) extent or room, esp. for printed or written matter; interval of time; (print.) (piece of type-metal making) blank between words etc. *v.* set (*out*) at intervals, put spaces between; make space between words etc. *a.* of, (used) in, (suitable) for, travelling outside earth's atmosphere. ~-**bar**, bar on typewriter depressed to make space. ~**craft**, ~-**ship**, craft for travelling in space. ~-**time**, four-dimensional continuum resulting from fusion of concepts of space and time. **spā'cious** *a.* having ample space; roomy.

spāde[1] *n.* tool for digging etc., usu. with flattish rectangular blade on long handle; anything resembling this in form or use. *v.t.* dig with spade. ~-**work**, hard work, preliminary drudgery.

spāde[2] *n.* (playing-card with) black figure(s) resembling pointed spade; (pl.) suit of these.

spaghett'ĭ (-gĕ-) *n.* pasta in long rods thinner than macaroni.

spake : see **speak**.

spăn[1] *n.* distance between tips of thumb and little finger of extended hand; nine inches; short distance or time; whole extent of period of time; full extent between abutments of arch, piers of bridge, wing-tips, etc.; arch of bridge. *v.* stretch from side to side of; extend, form arch, across; measure, cover, extent of with extended hand etc.

spăn[2] *n.* (U.S. etc.) pair of horses, mules, etc.; (S.-Afr.) team of oxen. *v.t.* harness, yoke.

span[3], *p.t.* of **spin**.

spăn'drel *n.* space between either shoulder of arch and surrounding rectangular framework.

spangle (spăng'gl) *n.* small round thin piece of glittering metal sewn to dress etc.; any small sparkling object. *v.t.* cover (as) with spangles.

Spăn'iard (-yard) *n.* native of Spain.

Spăn'ish *a.* & *n.* (language) of Spain or Spaniards.

spăn'iel (-yel) *n.* kinds of large-eared long-haired sporting dog freq. kept as pets.

spănk[1] *v.i.* move or travel quickly or dashingly. ~**er** *n.* (esp.) fast horse; fore-and-aft sail on mizen-mast. ~**ing** *a.* very large or fine; dashing, showy.

spănk[2] *v.t.* & *n.* slap or smack with open hand, esp. on buttocks.

spănn'er *n.* tool, usu. steel bar with jaw, socket, etc. at end(s), for turning nut of screw etc.

spār[1] *n.* stout pole esp. of kind used for ship's yards etc.

spār[2] *n.* kinds of crystalline mineral.

spār[3] *v.i.* use fists (as) in boxing, make motions of boxing; dispute, bandy words; (of cocks) fight. *n.* sparring; (practice) boxing-match; cock-fight.

spāre *v.* refrain from hurting, punishing, etc., refrain from taking (life); dispense with, do without; be frugal or grudging of; part with, give, etc. esp. without inconvenience or loss to oneself; *to* ~, that can be spared, spare, more than enough. *a.* scanty, frugal; lean; that can be spared, not required; reserved for future, emergency, etc. use. *n.* spare part etc. ~ **part**, substitute part of machine to replace loss, breakage, etc. ~-**rib**, part of closely-trimmed ribs of meat, esp. pork. ~ **room**, room not ordinarily used, guest-room. **spār'ing** *a.* (esp.) economical, frugal, grudging.

spārk *n.* fiery particle of burning substance; small bright object or point; flash of light accompanying electrical discharge; electric spark for firing explosive mixture in internal-combustion engine; flash, scintilla, particle (*of*); (pl., colloq.) radio operator. *v.* emit spark(s); produce sparks at point where electric circuit is broken; ~ *off*, set off (sudden or violent activity); ~*ing plug*, electrical device producing spark in motor-engine.

spār'kle *v.i.* (seem to) emit sparks; glitter, flash, scintillate. *n.* sparkling; spark, gleam, glitter. **spār'kler**

n. (esp., sl.) diamond. **spǎr'klǐng** *a.* (esp., of wines etc.) effervescing.

spǎ'rrow (-ō) *n.* kinds of small brownish-grey bird, esp. common house-sparrow. **~-hawk**, kinds of small hawk.

spǎrse *a.* thinly scattered.

spǎr'tan *a.* austere, hardy, unflinching, rigorous; *S~*, of ancient Sparta. *n.* person of courage and endurance; *S~*, native of Sparta.

spǎsm *n.* convulsive muscular contraction; violent access of emotion etc. **spasmŏd'ĭc** (-ăz-) *a.* sudden and violent; intermittent.

spǎs'tĭc *a.* caused by or subject to spasm(s); suffering from cerebral palsy. *n.* spastic person.

spǎt[1] *n.* spawn of shellfish, esp. oyster.

spǎt[2] *n.* short gaiter covering instep and ankle.

spǎt[3] *n.* (U.S.) tiff, quarrel.

spat[4], *p.t.* & *p.p.* of **spit**[2].

spǎtch'cǒck *n.* fowl split open and grilled immediately after being killed. *v.t.* cook as or like spatchcock; (colloq.) insert, interpolate (esp. something incongruous).

spāte *n.* sudden river-flood; rush, outpour.

spāthe (-dh) *n.* (bot.) large freq. bright-coloured bract enveloping inflorescence.

spā'tial *a.* of, in, relating to, etc., space.

spǎtt'er *v.* fly or send (mud etc.) flying in drops or splashes; splash, daub, sprinkle. *n.* spattering; pattering.

spǎt'ūla *n.* flat broad-bladed knife-shaped implement for spreading ointment, mixing pigments, etc. **spǎt'ūlate** *a.* with broadened rounded end.

spǎv'ǐn *n.* hard bony swelling on horse's hock. **~ed** *a.*

spawn *n.* eggs of fish, frogs, etc.; mass of thread-like tubes from which esp. mushrooms are produced; brood, offspring. *v.* cast spawn; produce or generate as spawn or in large numbers.

spay *v.t.* remove ovaries of (female animal).

S.P.C.K. *abbr.* Society for Promotion of Christian Knowledge.

speak *v.* (*spōke* & arch. *spāke*; *spōken*), utter words in ordinary (not singing) voice; say something; hold conversation; deliver speech; utter or pronounce; use (specified language) in speaking; reveal, indicate; *~ for*, be spokesman of or for; *~ of*, mention; *~ out*, *up*, speak freely, speak loud(er). **spea'ker** *n.* (esp.) person of specified skill in speech-making; official president of House of Commons etc.; loud-speaker.

spea'king *n.* (esp.) speech-making. *a.* (esp.) expressive, eloquent; (of likeness etc.) striking, faithful. *~ part*, part in play etc. containing words to be spoken. *~ terms*, degree of acquaintanceship, friendliness, etc. allowing exchange of conversation. *~-trumpet*, trumpet-shaped instrument for magnifying sound of voice. *~-tube*, tube for conveying voice from room to room, to driver of closed vehicle, etc.

spear *n.* thrusting or hurling weapon with long shaft and sharp-pointed head. *v.t.* pierce or strike (as) with spear. **~head**, (esp.) person(s) leading, forefront of, attack; *v.t.* be spearhead of (esp. attack). **~-mint**, common garden mint.

spĕc *n.* (sl.) speculation; *on ~*, experimentally, as a gamble.

spĕ'cial *a.* of peculiar or restricted kind; of or for particular person, occasion, or thing; not general; exceptional. *n.* special constable, train, etc. *~ constable*, person sworn in to assist police on special occasion etc. *~ licence*, licence allowing marriage to take place at time or place other than those legally appointed. *~ pleading*, (pop.) specious but unfair argument. *~ train*, extra train for special purpose. **spĕciǎl'itў** (-shǐ-), **~tў** *nn.* special feature or characteristic; special pursuit, product, etc.; thing to which special attention is given. **spĕ'ciallў** *adv.* in special manner, to special degree or extent; on purpose, expressly.

spĕ'cialist *n.* one who devotes himself to particular branch of profession etc., esp. medicine; authority, expert.

spē'cialīze v. be or become specialist; adapt for particular purpose; differentiate, be differentiated; ~ (in), make special study (of). ~īz'ā-tion n.

sp'ēcie (-shē) n. coin, coined money.

spē'cies (-shēz) n. (pl. same), class of things having common attribute(s) etc., esp. group of organisms having characteristic(s) not shared by other groups, subdivision of genus; kind, sort.

spécĭf'ic a. definite, distinctly formulated; of species; possessing properties characterizing species; of or for particular disease, condition, etc. n. specific remedy. ~ gravity, ratio of weight of substance to that of equal volume of water, hydrogen, etc., taken as standard.

spē'cĭfȳ v. name expressly, mention definitely; include in specification. spĕcĭfĭcā'tion n. specifying; specified detail, esp. detailed description of work undertaken, invention, patent, etc.

spē'cĭmén n. part or piece or individual as example of class or whole, esp. serving for investigation, scientific study, etc.

spē'cious a. fair-seeming; plausible. spēcĭŏs'ĭtȳ (-shĭ-) n.

spĕck n. small spot or stain or particle. v.t. mark with specks. spĕck'lèss a.

spĕck'le n. small speck, mark, or stain. v.t. mark with speckles.

spĕcs n.pl. (colloq.) spectacles.

spĕc'tacle n. public show, display, noteworthy scene; (pl.) pair of lenses set in frame supported on nose, to correct or assist defective eyesight. spĕc'tacled (-ld) a. wearing spectacles.

spĕctăc'ūlar a. of (nature of) spectacle or show; striking, imposing, flamboyant.

spĕctā'tor n. looker-on; person present at performance etc.

spĕc'tral a. ghost-like, unreal; of spectrum.

spĕc'tre n. ghost, apparition.

spĕc'troscōpe n. instrument for producing and examining spectra. ~scŏp'ic a.

spĕc'trum n. (pl. -ra) coloured band into which beam of light is decomposed by prism etc.

spĕc'ūlāte v.i. engage in esp. conjectural or theoretical thought or reflection; buy or sell commodities etc. in expectation of rise or fall in market value; engage in transaction, make investment, involving risk of loss. ~ā'tion, ~ātor nn.; ~ative a.

spĕc'ūlum n. (pl. -la), instrument for dilating cavities of human body for inspection; mirror, esp. in optical instruments. spĕc'ūlar a.

sped, p.t. & p.p. of speed.

speech n. act, faculty, or manner of speaking; thing said; public address; language, dialect. ~-day, annual prize-giving day in school. ~-therapy, remedial treatment of defective speech. spee'chĭfȳ v.i. make speeches; hold forth. speech'-lèss a. deprived of speech by emotion etc.

speed n. rapidity, quickness; rate of progress, motion, etc. v. (spĕd), go fast; travel at excessive or illegal speed; (arch.) be or make prosperous or successful; ~ up, increase speed (of). ~-boat, fast motor-boat. ~-up, speeding up of production etc. ~way, track for motor-cycle etc. racing; road intended for fast motor vehicles. speedŏm'eter n. instrument for registering speed of motor vehicle. spee'dȳ a. rapid, swift; prompt.

speed'well (-el) n. small blue-flowered herbaceous plant.

spēlēŏl'ogȳ (or -ĕl-) n. exploration and scientific study of caves etc. ~ogĭst n.

spĕll[1] n. words used as charm; fascination, attraction. ~binder, speaker who can hold audience spellbound. ~bound, bound (as) by spell, fascinated, entranced.

spĕll[2] v. (spĕlt or spĕlled, pr.-lt), name or write in order letters of word etc., form words etc. thus; form, make up (word); imply, involve, mean; ~ out, make out laboriously, spell aloud, state explicitly, explain in detail. spĕll'ing n.; ~ing-bee, competition in spelling.

spĕll[3] n. turn of work, activity, etc.;

short period; continuous period or stretch (*of*). *v.* relieve, take place of.

spelt, *p.t.* & *p.p.* of **spell²**.

spĕl'ter *n.* (commerc.) zinc.

spĕnd *v.* (*spĕnt*), pay out money for purchase etc.; use, use up, exhaust, wear out; live or stay through (period of time). ~**thrift**, wasteful (person).

spĕrm *n.* semen; sperm-whale. ~ **oil**, spermaceti. ~**-whale**, large whale yielding spermaceti.

spĕrmacē'tĭ (*or* -sĕ-) *n.* white soft scaly substance got from head of sperm-whale etc.

spĕrmăt'ĭc *a.* of sperm, seminal.

spĕrmatozō'ŏn *n.* (pl. -*zoa*), minute active fertilizing cell of male organism.

spew *v.* vomit.

S.P.G. *abbr.* Society for Propagation of Gospel.

sp. gr. *abbr.* specific gravity.

sphăg'num *n.* kinds of moss growing in swampy places.

sphēre *n.* figure or body having all points of its surface equidistant from point within it; ball, globe; any of (orig. 8) concentric transparent hollow globes formerly imagined as revolving round earth and carrying sun, stars, etc. with them; field of action, influence, etc.; place in society. **sphĕr'ical** *a.* sphere-shaped; of or concerned with spheres. **sphĕr'oid** *n.* & *a.* sphere-like but not perfectly spherical (body).

sphĭnc'ter *n.* ring of muscle guarding or closing orifice.

sphĭnx *n.* (Gk. myth.) winged monster with woman's head and lion's body; (ancient Egyptian) figure of recumbent lion with head of man, ram, etc.; enigmatic or mysterious person.

spīce *n.* aromatic or pungent vegetable substance used as flavouring; spices collectively; thing that adds zest, piquancy, excitement, etc. *v.t.* flavour with spice(s).

spĭck and spăn *adj. phr.* smart, trim, new-looking.

spī'cў *a.* of or like or flavoured with spice; pungent, sensational, somewhat improper.

spī'der *n.* kinds of eight-legged web-spinning animal; frying-pan with legs and long handle. **spī'derў** *a.* like spider or its long thin legs.

spiel *n.* (U.S. sl.) (esp. glib or persuasive) talk. *v.i.* talk volubly.

spĭg'ot *n.* peg or plug, esp. stopping vent-hole of cask or controlling flow of faucet or tap.

spīke *n.* sharp projecting point; large stout nail; inflorescence of sessile flowers on long common axis. *v.t.* furnish with spike(s); fix, pierce, (as) with spike(s); plug vent of (gun) with spike; ~ *guns of*, thwart, frustrate. **spī'kў** *a.*

spīke'nắrd (-kn-) *n.* (Eastern plant yielding) ancient costly aromatic substance.

spill¹ *v.* (*spilt* or *spilled*), (allow liquid etc. to) fall or run out from vessel, esp. accidentally or wastefully; shed (blood); cause to fall from horse or vehicle. *n.* throw or fall, esp. from horse or vehicle; tumble.

spill² *n.* strip of wood, paper, etc. for lighting candle etc.

spill'ĭkin *n.* one of heap of small slips of wood etc. used in game of *spillikins*.

spilt, *p.t.* & *p.p.* of **spill¹**.

spĭn *v.* (*spăn* or *spŭn*; *spŭn*), make yarn by drawing out and twisting together fibres of wool etc.; make (web etc.) by extrusion of fine viscous thread; (cause to) turn or revolve like top or wheel; fish with spinning bait; ~ *out*, prolong, last out. *n.* spinning motion, esp. of aircraft in diving descent, ball struck aslant, etc.; brisk or short run, drive, etc. ~**-drier**, machine for drying clothes etc. in rotating drum. **spinning-jenny**, early form of spinning-machine. **spinning-wheel** (hist.), spinning-apparatus with spindle driven by wheel worked by hand or foot.

spĭn'ach (-nĭj) *n.* (plant with) succulent leaves used as vegetable. ~ **beet**, kind of beet with leaves used like spinach.

spī'nal *a.* of spine. ~ **column**, spine. ~ **cord**, rope-like mass of nerve-cells etc. enclosed within spinal column.

spin'dle *n.* slender rod used to twist or wind thread in spinning; pin, axis, on which something revolves. ~-**berry**, -**tree**, (deep-pink fruit of) kinds of shrub. ~-**shanks**, (person with) long thin legs. **spin'dlў** *a.* slender, attenuated.

spin'drift *n.* spray blown along surface of sea.

spine *n.* backbone, articulated series of vertebrae extending from skull to hips; stiff sharp-pointed process, thorn, prickle; ridge, sharp projection, resembling backbone; part of book visible when it stands on shelf. ~-**less** *a.* (esp.) lacking backbone or character.

spin'el *n.* hard crystalline mineral, esp. ruby.

spin'et (*or* -ĕt') *n.* (mus.) small keyboard instrument of harpsichord kind.

spinn'aker *n.* large three-cornered extra sail of racing-yacht.

spinn'er *n.* (esp.) manufacturer engaged in spinning; spinning artificial bait.

spinn'eret *n.* spinning-organ in spider, silk-worm, etc.

spinn'ey *n.* copse.

spi'nous *a.* having spines.

spin'ster *n.* unmarried woman.

spir'acle *n.* (zool.) breathing-hole, blow-hole.

spirae'a *n.* kinds of garden plant allied to meadowsweet.

spir'al *a.* coiled in cylindrical or conical manner; curving continuously round fixed point at steadily increasing distance from it. *n.* spiral curve or course; thing of spiral form; progressive rise or fall. *v.i.* wind, move, ascend, descend, in spiral path or course.

spir'ant *a. & n.* (consonantal sound) formed by constriction but not closure of air-passage.

spire *n.* tapering structure in form of tall cone or pyramid rising above tower etc. esp. of church.

spir'it *n.* animating or vital principle, immaterial part, of man etc.; person viewed as possessing this; mental or moral nature or qualities; disembodied soul; incorporeal being; tone, general meaning or feeling

(*of*), mood; mettle, vigour, courage, dash; (usu. pl.) distilled alcoholic liquor; distilled extract, alcoholic solution *of*; *high, low,* ~*s,* gay or exalted, gloomy or depressed, mood. *v.t.* convey mysteriously *away* etc. **spi'rited** *a.* full of spirit, lively; courageous; having specified spirit(s). ~**ism** *n.* spiritualism; ~**ist** *a. & n.* ~**less** *a.*

spi'rituous *a.* containing much alcohol; produced by distillation.

spi'ritual *a.* of, concerned with, proceeding from, etc. spirit, soul, God, etc.; of sacred or religious things; ecclesiastical. *n.* characteristic religious song of Amer. Negroes. ~**ăl'itў**, ~**alizā'tion** *nn.*; ~**alīze** *v.t.*

spi'ritualism *n.* belief that spirits of dead can communicate with living, esp. through medium; doctrines or practices founded on this. ~**ist** *a. & n.*; ~**is'tic** *a.*

spit[1] *n.* pointed rod thrust into meat etc. for roasting; point of land runing out into water. *v.t.* pierce, transfix, (as) with spit.

spit[2] *v.* (*spăt*), eject saliva etc. (*out*) from mouth; utter vehemently; make spitting sound as sign of anger or hostility; (of rain etc.) fall thinly. *n.* spittle; act or instance of spitting; *the* (*very*) ~, exact counterpart (*of*). ~**fire**, fiery-tempered person.

spit[3] *n.* spade-depth.

spite *n.* ill will, malice; *in* ~ *of,* notwithstanding, in disregard or defiance of. *v.t.* thwart, annoy, mortify. ~**ful** *a.* animated or dictated by spite.

spitt'le *n.* saliva.

spittoon' *n.* receptacle for spittle.

spiv *n.* (flashily dressed) person living on his wits but not criminal.

splash *v.* dash, spatter, bespatter (*with* liquid); (cause liquid to) fly about in drops or scattered portions; step, fall, etc. *into, through,* etc. with splashing; mark, mottle, with irregular patches of colour etc.; (colloq.) display conspicuously esp. in print. *n.* splashing, sound or mark made by it; quantity splashed; dash of soda-water in spirits; large irregular patch of colour etc.; (colloq.) striking or ostentatious display or effect. ~-board, mud-guard in front of vehicle. splăsh'ў̆ a.

splăt n. flat piece of wood as central part of chair-back.

splătt'er v. & n. spatter, splash.

splay v. construct (aperture) with divergent sides; be so shaped or set; carry one's feet with toes turned abnormally out. n. extent to which aperture is splayed. a. splayed.

spleen n. abdominal organ concerned in formation of antibodies etc.; moroseness, irritability, spite. splĕn'ic a. of or in spleen.

splĕn'dĭd a. magnificent, admirable, glorious, excellent. splĕndif'erous a. (sl.) magnificent, splendid. splĕn'dour n. great brightness; magnificence, parade, pomp, brilliance.

splĕnĕt'ĭc a. morose, ill-tempered; of spleen.

splīce n. joining of two ends of rope etc. by untwisting and interweaving; overlapping join of two pieces of wood etc.; part of cricket-bat handle inserted in blade. v.t. join by splice; (colloq.) join in marriage.

splint n. strip of more or less rigid material holding broken bone etc. in position. v.t. put into, secure with, splint(s).

splĭn'ter n. rough, sharp-edged, or thin fragment broken or split off from some hard material. v. split into splinters; come off as splinter. ~ group, party, etc. small esp. political group that has split off from larger one. splĭn'terў̆ a. full of or like splinters; apt to splinter.

split v. (splĭt), break into parts, esp. with grain or plane of cleavage; divide into thicknesses, shares, factions, etc.; (sl.) reveal secret, inform on; ~ up, split, separate, part. n. splitting; fissure, rent; schism; something formed by splitting; half-bottle of mineral-water; split roll or bun; (pl.) acrobatic movement with body lowered to floor between legs widely separated at right angles to trunk. a. that has

split or been split. ~ infinitive, infinitive with adverb etc. inserted between to and verb. ~ personality, dissociation of personality in mental illness. ~ pin, pin with split end opening to keep it in position. ~ ring, ring with ends not joined but closely overlapped, esp. one consisting of two turns of spiral or helix pressed flat together. ~ second, very brief moment. ~-second, correct to minute fractions of time; extremely swift or rapid.

splŏtch n. large irregular spot or patch of colour etc., blotch. v.t. mark with splotches. ~ў̆ a.

splûrge n. ostentatious display of wealth etc.; splash; splotch. v. make ostentatious display (of); splash; spend extravagantly.

splŭtt'er v. utter, talk, hastily and indistinctly; scatter or fly in small splashes or pieces; make sputtering sound. n. spluttering noise; fuss; loud sputter or splash.

spoil n. (usu. pl. or collect.) plunder taken from enemy or acquired by violence etc.; booty; emoluments of office, etc. v. (spoilt or spoiled), (arch.) plunder, deprive of by force or stealth; destroy or impair good or effective qualities of; prevent full exercise or enjoyment of; injure character of by over-indulgence; cosset; deteriorate, decay, go bad. ~-sport, one who spoils sport or enjoyment of others.

spōke[1] n. any of radiating bars connecting wheel's hub and rim or of radial handles of steering-wheel; rung of ladder. ~shave, tool for planing curved surface etc.

spoke[2], spoken, p.t. & p.p. of speak.

spōkes'man (-ks-) n. (pl. -men), one who speaks for others, representative.

spōliā'tion n. pillaging, despoiling, depredation.

spŏn'dee n. metrical foot of two long syllables. spŏndā'ĭc a.

sponge (-ŭnj) n. kinds of aquatic animal or animal-colony; soft light porous skeleton of sponge used as absorbent in bathing, cleansing surfaces, etc.; pad of porous rubber etc. used similarly; thing of sponge-like absorbency or consistence, sponge-cake, soft porous dough, etc.; sponging, bath or swill with sponge; hard drinker; sponger. *v.* wet, wipe, soak up, etc. (as) with sponge; be meanly dependent *on*, cadge (*for* money etc.). ∼-bag, bag for holding sponge etc.; (of trousers) of checked material. ∼-cake, very light sweet cake of flour, eggs, and sugar. ∼-cloth, loose-textured cotton fabric with wrinkled surface. ∼-rubber, porous spongy rubber. spon'ger *n.* (esp.) one who sponges for money etc., parasite. spon'gy̆ *a.* (esp.) porous, compressible, absorbent, soft, light, etc. as sponge.

spŏn'son *n.* platform projecting from ship's side.

spŏn'sor *n.* godfather or godmother; person making himself responsible for another; advertiser paying cost of entertainment, radio programme, etc. *v.* act as sponsor for; support, favour, advocate.

spŏntā'nĕous *a.* resulting from natural impulse; not forced or suggested or caused from outside; not deliberate or laboured. spŏn-tanē'ĭty̆ *n.*

spōōf *n.* & *v.t.* (sl.) hoax, humbug. *a.* sham, false.

spŏōk (*or* -ŏŏ-) *n.* (colloq.) ghost. ∼ish, ∼y̆ *aa.*

spōōl *n.* bobbin or reel; roll of photographic film. *v.t.* wind on spool.

spōōn *n.* utensil consisting of shallow usu. oval bowl and handle, used for conveying food to mouth, cooking, etc.; wooden concave-faced golf-club (No. 3 wood); kind of artificial bait used in spinning for fish. *v.* take, lift, etc., with spoon; behave amorously, make love esp. in foolishly sentimental fashion. ∼-bill, kinds of wading-bird with long bill expanded and flattened at tip. ∼-fed, feed, fed, feed, with spoon like child; pamper(ed); supplied, supply, with instruction, information, etc. without effort or participation on part of pupil etc. ∼ful *n.* spōō'ny̆ *a.* silly; sentimentally amorous.

spōō'nerism *n.* accidental transposition of initial or other sounds of two or more words.

spoor *n.* track, trail.

spŏrăd'ĭc *a.* occurring in isolated instances or very small numbers; scattered; occasional.

spōre *n.* minute reproductive body in ferns, fungi, protozoa, etc.

spŏ'rran *n.* pouch worn with kilt.

spōrt *n.* amusement, diversion; pastime(s), game(s), esp. of outdoor or athletic kind; (pl.) (meeting for competition in) athletic pastimes; animal or plant that deviates from type; (sl.) sportsman, good fellow. *v.* gambol, play; toy, play, trifle, *with*; become or produce sport; wear, exhibit, esp. ostentatiously. ∼s car etc., open low-built fast car etc. ∼s coat etc., coat etc. for outdoor sports or informal wear. ∼sman, ∼swoman, person fond of sports, esp. hunting etc.; good fellow; person who is fair to opponents, cheerful in defeat, etc. spōr'ting *a.* (esp.) interested in sport; befitting, worthy of, sportsman; ∼ing chance, one involving some, but not great, risk. spōr'tĭve *a.* playful. spōr'ty̆ *a.* (sl.) sporting; of or like a sport, showy, flashy.

spŏt *n.* small esp. roundish mark or stain; discolouring or disfiguring mark; pimple; sun-spot; moral blemish; (billiards) marked place on table; particular or definite place or locality; *the* very place; (colloq.) small amount, drop, (*of*); *in a* ∼, in difficulties in an awkward situation; *in* ∼s, here and there, at intervals; *on the* ∼, at once, straightway, at place in question, equal to situation, wide awake; *put on the* ∼, mark for killing, assassinate. *v.* mark with spot(s); show spots readily; remove spot(s) from; (colloq.) pick out (esp. beforehand), detect, identify; act as spotter. ∼ cash, money paid immediately on sale etc. ∼light, lamp or projector throwing concentrated beam of light, light so thrown, on one spot, esp. of stage (freq. fig.); *v.t.* illuminate (as) with spotlight, throw into relief, concentrate attention etc. on. ~less *a.* (esp.) absolutely clean, unblemished. **spŏtt'ĕd** *a.* marked with spots; ~**ted dog**, Dalmatian dog, pudding spotted with currants. **spŏtt'er** *n.* (esp.) watcher, observer, noting approach or position of enemy forces, effect of gun-fire or bombing, etc. **spŏtt'ў** *a.*

spouse (-z) *n.* husband or wife.

spout *n.* projecting tube or lip through which rain-water is carried off from roof or liquid is poured or issues; whale's spiracle; jet of liquid; rush of water over ledge etc. esp. in detached stream, cascade; *down the* ~, irretrievably gone or lost; *up the* ~, in pawn, in a bad way or hopeless position. *v.* discharge, issue, forcibly in jet; (of whale) send up jet of water in breathing; utter in declamatory manner, speechify.

S.P.Q.R. *abbr., Senatus Populusque Romanus* [L], Roman Senate and People; small profits and quick returns.

sprain *v.t.* wrench (joint) so as to cause pain and swelling. *n.* such injury.

sprang, *p.t.* of **spring.**

sprăt *n.* small European herring or similar fish.

sprawl *v.* fall, lie, etc. with limbs spread out in careless or ungainly way; straggle, spread untidily. *n.* sprawling movement or attitude; straggling group or mass.

spray[1] *n.* liquid dispersed in small mist-like drops; preparation intended for spraying; instrument or apparatus for spraying. *v.* scatter, diffuse, as spray; sprinkle (as) with spray. ~**-gun**, apparatus for spraying esp. paint etc.

spray[2] *n.* slender shoot or twig, graceful branch with flowers etc.; jewel or other ornament in form of spray.

spread (-ĕd) *v.* extend surface of, cause to cover larger surface, by unrolling, unfolding, smearing, flattening, etc.; cover surface of; stretch or open *out*; extend, show extended or extensive surface; diffuse, be diffused. *n.* spreading,

being spread; extent or expanse, breadth, compass, span; anything spread or spread out; (colloq.) feast, meal; paste etc. for spreading on bread etc. ~ **eagle**, figure of eagle with wings and legs spread in heraldry, etc. ~**-eagle**, extend, fix, tie up, etc. in form of spread eagle.

spree *n.* bit of fun, carouse, bout of drinking etc.

sprig *n.* small usu. wedge-shaped headless nail; small branch, twig, spray. **sprĭgged** *a.* ornamented with (small) sprays.

spright'lў *a.* vivacious, lively, brisk.

spring *v.* (*sprăng, sprŭng*), well up from below ground; burst forth from soil, root, or stem; rise from base; originate; (cause to) leap, move rapidly or suddenly, esp. from constrained position or (as) by action of spring; produce, develop, suddenly or unexpectedly; explode (mine etc.); develop (leak). *n.* leap; power of springing, elasticity; place from which vault or arch springs; elastic contrivance with property of returning to normal shape after being compressed, bent, etc., used to lessen or prevent concussion, as motive power in clockwork, etc.; moving or actuating agency; source, origin; place where water, oil, etc. wells up from underground; flow of water etc. rising from earth; season of year between winter and summer, season in which vegetation begins. ~**-board**, elastic board, esp. one from end of which jump or dive is made. ~**bŏk**, S.-Afr. gazelle. ~**-clean**, clean house etc. thoroughly, esp. in spring. ~**-halt**, convulsive movement of horse's hind leg in walking. ~ **mattress**, one containing or consisting of springs. ~ **tide**, highest tide, occurring shortly after new and full moon. ~**time**, season of spring. ~**er** *n.* (esp.) support from which arch springs; medium-sized freq. black-and-white gun-dog of spaniel sort. ~**less**, ~**like**, ~**ў** *aa.*

sprĭnge (-nj) *n.* noose, snare, for catching small game.

sprĭnk'le *v.* (cause to) scatter or fall (on) in or with small drops or

particles. *n.* slight shower. **sprink'ler**
n. contrivance for sprinkling.
sprink'ling *n.* (esp.) a few here and
there.

sprint *v.i.* run etc. at top speed, esp.
for short distance. *n.* short fast race,
run, etc.

sprit *n.* small spar reaching diagonally from mast to upper outer
corner of sail. **~-sail,** sail extended
by sprit.

sprite *n.* elf or fairy.

sprock'et *n.* projection on rim of
wheel engaging links of chain.
~-wheel, wheel with sprockets.

sprout *v.* begin to grow, put forth
shoots; spring up; produce by
sprouting. *n.* shoot, new growth;
(pl.) Brussels sprouts.

spruce[1] (-ōōs) *a.* of trim smart appearance. *v.* smarten (*up*), make
spruce.

spruce[2] (-ōōs) *n.* (wood of) kinds of
fir with dense foliage.

sprung, *p.p.* of **spring.**

sprŭng *a.* (esp.) furnished with
springs; (of wood) warped, split;
(of verse-rhythm) resembling that
of natural speech.

sprȳ *a.* active, nimble, lively.

spŭd *n.* small sharp narrow spade or
prong for digging up weeds etc.;
(sl.) potato. *v.t.* dig (*out, up*) with
spud.

spūme *n.* & *v.i.* froth, foam. **spū'mȳ** *a.*

spun, *p.t.* & *p.p.* of **spin.**

spŭn *a.* (esp.) drawn out into threads.
~ glass, glass drawn into thread
while liquid. **~ silk,** thread or
fabric of waste silk and freq. cotton.

spŭnk *n.* mettle, spirit, pluck. **~ȳ** *a.*

spŭr *n.* pricking instrument worn
on horseman's heel; incentive,
stimulus; projection on back of
cock's leg or at base of flower;
range, ridge, etc. running out from
mountain mass; short branch or
shoot. *v.* prick (horse) with spurs;
incite, urge, prompt; provide with
spur(s); ride hard.

spŭrge *n.* kinds of plant with acrid
milky juice. **~ laurel,** kind of
daphne.

spūr'ious *a.* not genuine or authentic;
not what it appears, claims, or
pretends to be.

spŭrn *v.t.* repel, thrust back, with
foot; reject etc. with contempt or
disdain.

spŭrt *v.* (cause to) gush out in jet or
stream; make spurt. *n.* short
sudden violent effort, burst of
speed, esp. in racing; sudden
gushing out, jet.

sput'nĭk (-ōō-) *n.* Russian artificial
satellite.

spŭtt'er *v.* emit with, make, spitting
sound; splutter; speak, utter,
rapidly or incoherently. *n.* sputtering; sputtering speech.

spū'tum *n.* saliva, spittle.

spȳ *n.* person secretly collecting and
reporting information esp. relating
to another country, rival firm, etc.;
one who spies. *v.* act as spy (*on*);
discern, make out; **~ out,** explore
secretly, discover thus. **~-glass,**
small hand-telescope.

sq. *abbr.* square.

Sqn. Ldr *abbr.* Squadron-Leader.

sq(q). *abbr.* et seq.

squab (-ŏb) *n.* young esp. unfledged,
pigeon; thickly stuffed loose
cushion, esp. as (back of) car seat.
a. short and plump.

squabb'le (-ŏ-) *n.* & *v.i.* (engage in)
petty or noisy quarrel.

squad (-ŏd) *n.* (mil. etc.) small
number, organized party, or team
of persons; **flying ~,** small rapidly
available organized body, esp. of
police.

squad'ron (-ŏd-) *n.* division of cavalry
regiment, two troops; division of
fleet forming unit; division of air
force. **~-leader,** R.A.F. officer next
above flight-lieutenant.

squal'id (-ŏl-) *a.* dirty, filthy, mean in
appearance; marked by squalor.

squall (-awl) *n.* sudden violent gust
or storm; discordant cry; scream.
v. scream loudly or discordantly.
squall'ȳ *a.*

squal'or (-ŏl-) *n.* filth, dirt; wretched
poverty and neglect.

squan'der (-ŏn-) *v.t.* spend wastefully; scatter lavishly.

squāre *n.* plane rectangle with four
equal sides; object of (roughly) this
shape; open space, esp. enclosed by
houses etc., buildings surrounding
this; body of troops drawn up in

square formation; instrument, usu. triangular or T-shaped, for measuring or obtaining right angles; product of number or quantity multiplied by itself. *a.* of (approximate) shape of square; rectangular; (of measures etc.) equal in area to square whose side is specified length; angular, not round; solid, sturdy; fair, honest, straightforward; even, equal, level; (of meal) solid, substantial. *adv.* squarely. *v.* make square; mark (*out*), rule, in squares; multiply number etc. by itself; make or be consistent (*with*), reconcile; settle (*up*) account etc., make scores etc. equal or level; conciliate or satisfy, esp. with bribe; assume boxing attitude, move *up to* thus. ~ **dance**, one in which four couples face inwards from four sides; country dance; ~ **deal**, fair and honest dealing, transaction, etc. ~ **leg**, (position of) fielder on batsman's leg-side nearly in line with wicket. ~-**rigged**, having principal sails on horizontal yards slung to mast by middle. ~ **root**, number or quantity producing given number or quantity when multiplied by itself. ~ **sail**, four-sided sail slung at right angles to mast. **squār'ish** *a.*

squash[1] (-ŏ-) *v.* squeeze, be squeezed, flat or into pulp; force into small space; snub, suppress; crowd. *n.* crowded state; crowd; game like rackets played with soft ball; drink made of juice of crushed fruit. **squash'y̆** *a.*

squash[2] (-ŏ-) *n.* (gourd, used as vegetable etc., of) kinds of trailing plant.

squat (-ŏt) *v.i.* (make) sit with knees drawn up and heels close to or touching hams; crouch; (colloq.) sit; settle on or in unoccupied or unused land, building, etc. without title or payment of rent; take up land as squatter. *a.* short and thick, dumpy. *n.* squatting posture. **squatt'er** *n.* (esp., Austral.) person acquiring title to land by settling on it; sheep-farmer.

squaw *n.* Amer.-Ind. woman or wife.

squawk *n.* & *v.i.* (utter) harsh cry; (make) complaint.

squeak, *n.* short shrill cry or sound; *narrow* ~, narrow escape. *v.* emit squeak, utter in squeaking voice; (sl.) turn informer, peach. **squea'ky̆** *a.*

squeal *v.* utter (with), emit, more or less prolonged loud shrill cry or sound; (sl.) squeak, inform, complain. *n.* sharp shrill sound; squealing; complaint.

squea'mish *a.* fastidious; of delicate stomach or conscience.

squee'gee *n.* implement with rubber blade or roller for scraping, squeezing away moisture, etc. *v.t.* clean etc. with squeegee.

squeeze *v.* exert pressure on from opposite or all sides, esp. so as to crush, drain liquid from, etc.; force by pressure; force one's way; extort or obtain money etc. (from) by pressure; bring pressure to bear on, constrain; make squeeze of; (bridge) force (opponent) to discard important card(s). *n.* squeezing, application of pressure; crowd, crush; amount squeezed out; hardship, difficulty, etc. caused by squeezing; impression or cast of coin etc. made with wax or other plastic material; (bridge) forcing of discards.

squĕlch *v.* tread or walk heavily in water or wet ground, make sound (as) of this; crush, squash. *n.* (sound of) squelching.

squĭb *n.* small hissing firework thrown by hand; lampoon, short satire.

squĭd *n.* kinds of ten-armed cephalopod mollusc.

squĭff'y̆ *a.* (sl.) slightly drunk.

squĭgg'le *n.* wavy or curly line or mark, scrawl. *v.* scribble; wriggle, take form of squiggle. **squĭgg'ly̆** *a.*

squĭll *n.* kinds of scilla, esp. sea-onion.

squĭnch *n.* (archit.) straight or arched support across interior angle to carry dome etc.

squint *v.i.* have eyes turned in different directions; look sidelong or through small aperture. *n.* squinting set of the eyeballs;

(colloq.) look, glance; oblique opening through wall of church etc. *a.* squinting, looking different ways.

squire *n.* country gentleman, esp. chief landed proprietor in district; (hist.) attendant on knight; man escorting or attending on lady. *v.t.* escort (woman). **squire'archy** (-kǐ) *n.* class of landed proprietors; **~ar'chical** *a.*

squirm *v.i.* writhe, wriggle. *n.* squirming movement.

squi'rrel *n.* small bushy-tailed freq. arboreal rodent.

squirt *v.* eject liquid etc. (on), be ejected, (as) from syringe. *n.* syringe; small jet or spray; insignificant person, whippersnapper.

S.R. *abbr.* Southern Railway, Region.

Sr. *abbr.* Senior.

S.R.N. *abbr.* State Registered Nurse.

S.R.O. *abbr.* Statutory Rules and Orders.

SS. *abbr.* Saints.

S.S. *abbr., Schutz Staffel* [Ger.], protection patrol (Nazi police force); steamship.

SSE., SSW. *abbr.* south south--east, south south-west.

St. *abbr.* Saint; Strait; Street.

st. *abbr.* stone(s); stumped.

stab *n.* thrust or wound with sharp pointed implement or weapon; sudden acute pain or attack; (colloq.) try, 'shot.' *v.* pierce or wound with something pointed; aim stab (*at*).

stabil'ity *n.* being stable.

sta'bilize (*or* -ă-) *v.t.* make stable, esp. fix exchange rate of (currency). **~izā'tion** *n.* **sta'bilizer** *n.* (esp.) device for keeping ship, aircraft, etc. stable.

sta'ble[1] *a.* firmly fixed or established, not fluctuating or changing, not easily shaken, decomposed, destroyed, etc.

sta'ble[2] *n.* building in which horses are kept; collection of horses from one stable; establishment for training racehorses. *v.t.* put or keep in stable. **sta'bling** *n.* (esp.) accommodation for horses etc.

stacca'to (-kah-) *a. & adv.* (mus.) with breaks between successive notes.

stack *n.* (orderly) pile of hay, sheaves, wood, etc.; number of chimneys standing together; chimney; (building containing) compact arrangement of book-cases etc. *v.t.* pile in stacks; keep (number of aircraft) flying at different heights until they can land; shuffle or arrange (playing-cards) fraudulently or unfairly (*against* player; freq. fig.).

sta'dium *n.* (pl. -*ia* or -*s*), enclosed ground for athletic sports, games, etc. with tiers of seats for spectators.

staff (-ahf) *n.* (pl. -*s, stāves*), stick or pole as weapon or support or as symbol of office; (mus.) stave; body of officers attached to commander; body of assistants by whom institution, business, etc. is carried on; *general* **~**, body of officers controlling army from headquarters. *v.t.* provide with staff of officers, teachers, servants, etc. **~-officer**, member of general staff.

Staffs. *abbr.* Staffordshire.

stag *n.* male of (esp. red) deer; (St. Exch.) person who applies for new issue with view to selling at once. **~-beetle**, kinds of large beetle with antler-like mandibles. **~ party**, party of or for males only.

stage *n.* raised floor or platform; platform, esp. in theatre, on which plays etc. are exhibited or performed; *the* theatre or acting profession; scene of action; division of journey, process, development, etc.; point reached; stopping--place; interval between stopping--places. *v.* put (play etc.) on stage, organize (exhibition etc.); perform or present with view to dramatic effect; (of play etc.) lend itself to stage production. **~-coach**, (hist.) coach running regularly between two places. **~-door**, entrance to parts of theatre behind stage. **~ fright**, nervousness at appearing before audience. **~-manage**, arrange, control, etc. as or like stage-manager. **~-manager**, person in charge of stage-hands etc. & controlling stage during performance, rehearsals, etc. **~-struck**, smitten with love for stage, esp. with desire to become (professional) actor. **~ whisper**, whisper loud enough to be heard by audience or meant to be overheard. **stā′ger** n. old **~r**, experienced person, old hand. **stā′ging** n. (esp.) scaffolding, temporary platform or support; shelving, esp. for plants in greenhouse etc.; putting play on stage. **stā′gў** a. theatrical, dramatically artificial or exaggerated.

stăgg′er (-g-) v. go unsteadily as if about to fall; (cause to) totter, reel, hesitate, be unsettled or bewildered, etc.; arrange in zig-zag, slanting, or overlapping order; arrange (hours of work etc.) so that they do not coincide with those of others. n. act, effect, amount, of staggering; (pl.) diseased condition with unsteady gait etc. in animals.

stăg′nant a. not flowing or running, without motion or current; inert, sluggish, without activity. **~ancy**, **stagnā′tion** nn. **stăgnāte′** v.i. be stagnant.

stagy : see **stage**.

staid a. sober, steady, sedate.

stain v. discolour, soil; colour with pigment that penetrates; colour (glass) with transparent colours; sully, blemish; be stainable. n. discoloration, mark, esp. one not easily removable; dye etc. for staining; blot, blemish. **~lèss** a. (esp., of steel etc.) not liable to rust or tarnish under ordinary conditions.

stair n. each of succession of steps, esp. indoors; (pl.) set or flight of these; below **~s**, in or to basement, esp. as servants' part of house. **~case**, (part of building containing) flight or series of flights of stairs. **~-rod**, rod for securing stair-carpet in angle between steps. **~way**, staircase.

stāke n. stick or post pointed for driving into ground; post to which person was bound for burning alive; amount risked in wager or match; (pl.) amount staked by entrants to be contended for in horse-race etc., (pl.) such race; interest involved, something to be

gained or lost; at **~**, at issue, in question, risked. v.t. fasten, support, etc., mark out or off, with stake(s); risk (money, credit, etc.) on issue; furnish with money, supplies, etc., esp. in order to share gains; **~ a claim**, (esp., fig.) assert or secure title or right (to). **~-boat**, moored or anchored boat as starting-point or mark in boat-race.

stăl′actīte n. deposit of carbonate of lime hanging like icicle from roof of cavern etc. **stăl′agmīte** n. similar deposit rising from floor of cavern etc. **stălactīt′ĭc, stălagmīt′ĭc** aa.

stāle a. lacking freshness; the worse for age; overtrained, with vigour etc. impaired by overwork. n. urine of horses and cattle. v. make or become stale; (of horse etc.) urinate. **~mate**, (chess) position in which player can make no move without putting his king in check; deadlock, inconclusive position; v.t. place (player, king) in position of stalemate; bring to standstill.

stalk[1] (-awk) n. main stem of herbaceous plant; attachment or support of leaf, flower, animal organ, etc.; stem of wine-glass. **~ed** a. having stalk.

stalk[2] (-awk) v. steal up to game etc. under cover or unperceived; walk with stiff measured steps or in stately or imposing manner. n. stalking gait; attempt to stalk game etc. **~ing-horse**, screen etc. behind which hunter approaches game; (anything used as) pretext or concealment.

stall[1] (-awl) n. (division for one animal in) stable or cowhouse; fixed seat (partly) enclosed at back and sides in church, chapter-house, etc.; canonry etc. entitling holder to stall; one of seats in part of theatre nearest stage; booth, stand, table, etc. in market etc.; stalling. v. place or keep in stall, esp. for fattening; furnish with stalls; undesignedly stop internal combustion engine, be stopped accidentally; (cause to) lose flying-speed to point at which aircraft ceases to answer normally to controls.

stall[2] v. (sl.) stave off with trick,

plausible tale, etc., play for time thus.

stall′ion (-yon) *n*. uncastrated male horse.

sta′lwart (-awl-) *a*. sturdy, strong; courageous, resolute. *n*. resolute uncompromising partisan esp. of political party.

stā′men *n*. male or pollen-bearing organ of flowering plants.

stăm′ina *n*. staying power, power of endurance.

stămm′er *v*. falter or stumble in speech, esp. with rapid involuntary repetition of certain sounds in word etc.; utter with stammer. *n*. stammering speech, tendency to stammer.

stămp *v*. bring foot down heavily on ground etc.; crush (ore etc.) with downward blows; impress pattern, mark, etc. on with die etc.; affix stamp to; impress on memory; assign character to, characterize. *n*. (sound of) stamping; stamped impress; instrument for stamping; embossed or impressed mark, adhesive label, on document etc. to certify that duty, postage, etc. has been paid; mark, label, etc. on commodity as evidence of quality etc.; characteristic mark, impress (*of*); character, kind. **~ing-ground**, habitual place of resort, haunt. **~-paper**, gummed marginal paper of sheet of postage stamps.

stămpēde′ *n*. rush of horses or cattle or people under sudden common impulse, esp. panic. *v*. (cause to) take part in stampede.

stănce *n*. player's position for making stroke; pose, attitude.

stanch (-ah-) *v.t.* check flow of (esp. blood), check flow from (esp. wound).

stan′chion (-ahnshn) *n*. upright bar, stay, or support. *v.t.* provide, strengthen, etc. with stanchion(s).

stănd *v*. (*stood*), be in stationary upright position; rise up; assume stationary position; be set, placed, or situated; remain firm, valid, etc. or in specified condition; present firm front; offer oneself for election etc.; (naut.) steer, sail, in specified direction; place, set, in upright or specified position; successfully endure, put up with; provide at one's expense; **~** *by*, uphold, support, abide by, stand and look on, stand ready and waiting; **~** *down*, step down from witness-box, retire, withdraw; **~** *for*, represent, signify, (colloq.) tolerate; **~** *in*, cost (person) specified sum, deputize (*for*); **~** *off*, move away, keep one's distance; **~** *on* (ceremony etc.), observe scrupulously; **~** *out*, hold out, persist in opposition, be prominent or conspicuous; **~** *over*, be postponed; **~** *pat*, maintain one's position; **~** *to*, take up position in readiness; take up (attitude of attention); **~** *to gain*, *lose*, etc., be reasonably certain to win, lose, etc.; **~** *treat*, pay cost of entertainment; **~** *up*, rise to one's feet, maintain erect position, (sl.) fail to keep appointment with; **~** *up for*, side with, maintain; **~** *up to*, face courageously, stand (examination etc.). *n*. stationary condition or position; (period of) resistance to attack; pedestal, rack, etc. on or in which things may be placed; standing-place for vehicles etc.; stall in market etc.; raised structure for persons to sit or stand on; (U.S.) witness-box; standing growth or crop. **~-by**, thing or person that can be depended on. **~-in**, deputy, substitute; (cine.) person taking actor's place until lights, cameras, etc. are ready. **~-off half**, (Rugby footb.) half-back with position between scrum-half and three-quarters. **~-offish**, distant, reserved, not affable. **~-pipe**, vertical pipe esp. with spout or nozzle for hose, for attachment to water-main. **~-point**, point of view. **~-still**, halt, pause, cessation of progress or activity. **~-up**, (of collar) not turned down; (of fight) violent, hard-hitting, actual; (of meal etc.) taken standing.

stăn′dard *n*. distinctive flag; specimen or specification by which something may be tested or measured; required degree of some quality; degree of proficiency, class in primary school studying to reach this; average quality; upright support or holder, esp. for lamp; tree or shrub trained on erect stem. *a.* that is, acts as, or conforms to standard; of recognized merit or authority; accepted; of average or usual quality. **~-bearer**, prominent leader in cause. **~ of living**, degree of material comfort enjoyed by community, person, etc. **~ lamp**, lamp set on tall holder standing on floor etc. **~ time**, time established legally or by custom in region etc. **stăn'dardīze** *v.t.* make conform to standard; make uniform.

stăn'ding *a.* (esp.) of permanent kind; constantly ready for use; (of jump) made without run. *n.* (esp.) established repute or position; duration. **~ orders**, series of rules, instructions, etc. remaining in force until repealed or countermanded by proper authority. **~-room**, enough room to stand in.

stank, *p.t.* of **stink.**

stănn'ary *n.* tin-mine; tin-mining district. **stănn'ic** *a.* of tin.

stăn'za *n.* group of lines forming division of song or poem.

stăphȳlocŏcc'us *n.* kinds of micro--organism causing abscesses etc.

stā'ple[1] *n.* piece of wire or metal bent into U-shape for driving into wood etc.; various similar contrivances, esp. bent wire for fastening sheets of paper together. *v.t.* furnish, fasten, with staple(s).

stā'ple[2] *n.* important or principal product or article of commerce; textile fibre with respect to its quality or length. *a.* forming staple; standard; having important or principal place. *v.t.* sort, classify (wool etc.) according to fibre.

stăr *n.* celestial body appearing as point of light; planet etc. considered as influencing human affairs or person's fate; rayed figure or object representing star as ornament etc.; asterisk; brilliant or prominent person, esp. chief actor or actress; *falling, shooting,* **~,** small meteor looking like rapidly moving star; *fixed* **~,** star so far from earth as to appear

motionless. *v.* mark, adorn, set, with stars; present, perform, as star. **~-fish**, sea-animal with usu. five broad arms radiating from central disc. **~-gazer**, impractical idealist. **~light**, light of stars. **S~s and Stripes**, U.S. national flag. **~ sapphire**, cabochon sapphire. **~ turn**, principal item or attraction. **~less** *a.* **~let** *n.* young (esp. film-) star. **~dom** *n.* being star, status of star.

stăr'board (-berd) *n.* right side of ship etc. looking forward. *v.t.* turn (helm) to starboard.

stărch *n.* white odourless tasteless carbohydrate forming important constituent of human food; preparation of this for stiffening linen etc.; stiffness of manner or conduct. *v.t.* stiffen with starch. **~-reduced**, having smaller than normal proportion of starch. **star'chy** *a.*

stāre *v.* gaze fixedly with eyes wide open; open eyes in astonishment; be obtrusively conspicuous; **~** (person) *in the face*, be glaringly obvious to him. *n.* staring gaze. **stār'ing** *a.* (esp.) too conspicuous; (of eyes) fixed and wide open.

stărk *a.* rigid; stiff, sheer, downright. *adv.* completely.

stăr'ling *n.* small gregarious chattering lustrous-plumaged bird.

stărr'y *a.* set with stars; bright as star; star-like. **~-eyed**, (esp.) romantically enthusiastic; visionary.

stărt *v.* make sudden involuntary movement from pain, surprise, etc.; move suddenly; rouse (game) from lair; (cause timbers etc. to) be displaced by pressure, shrinkage, etc.; begin journey, operations, etc; set up or set going; (cause motor--engine etc. to) begin to run; give signal to start in race etc. *n.* sudden involuntary movement; beginning of journey, race, action, etc.; starting-place; opportunity for or assistance in starting; (amount of) advantage gained or allowed in starting; *by, in,* **~s,** fitfully, jerkily. **~ing-gate**, movable barrier for securing fair start in horse-race. **~ing-point**, place from which start is made, point of departure. **~ing-**

-post, post from which competitors start in race. **~ing-priçe,** odds on horse etc. at time of starting.

stär'ter *n.* (esp.) person giving signal to start race; competitor starting in race; apparatus for starting motor--engine.

stär'tle *v.t.* cause to start; alarm; take by surprise.

stärve *v.* (cause to) die or suffer acutely from lack or shortage of food etc.; (colloq.) feel hungry; deprive *of;* force *into, out,* etc. by starvation. **starvā'tion** *n.;* **~ diet, wages,** etc. not enough to live on. **~ling** *n.'* & *a.* starving (person etc.).

stāte *n.* position or condition; stage of process, work, etc.; (colloq.) excited or agitated condition of mind or feeling; rank, dignity; ceremonial pomp; organized political community under one government; civil government; *the S~s,* U.S.A. *a.* of, for, concerned with, State; reserved for, employed on, occasions of state or ceremony. *v.t.* express, esp. fully or clearly, in speech or writing; specify; put into form of statement. **S~ Department,** U.S. Department of Foreign Affairs. **S~-house,** (U.S.) building in which State legislature meets. **~ rights,** (U.S.) rights and powers not delegated to Federal Government but reserved to individual States. **~--room,** room reserved for ceremonial occasions; passenger's private cabin on ship.

stāte'ly (-tlĭ) *a.* dignified, imposing, grand.

stāte'ment (-tm-) *n.* stating; presentation of musical theme or subject; thing stated; formal account of facts, financial position, etc.

stātes'man (-tsm-) *n.* person skilled or taking leading part in management of State affairs. **~like** *a.;* **~ship** *n.*

stăt'ĭc *a.* of forces in equilibrium or bodies at rest; passive, not active or changing; (of electricity) stationary, produced by friction; (radio) atmospheric; (of water in tank etc.) having no pressure, requiring to be pumped. *n.* atmospherics. **stăt'ĭcs** *n.pl.* branch of physics concerned

with bodies at rest and forces in equilibrium; atmospherics.

stăt'ĭcė *n.* kinds of low-growing herbaceous plant including thrift.

stā'tion *n.* place in which person or thing stands or is placed, esp. habitually or for definite purpose etc.; (hist.) place where English officials etc. in India resided; (Austral.) sheep- or cattle-run with its buildings; position in life, (high) rank; stopping-place on railway etc. with buildings for passengers, goods, etc.; *S~s of the Cross,* 14 pictures or images of Christ's Passion before which devotions are performed. *v.t.* assign station or post to; post, place, in station. **~-house,** police station. **~-master,** official controlling railway station. **~ sergeant,** sergeant in charge of police station. **~ wagon,** car with van-like body and doors at back.

stā'tionarÿ *a.* remaining in one place, not moving or movable; not changing in condition, quality or quantity.

stā'tioner *n.* dealer in stationery. **stā'tionerÿ** *n.* writing-materials etc.

statĭs'tics *n.pl.* branch of study concerned with collection and classification of esp. numerical facts; facts so collected, numerical data. **~ĭcal** *a.;* **stătĭstĭ'cian** *n.*

stăt'ūarÿ *a.* of statues, sculptured. *n.* sculpture, statues.

stăt'ūe *n.* sculptured usu. (nearly) life-size figure of person etc. **stătūĕsque'** (-k) *a.* like statue, esp. in beauty or dignity. **stătūĕtte'** *n.* small statue.

stăt'ure (-yer) *n.* bodily height (freq. fig.).

stā'tus *n.* social or legal position or condition; rank, prestige. **~ symbol,** anything considered to show the high social status of its owner etc.

stā'tus quō (ăn'tė), unchanged position, previous position, of affairs. [L]

stăt'ūte *n.* written law of legislative body; permanent ordinance of corporation etc. **stăt'utorÿ** *a.* enacted, required, imposed, by statute.

staunch *a.* constant to obligations or purpose; untiring in service or loyalty. *v.t.* stanch.

stāve *n.* one of narrow shaped vertical strips forming sides of cask; stanza of song etc.; (mus.) set of (now five) parallel horizontal lines on and between which notes are placed to indicate pitch. *v.t.* (*stōve* or *staved*), break hole *in* (boat, cask, etc.); crush, bash, *in*; ~ *off*, ward off, defer.

stay¹ *n.* large rope from mast-head to another mast, spar, etc.; guy or rope supporting flagstaff etc.; tie-piece, cross-piece, holding parts together; prop, support; (pl.) corsets. *v.t.* support, steady, with stay(s); prop (*up*). ~-**sail**, triangular sail on stay.

stay² *v.* check, stop; postpone (judgement etc.); remain, dwell temporarily; pause; hold out (for), show powers of endurance; ~ *put*, remain in place, not leave or move; (*here* etc.) *to* ~, permanently, for good. *n.* (duration of) remaining, esp. living temporarily, in place; suspension of judicial proceedings. ~-**at-home**, (person) remaining habitually at home, unadventurous (person). ~-**ing-power**, endurance. ~-**in strike**, one in which strikers do not leave place of employment. **stay'er** *n.* (esp.) person etc. of great staying-power.

STD *abbr.* subscriber trunk dialling.

stead (stĕd) *n.* place; *in the* ~ *of*, as substitute for; *stand in good* ~, be of advantage or service to.

stead'fast (-ĕd-) *a.* constant, firm, unwavering.

stead'ing (-ĕd-) *n.* farmstead, homestead.

stead'y (-ĕdĭ) *a.* firm, stable, not faltering, shaking, rocking, etc.; unwavering, resolute; settled; regular, maintained at even rate of action, change, etc. *v.* make, become, steady. *adv.* steadily. ~-**going**, staid, sober.

steak (-āk) *n.* thick slice of beef etc., esp. cut from hind-quarters; thick slice of fish cut through backbone.

steal *v.* (*stōle*, *stōlen*), take dishonestly and esp. secretly what is another's;

obtain, win, etc., surreptitiously by insidious arts, by surprise, etc.; move secretly or silently; ~ *a march on*, gain advantage over unobserved. *n.* (colloq.) stealing, theft; bargain, easy gain.

stealth (-ĕl-) *n.* secrecy; secret, furtive, or underhand procedure; *by* ~, surreptitiously, clandestinely. ~**ў** *a.*

steam *n.* invisible vapour into which water is converted by heat, esp. used as motive-power; steam mixed with air etc. in form of white cloud or mist; (colloq.) energy, go; (attrib.) worked etc. by steam. *v.* subject to action of steam as method of cooking, softening etc.; emit, exhale, steam or vapour; cover, bedew, become covered, with condensed vapour; travel, move, by agency of steam. ~**boat**, steamship. ~-**engine**, locomotive or stationary engine worked by steam. ~ **radio**, (colloq.) radio as dist. from television. ~-**roller**, heavy locomotive engine with roller for crushing road-metal, levelling roads, etc.; *v.t.* crush, break down, drive *through* etc. as if with steam-roller. ~**ship**, ship driven by steam. **stea'mer** *n.* (esp.) vessel propelled by steam; vessel in which food is cooked by steam. **stea'mў** *a.*

stė'arĭn *n.* fatty substance in suet, etc.; substance derived from this used for making candles etc.

stė'atīte *n.* soapstone.

steed *n.* (poet.) (war-)horse.

steel *n.* kinds of very hard malleable alloy of iron with carbon or other elements; steel weapons or cutting tools; steel rod for whetting knives on; (attrib.) made of, hard as, steel. *v.t.* nerve, harden, fortify (*against*). ~ **engraving**, engraving on, impression taken from, steel plate. ~ **wool**, fine steel shavings used as abrasive. ~**yard**, weighing-apparatus with graduated arm along which weight slides. **stee'lў** *a.* of, hard as, steel; inflexible, obdurate.

steep¹ *v.* soak, be soaked, in liquid; permeate, impregnate. *n.* steeping.

steep² *a.* sloping sharply; (colloq., of price etc.) exorbitant; incredible, outrageous. *n*. (poet.) steep hill, precipice. **stee′pen** *v*.

stee′ple *n*. lofty structure, esp. tower with spire, rising above roof of church; spire. **~chase**, horse-race across country or on made course with hedges etc. **~-jack**, man who climbs steeples, tall chimneys, etc. to repair them etc.

steer[1] *n*. young esp. castrated male ox.

steer[2] *v*. guide vessel etc. by rudder, helm, etc. or by mechanical means; be steered; direct one's course; *~ clear of*, avoid. *n*. (U.S. colloq.) directions for steering; suggestion of course to be followed. **~ing-wheel**, wheel for steering car, ship, etc. **~sman**, helmsman. **steer′age** *n*. effect of helm on ship; part of ship allotted to passengers travelling at cheapest rate; **~age-way**, enough way for ship to answer helm.

stein (-īn) *n*. large earthenware mug for beer etc.

stēle *n*. (pl. *-lae*), upright slab with sculptured design or inscription.

stĕll′ar *a*. of stars; star-shaped.

stĕm[1] *n*. main body above ground of tree etc.; stalk of leaf, flower, or fruit; stem-shaped part or object; part of word to which inflexional suffixes are added; (arch.) line of ancestry, stock, race; curved upright timber etc. at fore end of vessel; bows. *v*. remove stem of; make headway against (tide etc.); *~ from*, originate in.

stĕm[2] *v*. check flow of, dam up; (skiing) force, check progress by forcing, heel of ski(s) outward. *n*. stemming on skis. *~* **turn**, turn made by stemming one ski.

stĕnch *n*. foul or offensive smell.

stĕn′cil *n*. plate of metal, cardboard, etc., punched with pattern reproduced on other surfaces by rolling, brushing, etc. pigment through holes; decoration, lettering, etc. so produced. *v.t.* produce, copy, etc. by use of stencil(s).

stĕnŏg′raphў *n*. shorthand. **~′grapher** *n*.; **~grăph′ic** *a*.

stĕntōr′ian *a*. (of voice) extremely loud.

stĕp *v*. lift and set down foot or alternate feet in walking etc.; go

short distance, progress, measure (distance), by stepping; (naut.) set up (mast) in step; *~ down*, retire, resign, lower voltage of (current) with transformer, decrease or lower (as) in steps; *~ in*, intervene; *~ on it*, *on the gas*, accelerate, hurry up; *~ out*, walk vigorously, stride; *~ up*, increase voltage of (current) with transformer, increase rate, volume, etc. of, speed up. *n*. movement or manner of, distance covered by, stepping; sound made by setting foot down; action towards result, (pl.) measures taken; flat-topped structure, esp. one of series, to facilitate movement from one level to another, rung of ladder, footboard of vehicle, etc.; (pl.) step-ladder; degree in scale, advance from one degree to another; (naut.) block or socket supporting mast etc.; step-like part; *in ~*, stepping in time with other persons or music, moving, acting, etc. in conformity or harmony or agreement (*with*); *out of ~*, not in step. **~-dance**, dance for display of special steps. **~-ins**, garments, esp. panties, easily slipped on and without fastenings. **~-ladder**, portable short ladder with flat steps and prop hinged to back. **~ping-stone**, stone set in or projecting above water or muddy place as help in crossing; means of advancement or progress.

stĕp- in comb., related by remarriage of parent. **stĕp′chīld**, **~daughter**, **~son**, child by previous marriage of one's wife or husband. So **~-brother**, **~father**, **~mother**, **~-parent**, **~sister**.

stĕphanō′tis *n*. kinds of tropical climbing plant with fragrant white waxy flowers.

stĕppe *n*. vast treeless plain, esp of S.E. Europe and Siberia.

stēr′ėo *n*. stereotype. *a*. stereoscopic; stereophonic; stereotyped.

stēr′ėo- in comb., solid; three-dimensional; stereoscopic; of stereochemistry. **stereochĕm′istrў** (-k-) *n*. (branch of chemistry dealing with) spatial arrangement of atoms etc. in molecule; **~chĕm′ical** *a*.

~grăph'ĭc *a.* delineating or representing solid body on plane surface. ~phŏn'ĭc *a.* (of sound) recorded or reproduced, (of apparatus) recording or reproducing sound, as by use of separate microphones or loud-speakers, to enhance actuality by giving effect of direction. ~scōpe *n.* instrument for combining two pictures of object etc. from slightly different points of view, to give effect of three dimensions. ~scŏp'ĭc *a.* of stereoscope; producing three-dimensional effect. stēr'ĕotȳpe (*or* stě-) *n.* (printing from) printing-plate cast from mould of forme of type; stereotyped thing; *v.t.* print from stereotype(s), make stereotypes of; fix or perpetuate in unchanging form, formalize.

stě'rīle *a.* barren; not producing, not capable of producing, fruit or off-spring; free from living micro-organisms. stĕrĭl'ĭtў, stĕrĭlĭzā'tion *nn.* stě'rĭlīze *v.t.* make incapable of producing offspring; make free from contamination by micro-organisms by treating with heat, antiseptic, etc.

stèr'lĭng *n.* English money. *a.* of sterling; genuine, of standard value or purity; solidly excellent, not showy or specious. ~ area, group of countries with currencies linked to sterling.

stern[1] *n.* after part of ship, aircraft, etc.; buttocks, rump; tail, esp. of fox-hound. ~ sheets, space in boat's stern aft of hindmost thwart. ~-wheeler, steamer with one large paddle-wheel at stern.

stèrn[2] *a.* severe, strict, not lenient, rigorous; hard, grim, harsh, gloomy.

stèr'num *n.* (pl. -*na*), breastbone.

stēr'ŏl *n.* one of class of complex solid alcohols.

stèr'torous *a.* (of breathing etc.) producing snoring or rasping sound.

stĕt, direction to printer etc. to disregard correction in MS. or proof.

stĕth'oscōpe *n.* instrument for auscultation esp. of heart or lungs. stĕthoscŏp'ĭc *a.*

stĕt'son *n.* man's slouch hat with wide brim.

stē'vĕdōre *n.* man employed in loading and stowing ships' cargoes.

stew *v.* cook by long simmering in closed vessel with liquid; make (tea) bitter or strong with too long standing; sweat or welter in hot close atmosphere. *n.* dish of stewed meat; (colloq.) state of great alarm or excitement.

stew'ard *n.* person paid to manage another's estate or house, or to cater for college, club, ship, etc.; official managing race-meeting, show, etc. ~ess *n.* (esp.) female attendant in ship or aircraft. ~-ship *n.* (esp.) charge committed to one.

stick *v.* (*stŭck*), thrust point or pointed thing *in*(*to*) or *through*; fix, be fixed, (as) by point or (as) by adhesion of surfaces; (cause to) adhere or cleave; (sl.) endure, bear; lose, deprive of, power of motion through friction, jamming, etc.; ~ *out, up,* etc. (cause to) protrude or project; ~ *up,* rob with violence, hold up; ~ *up for,* champion. *n.* short and relatively slender piece of wood, esp. as walking-cane, bludgeon, support for plant, etc.; (pl.) small pieces of wood as fuel; slender more or less cylindrical piece *of* chocolate, sealing-wax, etc.; number of aerial bombs released in quick succession; person of no liveliness or intelligence, poor actor. ~-insect, kinds of usu. wingless insect with stick-like body. ~-in-the-mud, slow, unprogressive (person). ~ing-plaster, adhesive plaster for cuts etc. ~ lac, lac in natural state, encrusting insects and small twigs. ~-up, hold-up. stick'er *n.* (esp.) adhesive label, paper etc. gummed on back.

stick'leback (-lb-) *n.* small spiny-finned fish.

stick'ler *n.* ~ *for,* one who insists on (trivial points of) accuracy etc.

stick'ў *a.* tending to stick or adhere, glutinous, viscous; (of ground) with yielding surface due to wet.

stiff *a.* rigid, not flexible; not working freely, sticking, not supple; thick and viscous, not fluid; hard to cope with, trying; unbending, unyielding; without ease, grace, or freedom; formal, constrained, haughty. *n*. (sl.) corpse. ~ **neck**, affection in which head cannot be moved without pain. ~**-necked**, obstinate. **stiff'en** *v*.

stī'fle[1] *v*. smother; (cause to) feel oppressed or unable to breathe. **sti'fling** *a*.

stī'fle[2] *n*. joint between hip and hock in horses etc.

stig'ma *n*. (pl. *-as*, *-ata*), moral spot or stain or brand; (pl.) marks resembling wounds on crucified body of Christ; identifying mark, characteristic. **stigmăt'ic** *a*. ~**tize** *v.t.* mark with stigmata; characterize; use opprobrious terms of.

stīle *n*. set of steps, bars, etc. to enable persons to pass over fence, wall, etc.

stilĕtt'ō *n*. (pl. *-os*), short dagger; small pointed implement for making eyelet-holes etc. ~ **heel**, high narrow pointed heel on shoe.

still[1] *n*. apparatus for distilling. ~**-room**, housekeeper's store-room in large house.

still[2] *a*. (almost) without motion or sound, silent, quiet, calm; (of wine etc.) not sparkling. *n*. deep silence; ordinary photograph, esp. single shot from motion film. *v*. quiet, calm, appease, make or grow still, *adv*. without motion or change; now, then, as before; even then, even now; nevertheless; even, yet; always. ~**-born**, born dead. ~ **life**, representation in painting etc. of inanimate things. **still'y** *a*. (poet.) still, quiet.

stilt *n*. one of pair of poles with brackets raising walker's feet above ground; (pl.) set of piles or posts supporting building etc.; kinds of marsh bird with long slender legs. **stil'tĕd** *a*. high-flown; stiff and pompous.

Stil'ton *n*. kind of cheese.

stim'ūlant *a*. producing temporary increase of activity or energy. *n*. stimulant drug etc., esp. alcoholic drink.

stim'ūlāte *v.t.* apply stimulus to; animate, make more vigorous or active. ~**ā'tion** *n*.; ~**ative** *a*.

stim'ūlus *n*. (pl. *-lī*), thing that rouses to activity or energy; rousing effect.

sting *n*. sharp-pointed organ in some insects etc., stiff sharp-pointed hair in some plants, capable of giving painful wound, causing itching rash, etc.; wound, puncture, or pain produced by sting; rankling or acute bodily or mental pain; pungency. *v*. (*stung*), wound with sting; (of plants) produce burning or itching rash etc. by contact with skin; feel or cause acute pain; be able to sting; (sl.) charge heavily, get money from. ~**ing nettle**, common nettle. ~**-ray**, kinds of ray with long tail armed with sharp-pointed serrated spine(s).

stin'gy (-ji) *a*. meanly parsimonious, niggardly.

stink *v*. (*stănk* or *stŭnk*; *stŭnk*), have foul or nasty smell; drive *out* with stench or suffocating smell. *n*. foul or nasty smell. ~**-horn**, kinds of ill-smelling fungus. ~**wood**, various trees with unpleasant-smelling wood. ~**er** *n*. (esp., colloq.) particularly annoying or unpleasant person; very difficult problem etc. ~**ing** *a*. that stinks; (sl.) obnoxious, objectionable.

stint *v.t.* keep on short allowance, supply or give in niggardly or grudging way. *n*. limitation of supply or effort; fixed or allotted amount of work etc.

stī'pĕnd *n*. salary, esp. of clergyman. **stīpĕn'diary** (*or* stĭ-) *a*. & *n*. (person) receiving stipend; ~**iary** (*magistrate*), paid magistrate.

stipp'le *v*. use dots or small spots to produce gradations of shade or colour in painting etc.; apply layer of paint etc. over another colour which shows through in places. *n*. (effect, result, of) stippling.

stip'ūlāte *v*. require or insist upon, make express demand *for*, as essential condition. ~**ā'tion** *n*.

stir *v*. set, keep, (begin to) be, in esp. slight motion; agitate soft or liquid mass with more or less circular motion; excite, animate, touch emotions of; ~ *up*, cause (trouble etc.), incite, rouse up. *n*. slight (sound of) movement; act of stirring; commotion, bustle, excitement. **stĭrr'ĭng** *a.* exciting, stimulating; moving.

stĭ'rrup *n.* support suspended by strap from saddle for rider's foot; U-shaped clamp or support. **~-bone,** stirrup-shaped bone of middle ear. **~-cup,** parting drink handed to rider on horseback. **~-pump,** small portable pump with stirrup-shaped foot-rest, for extinguishing small fires.

stĭtch *n.* (loop of thread etc. made or left by) each movement of threaded needle in and out of fabric etc. in sewing, or single complete movement of needle, hook, etc. in knitting, crochet, etc.; method of making stitch, kind of work produced; sudden sharp pain *in side. v.* sew; fasten, make, ornament, with stitches. **~wort,** kinds of chickweed, esp. with white starry flowers.

stoat *n.* animal of weasel kind, esp. ermine in its brown summer coat.

stŏck *n.* plant into which graft is inserted; base, holder, handle, for working parts of implement or machine; (source of) family or breed; (pl.) timbers on which ship rests while building; (pl., hist.) wooden framework set up in public place with holes for offender's feet; livestock; liquor made by stewing meat, bones, etc., as foundation for soup etc.; fund, store ready for drawing on; subscribed capital of company, public debt of State, etc., regarded as transferable property subject to fluctuation in market value; close-fitting wide band for neck; piece of silk etc. worn below clerical collar; goods or equipment for carrying on business; kinds of fragrant garden plant; solid hard brick pressed in mould; *take ~ (of),* make inventory of merchandise etc. in hand, reckon up, evaluate, estimate, scrutinize. *a.* kept regularly in stock for sale or use; commonly used, constantly recurring. *v.t.* equip with what is needful; keep (goods) in stock. **~ actor, company,** (member of) company regularly performing together at theatre etc.

~broker, person who buys and sells stocks on commission. **~ car,** racing car with chassis etc. of ordinary commercial model. **~dove,** wild pigeon. **~ exchange,** market, building, for buying and selling of stocks; association of brokers and jobbers doing business in particular place or market **~-in-trade,** goods kept in stock; all requisites for particular trade, occupation, etc. **~-jobber,** member of stock exchange dealing in stocks on his own account. **~-man,** man employed to look after livestock. **~-market,** traffic in stocks and shares. **~pile,** reserve supply of raw materials etc. **~piling,** accumulation of stockpile, esp. of materials which country cannot provide from its own resources. **~-pot,** cooking-pot in which stock is made and kept. **~ size,** (person able to wear) size of ready-made garments regularly kept in stock. **~-still,** quite motionless. **~-taking,** (time of) taking stock, esp. of goods in shop etc. **~-whip,** short-handled whip with very long lash. **~yard,** enclosure with pens for cattle etc. **stŏck'ĭst** *n.* one who stocks specified goods for sale.

stockāde' *n. & v.t.* (fortify, enclose, with) line of upright stakes as defence etc.

stŏck'ĭnĕt *n.* fine elastic knitted textile material.

stŏck'ĭng *n.* close-fitting usu. knitted covering for foot and leg up to or above knee; surgical appliance resembling this. **~ stitch,** knitting-stitch producing plain smooth surface.

stŏck'ў *a.* thickset.

stŏdge *n.* thick semi-solid mass of food. **stŏdg'ў** *a.* (of food) heavy, filling; dull, heavy, solid, uninspired.

stoep (-ōōp) *n.* (S.-Afr.) veranda at front (and occas. sides) of house.

stō'ĭc *n.* person of great self-control, fortitude, or austerity. **stō'ĭcal** *a.* **stō'ĭcĭsm** *n.*

stōke *v.* feed and tend fire or furnace (of); act as stoker; *~ up,* build up fire etc.; (colloq.) feed, eat, esp. in large quantities. **~hold,** apartment containing ship's boilers. ~-hole, opening through which furnace is tended; stokehold. sto'ker *n.* one who stokes furnace esp. of ship or locomotive.

stōle[1] *n.* vestment consisting of long narrow band hanging down in front from back of neck; woman's wrap of similar shape.

stole[2], stolen, *p.t. & p.p.* of steal.

stŏl'ĭd *a.* slow to feel or betray feeling; not easily moved; phlegmatic, dull. stolĭd'ĭtÿ *n.*

stom'ach (-ŭmak) *n.* cavity in which food is digested; (loosely) belly; appetite, inclination, courage, etc. *for. v.t.* brook, endure, tolerate. stom'acher *n.* (hist.) ornamental piece of female dress covering breast and pit of stomach. stomă'-chic (-k-) *a. & n.* (drug etc.) promoting digestion or appetite.

stōne *n.* piece of rock esp. of small or moderate size; stones or rock as substance or material; hard morbid concretion in kidney etc.; (hard wood-like case of) kernel in stone--fruit; seed of grape etc.; testicle; unit of weight (14 lb.). *v.t.* pelt with stones, esp. put to death thus; rid (fruit) of stone(s). S~ Age, stage of culture marked by use of stone implements and weapons. ~-blind, quite blind. ~-chat, small black--and-white singing bird. ~-cold, quite cold. ~-crop, kinds of creeping plant. ~-dead, deaf, quite dead, deaf. ~-fruit, fruit with seed enclosed in hard shell surrounded by pulp. ~-pine, kind of pine with wide-spreading branches and flat top. ~'s throw, short or moderate distance. ~-wall, obstruct by stone-walling. ~-walling, (crick.) excessively cautious batting; parliamentary obstructionism. ~-ware, hard dense pottery of flinty clay. stō'nÿ *a.* abounding in stones; hard or unfeeling; stony(-broke), (sl.) without any money.

stood, *p.t. & p.p.* of stand.

stōoge *n.* (theatr. sl.) person acting as foil for comedian etc.; subordinate, puppet. *v.i.* act as stooge; wander, fly, *about, (a)round,* esp. in aimless or routine way.

stōok *n.* bundle of corn sheaves. *v.t.* arrange in stooks.

stōol *n.* seat without arms or back; foot-stool; (place for) evacuation of bowels; faeces evacuated; stump of felled tree; stool-pigeon. *v.* throw up young shoots or stems; decoy, act as stool-pigeon. ~-pigeon, decoy; police-spy.

stōop[1] *v.* bend down; carry head and shoulders bowed forward; deign, condescend, lower oneself, *(to)*; (of hawk etc.) swoop down. *n.* stooping carriage of body; swoop of bird of prey on quarry.

stōop[2] *n.* (U.S., Can.) platform, porch, veranda, before door of house.

stŏp *v.* close or almost close aperture or cavity by plugging etc., esp. block mouth(s) of (fox's earth), fill cavity in tooth; prevent or forbid passage through; arrest (motion), check progress, motion, or operation of; hinder or prevent; prevent payment of; press down string, block hole, of musical instrument with finger etc. to alter pitch of note; cease (from), discontinue; make halt or pause; (colloq.) remain, stay; ~ *down,* reduce aperture of lens; ~ *off, over,* break journey *(at). n.* stopping, being stopped; pause, halt; punctuation--mark; peg, block, etc. meant to stop motion at fixed point; something stopping aperture; diaphragm in camera etc.; (handle or knob for turning on or off) graduated set of organ-pipes of like quality or tone; (closing of, key closing) hole in tube of wind instrument to alter pitch of note; consonant(-sound) in which passage of breath is completely obstructed. ~-cock, (key or handle for turning) tap or short pipe with externally operated valve to stop or regulate passage of liquid etc. ~-gap, makeshift, temporary substitute. ~-press, (news) inserted in paper after printing has begun. ~-watch, watch indicating fractions of a second by hand that may be instantly stopped at will. stŏpp'age *n.* stŏpp'er *n.* (esp.) plug for closing bottle etc.; *v.t.* close or provide with stopper. **stŏpp'ĭng** *n.* (esp.) filling of cavity in tooth.

stōr'age *n.* storing of goods; method of, space for, storing; cost of warehousing; *cold* ~, storage under refrigeration. ~ **battery**, accumulator. ~ **heater**, electric radiator storing heat accumulated in off-peak periods.

stōre *n.* abundance; provision, stock; large shop selling goods of many different kinds; (pl.) co-operative shop; (U.S.) shop; (pl.) articles of particular kind or for special purpose; (pl.) supply of things needed, stocks, reserves; storehouse; *in* ~, in reserve, to come, waiting *for*. *a.* (of animals) kept for breeding or bought for fattening; (U.S.) of store or shop, bought at shop, ready-made. *v.t.* equip or furnish (*with*); lay up for future use; deposit or keep in warehouse. ~**house**, place where things are stored; treasury, abundant source *of* information, etc. ~**-keeper**, person in charge of stores; (U.S.) shop-keeper.

stōr'ey, stōr'ў² *n.* each stage or portion into which building is divided horizontally.

stōr'ied (-ĭd) *a.* (esp.) celebrated in history or story.

stōrk *n.* kinds of large long-legged wading bird with long stout bill.

stōrm *n.* violent disturbance of atmosphere, with high winds and freq. rain, thunder, etc.; heavy discharge or shower (*of* blows etc.); violent disturbance, tumult, agitation, dispute, etc.; assault on, capture *of*, fortified place; *take by* ~, take by assault (freq. fig.). *v.* take by storm; rush violently; rage, be violent; bluster, fume, scold. ~ **centre**, comparatively calm central area of cyclonic storm; centre round which storm of controversy, trouble, etc. rages. ~**-cloud**, heavy rain-cloud. ~**-cock**, missel-thrush. ~**-cone**, tarred canvas cone hoisted as storm signal. ~**-lantern**, lantern with flame protected from wind and rain. ~**-signal**, any device signalling approach of storm; sign of

impending storm of argument, rage, etc. ~ **troops**, shock troops, esp. Nazi semi-military organization.

stor'mў *a.* like, characteristic of, marked by, associated or connected with, storm(s); ~**y petrel**, kinds of petrel supposed to be active before storms.

stōr'y¹ *n.* course of life of person, institution, etc.; narrative, tale, account, of real or fictitious events; legend, myth, anecdote, novel; plot of novel, play, etc.; (material for) article in newspaper; (colloq.) lie. ~ **-teller** *n.* one who tells stories; (colloq.) liar, fibber.

story²: see **storey**.

stoup (-ōōp) *n.* vessel, esp. stone basin in wall of church, for holy water; (arch.) flagon, beaker.

stout *a.* undaunted, resolute; of considerable thickness or strength; corpulent. *n.* heavy dark type of beer.

stōve¹ *n.* kinds of closed apparatus to contain burning fuel or consume gas, electricity, etc. for heating, cooking, etc. *v.t.* dry, heat, in stove; fumigate. ~**pipe**, pipe carrying off smoke etc. from stove; (colloq.) top hat.

stove², *p.t.* & *p.p.* of **stave**.

stow (-ō) *v.t.* pack (*away*), esp. closely or compactly; (*sl.*) desist from; ~ *away*, conceal oneself on ship etc., esp. to avoid paying fare. ~**away**, one who stows away. ~**age** *n.* stowing; room, price paid, for stowing.

strădd'le *v.* spread legs wide apart laterally; stand or sit across with straddled legs; drop bombs etc. across from side to side; bracket with shells etc. *n.* act or attitude of straddling.

strägg'le *v.i.* stray from main body, be dispersed or scattered, grow loosely. *n.* scattered or straggling group. **strägg'lў** *a.*

straight (-āt) *a.* without curves or angles; not curved or crooked; in straight line with, parallel or perpendicular to; correctly placed or in proper order; going direct to mark; unmixed, undiluted; (of cards etc.) in sequence, without gap; upright, honest, candid. *adv.* in straight line; direct; with good aim. **~ away**, immediately, at once. **~ face**, (colloq.) serious expression. **~ fight**, direct contest between two candidates. **~forward**, honest, open; presenting no complications. **~ off**, immediately; without hesitation etc. **~ out**, frankly, outspokenly. **~way**, (arch.) immediately. **straigh'ten** *v.*

strain[1] *n.* breed, stock; (inherited) tendency or quality.

strain[2] *n.* (injury or damage due to) straining or being strained; deformation or distortion due to stress; tension; melody; passage or snatch *of* music etc.; tone, style, character. *v.* stretch tightly; make taut or tense; injure by over--exertion etc.; wrest from true meaning; hold in tight embrace; over-task, injure or try or imperil by over-use etc.; make intense effort, strive intensely; clear liquid of solid matter by passing through sieve etc. **strained** *a.* (esp.) artificial, forced, constrained; (of relations) dangerously tense, nearly at breaking-point. **strai'ner** *n.* (esp.) utensil for straining or filtering.

strait *a.* narrow; strict. *n.* narrow water-passage connecting two seas or large bodies of water;(pl.) difficult position, need. **~jacket, ~ waistcoat**, strong garment for upper part of body, confining arms and used to restrain violent persons (freq. fig.). **~-laced**, severely virtuous, puritanical. **strai'ten** *v.t.* reduce to straits; **~ened circumstances**, inadequate means of living, poverty.

strāke *n.* continuous line of planking etc. from stem to stern of boat.

strănd[1] *n.* margin of sea, river, etc., esp. between tide-marks. *v.* run aground. **~ed** *a.* left without adequate resources or means of transport; in difficulties.

strănd[2] *n.* one of strings or wires twisted together to form rope etc.; thread, string of beads etc., tress of hair.

strănge (-j) *a.* foreign, alien; unfamiliar or not known (*to*); not one's own; queer, surprising, unexpected; fresh or unaccustomed *to*, bewildered.

strān'ger (-j-) *n.* person in place, company, etc. that he does not belong to; person strange to somebody or something.

străng'le (-nggl) *v.t.* kill by external compression of throat; hinder growth of by overcrowding; suppress. **~hold**, deadly grip (usu. fig.).

străng'ūlāte (-ngg-) *v.t.* constrict so as to prevent circulation or passage of fluid. **~ā'tion** *n.* strangling, being strangled; strangulating.

străp *n.* flat strip of leather etc., esp. with buckle etc. for holding things together; strapping; strip of metal etc. used to secure or connect. *v.t.* furnish, fasten, with strap; apply strapping to; thrash with strap. **~hanger**, passenger in bus, train, etc. standing and holding on to strap for want of seat. **~ hinge**, hinge with long flaps for fastening to surface. **~work**, ornamental work of narrow folded, interlaced, etc. band(s). **străpp'ing** *a.* stalwart; tall and strong; *n.* (esp.) strip(s) of adhesive plaster; flogging.

strata : see **stratum**.

străt'agėm *n.* device(s) for deceiving enemy; trick.

străt'ėgў *n.* art of war; art of planning and directing larger movements and operations of campaign or war. **stratē'gic** *a.* of, dictated by, serving ends of, strategy. **stratē'gical** *a.*; **străt'ėgist** *n.*

străth'spey (-ā) *n.* (music for) Sc. country dance.

străt'ĭfў *v.* form or divide into, arrange in, strata or layers. **~fĭcā'tion** *n.*

strātocū'mŭlus *n.* layer of low cloud in globular masses.

străt'osphēre *n.* region of atmosphere above troposphere in which temperature remains constant.

strā'tum (*or* -ah-) *n.* (pl. -*ta*), layer or bed of sedimentary rock; layer of deposits in excavation etc.; level or grade in social position, culture, etc.

strā'tus *n.* (pl. -*tĭ*), continuous horizontal sheet of cloud.

straw *n*. dry cut stalks of various cereals; stem of cereal plant; single stalk or piece of straw; insignificant trifle; straw hat. **~-board**, coarse yellow cardboard of straw pulp. **~-colour(ed)**, (of) pale light-yellow colour of straw. **~ vote**, unofficial, esp. sample, vote.

straw'berry *n*. (trailing white-flowered plant bearing) juicy edible pulpy usu. red fruit. **~ leaf**, leaf of strawberry as symbol of ducal rank. **~-mark**, reddish birth-mark. **~ roan**, red roan. **~-tree**, kind of arbutus.

stray *v.i.* wander, go aimlessly; deviate, get separated, from right way, companions, home, etc. *n*. strayed domestic animal; homeless friendless person. *a*. strayed; sporadic, isolated, occasional.

streak *n*. thin irregular line or band of different colour or substance from surface etc. in which it appears; flash (*of* lightning); strain, element, trait. *v*. mark with streak(s); go at full speed. **strea'ky** *a*. (esp., of bacon) with fat and lean in layers or streaks.

stream *n*. body of running water, esp. brook or small river; current or flow. *v*. flow or move as or in stream; emit stream of; run with liquid; float or wave in wind, current of water, etc. **~-line**, form, esp. of aircraft or car, offering minimum of resistance to air, water, etc.; *v.t.* give this shape to, make quicker, more efficient, etc. by simplifying, removing superfluities, etc. **strea'mer** *n*. (esp.) ribbon, strip of paper, etc., attached at one end and floating or waving at other. **~let** *n*.; **~y** *a*.

street *n*. road in town or village with houses on one side or both; *man in the* **~**, ordinary person; *on the* **~s**, living by prostitution. **~-car**, (U.S.) tram, bus. **~-walker**, prostitute.

strength *n*. being strong; degree of strongness; what makes strong; number of persons present or available; *on the* **~** *of*, relying on, arguing from. **streng'then** *v*. make, become, stronger.

stren'uous *a*. making or requiring great exertions.

streptococc'us *n*. (pl. *-cci*, pr. *-kī* or *-ksī*), (micro-organism of) genus of bacteria which form chains. **~cocc'-cal** *a*.

streptomy'cin *n*. antibiotic drug.

stress *n*. pressure, tension, strain; force exerted between contiguous bodies or parts; emphasis, accent. *v.t.* lay stress on; emphasize; subject to mechanical stress.

stretch *v*. make taut; tighten, straighten; lay or lie flat, extend; strain, exert to utmost or beyond legitimate extent; exaggerate; have specified length or extension; draw, be drawn, admit of being drawn, out into greater length, extension, etc.; (sl.) hang (person); extend limbs to tighten muscles; **~ out**, extend hand etc. by straightening arm or leg, reach out; **~ one's** *legs* straighten them by walking etc., esp. as relief from sitting. *n*. stretching, being stretched; continuous expanse, tract, or spell; (sl.) term of imprisonment, twelve months; *at a* **~**, without intermission, continuously. **stretch'er** *n*. (esp.) brick etc. laid with length in direction of wall; bar or rod used as tie or brace, esp. between legs of chair; board against which rower braces feet; oblong frame with handles at each end for carrying sick, injured, etc. person. **stretch'y** *a*. liable to stretch.

strew (-ōō) *v.t.* (p.p. *strewn, strewed*), scatter over surface; cover (surface etc.) with small objects scattered.

stri'ate, striā'ted *a*. marked with line(s), slight ridges or furrows, etc. **striā'tion** *n*.

strick'en *a*. afflicted with disease, grief, etc.; (of deer etc.) wounded; **~** *in years*, (arch.) of advanced age. **~ field**, (site of) pitched battle.

strict *a*. exact, precise, accurately defined or limited; rigorous, stringent; admitting no relaxation or indulgence.

stric'ture *n*. (usu. pl.), adverse criticism, critical remark.

stride *v*. (*strōde*), walk with long steps; pass over with one step; bestride. *n*. single walking or running step; (distance covered by) long step; striding gait; *take in one's* ~, clear obstacle without changing gait, deal with incidentally or without difficulty, effort, etc.

stri′dent *a.* loud and harsh, grating.

strid′ūlāte *v.i.* make shrill harsh grating sound esp. (of insects) by rubbing together hard parts of body. **strid′ūlant** *a.*; ~**ā′tion** *n.*

strife *n.* conflict, struggle, dispute.

strīke *v.* (p.t. *strŭck*, p.p. *strŭck* or occas. *strick′en*), hit, deliver blow(s) or stroke(s) (on); afflict, attack suddenly; (of lightning) descend upon and blast; produce, record, etc. by stroke(s) or striking; coin (money); touch string or key of instrument, produce (note) thus; sound hour with stroke(s) on bell etc.; reach gold, oil, etc. by drilling, digging, etc.; produce fire, spark, etc. by percussion of flint and steel, friction of match, etc.; arrest attention of, occur to mind of, produce impression on; lower or take down flag, tent, etc., remove (scene etc.); (cause to) penetrate, pierce, stab; turn in new direction, go, take specified direction; assume (attitude), esp. suddenly and dramatically; cease work esp. by common agreement to obtain remedy for grievance, better working conditions, etc.; ~ *home*, get blow well in (freq. fig.); ~ *in*, intervene in conversation etc.; ~ *off*, cancel, erase, remove from (*register* or other list); ~ *out*, erase, lay about one with fists etc., begin to swim, skate, etc.; ~ *up*, begin to play or sing, start (acquaintance, conversation, etc.). *n.* (esp. concerted) refusal to work; sudden discovery of oil, ore, etc.; sudden success, piece of luck, etc.; attack, raid; attempt to strike; *on* ~, taking part in strike. ~-**bound**, immobilized by strike. ~-**breaker**, one who works when others are on strike, esp. one of outsiders brought in to replace strikers. ~ **pay**, trade union allowance to workers on strike. **strī′ker** *n.* (esp.) worker on strike; blacksmith's assistant wielding heavy sledge-hammer.

strī′king *a.* (esp.) noticeable, arresting, impressive.

string *n.* twine or fine cord; length of this or some other material serving to tie, attach, lace, activate puppet, etc.; catgut, wire, etc. yielding musical tone(s) when stretched, in musical instruments; (pl., players of) stringed instruments played with bow; tough fibre etc.; things threaded on string; set or stud of horses; set of things etc. coming successively; *first, second*, etc. ~, person or thing that chief, alternative, etc. reliance is placed on. *v.* (*strŭng*), supply, fit, tie, with string(s); thread on string; connect; put together, arrange, in series, row(s), etc.; remove strings from (bean-pod etc.); ~ *out*, move into or in string or disconnected line; ~ *up*, brace up, make tense or taut. ~ **bean**, French or kidney bean. ~-**board**, board supporting ends of steps in staircase. ~-**course**, raised horizontal band running round or along building. ~-**piece**, long timber etc. connecting and supporting parts of framework. ~ **quartet**, (music for) quartet of stringed instruments, esp. two violins, viola and violoncello. **stringed** *a.* (esp.) having strings. **string′er** *n.* (esp.) string-board; string-piece. **string′y̆** *a.* (esp.) fibrous; like string.

strin′gent (-j-) *a.* strict, binding, requiring exact performance. ~**encў** *n.*

strip[1] *v.* denude; deprive *of* covering, property, etc.; undress; pull or tear off, *off*, etc., esp. thread from screw, teeth from wheel. ~-**tease**, entertainment of removing garments one by one before audience. **stripp′er** *n.* (esp.) performer of strip-tease.

strip[2] *n.* long narrow piece or tract; narrow flat bar of iron or steel, iron or steel in this form; set or line of drawings telling story or forming part of regularly-appearing series in newspaper etc. ~ **lighting**, lighting with usu. tubular lamps arranged in line. ~-**mill**, mill in which steel slabs are rolled into strips.

strĭp³ v. extract last milk from udder of (cow etc.).

strĭpe¹ n. long narrow band differing in colour or texture from surface on either side; narrow strip of cloth, braid, etc. sewn on, esp. chevron indicating non-commissioned rank. v.t. mark, ornament, with stripes. strĭ'pў a.

strĭpe² n. (arch.) stroke or lash with whip etc.

strĭp'lĭng n. youth approaching manhood.

strive v.i. (strōve, striven), try hard, struggle; engage in strife with; contend against.

strode, p.t. of stride.

strōke n. blow; shock given by blow; sudden favourable turn of luck; apoplectic or paralytic seizure; damaging or destructive discharge of lightning; movement of a recurrent or regulated kind; act or method of striking ball etc. in games; specially successful or skilful effort; sound made by striking clock; (mark made by) movement in one direction of pen, pencil, brush, etc.; oarsman rowing nearest stern and setting time of stroke. v.t. act as stroke to (boat, crew).

strōke² v.t. pass hand etc. softly in one direction over; (needlework) push (gathers) into place with blunt point; ~ the wrong way, irritate, ruffle. n. act, spell, of stroking.

strŏll v.i. walk in leisurely fashion. n. leisurely walk. strō'llĭng a. (of actors) travelling about and performing in temporary buildings etc.

strŏng a. physically, morally, or mentally powerful, vigorous, or robust; powerful in numbers, equipment, etc.; performed with muscular strength; difficult to capture, break into, escape from, etc.; energetic, effective, decided; powerfully affecting senses, mind, etc.; (of drink) with large proportion of alcohol, flavouring ingredient, etc.; (of verbs) forming inflexions by vowel change in root syllable. adv. strongly, vigorously, recklessly, etc.; going ~, thriving. strong-arm, bullying, violent. ~-box, strongly made box for money,

documents, etc. ~ drink, alcoholic liquors. ~hold, fortress, citadel. ~ language, swearing. ~-minded with vigorous or determined mind. ~ point, convincing argument; forte. ~-point, specially fortified position in defence system. ~-room, fire- and burglar-proof room for valuables. ~ suit, (cards) long suit containing high cards; thing in which one excels, forte. strŏng'er, strŏng'est (-ngg-) aa.

strŏn'tium (-shm) n. soft silver-white metallic element; ~ 90, radioactive isotope of this.

strŏp n. appliance, esp. strip of leather, for sharpening razor. v.t. sharpen on or with strop.

strove, p.t. of strive.

struck, p.t. & p.p. of strike.

strŭc'ture n. way in which building etc. is constructed; supporting framework or essential parts; thing constructed; complex whole; building. strŭc'tural a. of structure; ~ral engineering, design and construction of large structures, as bridges etc.

strŭgg'le v.i. throw limbs about in violent effort to get free; make one's way with difficulty; make great efforts under difficulties; contend with, against, etc. n. spell of struggling; effort under difficulties; hard contest. strŭgg'lĭng a. (esp.) finding difficulty in making a living, getting recognition, etc.

strŭm v. play unskilfully or monotonously on piano etc. n. strumming sound.

strŭm'pĕt n. (arch.) prostitute.

strung, p.t. & p.p. of string.

strŭt n. bar inserted in framework to resist pressure or thrust in direction of its length; strutting gait. v. walk in stiff pompous way; brace with strut(s).

'struth (-ōō-) int. (vulg. colloq.) expr. astonishment etc.

strўch'nine (-knēn; or -ĭn) n. highly poisonous vegetable alkaloid. strўch'nĭc a.

Sts. abbr. Saints.

stŭb n. stump of tree, tooth, etc. left projecting; short remnant of cigar, pencil, etc. v.t. rid (ground)

of stubs, grub up (root etc.);
bump (toe) painfully (*against, on*);
put *out* (cigarette) by crushing
lighted end against something.

stŭbb'le *n*. lower ends of grain-stalks
left in ground after harvest; short
stubble-like growth of hair, esp. on
unshaven face. **stŭbb'lў** *a*.

stŭbb'orn *a*. obstinate, unyielding;
not docile or amenable to control.

stŭcc'ō *n*. fine plaster for ceilings,
cornices, etc.; coarse plaster or
cement for covering exterior of
walls in imitation of stone. *v.t.* coat
or ornament with stucco.

stuck, *p.t.* & *p.p.* of **stick. stŭck** *a*. (of
animal) that has been stabbed or
had throat cut. **~-up,** (colloq.)
conceited, offensively superior in
manner.

stŭd¹ *n*. projecting nail-head or
similar knob on surface; kind of
two-headed button passed through
eyelet- or button-hole(s) in shirt-
-front etc.; upright post in framing
for lath-and-plaster wall. *v.t.* set
with studs; be scattered over or
about (surface). **stŭdd'ėd** *a*. thickly
set or strewn *with*.

stŭd² *n*. number of horses kept for
breeding, racing, etc.; place where
stud is kept. **~-book,** book giving
pedigree of thorough-bred horses.
~-farm, place where horses are
bred. **~-horse,** stallion.

stŭdd'ing *n*. woodwork of lath-and-
-plaster wall.

stū'dent *n*. person engaged in or
addicted to study; person undergoing instruction in university,
college, etc.; person receiving grant
to assist him to pursue studies.
~ship *n*.

stū'dĭō *n*. (pl. *-os*), work-room of
sculptor, painter, photographer,
etc.; room or premises used for
transmission of broadcasts etc.,
making films or recordings, etc.

stū'dĭous *a*. given to study, devoted
to learning; zealous, anxious, painstaking.

stŭd'ў *n*. devotion of time and
thought to acquiring information
esp. from books; pursuit of some
branch of knowledge; careful
examination or observation *of*;

thing that is or deserves to be
investigated; meditation; piece of
work, esp. in painting, done as
exercise or preliminary experiment;
(mus.) composition designed to
develop player's skill; room used
for literary occupation or owner's
private business. *v.* make object of
study; devote time and thought to
understanding subject etc. or assur-
ing desired result; scrutinize.

stŭd'ied (-ĭd) *a*. deliberate, intentional, artificial.

stŭff *n*. material; textile material,
esp. woollen fabric; substance or
things of uncertain kind or inferior
quality; trash, nonsense; *do one's*
~, do what is required or expected
of one. *v.* pack, cram; fill out skin
to restore original shape of (bird,
beast, etc.); fill (inside of bird,
piece of meat, etc.) with forcemeat,
breadcrumbs, herbs, etc. before
cooking; block *up*; eat greedily,
overeat oneself; (colloq.) gull, hoax.

stŭff'ing *n*. (esp.) seasonings etc.
used in stuffing meat etc.; padding
of furniture etc. **stŭff'ў** *a*. lacking
ventilation; close, oppressive, fusty;
without freshness, interest, etc.;
easily offended or shocked.

stŭl'tĭfў *v.t.* render worthless or
useless; reduce to foolishness or
absurdity. **~fĭcā'tion** *n*.

stŭm'ble *v.i.* lurch forward, have
partial fall, from catching or
striking foot etc.; make blunder(s)
in speaking etc.; come accidentally
across, (*up*)*on*. *n*. act of stumbling.
stumbling-block, obstacle, circumstance causing difficulty or hesitation.

stŭmp *n*. part of felled or fallen
tree that remains projecting from
ground; part remaining of broken
branch or tooth, amputated limb,
etc.; stub; (crick.) one of three
uprights of wicket; wooden leg;
(pl., colloq.) legs. *v.* walk stiffly,
clumsily, and noisily; (of wicket-
keeper) put out batsman while he
is out of his ground; nonplus,
cause to be at a loss; make stump
speeches, traverse (district doing
this; **~** *up,* produce, pay over,
money required. **~ speech,** open-

air speech. **stŭm′per** *n.* (crick.) wicket-keeper. **stŭm′py̆** *a.* thick-set, stocky, short in proportion to girth.

stŭn *v.t.* knock senseless; daze, bewilder, stupefy, with strong emotion, din, etc. **stŭnn′er** *n.* **stŭnn′ing** *a.* (sl.) splendid, delightful (person or thing).

stung, *p.t.* & *p.p.* of **sting**.

stunk, *p.t.* & *p.p.* of **stink**.

stŭnt[1] *v.t.* check growth or development of, dwarf, cramp.

stŭnt[2] *n.* (colloq.) special effort, feat; showy performance, skilful trick or manœuvre; device to obtain publicity. *v.i.* perform stunt, esp. with aircraft. **~-man,** man employed to perform dangerous feats in place of cinema actor.

stū′pefy̆ *v.t.* make stupid or torpid, dull wits or senses of. **stŭpĕfăc′-tion** *n.*

stŭpĕn′dous *a.* amazing; of vast size or importance.

stū′pid *a.* in state of stupor; dull by nature, slow-witted, unintelligent; uninteresting. **stūpĭd′ity̆** *n.*

stū′por *n.* dazed or torpid state; utter amazement.

stŭr′dy̆ *a.* robust, hardy, vigorous, strongly built.

stŭr′geon (-jn) *n.* kinds of large fish esteemed as food.

stŭtt′er *v.* & *n.* stammer.

sty̆[1] *n.* pen or enclosure for pigs; filthy room or dwelling.

sty̆[2], **sty̆e** *n.* inflamed swelling on edge of eyelid.

Sty̆′gian *a.* (as) of Styx or Hades; murky, gloomy, black.

sty̆le *n.* pointed rod with which ancients wrote on wax-coated tablet; pen or pencil; (bot.) narrowed prolongation of ovary supporting stigma; manner of writing, speaking, etc.; title, mode of address; kind, pattern, type; fashion; distinction, noticeably superior quality or manner. *v.t.* call by specified name or style; design, arrange, make, etc. in esp. fashionable style. **sty̆′lish** *a.* conforming to fashionable standard of elegance; showy, dashing; having good style. **sty̆′list** *n.* person having

or aiming at good style in writing etc.; one who styles esp. hair. **sty̆lis′tic** *a.* of literary or artistic style. **sty̆′līze** *v.t.* make conform to rules of conventional style, conventionalize; **sty̆līzā′tion** *n.*

sty̆′lus *n.* ancient writing-implement, style; tracing-point producing groove in record or following record-groove in reproducing sound.

sty̆′mie *n.* (golf) position on putting-green when opponent's ball lies between player's ball and hole. *v.t.* put into position of having to negotiate stymie (freq. fig.).

sty̆p′tic *a.* & *n.* (substance) that checks bleeding.

Sty̆x *n.* (Gk. myth.) river of Hades over which shades of dead were ferried.

suā′sion (sw-) *n.* persuasion.

suāve (sw-; *or* -ah-) *a.* bland, polite, soothing. **suăv′ity̆** *n.*

sŭb *n.* (colloq.) subaltern; submarine; subscription; substitute; advance on wages. *v.* pay or receive part of wages in advance; sub-edit; act as substitute.

sub- in comb., under, below; more or less, roughly, not quite, on the borders of; subordinate(ly), secondary, further. **sŭbă′cid** *a.* moderately acid or tart; somewhat biting. **~ā′quéous** *a.* existing, performed, taking place, used, etc. under water. **~ărc′tic** *a.* of or resembling regions somewhat south of Arctic Circle. **~atŏm′ic** *a.* of, concerned with, phenomena occurring within or particles smaller than atom. **~-bāse′ment** (-sm-) *n.* storey below basement. **~committee** *n.* committee formed from main committee for special purpose. **~cŏn′scious** *a.* & *n.* (part of mind) outside range of attention, or imperfectly or partly conscious. **~cŏn′tinent** *n.* land-mass of great extent not classed as continent. **~cŏn′tract** *n.* contract for carrying out (part of) previous contract. **~contrăct′** *v.* make subcontract (for); **~contrăc′tor** *n.* **~cūtā′néous** *a.* under the skin; hypodermic. **~divīde′** *v.* divide further. **~divi′sion** *n.* subdividing; subordinate division;

(mil.) half of division. ~dŏm'ĭnant
n. (mus.) fourth note of scale.
~-ĕd'ĭt v.t. act as assistant editor
of; prepare (copy) for supervision
of editor; ~-ĕd'ĭtor n. ~fŭsc' a.
dusky, dull, or sombre in colour.
~-head, ~-head'ing (-ĕd-) nn.
subordinate division of subject
etc.; subordinate heading or title.
~-hū'man a. less than human; not
quite human. ~jā'cent a. underlying, situated below. ~join' v.t.
add at end. ~lease n. lease granted
to subtenant; v.t. (-ēs'), sublet.
~lĕt' v.t. let to subtenant. ~-lieu-
tĕn'ant (-lĕft-, in navy -let-) n.
officer ranking next below lieutenant. ~lĭm'ĭnal a. below thres-
hold of consciousness, too faint or
rapid to be recognized. ~lu'narў
(-lo͞o-) a. between orbits of moon
and earth; subject to moon's
influence; of this world, earthly.
~-machine'-gŭn (-ēn-) n. machine-
-gun of inferior calibre and weight.
~mē'dĭant n. (mus.) sixth note of
scale. ~nŏr'mal a. less than
normal, below normal. ~-nŭ'clear
a. smaller than, occurring in,
atomic nucleus. ~-plŏt n. secondary plot in play etc. ~scrĭpt
a. written below. ~sĕction n. subordinate division of section. ~soil
n. soil immediately under surface
soil. subsŏn'ic a. less, having speed
less, than speed of sound. ~-
-stăn'dard a. inferior, of lower than
average standard. substrā'tum n.
(pl. -ta), lower layer; basis. ~-
tĕn'ant n. one who holds or leases
from a tenant; ~tĕn'ancў n.
~tĭtle n. subordinate or additional
title of literary work etc.; film
caption; v.t. add subtitles to.
~tŏn'ĭc n. (mus.) note next below
tonic, seventh in ascending scale.
~trŏp'ĭcal a. (characteristic of
regions) bordering on tropics.
~varī'etў n. subdivision of variety,
subordinate variety. ~way n.
underground passage, esp. for
pedestrians to cross below road(s)
etc.; (U.S.) underground railway.
sŭb'altern a. of inferior rank; subordinate. n. junior officer below
rank of captain.

subdūe' v.t. conquer, subjugate, overcome; soften, tone down. sub-
dū'al n.
sŭb'jĕct a. under government; politically dependent; owing obedience
to; liable or exposed or prone to;
~ to, conditional(ly) upon, on the
assumption of. n. person subject to
political rule; member of State or
of subject State; (gram. etc.)
thing about which something is
predicated; thinking or feeling
entity, conscious self; theme of
discussion, description, etc.; (mus.)
principal phrase of composition or
movement; person of specified
characteristics. v.t. (-ĕkt'), subdue,
make subject; ~ to, expose or make
liable to, treat with, cause to
suffer. ~-matter, matter treated
of in book etc., theme. subjĕc'-
tion n.
subjĕc'tĭve a. of, concerned with,
proceeding from, taking place
within, thinking subject; having
its source in the mind; imaginary,
illusory; (gram.) of subject, nominative. ~ĭvĭsm n. theory that all
knowledge is merely subjective.
~ĭvĭst n. & a.; subjectĭv'itў n.
sŭb ju'dĭcė (-jo͞o-), under judicial
consideration, not yet decided. [L]
sŭb'jugāte (-jo͞o-) v.t. bring into subjection, vanquish, conquer.
~gā'tion n.
subjŭnc'tĭve a. & n. (verbal mood)
expressing wish, imprecation, contingent or hypothetical events, etc.
sŭb'lĭmate n. (chem.) product of
sublimation; corrosive ~, mercuric
chlorate. v.t. transmute into something nobler, more refined, etc.;
(psycho-anal.) divert energy of
(primitive impulse) into activity
socially more useful, morally pre-
ferable, etc. sŭblĭmā'tion n. sub-
blimating; (chem.) conversion of
substance by heat to vapour which
on cooling is deposited in solid
form.
sublīme' a. of most exalted kind;
inspiring awe, deep reverence or
lofty emotion by beauty, vastness,
grandeur, etc. v.t. (cause to) undergo sublimation. sublĭm'itў n.
sŭb'marine (-ēn; or -ēn') a. existing,

lying, operating, constructed, etc. under surface of sea. *n.* vessel which can be submerged and navigated under water.

submerge' *v.* (cause to) sink or plunge under water. ~**gence** *n.*

submersed' (-st) *a.* submerged. ~**sible** *a.*; ~**sibil'ity, submer'sion** *nn.*

submi'ssion *n.* submitting, being submitted; theory etc. submitted; submissive attitude, conduct, etc. **submiss'ive** *a.* inclined to submit, yielding to power or authority, humble, obedient.

submit' *v.* surrender oneself, become subject, yield (*to* person, his authority, criticism, condition, etc.); bring under notice or consideration of person, refer *to* his decision etc.; urge or represent deferentially.

subor'dinate *a.* of inferior importance or rank, secondary, subservient; (gram., of clause) dependent, syntactically equivalent to noun, adj., or adv. *v.t.* (-āt), make subordinate; treat or regard as of minor importance. ~**ā'tion** *n.*; ~**ative** *a.*

suborn' *v.t.* bribe, induce, etc. to commit perjury or other unlawful act. ~**ā'tion** *n.*

subpoe'na (-pēn-) *n.* writ commanding person's attendance in court of justice. *v.t.* serve subpoena on.

sub rō'sa (-z-), in confidence, in secret. [L]

subscribe' *v.* sign (one's name or document); express one's agreement, acquiescence, etc.; make or promise contribution *to* common fund, party, etc., *for* common object, etc.; ~ *to*, undertake to buy (periodical) regularly. **subscrip'tion** *n.*

sub'sequent *a.* following in order, time, or succession, esp. coming immediately after. ~**ence** *n.*

subserve' *v.t.* be instrumental in furthering or promoting.

subser'vient *a.* serving as means to further end or purpose; subordinate, subject (*to*); cringing, obsequious. ~**ence** *n.*

subside' *v.i.* sink down, sink to low(er), esp. normal, level; go down; sink *into, on,* etc. chair etc.; cave in; abate, die away; cease

from activity or agitation. **sub'sidence** (*or* -sī'-) *n.*

subsid'iary *a.* serving to assist or supplement, auxiliary, supplementary; subordinate, secondary. *n.* subsidiary person, thing, or company. ~ **company,** one of which another company holds more than half issued share capital.

sub'sidize *v.t.* pay subsidy to; support by subsidies.

sub'sidy *n.* money grant from one State to another in return for military aid etc.; financial aid from government towards expenses of institution etc. held to be of public utility, or to producers of commodity etc. enabling goods or services to be provided at low(er) cost to consumer.

subsist' *v.i.* (continue to) exist, remain in being; maintain or support oneself. ~**ence** *n.* subsisting; means of supporting life; ~**ence diet,** minimum of food required to support life.

sub'stance *n.* essence or most important part of anything; purport, gist; particular kind or species of matter; theme, subject-matter, material; reality; solid or real thing; (arch.) possessions, wealth.

substan'tial *a.* having substance, not illusory; not inconsiderable; of solid material or structure; possessed of property, well-to-do, sound; essentially such, virtual, practical.

substan'tiate (-shǐ-) *v.t.* give substantial form to; give good grounds for. ~**ā'tion** *n.*

sub'stantive *a.* expressing existence; having separate existence; not subsidiary; of substantive rank. *n.* noun. ~ **rank,** permanent rank in army etc.

sub'stitute *n.* person or thing acting or serving in place of another. *v.* put in place of another; act as substitute. ~**tū'tion** *n.*

subsume' *v.t.* bring *under* (principle, rule, class, etc.).

subtend' *v.t.* (of line etc.) be opposite to (angle, arc).

sub'terfuge *n.* evasion, esp. in argument or excuse.

sŭbterrā′nėan *a.* underground.

subt′ilīze (sŭt-) *v.* make subtle; elevate, refine; argue or reason subtly.

subtle (sŭt′l) *a.* pervasive or elusive by reason of tenuity; fine or delicate, esp. as eluding observation or analysis; acute; ingenious, elaborate, clever; crafty, cunning. **~tȳ** *n.*

subtō′pïa *n.* (iron.) suburban paradise, spread of small houses over countryside.

subtrăct′ *v.t.* deduct (part, quantity, number) from whole, number, etc., esp. in arithmetic etc. **subtrăc′-tion** *n.*

sŭb′ŭrb *n.* residential district lying on or near outskirts of town. **subŭr′ban** *a.*; **subŭr′banīte** *n.*; **subŭr′banīze** *v.t.* **subŭr′bïa** *n.* suburbs esp. of London, their inhabitants etc.

subvĕn′tion *n.* grant in aid of institution etc., subsidy.

subvĕr′sion *n.* subverting, being subverted. **subvĕr′sive** *a.* tending to subvert.

subvĕrt′ *v.t.* overthrow, upset, effect destruction or ruin of (religion, government, etc.).

sŭb vō′cė, under the (specified) word. [L]

succeed′ (-ks-) *v.* come next after and take place of; come next (to), follow; come by inheritance or in due course to office, title, etc.; have success, be successful; prosper; accomplish one's purpose.

succĕss′ (-ks-) *n.* favourable issue; attainment of object, wealth, fame, etc.; person or thing that succeeds or is successful. **~ful** *a.*

succĕ′ssion (-ks-) *n.* following in order; series of things in succession; (right of) succeeding to inheritance, office, or esp. throne; set or order of persons with such right; *in* **~**, one after another in regular sequence; *apostolic* **~**, uninterrupted transmission of spiritual authority through bishops from apostles. **succĕss′ive** *a.* coming one after another in uninterrupted sequence. **succĕss′or** *n.*

succinct′ (-ks-) *a.* terse, brief, concise.

succ′our (-ker) *v.t.* come to assistance of. *n.* aid given in time of need.

succ′ūbus *n.* (pl. -bī), female demon supposed to have sexual intercourse with men in their sleep.

succ′ūlent *a.* juicy; having thick and fleshy or juicy tissues. **succ′ū-lence** *n.*

succŭmb′ (-m) *v.i.* be vanquished; give way *to*; die.

sŭch *a.* of kind, degree, or extent described, referred to, or implied; the previously described or specified; so great, so eminent, etc., so. *pron.* that; the action etc. referred to; other such thing(s); *as* **~**, as what has been specified. **~-and--~**, particular but unspecified. **~like**, of such a kind; *and* **~like**, and the like.

sŭck *v.* draw liquid, esp. milk from breast, into mouth by contracting muscles of lips etc.; apply lips, lips and tongue, etc. to breast, sweetmeat, etc. to obtain or absorb nourishment; perform sucking action, make sucking sound; imbibe, absorb; **~** *down*, (of whirlpool, quicksand, etc.) engulf; **~** *in, up*, absorb; **~** *up to*, (sl.) curry favour with. *n.* action, act, spell, of sucking; drawing action of whirlpool etc.; *give* **~**, suckle. **~ing** *a.* not yet weaned; budding, immature; **~ing-pig**, very young pig.

sŭck′er *n.* (esp.) shoot springing from root or lower stem; organ in animals, part of apparatus, adapted for adhering by suction to surfaces; (sl.) simpleton, person easily duped.

sŭck′le *v.t.* feed (young) at breast or udder. **sŭck′ling** *n.* unweaned child or animal.

sū′crōse *n.* kind of sugar obtained from cane, beet, etc.

sŭc′tion *n.* sucking; production of complete or partial vacuum so that external atmospheric pressure forces fluid into vacant space or causes adhesion of surfaces.

sŭdd′en *n.* coming, happening, performed, etc. unexpectedly or without warning, abrupt; *all of a* **~**, suddenly.

sūdorif′ic *a.* & *n.* (drug) promoting or causing sweating.

sŭds (-z) *n.pl.* water impregnated with soap; lather.

sūe *v.* institute legal proceedings, bring civil action, (against); plead, appeal (*for*).

suede (swād) *n.* kid-skin or other leather with flesh side rubbed into nap; **(-cloth)**, woven fabric imitating this.

sū'ét *n.* hard fat round kidneys of cattle and sheep, used in cooking etc. **sū'étў** *a.* of or like suet; pale--complexioned.

sŭff'er *v.* undergo, be subjected to, pain, loss, punishment, grief, etc.; permit (*to*), put up with, tolerate. **sŭff'ering** *n.* (esp.) pain etc. suffered.

suff'erance *n.* tacit permission or toleration; *on* ~, under conditions of bare tolerance or acquiescence.

suffīce' *v.* be enough; meet needs of.

suffi'cient (-shnt) *a.* sufficing; adequate, esp. in amount or number; enough. *n.* enough, a sufficient quantity. ~**encў** *n.* (esp.) sufficient supply, adequate provision.

sŭff'ix *n.* verbal element attached to end of word in inflexion, word--formation, etc. *v.t.* (-ĭks'), add as suffix.

sŭff'ocāte *v.* kill, stifle, choke, by stopping respiration; (cause to) feel suffocated. ~**cā'tion** *n.*

sŭff'ragan *a. & n.* (bishop) assisting diocesan bishop in particular part of diocese; bishop in relation to his archbishop or metropolitan.

sŭff'rage *n.* franchise. **sŭffragĕtte'** *n.* (hist.) woman militantly or violently advocating political enfranchisement of women. ~**gĭst** *n.* advocate of extension of franchise to women.

suffūse' (-z) *v.t.* overspread as with fluid, colour, etc. **suffū'sion** *n.*

su'gar (shŏŏ-) *n.* kinds of sweet crystalline substance obtained from juices esp. of sugar-cane and sugar--beet and forming important article of food; (chem.) any of group of soluble sweet carbohydrates; sweet words; (sl.) money. *v.t.* sweeten or coat with sugar; make sweet or agreeable or palatable. ~**-beet**, kind of white beet from which sugar is manufactured. ~**-cane**, tall stout perennial tropical and sub-tropical grass cultivated as source of sugar. ~**-loaf**, conical moulded mass of hard refined sugar; (thing, esp. hill) shaped like sugar-loaf. **su'garў** *a.* like sugar; containing (much) sugar; cloying, sentimental.

suggĕst' (suj-) *v.t.* cause (idea) to be present to mind; give hint or inkling of; propose for acceptance. ~**ible** *a.* (esp.) capable of being influenced by suggestion; ~**ibĭl'itў** *n.* **suggĕs'tion** *n.* suggesting; theory, plan, thought, etc. suggested; insinuation of belief or impulse by hypnosis or other means, belief or impulse so suggested; suggesting of prurient ideas. **suggĕs'tive** *a.* (esp.) suggesting something indecent.

sū'icīde *n.* person who intentionally kills himself; intentional self--slaughter; action destructive to one's own interests etc. **sūĭcī'dal** *a.*

sūī gĕn'erĭs, of its own kind, peculiar, unique. [L]

suit (sūt), *n.* suing, petition; seeking of woman's hand; prosecution of claim in law-court; any of four sets of playing-cards in pack; set of outer garments, usu. coat, (waistcoat), and trousers or skirt; set of pyjamas; set of armour; *follow* ~, play card of suit led, follow another's example. *v.t.* adapt or make appropriate *to*; meet requirements of; agree with; comport with; be agreeable, convenient, adapted, fitted, etc. to; be becoming to. ~**-case**, case for carrying clothes, usu. box-shaped with flat hinged lid. **sui'table** *a.* suited *to* or *for*; well fitted for purpose; appropriate to occasion. ~**abĭl'itў** *n.* ~**ing** *n.* cloth for suits.

suite (swēt) *n.* retinue; set of rooms, furniture, etc.; (mus.) set of movements, instrumental compositions, etc. related in key, theme, etc. freq. as music for ballet, play, etc.

sui'tor (sūt-) *n.* wooer; plaintiff or petitioner in law-suit.

sŭlk *v.i.* be sulky. *n.* sulky fit or state; light two-wheeled carriage for one person. **sŭl'kў** *a.* silent, inactive, or unsociable from resentment or ill temper; sullen.

sŭll′en *a*. ill-humoured, moody, morose, gloomy, dismal.

sŭll′y *v.t.* soil, tarnish; be stain on, discredit.

sŭlphanil′amīde *n*. antibacterial drug.

sŭl′phāte *n*. salt of sulphuric acid. **sŭl′phīde** *n*. compound of sulphur with element or radical. **sŭl′phīte** *n*. salt of sulphurous acid.

sŭl′phonal *n*. anaesthetic and hypnotic drug.

sŭl′phur (*-er*) *n*. pale-yellow nonmetallic element burning with blue flame and stifling smell; kinds of sulphur-coloured butterfly. **sŭl-phūr′éous** *a*. of or like sulphur; with qualities associated with (burning) sulphur; of or like fires of hell. **sŭlphūrĕtt′éd** *a*. combined with sulphur. **sŭlphūr′ĭc.** *a*. of, containing, sulphur; **~ic acid**, dense highly corrosive oily acid. **sŭl′phūrous** *a*. sulphureous; (-fūr′*us*), containing sulphur of lower valency than sulphuric compounds.

sŭl′tan *n*. sovereign of Moslem country, esp. (hist.) Turkey. **~ate** *n*.

sulta′na (-tah-) *n*. sultan's wife or concubine; small light-coloured seedless raisin.

sŭl′trў *a*. oppressively hot; hot with anger, lust, etc.; exercising strong sexual attraction; lurid.

sŭm *n*. total resulting from addition of items; summary; amount of money; arithmetical problem; **~ total**, total amount (*of*). *v*. find sum of; **~ up**, total up; summarize, epitomize; (of judge etc.) recapitulate evidence or arguments before jury considers verdict.

sū′mach (-k; *or* shoo-) *n*. (dried leaves used in tanning etc. of) kinds of shrub or small tree.

sŭm′marīze *v.t.* make or be summary of, sum up.

sŭmm′arў *a*. dispensing with details or formalities; done with dispatch. *n*. brief account or statement, abridgement, epitome.

sŭmmā′tion *n*. addition, summing (up); finding of total or sum.

sŭmm′er[1] *n*. warmest season of year; year of life or age. *v*. pass summer; pasture (cattle). **~-house** (usu. simple and light) building in park or garden for use in summer. **~ school,** course of lectures etc. held during summer vacation. **~-time,** season of summer; standard time one hour in advance of ordinary time.

sŭmm′er[2] *n*. horizontal beam, esp. main beam supporting girders, joists, etc.

sŭmm′ĭt *n*. highest point, top, apex; highest degree. **~ conference, meeting,** of heads of states.

sŭmm′on *v.t.* call together, require presence or attendance of; call upon (*to* do, appear, etc.); cite by authority to appear before court or judge; muster *up* (courage etc.)

sŭmm′ons (-z) *n*. (pl. -*ses*) authoritative call to attend or do something; citation to appear in court; *v.t.* take out summons against.

sŭmp *n*. pit or well for collecting water etc.; oil-reservoir at bottom of motor crank-case.

sŭmp′tūarў *a*. regulating expenditure. **~ law** etc., one restricting private expenditure.

sŭmp′tūous *a*. costly, splendid, magnificent.

sŭn *n*. star forming centre of system of worlds or planets, esp. central body of solar system; light or warmth of sun. *v*. expose to sun; **~ oneself,** bask (as) in sun. **~-bath,** exposure of skin to sun. **~-bathe,** take sun-bath. **~beam,** beam of sunlight. **~-blind,** external window-shade.' **~burn,** tanning or superficial inflammation of skin from exposure to sun. **~-deck,** upper deck of ship. **~dew,** small bog-plant with hairy leaves secreting viscid drops. **~dial,** contrivance for showing time by shadow cast by sun on surface. **~-dog,** parhelion. **~down,** sunset. **~downer,** (Austral.) tramp arriving at station at sunset. **~flower,** plant with large golden-rayed flowers. **~-glasses,** tinted spectacles to protect eyes from glare. **~-hat, -helmet,** hat with broad brim, double crown, to protect head from sun. **~-lamp,** lamp emitting ultra-violet rays. **~rise,** (time of) sun's rising. **~set,** (time of) sun's setting. **~shade,**

parasol. ~shine, sunlight, area illuminated by it; cheerfulness or bright influence. ~-spot, one of dark patches sometimes observed on sun's surface. ~stroke, acute prostration from excessive heat of weather. sŭn′lèss a.

Sun. abbr. Sunday.

sŭn′dāe n. confection of ice cream with fruit, nuts, syrup, etc.

Sŭn′day n. first day of week. ~-school, held on Sunday for religious instruction.

sŭn′der v.t. (rhet.) sever, keep apart.

sŭn′drў a. divers, several; all and ~, one and all. sŭn′dries (-ĭz) n.pl. oddments, small unspecified items.

sung, p.t. & p.p. of sing.

sunk, p.t. & p.p. of sink.

sŭnk, sŭnk′en aa. that has sunk, lying below general surface; (of eyes etc.) hollow, fallen in.

sŭnn′ў a. bright with or as sunlight; exposed to, warm with, sun; cheerful.

sŭp v. drink by sips; take supper. n. mouthful of liquid.

sup. abbr. superlative; supra [L], above.

sū′per (or soo-) n. (colloq.) supernumerary actor, superintendent. a. (of measure) superficial, in square measure; (sl.) excellent, unusually good.

sū′per- (or soo-) in comb., on top, over, beyond, besides, exceeding, transcending, of higher kind, more than usually. superabŭn′dant a. very or too abundant; ~abŭn′dance n. ~cārgō n. merchant ship's officer superintending (sales of) cargo. ~charger n. device increasing pressure of explosive mixture in cylinder of internal-combustion engine. ~cĭl′iarў a. of eyebrow, over eye. ~cōol v.t. cool below freezing-point without solidification or crystallization. ~ĕlĕvā′tion n. amount of elevation of outer above inner curve on road or railway. ~heat′ v.t. heat, esp. steam, to higher or very high temperature. ~hū′man a. beyond normal human capacity etc.; higher than (that of) man. ~impōse′ (-z) v.t. impose, place, on something else. ~incŭm′-

bent a. lying or resting on something else. ~măn n. ideal superior man of future; man of superhuman powers or achievement. ~market n. self-service store selling food and household goods of all kinds. ~nova n. nova of immense brightness or intensity. ~phŏs′phate n. fertilizer containing soluble phosphates. ~pōse′ (-z) v.t. place above or on something else, esp. so as to coincide; ~posi′tion n. ~săt′ūrātèd a. saturated to excess, having more of some substance etc. than is required for saturation. ~scrībe v.t. write or inscribe over, at top of, or outside something; ~scrĭp′tion n. ~sŏn′ĭc a. with velocity greater than that of sound. ~tăx n. (esp.) tax in addition to income-tax on incomes above certain amount. ~tŏn′ĭc n. (mus.) second note of ascending scale.

sūperănn′ūāte v.t. dismiss or discard as too old; discharge with pension. sūperānnūā′tion n.

sūpérb′ (or soo-) a. of most impressive or exalted kind, majestic, magnificent.

sūpercil′ious (or soo-) a. haughtily contemptuous, disdainful, or superior.

sūperĕrogā′tion n. doing of more than duty or circumstances require; (R.C. theol.) performance of good works beyond what God requires, constituting store of merit transferable to others.

sūperfi′cial (or soo-) a. of, on, surface; without depth; (of measures) involving two dimensions, square. ~ciăl′itў (-shĭ-) n.

sūperfi′cies (-shĭēz; or soo-) n. surface.

sū′perfīne (or soo-) a. extremely fine in quality, of very best kind.

sūperflu′itў (-loo-; or soo-) n. superfluous amount.

sūpér′fluous (-loo-; or soo-) a. more than enough, excessive; needless, uncalled-for.

sūperintĕnd′ (or soo-) v. have or exercise charge or direction (of), supervise. ~ence n. superĭntĕn′dent n. officer or official having control, oversight, or direction of institution etc.; police officer above rank of inspector.

sūpēr′ior (*or* sōō-) *a.* higher in place, upper; higher in rank, degree, quality, etc.; conscious, showing consciousness, of superior qualities, lofty, supercilious; ~ *to*, above influence or reach of, not affected or mastered by. *n.* person or thing of higher rank, authority, quality, value, etc.; head of religious community. **supēriŏ′ritў** *n.*

superl. *abbr.* superlative.

sūpēr′lative (*or* sōō-) *a.* & *n.* raised above or surpassing all others; of highest degree; (gram.) (degree, inflexional form, adjective or adverb) expressing highest or very high degree of quality etc. denoted by simple word.

sūpernă′tural (-cher-; *or* sōō-) *a.* due to, manifesting, some agency above forces of nature; outside ordinary operation of cause and effect. ~ism, ~ist *nn.*

sūpernū′merarў (*or* sōō-) *a.* & *n.* (person or thing) in excess of the normal number; (actor) with non-speaking part employed in addition to regular company.

sūpersēde′ *v.t.* appoint or adopt another person or thing in the place of; oust, take place of, supplant; set aside, cease to employ. ~sĕ′ssion *n.*

sūpersti′tion *n.* (habit or belief based on) irrational fear of unknown or mysterious, credulity regarding supernatural; false or pagan religion. **sūpersti′tious** *a.*

sū′perstrŭcture (*or* sōō-) *n.* (upper part of) building; any structure resting upon something else or with some other part as foundation; parts of vessel above main deck.

sūpervēne′ *v.i.* occur as an interruption in or change from some state. ~vĕn′tion *n.*

sū′pervīse (-z; *or* sōō-; *or* -īz′) *v.t.* oversee, superintend performance, movements, work, etc. of. ~vī′sion, ~vīsor *nn.*; ~vī′sorў *a.*

sū′pīne[1] *a.* lying face upwards; indolent, lethargic, inert.

sū′pīne[2] *n.* (gram.) Latin verbal noun used in special constructions.

sŭpp′er *n.* meal taken late in day, esp. evening meal less formal and substantial than dinner. ~lĕss *a.*

suppl. *abbr.* supplement.

supplant′ (-ah-) *v.t.* oust, esp. by dishonourable or treacherous means.

sŭpp′le *a.* easily bent, pliant, flexible; artfully or servilely complaisant or submissive. *v.t.* make supple.

sŭpp′lēment *n.* thing added to supply deficiency, amplify previous account, etc.; addition to complete literary work etc., esp. special number or part of periodical. *v.t.* (-ĕnt′), furnish supplement to. **sŭpplēmĕn′tal, ~ĕn′tarў** *aa.*

sŭpp′liant *n.* humble petitioner. *a.* supplicating; expressing supplication.

sŭpp′licāte *v.* make humble petition to or for. ~cā′tion *n.*; ~cā′tory *a.*

supplў′ *v.t.* furnish or provide (with) thing needed; make up for (deficiency etc.). *n.* provision of what is needed; stock, store; (pl.) necessaries; person, esp. teacher or minister, supplying vacancy or acting as substitute; ~ *and demand*, (pol. econ.) chief factors determining price of commodities; *Committee of S*~, House of Commons sitting to discuss public-service estimates.

suppŏrt′ *v.t.* carry (part of) weight of; prop up; give strength to, encourage; endure, tolerate; supply with necessaries; lend assistance or countenance to; back up, bear out, second. *n.* supporting or being supported; person or thing that supports. **suppŏr′ter** *n.* (esp., her.) each of pair of figures one on each side of shield.

suppōse′ (-z) *v.t.* assume as hypothesis; involve or require as condition; assume in default of knowledge, be inclined to think, accept as probable; *be* ~*d*, be required or expected or allowed *to* do. **suppōsed′** *a.* believed to exist or have specified character. **suppō′sēdlў** *adv.* **sŭpposi′tion** *n.* what is supposed or assumed.

sŭpposi′tious (-zit-) *a.* substituted for the real; spurious, false.

sŭppŏs′itorў (-z-) *n.* (med.) easily

melted cone or cylinder introduced into rectum, vagina, or
urethra.

suppress' *v.t.* put down, quell, put an
end to existence or activity of;
withhold or withdraw from publication; keep secret or unexpressed.
~ible *a.*; **suppre'ssion** *n.* ~or *n.*
(esp.) device to suppress electrical
interference.

supp'ūrāte *v.i.* form or secrete pus;
fester. ~ā'tion *n.*

sū'pra- (*or* soo-) in comb., super-.

sūprem'acy (*or* soo-), *n.* being
supreme, position of supreme authority or power.

sūprēme' (*or* soo-) *a.* highest in
authority or rank; greatest, of
highest quality, degree, or amount.

Supt. *abbr.* Superintendent.

sūr'ah *n.* soft twilled silk fabric.

surcease' (ser-) *v.i.* & *n.* (arch.) cease;
cessation.

sūr'charge *n.* extra load or charge;
extra charge on understamped
letter etc.; additional mark printed
on face of stamp, esp. to change its
value. *v.t.* (-ārj'), overload; charge
additional or excessive amount,
exact as surcharge; print surcharge
on (postage-stamp).

sūr'cingle (-nggl) *n.* band round
horse's body.

sūr'coat *n.* (hist.) rich outer garment,
esp. worn over armour.

sūrd *a.* & *n.* (math.) (quantity, esp.
root) that cannot be expressed in
finite terms of ordinary numbers or
quantities.

sure (shoor) *a.* confident, assured,
persuaded (*of*); having no doubt;
certain *to* do or be; reliable, unfailing; faithful; ~ *of*, certain to
get, keep, have, etc.; *make* ~, act
so as to be certain *of. adv.* assuredly,
undoubtedly; *as* certainly *as.*
~-footed, treading securely or
firmly. ~ly *adv.* with certainty or
safety; assuredly (freq. expr. belief
without proof or readiness to
maintain statement against possible
denial). **sure'ty** *n.* security; person
undertaking to be liable for
another's default, non-appearance,
etc.

surf *n.* swell and white foamy water

of sea breaking on rock or (esp.
shallow) shore. ~board, long
narrow board for riding over
heavy surf to shore. ~-riding,
sport of riding on surf-board.
sūr'fing *n.* surf-riding.

sūr'face *n.* outermost or uppermost
boundary of material body, water,
soil, etc. outward aspect or appearance of immaterial thing. *v.* put
special surface on; raise or rise
to surface of water etc. *a.* of or
on surface; travelling or carried on
surface of land or water, not airborne or underground or submarine. ~-water, water collecting
on and running off from surface of
ground etc.

sūr'feit (-fĭt) *n.* excess, esp. in eating
or drinking; satiety. *v.t.* overfeed;
satiate *with*, cloy.

surg. *abbr.* surgeon; surgery.

sūrge *v.i.* rise and fall, toss, move to
and fro (as) in waves or billows.
n. surging motion; waves.

sūr'geon (-jn) *n.* person skilled in
surgery; medical practitioner qualified to practise surgery.

sūr'gery *n.* manual treatment of
injuries or disorders of body;
correction of disorders etc. by
manual or instrumental operations;
consulting room of medical practitioner, dentist, etc. **sūr'gical** *a.* of
surgery or surgeons.

sūr'ly *a.* uncivil, churlishly ill-
-humoured.

sūrmise' (-z) *n.* conjecture, idea
formed on slight evidence. *v.* infer
doubtfully or conjecturally; guess.

sūrmount' *v.t.* overcome, prevail
over, get over; be on top of.

sūr'nāme *n.* name common to all
members of family. *v.t.* give (as)
surname to.

sūrpass' (-ahs) *v.t.* outdo, excel.
~ing *a.* greatly exceeding or
excelling others.

sūr'plice *n.* loose full-sleeved white
vestment worn by clergy etc.

sūr'plus *n.* amount left over when
requirements have been met. *a.* in
excess of what is taken, used, or
needed; ~ *value*, difference between
value of wages paid and work done
or commodities produced. ~age *n.*

surprise' (-z) *n.* catching of person(s) unprepared; emotion excited by the unexpected; thing or event exciting this. *v.t.* capture by surprise; attack or come upon unawares; astonish, be surprise to; lead unawares, betray, *into* doing etc. **surpri'sing** *a.* causing surprise, astonishing.

surre'alism *n.* movement in painting, literature, etc., seeking to express subconscious activities of mind by representing phenomena of dreams etc. **~ist** *n. & a.;* **~is'tic** *a.*

surren'der *v.* relinquish possession, control, etc. of esp. upon compulsion or demand; yield to enemy or assailant; submit, give oneself up, cease from resistance. *n.* surrendering, being surrendered.

surrep'ti'tious *a.* done by stealth; underhand, clandestine.

su'rrey *n.* (U.S.) light four-wheeled carriage with two seats facing forwards.

su'rrogate *n.* deputy esp. of bishop or his chancellor.

surround' *v.t.* come, lie, be, all round or on all sides; encompass, environ. *n.* border or edging esp. of boards round carpet etc. **surroun'dings** *n.pl.* environs, environment.

sur'tax *n.* graduated tax in addition to income-tax on incomes above certain level. *v.t.* impose surtax on.

survei'llance (serval-) *n.* supervision; close watch esp. on suspected person.

survey' (-vā) *v.t.* take general view of; scan; examine condition of (building etc.); determine form, extent, etc. of (tract of ground etc.) by linear and angular measurements, esp. to construct map etc. *n.* (ser'-) general or comprehensive view; examination in detail, account given of result of this; department etc. engaged in, operations constituting, map or plan showing results of, surveying of land etc. **survey'or** *n.* person professionally engaged in surveying; official inspector (of highways, weights and measures, etc.).

survi'val *n.* surviving; relic of earlier time.

survive' *v.* outlive, continue to live after death or end of, or after occurrence of (disaster, hardship, etc.); be still alive or existent. **survi'vor** *n.*

suscep'tible *a.* admitting *of*; accessible or sensitive *to*; impressionable; readily touched with emotion. **~bil'ity** *n.*

suspect' *v.t.* have suspicions or doubts about; imagine something, esp. something wrong, about; think guilty (*of*); imagine to be possible or likely; surmise. *a.* (sus'-), regarded with suspicion or distrust; of suspected character. *n.* (sus'-), suspected person.

suspend' *v.t.* deprive (temporarily) of office etc.; put (temporary) stop to, annul for a time; defer; refrain from forming (judgement etc.); hang up; hold, cause to be held, in suspension; *~ payment*, fail to meet financial engagements, become insolvent. **suspen'der** *n.* (esp.) device attached to top of sock or stocking to hold it up; (pl., chiefly U.S.) braces.

suspense' *n.* state of usu. anxious uncertainty, expectation, or waiting for information; undetermined state.

suspen'sion *n.* suspending, being suspended; diffusion as particles through fluid medium. **~ bridge**, bridge suspended from chains, wire cables, etc. between steel or masonry towers or other supports.

suspi'cion (-shn) *n.* suspecting, being suspected; feeling or state of mind of one who suspects; partial or unconfirmed belief, esp. that something is wrong or that person is guilty; inkling; slight trace, minute amount *of*. **suspi'cious** *a.* feeling, indicating, deserving of, exciting, suspicion; distrustful.

sustain' *v.t.* hold up, support, bear weight of; keep from failing or giving way; keep in being, in certain state, at proper level or standard, etc.; undergo, suffer (loss, etc.); uphold, allow validity, correctness, justice, etc. of; keep up

sus'tenance *n.* livelihood; means of sustaining life, food.

sŭt′ler *n.* camp-follower selling provisions etc. to soldiers.

sŭttee′ *n.* Hindu widow who immolates herself on husband's pyre; this custom.

sū′ture *n.* seam-like line of junction of two bones or parts at their edges; (surg.) stitching of edges of wound etc., stitch, thread, etc. used for this.

sū′zerain *n.* feudal overlord; sovereign or State having political control over another. **~tỹ** *n.*

s.v. *abbr., sub voce* [L], under the word.

svĕlte *a.* slim, slender, willowy.

SW *abbr.* south-west; south-western.

swab (-ŏb) *n.* mop or absorbent pad or cloth for cleansing, mopping up, etc.; specimen of morbid secretion etc. taken with swab. *v.t.* clean or wipe (as) with swab.

swadd′le (-ŏ-) *v.t.* swathe in bandages, wrappings, etc. **swadd′ling-clothes,** narrow bandages wrapped round new-born child to prevent free movement.

swăg *n.* ornamental festoon of flowers, fruit, etc. hung up by ends and hanging down in middle; (sl.) thief's booty; (sl.) dishonest gains; (Austral.) bundle carried by tramp, bush-traveller, etc. **~man,** (Austral.) one travelling with swag.

swăgg′er (-*ger*) *v.i.* walk or behave with superior, insolent, or blustering manner; talk boastfully. *n.* swaggering gait or manner.

swain *n.* (arch.) young rustic; bucolic lover; (joc.) suitor.

swall′ow¹ (-ŏlō) *v.* make or let pass down one's throat; engulf; accept credulously; recant (words); repress (emotion). *n.* gullet; act of, capacity for, swallowing. **~-hole,** hole through which stream disappears underground.

swall′ow² (-ŏlō) *n.* kinds of migratory insect-eating bird with long pointed wings and forked tail. **~ dive,** dive with arms spread sideways. **~tail,** forked tail; kinds of butterfly and humming-bird; man's full-dress evening coat.

swam, *p.t.* of **swim.**

swa′mi (-wah-) *n.* Hindu religious teacher.

swamp (-ŏ-) *n.* piece of wet spongy ground, marsh. *v.t.* submerge, inundate; cause to fill with water and sink; overwhelm with numbers or quantity. **~ỹ** *a.*

swan (-ŏn) *n.* large long-necked usu. white swimming bird. **~-neck,** curved tube or pipe. **~sdown,** swan's fine soft feathers or down; soft thick napped fabric. **~skin,** kind of thick soft flannel. **~-song,** last production or achievement. **swann′erỹ** *n.*

swănk *n.* (sl.) showing off; swagger. *v.i.* behave with swank. **~ỹ** *a.*

swap (-ŏ-), **swŏp** *v.* (sl.) exchange by way of barter. *n.* act of swapping; thing (to be) swapped.

sward (-ôrd) *n.* (expanse of) turf.

swarm¹ (-ôrm) *n.* cluster of bees leaving hive etc. with queen bee to establish new hive; large or dense body, multitude, of persons, insects, etc., esp. flying or moving about. *v.i.* move in or like swarm, congregate, cluster; be overrun or crowded; (of bees) leave hive in swarm.

swarm² (-ôrm) *v.* climb (*up*) clasping or clinging with arms and legs.

swar′thy (-ôrdhĭ) *a.* dark-complexioned, dark in colour.

swash¹ (-ŏ-) *v.i. & n.* (make) sound of water washing about. **~′buckler,** swaggering ruffian.

swash² (-ŏ-) *a.* inclined obliquely to axis; (of italic capitals) having flourished strokes at top and bottom. **~-plate,** rotating circular plate set obliquely to its shaft.

swas′tĭka (-ŏs-) *n.* cross with equal arms, each arm with limb of same length at right angles to its end.

swat (-ŏt) *v.t.* hit hard, crush (fly etc.) with blow.

swath (-aw-) *n.* (pl. pr. -dhs), row or line of grass, corn, etc. as it falls when cut; space covered, width of grass etc. cut, by sweep of scythe.

swāthe (-dh) *v.t.* wrap up or round, envelop, like bandage or (as) with wrapping. *n.* swath; wrapping, bandage.

sway *v.* have unsteady swinging

motion; waver; give swaying motion to; have influence over; rule over. *n.* swaying motion; rule, government.

swear (swār) *v.* (*swōre, sworn*), take oath; state or promise on oath; use profane oaths; cause to take oath; administer oath to; ~ *by*, (colloq.) profess or have great belief in; ~ *in*, admit to office etc. by administering oath; ~ *off*, forswear, renounce. ~-**word**, profane oath or word.

sweat (-ĕt) *n.* moisture exuded through pores, perspiration; drops of moisture on surface; condition or fit of sweating; (colloq.) state of impatience or anxiety; (colloq.) drudgery, laborious task. *v.* (cause to) exude sweat; (cause to) emit or exude, ooze *out*, as or like sweat; (cause to) exude or gather moisture in drops on surface; force moisture out of; work hard, toil; employ at starvation wages for long hours, exploit to the utmost. ~-**band**, band of leather etc. lining hat or cap. ~-**shirt**, kind of sweater worn by athletes before or after exercise. ~-**shop**, workroom in which workers are sweated. **sweat′er** *n.* (esp.) woollen etc. pullover. **sweat′y** *a.*

Swede *n.* native of Sweden; *s~*, large yellow variety of turnip. **Swe′dish** *a. & n.* (language) of Sweden.

sweep *v.* (*swĕpt*), glide swiftly; go majestically; extend in continuous curve, line, or slope; impart sweeping motion to; carry (*along, off,* etc.) in impetuous course; traverse or range swiftly, pass lightly, along, over, etc.; clear everything from; clear of dust, soot, litter, with broom; gather *up*, collect, (as) with broom; ~ *the board*, win all possible prizes etc. *n.* sweeping; moving in continuous curve; hostile reconnaissance by group of aircraft; sweeping motion or extension; curve in road etc.; long oar worked by standing rower(s); chimney-sweep; range, compass, stretch, expanse; sweepstake. ~-**stake**, form of gambling in which stakes go to drawer(s) of winning or placed

horse(s) etc. ~-**ing** *a.* (esp., of statement etc.) extreme, unqualified, careless of accuracy.

sweet *a.* tasting like sugar, honey, etc.; pleasing to sense of smell, fragrant; melodious; fresh; not sour or bitter; gratifying; dear, beloved; amiable, gentle; (colloq.) very pretty. *n.* sweetmeat; (usu. pl.) sweet dish(es) such as puddings tarts, jellies; (pl.) delights, gratifications; darling. ~-**bread**, pancreas or thymus-gland of animal, esp. calf, as food. ~-**brier**, kinds of single--flowered fragrant-leaved rose. ~ **chestnut**, Spanish or edible chestnut. ~ **corn**, sweet-flavoured kind of maize. ~-**heart**, darling; either of pair of lovers. ~-**meat**, small shaped piece of sugar or chocolate confectionery, bonbon; ~ **pea**, garden annual with showy scented flowers. ~ **pepper**, (mild-flavoured fruit of) kinds of capsicum. ~ **potato**, tropical plant with tuberous roots used for food. ~ **tooth**, taste for sweet things. ~-**william**, kind of pink with close clusters of sweet-smelling flowers. **swee′ten** *v.*; ~**ening** *n.* **swee′tie** *n.* sweetheart, darling; (chiefly Sc.) sweet. **swee′ting** *n.* kind of sweet apple.

swell *v.* (p.p. *swōllen,* occas. *swelled*), (cause to) grow bigger or louder; dilate, expand; rise or raise *up*; bulge *out*; increase in volume or force or intensity. *n.* act or state of swelling; (heaving of sea etc. with) long rolling waves that do not break; (mus.) increase followed by decrease in loudness, symbol ($<>$) denoting this; mechanism in organ etc. for gradually varying force of tone; (colloq.) fashionable or stylish persons, person of distinction or ability. *a.* (colloq.) smart, finely dressed; distinguished, first-rate. **swell′ing** *n.* (esp.) distension of injured cr diseased part of body.

swel′ter *v.i.* be oppressive or oppressed with heat.

swept, *p.t. & p.p.* of **sweep**.

swerve *v.* turn aside, (cause to) deviate from straight or direct course. *n.* swerving motion; divergence from course.

S.W.G., s.w.g. *abbr.* standard wire gauge.

swift *a.* rapid, speedy, quick, prompt, *adv.* swiftly. *n.* kinds of swift--flying long-winged insectivorous bird.

swig *v.* (sl.) take draughts (of). *n.* draught of liquor.

swill *v.* rinse (*out*), pour water over or through; drink greedily. *n.* swilling; (partly) liquid food given to pigs etc.; inferior liquor.

swim *v.* (*swăm, swŭm*), float on or at surface of liquid; progress in water by working limbs or body; make swim; be flooded with moisture; walk, etc. with gliding motion; have dizzy effect or sensation. *n.* spell of swimming; main current of affairs. **swimm'inglў** *adv.* (esp.) with easy unobstructed progress.

swin'dle *v.* cheat; defraud. *n.* piece of swindling; imposition; fraud.

swine *n.* (pl. same), kinds of non-ruminant hoofed mammal, esp. common domesticated species, regarded as type of greediness and uncleanness; person of greedy or bestial habits (esp. as strong term of abuse). **swi'nish** *a.*

swing *v.* (*swŭng*), move with to-and--fro motion; sway or hang like pendulum, door, etc.; oscillate; go with swinging gait; give (music) character of swing, dance to swing music. *n.* act of swinging; oscillation; swinging gait or rhythm; seat slung by ropes or chains for swinging in, swing-bòat; spell of swinging in this; swing music. ~-**boat**, boat-shaped swing at fairs etc. ~ **bridge**, bridge that swings on pivot(s) to let ships etc. pass. ~-**door**, door that swings in either direction and closes of itself when released. ~ **music**, jazz with time of melody freely varied over accompaniment in strict time. ~-**wing**, (of aircraft) having wings that can be swung back. **swing'ing** *a.* (esp.) gay, lively, vigorous, up--to-the-minute.

swin'geing (-jĭng) *a.* forcible; (colloq.) huge, thumping.

swing'le (-nggl) *n.* swinging bar of flail; flax-beating implement. *v.t.*

beat (flax). ~-**tree**, pivoted bar to which traces are attached in cart, plough, etc.

swipe *v.* hit hard and recklessly; (sl.) steal by snatching, seize, snatch. *n.* reckless hard (attempt to) hit; (pl.) inferior beer.

swirl *n.* eddying or whirling motion; twist, convolution; eddy. *v.* carry, be carried, flow, with swirling motion.

swish *n.* sound of switch etc. moved rapidly through air, of scythe cutting grass, etc.; swishing movement. *v.* make, move with, swish; flog with birch or cane.

Swiss *a.* & *n.* (native) of Switzerland. ~ **roll**, thin flat sponge cake spread with jam etc. and rolled up.

switch *n.* slender tapering whip; flexible shoot cut from tree; kinds of mechanism for making and breaking contact or altering connexions in electric circuit; (on railway etc.) movable rail(s) at junction of tracks to deflect train etc. from one track to another; tress of real or false hair tied at one end; act of switching, change, change-over. *v.* strike (as) with switch; flourish like switch, whisk, move with sudden jerk; deflect (train etc.) with switch; turn *on, off*, etc., change connexion (*over*) with switch; turn off, divert, change; change opinions, activities, allegiance, etc.; (bridge) change suit. ~-**back**, railway used for amusement at fairs etc. with series of alternate steep ascents and descents; road with alternate ascents and descents. ~**board**, board or frame with set of switches for varying connexions between electric circuits, esp. of telephones.

swiv'el *n.* ring and pivot or other device connecting two parts etc. so that one can turn freely without the other. *v.* turn (as) on swivel, swing round. ~ **bearing, coupling, gun,** etc. one provided with or mounted on swivel. ~ **chair,** chair turning horizontally on pivot. ~-**eye(d),** (with) squinting eye.

swizz'le *n.* kinds of mixed drink, esp. of rum etc. and bitters;

(colloq.) disappointment, 'sell'. ~-stick, stick or rod for stirring drink.

swollen, *p.p.* of **swell.**

swoon *v.i.* & *n.* (have) fainting fit.

swoop *v.i.* come down with rush of bird of prey; make sudden attack. *n.* act of swooping, sudden pounce; *at one (fell)* ~, at a single blow or stroke.

swop : see **swap.**

sword (sôrd) *n.* weapon with long blade for cutting or thrusting; *cross* ~*s,* engage in hostilities *with;* *put to the* ~, kill, esp. after victory. ~-arm, right arm. ~-fish, large sea-fish with upper jaw prolonged into sword-like point. ~-grass, kinds of grass with sharp-edged leaves. ~sman, one skilled in use of sword. ~-stick, hollow walking--stick containing sword-blade.

swore, sworn, *p.t.* & *p.p.* of **swear.**

swot *n.* (sl.) hard work or study; person who works hard, esp. at learning. *v.* work hard, esp. at books; ~ *up,* study hurriedly or for particular occasion.

swum, *p.p.* of **swim.**

swung, *p.t.* & *p.p.* of **swing.**

S.Y. *abbr.* Steam Yacht.

sybarite *n.* luxurious and effeminate person. ~it'ic *a.*

sycamore *n.* large species of maple; (bibl.) kind of fig-tree.

syce *n.* (Anglo-Ind.) groom.

sycophant *n.* flatterer, toady. ~ancy *n.*; ~an'tic *a.*

syllabary *n.* set of written characters representing syllables.

syllab'ic *a.* of, denoting, forming, etc. syllable(s); (of writing etc.) consisting of syllabic characters.

syllable *n.* vocal sound(s) forming whole word or part of it containing one vowel-sound; least mention or hint (*of*).

syllabub *n.* sillabub.

syllabus *n.* (pl. *-bī, -buses*), concise statement of subjects of lectures, course of study, etc.

syllogism *n.* form of reasoning in which conclusion is deduced from two premises containing common term which is absent from con-

clusion. **syllogis'tic** *a.* **syll'ogize** *v.* use syllogisms; put into syllogistic form.

sylph *n.* elemental spirit of air; slender graceful woman. ~like *a.* slender and graceful.

sylvan, silvan *a.* of wood(s); consisting of, abounding in, woods or trees.

symbiō'sis *n.* (pl. *-sēs*), association, advantageous to both, of two different organisms living attached to one another etc. **symbiōt'ic** *a.*

symbol *n.* thing standing for or representing something else, esp. material thing taken to represent immaterial or abstract thing; written character conventionally standing for object, process, etc. ~ism *n.* ~ize *v.t.* be symbol of; represent by symbol.

symm'etry *n.* (beauty resulting from) right proportion between parts, balance, harmony; structure allowing of object's being divided by line, plane, radiating lines, etc. into parts exactly similar in size, shape, and relative position; possession by whole of corresponding parts correspondingly placed. **symmet'rical** *a.*

sympathet'ic *a.* full of, expressing, feeling, etc. sympathy; capable of evoking sympathy, appealing, congenial; approving, not antagonistic; (of pain etc.) induced by similar or corresponding pain etc. in another organ, part, etc. ~ strike, strike in support of other strikers.

sym'pathize *v.i.* feel or express sympathy (*with*); share or understand feelings, ideas, etc. of another.

sym'pathy *n.* state of sharing or tendency to share emotion, sensation, condition, etc. of another person or thing; mental participation in another's trouble, compassion; disposition to agree (*with*) or approve, favourable attitude of mind.

sym'phony *n.* musical composition in several (usu. four) movements for full orchestra. **symphon'ic** *a.* of or like symphony; ~ poem, (usu.

descriptive or rhapsodic) orchestral work in one movement.

sўmpō'sium (-z-) *n*. (pl. *-ia*), meeting or conference for discussion of subject; collection of opinions delivered or articles contributed by number of persons on special topic.

sўmp'tom *n*. perceptible change in body or its functions indicating presence of disease or injury; evidence or token of existence of something. ~ăt'ic *a*.

sўn'agogue (-ŏg) *n*. (building for) regular assembly of Jews for religious instruction and worship.

sўn'chromĕsh (-k-) *a*. & *n*. (of, employing) device ensuring that parts of gear are revolving at same speed when brought into contact.

sўn'chronīze (-k-) *v*. be contemporary or simultaneous (*with*); (cause to) keep time (*with*), go at same rate, agree in time, etc. ~īzā'tion *n*. **sўn'chronous** *a*. contemporary, simultaneous; keeping time, proceeding at same pace, (*with*).

sўn'chrotron (-k-) *n*. apparatus for imparting very high speeds to electrons etc.

sўn'clīne *n*. (geol.) rock-bed forming trough.

sўn'copāte *v*. (gram.) shorten (word) by omitting syllable(s) or letter(s) in middle; (mus.) displace accent by beginning note on normally unaccented part of bar, putting strong in place of normally weak accent, etc. **sўncopā'tion** *n*.

sўn'copė *n*. fainting, faint; (gram.) syncopation.

sўn'crėtĭsm *n*. (attempted) reconciliation of differing philosophical or religious tenets etc. **sўncrĕt'ic** *a*.; **sўn'crėtīze** *v*.

sўn'dĭc *n*. member of special committee of senate in University of Cambridge; government officer, esp. one of four chief magistrates of Geneva.

sўn'dĭcalism *n*. movement for transfer of control and ownership of means of production and distribution to workers' unions. ~ist *a*. & *n*.

sўn'dĭcate *n*. combination of financiers etc. for promotion of financial or commercial undertaking; council,

body of syndics. *v*. (-āt), form into syndicate; publish simultaneously in number of periodicals. ~ā'tion *n*.

sўn'drōme *n*. concurrence of several symptoms, set of concurrent symptoms, in disease.

sўnĕc'doche (-kǐ) *n*. (gram.) figure of speech in which part or individual is put for whole or class.

sўn'od *n*. assembly of clergy of church, diocese, etc. for discussing and deciding ecclesiastical affairs; council, convention. ~al, **sўnŏd'ic(al)** *aa*.

sўn'onўm *n*. word having same meaning as another in same language. **sўnŏn'ўmous** *a*. **sўnŏn'ўmў** *n*. being synonymous.

sўnŏp'sis *n*. (pl. *-sēs*), summary; conspectus. **sўnŏp'tic** *a*. of, forming, furnishing, synopsis; taking, affording, comprehensive mental view. **synoptic gospels**, those of Matthew, Mark, and Luke, as giving account of events from same point of view. ~ŏp'tical *a*.

sўnovī'tis *n*. inflammation of membrane lining cavity of joint.

sўn'tăx *n*. arrangement of words in sentence; department of grammar dealing with usages of grammatical construction. **sўntăc'tic** *a*.

sўn'thėsis *n*. (pl. *-esēs*), putting together of parts or elements to make up complex whole; (chem.) formation of compound by combination of elements etc., esp. artificial production of naturally occurring compounds. **sўnthĕt'ic** *a*. produced by synthesis; artificial.

sўph'ilis *n*. venereal disease usu. communicated by direct contact with infected person. **sўphilĭt'ic** *a*. & *n*.

sў'phon *n*. siphon.

Sў'rĭăc *n*. & *a*. (of, in) language of ancient Syria.

sўrĭng'a (-ngg-) *n*. shrub with white scented flowers.

sў'rĭnge (-j) *n*. tube with nozzle and piston for drawing in quantity of liquid and ejecting it in stream or jet. *v.t.* sluice, spray, with syringe.

sў'rup *n*. water (nearly) saturated with sugar; condensed sugar-cane juice, part of this remaining un-crystallized. **sÿ′rupÿ** *a*.

sÿstǎl′tǐc *a*. having systole and diastole.

sÿs′tem *n*. complex whole; set, organized body of connected things or parts; *the* animal body as organized whole; comprehensive body of doctrines, theories, beliefs, etc., forming particular philosophy, form of government, etc.; scheme or method of classification, nota-tion, etc.; orderly arrangement or method. **sÿstemǎt′ic** *a*. of system(s); methodical; arranged, conducted, according to system. **~atīze** *v.t.*; **~atīzā′tion** *n*.

sÿs′tolė *n*. contraction of heart alternating with diastole.

T

T, t (tē) letter or its sound; *cross the t's*, be minutely accurate or par-ticular; *to a T*, exactly, to a nicety. **T-junction**, junction, esp. of two roads, in shape of T. **T-shirt**, usu. collarless short-sleeved (under)shirt. **T-square**, T-shaped instrument for measuring or obtain-ing right angles.

T. *abbr*. Tenor.

t. *abbr*. taken (betting); ton(s).

ta (tah) *int*. (nursery, colloq.) thank you.

T.A. *abbr*. Territorial Army.

tǎb *n*. short broad strap, flat loop, tag, etc. by which thing can be taken hold of, fastened, identified, etc.; (colloq.) account, check (esp. *keep ~s on*).

tǎb′ard *n*. (hist.) short surcoat with armorial bearings worn over armour; herald's or pursuivant's official dress of jerkin emblazoned with royal arms.

tabǎs′cō *n*. (sauce made with) pun-gent kind of pepper. **P.**

tǎbb′ÿ *n*. kind of watered silk; female cat; old maid or female gossip. **~ cat**, brownish, tawny, or grey cat with darker stripes.

tǎb′ernǎcle *n*. tent used as sanctuary by Jews during wanderings in the wilderness; nonconformist meeting-house; canopied niche or receptacle. **~nǎc′ūlar** *a*.

tā′bēs (-z) *n*. (path.) slow progressive emaciation.

tā′ble *n*. piece of furniture with flat top on which things may be placed, esp. one on which meals are laid out, work done, games played, etc.; provision or supply of food for meals; company of persons at table; flat usu. rectangular hori-zontal or vertical surface; flat elevated tract of land; slab of wood, stone, etc.; tabulated state-ment or arrangement; *at ~*, at meal(s); *lay, lie, on the ~*, postpone, be postponed, indefinitely; *turn the ~s*, cause complete reversal of state of affairs. *v.t.* lay on the table; bring, be brought, forward for dis-cussion. **~ land**, extensive elevated region with level surface. **~ tennis**, game resembling lawn tennis played on table with net stretched across.

tǎb′leau (-lō) *n*. (pl. *~eaux* pr. -ōz), presentation, esp. of group of persons etc., producing picturesque effect; dramatic or effective situa-tion suddenly brought about.

table d'hôte (tahbl-dōt′) *n*. meal in restaurant etc. served at fixed price and stated hour(s).

tǎb′lėt *n*. small thin flat piece of ivory, wood, etc. for writing on; pad of sheets of paper fastened together at top; small slab esp. with or for inscription; small flat sweet; small flat or compressed mass of medicated material; cake of soap.

tǎb′loid *n*. small concentrated tablet of medicated substance **(P.)**; any-thing in compressed or concen-trated form; (newspaper giving) news in concentrated and simplified form. *a*. of or like tabloid news-paper(s); concentrated and easily assimilated.

tabōō′, tabu′ (-ōō) *a*. set apart as sacred or accursed; forbidden by social convention etc., not to be mentioned, touched, used, etc. *n*. (institution, practice, state, of) setting or being set apart as taboo;

ban, prohibition. *v.t.* put under taboo.

tā'bor *n*. (hist.) small drum.

tabu : see **taboo**.

tăb'ūlar *a*. of, arranged in, etc. tables; broad, flat, and usu. comparatively thin; formed of, tending to split into, pieces of this form; (of crystal etc.) with flat base and top. **tăbū-lāte** *v.t.* arrange, summarize, exhibit, in form of table(s), esp. in columns and lines occupying single sheet(s), or of scheme or synopsis. **~ā'tion** *n.* **~ātor** *n.* (esp.) type-writer attachment for tabulating figures.

Tac. *abbr.* Tacitus.

tă'cĭt *a*. implied, understood, inferred, but not openly expressed or stated.

tă'cĭtūrn *a*. saying little, uncom-municative. **~tūr'nĭty** *n.*

tăck *n*. small sharp usu. broad-headed nail; long stitch used in fastening materials lightly or temporarily together; rope etc. for securing lower corner of some sails; boat's or ship's obliquely windward course as determined by position of sails, one of consecutive series of such courses with wind alternately on port and starboard side; course of action or policy. *v.* attach with tacks or in slight or temporary manner, esp. with long slight stitches; annex, append (*to, on to*); (make) run obliquely against wind, proceed to windward by series of tacks; change one's course, policy, etc.

tăck'le (*or* (naut.) tā-) *n*. gear or appliances esp. for fishing or other sport; rope(s) and pulley(s) etc. used in working sails, hoisting weights, etc.; (footb. etc.) tackling. *v.t.* grapple with, grasp, lay hold of, with endeavour to hold, manage, accomplish, overcome, etc.; (footb. etc.) seize and stop, obstruct, inter-cept (opponent in possession of ball etc.).

tăck'y *a*. (of nearly dry varnish etc.) slightly sticky or adhesive.

tăct *n*. delicate perception of right thing to do or say; adroitness in dealing with persons or circum-stances. **~ful, ~less** *aa.*

tăc'tĭc *n*. (piece of) tactics. **tăc'tĭcal** *a*. of tactics; adroitly planning or planned.

tăc'tĭcs *n*. (sing. or pl.), art of deploy-ing and manœuvring air, military or naval forces, esp. when in con-tact with enemy; procedure, de-vice(s) for gaining some end. **tactĭ'cian** *n.*

tăc'tĭle *a*. of, perceived by, connected with, appealing to, sense of touch; (painting etc.) producing effect of solidity. **tactĭl'ĭty** *n.*

tăd'pōle *n*. larva of frog, toad, etc. esp. when it seems to consist simply of a round head with a tail.

tăff'ėta *n*. fine plain-woven lustrous usu. silk fabric.

tăff'rail (-frĭl) *n*. rail round ship's stern.

tăg *n*. metal point of shoelace etc.; small pendent piece or part; label for tying on; loose or ragged end; brief and usu. trite quotation etc. *v.* furnish with tag(s); tack or fasten *on* etc.; follow, trail behind; **~** *along,* (colloq.) go *with,* follow.

tail[1] *n*. member prolonging animal's body backwards; slender prolonga-tion or appendage; rear end or part; outer corner of eye; reverse side of coin; weaker members of team etc.; (pl.) tail-coat. *v.* furnish with tail; follow (inconspicuously) and keep watch on; cut or pull off what is regarded as tail, esp. of fruit etc.; **~** *away, off,* fall away in tail or straggling line, diminish and cease. **~-board,** hinged or re-movable back of cart. **~-coat,** man's coat divided behind into tails. **~-light,** light carried at back of train, car, etc. **~-piece,** (esp.) small decoration at end of chapter, book, etc. **~-plane,** horizontal stabilizing surface of tail of air-craft. **~-race,** part of millrace below wheel. **~-skid,** small skid or runner supporting tail of aircraft on ground. **~-spin,** aircraft's spin-ning dive; (colloq.) panic, state of agitation. **~ wind,** following wind.

tail[2] *n*. limitation of estate etc. to person and (particular class of) heirs of his body. *a.* so limited.

tai'lor *n*. maker of men's outer garments, or similar clothes for women. *v.* be or work as tailor; make by tailor's methods; (of fabric) admit of being tailored; furnish with clothes; adapt, fit, *to* requirements etc. ~**-bird**, kinds of Asiatic passerine bird stitching leaves together for nest. ~**-made**, (suit etc.) made by tailor, usu. with little ornament and with special attention to exact fit; not ready-made; exactly fitted, suited or adapted *for* particular purpose etc. **tai'loring** *n.*

taint *n.* spot, trace, of decay, corruption, or disease; corrupt condition, infection. *v.* introduce corruption or disease into, infect, be infected.

tāke *v.* (*tŏok, tāken*), seize, grasp; capture, catch; appropriate, steal; receive into body or mind; accept, secure, obtain, get; deal with, use (up), consume; need (specified size) *in*; write *down*; face and (attempt to) get over, through, etc.; convey or conduct; catch or come upon; captivate; win; secure photograph (of); prove attractive, be in demand, be successful or effective; (gram.) have as proper construction; ~ *aim*, aim; ~ *alarm*, become alarmed; ~ *charge (of)*, make oneself responsible (for); ~ *care*, be careful *(of)*, be in charge *of*; ~ *care of*, look after, deal with; ~ *fire*, be kindled or ignited; ~ *hold (of)*, grasp, seize, take under one's control; ~ *it out of*, exhaust, fatigue, exact satisfaction from; ~ *place*, happen; ~ *possession*, enter into possession *(of)*; ~ *after*, show resemblance to (esp. parent); ~ *away*, remove, subtract, detract; ~ *back*, retract; ~ *in*, reduce to smaller size or compass, comprehend, deceive, cheat; ~ *off*, mimic, jump, spring, (of aircraft etc.) leave ground; ~ *on*, undertake, play (person *at* game etc.), (colloq.) show violent emotion; ~ *over*, succeed to or acquire possession or control of (esp. commercial company); ~ *to*, begin, begin to occupy oneself with, conceive liking for; ~ *up*, enter upon, begin to pursue, accept (challenge), subscribe for, subscribe

amount of, adopt as protégé etc., begin to consort *with*, interrupt, correct. *n.* amount (of fish etc.) taken or caught; takings; (cine.) (part of) scene photographed at one time without stopping camera. ~**-in**, fraud, deception. ~**-off**, caricature, mockery; place from which jump etc. is made; (time of) taking off or departure of aircraft. ~**-over**, taking control esp. of commercial company; ~*-over bid*, offer made to shareholders for their shares in attempt to take over company. **tā'ker** *n.* (esp.) one who accepts bet, offer, etc. **tā'king** *n.* (esp., pl.) money received, receipts; *a.* attractive, captivating, charming.

tălc *n.* soft translucent lustrous white, green, or grey mineral with greasy feel, freq. occurring in broad flat plates.

tăl'cum *n.* talc. ~ **powder**, toilet--powder of (usu. perfumed) powdered talc.

tāle *n.* narrative, story, esp. imaginative or fictitious; idle or mischievous gossip, malicious report.

tăl'ent *n.* ancient weight and money of account; special aptitude, gift *(for)*; high mental or artistic ability; (colloq.) talented person. ~**-money**, bonus to professional cricketer etc. for especially good performance. ~ **scout**, person engaged in searching for talented people, esp. theatrical etc. performers. **tăl'entĕd** *a.* gifted, having or showing talent.

tăl'ĭsman (-z-) *n.* charm, amulet; thing believed to bring good luck or protect from harm. **tălismăn'ĭc** *a.*

talk (tawk) *v.* convey or exchange ideas, information, etc. by speech, esp. familiar speech of ordinary intercourse; have or exercise faculty of speech, utter words; express, utter, discuss, in words; gossip; use (language); ~ *down*, silence by louder or more effective talking, bring (aircraft, its pilot) in to land by verbal instruction from ground; ~ *down to*, address in condescendingly simple language; ~ *into*, persuade by talking; ~ *over*, discuss, persuade to change opinion etc.; ~*to*, speak to, (colloq.) reprove. *n.* conversation; mere words; short conversational esp. broadcast address or lecture; rumour, (theme of) gossip. ~**ative** *a.* fond of talking, loquacious. **talk'ie** *n.* (colloq.) cinema sound-film.

tall (tawl) *a.* of more than average stature or height; high, lofty, higher than surroundings; (of talk etc.) high-flown, exaggerated, highly coloured. ~**boy**, tall chest of drawers. ~ **order**, thing difficult to do; unreasonable or excessive demand.

tăll'ow (-ō) *n.* fat of animals, esp. of sheep and ox kinds, melted down for use in making candles, soap, etc. **tăll'owy̆** *a.*

tăll'y̆ *n.* (hist.) piece of wood scored with notches for items of account and split into halves of which each party kept one; account or score so kept; distinguishing mark, ticket, label. *v.* record, reckon, by tally; agree, correspond, (*with*). ~**man**, one who sells goods paid for by instalments.

tălly̆-hō' *int.* & *n.* huntsman's view--halloo.

Tăl'mud *n.* body of Jewish civil and ceremonial law. **Talmŭd'ic(al)** *aa.*; ~**ist** *n.*

tăl'on *n.* claw, esp. of bird of prey.

tama'lĕ (-ah-) *n.* Mexican dish of crushed maize with meat, red pepper, etc. baked or steamed in corn-husks.

tăm'arĭnd *n.* (fruit-pod with seeds embedded in acid pulp of) large tropical tree.

tăm'arĭsk *n.* kinds of feathery--leaved evergreen shrub or small tree growing in sandy places.

tăm'bour (-oor) *n.* drum; circular frame for stretching embroidery--work on; cylindrical stone forming part of shaft or column; circular part of various structures.

tămbourine (-orēn) *n.* musical instrument of wooden hoop with skin stretched over one side and pairs of small cymbals in slots round circumference.

tăme *a.* (of animals) domesticated, tractable; lacking spirit; uninterest-

ing, insipid. *v.t.* make tame, domesticate; break in; humble, subdue, curb.

tăm-o'-shăn'ter *n.* round Scottish cap with flat baggy top.

tămp *v.t.* plug (blast-hole etc.) with clay etc.; block up; ram down.

tăm'per *v.i.* meddle or interfere *with*.

tăm'pon *n.* plug in wound etc. to stop bleeding, absorb secretions, etc. *v.t.* plug with tampon.

tăn¹ *n.* crushed or bruised bark of oak etc. used for tanning; spent bark from tan-pits used to cover riding-track etc.; track etc. covered with this; yellowish brown of tanned leather; bronzed colour of skin exposed to sun or weather. *a.* yellowish-brown. *v.* convert (hide) into leather by steeping in infusion of tan; make or become brown by exposure to sun or weather; (sl.) thrash. ~**-pit, -vat**, pit, cistern, etc. in which hides are tanned.

tan² *abbr.* tangent.

tăn'ager *n.* kinds of usu. bright--plumaged Amer. bird.

tăn'dem *adv.* (with two or more horses etc.) harnessed one behind another. *n.* vehicle driven tandem; bicycle etc. with two or more seats one behind the other.

tăng *n.* part of tool that fits into handle; strong or penetrating taste or smell; characteristic quality; trace or touch *of*.

tăn'gent (-j-) *n.* straight line touching but not intersecting curve; ratio of side of right-angled triangle opposite one acute angle to that opposite the other; *at a* ~, in course or direction diverging more or less acutely from that previously pursued. **tangĕn'tial** *a.*

tăngerine' (-jerēn) *n.* kind of small flattened sweet-scented orange.

tăn'gible (-j-) *a.* perceptible by touch; real, palpable. ~**bĭl'ity̆** *n.*

tang'le¹ (-nggl) *v.* intertwine, become twisted or involved, in confused mass; entangle; complicate. *n.* tangled condition or mass. **tăng'ly̆** *a.*

tăng'le² (-nggl) *n.* kinds of seaweed with long leathery fronds.

tăng'o (-nggō) *n.* (pl. -*os*), (music for)

slow S.-Amer. dance of Central African origin.

tănk *n.* large vessel for liquid, gas, etc.; part of locomotive tender containing water for boiler; receptacle for fuel in motor vehicle; reservoir; armoured car carrying guns and mounted on caterpillar tracks. ~-engine, railway engine carrying its own fuel and water instead of drawing tender. ~age *n.* (charge for) storage in tanks; capacity of tank(s).

tănk'ard *n.* large one-handled drinking-vessel, freq. with lid.

tănk'er *n.* ship, motor-vehicle, for carrying mineral oil etc. in bulk.

tănn'er[1] *n.* one who tans hides. **tănn'erў** *n.* place where hides are tanned.

tănn'er[2] *n.* (sl.) sixpence.

tănn'in *n.* kinds of complex substance extracted from tree-barks etc. and used in tanning etc. **tănn'ic** *a.* of or like, derived from, tan or tannin.

tăn'sy (-zĭ) *n.* kinds of aromatic herb.

tăn'talize *v.t.* torment, tease, by sight or promise of something desired that is out of reach or withheld. ~īzā'tion *n.*

tăn'talum *n.* rare hard ductile greyish--white metallic element.

tăn'talus *n.* decanter-stand with locking device.

tăn'tamount *pred.a.* equivalent *to.*

tăn'trum *n.* (colloq.) outburst or display of bad temper or petulance.

tăp[1] *n.* hollow plug with device for shutting off or controlling flow through which liquid is drawn from cask or through pipes; liquor from particular tap; (colloq.) tap-room; tool in shape of male screw for cutting thread of internal screw; *on* ~, on draught, ready for immediate consumption or use. *v.t.* prepare (cask, liquor) for draught by inserting tap; draw off fluid by incision; draw supplies or information from, furnish with screw-thread; connect electric circuit to another, esp. to overhear telephone conversation etc. ~room, room in public-house etc. where

liquors are kept on tap. ~-root, long straight root thick at top and tapering to a point.

tăp[2] *v.* strike (with) light or gentle blow; knock gently; do tap-dancing. *n.* light blow or sound; (pl., U.S.) signal on drum or bugle for lights out. ~-dance, kind of exhibition dance in which (esp. elaborate syncopated) rhythm is tapped out with feet. ~-shoes, shoes with metal plates.

tāpe *n.* narrow woven strip of cotton etc. used as string for tying garments etc., piece of tape stretched across race-course at winning-post; strip of tape, paper, flexible metal, magnetic material, etc. used as measuring-line, for recording telegraph messages, sounds, etc. *v.t.* furnish, measure, join or fasten, with tape(s); record on tape; *have* (thing, person) *taped*, have summed up, understand completely. ~-machine, receiving instrument of recording telegraph. ~-measure, strip of tape etc. marked for use as measure. ~-recorder, machine for recording and reproducing sounds on magnetic tape. ~worm, kinds of long flat worm parasitic in intestines of man etc.

tā'per *n.* wick with coat of wax etc. for lighting lamp etc.; slender wax candle; tapering. *a.* tapering. *v.* make, become, gradually smaller towards one end; ~ *off*, gradually diminish or cease.

tăp'ėstrў *n.* thick hand-woven usu. woollen fabric with pictorial or ornamental design formed by weft--threads; wall-hanging of this; embroidered, painted, or machine--woven fabric imitating or resembling tapestry. ~ carpet, carpet with design printed on warp before weaving. ~-needle, short thick needle. ~-stitch, embroidery stitch like cross-stitch with threads parallel with warp.

tăpiō'ca *n.* starchy granular food-stuff prepared from cassava.

tā'pir (-er) *n.* small pig-like mammal with flexible proboscis.

tăpp'ėt *n.* arm, cam, etc., used in

machinery to impart intermittent motion.

tăp′ster *n*. person employed at bar to draw and serve liquor.

tar *n*. thick viscid inflammable black or dark-coloured liquid distilled from wood or coal; (colloq.) sailor. *v.t.* coat, cover, smear, with tar. ~**mac (P)**, ~**-macadam**, road--making material of crushed stone etc. mixed or covered with tar or other bituminous binder; road, runway, etc. of this.

tă′radĭddle *n*. (sl.) fib.

tărantĕll′a, **tărantĕlle′** *nn*. rapid whirling S.-Ital. peasant dance; music for it; instrumental composition in rhythm of tarantella.

tarăn′tūla *n*. kinds of large venomous spider.

tarboōsh′ *n*. fez.

tar′dў *a*. slow to act, come, or happen; behind time.

tāre[1] *n*. kinds of vetch; (bibl.) darnel.

tāre[2] *n*. (allowance made for) weight of wrapping, box, conveyance, etc. in which goods are packed or carried.

tar′gĕt (-g-) *n*. shooting-mark, esp. with concentric circles round central ring or spot; anything aimed at.

tă′rĭff *n*. (schedule of) customs duties; duty on goods; list or scale of charges.

tar′latan *n*. thin stiff muslin.

tarmac : see **tar**.

tarn *n*. small mountain lake.

tar′nish *v*. dull lustre of, discolour by oxidation etc.; lose lustre; sully, taint, stain. *n*. tarnished state; stain, blemish.

tar′ō *n*. kinds of food-plant with starchy root.

tă′rot (-ō) *n*. pack of 78 playing--cards used in fortune-telling.

tarpau′lin *n*. (sheet or covering of) canvas coated with tar or other kinds of waterproof cloth.

tar′pon *n*. large silvery game-fish of W. Atlantic.

tă′rragon *n*. aromatic herb.

tarr′ў[1] *a*. of, like, impregnated or smeared with, tar.

tă′rrў[2] *v.i.* delay, be late; linger.

tar′sia *n*. wood mosaic.

tar′sus *n*. (pl. *tarsī*), collection of small bones forming ankle. **tar′sal** *a*.

tart[1] *a*. sharp-tasting, sour, acid; cutting, biting.

tart[2] *n*. pie, freq. small or open, containing fruit, jam, etc.; (sl.) girl, woman, prostitute. *v.t.* (colloq.) dress, deck, *up* gaudily or with cheap smartness. ~**lĕt** *n*. **tar′tў** *a*. of or like prostitute.

tar′tan *n*. (cloth woven in) distinctive pattern of Highland clan, with coloured stripes crossing at right angles; any similar pattern.

tar′tar[1] *n*. substance deposited in cask by fermentation of wine; incrustation of calcium phosphate on teeth; *cream of* ~, purified tartar used in cookery. **tartă′ric** *a*. of, derived from, tartar.

Tar′tar[2] *n*. native of Tartary; *t*~, intractable or violent-tempered person.

Tar′tarus *n*. (Gk. myth.) infernal regions; hell.

task (tah-) *n*. piece of work to be done; *take to* ~, find fault with, rebuke. *v.t.* assign task to; strain, tax. ~**-force**, armed force under unified command for specific operation. ~**master**, one who imposes heavy burden or labour.

tăss′el *n*. tuft of loosely hanging threads etc. as ornament; tassel--like head of plant, esp. maize. *v.t.* furnish with tassel(s).

tāste *n*. sensation excited in taste--buds by contact with some substances, flavour; sense by which this is perceived; small portion (*of* food etc.) taken as sample; liking, predilection, (*for*); sense of, faculty of discerning and enjoying, what is excellent or harmonious or fitting in art, literature, conduct, etc. *v*. perceive or learn flavour of; eat small portion of, sample; have taste (*of*). ~**-buds**, organs of taste in mouth, esp. on tongue. ~**ful** *a*. showing, having, done in, good taste. ~**less** *a*. insipid, without taste; lacking, not in, good taste. **tā′ster** *n*. (esp.) person who selects teas, wines, etc. by tasting. **tā′stў** *a*. savoury, not insipid.

tăt v. do, make by, tatting.

tătt'er n. rag, irregularly torn piece, esp. hanging loose. ~dĕmăl'ion (or -mā-) n. ragamuffin. tătt'ered a. ragged, reduced to tatters.

tătt'ing n. (making of) kind of knotted lace.

tătt'le v.i. gossip idly; repeat or discuss scandal. n. chatter, gossip, idle talk.

tattoo'[1] n. evening signal summoning soldiers to quarters; elaboration of this with music, marching, etc. as entertainment, esp. by artificial light; drumming, rapping; drum-beat. v.i. rap quickly and repeatedly.

tattoo'[2] v.t. mark skin by puncturing it and inserting pigment; make (design) thus. n. tattooing; tattooed design.

tătt'y a. (colloq.) ragged, shaggy; shabby, inferior.

taught, p.t. of teach.

taunt n. insulting or provoking gibe. v.t. reproach, mock at, insultingly or contemptuously.

Taur'us, Bull, second constellation and sign of zodiac.

taut a. drawn tight; stiff, tense; (of ship etc.) trim, neat. tau'ten v.

tautŏl'ogy n. repetition of same idea etc. in different words. tautolŏ'gi-cal, ~ogous aa.

tăv'ern n. inn, public-house.

taw[1] n. large freq. streaked or variegated marble.

taw[2] v.t. make into leather esp. by steeping in alum and salt.

taw'dry a. showy or gaudy without real value.

taw'ny a. & n. (of) brown with preponderance of yellow or orange. ~ owl, common European owl.

tawse (-z) n. (Sc.) kind of leather strap for chastising children.

tăx n. contribution levied on person, property, etc. for support of State; oppressive or burdensome charge etc.; strain, heavy demand (up)on. v.t. impose tax on, subject to taxation; make demands on, strain, burden; (law) fix proper amount of (costs); accuse, charge (with), call to account. ~able a.; ~abil'ity, taxā'tion nn.

tăx'i n. motor-cab, esp. with taxi-meter, plying for hire. v. go, convey, in taxi; (of aircraft) run along surface before taking off or after alighting.

tăx'idermy n. art of preparing and mounting skins of animals with lifelike effect. ~mist n.

tăx'imēter n. automatic device indicating fare due fitted to taxi.

tazza (tah'tsa) n. shallow ornamental bowl or cup mounted on base.

T.B. abbr. torpedo-boat; tubercle bacillus; tuberculosis.

T.B.D. abbr. torpedo-boat destroyer.

tē n. (mus.) seventh note of major scale in tonic sol-fa.

tea n. dried leaves of tea-plant; infusion of them as drink; meal at which this is served, esp. light meal in afternoon or evening meal when dinner is eaten at midday; tea-plant; infusion made from leaves etc. of other plants, beef extract, etc. ~-bag, small bag holding tea-leaves for infusion. ~-break, interruption of work allowed for drinking tea. ~-cake, kind of light flat freq. sweet bun or cake of bread. ~-chest, cubical chest lined with lead etc. in which tea is exported. ~-cloth, cloth used for drying cups etc. after washing; cloth for tea-table or tea-tray. ~-cup, (esp.) china cup holding about quarter-pint. ~-leaf, (esp., pl.) leaves of tea after infusion. ~-plant, kinds of Chinese and Indian shrub yielding tea. ~-pot, vessel with spout in which tea is made. ~-rose, kinds of delicate-scented rose. ~-spoon, small spoon for stirring tea etc.; as measure, about one-third table-spoon.

teach v. (taught, pr. tawt), impart knowledge or skill (to); give instruction or lessons (to); instil, inspire with. ~-in, (colloq.) kind of oral symposium on subject of topical interest. ~able a. (esp.) apt to learn, docile. tea'cher n. (esp.) one who teaches in school. tea'ching n. what is taught, doctrine.

teak n. (heavy durable oily wood of) large E.-Ind. tree.

teal *n.* (pl. same), kinds of small fresh-water duck.

team *n.* set of draught animals harnessed together (with vehicle they draw); side of players etc. in game or sport; set of persons working together. *v.* harness in, convey or transport with, team; join (*together*) as or in team; ~ *up*, join or collaborate or put (*with*), esp. for specific piece of work etc. ~-**work**, combined effort, organized co-operation. **team'ster** *n.* driver of team.

tear[1] (tār) *v.* (tōre, tōrn), pull apart, away, or asunder by force; make tear or rent in; lend itself to tearing, be torn; move violently or impetuously, rush. *n.* tearing; rent in cloth etc. **tear'ing** *a.* (esp.) vehement, violent, rushing.

tear[2] *n.* drop of limpid saline fluid appearing in or flowing from eye as result of emotion, esp. grief, or physical irritation etc.; (pl.) weeping, sorrow; something resembling tear. ~**gas**, lachrymatory vapour used to disable opponents. ~**ful** *a.* shedding, apt or ready to shed, tears; mournful, sad. ~**less** *a.*

tease (-z) *v.* assail playfully or maliciously, vex, with jests, petty annoyances, etc.; pull asunder fibres of (wool etc.); comb (cloth etc.) into nap with teasels etc. *n.* person addicted to teasing. **tea'ser** *n.* (esp., colloq.) difficult question, problem, task, etc.

tea'sel (-z-), **tea'zle** *n.* kinds of plant with prickly leaves and flower-heads; dried flower-head of species of this with hooked prickles, used for teasing cloth etc. into nap; contrivance used as substitute for this. *v.t.* dress (cloth) with teasel(s).

teat *n.* nipple, small protuberance at tip of breast in female mammals; artificial nipple of feeding-bottle etc.

tĕc *n.* (sl.) detective; technical.

Tech. *abbr.* Technical College.

tĕchnē'tium (-k-; -shm) *n.* artificially produced radioactive metallic element.

tech'nical (tĕk-) *a.* of, in, or peculiar to particular art, science, profession, etc.; esp. of, in, or for mechanical arts and applied science generally. **tĕchnical'itў** *n.* technical quality or character; technical term, detail, point, etc.; formality. **techni'cian** *n.* one skilled in technique of art or subject; expert in practical application of science. **tech'nics** *n.pl.* technology.

tĕchnique' (-knēk) *n.* manner of execution or performance in music, painting, etc.; mechanical part of art, craft, etc.; method of achieving purpose.

tĕchnŏc'racў (-kn-) *n.* government, control, by technical experts. **tĕch'nocrăt** *n.*; ~**crăt'ic** *a.*

tĕchnŏl'ogў (-k-) *n.* scientific study of industrial and mechanical arts; practical arts collectively; terminology of art or subject. ~**lŏ'gical** *a.*; ~**logist** *n.*

tĕctŏn'ic *a.* of building, construction, or structure. *n.pl.* art of producing useful and beautiful buildings, furniture, etc.

tĕd[1] *v.t.* turn over and spread out (grass, hay) to dry. **tĕdd'er** *n.* machine for drying hay.

tĕd[2] *n.* (sl.) Teddy-boy.

tĕdd'y-bear (-ār) *n.* soft toy bear.

Tĕdd'ў-boy *n.* youth, esp. delinquent or hooligan, affecting extreme, esp. Edwardian, style and fastidious taste in dress.

Tē Dē'um *n.* (musical setting of) ancient Latin hymn of praise and thanksgiving.

tē'dĭous *a.* tiresomely long, prolix, irksome. **tē'dĭum** *n.* weariness produced by tediousness, tedious circumstances.

tee[1] *n.* letter T; T-shaped thing or part. ~-**square**, T-square.

tee[2] *n.* small mound of sand, small shaped piece of wood etc., on which golf-ball is placed for driving off; place from which ball is played at beginning of each hole. *v.* place (ball) on tee; ~ *off*, play ball from tee.

teem[1] *v.i.* swarm *with*; be abundant.

teem[2] *v.i.* pour (esp. of rain).

teens *n.pl.* years of one's age from 13 to 19. **teen'-āge** *a.* in the teens; of or for teenagers. **teen'āger** *n.* person in the teens.

tee'nў *a.* (nursery) tiny.

tee'ter *v.* move like see-saw; stand, move, unsteadily.

teeth : see **tooth**.

teethe (-dh) *v.i.* grow or cut teeth, esp. milk-teeth. **teething troubles**, (esp., fig.) difficulties etc. of early stages of anything.

teetō'tal *a.* of or advocating total abstinence from intoxicants. **~ism**, **teetō'taller** *nn.*

teetō'tum *n.* top with four sides lettered to decide spinner's luck; any top spun with fingers.

tĕg *n.* sheep in its second year.

t.e.g. *abbr.* top edges gilt.

tĕg'ūment *n.* natural covering of (part of) animal body.

tĕl'ĕ- in comb., far; at a distance; of, by, etc. television. **tĕl'ĕcămera** *n.* television camera. **~cast** (-ahst) *n.* programme etc. broadcast by television. **~commūnicā'tions** *n.* (study of) means of communication at a distance. **~contrōl'** *n.* remote control. **~film** *n.* cinema film produced for television. **~kīnē'sis** *n.* movement at a distance from motive cause or agent without material connexion. **~print** *v.* send message etc., communicate, by teleprinter. **~printer** *n.* electrically operated typewriter transmitting and recording telegraphic messages. **~prŏmpter** *n.* device for prompting television speaker by displaying his text outside range of cameras. **~rĕcôr'ding** *n.* recording, record, of television programme. **~tȳpe** *v.* transmit by teleprinter.

tĕl'ĕgrăm *n.* message sent by telegraph.

tĕl'ĕgraph (-ahf) *n.* (apparatus for) instantaneous conveyance of messages to any distance by transmission of electrical impulses along wires; semaphore, signalling apparatus. *v.* send message by telegraph; make, convey by, signals. **~ēse'** (-z) *n.* elliptical style used in telegrams. **tĕlĕgrăph'ic** *a.*; **tĕlĕ'graphist** *n.* **tĕlĕg'raphў** *n.* communication by telegraph; *wireless* **~** : see **wireless**.

tĕl'ĕmărk *n.* swing turn in skiing

used to change direction or stop short.

tĕl'ĕmēter *n.* device for measuring and recording at a distance physical quantities. *v.t.* measure and record by telemetry. **telĕm'ĕtrў** *n.*

tĕlĕŏl'ogў *n.* doctrine of final causes, view that events etc. are due to purpose or design they serve. **~lŏ'gĭc(al)** *aa.*; **~logĭst** *n.*

tĕlĕp'athў *n.* communication of impressions from mind to mind without aid of senses. **~păth'ĭc** *a.*; **~pathĭst** *n.*; **~pathīze** *v.*

tĕl'ĕphōne *n.* instrument for transmitting speech etc. to a distance; system of communication by network of telephones. *v.* send message, speak, by telephone. **~ exchange**, office or central station of telephone system where connexion between various lines is effected. **tĕlĕphō'nĭc** *a.* **tĕlĕph'onĭst**-*n.* telephone operator. **tĕlĕph'onў** *n.*

tĕlĕphō'tō *a.* telephotographic; **~** *lens*, lens, combination of lenses, for photographing distant objects. **~graph** (-ahf) *n.* & *v.t.* photograph (made) with telephoto lens. **~gráph'ĭc** *a.* **tĕlĕphotŏg'raphў** *n.* photography of objects at a distance with telephoto lens.

tĕl'ĕscōpe *n.* optical instrument of tube(s) with arrangement of lenses or mirror(s) for making distant objects appear nearer and larger. *v.* force or drive, be forced, one into another like sliding-tubes of hand--telescope; close, slide together, in this way. **tĕlĕscŏp'ic** *a.* of, made with, telescope; consisting of sections that telescope; **~pic sight**, small telescope used as sight for firearm etc. **tĕlĕs'copў** *n.*

tĕl'ĕvision *n.* simultaneous visual reproduction of scenes, performances, etc. at a distance; apparatus for reception of televised images; televised programme(s) or matter. **tĕl'ĕvīse** (-z) *v.t.* transmit by television.

tĕl'fer *n.* telpher.

tĕll *v.* (*tōld*), relate or narrate; utter or express in words; inform, give information, *of* etc.; divulge, reveal; betray secret; ascertain, decide about, distinguish; instruct, order, (*to* do etc.); be of account or weight, produce impression or (marked) effect (*on*); (arch.) count; *all told*, altogether, including all; ~ one's *beads*, use rosary; ~ peron's *fortune*, forecast his future by occult means; ~ *fortunes*, be fortune-teller; ~ *off*, number (party etc.), pick out, *for* task etc. or *to* do, (sl.) rebuke, scold; ~ *tales* (*out of school*), reveal another's secrets, private affairs, misconduct, etc. ~**tale**, one who tells tales; thing, circumstance, revealing person's thoughts, conduct, etc. (esp. attrib.); kinds of automatic registering device; (naut.) index near wheel to show position of tiller. **tĕll'er** *n.* (esp.) person appointed to count votes, esp. one of two for each side counting votes in House of Commons etc.; person appointed to receive or pay out money in bank etc. **tĕl'-ling** *a.* (esp.) effective, impressive.

tĕllūr'ĭan *a.* & *n.* (inhabitant) of Earth.

tĕllūr'ĭum *n.* rare brittle lustrous silver-white non-metallic element. **tellūr'ic** *a.*

tĕll'ў *n.* (sl.) television.

tĕl'pher *n.* automatic esp. electrically--driven unit carrying goods etc. and travelling on overhead cable etc. ~**age** *n.*

tĕmerār'ĭous *a.* rash, reckless.

tĕmĕ'rĭtў *n.* rashness, audacity.

tĕmp. abbr., tempore [L], in the time of.

tĕm'per *v.t.* bring (clay etc.) to proper consistency by kneading etc.; toughen and harden (metal, glass) by heating, sudden cooling, and reheating; modify, mitigate, esp. by blending *with* another quality etc. *n.* consistency, degree of hardness, etc. obtained or produced by tempering; habitual or temporary disposition of mind; fit of anger; composure under provocation; *lose* one's ~, become angry.

tĕm'pera *n.* painting with colours mixed with natural or artificial emulsion.

tĕm'perament *n.* characteristic combination of physical, mental and moral qualities constituting per-

son's character; emotional character of artist etc.; (mus.) adjustment of tones of scale in fixed-tone instruments to adapt it for use in all keys. ~**mĕn'tal** *a.*

tĕm'perance *n.* moderation, self-restraint, esp. in eating and drinking; moderation in use of, total abstinence from, alcoholic beverages. *a.* non-alcoholic, aimed at restriction or prohibition of alcoholic drinks.

tĕm'perate *a.* moderate, self-restrained; (of climate) not exhibiting extremes of heat or cold.

tĕm'perature *n.* degree or intensity of heat of body or atmosphere, esp. as shown by thermometer; internal heat of body, abnormally high degree of this.

tĕm'pĕst *n.* violent storm; violent tumult or agitation. **tĕmpĕs'tūous** *a.* stormy, turbulent.

Tĕm'plar *n.* member of medieval military religious order (*Knights* ~*s*); occupant of chambers in Temple in London.

tĕm'plāte *n.* pattern, usu. thin board or plate, used as guide in cutting or drilling metal, stone, etc.; timber or plate used to distribute weight in wall, under beam, etc.

tĕm'ple[1] *n.* edifice dedicated to service of god; religious edifice of Jews in Jerusalem; place of Christian worship, esp. Protestant church in France; *T*~, two Inns of Court on former Templars' site in London.

tĕm'ple[2] *n.* flat part of side of head between forehead and ear.

tĕm'pō *n.* (mus.) speed or time of passage etc.; rate of movement, activity, etc.

tĕm'poral *a.* of or in or denoting time; (gram.) of time or tense; of this life only, secular, lay; of the temples.

tĕmporăl'itў *n.* (esp., pl.) secular possessions of religious body or ecclesiastic.

tĕm'porarў *a.* lasting or meant to last only for a time; held or occupied during limited time only, not permanent.

tĕm'porīze *v.i.* avoid committing oneself, act so as to gain time;

comply temporarily with requirements of occasion. ~izā'tion *n*.

tĕmpt *v.t.* entice, incite; allure, attract; (arch.) test or try resolution of. ~ā'tion *n*. tempting or being tempted; thing that attracts. ~er, ~rèss *nn.* tĕmp'ting *a*. alluring, attractive.

tĕn *a*. & *n*. one more than nine (10, X). ~pins, game like ninepins played with ten 'pins'. ~fold *a*. & *adv.*; tĕnth *a*. & *n*.; tĕnth'lў *adv*.

tĕn'able *a*. that can be maintained against attack or objection; that can be held *for* period, *by* person, etc. ~ bĭl'itў *n*.

tĕn'ace *n*. (whist etc.) (holding of) cards next above and next below opponents' highest of suit.

tĕnā'cious *a*. holding fast; keeping firm hold (*of*); retentive; adhesive; strongly cohesive. tĕnă'citў *n*.

tĕn'ancў *n*. (period of) holding property as tenant; property, land, etc. held by tenant.

tĕn'ant *n*. person who rents land or house from landlord; (law) person holding real property by private ownership; inhabitant, dweller. *v.t.* occupy as tenant. ~rў *n*. tenants.

tĕnch *n*. fresh-water fish of carp family.

tĕnd¹ *v.i.* move, be directed, in certain direction; be apt or inclined, conduce (*to*).

tĕnd² *v.t.* take care of, look after.

tĕn'dencў *n*. bent, leaning, inclination.

tĕndĕn'tious *a*. calculated to advance a cause, having underlying purpose.

tĕn'der¹ *v*. offer, hand in, present; offer as payment; make tender (*for*). *n*. offer, esp. to execute work or supply goods at fixed price; *legal* ~, currency legally recognized as acceptable in payment of debt.

tĕn'der² *n*. (esp.) vessel attending larger one to supply stores, convey orders, etc.; truck attached to locomotive and carrying fuel, water, etc.

tĕn'der³ *a*. not tough or hard; easily touched or wounded; delicate, fragile; solicitous, considerate; loving, affectionate. ~foot, (sl.)

newcomer in camp, settlement, etc., novice. ~loin, middle part of loin of pork; undercut of sirloin.

tĕn'don *n*. tough fibrous tissue connecting muscle to some other part. tĕn'dĭnous *a*.

tĕn'drĭl *n*. slender thread-like freq. spiral organ or appendage of some climbing plants by which they cling to support.

tĕn'ément *n*. dwelling-house; portion of house tenanted as separate dwelling; (law) property held of superior.

tĕn'ét *n*. belief, doctrine, of person, school, etc.

Tenn. *abbr.* Tennessee.

tĕnn'er *n*. (colloq.) £10 note.

tĕnn'ĭs *n*. ball-game played with rackets in walled court with net; lawn-tennis.

tĕn'on *n*. projection on end or side of piece of wood etc. fitting into mortise etc. *v.t.* cut into, join by means of, tenon. ~-saw, saw with thin blade, strong brass or steel back, and small teeth.

tĕn'or *n*. prevailing course or direction; general purport; (mus.) (music for, singer with) high adult male voice.

tĕnse¹ *n*. any form or modification in conjugation of verb indicating time etc. of action or state denoted by it.

tĕnse² *a*. stretched tight; strained or highly strung.

tĕn'sĭle *a*. of tension; capable of being drawn out or stretched.

tĕn'sion *n*. stretching, being stretched; tenseness; strained state; effect produced by forces pulling against each other; (electr.) voltage.

tĕn'sor *n*. (anat.) muscle that tightens or stretches part.

tĕnt *n*. portable shelter or dwelling of canvas etc.

tĕn'tacle *n*. slender flexible process in esp. invertebrate animals serving as organ of touch or attachment.

tĕn'tative *a*. done by way of trial, experimental. *n*. tentative proposal or step.

tĕn'terhooks *n.pl.* hooks on which cloth is fastened for setting or drying; *on* ~, in suspense, distracted by uncertainty.

tĕn'ūous *a.* thin, slender; subtle, over-refined. **tĕnū'itў** *n.*

tĕn'ure (-y*er*) *n.* (conditions or period of) holding *of* property or office.

tē'pee *n.* wigwam.

tĕp'ĭd *a.* slightly warm, lukewarm. **tĕpĭd'itў** *n.*

tĕratŏl'ogў *n.* study of monstrosities or abnormal formations, esp. in man. ~**lŏ'gĭcal** *a.*

tĕr'bĭum *n.* metallic element of rare--earth group.

tĕr'cel, tier'cel *n.* male falcon.

tĕrcĕntē'narў *a.* of 300 years. *n.* 300th anniversary. **tĕrcentĕnn'ĭal** *a.* & *n.* tercentenary.

tĕ'rĕbĭnth *n.* small S. European turpentine-yielding tree. **tĕrĕbĭn'-thĭne** *a.* of terebinth; of turpentine.

tĕrgĭvĕrsā'tion *n.* desertion of party or principles; shuffling, evasion.

tĕrm *n.* limited period; each period appointed for sitting of court of law, instruction and study in school, etc.; (math.) each of quantities composing ratio or fraction, forming series or progression, connected by signs of addition or subtraction, etc.; (pl.) stipulations made, conditions offered or accepted, payment offered or asked, footing or relation between parties; word or phrase considered as name or symbol of something; (pl.) language, mode of expression; figure, post, etc. marking boundary; ~*s of reference*, terms defining scope of inquiry, action, etc. *v.t.* denominate, call.

tĕr'magant *n.* virago, scold.

tĕr'mĭnable *a.* that may be terminated esp. after definite period.

tĕr'mĭnal *a.* of, forming, situated at, etc. limit, terminus, end, or extremity; of, lasting for, occurring in each, term. *n.* terminating thing, extremity, esp. each of free ends of open electric circuit; terminus.

tĕr'mĭnāte *v.* bring or come to an end; end *at, in*, etc. ~**ā'tion** *n.* (esp.) final syllable or letter(s) of word, ending, suffix.

tĕrmĭnŏl'ogў *n.* system of terms in science or subject; technical terms collectively. ~**lŏ'gĭcal** *a.*

tĕr'mĭnus *n.* (pl. *-uses*, *-ī*), (station at) end of railway line, bus-route, etc.; point to which motion or action tends.

tĕr'mĭte *n.* social insect destructive to timber. ~**mĭt'ĭc** *a.*

tĕrn *n.* kinds of sea-bird with long pointed wings and forked tail.

tĕr'narў *a.* of, in, set(s) of three; of three parts or elements.

Tĕrpsĭchorē'an (-k*o*-) *a.* of dancing.

tĕ'rrace *n.* raised level place, esp. in front of building on sloping ground; natural or artificial shelf in hillside etc.; row of houses built into one block.

tĕrracŏtt'a *n.* (brownish-red colour of) fine hard unglazed pottery. *a.* of, made of, of colour of, terracotta.

tĕ'rra fĭr'ma *n.* dry land.

tĕrrain' *n.* tract of country considered with regard to natural features, tactical advantages, etc.

tĕ'rra ĭncŏg'nĭta *n.* unknown or unexplored region. [L]

tĕ'rrapĭn *n.* kinds of N. Amer. edible turtle of fresh or brackish water.

tĕrrēne' *a.* of earth, earthy.

tĕrrĕs'trĭal *a.* of earth, of this world; of land as opp. to water.

tĕ'rrĭble *a.* exciting, fitted to excite, terror; grievous; (colloq.) very great or bad; excessive.

tĕ'rrĭer *n.* kinds of usu. small active hardy dog; (colloq.) member of Territorial Army.

tĕrrĭf'ĭc *a.* causing great terror; of tremendous intensity; violently impressive; (colloq.) very great, good, admirable, etc.

tĕ'rrĭfў *v.t.* fill with terror, frighten.

tĕ'rrĭne (-ēn; *or* -ēn') *n.* earthenware vessel for pâté de foie gras or other table delicacy; dish cooked or served in terrine.

tĕrrĭtōr'ĭal *a.* of territory; of particular territory or locality. *n.* member of Territorial Army. **T~ Army**, (hist.) military force of volunteers living at home and doing occasional periods of drill and other training. **~ waters**, waters, esp. parts of sea within minimum of three miles from low-water-mark, over which State claims jurisdiction.

tĕ′rrĭtorў *n*. land under jurisdiction of sovereign, State, etc.; (large) tract of land, region; area over which commercial traveller etc. operates; area defended, claimed, dominated, etc. by animal, side in game, etc.; sphere, realm, province; portion of country not yet admitted to full rights of State or Province.

tĕ′rror *n*. extreme fear; terrifying person or thing; (colloq.) exasperating, troublesome, or tiresome person, esp. child. **tĕ′rrorĭsm** *n*. policy or system of ruling, seeking to obtain political demands, etc. by violence and intimidation. **~ĭst** *n*. & *a*.; **~ĭs′tĭc** *a*. **tĕ′rrorīze** *v*. fill with terror; rule or maintain power by terrorism. **~īzā′tion** *n*.

tĕ′rrў *n*. & *a*. (pile-fabric) with loops left uncut.

tĕrse *a*. concise, curt; brief and forcible in style.

tĕr′tian *a*. & *n*. (fever, disease) with paroxysm recurring every other day.

tĕr′tiarў (-sha-) *a*. of third degree, order, class, etc.; of third great geological period, of rock-formations above Mesozoic; of third or last stage of syphilis. *n*. tertiary rock, period, etc.

tĕr′tium quĭd (-shĭ-) *n*. something (undefined) related to two (definite or known) things. [L]

tĕss′ĕllāte *v.t*. make (esp. pavement) of, pave with, small coloured blocks of marble, tile, etc. arranged in pattern. **~lā′tion** *n*.

tĕst *n*. (means of) critical examination or trial of qualities or nature of person or thing; standard, suitable circumstances, for comparison or trial; examination esp. in school etc. on limited subject, work done during limited period, etc. *v.t*. subject to test, make trial of; try severely, tax. **~-case**, case in which decision is taken as settling number of similar cases. **~ match**, (esp., crick.) one of series of games between representative sides as test of superiority. **~-pilot**, one who pilots aircraft on experimental

flights. **~-tube**, tube of thin glass closed at one end used to hold substance undergoing chemical tests etc.

tĕstā′cean *n*. shell-bearing mollusc etc.

tĕstā′ceous *a*. having esp. hard shell; of shells, shelly.

tĕs′tacў *n*. being testate.

tĕs′tament *n*. will; (colloq.) (written) statement, affirmation, of (political) beliefs, principles, etc.; *Old, New, T~*, main divisions of Bible; (colloq.) New Testament. **tĕstamĕn′tary** *a*. of (nature of), relating to, will or testament.

tĕs′tāte *a*. & *n*. (person) having left valid will.

tĕstā′tor, tĕstā′trĭx *nn*. man, woman, who makes or has died leaving a will.

tĕs′ter *n*. canopy esp. over bed.

testes, pl. of **testis.**

tĕs′tĭcle *n*. male organ in which gametes are produced; in man, each of two glandular sperm-forming bodies enclosed in scrotum.

tĕs′tĭfỹ *v*. bear witness; give evidence; affirm, declare, be evidence of.

tĕstĭmō′nial *n*. certificate or formal statement of character, conduct, or qualifications; gift presented as mark of esteem, in acknowledgement of services, etc.

tĕs′tĭmonў *n*. evidence, esp. statement made under oath or affirmation.

tĕs′tĭs *n*. (pl. -*tēs*), testicle.

tĕs′tў *a*. irascible, touchy.

tĕt′anus *n*. disease with tonic spasm and rigidity of voluntary muscles.

tĕtch′ў *a*. peevish, irritable.

tête-à-tête (tāt′atāt′) *n*. & *a*. (of) private conversation or interview between two persons. *adv*. in private, without presence of third person.

tĕth′er (-dh-) *n*. rope etc. by which grazing animal is confined; *end of one's ~*, extreme limit of one's resources of strength, patience, etc. *v.t*. fasten with tether.

tĕt′ra- in comb., four. **tĕt′rachŏrd** (-k-) *n*. series of four notes with interval of perfect fourth between lowest and highest. ~**gon** *n.* figure with four angles and four sides; **tetrăg'onal** *a.* ~**hē'dron** *n.* solid figure bounded by four plane triangles; triangular pyramid; ~hē'dral *a.* **tetrăl'ogў** *n.* set of four connected operas, plays, etc. **tetrăm'eter** *n.* verse of four feet.

tĕt'rad *n.* the number four; set or group of four.

tĕt'rarch (-k) *n.* (in Rom. Empire) governor of fourth part of country or province, subordinate ruler. ~**ate,** ~**ў** *nn.*

tĕtt'er *n.* (arch.) pustular skin--eruption.

Teutŏn'ic *a.* of Germans or ancient Teutons; of Germanic group of Indo-European languages.

tĕxt *n.* wording of anything written or printed, esp. opp. to translation, commentary, etc.; passage esp. of Scripture chosen as subject of sermon etc.; subject, theme; ~ (-*hand*), fine large kind of handwriting; sentence from Scripture. ~**book,** manual of instruction in any branch of study, work recognized as authority; (pl.) books prescribed for study. **tĕx'tūal** *a.* of or in text.

tĕx'tīle *a.* of weaving; woven, suitable for weaving. *n.* textile fabric or material.

tĕx'ture *n.* character of textile fabric resulting from way it is woven; structure, constitution; (representation in art etc. of) character of surface. **tĕx'tural** *a.*

thalĭd'omīde *n.* kind of tranquillizing drug. ~ **baby,** child born with malformation of limbs resulting from mother's use of thalidomide during pregnancy.

thăll'ĭum *n.* soft bluish-white metallic element.

than (dh*a*n) *conj.* introducing second member of comparison.

thāne *n.* (hist.) one holding land by military service, with rank between ordinary freemen and hereditary nobles or (Sc.) of earl's son.

thănk *v.t.* express gratitude to; ~ *you,* polite formula of gratitude etc. ~**s** *n.pl.* (expression of) gratitude; thank you; ~**s** *to,* owing to,

as result of. ~**-offering,** offering made as expression of gratitude to God. ~**sgiving,** expression of gratitude, esp. to God; *T~sgiving* (*Day*), U.S. annual festival and legal holiday on fourth Thursday of November. **thănk'ful** *a.* grateful; expressive of thanks. **thănk'less** *a.* not feeling or expressing gratitude; not likely to win thanks, unprofitable.

thăt (dh-) *dem. a.* & *pron.* (pl. *thōse,* pr. -z), the; the person or thing referred to, observed, understood, in question, etc., esp. the farther, less immediate or obvious, etc. of two; *and all* ~, and so forth; *at* ~, too, besides, at that standard, (even) in that capacity; ~ *is* (*to say*), in other words, or more correctly or intelligibly. *rel. pron.* (dh*a*t), introducing defining clause (regarded as) essential to identification, and now largely replaced by *who, which. conj.* (dh*a*t), introducing dependent clause, esp. expressing result or consequence. *adv.* (dhăt), (colloq.) so; ~ *far,* ~ *much,* as far, as much, as that.

thătch *n.* roof-covering of straw, reeds, etc. *v.t.* roof or cover with thatch; make (roof) of thatch.

thau'matūrge *n.* worker of miracles, wonder-worker. ~**tūr'gic(al)** *aa.;* ~**tūrgў** *n.*

thaw *v.* unfreeze, become unfrozen, become or make liquid, flexible, or limp by raising or rise of temperature; free, be freed, from coldness or stiffness, (cause to) unbend or become genial. *n.* thawing; melting of ice and snow after frost; warmth of weather that thaws.

the (*before vowel* dhĭ, *before consonant* dh*e, emphatic* dhē) *a.* 'definite article', applied esp. to person(s) or thing(s) already mentioned, under discussion, existent, unique, familiar, etc.; to singular nouns as repr. class etc.; with adjs. used abs.; emphatically to person or thing best known or best entitled to the name. *adv.* in that degree, by that amount; *the . . . the,* by how much . . . by so much.

the'atre *n.* building for dramatic spectacles, playhouse; room, hall, for lectures etc. with seats in tiers; scene, field of operation; operating--theatre; dramatic literature or art. **theăt'rical** *a.* of or suited to theatre; of acting or actors; calculated for effect, showy, affected, assumed, artificial. ~**rǐcăl'itў** *n.* **theăt'ricals** *n.pl.* (esp. amateur) theatrical performances.

thee (dh-) *pron.,* obj. case of *thou.*

theft *n.* stealing.

their (dhār) *pron. & a.,* poss. case of *they* and corresponding adj., with abs. form *theirs.*

the'ism *n.* belief in god(s), esp. in one God as creator and supreme ruler of universe. **the'ist** *n.;* **theis'tic(al)** *aa.*

them (dh-) *pron.,* obj. case of *they.*

theme *n.* subject of discourse, conversation, composition, etc.; school essay, exercise in translation; (mus.) tune on which variations are constructed; (gram.) inflexional base or stem of word. ~ **song** etc., recurrent melody in musical play, film, etc. **themăt'ic** *a.* of, belonging to, constituting, theme.

themselves' (dh-, -vz) *pron.,* emphat. and refl. form of *they.*

then (dh-) *adv.* at that time; after that, next; *now and* ~, at one time and another, from time to time. *conj.* in that case; therefore; it follows that; accordingly. *n.* that time. *a.* then-existing.

thence (dh-) *adv.* from there; from that. ~**forth,** ~**forward** *advv.* from that time forward.

the'o- in comb., God-, of god(s). **theocĕn'tric** *a.* having God as its centre. **theŏc'racў** *n.* government, State governed, by God directly or through priestly class etc.; ~**crăt** *n.,* ~**crăt'ic** *a.* **theŏg'onў** *n.* (poem etc. dealing with) genealogy of gods. ~**mŏr'phic** *a.* having form of a god. **theŏph'anў** *n.* manifestation of God or a god; Epiphany.

theŏd'olīte *n.* surveying instrument for measuring angles.

theŏl'ogў *n.* science of religion, study of God or god(s). **theolō'gian** *n.;* ~**lŏ'gical** *a.*

theŏr'bō *n.* (pl. -os), (hist.) large double-necked lute.

the'orĕm *n.* universal or general proposition, not self-evident but demonstrable by chain of reasoning.

theorĕt'ic(al) *aa.* of, relating or conforming to, consisting in, theory; existing only in theory, hypothetical; speculative.

the'orў *n.* scheme or system of ideas etc. held to explain observed facts etc.; (formulation of) abstract knowledge; systematic statement of general principles; (knowledge of) principles or methods of art, technical subject, etc., opp. *practice;* mere hypothesis, conjecture, individual view or notion. **the'orist** *n.;* **the'orīze** *v.*

theŏs'ophў *n.* philosophy professing to attain to knowledge of God by direct intuition, spiritual ecstasy, etc. **theosŏph'ic(al)** *aa.;* ~**opher,** ~**ophist** *nn.*

therapeu'tic(al) *aa.* of healing of disease, curative. **therapeu'tics** *n.pl.* branch of medicine concerned with remedial treatment of disease. **the'rapў** *n.* curative treatment.

there (dhār) *adv.* in or at that place; yonder; at that point; to that place or point. *n.* that place or point. *int.* drawing attention to anything. ~**about(s),** near that place or amount or time. ~**after,** thenceforward. ~**at,** (arch.) at that; at that place; on that account. ~**by,** (arch.) by that means or agency. ~**fore,** for that reason; accordingly, consequently. ~**in,** (arch.) in it or them; in that respect. ~**of,** (arch.) of that, of it. ~**upon,** in consequence of that, directly after that. ~**with,** (arch.) with it; thereupon.

therm *n.* unit of heat, esp. 100,000 B.Th.U. as basis of charge for coal-gas etc.

ther'mal *a.* of heat; determined, measured, operated, by heat. *n.* ascending current caused by local heating of air. ~ **springs,** hot springs. ~ **unit,** unit of heat; *British* ~ *unit,* heat required to raise temperature of one pound of water by one degree F.

thĕr'mion (*or* -ī-) *n.* electrically charged particle emitted by incandescent body. ~ŏn'ic *a.* of, emitting, thermions; ~onic valve, vacuum tube in which electrons are emitted from heated electrodes. ~ŏn'ics *n.pl.* branch of physics treating of thermionic phenomena etc.

thĕr'mīte *n.* mixture of powdered aluminium and iron oxide producing very high temperature on combustion.

thĕr'mō- in comb., heat-, thermoelectric. thĕrmochĕm'istrў (-k-) *n.* branch of chemistry dealing with relations between heat and chemical reactions; ~chĕm'ical *a.* ~couple (-kŭpl) *n.* thermoelectric device for measuring difference of temperature. ~dўnăm'ics *n.* science dealing with relationship between heat and all other forms of energy; ~dўnăm'ic *a.* ~ėlĕctri'citў *n.* electricity produced by action of heat at junction of two different metals; ~ėlĕc'tric *a.* ~gĕn'ėsis *n.* generation of heat in animal body. ~nū'clĕar *a.* of nuclear fusion, which requires temperatures of order generated by nuclear fission for its inception; ~nuclear bomb, hydrogen bomb. ~plăs'tic *a.* & *n.* (substance) becoming soft and plastic when heated. ~sĕtting *a.* becoming permanently hard and rigid when heated. ~stăt *n.* device for automatically maintaining constant temperature; ~stăt'ic *a.*

thermŏm'ėter *n.* instrument for measuring temperature, usu. by expansion of mercury, alcohol, etc. in sealed and graduated glass tube. thĕrmomĕt'ric(al) *aa.*; thermŏm'ėtrў *n.*

thĕr'mŏs *n.* vacuum flask. P.

thėsaur'us *n.* (pl. -rī), storehouse of information etc., esp. dictionary of synonyms etc.

these : see this.

thē'sis *n.* (pl. *theses*, pr. -ēz), proposition laid down or stated, esp. as theme to be discussed and proved; dissertation maintaining thesis esp. submitted by candidate for university degree.

Thĕs'pian *a.* of tragedy or dramatic art. *n.* actor or actress.

Thess. *abbr.* Thessalonians.

thews (-z) *n.pl.* sinews, muscles.

they (dhā) *pron.* (obj. *them*, poss. *their*), serving as pl. of *he, she, it.*

thick *a.* of considerable or specified thickness; (of line etc.) broad, not fine; made of thick material; closely set; numerous; crowded; abounding, packed, *with*; dense, viscid, stiff; turbid, muddy, not clear; dull, stupid; (of voice) muffled, indistinct; (colloq.) intimate; (sl.) going beyond what is reasonable, too much to tolerate. *n.* thick part of anything, esp. fight etc.; *through* ~ *and thin,* under all conditions, in spite of all opposition or difficulty. *adv.* thickly. ~-headed, stupid, slow-witted. ~set, set or growing close together; having stout limbs and sturdy frame. ~-skinned, not sensitive to criticism or rebuff. thick'en *v.* make or become thicker; make of stiffer consistence. thick'ish *a.* thick'nėss *n.* dimension other than length and breadth; being thick; layer.

thick'ėt *n.* dense growth of small trees, shrubs, etc.

thief *n.* (pl. -*ves*), one who steals, esp. secretly and without violence.

thieve *v.* be thief, practise stealing; steal. thie'verў *n.*; thie'vish *a.*

thigh *n.* upper part of human leg, from hip to knee.

thim'ble *n.* cap of metal etc. worn on end of finger to push needle in sewing. ~rigging, swindling game of betting which of three thimble-shaped cups covers a pea; trickery, dishonesty, swindle. ~ful *n.* very small quantity to drink.

thin *a.* of little thickness; (of line etc.) narrow, fine; of small diameter; slender; lean, spare, not plump; wanting body, fullness, volume, or substance; (of infusions etc.) weak; not crowded or numerous; (of excuse etc.) transparent, flimsy; (colloq.) wretched and uncomfortable *time. v.* make or become thin; reduce, be reduced, in bulk or number; ~ *out,* reduce number of.

adv. thinly. **~-skinned,** sensitive. **thin′ness** *n.*; **thinn′ish** *a.*

thine (dh-) *poss. pron.* & *a.* belonging to thee; what is thine.

thing *n.* what is or may be object of perception, knowledge, or thought; inanimate object; person or animal regarded in pity or contempt or affection; what is (to be) done, deed, occurrence; what is said; possession; (pl.) clothes, esp. outdoor garments; (pl.) implements, utensils; (pl.) affairs, concerns, matters. **thing′amy, ~amijig, thing′um(a)bŏb, thing′ummy** *nn.* (colloq.) person or thing whose name one forgets or does not wish to use.

think *v.* (*thought,* pr. -awt), consider, be of opinion; form conception of; exercise mind in active way, form connected ideas; reflect; conceive notion of doing, contemplate; **~** *about,* consider; **~** *of,* consider, imagine, intend, contemplate, entertain idea of, hit upon; **~** *out,* consider carefully, devise; **~** *over,* reflect upon. **think′er** *n.* (esp.) person of philosophic mind. **think′ing** *a.* (esp.) reflective; given to independent thought; rational.

third *a.* next after second. *n.* one of three equal divisions of whole; third thing, place, class, etc.; (mus.) interval between note and next but one in scale. **~ degree,** severe examination or interrogation esp. of prisoner to extort confession or information. **~ man,** (crick.) fielder between point and short slip. **~ party,** party in case other than two principals. **~-party insurance, risk,** insurance against, risk of, injury or damage sustained by person other than insured. **~-rate,** inferior, decidedly poor, in quality.

thirst *n.* uneasy or painful sensation caused by want of drink; desire for drink; ardent desire, craving (*for* fame, battle, etc.). *v.i.* feel thirst. **thirs′ty** *a.* feeling thirst; parched, arid; (colloq.) causing thirst; eager, greedy.

thirteen′ *a.* & *n.* one more than twelve (13, XIII). **~th** *a.* & *n.*

thir′ty *a.* & *n.* three times ten (30,

XXX). **~-two-mo, 32mo,** (size of) book with sheets folded into 32 leaves. **thir′tieth** *a.* & *n.*

this (dh-) *a.* & *pron.* (pl. *thēse,* pr. -z), the (person or thing) near, present, just mentioned.

thist′le (-sl) *n.* kinds of plant with stems, leaves, etc. thickly armed with prickles; Scottish national emblem and order of knighthood. **~down,** down by which 'seeds' of thistle are carried along by wind. **this′tly** (-sli) *a.*

thith′er (dhidh-) *adv.* (arch.) to that place.

thōle *n.* pin in gunwale of boat as fulcrum for oar; each of two such pins between which oar plays.

Thō′mism (t-) *n.* system of theology etc. of St. Thomas Aquinas. **~ist** *n.*

thŏng *n.* narrow strip of hide or leather used as lace, lash, etc. *v.t.* furnish with thong.

thōr′ax *n.* part of trunk between neck and abdomen. **thorǎ′cic** *a.*

thōr′ium *n.* radio-active metallic element.

thōrn *n.* stiff sharp-pointed process on plant; kinds of thorny plant, esp. hawthorn. **~less** *a.* **thōr′ny** *a.* (esp.) difficult to handle, ticklish, delicate.

thorough (thŭ′ro) *a.* complete, unqualified, not superficial, out-and-out. **~ bass,** figured bass. **~bred,** (animal, esp. horse) of pure breed; (person) with qualities associated with thoroughbred animal. **~fare,** public way open at both ends, esp. main road. **~-going,** extreme, thorough, out-and-out. **~-paced,** (fig.) complete, unqualified.

thōrp(e) *n.* (hist.) small village.

Thos. *abbr.* Thomas.

those : see **that.**

thou (dh-) *pron.* (obj. *thee,* poss. *thine* and *thy*), of 2nd pers. sing., now arch. or poet.

though (dhō) *conj.* in spite of the fact that; even if, granting that; *as* **~,** as if. *adv.* (colloq.) and yet, but yet, all the same, none the less.

thought[1], *p.t.* & *p.p.* of **think.**

thought[2] (-awt) *n.* process, power, faculty, etc. of thinking; what one thinks, what is or has been thought; idea, notion; consideration, heed;

meditation; intention, purpose. **~-reader, -reading,** (person capable of) direct perception of another's thoughts. **~-transference,** telepathy. **~ful** *a.* engaged in, given to, meditation; showing thought or consideration; considerate, kindly. **~less** *a.* unthinking, heedless, imprudent; inconsiderate.

thous'and (-z-) *a. & n.* ten hundred (1000, M); many. **~-and-one,** myriad, numberless. **~fold** *a. & adv.*; **~th** *a. & n.*

thrall (-awl) *n.* slave; bondage. **thral'dom** *n.*

thrăsh *v.t.* beat, esp. with stick or whip; conquer, surpass; thresh; **~** *out,* discuss exhaustively, argue thoroughly.

thread (-ĕd) *n.* length of spun and usu. twisted fibres or filaments of flax, silk, glass, etc.; thread-shaped or thread-like thing, esp. what connects successive points in narrative, train of thought, etc.; continuous or persistent feature running through pattern; spiral ridge of screw. *v.t.* pass thread through eye of (needle); string (beads etc.) on thread, make (necklace etc.) thus; pick one's *way* through street, crowded place, etc. **~bare,** with nap worn off and threads showing; shabby, seedy; commonplace, hackneyed.

threat (-ĕt) *n.* declaration of intention to punish or hurt; indication of coming evil. **threat'en** *v.* use threats (against); try to influence by threats; utter or use threat of; be source of danger to; presage, portend.

three *a. & n.* one more than two (3, III). **~-cornered,** having three angles or corners; (of contest etc.) between three persons. **~-decker,** ship with three decks; pulpit with three levels; (sandwich) with four slices of bread etc. and three layers of filling; novel in three volumes. **~-dimensional,** (producing effect or illusion of) having length, breadth, and height; realistic. **~halfpence,** 1½*d.* **~-handed,** (of games) played by three persons. **~-lane,** marked or designed for three lines of traffic.

~-legged, (of race) run by pairs with right leg of one tied to left leg of the other. **~-mile limit,** limit of zone of territorial waters extending three miles from coast. **~pence** (-rĕp- *or* -rĭp- *or* -rŭp-), 3*d.* **~penny,** worth or costing 3*d.*; **~penny bit,** coin worth 3*d.* **~-ply,** (yarn etc.) having, woven with, three strands; (plywood) of three layers. **~-point,** (of aircraft's landing) with landing--wheels or floats and tail-skid or -wheel touching surface simultaneously; (of motor-vehicle's turn) completed in two forward and one reverse movement. **~-quarter,** (Rugby footb. etc.) player with position between half-back and full--back. **~score,** sixty. **~some,** game esp. of golf played by three persons; party etc. of three persons. **~fold** *a. & adv.*

thrĕn'odў (*or* -ē-) *n.* song of lamentation.

thrĕsh *v.* beat out or separate grain from husks of corn etc.

thrĕsh'ōld *n.* plank or stone forming bottom of doorway; entrance; border, limit, point at which effect begins to be produced, idea enters consciousness, etc.

threw, *p.t.* of **throw.**

thrīce *adv.* three times.

thrĭft *n.* frugality, economical management; kinds of plant, esp. sea-pink. **~less, thrĭf'tў** *aa.*

thrĭll *n.* nervous tremor caused by intense emotion or sensation, wave of feeling or excitement. *v.* (cause to) experience thrill; quiver, throb, (as) with emotion. **thrĭll'er** *n.* (esp.) sensational play, story, etc.

thrīve *v.i.* (*thrōve, thrīven*), prosper; grow vigorously.

throat *n.* front of neck; gullet or windpipe; narrow passage or entrance. **~ў** *a.* guttural, hoarse.

thrŏb *v.i.* (of heart etc.) beat strongly, palpitate, pulsate, vibrate. *n.* throbbing, violent beat or pulsation.

thrōe *n.* (usu. pl.) violent pang(s); desperate or agonizing struggle, anguish.

thrŏmbō'sĭs *n.* localized clotting in heart or bloodvessel.

thrōne *n*. chair of state for sovereign, bishop, etc.; sovereign power; seat for painter's model; *T~s*, third of nine orders of angels. *v.t.* enthrone.

thrŏng *n*. crowd, multitude, esp. in small space. *v.* come, go, press, in multitudes; fill (as) with crowd.

thrŏst′le (-sl) *n*. song-thrush.

thrŏtt′le *n*. throat; valve controlling flow of steam, fuel, etc. in engine. *v.* choke, strangle; ~ (*down*), obstruct flow of steam, fuel, etc. in engine, slow down.

through (-rōō) *prep.* from end to end or side to side of; between sides, walls, parts, etc. of; from beginning to end of; by agency, means, or fault of· by reason of. *adv.* through something; from end to end; to the end; ~ *and* ~, all the way through, completely, utterly; *be, get,* ~, (*with*), finish (with), come to end (of). *a.* going, concerned with going, through; going all the way without change of line, etc. ~-**put**, amount of (raw) material put through process etc. ~**out′** *adv.* in every part or respect; *prep.* from end to end of; in every part of.

throve, p.t. of **thrive**.

throw (-ō) *v.* (*threw* pr. -ōō; *thrown* pr. -ōn), launch (object) into air with some force; use as missile; throw ball etc. with jerking motion of arm; bring to ground; cast (with) dice; put carelessly or hastily *on, off,* etc.; move quickly or suddenly; (sl.) give (party); twist (silk etc.) into thread; turn in lathe, shape (pottery) on wheel; ~ *away*, squander, waste, lose by neglect, discard (card), utter (esp. words in play etc.) extremely casually; ~ *in*, add to bargain without extra charge etc., utter in parenthesis or casually; ~ *in* one's *hand*, give up; ~ *in* one's *lot with*, decide to share fortunes of; ~ *off*, discard, get rid of, abandon (disguise), produce or utter in off-hand manner; ~ *out*, cast out, suggest, insinuate, reject, eject, disturb or distract from train of thought etc.; ~ *over*, desert, abandon; ~ *up*, vomit, resign (office), raise quickly or suddenly; ~ *up the sponge*, give

in, confess oneself beaten. *n.* throwing, cast; fall in wrestling. ~-**away**, printed paper, hand-bill, etc. not intended to be kept. ~-**back**, (example of) reversion to ancestral type or character. ~-**in**, (footb.) throwing in of ball after it has gone out of play.

thrŭm *v.* strum; sound monotonously, hum. *n.* (sound of) thrumming.

thrŭsh[1] *n.* kinds of song-bird.

thrŭsh[2] *n.* throat-disease in children; foot-disease in horses.

thrŭst *v.* (*thrust*), push, exert force of impact on or against; make lunge or stab with weapon; intrude oneself, force *upon*. *n.* stab or lunge; thrusting force of part of structure etc. on contiguous part, esp. horizontal or diagonal pressure against abutment etc.; driving force of propeller-shaft, engine, etc. ~**er** *n.* (esp.) one who rides too close to hounds.

thŭd *n.* & *v.i.* (make, fall with) low dull sound as of blow on soft thing.

thŭg *n.* cut-throat, ruffian; (hist.) Indian professional robber and strangler. **thŭgg′erў** *n.*

thū′lĭum *n.* rare metallic element.

thŭmb (-um) *n.* short thick inner digit, opposable to fingers, of human hand; opposable inner digit of other animals; part of glove covering thumb; *rule of* ~, method or procedure based on practice not theory. *v.t.* soil, wear, with thumb; make request for (lift) by sticking out thumb. ~-**nail** sketch, small or hasty sketch, brief word-picture. ~**screw**, instrument of torture squeezing thumb. ~-**tack**, drawing-pin.

thŭmp *n.* (sound of) heavy blow, bang. *v.* beat heavily, esp. with fist; deliver heavy blows. ~**ing** *a.* (esp., colloq.) very large, striking, impressive.

thŭn′der *n.* loud noise accompanying lightning; any loud deep rumbling or resounding noise; terrifying, threatening, or impressive utterance. *v.* sound with or like thunder; *it* ~*s*, there is thunder; utter, emit, in loud or impressive manner.

fulminate. ~bolt, lightning-flash
regarded as missile or destroying
agency; something very startling,
terrible, or destructive. ~-head,
rounded cumulus cloud near horizon
projecting above general body of
cloud. ~struck, amazed, terrified,
confounded. thun'derous, thŭn'-
derў aa.

thūr'ĭble n. censer.

Thurs. abbr. Thursday.

Thŭr'sday (-zdā or -zdĭ) n. fiftb day
of week.

thŭs (dh-) adv. in this way, like this;
accordingly, and so; to this extent,
number, or degree.

thwăck n. & v.t. whack.

thwart (-ôrt) v.t. frustrate, cross.
n. seat across boat for rower etc.

T.H.W.M. abbr. Trinity high-water
mark.

thy (dhī) poss. pron. & a., poss. case
of thou and corresponding adj.

thyme (tīm) n. kinds of shrubby
herb with fragrant aromatic leaves.
thȳ'mŏl n. phenol obtained from oil
of thyme and used as antiseptic.

thȳr'oid n. (extract prepared from)
large ductless gland lying near
larynx in vertebrates. a. of, connected with, thyroid. ~ cartilage,
large cartilage of larynx forming
Adam's apple. ~ gland, thyroid.

thyr'sus (-êr-) n. (pl. -sī), staff tipped
with pine-cone ornament as attribute of Dionysus.

thȳsĕlf' (dh-) pron., emphat. and
refl. form of thou.

tiâr'a n. Pope's official head-dress of
high pointed cap encircled by three
crowns; papal office; woman's
jewelled coronet.

tĭb'ĭa n. shin-bone.

tĭc n. habitual local spasmodic contraction of muscles, esp. of face.

tĭck[1] n. quick light dry distinct but
not loud recurring sound, esp. of
watch or clock; (colloq.) moment,
instant; small mark (√) set against
items in list etc. in checking.
v. mark (off) with tick; make
ticking sound; wear away etc. in
ticking; ~ off, (sl.) reprimand;
~ over, (of motor engine) run
slowly and quietly out of gear
(also fig.). tĭck'er n. (esp., colloq.)

watch; (joc.) heart; telegraphic
tape-machine.

tĭck[2] n. kinds of large blood-sucking
mite or other parasitic insects.

tĭck[3] n. case of mattress or bolster;
ticking. tĭck'ing n. strong hard
linen or cotton cloth used for
covering mattresses etc.

tĭck[4] n. (colloq.) credit.

tĭck'ĕt n. card or paper securing
admission etc. to holder, or serving
as label or notice; certificate of
qualifications of pilot, ship's mate,
etc.; pawnbrokers' receipt; (U.S.)
list of candidates of one party etc.,
principles of party; the ~, (sl.)
what is wanted, expected, etc. v.t.
put ticket on, label. ~-collector,
railway official taking or checking
passengers' tickets. ~ of leave,
licence giving convict restricted
liberty before expiration of sentence. ~-punch, tool for punching
holes in used tickets.

tĭck'le n. act, sensation, of tickling.
v. touch or stroke lightly so as to
excite nerves and usu. produce
laughter; cause, feel, peculiar
uneasy sensation as of being
tickled; excite agreeably, amuse.
tĭck'lĭsh a. sensitive to tickling;
difficult, critical, delicate.

tĭck'-tăck n., adv. & a. imitation of
ticking sound; of, practising, book-
-makers' system of signalling with
arms etc. at race-meetings.

t.i.d. abbr., ter in die [L], three times
a day.

tī'dal a. of, affected by, resembling,
etc. tides. ~ wave, exceptionally
large ocean wave or very high
water sometimes following earthquake etc.; widespread manifestation of feeling etc.

tĭdd'ler n. (nursery name for) stickle-
back.

tĭdd'lўwĭnks n. game of flipping smáll
counters into receptacle.

tīde n. rise and fall of sea occurring
twice in lunar day; something like
tide in ebbing and flowing etc.;
flood-tide; (arch.) time, season.
v. drift with tide; ~ over, (enable
or assist to) get through time, over
difficulty, etc. ~-mark, mark made
by tide at high water; (colloq.) line

between washed and unwashed parts of body. **~way**, tidal part of river.

ti'dings (-z) *n.pl.* (piece of) news.

ti'dy *a.* neat, orderly; neatly arranged; (colloq.) considerable. *n.* receptacle for odds and ends. *v.t.* make tidy; put in order.

tie *v.* (part. *tying*), attach, fasten with cord etc.; form into knot or bow; tie strings etc. of; bind by crosspiece etc.; (mus.) unite (notes) by tie; restrict, bind; make same score (as), be equal in score *with*; **~** *up*, restrict freedom, use, etc. of, esp. annex conditions to. *n.* necktie; uniting or connecting element or part; (U.S.) railway sleeper; (mus.) curved line over or under two notes indicating that sound is to be sustained; thing that hampers; draw or dead heat or equal score; match between winners of previous contests. **~-beam**, horizontal beam connecting rafters. **~d house**, public-house restricted to dealing with one firm of brewers etc. **~-pin**, ornamental pin worn in necktie. **~-up**, obstructed situation, standstill; link, connexion. **~-wig**, wig with hair tied in knot behind.

tier *n.* row, rank, esp. one of several placed one above another. *v.t.* arrange in tiers.

tierce *n.* (office said at) third hour of canonical day; third position in fencing.

tiff *n.* slight or petty quarrel. *v.i.* have a tiff.

tiff'in *n.* (Anglo-Ind.) light meal, lunch.

ti'ger (-g-) *n.* large striped feline beast of prey; other feline animals, esp. jaguar, puma; fierce, cruel, or rapacious person; formidable opponent in game etc.; (U.S. sl.) loud yell at end of burst of cheering. **~-cat**, kinds of smaller feline animal resembling tiger. **~-lily**, with dark-spotted orange flower. **ti'gerish** (-g-) *a.* like, cruel as, tiger. **ti'gress** *n.* female tiger.

tight *a.* close-textured, firmly constructed, so as to be impervious to fluid etc.; closely drawn, fastened,

fitting, etc.; tense, taut, stretched so as to leave no slack; produced by, requiring, great exertion or pressure; (colloq.) tight-fisted, (of money) difficult to come by, (of situation) difficult to deal with, escape from, etc.; (sl.) drunk. *adv.* tightly. **~ corner, spot**, dangerous or difficult position or situation. **~-fisted**, stingy, close-fisted. **~-laced**, having laces (esp. of stays) drawn tight; strict, strait-laced. **~-rope**, tightly stretched rope etc. on which acrobats etc. perform. **tigh'ten** *v.* **~s** *n.pl.* thin tightly fitting garment covering legs and (lower part of) body.

T.I.H. *abbr.* Their Imperial Highnesses.

til'de (-*e*) *n.* mark (~) placed over palatalized *n* in Spanish and nasalized *a* and *o* in Portuguese.

tile *n.* thin slab of baked clay for covering roof, floor, etc.; tiles collectively; (sl.) hat. *v.t.* cover, line, pave, etc. with tiles.

till[1] *prep.* up to, as late as. *conj.* up to time when; to degree that.

till[2] *n.* money-drawer, box, etc. usu. under and behind counter of bank, shop, etc.

till[3] *v.t.* cultivate (land). **till'age, till'er**[1] *nn.*

till'er[2] *n.* lever by which rudder is turned.

tilt[1] *v.* (cause to) incline abruptly from vertical to horizontal, assume or be in sloping or slanting position, heel over; engage in tilt, thrust or run *at* with lance etc. *n.* combat between two armed horsemen each trying to throw other with lance; (at) *full* **~**, at full speed, with full force or impetus. **~-hammer**, heavy forging hammer alternately tilted up and dropped by action of cam-wheel etc. **~-yard**, enclosed place for tilting.

tilt[2] *n.* awning of cart.

tilth, *n.* tillage, cultivation; cultivated soil.

Tim. *abbr.* Timothy.

tim'ber *n.* wood as material for building or carpentry; piece of wood, beam, esp. (naut.) rib of vessel; large standing trees; *stand-*

ing ~, trees, woods. *v.t.* support (sides and roof of tunnel etc.) with timber. ~-**wolf**, large grey wolf of northern N.America. **tim′bered** (-*er*d) *a.* made (partly) of wood; wooded.

timbre (tăm′b*er*) *n.* characteristic quality of musical or vocal sound depending on voice or instrument producing it.

tim′brel *n.* (bibl.) tambourine.

time *n.* indefinite continuous duration regarded as dimension; finite duration as dist. from eternity; more or less definite portion of this, historical or other period; (pl.) prevailing circumstances of period; allotted or available portion of time; definite or fixed point or portion of time; season; occasion; (payment for) amount of time worked; rhythm or measure of musical composition; (pl., preceded by numeral etc.) expressing multiplication, comparison, etc.; *at the same* ~ simultaneously, all the same; *at* ~*s*, now and then; *do* ~, (sl.) serve term of imprisonment; *from* ~ *to* ~, occasionally; *a good* ~, period of enjoyment; *in no* ~, rapidly, in a moment; *in* ~, not late, early enough, sooner or later, following time of music etc.; *on* ~, punctually. *v.t.* choose time for, do at chosen or appropriate time; take or record time of. ~ **bomb**, one designed to explode after predetermined interval. ~-**clock**, clock with device recording times e.g. of arrival of workmen etc. ~-**honoured**, respected on account of antiquity. ~-**keeper**, watch, clock, esp. in respect of accuracy; one who takes or records time. ~-**lag**, interval between cause etc. and result or consequence. ~**piece**, clock or watch. ~**server**, selfish opportunist. ~-**signal**, visible or audible signal announcing time of day. ~ **signature**, sign in written music, usu. in form of fraction, indicating time of passage etc. ~-**switch**, switch making or breaking electric contact at predetermined time. ~-**table**, tabular list or schedule of times of school classes,

arrival and departure of trains, etc. ~**less** *a.* unending, eternal; not subject to time. **time′ly** (-ml-) *a.* seasonable, opportune.

tim′id *a.* easily alarmed; shy. **timid′ity** *n.*

tim′orous *a.* timid.

tim′othy (grass) *n.* kind of meadow grass.

tin *n.* silvery-white malleable metallic element; vessel or box of tin or tinplate; tinplate; (sl.) money. *v.t.* cover, coat, with tin; seal up (fruit, meat, etc.) in tins for preservation. *a.* of tin; (colloq.) of corrugated iron. ~**foil**, thin sheet of tin or alloy of tin and lead used for wrapping, packing, etc. ~ **hat**, (sl.) steel helmet. ~-**pan alley**, world of composers, publishers, etc. of popular music. ~**plate**, sheet-iron coated with tin. ~-**pot**, resembling or suggesting pot made of tin in quality or sound; inferior, shabby, cheap. ~**tack**, tin-coated tack. **tinned** (-nd) *a.* (esp.) canned. **tinn′y** *a.* of or like tin; esp. (of sound) thin and metallic, (of taste), characteristic of food etc. preserved in tins.

tinctōr′ial *a.* of, used in, dying; yielding, using, dye.

tinc′ture *n.* (her.) colour or metal in coat of arms etc.; smattering, tinge, slight flavour; solution of medicinal substance. *v.t.* colour slightly; tinge, flavour; affect slightly.

tin′der *n.* dry inflammable substance readily taking fire from spark. ~**y** *a.*

tine *n.* prong, projecting sharp point of fork, harrow, etc.; pointed branch of antler.

tinge (-j) *v.t.* colour slightly (*with*); qualify, modify, slightly alter tone of. *n.* tint, slight colouring; flavour, touch.

ting′le (-nggl) *n.* & *v.i.* (feel) slight pricking or stinging sensation.

tink′er *n.* itinerant mender of kettles etc.; tinkering. *v.i.* work amateurishly or clumsily *at*, *with*, esp. to repair or improve.

tink′le *n.* & *v.* (make, cause to make) succession of short light sharp ringing sounds (as) of small bell.

tin′sel *n.* shining metallic material

used in sheets, threads, etc. to give sparkling effect; tawdry brilliance; flashiness. *a.* showy, gaudy, cheaply splendid. **tin'selled, tin'selly** *aa.*

tint *n.* (usu. slight or delicate) colour, esp. one of several tones of same colour. *v.t.* apply tint to, colour.

tintinnăbūlā'tion *n.* ringing of bells.

ti'ny *a.* very small.

tip[1] *n.* extremity, esp. of small or tapering thing; small piece or part attached to tip, esp. mouthpiece of cigarette. *v.t.* furnish with tip. ~-**toe**, (on) tips of toes, (standing or walking) with heels raised from ground; *v.i.* walk on tiptoe. ~-**top**, first-rate, of highest excellence.

tip[2] *v.* (cause to) lean or slant, topple, overturn, esp. with slight effort; discharge (contents of jug, wagon, etc.) thus; strike or touch lightly; give usu. small present of money to, esp. for service; (colloq.) give, communicate, in informal manner; predict (winner of race etc.); ~ *off*, ~ (person) *the wink*, (colloq.) give private signal, warning, information, etc. to; ~ *up*, (esp.) turn from horizontal to (nearly) vertical position, esp. to be out of the way. *n.* small present of money given esp. to servant etc. for service given or expected; piece of useful private or special information, prediction, given by expert; special device, good dodge; place where refuse etc. is tipped; light touch or blow. ~-**and-run**, form of cricket in which batsman must run if bat touches ball; (attrib.) marked by hasty attack and immediate withdrawal. ~-**cat**, (game with) small piece of wood tapered at both ends struck with stick and then knocked to a distance. ~-**staff**, (hist.) (metal- -tipped staff of) sheriff's officer. **tip'ster** *n.* one who gives tips about racing etc.

tipp'ét *n.* small cape or collar of fur etc.

tipp'le *v.* drink alcoholic liquor habitually or constantly in small quantities. *n.* alcoholic drink.

tip'sy *a.* (partly) drunk; unsteady in gait or speech with drink.

tirāde' (*or* tī-) *n.* piece of vehement denunciation or rant.

tire[1] *v.* make, grow, weary; ~ *out*, exhaust. **tired** *a.* weary, sick, (*of*). ~-**less** *a.* of inexhaustible energy. ~-**some** *a.* trying, annoying; tedious.

tire[2] : see **tyre**.

tire[3] *v.t.* (arch.) adorn, attire; dress (hair etc.).

tiro : see **tyro**.

tiss'ūe (*or* -shōō) *n.* (esp. rich or fine) woven fabric; network (*of* lies etc.); substance of (part of) animal or plant body; organized mass of similar cells; (piece of) tissue- -paper. ~-**paper**, thin soft unsized paper for wrappings etc.

tit[1] *n.* titmouse. ~-**lark**, meadow pipit.

tit[2] *n.* ~ *for tat*, equivalent in return, blow for blow, retaliation.

tit[3] *n.* (vulg. sl.) breast, teat.

Tit. *abbr.* Titus.

Ti'tan *n.* (Gk. myth.) one of twelve gigantic children of Uranus, from two of whom Zeus and Olympians descended; person of superhuman size, strength, etc. **tităn'ic** *a.* of Titans; gigantic, colossal.

titā'nium *n.* dark-grey metallic element.

tit'bit *n.* choice or delicate morsel or item.

tithe (-dh) *n.* tenth; tenth of annual produce of agriculture etc. payable for support of priesthood, religious establishments, etc., now converted into rent charge. *v.t.* subject to tithes. ~-**barn**, barn to hold tithes paid in kind.

Ti'tian(-)red *a.* (of hair) bright golden auburn.

tit'illāte *v.t.* tickle, excite agreeably. ~-**ā'tion** *n.*

tit'ivāte *v.* (colloq.) adorn, smarten, (oneself); put finishing or improving touches to appearance (of).

ti'tle *n.* name of book or other work of art; heading of chapter etc.; title-page; distinctive name or style, personal appellation denoting rank, office, etc ·; legal right to possession of (esp. real) property; just or recognized claim (*to*). ~-**deed**, document constituting evidence of ownership. ~-**page**, page at beginning of book bearing title, name of author, publisher, etc., publication date, etc. ~-role, part in play etc. from which title is taken. **tī'tled** (-ld) *a.* having title of nobility. **tī'tling** *n.* (esp.) impressing of title etc. of book on cover.

tĭt'mouse *n.* (pl. -*mīce*), kinds of small active bird.

tī'trāte (*or* tĭ-) *v.t.* find quantity of constituent in (solution) by adding measured amounts of reagent. ~**ā'tion** *n.* **tī'tre** *n.* quantity of constituent, strength of solution, found by titration.

tĭtt'er *v.i.* & *n.* (produce) laugh of suppressed or covert kind, giggle.

tĭtt'le *n.* (arch.) particle, whit.

tĭtt'le-tăttle *n.* & *v.i.* gossip, chatter.

tĭtt'up *v.i.* go, move, with up-and--down movement, mince, prance. ~**ў** *a.*

tĭt'ūlar *a.* held by virtue of title; such, existing, only in name; (of saint etc.) giving name to church. *n.* titular bishop, saint, etc. ~ **bishop**, (R.C.Ch.) one deriving title from see lost to Roman pontificate.

tĭzz'ў *n.* (sl.) dither.

T.N.T. *abbr.* trinitrotoluene (high explosive).

to *prep.* (tōō, tŏŏ, te), in direction of; as far as, not short of; also introducing indirect obj. of vb. etc., expressing purpose, consequence, etc., limiting meaning or application of adj., as sign of or substitute for inf. etc. *adv.* to or in normal or required position or condition, esp. to a standstill. ~ **and fro**, backwards and forwards; from place to place.

T.O. *abbr.* Transport Officer; turn over.

toad *n.* frog-like amphibian breeding in water but living chiefly on land; repulsive person. ~**flax**, kinds of yellow-flowered plant. ~-**in-the--hole**, sausage or other meat baked in batter. ~**stool**, fungus with round disc-like top and slender stalk. **toa'dў** *n.* sycophant; obsequious parasite; *v.i.* fawn, behave servilely (*to*); ~**ўism** *n.*

toast *n.* (slice of) bread browned at fire or other heat; person or thing drunk to; (hist.) reigning belle (*of*

the season, town, etc.). *v.* brown, cook, warm, esp. before fire; drink to health or in honour of. ~**ing--fork**, long-handled fork for toasting bread etc. ~-**master**, one who announces toasts at public dinner etc. ~-**rack**, for holding slices of dry toast. **toa'ster** *n.* (esp.) electrical device for toasting bread.

tobăcc'ō *n.* (pl. -*os*), (dried leaves, variously prepared for smoking, chewing, etc. of) kinds of plant; cigars, cigarettes, snuff, etc. ~**nist** *n.* dealer in tobacco.

tobŏgg'an *n.* & *v.i.* (ride on) long light narrow sledge curved up at forward end used esp. in sport of coasting down snow or ice slopes.

tō'bў jŭg *n.* mug or small jug in shape of man in three-cornered hat.

tocca'ta (-kah-) *n.* (mus.) composition for keyboard instrument designed to exhibit performer's touch and technique.

tŏc'sĭn *n.* (bell rung as) alarm or signal.

today' *adv.* & *n.* (on) this present day; nowadays, (in) modern times.

tŏdd'le *v.i.* go with small child's short unsteady steps; take casual or leisurely walk. *n.* toddling walk. **tŏdd'ler** *n.* (esp.) child just learning to walk.

tŏdd'ў *n.* sweetened drink of spirits and hot water; fresh or fermented sap of kinds of palm as beverage.

to-do' (-ōō) *n.* commotion, fuss.

tōe *n.* each digit of foot, forepart of foot; part of shoe, stocking, etc. covering toes. *v.t.* touch or reach with toes; furnish with toe, put new toe in; ~ *the line*, stand with tips of toes reaching line, conform strictly to standard or requirement. ~-**cap**, piece of leather etc. covering toe of boot or shoe. ~-**hold**, (esp.) very small foothold.

tŏff *n.* (sl.) distinguished or well--dressed person.

tŏff'ee (-fĭ) *n.* sweetmeat of boiled butter, sugar, etc. ~ **apple**, apple coated with toffee and stuck on stick.

tŏg *n.* (pl., sl.) clothes. *v.t.* dress (*out, up*). **togg'ery** *n.* togs.

tō'ga *n.* ancient Roman citizen's

outer garment of flowing cloak or robe covering whole body except right arm; gown etc. associated with (civil) profession.

togĕth′er (-dh-) *adv.* in(to) company, conjunction, union, etc.; simultaneously; in unbroken succession.

tŏgg′le *n.* short pin through eye or loop of rope etc., esp. as fastening; rod or bar with cross-piece etc. enabling it to pass through hole in one position but not in other.

togs : see **tog**.

toil *v.i.* work long or laboriously (*at*); make slow painful progress. *n.* labour; drudgery. **~some** *a.*

toi′lĕt *n.* process of dressing; (style of) dress; dressing-room; lavatory. **~-paper**, soft paper for use in lavatories. **~-powder**, dusting-powder used after bath etc. **~-roll**, roll of toilet-paper. **~ries** (-ĭz) *n. pl.* (shop-word) articles for use in toilet.

toils (-z) *n.pl.* net, snare.

Tokay′ (*or* -kī) *n.* rich sweet aromatic Hungarian wine.

tō′ken *n.* sign, symbol (*of*); evidence; keepsake; (hist.) piece of stamped metal issued by bank, tradesman, etc. and used instead of coin; anything used to represent something else, esp. money; gift coupon. **~ payment**, proportionately small payment as indication that debt etc. is not repudiated. **~ strike**, strike lasting a few hours only. **~ vote**, (parl.) vote of small sum proposed to enable public discussion to take place.

tōl′bōoth *n.* (Sc.) town hall; town prison.

told, *p.t.* & *p.p.* of **tell**.

tŏl′erable *a.* endurable; fairly good.

tŏl′erance *n.* willingness, capacity, to tolerate; permitted variation in dimension, weight, etc. **~ant** *a.*

tŏl′erāte *v.t.* endure, permit; allow to exist, be practised, etc. without interference or molestation; forbear to judge harshly; (med.) sustain use of (drug etc.) without harm. **~ā′tion** *n.*

tŏll[1] *n.* tax, duty, charge, for selling goods in market, passage along public road or over ferry, etc.;

(charge for) short-distance telephone trunk call; cost (esp. in suffering, loss, etc.). **~-bar, ~-gate,** barriers preventing passage without payment of toll. **~-bridge**, bridge at which toll is charged.

tōll[2] *v.* cause (bell) to ring, ring, with slow succession of strokes, esp. for death or funeral; announce, give out, thus. *n.* tolling sound.

tŏl′uēne *n.* colourless liquid hydrocarbon used in manufacture of explosives etc.

tŏm *n.* male animal, esp. cat. **~boy**, romping girl. **~cat**, male cat. **~fool**, witless person, buffoon; *a.* stupid, senseless. **~foolery**, foolishness, silliness. **~tit**, blue tit.

tŏm′ahawk (-*a*-h-) *n.* war-axe of N.-Amer. Indians. *v.t.* strike, kill, with tomahawk.

toma′tō (-ah-) *n.* (pl. -*oes*), (plant bearing) glossy red or yellow fleshy edible fruit.

tomb (tōom) *n.* grave; burial-vault; sepulchral monument. **~stone**, memorial stone over grave.

tŏmbō′la (*or* tŏ′-) *n.* kind of lottery.

tōme *n.* volume, esp. large heavy one.

tŏmm′ y̆ *n.* British private soldier. **~ rot**, (sl.) nonsense.

tŏmm′y-gŭn *n.* kind of sub-machine-gun.

tomŏ′rrow (-ō) *adv.* & *n.* (on) day after today; (in) future.

tŏm′tŏm *n.* kinds of primitive or barbaric drum, usu. beaten with hands.

ton (tŭn) *n.* measure of weight (20 cwt.); unit of internal capacity of ship (100 cu. ft.); (sl.) 100 m.p.h., esp. on motor-cycle; (pl., colloq.) large number or amount, lots.

tonn′age *n.* carrying capacity of ship expressed in tons; ships collectively, shipping; charge per ton on cargo or freight.

tō′nal *a.* of tone(s); (mus.) having tonic or key(s). **tonăl′ity̆** *n.* (esp.) tones of picture in relation to one another; (mus., observance of) key or key-scheme.

tōne *n.* sound, esp. with reference to pitch, quality, and strength; quality, pitch, intonation, etc. of voice, spoken sound, etc.; musical note, sound of definite pitch and character; degree of firmness or tension proper to strong and healthy bodily organs or tissues; tint or shade of colour; prevailing character of morals, sentiments, etc. *v.* give tone or quality to; harmonize; alter tone or colour of; ~ *down*, lower tone or quality of, make or become less emphatic, offensive, violent, etc.; ~ *up*, improve tone of, give higher or stronger tone to. ~-colour, timbre. ~-deaf, insensitive to differences in pitch. ~ poem, symphonic poem. ~less *a.* (esp.) dull, lifeless, unexpressive.

tŏngs (-z) *n.pl.* implement consisting of two limbs connected by hinge, pivot, etc. for grasping and lifting.

tongue (tŭng) *n.* muscular organ in mouth used in tasting, speaking, swallowing, etc.; faculty or manner of speaking; words, language; tongue-like piece or part. *v.* furnish with tongue; interrupt stream of air in wind instrument with tongue in playing. ~-tied, having tongue--ligament so short that distinct speech is difficult or impossible; speechless from embarrassment, shyness, etc. ~-twister, word(s) difficult to articulate.

tŏn'ĭc *a.* producing tension, esp. of muscles; of, maintaining, restoring, bodily tone; bracing, strengthening; (of, founded upon) tonic or key note. *n.* tonic medicine or agent; invigorating influence; (mus.) key--note. ~ major, ~ minor, major, minor, key with same tonic as given minor, major. ~ sol-fa, sol--fa system in which tonic of all major keys is doh. toni'cĭtў *n.* tonic quality or condition, tone.

tonight' *adv.* & *n.* (on) present night, (on) night of today.

tonnage : see ton.

tŏn'sil *n.* either of pair of small organs of lymphatic tissue at sides of root of tongue. tŏnsillĕc'tomў *n.* surgical removal of tonsils. tŏnsil-lī'tĭs *n.* inflammation of tonsils.

tŏnsŏr'ial *a.* (usu. joc.) of barber or his work.

tŏn'sure (-sher) *n.* shaving of head or of patch on crown esp. on admission to priesthood or monastic order. *v.t.* give tonsure to.

tŏn'tine (-ēn; *or* -ēn') *n.* financial arrangement by which benefits of remaining participants are increased on death or default of any one of them.

tōō *adv.* in addition, besides, also; in excess; more than is right or fitting; (colloq.) extremely, very.

took, *p.t* of take.

tōōl *n.* implement for working upon something, usu. one held in and operated by hand; (cutting-part of) machine-tool; person used as mere implement by another; small stamp or roller for impressing design on leather etc. *v.* work with tool; dress (stone) with large chisel; ornament (leather etc.) with tool; (colloq.) drive, ride, (*along*) esp. in casual or leisurely manner. tōō'ling *n.* (esp.) design(s) impressed with tools.

tōōt *n.* sound of horn etc. *v.* emit toot; sound (horn etc.).

tōōth *n.* (pl. *teeth*), any of hard processes with points, edges, or grinding surfaces rooted in jaws and used for biting, tearing, or chewing food or as weapons; elephant's tusk; taste, liking; projecting part or point resembling tooth; prong or tine of comb, saw, fork, etc.; cog; *in the teeth of*, in spite of, in opposition to, in the face of (wind etc.); ~ *and nail*, fiercely, with all one's might; *set* one's *teeth*, esp. clench teeth firmly from indignation, resolution, etc.; *show* one's *teeth*, (esp.) show hostility or malice, behave threateningly. *v.* furnish with tooth or teeth; give rough surface to; interlock. ~ache, ache in tooth or teeth. ~-pick, small pointed implement for removing matter lodged between teeth; (sl.) very narrow pointed boat. ~ful *n.* small mouthful, esp. of spirit. ~less *a.* ~some *a.* pleasant to eat.

tōō'tle *v.* toot gently or continuously, esp. on flute.

tŏp[1] *n.* summit, upper part, surface, of something; highest place, rank, degree, etc.; part or piece forming upper part or covering of something; platform on or round top of mast on ship; topsail; upper or turned-down part of leg of high boot, stocking, etc.; stopper of bottle; (pl.) part of plant, esp. vegetable, growing above ground; *on* ~, supreme, dominant. *a.* highest in position, degree, rank, etc.; that is at or on top. *v.t.* provide with top or cap; remove top of; reach, be at, top of; exceed in height; hit golf-ball above centre. ~**-boot**, boot with high top. ~ **brass**, officers of highest rank. ~**-coat**, overcoat; final coat of paint etc. ~ **drawer**, (esp.) high social position or origin. ~**-dress**, apply top-dressing to. ~**-dressing**, manure, road-metal, etc. applied to surface of land, road, etc. without working it in. ~**gallant**, mast, sail, yard, rigging, immediately above topmast and topsail. ~ **hat**, tall silk hat. ~**-heavy**, overweighted at top. ~**knot**, bow, tuft, crest, etc. worn or growing on top of head. ~**mast**, smaller mast on top of lower mast. ~**-notch**, (colloq.) first-rate, excellent. ~**sail** (-sl), sail next above lower sail in square--rigged vessel. ~ **secret**, most secret, extremely secret. ~**side**, part of ship's side above water-line or main deck; beef-joint cut from haunch between leg and aitch-bone. **tŏp′lĕss**, ~**most** *aa.* **tŏpp′er** *n.* (colloq.) top hat. **tŏpping** *a.* (sl.) tip-top, excellent.

tŏp² *n.* toy to which spinning motion is given by hand, spring, string, etc.; *sleep like a* ~, sleep soundly.

tō′păz *n.* semi-precious stone of various colours, esp. yellow.

tōpe *v.i.* drink to excess, esp. habitually. **tō′per** *n.*

tō′pee (-I), **tō′pĭ**, *n.* light pith hat or helmet.

Tō′phet *n.* Hell.

tō′pĭarў *a.* of art of clipping trees etc. into ornamental or fantastic shapes.

tŏp′ĭc *a.* subject of discourse, argument, etc. **tŏp′ĭcal** *a.* having reference to current events. ~**ăl′itў** *n.*

tŏp′mōst *a.* uppermost.

topŏg′raphў *n.* (description or delineation of) physical features of place or locality; (study of) local distribution. ~**grapher** *n.*; ~**grăph′ic(al)** *aa.*

tŏpp′le *v.* (cause to) tumble or fall headlong, as if top-heavy.

tŏpsў-tūr′vў *adv. & a.* with top where bottom should be, upside down; in(to) utter confusion.

tōque (-k) *n.* woman's small usu. swathed brimless hat.

tŏr *n.* craggy or rocky hill or peak.

tŏrch *n.* burning piece of resinous wood, length of resin-soaked flax etc., as light for carrying in hand; small portable electric lamp; (U.S.) blow-lamp; source of conflagration, enlightenment, etc.; *carry* ~ *for* (U.S. sl.) have unrequited passion for; *hand on the* ~, pass on tradition. ~**-bearer**, (esp.) one who guards or hands on light of truth, civilization, etc. ~**-singer**, singer of esp. jazz songs of unrequited love.

tore, *p.t.* of **tear**.

tŏ′readŏr, **torer′o** (-ārō) *nn.* bull--fighter.

tŏr′ment *n.* (cause of) severe bodily or mental suffering. *v.t.* (-ent′), subject to torment. ~**or** *n.*

tŏrnā′dō *n.* (pl. *-oes*), very violent storm; destructive rotatory storm advancing in narrow path for many miles.

tŏrpē′dō *n.* (pl. *-oes*), flatfish capable of inflicting electric shocks; self--propelled dirigible explosive submarine missile. *v.t.* attack, damage, destroy, (as) with torpedo. ~**-boat**, small fast armoured vessel carrying torpedoes. ~**-boat destroyer**, destroyer. ~**-net(ting)**, steel net to protect ship etc. against torpedoes. ~**-tube**, steel tube through which torpedoes are discharged.

tŏr′pĭd *a.* benumbed, dormant; sluggish; dull. **tŏrpĭd′itў**, **tŏr′por** *nn.*

tŏrque (-k) *n.* twisting or rotary force in mechanism etc.; (hist.) ancient British or Gaulish necklace or collar, usu. of twisted metal.

tŏ′rrent *n.* swift violent rushing stream of water etc.; downpour of rain; violent flow (of words etc.). **torrĕn′tial** *a.*

tŏ'rrĭd *a.* scorched, parched; intensely hot. **~ zone,** region between tropics of Cancer and Capricorn.

tŏr'sion *n.* twisting, twist. **~al** *a.*

tŏr'sō *n.* (pl. *-os*), statue lacking head and limbs; trunk of human body; mutilated or unfinished work.

tŏrt *n.* breach of duty imposed by law, making offender liable to action for damages. **tŏr'tious** *a.*

tŏr'toise (-*tus*) *n.* kinds of slow--moving four-footed reptile with body enclosed in shell and retractile head and legs. **~shell** (-t*e*shĕl), semi-transparent mottled yellowish--brown shell of tortoise used for ornament; (butterfly, cat) with brown, yellow and black mottled colouring.

tŏr'tūous *a.* full of twists or turns; devious, circuitous, not straight-forward. **tŏrtūŏs'ĭtў** *n.*

tŏr'ture *n.* infliction of severe bodily pain, esp. to extort something from victim; severe physical or mental pain. *v.t.* subject to torture; distort, strain, wrench.

Tŏr'ў *n. & a.* (member) of Conservative party. **~ism** *n.*

tŏsh *n.* (sl.) twaddle, nonsense.

tŏss *v.* throw, esp. lightly, carelessly, or easily; (of bull etc.) fling up with horns; throw (*up*) coin to decide choice etc. by way it falls, settle question or dispute (with) thus; throw back *head*, esp. in contempt or impatience; throw or roll about from side to side, restlessly or with fitful to-and-fro motion; **~ off,** drink off at a draught, dispatch (work etc.) or produce rapidly or without apparent effort. *n.* tossing; sudden jerk, esp. of head; throw from horseback etc.; *full* **~,** (crick.) ball which does not touch ground between wickets. **~-up,** tossing of coin; doubtful question; even chance.

tŏt¹ *n.* small child; small quantity (*of* drink, esp. spirits).

tŏt² *v.* add (*up*), mount *up* (*to*).

tō'tal *a.* complete; comprising or involving whole; absolute, un-qualified; (of warfare) in which all available resources are employed. *n.* sum of all items; total amount.

v. amount to, mount *up to*; reckon total of. **totăl'ĭtў** *n.*; **~īze** *v.*

totălitār'ĭan *a.* of regime permitting no rival loyalties or parties. **~ism** *n.*

tō'talīzātor, tōte¹ *nn.* device automatically registering number and amount of bets staked, amount due to winners, etc.

tōte² *v.t.* (U.S.) convey, carry.

tō'tĕm *n.* (image of) natural esp. animal object assumed as emblem of family or clan. **~-pole,** post with carved and painted totem(s), esp. in front of N.-Amer. Indian dwelling. **~ism** *n.* (stage of development, social relationships, associated with) cult of totems. **totĕm'ĭc, ~ĭs'tic** *aa.*

tŏtt'er *v.i.* walk with unsteady steps, go shakily or feebly; rock or shake as if about to overbalance or collapse. *n.* tottering gait. **~ў** *a.*

tou'can (tōō-) *n.* tropical Amer. bird with huge light thin-walled beak.

touch (tŭch) *v.* come into or be in contact (with); strike lightly; deal with (subject) momentarily; tint in parts or slightly *with*; concern; stir sympathy or other emotion in; affect slightly; produce slightest effect on; have to do with in slightest degree; reach, approach; eat or drink smallest quantity of; call *at* (port); **~ down,** alight on ground from air, make touch-down; **~ for,** (sl.) get (money) from; **~ on,** treat briefly; **~ off,** discharge (explosive etc.), set going, start (explosion etc.); **~ up,** give finishing, improving, etc. touches to, touch (horse etc.) with whip or spur; **~ wood,** touch (wooden object) to avert ill luck. *n.* act or fact of touching; sense of feeling; sensation conveyed by touching; light stroke with pencil etc., artistic detail, slight act or effort in work; artistic skill or style; manner of touching keys or strings of esp. keyboard musical instrument, instrument's response to this; communication, agreement, sympathy; (footb.) part of ground outside touch-lines. **~-and-go,** of uncertain result, risky. **~-down,** (Rugby footb.) touching ball on ground behind opponents' goal-line; contact with ground on landing of aircraft. ~-hole, (hist.) hole through which fire was set to charge in guns. ~-line, (footb.) either side-boundary of ground. ~-paper, paper steeped in nitre so as to burn slowly for igniting fireworks, etc. ~stone, black jasper etc. used for testing alloys of gold etc.; (fig.) standard, criterion. ~-typing, type-writing without looking at keys. ~wood, wood in soft rotten state usable as tinder. **touched** a. (esp., colloq.) crazy, 'cracked'. ~ing a. affecting, pathetic; *prep.* (arch.) concerning, about. **touch'ỹ** a. easily taking offence, over-sensitive.

tough (tŭf) a. of strongly cohesive substance or great endurance; hard to masticate; not easily injured or broken; hard to tackle or overcome; hardy, able to endure hardship; (colloq., of luck etc.) hard; (sl.) ruffianly, hardened in crime. n. street ruffian, tough person. **tough'en** v.

toupee (tōō'pā) n. false hair to cover bald spot.

tour (toor) n. journey through (part of) country from place to place; visit to noteworthy parts of exhibition, institution, etc.; (esp. mil.) spell of duty in service; *on* ~, touring. v. make tour (of); (of theatr. company etc.) travel, take (entertainment), from town to town or about (country etc.) fulfilling engagements. ~ing-car, usu. open--topped car for touring etc. ~ing **company**, theatrical company touring with play etc. **tour'er** n. touring-car. **tour'ism** n. organized touring; accommodation etc. of tourists as industry. **tour'ist** n. person who makes tour or travels for pleasure; a. of or for tourists or tourism; ~ist **camp**, place offering simple accommodation to motorists etc.; ~ist **class**, class on liner etc. inferior to first class.

tour de force (toor) n. feat of strength or esp. great skill. [F]

tour'maline (toor-; *or* -ēn) n. mineral, usu. crystalline and freq. richly coloured, used as gem etc.

tour'nament (toor- *or* tôr- *or* têr-) n. medieval sport of mounted combat with blunted weapons; contest between number of competitors playing series of selective games etc.

tournedos (toor'nedō) n. small piece of fillet of beef grilled or sauté.

tour'ney (têr- *or* toor-) n. & v.i. (hist.) (take part in) tournament.

tourniquet (toor'nĭkā) n. bandage etc. for arresting bleeding by compression of artery etc.

tou'sle (-zl) v.t. pull about; make (hair, person) untidy.

tout v.i. solicit custom; spy on horses in training. n. one who touts.

tow[1] (tō) n. (coarse and broken) fibres of flax etc. ready for spinning. ~-coloured, (of hair) flaxen, light yellow. ~-headed, -haired, having straight flaxen hair.

tow[2] (tō) v.t. draw along through water by rope or chain; pull along behind one. n. towing, being towed; *in* ~, being towed; *take in* ~, (fig.) take under one's guidance or patronage. ~ing-path, ~path, path beside canal or river for use in towing. **tow'age** n.

toward[1] (tō'erd) a. (arch.) docile, apt; about to happen, in train.

toward[2], **towards** (tôrd(z), tŏŏ-wôrd(z)') prep. in direction of; near, approaching; in relation to, as regards; as contribution to.

tow'el n. absorbent cloth, paper, etc. for drying or wiping after washing etc. v.t. rub or dry with towel; (sl.) beat, thrash. ~-horse, frame or stand for hanging towels on. **tow'elling** n. (esp.) material for towels.

tow'er, n. tall structure, freq. forming part of church or other large building; fortress etc. having tower; ~ *of strength*, steadfast person, strong or reliable support. v.i. reach high (*above*); soar, be poised, aloft. **tow'ering** a. high, lofty; (of rage etc.) violent.

town n. inhabited place usu. larger than village and having more complete and independent local government; inhabitants, business or shopping centre, of town; *T*~ (West End of) London; *go to* ~, work enthusiastically, spend lavishly, etc. (*on*); *man about* ~, fashionable idler, esp. in London. ~ **clerk**, secretary to corporation of town. ~ **council**, elective body administering town. ~ **hall**, municipal building of town. ~-**planning**, construction of plans for regulation of growth etc. of town(s), provision and siting of amenities, etc. ~s-**people**, people of town. ~**ship** *n.* (hist.) parish, small town or village forming division of original parish; (U.S.) division of county; (U.S. etc.) territorial unit (usu.) six miles square; (Austral., N.Z.) small **town**; (hist., village etc. on) site of prospective town. **townee'** *n.* (contempt.) inhabitant of town.

tŏxae'mia *n.* diseased condition due to presence of toxic substances in blood.

tŏx'ĭc *a.* of, caused by, or acting as poison. **tŏxĭcolŏ'gĭcal** *a.*; ~ŏl'ogĭst, ~ŏl'ogў *nn.*

tŏx'ĭn *n.* poisonous substance of animal or vegetable origin, esp. one produced by micro-organisms.

toxŏph'ĭlў *n.* archery.

toy *n.* plaything, esp. for child; trinket, knick-knack. *v.i.* trifle, amuse oneself (*with*); ~ *with*, deal with, handle, in careless, fondling, or trifling manner. ~ **dog**, dog of diminutive breed or variety.

trāce[1] *n.* track or mark left behind; indication of existence or occurrence of something; slight amount (*of*). *v.t.* delineate, mark out, write esp. laboriously; copy (drawing etc.) by following & marking its lines on tracing-paper etc.; follow track or path of; follow course, line, history, etc. of; observe or find traces of. ~r (**bullet** etc.), bullet, etc. emitting smoke etc. by which its course can be followed. ~r **element**, radioactive isotope that can be traced through organism, series of reactions, etc. **trā'cing** *n.* (esp.) copy made by tracing; record of self-registering instrument; **tracing-paper**, tough semi-transparent paper placed over drawings etc. to be traced.

trāce[2] *n.* each of pair of ropes, straps, etc. connecting collar of horse etc.

with swingle-tree of vehicle; *kick over the* ~s, rebel, act recklessly.

trā'cerў *n.* (pattern etc. resembling or suggesting) decorative stone open-work esp. in head of Gothic window, interlaced work of vault, etc.

trā'chėa (-k-) *n.* windpipe. **trā'chėal** *a.* **trāchėŏt'omў** *n.* (surg.) incision of trachea.

trachō'ma (-k-) *n.* contagious form of conjunctivitis.

trăck *n.* mark, series of marks, left by passage of anything; path, esp. one beaten by use; rough unmade road; line of travel or motion; prepared course for racing etc.; continuous line of railway; band of tracked vehicle; transverse distance between wheels of vehicle; *in one's* ~s, on the spot, instantly; *on the* ~ *of*, in pursuit of, having clue to; *keep* ~ *of*, follow course, sequence, etc. of; *make* ~s, make off, make for. *v.* follow track or footsteps (of); pursue, follow up; (of wheels) run in same track; furnish with tracks or caterpillars; ~ *down*, pursue until caught or found. ~**er dog**, dog used in pursuing fugitives. ~ **events**, races. **trăck'lėss** *a.* (esp.) pathless.

trăct[1] *n.* stretch, extent, region (*of*); region or area of esp. bodily organ or system.

trăct[2] *n.* short treatise, pamphlet, esp. on religious subject.

trăc'table *a.* easily managed; docile. ~**bĭl'itў** *n.*

trăc'tion *n.* pulling; drawing of vehicles or loads along road or track. ~ **engine**, steam or diesel engine for drawing loads.

trăc'tor *n.* traction-engine; motor vehicle for drawing heavy loads etc. esp. across fields or rough country.

trăd *a. & n.* (sl.) traditional (jazz).

trāde *n.* dealing in commodities for profit; particular branch of this or persons engaged in it; business, calling, skilled handicraft. *v.* deal in the way of trade; have commercial transaction(s) *with*; ~ *in*, barter, buy and sell, hand over (used article) in (part) payment (*for*); ~ *on*, take (esp. unscrupulous) advantage of. ~ **cycle,** recurrent alternation of trade conditions between prosperity and depression. **~-mark,** manufacturer's registered device or name to distinguish his goods. **~-name,** name of proprietary article; name by which thing is called in the trade; name under which person etc. trades. ~ **show,** showing esp. of cinema-film to exhibitors etc.; *v.t.* (usu. pass.) show thus. **~sman,** person engaged in trade, esp. shopkeeper; craftsman. **~(s) union,** organized association of employees etc. to protect and further common interests. ~ **wind,** constant wind blowing towards equator from NE. and SE.

trā'dĭng *n.* (esp.) buying and selling; commerce, traffic. **~-post,** station in sparsely populated area for exchanging local products for goods etc. ~ **stamp,** token given to customer with purchase and redeemable in merchandise or cash.

trădĭ'tion *n.* transmission of knowledge or belief from one generation to another, esp. by word of mouth; tale, belief, custom, etc. so transmitted. **tradĭ'tional** *a.*; **~alism,** **~ist** *nn.*

tradūce' *v.t.* calumniate, misrepresent.

trăff'ĭc *n.* trade (*in*) esp. in something which should not be subject of trade; transportation of goods, coming and going of persons, goods, or esp. vehicles or vessels, along road, canal, etc. *v.i.* trade (*in*), esp. illegally or reprehensibly. ~ **lights,** mechanical signals for controlling road traffic by coloured lights. ~ **policeman,** one engaged in controlling road traffic. ~ **warden,** person appointed to control esp. parking of vehicles. **trăff'ĭcātor** *n.* direction-indicator on motor vehicle.

trăg'acănth *n.* kinds of gum used as vehicle for drugs etc.

trage'dĭan *n.* author of or actor in tragedies. **tragēdĭĕnne'** *n.* tragic actress.

tră'gĕdў, *n.* literary composition, esp. play, of elevated theme and diction and with fatal or disastrous conclusion; branch of dramatic art dealing with sorrowful or terrible events; sad event, calamity, disaster. **tră'gĭc** *a.* of, in style of, tragedy; sad, calamitous, distressing. **trăgĭcŏm'ĕdў** *n.* drama of mixed tragic and comic elements; **trăgĭcŏm'ĭc(al)** *aa.*

trail *v.* draw, be drawn, along behind or in wake of something, esp. on ground; drag along, walk wearily; straggle; hang loosely; (of plant) grow or hang downwards, esp. so as to touch or rest on ground; (mil.) carry (rifle etc.) horizontally with arm extended downwards; track, shadow. *n.* trailing growth etc.; track, scent, or other sign of passage left by moving object; beaten path esp. through wild region; *at the* ~ (mil.) being trailed. ~ **ing edge,** rear edge of aircraft's wing. **trai'ler** *n.* (esp.) trailing plant; vehicle, esp. caravan, (designed to be) drawn along behind another; extracts from film exhibited in advance as advertisement.

train *v.* bring to desired standard of efficiency, obedience, etc. by instruction and practice; subject, be subjected, to course of instruction and discipline (*for*); teach and accustom (*to* do etc.); bring, bring oneself, to physical efficiency, esp. for sport or contest, by exercise and diet; cause (plant) to grow in desired shape; point, aim; (colloq.) travel by train. *n.* trailing prolongation of robe or gown; string of persons or animals; retinue; succession of events; set of parts in mechanism actuating one another in series; locomotive with the coaches or wagons it draws; railway travel; line of gunpowder laid as explosive charge; *in* ~, in proper order etc., in process. **~-bearer,** person holding up train of another's robe. **~--ferry,** ferry conveying railway--trains across water. **trainee'** *n.* person being trained (for occupation). **trai'ner** *n.* (esp.) one who trains persons or animals for racing etc. **trai'ning** *n.* (esp.) process of training for sport or contest by exercise, diet, etc.; *in* ~*ing*, undergoing this process, physically fit as result of it; *out of* ∼*ing*, in poor condition from lack or cessation of training; ∼**ing college,** college for training teachers; ∼**ing-ship,** ship on which boys are trained for naval service or merchant navy.

train′-oil *n.* whale-blubber oil.

tra(i)pse, trāpes (-ps) *v.i.* walk in trailing, slatternly, or untidy way; trudge wearily.

trait (trā) *n.* feature, distinguishing quality.

trai′tor *n.* one who is false to his allegiance or acts disloyally. ∼**ous** *a.*

trajĕc′torў *n.* path of body moving under given forces, esp. of projectile in flight through air.

trăm *n.* ∼(-*car*), passenger car running on rails on public road. *v.* convey in, travel by, tram. ∼**-line,** tram-car track with rails flush with road surface; tram-car route; (pl., colloq.) pair of long parallel lines bounding side of lawn-tennis court.

trămm′el *n.* kind of fishing-net; shackle, esp. one used in teaching horse to amble; (usu. pl.) hampering influence, restraint. *v.t.* hamper.

trămp *v.* walk with firm heavy tread; walk, go, traverse, on foot; be tramp. *n.* sound (as) of troops marching; long or tiring walk or march; person who tramps roads esp. as vagrant; freight-ship taking cargoes wherever obtainable and for any port.

trăm′ple *v.* tread heavily and (esp.) injuriously (on); crush or destroy thus (freq. fig.); put (fire) *out* by trampling.

trăm′polïne (*or* -ēn) *n.* springboard of canvas etc. attached by springs to horizontal frame, used for acrobatic exercises, etc.

trance (-ah-) *n.* sleep-like state, hypnotic or cataleptic condition esp. of spiritualist medium; mental abstraction from external things, absorption, ecstasy.

trăn′quil *a.* serene, calm, undisturbed. **trănquill′itў** *n.*; ∼**līze** *v.t.* **trăn′quillīzer** *n.* soothing drug.

trăns- in comb., across, beyond, over, to or on farther side of. **trănsăl′-**

pïne (-z-) *a. & n.* (person living) beyond Alps (usu. from Italian point of view). ∼**atlăn′tic** (-z-) *a.* across, on or from other side of, Atlantic; American; crossing Atlantic. ∼**cŏntïnĕn′tal** (-z-) *a.* extending or passing across continent. ∼**dū′cer** *n.* device or apparatus receiving electrical, acoustical, etc. waves from one system etc. and conveying related waves to another. **transhïp′** *v.* transfer, change, from one ship etc. to another; **transhïp′ment** *n.* ∼**lū′nary** (-z-; *or* -loo-) *a.* lying beyond moon; insubstantial, visionary. ∼**mïgrāte′** *v.i.* migrate; (of soul) pass after death into another body; ∼**mïgrā′tion** *n.*; ∼**mïgrā′torў** (*or* -mï′-) *a.* ∼**oceăn′ïc** (-zōsh-) *a.* situated or being beyond, crossing, ocean. ∼**pacïf′ïc** (-z-) *a.* situated or being beyond, crossing, Pacific. ∼**-shïp′** *v.* tranship. ∼**vĕs′tïsm** (-z-) *n.* practice of dressing in clothes of opposite sex; ∼**vĕs′tïte** *n.*

trănsăct′ (-z- *or* -s-) *v.t.* do, carry on, (action, business, etc.). **trănsăc′tion** *n.* transacting, being transacted; piece of business; (pl.) proceedings, dealings; (pl.) records of learned society's proceedings.

trănscĕnd′ *v.t.* go beyond, exceed, limits of; rise above, surpass, excel.

transcĕn′dent *a.* transcending ordinary limits, supreme, pre-eminent; outside, unrealizable in, experience. ∼**dĕn′tal** *a.* not derived from experience, *a priori*; recognizing transcendental element in experience; metaphysical, obscure, visionary. ∼**dencў,** ∼**dĕn′talism** *nn.*; ∼**dĕn′talïst** *n. & a.*

trănscrïbe′ *v.t.* copy out; reproduce in ordinary writing; (mus.) adapt for other than original instrument or voice. **trăn′scrïpt** *n.* written copy; (law) copy of legal record. **trănscrïp′tion** *n.*

trăn′sĕpt *n.* (either arm of) transverse part of cruciform church.

trănsfĕr′ *v.* convey, transmit, hand over, etc. from one person, place, etc. to another; (law) convey by legal process; convey (design etc.)

from one surface to another; change from one station, line, etc. to another to continue journey; transfer (esp. football-player) to another club, group, etc. n. (trăˈ-), transferring, being transferred; means or place of transfer; transfer ticket; transferred thing; design etc. (to be) transferred, design or picture on prepared paper from which it can be transferred. ~-fee, sum paid for transfer esp. of professional footballer to another club. ~ticket, ticket allowing journey to be continued on another line etc. ~able a. that can be transferred. ~abil'ity n. trăns'ference n. (esp., psychol.) transferring of emotions to new object; (psycho-anal.) development in patient of emotional attitude towards analyst.

trănsfig'ure (-ger) v.t. alter form or appearance of, esp. change so as to elevate or idealize. ~urā'tion n. (esp.) change in appearance of Jesus on the mountain; Church festival (6 August) commemorating this.

trănsfix' v.t. pierce with, impale on, sharp-pointed instrument; render motionless (with fear, grief, etc.).

trănsfōrm' v.t. change form, appearance, condition, function, etc. of esp. considerably; (electr.) change (current) in potential or type. transformā'tion n. transforming, being transformed; ~ation scene, elaborate spectacular scene in pantomime, esp. with scenery etc. changing in view of audience. transfōr'mer n. (esp. electr.) apparatus for changing potential or type of electric current.

trănsfūse' (-z) v.t. cause (fluid etc.) to pass from one vessel etc. to another; transfer (blood of one person etc.) into veins of another. transfū'sion n.

trănsgrĕss' v. infringe (law etc.); overstep (limit laid down); sin. transgrĕ'ssion, ~or nn.

tranship : see trans-.

trăn'sient (-z-) a. quickly passing away; fleeting; passing through, staying only briefly. n. temporary visitor, lodger, etc. ~ence n.

trănsĭs'tor n. very small semi-conductor device capable of replacing thermionic valve; radio receiver using transistors. ~ize v.t. equip with transistors.

trăns'ĭt (-z-) n. passing, passage, conveyance, etc. from one place to another; passage of planet across region or point of zodiac, of inferior planet across sun's disc, of satellite or its shadow across planet's disc, etc. v. make transit (across). ~-duty, duty on goods passing through country. ~ visa, visa allowing passage through but not stay in country.

trănsi'tion n. passage from one state, subject, set of circumstances, etc. to another; period of this; (mus., esp. brief) modulation. ~al, ~ary aa.

trăn'sĭtive a. (of verb) requiring direct object expressed or understood.

trăns'ĭtory a. not lasting; momentary, brief, fleeting.

trănslāte' v.t. turn (word, book, etc.) from one language into another; express sense of in other words; infer or declare or convey significance of; remove (bishop) to another see; (bibl.) convey to heaven without death. translā'tion, translā'tor nn.

trănslĭt'erāte (-z-) v.t. replace (letters of one alphabet or language) by those of another. ~ā'tion n.

trănslu'cent (-zlōō-) a. allowing passage of light but diffusing it. ~ence n.

trănsmĭss'ĭble (-z-) a. that may be transmitted. ~bĭl'ĭty n.

trănsmĭ'ssion (-z-) n. (esp.) gear transmitting power from engine to axle in motor-vehicle etc.; transmitting, programme etc. transmitted, by radio, television, etc.

trănsmĭt' (-z-) v.t. send, convey, etc. to another person, place, or thing; suffer to pass through, be medium for, send out, serve to communicate (heat, electricity, emotion, message, etc.). trănsmĭtt'er n. (esp.) (part of) radio etc. set or station for sending out wireless waves.

trănsmŏg'rĭfy (-z-) v.t. (joc.) transform utterly, grotesquely, etc. ~ifĭcā'tion n.

trănsmūte' (-z-) v.t. change form, nature, or substance of; convert (one substance, species, etc.) into another, esp. (alchemy) change (baser metal) into gold or silver. ~tā'tion n.

trăn'som n. cross-beam, cross-piece; horizontal bar across window; cross--bar between door and fan-light above it; window above transom, esp. of door.

trănspār'ent a. transmitting light so that bodies beyond are completely visible; pervious to specified form of radiant energy; easily seen through, obvious, clear; candid, open. trănspār'ence n. being transparent. ~encў n. transparence; transparent object or medium; esp. picture on glass etc. to be viewed by transmitted light.

trănspīre' v. emit, be emitted, as vapour or liquid through skin, tissue, etc.; leak out, come to be known; (misused for) occur, happen. trănspīrā'tion n.

trănsplant' (-lah-) v.t. remove and replant or establish elsewhere; transfer (living tissue) from one part of body or one person or animal to another; bear trans- planting. ~ā'tion n.

trănspōrt' v.t. carry, convey, from one place to another; (hist.) deport (convict) to penal colony; (usu. pass.) carry away by strong emotion. n. (tră'-) transporting of goods or passengers; means of conveyance, vehicles; vessel, air- craft, etc. used in transporting troops or military stores; vehement (usu. pleasurable) emotion; fit of joy, rage, etc. transportā'tion n. (esp.) deportation to penal settle- ment; (U.S.) means of transport. transpōr'ter n. (esp.) device or apparatus for conveying from one place to another; ~er bridge, high bridge with suspended platform or car for carrying traffic across navigable river etc.

trănspōse' (-z-) v.t. change order or serial place of; (mus.) put into different key. trănsposĭ'tion (-z-) n.

trănsubstăn'tiāte (-shĭ-) v.t. change into different substance. ~tiā'tion n. (esp.) conversion of eucharistic elements into body and blood of Christ.

trănsūrăn'ĭc a. belonging to group of artificially produced radioactive elements with atomic numbers and weights greater than those of uranium.

trănsvĕrse' (-z-) a. situated, lying, etc. across or athwart.

trăp[1] n. device, scheme, plan, etc. for catching, detecting, ensnaring, de- ceiving, etc.; trap-door; device for (suddenly) releasing bird to be shot at, greyhound at start of race, etc.; light esp. two-wheeled (horse-) carriage; device, esp. U-shaped section with standing water, for preventing escape of noxious gases from pipe; (sl.) mouth; (pl.) percus- sion instruments in esp. jazz or dance band etc. v.t. catch (as) in trap; set traps for game etc.; furnish with traps. ~-door, hinged or sliding door flush with surface of floor, roof, etc. ~-drum, bass drum with other percussion instru- ments attached. ~-drummer, per- cussion player in jazz band etc. ~-shooting, sport of shooting at balls etc. released from spring trap. trăpp'er n. (esp.) one who traps wild animals for their fur etc.

trăp[2] n. kind of dark volcanic rock.

trapes : see traipse.

trapēze' n. horizontal cross-bar suspended by ropes as apparatus for acrobatics etc. trapē'zĭum n. quadrilateral with (only) two sides parallel; (U.S.) trapezoid. trăp'ė- zoid n. quadrilateral with no sides parallel; (U.S.) trapezium.

trăpp'ings (-z) n.pl. ornamental cloth covering for horse; ornaments, ornamental accessories.

trăps n.pl. (colloq.) portable belong- ings, baggage.

trapse : see traipse.

trăsh n. waste or worthless stuff; nonsense; worthless or disreput- able people; white ~, poor white population esp. of southern U.S. trăsh'ў a.

trau'ma n. (pl. -ata, -as), wound,

injury; painful psychological experience etc., emotional shock, esp. as origin of neurosis. **traumăt'ĭc** *a.*

trăv'ail *n. & v.i.* (arch.) (suffer) pangs of childbirth; (make) laborious effort.

trăv'el *v.* make journey(s) esp. of some length or to foreign countries; act as commercial traveller; pass from one point or place to another; move, be capable of moving, along fixed course; journey through, pass over, traverse; (colloq.) bear transportation. *n.* travelling; (range, rate, etc. of) single movement of part of mechanism. **~ agency,** agency making arrangements, supplying tickets, etc. for travellers. **~ling crane,** crane travelling along esp. overhead support. **~ling fellowship, scholarship,** one enabling or requiring holder to travel for study or research. **trăv'elled** *a.* that has travelled (much or widely). **trăv'eller** *n.* person who travels or is travelling; commercial traveller; **~ler's cheques,** kind sold in fixed denominations by banks for convenience of travellers. **~ler's joy,** kinds of clematis trailing over wayside hedges. **trăv'elŏgue** *n.* usu. illustrated talk on travel.

trăv'erse *v.* travel or lie across; make traverse; turn (gun etc.), swivel, turn as on pivot; (of horse) walk obliquely; consider, discuss, whole extent of; deny, esp. in pleading; thwart, frustrate. *n.* thing, esp. part of structure, that crosses another; more or less horizontal crossing of face of precipice in climbing; (each leg or lap of) zigzag course or road; horizontal or lateral movement of gun etc.; (law) formal denial of matter of fact alleged.

trăv'ertīne (*or* -ĭn) *n.* light-coloured crystalline concretionary limestone used for building.

trăv'ĕstў *n.* gross parody, ridiculous imitation. *v.t.* make or be travesty of.

trawl *n.* large wide-mouthed net dragged by boat along bottom of sea etc.; (U.S.) long buoyed line supporting numerous baited lines,

for sea-fishing. *v.* fish with trawl or in trawler; catch with trawl. **traw'ler** *n.* vessel used in fishing with trawl-net.

tray *n.* flat shallow vessel used for carrying small articles etc.; shallow lidless box or drawer forming compartment of trunk etc.

treach'erous (-ĕch-) *a.* violating faith or betraying trust; perfidious; not to be relied on, deceptive. **~erў** *n.*

trea'cle *n.* uncrystallized syrup produced in refining sugar; molasses. **trea'clў** *a.*

tread (-ĕd) *v.* (*trŏd, trŏdden*), set one's foot down; (of foot) be set down; traverse on foot; press or crush with feet, trample (*on*); (of male bird) copulate (with); **~** *down,* press down with feet, trample on, crush; **~** *out,* stamp out, press out (wine etc.) with feet; **~** *water,* keep body erect and head above water by moving legs as in walking upstairs. *n.* manner or sound of walking; top surface of stair; piece of rubber etc. placed on step to lessen wear or sound; part of wheel, tyre, etc. coming in contact with ground. **~mill,** appliance for producing motion by treading on steps fixed to revolving cylinder, esp. kind formerly used in prisons as punishment; monotonous routine.

tread'le (-ĕd-) *n.* lever moved by foot and imparting motion to lathe, sewing-machine, etc. *v.i.* work treadle.

Treas. *abbr.* Treasurer.

trea'son (-z-) *n.* violation by subject of allegiance to sovereign or State; breach of faith, disloyalty. **~able, ~ous** *aa.* involving, guilty of, treason.

trea'sure (-ĕzher) *n.* accumulated wealth; precious metals, gems, etc. or hoard of them; valued thing or person; (colloq.) very efficient or satisfactory servant etc. *v.t.* set store on as dear or valuable; hoard, store (*up*). **~-house,** place where treasures are kept. **~-trove,** gold, silver, etc. found hidden in ground etc., owner of which is unknown. **trea'surer** (-ĕzhe-) *n.* person responsible for funds of institution, society, etc.

trea'sury (-ĕzhe-) *n.* place where treasure is kept; funds or revenue of State institution, society, etc.; *T~* (building of) department of State advising Chancellor of Exchequer, administering expenditure of public revenue, etc.

treat *v.* act or behave towards in specified way; deal with, apply process to, etc., esp. deal with disease etc. in order to relieve or cure; entertain, esp. with food and drink; negotiate (*with*); ~ *to*, indulge with. *n.* entertainment, esp. given gratuitously; treating, invitation to eat or esp. drink; great pleasure, delight, or gratification; *stand ~*, pay for another's drink, entertainment, etc.

trea'tise *n.* written or printed exposition of subject.

treat'ment *n.* (mode of) dealing with or behaving towards person or thing; esp. (method of) treating patient or disease.

trea'ty *n.* formally concluded and ratified agreement between States.

trĕb'le *a.* & *n.* threefold, triple (sum, quantity); (crochet stitch) with three loops on hook together; soprano (part, voice, singer, esp. boy); high-pitched, shrill (sound etc.); (string etc.) of treble pitch. *v.* multiply, be multiplied, by three.

tree *n.* perennial plant with self--supporting woody main stem (usu. developing woody branches at some distance from ground); erect bush or shrub with single stem; shaped piece of wood, esp. boot-tree; (arch.) gallows, cross of Christ; genealogical chart like branching tree. *v.i.* cause to take refuge in tree; stretch on boot-tree. ~--creeper, kinds of small bird that creep on tree-trunks etc. ~-fern, kinds of large fern with upright woody stem.

trĕ'foil (*or* -ē-) *n.* kinds of plant with three-lobed leaves; (archit.) opening divided by cusps suggesting three-lobed leaf.

trĕk *v.i.* travel, migrate, esp. by ox--wagon; make arduous journey,

esp on foot. *n.* trekking; (stage of) long and arduous journey.

trĕll'is *n.* grating of light wooden or metal bars, used as support for climbing plants, screen, etc. *v.t.* furnish, support, (as) with trellis. ~work, trellis.

trĕm'ble *v.i.* shake involuntarily with fear, cold, etc.; be affected with fear, suspense, etc. *n.* trembling, quiver, tremor. **trĕm'bler** *n.* (esp.) spring making electrical contact when shaken. **trĕm'bly** *a.* (colloq.).

trĕmĕn'dous *a.* awe-inspiring, terrible; extraordinarily great or large, immense, huge.

trĕm'olō *n.* & *a.* (mus.) (having, producing) tremulous or vibrating effects in voice or bowed instrument. [It.]

trĕm'or *n.* tremulous or vibratory movement or sound, vibration, shaking; quiver; thrill of fear or other emotion.

trĕm'ūlous *a.* trembling, quivering; timorous; tremblingly sensitive or responsive.

trĕnch (-sh) *n.* deep ditch, esp. one dug by troops as shelter from enemy's fire. *v.* make trench(es) or ditch(es) in, dig trench(es); make series of trenches so as to bring lower soil to surface; cut groove in wood etc.; encroach, border, verge, (*up*)*on*.

trĕnch'ant (-sh-) *a.* sharp, keen; incisive, decisive. **trĕnch'ancy** *n.*

trĕnch'er (-sh-) *n.* (esp.) wooden platter for cutting bread on. ~man, *good, valiant,* etc. eater.

trĕnd *v.i.* have specified direction, course, or general tendency. *n.* general direction, course, tendency. **trĕn'dy** *a.* following latest trends of fashion etc.

trĕpăn', trĕphine' (-ēn *or* -īn) *n.* surgeon's cylindrical saw for making opening in skull. *v.t.* use trepan on.

trĕpĭdā'tion *n.* agitation, alarm, anxiety.

trĕs'pass *v.i.* enter unlawfully on another's land, property, etc.; (arch.) transgress, sin; encroach *on*. *n.* act of trespassing; (arch.) sin, offence.

trĕss *n.* lock, braid, of hair; (pl.) hair.
trĕs'tle (-sl) *n.* horizontal beam with diverging legs or similar support for table etc.; open braced framework for supporting bridge etc. ~-**table**, table of board(s) laid across trestles.
T.R.H. *abbr.* Their Royal Highnesses.
tri- in comb., three, thrice. **trī'brăch** (-k; *or* -ĭ-) *n.* metrical foot of three short syllables. ~-**car** *n.* three-wheeled motor-car ~**cĕntē'nary**, -**centĕnn'ĭal** *aa. & nn.* tercentenary, tercentennial. ~**cĕps** *a. & n.* (muscle, esp. extensor of back of upper arm) with three points of origin. ~**chŏt'omȳ** (-k-) *n.* division into, classification etc. in, three. ~**chromăt'ĭc** (-k-) *a.* of or in three colours. ~**cŭs'pĭd** *a.* having three cusps or points. ~**ĕnn'ĭal** *a.* existing, lasting, for three years; occurring etc. every three years. ~**fō'lĭate** *a.* three-leaved; having three leaflets. ~**fōrm** *a.* having, appearing in, three forms. **trĭg'amy** *n.* having three wives or husbands at same time; ~**gamous** *a.* ~**graph** (-ahf) *n.* combination of three letters representing one sound. ~**lăt'eral** *a. & n.* three-sided (figure). ~**lĭng'ual** (-nggw-) *a.* speaking, using, expressed in, three languages. ~**nītrotŏl'ūēne** *n.* kind of high explosive. ~**nō'mĭal** *a. & n.* (esp.) (algebraical expression) of three terms. ~**ōde** *n.* thermionic valve with three electrodes. ~**pār'tīte** *a.* divided, of or involving division, into three parts or kinds; engaged in, concluded, between three parties. ~**rēme** *n.* ancient warship with three banks of oars. ~**sĕct'** *v.t.* divide into three esp. equal parts; ~**sĕc'tion** *n.* **trĭsȳll'able** (*or* trī-) *n.* word of three syllables; ~**syllăb'ic** *a.* ~**ūne** *a.* three in one. ~ **vā'lent** *a.* (chem.) having valency of three. ~-**wee'klȳ** *a. & adv.* (occurring, appearing, etc.) three times a week or every three weeks.
trī'ad *n.* group of three; (mus.) chord of note with its third and fifth.
trī'al *n.* examination by judicial tribunal; testing, putting to proof, investigation by experience; test of qualities, skill, efficiency, etc.; attempt, endeavour; being tried by suffering etc., painful test of endurance etc.; affliction, hardship; thing or person that tries one's patience etc.; *on* ~, undergoing trial(s), on approval.
trī'ăngle (-nggl) *n.* figure bounded by three straight lines; three-cornered object, space, etc., esp. musical percussion instrument of steel rod bent into triangle. **trĭăng'ūlar** *a.* triangle-shaped, three-cornered. **trĭăng'ūlāte** *v.t.* divide or convert into triangles; measure, map out, by triangulation. **trĭăngūlā'tion** *n.* (surveying etc.) measurement of sides and angles of series of triangles on determined base-line(s).
Trĭăss'ĭc *a. & n.* (of) system or period of rocks immediately above Permian.
tribe *n.* group of primitive or barbarous clans under recognized chiefs; one of twelve divisions of people of Israel claiming descent from sons of Jacob; group ranking below sub-family and above genus; (usu. contempt.) class, lot, set. ~**sman**, member of tribe. **trī'bal** *a.* **trī'balism** *n.* tribal life, system, or organization.
tribūlā'tion *n.* great affliction.
tribū'nal (*or* -ĭ-) *n.* court of justice, judicial assembly; board, committee, etc. set up to inquire into or adjudicate on particular question, claim, etc.
trib'ūne[1] *n.* platform, rostrum.
trib'ūne[2] *n.* (Rom. hist.) officer protecting interests and rights of plebeians from patricians; popular leader, demagogue.
trib'ūtarȳ *a. & n.* (person, State) paying or subject to tribute; auxiliary, contributory; (stream etc.) contributing its flow to larger stream or lake.
trib'ūte *n.* periodical payment exacted by one sovereign or State from another; thing done or said or given as mark of respect, affection, etc.
trice[1] *n.* instant, moment.
trice[2] *v.t.* (naut.) hoist *up* and secure with rope or lashing.

trichĭnō′sĭs (-k-) *n*. disease due to hair-like parasitic worms.

trick *n*. crafty or fraudulent, esp. mean or base, device or stratagem; hoax, joke; capricious, foolish, or stupid act; clever device or contrivance, feat of skill or dexterity; knack; habit, mannerism; (cards) cards played in, winning of, one round; (naut.) time of duty at helm. *v.t.* deceive by trick, cheat, beguile; dress, deck (*out*, *up*). **trick′erў**, **~ster** *nn*. **~sў** *a*. full of tricks or pranks, playful. **trick′ў** *a*. given to tricks, deceitful; skilful, adroit; (colloq.) requiring cautious or adroit action or handling, ticklish.

tric′kle *v*. (cause to) flow in drops or scanty halting stream; (cause ball to) run slowly over surface of ground. *n*. trickling, small fitful stream or flow. **~ charger**, (electr.) device for slow continuous charging of accumulator.

tric′olour (-ŭl*er*; *or* -ĭ-) *n*. & *a*. (flag, esp. French national flag) having three colours.

tricot (trē′kō; *or* trĭ-) *n*. knitted fabric, jersey. **~-stitch**, plain crochet stitch.

trī′cўcle *n*. three-wheeled pedal--driven vehicle. *v.i.* ride tricycle.

trī′dent *n*. three-pronged fish-spear borne as sceptre by Neptune and Britannia; three-pronged weapon used in Roman gladiatorial combats.

tried, *p.t.* & *p.p.* of **try**.

triennial : see **tri-**.

trī′fle *n*. thing, fact, circumstance, of slight value or importance; small amount or article; sweet dish of sponge-cakes with whipped cream etc. *v.i.* toy, play, dally, fidget, *with*; act or speak idly or frivolously.

trīfŏr′ĭum *n*. (pl. -*ia*), arcade or gallery above arches at sides of nave, choir, etc.

trig[1] *a*. trim, spruce, smart.

trig., trig[2] *abbr*. trigonometry.

trigg′er (-g-) *n*. lever or catch pulled or pressed to release spring or otherwise set mechanism in motion, esp. catch for releasing hammer of fire-arm. *v*. set *off* reaction, process,

etc. by comparatively small action etc. **~ finger**, forefinger of right hand. **~-happy**, (colloq.) impetuous or irresponsible in use of firearms (freq. fig.).

trigonŏm′etrў *n*. branch of mathematics dealing with measurement of sides and angles of triangles, and with certain functions of angles. **~mĕt′rical** *a*.

tril′bў *n*. soft felt hat with narrow brim and indented crown.

trī′lĭth, tril′ĭthon *nn*. prehistoric structure of horizontal stone resting on two upright ones.

trill *n*. (mus.) rapid alternation of two notes a tone or semitone apart; pronunciation of consonant, consonant pronounced, with vibration of tongue etc.; tremulous high-pitched sound or note(s). *v*. utter, sing, produce, with trill(s); make trill(s).

trill′ion (-yon) *a*. & *n*. third power of million, a million million millions; (U.S. etc.) square of million.

trī′lobīte (*or* trĭ-) *n*. kind of fossil crustacean.

tril′ogў *n*. set of three related dramatic or other literary works.

trim *a*. in good order, neat; not loose or ungainly. *v*. make neat or tidy; remove irregular, unsightly, etc. parts by planing, clipping, etc.; ornament; adjust balance of (vessel, aircraft) by distribution of weight; arrange (sails etc.) to suit wind; **~ one's** *sails*, adjust one's policy etc. to changing circumstances. *n*. state or degree of readiness, fitness, adjustment, etc.; balance; good order; trimming, being trimmed; trimmings. **trim′mer** *n*. (esp.) time-server, opportunist. **trimm′ing** *n*. (esp.) ornamental addition to dress, hat, etc.; (pl.) accessories, usual accompaniments; (pl.) pieces cut off in trimming.

trine *a*. & *n*. threefold, triple (group); (thing) made up of three parts; (astrol.) (aspect) of two heavenly bodies distant from each other by third part of zodiac.

Trĭnĭtār′ian *a*. & *n*. (holder) of doctrine of Trinity of Godhead.

trĭn′itў *n*. being three; group of three;

the T~, three persons of Godhead as conceived in orthodox Christian belief. **T~ Sunday**, Sunday after Whit Sunday. **T~ term**, university etc. term beginning after Easter.

trĭnk′ĕt *n*. small or trifling ornament, esp. piece of jewellery.

tri′o (-ēō) *n*. (pl. *-os*), group or set of three, esp. (mus.) performers; musical composition for three voices or instruments; middle division of minuet or scherzo.

trī′olĕt *n*. verse-form with eight lines and two rhymes.

trĭp *v*. go lightly and quickly along; catch one's foot and stumble; commit blunder or fault; cause (person) to stumble by entangling his feet; release (catch, lever, etc.) by contact with projection, operate thus; ~ *up*, (cause to) stumble, detect in error, inconsistency, etc. *n*. excursion for pleasure esp. at lower fare than usual; (short) voyage or journey, esp. one of series over particular route; stumble; projecting part of mechanism causing or checking movement by contact with another part. ~-**hammer**, massive machine hammer operated by trip. ~-**wire**, wire stretched close to ground and actuating warning device, working trap, etc. when tripped against.

trīpe *n*. first or second stomach of ox or other ruminant prepared as food; (pl., vulg.) entrails; (sl.) worthless or trashy product or thing, nonsense.

trĭp′le *a*. threefold, three times as much or as many, of three parts. *v*. increase threefold; be three times as great or as many as. ~ **crown**, papal tiara. ~ **time**, (mus.) rhythm of three beats in bar. **trĭp′lў** *adv*.

trĭp′lĕt *n*. set of three; esp. three successive lines of verse rhyming together; (mus.) group of three notes performed in time of two of same value; each of three children born at one birth.

trĭp′lĕx *a*. triple, threefold. ~ **glass**, kind of unsplinterable glass. **P.**

trĭp′lĭcate *a*. threefold, forming three exactly corresponding copies. *n*. each of three exactly corresponding copies or parts; *in* ~, in three identical copies etc. *v.t.* (-āt), multiply by three, make or provide in triplicate. ~**ā′tion** *n*.

trī′pod *n*. three-legged or three-footed stand, support, seat, etc.

trī′pŏs *n*. (Cambridge Univ.) final honours examination for B.A.

trĭpp′er *n*. (esp.) excursionist, one who goes on pleasure trip. ~**ish**, ~**ў** *aa*.

trĭpp′ingly *adv*. (esp.) fluently.

trĭp′tўch (-k) *n*. altar-piece etc. of three usu. folding panels.

trīte *a*. well-worn, hackneyed, commonplace.

trĭt′ĭum *n*. radioactive isotope of hydrogen with atomic weight 3.

Trī′ton *n*. (Gk. myth.) sea-god with body of man and tail of fish.

trĭt′ūrāte *v.t.* grind, rub, etc. to powder or fine particles. ~**ā′tion** *n*.

trī′umph *n*. (Rom. ant.) solemn processional entry into Rome of victorious general; triumphing; (glory of) victory; rejoicing in success. *v.i.* be victorious, prevail; rejoice in victory, exult (*over*); rejoice, glory. **trĭŭm′phal** *a*. of, celebrating, commemorating, triumph or victory. **trĭŭm′phant** *a*. victorious, successful; triumphing, exultant.

trĭŭm′vir *n*. (pl. *-rs*, *-rĭ*), one of group of three jointly exercising (supreme) power. ~**ate** *n*. office or function of triumvir; set of triumvirs.

trĭv′ĕt *n*. stand, esp. tripod, for pot, kettle, etc., placed over fire.

trĭv′ĭal *a*. of small value or importance, trifling, slight, inconsiderable. **trĭvĭăl′itў** *n*.

trŏ′chee (-k-) *n*. metrical foot of two syllables (— ◡).

trod, trodden, *p.t.* & *p.p.* of **tread**.

trŏg′lodўte *n*. cave-dweller, caveman.

troi′ka *n*. (Russian vehicle drawn by) three horses abreast.

Trō′jan *a*. & *n*. (inhabitant) of ancient Troy; *work like a* ~, work with great energy and endurance.

trŏll[1] *v*. sing (*out*) in carefree spirit, fish by drawing bait along in water.

tröll[2] *n.* kinds of supernatural being in Scandinavian mythology.

tröll'ey *n.* kinds of low truck, esp. running along rails; small table on wheels or castors; wheel running along overhead electric wire etc., usu. on pole down which current is conveyed to vehicle; (U.S.) electric tram-car. ∼-bus, bus with motive power derived from trolley.

tröll'op *n.* disreputable or slatternly woman.

trombōne' *n.* large brass wind-instrument with sliding tube. **trombō'nist** *n.*

trōop *n.* body of soldiers; (pl.) armed forces; (mil.) subdivision of cavalry regiment, artillery unit; company of Boy Scouts; number of persons or things collected together, company, herd, swarm. *v.* assemble, move, come or go, etc. in or as troop or in great numbers; ∼ *the colour(s)*, ceremonially escort regimental flag through regiment on parade. ∼-carrier, aircraft for transporting troops. **trōo'per** *n.* cavalryman, horse-soldier; troopship; mounted policeman, (U.S.) member of state police force usu. using motor vehicle(s).

trōpe *n.* figure of speech.

trō'phy *n.* (representation of) pile of spoils of war as memorial of victory; anything taken in war, hunting, etc.; prize, memento.

tröp'ic *n.* parallel of latitude 23° 28′ N. or S. of equator; (pl.) region lying between tropics, torrid zone. **tröp'ical** *a.* of, occurring in, etc. the tropics; very hot, ardent, or luxuriant.

tröp'osphēre *n.* layer of atmosphere extending from earth's surface to stratosphere.

tröt *n.* quadruped's gait between walk and gallop; gait between walking and running; spell of trotting. *v.* (make) go at trot; cover (distance) by trotting; ∼ *out*, produce, bring forward. **tröt'er** *n.* (esp.) horse specially trained for trotting; animal's foot, esp. as food.

tröth *n.* (arch.) faith, fidelity.

trou'badour (-ōō-, -oor) *n.* medieval romantic or amatory poet.

troub'le (trŭb-) *n.* (cause of) affliction, grief, bother, inconvenience, difficulty, unpleasant relations with authorities, etc.; discontent, public unrest; pains, exertion. *v.* disturb, agitate; distress, grieve; subject, be subjected, to inconvenience or exertion, bother. ∼-maker, one who stirs up trouble, agitator. ∼-shooter, person employed to trace and remove cause of defective working, discontent, etc. ∼some *a.* causing trouble, vexatious. **troub'lous** *a.* (arch.) full of troubles.

trough (-ŏf) *n.* long narrow box-like receptacle for liquid etc. to stand in; channel or hollow comparable to this; (meteor.) region of lower barometric pressure between two higher.

trounce *v.t.* beat severely; defeat heavily; scold, abuse.

troupe (-ōō-) *n.* company, esp. of actors etc. ∼r *n.* (esp.) theatrical performer.

trou'sers (-zerz) *n.pl.* loose two-legged outer garment from waist to ankles.

trou'sseau (-ōōsō) *n.* bride's outfit of clothes etc.

trout *n.* kinds of small fresh-water fish of salmon kind.

trow (-ō) *v.t.* (arch.) think, believe.

trow'el *n.* flat-bladed tool for spreading mortar etc.; gardener's short-handled hollow-bladed tool.

troy *n.* system of weights used for precious metals etc.

trs. *abbr.* transpose.

tru'ant (-ōō-) *n.* one who absents himself from duty etc., esp. child who stays away from school without leave. **tru'ancy** *n.*

truce (-ōō-) *n.* (agreement for) temporary cessation of hostilities; respite.

trŭck[1] *n.* (system of) payment of wages otherwise than in money; odds and ends, trash; (U.S.) market-garden produce; dealings.

trŭck[2] *n.* strong vehicle for heavy goods; open railway-wagon; barrow for moving luggage etc. *v.t.* carry, convey, on truck.

trŭck′le *v.i.* submit obsequiously, cringe (*to*).

trŭck′le-bed *n.* low wheeled bed that can be pushed under another.

trŭc′ūlent *a.* aggressive, fierce. **~ence** *n.*

trŭdge *v.i.* walk laboriously or without spirit. *n.* laborious or wearisome walk.

true (-ōō) *a.* in accordance with fact or reality; genuine, real, correct, proper; in good tune; accurately placed, fitted, or shaped; (of ground etc.) level, smooth, even; loyal, faithful, constant (*to*). *adv.* truly. *v.t.* make true or accurate.

trŭff′le *n.* rich-flavoured underground fungus esteemed as delicacy.

trŭg *n.* shallow usu. wooden garden--basket.

tru′ĭsm (-ōō-) *n.* self-evident or hackneyed truth.

tru′lў (-ōō-) *adv.* with truth; sincerely; loyally; accurately.

trŭmp¹ *n.* playing-card of suit ranking above others for one game; (colloq.) good fellow; *turn up* **~s**, (colloq.) turn out well or successfully, prove extremely kind, generous, etc. *v.* defeat, take, with trump; play trump; **~** *up*, (colloq.) fabricate, invent. **~-card,** card turned up to determine trump--suit; valuable resource, means of gaining one's end etc.

trŭmp² *n.* (arch.) (sound of) trumpet.

trŭm′perў *a.* showy but worthless, trashy; trumped-up.

trŭm′pĕt *n.* wind-instrument of bright ringing tone, with narrow straight or curved tube flared at end; trumpet-shaped thing, esp. corona of daffodil; sound (as) of trumpet, esp. elephant's loud cry. *v.* proclaim (as) by sound of trumpet; celebrate, extol loudly; (of elephant) make trumpet. **~er** *n.* player or sounder of trumpet, esp. cavalry--soldier giving signals with trumpet; **~er**(-*swan*), large N.-Amer. wild swan.

trŭncāte′ *v.t.* cut off top or end of; cut short; maim, mutilate. **~ā′tion** *n.*

trŭn′cheon (-chn) *n.* short thick staff or club, esp. that carried by policeman. *v.t.* strike or beat with truncheon.

trŭn′dle *v.* roll or bowl along; draw, be drawn, along on wheels or in wheeled vehicle.

trŭnk *n.* main stem of tree; body without head and limbs; shaft of column; main body or line of nerve, artery, etc. or of railway, telephone, road, etc. system, as dist. from branches; elephant's prehensile nose; travelling-box or portmanteau; (pl.) short close-fitting breeches worn by swimmers etc. **~ call,** telephone call to exchange at some distance. **~-hose,** (hist.) full puffed breeches reaching to mid-thigh. **~-line,** main line of railway, telephone system, etc. **~ road,** important main road.

trŭnn′ion (-yon) *n.* supporting cylindrical projection on either side of cannon etc.

Truron. *abbr.* (Bp.) of Truro.

trŭss *n.* bundle of hay or straw; supporting structure or framework of roof, bridge, etc.; surgical appliance for support in cases of hernia etc. *v.t.* make into trusses; support with truss(es); tie (*up*), fasten, bind, closely or securely; fasten limbs of (fowl etc. for cooking) close to body.

trŭst *n.* confidence in, reliance on, quality of person or thing, truth of statement, future state or happening, etc.; credit; being trusted; obligation of person given confidence or vested with authority; charge etc. committed to one; trusteeship; property committed to trustee(s); combination of producing or trading firms to reduce competition etc.; *in* **~**, held as trust, entrusted to person or body of persons; *take on* **~**, accept without question or investigation. *v.* put trust in; treat as reliable; commit to care of; hope; allow credit to. **~ful** *a.* full of trust, confiding. **~worthy** *a.* worthy of trust, reliable. **trŭs′tў** *a.* (arch.) trustworthy; *n.* trustworthy person, esp. (U.S.) convict given special privileges.

trŭstee' *n.* person to whom property is entrusted for benefit of another; one of number of persons appointed to manage affairs of institution. **~ship** *n.* position of trustee; status of area governed by another State under supervision of U.N.

truth (-ōō-) *n.* (pl. pr. -dhz), being true; loyalty, accuracy, integrity, etc.; what is true, true statement, account, belief, etc.; reality, fact. **~ful** *a.* habitually speaking truth; true.

trȳ *v.* examine and pronounce upon, determine guilt or innocence of, judicially; test; make severe demands on; make attempt (at); **~** *for*, attempt to attain or reach; **~** one's *hand*, make one's first attempt (*at*); **~** *it on*, (colloq.) attempt an imposition, begin doubtful action etc. experimentally to see how much will be tolerated; **~** *on*, test fit or style of (garment) by putting it on; **~** *out*, put to test, test thoroughly. *n.* attempt; (Rugby footb.) (points scored for) right of trying to kick goal obtained by touch-down. **~-on**, trying it on. **~-out**, experimental run, preliminary test, etc. **~sail**, small fore-and-aft sail set with gaff. **trȳ'ing** *a.* (esp.) exhausting; exasperating; difficult to bear.

trȳst (*or* -ī-) *n.* (arch.) appointed meeting, appointment.

tsär *n.* emperor of Russia. **tsari'na** (-ēn-), **tsarit'sa** *nn.* empress of Russia.

tsĕt'sė *n.* fly of central and southern Africa carrying disease to men and animals.

T-shirt, T-square : see **T.**

T.T. *abbr.* teetotal(ler); Tourist Trophy; tuberculin-tested.

T.U. *abbr.* Trade Union.

tŭb *n.* open cylindrical or concave wooden vessel used for washing and other purposes; (colloq.) bath-tub, bath; (mining) bucket, wagon, etc., for conveying coal to shaft or surface; slow clumsy ship; short broad boat, esp. for rowing practice. *v.* bathe in tub; plant, pack, in tub; coach, practise, in tub. **~-thumper**, ranting preacher or orator.

tū'ba *n.* large low-pitched brass wind-instrument of saxhorn family.

tŭbb'ў *a.* tub-shaped; short and fat.

tūbe *n.* long hollow cylinder esp. for conveying or holding liquids; main body of wind instrument; short cylinder of flexible metal for holding semi-liquid material; inner tube containing air in pneumatic tyre; hollow cylindrical organ in animal body; cylindrical tunnel of some electric railways; underground railway; cathode-ray tube of television receiver; (U.S.) thermionic valve. *v.t.* furnish with, enclose in, tube(s).

tū'ber *n.* short thick rounded root or underground stem of plant.

tū'bercle *n.* small rounded swelling in part or organ of body, esp. mass of granulation-cells characteristic of tuberculosis. **tūbĕr'cūlar, tubĕr'cūlous** *aa.* **tūbĕrcūlō'sis** *n.* infectious disease characterized by formation of tubercles in bodily tissues, esp. lungs.

tūbĕr'cūlin *n.* preparation from cultures of tubercle bacillus used for treatment and diagnosis of tuberculosis. **~-tested**, (of milk) from cows shown by tuberculin test to be free of tuberculosis.

tūbe'rōse (-brōz) *n.* tropical plant with creamy-white fragrant flowers.

tū'berous *a.* of, like, tuber; bearing tubers.

tū'bing *n.* (esp.) tubes; length or piece of tube; material for tubes.

tū'būlar *a.* tube-shaped; having or consisting of tubes.

T.U.C. *abbr.* Trades Union Congress.

tŭck *n.* flattened fold sewn in garment etc.; (sl.) eatables, esp. sweets and pastry. *v.* put tuck(s) in, shorten cr ornament with tuck(s); thrust or put *away*, esp. into secure place or concealment; thrust or turn (*in*, *up*), ends or edges of (anything pendent or loose, esp. bed-clothes) to restrain or confine them, be so disposed of; settle (person) in bed by tucking in bed-clothes; **~** *in*, (sl.) eat heartily. **~-in**, hearty meal; part to be tucked in; *a.* (esp. of blouse etc.) designed to be tucked into top of skirt etc. **~-out**, hearty meal. ~-shop, shop where tuck is sold.

tŭck'er *v.t.* (U.S.) tire (*out*), exhaust.

Tū'dor *a.* of Tudor sovereigns (Henry VII to Elizabeth I) of England; of, resembling, imitating, esp. domestic architecture of their period.

Tues. *abbr.* Tuesday.

Tūe'sday (-z-) *n.* third day of week.

tū'fa *n.* porous calcareous rock; tuff.

tŭff *n.* rock formed from volcanic ashes.

tŭft *n.* number of feathers, threads, hairs, grass-blades, etc. growing or joined together in cluster or knot. *v.t.* furnish with tuft(s); secure padding of (cushion, mattress, etc.) with thread drawn tightly through at regular intervals.

tŭg *v.* pull hard or violently (*at*); tow with tug. *n.* tugging, violent pull; small powerful steamboat for towing other vessels. ~-boat, tug. ~-of-war, athletic contest between two teams hauling on rope from opposite ends.

tūi'tion *n.* teaching, instruction. ~al, ~arȳ *aa.*

tū'lip *n.* (showy bell- or cup-shaped flower of) bulbous spring-flowering plant. ~-tree, kinds of tree with tulip-like flowers, esp. large N.-Amer. tree with large greenish-yellow flowers. ~-wood, light ornamental wood of tulip-tree etc.

tulle (tūl) *n.* thin soft fine silk net.

tŭm'ble *v.* (cause to) fall, esp. helplessly or violently; roll, toss; overthrow, demolish; be overthrown, fall into ruin; disorder, rumple; stumble, blunder; perform acrobatic feats, esp. somersaults; (of pigeon etc.) turn end over end in flight; ~ *to*, grasp, understand, realize. *n.* fall; tumbled condition, confused or tangled heap. ~down, falling or fallen into ruin; dilapidated. **tum'bler** *n.* (esp.) acrobat; kind of pigeon with tumbling flight; tapering cylindrical or barrel-shaped stemless drinking--glass; pivoted piece in lock moved into proper position by key; kinds of movable, pivoted, swivelling, etc. mechanism or part; ~r switch,

electric switch operated by pushing over small spring thumb-piece.

tŭm'brel, -il *n.* tip-cart, esp. for dung; cart in which condemned persons were carried to guillotine in Fr. Revolution; ammunition cart.

tū'mėfy̆ *v.* (cause to) swell; make, become, tumid. **tūmėfăc'tion** *n.*

tū'mid *a.* swollen, swelling; inflated, pompous. **tūmid'itў** *n.*

tŭm'(mў) *n.* (nursery or joc. form of) stomach.

tū'mour (-mer) *n.* swelling, esp. from morbid mass of new tissue.

tū'mŭlt *n.* commotion of multitude, esp. with confused cries and uproar; agitation, disorderly or noisy movement, confused and violent emotion. **tūmŭl'tūous** *a.*

tū'mŭlus *n.* (pl. -lī), ancient sepulchral mound, barrow.

tŭn *n.* large cask or barrel; measure of capacity (usu. about 210 gals.).

tū'na *n.* tunny, esp. of Californian coast.

tŭn'dra *n.* vast level treeless region with arctic climate and vegetation.

tūne *n.* rhythmical succession of musical tones forming melody or air; correct intonation in singing or instrumental music; harmony or accordance in other vibrations than those of sound; *in, out of,* ~, in or out of proper pitch, correct intonation, order, proper condition, or harmony (*with*), (not) correctly adjusted. *v.* adjust tones of (musical instrument) to standard of pitch; bring into accord, harmony, proper or desirable condition; adjust (engine etc.) to run smoothly, (wireless receiver) to desired wavelength etc.; ~ *in, out,* adjust wireless receiver to receive, cease to receive, signal; ~ *up,* (esp.) bring (instrument) up to proper pitch, adjust instruments for playing together. **tuning-fork,** small two-pronged steel instrument giving musical note of constant pitch when struck. **tūne'ful** *a.* melodious, musical. **tūne'lèss** *a.* **tū'ner** *n.* (esp.) one whose occupation is tuning pianos etc.

tŭng'sten *n.* heavy steel-grey ductile metallic element.

tū'nĭc *n.* ancient Gk. and Rom. short-sleeved body garment reaching to about knees; close-fitting short coat of police or military uniform; close-fitting upper garment reaching below waist; woman's garment of bodice and upper skirt worn over longer skirt; gym-tunic; (biol.) membranous sheath or lining of organ or part, esp. mantle of mollusc.

tŭnn'el *n.* subterranean passage under hill, river, roadway, etc.; burrowing animal's subterranean passage. *v.* make tunnel (through).

tŭnn'y *n.* large mackerel-like sea--fish esteemed as food and as game-fish.

tŭp *n.* male sheep, ram.

tŭpp'ence *n.*, **tuppenny,** (tŭp'enĭ) *a.* twopence, twopenny.

tū quō'quĕ *n.* the retort 'so are you' or 'so did you' etc.

tŭr'ban *n.* man's oriental head-dress of linen, silk, etc. wound round cap; woman's hat or head-dress resembling this.

tŭr'bĭd *a.* muddy, thick, not clear; confused, disordered. **tŭrbĭd'ĭtў** *n.*

tŭr'bĭne (*or* -ĭn) *n.* kinds of rotary motor driven by water, steam, etc.

tŭr'bō- in comb., turbine. **tŭrbo-jĕt'** *a.* & *n.* (jet engine) in which turbine drives air-compressor; (aircraft) powered by turbo-jet. **~-prŏp',** **~-propĕll'er** *aa.* & *nn.* (jet engine) having turbine-driven propeller; (aircraft) powered by turbo-prop engine.

tŭr'bot *n.* large flat-fish esteemed as food.

tŭr'būlent *a.* in commotion, troubled, stormy; disturbed by, causing, turbulence; tumultuous, unruly, violent. **~ence** *n.* (esp.) eddying or sinuous motion of air etc., departure from smoothness of flow.

tūreen' *n.* deep covered dish for serving soup.

tŭrf *n.* short grass with surface earth bound together by its roots; sod; slab or block of peat dug for fuel; *the T~,* institution, action, or practice of horse-racing. *v.t.* lay (ground) with turf; (sl.) throw *out.* **~ accountant,** bookmaker. **tŭr'fў** *a.*

tŭr'gĭd *a.* bombastic, rhetorical. **turgĭd'ĭtў** *n.*

Tŭr'key[1]. **~ carpet,** thick-piled woollen carpet with bold design in red, blue, and green. **~ red,** kind of scarlet dye. **~ towel,** rough towel with long nap.

tŭr'key[2] *n.* large gallinaceous bird esteemed as table fowl. **~-buzzard,** Amer. carrion vulture. **~-cock,** male of turkey; strutting pompous person.

Tŭr'kĭsh *a.* & *n.* (language) of Turks. **~ bath,** hot-air or steam bath followed by massage etc. **~ delight,** kind of sweetmeat.

tŭr'meric *n.* (pungent aromatic root--stock of) E. Indian herb of ginger kind.

tŭr'moil *n.* agitation, commotion.

tŭrn *v.* move on or as on axis; give rotary motion to, have rotary motion; change from one side to another, invert, reverse; give new direction to, take new direction; adapt, be adapted; move to other side of, go round, flank; cause to go, send, put; change in nature, form, condition, etc.; shape in lathe; give esp. elegant form to; revolve mentally; **~** *against,* become hostile to; **~** *down,* fold down, place upside down or face downwards, reduce flame etc. of esp. by turning tap, (sl.) reject; **~** *in,* (esp., colloq.) go to bed; **~** *off,* check flow of by turning tap, switch, etc., dismiss from employment, branch away from; **~** *on,* start flow, supply, etc. of, depend on, become hostile to, attack; **~** *out,* expel, (cause to) point or incline outwards, produce, clear contents out of, extinguish (light etc.), (cause to) assemble for duty etc., get out of bed, be found, prove; **~** *over,* (esp.) hand over, make over, do business to amount of; **~** *to,* apply oneself (to), set about; **~** *turtle,* capsize; **~** *up,* (esp.) appear, happen, (colloq.) nauseate, cause to vomit. *n.* turning; rotation, esp. single revolution of wheel etc.; (single) coil or twist; change of direction, course, colour, condition, etc.; angle, bend turning back (esp. of tide) character, tendency; (mus.) ornament consisting of principal note with those above and below it; (colloq.) momentary shock; act of good or ill will, service; attack of illness etc.; opportunity, occasion, etc. coming to several persons etc. in succession; appearance on stage, (performer of) item in entertainment; ~ (and ~) about, in turn; hand's ~, stroke, piece of work; in ~, in succession; on the ~, (of food etc.) turning sour; serve one's etc. ~, answer purpose or requirement. ~coat, person who changes principles or party. ~cock, one employed to turn on water from mains. ~key, one in charge of keys of prison. ~out, (esp.) equipage; muster, assemblage; (style of) equipment, outfit. ~over, (esp.) kind of pie etc. made by folding half of pastry over filling laid on other half; amount turned over in trade. ~pike, (hist.) toll-gate; road with gates etc. for collecting tolls; main road. ~-round, (time occupied by) arriving at destination, unloading, reloading, and leaving again. ~spit, (hist.) one who turned spit for roasting meat. ~stile, revolving barrier on footpath, in gateway, etc. ~table, revolving platform, table, etc., esp. for reversing railway vehicles etc. ~-up, turned-up part, esp. of end of trouser-leg; turning up of card etc.; (colloq.) commotion, row, fight. tŭr′ner n. (esp.) one who works with lathe; ~erў n. tŭr′ning n. place where road etc. turns or turns off from another; road etc. turning off; ~ing-point, point at which decisive change takes place.

tŭr′nĭp n. (cruciferous plant bearing) fleshy root used as vegetable and for feeding cattle and sheep.

tŭr′pentīne n. kinds of resin got from coniferous trees; volatile inflammable oil distilled from turpentines and used in mixing paints etc.

tŭr′pitūde n. baseness, wickedness.

tŭrps n. (colloq.) turpentine oil.

tŭr′quoise (-koiz; or -kw-) n. (blue-green colour of) opaque precious stone.

tŭ′rrĕt n. small tower, esp. rounded addition to angle of building; towerlike armoured structure in which guns are mounted or housed; rotating holder for dies or tools in lathe, drill, etc. tŭ′rrĕtĕd a.

tŭr′tle[1] n. kinds of wild dove noted for soft cooing and affection for its mate.

tŭr′tle[2] n. marine tortoise, esp. edible kinds used for soup etc. ~-neck(ed), (having) high close-fitting neck or collar.

Tŭs′can a. & n. (language, native) of Tuscany; (archit.) of simplest of five classical orders.

tŭsk n. long pointed tooth projecting beyond mouth in elephant, boar, etc.; tusk-like thing. ~er n. elephant, wild boar, with developed tusks.

tŭss′le n. & v.i. struggle, scuffle.

tŭss′ock n. tuft, clump, of grass etc. ~-grass, esp. stout tall-growing kinds of grass.

tŭss′ŏre n. strong coarse brownish wild silk.

tŭt, tŭt-tŭt′ ints., nn., & vv.i. (make) exclamation of impatience, dissatisfaction, or rebuke.

tū′tĕlage n. (being under) guardianship; instruction, tuition.

tū′tĕlarў a. of guardian, protective; serving as protector or patron.

tū′tor n. private teacher; university teacher directing studies of undergraduates; instruction book; (Rom. law) guardian. v. act as tutor (to); exercise restraint over, subject to discipline. ~age, ~ship nn. tūtōr′ĭal a. of tutor; n. period of instruction given to single student or small group.

tutti-fru′ttĭ (tōō-, frōō-) n. & a. (confection, esp. ice-cream) made of or flavoured with various fruits.

tut-tut : see tut.

tū′tū n. dancer's short skirt of layers of stiffened frills.

tŭxē′dō n. (U.S.) dinner-jacket.

TV, T.V. abbr. television.

twadd′le (-ŏ-) n. & v.i. (talk, write, etc.) silly nonsense.

twain n. & a. (arch.) two.

twăng n. sharp ringing sound (as) of plucking tense string, wire, etc.;

nasal intonation; peculiarity of pronunciation. *v.* (cause to) make twanging sound; play by plucking strings (of).

tweak *n.* twitch, sharp pull, pinch. *v.t.* seize and pull sharply with twisting movement, twitch.

tweed *n.* twilled woollen usu. rough-surfaced cloth; (pl.) tweed clothes. **twee'dy** *a.*

tweet (-tweet) *n. & v.i.* (utter) note of small bird.

twee'zers (-z) *n.pl.* small pincer-like instrument for picking up small objects, etc.

twelfth *a. & n.* next after eleventh; (that is) one of twelve equal parts; *the ~*, 12 Aug. as opening day of grouse-shooting. **T~-day, -night,** (evening of) Epiphany, 6 Jan., formerly last day of Christmas festivities.

twelve *a. & n.* one more than eleven (12, XII). **~mo, 12mo,** duodecimo. **~month,** year.

twen'ty *a. & n.* twice ten (20, XX). **~-five,** (space enclosed by) line across ground 25 yds. from each goal in Rugby footb. etc. **twen'tieth** *a. & n.*

twerp, twirp *n.* (sl.) silly fool, insignificant person.

twice *adv.* two times; on two occasions; doubly.

twidd'le *v.* trifle (with), twist idly about; *~ one's fingers, thumbs,* twirl them idly (for lack of occupation). *n.* slight twirl, quick twist; twirled mark or sign. **twidd'ly** *a.*

twig[1] *n.* small shoot or branch of tree or plant; divining-rod.

twig[2] *v.* (sl.) observe, notice; catch meaning (of).

twi'light (-īt) *n.* (period of) half light between daybreak and sunrise or (usu.) sunset and dark; faint light; period of approaching or growing decay, destruction, etc. **twi'lit** *a.* dimly illuminated (as) by twilight.

twill *n.* (textile fabric with) surface of parallel diagonal ribs. *v.t.* weave with twill.

twin *n.* one of two children or young born at one birth; each of closely related pair; counterpart. *a.* born as (one of) twins; consisting of two similar parts. *v.* bear twins; join or match closely, pair. **~-screw,** (esp.) having two screw propellers on separate shafts. **~-set,** woman's matching jumper and cardigan.

twine *n.* thread or string of thickness used for tying small parcels, sewing coarse materials, etc.; twining or trailing stem etc.; coil, twist. *v.* twist strands together to form cord; form by interlacing; wreathe, clasp; twist, coil, wind.

twinge (-j) *n.* transitory sharp pain.

twink'le *v.i.* shine with rapidly intermittent light, sparkle; wink, blink, quiver; move to and fro, in and out, etc. rapidly, flicker. *n.* wink, blink; quiver; intermittent or transient gleam.

twirl *v.t.* spin, swing, twist, quickly and lightly round; coil, twine; turn round and round idly. *n.* twirling, whirling; thing that twirls.

twirp : see **twerp.**

twist *v.* wind strands etc. about each other to form rope etc.; give spiral or winding form or course to; receive, grow in, take, spiral or winding form or course; wrench out of natural shape, distort. *n.* twisting, being twisted; manner or degree of twisting; peculiar tendency of mind, character, etc.; twisting strain, torque; distortion; unexpected development, turn, etc.; kinds of strong (esp. silk) thread etc; twisted thing, esp. tobacco twisted into tight roll; paper packet with screwed-up ends. **~er** *n.* (esp.) dishonest person, crook.

twit[1] *v.t.* taunt (*with*).

twit[2] *n.* (sl.) twerp.

twitch *v.* pull with light jerk, pull at; quiver or jerk spasmodically. *n.* twitching. **~y** *a.*

twitt'er *v.* (of bird) utter succession of light tremulous notes, chirp continuously (freq. fig.); utter or express thus. *n.* twittering; state of tremor.

two (tōō) *a. & n.* one more than one (2, II). **~-edged,** having two cutting edges; (fig.) cutting both ways, ambiguous. **~-faced,** (esp.) deceitful, insincere. **~fold,** double, doubly.

~-handed, wielded with both hands; worked or wielded by two persons; (of game etc.) for two players. **~pence** (tŭp′ens), 2d. **~penny** (tŭp′enĭ), costing 2d.; paltry, trumpery. **~penny-half-penny** (tŭp′nĭ-hāp′nĭ), (esp.) petty, cheap, worthless. **~-piece,** coat and skirt or coat and dress meant to be worn together; bathing-suit etc. in two separate pieces. **~-ply,** of two strands or layers. **~some,** two-handed game. **~-way,** (esp.) moving, allowing movement, in either of two directions; reciprocal; (of equipment etc.) capable of both sending and receiving signals.

tȳcoon′ n. business magnate.

tying : see **tie.**

tȳke n. dog, cur; low fellow; Yorkshireman.

tȳm′panum n. (pl. -na, -nums), ear-drum, (membrane closing) middle ear; (archit.) vertical recessed usu. triangular face of pediment; (carving etc. on) space between lintel and arch of door etc. **tȳm-păn′ic** a.

tȳpe n. person, thing, event, model, serving as illustration, symbol, characteristic specimen, etc.; general form, character, etc. distinguishing class or group; kind, class; small block with raised letter, figure, etc. on upper surface for use in printing; set, supply, kind, of these. v. typify; determine type of, classify according to type; write with typewriter. **~-cast,** cast performer in role of character he is supposed to resemble. **~script,** (matter) written with typewriter. **~setter,** compositor. **~write,** write with typewriter. **~writer,** machine for producing characters similar to those of print by striking keys which cause them to be impressed on paper through inked ribbon.

tȳ′phoid a. & n. typhus-like; ~ (fever), infectious eruptive febrile disease.

tȳphoon′ n. violent cyclonic storm, esp. of China seas etc. **tȳphŏn′ic** a.

tȳ′phus n. acute contagious fever transmitted to man by infected parasites. **tȳ′phous** a.

tȳp′ical a. serving as type; characteristic, distinctive.

tȳp′ifȳ v.t. represent by type; serve as type of. **~fica′tion** n.

tȳ′pist n. user of typewriter.

tȳpŏg′raphȳ n. art or practice of printing from types etc.; style, appearance, of printed matter **~grapher** n.; **~grăph′ic(al)** aa.

tȳrănn′ical (or tǐ-) a. acting like, characteristic of, tyrant; despotic, oppressive, cruel.

tȳrănn′icīde (or tǐ-) n. killer, killing, of tyrant.

tȳ′rannīze v.i. rule despotically or cruelly (over).

tȳ′rannous a. tyrannical.

tȳ′rannȳ n. government of, State ruled by, tyrant; oppressive or despotic government, arbitrary or cruel exercise of power.

tȳr′ant n. oppressive, unjust, or cruel ruler; person exercising power or authority arbitrarily or cruelly.

tȳre, tīre² n. metal rim or hoop round wheel; endless rubber solid or tubular cushion fitted on rim of wheel; tubeless ~, air-inflated tyre without inner tube.

tȳr′ō, tīr′ō n. beginner, novice.

U

U. abbr. universal (of cinema film licensed for all audiences).

ūbi′quitȳ n. being everywhere or in many places at once. **ūbi′quitous** a.

u.c. abbr. upper case.

U.D.C. abbr. Urban District Council.

ŭdd′er n. pendulous baggy milk-secreting organ in cows etc.

U.D.I. abbr. Unilateral Declaration of Independence.

U.F.O. abbr. unidentified flying object.

ugh (ŭ(h) or ŏŏ(h)) int. expressing disgust etc.

ŭg′lȳ a. unpleasing or repulsive to sight or hearing; vile; extremely awkward or unpromising (situation etc.); unpleasant, threatening, abusive. **ŭg'lĭfȳ** v.t. make ugly, disfigure. **ŭg'lĭness** n.

U.K. abbr. United Kingdom.

ūkāse' (-z) n. decree or edict of former Russian emperor etc.; arbitrary order.

ūkulele (-lā'lĭ) n. small four-stringed guitar.

ŭl'cer n. open sore on external or internal surface of body; corroding or corrupting influence. **~ous** a.; **~āte** v.

ŭll'age n. amount by which cask etc. falls short of being full.

ŭl'na n. (pl. -ae), large inner bone of fore-arm. **ŭl'nar** a.

ŭl'ster n. long loose usu. belted overcoat.

ult. abbr. ultimo.

ŭltēr'ior a. situated beyond; not immediate; beyond what is seen or avowed.

ŭl'tĭmate a. last, final; fundamental, elemental.

ŭltĭmā'tum n. final statement of terms, rejection of which may lead to rupture, declaration of war, etc.

ŭl'tĭmō adv. of last month.

ŭl'tra n. & a. (person) holding extreme views, esp. in religion or politics.

ŭl'tra- in comb., lying beyond, going beyond, surpassing, having quality etc. in extreme or excessive degree. **ŭltracĕn'trĭfūge** n. very high-speed centrifuge. **~mĭcroscŏp'ĭc** a. too small to be seen with microscope. **~mŏn'tāne** a. situated S. of Alps; Italian; favourable to absolute authority of Pope; n. person holding ultramontane views. **~-short** a. (of radio wave), having wave-length below ten metres. **~sŏn'ĭc** a. beyond range of human hearing. **~-vī'olėt** a. lying beyond violet end of visible spectrum.

ŭltramarine' (-ēn) a. & n. (of colour of) brilliant deep-blue pigment.

ŭl'tra vīr'ēs (-z), beyond one's power or authority. [L]

ŭl'ūlāte v.i. howl, wail. **~lā'tion** n.

ŭm'bel n. inflorescence with flower-stalks of nearly equal length springing from common centre. **ŭm'bellate, umbellif'erous** aa.

ŭm'ber n. brown earth used as pigment. a. umber-coloured.

ŭmbĭl'ĭcal a. of or near navel. **~ cord**, flexible tube attaching foetus to placenta.

ŭm'bra n. (pl. -ae), earth's or moon's (complete) shadow in eclipse.

ŭm'brage n. sense of slight or injury, offence. **ŭmbrā'geous** a. (esp.) giving shade.

ŭmbrĕll'a n. portable folding protection against rain etc., of silk etc. stretched on slender ribs attached radially to stick; light portable screen as protection against sun, symbol of rank, etc.; screen of fighter aircraft.

ŭm'pīre n. person chosen to decide between disputants etc., enforce rules of game or contest, etc. v. act as umpire (in).

ŭn- pref. freely used in comb. with adjj., advv., and nouns to express negation, not, in-, non-; in comb. with vbs., vbl. derivatives etc. to express contrary or reverse action, deprivation or removal of quality or property, etc. The number of words with this prefix being practically unlimited, many of those whose meaning is obvious are not listed here.

U.N. abbr. United Nations.

U.N.A. abbr. United Nations Association.

ŭnaccoun'table a. not accountable for, strange, inexplicable; not accountable.

ŭnadŏp'tėd a. (of road) not maintained by local authority.

ŭnalloyed' a. unmixed, pure.

ŭn-Amĕ'rĭcan a. not American; esp. not of, not worthy or characteristic of, opposed to, against interests of, etc. the U:S.A.

ūnăn'ĭmous a. all of one mind; held, given, etc. with general agreement or consent. **ūnanĭm'ĭtȳ** n.

ŭnassū'ming a. unpretentious.

unawares (ŭnawārz') adv. unexpectedly; unconsciously; by surprise.

ŭnbăcked' (-kt) a. (esp.) not backed by betting; (of horse) unbroken.

ŭnbăl'anced a. (esp.) mentally unstable or deranged.

ŭnbĕknown′ (-nōn) *a.* unknown (*to*). **~st (to)** *a. & adv.* (colloq.) without the knowledge (of).

ŭnbĕnd′ *v.* release, relax, from tension; straighten; be or become unconstrained or genial.

ŭnbĭdd′en *a.* (esp.) unasked, uninvited.

ŭnbo′som (-bōōz-) *v.t.* disclose; **~** *oneself*, disclose one's thoughts, feelings, etc.

ŭnbrī′dled *a.* unrestrained, uncontrolled.

ŭncalled′-for (-kawld-) *a.* not required or requested; impertinent, unprovoked.

ŭncănn′y̆ *a.* mysterious, uncomfortably strange or unfamiliar.

ŭncēr′tain *a.* not certain; not to be depended on; changeable. **~ty̆** *n.*

ŭn′cial (-shl) *a.* of, written in, form of script used in 4th-8th cent. MSS., resembling capitals but with some ascending and descending strokes. *n.* uncial letter or MS.

uncle (ŭng′kl) *n.* father's or mother's brother, aunt's husband; (sl.) pawnbroker. **U~ Sam**, Government or people of U.S.

ŭnc′ō *a. & adv.* (Sc.) extreme(ly), unusual(ly).

ŭncŏmm′on *a.* unusual, remarkable. *adv.* (colloq.) remarkably.

ŭncŏm′promīsĭng (-z-) *a.* refusing compromise; unyielding, stubborn, stiff.

ŭnconcĕrn′ *n.* freedom from anxiety; indifference.

ŭncŏn′scionable (-sho-) *a.* having no conscience, unscrupulous; not right or reasonable, excessive, shameless.

ŭncŏn′scious *a.* not aware (*of*); not conscious; not present to consciousness; done etc. without conscious action. *n.* unconscious mind or part of personality.

ŭnconsĭd′ered (-erd) *a.* not considered; not worth consideration, disregarded.

ŭncoup′le (-kŭ-) *v.t.* release from couples or coupling.

ŭncouth′ (-ōō-) *a.* awkward, clumsy, boorish.

ŭncov′ĕnantĕd (-kŭ-) *a.* not based on or subject to, not promised or secured by, covenant.

ŭnc′tion *n.* anointing with oil as religious rite or symbol; affected enthusiasm, gush; gusto. **ŭnc′tŭous** *a.* oily, greasy in feel, appearance, etc.; affectedly bland, smug, self--satisfied.

ŭncŭt′ *a.* (esp., of book) with leaves not cut open or margins not trimmed.

ŭndĕceive′ *v.t.* free from deception or mistake.

ŭn′der *prep.* in or to position lower than, below; inferior to, less than; subjected to, undergoing, liable to; governed, controlled, or bound by; in accordance with; in the time of. *adv.* in or to lower place or subordinate position. *a.* lower. **ŭn′dermōst** *a.*

ŭn′der- in comb., below; beneath, lower than; insufficient(ly), incomplete(ly); subordinate. **ŭnderăct′** *v.* act inadequately or with too much restraint. **~-āge′** *a.* not of full age. **~ärm** *a.* (of bowling, stroke, throw, etc.) made, delivered, etc. with arm lower than shoulder; placed or carried under arm; *adv.* with arm lower than shoulder. **~bĭd′** *v.* bid less than; bid too little (on); supplant, outdo, by offering services, goods, etc. at lower sum. **~brŭsh** *n.* undergrowth in forest. **~cărriage** *n.* supporting framework of vehicle etc.; landing--gear of aircraft. **~clothes** (-ōz *or* -ōdhz) *n.pl.* clothes worn under outer garments, esp. next to skin. **~cov′er** (-ŭv-) *a.* acting, done, surreptitiously or secretly. **~crŏft** *n.* crypt. **~cŭrrent** *n.* current flowing below surface or upper current; suppressed or underlying activity, force, etc. **~cŭt′** *v.t.* cut (away) below or beneath, esp. in carving; supplant by working for lower payment, selling at lower prices, etc.; strike (ball) obliquely downwards to give it backspin, make it rise, etc.; *n.* (ŭn′-), (esp.) under-side of sirloin. **~dŏg** *n.* loser in fight etc.; one in state of subjection or inferiority. **~done′** (-ŭn) *a.* incompletely or insufficiently cooked. **~ĕs′tĭmāte** *v.* form or make too low an estimate (of).

~foot *adv.* under one's feet; into state of subjection or inferiority. ~gō' *v.t.* be subjected to, suffer, endure. ~growth (-ōth) *n.* growth of plants or shrubs under trees etc. ~hǎnd' (*or* ŭn'-) *a. & adv.* clandestine(ly), secret(ly), not above--board; under-arm. ~hŭng' (*or* ŭn'-) *a.* (having lower jaw) projecting beyond upper jaw. ~lay' *v.t.* raise, support, line, etc., with something laid under, esp. (print.) to bring type, block, etc. to proper height for printing; *n.* (ŭn'-), something laid under esp. carpet or mattress. ~līe' *v.t.* lie, be situated, under; be basis or foundation of, lie beneath surface aspect of; ~lȳing *a.* ~mǎnned' *a.* furnished with too few men, short-handed. ~pass (-ahs) *n.* (crossing with) road etc. passing under another. ~pĭn' *v.t.* support or strengthen (esp. building) from beneath. ~prĭv'ĭlĕged *a.* relatively poor, not enjoying normal living standard or rights and privileges of civilized society. ~rāte' *v.t.* underestimate. ~sĕll' *v.t.* sell at lower price than. ~shoōt' *v.t.* (of aircraft) land short of runway. ~shǒt *a.* (of wheel) turned by water flowing under it. ~signed (-īnd) *a.; the* ~*signed,* person(s) whose signature(s) appear(s) below. ~sīzed *a.* of less than normal size. ~stātement (-tm-) *n.* statement falling below or coming short of truth or fact. ~stŭdy *n.* actor etc. who studies part in order to play it at short notice in absence of usual performer; *v.t.* study (part) thus, act as understudy to. ~tone *n.* low or subdued, underlying or subordinate, tone. ~tow (-ō) *n.* current below sea-surface in contrary direction to surface motion of breaking waves etc. ~trick *n.* (bridge) trick required to make bid or contract but not taken. ~wear (-wār) *n.* underclothes. ~wood *n.* undergrowth, brushwood, beneath trees. ~world (-wêr-) *n.* (esp.) infernal regions; lowest social stratum.

ŭndergrǎd'ūate *n.* member of university who has not yet taken degree.

ŭnderground' *adv.* below surface of ground; in(to) secrecy or concealment. *a. & n.* (ŭn'-), (railway) situated underground; (political movement etc.) conducted or existing in secret, hidden.

ŭnderlīne' *v.t.* draw line(s) under (words etc.) for emphasis, to indicate italics, etc.; emphasize, stress. *n.* descriptive line(s) under illustration.

ŭn'derlĭng *n.* (usu. contempt.) subordinate.

ŭndermīne' *v.t.* make mine or excavation under; wear away base or foundation of; injure, wear out, etc. insidiously, secretly, or imperceptibly.

ŭnderneath' *adv. & prep.* at or to lower place (than), below. *a. & n.* lower (surface, part).

ŭnderstǎnd' *v.* (-stoōd), comprehend, perceive meaning of; know how to deal with; infer, esp. from information received; take for granted. **ŭnderstǎnd'ĭng** *n.* (esp.) intelligence, intellect, insight; agreement, thing agreed upon; stipulation; sympathetic comprehension; *a.* intelligent, having understanding, sympathetic, tolerant.

ŭndertāke' *v.* (-toōk, -tāken), bind oneself to perform; engage in, enter upon; promise; guarantee; (colloq.) manage funerals. **ŭn'dertāker** *n.* (esp.) one who carries out arrangements for funerals. **ŭn'dertākĭng** *n.* (esp.) work etc. undertaken, enterprise; business of funeral undertaker.

ŭnderwrīte' *v.* (-wrōte, -wrĭtten), (esp.) accept risk of insurance by subscribing (policy); undertake esp. marine insurance; agree to take up unsold stock in (new company or issue). **ŭn'derwrīter** *n.* (esp.) marine insurer.

ŭndèsīr'able (-z-) *a.* not to be desired; objectionable. *n.* undesirable person.

ŭndo' (-oō) *v.t.* (-dĭd; -done, pr. -ŭn), annul, cancel; reduce to condition of not having been done etc.; unfasten and open; ruin.

ŭndoubt'ĕdly (-owt-) *adv.* without doubt.

ŭndrĕss' *v.* take off clothes (of). *n.* (ŭn'-), (esp., mil. etc.) uniform for ordinary occasions (freq. attrib.).

ŭndūe' *a.* improper; excessive, more or greater than is appropriate, warranted or natural. **undū'lў** *adv.*

ŭn'dūlāte *v.* (cause to) move in or like waves, (cause to) rise and fall, have wavy surface or outline, etc. ~ant *a.* undulating; ~ant **fever**, persistent remittent fever. ~ā'tion *n.* wavy motion or form, gentle rise and fall. ~ātorў *a.*

unduly : see **undue**.

ŭndў'ing *a.* immortal.

ŭnearth' (-ẽr-) *v.t.* dig up; force out of hole or burrow; bring to light, find by searching.

ŭnearth'lў (-ẽr-) *a.* not of this earth; supernatural, ghostly; (colloq.) extraordinary, odd, absurdly early or inconvenient.

ŭnea'sy (-zĭ) *a.* restless, disturbed, uncomfortable, in body or mind.

ŭnĕmploy'able *a.* & *n.* (person) unfitted or unsuitable for paid employment. **ŭnĕmployed'** (-oid) *a.* not employed; out of work; not in use. **ŭnĕmploy'ment** *n.*

U.N.E.S.C.O., Unĕs'cō (ū-) *abbr.* United Nations Educational, Scientific, and Cultural Organisation.

ŭnĕxcĕp'tionable *a.* with which no fault can be found.

ŭnfee'ling *a.* lacking sensibility, without feeling; harsh; cruel.

ŭnfĭt' *a.* not fit, unsuitable; in poor health. *v.t.* make unsuitable (*for*).

ŭnflĕdged' *a.* (fig.) undeveloped; immature; inexperienced.

ŭnfōld' *v.* open out; reveal; develop.

ŭnfôr'tūnate *a.* unlucky; unhappy; ill-advised. *n.* unfortunate person.

ŭnfrŏck' *v.t.* deprive of priestly function or office.

ŭnfũrl' *v.* unroll, spread out.

ŭngain'lў *a.* awkward, clumsy, ungraceful.

ŭngĕt-ăt'-able *a.* difficult or impossible to reach, inaccessible.

ŭngŏd'lў *a.* impious, wicked; (colloq.) outrageous, dreadful.

ŭngo'vernable (-gŭ-) *a.* uncontrollable.

ŭng'uent (-nggw-) *n.* ointment.

ŭng'ūlate (-ngg-) *a.* & *n.* hoofed (mammal).

ŭnhăll'owed (-ōd) *a.* unconsecrated; unholy, impious, wicked.

ŭnhănd' *v.t.* take one's hands off.

ŭnheal'thў (-hĕl-) *a.* sickly; diseased; prejudicial or hurtful to health; unwholesome; (sl.) dangerous.

ŭnhinge' (-j) *v.t.* derange, disorder (mind).

ŭnhō'lў *a.* profane, wicked; (colloq.) awful, dreadful.

ū'ni- in comb., one-; having, composed of, etc. one —. **ūnicăm'eral** *a.* having one (legislative) chamber. ~cĕll'ūlar *a.* (esp. of living organism) having, composed of, a single cell. **ū'nicўcle** *n.* one-wheeled pedal-propelled vehicle. ~lăt'eral *a.* of, on, affecting, done by, binding on, etc. one side only.

UNICEF, U'nicĕf (ū-) *abbr.* United Nations Children's Fund.

ū'nicôrn *n.* (heraldic representation of) fabulous animal with horse's body and single horn projecting from forehead.

ū'nifôrm *a.* unvarying; plain, unbroken; conforming to one standard, rule, etc. *n.* distinctive dress of uniform cut, colour, etc. worn by all members of military etc. organization. *v.t.* dress in uniform. **unifôr'mitў** *n.* being uniform, sameness, consistency, conformity.

ū'nifў *v.t.* make one or uniform. ~ficā'tion *n.*

ŭnintĕll'igible *a.* not such as can be understood.

ū'nion (-yon) *n.* uniting, being united; coalition; marriage; concord, agreement; whole resulting from combination of parts or members; trade union; (hist.) parishes consolidated for administration of poor laws, workhouse of such union; cloth of different yarns woven together; (premises of) general club and debating society open to all members of university; coupling for pipes etc. **U~ Jack**, national flag of Gt. Britain.

ū'nionist *n.* member of trade union, advocate of trade unions; one who desires or advocates union, esp. (*U~*) supporter of maintenance of union between Gt. Britain and Ireland; Conservative. *a.* of, supporting, or belonging to union, unionism, or unionists. **~ĭsm** *n.*

ūnique' (-ēk) *a.* of which there is only one; unmatched, unequalled; having no like, equal, or parallel.

ū'nĭson *n.* coincidence in pitch; combination of voices or instruments at same pitch; *in* **~**, at same pitch, (loosely) in octaves, (fig.) in concord or agreement or harmony.

ū'nĭt *n.* the number one; determinate quantity, magnitude, etc. as basis or standard of measurement; individual thing, person, or group. *a.* of, being, or forming unit; individual. **~arȳ** *a.*

Unĭtār'ĭan (ū-) *n.* one who maintains that Godhead is one person, not Trinity. *a.* of Unitarians or their doctrine. **~ĭsm** *n.*

ūnīte' *v.* join together; make or become one, combine; consolidate; agree, co-operate (*in*).

ū'nĭtȳ *n.* oneness, being one or single or individual; (thing showing) due interconnexion and coherence of parts, (thing forming) complex whole; numeral one as basis of number; harmony, concord.

Univ. *abbr.* University.

ūnĭvêr'sal *a.* of, belonging to used, or done by, etc. all persons or things in world or in class concerned; applicable to all cases; of universe. *n.* proposition in which predicate is affirmed or denied of entire subject. **~ joint**, joint or coupling permitting of free movement in any direction of parts joined. **~ suffrage**, suffrage extending to all persons, or all male persons, over specified age. **~săl'itȳ** *n.*, **~salīze** *v.t.*

ū'nĭvêrse *n.* all existing things; all creation; world or earth; cosmos; all mankind.

ūnĭvêr'sitȳ *n.* (colleges, buildings, etc. of) corporate institution with power of conferring degrees etc. and providing instruction in higher branches of learning; all members of university.

unkĕmpt' (ŭn-k-) *a.* dishevelled, untidy, neglected-looking.

ŭnleash' *v.t.* free from leash or restraint; set free in order to pursue, attack, etc.

ŭnlĕss' *conj.* if . . . not; except when.

ŭnlĭcked' (-kt) *a.* (esp.) not licked into shape.

ŭnlīke' *a. & prep.* not like, different (from).

ŭnlīke'lȳ *a.* improbable; unpromising.

ŭnlĭs'tĕd *a.* not included in list, esp. of Stock Exchange prices or of telephone numbers.

ŭnload' *v.* remove cargo or anything carried or conveyed (from); remove charge from (gun); relieve of burden; get rid of, sell (out).

ŭnlōoked'-fôr *a. & adv.* unexpected(ly).

ŭnlōose' *v.t.* loose; untie.

ŭnlŭck'ȳ *a.* unfortunate; unsuccessful; hapless; ill-contrived.

ŭnmăn' *v.t.* deprive of courage, strength, firmness, etc.

ŭnmănn'erlȳ *a.* rude; ill-bred.

ŭnmĕn'tionable *a.* not fit to be mentioned; unspeakable.

ŭnmĭstā'kable *a.* that cannot be mistaken or doubted.

ŭnmĭt'ĭgātĕd *a.* unqualified, absolute.

ŭnnă'tural (-cher-) *a.* contrary or doing violence to nature; lacking natural feelings; artificial.

ŭnnĕ'cĕssarȳ *a.* not necessary; more than necessary.

ŭnnêrve' *v.t.* deprive of nerve, courage, self-control, etc.

ŭnnŭm'bered (-erd) *a.* countless; not marked etc. with number.

U.N.O., UNO, U'nō (ū-) *abbr.* United Nations (Organisation).

ŭnpă'rallĕled *a.* having no parallel or equal.

ŭnpârliamĕn'tarȳ (-la-) *a.* contrary to parliamentary usage.

ŭnpĭck' *v.t.* undo stitches of (anything sewn or knitted).

ŭnplāced' *a.* not placed, esp. in race or list.

ŭnpleas'ant (-lĕz-) *a.* disagreeable. **~ness** *n.* (esp.) disagreeable situation, action, etc.; hostility, quarrel.

ŭnpŏp'ūlar *a.* not in popular favour, disliked.

ŭnprăc'tised *a.* not practised; inexperienced, inexpert.

ŭnpre'cĕdentĕd *a.* for which there is no precedent, unexampled, novel.

ŭnprĕj'udiced (-jōō-) *a.* impartial.

ŭnprĕsĕn'table (-z-) *a.* not fit to be presented to company; not fit to be seen.

ŭnprĭn'cĭpled (-ld) *a.* not having, based on, etc. sound or honest principles of conduct; unscrupulous.

ŭnprofĕ'ssional *a.* not professional; not worthy of member of profession.

ŭnprŏf'ĭtable *a.* without profit; serving no purpose.

ŭnqual'ĭfied (-ŏl-) *a.* not qualified; not modified or limited.

ŭnquĕs'tionable *a.* that cannot be questioned or doubted.

ŭn'quōte, direction in dictation etc. to mark end of quotation.

ŭnrăv'el *v.t.* separate threads of, disentangle; undo, esp. by pulling single thread(s); become or be unravelled.

ŭnrea'sonable (-z-) *a.* not reasonable; not in accordance with reason or good sense; excessive.

ŭnrĕhearsed' (-hēr-) *a.* not practised or prepared; spontaneous.

ŭnrĕlieved' *a.* not given relief, not aided or assisted; not diversified or varied (*by*), unvarying, monotonous.

ŭnrĕmĭtt'ing *a.* incessant.

ŭnrĕsĕrv'ĕdlў *adv.* without reservation.

ŭnrĕst' *n.* disturbance, turmoil, trouble.

ŭnrĭ'valled *a.* unequalled; incomparable.

UNRWA *abbr.* United Nations Relief and Works Agency (for Palestinian refugees).

ŭnru'lў (-ōō-) *a.* not amenable to rule or discipline; turbulent.

ŭnsā'vourў *a.* uninviting; disgusting.

ŭnscăthed' (-dhd) *a.* uninjured, unharmed.

ŭnscrĭp'tĕd *a.* not made, read, etc. from prepared script.

ŭnscru'pŭlous (-ōōp-) *a.* without scruples; unprincipled.

ŭnsea'sonable (-ēz-) *a.* not suited to or in accordance with time, occasion, or season of year.

ŭnseat' *v.t.* throw from saddle; dislodge, deprive of seat, esp. in House of Commons.

ŭnseen' *a.* not seen; invisible. *n.* unprepared passage for translation.

ŭnsĕl'fĭsh *a.* not selfish or self-regarding; generous.

ŭnsĕtt'led (-ld) *a.* not settled; restless, unquiet, disturbed; liable to change; not paid.

ŭnsĕx' *v.t.* (esp.) make unfeminine.

ŭnshĭp' *v.* detach or remove, be or admit of being detached, from fixed place or position.

ŭnsigh'tĕd *a.* unseen; (of gun) not furnished with sights; having view obscured.

ŭnsight'lў *a.* unpleasing to the eye, ugly.

ŭnsolĭ'cĭtĕd *a.* not asked for; given or done voluntarily.

ŭnsophis'tĭcātĕd *a.* artless, ingenuous, inexperienced.

ŭnsound' *a.* not sound; diseased; rotten; erroneous; unreliable.

ŭnspea'kable *a.* inexpressible, unutterable; indescribably repulsive, objectionable, etc.

ŭnstrĕssed' *a.* not bearing stress, unaccented, unemphasized.

ŭnstrŭng' *a.* with strings relaxed or removed; not threaded on string; weakened, unnerved.

ŭnstŭck' *a.* not stuck, not adhering; *come* ~, cease to stick, (colloq.) fail, go wrong.

ŭnstŭd'ied *a.* not premeditated; easy, natural, spontaneous.

ŭnthĭnk'able *a.* unimaginable; not to be thought of; incredible.

ŭntil' *prep. & conj.* till.

ŭntī'melў (-ml-) *a. & adv.* inopportune(ly); premature(ly).

ŭn'to (-ōō) *prep.* (arch.) to.

ŭntōld' *a.* not told; uncounted; beyond count.

ŭntouch'able (-tŭ-) *n.* non-caste Hindu (whom caste man may not touch).

ŭntō'ward (*or* -tōōwŏrd') *a.* (arch.) perverse; awkward; unlucky.

ŭn'truth (-rōō-) *n.* being untrue; falsehood, lie.

ŭnū'sual (-zhōō-) *a.* not usual; remarkable.

ŭnŭtt′erable *a.* above or beyond description.

ŭnvăr′nĭshed *a.* not covered (as) with varnish; not embellished, plain, direct, simple.

ŭnwa′rrantable (-wŏ-) *a.* unjustifiable. **ŭnwa′rrantĕd** *a.* unauthorized; not guaranteed.

ŭnwĕll′ *a.* not in gocd health; indisposed.

ŭnwĕpt′ *a.* not wept for, unlamented.

ŭnwiel′dў *a.* slow or clumsy of movement, awkward to handle etc., by reason of size, shape, or weight.

ŭnwĭtt′ĭng *a.* not knowing, unaware; unintentional.

ŭnwor′thy (-ĕr̄dhĭ) *a.* not worthy or befitting the character (*of*); discreditable.

ŭnwrĭtt′en *a.* not written (down); oral; traditional.

ŭnzĭp′ *v.* undo zip-fastener of, admit of being unzipped.

ŭp *adv.* to, in, high or higher place, amount, value, etc.; to or in capital, university, place further north or in question, etc.; to or in erect or vertical position, out of bed, out of lying or sitting or kneeling posture, in(to) condition of efficiency or activity; (with vbs., usu.) expressing complete or effectual result etc.; (colloq.) amiss, wrong; ~ *against*, in(to) contact or collision with, (colloq.) faced or confronted by; ~ *to*, as high or far as, up towards, until, as many or much as, fit or qualified for, capable of, able to deal with, on (to) a level with, engaged in, occupying oneself with, (colloq.) obligatory or incumbent on, at or in choice of; *well* ~, (colloq.) expert, well-informed, *in*; ~ *with*, so as to overtake, level with. *prep.* to higher point of, on or along in ascending direction; at or in higher part of. *a.* moving, sloping, going, etc. towards higher point or to capital. *n.* upward slope or movement; ~*s and downs*, rises and falls, undulating ground, alternations of fortune etc.; *on the* ~-*and*-~, honest(ly), continually improving. *v.* drive up (swans) for marking; rise or raise abruptly;

(colloq.) ~ *and*, begin abruptly or boldly (to do something).

ŭp- in comb. **ŭp-ăn′chor** (-ngk*er*) *v.i.* raise anchor before getting under way. **~-and-com′ĭng** (-kŭ-) *a.* active, alert, wide-awake. **~-beat** *n.* (mus.) unaccented beat, esp. at end of bar; *a.* cheerful, optimistic. **~brĭngĭng** *n.* bringing up, early rearing and training. **~cast** *n.* (fault caused by) upward dislocation of seam; *a.* turned upwards; (of shaft) through which air passes out of mine. **~-coun′trў** (-kŭn-) *n., a.,* & *adv.* (to, in, of) inland part of country. **~-dāte′** *v.t.* advance date of, bring up to date. **~-ĕnd′** *v.* set, rise up, on end. **~-grāde** *n.* upward slope; *on the* ~-*grade*, ascending, improving; *v.t.* (-ād′), raise status or price of; promote, raise to higher grade. **~hĭll** *a.* sloping upwards; arduous, difficult, laborious; *adv.* (-ĭl′), with upward slope, upwards on hill. **~keep** *n.* (cost of) maintenance in good condition or repair. **~land** *n.* (freq. pl.) piece of high ground, hilly or mountainous country; *a.* situated, living, etc. on high ground. **~lĭft′** *v.t.* raise up; elevate; raise spirits of; edify. **~lĭft** *n.* (colloq.) elevating or edifying effect, moral inspiration. **~raise′** (-z) *v.t.* raise up, elevate, rear. **~rōot′** *v.t.* tear up by the roots; eradicate, destroy. **~sĕt²** *a.* (of price) fixed as lowest at which property will be sold at auction. **~shŏt** *n.* final issue, conclusion. **~sīdes′** (-dz) *adv.* (colloq.) even or quits *with*. **~stāge′** *adv.* away from footlights or front of stage; ~*stage of*, further upstage than; *a.* (sl.) supercilious, haughty; *v.t.* force (actor) to face away from audience by getting or keeping upstage of him; behave haughtily or snobbishly towards. **~stairs** *a.*, **~stairs′** (-z) *adv.* on, to, an upper storey. **~stairs** (-z) *n.* upper part of house. **~stăn′dĭng** *a.* well set up, erect. **~stărt** *n.* one newly or suddenly risen in importance, position, etc. **~stream′** *adv.*, **~stream** *a.* (situated) higher up stream; (moving, done, etc.) against current. ~strŏke n. line made by upward movement of pen etc. ~swĕpt a. (of hair) brushed upwards towards top of head; curved or sloped upwards. ~tāke n. (colloq.) understanding, apprehension. ~thrŭst n. upward thrust, esp. (geol.) by volcanic or seismic action. ~ to date advb. phr., ~-to--date a. (extending) right up to present time; abreast of times in style, information, knowledge, etc. ~town a. (U.S.) of, situated in, upper or residential part of town.

U.P. abbr. United Presbyterian; United Press.

ū′pas (-tree) n. fabulous tree poisoning air and soil all around; (poison obtained from) Javanese tree yielding poisonous juice.

ŭpbraid′ v.t. chide, reproach.

ŭphea′val (-p-h-) n. sudden and violent heaving up, esp. of part of earth's crust; sudden esp. violent or radical change or disturbance.

ŭphōld′ (-p-h-) v.t. (-hĕld), give support or countenance to; maintain, confirm.

ŭphō′lster (-p-h-) v.t. furnish (room etc.) with hangings, carpets, etc.; provide (chair etc.) with textile covering, padding, etc. ~erer, ~erў nn.

upŏn′ prep. on; take ~ oneself, assume, assume responsibility for, venture, presume.

ŭpp′er a. higher in place; situated above; superior in rank, dignity, etc. n. upper part of shoe or boot; (down) on one's ~s, extremely poor, out of luck. ~ case, type-case containing capital letters; a. capital. ~ crust, (colloq.) aristocracy, highest social circles. ~-cut, (boxing) short-arm upward blow. ~ hand, mastery, control, advantage. ~ house, House of Lords or other higher legislative assembly. ~ ten, upper classes, aristocracy. ~most a. highest in rank or place; adv. on or to the top. ŭpp′ish a. self-assertive; pert.

ŭp′right a. & adv. erect, vertical; (of piano) with vertical frame; righteous, strictly honourable or honest. n. upright piano; post or rod fixed upright.

ŭprī′sing (-z-) n. (esp.) insurrection, popular rising against authority etc.

ŭp′roar n. tumult, violent disturbance, clamour. ŭproar′ious a.

ŭpsĕt′[1] v. (-sˇt), overturn, be overturned; disturb temper, digestion, composure, peace, etc. of. n. upsetting, being upset.

upset[2]: see up-.

ŭp′sīde-down′ adv. & a. with upper part under, inverted, in(to) total disorder.

ŭp′ward a. directed, moving, towards higher place, status, etc. ~(s) adv. in upward direction; ~s of, (rather) more than.

ūrae′mia n. presence in blood of matter normally eliminated by kidneys.

ūrā′nium n. heavy greyish metallic radioactive element capable of nuclear fission.

ūr′ban a. of, living or situated in, city or town. ~īze v.t. render urban; deprive of rural character. ~īzā′tion n.

ūrbāne′ a. courteous; suave. ūrbăn′itў n.

ūr′chin n. (roguish or mischievous) boy, little fellow; (dial.) hedgehog.

ūrē′ter n. either of two ducts conveying urine from kidney.

ūrē′thra n. duct through which urine is discharged from bladder.

ūrge v.t. drive forcibly, impel; entreat, exhort, earnestly or persistently; ply with argument or entreaty; advocate pressingly. n. impelling motive, force, pressure, etc., esp. from within. ūr′gencў n. ūr′gent a. pressing, calling for immediate action or attention; importunate, persistent.

ūr′ic a. of urine.

ūrī′nal (or ūr′i-) n. vessel for receiving urine; building etc. for urinating.

ūr′ināte v.i. pass urine. ~ā′tion n.

ūr′ine n. fluid excreted by kidneys and discharged from bladder. ūr′inarў, ūr′inous aa.

ūrn n. vase with foot, esp. as used for storing ashes of the dead; large vessel with tap in which water is kept hot or tea etc. made.

ŭr′sĭne (*or* -ĭn) *a.* of, like, bear.

us (ŭz, *uz*) *pron.* obj. case of *we*.

U.S. *abbr.* United States (of America).

U.S.A. *abbr.* United States of America; United States Army.

ū′sage (-z-) *n.* manner of using, treatment; habitual or customary practice, established use (esp. of word); quantity used.

ūse (-z) *v.* employ for purpose or as instrument or material; put into operation, avail oneself of; treat in specified manner; ~ *up*, use whole of, find use for remains of, exhaust, wear out. *n.* (ūs), (right or power of) using; employment; availability, utility, occasion for using, purpose for which thing can be used; custom, wont; ritual and liturgy of church, diocese, etc.; benefit or profit of property held by another for beneficiary. **ū′sable** *a.*; **ūsabil′ĭtў** *n.* **used**[1] (ūst) *p.t.* was or were accustomed, had as constant or frequent practice; *p.p.* accustomed. **used**[2] (ūzd) *a.* that has been used; secondhand. **ūse′ful** (-sf-) *a.* of use, serviceable; suitable for use; advantageous, profitable. **ūse′less** (-sl-) *a.* serving no useful purpose, unavailing; of inadequate or insufficient capacity etc., inefficient, incompetent; (sl.) fit for nothing.

ū′ser (-z-) *n.* one who uses anything; (law) (presumptive right arising from) continued use or exercise of right etc.

ŭsh′er *n.* official or servant acting as doorkeeper, showing persons to seats, or walking before person of rank; (arch. or contempt.) assistant schoolmaster. *v.t.* act as usher to; precede (person) as usher; show *in*, *out* (freq. fig.). ~**ĕtte′** *n.* female usher esp. in cinema.

U.S.M. *abbr.* United States Mail, Marine.

U.S.N. *abbr.* United States Navy.

ŭs′quèbaugh (-aw) *n.* whisky.

U.S.P.G. *abbr.* United S.P.G.

U.S.S. *abbr.* United States Senate; United States Ship.

U.S.S.R. *abbr.* Union of Soviet Socialist Republics.

ū′sual (-zhŏŏ-) *a.* commonly or ordinarily observed, practised, happening, etc.; current, ordinary, customary. **ū′suallў** *adv.*

ū′sŭfrŭct (-z-) *n.* right of enjoying use of another's property short of causing damage or prejudice to it; use, enjoyment (*of*).

ū′surer (-zhu-) *n.* one who practises usury.

ūsŭrp′ (-z-) *v.* seize or assume power, right, etc. wrongfully. ~**ā′tion**, ~**er** *nn.*

ū′surў (-zhu-) *n.* lending of money at exorbitant or illegal rate of interest; such interest. **ūsūr′ious** (-z-) *a.*

Ut. *abbr.* Utah.

ūtĕn′sĭl *n.* instrument, implement, vessel, esp. in domestic use.

ū′terus *n.* organ in which young of mammals are conceived and develop until birth, womb. **ū′terine** *a.*

ūtĭlĭtār′ian *a.* of, consisting in, based on, utility; esp., regarding greatest good of greatest number as chief consideration of morality. *n.* holder or supporter of utilitarian views; one devoted to mere utility or material interests. **U**~**ism** *n.* utilitarian principles, doctrines, etc.

ūtĭl′ĭtў *n.* usefulness, profitableness; power to satisfy human wants; useful thing; (*public*) *utilities*, (organizations supplying) gas, water, electricity, transport, etc. provided for community. *a.* reared, kept, made, etc. for useful ends as opp. to display or show.

ū′tĭlīze *v.t.* make use of, turn to account, use. ~**īzā′tion** *n.*

ŭt′most *a.* furthest, extreme; that is such in highest degree. *n.* utmost point, degree, limit, etc.; best of one's ability, power, etc.

Utō′pia (ū-) *n.* imaginary perfect social and political system. **Utō′pian** (ū-) *a.* & *n.*

ŭt′er[1] *a.* complete, total, unqualified. ~**mŏst** *a.*

ŭt′er[2] *v.t.* emit audibly; express in words; put (notes, base coin. etc.) in circulation. **ŭt′erance** *n.* (manner of) uttering; spoken words.

ū′vula *n.* (pl. -*ae*), conical fleshy prolongation hanging from middle of pendent margin of soft palate.

ū'vūlar a.

ŭxôr'ious a. excessively fond of one's wife; marked by such fondness.

V

V, v (vē), as Roman numeral, 5.

V abbr. volt.

v. abbr. verb; verse; versus; vide [L], see.

V.A. abbr. Vice-Admiral; (Order of) Victoria and Albert; Victoria and Albert Museum.

Va. abbr. Virginia.

văc n. (colloq.) vacation.

vā'cancÿ n. being vacant; vacant space, post, place, etc.; lack of intelligence, inanity.

vā'cant a. empty; without occupant or contents; unoccupied with thought, without intelligence. ~ **possession,** term offering immediate occupation and possession of house etc.

vacāte' v.t. leave vacant; give up possession or occupancy of; annul, cancel. **vacā'tion** n. vacating; time during which law-courts, schools, universities, etc., are closed; holiday.

văc'cināte (-ks-) v.t. inoculate with vaccine against smallpox, or with preparation of micro-organisms against infectious disease. ~**ā'-tion** n.

văc'cine (-ksēn) n. preparation of cow-pox virus used for inoculation against smallpox; any preparation similarly used.

vă'cĭllāte v.i. swing or sway unsteadily; hover doubtfully, waver. **vacillā'tion** n.

vacū'ĭtÿ n. state of emptiness; vacuousness, vacancy.

văc'ūous a. vacant, unintelligent.

văc'ūum n. (pl. -ums, -a), space entirely empty of matter; empty space; space, vessel, exhausted of air. v.t. (colloq.) clean with vacuum cleaner. ~ **brake,** brake operated by (partial) vacuum. ~ **cleaner,** apparatus for removing dust etc, by suction. ~**flask, jar, jug,** etc. vessel with double wall enclosing vacuum, used for keeping liquids etc. hot or cold. ~ **pump,** pump for producing vacuum. ~ **tube,** sealed glass or metal tube or bulb from which almost all air has been removed; radio valve.

V.A.D. abbr. (member of) Voluntary Aid Detachment.

văg'abŏnd a. wandering, having no settled habitation or home; straying; (as) of vagabond. n. vagabond person, esp. idle and worthless wanderer, vagrant. ~**age** n.

vagār'ÿ n. capricious or extravagant action etc.; freak.

vagī'na n. sheath-like part; passage from vulva to womb. **vagī'nal** a.

vā'grant n. one without settled home or regular work, wandering from place to place; (law) idle and disorderly person. a. (as) of vagrant; wandering. ~**ancÿ** n.

vāgue (-g) a. not clearly expressed or perceived, uncertain, ill-defined; not clear-thinking, inexact, indefinite.

vain a. empty, of no effect, unavailing; conceited, proud (of); in ~, to no effect or purpose, vainly. ~**glôr'ÿ** n. boastfulness, extreme vanity; ~**glôr'ious** a.

văl'ance n. short curtain round frame or canopy of bedstead, over window, etc.

vāle[1] n. valley.

vā'lė[2] int. & n. farewell. [L]

vălėdĭc'tion n. (words used in) bidding farewell. ~**torÿ** a. & n. (speech, oration) bidding farewell.

vā'lencÿ, vā'lence nn. combining-power of atoms; number of atoms of hydrogen which atom can combine with or replace.

văl'entīne n. sweetheart chosen on St. Valentine's day (14 Feb.); (usu. anonymous) letter or card sent to valentine on that day.

valēr'ĭan n. (root of) kinds of flowering herb.

văl'ėt (or -lā) n. man's personal servant. v. wait on, act, as valet; clean, mend, and press (clothes).

vălètūdĭnār'ĭan *n. & a.* (person) of infirm health, esp. (one) unduly concerned about health.

Vălhăll'a *n.* (Norse myth.) hall in which heroes who have died in battle feast with Odin.

văl'iant (-ya-) *a.* brave, courageous. **~ancў** *n.*

văl'ĭd *a.* sound, well-grounded; having legal force. **văl'ĭdāte** *v.t.* make valid, confirm. **~ā'tion, valĭd'itў** *nn.*

valise' (-ēs *or* -ēz) *n.* travelling-bag, suitcase.

vălkў'rĭe (*or* -ērĭ; *or* vă'-) *n.* (Norse myth.) any of Odin's war-maidens hovering over battlefields to select warriors for Valhalla etc.

văll'ey *n.* long depression or hollow between hills; any valley-like hollow, esp. trough between waves.

văll'um *n.* (Rom. ant.) rampart or wall as (esp. permanent) means of defence.

văl'our (-ler) *n.* (arch. or rhet.) courage, esp. in battle. **văl'orous** *a.*

valse (vahls) *n.* waltz. [F]

văl'ūable *a.* of great value, price, or worth. *n.* (usu. pl.) valuable thing, esp. small article.

vălūā'tion *n.* estimation (esp. by professional valuer) of thing's or person's worth; estimated value.

văl'ūe *n.* amount of commodity, money, etc. equivalent to something else or for which something else is readily available; worth, desirability, utility; number, quantity, relative duration, etc. represented by figure, note, etc.; (painting etc., usu. pl.) relation between parts, quality, in respect of light and shade, colour, etc. *v.t.* estimate value of; esteem, have high or specified opinion of. **văl'ūeless** *a.* worthless. **văl'ūer** *n.* (esp.) one who estimates or assesses values professionally.

valū'ta *n.* agreed or exchange value of currency; (foreign) currency.

vălve *n.* device for controlling flow of fluid, usu. acting by yielding to pressure in one direction only; membranous fold in heart etc. preventing reflux of blood etc.; (mus.) device for varying length

of tube in horn etc.; each half of hinged shell; thermionic valve used for detection and amplification of wireless waves. **văl'vūlar** *a.* of, like, acting as, valve.

vamōose' *v.i.* (sl.) make off.

vămp[1] *n.* upper front part of boot or shoe; something vamped up; (mus.) simple improvisation or accompaniment. *v.* repair, make *up*, produce, (as) by patching or piecing together; improvise.

vămp[2] *n.* (film actress playing part of) woman who exploits men. *v.t.* allure, entice (man).

văm'pīre *n.* reanimated corpse supposed to suck blood of sleeping persons; blood-sucking bat; person who preys on others. **~rĭsm** *n.*

văn[1] *n.* vanguard, forefront.

văn[2] *n.* covered vehicle, closed railway-truck, for conveyance of goods etc.

văn[3] *n.* (lawn tennis, colloq.) vantage.

vanā'dĭum *n.* hard steel-white metallic element.

V. & A. *abbr.* Victoria and Albert Museum.

văn'dal *n.* wilful or ignorant destroyer of anything beautiful, venerable, etc. **~ĭsm** *n.*; **~ĭstĭc** *a.*

văndўke' *n.* deeply-cut point of serrated or indented border or edge. *v.t.* cut (cloth etc.) in vandyke points. **~ beard,** small neat pointed beard. **~ brown,** deep-brown pigment. **~ collar,** broad lace or linen collar with deeply indented edge.

vāne *n.* weathercock; sail of windmill, blade of propeller, etc.

văn'guard (-gārd) *n.* front part, foremost division, of army, fleet, etc. moving forward or onward; leaders of movement etc.

vanĭll'a *n.* (podlike capsules of) kinds of climbing orchid; aromatic extract of this as flavouring or perfume.

văn'ish *v.i.* disappear from sight, esp. suddenly and mysteriously; fade away; cease to exist; (math.) become zero. **~ing point,** (perspective) point at which receding parallel lines appear to meet.

văn'itў *n.* what is vain or worthless; futility, emptiness; empty pride or self-conceit. **~-bag, -case,** woman's small handbag or case containing mirror, cosmetics, etc.

văn'quish v.t. (rhet.) conquer, overcome.

văn'tage n. advantage, esp. in lawn tennis; *coign of* ~, ~-*point*, etc. position giving superiority in defence or attack.

văp'ĭd a. insipid, flat. **vapĭd'ĭtў** n.

vā'porīze v. convert, be converted, into vapour. ~**īzā'tion** n. ~**īzer** n. (esp.) apparatus for vaporizing liquid, fine spray.

vā'pour (-er) n. matter diffused or suspended in air, esp. form into which liquids are converted by heat; vaporized substance; (pl., arch.) nervous irritability or depression. v.i. talk fantastically or boastingly. **vā'porous**, ~ў aa.

văquer'o (-kār'ō) n. (Sp.-Amer. etc.) herdsman, cowboy. [Sp.]

vār'iable a. apt or liable to vary, capable of variation; shifting, inconstant; (of star) varying periodically in brightness etc. n. variable quantity, star, etc. ~**bĭl'ĭtў** n.

vār'iance n. disagreement, difference of opinion, lack of harmony, discrepancy; *at* ~, disagreeing, out of harmony (*with*). **vār'iant** a. differing from something or from standard etc.; n. variant form, spelling, reading, etc.

vāriā'tion n. (extent of) varying or deviation esp. from normal condition etc. or standard or type; deviation of heavenly body from mean orbit, of magnetic needle from true north, etc.; (mus.) one of series of repetitions of theme etc. with changes which do not disguise its identity.

vār'icoloured (-kŭlerd) a. variegated in colour.

vā'rĭcōse a. (of vein) having permanent abnormal local dilatation; designed for treatment of varicose veins. ~**cŏs'ĭtў** n.

vār'iegāte (-rĭg-) v.t. diversify in appearance etc., esp. in colour. **vār'iegātéd** a.; **vāriegā'tion** n.

varī'etў n. diversity; absence of monotony or uniformity; collection of different things; different form, kind, sort (*of*); sub-division of

species; (pl.) variety entertainment. ~ **entertainment, performance,** etc. entertainment consisting of number of different independent turns. ~ **theatre,** music-hall.

vārĭōr'um a. & n. (edition) with notes of various editors or commentators.

vār'ious a. of several kinds; diverse; divers.

vār'lĕt n. (arch.) menial, low fellow.

vār'nĭsh n. resinous solution or other preparation applied to surface to produce translucent usu. glossy protective coating; superficial polish of manner etc. v.t. coat with varnish; gloss (*over*), disguise.

vār'sĭtў n. (colloq.) university.

vār'ў v. change, make or become different, modify, diversify; be different or of different kinds.

văs'cūlar a. (biol. etc.) of, containing, supplied with, tubular vessels.

vase (vahz) n. vessel, usu. of greater height than width, used as ornament, for holding flowers, etc.

văs'ĕline (-ēn) n. ointment and lubricant got from petroleum. **P.**

văss'al n. (hist.) holder of land by feudal tenure; humble servant or subordinate, slave. ~**age** n.

vast (vah-) a. immense, huge, very great.

văt n. large tub, cask, cistern, or other vessel for holding or storing liquids. ~ **dye,** one of class of water-insoluble usu. colour-fast dyes. ~-**dye,** dye with vat dye.

Văt'ican n. Pope's palace and official residence in Rome; papal government.

vati'cinăte v. prophesy, foretell. ~**ā'tion** n.

vau'devĭlle (vōdv-) n. variety entertainment.

vault[1] n. arched structure of masonry serving as roof or carrying other parts of building; room, cellar, tomb, etc. covered by vault; any underground room, cellar, strong-room; (partly) underground burial chamber; any vaultlike arched surface, esp. apparently concave surface of sky. v.t. construct with, cover (as) with, make in form of, vault; form vault over.

vault[2] v. leap, spring (over), esp.

while resting on hand(s) or with help of pole. *n.* leap, spring, performed by vaulting.

vaunt *n. & v.* (arch. or rhet.) boast.

V.C. *abbr.* Vice-Chancellor; Victoria Cross.

V.D. *abbr.* venereal disease.

v.d. *abbr.* various dates.

V.E. *abbr.* Victory in Europe.

veal *n.* flesh of calf as food.

vĕc'tor *n.* (math.) (representation of) quantity having both magnitude and direction; course or compass direction esp. of aircraft; carrier of disease. *v.t.* direct (aircraft in flight) on course, esp. from ground. **vĕctōr'ial** *a.*

veer *v.i.* change direction, esp. (of wind) in direction of sun's course; turn (ship), turn, with head away from wind; change, esp. gradually, be variable.

vĕ'gĕtable *a.* of (nature of), derived from, concerned with, comprising, plants. *n.* plant, esp. herbaceous plant cultivated for food. ~ **marrow**, kind of gourd used as vegetable etc.

vĕgĕtār'ian *n.* one who eats no animal food or none obtained by destruction of animal life. *a.* of vegetarian(s); living on, consisting of, vegetables. ~**ism** *n.*

vĕ'gĕtāte *v.i.* grow as or like plant(s); lead dull monotonous life. **vegetā'-tion** *n.* vegetating; plants collectively. **vĕ'gĕtative** *a.*

ve'hement (vēĭm-) *a.* intense, violent; showing, caused by, strong feeling or excitement. ~**ence** *n.*

ve'hicle (vēĭ-) *n.* carriage or conveyance for persons or goods, means of transport, esp. by land; liquid etc. used as medium for applying or administering drug, pigment, etc.; thing, person, as channel or instrument of expression, communication, etc. **vehĭc'ūlar** *a.*

veil (vāl) *n.* piece of linen etc. falling over neck and shoulders as part of nun's head-dress; piece of transparent material worn to hide or protect face; curtain; disguise, cloak, mask; *take the* ~, become nun; *beyond the* ~, in(to) next world. *v.t.* cover (as) with veil;

conceal, disguise, mask. ~**ing** *n.* (esp.) material for veils, net.

vein (vān) *n.* one of tubular vessels carrying blood from all parts of body back to heart; any blood-vessel; one of slender bundles of tissue forming framework of leaf etc.; anything suggesting or resembling vein, esp. streak of different colour in wood, marble, etc., crack or fissure in rock; fissure containing metallic ore; distinctive character or tendency, mood. *v.t.* fill or cover (as) with vein(s). ~**ing** *n.*

vē'lar *a.* (esp.) of soft palate; (of vocal sound) formed with back of tongue near soft palate.

veld(t) (-lt) *n.* fenced or unfenced grassland in S. Africa.

vĕllē'ĭtў *n.* wishful state not prompting to action.

vĕll'um *n.* calfskin dressed and prepared for writing etc.; smooth-surfaced writing-paper.

vĕlŏ'cĭpĕde *n.* light vehicle propelled by rider, esp. early kinds of bicycle etc.

vĕlŏ'cĭtў *n.* rapidity of motion, operation, or action; speed of motion in particular direction.

vĕlour(s)' (-oor) *n.* woven fabric with plush-like pile; (hat of) felt with similar surface.

vĕl'vĕt *n.* textile esp. silk fabric with dense smooth pile; surface or substance resembling this, esp. soft downy skin on newly grown antlers; *on* ~, in easy or advantageous position. *a.* of, soft as, velvet. **vĕlvĕteen'** (*or* vĕ'-) *n. & a.* (of) cotton fabric resembling velvet; (pl.) velveteen trousers. ~**ў** *a.*

Ven. *abbr.* Venerable.

vē'nal *a.* that may be bribed, mercenary; (of action etc.) characteristic of venal person. **vēnăl'ĭtў** *n.*

vĕnd *v.* sell; offer (esp. small articles) for sale. ~**ing machine**, slot-machine. **vĕn'dor** *n.*

vĕndĕtt'a *n.* blood-feud.

vĕneer' *v.t.* cover (furniture etc.) with thin layer of finer wood. *n.* thin sheet of fine wood; superficial appearance.

vĕn'erable *a.* entitled to veneration; title of archdeacon. ~**bĭl'ĭtў** *n.*

věn′erāte v.t. regard with respect and reverence; consider as exalted or sacred. **~ā′tion** n.

věnēr′eal a. of sexual desire or intercourse; (of disease) communicated by sexual intercourse with infected person.

Věnē′tian a. & n. (inhabitant) of Venice. **~ blind,** window-blind of horizontal slats that may be turned to admit or exclude light.

věn′geance (-jans) n. avenging oneself on another, hurt or harm inflicted in revenge; *with a ~,* in extreme degree, thoroughly, violently.

věnge′ful (-jf-) a. seeking vengeance, vindictive.

vē′nial a. pardonable, not grave or heinous, (theol.) not mortal.

věn′ison (-nzn or -nīzn) n. deer's flesh as food.

věn′om n. poison of snakes etc.; bitter or virulent feeling, language, etc. **~ous** a.

vē′nous a. of veins.

věnt[1] n. slit in garment, esp. in back of coat.

věnt[2] n. small outlet or inlet for air, smoke, etc.; anus esp. of lower animals; outlet, free passage, free play. v.t. give vent or free expression to.

věn′tilāte v.t. cause air to circulate in (room etc.); expose to fresh air, oxygenate; make public, discuss freely. **~ā′tion** n. **~ātor** n. (esp.) contrivance or opening for ventilating.

věn′tral a. of or on abdomen; of anterior or lower surface.

věn′tricle n. cavity of body, esp. cavity of heart from which blood is pumped into arteries. **~ic′ūlar, ~ic′ūlous** aa.

věntril′oquĭsm n. act or art of producing vocal sounds without visible movement of lips. **~lō′quĭal, ~loquĭs′tĭc** aa.; **~loquĭst** n.; **~loquĭze** v.i.

věn′ture n. undertaking of risk, risky undertaking; *at a ~,* at random. v. dare; make bold *to* do, hazard. **~some** a.

věn′ūe n. district in which case is to be tried; meeting-place, rendezvous.

Vē′nus n. Roman goddess of beauty and (esp. sensual) love; planet second in order from sun, morning or evening star.

verā′cious a. truthful; true. **verăc′itў** n.

verăn′da n. open roofed portico or gallery along side of house.

věrb n. part of speech which expresses action, occurrence, or being. **věr′bal** a. of or concerned with words; oral; word for word; of (nature of), derived from, verb. **~alism** n. (esp.) predominance of merely verbal over real significance. **~alīze** v. make (noun etc.) into verb; use, put into, words; **~alīzā′tion** n.

věrbā′tĭm adv. & a. word for word.

verbē′na n. kinds of chiefly Amer. herbaceous plant.

věr′biage n. needless array of words.

verbōse′ a. wordy; using, expressed in, too many words. **verbŏs′itў** n.

věr′dant a. abounding in green foliage; green. **~ancў** n.

věr′dĭct n. decision of jury; decision, judgement.

věr′digris (-ēs) n. green or greenish-blue deposit forming on copper or brass.

věr′dure (-dyer) n. (colour of fresh) green vegetation.

věrge n. extreme edge, brink, border; grass edging of path, etc.; limits, precincts (of). v.i. border *on.*

věr′ger n. official carrying rod etc. before dignitaries of cathedral, university, etc.; caretaker and attendant in church.

věrĭd′ical a. truthful, veracious.

vě′rĭfў v.t. (examine in order to) establish truth or correctness of; fulfil, bear out. **~fĭcā′tion** n.

vě′rĭlў adv. (arch.) in truth.

věrĭsĭmĭl′ĭtūde n. appearance of truth or reality; probability.

vě′rĭtable a. real, properly or correctly so called.

vě′rĭtў n. truth; true statement.

věr′juice (-ōōs) n. acid juice of unripe fruit.

věrmĭcěll′ĭ n. pasta in long slender threads.

věr′mĭcīde n. substance used to kill worms.

věrmĭc′ūlar a. of (nature of) worms;

worm-like; vermiculated. **vĕrmĭc'ū-latĕd** a. covered or ornamented with close wavy or sinuous markings. **~ūlā'tion** n. **vĕrmĭc'ūlīte** n. kinds of mineral expanded by heat into light--weight water-absorbent material used for insulation etc.

vĕr'mĭfŏrm a. worm-shaped. **~ appendix**, small blind tube extending from caecum in some mammals.

vĕr'mĭfūge n. substance that expels intestinal worms.

vermĭl'ion (-yon) n. (brilliant scarlet colour of) red crystalline mercuric sulphide. a. of this colour.

vĕr'mĭn n. (usu. collect.) animals and birds injurious to game, crops, etc.; noxious or offensive creeping or wingless, esp. parasitic, insects etc.; noxious, vile, or offensive persons. **~ous** a. (esp.) infested with vermin.

vĕr'mouth (-ōoth; or vār'mōot) n. white wine flavoured with wormwood or other herbs.

vernăc'ular a. (of language etc.) of one's own country, native, not learned or foreign. n. vernacular language or dialect; homely speech.

vĕr'nal a. of or in season of spring.

vĕr'nier n. small scale sliding along fixed scale for measuring fractional parts of divisions of larger scale.

verŏn'ĭca n. kinds of flowering herb or shrub.

vĕr'satīle a. turning easily or readily from one subject, occupation, etc. to another, showing facility in varied subjects, many-sided. **~tĭl'ĭtў** n.

vĕrse n. metrical composition, poetry; verse line; stanza, short poem; numbered subdivision of Bible chapter. **vĕrsed** (-st) a. experienced or skilled in. **vĕr'sĭcle** n. each of series of short sentences said or sung in liturgy.

vĕr'sĭfў v. turn into or relate in verse; make verses. **~fĭcā'tion** n.

vĕr'sion (or -shn) n. particular rendering of work etc. in another language; particular form of statement, account, etc.

vers libre (vār lēbr) n. free verse, verse with no regular metrical system, freq. unrhymed. [F]

vĕr'sō n. left-hand page of book, back of leaf.

vĕrst n. obsolete Russian measure of length, about ⅔ mile.

vĕr'sus prep. against.

vĕrt n. & a. (her.) green.

vĕr'tĕbra n. (pl. -ae), single segment of backbone. **vĕr'tĕbral** a.

vĕr'tĕbrate a. & n. (animal) having cranium and spinal column or spinal cord.

vĕr'tĕx n. (pl. usu. -tĭcēs), top; point opposite base of figure, point where axis meets curve or surface or where lines forming angle meet.

vĕr'tĭcal a. of, at, passing through, zenith; having position directly above given place or point; placed, moving, at right angles to plane of horizon, perpendicular. n. vertical line, plane, or circle.

vĕrtĭ'gĭnous a. of vertigo; causing, tending to cause, giddiness.

vĕr'tĭgō (or -tī'-) n. dizziness, condition with sensation of whirling and tendency to lose balance.

vĕr'vain n. kinds of herbaceous plant.

vĕrve n. enthusiasm, energy, vigour.

vĕ'rў a. real, true, properly so called etc. adv. in high degree, to great extent, extremely; **~ well**, formula of consent etc.

vĕs'ĭcant a. & n. (substance) causing formation of blisters.

vĕs'ĭcle n. small bladder-like vessel or cavity; bubble; small elevation of cuticle containing clear watery fluid.

vĕs'per n. (pl.) evensong, sixth of canonical hours of breviary. **~tīne** a. of, done, appearing, blooming, etc. in evening.

vĕss'el n. hollow receptacle for liquid etc., esp. domestic utensil for preparing, storing, or serving food or drink; ship or boat; duct, canal, holding or circulating blood, sap, etc.

vĕst[1] n. body-garment worn next to skin; (chiefly U.S.) waistcoat. **~-pocket**, waistcoat pocket; chiefly attrib., of small size.

vĕst[2] v. invest with power, authority, etc.; place or secure in full or legal possession of person etc.; become vested (in). **vĕs'tĕd** a. (of interest, right) invested or secured in hands or under authority of certain person(s).

věs'ta *n.* wax match.

věs'tal *a.* chaste, virginal, virgin. *n.* Vestal virgin, nun. **V~ virgin,** priestess, vowed to chastity, of Vesta, Roman goddess of hearth and household; woman of spotless chastity.

věs'tĭbūle *n.* antechamber, lobby; entrance-hall; (chiefly U.S.) enclosed platform at end of railway coach.

věs'tĭge *n.* trace, evidence; remnant; (biol.) small or degenerate remnant of organ or part fully developed in ancestors. **věstĭ'gĭal** *a.*

věst'ment *n.* (esp. ceremonial) garment; any of official garments worn by priest etc. during divine service etc.

věs'trў *n.* room or part of church for keeping of vestments etc., robing of clergy, parish meetings, etc.; (representatives of) ratepayers of parish assembled for dispatch of parochial business. **~man,** member of parochial vestry.

vět *n.* (colloq.) veterinary surgeon. *v.t.* examine, treat, (beast, person) medically; submit to careful and critical examination.

větch *n.* kinds of leguminous plant used for fodder.

vět'eran *a.* grown old in service, esp. in armed forces; experienced by long practice; (of army) composed of veteran troops; (of service) long-continued. *n.* veteran person, esp. soldier; (U.S.) ex-serviceman. **~ car,** car of date before 1904.

věterĭnār'ĭan *n.* veterinary surgeon.

vět'erĭnarў *a.* of or for (treatment of) diseases and injuries of domestic and other animals. *n.* veterinary surgeon.

vē'tō *n.* (pl. *-oes*), prohibition; (exercise of) constitutional right to prohibit passing or putting in force of enactment, resolution, etc. *v.t.* exercise veto against; forbid.

věx *v.t.* anger by slight or petty annoyance, irritate; (poet.) agitate, toss about. **věxā'tion** *n.* being vexed; annoying thing. **věxā'tious** *a.*

věxed (-kst) *a.* (of question etc.) much discussed or contested.

v.f. *abbr.* very fair.

v.g. *abbr.* very good.

V.H.F. *abbr.* very high frequency.

vī'a *prep.* by way of, through.

vī'able *a.* capable of living or surviving.

vī'adŭct *n.* bridge-like structure carrying railway or road over valley, river, etc.

vī'al *n.* small glass bottle.

vī'ands (-z) *n.pl.* articles of food; victuals.

vĭăt'ĭcum *n.* Eucharist as administered to the dying.

vī'brant *a.* vibrating, thrilling, resonant. **~ancў** *n.*

vī'braphōne *n.* percussion instrument with electrically produced pulsating effect.

vībrāte' *v.* (cause to) swing to and fro periodically, oscillate, quiver; set, be, in state of vibration; thrill; (of sound) have quivering or pulsating effect. **vībrā'tion** *n.* (esp.) rapid reciprocating motion of particles of elastic body produced by disturbance of its equilibrium. **~ā'tional, vī'bratorў** *aa.*; **~ā'tor** *n.*

vĭbra'tō (-ah-) *n.* (mus.) pulsating effect or slight undulation of pitch in singing etc. [It.]

Vic. *abbr.* Victoria.

vĭc'ar *n.* incumbent of parish receiving only part of tithes or none; *V~ of Christ,* Pope. **~ choral,** clerical or lay assistant in musical parts of cathedral service. **~age** *n.* vicar's house or office. **vĭcār'ĭal** *a.*

vĭcār'ĭous (*or* vĭ-) *a.* deputed, delegated; acting, done, etc. for another.

vīce[1] *n.* evil, esp. grossly immoral, habit or conduct; depravity, serious fault; defect, blemish; fault, bad trick (of horse etc.).

vīce[2], **vīse** *n.* appliance with two jaws in which things may be gripped and held steady.

vī'cė[3] *prep.* in place of, in succession to.

vīce- in comb., person acting in place of, assistant, person next in rank to. **vīce-chan'cellor** (-ah-) *n.* (esp.) acting representative of university

Chancellor, discharging most administrative duties; ~-chan'cellorship n. ~gĕ'rent n. person exercising delegated power, deputy. ~-prĕs'ident (-z-) n. president's deputy; ~presidĕn'tial a. ~rē'gal a. of viceroy. ~-rē'gent n. one acting in place of regent. ~reine (-ān) n. wife of viceroy. ~roy n. person acting as governor in name and by authority of supreme ruler; (hist.) representative of British Crown in India.

vī'cė vẽr'sa *advb. phr.* the other way round.

vi'cĭnage n. neighbourhood, surrounding district.

vĭcĭn'itў (*or* vī-) n. surrounding district; nearness in place; *in the* ~ (*of*), in the neighbourhood (of).

vĭ'cĭous a. of the nature of, addicted to, vice; evil; depraved; bad-tempered, spiteful. ~ circle, fallacious reasoning by which proposition is proved by conclusion it has established; (colloq.) chain of circumstances etc. leading back to or aggravating original one.

vĭcĭss'ĭtūde (*or* vī-) n. change of circumstances, esp. of condition or fortune.

vĭc'tĭm n. living creature sacrificed to deity etc.; person killed or made to suffer by cruelty or oppression; one who suffers injury, hardship, etc. vĭc'tĭmīze *v.t.* treat unjustly or with undue harshness, esp. by dismissal as result of strike etc.; make victim of cruelty, swindle, spite, etc. ~īzā'tion n.

vĭc'tor n. conqueror; winner of contest.

vĭctōr'ĭa n. light open four-wheeled carriage with seat for two; Victoria lily, victoria plum. V~ Cross, military decoration for conspicuous bravery. V~ lily, kinds of gigantic S.-Amer. water-lily. ~ plum, large red luscious variety. Vĭctōr'ĭan a. & n. of, (person) living in, characteristic of, reign of Queen Victoria; ~ĭanĭsm n.

vĭc'torў n. winning of battle, war, or contest. victōr'ĭous a. conquering, triumphant; marked by, producing, victory.

victual (vĭt'l) n. (usu. pl.) food, provisions. v. supply with victuals, lay in supply of victuals. victualler (vĭt'ler) n. purveyor of victuals, esp. (*licensed* ~), licensee of public-house.

vĭcu'ña (-ōōnya; *or* vī-) n. S.-Amer. mammal with fine silky wool; (imitation of) soft cloth of vicuña wool.

vī'dė, refer to, consult. [L]

vĭdē'lĭcĕt, that is to say; namely. [L]

vĭd'ėō a. & n. (U.S.) television. ~ recording, ~ tape, recording, record on magnetic tape, of television programme etc.

vīe *v.i.* contend or compete (with) for superiority.

view (vū) n. inspection by eye or mind; what is seen, scene, prospect; picture etc. of view; range of vision; mental survey, mental attitude; *in* ~ *of*, having regard to, considering; *on* ~, open to inspection; *point of* ~, position from which thing is viewed, way of looking at matter; *private* ~, view of exhibition open only to invited guests; *with a* ~ *to*, for the purpose of, as a step towards, with an eye to. *v.t.* survey with eyes or mind; regard, consider. ~-finder, device showing view in range of camera lens. ~-hallōō', huntsman's shout on seeing fox break cover. ~-point, point of view. ~er n. one who watches television. ~lėss a. (esp., poet.) invisible.

vĭgĕs'ĭmal a. of or pertaining to, based on, (the number) twenty.

vĭ'gĭl n. (watch kept on) eve of festival; watching, keeping awake; *keep* ~, keep watch.

vĭ'gĭlance n. watchfulness against danger or action of others, caution, circumspection. ~ committee, (U.S.) self-appointed committee for maintenance of justice and order, esp. when processes of law are considered inadequate. ~ant a. vĭgĭlán'tė n. (U.S.) member of vigilance committee.

vignette (vēnyĕt') n. decorative design, photograph, etc. with edges shading off into surrounding paper background, etc.; short description,

word-sketch. *v.t.* make vignette of,
esp. by shading off or softening
away edges.

vig′our (-ger) *n.* activity and strength
of body or mind. **vig′orous** *a.*
active; forcible.

Vī′king *n.* & *a.* (one) of Scandinavian
sea-adventurers, traders, pirates,
etc. of 8th–11th cc.

vīle *a.* despicable on moral grounds,
depraved, base; worthless, of poor
or bad quality; disgusting, filthy;
shameful.

vil′ifȳ *v.t.* speak ill of, defame.
~fica′tion *n.*

vill′a *n.* detached or semi-detached
small house in suburban or residential district; country residence, esp.
in Italy, southern France, etc.;
(hist., esp. Roman) country estate
with house(s), farm(s), etc.

vill′age *n.* assemblage of houses etc.
in country district, larger than
hamlet and smaller than town.
vill′ager *n.* dweller in village;
rustic.

vill′ain (-an) *n.* person guilty or
capable of great wickedness;
character in play, novel, etc. whose
evil motives or actions are important element of plot. **vill′ainous**
a. worthy of a villain, wicked, vile;
(colloq.) abominably bad. **vill′-
lainȳ** *n.*

villanĕlle′ *n.* poem of (usu.) five
three-line stanzas and final quatrain, with two rhymes throughout.

vill′ein (-in) *n.* (hist.) peasant culti-
vator entirely subject to lord or
attached to manor. **~age** *n.*

vim *n.* (colloq.) vigour, energy.

vinaigrĕtte′ (-nig-) *n.* smelling-salt
bottle; ~ (*sauce*), sauce of oil,
vinegar, etc.

vin′dicāte *v.t.* establish existence,
merits, justice, etc. of; successfully
maintain cause of. **~ā′tion** *n.*
~atorȳ *a.* tending to vindicate;
punitive.

vindic′tive *a.* revengeful, avenging,
given to revenge; punitive.

vīne *n.* trailing or climbing woody-
-stemmed plant bearing grapes; any
trailing or climbing plant. **vī′nerȳ**
n. glass-house for growing grapes.

vin′egar *n.* sour liquid produced by
fermentation of wine, malt liquors,
etc. **vin′egarȳ** *a.* sour, acid.

vine′yard (-ny-) *n.* plantation of
grape-vines, esp. for wine-making.

vingt-et-un (vănt ā ŭṅ) *n.* card-game
in which object is to score 21. [F]

vī′nous *a.* of, like, due or addicted to,
wine.

vin′tage *n.* (season of) grape-harvest;
wine, esp. of good quality; wine
from grapes of particular district
(in particular year); date of wine
as indication of quality. **~ car,** car
of date between 1904 and 1931.
vin′tager *n.* grape-harvester.

vint′ner *n.* wine-merchant.

vī′nȳl *n.* (chem.) radical forming
basis of many plastics etc.

vī′ol *n.* medieval stringed musical
instrument (now again in use)
similar in shape to violin. **~(a) da
gamba,** bass viol, held like violoncello. **~ist** *n.* player of viol.

vīō′la[1] (*or* vī-) *n.* (player of) tenor
member of violin family of musical
instruments, slightly larger and of
lower pitch than violin.

vī′ola[2] *n.* kinds of herbaceous plant
including violets and pansies;
hybrid garden-plant more uniformly and delicately coloured than
pansy.

vīolā′ceous *a.* (bot.) of violet family.

vī′olāte *v.t.* transgress; infringe;
break in upon; commit rape upon.
~ā′tion *n.*

vī′olence *n.* violent conduct or treatment; violent feeling or language,
vehemence; intensity (*of*); (law)
(intimidation by threat of) unlawful exercise of physical force.
vī′olent *a.* marked or caused by,
acting with, great physical force or
unlawful exercise of force; intense,
vehement, passionate, furious, etc.

vī′olet *n.* (esp. sweet-scented purplish-
-blue or white) plant of viola kind;
purplish-blue colour of violet,
colour at opposite end of spectrum
from red. *a.* of this colour.

violin′ *n.* (player of, part for) four-
stringed musical instrument played
with bow. **~ist** *n.* player of
violin.

violoncell′ō (-chĕ-) *n.* (pl. *-os*), large

instrument of violin family supported on floor between performer's knees. ~cĕll'ist *n*.

V.I.P. *abbr*. very important person.

vī'per *n*. kinds of small venomous snake, esp. adder; malignant or treacherous person. ~ish, ~ous *aa*.

vĭrā'gō (*or* -ah-) *n*. (pl. -os), fierce or abusive woman, termagant.

Virg. *abbr*. Virgil.

vīr'gĭn *n*. person, esp. woman, who has had no sexual intercourse; *the* (*Blessed*) *V*~ (*Mary*), (image or picture representing) mother of Christ. *a*. that is a virgin; of, befitting, virgin; undefiled, spotless, not previously touched, used, etc. ~ **soil**, soil not yet brought into cultivation. **vīrgĭn'itў** *n*.

vīr'gĭnal *a*. being, befitting, belonging to, virgin. *n*. (freq. pl.) keyboard instrument, earliest form of harpsichord.

Vīrgĭn'ĭa *n*. tobacco from Virginia; any Amer. tobacco. ~ **creeper**, kinds of ·N. Amer. ornamental climbing plant.

Vīr'gō, Virgin, sixth constellation and sign of zodiac.

vĭrĭdĕs'cent *a*. greenish, verdant. ~ence *n*.

vĭrĭd'ĭan *n*. emerald-green pigment.

vĭ'rīle *a*. of, characteristic of, a man; capable of procreation; having masculine vigour or strength. **vĭrĭl'itў** *n*.

vīrŏl'ogў *n*. science or study of viruses. ~ogist *n*.

vĭrtu' (-ōō) *n*. (arch.) knowledge of, taste for, fine arts; *article, object*, etc. *of* ~, curio, antique.

vĭrt'ŭal *a*. that is so in essence or effect, although not formally or actually.

vīr'tūe *n*. moral goodness; particular moral excellence; chastity, esp. of women; good quality or influence, efficacy; (pl.) seventh order of angels; *by, in,* ~ *of*, on strength or ground of. **vĭr'tūous** *a*. possessing, showing, moral rectitude; chaste.

vĭrtūō'sō (*or* -z-) *n*. (pl. -si, pr. -sē), person skilled in technique of an art, esp. of performance on musical instrument; person with special interest in or knowledge of fine arts. ~ŏs'itў *n*.

vĭ'rūlent (*or* -rōō-) *a*. poisonous; malignant, bitter; (of disease) extremely violent. ~ence *n*.

vīr'us *n*. kinds of ultramicroscopic esp. disease-producing organism capable of growth and multiplication only within living cells; moral poison, malignity.

Vis., Visct. *abbr*. Viscount.

visa (vē'za) *n*. endorsement on passport permitting holder to enter certain countries etc. *v.t.* mark with visa.

vĭs'age (-z-) *n*. (literary) face.

vĭs-à-vĭs (vēzavē') *prep*. & *adv*. over against, in comparison with; facing, face-to-face (with). *n*. either of two persons or things placed opposite each other; person facing one.

vĭs'cera *n.pl*. internal organs of principal cavities of body. **vĭs'ceral** *a*.

vĭs'cĭd *a*. glutinous, sticky. **vĭscĭd'itў** *n*.

vĭs'cōse *n*. viscous solution of cellulose used in making rayon etc.

vĭscŏs'itў *n*. quality, degree, of being viscous; body's property of resisting alteration of relative position of its parts.

vĭ'scount (vīk-) *n*. peer ranking between earl and baron; courtesy title of earl's eldest son. ~cy, ~ėss, ~ў *nn*.

vĭs'cous *a*. glutinous, sticky; having viscosity; intermediate between solid and fluid.

vise : see **vice²**.

vĭs'ible (-z-) *a*. capable of being seen, that can be seen; in sight; apparent, open, obvious. **vĭsĭbil'itў** *n*. (esp.) conditions of light, atmosphere, etc. as regards distinguishing objects by sight; possibility of seeing, range of vision.

vĭ'sion *n*. act or faculty of seeing; power of discerning future conditions etc.; thing, person, etc. seen in dream or trance; supernatural apparition, phantom; person, sight, of unusual beauty. ~arў *a*. given to seeing visions or indulging in fanciful theories; seen (only) in a vision, existing only in imagination; unreal, fantastic, unpractical; *n*. visionary person.

vĭs'ĭt (-z-) *v.* go, come, to see (person, place, etc.), esp. as act of friendship or social ceremony; stay with or at; (bibl.) punish, avenge (*upon*), afflict. *n.* call on person or at place; temporary residence; occasion of going *to* doctor etc. for examination or treatment; doctor's professional call. **~ant** *n.* (esp.) migratory bird as temporarily frequenting place etc.

visĭtā'tion (-z-) *n.* official visit of inspection etc., esp. bishop's inspection of churches of his diocese; divine dispensation of punishment or award; notable affliction; *V~* (*of Our Lady*), visit of Virgin Mary to Elizabeth, day (2 July) commemorating this.

vĭs'ĭtor (-z-) *n.* one who visits; person with right or duty of supervision over university, college, etc.

vī'sor (-z-) *n.* (hist.) movable front part of helmet, covering face; mask; (U.S.) peak of cap.

vĭs'ta *n.* view, prospect, esp. through avenue of trees or other long narrow opening; mental view of extensive period, series of events, etc.

vĭs'ūal (-z- *or* -zh-) *a.* of, concerned with, used in, seeing; received through sight. **~ize** *v.t.* make mental vision or image of. **~īzā'- tion** *n.*

vī'tal *a.* of, concerned with, essential to, organic life; essential to existence, success, etc.; fatal. **~ statistics**, those relating to births, deaths, health, etc.; (colloq.) measurements of woman's bust, waist, and hips. **vītăl'itў** *n.* vital power; hold on life; persistent energy, animation, liveliness. **~ize** *v.t.* put life or animation into, infuse with vitality or vigour; **~īzā'tion** *n.* **vī'tals** *n.pl.* vital parts of body.

vī'tamĭn (*or* vī-) *n.* kinds of substance occurring in certain foodstuffs and essential in small quantities to health, normal growth, etc. **~ize** *v.t.* introduce vitamin(s) into (food).

vĭ'tiāte (-shǐ-) *v.t.* impair quality of, corrupt, debase, spoil. **~ā'tion** *n.*

vĭt'ĭcŭlture *n.* vine-growing.

vĭt'rēous *a.* of (nature of) glass; resembling glass in composition, brittleness, hardness, lustre, etc. **vĭt'rĭfў** *v.* convert, be converted, into glass or glass-like substance; make or become vitreous; **vitrĭfăc'tion, vĭtrĭfĭcā'tion** *nn.*

vĭt'rĭŏl *n.* various metallic sulphates used in arts etc.; (*oil of*) **~**, concentrated sulphuric acid; causticity, acrimony, of feeling etc. **vĭtrĭŏl'ĭc** *a.* (esp.) caustic, scathing, malignant, bitter.

vītū'perāte (*or* vĭ-) *v.t.* revile, abuse **~ā'tion** *n.*; **~ative** *a.*

vī'va¹ (vē-) *int.* & *n.* (salute, greeting, cry, of) long live . . . ! [It.]

vī'va² *n.* (colloq.) viva voce.

vĭvā'cious (*or* vī-) *a.* lively, animated. **vivă'citў** *n.*

vīvār'ĭum *n.* (pl -*ia*), place for keeping living animals etc. in natural conditions.

vī'va vō'cė *adv.* orally. *a.* oral. *n.* oral examination.

vĭv'ĭd *a.* bright; intense; lively; incisive; graphic.

vĭv'ĭfў *v.t.* give life to, animate.

vĭvĭp'arous *a.* bringing forth young alive.

vĭv'ĭsĕct *v.t.* perform vivisection on. **vĭvĭsĕc'tion** *n.* performance of surgical experiments on living animals. **~tionĭst** *n.*

vĭx'en *n.* she-fox; spiteful woman. **~ish** *a.*

viz. *abbr.* videlicet.

vĭz'ard *n.* (arch.) mask; visor.

vĭzier' (-ēr) *n.* high administrative official in some Moslem countries.

v.l. *abbr.*, *varia lectio* [L], variant reading.

V.O. *abbr.* Royal Victorian Order.

voc. *abbr.* vocative.

vō'cable *n.* word.

vocăb'ūlarў *n.* list of words with their meanings; sum of words used in language etc. or by person, class, etc.

vō'cal *a.* of, with, for, voice; uttered by voice; endowed (as) with voice; expressive, eloquent. **~ cords**, voice-producing organs, two strap- -like membranes stretched across larynx. **~ score**, musical score

showing voice parts in full. **vocăl'ĭc**
a. of (nature of), concerning,
vowel(s). **~ĭsm** *n.* use of voice;
system of vowels in language etc.
~ĭst *n.* singer. **~īze** *v.* utter, make
vocal; convert into, use as, vowel;
sing, esp. on vowel-sound(s);
~īzā'tion *n.*

vocā'tion *n.* divine call to, sense of
fitness for, career or occupation;
occupation, calling. **~al** *a.* of or
for career or occupation.

vŏc'ative *a.* & *n.* (case, word) used
in address or invocation.

vocif'erāte *v.* shout, clamour, bawl;
speak loudly. **vocif'erous** *a.* clamo-
rous, noisy.

vŏd'ka *n.* alcoholic spirit distilled
esp. in Russia from rye etc.

vōgue (-g) *n.* popular favour, general
acceptance or currency; prevailing
fashion.

voice *n.* sound uttered by mouth,
esp. human utterance; use of voice,
expression in words, opinion etc.
expressed, vote; sound uttered
with vibration or resonance of vocal
cords; (quality of) singing voice;
(gram.) set of forms of verb showing relation of subject to action.
v.t. give voice to; utter with voice.
~d *a.* (esp., phonet.) uttered with
voice. **~lĕss** *a.*

void *a.* empty, vacant; not valid.
n. empty space; sense of loss.
v.t. invalidate; discharge, excrete.

voile *n.* thin semi-transparent dress
material.

vol. *abbr.* volume.

vŏl'atile *a.* readily evaporating at
ordinary temperatures; changeable, flighty, lively, gay; transient.
~tĭl'itỹ *n.* **volăt'ĭlīze** *v.* (cause to)
evaporate; make, become, volatile;
~tĭlīzā'tion *n.*

vŏl'-au-vent' (-ō-vahṅ) *n.* pie of
light puff pastry filled with sauce
containing meat, fish, etc.

vŏlcā'nō *n.* (pl. *-oes*), mountain or
hill with opening(s) through which
ashes, gases, (molten) rocks, etc.
are or have been periodically
ejected. **volcăn'ĭc** *a.* of, produced
by, volcano; characterized by
volcanoes; violent, intense, passionate, fervid.

vōle *n.* kinds of small rodent with
short ears and tail.

voli'tion *n.* act or faculty of willing,
exercise of will. **~al** *a.*

vŏll'ey *n.* salvo, simultaneous discharge, shower, of missiles etc.;
(tennis, etc.) return stroke at ball
before it touches ground. *v.* discharge, return, hit, fly, etc., in
volley(s). **~ball**, game in which
large inflated ball is struck with
hands over net without touching
ground.

vōlt *n.* unit of electromotive force,
difference of potential capable of
sending current of one ampere
through conductor with resistance
of one ohm. **~meter**, instrument
for measuring voltage. **vōl'tage** *n.*
electromotive force expressed in
volts.

vŏltā'ĭc *a.* producing electricity,
generated, by chemical action.

vŏlte-face' (-tfahs) *n.* complete
change of front.

vŏl'ūble *a.* fluent, glib; speaking,
spoken, with great fluency. **~-
bĭl'itỹ** *n.*

vŏl'ūme *n.* set of written or esp.
printed sheets bound together and
forming book; bulk, mass, (large)
quantity; space occupied, esp. as
measured in cubic units; size,
amount, (*of*); moving mass of water
or smoke; quantity, power, fullness,
of tone or sound. **vŏlūmĕt'rĭc** *a.* of,
concerned with, etc. measurement
of volume.

volū'mĭnous *a.* of great volume
bulky, ample; consisting of, enough
for, many volumes; copious.

vŏl'untarỹ *a.* having free will; done,
acting, able to act, of one's own
free will; controlled by the will;
brought about, maintained, etc.,
by voluntary action. *n.* organ solo
played before, during, or after
church service.

vŏlunteer' *n.* one who voluntarily
offers services or enrols himself for
enterprise, esp. for service in any
of armed services. *v.* undertake,
offer, voluntarily; make voluntary
offer of one's services.

volŭp'tūarỹ *n.* person given up to

indulgence in luxury and gratification of senses. **volŭp'tūous** *a.* of, marked by, addicted to, promising or suggesting, etc. gratification of the senses.

volūte' *n.* spiral scroll as ornament of Ionic or other capitals; spiral conformation, convolution, esp. of spiral shell.

vŏm'ĭt *v.* eject contents of stomach through mouth; bring up, eject, (as) by vomiting, belch forth, spew out. *n.* matter vomited.

vōō'doo *n.* system of religious or magical beliefs and practices among Negroes etc. of W. Indies and America. *v.t.* bewitch, put voodoo spell on. ~**ism** *n.*

vorā'cious *a.* greedy in eating, ravenous. **vorá'cĭtў** *n.*

vōr'tĕx *n.* (pl. -*ĭcēs* or -*ĕxes*) whirlpool; anything resembling this esp. in rush or excitement, absorbing or engulfing effect, etc. **vōrt'ĭcal** *a.* **vōr'tĭcĭsm** *n.* artistic movement or theory developed from cubism, futurism, etc.; **vōr'tĭcĭst** *n.* & *a.*

vō'tarў *n.* one bound by vow(s), esp. to religious life; devotee, devoted worshipper, ardent follower (*of*). **vō'tarĕss** *n.* female votary.

vōte *n.* expression of preference, acceptance, rejection, etc. signified by ballot, show of hands, etc.; right to vote; opinion expressed, resolution or decision carried, by voting; number of votes given. *v.* give vote; decide by majority of votes; (colloq.) pronounce, declare, by general consent; (colloq.) suggest; ~ *down*, defeat, reject, by voting. **vō'ter** *n.* (esp.) person entitled to vote.

vō'tĭve *a.* given, consecrated, etc. in fulfilment of vow.

vouch *v.i.* answer, be surety or confirmation, *for.* **vou'cher** *n.* document establishing payment of money, correctness of accounts, etc.; esp. document exchangeable for goods or services as token of payment made or promised.

vouchsāfe' *v.t.* give, grant, etc. in condescending or gracious manner; deign, condescend, *to* do.

vow *n.* solemn promise or engagement, esp. to deity or saint. *v.t.* promise or undertake solemnly, esp. by vow; make solemn resolve to exact (vengeance) etc.

vow'ĕl *n.* (letter representing) speech-sound produced by vibrations of vocal cords, but without audible friction.

vŏx hūma'na (-mā- *or* -mah-), organ reed-stop resembling human voice in quality and tone. [L]

vŏx pŏp'ūlĭ, voice of the people; public opinion, general verdict. [L]

voy'age *n.* & *v.i.* journey, travel, esp. to some distance, by water. **voy'ager** *n.*

voyeur (vwahyēr') *n.* one who derives gratification from looking at sexual organs or acts of others. [F]

V.R. *abbr.*, *Victoria Regina* [L], Queen Victoria.

V.S. *abbr.* Veterinary Surgeon.

Vt. *abbr.* Vermont.

vŭl'canīte *n.* black rubber hardened by treatment with sulphur at high temperatures. **vŭl'canīze** *v.t.* harden (rubber etc.) esp. by combining with sulphur. ~**īzā'tion** *n.*

Vulg. *abbr.* Vulgate.

vŭl'gar *a.* of common people, plebeiaǹ, coarse, low; in common use; offending against good taste. ~ **fraction**, fraction represented by numbers above line for numerator and below for denominator. ~ **tongue**, popular or native language, esp. opp. to Latin. **vŭlgār'ian** *n.* vulgar (esp. rich) person. **vŭlgă'rĭtў** *n.* ~**īze** *v.t.* make vulgar or commonplace; reduce to level of the usual or ordinary; ~**īzā'tion** *n.*

Vŭl'gate *n.* fourth-century Latin version of Bible.

vŭl'nerable *a.* that may be wounded, open to or not proof against attack, injury, criticism, etc.; (contract bridge) having won one game towards rubber.

vŭl'pīne *a.* of or like fox; crafty, cunning.

vŭl'ture *n.* kinds of large bird of

prey feeding on carrion; rapacious person. **vŭl′turīne** a.

vŭl′va n. external opening of vagina.

vv. abbr. verses.

vying, pres. p. of **vie.**

W

W. abbr. Welsh; West.

w. abbr. watt; wicket; wide; wife; with.

wăck′y̆ a. (sl.) whacky.

wad (wŏd) n. small bundle or mass of soft material used as pad, plug, etc., esp. disc of felt etc. keeping powder or shot compact in gun; (U.S.) tight roll, esp. of bank-notes, (colloq.) wealth, money. v.t. press, roll, etc. into wad; line, pad, with wadding; furnish, plug, with wad. **wadd′ing** n. (material for) wads; loose soft fibrous material for padding, packing, quilting, etc.

wadd′le (wŏ-) v.i. walk with short steps and swaying motion. n. waddling gait.

wāde v. walk through water or other impeding medium; progress slowly or with difficulty (through). n. act or spell of wading. **wā′der** n. (esp.) long-legged bird that wades in shallow water; (pl.) high water-proof fishing-boots.

wa′dĭ, wa′dy̆ (wah- or wŏ-) n. in N. Africa etc., rocky water course or ravine dry except in rainy season.

w.a.f. abbr. with all faults.

wā′fer n. very thin light crisp biscuit; thin disc of unleavened bread used at Eucharist; small disc of gelatine, flour, etc., formerly used for sealing letters; disc of red paper used as seal on legal document. v.t. fasten or seal with wafer. **wā′fer̆y** a.

waff′le[1] (wŏ-) n. small soft crisp batter-cake. ~-iron, utensil usu. of two metal plates etc. hinged together for cooking waffles.

waff′le[2] (wŏ-) v.i. & n. (utter) vague wordy nonsense.

waft (-ŏ- or -ah-) v. convey, float, smoothly and lightly along (as) through air or over water. n. whiff of perfume etc.; waving movement.

wăg[1] v. shake or move briskly to and fro. n. single wagging motion. ~tail, kinds of long-tailed small bird.

wăg[2] n. facetious person, habitual joker. **wăgg′er̆y** n.; **wăgg′ish** a.

wāge[1] n. (freq. pl.) amount paid periodically, esp. by day or week, for work or service of employee or servant; (usu. pl.) requital, reward; (pl.) that part of total production which is reward of all forms of labour. ~ freeze, ban on wage-increases.

wāge[2] v.t. carry on (war etc.).

wā′ger v.t. bet, stake. n. instance of wagering; amount staked.

wăgg′le v. move, be moved, to and fro or from side to side with short quick motions. n. act of waggling.

wăg(g)′on n. four-wheeled vehicle for heavy loads; open railway truck; vehicle for carrying water; on the ~, (sl.) abstaining from alcohol. **wăg(g)′oner** n. driver of wagon. **wăg(g)onĕtte′** n. four-wheeled open horse-drawn carriage with facing side-seats.

waif n. (law) object or animal found ownerless; homeless and helpless person, esp. abandoned child.

wail n. prolonged plaintive inarticulate cry of pain, grief, etc.; sound resembling cry of pain; lamentation. v. utter wail(s) or persistent lamentations or complaints.

wain n. (poet. etc.) wagon.

wain′scot n. wooden panelling or boarding on room-wall. v.t. line with wainscot. ~ing n. (material for) wainscot.

waist n. part of human body between ribs and hip-bones; (narrowed) part of garment approximately covering this; (U.S.) bodice, blouse; middle narrower part of anything; (naut.) middle part of (upper deck of) ship. ~coat, usu. sleeveless and collarless garment covering upper part of body down to waist and worn under jacket etc. ~line, line of waist. **wai′stĕd** a. narrowed or close-fitting at waistline.

wait *v.* defer action until expected event occurs; pause; be expectant or on the watch (*for*); await, bide; defer (meal) until someone arrives; act as attendant *on*; serve food and drink etc. at table; ~ (*up*)*on*, pay respectful visit to. *n.* act or time of waiting; (pl.) street singers of Christmas carols. **wai'ter** *n.* (esp.) man employed in restaurant etc. or (U.S.) private house to wait at table etc. **wai'ting** *n.* (esp.) (period of) official attendance at court; *in* ~, on duty, in attendance; ~**ing-list**, list of persons waiting for appointment, next chance to obtain something, etc.; ~**ing-room**, room provided for persons to wait in, esp. at railway-station etc. or house of doctor etc. **wai'tress** *n.* woman employed to wait at table in restaurant etc.

waive *v.t.* forbear to insist on or exercise; forgo. **wai'ver** *n.* (law) waiving.

wāke[1] *n.* track left by ship etc. on surface of water; *in the* ~ *of*, following close behind, in imitation of, following as result or consequence.

wāke[2] *v.* (p.t. *wōke*, *wāked*; p.p. *wāked*, *wōken*), cease to sleep, rouse from sleep; (arch.) be awake; cease, rouse, from sloth, inactivity, etc.; rise, raise, from the dead; arouse, excite; hold wake over (corpse). *n.* (chiefly in Ireland) watch by corpse before burial, drinking, lamentation, etc. associated with this; (pl.) annual holiday in (industrial) north of England. ~**ful** *a.* unable to sleep; vigilant; sleepless. **wā'ken** *v.* cause to be, become, awake.

wāle *n.* (naut.) one of broader thicker strakes; weal. *v.t.* mark with weals.

walk (wawk) *v.* travel, go (over, along, etc.) on foot; progress by alternate movement of legs so that one foot is always on ground, (of quadruped) go at gait in which two feet are always on ground; (of ghost etc.) appear; cause to walk with one; take charge of (hound-puppy); ~ *away with*, win easily; ~ *off with*, steal, carry off; ~ *on*, play non-speaking part on stage; ~ *out*, (esp., colloq.) strike; ~ *over*, (esp.) win with little or no effort; ~ *the streets*, (esp.) be prostitute. *n.* walking gait, walking pace; manner of walking; journey on foot; place for walking, avenue, broad path, side-walk; beat or round; place where game-cock is kept; *cock of the* ~, person of unchallenged superiority etc.; ~ *of life*, department of action, calling, occupation. ~**ing-stick**, stick carried for support or display when walking. ~**ing-tour**, pleasure journey on foot. ~**-out**, (colloq.) strike. ~**-over**, (esp.) easy victory. ~**-up**, (U.S. colloq.) (flat, block of flats) not served by lift.

walk'ie-talk'ie (waw-, taw-) *n.* two-way radio set carried on the person.

wall (wawl) *n.* structure of stone, earth, etc. of some height serving as rampart, defensive enclosure, or to enclose or divide off house, room, field, etc.; something resembling wall in appearance or function; investment or lining tissue of bodily organ or cavity, cell, etc. *v.t.* provide or protect with wall; shut *in*, *off*, etc., block *up*, with wall(s). ~**flower**, kinds of fragrant--flowered wild or garden plant; (colloq.) woman sitting out dances for lack of partners. ~**-game**, kind of football played at Eton. ~**-paper**, paper for covering interior walls of rooms.

wa'llaby (wŏ-) *n.* kinds of small kangaroo.

wall'ah (wŏ-) *n.* (Anglo-Ind.) person employed about or concerned with something; (colloq.) man, person.

wall'et (wŏ-) *n.* (arch.) bag for holding provisions etc. on journey; flat usu. leather case for holding paper money, documents, etc.; bag for holding small tools, items of equipment, etc.

wall-eye (waw'lī) *n.* eye with iris whitish, streaked, etc. or with divergent squint.

wall'op (wŏ-) *v.t.* (sl.) thrash, beat. *n.* whack; (sl.) beer. **wall'oping** *a.* big, strapping, thumping.

wallow (wŏl'ō) *v.i.* roll about in mud,

sand, water, etc.; take gross delight *in*. *n*. act of wallowing; place where animals wallow.

Wall (wawl) **Street**, name of street in New York City; U.S. money--market.

wal'nŭt (wawl-) *n*. (edible nut in spheroidal shell of) kinds of tree; wood of walnut-tree, used in cabinet-making.

wal'rus (wawl-) *n*. large long-tusked carnivorous amphibious mammal. ~ **moustache**, long thick moustache hanging down over mouth.

waltz (wawls *or* wŏ-) *n*. (music in triple time for) dance performed by couples swinging round and round as they progress with smooth gliding steps. *v*. dance waltz; move lightly, trippingly, etc.; whirl (person) round (as) in waltz.

wam'pum (wŏ-) *n*. shell-beads formerly used by N.-Amer. Indians for money, ornament, etc.

wan (wŏn) *a*. pale, pallid, colourless, sickly.

wand (-ŏ-) *n*. slender rod or staff carried as sign of office etc.; fairy's or magician's magic staff.

wan'der (wŏ-) *v*. move idly, restlessly, or casually about; go from place to place without settled route or destination; diverge from right way; stray; wind, meander; be unsettled or incoherent in mind, talk, etc., be inattentive or delirious, rave. **wan'derer**, ~**ing** *nn*. **wan'derlŭst** *n*. strong or irresistible desire to travel or wander.

wāne *v.i.* decrease in brilliance, size, etc., lose power, vigour, importance, etc.; (of moon) undergo periodical decrease in extent of visible illuminated surface. *n*. (period of) waning, decline.

wăng'le (-nggl) *v.t.* accomplish, obtain, bring about, etc. by scheming or contrivance. *n*. act of wangling.

want (wŏ-) *n*. lack or need (*of*), deficiency; lack of necessaries of life, penury, destitution; need; something needed or desired. *v*. be without or insufficiently provided with; be in want; require; desire, wish for possession or presence of;

~ *for*, lack, be without. **wan'tĕd** *a*. (esp.) sought for by police. **wan'tĭng** *a*. (esp.) lacking *in*; lacking, minus, without; (colloq.) mentally deficient.

wan'ton (wŏ-) *a*. sportive, capricious; luxuriant, wild; licentious, unchaste; unprovoked, reckless, arbitrary. *n*. unchaste woman. *v.i.* (arch.) gambol, frolic; luxuriate *in*; sport amorously.

wap'ĭtĭ (wŏ-) *n*. large N.-Amer. deer.

war (wōr) *n*. quarrel usu. between nations conducted by armed force; hostility between persons; *civil* ~, war between parties within one nation; *cold* ~, enmity, suspicion, etc. between nations without actual hostilities. *v.i.* make war, be at war. ~**-cry**, phrase or name formerly shouted in battle; party catchword. ~**-head**, explosive head of torpedo, rocket, etc. ~**monger**, one who seeks to bring about war. ~**-paint**, paint applied by savages to face and body before battle; one's best clothes and finery. ~**-path**, (route taken by) warlike expedition of N. Amer. Indians; *on the* ~**-path**, seeking occasion for quarrel etc., belligerent. ~**ship**, ship armed and manned for war. ~ **widow**, woman whose husband has been killed in war. ~**fāre** *n*. state of war; being engaged in war, conflict. ~**līke** *a*. martial; skilled in, fond of, war; of, for use in, war; bellicose. **warr'ĭng** *a*. (esp.) contending, discordant.

War. *abbr.* Warwickshire.

war'ble[1] (wōr-) *v*. sing in sweet gentle continuous trilling manner. *n*. warbling sound. **war'bler** *n*. kinds of small bird.

war'ble[2] (wōr-) *n*. (swelling caused by) maggot of ~**-fly**, kinds of dipterous insect with maggots burrowing under skin of cattle etc.

ward (-ōr-) *n*. guardianship of minor or other person legally incapable of conducting his affairs; minor etc. under care of guardian or Court of Chancery; separate room or division of hospital, prison, etc.; administrative division of borough, city, and some counties; ridge projecting from inside plate of lock preventing passage of key not having corresponding incision; corresponding incision in bit of key; *keep watch and ~,* guard, keep watch (over). *v.t.* parry or keep *off.* **~-maid,** maidservant in hospital ward. **~room,** mess-room or living-space of naval commissioned officers below commanding officer. **~ship** *n.*

war'den (-ōr-) *n.* president, governor (*of* certain colleges, schools, etc.); churchwarden; member of civil organization for assisting civilian population in war etc.; traffic warden. **~ship** *n.*

war'der (-ōr-) *n.* (arch.) sentinel, watchman on tower; official in charge of prisoners in jail. **ward'rèss** *n.*

war'drōbe (wōr-) *n.* place, esp. large cupboard, where clothes are kept; room where theatrical costumes and properties are kept; stock of clothes. **~ dealer,** dealer in second-hand clothes. **~ mistress,** woman in charge of theatrical wardrobe or costumes.

wāre[1] *n.* articles made for sale, goods, esp. vessels etc. of baked clay; (pl.) things person has for sale.

wāre[2] *pred. a.* (poet.) aware. *v.t.,* usu. imper. (wōr *or* wār), beware of, look out for.

wāre'house (-ār-h-) *n.* (part of) building used for storage of merchandise, wholesaler's goods for sale, property temporarily stored for owner etc.; bonded warehouse. *v.t.* store in warehouse. **~man,** wholesaler; person storing furniture etc. for owner.

warfare, warlike : see **war.**

war'lock (wōr-) *n.* (arch.) wizard.

warm (-ōr-) *a.* of, at, rather high temperature, moderately hot; glowing with exercise, excitement, etc.; (of clothes etc.) serving to keep wearer warm; (of feelings etc.) hearty, excited, sympathetic, affectionate, heated, eager; (in children's games) near object, answer, etc. sought; (of colour) suggesting warmth, esp. of or containing rich eds and yellows. *n.* warming,

being warmed. *v.* make warm; excite; become warm, animated or sympathetic; **~ up,** (esp.) re-heat (food etc.). **~-blooded,** (of birds and mammals) having constant body-temperature normally higher than that of surrounding medium; passionate, amorous, emotional. **~ front,** (meteor.) line between cold air and advancing warm air. **~-hearted,** of, showing, proceeding from, generous and affectionate disposition. **~ing-pan,** long-handled covered metal pan for holding live coals etc. formerly used for warming beds. **warmth** *n.*

warn (-ōr-) *v.t.* give timely notice of impending danger or misfortune, put on guard, caution *against*; give cautionary notice or advice with regard to actions, conduct, belief, etc.; **~ off,** give notice to keep at distance, off private ground, etc., prohibit from taking part in race-meeting etc. **war'ning** *n.* (esp.) thing that serves to warn; notice of, caution against, danger etc.; notice of termination of business relation, esp. between master and servant.

warp (-ōr-) *n.* threads stretched in loom to be crossed by weft; rope used in towing or warping; distortion, perversion, crookedness, produced by warping. *v.* make or become crooked or bent or perverted, change from straight or right or natural state; (of timber etc.) become bent or crooked through uneven shrinking etc.; move ship etc. by hauling on rope attached to fixed point.

wa'rrant (wŏ-) *n.* sanction, authority, justifying reason or ground; document conveying authority or security, esp. writ or order for arrest, search, etc.; official certificate of rank issued to officer lower than commissioned officer. *v.t.* serve as warrant for, justify; guarantee. **~ officer,** officer of rank between commissioned and non-commissioned officers. **wa'rranty** *n.* (esp.) express or implied undertaking that vendor's title is secure, that certain conditions are fulfilled, etc.

wa'rrėn (wŏ-) *n.* piece of land where rabbits breed or abound; densely populated building or district.

wa'rrior (wŏ-) *n.* distinguished or veteran soldier; fighting man of past ages or primitive peoples.

wart (-ôr-) *n.* small round dry excrescence on skin; protuberance on skin of animal, surface of plant, etc. **~-hog**, African wild hog with large warty excrescences on face. **war'tў** *a.*

wār'ў *a.* (habitually) on one's guard, cautious, circumspect.

was : see **be**.

wash (wŏ-) *v.* cleanse with liquid; wash oneself or esp. one's hands (and face); wash clothes; take *away, off, out*, by washing; (of material etc.) bear washing; purify; moisten, (of water) flow past, beat upon, sweep *over*, surge *against*, carry *along, away*, etc.; sift ore, sand, etc. (*for* gold etc.) by action of water; brush watery colour over; coat thinly with metal etc.; (colloq.) bear scrutiny, investigation, etc.; ~ *down*, (esp.) accompany or follow (solid food) *with* draughts of liquid; ~ one's *hands of*, decline responsibility for; ~ *out*, (esp.) wash (small article(s) of clothing), (of flood) carry away (part of hill-side, road, etc.), (of rain etc.) cause cancellation of, (colloq.) cancel; ~*ed out*, (esp.) enfeebled, limp, exhausted; ~ *up*, wash (table utensils etc.) after use, (U.S.) wash one's face and hands, (sl.) finish. *n.* washing, being washed; process of being laundered, quantity of clothes etc. (to be) washed; thin even layer, coating of colour etc.; visible or audible motion of agitated water; waves, disturbance of air, caused by passage of vessel or aircraft; lotion; swill or liquid food for pigs etc.; malt etc. steeped in water to ferment before distillation; thin solution, watery liquid. **~-basin**, bowl for washing hands etc. **~-day**, day for washing clothes. **~-drawing**, (drawing produced by)

method of using washes of colour etc. **~-house**, outbuilding for washing clothes. **~-leather**, soft kind of leather used for dusting, cleaning, etc. **~-out**, (esp.) place where flood has washed out road, etc.; (sl.) disappointing failure, fiasco. **~-room**, (U.S.) room with toilet facilities, lavatory. **~-stand**, piece of furniture for holding wash-basin, soap-dish, etc. **~-tub**, tub for washing clothes etc. **wash'-able** *a.* that may be washed without damage. **wash'er**[1] *n.* person or thing that washes; washing-machine; **~erman**, **~erwoman**, man or woman whose occupation is washing clothes. **wash'ing** *n.* (esp.) clothes etc. (to be) washed; **~ing--day**, wash-day; **~ing-machine**, machine, esp. power-driven, for washing clothes etc.; **~ing-soda**, crystalline sodium carbonate used in washing clothes etc. **wash'ў** *a.* dilute, weak, sloppy, thin; faded--looking, pale; feeble, diffuse, wanting force or vigour.

Wash. *abbr.* Washington.

wash'er[2] (wŏ-) *n.* disc or flattened ring of metal, leather, rubber, etc. placed between two surfaces or under plunger of tap, nut, etc. to prevent lateral motion or leakage, relieve friction, etc.

wasp (wŏ-) *n.* kinds of winged insect with freq. formidable sting. **~--waisted**, having very small or slender waist. **was'pish** *a.* irritable, petulantly spiteful, ill-tempered.

wassail (wŏ'sl, wă'sl; *or* -āl) *n.* (arch.) liquor in which healths were drunk, esp. spiced ale drunk at Christmas etc. *v.i.* make merry; sit carousing and drinking healths.

wast : see **be**.

wā'stage *n.* loss or diminution by use, wear, decay, etc.; amount wasted.

wāste *a.* desert, barren; not inhabited or cultivated; superfluous, refuse; left over; *lay* ~, devastate, ravage. *v.* lay waste; squander; use extravagantly; wear away, be used up, lose substance or volume by gradual loss, decay, etc.; reduce one's weight by training etc. *n.*

waste region; dreary scene or expanse; loss or diminution from use, wear and tear, etc.; extravagance, squandering; waste matter; remains, scraps, shreds; scraps, remnants, from manufacture of yarns etc. used for cleaning machinery etc.; *run to* ~, (of liquid) flow away so as to be wasted, be expended uselessly. ~ land, land not utilized for cultivation or building. ~ **paper**, paper thrown away as spoiled, useless, etc. ~-**pipe**, pipe carrying off superfluous or used water or steam. ~ **product**, useless by--product of manufacture, physiological process, etc. **wā′steful** (-tf-) *a.* extravagant; not economical. **wā′ster** *n.* (esp., colloq.) dissolute or good-for-nothing person. **wā′sting** *a.* (esp., of disease etc.) causing loss of strength, vitality, weight, etc. **wā′strėl** *n.* waster; spendthrift.

watch (wǒ-) *v.* remain awake, keep vigil; be on the alert *for*, be vigilant; exercise protecting care *over*; keep eyes fixed on, keep under observation, follow observantly. *n.* watching, keeping awake and vigilant at night; (hist.) each of several periods into which night was anciently divided; period (usu. four hours) for which division of ship's company remains on duty, sailor's turn of duty, part (usu. half) of ship's company on duty during a watch; watching, observing, continued look-out, guard; look--out man; (hist.) man, body of men, patrolling and guarding streets at night; small time-piece worn or carried on person. ~-**dog**, dog kept to guard house, property, etc. ~**ing** **brief**, brief of barrister watching case for client not directly concerned. ~**man**, (hist.) member of watch, one who patrolled streets at night; man employed to guard building etc. esp. at night. ~-**night**, New Year's Eve. ~-**tower**, tower from which observation is kept of approach of danger. ~**word**, (hist.) military password; word or phrase expressing guiding principle or

rule of action. **watch′ful** *a.* vigilant, showing vigilance, watching.

wa′ter (waw-) *n.* transparent colourless tasteless inodorous liquid forming seas, rivers, etc., falling as rain, etc.; this as supplied for domestic use; sheet or body of water; **tears**, **saliva**, **urine**, etc.; aqueous decoction, infusion, etc.; (freq. pl.) water of mineral spring(s); state of tide; transparency and lustre of diamond or pearl. *v.* sprinkle or adulterate or dilute with water; provide or fill (horse, engine, etc.) with water; (of mouth, eyes) secrete or run with water; increase nominal amount of (stock, capital) by issuing shares without adding to assets; (*p.p.*, of silk fabric etc.) having wavy lustrous finish. ~--**closet**, place for evacuation of bowels etc. with water-supply for flushing pan. ~-**colour**, (picture painted, art or method of painting, with) artists' paint of pigment mixed with gum etc. and diluted with water. ~**course**, (bed or channel of) stream of water. ~**cress**, kind of cress with pungent leaves growing in springs and clear running streams. ~**fall**, more or less perpendicular fall of water from height. ~**fowl**, bird(s) frequenting water. ~-**front**, (U.S.) land or buildings abutting on river, sea, etc. ~-**glass**, aqueous solution of sodium or potassium silicate used as cement, for preserving eggs, etc. ~-**hen**, kinds of water-bird, esp. moorhen and Amer. coot. ~-**ice**, frozen confection of flavoured water and sugar ~**ing-can**, portable vessel with long tubular spout for watering plants. ~**ing-place**, drinking-place for animals; spa; seaside holiday or health resort. ~-**level**, (height of) surface of water; upward limit of saturation by water. ~-**lily**, kinds of water-plant with broad floating leaves and showy flowers. ~-**line**, line along which surface of water touches ship's side, esp. proper line of flotation when ship is fully loaded. ~**logged**, filled or saturated with water so as to be unbuoyant; (of ground etc.) made useless by saturation with water. ~man, boatman plying for hire. ~mark, distinguishing mark or design in paper visible when it is held up to light. ~-meadow, meadow periodically inundated by stream. ~-melon, elliptical smooth kind with watery juice. ~ polo, game played by teams of swimmers with ball like football. ~-power, mechanical force derived from weight or motion of water. ~proof, (garment, material) impervious to water; *v.t.* make waterproof. ~-rate, charge for use of public water-supply. ~-shed, summit or boundary-line separating river-basins. ~-splash, shallow stream or ford across road. ~spout, (esp.) gyrating column of water, spray, etc. produced by action of whirlwind on sea and clouds above it. ~-table, level at which porous rock etc. is saturated by underground water, height to which such water naturally rises in well etc. ~tight, so closely constructed or fitted that water cannot leak through; (of argument etc.) unassailable. ~tight compartment, each of compartments into which interior of ship etc. is divided by watertight partitions; division of anything regarded as kept entirely separate from rest. ~way, navigable channel. ~weed, any aquatic plant with inconspicuous flowers. ~-wheel, wheel rotated by action of water and driving machinery; wheel for raising water in boxes or buckets fitted on circumference. ~-wings, inflated floats used as supports in learning to swim. ~works, assemblage of machinery, buildings, etc. for supplying water through pipes; (sl.) tears. **wa′terless** *a.* **wa′tery** *a.* of, consisting of, water; full of, covered or running with, containing too much, water; pale, washed out, diluted, vapid, insipid.

watt (wŏt) *n.* unit of electric power. ~**age** *n.* amount of electric power expressed in watts.

watt′le[1] (wŏ-) *n.* interlaced rods and twigs or branches used for fences, walls, or roofs; kinds of Australian acacia with fragrant golden-yellow flowers. *v.t.* construct of wattle; interlace (twigs etc.) to form wattle.

watt′le[2] (wŏ-) *n.* fleshy appendage pendent from head or neck of turkey etc. **watt′led** *a.*

wāve *n.* moving ridge or swell of water between two troughs; undulating configuration, line, or movement; something resembling wave, esp. temporary heightening of emotion, influence, etc.; act or gesture of waving; oscillatory condition propagated from place to place, with same type of vibration occurring all along path; *heat, cold,* ~, spell of hot or cold weather. *v.* move in waves; move to and fro; impart waving movement to; wave hand, motion (person) *away, back,* etc. or give (greeting, signal, etc.) by waving hand; make or be wavy, give to or have undulating surface, course, or appearance. ~**length**, distance between successive points of equal phase in direction of propagation of wave. **wāve′lėt** (-vl-) *n.* small wave, ripple. **wā′vў** *a.* undulating; forming undulating line or series of wave-like curves.

wā′ver *v.i.* oscillate unsteadily, flicker, fluctuate, vary; be irresolute, show doubt or indecision; falter, show signs of giving way. **wā′verer** *n.*; **wā′vering** *a.*

wavy : see **wave**.

wăx[1] *v.i.* (of moon) undergo periodical increase in extent of visible illuminated surface; (arch.) become.

wăx[2] *n.* sticky plastic yellowish substance secreted by bees and used as material of honeycomb or, bleached and purified, for candles, as basis of polishes, etc.; kinds of substance resembling wax; sealing-wax; cobblers'-wax; yellow waxy secretion in external canal of ear; (attrib.) made of wax. *v.t.* smear, coat, polish, treat, with wax. ~**bill**, kinds of small bird with waxy-looking pink, red, or white beak. ~ **doll**, doll with wax head etc.; person with pretty but unexpressive face. **~-end,** shoemaker's wax-coated thread. **~ paper,** paper coated with wax. **~wing,** kinds of small bird. **~work,** modelling, object modelled, in wax, esp. figure of person coloured and clothed to look like life; (pl.) exhibition of such works. **wăx′en** *a.* made of wax; resembling wax in smooth and lustrous surface, pallor, softness, etc. **wăx′ў¹** *a.*

wăx′ў² *a.* (sl.) angry.

way *n.* road, track, path, street; place of passage; track, inclined structure, etc., for launching, sliding, etc.; course, route; opportunity for passage, advance, progress, etc.; (direction of) travel or motion; distance (to be) travelled; (rate of) progress through water; device, method, means; habitual course or manner of action; (pl.) habits; condition; *~s and means,* methods esp. of providing money; *by the ~,* by the road-side, while going along, incidentally, in passing; *by ~ of,* via, in capacity or function of, in habit of, having reputation for; *give ~,* retreat, fail to resist, make concessions, break down, collapse; *give ~ to,* yield to, be superseded by; *lead the ~,* act as guide or leader; *make ~,* open passage (*for*), leave place vacant *for*; *make one's ~,* proceed, make progress in career, advance in wealth, reputation, etc.; *the other ~ round,* conversely, vice versa; *out-of-the-~,* uncommon, remarkable, remote, inaccessible; *pay one's ~,* pay expenses as they arise, contrive to avoid debt; *see one's ~,* (esp.) feel justified in deciding (*to* do etc.); *under ~,* (of vessel) having begun to move through water, in progress. *adv.* at or to great distance, far; *~ back,* (colloq.) long ago. **~-bill,** list of passengers or goods on conveyance. **~farer,** traveller, esp. on foot. **~faring,** travelling, itinerant. **~lay,** lie in wait for; wait for and accost or stop (person) to rob or interview him. **~leave,** (rent or charge for) permission to convey minerals etc. across person's land, telephone

wires over buildings, etc. **~side,** (land bordering) side of road or path; *a.* situated on, growing at, etc. wayside.

way′ward *a.* childishly self-willed; capricious, erratic, perverse, freakish.

wayz′gōōse *n.* annual feast or holiday of printing-house.

W.C. *abbr.* West Central (postal district).

w.c. *abbr.* water-closet.

W.D. *abbr.* War Department.

wē *pron.* (obj. *us,* poss. *our*), 1st pers. nom. pl. pronoun; used by sovereign, newspaper editor, etc. instead of *I.*

W.E.A. *abbr.* Workers' Educational Association.

weak *a.* wanting in strength, power, or number; fragile; feeble; unsound; (gram., of Germanic verbs) forming p.t. by addition of suffix. **~ ending,** (in verse) unstressed monosyllable in normally stressed place at end of line. **~-kneed,** (esp.) wanting in resolution or determination. **~-minded,** (esp.) mentally deficient. **wea′ken** *v.* make or become weaker. **~ling** *n.* weak or feeble person or animal. **~lў** *a.* not robust, ailing. **~nèss** *n.* (esp.) weak point, failing, defect; foolish or self-indulgent liking *for.*

weal¹ *n.* ridge or mark raised on flesh by stroke of lash, rod, etc. *v.t.* raise weals on.

weal² *n.* (arch.) welfare, well-being.

weald *n.* tract of formerly wooded country in SE. England. **~en** *n.* series of lower Cretaceous fresh-water strata above Oolite and below chalk; *a.* of weald or wealden.

wealth (wĕl-) *n.* riches; being rich; abundance, a profusion *of.* **weal′thў** *a.*

wean *v.t.* accustom (young mammal) to food other than mother's milk; detach, alienate *from,* reconcile gradually to privation of something.

weap′on (wĕp-) *n.* instrument, part of (esp. bird's or beast's) body, used in war or combat as means of attack or defence; action or means used against another in conflict.

wear[1] (wār) *v.* (*wōre, wōrn*), be dressed in, have on; carry or exhibit on person; waste, damage, deteriorate, gradually by use or attrition; make (hole etc.) by attrition; exhaust, tire or be tired *out*; endure continued use (*well* etc.), last; (of time) go slowly *on*, pass, be passed, gradually *away*; ~ *down*, put or break down, tire, overcome, etc. by persistence; ~ *out*, use or be used until usable no longer. *n.* use as clothes; things to wear; capacity for resisting effects of wear or use; damage or deterioration due to ordinary use. **wear'able** *a.*; **wear'er** *n.*

wear[2] (wār) *v.* (p.t. & p.p. *wore*), bring (ship), come, about by turning head away from wind.

wear'isome *a.* causing weariness, monotonous, fatiguing.

wear'y *a.* tired, worn out, intensely fatigued; sick *of*; dispirited; tiring, toilsome, tedious. *v.* make or grow weary.

wea'sel (-zl) *n.* small slender-bodied reddish-brown carnivorous mammal; tracked motor vehicle for use on snow in arctic conditions. ~-**faced**, having sharp thin features.

weath'er (wĕdh-) *n.* atmospheric conditions prevailing at specified time or place with respect to heat or cold, sunshine, fog, strength of wind, etc.; rain, frost, wind, etc. as hurtful or destructive agents; *make heavy* ~ *of*, find trying or difficult; *under the* ~, indisposed, not very well, in adversity. *a.* (naut.) windward; *keep one's* ~ *eye open*, be watchful and alert. *v.* expose to atmospheric changes; wear away, discolour, etc. by exposure to weather; get to windward of; come safely through (storm etc.). ~-**beaten**, worn, damaged, bronzed, etc. by exposure to weather. ~-**board**, sloping board attached at bottom of door to keep out rain; one of series of horizontal boards with overlapping edges covering walls etc. ~**bound**, kept from proceeding by bad weather. ~-**chart**, diagram of weather over wide area. ~**cock**, plate of metal, freq. in form of cock

fixed on vertical spindle and turning readily with wind to show direction from which this is blowing; changeable or inconstant person. ~-**glass**, barometer. ~-**vane**, weathercock.

weave *v.* (*wōve*; *wōven* and *wōve*), form fabric by interlacing threads, form fabric out of (threads), esp. in loom; intermingle, form or introduce *into* whole, as if by weaving; (cause to) move from side to side or in devious or intricate course. *n.* style, method, of weaving. **wea'ver(-bird)** *n.* kinds of tropical bird building elaborately interwoven nests.

weazen(ed) : see **wizen(ed)**.

wĕb *n.* woven fabric, esp. whole piece on or after coming from loom; cobweb or similar tissue; tissue, membrane, fold of skin, esp. connecting toes of aquatic bird or beast, forming palmate foot; (paper-making) (large roll of paper made on) endless wire-cloth on rollers carrying pulp. ~-**footed**, having webbed feet. ~-**offset**, method of printing by offset process on continuous roll of paper. **wĕbb'ing** *n.* (esp.) stout strong closely woven material in form of narrow bands, used in upholstery.

wĕd *v.* (p.t. *wedded*; p.p. *wedded* or *wed*), marry; unite, join, *to, with*; *wedded to*, obstinately attached to (pursuit etc.).

wĕdd'ing *n.* marriage ceremony with its attendant festivities. ~-**ring**, that used at wedding and usu. worn constantly by married woman.

wĕdge *n.* piece of wood, metal, etc. thick at one end and tapering to thin edge at the other, used for splitting stone etc., forcing things apart, fixing them immovably, etc.; wedge-shaped thing; *thin end of the* ~, small beginning that may lead to something greater. *v.t.* force open or apart, fix firmly, with wedge(s); drive, push (object) into position where it is held fast; pack or crowd (*together*) in close formation or limited space.

wĕd'lŏck *n.* married state; *born in, out of,* ~, legitimate, illegitimate.

Wednesday (wĕnz′dǐ) *n.* fourth day of week; *Ash* ~: see **ash**[2].

wee *a.* tiny, very small.

weed *n.* herbaceous plant not valued for use or beauty and growing wild or rank, esp. as hindering growth of more valued plants; (colloq.) tobacco, *a* cigar; lanky and weakly horse or person. *v.* remove, clear ground or crop of, weeds; eradicate, remove, clear *out* (faults, inferior individuals, etc.). **wee′dy** *a.* full of weeds; weak and lanky.

weeds (-z) *n.pl.* deep mourning worn by widow.

week *n.* cycle of seven days beginning with Sunday; any period of seven days; the six days other than Sunday. ~**day**, day other than Sunday. ~**-end**, holiday period at end of week, from Friday or Saturday to Monday; *v.i.* make week-end visit or stay. **wee′kly** *a.* occurring, done, etc. once a week; of, for, lasting, a week; *adv.* once a week, every week; *n.* weekly periodical.

ween *v.t.* (arch.) think.

wee′ny *a.* (colloq.) tiny.

weep *v.* (*wĕpt*), shed tears (over); lament for; shed moisture in drops, exude. **wee′ping** *a.* (esp.) drooping; ~**ing willow**, large Asian willow with long slender drooping branches. **wee′py** *a.* inclined to weep, given to weeping.

wee′vil *n.* kinds of small beetle, any insect, damaging stored grain etc.

wĕft *n.* (one of) threads crossing from side to side of web and interwoven with warp.

weigh (wā) *v.* find weight of; take definite weight (*out*) of; balance in hand (as if) to guess weight of; estimate relative value or importance of, consider, ponder; be of specified weight or importance; have influence (*with*); heave up (anchor) before sailing; ~ *down*, bend or force down by pressure of weight, depress, oppress, lie heavy on; ~ *in*, be weighed before boxing-match, after horse-race, etc., intervene; ~ *in with*, introduce, produce; ~ *on*, be burdensome, oppressive, etc. to; ~ *up*, (colloq.) appraise, form estimate of; ~ one's *words*, speak with deliberation. *n.* process or occasion of weighing. ~**-bridge**, platform scale flush with road for weighing vehicles etc. ~**man**, man employed to weigh goods, esp. tubs of coal at pit-mouth.

weight (wāt) *n.* mass or relative heaviness as property of material substances; amount thing etc. weighs; portion or quantity weighing definite amount; piece of metal etc. of known weight for use in weighing; heavy body used to pull down something, act as counterpoise, etc.; heavy stone thrown with one hand in athletic sport; load or burden; influence; importance; persuasive or convincing power, preponderance (*of* evidence etc.). *v.* attach weight to, hold down with weight(s); impede or burden with load; add weight to (textile etc.) by addition of adulterant etc.; adjust figures of statistical tables etc. by use of factors indicating relative importance etc. of various items; bias, give particular tendency etc. to, by manipulation. ~**-lifting**, athletic sport or exercise of lifting heavy weights. **weight′less** *a.* **weigh′ty** *a.* heavy; momentous, important; requiring, giving evidence of, earnest thought etc.; influential, authoritative.

weir (wēr) *n.* dam or barrier across river etc. to retain water and regulate its flow.

weird (wērd) *a.* uncanny, supernatural; (colloq.) queer, fantastic.

wĕl′come *int.* of greeting. *n.* kind or glad reception or entertainment. *v.t.* give welcome to, receive gladly; greet. *a.* gladly received; acceptable as visitor; ungrudgingly permitted or given right to; *make* ~, receive hospitably.

wĕld *v.* unite (pieces of esp. heated metal etc.) into solid mass by hammering or pressure; admit of being welded; unite intimately or inseparably. *n.* joint made by welding. **wĕl′der** *n.*

wĕl'fāre *n.* good fortune, happiness, or well-being. **W~ State**, State with highly-developed social services controlled or financed by government. **~ work**, work for welfare of class or group, esp. of employees of factory etc.

wĕl'kĭn *n.* (poet.) sky.

wĕll[1] *n.* (usu. circular) pit or shaft sunk in ground to obtain water, oil, gas, etc.; enclosed space more or less resembling well-shaft, esp. central open space of winding or spiral staircase, lift-shaft, deep narrow space between surrounding walls of building(s); receptacle for liquid, esp. ink. *v.i.* spring *up, out*, etc. (as) from fountain. **~-head**, original or chief source. **~-spring**, head-spring of stream etc.

wĕll[2] *adv.* in good manner or style, rightly; thoroughly, carefully, completely; to considerable distance, degree, or extent; heartily, kindly, approvingly, on good terms; probably, easily, with reason, advisably; *as ~*, with equal reason, preferably, in addition, also; *as ~ as*, (esp.) to the same extent, in the same degree, in addition to, both ... and, not only ... but also. *a.* in good health; in satisfactory state or position, satisfactory; advisable, right and proper. *int.* introducing remark or statement; expressing astonishment, relief, qualified recognition, expectation, etc.; *very ~*, denoting agreement, approval, or acquiescence.

wĕll- in comb. **well-advised'** *a.* (esp.) prudent, wary, wise. **~-appoin'ted** *a.* properly equipped or fitted out. **~-balanced** *a.* sensible, sane; equally matched. **~-being** *n.* happy, healthy, or prosperous condition, moral or physical welfare. **~-bŏrn'** *a.* of noble or distinguished family. **~-brĕd'** *a.* having or displaying good breeding or manners; of good breed or stock. **~-connĕc'ted** *a.* (esp.) of good family and connections. **~-dō'ing** (-ōō-) *n.* virtuous conduct. **~-fā'voured** *a.* comely. **~-informed'** *a.* having well-stored mind or access to best information. **~-**-grōōmed'** *a.* (esp., of persons) with hair, skin, etc. carefully tended. **~-jŭdged'** *a.* opportunely or skilfully done. **~-knĭt'** *a.* compact. **~-mea'ning** *a.* having or showing good intentions (freq. implying inefficient or unwise). **~-ŏff'** *a.* fortunately situated; fairly or sufficiently rich. **~-spō'ken** *a.* (esp.) ready or refined in speech. **~-tīmed'** *a.* timely, opportune. **~-to-do'** (-ōō) *a.* prosperous, in easy circumstances. **~-trīed'** *a.* often tried or tested with good result. **~-tŭrned'** *a.* (esp.) neatly made or finished; happily expressed. **~-wisher** *n.* one who wishes well to another, a cause, etc. **~-wŏrn'** *a.* (esp.) trite, hackneyed.

wĕll'ingtons *n.pl.* waterproof rubber boots reaching to knee.

Wĕlsh[1] *a. & n.* (people, Celtic language) of Wales. **~ rabbit**, dish of melted or toasted cheese with seasoning, on buttered toast.

wĕlsh[2] *v.* (of bookmaker etc.) decamp without paying winner(s) of bet(s). **~er** *n.*

wĕlt *n.* strip of leather sewn between edge of sole and turned-in edge of upper of boot or shoe; ribbed or reinforced border of knitted garment; mark of heavy blow, weal. *v.t.* provide with welt; raise weals on, beat, thrash.

wĕl'ter *v.i.* wallow; be tossed or tumbled about; lie prostrate, be sunk or deeply involved, *in. n.* state of turmoil or upheaval; surging or confused mass.

wel'ter-weight *n.* boxing-weight (10 st. 7 lb.).

wĕn *n.* more or less permanent benign tumour on scalp etc.

wĕnch *n.* (joc.) girl or young woman. *v.i.* associate with whores.

wĕnd *v.* direct (one's *way*); (arch.) go.

went, *p.t.* of **go**.

wept, *p.t. & p.p.* of **weep**.

were : see **be**.

wer(e)wolf (wēr'wŏŏlf) *n.* (folk-lore) human being who changes into wolf.

Wĕs'leyan (*or* -z-) *a. & n.* (follower)

of John Wesley, founder of Methodism; (member) of Wesleyan Methodist Church.

wĕst *n.* point in heavens where sun sets on equator at equinox, corresponding point on earth; western part of world or of country, region, etc., esp. Europe and America as dist. from Asia etc., or America and western Europe opp. Communist States; western hemisphere; western States of U.S.; West End of London. *a.* lying towards, situated in, of, the west; (of wind) blowing from west. *adv.* towards, in direction or region of, west; *go* ~ (esp., colloq.) die, perish, be destroyed or finished. ~ **country**, (esp.) south-western counties of England. **W. End**, part of London west of Charing Cross and Regent Street, including fashionable shopping district, Mayfair, etc.; fashionable or aristocratic quarter of any town. **wĕs'tering** *a.* tending, declining, towards west. **wĕs'ting** *n.* westward progress or deviation, esp. in sailing. **wĕs'terlȳ** *a.* & *adv.* towards, coming from, west. ~**ward** *adv., a.,* & *n.*; ~**wards** *adv.*

wĕs'tern *a.* living or situated in, coming from, west; of Western countries or races; of, constituting, West of U.S. *n.* film, novel, etc. dealing with frontier life, cowboys, etc. in Amer. West. ~**er** *n.* ~**īze** *v.t.* make (more) Western in institutions, ideas, etc.; ~**īzā'tion** *n.*

wĕt *a.* soaked, covered, supplied with, employing, etc. water or other liquid; rainy; addicted to, concerned with, supplying, permitting sale of, etc., alcoholic drinks; (sl.) lacking vitality, feeble. *v.t.* make wet; moisten. *n.* liquid that wets something; rainy weather; (sl.) drink; (sl.) feeble or spiritless person. ~ **blanket**, person or thing damping or discouraging enthusiasm, cheerfulness, etc., spoil-sport. ~**-nurse**, woman employed to suckle another's child; *v.t.* act as wet-nurse to; foster, coddle. **wĕtt'ish** *a.*

wĕth'er (-dh-) *n.* castrated ram.

w.f. *abbr.* wrong fount.

W.F.T.U. *abbr.* World Federation of Trade Unions.

whăck *n.* heavy resounding blow, esp. with stick; (colloq.) portion, share. *v.t.* beat or strike vigorously. **whăcked** (-kt) *a.* (sl.) beaten; exhausted. **whăck'ing** *a.* (sl.) huge, 'thumping', 'whopping'.

whăck'ȳ *a.* (sl.) crazy, eccentric.

whāle[1] *n.* large fish-like marine mammal; (colloq.) something impressive in size, amount, etc.; expert, 'dab' (*at*). *v.i.* hunt whales. ~**-boat**, long narrow rowing-boat, sharp at both ends, used in whale-fishing, as lifeboat, etc. ~**bone**, elastic horny substance in upper jaw of some whales; strip of this as stiffener etc. ~**-oil**, oil obtained from whales' blubber. **whā'ler** *n.* ship, man, engaged in whale-fishing.

whāle[2] *v.* (colloq.) beat, thrash; perform action vigorously or vehemently.

whăng *v., n.,* & *int.* bang.

wharf (wôrf) *n.* (pl. *-ves, -fs*), structure at water's edge for loading or unloading of vessels lying alongside. *v.* discharge (cargo), anchor, at wharf. ~**age** *n.* wharf accommodation or dues. **whar'finger** (wôrfĭnj-) *n.* owner or keeper of wharf.

what (wŏt), *a.,* (interrog.) asking for selection from indefinite number or for specification of amount, kind, etc.; (excl.) how great, how strange, how remarkable! etc.; how; (rel.) the . . . that, as much or many . . . as. *pron.*(interrog.) what thing(s)?; what did you say?; *know* ~*'s* ~, have good judgement or apprehension, know the matter in hand, what is fitting, etc.; (excl.) what thing(s)!, how much!; (rel.) that or those which; thing(s) that, anything that. ~ **not**, other things of the same kind, anything; ~**-not**, a (trivial or indefinite) something; piece of furniture with shelves for knick-knacks. **whatev'er** *pron.* & *a.* any(thing) at all (that); no matter what; (colloq.) as emphatic extension of *what* implying perplexity or surprise. **whatsŏĕv'er** *pron.* & *a.* (more emphatic for) whatever.

whaup *n.* (Sc.) curlew.

wheat *n.* cereal plant; its grain furnishing chief bread-stuff in temperate countries. **~meal,** (esp.) wholemeal. **~en** *a.* of (grain or flour of) wheat.

whea'tear *n.* kinds of small migratory bird.

whee'dle *v.t.* cajole, persuade, fool, by flattery or coaxing; get *out of* by wheedling.

wheel *n.* circular spoked frame or disc revolving on axis; wheel-like structure or thing; instrument or appliance with wheel as essential part; ancient instrument of torture; motion as of wheel; motion of line as on pivoted end; **~s within ~s,** intricate machinery, complex indirect or secret agencies. *v.* turn on axis or pivot, (cause to) move in circle or spiral; change direction, turn *about, round*; push or pull (bicycle, wheel-chair, etc.). **~barrow,** shallow open box ·with shafts and one wheel for carrying small loads on. **~-base,** distance between points of contact with ground etc. of front and back wheels of vehicle. **~-chair,** invalid's chair on wheels. **~-load,** part of load of vehicle borne by single wheel. **~-spin,** rotation of wheels without traction. **~wright,** maker and repairer of (wooden) wheels. **whee'ler** *n.* pole- or shaft-horse.

wheeze *v.* breathe hard with audible whistling or piping sound; utter with wheezing. *n.* sound of wheezing; (sl.) trick, dodge. **whee'zy** *a.*

whělk *n.* kinds of spiral-shelled marine mollusc.

whělp *n.* young dog, puppy; (arch.) young of lion, tiger, etc.; unmannerly child or youth. *v.* bring forth whelp(s).

whěn *adv.* & *conj.* at what time, on what occasion, in what case or circumstances; at the time, on the occasion, etc. that; at which time etc., and (just) then; seeing that, considering that; whereas. *n.* time, date, occasion. **whěněv'er** *adv.* & *conj.* at whatever time, on whatever occasion every time that. **when-**

soěv'er *adv.* & *conj.* (arch., emphat.) whenever.

whěnce *adv.* & *conj.* (arch.) from where, from what place or source; (*place* etc.) from which.

where (wār) *adv.* & *conj.* at or in what place, position, or circumstances; in what respect, from what source, etc.; to what place; in, at, to, etc. place in or at which; and there. *n.* place, locality. **~abouts'** *adv.* in or near what place? **~'abouts** *n.* (approximate) position or situation, place in or near which thing or person is. **~as'** *conj.* taking into consideration the fact that; in contrast or comparison with the fact that. **~bȳ'** *adv.* (arch.) by which; by what. **wherěv'er** *adv.* at or to whatever place etc. **~fōre** *adv.* for what; why; and therefore; (arch.)·because of, in consequence etc. of, which. **~ĭn', ~ŏf', ~ŏn', ~with'** *adv.* (arch. or formal) in, of, on, with, what or which. **~soěv'er** *adv.* (arch.) wherever. **~upŏn'** *adv.* (esp.) after which, and thereupon. **~withal'** (-dhawl) *n.* (colloq.) means, esp. pecuniary means (for or *to* do).

whě'rrȳ *n.* large light barge, lighter, etc., esp. with single sail; light rowing-boat.

whět *v.t.* sharpen; make (more) acute. *n.* whetting; dram, etc. taken to whet appetite. **~stone,** stone for sharpening cutting tools.

wheth'er (wědh-) *conj.* introducing dependent question etc. and expressing doubt, choice, etc. between alternatives. *pron.* (arch.) which of the two.

whew (hwū) *int.* expressing astonishment, consternation etc.

whey (wā) *n.* watery liquid left after separation of curd from milk.

which *a.* & *pron.* (interrog.) what one(s) of stated or implied set of persons, things, or alternatives; (rel.) and that, it, they, etc.; that. **whichěv'er** *a.* & *pron.* any or either that; no matter which. **~soěv'er** *a.* & *pron.* (arch., emphat.) whichever.

whiff *n.* puff, breath, of air, smoke, odour, etc.; light narrow out-

rigged sculling-boat; small cigar.
v. blow or puff lightly.

whiff′le *v.* blow in puffs; veer or shift
about; make light whistling sound.

Whig *n. & a.* (member) of political
party that preceded Liberals.
Whigg′erў, ~gism *nn.*; **~gish** *a.*

while *n.* space of time, esp. time
spent in doing something; *all the ~*,
during the whole time (that); *at ~s*,
sometimes, at intervals; *once in
a ~*, occasionally, at long intervals;
worth (one's) *~*, worth doing,
advantageous, profitable. *adv. &
conj.* during the time that; for as
long as; although; and at the same
time, besides that. *v.t.* pass (time
etc.) *away* in leisurely manner or
without wearisomeness. **whilst** *adv.
& conj.* while.

whi′lom *adv. & a.* (arch.) former(ly);
(existing, being such) at some past
time.

whim *n.* sudden fancy, caprice,
freakish notion.

whim′brel *n.* kinds of small curlew.

whim′per *v.i.* cry querulously; whine
softly. *n.* feeble whining broken
cry.

whim′sical (-z-) *a.* capricious; fantastic. **~căl′itў** *n.*

whim′sy (-zĭ) *n.* whim, crotchet.

whin[1] *n.* gorse. **~-chat**, small song-
-bird.

whin[2], **whin′sill**, **whin′stone** *nn.*
(boulder or slab of) kinds of very
hard dark-coloured esp. basaltic
rock.

whine *n.* long-drawn complaining cry
(as) of dog; querulous tone; feeble,
mean, or undignified complaint.
v. utter whine(s); utter whiningly,
complain.

whinn′ў *n.* gentle or joyful neigh.
v. emit whinny.

whip *n.* instrument, usu. stick with
lash attached, for urging on horse
etc. or for flogging or beating;
whipping or lashing motion; official
responsible to huntsman for managing hounds; official appointed to
maintain discipline of political
party in House of Parliament;
whip's written notice requesting
member's attendance. *v.* apply
whip to; urge on thus; lash, beat;

make (eggs, cream, etc.) light and
frothy by stirring or beating in air;
flick line or bait on water with
movement like stroke of whip, fish
stream etc. with fly; bind round
closely with twine, thread, etc.;
overcast, sew over and over; move
suddenly or briskly, dart; snatch;
make *up* quickly or hastily; bend
or spring like whip or switch.
~cord, thin tough hempen cord;
close-woven fabric with fine close
diagonal ribs. **~-hand**, upper hand,
control (*of*), advantage. **~per-in**,
whip of pack of hounds. **~ping-boy**,
(hist.) boy educated with young
prince and chastised in his stead;
scapegoat. **~ping-top**, top kept
spinning by strokes of lash. **~-
-round**, appeal to number of persons
for contribution to fund etc. **~saw**,
saw with very long narrow tapering
blade. **~-stitch**, (sew with) whipping stitch. **whipp′ў** *a.* flexible;
springy.

whipp′er-snăpper *n.* young and
insignificant but impertinent person.

whipp′ĕt *n.* small dog like greyhound; (mil.) fast light tank.

whipp′oorwill *n.* N. Amer. nocturnal
bird allied to nightjar.

whirl *v.* swing round and round
revolve rapidly; send, travel, go,
swiftly in orbit or curve, rapidly
in wheeled conveyance, etc.; be
giddy, seem to spin round. *n.*
whirling, swift, or violent movement; rush; distracted or dizzy
state. **~pool**, circular eddy in sea,
river, etc. **~wind**, whirling mass or
column of air moving over land or
water. **whir′ligig** (-g-) *n.* spinning
toy like sails of windmill on stick;
merry-go-round.

whirr *n. & v.i.* (make) continuous
buzzing or vibratory sound (as) of
swiftly turning wheel etc.

whisk *n.* bunch of twigs, hair, etc. for
brushing or dusting; instrument for
whipping eggs, cream, etc.; whisk-
ing movement (as) of tail etc.
v. convey, go, move, with light rapid
sweeping motion; brush or sweep
lightly and rapidly from surface;
beat esp. with whisk.

whis′ker *n.* hair on cheeks or sides of

face of adult man; projecting hair or bristle on upper lip or near mouth of cat etc. **~ed**, **~y** *aa*.

whis'key *n*. Irish whisky.

whis'ky *n*. spirit distilled from malted barley, rye, etc.

whis'per *n*. (remark made in) speech or vocal sound without vibration of vocal cords; soft rustling sound; insinuation, rumour, hint. *v.* make, utter in, whisper; communicate etc. quietly or confidentially.

whist *n*. card-game, usu. for two pairs of opponents. **~ drive**, whist-party with players moving on from table to table.

whist'le (-sl) *n*. clear shrill sound made by forcing breath through lips contracted to narrow opening; similar sound made by bird, wind, or missile, or produced by pipe etc.; tubular instrument producing shrill tone by forcing air or steam against sharp edge or into bell. *v.* emit whistle; summon or give signal thus; produce, utter, call or send (*away*, *up*, etc.), by whistling; **~ for**, (colloq.) seek or expect in vain, go without. **~-stop**, (U.S.) pause of train at station, esp. to allow political candidate to show himself, etc.; (small town with) station at which trains stop only on signal.

whit[1] *n*. particle, jot.

Whit[2], **Whit'sun** *aa*. connected with, belonging to, following, **Whit Sunday**, seventh Sunday after Easter, Pentecost. **Whit'suntide**, week-end or week including Whit Sunday.

white *a*. of colour of snow or milk; of colour produced by reflection or transmission of light without sensible absorption; pale; innocent, unstained; of royalist, legitimist, counter-revolutionary, or reactionary political tendency, allegiance, etc. *n.* white or light-coloured part of anything; (nearly) white colour; white pigment, clothes, material, etc.; translucent viscid fluid round yolk of egg; white part of eyeball; white man, butterfly, etc.; member or supporter of white political party etc.; chess-

-player having lighter-coloured pieces. **~ ant**, termite. **~bait**, small silvery-white fry of various fishes esteemed as delicacy. **~beam**, small tree with white silky hairs on underside of leaves. **~cap**, kinds of bird with light-coloured patch on head; white-crested wave. **~-collar**, engaged in, being, non-manual work. **~ dwarf**, one of class of small extremely dense stars radiating white light. **~ elephant**, burdensome or useless possession. **~ ensign**, flag of British Navy etc., with St. George's cross on white ground. **~ feather**, symbol or emblem of cowardice. **~ flag**, plain white flag of truce or surrender. **~-heart (cherry)**, yellowish-white cultivated cherry. **~ heat**, degree of heat making metal etc. glow white; intense anger or passion. **~ horses**, white-crested waves. **~-hot**, at white heat. **~ lead**, basic lead carbonate as white pigment. **~ lie**, harmless or trivial lie, fib. **~-livered**, cowardly, dastardly. **~ man**, member of race with light-coloured skin or complexion, esp. of European extraction; (colloq.) honourable or trustworthy person. **~ paper**, (esp. English) government report. **~ slave**, woman held unwillingly for purpose of prostitution. **~thorn**, hawthorn. **~throat**, kinds of warbler. **~wash**, liquid composition of lime or whiting and water etc. for whitening ceilings, walls, etc.; glossing over of faults; *v.* apply whitewash (to); gloss over, clear of blame etc. **~ wine**, wine of (pale) yellow colour. **whi'ten** *v.* make, become, white or whiter. **whi'tening**, **whi'ting**[1] *nn*. preparation of finely powdered chalk. **whi'tish** *a*.

White'hall (-t-hawl) *n*. British Government or its policy; Civil Service, bureaucracy.

whith'er (-dh-) *adv. & pron.* (arch.) to where or which. **~soev'er** *adv.* (arch.) to whatever place.

whiting[1] : see **white**.

whi'ting[2] *n*. kinds of small edible sea-fish.

whit'low (-ō) *n.* small abscess esp. under or near nail.

Whitsun etc.: see **Whit²**.

whitt'le *v.* pare or shape wood by cutting thin slices or shavings from surface; reduce amount or effect of, pare *down*, take *away*, by degrees.

whiz(z) *v.* (cause to) make sound as of body rushing through air; move swiftly (as) with such sound. *n.* act or sound of whizzing.

who (hōō) *pron.* (obj. *whom*, pr. hōōm; poss. *whose*, pr. hōōz), what or which person(s), what sort of person(s) in regard to origin, position, etc.; (person or persons) that; and or but he (she, they). **whoěv'er** *pron.* whatever person(s), any (one) who; no matter who. **~sōěv'er** *pron.* (arch., emphat.) whoever.

W.H.O. *abbr.* World Health Organization.

whoa (wō) *int.* command to horse etc. to stop or stand still.

whodŭn(n)'it (hōō-) *n.* (sl.) mystery or detective story.

whole (hōl) *a.* in uninjured, intact, undiminished, undivided, etc. state; all, all of. *n.* full, complete, or total amount (*of*); complete thing; organic unity, complex system, total made up of parts; *go the ~ hog*, act etc. without reservation; *on the ~*, all things considered, in general, for the most part. **~-hearted**, given, done, acting, etc. with all one's heart; sincere, heartfelt. **~meal**, meal or flour made from whole grain of wheat. **whōl'lỹ** (-l-lǐ) *adv.* entirely, to the full extent, altogether; exclusively.

whole'sāle (hōls-) *n.* selling in large quantitites, esp. for retail by others. *a.* selling wholesale; of sale in gross; unlimited, indiscriminate; doing, done, largely or profusely. *adv.* in large quantities or gross; at wholesale price; in abundance, extensively, indiscriminately. **~r** *n.* one who sells wholesale.

wholesome (hōl'sum) *a.* promoting, conducive to, health or well-being; healthy; not morbid, corrupt, etc.

wholly : see **whole**.

whom (hōōm) *pron.*, obj. case of *who*.

~soěv'er *pron.* (arch.), obj. case of *whoever*.

whōōp (h-) *n. & int.* (cry) expressing excitement, exultation etc.; characteristic drawing-in of breath after cough in **~ing-cough**, infectious disease esp. of children, with violent convulsive cough. **whōōpee'** (h- *or* w-; *or* -ōō-) *n. & int.* (cry) expressing wild joy, excitement etc.; *make ~* rejoice noisily or hilariously, have a good time.

whŏp *v.* (sl.) thrash, defeat. **whŏpp'er** *n.* (sl.) big specimen; monstrous lie. **whŏpp'ing** *a.* (sl.) very big, 'thumping'.

whōre (h-) *n.* prostitute.

whŏrl *n.* convolution, coil, esp. complete circle formed by central papillary ridges in finger-print; each turn of spiral shell or any spiral structure; ring of leaves etc. springing from stem or axis at same level.

whor'tleberrỹ (wer-) *n.* bilberry.

whose (hōōz) *pron.*, poss. case of *who* and occas. of *which*.

whỹ *adv.* (interrog.) on what ground? for what reason or purpose? (rel.) on account of which. *int.* expressing esp. mild or slight surprise, slight protest, etc. *n.* reason, explanation.

W.I. *abbr.* West Indies; Women's Institute.

wick *n.* (usu. loosely twisted or woven) bundle of fibre drawing up oil or grease to maintain flame of lamp, candle, etc.

wick'ěd *a.* sinful, vicious, morally depraved; (colloq.) very or excessively bad, malicious, mischievous.

wick'er *n.* plaited osiers etc. as material of baskets, chairs, etc. **~work**, things made, craft of making things, of wicker.

wick'ět *n.* small gate or door, esp. beside or in larger one; (crick.) set of three upright stumps surmounted by two bails: time during which batsman defends wicket, esp. as measure of progress of game; ground between and about wickets, pitch. **~-keeper**, fieldsman stationed behind wicket.

wīde *a.* measuring much, having

specified measurement, from side to side; broad, not narrow; extending far, embracing much, of great extent; not tight, close, restricted, etc.; open to full extent; far from, not within reasonable distance *of*, point or mark; (crick., of ball) out of batsman's reach. *adv.* at or to many points; with wide interval or opening; so as to miss mark or way; *far and ~*, over or through large space or region. *n.* (crick.) wide ball. *~ awake*, fully awake; (colloq.) fully aware of what is going on, alert, sharp-witted. *~- -awake*, broad-brimmed soft felt hat. *~spread*, widely disseminated. **wi'den** *v.* make or become wide(r).

widgeon (wĭj'on) *n.* kinds of wild duck.

wid'ow (-ō) *n.* woman whose husband is dead. *v.t.* make widow or widower of. **wid'ower** (-ōer) *n.* man whose wife is dead. *~hood n.*

width *n.* distance or measurement from side to side; large extent; piece of material of same width as when woven.

wield *v.t.* hold and use, control, manage.

wife *n.* (pl. *wives*), married woman esp. in relation to her husband; *old wives' tale*, foolish or superstitious tradition. *~less, ~ly aa.*

wig *n.* covering of hair etc. for whole or part of head.

wigg'ing (-g-) *n.* severe rebuke, scolding.

wigg'le *v.* (colloq.) (cause to) move rapidly, jerk, shake, from side to side or up and down. *n.* wiggling movement.

wight (wīt) *n.* (arch.) person.

wig'wăm *n.* N. Amer. Indian's tent or cabin.

wil'cō *abbr.* of phr. 'will comply' used in signalling etc. to indicate that directions received will be carried out.

wild *a.* in original natural state; not domesticated, tame, or cultivated; uncivilized; tempestuous; lawless; out of control; violently excited or agitated; passionately desirous (*to* do); elated, enthusiastic; rash, ill-aimed, random;

run ~, be out of control or free from restraint, take one's own way, live in or revert to state of nature. *n.* wild or waste place, desert. *~cat*, reckless, unsound; (of strike) unofficial. *~fire*, highly inflammable composition formerly used in warfare etc.; *like ~fire*, with immense rapidity. *~-goose chase*, foolish, fruitless, or hopeless quest. *~ oats: sow one's ~ oats*, commit youthful indiscretions etc. *W~ West*, western States of U.S. during period when they were lawless frontier districts. **wil'ding** *n.* (fruit of) wild plant, esp. crab-apple.

wildebeest (vĭl'debäst; *or* -ēst) *n.* gnu.

wil'derness *n.* desert, uncultivated and uninhabited land or tract; mingled, confused, desolate, or vast assemblage *of*; *in the ~*, (of political party) out of office, (of person) in exile or disgrace, out of favour.

wile *n.* trick, cunning procedure, artifice. *v.t.* while *away* (time etc.).

wil'ful *a.* deliberate, intentional; obstinately selfwilled; wayward.

will[1] *v.aux.* (pres. *I, he, we, you, they, will, thou wilt*; past & cond. *I, he, we, you, they, would, thou wouldst or wouldest*; neg. *will not, wōn't; would not, wouldn't*), forming (in 2nd & 3rd, & now freq. 1st, pers.) plain future or conditional statement or question, or (in 1st pers.) future or conditional statement expressing speaker's will or intention. *v.t.* want, desire, choose, consent, to; intend unconditionally to; be accustomed, be likely, be observed from time to time, to.

will[2] *n.* faculty or function directed to conscious and intentional action; act or action of willing; intention, determination; desire, wish; (document expressing) formal declaration, esp. in writing, of person's intention as to disposal of his property etc. after his death; *against* one's *~*, unwillingly; *at ~*, according to one's volition or choice, as one pleases, (of estate etc.) held during owner's pleasure, (of tenant) that may be ousted at any time; *of* one's *own free ~*, of one's own accord, voluntarily; *with a* ~, resolutely, determinedly, energetically. *v.* choose or decide to do something or that something shall be done; exercise will; (try to) influence, induce (*to* do), by exercise of will; direct by will or testament; bequeath. ~-**power**, (strength of) will, esp. power to control one's own actions etc.

will'ing *a.* not reluctant (*to* do), ready to be of use or service; given, rendered, performed, etc. willingly.

will-o'-the-wisp' (-dh-) *n.* phosphorescent light seen on marshy ground; elusive or delusive thing or person.

will'ow (-ō) *n.* kinds of tree or shrub with pliant branches, usu. growing by water; (willow-wood) cricket or baseball bat. ~-**herb**, kinds of common weed with showy purplish-pink flowers. ~ **pattern**, blue orig. Chinese pattern on white china, including willow-tree etc. ~-**warbler**, ~-**wren**, kinds of small European song-bird. **will'owỹ** *a.* abounding in, shaded by, willows; lithe and slender.

willỹnill'ỹ *adv.* whether one likes it or not.

wilt[1] : see **will**.

wilt[2] *v.* (cause to) fade, droop, become limp.

Wilts. *abbr.* Wiltshire.

wi'lỹ *a.* crafty, cunning.

wim'ple *n.* head-dress covering neck and sides of face worn by nuns etc.

win *v.* (*won*, pr. wŭn), be victorious in (game, battle, race, etc.), gain victory; get, gain as result of fight, contest, bet, etc.; gain affection or allegiance of, bring *over* to one's cause etc.; make one's way *to*, *through*, etc.; ~ *through*, gain one's end, be successful. *n.* victory in game or contest; (pl.) winnings, gains. **winn'er** *n.* **winn'ing** *a.* attractive, charming; *n.pl.* money won by gambling, betting, etc. ~**ning-post**, post marking end of race-course.

wince *v.i.* & *n.* (make, give) start or involuntary shrinking movement of pain etc., flinch.

winceyĕtte' (-sĭ-) *n.* kind of light-weight napped flannelette used for night-clothes etc.

winch *n.* crank of wheel or axle; revolving horizontal drum turned by crank, used for hauling or hoisting.

Win'chĕster[1] *n.* (bottle holding) half gallon or 2½ litres.

Win'chĕster[2] *n.* breech-loading repeating rifle.

wind[1] (*in verse also* -ī-) *n.* current of air occurring naturally in atmosphere or put in motion by passage of missile, action of bellows, etc.; wind in reference to direction from which it blows, in relation to ship, etc.; gas in stomach or intestines; breath as needed in exertion, used in speech or for sounding musical instrument, etc.; part of body in front of stomach; (players of) wind instruments of orchestra; *get* ~ *of*, hear rumour or hint of; *get, have, put, the* ~ *up*, (sl.) be in, put into, state of alarm or 'funk'; *in the* ~, astir, afoot, happening or ready to happen; *raise the* ~, (colloq.) obtain money needed; *sail* etc. *close to the* ~, come very near indecency or dishonesty; *second* ~, regular breathing regained after breathlessness during continued exertion; *take the* ~ *out of* person's *sails*, put him at a disadvantage. *v.* (-ī-), detect presence of by scent; deprive of breath, make out of breath; (-ĭ-), sound (horn or bugle), blow (note etc.) on horn etc. ~-**băg**, wordy talker. ~**break**, thing, esp. row of trees etc., used to break force of wind. ~-**cheater**, windproof jacket. ~**fall**, something, esp. fruit, blown down by wind; piece of unexpected good fortune, esp. legacy. ~ **instrument**, musical instrument in which sound is produced by current of air. ~**jammer**, (colloq.) sailing-ship. ~**mill**, mill worked by action of wind on sails. ~**pipe**, air-passage between throat and lungs. ~**screen**, screen to keep off wind, esp. sheet of glass in front of driver of car etc. ~**shield**, (U.S.) windscreen. ~-**sleeve**, ~-**sock**, canvas cylinder or cone flown from mast-head etc. to show

aircraft etc. direction of wind. ~
tunnel, enclosed chamber for
testing (models, parts, of) aircraft
in winds of known velocities. ~-
ward, (region) lying in direction
from which wind blows, facing the
wind. ~**less** *a.*

wind² *v.* (*wound*), move, go, in
curved or sinuous course; coil,
wrap closely around something or
upon itself, enclose or encircle thus;
haul or hoist by turning windlass
etc.; tighten *up* coiled spring of
clock etc., or tension, efficiency,
etc. of; ~ *up*, bring or come to an
end, arrange and adjust affairs of
(company etc.) on its dissolution.
winding-sheet, linen in which
corpse is wrapped. **win'der** *n.*

wind'lass *n.* mechanical contrivance
with horizontal roller or beam
wound round with rope or chain,
for hoisting or hauling.

win'dow (-ō) *n.* opening, usu. filled
with glass, in wall etc. to admit
light and air, afford view, etc.;
window space or opening esp. used
for display of goods etc.; opening
resembling window in shape or
function. ~**-box,** box placed outside window for cultivating plants.
~**-dressing,** art of arranging display
in shop-window etc.; adroit presentation of facts etc. to give
falsely favourable impression. ~-
-seat, seat below window. ~**-shop-**
ping, looking at displays in shop-
-windows without buying anything.

Wind'sor (-z-). ~ **chair,** strong plain
chair of polished wood with curved
back. ~ **soap,** brown scented kind.

wind'y *a.* exposed to or stormy with
wind; in which wind is frequent
or prevalent; wordy; generating,
characterized by, flatulence; (sl.)
frightened, apprehensive.

wine *n.* fermented grape-juice as
drink; fermented drink resembling
it made from other fruits etc.; colour
of red wine. *v.* drink wine, entertain
to wine. ~**bibber,** tippler. ~-
-cellar, (contents of) cellar used for
storing wine. ~**-cooler,** vessel in
which wine-bottles are cooled with
ice. ~**glass,** small glass for wine,
usu. with stem and foot. ~**press,**

press in which grape-juice is extracted for wine. ~**sap,** large red
Amer. winter apple. **wī'nÿ** *a.*

wing *n.* one of the limbs or organs by
which flying is effected; power or
means of flight; flying man's badge
of representation of bird's wing(s);
anything resembling wing in form
or function, esp. one of main supporting surfaces of aircraft; mud-
guard of motor vehicle; either of
two divisions at side of main body
in battle; division of military air-
-force; (player occupying) position
of forwards on either side of centre
in football etc.; section of political
party etc. with views deviating
from centre; subordinate part of
building on one side of main part;
(pl.) side-scenes on stage, space
where these stand. *v.* equip with
wings; send in flight, lend speed to;
travel, traverse, on wings; wound
in wing or arm. ~**-case,** horny
covering of some insects' wings.
~ **chair,** chair with projecting side-
-pieces at top of high back. **W~**
Commander, officer of R.A.F.
ranking next to Group Captain.
~**-coverts,** small feathers overlying
flight-feathers of bird's wing. ~-
-nut, nut with projections to turn
it by. ~**-span,** ~**-spread,** extreme
measurement between tips of wings.
winged, ~**less** *aa.*

wink *v.* blink; close eye(s) for a
moment; close one eye momentarily; (cause to) flicker like eyelid,
twinkle; convey signal, message,
hint, etc. by winking, flashing
lights, etc.; ~ *at*, affect not to
notice, connive at; *like ~ing*, in a
flash, in a twinkling. *n.* act of
winking, esp. as signal, hint, etc.;
forty ~s, nap; *not a ~ (of sleep)*, no
sleep at all; *tip the ~*, give signal
or intimation. **wink'ers** *n.pl.*
(colloq.) motor vehicle's flashing
signal-lights.

wink'le *n.* edible sea snail. *v.t.* ~ *out*,
extract, prise out.

winn'ow (-ō) *v.t.* fan (grain) free of
chaff etc.; fan (chaff, etc.) *away* or
from; sift, separate (*out*) from
worthless or inferior elements.

win'some *a.* winning, engaging.

wĭn'ter *n*. coldest season of year; colder half of year. *v*. spend the winter *at, in,* etc.; keep, feed, during winter. *a*. of, occurring or used in, keeping until, lasting for, etc., winter. ~ **aconite**, small perennial winter-flowering plant with bright--yellow starry flowers. ~ **garden**, glass-covered space with plants, esp. as public lounge in hotel etc. ~**green**, kinds of low shrubby plant with leaves green in winter, esp. N. Amer. kind yielding aromatic oil. ~ **sports**, skiing, skating, and other open-air sports practised on snow or ice. ~ **wheat** etc., wheat etc. sown in autumn and remaining in ground all winter. **wĭn'trў** *a*. characteristic of winter; cold, windy, cheerless; devoid of warmth, chilly, dreary.

Winton. *abbr*. (Bishop) of Winchester.

wīpe *v*. clean or dry surface by rubbing with something soft; get rid of (tears), clean (vessel) *out*, make *clean*, etc. by wiping; (sl.) aim sweeping blow at; ~ *out*, destroy, annihilate, exterminate. *n*. act of wiping. **wī'per** *n*. esp. = *windscreen* ~, device for keeping windscreen clear.

wīre *n*. (piece of) metal drawn out into slender flexible rod or thread; length or line of this used for fencing, as conductor of electric current, etc.; wire-netting, framework of wire, snare made of wire, etc.; (colloq.) telegram; *pull (the)* ~*s*, exert private influence (as though working puppets). *v*. furnish, support, stiffen, secure, with wires; snare with wire; (colloq.) telegraph. ~**-drawn**, fine--spun, elaborately subtle or refined. ~ **edge**, turned-over strip of metal on edge of faultily sharpened tool etc. ~**-haired**, (of dogs) having rough hard wiry coat. ~**-tapping**, tapping of telephone lines. ~**-walker**, acrobat performing feats on wire rope. ~ **wool**, very fine wire used for scouring kitchen utensils etc. ~**worm**, slender yellow larva of kinds of beetle, millipede, destructive to plant roots. ~**-wove**, (of

paper) made in wire-gauze frame. **wīr'ў** *a*. made of wire; tough and flexible like wire; tough, sinewy, untiring.

wīre'less *a*. without wire(s), esp. (of telegraphy, telephony) with no connecting wire between transmitting and receiving stations; radio. *n*. radio receiver or transmitter; wireless telegraphy or telephony. *v*. send message etc., inform, by wireless. ~ **set**, radio receiver.

Wisc. *abbr*. Wisconsin.

Wisd. *abbr*. Wisdom (of Solomon).

wĭs'dom (-z-) *n*. being wise; soundness of judgement in matters relating to life and conduct; knowledge, learning. ~ **tooth**, hindmost molar tooth on each side of upper and lower jaws, usu. cut at age of about 20.

wīse[1] (-z) *a*. having, showing, dictated by, etc., sound judgement resulting from experience and knowledge; sagacious, prudent, sensible; having knowledge; (sl.) alert, crafty, smart; ~ *to*, aware or informed of. ~**crăck**, (colloq.) smart remark, witticism; *v*. make wisecracks. ~ **man**, (esp., arch.) wizard, esp. (pl.) the three Magi. ~ **woman**, (esp. harmless or benevolent) witch, female soothsayer.

wīse[2] (-z) *n*. (arch.) way, manner, guise.

wī'seacre (-zāk*er*) *n*. sententious dullard.

wĭsh *n*. (expression of) desire or aspiration; request; (pl.) expression of desire for another's happiness, success, etc. *v*. have or express wish *for* or for; want, want (person), *to* do; request; desire esp. something good for (person etc.). ~**bone**, forked bone between neck and breast of cooked bird. ~**-fulfilment**, supposed tendency of esp. unconscious wishes to seek gratification in reality or fantasy. **wĭsh'ful** *a*. wishing, desirous; ~**ful thinking**, believing a thing to be so because it is desired or desirable.

wĭsh'ў-washў (-wŏ-) *a*. thin, sloppy; feeble or poor in quality or character.

wisp *n.* small bundle or twist of hay, straw, etc.; thin, filmy, or slight piece or scrap (*of*). **wis'py** *a.*

wist, *p.t.* of **wit²**.

wistār'ia, -ēria *n.* kinds of climbing shrub with blue-lilac, purple, or white flowers.

wist'ful *a.* yearningly or mournfully expectant or wishful.

wit¹ *n.* (sing. or pl.) intelligence, understanding; imaginative and inventive faculty; amusing ingenuity of speech or ideas; person noted for this; (arch.) person of great mental ability; *five ~s*, five senses; *have one's ~s about one*, be mentally alert; *at one's ~'s end*, utterly perplexed; *out of one's ~s*, mad, distracted. **~less** *a.* foolish, unintelligent.

wit² *v.* (arch.; pres. *wŏt, wŏttest*; *p.t. & p.p. wist*), know; *to ~*, that is to say, namely.

witch *n.* woman supposed to have dealings with devil or evil spirits; hag; fascinating or bewitching woman. **~ ball,** coloured glass ball of kind formerly hung up to keep away witches. **~craft,** use of magic, sorcery. **~-doctor,** sorcerer of primitive people. **~-hunt, ~-hunting,** searching out and persecution of supposed witches, persons suspected of unpopular or unorthodox political views, etc. **witch'ery** *n.* witchcraft; power of beauty, eloquence, or the like.

witch² *n.* flat-fish used for food.

witch³ : see **wych**.

witėnagėmōt' (-g-) *n.* (hist.) Anglo--Saxon national council.

with (-dh) *prep.* against, in opposition to; in or into company of or relation to, among, beside; having, carrying, characterized by, possessed of; by means or operation of, owing to; on the side of; in the care or charge of; despite, notwithstanding, presence of; in same way, degree, etc., or at same time, as; in regard to, concerning, in mind or view of; so as to be separated from; *~ it*, up-to-the--minute, (capable of) understanding new ideas etc.

withal' (-dhawl) *adv.* (arch.) moreover; as well.

withdraw' (-dh-) *v.* (-*drew*, pr. -ōō; -*drawn*), pull aside or back; take away, remove; retract; retire or go apart. **withdraw'al** (-dh-) *n.*

withe (-dh; *or* with), **with'y** (-dhĭ) *n.* tough flexible branch or shoot, esp. of willow.

with'er (-dh-) *v.* make, become, dry or shrivelled; deprive of or lose vigour, freshness, etc.; decline, decay; blight, paralyse (*with* look etc.).

with'ers (-dherz) *n.pl.* ridge between shoulder-blades of horse etc.

withhōld' (-dh-h-) *v.t.* (-*hěld*), refuse to give, grant, or allow; hold back, restrain.

within' (-dh-) *adv.* inside, inwardly; indoors. *prep.* inside; not out of or beyond; not transgressing or exceeding; in limits, scope, sphere of action, etc. of.

without' (-dh-) *adv.* (arch.) outside; out-of-doors. *prep.* not having or feeling or showing; in want of; free from; in absence of; (arch.) outside. *conj.* (arch. or illiterate) unless.

withstănd' *v.t.* (-*stood*), resist, oppose (successfully).

withy : see **withe**.

witless : see **wit¹**.

wit'nėss *n.* testimony, evidence, confirmation; person giving sworn testimony; person attesting another's signature to document; person present, spectator; person or thing whose existence, position, etc., is testimony *to* or proof *of*; *bear ~ (to)*, give or be evidence (of), be confirmation (of). *v.* sign (document) as witness; see, be spectator of; serve as evidence or indication of; bear witness. **~-box,** (U.S.) **~-stand,** enclosed space, stand, from which witness gives evidence.

wit'icĭsm *n.* witty saying, piece of wit, esp. jeer, witty sarcasm.

wit'inglỹ *adv.* knowingly, intentionally.

wit'ỹ *a.* full of wit; capable of, given to, saying or writing brilliantly or sparklingly amusing things.

wivern : see **wyvern**.

wives, pl. of **wife**.

wiz'ard *n*. magician, sorcerer, male witch; person who effects seeming impossibilities. *a*. (colloq.) marvellous, wonderful. ~**ry** *n*.

wiz'en(ed) *aa*. of shrivelled or dried--up appearance.

W.J.C. *abbr*. World Jewish Congress.

W/L *abbr*. wave-length.

Wm *abbr*. William.

wō *int*. whoa.

W.O. *abbr*. War Office; Warrant Officer.

woad *n*. (blue, black, or green dye--stuff obtained from) European biennial plant.

wŏbb'le *v.i*. move unsteadily or uncertainly from side to side or backwards and forwards; rock, quiver, shake; hesitate, waver. *n*. wobbling motion. **wŏbb'lў** *a*.

wōe *n*. affliction, bitter grief; (pl.) calamities, troubles. ~**begone**, dismal-looking. ~**ful** *a*.

wŏg *n*. (sl., contempt.) native of Middle East.

woke, *p.t.* of **wake**².

wōld *n*. rolling uplands.

wolf (wŏo-) *n*. (pl. *-ves*), kinds of largish mammal of dog tribe; rapacious or greedy person; (sl.) man who pursues women; *keep the ~ from the door*, ward off hunger or starvation. *v.t.* (sl.) devour greedily. ~**-cub**, young wolf; junior Boy Scout. ~**-hound**, kinds of dog kept for hunting wolves; Alsatian. ~**'s-bane**, aconite. ~**-whistle**, whistle or other sound expressing admiration of woman's appearance.

wol'fram (wŏo-) *n*. tungsten; tungsten ore.

wolverene, **-ine** (wŏol'verēn) *n*. (fur of) N.-Amer. glutton.

wo'man (wŏo-) *n*. (pl. *women*, pr. wĭm'ĭn), adult human female; female servant or attendant; average or typical woman, female sex; (attrib.) female. *v.t.* address as 'woman'. ~**kind**, women in general. **womenfolk**, **womenkind**, women; women of one's family. **women's rights**, rights of equal privileges and opportunities with men. ~**hood** *n*. being a (grown) woman; womankind; character or qualities natural to woman. ~**ish** *a*. effeminate, unmanly. ~**īze** *v.i.* consort illicitly with women. **wo'manlў** *a*. having, showing, qualities befitting (grown) woman; not masculine or girlish.

womb (wŏom) *n*. organ in female mammals in which child is conceived and nourished till birth; place where anything is generated or produced.

wŏm'băt *n*. burrowing herbivorous bear-like Australian marsupial.

won, *p.t.* & *p.p.* of **win**.

won'der (wŭ-) *n*. marvel, miracle, prodigy; strange or remarkable thing, specimen, event, etc.; emotion excited by novel and unexpected thing; astonishment mixed with perplexity, curiosity, or admiration. *v*. marvel, be affected with wonder; feel doubt or curiosity, be desirous to know or learn; *I shouldn't ~*, (colloq.) I should not be surprised. ~**ful** *a*. marvellous, surprising; surprisingly fine, large, excellent, etc. ~**ment** *n*. **won'drous** *a*. & *adv*. (poet.) wonderful(ly).

wŏnk'ў *a*. (sl.) shaky, unsteady; not well.

wōnt *a*. (arch.) accustomed, used (*to* do). *n*. custom; habit. **wō'ntěd** *a*. habitual.

won't, contr. of *will not*.

wŏo *v*. seek love of, make love (to); seek to win, court, invite. **wŏo'er**, **wŏo'ing** *nn*.

wŏod *n*. growing trees covering piece of ground; hard compact fibrous substance of tree, whether growing or cut for timber or fuel; something made of wood, esp. *the* cask used for storing wine etc., bowl in game of bowls, wooden-headed golf-club; *out of the ~*, clear of danger, difficulty, etc. ~ **alcohol**, alcohol got by distillation of wood. ~**bine**, honeysuckle; (U.S.) Virginia creeper. ~**cock**, game-bird allied to snipe. ~**craft**, knowledge of and skill in woodland conditions. ~**cut**, print from design cut in relief on wood block. ~**land**, woodeᵈ country. ~**-louse**, small terrestrial crustacean found in old wood etc. ~man, forester. ~-nymph, dryad. ~pecker, kinds of bird pecking holes in tree-trunks etc. to find insects etc. ~-pulp, wood-fibre prepared as material for paper etc. ~sman, man living in or frequenting woods, one skilled in woodcraft. ~wind, wind instruments of orchestra (usu. or formerly) made of wood. ~work, work done in wood; wooden part (of), esp. wooden interior parts of building. wŏŏ'dĕd a. covered with growing trees; abounding in woods. wŏŏ'dĕn a. made or consisting of, resembling, wood; dull, stiff and lifeless, inexpressive. wŏŏ'dў a.

wŏŏd'chŭck n. thick-bodied reddish--brown N. Amer. marmot.

wŏŏf n. (arch.) weft.

wŏŏl n. fine soft wavy hair forming fleecy coat of domesticated sheep etc.; woollen yarn or cloth or garments; Negro's short crisp curly hair; hair; downy substance found on some plants; any fine fibrous substance; dyed in the ~, dyed before spinning, thoroughgoing, out-and-out; pull the ~ over person's eyes, hoodwink, deceive. ~gathering, absentmindedness. ~sack, Lord Chancellor's seat in House of Lords; his office. ~work, wool embroidery, esp. on canvas. wŏŏ'llen a. & n. (fabric) made of wool or yarns containing wool fibres. wŏŏ'llў a. bearing, naturally covered with, wool or wool-like hair; resembling or suggesting wool in softness, texture, etc.; confused, blurred, hazy; wild and ~ly, uncivilized, barbarous, lawless; n. woollen, esp. knitted, garment.

wŏp n. (sl., contempt.) Italian or other S. European.

Worcs. abbr. Worcestershire.

word (wĕrd) n. (written or printed symbol(s) representing) sound(s) constituting minimal element of speech having meaning and capable of independent grammatical use; (usu. pl.) thing(s) said, speech, verbal expression, text of song, actor's part, etc.; (pl.) quarrelsome talk, altercation; watchword, pass-

word; report, tidings; command· order; promise, assurance; ~ for ~, verbatim, exact(ly); last ~, final utterance esp. in dispute or (pl.) before death, final or conclusive statement, the latest thing; man of his ~, one who keeps his promises; the W~ (of God), Bible. v.t. put into words; select words to express. ~-perfect, knowing perfectly every word of lesson, theatrical part, etc.; so known. wor'ding n. (esp.) form of words used, phrasing. ~lĕss a. wor'dў a. verbose, using or containing (too) many words.

wore, p.t. of wear.

work (wĕrk) n. action involving effort or exertion, esp. as means of livelihood; operation of force in producing movement etc.; something to do or be done; employment; thing done or made; book, picture, or other product of art; writings, paintings, etc. as whole; needlework; (pl.) operations in building or engineering; (pl.) operative parts of machine; (pl.) establishment where industrial process is carried on; at ~, engaged in work, at place of employment, working, operating; in ~, in regular occupation, gainfully employed; out of ~, unemployed; set to ~, set (person), apply oneself, to working or doing something. v. engage, be engaged, in bodily or mental work; make efforts; (cause to) operate, act; be in (agitated) motion or fermentation; effect or bring about; excite artificially into mood etc.; knead, hammer, fashion, into shape, desired consistency etc.; do, make by, needlework etc.; (cause to) make way or become tight, free, etc., gradually or with difficulty; solve (sum); ~ off, get rid of, finish working at; ~ out, find or solve by calculation, be calculated at, exhaust by working, develop, plan or provide for details of, discharge (debt) or pay for by labour instead of money; ~ up, bring to efficient or desired or finished state, advance gradually to, stir up, make up, excite. ~aday, concerned with ordinary everyday

life. ~bag, ~basket, ~box, receptacles esp. for holding sewing-
-materials. ~day, day on which
work is ordinarily performed. ~-
house, (hist.) public institution for
maintenance of paupers, in which
able-bodied were set to work.
~man, man hired to do work or
(usu.) manual labour; craftsman;
one who works in specified manner.
~manlike, showing practised skill.
~manship, degree of skill in workman or of finish in his product.
~-out, (colloq.) spell of exercise or
practising; practice game, bout,
run, etc. ~people, people engaged
in manual or industrial labour for
wages. ~shop, room or building
in which manufacture, manual
work, etc. is carried on. ~shy a.
disinclined for work, lazy. ~able a.
(esp.) practicable, that can be
worked or will work; ~abil'ity n.
~er n. (esp.) one employed for
wage; one who works with hand
or brain; neuter or undeveloped
female ant, bee, etc. ~less a. & n.
• wor'king (wer-) n. (esp.) way thing
works; action, operation; (freq. pl.)
place in which mineral is or has
been extracted; excavation(s) made
in mining, tunnelling, etc. a. that
works; of, at, in, for, work; spent in
work; engaged in manual or industrial work. ~ capital, capital used
in conduct of business, not invested
in buildings etc. ~ class(es), class
of those employed for wages, esp. in
manual or industrial work. ~-class,
of, for, working class. ~-day,
workday; number of hours constituting day's work, part of day
devoted to work. ~ drawing(s),
scale drawing(s) for carrying out
construction, manufacture, etc.
~ man, working-class man. ~
model, model of machine etc.
capable of being operated. ~ party,
committee appointed to investigate
means of securing efficiency in
industry etc.
world (-er-) n. human existence, this
present life; secular or lay life and
interests; earth; planet or other
heavenly body, esp. viewed as
inhabited; universe; everything,

all people; (esp. high or fashionable section of) human society;
sphere of interest, action, or
thought; (freq. pl.) great quantity,
vast or infinite amount or extent;
for all the ~, in every respect (like);
not for (all) the ~, not for ~s, not on
any account; the next, other, a
better ~, the future state, life after
death; ~ without end, eternally,
for ever. ~ power, any of powers
dominating international politics.
~ war, war affecting (most of)
world. ~wide, spread over the
world, known or found everywhere;
universal. ~ling n. worldly person.
world'ly a. temporal, earthly; concerned with or devoted to affairs of
this life, esp. to pursuit of wealth
or pleasure; ~ly goods, property;
~ly-minded, intent on worldly
things; ~ly-wise, (esp.) prudent in
advancing one's own interests.
worm (-er-) n. kinds of invertebrate
limbless creeping animal; internal
parasite; larva, maggot, grub;
maggot supposed to eat bodies in
grave; long slender marine mollusc
boring into timber; abject, miserable or contemptible person; spiral
of screw, screw whose thread gears
with teeth of toothed wheel etc.;
long spiral or coiled tube in which
vapour from still is condensed.
v. convey oneself, progress, with
crawling or wriggling motion; insinuate oneself into favour etc., make
one's way insidiously; draw out
(secret etc.) by craft. ~-cast, mass
of mould voided by earthworm and
left on surface of ground. ~-eaten,
eaten into by worm(s), full of holes
made by burrowing insect larva;
decayed, decrepit, antiquated. ~-
-wheel, toothed wheel gearing with
worm. wor'my a.
worm'wood (wer-) n. woody herb
with bitter aromatic taste; (cause
of) bitter humilation.
worn a. impaired by use, exposure,
or wear; enfeebled, exhausted.
~-out, no longer of use or service;
utterly wasted in strength or
vitality; stale, trite.
wo'rry (wu-) v. shake or pull about
with teeth, kill or injure thus;

harass, vex, pester, importune; be trouble or anxiety to; make or be anxious and ill at ease. *n.* (cause of) harassing anxiety or solicitude; (pl.) cares, troubles.

worse (wers) *a.* & *adv.*, used as comp. of *bad*, *evil*, *badly*, *ill*, or as opposite of *better*; in worse condition, manner, etc.; less good or well. *n.* worse thing(s); worse condition. **wor'sen** *v.* make or become worse, deteriorate.

wor'ship (wer-) *n.* homage or service paid to being or power regarded as divine; acts, rites, or ceremonies displaying this; adoration, devotion; title of respect for magistrate, esp. mayor. *v.* adore as divine; honour with religious rites; idolize; attend public worship. **~ful** *a.* honorific title of justices of the peace, aldermen, recorders, etc.

worst (wer-) *a.* & *adv.* used as sup. of *bad(ly)*, *evil*, *ill*; least good or well. *n.* worst part, state, issue, etc.; *at (the)* ~, in the most evil or undesirable possible state, even on the most unfavourable view or surmise; *if the* ~ *comes to the* ~, if things fall out as badly as possible or conceivable; *do one's* ~, do the utmost evil or harm possible; *get the* ~ *of*, be defeated in. *v.t.* get the better of, defeat, outdo.

wor'sted (woos-) *n.* (fabric made from) fine smooth-surfaced long--staple woollen yarn. *a.* made of worsted.

wort (wert) *n.* infusion of malt or other grain before it is fermented into beer.

worth (wer-) *a.* of value of (specified amount, sum, etc.), equivalent to or good return for; deserving or worthy of; possessed of. *n.* value; equivalent (*of*). ~ **while**, worth the time or effort spent. **~-while**, that is worth while. **~less** *a.*

worthy (wer'dhi) *a.* estimable, deserving respect; deserving *of*; of sufficient worth, desert, merit, etc. (*to*). *n.* worthy, eminent, or famous person, esp. hero of antiquity.

wot : see **wit²**.

would (-ood): see **will¹**. **~-be**, desiring or professing to be.

wound¹ (woo-), *n.* injury done by cut, stab, blow, or tear to animal or vegetable tissues; injury to reputation, pain inflicted on feelings. *v.* inflict wound (on); pain, grieve deeply.

wound², *p.t.* & *p.p.* of **wind²**.

wove¹, *p.t.* of **weave**.

wove² *a.* (esp., of paper) made on mould of closely woven wire.

woven, *p.p.* of **weave**.

wow *n.* (sl.) striking or 'howling' success. *v.t.* have immense success with.

W.P. *abbr.* weather permitting.

W.P.B. *abbr.* waste-paper basket.

W.R. *abbr.* West Riding.

W.R.A.C. *abbr.* Women's Royal Army Corps.

wrack (r-) *n.* seaweed etc. cast up or growing on seashore.

W.R.A.F. *abbr.* Women's Royal Air Force.

wraith (r-) *n.* ghost; spectral appearance of living person supposed to portend his death.

wrangle (rang'gl) *n.* & *v.i.* brawl; (engage in) noisy argument or dispute. **wrang'ler** *n.* (esp., at Cambridge University) candidate placed in first class in mathematical tripos.

wrap (r-) *v.* envelop, pack, swathe, (*up*) in garment or folded or soft encircling material; arrange or draw (pliant covering) *round*, *about*, etc.; ~ *over*, overlap; ~ *up*, put on wraps; **~ped up**, (esp.) engrossed, centred, absorbed, *in*. *n.* wrapper, covering; shawl, scarf, blanket, rug, etc. **wrapp'er** *n.* (esp.) protective covering for parcel etc.; paper enclosing newspaper etc. for posting; paper cover, esp. detachable outer paper cover of book etc.; loose enveloping robe or gown. **wrapp'ing** *n.* (esp., pl.) wraps, enveloping garments; **~ping paper**, (esp.) strong paper for packing or wrapping up parcels.

wrasse (ras) *n.* kinds of spiny-finned usu. brilliant-coloured edible sea--fish.

wrath (raw- *or* ro-) *n.* anger, indignation. **~ful** *a.*

wreak (r-) *v.t.* gratify (anger etc.), inflict (vengeance etc.), (*up*)*on*.

wreath (r-) *n.* (*pl. pr.* -dhz), flowers, leaves, etc. strung, woven, or wound together into ring for wearing on head, decorating coffin or grave, etc.; curl or ring of smoke, cloud, etc. **wreathe** (-dh) *v.* encircle as or (as) with wreath; form into wreath; wind (flexible object) round or over something; move in wreath-like shape.

wrĕck (r-) *n.* destruction or disablement, esp. of ship; ship that has suffered wreck. *v.* cause wreck of (ship, hopes, etc.); suffer wreck. **~age** *n.* fragments or remains of wrecked or shattered vessel, structure, etc. **~er** *n.* (esp.) one who tries from shore to bring about shipwreck in order to plunder or profit by wreckage; one who tears down or demolishes old buildings etc.

wren[1] (r-) *n.* kinds of small usu. brown song-bird.

Wrĕn[2] (r-) *n.* member of W.R.N.S.

wrĕnch (r-) *n.* violent twist, pull, or turn; tool for gripping and turning nuts, etc.; (fig.) pain caused by parting etc. *v.t.* twist, turn; pull (*away, off*, etc.) violently or with effort; injure, pain, by straining or stretching.

wrĕst (r-) *v.t.* twist, distort, pervert; force or wrench away from person's grasp.

wrĕs'tle (-sl) *n.* contest in which two opponents grapple and try to throw each other to ground; tussle, hard struggle. *v.* have wrestling-match (with); struggle *with* or *against*; (western U.S.) throw (cattle) for branding.

wrĕtch (r-) *n.* miserable, unhappy, or unfortunate person; one without conscience or shame, vile or contemptible person. **wrĕtch'ĕd** *a.* miserable, unhappy, afflicted; of poor quality, of no merit; contemptible; causing discontent, discomfort, or nuisance.

wrigg'le (r-) *v.* twist or turn body about with short writhing movements; move, make way, etc. with wriggling motion; be slippery, practise evasion. *n.* wriggling movement.

wrĭng (r-) *v.t.* (*wrŭng*), press, squeeze or twist, esp. so as to drain or make dry; distress, rack; extort, get (money, concession) *out of* or *from* by exaction or importunity; clasp (person's *hand*) forcibly or with emotion; ~ one's *hands*, twist them together in distress or pain. *n.* squeeze, act of wringing. **~ing wet**, so wet that moisture may be wrung out. **wrĭng'er** *n.* (esp.) device for wringing water from laundered clothes etc.

wrĭnk'le (r-) *n.* crease or furrow of skin or other flexible surface; useful hint, clever expedient. *v.* make wrinkles in; acquire or assume wrinkles. **wrĭnk'lȳ** *a.*

wrĭst (r-) *n.* joint connecting hand and forearm; part of garment covering wrist. **~band**, band of sleeve covering wrist; wristlet. **~-watch**, small watch worn on wristlet. **wrĭst'let** *n.* band, bracelet, strap, worn on wrist to strengthen it, as ornament, to hold watch, etc.; handcuff.

wrĭt *n.* formal written court order to do or refrain from doing specified act; Crown document summoning lord to attend Parliament or directing sheriff to hold parliamentary election; *Holy W* ~, Bible.

wrīte *v.* (*wrōte, wrĭtten*), form symbol(s) representing letter(s) or word(s) with pen, pencil, brush, etc., esp. on paper, parchment, etc. set down, express, in writing; make record or account of; convey (message etc.) by letter; engage in writing or authorship; produce writing; ~ *down*, set down in writing, write in disparagement or depreciation of, reduce to lower amount; ~ *off*, cancel (debt etc.), reckon as lost; ~ *up*, write or give full account, elaborate description, etc. of, praise in writing. **~-off**, something that must be written off as total loss, wreck. **~-up**, laudatory description in newspaper etc. **wrī'ter**, *n.* one who writes, clerk in certain offices; author; *W~ to the Signet*, Scottish solicitor. **wri′ting** n. (esp.) hand-writing; document; (piece of) literary work; *put in writing*, write down. **writt′en** a. that is in writing, esp. opp. *oral* or *printed*.

writhe (rīdh) v. twist or roll oneself about (as) in acute pain; twist about, contort; squirm. n. act of writhing.

written : see **write**.

W.R.N.S. *abbr.* Women's Royal Naval Service.

wrŏng (r-) a. not morally right or equitable; not correct or proper; not true, mistaken; in error; not in good order or condition; not what is required, intended, or expected; ~ *side*, side of fabric etc. not meant to be shown, disadvantageous or undesirable side *of*; *on the* ~ *side of*, older than; ~ *side out*, in bad temper, peevish, irritable; *the* ~ *way*, in contrary or opposite way to proper or usual one. *adv.* amiss; in wrong course, direction, or way; with incorrect result; *go* ~, go astray, happen amiss or unfortunately, get out of order, take to evil courses. n. what is morally wrong; wrong action; injustice; being wrong; *in the* ~, wrong in attitude, belief, etc. v. treat unjustly, do injustice to; dishonour. ~**doer**, offender. ~**doing**, transgression. ~**-headed**, perverse and obstinate. **wrŏng′ful** a. unwarranted, lacking justification; illegal; holding office etc. unlawfully or without right.

wrote, *p.t.* of **write**.

wrŏth (*or* rŏ-) a. (arch.) roused to wrath, angry.

wrought (rawt) a. worked, manufactured; (of metals) beaten out or shaped with hammer etc. ~**-up**, stirred up, excited or agitated.

wrung, *p.t. & p.p.* of **wring**.

W.R.V.S. *abbr.* Women's (Royal) Voluntary Service(s).

wrȳ (r-) a. distorted, turned to one side; contorted in disgust, disrelish, etc. ~**neck**, kinds of small migratory bird allied to woodpecker.

W.S. *abbr.* Writer to the Signet.

W/T *abbr.* wireless telegraphy, telephony.

wt. *abbr.* weight.

wўch, witch[3] n. in names of trees etc. with pliant branches. ~**-elm,** kind of elm with broader leaves and more spreading branches than common elm. ~**-hazel,** N. Amer. shrub; astringent extract of its bark.

Wyo. *abbr.* Wyoming.

wȳ′vern, wī′vern n. (her.) winged dragon with eagle's feet.

X

X, x (ĕks), as Roman numeral, 10; (alg. etc., *x*) (first) unknown or variable quantity, incalculable or unknown factor or influence. **x-height,** (typ.) height of body of letter.

X *abbr.* Christ.

x-cp. *abbr.* ex coupon.

xd, x-d., x-div. *abbr.* ex dividend.

xē′bĕc (z-) n. small three-masted Mediterranean ship formerly much used by corsairs.

Xen. *abbr.* Xenophon.

xĕn′on (z-) n. (chem.) heavy almost inert gaseous element.

xĕnophō′bia (z-) n. strong dislike of foreigners. **xĕn′ophōbe** n.

x-i. *abbr.* ex interest.

Xmas *abbr.* Christmas.

X-ray (ĕks-) n. (pl.) electromagnetic radiations of very short wavelength capable of passing through extensive thickness of any body; (sing.) X-ray photograph. *v.t.* photograph, examine, treat, with X-rays. ~ **photograph,** shadow--photograph, esp. of bodies impervious to light, made with X-rays.

Xt, Xtian *abbr.* Christ, Christian.

xȳ′lophōne (z-) n. musical instrument of graduated series of flat wooden bars played by striking with small wooden hammer(s).

Y

Y, y (wī), thing, marking, etc. in shape of letter Y; (alg. etc., *y*) second unknown or variable quantity.

Y. *abbr.* Yeomanry.

yacht (yŏt) *n.* light sailing-vessel for racing; vessel used for private pleasure excursions, cruising, etc. *v.i.* race or cruise in yacht. **~sman,** person who yachts.

yaff'le *n.* green woodpecker.

yah *int.* of derision, defiance, etc.

yahoo' (-a-h-) *n.* bestial person.

yăk *n.* large humped bovine mammal of Tibet etc.

yăm *n.* (starchy tuberous root used for food of) kinds of twining herb or shrub; (U.S.) sweet potato.

yănk[1] *n. & v.* (sl.) (pull with) sudden sharp tug or jerk.

Yănk[2] *n.* (colloq.) Yankee.

Yănk'ee (-kĭ) *n.* (colloq.) native or inhabitant of New England or northern U.S.; any inhabitant of U.S. *a.* of Yankees; that is a Yankee.

yaourt : see **yog(h)urt.**

yăp *n.* shrill or fussy bark, yelp; yapping talk. *v.i.* utter yap(s); talk noisily, excitedly, incessantly, etc.

yăpp *n.* limp-leather book-binding with overlapping edges or flaps.

yăr'borough (-boro) *n.* whist or bridge hand with no card above nine.

yărd[1] *n.* unit of long measure (3 ft.); yard-length of material; cubic yard of gravel, soil, etc.; spar slung from mast to support and extend sail. **~-arm,** either end of yard of square-rigged vessel. **~stick,** stick as yard-measure; standard, criterion. **yăr'dage** *n.* number of yards.

yărd[2] *n.* piece of enclosed ground, esp. surrounded by or attached to building(s); (U.S.) garden; farm-yard; ground near railway station where rolling-stock is kept, trains are made up, etc.; *the Y~,* Scotland Yard.

yărn *n.* fibre spun and prepared for weaving, knitting, etc.; (colloq.) story, tale. *v.i.* (colloq.) tell yarn(s).

yă'rrow (-ō) *n.* kinds of common herb of waysides etc.

yăsh'măk *n.* Moslem woman's veil concealing face below eyes.

yăt'aghan (-găn) *n.* short slightly curved sword of Moslem countries.

yaw *v.i.* (of ship, aircraft) deviate from straight course through action of heavy sea or strong winds. *n.* yawing.

yawl *n.* ship's boat like small pinnace; kinds of yacht and fishing-boat.

yawn *v.i.* breathe in involuntarily with mouth wide open, as from drowsiness, boredom, etc.; gape, have wide opening. *n.* act of yawning.

yaws (-z) *n.* contagious tropical skin-disease.

yd. *abbr.* yard.

ye (yē, yĭ) *pron.* (arch.) you.

yea (yā) *adv. & n.* (arch.) yes.

yeah (yĕa) *adv. & n.* (U.S. colloq.) yes.

year (yēr *or* yēr) *n.* time occupied by one revolution of earth round sun (about 365¼ days); period from 1 Jan. to 31 Dec. inclusive, any period of twelve calendar months; (pl.) age, old age; (pl.) period, times, a very long time; *~ in (and) ~ out,* right through the year (and successive years), continually. **~-book,** annual publication containing information for the year. **~ling** *n. & a.* (animal, esp. sheep, calf, or foal) a year old. **year'ly** *a. & adv.* (occurring, observed, done, etc.) once a year or every year, annual(ly).

yearn (yĕrn) *v.i.* long; be moved with compassion or tenderness.

yeast *n.* greyish-yellow substance, got esp. from fermenting malt liquors and used as fermenting agent, in raising bread, etc. **yea'stў** *a.* frothy, fermenting or working like yeast.

yĕll *n.* sharp loud outcry of strong and sudden emotion; shout of pain, anger, laughter, etc. *v.* make, utter with, yell(s).

yĕll'ow (-ō) *a.* of the colour of gold, lemons, buttercups, etc.; having yellow skin or complexion; (of newspaper etc.) recklessly or unscrupulously sensational; cowardly, craven. *n.* yellow colour or pigment. *v.* turn yellow. **~ fever,** tropical fever with jaundice etc.

~-hammer, common European bunting with bright-yellow head, throat, etc. ~ peril, danger that yellow races may overwhelm white. yĕll'owĭsh, yĕll'owў *aa*.

yĕlp *n. & v.i.* (utter) sharp shrill bark or cry (as) of dog in excitement, pain, etc.

yĕn *n.* (U.S. sl.) intense desire or longing.

Yeo(m). *abbr.* Yeomanry.

yeo'man (yō-) *n.* man owning and farming small estate; middle-class farmer or countryman; member of yeomanry force; *Y~ of the Guard*, member of bodyguard of English sovereign, now acting chiefly as warders of Tower of London; *~ of the signals*, petty officer in signals branch of Royal Navy. ~ service, efficient (and long-continued) service; help in need. ~rў *n.* (hist.) volunteer cavalry force in British army.

yĕs *adv. & n.* (utterance of) word expressing affirmative reply to question, command, etc. ~-man, (colloq.) one who endorses or supports all opinions or proposals of a superior.

yĕs'terday *n. & adv.* (on) the day immediately preceding today. yĕs'ter-year *n.* (poet) last year.

yĕt *adv.* up to this or that time; at some time in the future; even now (though not till now); in addition or continuation, again; (with comp.) even, still; *as ~*, hitherto; *nor ~*, and also not; *not ~*, still not, not by this (or that) time. *conj.* in spite of that, nevertheless.

yĕt'ĭ *n.* either of two unidentified animals occas. reported on high slopes of Himalayas.

yew *n.* dark-leaved evergreen coniferous tree or its wood.

Y.H.A. *abbr.* Youth Hostels Association.

Yĭd *n.* (sl. contempt.) Jew.

Yĭdd'ĭsh *a. & n.* (of) form of German used by Jews in Europe and America.

yield *v.* produce or return as fruit, profit, or result; surrender or make submission (*to*); concede; give way *to* persuasion, entreaty, etc., give consent; give right of way (*to*); ~ *to*, give way under, be affected by, physical action or agent. *n.* amount yielded or produced, output, return.

Y.M.C.A. *abbr.* Young Men's Christian Association.

yŏb *n.* (sl., contempt.) boy, lout.

yō'del *v.* sing or warble with interchange of ordinary and falsetto voice in manner of Swiss etc. mountaineers. *n.* yodelling cry.

Yō'ga *n.* Hindu system of meditation, asceticism, etc. as means of attaining union with Supreme Spirit. yō'gi (-gĭ) *n.* devotee of yoga.

yŏg(h)'urt (-gert), yaourt (yah'-oort) *nn.* semi-solid junket-like food made from fermented milk.

yoicks *int.* used in foxhunting to urge on hounds.

yōke *n.* wooden neckpiece for coupling pair of draught oxen etc.; marriage tie or other bond of union; pair *of* oxen etc.; sway, dominion, servitude; wooden shoulder-piece for carrying pair of pails; part of garment fitting shoulders (or hips) and supporting depending part. *v.* put yoke upon; harness (draught animal) *to* vehicle or plough; couple, join, link (*together*).

yō'kel *n.* (contempt.) country bumpkin.

yolk (yōk) *n.* yellow part of egg.

yŏn'der *adv. & a.* (situated) over there; at some distance (but within sight).

yōre *n.*: *of ~*, in or of time long past.

yörk *v.t.* (crick.) bowl with yorker. yör'ker *n.* ball pitching immediately under bat.

Yör'kĭst *n. & a.* (adherent) of House of York, esp. in Wars of the Roses.

Yorks. *abbr.* Yorkshire.

Yörk'shire (-er). ~ pudding, light baked batter pudding usu. eaten with or before roast meat. ~ terrier, small long-haired terrier.

you (yōō, yŏō) *pron.* (obj. same, poss. *your*), 2nd pers. sing. (with pl. verb) and pl. pronoun: the person(s) or thing(s) addressed; (in general statements) one, a person.

young (yŭ-) *a.* that has lived, existed, etc. relatively short time; lately begun, formed, etc., recent, new; of youth or young person(s); youthful. *n*. (collect.) young ones of animals; young people. **young′ish** *a*. **young′ster** *n*. young person, esp. young man; child. esp. boy.

your (ūr, yôr, yer) *pron. & a.*, poss. case of *you* and corresponding adj., with abs. form *yours*. **yoursĕlf′, yoursĕlves** *prons.*, emphat. and refl. forms of *you*.

youth (yōō-) *n*. (pl. pr. -dhz), being young; early part of life, esp. adolescence; the young; young person, esp. young man between boyhood and maturity; quality or condition characteristic of the young. **~ hostel**, place where young holiday-makers etc. put up for night. **youth′ful** *a*.

yowl *n. & v.* howl.

yr., yrs. *abbr*. year, years; your, yours.

ÿttĕr′bium *n*. metallic element of rare-earth group.

ÿtt′rium *n*. rare metallic element.

yŭcc′a *n*. kinds of plant of Mexico etc., with crown of usu. rigid narrow pointed leaves and cluster of white flowers.

Yu′goslav, Jugo- (yōō-, -ahv) *a. & n.* (native, inhabitant) of Yugoslavia; South Slav.

yule (yōōl) *n*. festival of Christmas. **~-log**, large log burnt at Christmas. **~tide**, period of yule.

Y.W.C.A. *abbr*. Young Women's Christian Association.

Z

z (zĕd), (alg.) third of set of unknown or variable quantities.

Z *abbr*. zero.

zā′nÿ *n*. buffoon, simpleton.

zarē′ba, -iba (-rē-) *n*. fence, stockade, protecting camp or village in Sudan etc.

zeal *n*. ardour, eagerness, in pursuit of end or in favour of person or cause. **zeal′ous** (zĕl-) *a*.

zeal′ot (zĕl-) *n*. fanatical enthusiast; *Z~*, (hist.) member of Jewish sect

aiming at Jewish theocracy over world.

zē′bra (*or* zĕ-) *n*. African striped horse-like quadruped. **~ crossing**, street-crossing with black and white stripes where pedestrians have precedence. **~-wood**, kinds of ornamentally striped wood.

zē′bū *n*. humped ox domesticated in India etc.

Zech. *abbr*. Zechariah.

zėna′na (-ah-) *n*. part of dwelling--house in which women of family are or were secluded in India etc.

zĕn′ith *n*. point of heavens directly overhead; highest point or state, culmination.

Zeph. *abbr*. Zephaniah.

zĕph′yr (-er) *n*. west wind esp. personified; soft mild gentle wind or breeze.

zēr′ō *n*. (pl. -*os*), figure 0, nought, nil; point marked 0 on graduated scale, esp. in thermometer etc.; temperature corresponding to zero of thermometer; lowest point, bottom of scale, nullity, nonentity; zero-hour. **~-hour**, hour at which planned esp. mil. operation is timed to begin; crucial or decisive moment.

zĕst *n*. piquancy; keen interest or enjoyment, relish, gusto.

zĭg′zăg *n*. succession of straight lines with abrupt alternate right and left turns; something having such lines or sharp turns. *a*. having form of zigzag; with abrupt alternate right and left turns. *adv*. in zigzag manner or course. *v.i.* move in zigzag course.

zĭnc *n*. hard bluish-white metallic element.

zĭnn′ia *n*. kinds of tropical Amer. composite plant with showy flowers.

Zī′on *n*. hill in Jerusalem, centre of Jewish life and worship; the Jewish religion; the Christian Church; the Kingdom of Heaven; Christian (esp. nonconformist) place of worship. **~ism** *n*. movement resulting in re-establishment of a Jewish nation in Israel. **~ist** *n. & a.*

zĭp *n*. (colloq.) (movement accompanied by) light sharp sound as of tearing canvas etc.; energy, force, impetus; zip-fastener. *v.* close or fasten (*up*) with zip-fastener; move or go with sound of zip or with great rapidity or force. **~-fastener**, fastening device of two flexible stringers engaged and disengaged by means of sliding cam pulled between them. **zipp'er** *n.* zip- -fastener. **zipp'ÿ** *a.* lively; quick.

zir'con *n.* translucent crystalline native silicate of zirconium used as gem.

zir'cō'nium *n.* metallic element.

zith'er (*or* -dh-) *n.* musical instrument with flat sound-box and numerous strings, held horizontally and played by plucking.

zō'diăc *n.* (now chiefly astrol.) belt of heavens including all apparent positions of sun and planets as known to ancient astronomers and divided into twelve equal parts called *signs of the ~*.

zō'ētrōpe *n.* mechanical toy with series of images on inner surface of cylinder appearing to move when it is rotated.

zŏm'bie *n.* in voodoo, supernatural force or spirit reanimating and con- trolling corpse; corpse so revived; person thought to resemble zombie, mindless or will-less automaton.

zōne *n.* (arch.) girdle or belt; band or ring, esp. one of series of concentric or alternate stripes of colour, light etc.; each of five encircling regions into which surface of earth is divided by tropics and polar circles; any well-defined tract, region, part of town, etc., esp. one divided off from other parts for particular use or purpose. *v.t.* mark, encircle, with zone; divide into zones, esp. in town planning etc. **zō'nal** *a.*

zōō *n.* place where wild animals are kept for public exhibition.

zōōl'ogÿ *n.* scientific study of animals. **zōōlŏ'gical** *a.*; **~gist** *n.*

zōōm *v.* make, move with, loud low- -pitched buzzing sound; climb, make (aircraft) climb, for short time at high speed and very steep angle; (of cinema or television camera) move rapidly towards or away from object while keeping it in focus, (of image) appear to advance or recede rapidly; make (camera, image) zoom. *n.* act or action of zooming. **~ lens**, camera lens with continuously variable focal length.

zōōmor'phic *a.* representing or imitating animal forms; having form of animal; attributing form or nature of animal to deity etc. **~ism** *n.*

zō'ophÿte *n.* animal resembling plant or flower in form. **zōophÿt'ic** *a.*

zȳ'gote *n.* fertilized ovum, cell arising from union of two gametes.

ADDENDA

ABM *abbr.* anti-ballistic missile.

abort. Also: bring or come to premature end.

ăb'seil (-sāl *or* -zīl) *n.* & *v.i.* (use) climber's method of descending steep slope by sliding down doubled rope.

abstract[1] *a.* Also: (of painting etc.) non-representational.

accelerator. Also: apparatus imparting high velocities to free electrons etc.

acid *n.* Also: (sl.) L.S.D. **~-head,** one who habitually takes L.S.D.

acrȳl'ĭc *a.* **~** *fibre, resin, plastic,* kinds of freq. transparent synthetic thermoplastic substance.

addĭc'tĭve *a.* causing addiction.

ăd'măss *n.* part of community easily influenced by mass publicity, etc.

aero-. **~space** *n.* earth's atmosphere and outer space as field of travel.

ăfrormō'sia (-z-) *n.* ornamental African wood used for furniture.

air. **~space,** air above a country, esp. considered as subject to its jurisdiction.

Al'gŏl (ă-), **ALGOL** *n.* algebraic computer language.

ăl'gorĭthm (-dh-) *n.* process or rules for computing, machine translation, etc.

ămp *n.* ampere.

anti-freeze *n.* & *a.* (additive) lowering freezing-point of water.

approve. **~d school,** training establishment for young people exposed to moral danger or found guilty of offences.

ărcāne' *a.* secret, mysterious.

ăr'tĕfăct *n.* product of human workmanship.

ăr'thropŏd *n.* animal with jointed limbs and hard jointed external skeleton.

audiō- in comb., of sound or hearing. **audio-frē'quencў** *n.* frequency capable of being aurally perceived.

~ typist *n.* one typing direct from tape or other recording. **~-visual** *a.* both aural and visual, esp. of mechanical aids to teaching.

au'todĭdăct *n.* self-taught person.

ăv'ant-gȧrde' (-vahṅ-) *n.* pioneers, innovators, esp. in arts.

back. **~ bench,** any of benches in House of Commons etc. for those not entitled to sit on front benches. **~ bencher,** one who sits on back bench. **~lash,** sudden recoil; slack or play between parts of mechanism etc.; reaction, esp. violent or excessive. **~ projection,** projection from rear on to translucent screen of still or moving background for scene etc.

băng'er *n.* (sl.) sausage; noisy old car.

beat *v.* Also; give light and fluffy consistency to, mix smoothly, by beating or rapid stirring.

bĭdet (bē'dā) *n.* narrow washing-bowl that can be bestridden.

bīōdĕgrā'dable *a.* susceptible to decomposing action of living organisms.

black. **~ box,** (esp.) flight recorder.

blast. Also: *v.i.* (of rocket, etc.) take *off.* **~-off,** blasting off.

bloody. **~-minded,** perverse, tiresome, stubbornly obstructive.

body. **~-stocking,** one-piece undergarment covering body from neck to toes.

bŏng'ō(-drŭm) (-ngg-) *n.* either of pair of small drums played with fingers.

break. **~-through,** breaking through obstacle, enemy's line, etc.; major advance in scientific knowledge etc.

breath'alȳser (brĕ-; -z*er*) *n.* device for measuring amount of alcohol in breath.

bug. Also: flaw, snag; hidden eavesdropping device, e.g. microphone. *v.t.* conceal bug(s) in.

butch (-ŏŏ-) *n.* tough (young) man; lesbian of masculine appearance or behaviour.

bygones. Also: domestic, industrial, etc. objects belonging to past.

caftan. Also: wide-sleeved loose--fitting shirt or dress.

calăn'drĭa *n.* in nuclear reactor, tank containing heavy-water moderator etc.

candē'la *n.* SI unit of luminous intensity.

cănn'abĭs *n.* preparation of Indian hemp, esp. for smoking.

capă'cĭtor *n.* device for obtaining (esp. specified) capacitance.

casual. Also: suitable for informal wear. *n.pl.* casual shoes, clothes.

ceramic. Also: of (making of) substances or objects produced by very-high-temperature firing of non--metallic minerals, esp. clay.

cẽr'mĕt *n.* alloy of ceramic substance with metal.

chalet. Also: small usu. wooden building as beach hut, holiday--camp unit, etc.

chăl'ōne (k-; *or* kā-) *n.* one of group of endocrine secretions having inhibiting effect on physiological process.

clămp[2] *n.* low compact mound, esp. of earth and straw for protecting stored potatoes from frost.

clŏbb'er[1] *n.* (sl.) clothes; equipment, gear.

clŏbb'er[2] *v.t.* (sl.) set on; hit; thrash, beat up.

clōne *n.* group of organisms produced asexually from one individual.

Cō'bŏl, COBOL *n.* computer language for general commercial purposes, using standardized English terms.

colŭm'bĭum *n.* niobium.

computer. ~ **language,** system of characters or symbols and rules used to supply information or instructions to computer. **cŏmpū'terīze** *v.t.* furnish with computer(s); deal with or solve by computer.

cŏnsōr'tĭum (*or* -shĭ-) *n.* (temporary) association or combination, esp. of business, banking, etc. organizations for common purpose.

container. Also: (large, esp. metal) unit of standard shape and size for transporting or storing goods. ~ **ship,** one designed to carry containers. ~ **system,** use of containers for transport of goods.

cŏntĭn'ūō *n.* figured bass as indication to (17th–18th c.) keyboard accompanist of chord-series for improvisation.

cŏnvĕc'tion *n.* conveyance of heat or electricity by movement of heated or electrified air, water, etc. **cŏnvĕc'tor** (**heater**) *n.* appliance that warms room by convection.

cordon. ~ **bleu** (-ẽr), first-class cook.

corps. ~ **de ballet** (kōrdebăl'ā) *n.* ballet company excluding principals.

count. ~**-down,** counting down esp. before missile etc. is launched.

cuff[1]. ~**-link,** pair of linked buttons for fastening cuff.

cūrĕtt'age (-ahzh) *n.* curetting.

dē-brie'fing *n.* examination or interrogation after completion of mission etc.

dēĕscala'tion *n.* reversal, reverse, of escalation.

dĕm'ō *n.* (colloq.) demonstration.

dēsĕg'rēgāte *v.t.* reunite (segregated races, classes, etc.), abolish racial segregation in (schools etc.). ~**ā'tion** *n.*

dī'cey *a.* (sl.) risky, dangerous.

dĭdjerĭdōō' *n.* Australian aboriginal musical wind instrument of tubular shape.

disadvantage. Also: *at a* ~, in disadvantageous position.

D.J. *abbr.* disc jockey.

do[2]. ~**-it-yourself,** applied to work of home handyman etc.

D.O.A. *abbr.* dead on arrival.

dŏdg'ў *a.* (sl.) cunning, artful; awkward, ticklish.

drop. Also: ~ **out,** abandon course or career embarked on, way of life, etc. ~**-out,** one who has dropped out.

duchy. Also: dukedom of Cornwall or Lancaster.

dū'vet (-vā) *n.* quilt (esp down--filled) used in place of upper bedclothes.

dye'līne (dīl-) *n.* (print or copy made

by) method of photographic copying.

èlăs'tomer *n.* substance tending to return to original form after stretching.

electro-. **~motive force** *n.* force set up by difference of potential in electric circuit.

ènăn'tiomōrph *n.* form related to another as object to its mirror image. **~mōr'phic,** **~mōr'phous** *aa.*

E.N.T. *abbr.* ear, nose, and throat.

epilogue. Also: (radio etc.) religious broadcast towards end of day's programmes.

èpŏx'y rĕs'ĭn (-z-) *n.* kinds of usu. thermosetting flexible chemically resistant · synthetic resins, used chiefly in coatings and adhesives.

Er'nĭe (ēr-) *n.* device for drawing prize-winning numbers of Premium Bonds.

E.S.P. *abbr.* extrasensory perception.

estate. **~ car,** passenger car constructed or adapted to carry goods also.

E.T.A. *abbr.* estimated time of arrival.

Expo. *abbr.* Exposition.

fibre. **~-glass :** also, compound plastic with glass fibre as fibrous component.

fish. **~ fingers,** small finger-shaped pieces of fish cooked in breadcrumbs or batter.

flight[1]. **~ recorder,** device in aircraft automatically recording technical details of any flight.

flip. **~ side,** reverse side (of disc).

Fōr'trăn, FORTRAN *n.* computer language for programming scientific problems.

franchise. Also: right to use or market company's goods, services, etc. in particular place.

fraught. Also: tense; distressed, distressing.

front. **~ bench,** in House of Commons etc. one of those traditionally reserved for members of Government and leaders of Opposition.

fŭzz[2] *n.* (sl.) police.

gĭ'ga (*or* jĭ-) in comb., a thousand million (times).

girl. **~ friend,** boy's or man's preferred or usual female companion.

glitch *n.* (sl.) hitch, snag; surge of current or spurious electrical signal; brief irregularity in function or behaviour.

hallū'cĭnogĕn'ĭc (*or* -loo-) *a.* (esp of drugs) inducing hallucination.

hăpp'enĭng *n.* improvised or spontaneous (pseudo-)theatrical entertainment.

hard. Also: (of drugs) addictive. **~ core,** rubble, clinker, etc. used as foundation of road etc.; irreducible minimum. **~ shoulder,** firm level surface for emergency use at side of motorway. **~ware :** also, (colloq., parts of) machine(s), items of equipment, etc. made of metal or opp. to men etc.; esp. (of computer), machine as opp. to programmes etc.

heat. Also: (in female mammals) period of readiness to receive male.

hĕrtz (-ts) *n.* SI unit of frequency, one cycle per second.

HGV *abbr.* Heavy Goods Vehicle(s).

high-rise *a.* tall, multi-storey.

hĭpp'ў *n.* (sl.) person (appearing to be) given to use of hallucinogenic drugs; hipster.

hĭp'ster[2] *n.* person alive to or following the most up-to-date fashions in dress, music, etc.

hot. Also: (of music) performed with vigour, virtuosity, and excitement. **~ line,** permanently open telephone connection.

huddle. Also: (colloq.) close or secret conference.

hў'drofoil *n.* (fast motor-boat, seaplane, etc. with) plate or fin for lifting hull out of water at speed.

hyper-. **~market** *n.* very large self--service store, usu. outside a town.

Hz *abbr.* hertz.

ice. **~-pack,** closely packed field of floating ice; crushed ice in bag or towel applied to head etc.

I.M.F. *abbr.* International Monetary Fund.

initial. **~ĭsm** *n.* abbreviation consisting of initial letters.

instant *a.* Also: (that can be) prepared in an instant.

I.R.O. *abbr.* International Refugee Organization.

iron *n.* Also: steel-headed golf-club.

island *n.* Also: raised place for

pedestrians in roadway, esp. between lines of traffic.

junk[1]. Also: narcotic drug, esp. heroin. ～**ie** *n.* (sl.) drug addict.

K *abbr.* kelvin.

kara′tĕ (-rah-) *n.* Japanese system of unarmed combat using hands, feet, etc. as weapons.

kĕl′vĭn *n.* S.I. unit of thermodynamic temperature.

kick *n.* Also: *for* ～*s*, for thrills, for excitement.

language. Also: computer language.

L(E)M *abbr.* Lunar (Excursion) Module.

lĕx′ĭcal *a.* of vocabulary of a language.

Lib *abbr.* liberation.

lift. ～**-off**, vertical take-off.

lŏg′ō (*or* lō-), **lŏg′otȳpe** *n.* two or more separate letters or figures cast as one type, esp. as trade--name, distinguishing device, etc.

mari′na (-rē-) *n.* basin or dock for mooring pleasure craft.

măs′cŏn *n.* supposed massive concentration of dense matter beneath surface of moon.

mĕl′anĭn *n.* dark-brown pigment in hair, skin, etc.

mĕl′ba toast *n.* very thin crisp toast.

mĕths *n.* (colloq.) methylated spirit.

mĕtrĭcā′tion *n.* conversion to metric system.

micro-. ～**climate** *n.* climate of small area or of organism's immediate surroundings.

mint[2]. Also: (*in*) ～ *condition, state,* (as if) newly issued from mint, perfect.

M.I.R.V. *abbr.* multiple independently targeted re-entry vehicles.

module. Also: standardized unit used esp. in building etc.; independent unit forming part of space-craft.

moon. ～**quake**, tremor of moon's surface analogous to earthquake.

MRCA *abbr.* multi-role combat aircraft.

multi-. ～**-storey** *a.* many-storeyed.

N.E.D.C., colloq. **Nĕdd′ȳ** *abbr.* National Economic Development Council.

O.A.P. *abbr.* old age pensioner.

O.E.C.D. *abbr.* Organization of European Co-operation and Development.

off. ～**-peak**, not at or of (time of) greatest use, intensity, etc.

one. ～**-off**, (colloq.) single example, one only.

open. ～**-plan**, (almost) without partition walls.

ōr′acȳ *n.* ability to hear and understand words.

ōrienteer′ĭng *n.* (competitive sport of) finding and making one's way across rough country with aid of maps and compasses.

over-. ～**-steer** *n.* & *v.i.* (motor vehicle's tendency to) increase sharpness of turn when steered away from straight line.

paĕll′a (pah-) *n.* Spanish dish of rice with chicken, mussels, etc. cooked and served in large flat pan.

pallet[2]. Also: flat board or plate, esp. kind of tray for supporting loads being lifted or in storage.

pă′ratrōōps *n.pl.* airborne troops landing by parachute.

passive. ～ **resistance**, resistance without resort to violence or active opposition.

p.d.q. *abbr.* (sl.) pretty damn quick.

P.E. *abbr.* physical education.

pĕl′ĭcan[2] **crossing** *n.* pedestrian crossing with traffic lights controlled by pedestrians.

perfect. Also: ～ *interval*, (mus.) fourth, fifth, or octave.

permissive. Also: tolerant, indulgent.

phō′tocŏpȳ *n.* & *v.t.* (make) photographic copy (of).

pĭzz′a (-ts*a*; *or* pē-) *n.* Italian open pie of cheese, tomato, etc.

poly-. ～**ester** (**fibre, resin, plastic**) *nn.* kinds of synthetic fibre, resin, plastic, used in paint, moulds, recording tapes, etc. ～**vinyl chloride** *n.* kinds of tough, rigid, chemically inert, electrically resistive thermoplastic resin.

pŏrn *abbr.* (colloq.) pornography.

print. ～**-out**, computer's printed output.

pŭl′săr *n.* pulsating radio star.

P.V.C. *abbr.* polyvinyl chloride.

răd *abbr.* unit of absorbed dose of ionizing radiation.

radio. ～**sonde**, sonde with radio for transmitting information obtained to observer(s) on ground.

radio-. ∼ **star** *n.* source of radiation in space.

R & D *abbr.* Research and Development.

rap[1]. Also: *take the* ∼, take the blame or punishment.

reaction. Also: (colloq.) response to statement, situation, etc.

rēcȳ′cle *v.t.* (esp.) convert (waste) into re-usable material.

rēdĭffū′sion (-zhn) *n.* rebroadcasting of second-hand radio or television material.

rĕgg′ae (-gā) *n.* kind of West Indian music with strongly accented off--beat.

Rie′sling (rēz-; *or* -s-) *n.* (grape used for) dry white wine from Alsace, Hungary, etc.

r.p.m. *abbr.* revolutions per minute.

sacred. ∼ **cow,** idea etc. held to be immune from questioning or criticism.

S.A.E. *abbr.* stamped addressed envelope.

SALT *abbr.* strategic arms limitation talks.

sĕll′otāpe *n.* kind of usu. transparent synthetic adhesive tape. **P.**

sĕm′ĭ *abbr.* (colloq.) semi-detached house.

sĕmĭŏt′ĭcs *n.* study of signs and symbols in relation to meaning as branch of linguistics.

S.E.N. *abbr.* State Enrolled Nurse.

set[2]. Also: setting, stage properties, etc. of theatre or cinema scene.

shock. ∼ **wave,** disturbance produced when body travels through medium at speed greater than that at which medium transmits sound.

SI *abbr. Système International,* International System (of units).

side. ∼-**effect,** any effect of drug etc. other than that it was intended to produce; indirect or secondary consequence.

S.L.B.M. *abbr.* submarine-launched ballistic missile.

slip[3]. ∼-**road,** road giving access to or exit from motorway.

sŏnde *n.* device for obtaining information on atmospheric conditions at high altitudes.

sonic. ∼ **barrier,** sudden large increase in resistance of air to objects moving at speed near that of sound.

sour. ∼**puss,** (orig. U.S.) sour-faced person.

splash. ∼-**down,** landing of spacecraft in sea.

split. ∼-**level,** (of building) in which parts of storey or room are on visibly lower level than adjacent parts.

square *sl.* Also: old-fashioned person.

S.S.R.C. *abbr.* Social Science Research Council.

stage *n.* Also: section of rocket with its own engines and propellant.

state. ∼**craft,** statesmanship.

straight *a.* ∼ **play,** one having plain dialogue without music etc.

stream *n.* Also: any of groups to which in some schools children considered to have similar ability in relation to their age are assigned. ∼**ing** *n.* practice of dividing schoolchildren into streams.

strōbe *n.* apparatus for producing rapidly flashing bright light (∼ *lighting*).

sŭbôr′bĭtal *a.* of less duration or distance than one orbit.

swept. ∼-**back,** (of aircraft wing) with axis running backwards at acute angle to that of aircraft. ∼-**up,** (of hair) brushed up towards top of head.

tăch′ograph (-k-) *n.* device automatically recording speed and running time of motor vehicle.

taxŏn′omȳ *n.* (principles of) scientific classification of organisms. ∼**omer,** ∼**omist** *nn.* ∼**onŏm′ic** *a.*

tĕllūr′ĭc[2] *a.* of the earth.

tĕ′ra- in comb., a million million (times).

tĭm′pani, tȳm- *n.pl.* kettle-drums of orchestra. ∼**ĭst** *n.*

T.I.R. *abbr. Transports Internationaux Routiers,* International Road Transport.

tonne (tŭn) *n.* metric ton, 1000 kilogrammes.

touché (tōō′shā) *int.* acknowledging hit in fencing, telling retort, etc.

town. ∼**scape** *n.* (pictorial representation of) urban scene.

tran′splant (-ahn-) *n.* transplanting, esp. by surgery.

transport, ～cafe, café providing meals for drivers of heavy goods-vehicles.

trĭbŏl′ogy (-jĭ; *or* -ī-) *n.* science and technology of interacting surfaces in relative motion.

trī′marăn *n.* boat with three hulls side by side.

trip *n.* Also: experience induced by hallucinatory or other drug.

U *abbr.* upper-class.

ŭnder-. ～-steer *n.* & *v.i.* (motor vehicle's tendency to) veer back to straight line when steered away from it.

ŭnflăpp′able *a.* imperturbable.

ŭnwīnd′ *v.i.* relax.

ŭp′tight (*or* -īt′) *a.* (colloq.) tense, worried.

Ur′anus (ūr-; *or* -ā′nus) *n.* planet with orbit next outside Saturn's.

U-turn *n.* turning, without reversing, of vehicle to face in opposite direction.

V.A.T., VAT (văt) *abbr.* value-added tax.

V.T.O. *abbr.* vertical take-off (and landing).

WASP *abbr.* White Anglo-Saxon Protestant.

W.(R.)V.S. *abbr.* Women's (Royal) Voluntary Service.

PRONUNCIATION OF PROPER NAMES

THIS list is intended as a guide to the pronunciation of some difficult proper names frequently met with. It makes no claim to completeness, and many geographical names in particular have had to be omitted.

One or two general points may perhaps be noted here: Classical names ending in -*es* are usually pronounced (-ēz). In New Zealand etc. native names are pronounced with all vowels sounded (and pronounced as Italian vowels, i.e. *a* = ah, *e* = ā or ĕ, *i* = ē or ĭ, *u* = ōō). The U.S. pronunciation of some American place-names differs from the usual English pronunciation; in the following list such specifically U.S. pronunciations are preceded by an asterisk.

There are many proper names (e.g. Kerr, Smyth) the pronunciation of which varies according to the family or individual referred to; such names have usually been omitted.

The symbol *ğ* (= 'soft' *g* in *ginger*) has been employed in this list, in addition to those used in indicating pronunciation in the body of the dictionary.

Aar'on (ār-)
Abbeville (ăb'vēl)
Abĕd'nĕgō
A'bel (ā-)
Ab'ĕlărd (ă-)
Aberfan (ăbervăn')
Abergavĕnn'ğ [place] (ă-)
Abergavĕnny [surname] (ăbergĕn'ĭ)
Abĭ'jah (-*a*)
Aboukir (ahbōōkēr')
A'brahăm (ā-)
Abruz'zi (-brōōtsĭ)
Abȳ'dŏs
Accra (akrah')
Acĕl'dama (-k- *or* -s-)
Achates (akā'tēz)
Ach'erŏn (ăk-)
Achilles (akĭl'ēz)
Achĭt'ophĕl (*ak*-)
Ad'ĕlaide (ă-)
A'den (ā-)
Adĭrŏn'dăck (ă-)
Adonā'ĭs (ă-)
Adō'nĭs
Adrĭăt'ĭc (ā-)
Æğē'an
Æğī'na
Æl'frĭc (ă-; *or* -ch)
Ænē'ăs
Æ'nĕĭd
Æ'olus
Æ'schўlus (-k-)

Æ'sŏp
Afghan (ăf'găn)
Afghăn'ĭstăn (ăfg-; *or* -ahn)
A'găg (ā-)
Agincourt (ăj'ĭnkôrt)
A'gra (ah- *or* ă-)
Aï'da (ah-ē-)
Aix-la-Chapelle (ā'ks-lah-shăpĕl')
Aix-les-Bains (ā'ks-lā-băṅ)
A'jax (ā-)
Alabama (ălabah'ma; *-bă-)
Alădd'ĭn
Albani (ălbah'nĭ)
Al'banў (awl-)
Alcan'tara (ălkahn-)
Alcĕs'tĭs (ă-)
Alcĭbī'adēs (ă-; -z)
Aldĕb'aran (ă-)
Aldeburgh (awld'boro)
Alğecīr'as (ă-; *or* -sēr-)
Alğēr'ĭa (ă-)
Algiers (ăljērz')
Allahabad (ăla-habăd')
Alleghany (ălĭgā'nĭ; *or* -ănĭ)
Almerĭ'a (ă-)
Alnwick (ăn'ĭk)
Aloysius (ălōĭsh'*u*s)
Alsace (ăl'săs; *or* -ăs')
Amiens [French city] (ăm'ĭăṅ)
Amiens [in Shakespeare] (ăm'ĭens)
A'mŏs (ā-)
Amphĭt'rўon (ă-)

Anăc'rèon
Ananī'as (ă-)
Anchises (ăngkī'sēz)
Andes (ăn'dēz)
An'droclēs (ă-; -z)
Andrŏm'ache (ă-; -akĭ)
Andrŏm'èda (ă-)
Andrŏn'ĭcus [in Shakespeare] (ă-)
Anğĕl'ĭcō (ă-)
An'ğèvĭn (ă-)
Angōr'a (ăngg-; or ăng'gora)
Ank'ara (ă-)
Antæ'us (ă-)
Anthæa (ăn'thĭa)
Anthony (ăn'tonĭ)
Antĭg'onè (ă-)
Antĭg'ūa (ă-; or -ēgwa or -ēga)
Antĭn'ōus (ă-)
Antonī'nus (ă-)
Apĕll'ēs (-z)
Aphrodī'tè (ă-)
Apŏllĭnār'ĭs (or -nār̄-)
Apŏll'yon
Appalā'chĭan (ă-; or -ăch-)
Aquī'năs
Arăch'nè (-kn-)
Archimedes (ār̄kĭmē'dēz)
Arctūr'us (ār̄-)
Arèŏpağĭt'ĭca (ă-; or -g-)
Arèthū'sa (ă-; -za)
Arğenti'na (-ēna)
Ar'ğentīne (ār̄-)
Argyll (ār̄gĭl')
Arĭăd'nè (ă-)
Ar'ĭel (ār̄-)
Aries (ār̄'ĭēz)
Arĭmathæ'a (ă-)
Arĭstī'dēs (ă-; -z)
Arĭstŏph'anēs (ă-; -z)
A'rĭstŏtle (ă-)
Arizō'na (ă-)
Arkansas (ār̄'kansaw)
Armē'nĭa (ār̄-)
Artaxerxes (ār̄tagzér̄'ksēz)
Ar'tèmĭs (ār̄-)
A'run (ă-)
A'rundel (ă-)
Ascham (ăs'kam)
Asia (ā'sha)
Assisĭ (ăsē'zĭ)
Assouan (ăsōŏăn')
Astār̄'tè (ă-)
Astrakhan (ăstrakăn')
Atalăn'ta (ă-)
A'tè (ā- or ah-)
Athènæ'um (ă-)

Athē'nè
Athens (ă-; -z)
At'ropŏs (ă-)
Au'chĭnlèck (-k-; or ŏch-)
Auğē'ăs
Augŭs'tĭne
Aurē'lĭus
Autŏl'ўcus
Av'alon (ă-)
Avignon (ă'vēnyawṅ)
A'von (ā-)
Ayscough (ăs'kū)
Azores' (-ōr̄z)
Az'rāel (ă-)

Bā'al
Bā'bel
Băb'ўlon
Băcch'us (-k-)
Bach (bahch)
Ba'den (bah-)
Bā'den-Pow'ell (-ōel)
Bae'dèker (bā-)
Bagehot (băğ'et)
Bahamas (ba-hah'maz)
Baikal (bīkahl')
Bălèă'rĭc (or balēr̄'ĭc)
Bal'kan (bawl-)
Bā'llĭol
Bălmŏ'ral
Bălthazār̄' [in Shakespeare]
Balu'chĭstăn (-lōōk-; or -ăn' or -ahn')
Băn'tu (-tōō)
Barăbb'as
Bār̄bā'dos (-ōz)
Bār̄cèlō'na
Bār̄'mècīde
Barō'da
Bā'shăn
Băs'ra (-z-; or bŭs-)
Bassa'nĭō (-ahn-)
Băstille' (-tēl)
Basu'tōlănd (-ōō-)
Băt'on Rouge (rōōzh)
Bau'cĭs
Bayeux (bīyêr̄', bā-yōō')
Bayreuth (bī'roit)
Bea'consfield (bĕ- or bē-)
Beauchamp (bē'cham)
Beaulieu (bū'lĭ)
Beaune (bōn)
Bĕchua'na (-kūahna; or bĕch-)
Bèĕl'zèbŭb
Beethoven (bā'tōven)
Beh'rĭng (bār̄-)
Beirut (bārōōt'; or bā'-)

Bĕl'gium (-jum)
Bē'lĭal
Bĕllăgg'ĭō (-j-)
Bĕllĕ'rophon
Bĕll'ĭngham (-jam)
Bĕlli'nĭ (-lē-)
Belvoir (bē'ver)
Bénār'ēs (-z)
Bengal (bĕnggawl')
Bĕn'tham (-tam)
Berkeley (bark'lĭ)
Bĕrk'eley [America] (-kl-)
Berkshire (bark'sher)
Bĕrlĭn'
Berlioz (bar'lĭōz)
Bĕrmū'da
Berwick (bĕ'rĭk)
Bethune [English surname] (bē'ten)
Bĭăf'ra (or bī-)
Bicester (bĭs'ter)
Bĭd'ĕford
Bĭhar'
Bĭlba'ō (-ah- or -ā-)
Blanc (-ahṅ)
Blĕn'heim (-nĭm)
Blériot (blĕ'rĭō)
Bloem'fŏntein (-ōō-; -ān)
Blücher (blōō'ker)
Blȳth (or -dh; or blī)
Bōadĭcĕ'a
Bōanĕr'ğēs (-z)
Bocca'cciō (-kahch-)
Bō'diham (-dĭam)
Bō'er (or boor)
Bōē'thĭus
Bohun (bōōn)
Boleyn (bōōl'ĭn; or -ĭn')
Bō'naparte
Boötes (bō-ō'tēz)
Bŏrdeaux' (-dō)
Bŏrdō'nĕ
Bŏr'ĕăs
Bŏs'ton (or *baws-)
Bŏtswa'na (-wah-)
Bŏttĭcell'ĭ (-chĕlĭ)
Boulogne (bōōlōn'; or -oin')
Bour'bon (boor-)
Bourchier (bow'cher)
Bow (bō)
Bŏz (or bōz)
Braemar' (brā-)
Bra'senōse (-zn-; -z)
Brazĭl'
Breadal'bane (-ĕdawl-)
Brough (brŭf)
Brougham (brōōm or brōō'am)

Bruges (brōōzh)
Buccleuch (buklōō')
Būcĕph'alus
Buch'an (bŭk-)
Būchăn'an (-k-)
Bū'charĕst' (-ker-)
Būdapĕst'
Buenos Aires (bwĕn'osar'ĭz; or bwā- or -sīr-)
Būr'leigh (-lĭ)
Bȳr'on
Bysshe (bĭsh)
Bȳzăn'tĭum (or bī-)

Căb'ot
Cā'dĭz (or kadĭz')
Cadog'an (-ŭg-)
Cæd'mon (kă-)
Caen (kahṅ)
Cæsar (sē'zer)
Cagliostro (kălĭŏs'trō)
Cai'aphăs (kī-)
Cairo (kīr'ō)
Caius [Roman name] (kī'us)
Caius [Cambridge] (kēz)
Căl'ais (-ā or -ĭ or -ĭs)
Călĕdō'nĭa
Calĭg'ūla
Callī'opĕ
Căm'brĭdge
Cămbȳ'sēs (-z)
Cămpa'gna (-ahnya)
Campbell (kăm'bl)
Cā'naan (-nan)
Căn'berra
Căndā'cĕ
Canō'pus
Carăc'tacus
Carew' (-ōō)
Carew [Thomas, 1589–1639] (kar'ĭ)
Car'ey
Carlisle' (-ĭl)
Carmar'then (-dh-)
Carnar'von
Carnĕg'ie (-gĭ; or -āgĭ)
Caroli'na
Căsabĭăn'ca
Căssĭopei'a (-ĭa)
Căstile' (-ēl)
Căthay'
Catrĭ'ona (or kătrĭō'na)
Catŭll'us
Căv'ell (or kavĕl')
Cavour' (-oor)
Cecil (sĕsl or sĭsl)
Cĕcĭl'ĭa

Cellini (chĕlē'nĭ)
Cenci (chĕn'chĭ)
Cĕr'ēs (-z)
Cĕr̆văn'tēs (-z)
Césăr̆'ĕwĭtch (-z-)
Ceylŏn' (sĭ-)
Cĕzănne' (sā-)
Chablis (shăb'lē)
Chăl'dees (k-; -z)
Chăl'kĭs (k-)
Chamonix (shăm'onē)
Chapultĕpĕc' (chahpool-)
Chă'rĭng Crŏss (or chār̆-)
Charlemagne (shār̆l'emān)
Chār̆'on (k-)
Chār̆'teris (-terz)
Charўb'dĭs (k-)
Chăt'ham (-tam)
Chautau'qua (sha-; -kwa)
Chekhov (chĕch'ov)
Cherbourg (shĕr̆'boorg)
Cher'wĕll (chár̆-)
Cheyne (chā'nĭ; or -n)
Chicago (shĭkah'gō, *shĭkaw'gō)
Chĭl'ė
Chiswick (chĭz'ĭk)
Chloe (klō'ĭ)
Cholmondeley (chŭm'lĭ)
Chopin (shŏp'ăṅ or shō-)
Cicero (sĭs'erō)
Cimabu'e (chē-; ōōĭ)
Cimarō'sa (chē-; -z-)
Cĭncĭnnăt'ĭ (or -ah-)
Cĭr̆'cė
Cĭr̆'encĕster (or sĭs'ĭster)
Clār̆'a (or -âr̆-)
Clā'verhouse (or klā'verz)
Cler'kenwĕll (klár̆-)
Clĭ'ō
Clough (klŭf, klōo)
Cockaigne' (-ān)
Cockburn (kō'bern)
Cœur de Lion (kĕr̆delē'awṅ)
Colbourne (kō'bern)
Cŏl'chĭs (-k-)
Cologne' (-ōn)
Colom'bō (-ŭm- or -ŏm-)
Colōn'
Cŏlora'dō (-ah-; *-ă-)
Colquhoun (ko-hōōn')
Cō'mō
Comte (kawṅt)
Connect'ĭcut (-nĕt-)
Con'stable (kŭn-)
Cophĕt'ūa
Cŏr̆dĭller'a (-lyāra)

Cŏr̆neille' (-nā)
Cŏ'rot (-rō)
Cŏrrĕgg'ĭō (-j-)
Cŏr̆'tĕs (-z; or -ĭz)
Cŏs'ta Rĭ'ca (rē-)
Cow'per (kōō-)
Creusa (krēōō'za)
Crichton (krĭ'ton)
Crĭmė'a
Crŏ'ce (-chĭ)
Crœ'sus (krē-)
Cruick'shănk (krōōk-)
Cullŏd'en
Cўm'beline (-lēn)
Cўn'ĕwulf (k-; -ōōlf)
Cўp'rĭan
Cўrē'nė
Cўthēr̆'a
Czech (chĕk)

Dæ'dalus
Dahō'mey (da-h-)
Dakō'ta
Dăl'ai La'ma (-lĭlah-)
Dăl'zĭel (or dĕĕl')
Dăm'oclĕs (-z)
Dā'mon
Dăn'āë (-ĭ)
Dăn'tė
Dăph'nė
Darĭ'us
Daudet (dō'dā)
Dăv'entrў (or dā'ntrĭ)
Da'vŏs (dah-; or davōs')
Debū'ssy (-ē)
Décăm'eron
De Crespigny (dekrĕp'ĭnĭ; or -krĕs-)
Degas (dā'gah or degah')
Dĕlagō'a
De la Mare (dĕlamār̆')
Delhi (dĕl'ĭ)
Dē'lĭus
Dĕl'phĭ
Dĕmē'ter
Dĕmē'trĭus (or -mĕt-)
Dĕmŏc'rĭtus
Dē'mŏs
Dĕmŏs'thenĕs (-z)
Dĕn'bigh (-bĭ)
Der'bў (dár̆-; *dĕr̆-)
De Reszke (derĕs'kĭ)
Dĕr̆'went
Descartes (dā'kār̆t)
Desdĕmō'na (dĕz-)
Des Moines (dĭmoin')
Dĕtroit'

Deuterŏn'omў
Dĭăn'a
Diderot (dĕ'derō)
Dĭ'dō
Dieppe (dēĕp')
Dijon (dē'zhawṅ)
Dĭŏclē'tian (-shĭan)
Dĭŏg'ĕnēs (-z)
Dĭomē'dēs (-z)
Dĭonў'sĭus (or -ĭs-)
Dĭonў'sus
Dĭsrae'lĭ (-zrāl-)
Dĭ'vĕs (-z)
Domĭ'tian (-shĭan)
Dŏn Giova'nnĭ (jōvah-)
Dŏn Ju'an (jōōan)
Dŏnne
Donne [John, 1573–1631] (dŭn)
Dŏn Quĭx'ōte
Do'theboys (dōōdhe-)
Doug'las (dŭg-)
Drey'fus (drā-)
Dŭb'lĭn
Dŭl'wich (-lĭj)
Dū'mas (-mah)
Dū Maurier (mŏr'ĭă)
Dŭmfries' (-ēs)
Dŭnē'dĭn
Dŭnlaoghaire (-lār'e)
Durham (dŭ'ram)
Dvorak (dvŏr'zhăk)
Dўm'oke

Ebbw (ĕb'ōō)
Ecclēsĭăs'tēs (ĭk-; -zĭ-; -z)
Ed'ĭnburgh (ĕ-; -buru)
Eğēr'ĭa (ĭ-)
Ei'ffel Tower (ĭf-)
Einstein (īn'stīn)
Eire (ār'e)
El Dorado (ĕldorah'dō)
El'gĭn (ĕ-)
E'lĭ (ē-)
E'lĭa (ē-)
E'lў (ē-)
Empĕd'oclēs (ĕ-; -z)
Endўm'ĭon (ĕ-)
Eng'land (ĭngg-)
Entĕbb'ė (ĕ-)
Eph'ėsus (ĕf-)
Epĭcūr'us (ĕ-)
E'rėwhŏn (ĕ-)
Erie (ēr'ĭ)
Erin (ĕ'rĭn or ēr'-)
Er'ŏs (ēr- or ĕr-)
Es'tė (ĕ-)

Esthō'nĭa (ĕst-)
Etherege (ĕth'erĭj)
E'ton (ē-)
Eubœa (ūbĭ'a)
Eu'clĭd
Euphrā'tēs (-z)
Eu'phūēs (-z)
Eurĭp'ĭdēs (ūr-; -z)
Europe (ūr'op)
Eurўd'ĭcē (ūr-)
Eutēr'pė
Evėli'na (ĕ-; -ēna)
E'velўn (ē- or ĕ-)
Eyck (īk)
Ezē'kĭel (ĭ-)

Fā'gĭn
Făll'odon
Făr'quhar (-kwer or -ker)
Făt'ĭma
Fa(u)lk'land (fawk-)
Faust (fowst)
Featherstonehaugh (făn'shaw)
Fēr'măn'agh (-na)
Fĭde'lĭō (-dā-)
Fiennes (fĭnz)
Fie'solė (fēāz-)
Fĭg'arō
Fiji (fē'jē)
Fĭnĭsterre' (-ār)
Flŏr'ēs (-z)
Flŏ'rĭda
Foch (fŏsh)
Folkes'tone (fōks-)
Fŏrtūnā'tus
Fowey (foi)
Frăncĕs'ca (or -chĕs-)
Freud (froid)
Frö'bel (frēr-)
Frŏ'bĭsher
Frome (-ōōm)
Froude (frōōd)
Frowde (-owd or -ōōd)

Gael (gāl)
Galăp'agos
Gā'lėn
Gălĭle'o (-āō or -ēō)
Gallĭp'olĭ
Galsworthy (gaw'lzwerdhĭ)
Găm'bĭa
Găn'ğēs (-z)
Gĕdd'ės (g-)
Gĕm'ĭnĭ (ğ-)
Gĕn'ėsĭs (ğ-)
Gėnē'va (ğ-)

Gĕn′ŏa (ğ-)
Geoff′rey (ğĕf-)
Gha′na (gah-)
Ghirlăndai′o (gēr-; -dĭ′yō)
Giaour (jowr)
Gĭbral′tar (ğ-; -awl-)
Gĭd′ėa (g-)
Gĭl′ĕăd (g-)
Gĭllĕtte′ (ğ-)
Giŏr̄ĝiō′nė (ğ-)
Gĭŏtt′ō (ğ-)
Giovanni (ğōvah′nĭ)
Glamis (glahmz)
Glăs′gow (-zgō)
Gloucester (glŏs′ter)
Gluck (-ōōk)
Glȳnde′bourne (-n(d)b-)
Gō′a
Gŏd′almĭng
Gōda′varĭ (-dah-)
Godĭ′va
Goethe (gĕr′te)
Golĭ′ath
Gotham [Notts.] (gŏt′am)
Gō′tham [New York]
Gounod (gōō′nō)
Gough (gŏf)
Gracchus (grăk′us)
Grătia′nō (-shĭah-)
Greenwich (grĭn′ĭj)
Greuse (grēr̄z)
Grieg (grēg)
Grĭn′delwald (-vahld)
Groote Schoor (grō′tskoor)
Grosvenor (grō′vner)
Guadeloupe (gwahdėlōōp′)
Guăr̄nēr̄′ius (gw-)
Guatemala (gwahtĭmah′la)
Gudrun (gōōd′rōōn)
Guelph (gwĕlf)
Guernsey (gēr̄n′zĭ)
Guiana (gĭah′na)
Guinea (gĭn′ĭ)
Guinness (gĭn′ĭs)
Gŭsta′vus (-tah-)
Guyana (gĭah′na)

Haar′lem (har̄-)
Hā′dĕs (-z)
Hā′gar̄
Hăgg′āī
Hague (hāg)
Haifa (hī′fa)
Hai′nault (-awt)
Hai′tĭ (or hī-)
Hăk′luyt (-ōōt)

Hănsĕăt′ĭc
Hare′wōōd (har̄-; locally har̄-)
Har̄′lĕch (-k)
Hă′run-ăl-Răsch′id (-rōō-; -shĭd)
Harwich (hă′rij)
Har̄′wĭch [America]
Hausa (hou′za)
Havăn′a
Havre (hah′vr)
Hawaii (hawĭ′ē)
Haw′arden (-erd-; or har̄d-)
Haw′orth (or how′erth)
Hay′dn (hī-)
Hē′bė
Hĕb′rĭdĕs (-z)
Hĕc′atė
He′gel (hāg-)
Hĕğ′ĭra (or hĭjĭr̄′a)
Hei′delbēr̄g (hī-)
Heine (hī′ne)
Hĕll′ėspŏnt
Hĕm′ans (-z)
Hĕn′gĭst (-ngg-)
Hepb′urn (hĕb-)
Hē′raclĕs (-z)
Hĕraclī′tus
Hēr̄cūlā′nĕum
Hēr̄′cūlĕs (-z)
Hĕ′rėford
Hĕ′rėward
Hēr̄′mĕs (-z)
Hēr̄mī′onė
Hĕrō′dĭăs
Hĕrŏd′otus
Hert′ford [England] (har̄f-)
Hēr̄t′ford [America]
Herts (har̄ts)
Hĕspĕ′rĭdĕs (-z)
Hiawath′a (-wŏ-)
Hĭl′dėbrănd
Hĭmalay′a (or hĭmah′lĭa)
Hĭppŏc′ratĕs (-z)
Hĭppŏl′y̆ta
Hŏbb′ėma
Hō′bōken
Hoh′enlĭn′den (hōen-)
Hŏl′bein (-bīn; or hō-)
Hol′born (hōben)
Hŏlōfĕr̄′nĕs (-z)
Hŏl′y̆rōōd
Hŏl′y̆wĕll
Home (hŭm or hōm)
Hō′mer
Hŏndūr̄′ăs
Hŏnolu′lu (-lōōlōō)
Hou′ston (hŭs-)

Houyhnhnm (hwĭn'ĭm)
Hū'dĭbrăs
Hūr'on
Hȳ'derabăd
Hȳğei'a (-ĭa)
Hȳmĕtt'us
Hȳpā'tia (-shĭa)
Hȳpēr'ĭon (or -ĕr-)

Iago (ĭah'gō)
Ian (ĭ'an)
Iăn'thė (ī-)
Ibēr'ĭa (ī-)
Ic'arus (ĭ- or ī-)
Idaho (ī'da-hō)
Idūmė'a (ī-)
Illĭnois' (ĭ-; -noi)
Illȳ'rĭa (ĭ-)
Indĭăn'a (ĭ-)
Indĭanăp'olĭs (ĭ-)
Indonē'sia (ĭ-; -zha or -sha or -sĭa)
Inge [surname] (ĭng or ĭnj)
Ingelow (ĭn'ğĭlō)
In'ĭgō (ĭ-)
In'terlaken (ĭ-; -lah-)
Iōlăn'thė (ī-)
Iŏl'chus (ĭ-; -k-)
Iō'na (ī-)
I'owa (ī-)
Iphĭğēnī'a (ĭ-)
Iran (ĭrahn')
Iraq (ĭrahk')
I'roquois (ĭ-; -kwoi or -kwah)
Isaac (ī'zac)
Isaiah (īzī'a)
I'sĭs (ī-)
Islam (ĭz'lahm)
I'sleworth (īzelw-)
Ismailia (ĭzmah-ē'lĭa)
Isŏc'ratēs (ĭ-; -z)
Isolde (ĭzŏl'da)
Ispahan (ĭspa-hahn')
Is'rāel (ĭz-; or -rĭ-)
Ith'aca (ĭ-)
Ixī'on (ĭ-)

Jaeger (yā'ger)
Jā'ĕl
Jaipur (jīpoor')
Jāĭr'us (or jīr'us)
Jakār'ta
Jamai'ca
Jā'nus
Jā'phĕth
Jā'ques [in Shakespeare] (-kwĭz)
Ja'va (jah-)

Jėhō'vah (-va)
Jē'hū
Jĕk'ўll
Je'na (yā-)
Jĕ'rome (or jerōm')
Jĕr'vaulx (-vō)
Jōb
Jōhănn'ėsbūrg
Jō'lĭĕt
Jōsē'phus
Jungfrau (yōōng'frou)

Kabul (kah'bōōl)
Kălahār'ĭ
Kănsas (-nz-)
Kara'chĭ (-rah-)
Kăshmir' (-ēr)
Kăttėgăt'
Kauff'mann (kow-)
Kē'ble
Kē'dār
Kĕntŭck'ў
Kĕn'ўa (or kē-)
Kēr'guelėn (-gĭl- or kêrgū')
Keswick (kĕz'ĭk)
Keynes (kānz)
Khārt(o)um' (k-; -ōōm)
Khayyam (kī-ahm')
Khȳ'ber (k-)
Kiel (kēl)
Kiev (kē'ef)
Kil'ĭmanjār'ŏ
Kĭrkcud'bright (-kōō'brĭ)
Knollys (nōlz)
Kodaly (Kodah'ē)
Kreisler (krī'sler)
Kreutzer (kroi'tser)

Lăbouchère' (-bōōshār)
Lăch'ėsĭs (-k-)
Lāēr'tēs (-z)
Lafitte (lahfēt')
Lā'gŏs
L'Alle'grō (lălā-)
Lancelot (lahnslet)
Lāŏc'ōōn
Lapū'ta
Lascelles (lăs'els)
Las Pal'mas (lahs pahl-)
Lau'rence (lŏ-)
Lausănne' (lōz-)
Lăv'ėngrō
Lăvoi'sier (-vwahzyā)
Law'rence (lŏ-)
Lea'mĭngton (lĕm-)
Lĕăn'der (or lĭ-)

Lĕ′da
Le Fanu (lēv′anu; or lĕf-)
Le Fevre (fĕ′ver)
Leicester (lĕs′ter)
Leigh (lē)
Lein′ster (lĕn-)
Leip′zĭg (līp-)
Leith (lē-)
Lĕ′land
Lĕ′lў
Lĕn′ĭn
Leominster (lĕm′ster)
Lesō′tho (-tō)
Leonâr′dō (lā-on-)
Lĕ′thė (or -ē)
Lew′ės
Ley′den (lā- or lī-)
Lha′sa (lah-)
Liège (-āzh)
Li′ma (lē-)
Lĭmoges′ (-ōzh)
Lincoln (lĭng′kon)
Lĭszt (-st)
Lĭv′ў
Llewĕll′ўn (lōō-)
Loh′engrĭn (lōĭ-)
Lon′don (lŭn-)
Lŏngĭ′nus (-nj-)
Lôr′ėlei (-ī)
Lŏs An′ğėlēs (ănj-; * or ăngg-; -z)
Louisĭăn′a (lōō-ēz-)
Louisville (lōō′ĭvĭl)
Lourdes (loord)
Lou′vre (lōō-)
Lў′cĭdăs
Lўcûr′gus
Lўm′ĭngton
Lympne (lĭm)
Lўsăn′der

Mă′cėdon
Măcėdō′nĭa
Machĭavĕll′ĭ (măk-)
Mackay (makī′)
Maclean (maklān′)
Macleod (maklowd′)
Madeir′a (-ēra)
Madrăs′ (or -ahs)
Madrĭd′
Maecē′năs (mī-)
Mae′lström (māl-)
Mae′terlĭnck (mah-)
Măf′ėkĭng
Măg′dalėn [Biblical name]
Magdalen [Oxford] (mawd′lĭn)
Măgdalē′nė [Biblical name]

Magdalene [Cambridge] (mawd′lĭn)
Magĕll′an
Măggĭôr′ė (-j-)
Mag′yar (măg- or mŏd-)
Mahōn (ma-h-; or -ōōn; or mahn)
Mahony (mah′nĭ)
Măl′achī (-k-)
Mala′wĭ (-lah-)
Malay′sĭa (-z-)
Măl′herbe (-lârb)
Măll
Măl′orў
Mal′ta (mawl-)
Mal′vern (mawl-)
Măn′et (-ā)
Maori (mowr′ĭ)
Marī′a [English name]
Mari′a (-ēa) [Latin name]
Mâr′ĭon (or mă-)
Marjoribănks (mârch′b-; or -sh-)
Mârque′sas (-kā-)
Mârseilles′ (-āls)
Mâr′tĭneau (-nō)
Mârtĭnique′ (-ēk)
Mâr′ўland (*mĕ′rĭland)
Mărylebone (-ĭlebon; or mă′rĭbon)
Măssachu′sĕtts (-ōō-)
Măss′enet (-enā)
Mătabē′lė
Maurī′tius (-shus)
Mazzini (mădzē′nĭ)
Mĕch′lĭn (-kl-)
Mĕdė′a
Mĕd′ĭci (-chĭ)
Mĕdi′na (-ē-)
Mei′stersĭnger (mī-)
Mĕlpŏm′ėnė
Mĕn′ai (-nī)
Mĕn′delssohn (-son or -sōn)
Mĕnėlā′us
Mêrcā′tor
Mêrcē′dēs (-z)
Mêrcū′tiō (-shĭ-)
Mĕ′rėdĭth (or -rĕd′-)
Mĕrĭon′ėth
Mĕssi′na (-sē-)
Mĕtt′ernĭch (-k-)
Mey′nell (mĕ- or mā-)
Mĭăm′ĭ
Mĭch′ĭgan (-sh-)
Mi′dăs
Mĭlăn′ (or mĭl′an)
Mĭll′ais (-ā)
Minnėăp′olĭs
Minnėsō′ta
Mĭnn′ėsĭnger

Mĭrăn′da
Mĭssour′ĭ (-oor-; *mĭz-)
Mĭthrĭdā′tēs (-z)
Mĭtўlē′nė
Mōbile′ (-ēl)
Moh′ĭcan (mōĭ-; *properly* mō-hē′-)
Mohun (mōōn)
Mō′lière (-lĭār; *or* mŏ-)
Mŏn′acō (*or* mŏnah′-)
Mŏntaigne′ (-ān)
Mŏntăn′a
Mŏntrėal′ (-awl)
Môr′pheus (-fūs)
Mŏs′cow (-ō)
Moulmein′ (-mān)
Mōzambique′ (-bĕk)
Multan (mōōl′tahn)
Mū′nĭch (-k)
Mūrĭll′ō
Mўcē′næ
Mўtĭlē′ne (*or* -ē)

Nairō′bĭ (nīr-)
Nā′mĭer (*or* namēr′)
Nā′omĭ
Nā′pĭer (*or* napēr′)
Napō′lėon
Natăl′
Năv′ajo (-a-hō)
Nĕm′ėsĭs
Nėpal′ (awl)
Nĕva′da (-vah-; *-ă-)
New′foundland (-fund-; *or* nūfow′-)
New Or′leans (ôrlēnz)
Nĭăg′ara
Nibelung (nē′belōōng)
Nietzsche (nē′che)
Nĭ′ģer
Nĭģēr′ĭa
Nĭl′gĭrĭ
Nĭn′ėveh (-vĭ)
Nĭ′obė
Norwich (nŏ′rĭj)
Nўăs′a

O′ban (ō-)
Oberămm′ergau (ō-; -gow)
O′beron (ō-)
Odўss′eus (-ūs)
Od′ўssey (ŏ-)
Œ′dĭpus (ē-)
Œnō′nė (ē-)
Ohĭ′ō (ŏ-h-)
Oklahō′ma (ō-)
Omaha (ō′ma-hah; *-aw)
Oman (ōmahn′ *or* ō′măn)

On′ions (ŭn-; *or* onĭ′-)
Ontār′ĭo (ŏ-)
Ophē′lĭa (ō-)
Orĕs′tēs (ŏ-; -z)
Orĭ′on (ŏ-)
Orlė′ans (ôr-; -z)
Orpheus (ôr′fūs)
Orsi′no (-sē-)
Osīr′ĭs (ō-)
O′sler (ō-)
Ota′gō (ōtah-)
Othĕll′ō (ō-)
Ottawa (ŏt′awa)
Ouida (wē′da)
Ouse (ōōz)
Ov′ĭd (ŏ-)

Păderew′skĭ (-ĕvskĭ)
Păgani′nĭ (-nē-)
Pagliacci (păliăch′ĭ)
Pakĭstan′ (pah-; -ahn)
Păl′amon
Pălĕstri′na (-ēn-)
Păll′ăs
Păll′ Măll′ (*or* pĕl′mĕl′)
Pălmȳr′a
Pănama′ (-ah)
Pā′phŏs
Pā′raguay (-gwĭ *or* -gwā; *or* -gwĭ′)
Pârnăss′us
Parŏll′ės
Păsteur′ (-êr)
Patrŏc′lus
Pau (pō)
Pausā′nĭăs
Pavĭ′a
Pĕg′asus
Pēkĭn′
Pē′leus (-lūs)
Pĕloponnē′sus
Pē′lŏps
Pėnĕl′opė
Pĕnnsўlvā′nĭa
Pĕnthĕsĭlė′a
Pepys (pēps *or* pĕps *or* pĕp′ĭs)
Pêr′dĭta
Pêrgole′sė (-lāz-)
Pĕ′rĭclēs (-z)
Pĕ′rrault (-rō)
Pêrsĕph′onė
Pêrsĕp′olĭs
Pêr′seus (-ūs)
Peru′ (-ōō)
Pĕrugi′nō (-ōōjē-)
Peshawar (pėshôr′)
Pĕstalŏzz′i (-tsĭ)

Pĕsth (-st)
Pĕt′ra
Pĕt′rȧrch (-k)
Pĕtru′chĭo (-ōōk- or -ōōch-)
Phæ′dra
Phā′ĕthon
Phȧr′aoh (-rō)
Phȧrsā′lĭa
Phĭlē′mŏn (or fī-)
Phō′cĭs
Phœ′bė (fē-)
Phœnicia (fēnĭsh′ĭa)
Phrȳ′nė
Pie′dmont (pē- or pyā-)
Pīēr′ĭan
Pĭla′tus (-ah-)
Pĭnēr′ō
Pīræ′us
Pisces (pĭs′ēz; or pī-)
Plăntăg′ėnĕt
Plā′tō
Plei′ad (plī- or plē-)
Plĭn′ў
Plotī′nus
Plu′tȧrch (-ōō-; -k)
Plўm′outh (-uth)
Pŏlĭx′enēs (-z)
Pŏllaiuo′lō (-lī-ōō-ō-)
Pŏlўb′ĭus
Pŏlўc′ratēs (-z)
Pŏlўphē′mus
Pom′frėt (pŭm-)
Pŏmpei′i (-ēī or -āē)
Pŏn′tėfrăct
Pȯrt Said (sah′ĭd or sād)
Pŏsei′don (-sī-)
Potō′măc
Poughkeep′sĭe (pokĭp-)
Poussin (pōō′săṅ)
Pō′wўs
Prăxĭt′elēs (-z)
Prėtōr′ĭa
Prī′am
Promē′theus (-ūs)
Prosĕr′pĭna
Prō′teus (-ūs)
Proust (prōōst)
Psȳchė (s-)
Ptŏl′emў (t-)
Puccini (pōōchē′nĭ)
Pŭnjab′ (-ahb)
Pў′ramus
Pȳtch′ley
Pȳthăg′orăs

Quėbĕc′

Quĭll′er-Couch′ (-ōōch)
Quĭ′rĭnal (kw-)
Quĭx′ōte (or -ot)

Răb′elais (-elā)
Ră′cine (-sēn)
Raeburn (rā′bern)
Rajputana (rahjpōōtah′na)
Raleigh (raw′lĭ; or rah- or ră-)
Răm′ēsēs (-z)
Răn′élagh (-la)
Răph′āel
Read′ĭng (rĕd-)
Reger (rā′ger)
Reu′ter (roi-)
Rey′kjavĭk (rākya-)
Rheims (rēmz)
Rhōdē′sĭa (rō-; -z- or -s-; or -zha)
Rhondda (rŏn′da)
Richelieu (rē′shelyēr)
Rio de Janeir′o (rē′ō; -ērō)
Rĭ′o Grănde (or rē′ō grahn′dā)
Rĭvĭer′a (-āra)
Robespierre (rö′bzpyār)
Rŏck′ėfĕller
Rōma′nēs (-ah-; -z)
Rŏm′ney (or rŭm-)
Rōō′sevĕlt (-sv-; *rō′ze-)
Rossĕtt′ĭ (rōz-)
Rōtoru′a (-ōōa)
Rouen (rōō′ahṅ)
Rousseau (rōō′sō)
Rŏx′burgh (-bru)
Ruy Blas (rwē blahs)
Ru′ў Lō′pėz (rōō-)

Sachĕv′erell (-sh-)
Sahȧr′a°(sa-h-)
Sainte-Beuve (săṅt bērv)
Saint-Saens (săṅ sahṅs)
Sā′lĕm
Salisbury (saw′lzbrĭ)
Salō′mė
Salŏn′ĭca (or sălonē′-)
Săn′chō Păn′za (-ngk-)
Săn Diego (dĭā′gō)
Săn Jose (hōzā′)
Săn Juan′ (hwahn)
Săn′ta Fé (fā)
Săntĭa′gō (-ah-)
Sȧr′a(h) (or sȧr-)
Sărasa′tė (-ah-)
Săratō′ga
Săskătch′ėwan
Săskatōōn′
Sau′dĭ (saōō- or sow-)

Sault Sainte Marie (sōō′ sānt marē′)
Săvonarō′la
Sca′fĕll′ (scaw-)
Scăl′iğer
Schéhē̇raza′dė (sh-; -azah-; or -hĕ-)
Scheldt (skĕlt)
Schènĕc′tadў (sk-)
Schu′bĕrt (shōō-)
Schuyler (skī-)
Schuyl′kĭll (skōōl-)
Scĭll′ў (s-)
Scĭp′ĭō (s-)
Scrĭ′abĭn
Scўll′a (s-)
Sĕătt′le
Sĕdăn′
Sĕd′bĕr̄gh [school] (-rg)
Sĕd′bergh [town] (-ber)
Seine (sān)
Sĕm′élé
Sĕmĭ′ramĭs
Sĕn′éca
Sĕnégal′ (-awl)
Sĕnnăch′erĭb (-k-)
Sėquoi′a
Sĕt′ėbŏs
Sèvres (sā′vr)
Shănghai′ (-ng-hī)
Shrews′burў (-ōōz- or -ōz-)
Sĭăm′
Sĭbe′lĭus (-bā-)
Siegfried (sē′gfrĕd)
Sĭerr′a Lėone′ (-ār̄-; -ōn)
Sikh (sēk)
Sĭlē′nus
Sĭm′èon
Sĭ′mon
Sĭm′plon (or săṅ′plawṅ)
Sĭ′nai (-nĭī)
Sioux (sōō)
Sĭs′ўphus
Si′va (shĕ- or sē-)
Skĭdd′aw (or skĭdaw′)
Slough (slow)
Smĕth′wick (-dhĭk)
Sŏc′ratēs (-z)
Sofi′a (-fēa)
Sō′lŏn
Soma′lĭ (-ah-)
Som′ersĕt (sŭm-)
Sŏph′oclēs (-z)
Soth′ebў (sŭdhe-)
Southey (sow′dhĭ or sŭdh′ĭ)
Southwark (sŭdh′erk)
Sou′za (-ōō-)
Srĭna′gar (-ah-; or -nŭ-)

St. Al′bans (awl-)
Stendhal (stahṅ′dahl)
St. John [saint, place] (snt jŏn′)
St. John [surname] (sĭn′jon)
St. Lou′ĭs (lōō-)
St. Ma′lō (-ah-)
St. Neots (nēts)
Stōke Pŏ′ğės (-z)
Strachan (strawn; or stră′chan)
Strădĭvār̄′ĭus (or -vār̄-)
Strauss (-ows)
Streatham (strĕt′am)
Stuy′vėsant (stī-)
Sudăn′ (sōō- or sōō-)
Su′éz (-ōō-)
Suma′tra (sōōmah-)
Sŭsquėhănn′a (-kw-)
Swahi′lĭ (swah-hē-)
Swa′zĭlănd (swah-)
Sўnge (-ng)
Sȳr̄′acūse (-z)
Sў′racūse [U.S.]

Tā′gus
Tahi′tĭ (ta-hē-)
Taj Mahal (tahj mahahl′)
Tăngănyi′ka (-ngg-; -yē-)
Tănğier′ (-jēr̄)
Tănnhäu′ser (-hoiz-)
Tănzani′a (-ĭa)
Tărragō′na
Tchaikovsky (chĭkŏv′skĭ)
Teh′erăn (tāer-)
Teignmouth (tĭn′muth)
Tėlĕm′achus (-kus)
Tĕm′pė
Tĕneriffe′ (-ĕf)
Tĕr̄psĭch′orė (-k-)
Tĕr̄tŭll′ĭan
Thai′land (tī-)
Thalĭ′a
Thame (tām)
Thames (tĕmz)
Thăn′ĕt
Thēbes (-bz)
Thĕmĭs′toclēs (-z)
Thė′obald (-awld; or tĭb′ald)
Thėŏc′rĭtus
Thėŏd′orĭc
Thĕr̄mŏp′ўlae
Thĕr̄sĭ′tēs (-z)
Thė′seus (-ūs)
Thĕs′pĭs
Thĕssalonĭ′ca
Thĕss′alў
Thĭs′bė (-z-)

Thŏm′as (t-)
Thomas [Ambroise] (tō′mah)
Thôr′eau (-ō)
Thŭcўd′ĭdēs (-z)
Thŭ′lĕ
Tĭbēr′ĭus
Tĭbĕt′
Tĭbŭll′us
Tĭci′nō (-chē-)
Tĭerr′a dĕl Fuego (-āra; fōōā′gō)
Tĭf′lĭs
Tĭ′grĭs
Tĭ′mon
Tĭntăğ′el
Tĭtā′nĭa (or -ah-)
Tĭ′tian (-shĭ-)
Tĭ′tus
Tĭv′olĭ
Tobā′gō
Tōbĭ′as
Tō′kўō
Tolē′dō (or -ā′dō)
Tŏ′rrĕs
Tŏt′nĕs
Toulon (tōōlawṅ′)
Toulouse (tōōlōōz′)
Touraine′ (toor-)
Tours (toor)
Towcester (tō′ster)
Trafăl′gar (or trăfalgär′)
Trā′jan
Trănsvaal′ (-ahl)
Trĭchĭnŏp′olў
Trĭĕste′ (-st)
Trĭn′ĭdăd
Trĭs′tan da Cun′ha (kōōnya)
Trī′ton
Trŏll′ope (-op)
Trŏss′achs (-ks)
Trou′vĭlle (-ōō-)
Tucson (tōō′son)
Tuileries (twē′lerē)
Turgenev (toorgā′nyef)
Tūrĭn′ (or tūr′ĭn)
Tûrkĕstăn′ (or -ahn)
Tŭssaud′s′ (-z; or tōōsōz)
Tutankha′mĕn (tōō-; -kah-)
Tў′chō (-k-)
Tўn′dale (-dl)
Tў′rol (or tĭrōl′; or -ŏl′)
Tў′rrwhit (-rĭt)

Ugăn′da (ū-)
U′ĭst (ōō-; or wĭst)
Ukraine′ (ū-; -ān or -ah-ēn)
Ulўss′ēs (ū-; -z; or ū′-)

Ur′anus (ūr-; or ūrā′nus)
Ur′du (ūrdōō; or oor-; or -ōō′)
Urī′ah (ūr-)
Ur′ĭel (ūr-)
Urquhart (ûr′kert)
Uruguay (ōō′rōōgwī; or -ā)
Ush′ant (ŭ-)
Utah (ū′tah, *ū′taw)
U′ther (ū-)
Utrecht (ūtrĕkt′)
Utrĭll′ō (ū-)

Valĕn′cia (-shĭa or -sĭa)
Vălenciennes′ (-syĕn)
Vălhăll′a
Vălkӯr′ĭe (or -kēr-; or văl′kĭrĭ)
Văl′ois (-wah)
Vălparai′sō (-z-; or -rī′zō)
Văn′burgh (-bru)
Văn Dӯck
Văn Eyck (īk)
Văsär′ĭ
Văs′cō da Ga′ma (gah-)
Văth′ĕk (or vā-)
Vaughan (vawn)
Vauxhall (vŏks′hawl)
Ve′da (vā-)
Ve′ga [Lope de, 1562–1635] (vā-)
Vē′ga [star]
Vĕlăs′quez (-kwĭz or -kĭz)
Vĕnĕzue′la (-zwā-)
Vērde
Ver′dĭ (vār-)
Vērdŭn′ (or vārdŭṅ)
Vēr′ğĭl
Vērne (or vārn)
Vĕrone′se (-āzĭ)
Versailles (vārsī′)
Vĕ′rulam (-ōō-)
Vichy (vē′shē)
Vi′cō (vē-)
Vĭenn′a
Vĭĕtnăm′ (or vēĕt- or vĕt-)
Villon (vē′yawṅ)
Vĭn′ci (-chĭ)
Vĭ′ola
Vĭr′ğĭl
Vosges (vōzh)

Wa′băsh (waw-)
Wadham (wŏd′am)
Wag′ner (vah-)
Walde′grāve (wawlg-)
Walpurgis (vălpoor′gĭs)
Wan′tage (wŏn-)

Wapp'ing (wŏ-)
Wār'ing
Warwick (wŏ'rĭk)
Watteau (wŏt'ō)
Wear [river] (wēr)
We'ber (vā-)
Wednes'burў (wĕnzb-)
Wei'mȧr (vī-)
Weiss'hŏrn (vīs-h-)
Welwyn (wĕl'ĭn)
Wemyss (wēmz)
We'ser (vāz- or wēz-)
Whewell (hūl)
Wies'baden (vēzbah-)
Wĭnd'sor (-nz-)
Wĭs'bĕch (-z-)
Wĭscŏn'sĭn
Wŏŏl'wich (-lĭj)
Wŏŏtt'on
Worcester (wŏŏs'ter)
Wŏrms (v-; -z)
Wrĕ'kĭn (r-)
Wrotham (rōō'tam)
Wўch'erley
Wўc'lĭf(fe)
Wўc'ombe (-om)
Wykeham (wĭk'am)

Wymondham (wĭn'dam)
Wўō'mĭng

Xăv'ĭer (z-; or zā-)
Xĕn'ophon (z-)
Xêr'xĕs (z-; -z)

Yeats (yāts)
Ye'men (yā-)
Yeo'vĭl (yŏ-)
Yōkōha'ma (-hah-)
Yonge (yŭng)
Yōsĕm'ĭtė
Ypres (ēpr; or wĭ'perz)
Ysaye (ĭsī'ĭ)
Yucatan' (ū-; -ahn)

Zăcharī'ah (-karīa)
Zăm'bĭa
Zē'nō
Zeus (zūs)
Zō'ė
Zō'la
Zŏrōăs'ter
Zurich (zūr'ĭk)
Zuy'der Zee' (zī- or zoi-; or -zā)

NOTES

NOTES

NOTES

NOTES

NOTES